W9-CUH-147

ST. JAMES ENCYCLOPEDIA OF

POPULARCULTURE

ST. JAMES ENCYCLOPEDIA OF
POPULARCULTURE

VOLUME 5: U-Z/INDEXES

EDITORS: Tom Pendergast   Sara Pendergast

with an introduction by Jim Cullen

ST. JAMES PRESS

AN IMPRINT OF THE GALE GROUP

DETROIT • SAN FRANCISCO • LONDON
BOSTON • WOODBRIDGE, CT

Tom Pendergast, Sara Pendergast, *Editors*

Michael J. Tyrkus, *Project Coordinator*

Laura Standley Berger, Joann Cerrito, Dave Collins,
Steve Cusack, Nicolet V. Elert, Miranda Ferrara, Jamie FitzGerald,
Kristin Hart, Laura S. Kryhoski, Margaret Mazurkiewicz
St. James Press Staff

Peter M. Gareffa, *Managing Editor, St. James Press*

Maria Franklin, *Permissions Manager*
Kimberly F. Smilay, *Permissions Specialist*
Kelly A. Quin, *Permissions Associate*
Erin Bealmear, Sandy Gore, *Permissions Assistants*
Mary Grimes, Leitha Etheridge-Sims, *Image Catalogers*

Mary Beth Trimper, *Composition Manager*
Dorothy Maki, *Manufacturing Manager*
Wendy Blurton, *Senior Buyer*

Cynthia Baldwin, *Product Design Manager*
Martha Schiebold, *Graphic Artist*

Randy Bassett, *Image Database Supervisor*
Robert Duncan, Michael Logusz, *Imaging Specialists*
Pamela A. Reed, *Imaging Coordinator*

Library of Congress Cataloging-in-Publication Data
St. James Encyclopedia of Popular Culture / with an introduction by Jim Cullen; editors,
Tom Pendergast and Sara Pendergast.
    p. cm.
    Includes bibliographical references and index.
    ISBN 1-558-62400-7 (set) — ISBN 1-558-62401-5 (v.1) — ISBN 1-558-62402-3 (v.2) —
ISBN 1-558-62403-1 (v.3) — ISBN 1-558-62404-x (v.4) — ISBN 1-558-62405-8 (v. 5)
    1. United States—Civilization—20th century—Encyclopedias. 2. Popular culture—United
States—History—20th century—Encyclopedias. I. Pendergast, Tom. II. Pendergast, Sara.
E169.1.S764 1999
973.9 21—dc21   99-046540

Printed in the United States of America

St. James Press is an imprint of Gale Group
Gale Group and Design is a trademark used herein under license

10 9 8 7 6 5 4 3

CONTENTS

EDITORS' NOTE   PAGE VII

INTRODUCTION   XI

ADVISORS   XV

CONTRIBUTORS   XVII

LIST OF ENTRIES   XXI

ENCYCLOPEDIA OF POPULAR CULTURE   **1**

    VOLUME 1: A-D

    VOLUME 2: E-J

    VOLUME 3: K-O

    VOLUME 4: P-T

    VOLUME 5: U-Z, INDEXES

READING LIST   239

ACKNOWLEDGMENTS   243

NOTES ON ADVISORS AND CONTRIBUTORS   251

TIME-FRAME INDEX   267

CATEGORY INDEX   313

INDEX   351

EDITOR'S NOTE

Thirty some years ago Ray Browne and several of his colleagues provided a forum for the academic study of popular culture by forming first the *Journal of Popular Culture* and later the Popular Culture Association and the Center for the Study of Popular Culture at Bowling Green State University. Twenty some years ago Thomas Inge thought the field of popular culture studies well enough established to put together the first edition of his *Handbook of Popular Culture*. In the years since, scholars and educators from many disciplines have published enough books, gathered enough conferences, and gained enough institutional clout to make popular culture studies one of the richest fields of academic study at the close of the twentieth century. Thirty, twenty, in some places even ten years ago, to study popular culture was to be something of a pariah; today, the study of popular culture is accepted and even respected in departments of history, literature, communications, sociology, film studies, etc. throughout the United States and throughout the world, and not only in universities, but in increasing numbers of high schools. Thomas Inge wrote in the introduction to the second edition of his *Handbook*: "The serious and systematic study of popular culture may be the most significant and potentially useful of the trends in academic research and teaching in the last half of this century in the United States."[2] It is to this thriving field of study that we hope to contribute with the *St. James Encyclopedia of Popular Culture.*

The *St. James Encyclopedia of Popular Culture* includes over 2,700 essays on all elements of popular culture in the United States in the twentieth century. But what is "popular culture?" Academics have offered a number of answers over the years. Historians Norman F. Cantor and Michael S. Werthman suggested that "popular culture may be seen as all those things man does and all those artifacts he creates for their own sake, all that diverts his mind and body from the sad business of life."[1] Michael Bell argues that:

> At its simplest popular culture is the culture of mass appeal. A creation is popular when it is created to respond to the experiences and values of the majority, when it is produced in such a way that the majority have easy access to it, and when it can be understood and interpreted by that majority without the aid of special knowledge or experience.[3]

While tremendously useful, both of these definitions tend to exclude more than they embrace. Was the hot dog created for its own sake, as a diversion? Probably not, but we've included an essay on it in this collection. Were the works of Sigmund Freud in any way shaped for the majority? No, but Freud's ideas—borrowed, twisted, and reinterpreted—have shaped novels, films, and common speech in ways too diffuse to ignore. Thus we have included an essay on Freud's impact on popular culture. Our desire to bring together the greatest number of cultural phenomena impacting American culture in this century has led us to prefer Ray Browne's rather broader early definition of popular culture as "all the experiences in life shared by people in common, generally though not necessarily disseminated by the mass media."[4]

Coverage

In order to amass a list of those cultural phenomena that were widely disseminated and experienced by people in relatively unmediated form we asked a number of scholars, teachers, librarians, and archivists to serve as advisors. Each of our 20 advisors provided us with a list of over 200 topics from their field of specialty that they considered important enough to merit an essay; several of our advisors provided us with lists much longer than that. Their collective lists numbered nearly 4,000 potential essay topics, and we winnowed this list down to the number that is now gathered in this collection. We sought balance (but not equal coverage) between the major areas of popular culture: film; music; print culture; social life; sports; television and radio; and art and perfomance (which includes theatre, dance, stand-up comedy, and other live performance). For those interested, the breakdown of coverage is as follows: social life, 23 percent (a category which covers everything from foodways to fashion, holidays to hairstyles); music, 16 percent; print culture, 16 percent; film, 15 percent; television and radio, 14 percent; sports, 10 percent; and art and performance, 6 percent. A variety of considerations led us to skew the coverage of the book in favor of the second half of the century. The massive popularity of television and recorded music, the mass-marketing of popular fiction, and the national attention given to professional sports are historical factors contributing to the emphasis on post-World War II culture, but we have also considered the needs of high school and undergraduate users in distributing entries in this way.

The Entries

The entries in this volume vary in length from brief (75 to 150-word) introductions to the topic to in-depth 3,000-word explorations. No matter the length, we have asked our contributors to do two things in each entry: to describe the topic and to analyze its significance in and relevance to American popular culture. While we hope that users will find the basic factual information they need concerning the topic in an entry, it was even more important to us that each user gain some perspective on the cultural context in which the topic has importance. Thus the entry on MTV, for example, chronicles the channel's rise to world popularity, but also analyzes the relationship between MTV, youth culture, and consumerism. The entry on John Ford, while tracing the outlines of the film director's long career, assesses the impact Ford's films have had on the film Western and on Americans' very perceptions of the West. Given the brevity of the entries, we chose to emphasize analysis of a topic's contribution to popular culture over a full presentation of biographical/historical information. The entry on World War I, for example, offers an analysis of how the war was understood in popular film, print culture, and propaganda rather than a blow-by-blow description of the actual military conflict.

Entries are accompanied by a list of further readings. These readings are meant to provide the user with readily accessible sources that provide more information on the specific topic. As befits a multimedia age, these "further readings" come not just from books and magazines, but also from albums, liner notes, films, videos, and web sites. Users of the Internet know well the perils of trusting the information found on the World Wide Web; there are as yet few filters to help browsers sift the useful from the absurd. We cited web sites when they provided information that was unavailable in any other known form and when our reasonable efforts to determine the veracity of the information led us to believe that the information provided was valid and useful. We have occasionally provided links to "official" web sites of performers or organizations, for the same reason that we provide citations to autobiographies. All web links cited were accurate as of the date indicated in the citation.

Organization and Indexing

Entries are arranged alphabetically by the name under which the topic is best known. For topics which might reasonably be sought out under differing names, we have provided in-text cross references. For example, a user seeking an entry on Huddie Ledbetter will be referred to the entry on Leadbelly, and a user seeking an entry on Larry Flynt will be referred to the entry on *Hustler* magazine. Far more powerful than the cross references, however, are the indexes provided in the fifth volume of the collection. The general index is by far the most powerful, for it leads the user searching for information on Humphrey Bogart, for example, to the entries on Lauren Bacall, *Casablanca, The Maltese Falcon, The African Queen,* and several other entries that contain substantive information about Bogie. Equally powerful is the subject index, a list of categories under which we listed all pertinent entries. Consulting the subject index listing for Sex Symbols, for example, will lead the user to entries on Marilyn Monroe, the Varga Girl, *Playboy* magazine, David Cassidy, Mae West, and a long entry on the Sex Symbol, among others. Finally, a time index, organized by decades, provides a list of the entries that concern each decade of the twentieth century. Those entries that concern nineteenth-century topics are indexed by the first decade of the twentieth century.

We encourage readers to use the indexes to discover the fascinating intertwinings that have made the development of popular culture in the twentieth century such a vital field of study. Using the indexes, it is possible to uncover the story of how the American humor that was first made popular on the vaudeville stage evolved into first the radio comedies that entertained so many Americans during the Depression and War years and later the sitcoms that have kept Americans glued to their television screens for the last 50 years. That story is here, in the entries on Vaudeville, the Sitcom, *Amos 'n' Andy,* and the many other programs and comedians that have defined this tradition. A teacher who wishes students to uncover the similarities between sitcoms of the 1950s, 1960s, 1970s, 1980s, and 1990s might well ask the students to use this collection to begin their research into such comedies. Similarly, a teacher who asks students to explore the cross-pollination between musical genres will find that the indexes reveal the mixing of "race music," rhythm and blues, gospel, soul, and rock 'n' roll. It is hoped that this collection will be of particular use to those instructors of high school and undergraduate courses who challenge their students to discover the real cultural complexity of the music, films, magazines, and television shows that they take for granted. This collection should also be of use to those more advanced scholars who are beginning new research into an area of popular culture or who are looking for some context in which to place their existing research.

Acknowledgments

The *St. James Encyclopedia of Popular Culture* represents the work of hundreds of people, and we owe our thanks to all of them. We have had the privilege of working with 20 advisors whose experience, knowledge, and wisdom have truly helped shape the contents of this collection. Each of our advisors helped us to discover hidden corners of popular culture that we would not have considered on our own, and the breadth of coverage in this collection is a tribute to their collective knowledge. Several of our advisors deserve special thanks: Paul Buhle, George Carney, B. Lee Cooper, Jerome Klinkowitz, and Ron Simon all showed an extraordinary level of commitment and helpfulness.

It has been a pleasure to work with the nearly 450 contributors to this collection; we've appreciated their expertise, their professionalism, and their good humor. Several of our contributors deserve special mention for the quality of their contributions to this collection: Jacob Appel, Tim Berg, Pat Broeske, Richard Digby-Junger, Jeffrey Escoffier, Bryan Garman, Tina Gianoulis, Milton Goldin, Ian Gordon, Ron Goulart, Justin Gustainis, Preston Jones, Robyn Karney, Deborah Mix, Leonard Moore, Edward Moran, Victoria Price, Bob Schnakenberg, Steven Schneider, Charles Shindo, Robert Sickels, Wendy Woloson, and Brad Wright. Our team of copyeditors helped us bring a uniformity of presentation to the writings of this mass of contributors, and spotted and corrected innumerable small errors. Heidi Hagen, Robyn Karney, Edward Moran, and Tim Seul deserve special thanks for the quality and quantity of their work; we truly couldn't have done it without them. The contributors and copyeditors provided us with the material to build this collection, but it has been the editors' responsibility to ensure its accuracy and reliability. We welcome any corrections and comments; please write to: The Editors, *St. James Encyclopedia of Popular Culture,* St. James Press, 27500 Drake Road, Farmington Hills, MI 48331-3535.

Gathering the photos for this collection was an enormous task, and we were helped immeasurably by the knowledgeable and efficient staff at several photo agencies. We'd like to thank Marcia Schiff at AP/Wide World Photos; Eric Young at Archive Photos; and Kevin Rettig at Corbis Images. Lisa Hartjens of ImageFinders, Inc. also helped us acquire a number of photos.

We would like to thank Shelly Andrews, Anne Boyd, Melissa Doig, Tina Gianoulis, Heidi Hagen, Robyn Karney, Edward Moran, Victoria Price, Rebecca Saulsbury, Tim Seul, and Mark Swartz for their careful copyediting of the entries.

At the St. James Press, we'd like to thank Mike Tyrkus for his good humor and efficiency in helping us see this project to completion; Peter Gareffa for his usual wise and benevolent leadership; Janice Jorgensen for helping us shape this project at the beginning; the permissions department for smiling as we piled the photos on; and the staff at the St. James Press for their careful proofreading and for all their work in turning so many computer files into the volumes you see today.

Finally, we'd like to thank Lee Van Wormer for his sage management advice and our children, Conrad and Louisa, for their warm morning cuddles and for the delightful artwork that adorns our office walls.

—Tom Pendergast and Sara Pendergast,
Editors

NOTES

1. Cantor, Norman F. and Michael S. Werthman. *The History of Popular Culture to 1815.* New York, Macmillan, 1968, xxiv.
2. Inge, M. Thomas, editor. *Handbook of American Popular Culture.* 2nd edition. Westport, Connecticut, Greenwood Press, 1989, xxiii.
3. Bell, Michael. "The Study of Popular Culture," in *Concise Histories of American Popular Culture,* ed. Inge, M. Thomas. Westport, Connecticut, Greenwood Press, 1982, 443.
4. Browne, Ray B. *Popular Culture and the Expanding Consciousness.* New York, Wiley, 1973, 6.

INTRODUCTION

The Art of Everyday Life

Sometimes, when I'm wandering in an art museum looking at the relics of an ancient civilization, I find myself wondering how a future society would represent a defunct American culture. What objects would be chosen—or would survive—to be placed on display? Would I agree with a curator's choices? Were I to choose the items that some future American Museum of Art should exhibit to represent twentieth-century American culture, here are some I would name: an Elvis Presley record; a Currier & Ives print; a movie still from *Casablanca.* To put it a different way, my priority would *not* be to exhibit fragments of an urban cathedral, a painted landscape, or a formal costume. I wouldn't deny such objects could be important artifacts of American culture, or that they belong in a gallery. But in my avowedly biased opinion, the most vivid documents of American life—the documents that embody its possibilities and limits—are typically found in its popular culture.

Popular culture, of course, is not an American invention, and it has a vibrant life in many contemporary societies. But in few, if any, of those societies has it been as central to a notion of national character at home as well as abroad. For better or worse, it is through icons like McDonald's (the quintessential American cuisine), the Western (a uniquely American narrative genre), and Oprah Winfrey (a classic late-twentieth century embodiment of the American Dream) that this society is known—and is likely to be remembered.

It has sometimes been remarked that unlike nations whose identities are rooted in geography, religion, language, blood, or history, the United States was founded on a democratic ideal—a notion of life, liberty, and the pursuit of happiness elaborated in the Declaration of Independence. That ideal has been notoriously difficult to realize, and one need only take a cursory look at many aspects of American life—its justice system, electoral politics, residential patterns, labor force, et. al.—to see how far short it has fallen.

American popular culture is a special case. To be sure, it evinces plenty of the defects apparent in other areas of our national life, among them blatant racism and crass commercialism. If nothing else, such flaws can be taken as evidence of just how truly representative it is. There is nevertheless an openness and vitality about pop culture—its appeal across demographic lines; its interplay of individual voices and shared communal experience; the relatively low access barriers for people otherwise marginalized in U.S. society—that give it real legitimacy as the art of democracy. Like it or hate it, few dispute its centrality.

This sense of openness and inclusion—as well as the affection and scorn it generated—has been apparent from the very beginning. In the prologue of the 1787 play *The Contrast* (whose title referred to the disparity between sturdy republican ideals and effete monarchical dissipation), American playwright Royall Tyler invoked a cultural sensibility where "proud titles of 'My Lord! Your Grace/To the humble 'Mr.' and plain 'Sir' give place." Tyler, a Harvard graduate, Revolutionary War officer, and Chief Justice of the Vermont Supreme Court, was in some sense an unlikely prophet of popular culture. But the sensibility he voiced—notably in his beloved character Jonathon, a prototype for characters from Davy Crockett to John Wayne—proved durable for centuries to come.

For much of early American history, however, artists and critics continued to define aesthetic success on European terms, typically invoking elite ideals of order, balance, and civilization. It was largely taken for granted that the most talented practitioners of fine arts, such as painters Benjamin West and John Singleton Copley, would have to go abroad to train, produce, and exhibit their most important work. To the extent that newer cultural forms—like the novel, whose very name suggests its place in late eighteenth- and early nineteenth-century western civilization—were noted at all, it was usually in disparaging terms. This was especially true of novels written and read by women, such as Susanna Rowson's widely read *Charlotte Temple* (1791). Sermons against novels were common; Harvard devoted its principal commencement address in 1803 to the dangers of fiction.

The industrialization of the United States has long been considered a watershed development in many realms of American life, and popular culture is no exception. Indeed, its importance is suggested in the very definition of popular culture coined by cultural historian Lawrence Levine: "the folklore of industrial society." Industrialization allowed the mass-reproduction and dissemination of formerly local traditions, stories, and art forms across the continent, greatly intensifying the spread—and development—of culture by, for, and of the people. At a time when North America remained geographically and politically fragmented, magazines, sheet music, dime novels, lithographs, and other print media stitched it together.

This culture had a characteristic pattern. Alexis de Tocqueville devoted 11 chapters of his classic 1835-40 masterpiece *Democracy in America* to the art, literature, and language of the United States, arguing that they reflected a democratic ethos that required new standards of evaluation. "The inhabitants of the United States have, at present, properly speaking, no literature," he wrote. This judgment, he made clear, arose from a definition of literature that came from aristocratic societies like his own. In its stead, he explained, Americans sought books "which may be easily procured, quickly read, and which require no learned researches to be understood. They ask for beauties self-proffered and easily enjoyed; above all they must have what is unexpected and new." As in so many other ways, this description of American literature, which paralleled what Tocqueville saw in other arts, proved not only vivid but prophetic.

The paradox of American democracy, of course, is that the freedom Euro-Americans endlessly celebrated co-existed with—some might say depended on—the enslavement of African Americans. It is therefore one of the great ironies of popular culture that the contributions of black culture (a term here meant to encompass African, American, and amalgamations between the two) proved so decisive. In another sense, however, it seems entirely appropriate that popular culture, which has always skewed its orientation toward the lower end of a demographic spectrum, would draw on the most marginalized groups in American society. It is, in any event, difficult to imagine that U.S. popular culture would have had anywhere near the vitality and influence it has without slave stories, song, and dance. To cite merely one example: every American musical idiom from country music to rap has drawn on, if not actually *rested* upon, African-American cultural foundations, whether in its use of the banjo (originally an African instrument) or its emphasis on the beat (drumming was an important form of slave communication). This heritage has often been overlooked, disparaged, and even satirized. The most notable example of such racism was the minstrel show, a wildly popular nineteenth century form of theater in which white actors blackened their faces with burnt cork and mocked slave life. Yet even the most savage parodies could not help but reveal an engagement with, and even a secret admiration for, the cultural world the African Americans made in conditions of severe adversity, whether on plantations, tenant farms, or in ghettoes.

Meanwhile, the accelerating pace of technological innovation began having a dramatic impact on the form as well as the content of popular culture. The first major landmark was the development of photography in the mid-nineteenth century. At first a mechanically complex and thus inaccessible medium, it quickly captured American imaginations, particularly by capturing the drama and horror of the Civil War. The subsequent proliferation of family portraits, postcards, and pictures in metropolitan newspapers began a process of orienting popular culture around visual imagery that continues unabated to this day.

In the closing decades of the nineteenth century, sound recording, radio transmission, and motion pictures were all developed in rapid succession. But it would not be until well after 1900 that their potential as popular cultural media would be fully exploited and recognizable in a modern sense (radio, for example, was originally developed and valued for its nautical and military applications). Still, even if it was not entirely clear how, many people at the time believed these new media would have a tremendous impact on American life, and they were embraced with unusual ardor by those Americans, particularly immigrants, who were able to appreciate the pleasures and possibilities afforded by movies, records, and radio.

Many of the patterns established during the advent of these media repeated themselves as new ones evolved. The Internet, for example, was also first developed for its military applications, and for all the rapidity of its development in the 1990s, it remains unclear just how its use will be structured. Though the World Wide Web has shown tremendous promise as a commercial enterprise, it still lacks the kind of programming—like *Amos 'n' Andy* in radio, or *I Love Lucy* in television—that transformed both into truly mass media of art and entertainment. Television, for its part, has long been the medium of a rising middle class of immigrants and their children, in terms of the figures who have exploited its possibilities (from RCA executive David Sarnoff to stars like Jackie Gleason); the new genres it created (from the miniseries to the situation-comedy); and the audiences (from urban Jews to suburban Irish Catholics) who adopted them with enthusiasm.

For much of this century, the mass appeal of popular culture has been viewed as a problem. "What is the jass [*sic*] music, and therefore the jass band?" asked an irritated New Orleans writer in 1918. "As well as ask why the dime novel or the grease-dripping doughnut. All are manifestations of a low stream in man's taste that has not come out in civilization's wash." However one may feel about this contemptuous dismissal of jazz, now viewed as one of the great achievements of American civilization, this writer was clearly correct to suggest the demographic, technological, and cultural links between the "lower" sorts of people in American life, the media they used, and forms of expression that were often presumed guilty until proven innocent.

Indeed, because education and research have traditionally been considered the province of the "higher" sorts of people in American life, popular culture was not considered a subject that should even be discussed, much less studied. Nevertheless, there have always been those willing to continue what might be termed the "Tocquevillian" tradition of treating popular culture with intellectual seriousness and respect (if not always approval). In his 1924 book *The Seven Lively Arts* and in much of his journalism, critic Gilbert Seldes found in silent movies, cartoons, and pop music themes and motifs fully worthy of sustained exploration. Amid the worldwide crisis of the 1930s and 1940s, folklorist Constance Rourke limned the origins of an indigenous popular culture in books like *American Humor* (1931) and *The Roots of American Culture* (1942). And with the rise of the Cold War underlining the differences between democratic and totalitarian societies, sociologists David Riesman and Reuel Denny evaluated the social currents animating popular culture in Denny's *The Astonished Muse* (1957), for which Riesman, who showed a particular interest in popular music, wrote the introduction.

European scholars were also pivotal in shaping the field. Johan Huizinga's *Homo Ludens* (1938), Roland Barthes's *Mythologies* (1957), and Antonio Gramsci's prison letters (written in the 1920s and 1930s but not published until the 1970s) have proved among the most influential works in defining the boundaries, strategies, and meanings of popular culture. While none of these works focused on American popular culture specifically, their focus on the jetsam and flotsam of daily life since the medieval period proved enormously suggestive in an American context.

It has only been at the end of the twentieth century, however, that the study of popular culture has come into its own in its own right. To a great extent, this development is a legacy of the 1960s. The end of a formal system of racial segregation; the impact of affirmative action and government-funded financial aid; and the end of single-sex education at many long-established universities dramatically transformed the composition of student bodies and faculties. These developments in turn, began having an impact on the nature and parameters of academic study. While one should not exaggerate the impact of these developments—either in terms of their numbers or their effect on an academy that in some ways has simply replaced older forms of insularity and complacency with new ones—it nevertheless seems fair to say that a bona fide democratization of higher education occurred in the last third of the twentieth century, paving the way for the creation of a formal scholarly infrastructure for popular culture.

Once again, it was foreign scholars who were pivotal in the elaboration of this infrastructure. The work of Raymond Williams, Stuart Hall, and others at Britain's Centre for Contemporary Cultural Studies in the 1950s and 1960s drew on Marxist and psychoanalytic ideas to explain, and in many cases justify, the importance of popular culture. Though not always specifically concerned with popular culture, a panoply of French theorists—particularly Jacques Derrida, Louis Althusser, and Michel Foucault—also proved highly influential. At its best, this scholarship illuminated unexamined assumptions and highly revealing (and in many cases, damning) patterns in the most seemingly ordinary documents. At its worst, it lapsed into an arcane jargon that belied the directness of popular culture and suggested an elitist disdain toward the audiences it presumably sought to understand.

Like their European counterparts, American scholars of popular culture have come from a variety of disciplines. Many were trained in literature, among them Henry Nash Smith, whose *Virgin Land* (1950) pioneered the study of the Western, and Leslie Fiedler, who applied critical talents first developed to study classic American literature to popular fiction like *Gone with the Wind*. But much important work in the field has also been done by historians, particularly social historians who began their careers by focusing on labor history but became increasingly interested in the ways American workers spent their free time. Following the tradition of the great British historian E. P. Thompson, scholars such as Herbert Gutman and Lawrence Levine have uncovered and described the art and leisure practices of African Americans in particular with flair and insight. Feminist scholars of a variety of stripes (and sexual orientations) have supplied a great deal of the intellectual energy in the study of popular culture, among them Ann Douglas, Carroll Smith-Rosenberg, and Jane Tompkins. Indeed, the strongly interdisciplinary flavor of popular culture scholarship—along with the rise of institutions like the Popular Press and the Popular Culture Association, both based at Bowling Green University—suggests the way the field has been at the forefront of an ongoing process of redrawing disciplinary boundaries in the humanities.

By the 1980s, the stream of scholarship on popular culture had become a flood. In the 1990s, the field became less of a quixotic enterprise than a growing presence in the educational curriculum as a whole. Courses devoted to the subject, whether housed in communications programs or in traditional academic departments, have become increasingly common in colleges and universities—and, perhaps more importantly, have become integrated into the fabric of basic surveys of history, literature, and other fields. Political scientists, librarians, and curators have begun to consider it part of their domain.

For most of us, though, popular culture is not something we have to self-consciously seek out or think about. Indeed, its very omnipresence makes it easy to take for granted as transparent (and permanent). That's why trips to museums—or encyclopedias like this one—are so useful and important. In pausing to think about the art of everyday life, we can begin to see just how unusual, and valuable, it really is.

—Jim Cullen

FURTHER READING:

Barthes, Roland. *Mythologies.* Translated by Annette Lavers. 1957. Reprint, New York, The Noonday Press, 1972.

Cullen, Jim. *The Art of Democracy: A Concise History of Popular Culture in the United States.* New York, Monthly Review Press, 1996.

Fiske, John. *Understanding Popular Culture.* Boston, Unwin/Hyman, 1989.

Levine, Lawrence. *The Unpredictable Past: Explorations in American Cultural History.* New York, Oxford University Press, 1993.

Storey, John. *An Introductory Guide to Cultural Theory and Popular Culture.* Athens, University of Georgia Press, 1993.

Susman, Warren. *Culture as History: The Transformation of American Society in the Twentieth Century.* New York, Pantheon, 1984.

ADVISORS

Frances R. Aparicio
University of Michigan

Paul Buhle
Brown University

George O. Carney
Oklahoma State University

B. Lee Cooper
University of Great Falls

Corey K. Creekmur
University of Iowa

Joshua Gamson
Yale University

Jerome Klinkowitz
University of Northern Iowa

Richard Martin
Metropolitan Museum of Art
Columbia University
New York University

Lawrence E. Mintz
University of Maryland
Art Gliner Center for Humor Studies

Troy Paino
Winona State University

Grace Palladino
University of Maryland

Lauren Rabinovitz
University of Iowa

T. V. Reed
Washington State University

William L. Schurk
Bowling Green State University

Alison M. Scott
Bowling Green State University

Randall W. Scott
Michigan State University Libraries

Ron Simon
Museum of Television & Radio
Columbia University

Erin Smith
University of Texas at Dallas

June Sochen
Northeastern Illinois University

Colby Vargas
New Trier High School

CONTRIBUTORS

Nathan Abrams
Frederick Luis Aldama
Roberto Alvarez
Byron Anderson
Carly Andrews
Jacob M. Appel
Tim Arnold
Paul Ashdown
Bernardo Alexander Attias
Frederick J. Augustyn, Jr.

Beatriz Badikian
Michael Baers
Neal Baker
S. K. Bane
Samantha Barbas
Allen Barksdale
Pauline Bartel
Bob Batchelor
Vance Bell
Samuel I. Bellman
James R. Belpedio
Courtney Bennett
Timothy Berg
Lisa Bergeron-Duncan
Daniel Bernardi
R. Thomas Berner
Charlie Bevis
Lara Bickell
Sam Binkley
Brian Black
Liza Black
Bethany Blankenship
Rebecca Blustein
Aniko Bodroghkozy
Gregory Bond
Martyn Bone
Austin Booth
Gerry Bowler
Anne Boyd
Marlena E. Bremseth
Carol Brennan
Tony Brewer
Deborah Broderson
Michael Brody
Pat H. Broeske
Robert J. Brown
Sharon Brown
Craig Bunch
Stephen Burnett
Gary Burns
Margaret Burns

Manuel V. Cabrera, Jr.
Ross B. Care

Gerald Carpenter
Anthony Cast
Rafaela Castro
Jason Chambers
Chris Chandler
Michael K. Chapman
Roger Chapman
Lloyd Chiasson, Jr.
Ann M. Ciasullo
Dylan Clark
Frank Clark
Randy Clark
Craig T. Cobane
Dan Coffey
Adam Max Cohen
Toby I. Cohen
Susann Cokal
Jeffrey W. Coker
Charles A. Coletta, Jr.
Michael R. Collings
Willie Collins
Mia L. Consalvo
Douglas Cooke
ViBrina Coronado
Robert C. Cottrell
Corey K. Creekmur
Richard C. Crepeau
Jim Cullen
Susan Curtis

Glyn Davis
Janet M. Davis
Pamala S. Deane
S. Renee Dechert
John Deitrick
Gordon Neal Diem, D.A.
Richard Digby-Junger
Laurie DiMauro
John J. Doherty
Thurston Domina
Jon Griffin Donlon
Simon Donner
Randy Duncan
Stephen Duncombe
Eugenia Griffith DuPell
Stephanie Dyer

Rob Edelman
Geoff Edgers
Jessie L. Embry
Jeffrey Escoffier
Cindy Peters Evans
Sean Evans
William A. Everett

Alyssa Falwell
Richard Feinberg
G. Allen Finchum
S. Naomi Finkelstein
Dennis Fischer
Bill Freind
Bianca Freire-Medeiros
Shaun Frentner
James Friedman
Adrienne Furness

Paul Gaffney
Milton Gaither
Joan Gajadhar
Catherine C. Galley
Caitlin L. Gannon
Sandra Garcia-Myers
Bryan Garman
Eva Marie Garroutte
Frances Gateward
Jason George
Tina Gianoulis
James R. Giles
Milton Goldin
Ilene Goldman
Matthew Mulligan Goldstein
Dave Goldweber
Ian Gordon
W. Terrence Gordon
Ron Goulart
Paul Grainge
Brian Granger
Anna Hunt Graves
Steve Graves
Jill A. Gregg
Benjamin Griffith
Perry Grossman
Justin Gustainis
Dale Allen Gyure

Kristine J. Ha
Elizabeth Haas
Ray Haberski, Jr.
Jeanne Lynn Hall
Steve Hanson
Jacqueline Anne Hatton
Chris Haven
Ethan Hay
Jeet Heer
Andrew R. Heinze
Mary Hess
Joshua Hirsch
David L. Hixson
Scott W. Hoffman
Briavel Holcomb

Peter C. Holloran
David Holloway
Karen Hovde
Kevin Howley
Nick Humez

Judy L. Isaksen

Jennifer Jankauskas
E. V. Johanningmeier
Patrick Jones
Patrick Jones
Preston Neal Jones
Mark Joseph
Thomas Judd

Peter Kalliney
Nicolás Kanellos
Robyn Karney
Stephen Keane
James D. Keeline
Max Kellerman
Ken Kempcke
Stephen C. Kenny
Stephen Kercher
Matt Kerr
M. Alison Kibler
Kimberley H. Kidd
Matthew A. Killmeier
Jason King
Jon Klinkowitz
Leah Konicki
Steven Kotok
Robert Kuhlken
Andrew J. Kunka
Audrey Kupferberg
Petra Kuppers

Emma Lambert
Christina Lane
Kevin Lause
Nadine-Rae Leavell
Christopher A. Lee
Michele Lellouche
Robin Lent
Joan Leotta
Richard Levine
Drew Limsky
Daniel Lindley
Joyce Linehan
Margaret Litton
James H. Lloyd
David Lonergan
Eric Longley
Rick Lott
Bennett Lovett-Graff
Denise Lowe

Debra M. Lucas
Karen Lurie
Michael A. Lutes
James Lyons
John F. Lyons

Steve Macek
Alison Macor
David Marc
Robin Markowitz
Tilney L. Marsh
Richard Martin
Sara Martin
Linda A. Martindale
Kevin Mattson
Randall McClure
Allison McCracken
Jennifer Davis McDaid
Jason McEntee
Cheryl S. McGrath
Daryna McKeand
Jacquelyn Y. McLendon
Kembrew McLeod
Josephine A. McQuail
Alex Medeiros
Brad Melton
Myra Mendible
Jeff Merron
Thomas J. Mertz
Nathan R. Meyer
Jonathan Middlebrook
Andre Millard
Jeffrey S. Miller
Karen Miller
P. Andrew Miller
Dorothy Jane Mills
Andrew Milner
Deborah M. Mix
Nickianne Moody
Richard L. Moody
Charles F. Moore
Leonard N. Moore
Dan Moos
Robert A. Morace
Edward Moran
Barry Morris
Michael J. Murphy
Jennifer A. Murray
Susan Murray
Pierre-Damien Mvuyekure

Michael Najjar
Ilana Nash
Mary Lou Nemanic
Scott Newman
Joan Nicks
Martin F. Norden
Justin Nordstrom
Anna Notaro

William F. O'Connor
Paul O'Hara
Angela O'Neal
Christopher D. O'Shea
Lolly Ockerstrom
Kerry Owens
Marc Oxoby

D. Byron Painter
Henri-Dominique Paratte
Leslie Paris
Jay Parrent
Felicity Paxton
Sara Pendergast
Tom Pendergast
Jana Pendragon
Geoff Peterson
Kurt W. Peterson
Emily Pettigrew
Daniel J. Philippon
S. J. Philo
Allene Phy-Olsen
Ed Piacentino
Jürgen Pieters
Paul F. P. Pogue
Mark B. Pohlad
Fernando Porta
Michael L. Posner
John A. Price
Victoria Price
Luca Prono
Elizabeth Purdy
Christian L. Pyle

Jessy Randall
Taly Ravid
Belinda S. Ray
Ivan Raykoff
Wendy Wick Reaves
James E. Reibman
Yolanda Retter
Tracy J. Revels
Wylene Rholetter
Tad Richards
Robert B. Ridinger
Jeff Ritter
Thomas Robertson
Arthur Robinson
Todd Anthony Rosa
Ava Rose
Chris Routledge
Abhijit Roy
Adrienne Russell
Dennis Russell

Lisa Jo Sagolla
Frank A. Salamone
Joe Sutliff Sanders

Andrew Sargent
Julie Scelfo
Elizabeth D. Schafer
Louis Scheeder
James Schiff
Robert E. Schnakenberg
Steven Schneider
Kelly Schrum
Christine Scodari
Ann Sears
E. M. I. Sefcovic
Eric J. Segal
Carol A. Senf
Tim Seul
Alexander Shashko
Michele S. Shauf
Taylor Shaw
Anne Sheehan
Steven T. Sheehan
Pamela Shelton
Sandra Sherman
Charles J. Shindo
Mike Shupp
Robert C. Sickels
C. Kenyon Silvey
Ron Simon
Philip Simpson
Rosemarie Skaine
Ryan R. Sloane
Jeannette Sloniowski
Cheryl A. Smith

Kyle Smith
John Smolenski
Irvin D. Solomon
Geri Speace
Andrew Spieldenner
tova stabin
Scott Stabler
Jon Sterngrass
Roger W. Stump
Bob Sullivan
Lauren Ann Supance
Marc R. Sykes

Midori Takagi
Candida Taylor
Scott Thill
Robert Thompson
Stephen L. Thompson
Rosemarie Garland Thomson
Jan Todd
Terry Todd
John Tomasic
Warren Tormey
Grant Tracey
David Trevino
Marcella Bush Trevino
Scott Tribble
Tom Trinchera
Nicholas A. Turse

Anthony Ubelhor
Daryl Umberger

Rob Van Kranenburg
Robert VanWynsberghe
Colby Vargas

Sue Walker
Lori C. Walters
Nancy Lan-Jy Wang
Adam Wathen
Laural Weintraub
Jon Weisberger
David B. Welky
Christopher W. Wells
Celia White
Christopher S. Wilson
David B. Wilson
Kristi M. Wilson
Jeff Wiltse
Wendy Woloson
David E. Woodward
Bradford W. Wright

Sharon Yablon
Daniel Francis Yezbick
Stephen D. Youngkin

Kristal Brent Zook

LIST OF ENTRIES

A&R Men/Women
Aaron, Hank
AARP (American Association
  for Retired Persons)
ABBA
Abbey, Edward
Abbott and Costello
Abdul-Jabbar, Kareem
Abortion
Abstract Expressionism
Academy Awards
AC/DC
Ace, Johnny
Acker, Kathy
Acupuncture
Adams, Ansel
Addams, Jane
Addams Family, The
Adderley, Cannonball
Adidas
Adler, Renata
*Adventures of Ozzie and
  Harriet, The*
Advertising
Advice Columns
Advocate, The
Aerobics
Aerosmith
African American Press
African Queen, The
Agassi, Andre
Agents
AIDS
Ailey, Alvin
Air Travel
Airplane!
Alabama
Alaska-Yukon Exposition
  (Seattle, 1909)
Albert, Marv
Album-Oriented Rock
Alda, Alan
Ali, Muhammad
Alice
Alien
Alka Seltzer
All About Eve
All in the Family
All My Children
All Quiet on the Western Front
Allen, Steve
Allen, Woody
Allison, Luther
Allman Brothers Band, The
Ally McBeal

Alpert, Herb, and the
  Tijuana Brass
Altamont
Alternative Country Music
Alternative Press
Alternative Rock
Altman, Robert
Amazing Stories
American Bandstand
American Girls Series
American Gothic
American Graffiti
American International Pictures
American Mercury
American Museum of Natural
  History
Amos 'n' Andy Show, The
Amsterdam, Morey
Amtrak
Amusement Parks
Amway
Anderson, Marian
Anderson, Sherwood
Andretti, Mario
Andrews Sisters, The
Androgyny
Andy Griffith Show, The
Andy Hardy
Angell, Roger
Angelou, Maya
Animal House
Animated Films
Anita Hill-Clarence Thomas
  Senate Hearings
Anka, Paul
*Anne Frank: The Diary of a
  Young Girl*
Annie
Annie Get Your Gun
Annie Hall
Another World
Anthony, Piers
Aparicio, Luis
Apocalypse Now
Apollo Missions
Apollo Theatre
Apple Computer
Arbuckle, Fatty
Archie Comics
Arden, Elizabeth
Argosy
Arizona Highways
Arledge, Roone
Armani, Giorgio
Armed Forces Radio Service
Armory Show

Armstrong, Henry
Armstrong, Louis
Army-McCarthy Hearings
Arnaz, Desi
Arrow Collar Man
Arthur, Bea
Arthurian Legend
As the World Turns
Ashcan School
Ashe, Arthur
Asimov, Isaac
Asner, Ed
Astaire, Fred, and Ginger
  Rogers
Astounding Science Fiction
Astrology
AT&T
A-Team, The
Athletic Model Guild
Atkins, Chet
Atlantic City
Atlantic Monthly
Atlantic Records
Atlas, Charles
Auerbach, Red
Aunt Jemima
Automobile
Autry, Gene
Avalon, Frankie
Avedon, Richard
Avengers, The
Avery, Tex
Avon
Aykroyd, Dan

''B'' Movies
Babar
Baby Boomers
Babyface
Bacall, Lauren
Bach, Richard
Back to the Future
Bad News Bears, The
Baez, Joan
Bagels
Baker, Josephine
Baker, Ray Stannard
Bakker, Jim and Tammy Faye
Balanchine, George
Baldwin, James
Ball, Lucille
Ballard, Hank
Ballet
Bambaataa, Afrika
Band, The

Bara, Theda
Baraka, Amiri
Barbecue
Barber, Red
Barbershop Quartets
Barbie
Barker, Clive
Barkley, Charles
Barney and Friends
Barney Miller
Barry, Dave
Barry, Lynda
Barrymore, John
Barton, Bruce
Baryshnikov, Mikhail
Baseball
Baseball Cards
Basie, Count
Basketball
Bathhouses
Batman
Baum, L. Frank
Bay, Mel
Bay of Pigs Invasion
Baywatch
Bazooka Joe
Beach Boys, The
Beach, Rex
Beanie Babies
Beastie Boys, The
Beat Generation
Beatles, The
Beatty, Warren
Beau Geste
Beauty Queens
Beavers, Louise
Beavis and Butthead
Bee Gees, The
Beer
Beiderbecke, Bix
Belafonte, Harry
Bell Telephone Hour, The
Bellbottoms
Belushi, John
Ben Casey
Bench, Johnny
Benchley, Robert
Ben-Hur
Benneton
Bennett, Tony
Benny Hill Show, The
Benny, Jack
Bergen, Candice
Bergen, Edgar
Bergman, Ingmar
Bergman, Ingrid
Berkeley, Busby
Berle, Milton
Berlin, Irving
Bernhard, Sandra

Bernstein, Leonard
Berra, Yogi
Berry, Chuck
Best Years of Our Lives, The
Bestsellers
Better Homes and Gardens
Betty Boop
Betty Crocker
Beulah
Beverly Hillbillies, The
Beverly Hills 90210
Bewitched
Bicycling
Big Apple, The
Big Bands
Big Bopper
Big Little Books
Big Sleep, The
Bigfoot
Bilingual Education
Billboards
Bionic Woman, The
Bird, Larry
Birkenstocks
Birth of a Nation, The
Birthing Practices
Black, Clint
Black Mask
Black Panthers
Black Sabbath
Black Sox Scandal
Blackboard Jungle, The
Blackface Minstrelsy
Blacklisting
Blade Runner
Blades, Ruben
Blanc, Mel
Bland, Bobby Blue
Blass, Bill
Blaxploitation Films
Blob, The
Blockbusters
Blondie (comic strip)
Blondie (rock band)
Bloom County
Blount, Roy, Jr.
Blue Velvet
Blueboy
Bluegrass
Blues
Blues Brothers, The
Blume, Judy
Bly, Robert
Board Games
Boat People
Bob and Ray
Bobbsey Twins, The
Bobby Socks
Bochco, Steven
Body Decoration

Bodybuilding
Bogart, Humphrey
Bok, Edward
Bomb, The
Bombeck, Erma
Bon Jovi
Bonanza
Bonnie and Clyde
Booker T. and the MG's
Book-of-the-Month Club
Boone, Pat
Borge, Victor
Borscht Belt
Boston Celtics, The
Boston Garden
Boston Marathon
Boston Strangler
Boston Symphony Orchestra, The
Bouton, Jim
Bow, Clara
Bowie, David
Bowling
Boxing
Boy Scouts of America
Bra
Bradbury, Ray
Bradley, Bill
Bradshaw, Terry
Brady Bunch, The
Brand, Max
Brando, Marlon
Brat Pack
Brautigan, Richard
Breakfast at Tiffany's
Breakfast Club, The
Breast Implants
Brenda Starr
Brice, Fanny
Brideshead Revisited
Bridge
Bridge on the River Kwai, The
*Bridges of Madison
     County, The*
Brill Building
Bringing Up Baby
Brinkley, David
British Invasion
Broadway
Brokaw, Tom
Bronson, Charles
Brooklyn Dodgers, The
Brooks, Garth
Brooks, Gwendolyn
Brooks, James L.
Brooks, Louise
Brooks, Mel
Brothers, Dr. Joyce
Brown, James
Brown, Jim
Brown, Les

Brown, Paul
Browne, Jackson
Brownie Cameras
Brubeck, Dave
Bruce, Lenny
Bryant, Paul "Bear"
Brynner, Yul
Bubblegum Rock
Buck, Pearl S.
Buck Rogers
Buckley, William F., Jr.
Buckwheat Zydeco
Budweiser
Buffalo Springfield
Buffett, Jimmy
Bugs Bunny
Bumper Stickers
Bundy, Ted
Bungalow
Burger King
Burlesque
Burma-Shave
Burnett, Carol
Burns, George, and Gracie
    Allen
Burns, Ken
Burr, Raymond
Burroughs, Edgar Rice
Burroughs, William S.
Buster Brown
*Butch Cassidy and the
    Sundance Kid*
Butkus, Dick
Butler, Octavia E.
Butterbeans and Susie
Buttons, Red
Byrds, The

Cabbage Patch Kids
Cable TV
Cadillac
Caesar, Sid
Cagney and Lacey
Cagney, James
Cahan, Abraham
Cakewalks
Caldwell, Erskine
Calloway, Cab
Calvin and Hobbes
Camacho, Héctor "Macho"
Camelot
Camp
Campbell, Glen
Campbell, Naomi
Camping
Cancer
Candid Camera
Caniff, Milton
Canova, Judy
Canseco, Jose

Cantor, Eddie
Capital Punishment
Capone, Al
Capote, Truman
Capra, Frank
Captain America
Captain Kangaroo
Captain Marvel
Car 54, Where Are You?
Car Coats
Caray, Harry
Carey, Mariah
Carlin, George
Carlton, Steve
Carmichael, Hoagy
Carnegie, Dale
Carnegie Hall
Carpenters, The
Carr, John Dickson
Cars, The
Carson, Johnny
Carter Family, The
Caruso, Enrico
Carver, Raymond
Casablanca
Cash, Johnny
Caspar Milquetoast
Cassette Tape
Cassidy, David
Castaneda, Carlos
Castle, Vernon and Irene
Castro, The
Casual Friday
Catalog Houses
Catch-22
Catcher in the Rye, The
Cather, Willa
Cathy
Cats
Cavett, Dick
CB Radio
*CBS Radio Mystery
    Theater, The*
Celebrity
Celebrity Caricature
Cemeteries
Central Park
Century 21 Exposition
    (Seattle, 1962)
Century of Progress
    (Chicago, 1933)
Challenger Disaster
Chamberlain, Wilt
Chandler, Raymond
Chandu the Magician
Chanel, Coco
Chaplin, Charlie
Charles, Ray
Charlie Chan
Charlie McCarthy

Charlie's Angels
Charm Bracelets
Chase, Chevy
Chautauqua Institution
Chavez, Cesar
Chavis, Boozoo
Chayefsky, Paddy
Checker, Chubby
Cheech and Chong
Cheerleading
Cheers
Chemise
Chenier, Clifton
Cherry Ames
Chessman, Caryl
Chicago Bears, The
Chicago Bulls, The
Chicago Cubs, The
Chicago Jazz
Chicago Seven, The
Child, Julia
Child Stars
China Syndrome, The
Chinatown
Chipmunks, The
Choose-Your-Own-Ending
    Books
Christie, Agatha
Christmas
Christo
Chrysler Building
Chuck D
Chun King
Church Socials
Cigarettes
Circus
Cisneros, Sandra
Citizen Kane
City Lights
City of Angels, The
Civil Disobedience
Civil Rights Movement
Civil War Reenactors
Claiborne, Liz
Clairol Hair Coloring
Clancy, Tom
Clapton, Eric
Clark, Dick
Clarke, Arthur C.
Clemente, Roberto
Cleopatra
Clift, Montgomery
Cline, Patsy
Clinton, George
Clockwork Orange, A
Clooney, Rosemary
*Close Encounters of the
    Third Kind*
Closet, The
CNN

Cobb, Ty
Coca, Imogene
Coca-Cola
Cocaine/Crack
Cocktail Parties
Cody, Buffalo Bill, and his
    Wild West Show
Coffee
Cohan, George M.
Colbert, Claudette
Cold War
Cole, Nat ''King''
College Fads
College Football
Collins, Albert
Coltrane, John
Columbo
Columbo, Russ
Comic Books
Comics
Comics Code Authority
Coming Out
Commodores, The
Communes
Communism
Community Media
Community Theatre
Como, Perry
Compact Discs
Concept Album
Conceptual Art
Condé Nast
Condoms
Coney Island
Confession Magazines
Coniff, Ray
Connors, Jimmy
Consciousness Raising Groups
Conspiracy Theories
Consumer Reports
Consumerism
Contemporary Christian Music
Convertible
Conway, Tim
Cooke, Sam
Cooper, Alice
Cooper, Gary
Cooperstown, New York
Coors
Copland, Aaron
Corbett, James J.
Corman, Roger
Corvette
Corwin, Norman
Cosby, Bill
Cosby Show, The
Cosell, Howard
Cosmopolitan
Costas, Bob
Costello, Elvis

Costner, Kevin
Cotten, Joseph
Cotton Club, The
Coué, Emile
Coughlin, Father Charles E.
Country Gentlemen
Country Music
Cousteau, Jacques
Covey, Stephen
Cowboy Look, The
Cox, Ida
Crawford, Cindy
Crawford, Joan
Cray, Robert
Creationism
Credit Cards
Creedence Clearwater Revival
Crichton, Michael
Crime Does Not Pay
Crinolines
Crisis, The
Croce, Jim
Cronkite, Walter
Crosby, Bing
Crosby, Stills, and Nash
Crossword Puzzles
Cruise, Tom
Crumb, Robert
Crystal, Billy
Cukor, George
Cullen, Countee
Cult Films
Cults
Cunningham, Merce
Curious George
Currier and Ives

Dahmer, Jeffrey
Dallas
Dallas Cowboys, The
Daly, Tyne
Dana, Bill
Dance Halls
Dandridge, Dorothy
Daniels, Charlie
*Daredevil, the Man
    Without Fear*
Dark Shadows
Darrow, Clarence
Davis, Bette
Davis, Miles
Davy Crockett
Day, Doris
Day the Earth Stood Still, The
Days of Our Lives
Daytime Talk Shows
Daytona 500
DC Comics
De La Hoya, Oscar
De Niro, Robert

Dead Kennedys, The
Dean, James
Death of a Salesman
Debs, Eugene V.
Debutantes
Deer Hunter, The
DeGeneres, Ellen
Del Río, Dolores
DeMille, Cecil B.
Dempsey, Jack
Denishawn
Denver, John
Department Stores
Depression
Derleth, August
Detective Fiction
Detroit Tigers, The
Devers, Gail
Devo
Diamond, Neil
Diana, Princess of Wales
DiCaprio, Leonardo
Dick and Jane Readers
Dick, Philip K.
Dick Tracy
Dickinson, Angie
Diddley, Bo
Didion, Joan
Didrikson, Babe
Dieting
Dietrich, Marlene
Diff'rent Strokes
Dilbert
Dillard, Annie
Diller, Phyllis
Dillinger, John
DiMaggio, Joe
Dime Novels
Dime Stores/Woolworths
Diners
Dionne Quintuplets
Dirty Dozen, The
Disability
Disaster Movies
Disc Jockeys
Disco
Disney (Walt Disney Company)
Ditka, Mike
Divine
Divorce
Dixieland
Do the Right Thing
Dobie Gillis
Doby, Larry
Doc Martens
Doc Savage
Doctor Who
Doctor Zhivago
Doctorow, E. L.
Docudrama

Do-It-Yourself Improvement
Domino, Fats
Donahue, Phil
Donovan
Doobie Brothers, The
Doonesbury
Doors, The
Doo-wop Music
Dorsey, Jimmy
Dorsey, Tommy
Double Indemnity
Douglas, Lloyd C.
Douglas, Melvyn
Douglas, Mike
Downs, Hugh
Doyle, Arthur Conan
Dr. Jekyll and Mr. Hyde
Dr. Kildare
Dr. Seuss
*Dr. Strangelove or: How I
    Learned to Stop Worrying
    and Love the Bomb*
Dracula
Draft, The
Drag
Drag Racing
Dragnet
Dragon Lady
Dream Team
Dreiser, Theodore
Drifters, The
Drive-In Theater
Drug War
Du Bois, W. E. B.
Duck Soup
Dukes of Hazzard, The
Duncan, Isadora
Dungeons and Dragons
Dunkin' Donuts
Dunne, Irene
Duran, Roberto
Durbin, Deanna
Durocher, Leo
Duvall, Robert
Dyer, Wayne
Dykes to Watch Out For
Dylan, Bob
Dynasty

Eames, Charles and Ray
Earth Day
Earth Shoes
Eastwood, Clint
Easy Rider
Ebbets Field
Ebony
EC Comics
Eckstine, Billy
Eco-Terrorism
Eddy, Duane

Eddy, Mary Baker
Eddy, Nelson
Edge of Night, The
Edison, Thomas Alva
Edsel, The
Edwards, James
Edwards, Ralph
Eight-Track Tape
Einstein, Albert
Eisner, Will
El Teatro Campesino
El Vez
Electric Appliances
Electric Guitar
Electric Trains
Elizondo, Hector
Elkins, Aaron
Ellington, Duke
Ellis, Brett Easton
Ellis, Perry
Ellison, Harlan
Elway, John
E-mail
Emmy Awards
Empire State Building
Environmentalism
Equal Rights Amendment
ER
Erdrich, Louise
Erector Sets
Ertegun, Ahmet
Erving, Julius "Dr. J"
Escher, M. C.
ESPN
Esquire
est
E.T. The Extra-Terrestrial
Etiquette Columns
Evangelism
Everly Brothers, The
Everson, Cory
Evert, Chris
Existentialism
Exorcist, The

Fabares, Shelley
Fabian
Fabio
Facelifts
Factor, Max
Fadiman, Clifton
Fail-Safe
Fairbanks, Douglas, Jr.
Fairbanks, Douglas, Sr.
Fallout Shelters
Family Circle
Family Circus, The
Family Matters
Family Reunions
Family Ties

Fan Magazines
Fantasia
Fantastic Four, The
Fantasy Island
Far Side, The
Fargo
Farm Aid
Farr, Jamie
Fast Food
Fatal Attraction
Father Divine
Father Knows Best
Father's Day
Faulkner, William
Fauset, Jessie Redmon
Fawcett, Farrah
Fawlty Towers
FBI (Federal Bureau of
    Investigation)
Feliciano, José
Felix the Cat
Fellini, Federico
Feminism
Fenway Park
Ferrante and Teicher
Fetchit, Stepin
Fibber McGee and Molly
Fiddler on the Roof
Fidrych, Mark "Bird"
Field and Stream
Field of Dreams
Field, Sally
Fields, W. C.
Fierstein, Harvey
Fifties, The
Film Noir
Firearms
Firesign Theatre
Fischer, Bobby
Fisher, Eddie
Fisher-Price Toys
Fisk, Carlton
Fistful of Dollars, A
Fitzgerald, Ella
Fitzgerald, F. Scott
Flack, Roberta
Flag Burning
Flag Clothing
Flagpole Sitting
Flappers
Flash Gordon
Flashdance Style
Flatt, Lester
Flea Markets
Fleetwood Mac
Fleming, Ian
Fleming, Peggy
Flintstones, The
Flipper
Florida Vacations

Flying Nun, The
Flynn, Errol
Foggy Mountain Boys, The
Folk Music
Folkways Records
Follett, Ken
Fonda, Henry
Fonda, Jane
Fonteyn, Margot
Ford, Glenn
Ford, Harrison
Ford, Henry
Ford, John
Ford Motor Company
Ford, Tennessee Ernie
Ford, Whitey
Foreman, George
Forrest Gump
Forsyth, Frederick
Fortune
42nd Street
Fosse, Bob
Foster, Jodie
Fourth of July Celebrations
Foxx, Redd
Foyt, A. J.
Francis, Arlene
Francis, Connie
Francis the Talking Mule
Frankenstein
Franklin, Aretha
Franklin, Bonnie
Frasier
Frawley, William
Frazier, Joe
Frazier, Walt "Clyde"
Freak Shows
Freaks
Frederick's of Hollywood
Free Agency
Free Speech Movement
Freed, Alan "Moondog"
Freedom Rides
French Connection, The
French Fries
Freud, Sigmund
Friday, Nancy
Friday the 13th
Friedman, Kinky
Friends
Frisbee
Frizzell, Lefty
From Here to Eternity
Frost, Robert
Frosty the Snowman
Frozen Entrées
Fu Manchu
Fugitive, The
Fuller, Buckminster
Fundamentalism

Funicello, Annette
Funk
Fusco, Coco

Gable, Clark
Gambling
Game Shows
Gammons, Peter
Gangs
Gangsta Rap
Gap, The
Garbo, Greta
Gardner, Ava
Garfield, John
Garland, Judy
Garner, James
Garvey, Marcus
Garvey, Steve
Gas Stations
Gated Communities
Gay and Lesbian Marriage
Gay and Lesbian Press
Gay Liberation Movement
Gay Men
Gaye, Marvin
Gehrig, Lou
General, The
General Hospital
General Motors
Generation X
Gentlemen Prefer Blondes
Gere, Richard
Gernsback, Hugo
Gertie the Dinosaur
Get Smart
Ghettos
GI Joe
Giant
Gibson, Althea
Gibson, Bob
Gibson Girl
Gibson, Mel
Gibson, William
Gifford, Frank
Gillespie, Dizzy
Gilligan's Island
Ginny Dolls
Ginsberg, Allen
Girl Groups
Girl Scouts
Gish, Dorothy
Gish, Lillian
Glass Menagerie, The
Gleason, Jackie
Glitter Rock
Gnagy, Jon
Godfather, The
Godfrey, Arthur
Godzilla
Gold, Mike

Goldberg, Rube
Goldberg, Whoopi
Golden Books
Golden Gate Bridge
Golden Girls, The
Goldwyn, Samuel
Golf
Gone with the Wind
Good Housekeeping
*Good, the Bad, and the
     Ugly, The*
Good Times
Goodbye, Columbus
Gooden, Dwight
GoodFellas
Goodman, Benny
Goodson, Mark
Gordy, Berry
Gospel Music
Gossip Columns
Goth
Gotti, John
Grable, Betty
Graceland
Graduate, The
Graffiti
Grafton, Sue
Graham, Bill
Graham, Billy
Graham, Martha
Grandmaster Flash
Grand Ole Opry
Grant, Amy
Grant, Cary
Grapes of Wrath, The
Grateful Dead, The
Gray Panthers
Great Depression
Great Train Robbery, The
Greb, Harry
Greed
Greeley, Andrew
Green, Al
Green Bay Packers, The
Green Lantern
Greenberg, Hank
Greene, Graham
Greenpeace
Greenwich Village
Greeting Cards
Gregory, Dick
Gretzky, Wayne
Grey, Zane
Greyhound Buses
Grier, Pam
Griffin, Merv
Griffith, D. W.
Griffith, Nanci
Grimek, John
Grisham, John

Grits
Grizzard, Lewis
Groening, Matt
Grunge
Grusin, Dave
Guaraldi, Vince
Guardian Angels, The
Gucci
Guiding Light
Gulf War
Gunsmoke
Guthrie, Arlo
Guthrie, Woodie
Guy, Buddy
Gymnastics

Hackett, Buddy
Hackman, Gene
Haggard, Merle
Hagler, Marvelous Marvin
Haight-Ashbury
Hair
Hairstyles
Halas, George ''Papa Bear''
Haley, Alex
Haley, Bill
Hall and Oates
Hallmark Hall of Fame
Halloween
Halston
Hamburger
Hamill, Dorothy
Hammett, Dashiell
Hancock, Herbie
Handy, W. C.
Hanks, Tom
Hanna-Barbera
Hansberry, Lorraine
Happy Days
Happy Hour
Hard-Boiled Detective Fiction
Harding, Tonya
Hardy Boys, The
Hare Krishna
Haring, Keith
Harlem Globetrotters, The
Harlem Renaissance
Harlequin Romances
Harley-Davidson
Harlow, Jean
Harmonica Bands
Harper, Valerie
Harper's
Hate Crimes
Havlicek, John
Hawaii Five-0
Hawkins, Coleman
Hawks, Howard
Hayward, Susan
Hayworth, Rita

Hearst, Patty
Hearst, William Randolph
Heavy Metal
Hee Haw
Hefner, Hugh
Hellman, Lillian
Hello, Dolly!
Hell's Angels
Hemingway, Ernest
Hemlines
Henderson, Fletcher
Hendrix, Jimi
Henry Aldrich
Henson, Jim
Hep Cats
Hepburn, Audrey
Hepburn, Katharine
Herbert, Frank
*Hercules: The Legendary
    Journeys*
Herman, Woody
Herpes
Hersey, John
Hess, Joan
Heston, Charlton
Higginson, Major Henry Lee
High Noon
Highway System
Hijuelos, Oscar
Hiking
Hill Street Blues
Hillerman, Tony
Himes, Chester
Hindenberg, The
Hippies
Hirschfeld, Albert
Hispanic Magazine
Hiss, Alger
Hitchcock, Alfred
Hite, Shere
Hockey
Hoffman, Abbie
Hoffman, Dustin
Hogan, Ben
Hogan, Hulk
Hogan's Heroes
Holbrook, Hal
Holden, William
Holiday, Billie
Holiday Inns
Holliday, Judy
Holly, Buddy
Hollywood
Hollywood Squares
Hollywood Ten, The
Holocaust
Holyfield, Evander
Home Improvement
Home Shopping Network/QVC
Honeymooners, The

Hooker, John Lee
Hoosiers
Hoover Dam
Hoover, J. Edgar
Hopalong Cassidy
Hope, Bob
Hopkins, Sam "Lightnin'"
Hopper, Dennis
Hopper, Edward
Hopscotch
Horne, Lena
Horror Movies
Hot Dogs
Hot Pants
Hot Rods
Houdini, Harry
Houston, Whitney
How the West Was Won
Howdy Doody Show, The
Howe, Gordie
Howlin' Wolf
Hubbard, L. Ron
Hudson, Rock
Hughes, Howard
Hughes, Langston
Hula Hoop
Hull, Bobby
Hunt, Helen
Hunter, Tab
Huntley, Chet
Hurston, Zora Neale
Hustler
Huston, John
Hutton, Ina Ray

I Dream of Jeannie
I Love a Mystery
I Love Lucy
I Spy
I Was a Teenage Werewolf
Iacocca, Lee
IBM (International Business
    Machines)
Ice Cream Cone
Ice Shows
Ice-T
In Living Color
Incredible Hulk, The
Independence Day
Indian, The
Indianapolis 500
Industrial Design
Ink Spots, The
Inner Sanctum Mysteries
International Male Catalog, The
Internet, The
Intolerance
Invisible Man
Iran Contra
Iron Maiden

Ironman Triathlon
Irving, John
It Happened One Night
It's a Wonderful Life
It's Garry Shandling's Show
Ives, Burl
Ivy League

J. Walter Thompson
Jack Armstrong
Jackson Five, The
Jackson, Jesse
Jackson, Mahalia
Jackson, Michael
Jackson, Reggie
Jackson, Shirley
Jackson, "Shoeless" Joe
Jakes, John
James Bond Films
James, Elmore
James, Harry
Japanese American
    Internment Camps
Jaws
Jazz
Jazz Singer, The
Jeans
Jeep
Jefferson Airplane/Starship
Jeffersons, The
Jell-O
Jennings, Peter
Jennings, Waylon
Jeopardy!
Jessel, George
Jesus Christ Superstar
Jet
Jet Skis
Jewish Defense League
JFK (The Movie)
Jogging
John Birch Society
John, Elton
Johns, Jasper
Johnson, Blind Willie
Johnson, Earvin "Magic"
Johnson, Jack
Johnson, James Weldon
Johnson, Michael
Johnson, Robert
Jolson, Al
Jones, Bobby
Jones, George
Jones, Jennifer
Jones, Tom
Jonestown
Jong, Erica
Joplin, Janis
Joplin, Scott
Jordan, Louis

Jordan, Michael
Joy of Cooking
Joy of Sex, The
Joyner, Florence Griffith
Joyner-Kersee, Jackie
Judas Priest
Judge
Judson, Arthur
Judy Bolton
Juke Boxes
Julia
Juliá, Raúl
Jurassic Park
Juvenile Delinquency

Kahn, Roger
Kaltenborn, Hans von
Kansas City Jazz
Kantor, MacKinlay
Karan, Donna
Karloff, Boris
Kasem, Casey
Kate & Allie
Katzenjammer Kids, The
Kaufman, Andy
Kaye, Danny
Keaton, Buster
Keillor, Garrison
Keitel, Harvey
Kelley, David E.
Kelly Bag
Kelly, Gene
Kelly Girls
Kelly, Grace
Kennedy Assassination
Kent State Massacre
Kentucky Derby
Kentucky Fried Chicken
Kern, Jerome
Kerrigan, Nancy
Kershaw, Doug
Kesey, Ken
Kewpie Dolls
Key West
Keystone Kops, The
King, Albert
King, B. B.
King, Billie Jean
King, Carole
King, Freddie
King Kong
King, Larry
King, Martin Luther, Jr.
King, Rodney
King, Stephen
Kingston, Maxine Hong
Kingston Trio, The
Kinison, Sam
Kinsey, Dr. Alfred C.
Kirby, Jack

KISS
Kitsch
Kiwanis
Klein, Calvin
Klein, Robert
Kmart
Knievel, Evel
Knight, Bobby
Knots Landing
Kodak
Kojak
Koontz, Dean R.
Koresh, David, and the Branch
    Davidians
Korman, Harvey
Kosinski, Jerzy
Kotzwinkle, William
Koufax, Sandy
Kovacs, Ernie
Kraft Television Theatre
Krantz, Judith
Krassner, Paul
Krazy Kat
Krupa, Gene
Ku Klux Klan
Kubrick, Stanley
Kudzu
Kuhn, Bowie
Kukla, Fran, and Ollie
Kung Fu
Kwan, Michelle

L. A. Law
L. L. Cool J.
"La Bamba"
Labor Unions
Lacoste Shirts
Ladd, Alan
Laetrile
Lahr, Bert
Lake, Ricki
Lake, Veronica
LaLanne, Jack
Lamarr, Hedy
LaMotta, Jake
Lamour, Dorothy
L'Amour, Louis
Lancaster, Burt
Landon, Michael
Landry, Tom
Lang, Fritz
lang, k.d.
Lansky, Meyer
Lardner, Ring
Larry Sanders Show, The
LaRussa, Tony
Las Vegas
Lasorda, Tommy
Lassie
Late Great Planet Earth, The

Latin Jazz
Laugh-In
Lauper, Cyndi
Laura
Laurel and Hardy
Lauren, Ralph
Laver, Rod
Laverne and Shirley
Lavin, Linda
Lawn Care/Gardening
Lawrence of Arabia
Lawrence, Vicki
La-Z-Boy Loungers
le Carré, John
Le Guin, Ursula K.
Leachman, Cloris
Leadbelly
League of Their Own, A
Lear, Norman
Leary, Timothy
Least Heat Moon, William
Leather Jacket
Leave It to Beaver
Led Zeppelin
Lee, Bruce
Lee, Gypsy Rose
Lee, Peggy
Lee, Spike
Lee, Stan
Legos
Lehrer, Tom
Leisure Suit
Leisure Time
LeMond, Greg
L'Engle, Madeleine
Lennon, John
Leno, Jay
Leonard, Benny
Leonard, Elmore
Leonard, Sugar Ray
Leone, Sergio
Leopold and Loeb
Les Miserables
Lesbianism
*Let Us Now Praise
    Famous Men*
Let's Pretend
Letterman, David
Levin, Meyer
Levi's
Levittown
Lewinsky, Monica
Lewis, C. S.
Lewis, Carl
Lewis, Jerry
Lewis, Jerry Lee
Lewis, Sinclair
Liberace
Liberty
Lichtenstein, Roy

Liebovitz, Annie
Life
Life of Riley, The
Like Water for Chocolate
Li'l Abner
Limbaugh, Rush
Lincoln Center for the
    Performing Arts
Lindbergh, Anne Morrow
Lindbergh, Charles
Linkletter, Art
Lion King, The
Lionel Trains
Lippmann, Walter
Lipstick
Liston, Sonny
Little Black Dress
Little Blue Books
Little League
Little Magazines
Little Orphan Annie
Little Richard
Live Television
L.L. Bean, Inc.
Lloyd Webber, Andrew
Loafers
Locke, Alain
Lolita
Lollapalooza
Lombard, Carole
Lombardi, Vince
Lombardo, Guy
London, Jack
Lone Ranger, The
Long, Huey
Long, Shelley
Long-Playing Record
Loos, Anita
López, Nancy
Lorre, Peter
Los Angeles Lakers, The
Los Lobos
Lost Weekend, The
Lottery
Louis, Joe
Louisiana Purchase Exposition
Louisville Slugger
Love Boat, The
Love, Courtney
Lovecraft, H. P.
Low Riders
Loy, Myrna
LSD
Lubitsch, Ernst
Lucas, George
Luce, Henry
Luciano, Lucky
Ludlum, Robert
Lugosi, Bela
Lunceford, Jimmie

Lupino, Ida
LuPone, Patti
Lynch, David
Lynching
Lynn, Loretta
Lynyrd Skynyrd

Ma Perkins
Mabley, Moms
MacDonald, Jeanette
MacDonald, John D.
Macfadden, Bernarr
MacMurray, Fred
Macon, Uncle Dave
Macy's
MAD Magazine
Madden, John
Made-for-Television Movies
Madonna
Mafia/Organized Crime
Magnificent Seven, The
Magnum, P.I.
Mah-Jongg
Mailer, Norman
Malcolm X
Mall of America
Malls
Maltese Falcon, The
Mamas and the Papas, The
Mamet, David
Man from U.N.C.L.E., The
*Man Who Shot Liberty
    Valance, The*
Manchurian Candidate, The
Mancini, Henry
Manhattan Transfer
Manilow, Barry
Mansfield, Jayne
Manson, Charles
Mantle, Mickey
Manufactured Homes
Mapplethorpe, Robert
March on Washington
Marching Bands
Marciano, Rocky
Marcus Welby, M.D.
Mardi Gras
Mariachi Music
Marichal, Juan
Marie, Rose
Marijuana
Maris, Roger
Marlboro Man
Marley, Bob
Married . . . with Children
Marshall, Garry
Martha and the Vandellas
Martin, Dean
Martin, Freddy
Martin, Quinn

Martin, Steve
Martini
Marvel Comics
Marx Brothers, The
Marx, Groucho
Mary Hartman, Mary Hartman
Mary Kay Cosmetics
Mary Poppins
Mary Tyler Moore Show, The
Mary Worth
*M*A*S*H*
Mason, Jackie
Mass Market Magazine
    Revolution
Masses, The
Masterpiece Theatre
Masters and Johnson
Masters Golf Tournament
Mathis, Johnny
Mattingly, Don
Maude
Maupin, Armistead
Maus
Max, Peter
Mayer, Louis B.
Mayfield, Curtis
Mayfield, Percy
Mays, Willie
McBain, Ed
McCaffrey, Anne
McCall's Magazine
McCarthyism
McCartney, Paul
McCay, Winsor
McClure's
McCoy, Horace
McCrea, Joel
McDaniel, Hattie
McDonald's
McEnroe, John
McEntire, Reba
McGwire, Mark
McHale's Navy
McKay, Claude
McKuen, Rod
McLish, Rachel
McLuhan, Marshall
McMurtry, Larry
McPherson, Aimee Semple
McQueen, Butterfly
McQueen, Steve
Me Decade
Meadows, Audrey
Mean Streets
Media Feeding Frenzies
Medicine Shows
Meet Me in St. Louis
Mellencamp, John
Mencken, H. L.
Mendoza, Lydia

Men's Movement
Merton, Thomas
Metalious, Grace
Metropolis
Metropolitan Museum of Art
MGM (Metro-Goldwyn-Mayer)
Miami Vice
Michener, James
Mickey Mouse Club, The
Microsoft
Middletown
Midler, Bette
Midnight Cowboy
Mildred Pierce
Militias
Milk, Harvey
Millay, Edna St. Vincent
Miller, Arthur
Miller Beer
Miller, Glenn
Miller, Henry
Miller, Roger
Milli Vanilli
Million Man March
Milton Bradley
Minimalism
Minivans
Minnelli, Vincente
Minoso, Minnie
Minstrel Shows
Miranda, Carmen
Miranda Warning
Miss America Pageant
Mission: Impossible
Mister Ed
Mister Rogers' Neighborhood
Mitchell, Joni
Mitchell, Margaret
Mitchum, Robert
Mix, Tom
Mod
Mod Squad, The
Model T
Modern Dance
Modern Maturity
Modern Times
Modernism
Momaday, N. Scott
Monday Night Football
Monkees, The
Monopoly
Monroe, Bill
Monroe, Earl "The Pearl"
Monroe, Marilyn
Montalban, Ricardo
Montana, Joe
Montana, Patsy
Monty Python's Flying Circus
Moonies/Reverend Sun
    Myung Moon

Moonlighting
Moore, Demi
Moore, Michael
Moral Majority
Moreno, Rita
Mork & Mindy
Morris, Mark
Morrissette, Alanis
Morrison, Toni
Morrison, Van
Morse, Carlton E.
Morton, Jelly Roll
Mosley, Walter
Moss, Kate
Mother's Day
Mötley Crüe
Motley, Willard
Motown
Mount Rushmore
Mountain Biking
Mouseketeers, The
Movie Palaces
Movie Stars
Mr. Dooley
Mr. Smith Goes to Washington
Mr. Wizard
Ms.
MTV
Muckraking
Multiculturalism
Mummy, The
Muni, Paul
Munsey's Magazine
Muppets, The
Murder, She Wrote
Murphy Brown
Murphy, Eddie
Murray, Anne
Murray, Arthur
Murray, Bill
Murray, Lenda
Murrow, Edward R.
Muscle Beach
Muscle Cars
Muscular Christianity
Musical, The
Mutiny on the Bounty
Mutt & Jeff
Muzak
My Darling Clementine
My Fair Lady
My Family/Mi familia
My Lai Massacre
My So Called Life
My Three Sons

Nader, Ralph
Nagel, Patrick
Naismith, James
Namath, Joe

Nancy Drew
NASA
Nation, The
National Basketball
    Association (NBA)
National Collegiate Athletic
    Association (NCAA)
National Enquirer, The
National Football League (NFL)
National Geographic
National Hockey League (NHL)
National Lampoon
National Organization for
    Women (N.O.W.)
National Parks
Natural, The
Natural Born Killers
Nava, Gregory
Navratilova, Martina
Naylor, Gloria
Neckties
Negro Leagues
Neighborhood Watch
Nelson, Ricky
Nelson, Willie
Nerd Look
Network
Networks
New Age Music
New Age Spirituality
New Deal
New Kids on the Block, The
New Left
New Look
New Orleans Rhythm and Blues
New Republic
New Wave Music
New York Knickerbockers, The
New York Mets, The
New York Times, The
New York Yankees, The
New Yorker, The
Newhart, Bob
Newlywed Game, The
Newport Jazz and Folk
    Festivals
Newsweek
Newton, Helmut
Niagara Falls
Nichols, Mike, and Elaine May
Nickelodeons
Nicklaus, Jack
Night of the Living Dead
Nightline
Nike
1980 U.S. Olympic
    Hockey Team
1968 Mexico City Summer
    Olympic Games
Nirvana

Nixon, Agnes
Noloesca, La Chata
Norris, Frank
North by Northwest
Northern Exposure
Novak, Kim
Nureyev, Rudolf
Nylon
NYPD Blue

Oakland Raiders, The
Oates, Joyce Carol
Objectivism/Ayn Rand
O'Brien, Tim
Ochs, Phil
O'Connor, Flannery
Odd Couple, The
O'Donnell, Rosie
O'Keeffe, Georgia
Oklahoma!
Old Navy
Oliphant, Pat
Olivier, Laurence
Olmos, Edward James
Olsen, Tillie
Olympics
Omnibus
On the Road
On the Waterfront
Onassis, Jacqueline Lee Bouvier
    Kennedy
One Day at a Time
*One Flew Over the Cuckoo's
    Nest*
One Man's Family
O'Neal, Shaquille
O'Neill, Eugene
Op Art
Opportunity
Orbison, Roy
Organization Man, The
Original Dixieland Jass
    (Jazz) Band
O'Rourke, P. J.
Orr, Bobby
Osborne Brothers, The
Osbourne, Ozzy
Ouija Boards
Our Gang
Outer Limits, The
Outing
Outline of History, The
Owens, Buck
Owens, Jesse
Oxford Bags

Paar, Jack
Pachucos
Pacino, Al
Paglia, Camille

Paige, Satchel
Paley, Grace
Paley, William S.
Palmer, Arnold
Palmer, Jim
Pants for Women
Pantyhose
Paperbacks
Parades
Paretsky, Sara
Parker Brothers
Parker, Charlie
Parker, Dorothy
Parks, Rosa
Parrish, Maxfield
Parton, Dolly
Partridge Family, The
Patinkin, Mandy
Patton
Paul, Les
Paulsen, Pat
Payton, Walter
Peale, Norman Vincent
Peanuts
Pearl Jam
Pearl, Minnie
Peck, Gregory
Peep Shows
Pee-wee's Playhouse
Pelé
Penn, Irving
Penthouse
People
Peppermint Lounge, The
Pepsi-Cola
Performance Art
Perot, Ross
Perry Mason
Pet Rocks
Peter, Paul, and Mary
Peters, Bernadette
Pets
Petting
Petty, Richard
Peyton Place
Pfeiffer, Michelle
Phantom of the Opera, The
Philadelphia Story, The
Philco Television Playhouse
Phillips, Irna
Phone Sex
Phonograph
Photoplay
Picasso, Pablo
Pickford, Mary
Pill, The
Pink Floyd
Pin-Up, The
Piper, ''Rowdy'' Roddy
Pippen, Scottie

Pittsburgh Steelers, The
Pizza
Place in the Sun, A
Planet of the Apes
Plastic
Plastic Surgery
Plath, Sylvia
Platoon
Playboy
Playgirl
Playhouse 90
Pogo
Pointer Sisters, The
Poitier, Sidney
Polio
Political Bosses
Political Correctness
Pollock, Jackson
Polyester
Pop Art
Pop, Iggy
Pop Music
Pope, The
Popeye
Popsicles
Popular Mechanics
Popular Psychology
Pornography
Porter, Cole
Postcards
Postman Always Rings
    Twice, The
Postmodernism
Potter, Dennis
Powell, Dick
Powell, William
Prang, Louis
Preminger, Otto
Preppy
Presley, Elvis
Price Is Right, The
Price, Reynolds
Price, Vincent
Pride, Charley
Prince
Prince, Hal
Prinze, Freddie
Prisoner, The
Professional Football
Prohibition
Prom
Promise Keepers
Protest Groups
Prozac
Pryor, Richard
Psychedelia
Psychics
Psycho
PTA/PTO (Parent Teacher
    Association/Organization)

Public Enemy
Public Libraries
Public Television (PBS)
Puente, Tito
Pulp Fiction
Pulp Magazines
Punisher, The
Punk
Pynchon, Thomas

Quayle, Dan
Queen, Ellery
Queen for a Day
Queen Latifah
Queer Nation
Quiz Show Scandals

Race Music
Race Riots
Radio
Radio Drama
Radner, Gilda
Raft, George
Raggedy Ann and Raggedy
    Andy
Raging Bull
Ragni, Gerome, and James
    Rado
Raiders of the Lost Ark
Rainey, Gertrude ''Ma''
Rains, Claude
Raitt, Bonnie
Rambo
Ramones, The
Ranch House
Rand, Sally
Rap/Hip Hop
Rather, Dan
Reader's Digest
Reagan, Ronald
Real World, The
Reality Television
Rear Window
Rebel without a Cause
Recycling
Red Scare
Redbook
Redding, Otis
Redford, Robert
Reed, Donna
Reed, Ishmael
Reed, Lou
Reese, Pee Wee
Reeves, Steve
Reggae
Reiner, Carl
Religious Right
R.E.M.
Remington, Frederic
Reno, Don

Renoir, Jean
Replacements, The
Retro Fashion
Reynolds, Burt
Rhythm and Blues
Rice, Grantland
Rice, Jerry
Rich, Charlie
Rigby, Cathy
Riggs, Bobby
Riley, Pat
Ringling Bros., Barnum &
    Bailey Circus
Ripken, Cal, Jr.
Ripley's Believe It Or Not
Rivera, Chita
Rivera, Diego
Rivera, Geraldo
Rivers, Joan
Rizzuto, Phil
Road Rage
Road Runner and Wile E.
    Coyote
Robbins, Tom
Roberts, Jake "The Snake"
Roberts, Julia
Roberts, Nora
Robertson, Oscar
Robertson, Pat
Robeson, Kenneth
Robeson, Paul
Robinson, Edward G.
Robinson, Frank
Robinson, Jackie
Robinson, Smokey
Robinson, Sugar Ray
Rock and Roll
Rock, Chris
Rock Climbing
Rockefeller Family
Rockettes, The
Rockne, Knute
Rockwell, Norman
Rocky
Rocky and Bullwinkle
Rocky Horror Picture
    Show, The
Roddenberry, Gene
Rodeo
Rodgers and Hammerstein
Rodgers and Hart
Rodgers, Jimmie
Rodman, Dennis
Rodriguez, Chi Chi
Roe v. Wade
Rogers, Kenny
Rogers, Roy
Rogers, Will
Rolle, Esther
Roller Coasters

Roller Derby
Rolling Stone
Rolling Stones, The
Romance Novels
Romero, Cesar
Roots
Rose Bowl
Rose, Pete
Roseanne
Rosemary's Baby
Rosenberg, Julius and Ethel
Ross, Diana, and the Supremes
Roswell Incident
Roundtree, Richard
Rouse Company
Route 66
Royko, Mike
Rubik's Cube
*Rudolph the Red-Nosed
    Reindeer*
Run-DMC
Runyon, Damon
RuPaul
Rupp, Adolph
Russell, Bill
Russell, Jane
Russell, Nipsey
Russell, Rosalind
Ruth, Babe
RV
Ryan, Meg
Ryan, Nolan
Rydell, Bobby
Ryder, Winona

Safe Sex
Sagan, Carl
Sahl, Mort
Saks Fifth Avenue
Sales, Soupy
Salsa Music
Salt-n-Pepa
Sam and Dave
Sandburg, Carl
Sanders, Barry
Sandman
Sandow, Eugen
Sanford and Son
Santana
Sarandon, Susan
Saratoga Springs
Sarnoff, David
Sarong
Sassoon, Vidal
Sassy
Satellites
Saturday Evening Post, The
Saturday Morning Cartoons
Saturday Night Fever
Saturday Night Live

Savage, Randy ''Macho Man''
Savoy Ballroom
Schindler's List
Schlatter, George
Schlessinger, Dr. Laura
Schnabel, Julian
Schoolhouse Rock
Schwarzenegger, Arnold
Science Fiction Publishing
Scientific American
Scopes Monkey Trial
Scorsese, Martin
Scott, George C.
Scott, Randolph
Scream
Screwball Comedies
Scribner's
Scruggs, Earl
Sculley, Vin
Sea World
Seals, Son
Search for Tomorrow
Searchers, The
Sears Roebuck Catalogue
Sears Tower
Second City
Sedona, Arizona
Seduction of the Innocent
Seeger, Pete
Seinfeld
Selena
Seles, Monica
Sellers, Peter
Selznick, David O.
Sennett, Mack
Serial Killers
Serling, Rod
Sesame Street
Seven Days in May
Seven Year Itch, The
Seventeen
Sex and the Single Girl
Sex Scandals
Sex Symbol
Sexual Harassment
Sexual Revolution
Shadow, The
Shaft
Shakur, Tupac
Shane
Shaw, Artie
Shawn, Ted
She Wore a Yellow Ribbon
Sheldon, Sidney
Shepard, Sam
Sherman, Cindy
Shirelles, The
Shirer, William L.
Shock Radio
Shore, Dinah

Shorter, Frank
Show Boat
Shula, Don
Shulman, Max
SIDS (Sudden Infant Death
    Syndrome)
Siegel, Bugsy
Silence of the Lambs, The
Silent Movies
Silver Surfer, The
Simon and Garfunkel
Simon, Neil
Simon, Paul
Simpson, O. J.
Simpson Trial
Simpsons, The
Sinatra, Frank
Sinbad
Sinclair, Upton
Singer, Isaac Bashevis
Singin' in the Rain
Singles Bars
Sirk, Douglas
Siskel and Ebert
Sister Souljah
Sitcom
Six Million Dollar Man, The
60 Minutes
$64,000 Question, The
Skaggs, Ricky
Skateboarding
Skating
Skelton, Red
Skyscrapers
Slaney, Mary Decker
Slang
Slasher Movies
Slinky
Sly and the Family Stone
Smith, Bessie
Smith, Dean
Smith, Kate
Smith, Patti
Smithsonian Institution
Smits, Jimmy
Smothers Brothers, The
Snoop Doggy Dogg
*Snow White and the Seven
    Dwarfs*
Soap Operas
Soccer
Social Dancing
Soda Fountains
Soldier Field
Some Like It Hot
Sondheim, Stephen
Sonny and Cher
Sosa, Sammy
Soul Music
Soul Train

Sound of Music, The
Sousa, John Philip
South Pacific
South Park
Southern, Terry
Spacek, Sissy
Spaghetti Westerns
Spalding, Albert G.
Spartacus
Spawn
Special Olympics
Spector, Phil
Spelling, Aaron
Spice Girls, The
Spider-Man
Spielberg, Steven
Spillane, Mickey
Spin
Spitz, Mark
Spock, Dr. Benjamin
Sport Utility Vehicles (SUVs)
Sporting News, The
Sports Hero
Sports Illustrated
Spring Break
Springer, Jerry
Springsteen, Bruce
Sprinkle, Annie
Sputnik
St. Denis, Ruth
St. Elsewhere
Stadium Concerts
Stagecoach
Stagg, Amos Alonzo
Stallone, Sylvester
Stand and Deliver
Standardized Testing
Stand-up Comedy
Stanley Brothers, The
Stanwyck, Barbara
Star System
Star Trek
Star Wars
Starbucks
Starr, Bart
Starr, Kenneth
Starsky and Hutch
State Fairs
Staubach, Roger
Steamboat Willie
Steel Curtain
Steffens, Lincoln
Steinbeck, John
Steinberg, Saul
Steinbrenner, George
Steinem, Gloria
Stengel, Casey
Steppenwolf
Stereoscopes
Stern, Howard

Stetson Hat
Stevens, Ray
Stewart, Jimmy
Stickball
Stiller and Meara
Stine, R. L.
Stock-Car Racing
Stock Market Crashes
Stockton, ''Pudgy''
Stokowski, Leopold
Stone, Irving
Stone, Oliver
Stonewall Rebellion
Stout, Rex
Strait, George
Stratemeyer, Edward
Stratton-Porter, Gene
Strawberry, Darryl
Streaking
Streep, Meryl
Street and Smith
Streetcar Named Desire, A
Streisand, Barbra
Strip Joints/Striptease
Stuart, Marty
Stuckey's
Student Demonstrations
Students for a Democratic
    Society (SDS)
Studio 54
Studio One
Studio System
Sturges, Preston
Styron, William
Suburbia
Suicide
Sullivan, Ed
Sullivan, John L.
Summer Camp
Summer, Donna
Sun Records
Sundance Film Festival
Sunday, Billy
Sunday Driving
Sunset Boulevard
Super Bowl
Superman
Supermodels
Surf Music
Susann, Jacqueline
Susskind, David
Swaggart, Jimmy
Swann, Lynn
Swatch Watches
Sweatshirt
Swimming Pools
Swing Dancing
Swinging
Sylvia
Syndication

Tabloid Television
Tabloids
Tales from the Crypt
Talk Radio
Talking Heads
Tang
Tanning
Tap Dancing
Tarantino, Quentin
Tarbell, Ida
Tarkanian, Jerry
Tarkington, Booth
Tarzan
Taxi
Taxi Driver
Taylor, Elizabeth
Taylor, James
Taylor, Robert
Teddy Bears
Teen Idols
Teenage Mutant Ninja Turtles
Teenagers
Tejano Music
Telephone
Televangelism
Television
Television Anchors
Temple, Shirley
Temptations, The
Ten Commandments, The
Tennis
Tennis Shoes/Sneakers
10,000 Maniacs
Tenuta, Judy
Terkel, Studs
Terminator, The
Terry and the Pirates
Thalberg, Irving G.
Thanksgiving
Tharp, Twyla
Them!
Thing, The
Third Man, The
This Is Your Life
Thomas, Danny
Thomas, Isiah
Thomas, Lowell
Thomas, Marlo
Thompson, Hunter S.
Thompson, John
Thomson, Bobby
Thorogood, George
Thorpe, Jim
Three Caballeros, The
Three Investigators Series
Three Stooges, The
Three's Company
Thurber, James
Tierney, Gene
Tiffany & Company

Tijuana Bibles
Time
Times Square
Timex Watches
Tiny Tim
Titanic, The
To Kill a Mockingbird
To Tell the Truth
Today
Toffler, Alvin
Toga Parties
Tokyo Rose
Tolkien, J. R. R.
Tom of Finland
Tom Swift Series
Tomlin, Lily
Tone, Franchot
Tonight Show, The
Tootsie
Top 40
Tora! Tora! Tora!
Torme, Mel
Touched by an Angel
Tour de France
Town Meetings
Toy Story
Toys
Tracy, Spencer
Trading Stamps
Trailer Parks
Tramps
Traveling Carnivals
Travolta, John
*Treasure of the Sierra
    Madre, The*
Treviño, Lee
Trevor, Claire
Trillin, Calvin
Trivial Pursuit
Trixie Belden
Trout, Robert
True Detective
True Story Magazine
T-Shirts
Tupperware
Turner, Ike and Tina
Turner, Lana
Turner, Ted
TV Dinners
TV Guide
Tweetie Pie and Sylvester
Twelve-Step Programs
Twenties, The
23 Skidoo
20/20
Twiggy
Twilight Zone, The
Twin Peaks
Twister
2 Live Crew

2001: A Space Odyssey
Tyler, Anne
Tyson, Mike

Uecker, Bob
UFOs (Unidentified Flying
    Objects)
Ulcers
Underground Comics
Unforgiven
Unitas, Johnny
United Artists
Unser, Al
Unser, Bobby
Updike, John
Upstairs, Downstairs
U.S. One
USA Today

Valdez, Luis
Valens, Ritchie
Valentine's Day
Valentino, Rudolph
Valenzuela, Fernando
Valium
Vallee, Rudy
Vampires
Van Dine, S. S.
Van Dyke, Dick
Van Halen
Van Vechten, Carl
Vance, Vivian
Vanilla Ice
Vanity Fair
Vardon, Harry
Varga Girl
Variety
Vaudeville
Vaughan, Sarah
Vaughan, Stevie Ray
Velez, Lupe
Velveeta Cheese
Velvet Underground, The
Ventura, Jesse
Versace, Gianni
Vertigo
Viagra
Victoria's Secret
Vidal, Gore
Video Games
Videos
Vidor, King
Vietnam
Villella, Edward
Vitamins
Vogue
Volkswagen Beetle
von Sternberg, Josef
Vonnegut, Kurt, Jr.

Wagner, Honus
Wagon Train
Waits, Tom
Walker, Aaron ''T-Bone''
Walker, Aida Overton
Walker, Alice
Walker, George
Walker, Junior, and the
    All-Stars
Walker, Madame C. J.
Walkman
Wall Drug
Wall Street Journal, The
Wallace, Sippie
Wal-Mart
Walters, Barbara
Walton, Bill
Waltons, The
War Bonds
War Movies
War of the Worlds
Warhol, Andy
Washington, Denzel
Washington Monument
Washington Post, The
Watergate
Waters, Ethel
Waters, John
Waters, Muddy
Watson, Tom
Wayans Family, The
Wayne, John
Wayne's World
Weathermen, The
Weaver, Sigourney
Weavers, The
Webb, Chick
Webb, Jack
Wedding Dress
Weekend
Weird Tales
Weissmuller, Johnny
Welcome Back, Kotter
Welk, Lawrence
Welles, Orson
Wells, Kitty
Wells, Mary
Wertham, Fredric
West, Jerry
West, Mae
West Side Story
Western, The
Wharton, Edith
What's My Line?
Wheel of Fortune
Whisky A Go Go
Whistler's Mother
White, Barry
White, Betty

White Castle
White, E. B.
White Flight
White, Stanford
White Supremacists
Whiteman, Paul
Whiting, Margaret
Who, The
Whole Earth Catalogue, The
Wide World of Sports
Wild Bunch, The
Wild Kingdom
Wild One, The
Wilder, Billy
Wilder, Laura Ingalls
Wilder, Thornton
Will, George F.
Williams, Andy
Williams, Bert
Williams, Hank, Jr.
Williams, Hank, Sr.
Williams, Robin
Williams, Ted
Williams, Tennessee
Willis, Bruce
Wills, Bob, and his Texas
    Playboys
Wilson, Flip
Wimbledon
Winchell, Walter
Windy City, The
Winfrey, Oprah
Winnie-the-Pooh
Winnie Winkle the Breadwinner
Winston, George
Winters, Jonathan
Wire Services
Wister, Owen
Wizard of Oz, The

WKRP in Cincinnati
Wobblies
Wodehouse, P. G.
Wolfe, Tom
Wolfman, The
Wolfman Jack
Woman's Day
Wonder, Stevie
Wonder Woman
Wong, Anna May
Wood, Ed
Wood, Natalie
Wooden, John
Woods, Tiger
Woodstock
Works Progress Administration
    (WPA) Murals
World Cup
World Series
World Trade Center
World War I
World War II
World Wrestling Federation
World's Fairs
Wrangler Jeans
Wray, Fay
Wright, Richard
Wrigley Field
Wuthering Heights
WWJD? (What Would
    Jesus Do?)
Wyeth, Andrew
Wyeth, N. C.
Wynette, Tammy

X Games
Xena, Warrior Princess

X-Files, The
X-Men, The

Y2K
Yankee Doodle Dandy
Yankee Stadium
Yankovic, ''Weird Al''
Yanni
Yardbirds, The
Yastrzemski, Carl
Yellow Kid, The
Yellowstone National Park
Yes
Yippies
Yoakam, Dwight
Young and the Restless, The
Young, Cy
Young, Loretta
Young, Neil
Young, Robert
Youngman, Henny
Your Hit Parade
Your Show of Shows
Youth's Companion, The
Yo-Yo
Yuppies

Zanuck, Darryl F.
Zap Comix
Zappa, Frank
Ziegfeld Follies, The
Zines
Zippy the Pinhead
Zoos
Zoot Suit
Zorro
Zydeco
ZZ Top

U

Uecker, Bob (1935—)

No baseball player ever built more around a lifetime batting average of .200 than sportscaster/humorist Bob Uecker. The former catcher for three National League teams parlayed his limited on-field abilities into a lucrative second career, becoming visible through his play-by-play commentary, roles in sitcoms and movies, and a series of commercial endorsements. "Anybody with ability can play in the big leagues," he once remarked. "But to be able to trick people year in and year out the way I did, I think that's a much greater feat."

A Milwaukee native, Uecker was signed by the hometown Braves (National League pennant winners in 1957 and 1958) for $3,000. "That bothered my dad at the time," Uecker later joked, "because he didn't have that kind of money to pay out." Contrary to his public persona, Uecker actually hit very well in the Braves' minor league system, batting over .300 in three different seasons. He eventually joined the parent Braves in 1962, where he was used for his defensive skills.

During the 1964 season Uecker was traded to the St. Louis Cardinals, and was part of a World Series team. "I made a major contribution to the Cardinals' pennant drive," he told Johnny Carson. "I came down with hepatitis. The trainer injected me with it." Before the first game of the World Series, Uecker stole a tuba from a Dixieland band and caught outfield flies with it during batting practice. Teammate Tim McCarver later credited Uecker's infectious humor with the Cardinals' upset win over the Yankees in the Series: "If Bob Uecker had not been on the Cardinals, then it's questionable whether we could have beaten the Yankees." He practiced doing play-by-play by broadcasting into beer cups in the Cardinals' bullpen ("Beer cups don't criticize," he later observed). While Uecker's offensive skills were weak, he had his greatest batting success, ironically, off the top pitcher of his generation, Sandy Koufax. Uecker was traded to the Philadelphia Phillies in 1966, retiring a year later.

In 1971 Uecker was hired to do play-by-play for the new Milwaukee Brewers team in the American League, and quickly became a fan favorite for his self-deprecating humor as well as his observant commentary. In 1976 he was picked to announce games for ABC's *Monday Night Baseball* program, where he was paired with the ubiquitous Howard Cosell. Cosell, who possessed a large vocabulary and a thinly-veiled contempt for baseball, was a worthy companion for the unpretentious Uecker. When Cosell asked Uecker to use the word "truculent" in a sentence, Uecker quickly replied, "If you had a truck and I borrowed it, that would be a truck-you-lent." Uecker also became a favorite guest on Johnny Carson's *The Tonight Show.*

Uecker enjoyed popularity as a commercial spokesman for Miller Lite beer in the 1970s and 1980s, poking fun at his athletic inability. In the most famous spot, Uecker was shown in the stands touting Miller Lite while waiting for his complimentary tickets from the team management ("I must be in the front row!"). As the commercial faded to black, Uecker was seen in his free seats—in the uppermost part of the upper deck.

Uecker wrote a bestselling autobiography in 1982 titled *Catcher in the Wry.* From 1985 to 1990 he costarred on the popular ABC situation comedy *Mr. Belvedere,* where his irreverent sportswriter character proved a perfect foil for Christopher Hewitt's title role of a stuffy, English-born butler. In 1989 he enjoyed his greatest success as Harry Doyle, the comical announcer for the woebegone Cleveland Indians in *Major League,* a surprise movie comedy hit. Uecker's ironic play-by-play—when Charlie Sheen's pitches land ten rows up in the grandstand, Uecker remarks, "Jusssst a bit outside"—chronicled the Indians' improbable rise to clinch the American League pennant.

Uecker returned to network baseball coverage in 1997, joining Bob Costas and Joe Morgan on NBC's broadcasts of playoff and World Series games. Again, Uecker's self-effacement played well off the erudition of both his colleagues. When asked to describe his greatest moment as a player, Uecker said with pride, "Driving home the winning run by walking with the bases loaded."

—Andrew Milner

FURTHER READING:

Green, Lee. *Sportswit.* New York, Harper and Row, 1984.

Shatzkin, Mike. *The Ballplayers: Baseball's Ultimate Biographical Reference.* New York, William Morrow, 1990.

Smith, Curt. *The Storytellers.* New York, Macmillan, 1995.

Uecker, Bob, with Mickey Herskowitz. *Catcher in the Wry.* New York, Putnam, 1982.

UFOs (Unidentified Flying Objects)

The concept of the Unidentified Flying Object (UFO), ostensibly the vehicle of choice for alien visitors from outer space, originated in the United States in the 1940s and, over the course of five decades, has attracted a sizable cult of adherents stimulated by the phenomenon's embodiment of both antigovernment social protest and romantic secular humanism.

The first mass sightings of UFOs in the United States came in 1896, when a number of people from California to the Midwest reported seeing mysterious aircraft. According to reports, these dirigible-like machines were cigar-shaped and featured a host of intense colored lights. Another wave of UFO sightings were reported in 1909 and 1910, and, during World War II, several Allied pilots claimed to have spotted glowing objects that paced their airplanes. A Gallup Poll taken in 1947, though, indicated that few Americans associated flying disks with extraterrestrial spaceships; by and large, people attributed the reported sightings to optical illusions, misinterpreted or unknown natural phenomena, or top-secret military vehicles not known to the public.

A rash of sightings between 1947 and 1949 radically recast public perceptions of UFOs. A celebrated incident in which pilot Kenneth Arnold allegedly intercepted nine saucer-like objects flying at incredible speeds over Mt. Rainier in Washington landed UFOs on the front pages of newspapers across the nation. A landmark *True* magazine article by Donald Keyhoe entitled "The Flying Saucers Are Real" postulated that UFOs, such as those encountered by Arnold, were actually extraterrestrial spaceships. Pulp magazines and Hollywood producers seized upon this image, and, not long after the

Purported UFO shot off San Pedro, California, 1957.

article's publication in 1949, the UFO as an alien vehicle became the dominant public interpretation of these phenomena. The shift in public perception was accompanied by a massive increase in the number of UFO sightings.

The government quickly became involved in this cultural phenomenon, inaugurating committees to investigate the sightings. The air force's Project Sign, which began its work in 1948, concluded that UFOs were real, but were easily explained and not extraordinary. UFOs, the committee concluded, were not extraterrestrial spaceships, but rather astronomical objects and weather balloons. Amid the growing public obsession with UFOs, a second project, Grudge, published similar findings, but engendered little public belief. The CIA-sponsored Robertson panel, named after H. P. Robertson, a director in the office of the Secretary of Defense, convened in January of 1953 and drastically changed the nature of the air force's involvement in the UFO controversy. Heretofore, the government had sought the cause of sightings. The Robertson panel charged the air force with keeping sighting reports at a minimum. The air force would never again conduct a program of thorough investigations with regard to UFOs; the main thrust of their efforts would be in the field of public relations. Government officials thus embarked on a series of educational programs aimed at reducing the gullibility of the public on matters related to UFOs. This policy has remained largely unchanged for the past 40 years.

Much to the government's consternation, adherents to the extraterrestrial theory formed a host of organizations that disseminated the beliefs of the UFO community through newsletters and journals; among these groups were the Civilian Saucer Committee, the Cosmic Brotherhood Association, and the Citizens Against UFO Secrecy. Some of the larger organizations funded UFO studies and coordinated lobbying efforts to convince Congress to declassify UFO-related government documents. In the eyes of many UFO fanatics, government officials were conspiring to shield information on extraterrestrial UFOs for fear of mass panic, as in the case of Orson Welles's famed *War of the Worlds* broadcast. The government conspiracy theory took many forms, from the belief in secret underground areas—most notably the mythical Area 51 in Nevada where alien bodies recovered from UFO crashes allegedly were preserved—to the concept of ''men in black,'' government officials who silenced those who had come in contact with UFOs and aliens.

The UFO craze continued throughout the latter decades of the twentieth century. Numbers of sightings increased steadily, and, as of the late 1990s, almost half of Americans believed that UFOs were in fact extraterrestrial spaceships. A host of reputable citizens, among them Georgia Governor Jimmy Carter of Georgia, later U.S. president, stepped forward to say that they had witnessed extraterrestrial aircraft hurtling through the sky. UFOs and aliens also had become an indelible part of popular culture. Movies from *The Day the Earth Stood Still* (1951) to *Close Encounters of the Third Kind* (1977) portrayed extraterrestrial visitations via spaceships, while television series such as *The X-Files* and *Unsolved Mysteries* capitalized on public interest with weekly narratives on encounters with aliens and UFOs.

The form of the UFO myth changed shape somewhat in the 1980s and 1990s, as individuals began to claim that they not only had seen UFOs, but that they actually had been on board the spacecraft, as aliens had abducted them and performed experiments on them before returning them to Earth. One ''abducted'' 18-year-old claimed to have had sex with an extraterrestrial, while most others offered distinct remembrances of having sperm and eggs removed from their bodies by alien doctors, ostensibly so that human reproduction could be studied in extraterrestrial laboratories. By 1997, nearly 20 percent of adult Americans believed in alien abduction theories, and abduction came to supersede sightings of ''lights in the sky'' as the dominant image associated with UFOs.

Scholars believe that the UFO myth contains religious-like elements that do much to explain its massive appeal. In postulating the existence of superhuman beings, by promising deliverance through travel to a better planet, and by creating a community fellowship engaged in ritualized activities such as the various UFO conventions popular with believers, the UFO myth embodies much of popular religious belief. At the same time, the UFO myth, with its government conspiracy dimensions, resonates with an American public increasingly distrustful of its government. UFO ''flaps,'' periods of high numbers of UFO sightings, have corresponded to a number of broadly defined crises in government faith, among them the McCarthy hearings, the Vietnam War, and Watergate.

The public fascination with UFOs has shown no signs of abating in the 1990s. In 1997, the fiftieth anniversary of the Roswell incident, in which the government purportedly covered up the existence of a crashed UFO, nearly 40 thousand people flocked to Roswell, New Mexico, to pay homage to the alleged crash site. A number of Hollywood's biggest blockbusters were standard UFO and alien fare; these films included the box-office smashes *Independence Day* (1996), *Contact* (1997), and *Men in Black* (1997). Most tragically, the

Heaven's Gate UFO cult committed mass suicide in 1997 as part of an effort to gain the attention of a UFO they believed to be associated with the Hale-Bopp comet. Like other believers in UFOs, the Heaven's Gate cult located its hopes and fears about the world in the idea of disk-shaped alien spaceships, but, as scholar Curtis Peebles has aptly noted, ''We watch the skies seeking meaning. In the end, what we find is ourselves.''

—Scott Tribble

FURTHER READING:

Jacobs, David Michael. *The UFO Controversy in America.* Bloomington & London, Indiana University Press, 1975.

Keyhoe, Donald. *The Flying Saucers Are Real.* New York, Fawcett Publications, 1950.

Peebles, Curtis. *Watch the Skies! A Chronicle of the Flying Saucer Myth.* Washington and London, Smithsonian Institution Press, 1994.

Sagan, Carl, and Thornton Page, editors. *UFOs—A Scientific Debate.* Ithaca and London, Cornell University Press, 1972.

Saler, Benson, Charles A. Zeigler, and Charles B. Moore. *UFO Crash at Roswell: The Genesis of a Modern Myth.* Washington and London, Smithsonian Institution Press, 1997.

Ulcers

Peptic ulcers are painful open sores or lesions in either the stomach (gastric ulcers) or duodenal lining (duodenal ulcers). Ulcers affect more than four million people each year and account for approximately 40,000 surgeries and six thousand deaths. With 10 percent of the population suffering from ulcers, they are responsible for an estimated three to five million doctor's office visits and two million prescriptions each year. Until the early 1980s, ulcers were believed to be caused primarily by such factors as stress and spicy foods, but a new link was found in 1982 that has changed attitudes about the causes of this common and painful condition. With the discovery of a bacterium called Helicobacter Pylori (H. Pylori), researchers have found increasing evidence that the majority of ulcers may be caused by this bacteria, and research suggests these ulcers can be treated with antibiotics.

Duodenal ulcers occur in the first section of the intestine after the stomach. The first occurrence of these ulcers is usually between the ages of 30 and 50, and is more common in men than in women. Gastric ulcers occur in the stomach itself, and are more common in those over 60, and affect more women than men. Ulcer symptoms may be mild, severe, or nonexistent and include weight loss, heartburn, loss of appetite, bloating, fatigue, burping, nausea, vomiting, and pain. The pain associated with ulcers is often an intermittent dull or gnawing pain, usually occurring two to three hours following a meal or when the stomach is empty, and is often relieved by food intake. While most of these symptoms require only a visit to the doctor, others require immediate medical attention. These symptoms include sharp, sudden pain; bloody or black stools; or bloody vomit sometimes resembling coffee grounds. Any or all of these symptoms

could signal a perforation, bleeding, or an obstruction in the gastrointestinal tract. H. Pylori is now considered a major contributing factor in both gastric and duodenal ulcers, with the remainder of the cases caused by damage from nonsteroidal anti-inflammatory drugs such as aspirin and ibuprofen.

Ulcers are diagnosed by such methods as an upper gastrointestinal (Upper GI) series or an endoscopy. Doctors who suspect an ulcer is caused by H. Pylori will often perform blood, breath, and stomach tissue tests after one of these procedures detects the presence of an ulcer. Since the discovery of H. Pylori, doctors try to determine if the ulcer is caused by this bacterium or if other factors such as the use of NSAIDs have contributed to the formation of the ulcer. Until the 1980s, medical professionals believed ulcers were caused mainly by stress, spicy foods, alcohol consumption, and excess stomach acids, and treated most ulcers with bland diets, antacids, and rest or reduced stress levels. In the early years of the twentieth century, physicians and psychologists considered overwork the cause of most ulcers. It was in the 1970s that researchers caused a stir with the idea that ulcers are caused by stress, creating a new buzzword in both the medical and business worlds. This theory led to an emphasis on stress management in the 1980s, and experts in every field from psychology to the New Age movement began to advance new theories on the causes and treatment of ulcers.

In 1982, when the H. Pylori bacterium was discovered, medical researchers began to think differently about the causes and treatment of ulcers. A pathologist in Perth, Australia, found that a significant number of ulcer patients were infected with the same unknown bacterium, later named H. Pylori. Research has found that the spiral-shaped H. Pylori bacteria are able to survive corrosive stomach acids because of their acid neutralizing properties. The bacteria work by weakening the mucous coating of the stomach or duodenum and allowing stomach acid to attack the more sensitive stomach or duodenal lining, leading to the formation of an ulcer. Possible causes of infection by H. Pylori include intake of contaminated food or water or possibly through saliva.

Many researchers in the late 1990s believe H. Pylori causes the majority of ulcers, with an estimated 80 percent of stomach ulcers and 90 percent of duodenal ulcers caused by the bacteria. Research suggests that 20 percent of Americans under 40 and 50 percent of Americans over 60 are infected with it. Further research has shown that 90 percent of ulcers traced to H. Pylori have been healed by the use of antibiotics and do not recur when treated with them.

Despite a statement by the National Institute of Health that most ulcers may be caused by H. Pylori, the issue remains a controversial one. By the final years of the 1990s, the Food and Drug Administration had not officially sanctioned the use of antibiotics to treat ulcers believed to be caused by H. Pylori. The predominant treatment of ulcers remains the use of medication such as antacids and drugs like Zantac, Tagamet, or Pepcid that inhibit the production of stomach acid, and lifestyle changes. If H. Pylori is indicated as a cause of ulcers, doctors often use a combination of drugs including antibiotics, H2 blockers such as rantidine, proton pump inhibitors such as omeprazole, and stomach lining protectors.

While research continues to examine the causes and treatment of ulcers, doctors and patients have a wider range of treatments than ever before for ulcers, as well as related conditions such as heartburn and acid-reflux disease. The last two decades of the twentieth century have afforded a greater understanding of the formation of ulcers and provided a promising outlook in identifying a cure for this common and potentially dangerous disease.

—Kimberley H. Kidd

FURTHER READING:

Berland, Theodore, and Mitchell A. Spellberg, M.D. *Living with Your Ulcer.* New York, St. Martin's Press, 1971.

Monmaney, Terence. "Second Opinion: The Bunk Stops Here: The Truth about Ulcers." *Forbes.* Vol. 150, No. 150, 1992, 31.

Soll, A. H. "Medical Treatment of Peptic Ulcer Disease: Practical Guidelines." *Journal of the American Medical Association.* Vol. 275, No. 8, 1996, 622-628.

Underground Comics

Underground Comics (or "Comix," with the X understood to signify X-rated material) include strips and books heavily dosed with obscenity, graphic sex, gory violence, glorification of drug use, and general defiance of convention and authority. All are either self-published or produced by very small companies which choose not to follow the mainstream Comics Code. Some undergrounds are political, carrying eco-awareness, anti-establishment messages, and general revolutionary overtones. Others are just meant for nasty, subversive fun. All have elements of sensation and satire. The origins of underground comics can be traced to the so-called "Tijuana Bibles" of the 1930s and 1940s: illegally produced 8-page mini-comics that depicted mainstream comic strip characters getting drunk and having sex (Popeye, Mickey Mouse, Dick Tracy, etc.). The legacy of underground comics are the Alternative and Independent of the 1980s and 1990s.

Underground comics truly came into their own during the 1960s, thanks to the talents of artist/writers such as Robert ("R.") Crumb, Gilbert Shelton, and S. Clay Wilson. The first underground strips appeared in underground papers such as New York's *East Village Other,* Berkeley's *Barb,* the Los Angeles *Free Press,* and the Detroit *Fifth Estate.* The first recognizable underground comic book is *God Nose (Snot Reel)* put out by Jack ("Jaxon") Jackson in 1963. Undergrounds proliferated in the mid and late 1960s, with printing and distribution by companies such as San Francisco's Rip-Off Press, Milwaukee's Kitchen Sink Enterprises (a.k.a. Krupp), and Berkeley's Print Mint. These companies sold their books not through newsstands but through Head Shops.

The first issues of R. Crumb's *Zap* (1967) were a milestone in underground comics. *Zap* featured the catchy Keep On Truckin' image and introduced characters such as the hedonistic guru Mr. Natural and the outwardly proud but inwardly repressed Whiteman. Crumb's intense and imaginative artwork, strange and often shocking images, unsparing satires, and unflattering self-confessions still remain perhaps the most impressive work in the history of underground comics. Crumb's very popular comics and illustrations have become widely available in compilations, anthologies, and even coffee table

books. Crumb's life and work are the subject of the excellent 1995 documentary film, *Crumb.*

Gilbert Shelton found his greatest success with his *Fabulous Furry Freak Brothers* comic, more than a dozen issues of which have been infrequently published since #1 in 1968. The Freaks include Phineas, Freewheelin Franklin, and Fat Freddy (the most popular of the three): fun-loving hippy buddies out looking for sex, drugs, and rock n' roll—especially drugs. The comic also features the adventures of Fat Freddy's cat, who must sometimes fight off suicidal cockroaches in Freddy's apartment. Shelton also writes and draws the superhero parody strip "Wonder Wart-Hog."

S. Clay Wilson holds the distinction of being the most perverse and most disgusting of any underground comic artist. His work is filled with orgies and brawls, molestations and mutilations. His characters are usually pirates, lesbians, motorcycle gangs, or horned demonic monsters. All his characters are drawn in anatomically correct detail, complete with warts, nosehair, sweat, saliva, and wet rubbery genitalia. Comics featuring his work include *Zap* and *Yellow Dog.*

Other important and popular underground artist/writers include: Kim Deitch whose playful and humorous work appeared (among elsewhere) in the *East Village Other* and *Gothic Blimp Works;* Greg Irons whose frightening bony faces and horror stories appeared in *Skull;* Rick Griffin whose psychedelic-organic art appeared in *Zap,* countless posters, and some of the more famous Grateful Dead album covers; Victor Moscoso whose space/time distortions show the influence of M.C. Escher; George Metzger who was the most important sci-fi/fantasy underground artist with his dreamy *Moondog* book; and Richard Corben (later famous for the Den series in *Heavy Metal*), whose fleshy, muscular, scantily-clad men and women appeared under the pseudonym "Gore" in *Slow Death* and *Death Rattle.* Mainstream artists who got their start with early undergrounds include Bill Griffith (*Zippy*) and Art Spiegelman (*Maus,* covers for *The New Yorker*). There have been few women in underground comics, but notable exceptions include Trina Robbins and Lee Marrs, both of whom worked as artists, writers, and editors. Robbins edited *It Ain't Me Babe Comix*—the first all-women comic—in the early 1970s.

In the 1960s and 1970s, the most popular underground sex comics included *Snatch Comics, Jiz Comics, Big Ass Comics, Gay Comics, Young Lust,* and *Bizarre Sex.* Popular pro-drug comics included *Freak Brothers, Dope Comix,* and *Uneeda Comix.* Popular political compilations included the anti-pollution *Slow Death* and the anti-government *Anarchy Comics.* Small print-runs and low distributions kept most of these comics away from the eyes of civil and political authorities. But there were some notable legal battles, the biggest of which erupted in 1969 over *Zap Comics* #4, which featured Crumb's infamous "Joe Blow" story about an incestuous S&M family orgy. A New York State judge ruled the comic obscene and therefore illegal, holding publisher Print Mint liable for fines.

When Head Shops died out in the early 1970s, many underground comics vanished entirely, the survivors becoming available only through mail order. But with the dawn of comic speciality shops in the early 1980s, undergrounds once again had a place on the shelves. In the 1990s, reprints and compilations of early undergrounds are found alongside conventional mainstream books.

The influence of underground comic books and the openness of comic specialty shops helped make possible the so-called Alternative or Independent comics that flourished in the 1980s and continue to reach wide audiences through the late 1990s. Some of the most popular Alternatives are the Hernandez brothers' *Love and Rockets,* Chester Brown's *Yummy Fur,* Roberta Gregory's *Bitchy Bitch,* Peter Bagge's *Hate,* Dave Sim's *Cerebus,* Dan Clowes's *Eightball,* Charles Burns' *Black Hole,* and compilations *Weirdo, Raw,* and *Drawn & Quarterly.* Like the early undergrounds, these new books are uncompromising in their treatment of sex and violence, and often hold skeptical and subversive undertones. Most Alternatives avoid the extremism of their 1960s and 1970s predecessors, but without these earlier books, the widely-read and widely-praised Alternative books would not have been possible.

—Dave Goldweber

FURTHER READING:

Adelman, Bob, editor. *Tijuana Bibles: Art and Wit in America's Forbidden Funnies.* New York, Simon & Schuster, 1997.

Estren, Mark James. *A History of Underground Comics.* Berkeley, Ronin, 1993 (1974).

Griffith, Bill, editor. *Zap to Zippy: The Impact of Underground Comix.* San Francisco, Cartoon Art Museum, 1990.

Juno, Andrea, editor. *Dangerous Drawings: Interviews with Comix and Graphix Artists.* New York, Juno, 1997.

Sabin, Roger. *Comics, Comix, and Graphic Novels.* London, Phaidon, 1996.

Unforgiven

Of his 1992 film *Unforgiven,* director and star Clint Eastwood said "the movie summarized everything I feel about the Western." Despite this, the film sparked considerable debate about exactly what it had to say about the Western. Some critics have argued for the film as an anti-Western, tearing down the icons of the genre, while others have insisted that it is simply a continuation of the genre, but with slight variation. Whatever deeper meanings the film may have intended, it meant for many, including the filmmakers, a restoration. Not only did the film give a needed career boost to actors like Eastwood, Gene Hackman, Morgan Freeman, and Richard Harris, but it also was credited with revitalizing the Western genre. Interestingly, the film was also touted by some critics as the final word on the Western. Indeed, none of the Westerns released in *Unforgiven*'s wake have matched the impact of Eastwood's dark, brooding film. Certainly, none matched *Unforgiven*'s critical and commercial success. It broke box office records, not only for a Western, but for an August

Gene Hackman (left) and Clint Eastwood in a scene from the film *Unforgiven*.

release, and won four Academy Awards: Best Picture, Best Director, Best Supporting Actor (for Hackman), and Best Editing.

These accomplishments were all the more remarkable given the state of the genre. Within the film industry, the Western was largely considered dead and gone, and earlier attempts to resuscitate it had been tepidly received, with the exception of Kevin Costner's 1990 Western-of-a-sort, *Dances with Wolves*. David Webb Peoples penned the *Unforgiven* script (originally entitled "The Cut-Whore Killings") in 1976, but it had attracted only slight interest. Francis Ford Coppola had optioned the script but allowed the option to lapse. Eventually it was picked up by Eastwood, who sat on the script for some time, claiming that he needed to age into the lead role of William Munny.

At the beginning of the film, Munny is a struggling hog farmer raising two young children. A prologue scrolling across the screen tells of a less domestic Munny, a drunk, an outlaw, and a killer, now reformed, according to Munny, by his dead wife. But Munny's reputation brings to the ranch the Schofield Kid (Jaimz Woolvett), who lures Munny away in pursuit of a bounty on two cowboys involved in the mutilation of a prostitute. Munny, in turn, recruits his partner from the old days, Ned Logan (Freeman). What follows is the story of their search for the cowboys and their conflict with the law of the Wyoming town, Big Whisky, and a brutal sheriff named Little Bill Daggett (Hackman). The killings of the cowboys are pivotal. The first is that of Davey Boy, whose crime is largely to have been on the scene at the time of the attack on the prostitute. This is a drawn out and painful scene in which Munny shoots the cowboy from a distance. Rather than dropping to a quick death, the cowboy's life slowly ebbs while he calls out to his friends for water. Logan is left too rattled by the murder to continue in pursuit of the other cowboy. The Schofield Kid, finally living up to his bravado, kills the second cowboy, who is squatting in an outhouse at the time. The Kid is consequently reduced to trembling and tears by the gravity of what he has done, realizing that he isn't the Billy the Kid figure he has pretended to be.

The final scene is one that critics have found more troubling. It is a scene that might well be out of the penny dreadfuls of the Old West. Munny confronts Daggett and his deputies, single handedly killing five armed men. Munny's attack is motivated by vengeance against those who killed his friend, and this, combined with the incredible odds, turns Munny into a kind of mythological force for vengeance, despite the film's earlier attempts to reduce Munny to a very human and fallible man. Still, it can be argued that the final scene doesn't come off quite the way it might in another Western. Given the unpleasantness of the earlier killings, this scene is tainted, polluted with the knowledge that, as Munny puts it, "It's a hell of a thing killing a man."

Certainly, *Unforgiven* employs many of the genre's clichés while simultaneously undercutting the comfort that comes with such clichés. This had been done before, particularly in spaghetti Westerns, but whereas these presented a parody of the Western myth with almost cartoonish violence, the violence in *Unforgiven* is decidedly more realistic. Moreover, whereas many earlier Westerns were brightly lit, the action in *Unforgiven* is often shrouded in darkness and haze.

Eastwood dedicated the film to Sergio Leone and Don Siegel, suggesting a nod to his mentors and influences. *Unforgiven* is certainly in the tradition of Leone's spaghetti Westerns, but Eastwood carried the tradition to a new level. Putting his own spin on the genre, he created a new standard, a Western for an era in which the invented heroics of the past seem less convincing than they may have in the heyday of the genre. *Unforgiven* reflects the skepticism of its time, wherein the old John Ford adage "When the legend becomes fact,

print the legend" doesn't quite hold up any more. Eastwood's film suggests that the legend is a frail thing and that perhaps truer things have a way of showing though.

—Marc Oxoby

FURTHER READING:

O'Brien, Daniel. *Clint Eastwood: Film-Maker*. London, Batsford, 1996.

Schickel, Richard. *Clint Eastwood: A Biography*. New York, Knopf, 1996.

Smith, Paul. *Clint Eastwood: A Cultural Production*. Minneapolis, University of Minnesota Press, 1993.

Unidentified Flying Objects
See UFOs (Unidentified Flying Objects)

Unitas, Johnny (1933—)

The gaudiest names on the gridiron often are quarterbacks. In the 1990s, such glamour boys as Joe Montana and Steve Young, Dan Marino and John Elway and Bret Favre have earned the bulk of National Football League fame. However, none of these superstar signal callers have anything on Johnny Unitas, otherwise known as "Mr. Quarterback," "The Golden Arm," and simply "Johnny U.," who played for the Baltimore Colts between 1956 and 1972. In his prime, Unitas was the league's most renowned, respected, and feared quarterback. As noted in his enshrinee data at the Football Hall of Fame, he was a "legendary hero," and an "exceptional field leader [who] thrived on pressure."

Johnny U.'s career is defined by a combination of luck, persistence, and hard work. He was born John Constantine Unitas in Pittsburgh, and began his quarterbacking career as a sophomore at St. Justin's High School when the first-string signal caller busted his ankle. He had a scant seven days to master his team's complete offense. As he neared graduation, the lanky six-footer with the signature crew cut hoped to be offered a scholarship to Notre Dame, but was denied his wish as the school determined that he probably would not add weight to his 138-pound frame. Instead, he attended the University of Louisville, from which he graduated in 1955.

While no college gridiron luminary, Unitas had impressed people enough to be drafted in the ninth round by the Pittsburgh Steelers. Unfortunately, the team was overloaded with signal callers—and its coach believed Unitas was "not intelligent enough to be a quarterback"—and so he was denied a slot on the Steelers' roster. Unable to hook up with another NFL team, he settled for work on a construction gang and a spot on the semi-pro Bloomfield Rams, where he earned $3 per game. Fortuitously, the Baltimore Colts called him in early 1956 and invited him to a try out the following season. He was signed to a $7,000 contract, and played for the Colts for the next 17 years before finishing his career in 1973 with the San Diego Chargers.

Unitas was the Babe Ruth, Michael Jordan, and Wayne Gretsky of quarterbacks. Upon his retirement, he held the NFL records for making 5,186 pass attempts and 2,830 completions, throwing for 40,239 total yards and 290 touchdowns, tossing touchdown passes in 47 consecutive games, and having 26 300-yard games. He also threw for 3,000 yards or more in three seasons, and piloted his team to three

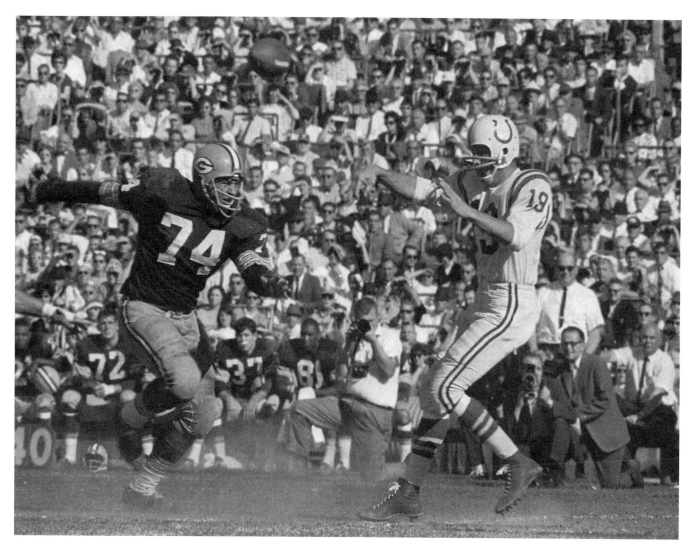

Baltimore Colts quarterback Johnny Unitas (right) passes against the Green Bay Packers, 1964.

NFL championships (in 1958, 1959, and 1968) and one Super Bowl title (in 1971). Unitas was one of the stars of what is arguably the greatest game in NFL history: the Colts' 1958 title victory over the New York Giants, a 23-17 overtime win in which he completed 26 of 40 passes for 349 yards. Down 17-14 in the final minutes of the fourth quarter, he marched the Colts 85 yards; with seven seconds remaining on the clock, Steve Myhra booted a 20-yard, game-tying field goal. Then in overtime, Unitas spearheaded his team to 80 yards on thirteen plays, with Alan Ameche rushing for the game-winning touchdown.

Unitas was a five-time All-NFL selection, a three-time NFL Player of the Year, a ten-time Pro Bowl pick—and a three-time Pro Bowl MVP. He was named "Player of the Decade" for the 1960s, and was cited as the "Greatest Player in the First 50 Years of Pro Football." He was one of four quarterbacks—the others are Otto Graham, Sammy Baugh, and Joe Montana—named to the NFL's 75th Anniversary Team. He was inducted into the Football Hall of Fame in 1979.

In retirement, Unitas sported a crooked index finger on his passing hand: a souvenir of his playing career. He was fiercely proud of his reputation as a hard-nosed competitor who once declared, "You're not an NFL quarterback until you can tell your coach to go to

hell!" He also has noted that playing in the NFL of the 1990s would be "a piece of cake. The talent's not as good as it once was.... [Defensive backs] used to be able to come up and knock you down at the line of scrimmage. If you tried to get up, they'd knock you down again, then sit on you and dare you to get up."

And he has been quick to declare that he should not be censured for his team's shocking 16-7 loss to Joe Namath and the underdog New York Jets in Superbowl III—the game that established the upstart American Football League as a rival of the NFL. For most of the 1968 season, Unitas had been plagued by a sore elbow. Earl Morrall, who had replaced Unitas in training camp and was the league MVP, started the game for the Colts. In the first half, the Jets' secondary intercepted three of his passes. Unitas, the aging, injured veteran of the football wars, heroically came off the bench in the fourth quarter to complete 11 of 24 passes, for 110 yards. Unfortunately, the Colts could muster only a single touchdown.

"I always tell people to blame [Colts coach Don] Shula for that," he once observed, "because if he had started me in the second half, I'd have got it."

—Rob Edelman

7

FURTHER READING:

Fitzgerald, Ed. *Johnny Unitas: The Amazing Success Story of Mr. Quarterback,* New York, Nelson, 1961.

Unitas, Johnny, and Ed Fitzgerald. *Pro Quarterback, My Own Story.* New York, Simon and Schuster, 1965.

———, with Harold Rosenthal. *Playing Pro Football to Win.* Garden City, New York, Doubleday, 1968.

United Artists

Founded in 1919 by Douglas Fairbanks, Charlie Chaplin, Mary Pickford, and D.W. Griffith, United Artists (UA) began as a distributor and financier of independent films and their producers; it was not a studio and never had stars under contract. UA was a unique entity in the early history of Hollywood, never losing sight of its goal—to make and distribute quality work.

The idea for United Artists began when Fairbanks, Chaplin, Pickford, and cowboy star William S. Hart were traveling around the country selling Liberty bonds to help the World War I effort in 1918. The four began to discuss the possibility of forming their own company to protect them from rumored studio mergers and the loss of control and salary this might cause. Hart eventually bowed out, but was soon replaced with the world's premier director, D. W. Griffith. When the company was officially formed in February of 1919, many felt that ''the idiots had taken over the asylum.''

The company was an immediate success. UA brought audiences hits such as Pickford in *Pollyanna* (1920), Griffith's *Broken Blossoms* (1919), Fairbanks as *Robin Hood* (1923), and Chaplin's masterpiece, *The Gold Rush* (1925). With such quality work, UA's only problem in the early years was providing enough product to meet the demand of the audiences.

UA began courting other stars to have their work distributed through the company. While many declined, some of the top stars of silent films agreed, including Gloria Swanson, Norma Talmadge, and Buster Keaton. The company also brought in Joseph Schenck as a partner and chairman of the board in 1924. He secured producers like Samuel Goldwyn, Walt Disney, and Howard Hughes, all of whom added to the roster of successful films released through UA.

UA was temporarily hurt by the advent of ''talking pictures.'' While initially there were hits such as *Coquette* (1929), for which Mary Pickford won an Academy Award, as ''talkies'' became more the rule than the exception, the company found its product in less demand. One notable exception was *Hell's Angels* (1930), produced by Howard Hughes. After silent screen star Greta Nissen had to be replaced, Hughes introduced to the screen the sex symbol of the 1930s, Jean Harlow. The result made *Hell's Angels* one of UA's biggest hits.

But UA was beginning to lose some of its creative talent as Griffith, Disney, Schenck, and others left. The company managed, however, to stay afloat with hits such as *The Scarlet Pimpernel* (1935), *Dodsworth* (1936), and *Algiers* (1938). The star founders of UA had all but faded by this time. Griffith was gone, Fairbanks was dead, and Pickford's career was over, although she was still a stockholder in the company. Charlie Chaplin continued to be successful, however, particularly with *Modern Times* in 1936.

UA fell on hard times in the 1940s. The hits were fewer and more creative forces such as David O. Selznick and Alexander Korda left

the company. In 1950 a syndicate led by Arthur Krim and Robert Benjamin took over operations. As the old studio system died, Hollywood changed and the independents, including UA, had the upper hand. The old production code and puritanical limits to motion picture making were also disappearing. One of the first and biggest reasons for this was Otto Preminger's *The Moon is Blue* (1953). UA released the film without the seal of approval from the Production Code Administration. Despite, or perhaps because of this, the film was a box office and critical success. The 1950s, however, marked the end of an era at UA for another reason. By 1956 founders Chaplin and Pickford gave in to pressure and sold their shares in the company. UA then had a public stock offering in 1957.

Following the public sale of UA, *The Apartment* (1960) was released and won five Academy Awards, signaling a prosperous time for the studio. In 1961 UA announced what turned out to be a brilliant decision: the company was going to release seven James Bond films, all of which went on to be big hits. The spy series proved to be one of the most successful in motion picture history.

If a motion picture company is to stay afloat, it must, in some way, reflect changes in society. Things were clearly changing with the Vietnam War, the generation gap, and the beginning of the sexual revolution. UA continued its success with violent and controversial hits like *The Dirty Dozen* (1967) and *The Wild Bunch* (1969). In the late 1960s, UA experienced the first of many shakeups in ownership when in 1967 Transamerica took over the company. By 1969, millionaire Kirk Kerkorian was the largest shareholder. While UA continued to have hits such as *One Flew Over the Cuckoo's Nest* (1975), many were not happy with the way the company was being run. In 1978 several executives, including Krim and Benjamin, resigned from the company to form Orion Pictures.

In November of 1980, UA released a film that has become known as the biggest box office disaster in motion picture history—*Heaven's Gate*—which lost $40 million. In 1981 MGM (Metro-Goldwyn-Mayer) bought UA and it became MGM/UA. The company continued to be sold and resold throughout the 1980s, and in the 1990s it no longer existed in its original form.

Nevertheless, United Artists will be remembered for its part in changing the face of Hollywood, for offering more control to the creative forces of motion pictures and less to the businessmen. In addition to producing many hit films throughout the years, UA is also largely responsible for the way in which the motion picture industry evolved as the studio system began to fade.

—Jill A. Gregg

FURTHER READING:

Balio, Tino. *United Artists: The Company that Changed Film History.* Wisconsin, University of Wisconsin Press, 1987.

Bergan, Ronald. *The United Artists Story.* New York, Crown, 1986.

Unser, Al (1939—)

Al Unser, Sr., one of the foremost names in the sport of auto racing, is known primarily for his remarkable success at the Indianapolis 500. He is the second of three generations of racecar drivers, and it is arguable that no other family has left such an indelible mark on a sport as the Unser family has done on auto racing. Al's uncle, Louie Unser, attempted qualification at the Indianapolis 500 in 1940;

Al Unser

his brother Jerry was national stock car champion in 1956 but was killed in 1959 while on a practice lap at Indianapolis. The two surviving brothers, Al and Bobby Unser, went on to win a total of seven Indianapolis 500 races, while Al's son, Al Unser, Jr., is successful in his own right, having twice won at Indianapolis by the late 1990s. Johnny Unser (Jerry's son) and Robby Unser (Bobby's son) are also third generation drivers at Indianapolis.

Al Unser, Sr. was born in Albuquerque, New Mexico, on May 29, 1939. At age 18 he began competitive auto racing with modified roadsters before progressing to Midgets, Sprints, Stock Cars, Sports Cars, Formula 5000, Championship Dirt Cars, and Indy Cars. His dominance in the sport is seen in the fact that he placed third in the national standings in 1968, second in 1969, 1977, and 1978, first in 1970, and fourth in 1976. He is one of the few drivers who can boast of a career that spans five decades.

Most drivers of Unser's generation are, however, judged by their success at Indianapolis, where Unser ranks first in points earned and second in miles driven and total money won. He is tied for second in a total number of 500 starts and is ranked fourth in money earned

leading the race. Although A. J. Foyt was the first driver to win four times at Indianapolis, Unser matched that feat in 1987, with Rick Mears the only other driver to do so subsequently. In 1988, Unser surpassed the long-standing record for the most laps led during a career at the 500, having achieved a staggering laps total of 644.

In addition to winning Indianapolis four times (1970, 1971, 1978, and 1987), Unser won the Pocono 500 and the Ontario 500 twice each. When he won at Indianapolis, Pocono, and Ontario all in the same year (1978) he achieved the unique distinction of sweeping this "Triple Crown" of Indy car racing. The 1970 season was perhaps his most remarkable of all, with 10 wins on ovals, road courses, and dirt tracts to capture the national championship. Al Unser also won the prestigious "Hoosier Hundred" four years in a row, making him a dirt-car champion, and had his share in the Unser family dominance of the Pikes Peak Hill Climb, taking back-to-back victories in 1964 and 1965.

Even as Unser approached the end of his career, he was still able to win two more national championships, in 1983 and in 1985. His main competitor in 1985 was his own son, who lost to his father by only one point. Thus, at the age of 46, Al Unser enjoyed the distinction of becoming the oldest Indy Car champion.

Al Unser, Sr., an avid snowmobile enthusiast, retired to his home in New Mexico. Thanks to the particular popularity of Unser and his family within a sport of generally popular practitioners, everything from diecast racecars to CD-ROM computer games have been marketed with the Unser name.

—James H. Lloyd

FURTHER READING:

"Al Unser." In "Motor Sports Hall of Fame." http://www.mshf.com/hof/unsera.htm. April 1999.

Bentley, Karen. *The Unsers.* Broomall, Pennsylvania, Chelsea House, 1996.

Dregni, Michael. *The Indianapolis 500.* Minneapolis, Capstone Press, 1994.

Walker, Mark H. *Official ABC Sports Indy Racing: Road to the Indianapolis 500 Official Strategies and Secrets.* San Francisco, Sybex, 1998.

Unser, Bobby (1934—)

The Unser family has produced many superb race-car drivers, amongst them Bobby Unser, who recorded 35 Indy car victories and two United States Auto Club (USAC) national driving championships over his 32-year career.

Robert William Unser was born in Albuquerque, New Mexico, on February 20, 1934 and began racing at the age of fifteen. The dream of most race-car drivers at the time was to drive in the Indianapolis 500; Unser won at Indianapolis in 1968, 1975, and 1981. In addition to Indy cars, he claimed victories in sprint cars, stock cars, and midget racers. After retirement he won USAC's Fast Masters Tournament for drivers over the age of 50.

During the height of his career, race cars and other toys were marketed with his name. In the 1990s, Unser worked for ABC Sports and was one of the most respected color commentators for the sport of motor racing.

—James H. Lloyd

FURTHER READING:

Bentley, Karen. *The Unsers.* Broomall, Pennsylvania, Chelsea House, 1996.

Scalzo, Joe, and Bobby Unser. *The Bobby Unser Story.* Garden City, New York, Doubleday, 1979.

Walker, Mark H. *Official ABC Sports Indy Racing: Road to the Indianapolis 500 Official Strategies and Secrets.* San Francisco, Sybex, 1998.

Updike, John (1932—)

Considered by critics to be one of the most significant American writers of the latter half of the twentieth century, John Updike is best known for his tetralogy of Rabbit novels (*Rabbit, Run,* 1960; *Rabbit Redux,* 1971; *Rabbit is Rich,* 1981; and *Rabbit at Rest,* 1990), which chronicles four decades of American culture through the eyes of Everyman protagonist Harry Angstrom. His depictions of everyday middle-class life and the stifling atmosphere of marriage have, in the minds of many readers, vividly captured the emptiness of middle America. Prolific and versatile, Updike has published 50 volumes, including novels, short stories, essays, reviews, poems, memoirs, and drama.

Updike was born in Reading, Pennsylvania, on March 18, 1932 and grew up in the small town of Shillington. He later lived on a family farm in nearby Plowville. Through early academic success, Updike earned a scholarship to Harvard, where he continued the writing and drawing he had begun as a child. Following graduation from Harvard, Updike spent a year in Oxford, England, studying drawing on a fellowship, and two years in New York City working as a staff writer for *The New Yorker.*

In 1957 Updike and his young family, which would grow to four children by 1960, left New York City and moved to the small town of Ipswich, Massachusetts. Big-city life had proved too distracting, expensive, and overwhelming. By returning to a small town, not so unlike the Shillington of his youth, Updike found an atmosphere conducive to writing that would allow him to experience firsthand the middle-class everyday life that would become the great subject of his work.

In Ipswich, Updike began publishing books, beginning with a volume of poetry, *The Carpentered Hen* (1958); a first novel, *The Poorhouse Fair* (1959); and a collection of stories, *The Same Door* (1959). Most of Updike's early work, written between the early 1950s and mid-1960s, depicts and lyrically celebrates a mythically endowed Pennsylvania that the author knew intimately from childhood. His most famous novel, *Rabbit, Run* (1960), depicting the angst and entrapment of early married life, appeared in 1960 and would go on to sell more than 2.5 million copies. Before he turned 30, Updike had established himself as one of his generation's foremost writers.

Updike's break with his early work came in 1968 with the publication of the novel *Couples,* set in a small New England town, that dealt with the adulterous interactions of a circle of 10 couples. The novel, the author's first and only number-one best-seller, landed Updike on the cover of *Time* magazine (he would appear there again in 1982) and greatly enlarged his readership. Over the subsequent decade Updike became America's best-known chronicler of marriage and adultery, producing such works as *A Month of Sundays* (1975), *Marry Me* (1976), and *Too Far to Go* (1979). During this same period, Updike divorced his first wife of 20 years and remarried.

The next phase of Updike's writing was signaled by the publication of *The Coup* (1978), one of the most radical departures of his career. Set in a fictional African country and told from the perspective of a black African leader in exile, *The Coup* was a breakthrough novel, demonstrating that Updike could extend his vision beyond suburban adultery or a Pennsylvania boyhood.

Updike went on to write some of his finest and most exuberant fiction during the late 1970s and early 1980s, including *Problems and Other Stories* (1979), *Rabbit is Rich* (1981), and *The Witches of Eastwick* (1984). In addition, he emerged as one of America's finest and most prolific literary critics through the publication of his award-winning critical tome *Hugging the Shore* (1983).

In his later novels, such as *Roger's Version* (1986), an intellectually demanding novel about a divinity professor and his battle with a computer scientist, *Rabbit at Rest* (1990), and *Toward the End of*

Time (1997), Updike has revealed his concerns with aging and displayed a bleakness and detachment that stand in contrast to the lyrical celebration of much of his early work. *Roger's Version* also signaled the increasing use of research in Updike's writing, to the extent that he began appending bibliographies to his novels. More heavily intertextual and loaded with information, these novels reveal a more erudite author.

Despite his large following, Updike has had his share of critics. Some have argued that while he may be a brilliant verbal performer, he allows himself to be carried away by his prose, to the point that his language becomes excessive in description and detail. In addition, some have found his graphic depictions of human sexuality to be gratuitous, and several feminist critics have accused him of misogyny.

Updike is considered by many to be America's greatest poetic novelist—a master of metaphor, scene, description, and image. With his verbal gifts, his eye for detail, and his lyric love of the surface world, Updike has created moments and scenes of extraordinary beauty and freshness. Like Walt Whitman, the great nineteenth-century poet, Updike has attempted to celebrate and sing America, delighting in its textures and surfaces, its objects and gestures. His subject, in his own words, is "the whole mass of middling, hidden, troubled America," and the purpose of his books, which together form "a continental *magnum opus*," has been "the hymning of this great roughly rectangular country."

—James Schiff

FURTHER READING:

Baker, Nicholson. *U & I: A True Story.* New York, Random House, 1991.

Broer, Lawrence R., editor. *Rabbit Tales: Poetry and Politics in John Updike's Rabbit Novels.* Tuscaloosa, University of Alabama Press, 1998.

Detweiler, Robert C. *John Updike.* Boston, Twayne, 1984.

Greiner, Donald J. *John Updike's Novels.* Athens, Ohio University Press, 1984.

Luscher, Robert M. *John Updike: A Study of the Short Fiction.* New York, Twayne, 1993.

Newman, Judie. *John Updike.* New York, St. Martin's Press, 1988.

Schiff, James. *John Updike Revisited.* New York, Twayne, 1998.

Upstairs, Downstairs

Upstairs, Downstairs, a popular British-import television program about servants and their masters in an early twentieth-century London household, has been watched by an estimated one billion people in 40 countries since it was first broadcast on *Masterpiece Theatre* during the 1974 season. Produced by London Weekend Television, its 68 episodes follow the wealthy Bellamy family ("upstairs") and their servants ("downstairs") from 1903 until the stock market crash of 1929. Rigorous period detail, distinguished acting, and the equal time given to lower-class characters are hallmarks of the series. In depicting the erosion of the British class system during and after the Edwardian era, *Upstairs, Downstairs* bolstered the reputation of British television around the globe. The show won eight Emmy Awards and garnered high ratings for the Public Broadcasting

System in the United States, besides helping assure the success of *Masterpiece Theatre* as a PBS showcase synonymous with quality programming.

—Neal Baker

FURTHER READING:

Flaherty, Terrence. *Masterpiece Theatre: A Celebration of 25 Years of Outstanding Television.* San Francisco, KQED Books, 1996.

Floyd, Patty Lou. *Backstairs with Upstairs, Downstairs.* New York, St. Martin's, 1988.

Hardwick, Mollie. *The World of Upstairs, Downstairs.* New York, Holt, Rinehart, and Winston, 1976.

U.S. One

Running from Fort Kent, Maine, to Key West, Florida, U.S. One has served as the site and symbol for East Coast travel for much of the twentieth century. Stretching 2,377 miles, Route One got its name in 1925—when federal highway numbering began—as a recognition of the road's history as the primary conduit for passengers, commerce, information, and culture along the Atlantic seaboard. Much like Route 66, Route One became a popular site for exploring "local color" and roadside excursions. In 1938, the Federal Writers' Project published a popular guidebook highlighting distinctive landmarks, historical sites, and even local foods found along the route. Although still in active use by the late 1990s, U.S. One has lost much of its traffic to newer Interstates that allow travel at faster speeds.

—Justin Nordstrom

FURTHER READING:

Malcolm, Andrew, and Roger Straus. *U.S. 1: America's Original Main Street.* New York, St. Martin's Press, 1991.

USA Today

Debuting during an era when most newspapers saw sharp circulation declines, *USA Today* became the first successful national daily general-interest newspaper in the 1980s. Its stylish innovations, originally lampooned and mocked, were eventually adopted by most of the newspaper industry.

USA Today was the brainchild of Allen H. Neuharth, who became chairman of the Gannett newspaper chain during the 1970s. He began his publishing career in 1952 by starting a statewide sports newspaper in his native South Dakota, and joined Gannett in the 1960s by creating a statewide daily in Florida. He helped lead Gannett from its initial holdings in small upstate New York newspapers to a more national base. During his tenure at Gannett, the company bought the Louis Harris and Associates polling organization. Upon being named chairman of Gannett in 1978, he began developing the idea of a national daily newspaper; in December 1980, Gannett began a satellite information system, which would allow publishing plants on the East and West coasts to simultaneously publish the same information from one satellite. Neuharth insisted that there was also a growing market for a national newspaper—by the early 1980s, the rise of business travel meant that millions of people on business trips would tire of reading out-of-town newspapers, and want a standard newspaper from one city to another. A Neuharth associate said, "When (a traveler) wakes up in the morning his first thought is, 'What city am I in?'... The local newspaper doesn't mean a thing to him."

Neuharth oversaw the development of the newspaper, which was introduced in select markets on September 15, 1982 (it did not saturate the entire country until late 1983). *USA Today*'s staff had a dilemma as the deadline for the first edition neared, when three breaking news stories jockeyed for top coverage—Lebanese president-elect Bashir Gemayel was assassinated, a plane crash in Spain killed 55, and Princess Grace of Monaco had died in an automobile accident at age 53. The newspaper's editors spent much of September 14 on the streets and in offices in suburban Washington, D.C., determining that the public was most interested in Princess Grace's death; as Grace Kelly, she had been a major American film star during the 1950s. As a result, *USA Today*'s inaugural front page trumpeted the death of "America's Princess," relegating Gemayel's death to one paragraph on page one. Significantly, the coverage of the plane crash emphasized the "miracle" of 327 surviving passengers, not the 55 dead. The new paper was roundly castigated by media critics and competing newspapers for focusing on celebrity over international politics. In 1997, a subsequent *USA Today* editor, David Mazzarella, admitted that he would have led with the plane crash, featured a larger story on the assassination, and merely played Kelly's death as a small page one feature.

Criticism of *USA Today* began almost immediately. "A national daily newspaper seems like a way to lose a lot of money in a hurry," media analyst John Morton wrote upon *USA Today*'s debut. Complaints started with the newspaper's very look. It was sold in vending machines designed to resemble television sets, leading critics to accuse the newspaper of coverage as shallow as television (unlike established newspapers, *USA Today* used flashy national commercials in its first years, with celebrities from Willard Scott to Willie Mays and Mickey Mantle promoting the newspaper). Many derisively compared *USA Today* to fast food, calling it "McPaper." The newspaper ran full-color photographs on the front pages of each of its four sections at a time when color photography was prohibitively expensive for many newspapers, and seen as too garish by many editors. The *New York Times,* for example, was known as "The Gray Lady" for its steadfast black-and-white pages. The back of the news section was a full-page, full-color weather map, while most of its rivals printed a small, black-and-white map of the weather on an inside page. Each section—"News," "Money," "Sports," and "Life"--had only one story jump from the first page to the inside. Neuharth and his editors made a conscious decision to replace long newspaper stories with shorter pieces, accompanied by sidebars, and a greater use of charts and tables, and the paper's motto became, "An economy of words. A wealth of information." Each section also published polls every day, and invariably referred to "America" in its news stories as "the USA."

In an editorial mission statement in *USA Today*'s first issue, Neuharth wrote that he wanted his newspaper "to serve as a forum for better understanding and unity to help make the USA truly one nation." Each section of his paper was a deliberate attempt to fulfill this belief. The news section featured a state-by-state breakdown of top news stories, giving readers a cross-section of news events from across the country. The daily editorial was frequently accompanied by a differing viewpoint ("Another View") from a guest writer (in its early years, *USA Today* would include four editorials from various regional writers alongside its main editorial). The newspaper also developed a middle-of-the-road op-ed section, with regular national commentary from veteran journalists Richard Benedetto and Walter Shapiro. More politically pointed opinion makers (such as conservative writer Cal Thomas) tended to fare less successfully, as the newspaper adopted a populist, rather than elitist, approach. One 1998 editorial, published after the Modern Library's list of the top 100 American novels of the twentieth century, maintained that the truly great novels were the most commercially successful ones, not the most critically or intellectually acclaimed works.

USA Today's "Money" section (symbolized by a green title), introduced a regular feature, "Ad Watch," where popular television commercial campaigns were analyzed not by ad executives, but by focus groups of average American viewers. Eventually, *USA Today* ran "Ad Watch" features to judge commercials produced for the Super Bowl. The newspaper also began annual telephone public services during preparations for filing IRS (Internal Revenue Service) forms, as well as during college admissions and financial aid seasons, where money experts could provide free advice for readers.

USA Today's sports section had the most impact upon the newspaper industry. It published daily notes on all professional sports (during football season, for example, it ran daily notes on each National Football League team), and introduced a top 25 ranking for college sports (the Associated Press and UPI lists had previously gone only to 20), as well as top 25 lists for high school sports. Their major league baseball coverage featured expanded boxscores, offering play-by-play accounts on how every run in each major league baseball game was scored, and extensive, week-by-week, team-by-team statistical charts. The expanded sports coverage was welcomed by Rotisserie league team owners, who rated their teams on how the players they "owned" performed day by day. In 1991, *USA Today* introduced a successful weekly spin-off devoted to baseball. In both incarnations, *USA Today* successfully challenged *The Sporting News*, which since 1886 had provided weekly coverage of baseball and other major sports. Significantly, the only major national daily newspaper formed after *USA Today*'s debut was a sports newspaper. *The National,* edited by former *Sports Illustrated* senior writer Frank Deford, debuted in 1989. Despite a roster of nationally-known columnists and a series of high-profile scoops, *The National* lost its investment and folded within two years.

The sports section also supplied *USA Today* with its greatest professional controversy. In 1992, *USA Today* sportswriters learned that tennis great/political activist Arthur Ashe was suffering from AIDS (Acquired Immune Deficiency Syndrome)—the result of a tainted blood transfusion in 1988—a fact he had told only family and close friends. The reporters contacted Ashe and told him they were planning a story on his health. Ashe responded by holding an emotional press conference, where he made his AIDS status public. *USA Today* came under intense criticism from inside and outside the journalism community. Many observers felt that the newspaper had violated Ashe's privacy and had engaged in emotional blackmail, while others (such as Phil Mushnick) maintained that Ashe's health was a legitimate news story, and that by Ashe coming forward and admitting he had AIDS—rather than staying silent—he was able to raise both awareness and financial support for the disease, which he would die from in early 1993.

USA Today's "Life" section included a weekly column by radio and television talk show host Larry King, written much in the style of legendary gossip columnist Walter Winchell. King recommended movies and books, while also making occasional political commentary and noting events in his personal life, most memorably his heart surgery, frequent marriages, and the birth of his son in 1999, when King was 65. The Life section featured annual high school and collegiate "Academic All-Stars," honoring the brightest students in the nation. *USA Today*'s television coverage included nightly listings for national cable channels, several years before more traditional newspapers acknowledged cable's growing presence. The newspaper initiated the weekly list of top ten films at the box office, which was widely imitated by other venues, and provided complete Nielsen ratings for all prime-time television series. The Life section also developed one of the most respected book review sections in the country, with lengthy book reviews from freelancers and a bestseller list (eventually listing the top 150 books) drawn from national bookstore chains. This was in opposition to the *New York Times* bestseller list, which listed only the top 15 books, and kept its listing methodology secret.

Cynicism towards the press grew during the 1980s and 1990s, fueled by political scandals, perceived ideological and cultural bias, and paparazzi reporting tactics (including those implicated in Princess Diana's 1997 death). Neuharth saw his newspaper's role as helping to alleviate the cynicism. The idiosyncratic Neuharth—whose autobiography, *Confessions of an S.O.B.,* included commentary from his two ex-wives—embarked on a cross-country "BusCapade" during 1987, writing a regular column from each of the 50 states to celebrate the bicentennial of the Constitution. Neuharth celebrated the down-home common sense of average Americans from the heartland, as opposed to out-of-touch politicians and academics from the East and West Coasts. Some dismissed Neuharth's trek as a mere publicity stunt, but others appreciated his willingness to meet with his readers.

After a decade of losing money, *USA Today* finally turned a profit in 1993. The management spent their newfound prosperity on emphasizing its editorial content over its presentation. Executive editor Bob Dubill acknowledged that *USA Today*'s editors were "following TV.... Now, we're trying to lead TV." Within a 15 month span in 1996-1997, *USA Today* added an additional 25 reporting and editing slots for an editorial staff of 440. Publisher Tom Curley added, with pride, that many seasoned editors had returned to reporting beats. "We've taken some from the back room and put them on the street." Having begun in 1982 with no international bureaus and only two domestic bureaus, by the late 1990s, *USA Today* was also starting four domestic bureaus and several foreign bureaus—coinciding with the closing of domestic and international news bureaus by the major television networks.

By the mid-1990s, much of the early criticism of *USA Today* had abated. Media critic Ben Bagdikian (author of *The Media Monopoly*), who in 1982 called *USA Today* a "mediocre piece of journalism (presenting) a flawed picture of the world every day," recanted 15 years later. "It has become a much more serious newspaper ... I don't think it's a joke anymore." Veteran Washington reporter David Broder said, "*USA Today* has become a pretty damn good newspaper. They are spending money, and it is making a difference. And they are

everywhere." John Morton, who had initially criticized Neuharth's venture, said in 1997, "There is no question that they are a success. . . . You are less likely to find a front page article on some silly topic than on more serious issues. They have made it a more serious vehicle than it ever has been." Thomas Frank of *The Baffler,* while attacking the daily's middlebrow mindset, readily conceded that "*USA Today* is arguably the nation's most carefully edited and highly polished newspaper," concluding that it "has charted the course that almost every paper in the country is presently following." In 1997, even The Gray Lady, the *New York Times,* began running color photographs in every section of its daily editions (*The Washington Post* followed suit two years later).

While the circulation of most daily newspapers declined in the 1980s and 1990s (as New York, Philadelphia, Dallas, and Los Angeles all lost papers), *USA Today* enjoyed the second highest circulation of any paper in the country, with 1.62 million readers as of March 31, 1997. Analysts hailed *USA Today*'s strategies to keep its circulation base by appealing to common demographic interests. Some, however, lamented that *USA Today* simply pandered to its readership's pre-existing tastes, rather than helping its audience cultivate new ones; performance artist Jello Biafra dismissed the newspaper as providing "happy news for happy people with happy problems." Others maintained that *USA Today* treated its readers as consumers, not public citizens, and were upset that Neuharth denied any professional obligation, as a newspaper publisher, to call for sustained political and social change.

Neuharth retired from Gannett in 1989 upon his 65th birthday, and helped found the Freedom Forum, a media think-tank which produces a quarterly magazine—*Media Studies Journal.* Neuharth wrote that the Forum's principles were based upon "free press, free speech and free spirit." In 1996, the Forum opened the Newseum, directly across the street from *USA Today*'s Arlington, Virginia, headquarters. The Newseum hosts seminars and is the backdrop for the Cable News Network (CNN) media analysis program "Reliable Sources," and features many interactive media displays, allowing visitors to generate their own news broadcast, or select from newspapers across the country. Among the Newseum's archival documents is one of only three surviving rough drafts of the Declaration of Independence, which includes Thomas Jefferson's meticulous editing marks. Over 800,000 visitors toured the Newseum within its first two years, and in 1999, the Newseum began a coast-to-coast tour which, like the BusCapade, will visit each of America's 50 states.

—Andrew Milner

FURTHER READING:

Hartman, John K. *The USA Today Way: A Candid Look at the National Newspaper's First Decade, 1982-1992.* Mount Pleasant, Michigan, John K. Hartman, Department of Journalism, Central Michigan University, 1992.

Neuharth, Al. *Confessions of an S.O.B.* New York, Doubleday, 1989.

Prichard, Peter S. *The Making of McPaper: The Inside Story of USA Today.* New York, Andrews, McMeel & Parker, 1987.

V

Valdez, Luis (1940—)

Luis Valdez is considered to be the father of Chicano theater. He is the instigator of the contemporary Chicano theatrical movement and its most outstanding playwright. Valdez has distinguished himself as an actor, director, playwright, and film maker. However, it was in his role as the founding director of El Teatro Campesino, a theater of farm workers in California, that his efforts inspired young Chicano activists across the country to use theater as a means of organizing students, communities, and labor unions.

Luis Valdez was born on June 26, 1940, into a family of migrant farm workers in Delano, California. The second of ten children, he began to work the fields at the age of six and to follow the crops. Although Valdez's education was constantly interrupted, he nevertheless finished high school and went on to San Jose State College, where he majored in English and pursued his interest in theater. While there he won a playwriting contest with his one-act *The Theft* (1961). In 1963 the Drama Department produced his play *The Shrunken Head of Pancho Villa.* After graduating from college in 1964, Valdez joined the San Francisco Mime Troupe and learned the techniques of agitprop (agitation and propaganda) theater and Italian *commedia dell'arte* (comedy of art), both of which influenced Valdez's development of the basic format of Chicano theater: the one-act presentational *acto* or ''act.'' In 1965 Valdez enlisted in César Chávez's mission to organize farm workers in Delano into a union. It was there that Valdez brought together farm workers and students into El Teatro Campesino to dramatize the plight of the farm workers. The publicity and success gained by the troupe led to the spontaneous appearance of a national Chicano theater movement.

In 1967 Valdez and El Teatro Campesino left the unionizing effort to expand their theater beyond agitprop and farm worker concerns. From then on, Valdez and the theater have explored most of the theatrical genres that have been important to Mexicans in the United States, including religious pageants, vaudeville with the down-and-out *pelado* or underdog figure, and dramatized *corridos,* or ballads. The new type of socially engaged theater that El Teatro Campesino pioneered led to the creation of a full-blown theatrical movement in fields and barrios across the country. For more than three decades, El Teatro Campesino and Luis Valdez have dramatized the political and cultural concerns of Hispanics, initially among workers and their supporters and later among students in universities and the general public through stage, television, and film. In establishing the canon of what *teatro chicano* should be, Valdez and El Teatro Campesino published their *actos* (short one-act agitprop pieces) in 1971 with a preface in which Valdez outlined their theatrical principals: (1) Chicanos must be seen as a nation with geographic, religious, cultural, and racial roots in the Southwest; teatros must further the idea of nationalism and create a national theater based on identification with the Amerindian past; (2) the organizational support of the national theater must be from within and totally independent; (3) ''Teatros must never get away from La Raza. . . . If the Raza will not come to the theater, then the theater must go to the Raza. This, in the long run, will determine the shape, style, content, spirit and form of *el teatro chicano.*'' Valdez and his theater did expand by taking Chicano theater to Broadway and more commercial venues and by moving into commercial cinema and television.

During the late 1960s and the 1970s, El Teatro Campesino produced many of Valdez's plays, including *Los vendidos* (1967, The Sell-Outs), *The Shrunken Head of Pancho Villa* (1968), *Bernabé* (1970), *Dark Root of a Scream* (1971), *La Carpa de los Rascuachis* (1974), and *El Fin del Mundo* (1976). In 1978, Valdez broke into mainstream theater in Los Angeles with the Mark Taper Forum's production of his *Zoot Suit* and, in 1979, with the Broadway production of the same play. In 1986 he had a successful run of his play *I Don't Have to Show You No Stinking Badges* at the Los Angeles Theater Center.

In *Bernabé*, one of Valdez's most poetic plays, a young village idiot is transformed into a natural man by his marriage to La Tierra (The Earth) and his subsequent death. Employing Aztec mythology and symbols in a tale about contemporary barrio characters, the play explores the pre-Colombian heritage of Chicano society. The Mayan theme of "death is life, and life is death" was developed here and continued to appear in Valdez's later works. The writing of *Bernabé* marked the beginning of Valdez's search for the meaning of Aztec and Mayan legends, history, and philosophy, but also revealed the influence of Spanish playwright Federico García Lorca, who also strove to elevate the country folk to heroic and mythic stature.

Valdez's screenwriting career began with early film and television versions of Corky González's poem ''I Am Joaquín'' (1969) and with his own ''Los Vendidos.'' Later, he wrote a film adaptation of *Zoot Suit* (1982). However, his real incursion into major Hollywood productions and success came with his writing and directing of *La Bamba*, the screen biography of Chicano rock 'n' roll star Ritchie Valens. Other screen plays include *Corridos* (1987) and the successful television movies *La Pastorela* (1991) and *The Cisco Kid* (1993). Valdez's plays, essays, and poems have been widely anthologized. He published two collections of plays: *Luis Valdez—The Early Works* (1990) and *Zoot Suit and Other Plays* (1992). Valdez's awards include an Obie (1968), Los Angeles Drama Critics Awards (1969, 1972 and 1978), a special Emmy Award (1973), the San Francisco Bay Critics Circle for Best Musical (1983), and honorary doctorates from San Jose Sate University, Columbia College, and the California Institute of the Arts.

—Nicolás Kanellos

FURTHER READING:

Broyles-González, Yolanda. *El Teatro Campesino: Theatre in the Chicano Movement.* Austin, University of Texas Press, 1994.

Kanellos, Nicolás. *The Hispanic American Almanac.* Detroit, Gale Research, 1997.

Kanellos, Nicolás, and Claudio Esteva Fabregat, editors. *Handbook of Hispanic Cultures in the United States.* Houston, Arte Público Press, 1994-95.

Valens, Ritchie (1941-1959)

The Latino teen rock sensation had a brief but brilliant career. Most famous for his song "La Bamba," a rock 'n' roll version of a traditional Mexican ballad, Ritchie Valens fused different kinds of music together to form his own remarkable style. Influenced by some of the biggest names in rock 'n' roll, including Elvis Presley, Bo Diddley, and Little Richard, he earned himself the nickname "The Little Richard of San Fernando." Although his career was cut short by a fatal plane crash, Ritchie wrote and recorded songs that would influence future generations of rock musicians, including the Beatles and Led Zepellin.

Born Richard Steve Valenzuela in the San Fernando Valley suburb of Pacoima, California, Ritchie received a good Catholic upbringing from his parents despite money being tight. As a child, Ritchie made himself a guitar out of a cigar box and a broom handle and strung it with household string. His home life gave him a grounding in traditional Mexican mariachi music played by his relatives, and the radio exposed him to the rhythm and blues sound. In 1956 Ritchie joined a band called The Silhouettes who performed at "hops" around the San Fernando Valley area. The Silhouettes were a multiracial band featuring two African Americans, a Japanese American, and Ritchie, a Mexican American. After various reshuffles in the band, Ritchie sang lead vocals and played the guitar.

Ritchie was discovered at the tender age of 16 by Bob Keane of Del-fi Records at one of the San Fernando garage hops. Once Keane saw how audiences responded to the band's charismatic lead singer he gave him a recording contract. Keane changed his name to Ritchie Valens: a catchier, rockier, and Anglicized version of his real name. Ritchie's first hit was a rock 'n' roll number "Come On Let's Go," which he wrote himself. It reached number 42 on the U.S. charts. In October 1958, Del-fi released "La Bamba" with a lovesong entitled "Donna" on the other side. This lovesong was written by Ritchie about his high school sweetheart, who was forbidden by her father to go out with "that Mexican." It turned out to be the more successful track, selling over a million copies and reaching number two on the U.S. charts. "La Bamba" only climbed as high as number 22.

Keane found Ritchie an unorthodox musician to work with; Ritchie would make up songs and then forget them, or he would base a whole song on just eight guitar chords and two lines of lyrics. The pair successfully recorded a large number of songs in Keane's basement studio at his home in Silverlake, California. Keane wanted to get Ritchie out on the road on tour since his major talent was in performing. He assessed that Ritchie "could rock like a rough street kid while simultaneously exuding a shy, appealing vulnerability," a combination that dazzled his teenage audiences.

Ritchie's final tour was called "The Winter Dance Party." He headlined with Buddy Holly and the Big Bopper. Ritchie, with the success of "Donna" under his belt, was not obliged to play low profile concerts in the Midwest but reportedly did so out of loyalty to his fans. The weather was bitterly cold and the heating had broken on their tour bus. Buddy Holly chartered a plane with space for himself, his guitarist, and the Big Bopper. Ritchie could not cope with the sub-zero temperature levels and talked Buddy's guitarist into tossing a coin for the last seat. Ritchie won the toss. The plane crashed shortly after takeoff in a field outside of Fargo, North Dakota. All passengers were killed. The occasion was dubbed by the press as "The Day the Music Died."

Had he lived longer, Ritchie would have likely become one of the most significant musicians of the 1960s. The cultural critic George Lipsitz wrote that "Valens' tragic death at the age of seventeen deprived the Los Angeles Chicano community of its biggest star, and it cut short the career of one of rock and roll's most eclectic synthesizers." Ritchie's talent lay in his ability to mix radically different types of music: black rhythm and blues, white folk music, and Mexican mariachi songs—the sounds that surrounded him as he grew up in postwar California. Despite being the only musician of Mexican ancestry to make it in the mainstream pop scene, Ritchie regarded himself as first and foremost American. He did not speak Spanish and had to be coached for singing the Spanish lyrics of "La Bamba." In 1987 a bioptic called La Bamba, made by the Chicano film director Luis Valdez was released, regenerating interest in Ritchie's music, demonstrating how Ritchie's music continued to touch young people. Ritchie's music didn't die with him.

—Candida Taylor

FURTHER READING:

Culler, Jim. The Art of Democracy: A Concise History of Popular Culture in the United States. New York, Monthly Review Press, 1996.

Lipsitz, George. "Cruising Around the Historical Block." Time Passages: Collective Memory and American Popular Culture. Minneapolis, University of Minnesota Press.

Stambler, Irwin. The Encyclopedia of Pop, Rock and Soul. New York, St. Martin's Press, 1974.

Valentine's Day

Valentine's Day, February 14, is a day consecrated by custom to the celebration of romantic love. The observance dates back to medieval times but, in twentieth-century America, Valentine's Day—like other occasions that are linked to sentiment, such as Mother's Day—has become a ritual appendage of consumer culture. Attempts to link Valentine's Day and its emphasis on worldly love to an early martyr (or pair of martyrs) of the Christian church have been discredited, and historians have come to attribute the connection between romance and February 14 to Geoffrey Chaucer (1340?-1400), the English poet and author of The Canterbury Tales.

In his work The Parliament of Foules, Chaucer wrote: "For this was Seynt Valentyne's Day. When every foul cometh ther to choose his mate." Throughout the late Middle Ages and the early modern period, Valentine's Day was an occasion for declaring one's affections or using divination to determine the identity of one's lover or future spouse. Sleeping on a pillow to which five bay leaves were pinned, for example, would produce a dream in which a lover would be revealed. Observances of the day could be elegant and courtly or a raucous and vulgar charivari (mock serenade, usually of newlyweds). The first Valentine's day cards were hand-made, but by the early nineteenth century in England printed cards were common. When this fashion was exported to the United States in the 1840s a veritable Valentine mania broke out.

The industrialized world of the early 1800s suffered from a shortage of holidays. Where once the feasting and fasting days of the

Christian year had provided the occasion for a host of holidays, festivals, and fairs, the Enlightenment and the Industrial Revolution had, in the names of efficiency and the economy, produced a calendar almost empty of special days. (In 1761 there were 47 bank holidays in England; by 1834 there were only four.) By popularizing and commercializing Valentine's Day in the United States the merchant class reshaped, romanticized, and tamed the day for their own purposes. Valentine's Day (and slightly later, Christmas) demonstrates how business could profit from creating new meaning for an old holiday.

Printing companies were not the only ones to profit from the new popularity of the day as other business interests rapidly attached themselves to the successful annual marketing of romance. Confectioners sold candies and chocolates in great quantities, while florists, jewelers, photographers, and makers of pens, pins, and knick-knacks of all kinds found they could increase sales by linking their product to Valentine's Day. Women and children were prime targets for this commercialization of sentiment.

In the twentieth century the Valentine's Day industry grew even more vast. By the 1990s, sales of candy for the occasion had risen to over $600 million; 70 million roses are given on the day; restaurants are filled with couples seeking romantic dining; over a billion cards are exchanged every year in the United States alone, with school children leading the way. Hallmark Cards, the largest American manufacturer, produces over 2,000 different designs, which are changed annually. Most of these cards are plainer than they once were, shorn of the peacock feathers, real lace, and jewels that once adorned those of the nineteenth century. It is interesting to note that Valentine cards were not always necessarily sent as straightforward declarations of love. A widespread custom was the anonymous sending of insulting or sarcastic cards, often aimed at women to keep them in their place, and comic or satirical, even vulgar, cards were still bought and sent in the late twentieth century.

Valentine's Day is celebrated in song and film as synonymous with romantic love. It is a day for dances and gala balls, the advertising of ''honeymoon suites'' for married couples whose ardor may have waned over the years, and for decorating public places with heart shapes pierced by the arrow of an often visible and cherubic Cupid. Over the years the holiday has spread beyond England and America to Europe, Asia, and other English-speaking countries such as South Africa and Australia, and production and sales of Valentine cards have become a world-wide phenomenon.

—Gerry Bowler

FURTHER READING:

MacDonald, Margaret Read. *The Folklore of World Holidays*. Detroit, Gale Research, 1992.

Schmidt, Leigh Eric. *Consumer Rites: The Buying and Selling of American Holidays*. Princeton, Princeton University Press, 1995.

Valentino, Rudolph (1895-1926)

''The Great Lover'' was the nickname given to Rudolph Valentino when he became a motion picture star in 1919. While the nickname is still synonymous with Valentino, his last name is sufficient to evoke the same picture, that of a handsome, suave man who is irresistible to women. His female fans copied styles from his movies, and some men copied his hairstyles. During his brief stardom, he was often the butt of criticism from men. Despite this, women of the era literally fainted at the sight of him and worshipped him at the altar of their local movie theater.

For someone who had such a profound effect on popular culture during his lifetime, Valentino came from rather humble beginnings. He was born in Castellaneta, Italy, with the impossible name of Rudolpho Alfonzo Ralfaelo Pierre Filibert Gugllielmi di Valentina d'Antonguolla. Ironically, the year of his birth, 1895, is also generally looked on as the year motion pictures were born. His father, Giovanni, was a veterinarian who died of malaria in 1906. While the young Valentino longed to become a cavalry officer, his family felt that after the death of his father he needed a better paying career to help take care of the family. His mother was finally persuaded to allow him to apply to the Royal Naval Academy, but he failed the physical. Eventually he attended the Royal Academy of Agriculture, where he graduated with honors. He planned to become a gentleman farmer, but fate had other plans.

After graduation, he went on a trip outside Italy and proceeded to lose all his money gambling. To ease the family's embarrassment, Rudolpho was sent to America on the U.S.S. Cleveland in 1913. After some difficult times in New York, Valentino began to find work as a taxi dancer. Shortly thereafter, he got a job with the millionaire Cornelius Bliss as a gardener. Unfortunately, he was soon fired when he wrecked a motorcycle owned by his employer.

Unemployed again, Valentino received help from a friend who was the head waiter at Maxim's Restaurant. He was hired for a position as a dancer there. He later met and signed as a partner to dancer Bonnie Glass who was replacing her current partner, Clifton Webb (soon to be an actor). After Glass retired, he danced with another partner, Joan Sawyer, on the vaudeville circuit. Valentino soon grew tired of touring and resolved to give up dancing and become a farmer in California. To get there, he took a part in a play called *The Masked Model* that was to tour the West Coast. Unfortunately the play closed in Utah, but he was paid with a ticket to San Francisco.

Once there, he met Norman Kerry, Mary Pickford's leading man, who persuaded him to try his luck in Hollywood. By 1917, he made his first screen appearance as an extra in *Alimony* and had played several villains in other films. A chance meeting with screen star Mae Murray resulted in work on two of her films. It was this exposure that led to more work.

While working on *Once to Every Woman* in 1919, he impulsively married actress Jean Acker. Jean locked him out of her apartment that night, and they separated with the marriage never being consummated. This was to be a source of embarrassment to studio executives when Valentino became a sex symbol. Despite their brief marriage, Valentino and Acker remained good friends to the end of his life.

Valentino made an important fan with his next project, *The Eyes of Youth*, with Clara Kimball Young, released in 1919. He impressed the head Scenarist for Metro Studios, June Mathis. Currently working on the project, *The Four Horsemen of the Apocalypse*, based on the novel by Blasco-Ibanez, she was convinced she had found the perfect actor for the part of Julio. Studio executives, however, were not as impressed. But after much lobbying, both by Mathis and Valentino

Rudolph Valentino (right) in a scene from the film _The Four Horsemen of the Apocalypse_.

himself, he was given the part. He so impressed Mathis and director Rex Ingram during early footage that they expanded his part, and a star was born. From his first appearance in the film, when he tangos with Beatrice Dominguez, he enthralled the audience. Details of the film were copied by fans. The tango became a dance craze, men copied his slicked back hair, and women copied the bolero costume he wore.

If Valentino had expected the studio heads to now give him better parts and pay him accordingly, he was wrong. He appeared in several more films, such as _Camille_ and _The Conquering Power_. The executives refused his demand for a raise, and then declined to renew his contract when it expired. A new contract, however, was eventually signed with the Famous Players-Lasky Paramount Studio, and Valentino began filming _The Sheik_ with Agnes Ayres; this film cemented his stardom. During this time, his friend and supporter, June Mathis, had also left Metro and joined Famous Players studio. It would be almost impossible to imagine the kind of hysteria that greeted him after this film was released in 1921. Audiences were much less sophisticated and blasé in the early days of film than in the late twentieth century, and pandemonium reigned whenever he made an appearance.

Valentino experienced a good year in 1922 with the release of the original _Blood and Sand_ and _The Young Rajah_. After the latter film was released, women began wearing their hair in turban style.

That year, Valentino was also granted an interlocutory divorce from Jean Acker. Unfortunately, he neglected to wait a year before marrying Natacha Rambova (Winifred Hudnut) in Mexico. When he returned to California, he was arrested and jailed for bigamy. He was fined $10,000 and released. The resulting scandal actually increased Valentino's popularity instead of ruining him. He and Rambova remarried in 1923 after waiting the required year.

In 1924, he filmed several pictures, including _Monsieur Beaucaire_ and _The Eagle_. For the film _The Hooded Falcon,_ he grew a beard that not only infuriated his fans, but also the Barbers of America Organization, which threatened to boycott his films; needless to say, he shaved the beard. Unfortunately, Rambova had tremendous influence over Valentino's career, but did not have the best taste in selecting projects for him. His image began to tarnish, at least among the male half of the audience. Rambova bought him a slave bracelet that he wore constantly, and began choosing projects for him that made his androgynous qualities appear more feminine; she was eventually barred from working in any capacity on his films. Shortly thereafter, Rambova left him and they eventually divorced.

In 1926, he filmed _Son of the Sheik,_ supposedly a sequel to his earlier hit film. The film was not as successful, although his female fans were steadfast. His most steady date in this, the last year of his life, was eccentric Polish actress, Pola Negri. She saw him off on a train to New York for the East Coast premiere of *Son of the Sheik*. On August 15, however, he became seriously ill and was taken to the hospital. Diagnosed with a perforated ulcer, surgery was performed on him. The surgery went well and Valentino appeared to be doing well, but peritonitis set in and the infection spread throughout his body; he died on August 23, 1926.

The events surrounding the viewing of the body and the funeral took on a circus-like atmosphere—it probably was the first such celebrity funeral that had so much chaos surrounding it. There were riots in the street near the Campbell's Funeral Parlour; approximately 100,000 people viewed his body and it took three days for everyone in line to pass by the coffin. Rumors also began circulating about Valentino's death, the most persistent being that he was murdered, either by the Black Hand gang or by a jealous husband.

The funeral service in New York was conducted at St. Malachi's Church, with over 6,000 people in attendance. His body was then transported by train back to California, and crowds of people gathered as the train passed through each town. The service in California was at the Church of the Good Shepherd in Hollywood, and only 300 people attended his second funeral. Pola Negri, never one to give up an opportunity for publicity, threw herself on the coffin and then fainted. Although she had no proof of it, she claimed that she and Valentino were engaged. The day following the funeral, 5,000 people visited the mausoleum.

Valentino was buried in a crypt borrowed from June Mathis. When she died two years later, her husband, Sylvano Balboni, solved the problem of what to do with Valentino's body when he sold his adjoining crypt to the Valentino family. Valentino was then moved to his final resting place above June Mathis' mother.

In 1927, a commemorative service was attended by faithful fans and the tradition continued for many years—even in the late 1990s there were Valentino fan clubs. Another tradition that helped keep Valentino's name alive for so many years after his death was the annual appearances of the so-called "Lady in Black." For many years (over 50) she appeared, dressed in black with a veil covering her face and carrying red roses to his grave on the anniversary of his death. Speculation on the identity of the woman varied from a publicity stunt with various women playing the part, to a brokenhearted lover who could not forget him. The truth of the story was never established, and the lady finally disappeared.

For women of the Jazz Age of the Roaring Twenties, Valentino was the first sex symbol of the dangerous kind. He represented all that was enticing to repressed women, who had only recently started to make gains in emancipation by getting the vote. Despite his short life, he represented something they had not dared long for in the Victorian and Edwardian eras. In spite of rumors which surfaced many years after his death regarding his sexual orientation and that of his ex-wives, the effect Valentino had on the 1920s cannot be minimized or overlooked.

—Jill A. Gregg

FURTHER READING:

Bothan, Noel. *Valentino: The Love God.* New York, Ace Books, 1977.

Morris, Michael. *Madam Valentino: The Many Lives of Natacha Rambova.* New York, Abbeville Press, 1991.

Scagnetti, Jack. *The Intimate Life of Rudolph Valentino.* New York, Jonathon David Publishing, 1975.

Tajiri, Vincent. *Valentino.* New York, Bantam Books, 1977.

Walker, Alexander. *Rudolph Valentino.* New York, Stein and Day, 1976.

Valenzuela, Fernando (1960—)

Few baseball players have captured the popular imagination as Fernando Valenzuela did in the summer of 1981, when the word "Fernandomania" came into the English lexicon, as the young lefthander with the incredible screwball astounded the baseball world by tossing five shutouts during an eight game winning streak to start the season. In a career that lasted from 1980 to 1996, Valenzuela was known almost as much for his burly physique and unorthodox windup as for his effectiveness and durability.

Fernando Valenzuela was born in Etchohaquila, in the Mexican state of Sonora, about 350 miles south of the Arizona border. The youngest of twelve children, by the age of sixteen Fernando was earning $80 a month as a pitcher in the Mexican leagues. Beating out the Yankees by half a step, the Los Angeles Dodgers bought the lefthander's contract from Puebla for $120,000 in 1979. The following year, Valenzuela made his debut with the Dodgers, pitching eighteen scoreless innings during the season's final weeks.

In 1981, twenty-year-old rookie Fernando Valenzuela exploded on the baseball scene. Fernandomania began in Los Angeles soon after the screwball-throwing lefthander started the season with a shutout, and it spread across the North American continent as Valenzuela managed to notch seven more victories (including four more shutouts) before registering his first loss. Although the league caught up with him in the second half of a strike-torn season, Valenzuela nevertheless finished the year as baseball's strikeout king, while also boasting the league's second-highest win total (13) and an impressive 2.48 ERA. In his first full season in the major leagues, the boy from Mexico had led his team to a World Series championship, while being recognized as both the National League's Rookie of the Year and its Cy Young Award winner.

Valenzuela's face appeared on the covers of numerous sports magazines in the summer of 1981, while he charmed the sports world with his modesty, his eyes-to-the-sky windup, and his virtual ignorance of English. His age also kept people guessing, as many observers supposed that he was significantly older than his twenty years. Although Valenzuela went on to have a successful career with the Dodgers, Fernandomania faded by season's end; afterwards he was just a very good pitcher. But good enough to win 19 games in 1982 and register a league leading 21 victories in 1986. Along the way he received baseball's first million-dollar salary arbitration award in 1983.

Valenzuela pitched for the Dodgers for eleven seasons, during which he won 141 games while losing 116. One of his most appealing features was his durability, as he led the league in complete games in three seasons and twice in innings pitched. During the 1980s he was also one of the league's most consistent strikeout pitchers, finishing among the top five for seven years in a row. During the late 1980s, his

Fernando Valenzuela

FURTHER READING:

Littwin, Mike. *Fernando!* New York, Bantam, 1981.

McNeil, William F. *Dodger Chronicles.* Pittsfield, Massachusetts, W.F. McNeil, 1993.

———. *The Dodgers Encyclopedia.* Champaign, Illinois, Sports Publishing, 1997.

Sahadi, Lou. *The L.A. Dodgers: The World Champions of Baseball.* New York, Quill, 1982.

Thorn, Jim, and Pete Palmer, ed. *Total Baseball.* New York, Warner, 1989.

Valium

career began to be hobbled by shoulder soreness—an ailment no doubt caused by a decade of subjecting his arm to the strain of throwing his famed screwball. In addition to being a star hurler during his years with the Dodgers, Valenzuela was also recognized for his excellent defense and a dangerous bat.

His years with the Dodgers were capped by a no-hitter on June 26, 1990, but his career was thrown into doubt after the Dodgers released him the following spring. For the next seven years Valenzuela bounced from team to team, including a stint in the Mexican leagues in 1992. Although his comebacks always seemed to draw a fair amount of attention, they were rarely successful (a 13-8 record in San Diego in 1996 being the only exception), as Valenzuela managed to compile a meager record of only 32 wins and 35 losses during his post-Dodger career.

With 173 career victories, Valenzuela retired as the leading Mexican-born pitcher in Major League history. Despite his considerable achievements with the Dodgers, he is nevertheless best remembered for setting the baseball world on its ear during the spring and summer of 1981.

—Kevin O'Connor

Little over a decade after its 1963 debut on the prescription-drug market in the United States, Valium had become a widely prescribed tranquilizer and began attracting media attention for what was seen as its rampant abuse. Reports found that many prescriptions for diazepam, Valium's generic name, were written by general practitioners, not mental-health professionals, and that a disproportionate number were given to women over 30 to control so-called "free-floating" anxiety.

Valium, taken from the Latin word meaning "to be strong and well" and classified as an anxiolytic, or anxiety-dissolving drug, was developed in the New Jersey labs of pharmaceutical giant Hoffman-LaRoche by Dr. Leo Sternbach, who had also synthesized the compound that came on the market as Librium in 1960. Librium had been developed to compete with a rival company's popular tranquilizer, Miltown. All of these new drugs were targeted at middle-class Americans, many of whom were unlikely to visit a psychologist or psychiatrist for non-threatening depression or anxiety disorders because of the stigma attached to "mental illness." Valium, stronger than Librium and less bitter in taste, acted on the limbic system, the part of the brain that regulates emotional response and reaction. Because it was so potent, it could be formulated into much smaller doses than Librium, and unlike other tranquilizers, soothed without inducing drowsiness.

"Some Roche executives did not expect much of it," wrote Gilbert Cant of the *New York Times Magazine* about Sternbach's synthesizing of diazepam, "but a couple of them tried it on postmenopausal mothers-in-law whom they found insufferable, and were delighted by its calming effects." Valium came on the market in the United States in 1963. Users were cautioned not to operate heavy machinery or drive a car while taking it, and warnings about mixing it with alcohol were also blatant—the effects of both substances on the central nervous system were doubled when ingested together. Part of Valium's appeal lay in the belief that it was nonaddictive, and unlike other tranquilizers, almost impossible to be taken in a lethal dose by a suicidal person.

By 1974, 59.3 million Valium prescriptions were being written by doctors, and this figure, taken in conjunction with Hoffman-LaRoche's patent on diazepam, meant that Sternbach's employer had cornered 81 percent of the tranquilizer market in the country. The following year, a *Vogue* article entitled "Danger Ahead! Valium—The Pill You Love Can Turn on You," quoted extensively from Dr.

Marie Nyswander, a New York City psychiatrist, who warned of its addictive properties. "Probably it would be very hard to find any group of middle-class women in which some aren't regularly on Valium," Nyswander declared. "Valiumania," as a 1976 piece authored by Cant in the *New York Times Magazine* was titled, termed it the most profitable drug in history, and questioned whether it had been "overmarketed" by Hoffman-LaRoche. Tellingly, only about 10 percent of prescriptions for Valium written in 1974 came from mental health professionals; 60 to 70 percent of Valium prescriptions came from the family doctor, gynecologists, or even more alarmingly, pediatricians. "Women, mostly those over 30, outnumber male users of Valium by 2-1/2 to one," Cant pointed out.

Valium also began to appear as an illegal "street" drug around 1975, the same year overall tranquilizer usage in the United States peaked. In 1978, it was estimated that about 20 percent of American women were taking Valium; nearly 2.3 billion of the pills were prescribed that year alone. The drug was so pervasive—and still considered relatively harmless—that it began to enter the vernacular. It was jokingly referred to as "Executive Excedrin," and made its way into comic scenes in movies such as *Starting Over,* as well as Woody Allen films and Neil Simon plays. An autopsy report found it in Elvis Presley's system when he died in 1977.

A 1979 bestseller, *I'm Dancing as Fast as I Can,* did much to alert the public to Valium's dangers. Its author, Barbara Gordon, was a successful, educated Manhattan career woman who became hooked on the drug over a nine-year period, and had to be hospitalized for her withdrawal symptoms. Reports of "rebound insomnia" from even light Valium usage began to appear in the press, and Senate subcommittee hearings later that year received widespread media coverage. Dr. Joseph Pursch—who, as head of the drug and rehabilitation program at Long Beach (California) Naval Regional Medical Center had treated former First Lady Betty Ford for her substance abuse problems—testified on the dangers of Valium. Physicians publicly confessed they had become addicted to the free samples mailed to them by Hoffman-LaRoche. An executive at the company defended the drug before the Senate committee, and asserted that its abuse was not Hoffman-LaRoche's fault, but lay rather at the feet of the doctors who overprescribed it and in the percentage of patients who became addicted to almost any substance. A physician also spoke on behalf of Hoffman-LaRoche, and asserted with complete seriousness that "to imply that the medicine is dangerous or highly addictive is not only incorrect, but it is a great disservice to millions of people whose lives are already troubled," *Time* quoted Dr. Michael Halberstam as saying.

As a compromise, the Food and Drug Administration forced Hoffman-LaRoche to include the caveat in its medical-journal advertisements for Valium as well as in the information provided to physicians stating that "anxiety or tension associated with the stress of everyday life usually does not require treatment with an anxiolytic drug." This warning went into effect in the summer of 1980, but a 1981 report on the possible link between Valium use and the rapid growth of cancer cells probably spelled a far worse death knell for the drug's popularity with the general public. The author of the study, Dr. David Horrobin, claimed he was forced out of a job at the University of Montreal because of his findings and his attempt to make them public. By 1982, the most prescribed medication in America was Tagamet, the anti-ulcer drug.

—Carol Brennan

FURTHER READING:

Cant, Gilbert. "Valiumania." *New York Times Magazine.* February 1, 1976, 34-44.

"Danger Ahead! Valium—The Pill You Love Can Turn on You." *Vogue.* February, 1975, 152-153.

"The Drugging of America." *Science News.* February 25, 1978, 119.

Kent, Letitia. "Leo Sternbach: The Tranquil Chemist." *SciQuest.* December, 1980, 22-24.

"Tranquil Tales." *Time.* September 24, 1979, 78.

"Valium Abuse: The Yellow Peril." *Newsweek.* September 24, 1979, 66.

"Valium Alarm." *Time.* January 19, 1981, 74-75.

"Yellow Light for Tranquilizers." *Time.* July 21, 1980, 53.

Vallee, Rudy (1901-1986)

One of the most popular American singers in the 1920s and 1930s, Rudy Vallee became a sought-after supporting actor in Hollywood films, an important pioneer in radio variety shows, and much later a musical comedy star on Broadway.

Born Hubert Prior Vallée in Island Pond, Vermont, he was a self-taught drummer in his high school band. In 1919 he began a self-study

Rudy Vallee

of the clarinet and saxophone, frequently spending six to eight hours a day practicing, and within a year was performing publicly at the Strand Theater in Portland, Maine. After a year at the University of Maine, he transferred to Yale in the fall of 1922, where he earned tuition by playing his sax at country clubs and college dances. While playing with the Yale Collegians he began using a hand-held megaphone to amplify his crooning, light-tone voice. The megaphone— similar to the ones used by cheerleaders—became his trademark and was soon copied by other vocalists.

In 1924 Vallee dropped out of Yale and went to London, where he played sax at the Savoy Hotel with Vincent Lopez and the Savoy Havana Band. Returning to Yale, he continued his studies and graduated with a Bachelor of Philosophy degree in 1925. Moving to New York City, Rudy formed a small band called The Connecticut Yankees, consisting of two violins, two saxophones, and a piano. The primary purpose of the orchestra was to accompany their leader's suave, but somewhat nasal vocals. An engagement at the Heigh-Ho Club in Manhattan in 1928 brought Vallee his first real fame. He was soon broadcasting on radio as many as 25 times a week, beginning each one with "Heigh-ho everyone, this is Rudy Vallee." His sudden success brought him engagements at New York's Paramount and Palace Theaters.

Rudy and the Connecticut Yankees went to Hollywood to film *Vagabond Lover* in 1929, returning immediately to New York for more radio work and regular appearances at Villa Vallee, a nightclub Rudy owned. He soon evolved a busy routine, starting with daily shows at the Paramount and other theaters, then nightly shows at the Villa Vallee, and three broadcasts, along with recording sessions and filming musical short subjects.

In 1929 Rudy also began broadcasting a weekly one-hour variety show on NBC radio. Stars such as Fred Allen, Jack Benny, Edgar Bergen, and Kate Smith made their debuts on *Vallee's Fleischmann Hour* and later became radio stars themselves. Other outstanding guests included George Gershwin, George Burns and Gracie Allen, Eddie Cantor, Red Skelton, and Fannie Brice. Vallee also invited black performers, rarely used on network shows, to appear, including Bill "Bojangles" Robinson, Maxine Sullivan, and Fats Waller. At its peak, the show featured America's top stars. On December 13, 1934, for example, Vallee broadcast from the Radio City Music Hall, featuring announcer Jimmy Wallington, guests Henry Fonda and June Walker playing a scene from *The Farmer Takes a Wife,* and interviews with Cole Porter, Buck and Bubbles, William S. Hart, and Bea Lillie.

After ten years, Vallee ended his popular radio show. In 1942, he played the bumbling millionaire in one of director Preston Sturges' best films, *Palm Beach Story,* starring Claudette Colbert. When World War II began, Vallee joined the U.S. Coast Guard Service and led a forty-piece band on an extensive tour. He then returned to radio in 1944, broadcasting for two years with co-star Monty Woolley. Hollywood beckoned in 1947, and Vallee played light comedy and character roles in such films as *Bachelor and the Bobby-Soxer,* with Cary Grant and Myrna Loy; *I Remember Mama,* with Irene Dunne; *Unforgettably Yours,* with Rex Harrison; and *The Beautiful Blonde from Bashful Bend,* with Betty Grable. From 1961-64, he played in the Broadway musical, *How to Succeed in Business Without Really Trying*, and his final film was the Hollywood version of that show in 1967.

—Benjamin Griffith

FURTHER READING:

Lackmann, Ron. *Same Time . . . Same Station: A-Z Guide to Radio from Jack Benny to Howard Stern.* New York, Facts on File, 1996.

Ragan, David. *Who's Who in Hollywood, 1900-1976.* New Rochelle, Arlington, 1976.

Quinlan, David. *The Illustrated Directory of Film Stars.* New York, Hippocrene, 1982.

Vampires

No creature haunting Western society's collective imagination has proven more enduring, more compelling, or more alluring than the vampire. But it was only with the his transformation from emaciated, plague-carrying "nosferatu" (literally, "not dead") to suave, sexually appealing anti-hero that the vampire's status as pop cultural icon was assured. Authors and poets ranging from Byron, Goethe, Baudelaire, and Le Fanu to Poe, Wells, King, and Rice have made contributions to vampire lore. Dracula, the best-known and most resilient vampire, has appeared in more films than any other fictional character save perhaps for Sherlock Holmes. On television, vampires have starred in dramas (*The Kindred,* 1996), sitcoms (*The Munsters,* 1964-1966), soaps (*Dark Shadows,* 1966-1971), and countless made-for-television movies. On the radio, Orson Welles' portrayal of Dracula for *The Mercury Theatre* in 1938 became an instant classic. In addition, vampires have been made the subject of such cultural castoffs as stamps, comic books, lunchboxes, breakfast cereals, cartoons, role-playing games, and do-it-yourself makeup kits—in short, just about anything capable of sustaining an image or supporting a narrative.

In pre-Christian times, the vampire was a regular in Middle European folklore. Typically portrayed as an unkempt peasant with terrible breath and a craving for the blood of farm animals, his taste underwent a profound change in the seventeenth century— instead of sheep and oxen, he began turning to members of his own family in search of nourishment. This shift in sensibility most likely occurred because distraught villagers needed a face to attach to the deadly plague infecting their neighbors.

The vampire entered the literary realm by way of German gothicism: in Ossenfelder's "The Vampire" (1748), Bürger's *Lenore* (1773), and Goethe's *The Bride of Corinth* (1797) the once-shy bloodsucker slowly made the transition to sexual predator. But the first truly modern vampire appeared in John Polidori's extended revision of a fragment written by the English poet Lord Byron in 1816; amazingly, it was during the same session of story-telling at a villa near Geneva that Mary Shelley conceived the plot of *Frankenstein.* In Polidori's *The Vampyre* (1819), the dashing Lord Ruthven quenches his thirst with the blood of attractive young women. To cash in on Ruthven's surprising popularity, a number of plays, burlesques, and operas were quickly brought to stage in France, Germany, and England.

With the publication of James Malcolm Rymer's 868 page penny-dreadful, *Varney the Vampire, or the Feast of Blood* in 1847, the vampire became a pop culture phenomenon. Many elements of Varney's comic-book adventures were appropriated by Bram Stoker

Christopher Lee as the vampire Dracula in a scene from the film *Horror of Dracula*.

for use in his celebrated gothic novel, *Dracula* (1897). Female vampires also came into their own around this time; Sheridan Le Fanu's novella *Carmilla* (1871) recounts a destructive lesbian affair, a theme exploited years later in such films as *Dracula's Daughter* (1936) and *The Velvet Vampire* (1971), as well as in the homoerotic vampire fantasies of novelist Anne Rice.

In preparation for his novel, Stoker read everything he could find on vampires at the British Museum. He was fascinated by stories of Vlad the Impaler, a fifteenth century Romanian prince with a penchant for staking his victims. This real-life Dracula (Vlad's father was a member of the paramilitary group, "Dracul") provided Stoker with a historical basis for his monster. *Dracula* effectively synthesized the vampire legend's major motifs (including shape-shifting, mind control, avoidance of daylight, lack of reflection, and talismans such as garlic and crosses), and moved the Count out of his castle and into a bustling urban locale. Stoker's rendition of the vampire as a sexual oppressor roaming the streets of London tapped into the public's fear of serial killers such as Jack the Ripper, who not 10 years earlier murdered six women in the city's East End.

In 1922, German director F.W. Murnau brought the folkloric vampire back to life with his silent expressionist masterpiece, *Nosferatu: A Symphony of Horror*. Max Schreck stars as Count Orlock, a gaunt, bald, rat-like vampire who bears almost no resemblance to Bela Lugosi's suave, aristocratic Count Dracula. Four years before gracing the silver screen in Tod Browning's 1931 classic, *Dracula,* the Hungarian-born Lugosi established his reputation as the world's leading vampire by starring in a Broadway production of Stoker's tale (a half-century later, Frank Langella would play the Count in a successful New York revival). Lugosi's exotic accent, distinctive mannerisms, and sinister charm captivated audiences, and Universal Studios contracted him to reprise his role in a slew of horror films.

Celluloid vampires suffered from burnout until 1958, when Christopher Lee reprised the role of the Count in Hammer Films' elegant bloodfest, *Horror of Dracula*. Numerous sequels, also starring Lee, soon followed. Other notable vampire pictures include Carl Dreyer's *Vampyre* (1931), Roman Polanski's *Fearless Vampire Killers* (1969), a 1972 blaxploitation film entitled *Blacula,* Werner Herzog's remake of *Nosferatu* (1979), campy satires by Mel Brooks and Andy Warhol, a porno (*Dracula Sucks,* 1979), Coppola's big-budget rendition of *Bram Stoker's Dracula* (1992), and a 1994 adaptation of Rice's *Interview with the Vampire.* Vampires even turned up in such unlikely genres as science fiction (*Lifeforce,* 1985) and Westerns (*Billy the Kid vs. Dracula,* 1966).

Vampire iconography has exerted a powerful influence on communal style and behavior. A whole "Gothic" youth culture, complete with all-black clothing, somber music, and atmospheric nightclubs, arose as an offshoot of punk in the 1970s, and an underground cult of real-life blood drinkers has steadily increased in numbers. The socially-revealing image of vampire as obsessive blood-junkie has been thematized in such films as *Deathdream* (1972), *Martin* (1978), and *The Addiction* (1995).

There are many reasons for the vampire's enduring popularity. While most monsters are portrayed as ugly, even grotesque, vampires are often handsome or beautiful. They are surrounded by large and arcane bodies of knowledge concerning their origins, powers, and weaknesses. Foreign, well-traveled, aristocratic, charming, even magnetic, they possess an undeniable erotic appeal. What is more, they are subversive, challenging traditional ideas about death, religion, science, sexual mores, and patriarchy. And lest we forget, they have what we all want: money, power, sexual attractiveness, and, above all, eternal youth.

—Steven Schneider

FURTHER READING:

Carter, Margaret, editor. *The Vampire in Literature: A Critical Biography.* Anne Arbor, UMI Research Press, 1989.

Dresser, Norine. *American Vampires: Fans, Victims, and Practitioners.* New York, Norton, 1989.

Melton, Gordon. *The Vampire Book: The Encyclopedia of the Undead.* Detroit, Visible Ink Press, 1998.

Pirie, David. *The Vampire Cinema.* New York, Crescent Books, 1977.

Silver, Alain, and James Ursini. *The Vampire Film: From Nosferatu to Bram Stoker's Dracula.* New York, Limelight, 1993.

Twitchell, James. "The Rise and Fall and Rise of Dracula." *Dreadful Pleasures: An Anatomy of Modern Horror.* New York, Oxford University Press, 1985, 105-159.

Waller, Gregory. *The Living and the Undead: From Stoker's Dracula to Romero's Dawn of the Dead.* Urbana, University of Illinois Press, 1986.

Van Dine, S. S. (1888-1939)

The "Golden Age" of the detective novel is generally considered to have been the years between World Wars I and II. S. S. Van Dine's first Philo Vance detective novel, *The Benson Murder Case* (1926), is often cited as the book that began this era. Although there were only 12 Vance novels and his popularity fell as quickly as it rose, Vance was by far the bestselling mystery character of his time. Born Willard Huntington Wright in Charlottesville, Virginia, Van Dine

first became known as an editor and literary critic for the *Los Angeles Times* and then for *Smart Set* magazine. By the 1930s Van Dine's following as a mystery writer was already beginning to fade. He began writing for motion pictures and contributed a chapter to *The President's Mystery Story,* published by Franklin D. Roosevelt in 1935.

—Jill A. Gregg

FURTHER READING:

Loughery, John. *Alias S. S. Van Dine.* New York, Scribners, 1992.

Van Dyke, Dick (1925—)

Dick Van Dyke is best remembered as a television comedian in the 1960s and 1970s, but this performer's career has included everything from Broadway to motion pictures to drama, in which he has excelled portraying likeable and sensible characters. His most successful role was as the star of *The Dick Van Dyke Show,* an Emmy-award-winning sitcom that appeared on the CBS-TV network from 1961 to 1966; he played the role of Rob Petrie, the head writer for the

Dick Van Dyke

fictional "*Alan Brady Show*" who lives with his wife (played by Mary Tyler Moore) and son in suburban New Rochelle, New York. The show was unusual for a sitcom of the period in that it allowed its star to portray a "TV Dad" both at home and at work while offering an insightful, behind-the-scenes glimpse of a television sitcom from the inside out.

Van Dyke was born in West Plains, Missouri, on December 13, 1925, the son of a trucking agent. His younger brother, Jerry, also became a comedian. It was while he was serving in the U.S. Air Force during World War II that Van Dyke began performing in shows; one of his buddies, Byron Paul, later became his personal manager. After a failed attempt, with a friend, to start an advertising agency after the war, Van Dyke formed a comedy pantomime act, *The Merry Mutes,* with his friend Philip Erickson. "Eric and Van" broke up in 1953 and Van Dyke continued to appear solo in nightclubs around the country until he became emcee of two daytime programs for an Atlanta television station: *The Merry Mutes Show* and *The Music Shop.* In 1955, he originated a variety program he called *The Dick Van Dyke Show* for a New Orleans television station, and went to New York as emcee for CBS's *The Morning Show,* following in the footsteps of Walter Cronkite and Jack Paar. He was emcee of *CBS Cartoon Theater* in 1956 and NBC's *Laugh Line* in 1959.

Disappointed with CBS's refusal to offer him a daily show, Van Dyke appeared as a guest performer on a variety of television shows, including *The United States Steel Hour,* but it was on Broadway that he had his first major starring role. From April 1960 to September 1961, he attracted much critical and popular attention and won a Tony award for the role of Albert Peterson in the musical comedy *Bye Bye Birdie.* A month after leaving that cast, he debuted as TV writer Rob Petrie in his own weekly TV sitcom, *The Dick Van Dyke Show,* which premiered on October 3, 1961 with Van Dyke and Mary Tyler Moore as the leads, and Rose Marie, Morey Amsterdam, and Richard Deacon playing the supporting roles. The episode, titled "Head of the Family" was the title of the pilot episode that writer-producer Carl Reiner had earlier made with himself in the leading role—Johnny Carson was also briefly considered for the part—until he agreed that Van Dyke was a better choice. Reiner, who appeared on the show in the role of Alan Brady, based many of the episodes on his own experience as a writer for the 1950s comedy series *Your Show of Shows. The Dick Van Dyke Show* was also a vehicle for the relatively unknown Mary Tyler Moore, who had appeared mostly in commercials before assuming the role of Rob Petrie's wife.

The Dick Van Dyke Show stands as an icon to the times, a mirror for the world of television in the early 1960s and for the suburban lifestyle that was then somewhat more idyllic than it would become in later years. It was popular largely because of Van Dyke's ability to play both light, sophisticated, domestic comedy and engage in clownish, farcical pratfalls. The stories endure because they present believable characters in unusual but ultimately explainable situations. The producers and cast deliberately ended production after just five seasons, and so the quality of this series remains consistently high throughout; it won fifteen Emmys in five consecutive years.

Beginning in the 1960s Van Dyke starred in a number of memorable films. He reprised his Broadway role in a film adaptation of *Bye, Bye, Birdie* (1963), then played the Chimney Sweep alongside Julie Andrews in *Mary Poppins* (1965). He next starred in *Lt. Robin Crusoe U.S.N.* (1966) and *Divorce American Style* (1967), and played

an eccentric inventor in *Chitty Chitty Bang Bang* (1968). In 1971, he tried a different type of role in the satire *Cold Turkey,* that of a minister in a town undergoing withdrawal symptoms as it tries to give up smoking for a month to win a bounty from a tobacco company.

Carl Reiner and Dick Van Dyke were reunited in *The New Dick Van Dyke Show* in 1971 by a CBS network anxious to try to recapture the viewers and quality of their first sitcom a decade earlier. By this time *The Mary Tyler Moore Show* had become a hit, and the trend was toward the sophisticated, more adult comedies, like the original *Dick Van Dyke Show* had been. In *The New Dick Van Dyke Show,* Van Dyke was cast in the role of Dick Preston, the host of a local talk show in Phoenix, Arizona, and a happily married family man with loving young daughter and college-age son. For the final twenty-four episodes, the scene shifted to Hollywood as Dick Preston accepted a major role in a daytime soap opera. This venue seemed a more deliberate attempt to duplicate the earlier show, with its faster pace and more emphasis on behind-the-scenes banter among the performers, writers, and producer.

Despite these devices, *The New Dick Van Dyke Show* was not overly popular with audiences and it was almost canceled by the network until a flap over one episode in which the Prestons' teenaged daughter accidentally walked in on them while they were having sex. Though the bedroom scene was not shown on camera, the network refused to air the episode as it was filmed and Reiner quit. It was after his departure that the show's setting moved to Hollywood, and the show's new soap-opera situation, plus publicity over the earlier flap, helped raise its ratings somewhat. By 1974 Van Dyke decided not to continue the show, which still won an Emmy. He returned later in the 1970s with a briefly-running variety show called *Dick Van Dyke and Co.* that won another Emmy for him.

Following this show, Van Dyke continued to make occasional movies and is perhaps best known for a series of public-service announcements aimed at fire safety for children that advised them to: "Stop, Drop and Roll." He, along with Pearl Bailey and Hermione Gingold, supplied voices for the British-made children's movie *Tubby the Tuba* (1977), and he appeared as the star of *The Runner Stumbles* (1979) and in the supporting cast of *Dick Tracy* (1990). In the early 1990s Van Dyke reappeared before television audiences as the "Chairman" of *Nick-at-Nite,* the cable network program that shows reruns of classic TV shows including his own 1960s series. Around this time, he also appeared in episodes of the show *Jake and the Fatman* and in several television movies. His most notable role in this period was that of Dr. Mark Sloan in the hour-long CBS-TV dramatic series *Diagnosis Murder.* In this show, Dr. Sloan is portrayed as a Los Angeles crime-solving physician with a police detective son, played by Van Dyke's real-life son, Barry. This show captured a strong following and benefited from a new writing team that allowed it to grow and expand. Despite its serious subject, the show was directed with a playful and human feel that reflected Van Dyke's combination of sophistication and humor. In early 1999, he was cast as Ted Danson's father in a "Becker the Elder" episode of another CBS-TV series, *Becker.*

—Frank E. Clark

FURTHER READING:

"Becker." http://members.theglobe.com/Becker_TV/dickvan1.htm. June 1999.

Castleman, Harry, and Walter J. Podrazik. *Harry and Wally's Favorite Shows: A Fact-filled Opinionated Guide to the Best and Worst on TV*. New York, Prentice Hall Press, 1989.

Marc, David, and Robert J. Thompson. *Prime Time, Prime Movers: From I Love Lucy to L. A. Law—America's Greatest TV Shows and the People Who Created Them*. Boston, Little Brown, 1992.

McNeil, Alex. *Total Television: A Comprehensive Guide to Programming from 1948 to the Present*. 3rd edition. New York, Penguin Books, 1991.

Putterman, Barry. *On Television and Comedy: Essays on Style, Theme, Performer and Writer*. Jefferson, North Carolina, McFarland, 1995.

''VideoFlicks.'' http:www.videoflicks.com. June 1999.

Waldron, Vince. *Classic Sitcoms: A Celebration of the Best in Prime-Time Comedy*. 2nd edition. Los Angeles, Silman-James Press, 1997.

Van Halen

The rock quartet Van Halen exploded into the American mainstream in 1978 with an eponymously titled debut album that soon went platinum, thanks to its blend of musical experimentation and an old-fashioned rock 'n' roll aesthetic. Named for Eddie Van Halen, the group's guitar virtuoso, the band's image promoted a hedonistic lifestyle and immediately captured the imagination of many young fans. Drawing from traditions of Southern blues, European baroque, and 1980s America, the band, over the next two decades, weathered major lineup changes and stylistic reinvention to remain one of the nation's most innovative musical groups.

Van Halen came together in Pasadena, California, in the mid-1970s, one of the first of the new wave of West Coast hard rock and heavy metal bands that had grown up on and would eventually replace British acts like Black Sabbath and Led Zeppelin. The band's first incarnation centered on Alex and Eddie Van Halen, sons of an accomplished Dutch musician. The boys' intense classical training helped them produce distinctive and innovative music in an era when many metal bands were surrendering to formula. The band added Michael Anthony as bass player and David Lee Roth as vocalist and gigged locally under the name Mammoth before choosing to call itself Van Halen.

Van Halen paid its dues in the highly competitive Los Angeles music scene, where it was discovered first by Gene Simmons of the band KISS and later by a Warner Brothers executive. Its debut album, with Roth's lewd, growling vocals on songs like ''Dance the Night Away'' and ''Runnin' With the Devil'' grounded the band firmly in blues and heavy metal traditions, while Eddie Van Halen's creative guitar work, showcased on the extended pseudo-classical solo ''Eruption,'' appealed to other traditionalists.

The band's next five albums all went multi-platinum, even when the band experimented with organs, synthesizers, saxophone, and *a capella* crooning, as on 1982's *Diver Down* and 1984's *1984*. The latter album showed the band's more lighthearted, pop-friendly approach, as with the single ''Jump'' and its video that took advantage of David Lee Roth's high-kicking manic stage presence. In 1985,

at the height of the band's popularity, David Lee Roth left the group to pursue a moderately successful solo career. Van Halen continued with new lead vocalist Sammy Hagar, already well-known from his work with Montrose and as a solo performer. The band released three hugely successful albums with Hagar at the helm, maintaining its exuberance while adding a nuance of socially meaningful music, as with ''Right Here Right Now,'' a powerful song and carefully crafted video about taking care of one's own life in the midst of problems abroad. In 1996, Hagar himself left and Van Halen responded by releasing live and greatest-hits albums and attempting a reunion with David Lee Roth at the 1996 MTV Music Video Awards. Van Halen resurfaced in 1998 with new lead vocalist Gary Cherone; ''Without You,'' the first single with this new lineup, debuted at #1 on the Billboard charts.

Still, it is Eddie Van Halen who has been recognized as the force behind most of Van Halen's music. From the beginning, his technical mastery and innovation set new parameters for the iconic Guitar Hero. In his unending quest for superb sound, he rewired amps, assembled guitars backwards, converted arias and concertos into searing solos, and tapped the fret board of his instrument with both hands at once. His solo on Michael Jackson's smash hit ''Beat It'' gave the song a hard edge, a certain legitimacy in a decade where dance and heavy metal fought for control of the airwaves. Eddie Van Halen, who had married teen idol Valerie Bertinelli, spent the 1990s overcoming substance-abuse problems, but he is remembered for having provided the blueprint for rock idols of his era—beautiful, long-haired, positive, and talented.

—Colby Vargas

FURTHER READING:

Considine, J. D. *Van Halen*. New York, Quill, 1985.

Kitts, Jeff, editor. *Guitar World Presents Van Halen: Eddie Van Halen In His Own Words*. Milwaukee, Hal Leonard Publishing, 1997.

Morison, Buzz. *The Mighty Van Halen*. Port Chester, New York, Cherry Lane Books, 1984.

Shearlaw, John. *Van Halen: Jumpin' for the Dollar*. Port Chester, New York, Cherry Lane Books, 1984.

Walser, Robert. *Running With the Devil: Power, Gender, and Madness in Heavy Metal Music*. Hanover, Wesleyan University Press, 1993.

Van Vechten, Carl (1880-1964)

Carl Van Vechten was, in the course of his lifetime, a music, dance, and literary critic, a novelist, and a photographer. He was an early aficionado of ragtime and jazz and during the Harlem Renaissance of the 1920s wrote numerous articles in support of the movement. In his fifth and best-known novel, *Nigger Heaven* (1926), he meant to portray the life of Harlem in a realistic and sympathetic fashion. Though controversial, the book was generally praised by white critics; it was condemned and dismissed by black critics

Van Halen: (from left) Michael Anthony, Eddie Van Halen, Alex Van Halen, and Sammy Hagar, 1987.

because of its ill-chosen title. Van Vechten sought to ensure that the African American contribution to American culture would be recognized and appreciated in perpetuity by founding, in 1941, the James Weldon Johnson Collection at Yale University.

—Laural Weintraub

FURTHER READING:

Kellner, Bruce. *Carl Van Vechten and the Irreverent Decades.* Norman, University of Oklahoma Press, 1968.

Lueders, Edward. *Carl Van Vechten.* New York, Twayne Publishers, 1964.

Vance, Vivian (1909-1979)

In the early days of television when millions of Americans viewed small screen stars as personal friends, Vivian Vance became the nation's most celebrated neighbor. Vance, a Broadway veteran with credits for *Voice of the Turtle* and Jerome Kern's *Music in the Air,* rocketed to stardom as Lucille Ball's landlady and confidante on the immensely popular *I Love Lucy* show. Her character, Ethel Mertz, by nature homespun and pragmatic, wavers just enough in her resolve to be cajoled into participating in the hair-brained schemes of Ball's antic Lucy Ricardo. She also struggles to pump life into her happy but conventional existence with husband Fred (William Frawley). Vance proved to be Ball's ideal foil; their interaction helped make the sitcom the country's number one show from 1951 to 1957.

Vance's perennial good cheer on screen masked her personal frustrations and several bouts with mental illness. She resented the ease with which the public accepted her as Ethel Mertz. "Ethel is a frump," she lamented. "She's frowsy, she's blowsy, and talks like a man." Vance also grew increasingly dissatisfied with co-star Frawley; he was twenty-five years her senior and she complained, "He should be playing my father." Remarkably, the public remained entirely ignorant of the backstage feud between Frawley and Vance. Even after the secret leaked during the 1960s, an increasingly suburban

27

Vivian Vance and Desi Arnaz

America continued to view Fred and Ethel as representatives of a bygone era of neighborliness. Ironically, Vance's efforts on the *I Love Lucy* show helped popularize television, then a fledgling medium, and went a long way toward breaking down the traditional social patterns which Fred and Ethel Mertz represented.

—Jacob M. Appel

FURTHER READING:

Andrews, Bart. *Lucy & Ricky & Fred & Ethel: The Story of "I Love Lucy."* New York, Dutton, 1976.

McClay, Michael. *I Love Lucy: The Complete Picture History of the Most Popular TV Show Ever.* New York, Warner Books, 1995.

Wyman, Ric B. *For The Love of Lucy: The Complete Guide For Collectors and Fans.* New York, Abbeville Press, 1995.

Vanilla Ice (1968—)

White rapper Vanilla Ice burst on the music scene in 1990 with his hit single "Ice Ice Baby," a danceable tune with a bass line lifted from the David Bowie/Queen collaboration "Under Pressure." The single, from the album *To the Extreme,* became the first rap song to reach number one on the pop singles chart, where it stayed for sixteen weeks. Critics slammed Vanilla Ice (whose real name is Robert Van Winkle) for his rip-off of black culture, but apologists credited him

with bringing rap to a larger audience. Vanilla Ice's popularity lasted just a few months—long enough to earn him a starring role in the movie *Cool As Ice* but not long enough to propel sales of his subsequent albums beyond a small core of dedicated fans.

—Tom Pendergast

FURTHER READING:

Bego, Mark. *Ice, Ice, Ice: The Extraordinary Vanilla Ice Story.* New York, Dell, 1991.

Vanilla Ice. *Ice, by Ice.* New York, Avon, 1991.

Vanity Fair

The original *Vanity Fair,* superbly edited by the inimitable Frank Crowninshield from 1914 to 1936, was the epitome of elan during the teens and twenties. A unique amalgam of art, literature, humor, fashion, and social commentary, *Vanity Fair* attracted a loyal audience and became the model of sophisticated success in the publishing industry, even after it was felled by the Depression. Revitalized in the early 1980s, the *Vanity Fair* of the late twentieth century is a slick, celebrity-driven monthly that has become the last word on American popular culture among the upwardly mobile. Amidst the celebrity mania of the late twentieth century, *Vanity Fair* is the bible of the stars.

Vanity Fair's emergence during the teens, as a "smart magazine" aimed at an urban leisure class, was the direct result of a number of changes in America in general and in the publishing business in specific. Following the Civil War, America underwent many sweeping metamorphoses, among which was a gradual shift from a rural society to an urban one. As the population became gentrified during the second half of the nineteenth century, as rural communities diminished and the cities grew, as Americans began to conceive of themselves as a cultured nation, and as the upper middle classes swelled and reveled in their new wealth, smart magazines began to appear. According to George H. Douglas, "smart magazines were written and edited for the leisured classes (although not necessarily the very rich)—for sophisticated urbanites, the kind of person who was well traveled, well read, well acquainted; for people who wanted to be entertained, but on an exalted plane." These magazines, he added, were "general magazines intended for the entertainment of cultural elites . . . rooted in . . . contrivances of humor, of gaiety, of urbanity, of high style and fashion. The rich, it seemed, were not usually interested in 'uplift,' in the birth pangs of reform and good works; as often as not they enjoyed the demimonde, even low life; they wanted to hear about the lives of actors, poets, of theatre people, pugilists, polo players. They loved gossip and scandal."

Major changes in the printing process during the 1880s and 1890s made faster typesetting and printing possible, allowing for more publications of higher quality. After the halftone process, chromolithography, and rotogravure printing were invented, magazines took on a new glossy format, filled with full-page color illustrations and advertisements. The vast changes in advertising, which metamorphosed from simple classified-type ads to colorful images and slogans thought out by prestigious firms, contributed to the evolution of a whole new kind of magazine, leading to an era which Douglas calls "a renaissance or high-water mark of the

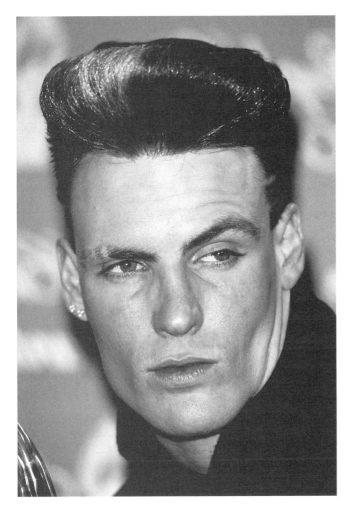

Vanilla Ice

American magazine with many new giants entering the field, and many older ones becoming bigger and more affluent than they would have dreamed possible before . . . By the 1890s magazines had become big business.''

Into a field that included the *Saturday Evening Post, Ladies' Home Journal,* and *Harper's Monthly* entered the first of these smart magazines, aptly called *The Smart Set* and subtitled ''A Magazine of Cleverness.'' A huge success during the first decade of the twentieth century, this literary and artistic monthly catering to cosmopolitan café society became a model periodical, featuring the writing of such brilliant young literary bucks as H. L. Mencken and George Jean Nathan, who later became its joint editors. *The Smart Set* set the tone for all the smart magazines that followed.

Vanity Fair, the quintessential smart magazine, however, came into being by a rather circuitous route. In the 1890s a publication by the same name had a limited success in New York as a ''peekaboo magazine'' of dubious quality. In 1913, Condé Nast, a successful entrepreneur who had made his first success in the publishing field with *Vogue,* a high-tone, women's fashion magazine, bought another fashion rag called *Dress.* He then purchased the rights to the name *Vanity Fair* and, in 1913, put out the first issue of *Dress and Vanity Fair* to limited success. It stumbled around for a year, without finding its niche, until Nast brought in his friend Frank Crowninshield as

editor. In March 1914, Frank Crowninshield's *Vanity Fair* found its way to the newsstands where it made a very big splash.

In his first editorial, Crowninshield wrote, ''*Vanity Fair* has but two major articles in its editorial creed: first, to believe in the progress and promise of American life, and, second, to chronicle that progress cheerfully, truthfully, and entertainingly . . . At no time in our history has the wonder and variety of American life been more inspiring, and, probably as a result of this, young men and young women, full of courage, originality, and genius are everywhere to be met with.'' With these young people as both audience and contributors, Crowninshield set about to create a magazine that would chronicle the cutting edge in art, literature, drama, sport, film, and dance.

Crowninshield himself was in his early forties, raised and educated in Europe, of aristocratic background, but a working man who had been the editor of a number of top magazines. He was also a devotee of modern art—one of the organizers of the Armory Show, Crowninshield had a superb art collection himself. Thus, he knew how to appeal to the upper classes, the intelligentsia, and the avant-garde. Under Crowninshield, *Vanity Fair* contained the writing of such diverse young talents as Edna St. Vincent Millay, Edmund Wilson, P. G. Wodehouse, e. e. cummings, and Aldous Huxley, as well as more established writers such as F. Scott Fitzgerald, art by Picasso, Matisse, and Jacob Epstein, and photography by Edward Steichen. As Cleveland Amory wrote in his introduction to an anthology of the magazine, ''*Vanity Fair* was a pioneer in so many areas that it can be said to be a significant yardstick of American culture. Not only did it publish many pieces by first-rate writers and artists before—and after—they became known, but it set a new standard for photography and picture journalism. Another thing it did 'first' was to give due recognition to Negro personalities and artists.''

Although *Vanity Fair* never had more than 100,000 annual subscribers, it succeeded largely by being unique. Charming, witty, insouciant, aesthetically appealing, *Vanity Fair* was the genuine article and thus attracted a loyal following. For young writers it was the place to work, even if it paid less than other magazines. Dorothy Parker, Robert Benchley, Robert E. Sherwood, and Edmund Wilson all found their start at *Vanity Fair.* A conversation piece among the Smart Set, *Vanity Fair* was the place to find out who was who and what was what, from articles on silent movie stars and dashing polo players to photographs of French poets and English royalty. There were essays by D. H. Lawrence and Harry Houdini, poems by Theodore Dreiser and Amy Lowell, paintings by Raoul Dufy and August Renoir, and, of course, Miguel Covarrubias's wonderful caricatures. Regular features included the yearly Hall of Fame, a popular section on men's fashion, humorous sketches, and theatre reviews.

Throughout the Roaring Twenties, *Vanity Fair* was the most successful of the smart magazines, but when the Depression hit in 1929, it began to slip from favor. As Americans struggled to make ends meet, advertisements were withdrawn, and fewer and fewer people wanted to read about café society. By 1936, Condé Nast decided to merge *Vanity Fair* into *Vogue,* calling it a ''heartbreaking decision.'' For more than forty-five years, all that remained of the magazine was a memory.

In 1982, two years into the glamorous excess of the Reagan years, Condé Nast Publications decided to reissue *Vanity Fair* as an upscale publication for the elite of the eighties. The new *Vanity Fair* hoped to follow the format of the original smart magazines. Initially, however, it floundered, and many believed the magazine would never be able to live up to the verve, wit, and genuine charm of its forebear.

In 1984, Tina Brown, the young Oxford graduate who had resurrected London's *Tatler,* was brought in to punch up the publication. Brown immediately put her mark on *Vanity Fair,* bringing in top writers from around the world by paying them unheard-of six-figure contracts. She turned her staff into stars and the magazine into a money earner. Under Brown, the second incarnation of *Vanity Fair* became a slick publication with a celebrity buzz. Its approach, however, was formulaic. Filled with seductive advertisements for luxury products, photographs of movie stars, articles about the rich, the famous, or the bizarre, the new *Vanity Fair*'s audience purported to be the Eighties Smart Set. In fact, the magazine became a mass-market publication aimed at the entire upwardly mobile population of the United States.

During the late eighties and early nineties, the covers of *Vanity Fair* seemed to feature many of the same actors in various poses—Demi Moore in multiple states of nudity, Tom Cruise with a sly smirk or a toothy grin, Arnold Schwarzenegger clothed or unclothed, all shot with Annie Leibowitz's unerring lens. But by the mid-nineties, with Brown departed for the *New Yorker, Vanity Fair* began to compete with more cutting-edge magazines, such as *Interview,* by featuring cover stories about young Hollywood. Where once *Vanity Fair* signaled mainstream success, the magazine has now become a star maker, as cover stories about Matthew McConaughey, Matt Damon, and Renee Zellweger brought these young actors to the attention of the mainstream and boosted their status in Hollywood.

If the original *Vanity Fair* set a sophisticated standard for American culture, its second incarnation is the quintessence of late-twentieth-century popular culture—slick, global, and all about money and fame.

—Victoria Price

FURTHER READING:

Amory, Cleveland. *Vanity Fair: A Cavalcade of the 1920s and 1930s.* New York, Viking Press, 1960.

Douglas, George H. *The Smart Magazines: 50 Years of Literary Revelry and High Jinks at Vanity Fair, The New Yorker, Life, Esquire, and The Smart Set.* Connecticut, Archon Books, 1991.

Handelman, David. "Run for Cover!" Salon: Media. http://www.salonmagazine.com/media/1997/12/11media.html. October 27, 1998.

Mitchell, Deborah. "Is Anna Wintour Really Worth a Million Bucks?" Salon: Media Circus. http://www.salon1999.com/media/1997/10/27/money.html. October 27, 1998.

Vardon, Harry (1870-1937)

Golf's first international celebrity, Harry Vardon may be best remembered for something he popularized but did not invent: the overlap golf grip that bears his name. Vardon's name, however, was well-known long before he became famous for the grip. Not only was he the first Englishman to win the British Open, he claimed the title six times, winning in 1896, 1898, 1899, 1903, 1911, and 1914. In 1900 Vardon added the United States Open to his list of major championships, and was arguably the most famous golfer in the world at the time. Although a bout with tuberculosis in 1903 affected his health, his game was still strong enough to earn him second place in

the 1920 United States Open. Vardon's legacy is tied to the Vardon Trophy, emblematic of the lowest scoring average each year on the Professional Golfers' Association tour.

—Lloyd Chiasson, Jr.

FURTHER READING:

Atha, Anthony. *World of Golf: The History, the Classic Players, the Major Tournaments.* New York, Smithmark, 1997.

Browning, Robert. *History of Golf.* Norwalk, Connecticut, Classics of Golf, 1985.

Concannon, Dale. *Golf: The Early Days.* New York, Smithmark, 1995.

Gibson, Nevin H. *The Encyclopedia of Golf.* New York, A. S. Barnes, 1958.

Grimsley, Will. *Golf: Its History, People and Events.* Englewood Cliffs, New Jersey, Prentice-Hall, 1966.

Varga Girl

During World War II, the Varga Girl pinup, with her long legs, narrow waist, and "sumptuous" figure, was a major military morale booster. As Jamie Malanowski notes, her image "hung in billets and on bulkheads, was unfolded in foxholes, and was lovingly imitated on fuselages throughout Europe and the Pacific." Above all, the "Varga Girl" was timely. Her success derived from the confluence of a World War, the coming of age of "mass culture," and changing sexual mores. Drawn by Alberto Vargas, she was part of a new set of myths, which Leo Lowenthal of the Frankfurt School called a byproduct of twentieth century capitalism. Mass culture, according to Lowenthal, was manufactured in assembly line style by agents of mass media communication and was widely distributed.

Thousands of servicemen treasured the Varga Girl pinup. They were the pleased consumers of a product ingeniously distributed by *Esquire* magazine, which along with *Life* and *Reader's Digest* had been designated as wartime "morale boosters." The upbeat image of the Varga Girl provided a counter to the unpleasantness of the war and the loneliness of the trenches. One letter written to the pinup's artist Alberto Vargas by a serviceman suggested that regardless of what "the girl back home" looked like, "we can see her in each of your drawings." As Kurt Vonnegut once observed, "The American male's capacity to make do with imaginary women gave our military forces a logistical advantage I have never seen acknowledged anywhere."

The Varga Girl and her predecessor, the Petty Girl, evolved from the more modestly clad Gibson Girl. Both "girls" were also directly related to the women drawn by Raphael Kirchner for the turn-of-the-century avant-garde publication, *Le Parisienne.* The airbrush technique used by George Petty and Vargas allowed the impression of flawless women, suggestively clad and sultry-looking. In 1940, after Petty objected to the high-handed manner of *Esquire*'s publisher David Smart, he was replaced by Vargas. The Varga Girl (a name suggested as more "euphonious" by Smart) became a monthly staple in *Esquire* and in the popular "Varga Calendar" and other spin-off products.

Although appreciated by a significant portion of the U.S. male population, the pinup stirred up controversy in the areas of sexuality, gender exploitation, cultural representation, mass (popular) culture, and consumerism. According to Jeanne Meyerowitz, ''The proliferation in the mass media of sexual representations of women is arguably among the most important developments in twentieth century popular culture.'' Meyerowitz further notes that the genres of ''cheesecake'' (suggestive) and ''borderline'' (more than suggestive) material ''arose in the confluence of rising consumerism, burgeoning mass production, and changing sexual mores.'' There was strong resistance to these cultural changes. In 1943, the U.S. Post Office brought charges of obscenity against *Esquire,* specifically citing a number of Varga Girl illustrations. At the trial, one female witness asserted that the pinups and other cartoons in the magazine exploited and demeaned women, while another female witness argued that the Varga images ''beautifully portrayed'' the female form. *Esquire* won the suit and a lot of free publicity. Into the late 1990s, the debate about whether erotic representations of women celebrate or degrade women is part of the discourse of feminists, lesbians, sexual libertarians, and anti-pornography and free speech advocates.

The Varga Girl was the work of Peruvian-born illustrator Alberto Vargas (1896-1982). Educated in Europe, Vargas was influenced by the work of Ingres and Kirchner. When he arrived in New York in 1916, Vargas was struck by the confident, vivacious women he saw. For a time he worked for producer Florenz Ziegfeld and once said that from Ziegfeld he learned the difference between ''nudes and lewds.'' He later worked as an illustrator and set designer for several major Hollywood studios. In 1939, after Vargas walked out in solidarity with union advocates at Warner Brothers, he was blacklisted. A year later, David Smart hired Vargas for a pittance, and without the right to royalties for his own work. Like Petty, Vargas was eventually driven to sue Smart. Vargas lost on appeal (he maintained that the judge was bribed), and he was enjoined from using the trademark name ''Varga.''

In the mid-1950s, Hugh Hefner hired Vargas to resurrect the Varga Girl under the artist's own name. The Vargas Girl appeared in *Playboy* on a monthly basis into the 1970s, until it was eclipsed by more prurient fare. *Playboy* pushed the envelope by using photography to convey a new image of the desirable woman. According to writer Hugh Merrill, whereas *Esquire*'s images had been ''grounded'' in burlesque shows patronized by the upper classes, *Playboy* had its cultural roots in the movies, an art form accessible to the masses. Photos of actress Marylyn Monroe graced the first issue *Playboy.* Eventually Vargas' idealized depictions gave way to centerfold photography that left nothing to the imagination. Yet according to Merrill, Vargas' work had helped set the stage for this change. In the 1940s the center of glamour had moved from New York City (the stage) to Hollywood (the movies). The ''new cinematic standard of beauty of the 1950s did not come from nowhere. It was a real-life extension of the imaginary women in the Vargas paintings of the 1940s.'' Some of these paintings had even been showcased in the film, *Dubarry Was a Lady.*

Personally, Vargas was quite different from the sexually heady atmosphere he worked in. He was an unassuming, courtly gentleman, born during the Victorian era, who was devoted to his wife, Anna Mae. His primary (some say, naive) desire was to ''immortalize the American girl.'' In his time, he succeeded. One admirer described his monthly pinup calendar as ''an icon of popular culture,'' while another described him as ''the finest watercolorist of the female form.'' Vargas' girls remain embedded in the collective psyche of the

generations of the 1940s and 1950s, and they also remain as one of the cultural signifiers of those eras.

—Yolanda Retter

FURTHER READING:

Malanowski, Jamie. ''Vivat, Vivat, Varga Girl!'' *Esquire.* November 1994, 102-107.

Merrill, Hugh. *Esky: The Early Years at Esquire.* New Brunswick, New Jersey, Rutgers University Press, 1995.

Meyerowitz, Jeanne. ''Women, Cheesecake and Borderline Material: Responses to Girlie Pictures in the Mid-Twentieth Century U.S.'' *Journal of Women's History.* Fall 1996, 9-35.

''Vargas.'' http://www.vargasgirl.com/artists/vargas/index.html. March 1999.

Vargas, Alberto, and Reid Austin. *Vargas.* New York, Harmony Books, 1978.

Variety

A weekly trade newspaper focusing on theater and film, *Variety* has been a bible of the entertainment industry since the turn of the century. Founded in 1905 by Sime Silverman, a former vaudeville critic for a New York newspaper, *Variety*'s origins can be traced to a dispute between Silverman and a former editor, who asked the critic to soften a scathing review. Silverman promptly quit, and set about launching *Variety,* whose distinctive, trademark ''V'' was designed by his wife on a nightclub tablecloth.

From its earliest days, *Variety* became embroiled in a feud with the powerful Keith-Albee theater chain over what the paper considered its stranglehold over vaudeville entertainment in the United States. The newspaper supported protests by a group of actors called the White Rats of America, a fledgling performers' union modeled after the Water Rats, a similar organization in London. Keith-Albee replied by forbidding its actors and agents to read or advertise in the publication, and warned music publishers to withdraw their advertisements or face a blacklist of their songs in Keith-Albee theaters. A famous editorial on March 28, 1913 established Silverman as a crusading editor in the tradition of ''Dana, Pulitzer, and Bennett,'' wrote one show-business historian. *Variety*'s support for these unionization activities laid the groundwork for what would become today's Actors Equity Association.

Variety reached its peak of popularity during the golden age of vaudeville in the 1920s and 1930s. ''There were only two media'' at that time, noted Syd Silverman, who was once heir apparent to his father's dynasty. ''Legit theater and vaudeville.'' Long known as the industry paper of record, along with its primary competitor, *The Hollywood Reporter,* established in 1930, *Variety* specialized in coverage of Broadway and off-Broadway theater in New York, and was, for many years, the only trade publication to provide crucial data in the form of weekly box-office reports for stage productions.

Although they share the same roots, *Variety* is not be confused with the more West Coast-oriented *Daily Variety,* founded by the elder Silverman in 1933, whose readership has traditionally been vastly different. *Daily Variety*'s subscribers are generally comprised of a select demographic of upper-income entertainment executives residing almost exclusively in Los Angeles. *Variety*'s readership, in

The Cover of *Variety*, 1929.

contrast, has been scattered throughout the United States, Europe, and the world.

During its heyday in the 1920s and 1930s, *Variety* affected a light and breezy style with its own slang and locutions that gave it a distinctive voice, not unlike the "Guys and Dolls" patter of Damon Runyon and other Broadway denizens. Two of its most famous headlines during the period are considered journalistic classics of wit and brevity: on October 30, 1929, the day after the stock-market crash, *Variety*'s banner headline read: "Wall Street Lays an Egg," after the slang term for a failed theatrical production; on July 17, 1935, a front-page report on the unpopularity of vapid films in small Midwestern towns was headlined, "Sticks Nix Hick Pix." *Variety* peppered its prose with hundreds of examples of theatrical argot and invented terms, like "boff" for hit show, "cleffer" for songwriter, "deejay" for disk jockey, "strawhat" for summer-stock company, and "whodunit" for mystery show. *Variety* rarely used the term "talkies" to describe motion pictures with sound, instead preferring its own term "talkers," and referred to television in its early days as "video." *Variety* also popularized the term "Tin Pan Alley" to describe New York City's songwriting district.

The popularity of new media took its toll on *Variety* in later years, and its theater coverage began to seem increasingly less relevant in a world dominated by motion pictures, television, and

video. In 1987, Syd Silverman made a difficult decision. After 82 years of family ownership, he resolved to sell his father's publication (along with *Daily Variety*) to Cahners Publishing Company, a subsidiary of the British-based Reed International. The sale was valued at approximately $56.5 million, and Cahners, which already published some 52 trade magazines, quickly set about making massive internal changes to resuscitate the paper.

Following the sale, Silverman announced that the publication's day-to-day editorial responsibilities would be handed over to Roger Watkins, a former general manager of *Variety* in London. The magazine, it soon became clear, was about to be ushered into a new technological era of corporate media. Within months, *Variety*'s staff was moved from the cramped, theater-district offices they had inhabited since 1919 to sparkling new cubicles on Park Avenue South. One editor even noted that some *Variety* reporters had still been "banging out stories" on vintage Underwood manual typewriters. All this would change under the Cahners management, which advised staff members of new dress codes—coats and ties only for men—to go with the publication's spiffy corporate look. Other changes included a consolidation of staff members in the East and West Coast offices of *Variety* and *Daily Variety,* a move that ruffled more than a few feathers; the sister publications were long known for harboring bitter rivalries and jealousies over story assignments and advertising accounts. Despite these changes, at least one *Variety* institution remained unchanged: columnist Army Archerd, who had written the "Just for Variety" column since the 1950s, and described as "a throwback to Walter Winchell, without the ego" and the paper's "most treasured asset" by Liz Smith.

Perhaps the most controversial shift came about with the 1989 hiring of Peter Bart as editor of the weekly *Variety*—he became editorial director of both *Variety* and *Daily Variety* in 1991. Because Bart had been a studio executive as well as a *New York Times* correspondent for two decades prior to joining *Variety,* there was much speculation as to whether or not he could maintain an objective critical stance toward the industry that had long provided his bread and butter (and caviar). Even the *New York Times* and the *Washington Post* got in on the debate, asking in one headline if Peter Bart was simply "too solicitous of the industry he covers." The *Post* highlighted what became known as the "Patriot Games" incident as an especially egregious example of Bart's lack of journalistic boundaries. The incident occurred following *Variety*'s acerbic review of the film *Patriot Games,* written by 18-year veteran critic, Joseph McBride. Not only did Bart dash off an apologetic letter to Martin Davis, chairman of Paramount studios, following the review, he also demoted McBride, who resigned soon afterward, to reviewing children's movies. Bart's supporters countered that *Variety* was, after all, a trade paper, with some eighty percent of its subscriber base and fifty percent of its ads coming from studios. It was no secret, they maintained, that the publication was mutually dependent upon, and accountable to, the entertainment industry. In 1991, Steve West was named executive editor of *Daily Variety.*

In the 1990s, the entertainment industry continued to share a cozy relationship with its chief trade publications, *Variety* and *Daily Variety.* Buoyed by increasing revenues and profits, *Variety* established several new ventures. In October 1997, it began publishing *Variety Junior,* a five-time-a-year paper covering the children's entertainment business; in November it reintroduced *On Production,* a paper about the making of film, television, and commercials; and in January 1998, it opened its *variety.com* website. In May of that year, *Daily Variety* started putting out a five-day-a-week New York edition known as *Daily Variety Gotham.* The paper carried news about Broadway and the publishing and entertainment business while continuing its heavy coverage of the Hollywood film industry. Peter Bart said that *Variety* hoped to attract another 14,000 subscribers with the new edition. In 1997, the *New York Times* reported that *Daily Variety* had advertising revenues of $27 million, up from $12 million in 1992, with profits increasing from $2 to $20 million between it and *Variety* itself.

—Kristal Brent Zook

FURTHER READING:

Carmody, Deirdre. "Technology Opens Doors for Cahners Magazine." *New York Times.* July 19, 1993, D5.

Fabrikant, Geraldine. "Executive Editor is Appointed at *Daily Variety.*" *New York Times.* August 16, 1991, C22.

Green, Abel, and Joe Laurie, Jr. *Show Biz: From Vaude to Video.* New York, Henry Holt and Company, 1951.

Mathews, Jay. "The Protective Paws of Variety's Top Dog." *The Washington Post.* April 26, 1993.

Peterson, Iver. "For *Variety*: A New York State of Mind." *New York Times.* March 16, 1998, D7.

Pogebrin, Robin. "That's Entertainment: *Variety* Goes Bicoastal." *New York Times.* February 3, 1998, E4.

Smith, Liz. "Tricks of the Trade." *Vanity Fair.* April 1995, 118-21.

Sragow, Michael. "Execs, Checks, Sex, FX." *New York Times Book Review.* Feb. 21, 1999, 28.

"*Variety* Official Website." http://www.variety.com. June 1999.

Vaudeville

Vaudeville, a collection of disparate acts (comedians, jugglers, and dancers) marketed mainly to a family audience, emerged in the 1880s and quickly became a national industry controlled by a few businessmen, with chains of theaters extending across the country. The term vaudeville originates either from the French Val de Vire (also Vau de Vire), the valley of the Vire River in Normandy, known as the location of ballads and comic songs, or from the French name for urban folk songs, "voix de ville" or "voice of the city." By the late nineteenth century, entertainment entrepreneurs adopted the exotic title of "vaudeville" to describe their refined variety performances. Whereas variety shows had a working class, masculine and somewhat illicit reputation in the nineteenth century, early vaudeville innovators eliminated blue material from performances, remodeled their theaters, and encouraged polite behavior in their auditoriums to attract middle-class women and their children in particular. This pioneering process of expansion and uplift laid the foundation for the establishment of a national audience for mass-produced American culture.

It is difficult to define the content of vaudeville entertainment because it was so eclectic. The average vaudeville bill, which usually included between nine and twelve acts, offered something for everyone. Indeed, vaudeville primarily provided an institutional setting for attractions from other show business and sports venues of the day. Circus acrobats, burlesque dancers, actors from the legitimate dramatic stage, opera singers, stars from musical comedies, baseball players and famous boxers all made regular appearances on vaudeville bills. Vaudeville bills also featured motion pictures as standard acts around the turn of the century, providing one of the key sites for the exhibition of early films.

Despite the diversity and cultural borrowing at the heart of vaudeville, this industry had its own aesthetic, standard acts, and stars. It featured a rapid pace, quick changes, and emotional and physical intensity; the personality of individual performers was paramount. Vaudeville demanded affective immediacy (performers tried to draw an outward response from the audience very quickly), as opposed to the more reserved, intellectual response advocated in the legitimate theater. On the vaudeville stage, the elevation of spectacle over narrative and the direct performer/audience relationship contrasted with legitimate drama's emphasis on extended plot and character development and the indirect (or largely unacknowledged) relationship between performers and the audience. And players retained creative authority in vaudeville acts, often writing their own routines, initiating innovations in the acts, and maintaining their own sets, while directors were gaining power over productions in the legitimate theater.

Standard acts included the male/female comedy team, in which the woman usually played the straight role and the man delivered the punch lines. One such pair, Thomas J. Ryan and his partner (and wife) Mary Richfield, starred in a series of sketches about the foibles of Irish immigrant Mike Haggerty and his daughter Mag. Many women, such as Nora Bayes and Elsie Janis, rose to stardom in vaudeville as singing comediennes. Perhaps the most famous singing comedienne was Eva Tanguay. Famous for her chunky physique, her frizzy, unkempt hair and her two left feet, she earned huge salaries for her sensual, frenetic, and often insolent performances. Her hit songs included "I Don't Care" and "I Want Someone to Go Wild with Me." W. C. Fields and Nat Wills were among the many tramp comedians who became headliners in vaudeville and Julian Eltinge, a man who excelled in his portrayal of glamorous women, led the field of female impersonators in vaudeville.

Between approximately 1880 and 1905 most vaudeville bills included at least one and as many as three acts of rough ethnic comedy. Joe Weber and Lew Fields, well-known German (also called Dutch) comedians, spoke with thick accents and fought each other vigorously on stage, while Julian Rose succeeded in vaudeville with his comic monologues about a Jewish immigrant's mishaps. Kate Elinore joined the male-dominated ranks of slapstick ethnic comedy with her portrayal of uncouth Irish immigrant women. Along with being a showcase for ethnic stereotypes, vaudeville also was the main outlet for blackface comedy following the decline of the minstrel show. But it was not only white performers who donned the black mask; black comedians like the well-known Bert Williams also blacked up to fit the caricature of a "shiftless darky."

Vaudeville's styles and standards were embedded in the social and political changes of the era. Bold women like Eva Tanguay reflected (and energized) women's increasing rejection of Victorian codes of conduct around the turn of the century. Women on stage, who sometimes championed divorce and women's suffrage, and women who flocked to the exciting environment of vaudeville theaters participated in the expansion of public roles for women. Ethnic themes and caricatures in comedy sketches provided a crude code of identification in cities that were becoming more diverse as immigration increased in late nineteenth century. Vaudeville's ethnic comedy addressed anxieties about immigration, including the xenophobia of native-born Americans as well as tensions surrounding

An exterior view of the Automatic Vaudeville and Crystal Hall Theater on Broadway in New York City.

upward mobility and assimilation within immigrant families. Although many vaudeville performances were titillating and impertinent, the emphasis on propriety and respectability in the major vaudeville circuits was, according to Robert Allen, ''another chapter in the history of the consolidation of the American bourgeoisie.'' Administrators such as B. F. Keith emphasized the opulence of their theaters, their well-mannered patrons, and the clean, even educational acts on stage: their mixed audience seemed to be led by the middle classes.

Vaudeville entrepreneurs drew most of the raw material for their entertainment from nineteenth century popular theater, namely the heterogeneous offerings in the minstrel show, concert saloon, the variety theater, and the dime museum. In fact, vaudeville theater managers often remodeled concert saloons and dime museums into new vaudeville establishments. Concert saloons and variety theaters (terms often used interchangeably) combined bars with cheap (or free) amusements in connected rooms or auditoriums. These largely disreputable institutions were smoky, noisy and crowded; patrons were likely to be drunk; and waitresses, jostling among the men, were often willing to sell sex along with liquor. After running one of the few respectable concert saloons on the Bowery (a street in New York City well-known for its tawdry amusements), Tony Pastor opened a ''variety'' theater. He eliminated the smoking, drinking and lewd

performances that had previously characterized variety entertainment within the setting of the concert saloon. Pastor's variety theater, one of the most successful and famous establishments of its kind between 1880 and 1890, was a pivotal establishment in the early history of vaudeville because other entrepreneurs copied Pastor's reform efforts to popularize variety as ''vaudeville.''

Benjamin Franklin Keith, the most powerful vaudeville innovator, adopted Pastor's philosophy in his efforts to make dime museums in Boston into respectable vaudeville establishments. Whereas Pastor operated only one theater, Keith eventually mass produced vaudeville for a nation. Born on January 6, 1846, Benjamin Franklin Keith began his career in popular entertainment as a circus performer and promoter in the 1870s and then opened a dime museum in Boston in 1883. Many dime museums, a combination of pseudo-scientific displays and stage entertainment, were housed in storefronts in inexpensive urban entertainment areas and attracted working-class and lower-middle class audiences. Keith, with his colleague Edward F. Albee (also previously a circus performer) worked to remove the working-class reputation of the dime museum. At the museum they displayed circus ''freaks'' for an admission charge of ten cents, and they soon opened a second-floor theater where they presented a series of singers and animal acts—their first vaudeville bill. He touted his clean variety and dramatic stage productions, such as a burlesque of Gilbert and

Sullivan's *HMS Pinafore*, to draw more middle-class patrons to his theaters. After combining light opera with variety acts in the late 1880s and early 1890s, Keith eventually offered exclusively vaudeville after 1894.

Vaudeville theaters, depending on whether they were classified as "big time" or "small time," served different clientele. With expensive interior designs and stars who demanded high salaries, big time theaters had higher production costs and, consequently, more expensive admission prices than small-time vaudeville did. Big-time theaters were also more attractive to performers because these theaters offered two shows a day and maintained one bill for a full week. Small-time theaters, on the other hand, demanded a more grueling schedule from performers who had to offer three to six shows a day and only stayed in town for three or four days, as small-time theaters maintained a single bill for only half a week. For performers, according to Robert Snyder, "small-time was vaudeville's version of the baseball's minor leagues." Small-time theaters catered primarily to working-class or immigrant audiences, drawing particularly from the local neighborhoods, rather than attracting middle-class shoppers and suburbanites who would frequently arrive at big-time theaters via trolleys and subway lines. One of the leaders of small-time vaudeville was Marcus Loew, who began to offer a combination of films and live performances in run-down theaters in 1905. Over the next decade he improved his existing theaters and acquired new ones, establishing a circuit of 112 theaters in the United States and Canada by 1918.

Whereas before 1900 vaudeville theaters were owned independently or were part of small chains, after 1907 the control of vaudeville rested in the hands of a few vaudeville magnates, including B. F. Keith. In 1923 there were 34 big-time vaudeville theaters on the Keith Circuit, 23 owned by Keith and eleven others leased by Keith. F. F. Proctor and Sylvester Poli each controlled chains of theaters in the East, and Percy G. Williams and Martin Beck, the head of the Orpheum circuit, had extensive vaudeville interests in the West. Another vaudeville organization, the Theater Owners' Booking Association (TOBA), catered to black audiences in the South and employed black performers, including the great blues queens Ma Rainey and Bessie Smith.

During the first decade of the twentieth century, big-time vaudeville in the United States was consolidated under the guidance of Keith largely because of his extensive control of booking arrangements. In 1906 Keith established a central booking office, the United Booking Office (UBO), to match performers and theaters more efficiently. Performers and theater managers subsequently worked through the UBO to arrange bookings and routes. The UBO had tremendous leverage over performers because it was the sole entryway to the most prestigious circuit in the country: if performers rejected a UBO salary, failed to appear for a UBO date, or played for UBO competition, they could be blacklisted from performing on the Keith circuit in the future. When *Equity*, a trade publication for actors, surveyed the history of vaudeville in 1923, it emphasized the power of central booking agencies, including the UBO (the most prominent booking firm): "It is in the booking office that vaudeville is run, actors are made or broken, theaters nourished or starved. It is the concentration of power in the hands of small groups of men who control the booking offices which has made possible the trustification of vaudeville."

Vaudeville performers tried to challenge the centralized authority of vaudeville through the establishment of the White Rats in 1900. Initially a fraternal order and later a labor union affiliated with the American Federation of Labor, the White Rats staged two major strikes, the first in 1901 and the last in 1917. The White Rats never won any lasting concessions from vaudeville theater owners and managers and the union was defunct by the early 1920s.

The leaders of vaudeville organized theaters into national chains, developed centralized bureaucracies for arranging national tours and monitoring the success of acts across the country, and increasingly focused on formulas for popular bills that would please audiences beyond a single city or neighborhood. In these ways, vaudeville was an integral part of the growth of mass culture around the turn of the century. After approximately 1880 a mass culture took shape in which national bureaucracies replaced local leisure entrepreneurs, mass markets superseded local markets, and new mass media (namely magazines, motion pictures and radio) targeted large, diverse audiences.

Vaudeville began to decline in the late 1920s, falling victim to cultural developments, like the movies, that it had initially helped promote. There were a few reports of declining ticket sales (mainly outside of New York City) and lackluster shows in 1922 and 1923 but vaudeville's troubles multiplied rapidly after 1926. Around this time, many vaudeville theaters announced that they would begin to advertise motion pictures as the main attractions, not the live acts on their bills; by 1926 there were only fifteen big time theaters offering straight vaudeville in the United States. The intensification of vaudeville's decline in the late 1920s coincides with the introduction of sound to motion pictures. Beginning with *The Jazz Singer* in 1927, the innovation of sound proved to be a financial success for the film industry.

In 1928 Joseph P. Kennedy, head of the political dynasty, bought a large share of stock in the Keith-Orpheum circuit, the largest organization of big-time theaters in the country. Kennedy planned to use the chain of theaters as outlets for the films he booked through his Film Booking Office (FBO) which he administered in cooperation with Radio Corporation of American (RCA). Two years later Kennedy merged Keith-Orpheum interests with RCA and FBO and formed Radio-Keith-Orpheum (RKO). Keith-Orpheum thus provided the theaters for the films that were made and distributed by RCA and FBO. The bureaucratic vaudeville circuits had worked to standardize live acts and subsume local groups into a national audience but vaudeville did not have the technology necessary to develop a mass-production enterprise fully. As Robert Snyder concludes in *The Voice of the City*, "A major force in the American media had risen out of the ashes of vaudeville."

Vaudeville was also facing greater competition from full length revues, such as the Ziegfeld Follies. While vaudeville bills often included spectacular revues as a single act on the bill, full-length revues increased in popularity after 1915, employing vaudevillians and stealing many of vaudeville's middle-class customers along the way. Between 1907 and 1931, for example, there were twenty-one editions of the Follies. Such productions, actually reviewed as vaudeville shows through the early twentieth century, used thin narratives (like a trip through New York City) to give players the opportunity to do a comic bit or song and dance routine, borrowing the chain of intense performances from the structure of a vaudeville bill.

Just as the revue borrowed vaudeville performers and expanded on spectacles that had been popular as part of a vaudeville bill, the motion picture industry also incorporated elements of the vaudeville aesthetic. Vaudeville performers such as Eddie Cantor, the Marx Brothers, Bert Wheeler, Robert Woolsey and Winnie Lightner took leading roles in film comedies of the 1920s and early 1930s. They brought some of vaudeville's vigor, nonsense, and rebelliousness with them to the movies. Motion pictures, therefore, drew on the traditional acts of vaudeville and, with the aid of technology, perfected vaudeville's early efforts at mass marketing commercial leisure. Vaudeville had helped create a world that made it obsolete.

Vaudeville helped recast the social and cultural landscape of the United States at the turn of the century. From a scattered array of commercial amusements, vaudeville helped build a national system of entertainment. From a realm of raunchy, male-dominated popular entertainment, vaudeville crafted a respectable culture that catered to the female consumer. From a fragmented theatrical world, this entertainment industry forged a mass audience, a heterogeneous crowd of white men and women of different classes and ethnic groups. Vaudeville was thus a key institution in the transition from a marginalized sphere of popular entertainment, largely associated with vice and masculinity, to a consolidated network of commercial leisure, in which the female consumer was not only welcomed but pampered.

—M. Alison Kibler

FURTHER READING:

Allen, Robert. *Vaudeville and Film, 1895-1915: A Study in Media Interaction*. New York: Arno Press, 1980.

Bernheim, Alfred. ''The Facts of Vaudeville.'' *Equity* 8 (September, October, November, December 1923): 9-37; 13-37; 33-41, 19-41.

Distler, Paul Antonie. ''Exit the Racial Comics.'' *Educational Theatre Journal* 18 (October 1966): 247-254.

''The Facts of Vaudeville.'' *Equity* 9 (January, February, March, 1924): 15-47; 19-45; 17-44.

Gilbert, Douglas. *American Vaudeville: Its Life and Times*. New York: Dover Publications, 1940, 1968.

———. *Horrible Prettiness: Burlesque and American Culture*. Chapel Hill: University of North Carolina Press, 1991.

Jenkins, Henry. *What Made Pistachio Nuts?: Early Sound Comedy and the Vaudeville Aesthetic*. New York: Columbia University Press, 1992.

Kibler, M. Alison. *Rank Ladies: Gender and Cultural Hierarchy in American Vaudeville*. Chapel Hill: University of North Carolina Press, 1999.

McLean, Albert F., Jr. *American Vaudeville as Ritual*. Lexington: University of Kentucky Press, 1965.

Snyder, Robert. *The Voice of the City: Vaudeville and Popular Culture in New York*. New York: Oxford University Press, 1989.

Staples, Shirley. *Male/Female Comedy Teams in American Vaudeville, 1865-1932*. Ann Arbor: UMI Research Press, 1984.

Vaughan, Sarah (1924-1990)

Sarah Vaughan is one of a handful of legendary jazz singers who brought the same level of creativity and musicianship to the vocal line that her colleagues brought to sax, bass, and drums. Vaughan was one of the first singers to be associated with the progressive sounds of bebop in its earliest incarnation. ''It's Magic,'' ''Make Yourself Comfortable,'' ''Broken-Hearted Melody,'' ''Misty,'' and ''Send in the Clowns'' are among her best-known songs.

Sarah Vaughan

Vaughan was born in Newark, New Jersey in 1924. Both of her parents were musical. Her father played guitar, and her mother sang in the choir of their Baptist church. Vaughan was a serious student of piano as a young girl, and she often served as organist for the church. She maintained these skills throughout her career, along with her love for sacred music. But she also took an early interest in that ''sinful'' music called jazz. As a teenager, she would sneak out with a girlfriend into the burgeoning music scene in Newark and New York City. After watching her friend take a prize as runner-up in the talent contest at Harlem's Apollo Theater, Vaughan decided to give the contest a try. Her rendition of ''Body and Soul'' took first place and launched her musical career.

Soon thereafter, on the recommendation of singer Billy Eckstine, one of her earliest admirers and a lifelong friend, she took her first professional singing job with the Earl Hines big band in 1943 and went on to perform and record with the major innovators of the day, including Charlie ''Bird'' Parker and Dizzy Gillespie. During her early days in the music business, Vaughan was known for her shyness and lack of physical glamour. With her very dark skin, her unspectacular figure, and her pronounced overbite, she lacked the beauty-queen allure of Lena Horne, but she quickly earned the respect of her musical colleagues. It was clear from the start that her talent and inventiveness would make it possible for them to do their best work. If any one jazz singer personified the capacity of the human voice to behave like a horn, Vaughan was it. Carl Schroeder, one of Vaughan's pianists in the sixties and seventies, said to Gourse, "She could walk the line between the melody and improvisation exactly the way a great saxophone player could."

Vaughan was grateful for the camaraderie of the boys in the band. Their good times together softened some of the difficulties of life on the road for black musicians in an era where racial segregation and bias remained the norm. She was less fortunate in matters of romance. She was often drawn to flashy, agressive men who ultimately "did her wrong," both personally and professionally. Showing no interest in the business side of her career, she would always tell her associates, "I sing. I just sing." She liked to have a manager with her on the road to take care of all the incidentals of bookings and hiring of personnel, and, to her way of thinking, no better person could do the job than the one who shared her bed. On several occasions, her lack of interest in practical matters lost her a great deal of money when the romance had also gone.

Vaughan maintained an active career on the road and in clubs like New York's famous Café Society from the 1940s through the 1960s. During these years, she recorded many of her landmark albums, often using potentially commercial pop songs to offset the commercial riskiness of straight-ahead jazz. The album *Sarah Vaughan and Count Basie* (Roulette, 1960) was named one of the 101 best jazz albums by critic Len Lyons. Like many jazz musicians, she suffered through rock's encroachment on the commercial music scene but kept a loyal cadre of fans. In her later years, her venues moved from the club to the concert stage, where she performed as guest soloist with several major symphony orchestras, developing an artistic relationship with conductor Michael Tilson Thomas of which she was particularly proud.

According to jazz historian Martin Williams, "Sarah Vaughan has an exceptional range (roughly of soprano through baritone) . . . a variety of vocal textures, and superb and highly personal vocal control. Her ear and sense of pitch are just about perfect, and there are no 'difficult' intervals for Sarah Vaughan." The same abilities that many have found praiseworthy, however, could be problematic to others. Vaughan was frequently taken to task by critics for allowing her facility for vocal pyrotechnics to obscure the lyrics of the great American popular standards in her repertoire. This criticism may have been exacerbated by the nature of the competition. Sarah Vaughan carried on most of her musical career in the shadow of Ella Fitzgerald, whose supreme gift among many was a precise and natural diction that made her the ideal singer for the sophisticated and witty lyrics of Ira Gershwin, Cole Porter, and Larry Hart, among others. But where Ella offered an almost childlike clarity, Sarah offered dramatic highlights and greater emotional depth.

Vaughan often joked with friends that she was born in "Excess" (as opposed to "Essex") County, New Jersey. She was in fact prone to excess in many areas of her life: she smoked two packs of cigarettes a day (to the astonishment of fellow singers), loved a good cognac, and dabbled in cocaine. Nevertheless, she kept up a rigorous schedule of performances and recording dates well into her sixties, when she was diagnosed with an advanced stage of lung cancer and died a few months later. Leontyne Price sent a message of sympathy to the First Mount Zion Baptist Church in Newark, New Jersey, where the funeral

was held. Rosemary Clooney and Joni Mitchell were among those who attended a memorial service at Forest Lawn on the West Coast. Carmen McRae released the album *A Tribute to Sarah* in 1991.

—Sue Russell

FURTHER READING:

Gourse, Leslie. *Sassy: The Life of Sarah Vaughan.* New York, Scribner, 1993.

Lyons, Len. *The 101 Best Jazz Albums: A History of Jazz on Records.* New York, William Morrow, 1980.

Williams, Martin. *The Jazz Tradition* (new and revised edition). New York, Oxford University Press, 1983.

Vaughan, Stevie Ray (1954-1990)

The most influential guitarist of his generation, Stevie Ray Vaughan's power and soul brought blues into mainstream rock and helped spark the blues revival of the 1980s. He combined the power of Albert King with the flamboyance of Jimi Hendrix to create a style easily accessible to a generation of young fans and copycat guitar players.

Vaughan was born in Dallas, Texas, into a family that included brother Jimmie, three and a half years his senior. Jimmie, who would later gain fame as the founder and guitarist of the Fabulous Thunderbirds, was Stevie Ray's earliest influence through his record collection. The brothers soaked up Albert, B. B., and Freddie King; Kenny Burrell; Albert Collins; Lonnie Mack; and Jimmy Reed. By the age of eight, Stevie Ray was playing hand-me-down guitars from his brother.

As a teenager, Vaughan fell under the spell of Jimi Hendrix. Vaughan would later take his 1960s psychedelic twist on blues and reinterpret it for the youth of the 1980s. Vaughan's cover of the Hendrix song "Voodoo Chile (Slight Return)" became a high point of his live shows.

After playing in several Dallas bands, Vaughan dropped out of school and moved to Austin in 1972, where a large blues scene was developing. Vaughan continued to play in various bands until forming his own group, Double Trouble, named for an Otis Rush song, in 1979. The original lineup included singer Lou Ann Barton, but as Vaughan gained confidence, the group was pared down to a power trio including Tommy Shannon on bass and Chris Layton on drums. Double Trouble quickly rose to the top of the Austin music scene.

Vaughan's reputation spread to R & B producer Jerry Wexler, who viewed a performance in 1982. Wexler, considerably impressed, used his pull to get Vaughan booked at the Montreux Jazz Festival in Switzerland, a feat almost unheard of for an unsigned artist. One member of the Montreux audience was British rocker David Bowie, who asked Vaughan to play on his *Let's Dance* album and join his 1983 world tour. Vaughan added some stunning Albert King-tinged licks to the album, but pulled out of the tour due to money and other disputes. Vaughan returned to Austin and resumed playing the club circuit.

Stevie Ray Vaughan

Another audience member at Montreux was Jackson Browne, who offered the use of his studio for the band to record a demo tape. The tape eventually found its way to John Hammond, Sr., the legendary talent scout and producer who had discovered Bob Dylan, Bruce Springsteen, Aretha Franklin, and Billie Holiday.

"He brought back a style that had died, and he brought it back at exactly the right time," Hammond said in *Stevie Ray Vaughan: Caught in the Crossfire.* "The young ears hadn't heard anything with this kind of sound."

Hammond produced the band's first album, *Texas Flood,* released by Epic Records in 1983. Although only peaking at No. 38 on the *Billboard* album charts, the record went gold with over 500,000 copies sold. Vaughan's 1984 follow up, *Couldn't Stand the Weather,* sold over one million copies and spent 38 weeks on the *Billboard* top 200 album chart. Organist Reese Wynans joined Double Trouble for the 1985 release *Soul to Soul.*

Vaughan had always boosted his performances by using cocaine and alcohol, but his newfound success exacerbated the problem. "Whereas his cocaine habit had always previously been kept in check by his bank account, that constraint vanished with sold-out concerts," Joe Nick Patoski and Bill Crawford said in their biography *Stevie Ray Vaughan: Caught in the Crossfire.* "He was rock royalty, a gentleman of privilege, who could have anything he wanted, before, during

and after a show, as long as he gave the customers their money's worth." In 1986, all-night mixing sessions for the *Live Alive* double live album coupled with constant touring pushed Vaughan's drug abuse over the edge. After collapsing on stage during a London concert in October, it seemed Vaughan was headed for an early death like his idol, Jimi Hendrix.

Vaughan was determined to survive his addictions, entering a rehabilitation clinic and joining Alcoholics Anonymous. After four months of treatment, Vaughan emerged a new man. Double Trouble's 1989 album *In Step* was the band's most focused and critically acclaimed release, selling over one million copies and winning a Grammy Award for Best Contemporary Blues Album. Days after winning the award, Vaughan appeared on MTV's *Unplugged* program, showcasing his acoustic guitar mastery.

Vaughan's live performances were infused with a new vigor, and he was at the top of his game. His next project was an album with his older brother, Jimmie, called *Family Style,* recorded during the summer of 1990. The brothers planned to tour together in support of the album. Before the release of *Family Style,* Vaughan began a tour with Eric Clapton and Robert Cray. Buddy Guy, Bonnie Raitt, Jeff Healey, and brother Jimmie joined in for an appearance at Alpine Valley Music Theater in East Troy, Wisconsin, on August 25 and 26. The concert on the 26th concluded with Stevie Ray, Jimmie, Clapton, and Guy dazzling the crowd of 35,000 with ''Sweet Home Chicago.'' Afterwards, a helicopter carrying Vaughan and three members of Clapton's entourage to Chicago crashed into a fog-shrouded hillside near the theater. All aboard were killed. The accident was blamed on pilot error.

Family Style was released on September 25 and broke the top ten on *Billboard*'s album chart. The album was a departure for Vaughan, who showed more restraint than on his solo efforts. Vaughan's career appeared to be moving into a more mature phase, demonstrated in songs like ''Tick Tock,'' which showcased Vaughan's vocals rather than his guitar. *Family Style* won a Grammy Award for Best Contemporary Blues Album, and the instrumental ''D/FW'' won for Best Rock Instrumental.

Vaughan's death sparked interest in his earlier albums as well, and each quickly shot over one million in sales. *The Sky is Crying*, an album of previously unreleased out-takes and masters, was released in 1991 and won two more Grammy Awards. Several live recordings of varying quality were released in later years, proving Vaughan's enduring legacy.

—Jon Klinkowitz

FURTHER READING:

Kitts, Jeff, Brad Tolinski, and Harold Steinblatt. *Guitar World Presents Stevie Ray Vaughan*. Wayne, New Jersey, Music Content Developers, 1997.

Leigh, Keri. *Stevie Ray: Soul to Soul*. Dallas, Taylor Publishing Company, 1993.

Patoski, Joe Nick and Bill Crawford. *Stevie Ray Vaughan: Caught in the Crossfire*. Boston, Little, Brown and Company, 1993.

Rhodes, Joe. ''Stevie Ray Vaughan: A White Boy Revives the Blues.'' *Rolling Stone*. September 29, 1983, 57-59.

Velez, Lupe (1908-1944)

Lupe Velez was ''the Mexican Spitfire'' in a series of successful films in the late 1930s and early 1940s with RKO Studios. Despite her screen charisma and gift for comedy, Velez is best remembered for her tumultuous love life. She had turbulent and often violent relationships with actor Gary Cooper and the movies' most famous Tarzan, Johnny Weissmuller, to whom she was married for five years. A former nightclub performer, her first appearance in a full-length film was opposite Douglas Fairbanks, Sr. in *The Gaucho* (1927). By the 1940s moviegoers' tastes had begun to change and Velez's star began to fade. She became pregnant by bit player Harald Raymond who would not marry her. A devout Catholic, Velez would not have an abortion and Hollywood of that era would not tolerate an unwed mother. She took what she felt was the only way out and committed suicide in 1944.

—Jill A. Gregg

FURTHER READING:

Conner, Floyd. *Lupe Velez and Her Lovers*. New York, Barricade Books, 1993.

Shipman, David. *Great Movie Stars: The Golden Years*. London, Warner Books, 1989.

Velveeta Cheese

Introduced by Kraft Foods in 1928, this cheese food product is a blend of Colby and cheddar cheeses with emulsifiers and salt. The ingredients are heated until liquefied, squirted into aluminum foil packaging, and then allowed to cool into half-pound, one-pound, or two-pound bricks. Velveeta is part of a uniquely American group of highly processed foods, including such favorites as Spam and Jell-O, that have become the building blocks for a remarkably inexpensive though nutritionally dubious popular cuisine. Revered for its plastic-like meltability, it is a favored topping for macaroni, omelettes, and grilled sandwiches, though some prefer to eat it sliced. The single most popular brand of processed cheese, Velveeta controls some 20 percent of the $300 billion United States processed-cheese market (as well as another three percent with its ''Lite'' brand). Some of the most requested Velveeta recipes developed by Kraft include those for Cheese Fudge and Cheesy Broccoli Soup. In the 1980s, several pre-flavored Velveetas were introduced, including Mexican Salsa and Italian.

—David Marc

The Velvet Underground

In an oft-repeated declaration, Roxy Music co-founder Brian Eno once said that the Velvet Underground only sold a few records, but everyone who bought their albums started their own band. While Eno's claim most certainly is hyperbole, the avant-garde guitar stylings the Velvet Underground developed during their period of activity in the second half of the 1960s was extremely influential. Their music shaped the sound and attitude of the New York Dolls, the Modern Lovers, REM, Suicide, Television, David Bowie, Patti Smith, Sonic Youth, Galaxie 500, Yo La Tengo, and countless other post-punk and indie-rock bands. Each of Velvet Underground's periods—their innovative noise, beautifully sparse neo-folk, and straightforward rock phases—laid the blueprint for a number of entire sub-genres of rock 'n' roll. And while the Velvet Underground did not sell many records by most commercial standards (for instance, their third album had only sold 50,000 copies over 20 years after it was released), their influence has been widespread enough to secure their entry in the Rock and Roll Hall of Fame.

In the early-to-mid 1960s, rhythm guitarist Lou Reed met lead guitarist Sterling Morrison and bassist/violist John Cale, and the three of them—along with original percussionist Angus MacLise—began playing at Lower Manhattan poetry readings and happenings under the various names of the Warlocks, Falling Spikes, and the Primitives. As the Primitives, the group recorded a number of commercial dance-oriented singles for Pickwick Records, the company for which Reed was a staff songwriter. When Lou Reed met John Cale, Cale was playing in an avant-garde group founded by famed minimalist La Monte Young, and the two became intrigued by the idea of bringing Cale's avant-garde concepts to a rock 'n' roll format. In 1965, MacLise left to be replaced by Maureen Tucker, who became known for her peculiar standup style of primitive drumming.

The Velvet Underground soon began playing a regular gig at Greenwich Village's Cafe Bizarre—an engagement that abruptly ended when they played their screeching ''Black Angel's Death Song'' immediately after being told by the management never to play

The Velvet Underground: (from left) Sterling Morrison, Maureen Tucker, Lou Reed, and John Cale.

it again. Before the group was fired, they impressed Pop art svengali Andy Warhol, who invited them to play at a series of his film screenings called ''Cinematique Uptight,'' and later in a multimedia spectacle called ''The Exploding Plastic Inevitable.'' During this time, Warhol arranged for European chauntesse/aspiring movie star Nico to sing with the Velvet Underground for the Exploding Plastic Inevitable, something that caused a certain amount of resentment among members of the band.

In 1966, Andy Warhol took them into the studio to have them recorded—a series of sessions that resulted in two singles and the entirety of their first album, *The Velvet Underground and Nico,* which sported an Andy Warhol-designed peelable banana album cover. The album featured three songs sung by Nico, as well as Reed's infamous drug song, ''Heroin.'' The Teutonic, monotone voice of Nico, and Reed's equally monotone voice, combined with lyrics about sadomasochism, hard drugs, and death made this album extremely uncommercial, particularly during a time dominated by the positive vibes of hippy flower-power.

Rather than going a more commercial route, the group instead followed their muse (and the path that was driven by taking an extreme amount of amphetamines) by making *White Light/White Heat,* their second album. This uncompromisingly noisy album whose lyrics dealt with prostitutes, sailors, and other sundry topics

(and which culminated in a 17 minute noise-jam called ''Sister Ray'') was too dissonant to be heavy metal and too heavy to be psychedelic.

After a long-time power struggle with Reed, Cale quit the group and was replaced by Doug Yule, who only filled Cale's bass duties—the group never had another violist. After recording what would be called their great ''lost'' album, Reed radically changed the group's direction with their self-titled third album, which featured almost uniformly pretty, quiet songs like ''Pale Blue Eyes'' and ''Candy Says.'' Their last studio album, *Loaded,* contained the oft-covered classics ''Rock and Roll'' and ''Sweet Jane,'' and was the first to be recorded for Atlantic Records (after a commercially unsuccessful three-album stint at Verve Records). *Loaded* was their most conventional rock-oriented album, which was partially caused by Maureen Tucker's absence from most of the recording sessions due to pregnancy (Doug Yule's little brother, Billy Yule, filled in on drums). Reed quit the group before the album was mixed, and Reed claims that two songs—''Sweet Jane'' and ''New Age''—were significantly changed by Doug Yule and the rest of the group. (Reed's original vision was later restored on the 1995 Velvet Underground box set, *Peel Slowly and See*).

The group continued to tour without Reed, with Morrison and Tucker eventually quitting, before Doug Yule put the name to rest in 1973 after releasing what amounted to a Yule solo album, *Squeeze.*

Morrison went on to teach English at the University of Texas and drive a tugboat in his spare time. Tucker raised a family and released a number of critically praised solo albums. Cale also released numerous solo albums and produced important albums by Jonathan Richman's Modern Lovers, Patti Smith, the Stooges, Squeeze, and Nico (the Cale-produced Nico solo albums, *Desert Shore* and *Marble Index,* are considered classics). While all the members of the Velvet Underground have maintained a substantial cult following, it is Reed who has occasionally had the highest profile, as well as the only hit, with 1972's "Walk on the Wild Side." (Reed even made the mainstream, playing at the White House in front of President Clinton and a number of foreign dignitaries in 1998). In 1993, the group finally patched up their differences to do a brief tour of Europe in 1993 (sans Nico, who died in a bike accident in 1989), which resulted in the live recording *Live MCMXCIII.* But their egos soon clashed and they went their separate ways again; the group dissolved before they recorded a planned studio album. Sterling Morrison died in 1995, putting an end to speculation that the group might again record under the Velvet Underground moniker.

—Kembrew McLeod

FURTHER READING:

Bockris, Victor, and Gerald Malanga. *Up-Tight: The Velvet Underground Story.* New York, Omnibus, 1983.

Heylin, Clinton. *From the Velvets to the Voidoids: A Pre-Punk History for a Post-Punk World.* New York, Penguin, 1993.

Thompson, Dave. *Beyond the Velvet Underground.* New York, Omnibus, 1989.

Zak, Albin. *The Velvet Underground Companion: Four Decades of Commentary.* New York, Schirmer Books, 1997.

Ventura, Jesse (1951—)

With his surprise election as Governor of Minnesota in 1998, former professional wrestler Jesse "The Body" Ventura (whose real name is James Janos) captured the attention of the nation. Representing the Reform Party, Ventura parlayed his gift for gab, his celebrity status, and public disgust with "politics as normal" to become an instant icon. Within days of his election, Ventura was the talk of the nation—appearing on countless talk shows (where he announced that he should now be dubbed "The Mind"), becoming the subject of both serious news analyses and numerous jokes, and morphing into a *Doonesbury* character. The A&E cable channel quickly put together an episode of *Biography,* two networks started work on TV movies, and Ventura found time to pen a political autobiography called *Ain't Got Time to Bleed.*

Ventura's diverse resume includes time as a Navy Seal, TV broadcaster, radio talk show host, and a very successful stint in professional wrestling. Ventura was named the "The Body" due to his impressive physique, but when a blood clot forced his early retirement from the ring, it was his ability behind the microphone as a color commentator, coupled with a penchant for boas and outrageous costumes, which earned him an impressive fan base and won notice by Hollywood producers. Ventura acted respectably in roles in *Predator* (1987), *The Running Man* (1987), and *Batman & Robin*

Jesse "The Body" Ventura

(1997). As typifies late twentieth century American popular culture, the road to politics was only a step away.

—Patrick Jones

FURTHER READING:

Gray, Paul. "Body Slam." *Time.* November 16, 1998.

Lentz, Harris M. *Biographical Dictionary of Professional Wrestling.* Jefferson, North Carolina, McFarland & Company, 1997.

Tapper, Jake. *Body Slam: The Jesse Ventura Story.* New York, St. Martins, 1999.

Ventura, Jesse. *I Ain't Got Time to Bleed: Rebuilding the Body Politic from the Bottom Up.* New York, Villard Books, 1999.

Versace, Gianni (1946-1997)

As a boy, Versace observed his mother's dressmaking studio in Reggio Calabria, Italy; as a man, Versace moved to Milan to design for other companies from 1972 to 1977 and established his own company in 1977. A consummate dressmaker, Versace rocked the world of fashion by other principles: featuring hot models; packing runway shows with celebrities; dressing famous men and women from Elton John to Princess Diana to model Elizabeth Hurley; and creating body-conscious clothing for the most self-confident clients. His body-exposing black safety-pin dress worn by Hurley to a London movie premiere was the most photographed dress of 1994. Leather and metal-mesh dresses from his last collection in 1997 referred to Byzantine art, but clung to the body. In sensibility and life, Versace was flamboyant and larger-than-life. He realized fashion as media and created Cinderella fantasies for the 1980s and 1990s. He was murdered on the steps of his Miami mansion in July 1997.

—Richard Martin

FURTHER READING:

Martin, Richard. *Gianni Versace.* New York, Metropolitan Museum of Art/Abrams, 1997.

———. *Versace.* New York, Universe, 1997.

Vertigo

Released in 1958, *Vertigo* is often singled out as Alfred Hitchcock's most important film. The film combined a complex storyline with equally complex cinematography. *Vertigo* debuted Hitchcock's now famous combination of forward zoom and reverse tracking. His unique zoom and tracking method along with other

James Stewart and Kim Novak in a scene from the film *Vertigo*.

creative and technical complexities of the film exerted a tremendous influence on an entire generation of filmmakers, especially the French New Wave. *Vertigo*'s presence is felt in films as diverse as *Jules et Jim* (1961), *High Anxiety* (1977), *Body Double* (1984), and *Twelve Monkeys* (1995). *Vertigo* was unavailable for decades because its rights, along with those of four other films, were left by Hitchcock as a legacy to his daughter. *Vertigo* and the other four films were re-released in 1984 to much popular and critical acclaim. Because the films are so popular as well as creatively and technically complex, Hitchcock's films complicate the distinction between high and low art.

Vertigo is a complex psychological thriller—it opens with San Francisco police detective Scottie Ferguson's letting a fellow officer fall to his death during a rooftop chase of a suspect. After the accident, Ferguson is hired by an old friend to investigate the friend's wife, Madeleine, who believes herself to be the reincarnation of a turn-of-the-century belle, Carlotta. Madeleine reenacts Carlotta's suicide by jumping off a mission bell tower while Scottie stands by helplessly, paralyzed by his vertigo. The remainder of the film details Scottie's nervous breakdown and his discovery of a woman named Judy who uncannily resembles Madeleine. Scottie recreates Madeleine in Judy, forcing Judy to adopt Madeleine's makeup, clothing, hairstyle, and speech. When Scottie realizes he has been the dupe of a complex murder plot he attempts to cure himself of his vertigo by revisiting the scene of Madeleine's death. Able to conquer his vertigo, Scottie is nevertheless unable to save Judy, who falls to her death.

The overwhelming critical and popular response to *Vertigo*'s re-release raises the question of why the film is such a vital text for film criticism and theory. The film itself has been interpreted in a variety of ways: as an allegorical tale of man's descent into the underworld in search of a lost love; as a psychological parable of guilt, obsession, and repression; and as an experiment in generic collage, drawing on the generic conventions of realism, fantasy, and the women's film. Together with *Rear Window, Vertigo* has often been discussed as a document of late 1950s culture, as a portrayal of the alienation and rootlessness of the 1950s, as well as of the constructions of 1950s femininity. It is these latter issues—the representation of women and the relationships among power, sexuality, and gender—which have garnered the most critical attention.

Hitchcock is frequently understood as a misogynist whose films entice audiences to participate in sadistic fantasies about women (such as Scottie's efforts to make over Judy into Madeleine, despite Judy's plea that he love her the way she is). Certainly Hitchcock's films are both fascinated by and horrified by women's (potential) power. Hitchcock's films can also be read, however, as exposures of the mechanisms of patriarchy—*Vertigo* can be read, for example, as a critique of the ways in which femininity in our culture is largely a masquerade and a male construct.

Hitchcock's films are central to film theory and feminist criticism because they are all about scopophilia—voyeurism, fetishism, and the interrelated questions of epistemology, identification, and spectatorship. One of the most important essays of feminist film criticism, Laura Mulvey's 1974 essay "Visual Pleasure and the Narrative Cinema," uses readings of Hitchcock's *Rear Window* and *Vertigo* to argue that classic Hollywood movies inevitably transform women into passive objects of male voyeurism and sadism. Mulvey's essay also claims that Hitchcock's female characters both represent and assuage male spectators' anxieties and desires, while female spectators are trapped into a masochistic identification with the female victims on screen. Later feminist film critics also turned to *Vertigo* as a central text. Tania Modleski, for example, uses *Vertigo* to elaborate upon the notion of the female spectator. She argues that identification is a more complex mechanism than heretofore considered and suggests that the female spectator is implicated in a split position, identifying with both the passive female object and the active male subject. Hitchcock himself seems to suggest this position, when, in a pivotal scene in the movie, we see things from Judy's point of view as well as Scottie's. Indeed, it is *Vertigo*'s multiple points of view, and hence of knowledge and of identification, that suggests that the movie's appeal lies in its very ambivalence toward women and their potential to upset the male spectator's position.

—Austin Booth

FURTHER READING:

Modleski, Tania. *The Women Who Knew Too Much: Hitchcock and Feminist Theory.* New York, Methuen, 1988.

Mulvey, Laura. "Visual Pleasure and Narrative Cinema." *Screen,* Vol. 16, No. 3., 1975, 6-18.

Sloan, Jane. *Alfred Hitchcock: A Guide to References and Resources.* New York, G. K. Hall, 1993.

Viagra

Viagra, a little blue pill made by the pharmaceutical company Pfizer Inc., became the first oral medicine approved for male impotence by the U.S. Food and Drug Administration. Its approval in March 1998 set off a worldwide demand and sent Pfizer stock soaring. Hardly a day went by when newspapers, radio, and television did not have stories of the Viagra craze. The pill, which sold by prescription for about $10 apiece retail, was taken by men with sexual problems about an hour before they expected to have sexual activity. Their performance during the sex act improved dramatically. The drug, chemically named sildenafil, had been used unsuccessfully as a medicine for heart problems. When some heart patients reported to doctors they were getting erections after taking the pill, it was developed to treat sexual impotence.

Clinical studies of about 4,000 men with erectile dysfunction showed that up to 72 percent reported they had successful intercourse after using Viagra, against 23 percent of men who took a placebo. Viagra works by improving the blood flow to the penis. More specifically, it inhibits the effects of an enzyme that acts to reverse erections after sex. Before Viagra came along, men with erectile problems had to forego sex, rely on mechanical devices such as a small pump to produce an erection, have surgical penile implants, or inject medicines directly into the penis.

Once the Viagra craze spread, so did reports of problems associated with taking the pill. Some men reported problems with their vision, seeing green or blue. There were stories of dizziness and headaches or upset stomachs. Men with heart problems who took nitroglycerin or nitrates were warned not to use Viagra because it could act to reduce blood pressure. By late 1998, the Food and Drug Administration issued warnings that Viagra could be hazardous to some men with heart ailments, and that using the pill could lead to

heart attacks or strokes. The drug watchdog agency said that although Viagra was still considered safe and effective, it posed potential problems for men with very high or very low blood pressure, so that patients should get careful examinations before taking the pill. The FDA also said that 130 reported deaths of men who had taken Viagra could not be attributed directly to the drug. The average age of those who died was 64 and many of the men who died had had serious health problems aggravated by sexual activity, which ended in heart attacks or strokes. "The people who died had underlying cardiovascular problems," Dr. Lisa Rarick, director of an FDA division, told reporters during late 1998. She added that men with heart problems should ask their doctors, "Is sex good for me?" Many of the men who died had impotence problems because of their medical conditions. By the time of the warning some six million prescriptions had been written for about three million men.

The underlying demand for Viagra could be linked to a major study, released in 1999 by the *Journal of the American Medical Association,* of the sexual habits of nearly 5,000 people, the largest such study since the report of biologist Alfred Kinsey some 50 years earlier. The new research revealed that sexual problems were widespread in the United States. On the basis of personal interviews with 1,749 women and 1,410 men, the research showed that about two out of five women and one out of three men had some forms of sexual dysfunction.

The clamor for Viagra in other countries spurred some swindlers to peddle pills made to look like Viagra. But cashing in on demands for a silver bullet to cure sex problems was not new. The search for a magic potion that could produce erections on demand has gone on for centuries, encouraging charlatans who sold bogus remedies to unwitting, desperate men. Among the miracle cures thus ballyhooed to have been miracle cures have been underwear electrified to stimulate the penis, rhinoceros horns pounded into powder, and tiger penises made into soups.

—Michael L. Posner

FURTHER READING:

Katzenstei, Larry. *Viagra: The Potency Promise.* New York, St. Martin's, 1998.

Vaughn, Susan C. *Viagra: A Guide to the Phenomenal Potency-Promoting Drug.* New York, Pocket Books, 1998.

Victoria's Secret

Perhaps given a boost by the openness of the Sexual Revolution, the Victoria's Secret retail chain almost single-handedly redefined America's conception of lingerie beginning in the early 1980s. Despite the secrecy promised in the franchise's moniker, each of its stores replaced the modest, tucked-away, department-store displays of women's underwear with an openly luxurious atmosphere that recreated a nineteenth-century boudoir. At the same time, Victoria's Secret decidedly built its image with a fairly conservative, middle-class shopper in mind and avoided any connotations of sleaziness which lingerie might carry. While some critics have contested the sometimes reactionary portrait of femininity developed in the store's

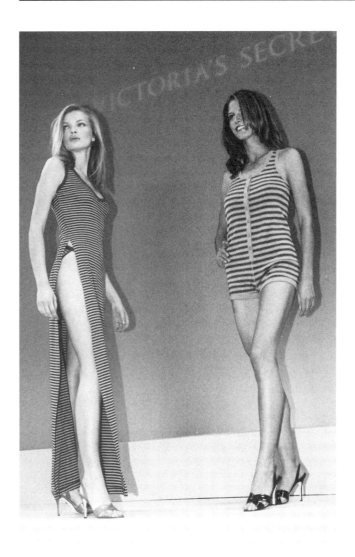

Models display the latest fashions from Victoria's Secret, 1997.

and Warner's. Although subsequent stores were less customized than Raymond's prototype, this balance of seduction and ''classy'' charm continued to rule the sensibilities of Victoria's Secret.

In its first year of business, the San Francisco store had amassed sales of an impressive half a million dollars, allowing Raymond to expand Victoria's Secret into four new locations, in addition to a headquarters and warehouse. Raymond's creative vision was not equaled by financial mastery, however, and in 1982 he was forced to sell Victoria's Secret to the Columbus, Ohio-based conglomerate The Limited for the relatively slight sum of four million dollars. Although it was already a nationally known fashion enterprise, The Limited kept the personalized image of Victoria's Secret intact, albeit in a mass-produced, cost-efficient manner. Rapidly expanding into the terrain of America's malls throughout the 1980s, Victoria's Secret blossomed from a handful of stores to more than four hundred and solidified its exclusive image by appending its own label to all of its offerings as a brand name. In addition to volume growth, the company was able to vend a widened range of products with the aid of a popular mail catalog issued eight times annually. While corsets, teddies, and silk pajamas remained at the hub of the Victoria's Secret wheel, home shoppers could buy shoes, evening wear, and perfumes—such as Wild English Gardens and Heather's Embrace—all under a single banner promising both middle-class refinement and daring sexuality.

By the early 1990s, Victoria's Secret had become the largest American lingerie outfitters, easily surpassing both the even higher-priced Cacique chain and the racier Frederick's of Hollywood. However, despite the fact that the company had topped the billion dollar mark, its growth showed signs of stagnation. In 1993, Grace Nichols took over the executive helm from former president Howard Gross and immediately addressed allegations that the quality of Victoria's Secret's merchandise did not match its elevated price tags. In addition, Nichols placed added emphasis upon an older age group as the company's target concern. Nevertheless, while Nichols stressed that thirty- to forty-year-old women need not feel out of place in sexy underwear, the company's advertising campaigns continued to exclusively portray younger models with svelte, busty figures. Indeed, some critics saw the Victoria's Secret formula of femininity as a limitation to the majority of American women and argued that the company's image (highlighted in design series such as their English Lace line) implicitly promoted an overly bourgeois conception of ''good taste.'' Whatever class and gender ramifications Victoria's Secret might have entailed, the company grew once again under Nichols's care throughout the 1990s, as millions of women—and men--continued to fill out their fantasies with the satin-lined aid of offerings such as the Angels bra series and, perhaps Victoria's Secret's single biggest contribution to the public imagination, the uplifting Miracle Bra.

—Shaun Frentner

FURTHER READING:

Schwartz, Mimi. ''A Day in the Life of Victoria's Secret.'' *Mademoiselle.* Vol. 96, April 1990, 238–39.

Woodman, Sue. ''Victoria Reigns . . . Again.'' *Working Woman.* Vol. 16, September 1991, 77.

Workman, Nancy V. ''From Victorian to Victoria's Secret: The Foundations of Modern Erotic Wear.'' *Journal of Popular Culture.* Vol. 30, Fall 1996, 61-73.

designs and advertising campaigns, Victoria's Secret helped women of all shapes and sizes, if not tax brackets, feel that sensuality need not be limited to models and celebrities.

Victoria's Secret was launched through the personal vision of entrepreneur Roy Raymond, an ambitious graduate of Stanford University who found himself dissatisfied working in the lower rungs of large corporations. Raymond's brainchild came to him in the mid-1970s as the result of his own experiences of buying lingerie for his wife. A shy man by nature, Raymond found himself made uncomfortable by the probing glances of lingerie salespeople in department stores and moreover thought the wares of such stores to be either excessively frilly or blandly conservative. Believing that many men and women alike shared in his desire for a middle ground between these two poles, Raymond decided to embark on the risky venture of creating his own boutiques. In 1977, he borrowed a total of eighty thousand dollars—half of it from his parents—and opened the doors of the first Victoria's Secret in a shopping center in the southern outskirts of San Francisco. Decorated to resemble a popularized Victorian bedroom, the premiere outlet was furnished with opulent Oriental rugs and period vanities whose drawers housed fittingly plush bras and panties made by upscale designers such as Vanity Fair

Vidal, Gore (1925—)

Thanks to the broadcast media, which continually gives public platform to the curmudgeonly wit and iconoclastic political observations of Gore Vidal, he has become one of those rare authors who is as famous for what he says as for what he writes. Considered to be one of the most promising members of the generation of writers emerging from World War II (a group which included his arch-rival and eventual sparring partner, Norman Mailer), Vidal first made his mark with a fairly well received novel based on his army experiences, *Williwaw*, in 1946, then followed up with two more books, the second of which, *The City and the Pillar* (1948), stirred waves of controversy because of its frank treatment of homosexuality. "Not until that third book," Vidal has recalled, "did I begin to get bored with playing safe." Ever since, "playing safe" is a charge which has never been leveled against Vidal, by himself or by anyone else. With his literary career in a slump, he supported himself by writing television plays, finding in that infant medium great success which he soon was able to transpose to Broadway. This in turn led to screenwriting assignments, and in due time Vidal was able to return, with mixed success, to novel writing. His most notorious book was 1968's story of transsexuality, *Myra Breckinridge,* a personal favorite of the author's. While penning historical novels and essays, Vidal has also kept himself in the public eye through appearances on TV interviews and talk shows, and even an occasional acting stint on film. In his TV appearances, Vidal's gadfly manner and contentious political views have entertained and, some would say, enlightened the public in a forum denied to most other scribblers. Vidal has even run for public office and, though never elected, was one of those unsuccessful candidates—Barry Goldwater, Vidal's political opposite, was another—whose views have nonetheless had an influence upon the electorate.

The man who would later christen himself Gore Vidal was born Eugene Luther Vidal at West Point, New York, on October 3, 1925. A greater influence on his childhood than his parents, who soon divorced, was the boy's blind grandfather, Thomas Pryor Gore, Oklahoma's first senator. Young Vidal read to his grandfather the Congressional Record and constitutional history, a formative experience that instilled political ambitions in the lad. As a young man, Vidal decided to forgo Harvard in favor of the military, a decision he claims never to have regretted. The army at least provided fodder for Vidal's first novel and also his most successful teleplay, the satirical *Visit to a Small Planet,* which concerns the misadventures of an alien from outer space who wants to start a war because, he says, "it's the one thing you people down here do *really* well." *Planet* made a successful transition from TV to stage, as did Vidal's trenchant melodrama about rivalry between would-be presidential candidates at their party's convention, *The Best Man.* The latter play also made for a fine film starring Henry Fonda, but Vidal was so displeased with the rewriting and the miscasting of Jerry Lewis in the film version of *Planet* that he has disowned the movie. (Subsequently, Vidal would be equally displeased with the film version of *Myra Breckinridge*; he would also sue to have his name removed from Bob Guccione's infamous production of *Caligula*). Vidal was responsible for the screenplay of his friend Tennessee Williams's play *Suddenly, Last Summer* and made some major, although uncredited, contributions to the script of *Ben-Hur.* (To the continued annoyance and denials of Charlton Heston, Vidal insists that he persuaded director William Wyler to insert a homo-erotic subtext into the film's key relationship between Judah Ben-Hur and his boyhood friend, Messala.)

Vidal, who once criticized the United States as "the land of the dull and the home of the literal," nevertheless always wanted to be its president. He campaigned for representative in 1960 and senator in 1982, losing both battles but nevertheless winning many converts to his somewhat extreme positions (such as his proposal to tax church income).

Although he dabbled with science fiction in one of his novels (*Messiah,* 1954), most of his latter-day books have been such historical novels as *Julian* (1964), *Burr* (1973), and *Lincoln* (1984). *The Smithsonian Institution* (1998) manages to combine both the science fictional and the historical.

There was a time in Vidal's own history when his public spats with other literary figures, such as Truman Capote and William F. Buckley, Jr., led to much-publicized lawsuits. In the case of his feud with Norman Mailer, it even led to flung drinks and fisticuffs. (Covering the 1968 Democratic Convention for ABC-TV, the unlikely team of Vidal and Buckley ended up calling each other, respectively, "crypto-Nazi" and "queer.") Vidal in his later years, however, can hardly be said to have mellowed. "There is no warm loveable person inside," he proclaims, "beneath my cold exterior, once you break the ice, you find cold water."

—Preston Neal Jones

Further Reading:

Parini, Jay, editor. *Gore Vidal: Writer against the Grain.* New York, Columbia University Press, 1992.

Vidal, Gore. *The Essential Gore Vidal.* Edited by Fred Kaplan. New York, Random House, 1999.

Vidal, Gore and Robert J. Stanton, editors. *Views from a Window: Conversations with Gore Vidal.* Seacaucus, New Jersey, L. Stuart, 1980.

Video Games

When the basic "electronic tennis" game, Pong, first appeared in American bars in 1972 it created a sensation that has only since been replicated by the 1990s Karaoke boom in Japan. In relative terms, of course, Pong was as fun and innovative in the 1970s as any video game now, but the basic principles of video gaming have always, in any case, remained the same—score the points, beat the enemy, come back for more. The term "video game" could only really be applied when Atari and Nintendo introduced game consoles into the home throughout the 1970s; the idea being that you would slot your Pong cartridges into the console and play the games through your television set—hence video rather than computer games. But the term has come to cover the main aspect of the medium, playing sight-and-sound games through any convenient screen.

In some sense, the arcade boom that began in 1978 took the group appeal out of video gaming. School children were still taking part in a mass fad, perhaps, but they were also cutting themselves off from others, with the distinction that while Pong required a human opponent, battling against pixelated aliens just pitched the player

A boy playing the arcade video game Q-bert.

against the machine. Of course, after the release of George Lucas's blockbuster movie *Star Wars* in 1977, battling aliens became the rage in the first popular coin-operated machines, such as Space Invaders, Asteroids, and Galaxians. Breakout may have introduced a puzzle element and Pac Man offered a maze race, but video games have essentially always been based on the same principle: "your" pixels blasting, avoiding, or racing against "their" pixels. Technological developments, however, have made the experience of playing these games more visually and aurally realistic, to such an extent that you will not notice that you are only rearranging pixels.

With the introduction of Donkey Kong in 1981, there was an attempt to make a "story" as attractive as the "action." Hence the player now had a character to portray, in this case that of a boy rescuing a princess from an ape monster, as opposed to the previous standard of the player as "thing"—a tennis racquet, a spaceship, or a pac man. It is because of this sort of narrative appeal that Nintendo was able dominate the console market throughout the 1980s. Their 8-bit Nintendo Entertainment System (NES), released in 1983, took away the market from the Atari 2600, even managing to compete with the personal computer boom—in fact, it is estimated that, by 1990, a third of American homes owned Nintendo consoles. Part of the success of Nintendo in the 1980s was not only their 8-bit monopoly but also the blanket marketing of their games. Again, part of the

"humanizing" factor was to bring in a character as appealing as Mickey Mouse or Ronald McDonald, hence the introduction of Mario, the cute Italian-American plumber who would go on to save the world in as many imaginative variations on the platform game formula as possible. First appearing in the Mario Bros. coin-op in 1983, the NES Super Mario Bros. became the "greatest video game" of its generation in 1984, only to be surpassed by Super Mario 3 in 1988.

Following advances in video gaming is just a matter of tracing developments in the game consoles themselves (bearing in mind that, throughout the 1980s and 1990s, arcade machines and personal computers were also advancing the cause). When Sega introduced their 16-bit Mega Drive in 1989, Nintendo was caught off-guard in the "next generation" of console wars. Sega began the 1990s with the christening of a new hero, Sonic the Hedgehog, but Nintendo released their own 16-bit machine, the Super NES in 1990 and was able to win ground with the "greatest video game" of this next generation, Super Mario World. Such were the advances in technology, however, that the mid-1990s came to be characterized by the 32-bit wars, Nintendo seemingly missing out in 1994 when Sega introduced their Saturn and Sony entered the market with the Playstation. And it is the Playstation which came to dominate the market in America, Japan, and Europe, making games "trendy," fun, violent, and often intelligent enough to appeal to "children" of all ages, from three to 33.

For every quick-fire arcade variant, the Playstation also managed to follow the PC (Personal Computer) route into adventure gaming; and altogether combining both speed and strategy with "filmic" production values. Between 1994 and 1998, titles like Doom and Wipeout 2097 became instant classics, and for the growing number of Playstation fans, the Tomb Raider and Final Fantasy series became ways of life. Although missing out on the 32-bit market, Nintendo headed the next "next generation" war with their Nintendo 64 in 1996. With 64-bits to play with, Nintendo's flagship title, Super Mario 64, took Mario out of the 2-dimensional platform world and into a whole new 3-dimensional environment. That games were becoming more like movies was demonstrated by one of the most successful film tie-ins ever, the intelligent and action-packed James Bond spy simulation, Goldeneye (1997); and that Nintendo could corner the same adult market as the Playstation was demonstrated by the glorious prehistoric gore of Turok 2: Seeds of Evil (1998).

Clearly, the basic generic patterns of video gaming have been set—shoot-em-ups, sport, and simulations—but the presentation of video games, sound, graphics, and game play has become nothing short of spectacular. In 1998, Sega launched their Dreamscape, and in 1999 the Playstation 2 completes the 64-bit circuit. With the next 128-bit cycle, however, players will want whole rooms full of equipment in order to experience completely the sights, sounds, and total immersive capacity of these games, the hardware finally expanding to match the immense virtual horizons of the software itself.

—Stephen Keane

FURTHER READING:

Bukatman, Scott. *Terminal Identity: The Virtual Subject in Postmodern Science Fiction.* Durham and London, Duke University Press, 1993.

Jones, Steven G. *CyberSociety.* Thousand Oaks, Sage, 1995.

Trushell, John. "Interactive Games and Other Fairy Tales: Or, Player(s) in Search of Authority." *Foundation: The International Review of Science Fiction.* No.70, Summer 1997, 58-70.

Videos

By late 1987, over one-half of American households owned a videocassette recorder (VCR). With unprecedented speed, the small device had entered the home and taken up its place alongside the television as the premiere electronic consumer item. As with many other consumer products, videocassette recording technology had a long development period, and one that dovetailed with the development of other forms of media. Necessary innovations came in the first half of the twentieth century. Dr. Fritz Pfleumer received a 1928 German patent for the deposition of magnetic powders on paper or plastic backing media. The German companies, Allegemeine Elektrizitats Gelleschaft (AEG) and BASF, produced quantities of magnetic tape between 1934 and 1944 exclusively for the German radio broadcasting stations. In 1944, the American 3M corporation began its own experiments with magnetic coatings, but it was not until after World War II that John T. Mullin, a United States electronic specialist, went to Germany and returned home with four "Magnetophon" recorders. These audiotape recorders were scrutinized, re-wired with parts from the United States, and finally demonstrated to the Institute of Radio Engineers in 1946. Mullin joined the Ampex Electric Corporation in 1948, which later that year introduced the first successful American audiotape recorder. Although other American companies, including RCA, experimented with videotape recording during the late 1940s and early 1950s, Ampex, due largely to its advanced research in audiotape recording, was able to develop the first feasible professional videotape recorder—the VR-1000, which premiered in 1956, weighing 900 pounds and sporting a price tag of $75,000 a unit.

The vast majority of these recorders were purchased by stations and studios affiliated with one of the three major television broadcasting companies—ABC, NBC, and CBS—who employed them in the retransmission, delay, and temporary archiving of programming. Technological innovations during the 1950s largely served the ends of professional engineers and included enhancements in mobility, advanced editing capability, and the addition of color recording. CBS was the first to broadcast from videotape, presenting *Douglas Edwards and News* in 1956 using Ampex recorders. Quickly, the technique diminished the need for "live" broadcasting. Stations could now provide uniform "clock-times" for shows coast-to-coast, functionally eliminating differences introduced by time zones and the erratic adoption of Daylight Savings Time in some regions. Videotape recording also freed performers from the anxiety of "live" performances. Errors could be corrected and re-taped as in film production, and the possibility of the "re-run" was created. Recording technology allowed the networks to concentrate on technical quality and the consolidation of viewing markets. Little attention was yet paid to the development of a viable consumer videotape recorder, although videotape's impact on television viewing was already being felt.

The 1960s marked the beginning of "consumer" videotape recording. The high cost of the Ampex VR-1000 provoked Japanese manufacturing into developing a domestic alternative. Research had begun at Sony as early as 1953, but no significant gains were made until the Japanese company Toshiba developed a helical-scanning recording head in 1959. Helical-scanning technology, the basis of today's VCR, wound its tape around a spinning, drum-like recording head, a novel method which avoided restrictions imposed by Ampex's numerous patents. In 1961, the Victor Company of Japan (JVC) introduced an improved dual, helical-scan head. These innovations allowed for an increased recording quality with a slower tape transport, resulting in decreased tape use and cost savings. Yet, these early units were inferior in image quality and unacceptable for broadcast use.

In 1959, the Society of Motion Picture and Television Engineers (SMPTE) adopted standards for the manufacture of videotape recorders, thus potentially allowing any manufacturer to enter the marketplace. The early 1960s also saw the use of transistorized electronic components, resulting in more compact recorders and potential portability. Nevertheless, the 1963 Nieman Marcus Christmas catalog offered the gigantic $30,000 Ampex VR-1500 videotape recorder / "entertainment center." In 1965, Sony introduced the helical-scan, black-and-white, reel-to-reel, CV-2000 which used an extremely compact 1/2" tape (as compared to the 2" tape of the older Ampex VR-1000). Briefly offered as a consumer model, marketers later emphasized its sale to broadcast and industrial markets. By 1967, Ampex claimed to have sold 500 recorders for "home-use," and by 1968, a number of consumer machines were available in the $800 to $4,000 price range. Most of these, however, such as Cartrivision, failed to capture a significant home market due to either high price or technical shortcomings.

Significant inroads were finally made in the 1970s when Sony introduced the 3/4" tape U-Matic VCR to the American market in 1972. The development of the video-cassette served as a significant leap beyond older reel-to-reel tape formats and completely removed the need for a skilled engineer/operator. Although consumers still resisted the notion of a home videocassette recorder, broadcast engineers began to utilize the Sony U-Matic for news reportage, an area still dominated by film recording. The 1968 Mexico City Olympics games had been covered by at least one older-generation Ampex videotape recorder, and in 1974, a U-Matic was used to document Nixon's historic trip to Moscow. Sony followed in 1975 with the 1/2" Betamax recorder/television combination ($2,300) and the 1976 Betamax stand-alone model ($1,300), each capable of recording one hour of programming. Whereas the U-Matic tape had been the size of a large hardcover book, the Betamax cassette was now that of a paperpack. Coupled with improvements in tape media and recording method (Beta being a term in Japanese for a calligraphic stroke so rich that completely covers the material below; in this case, where the video signal completely saturates the tape), Betamax was strongly posed to enter a market already cluttered with competitors. The result was revolutionary.

Betamax launched its United States marketing program in fall of 1975. The pitch was simple: "any time is prime time." This was a "time-shift machine," one capable of recording a single program while you watched another, and could begin a pre-set recording even when the user was not at home. A total of 55,000 home VCRs were sold by the end of 1976, 160,000 by the end of 1977, and over 400,000 by the close of 1978. According to a trade magazine poll in January 1977, 40 percent of Americans knew what a Betamax was. Yet, according to a 1979 Nielsen poll, the total number of households in the United States owning VCRs was only 475,000, a mere one-half of one percent of the total homes owning televisions. Although other polls placed the number at closer to 800,000, the situation was not yet considered threatening by the majority of the commercial broadcast executives. Sales of prerecorded videocassettes hovered at approximately one tape for every two VCRs. Sales of blank videocassettes continued to climb sharply, prompting some in the industry to ask to what use these tapes were being put.

In 1977, RCA had introduced the Video Home System (VHS) VCR, capable of recording two hours of programming on its slightly larger tape cassette. This increase in allowable recording time was followed by a two-hour Betamax recorder in 1977. RCA responded with a four-hour VHS in 1977, and again in 1979 with a six-hour model. Stiff competition erupted between the two incompatible formats although sales of prerecorded material continued to stagnate. By the end of 1979, VHS had captured 55 percent of the VCR market, a share which would only increase over the next seven years when production of the Betamax recorder was discontinued. Although JVC and other manufacturers rushed to augment their models with features such as ''stop-action'' and ''pause,'' it was not until Sony's introduction of the Betascan in 1979 that the VCR threatened to severely alter the viewing patterns of American households. By allowing the viewer of recorded broadcast material to ''scan'' across the tape while simultaneously viewing it, Betascan users could easily skip commercial advertisements. This feature was rapidly incorporated into JVC's VHS model released in 1979.

In 1984, a major Nielsen survey stated that 36 of the respondents used the ''stop'' or ''pause'' feature of their VCR to delete commercials from shows they where both watching and taping. Nearly half said that they ''frequently'' used the ''fast-forward'' capability to skip taped commercials. Debate raged over what this meant for the future of commercial viewing. Some analysts adopted an almost apocalyptic tone, saying that the VCR would mean the end of viable commercial broadcasting. Others adopted the more modest stance that while VCRs increased the difficulties of directing commercials at specific target audiences (children, female homemakers, etc.), they had potentially opened an entirely new group of viewers for their programming. While television viewing did decrease on Friday and Saturday evenings as viewers turned to other prerecorded materials or shows taped earlier in the week, the overall time spent viewing television increased from six hours and 10 minutes in 1977 to seven hours and seven minutes in 1986.

The sales of prerecorded materials got off to a slow start. Andre Blay founded the Video Club of America in 1977, offering a slim catalog of 50 films on video mostly licensed from Twentieth Century Fox; none of the titles were more recent than 1973, and all had been sold to television. Nevertheless, Blay's Club was the first serious offering of prerecorded feature films at a time when adult films comprised the vast majority of videocassettes publicly available. Warner Home Video began releasing prerecorded videotapes of Hollywood films in 1980. Starting with a very modest 25 titles, this number increased as consumer demand climbed. Warner Brothers, like other film producing companies, had originally expected that consumers would purchase these recordings outright. Yet, much to their chagrin, stores had sprouted up which offered to rent titles to viewers. These ''middlemen'' were perceived as a potential threat, much like television production companies had considered the VCR itself. Copyright was, for them, the right to completely dominate and control the marketing and distribution of their programming and films. MCA/Universal Studios and Walt Disney Production had attempted to sue Sony beginning in 1975, just after the release of the Betamax recorder in the United States. The case had wound its way though the Federal court system until the Supreme Court decided in

January 1985 that ''neither the consumers who tape television programs for their own use nor companies that make and sell video recorders violate Federal copyright law.'' In light of the ''Betamax case,'' film companies opted for the creation of licensing agreements over expensive litigation which, in turn, paved the way for a widespread increase in available titles.

Tom Shales wrote in the Washington Post in 1985: ''The Thing of the Year: the videocassette, which in the past twelve months has had a tremendous effect on American television viewing and American family life. We have gone from being a television nation to being a video nation. . . . By 1955, you felt naked if you didn't own a TV set. By 1965, you felt a tad underdressed if you haven't gone to color. In 1975, it began feeling a little nippy if you didn't have cable TV. And 1985 was the year you felt positively indecent unless you had a VCR.'' In the 1980s, video made itself felt in other ways. The cable station Music Television (MTV) was launched in August 1981 with the appropriately titled ''Video Killed the Radio Star'' by The Buggles. It soon became a market force in the music industry and a serious creator of youth culture. Performers, once content with the studio/radio/tour mode of production and promotion, now had to consider visual elements often unrelated to the music itself. In 1983, Sony introduced the Betamovie camera, the first camcorder. Although Sony had introduced the bulky ''PortaPack'' several years earlier, the Betamovie was the first truly portable video camera. Largely due to the public's penchant for creating documentary ''home movies,'' camcorder sales increased throughout the 1980s, eventually displacing the traditional 8mm film camera in that role. Although never ubiquitous as the VCR, the video camera enjoyed a higher profile in the late 1980s and 1990s. Through television shows, such as *America's Funniest Home Videos,* and the increasing use of ''amateur'' footage in news broadcasts, the videotaped events became common viewing. Their importance would perhaps become most clear as the public witnessed the tapes of the Rodney King beating and the Los Angeles riots of 1992.

—Vance Bell

FURTHER READING:

Cubitt, Sean. *Timeshift: On Video Culture.* London/New York, Routledge, 1991.

Frith, Simon, editor. *Sound and Vision: The Music Video Reader.* London, Routledge, 1993.

Hall, Doug, and Sally Jo Fifer. *Illuminating Video: An Essential Guide to Video Art.* New York, Aperture, 1990.

Lardner, James. *Fast Forward: Hollywood, the Japanese, and the Onslaught of the VCR.* New York/London, W.W. Norton Company, 1987.

Marlow, E., and E. Secunda. *Shifting Time and Space: The Story of the Videotape.* New York, Praeger Publishers, 1991.

Vidor, King (1894-1982)

In a 40 year career, Texan-born pioneer film director King Vidor necessarily adapted to commercial considerations, but his personal vision, and his concern with the problems of society and the individuals within it, resulted in two silent masterpieces (both his wives, Florence Vidor and Eleanor Boardman, were leading silent stars) and a handful of significant sound films. He established his reputation with a powerful anti-war statement, *The Big Parade* (1925), and secured it with *The Crowd* (1928). This profoundly realistic examination of struggle and alienation in the big city revealed a virtuoso use of the camera. Vidor's eclectic tastes and wide interests informed the watershed all-black musical *Hallelujah* (1929), the huge hit *The Champ* (1931), and the Depression drama *Our Daily Bread* (1934). Later work ranged from *Stella Dallas* (1937) and *The Fountainhead* (1949), to Westerns *Duel in the Sun* (1947) and *Man Without a Star* (1955) and the epic *War and Peace* (1956). A five-time Academy nominee, he retired in 1959 and received an honorary Oscar in 1979 for "incomparable achievements as a cinematic creator and innovator."

—Robyn Karney

FURTHER READING:

Brownlow, Kevin. *Behind the Mask of Innocence: Films of Social Conscience in the Silent Era.* London, Jonathan Cape, 1990.

Finler, Joel W. *The Movie Directors Story.* New York, Crescent Books, 1986.

Vidor, King. *On Filmmaking.* New York, Daniel McKay Co., 1972.

———. *A Tree is a Tree.* New York, Longman's, Green & Co. Ltd., 1954.

Vietnam

American involvement in Vietnam began in the mid-1950s, as the French, defeated on the battlefield by the communist Viet Minh, began to withdraw all military forces out of their former colony. Fearing a vacuum that the communists might soon fill, the United States helped establish the Republic of Vietnam in the southern half of the country. In the face of North Vietnam's determination to unite all of Vietnam under its control, a series of U.S. administrations provided support to the South Vietnamese government—first with economic and military aid under President Dwight D. Eisenhower, then military advisors under President John F. Kennedy, then combat troops under President Lyndon Johnson, and finally by invading Cambodia under President Richard Nixon.

As the commitment to Vietnam grew, so did protest at home. Many Americans (often, but not always, college students) opposed the war on moral grounds, frequently extending their opposition to the Selective Service system whereby young men were "drafted" into military service. Other (often older) Americans, motivated by patriotism, anti-communism, or the conviction that "our leaders know best," supported the war effort and often disdained those who protested. The nation was thus polarized as it had not been since the Civil War a century earlier. Eventually, U.S. combat casualties and the lack of significant military progress eroded much of the support for the war. President Richard Nixon gradually disengaged and withdrew most American troops. Under his "Vietnamization" policy, all fighting was gradually turned over to the South Vietnamese army, which, Nixon said, was fully capable of achieving victory. South Vietnam fell to the communists in April 1975.

Vietnam first entered American popular culture through articulation of what became known as the "domino theory." At a press conference in April 1954, President Dwight Eisenhower was asked by a reporter to assess the importance of French Indochina for American

An American soldier in Vietnam.

national security. Eisenhower replied, "You have a row of dominos set up, you knock over the first one, and what will happen to the last one is the certainty that it will go over very quickly. So you could have the beginning of a disintegration that would have the most profound influences."

The image of falling dominos as a metaphor for the consequences of a communist victory in Vietnam was a compelling one, and many leaders who followed Eisenhower made use of it in policy discussions. It was endorsed by Presidents Kennedy, Johnson, and Nixon, as well as their surrogates and spokesmen. Scholars and pundits debated the domino theory's merits in print and in person, and it even showed up in an episode of the popular late-1960s television show, *The Monkees*: the boys have an arrangement of dominos set up on a table. One of them says, "Look, Southeast Asia," and pushes the first domino over, with predictable results for the others.

One of the earliest literary discussions of Vietnam also appeared during Eisenhower's time with William Lederer and Eugene Burdick's 1959 book *The Ugly American.* Less a novel than a collection of loosely-related stories, it is a stinging indictment of U.S. diplomacy throughout Asia—especially in the fictional country of Sarkhan, a thinly-disguised Vietnam. The book depicts U.S. diplomats throughout the region as ignorant, incompetent political hacks, who spend their time at embassy cocktail parties while the communist agents move among the people, speaking their language, respecting their culture, and gaining their allegiance. Several scholars claim that *The Ugly American* inspired President John F. Kennedy (who had read and endorsed the book when it first appeared) to create the Peace Corps; others contend that reading it led Kennedy to transform a small, neglected U.S. Army unit called the Special Forces into those fabled champions of counterinsurgency, the Green Berets.

That elite commando force is also the subject of one of the few fictional works about Vietnam written while the U.S. was militarily engaged there: Robin Moore's *The Green Berets* (1965). Although the book was published during the Johnson Administration, it was Kennedy who gave Moore permission to accompany a Special Forces ''A'' team to Vietnam—provided the author first went through Special Forces training himself. The resulting book was hugely popular, inspiring both a song and a motion picture.

The film, John Wayne's 1968 production *The Green Berets,* was blatant propaganda on behalf of the war and against its critics. Wayne, whose right-wing sympathies were well known, starred, directed, and installed his own son as producer. The Pentagon, on President Johnson's orders, loaned Wayne immense amounts of military equipment and charged him cut rates for its use. In return, the Defense Department had approval rights on the script, and it was not displeased with the result. The film glorifies the Special Forces, vilifies the Viet Cong, and portrays the war's American opponents as uninformed and misguided.

The music that accompanies the film's opening credits is a choral version of Barry Sadler's ''The Ballad of the Green Berets.'' Sadler, a Special Forces NCO, wrote the song while serving in Vietnam and later saw his recording of it reach number one on the singles chart.

In addition to using Wayne's film to influence public opinion on the war, the Johnson Administration also produced a film of its own. *Why Vietnam?* was released in 1965 by the Defense Department and a copy was made available for loan to any school, club, or civic organization that was interested in screening it. The 40-minute documentary was done in the melodramatic, end-of-the-world style of Frank Capra's *Why We Fight* films that was effective in the 1940s. But 1960s audiences often found the approach hokey. In addition, the historical perspective that the film gave of the reasons for U.S. involvement in Vietnam was not only one-sided but at times simply untrue—as when the film's narrator claimed that the planned 1954 national plebiscite that would have united Vietnam was sabotaged by the communists in the North (South Vietnam was actually responsible, with U.S. concurrence).

A very different documentary was released in 1974, just as the war was nearing its end. *Hearts and Minds,* directed by Peter Davis, was an uncompromising indictment of American involvement in Vietnam. The winner of an Academy Award for Best Feature-length Documentary, the film uses juxtaposition—for example, Nixon justifying his ''Christmas bombing'' of 1972 followed by footage of a Hanoi hospital destroyed in that bombing—and interviews with Vietnamese peasants to show the devastating damage that the United States inflicted on Vietnam.

News coverage, especially on television, was of vital concern to the several U.S. administrations that waged war in Vietnam. It was believed, not without reason, that the focus and tone of the news might well have an effect on public support for the war. Consequently, both civilian and military officials tried to influence the coverage—they emphasized some aspects of the war, downplayed others, withheld

some and lied about more than a few. These efforts at news management were fairly successful for several years; many journalists, both print and electronic, produced stories that were generally favorable to both the American goals in Vietnam and the ways those goals were pursued.

The Tet Offensive changed everything. At 3:00 a.m. Saigon time on January 30, 1968, the traditional Lunar New Year truce was broken when Viet Cong and North Vietnamese Army units simultaneously attacked targets all across South Vietnam. A number of images arising out of this campaign found their way into America's living rooms, and they did not help the Johnson Administration's cause: dead Viet Cong on the grounds of the U.S. embassy in Saigon, the walls of which had never before been breached; the head of the South Vietnamese National Police, General Loan, drawing his pistol and shooting a bound Viet Cong prisoner in the head; a U.S. army Major, explaining the devastation of a hamlet called Ben Tre by saying, ''We had to destroy the village in order to save it.''

Tet marked a turning point in media coverage of the war. Reporters, who had listened for months to the claims of American officials that the Viet Cong were defunct, now grew cynical in the face of clear evidence to the contrary. News stories began to be more critical of the ''official'' version of events. CBS News anchorman Walter Cronkite, who polls showed to be the must trusted man in America, said on television that he thought the war to be hopelessly stalemated and that the United States should negotiate with the communists.

Meanwhile, U.S. antiwar protesters were receiving media coverage, too; much of it was unsympathetic. News reports tended to focus on the most dramatic or shocking aspects of antiwar activity—if 500 people demonstrated peacefully and three others burned a U.S. flag, then the latter group would almost certainly be featured on the evening news. Further, as antiwar protests became more common, many journalists declined even to cover them, unless they involved large numbers of people or were likely to turn violent. Astute demonstrators thus learned how to draw media attention through destructive or shocking behavior—but the very acts that brought news coverage also alienated most of the middle-class audience watching or reading at home.

Although many popular musicians of the period appeared oblivious to the war, there were some who became known for their antiwar material: Joan Baez, Pete Seeger, Phil Ochs, and Barbara Dane were prominent among these. Other individuals and bands recorded a song or two critical of the war effort, including Country Joe McDonald's ''Feel Like I'm Fixin' To Die Rag,'' The Animals' ''We Gotta Get Out of This Place,'' Buffalo Springfield's ''For What It's Worth,'' The Association's ''Requiem for the Masses,'' Barry McGuire's ''Eve of Destruction,'' The Doors' ''Unknown Soldier,'' and Crosby, Stills, Nash and Young's ''Ohio.''

But there was reaction against protest, even on the radio. Some country artists, in particular, whose fan base tended to be more conservative than that of rock musicians, recorded songs that were supportive of the war, or critical of protesters, or both. These included two Merle Haggard records, ''Okie from Muskogee'' and ''The Fightin' Side of Me,'' as well as Maybelle Carter's ''I Told Them What You're Fightin' For,'' Johnny Wright's ''Hello, Vietnam,'' and Dave Dudley's ''Vietnam Blues.''

Although the war's end in 1975 also brought a halt to the musical battle being waged over the airwaves, most other aspects of American popular culture continued to find the Vietnam conflict a worthy subject. One of these manifestations involved memoirs: a number of veterans published personal accounts of their experiences in the war, including Tim O'Brien's *If I Die in a Combat Zone* (1973), Ron Kovic's *Born on the Fourth of July* (1976), Michael Herr's *Dispatches* (1977), and William Broyles' *Brothers in Arms* (1986). A number of "oral histories" from veterans were also collected and published, such as Al Santoli's *Everything We Had* (1981) and *To Bear Any Burden* (1986), Wallace Terry's *Bloods: An Oral History of the Vietnam War by Black Veterans* (1984), and Kathryn Marshall's *In the Combat Zone: An Oral History of American Women in Vietnam* (1984).

The postwar period also saw no shortage of novels about the conflict in Vietnam. Some of the most important are Tim O'Brien's books *Going after Cacciato* (1978) and *The Things They Carried* (1990), James Webb's *Fields of Fire* (1978), Winston Groom's *Better Times than These* (1978), John DelVecchio's *The Thirteenth Valley* (1982), and Philip Caputo's *Indian Country* (1987).

The dearth of war-related motion pictures made while the conflict was in progress was more than made up afterwards. Ted Post directed 1978's *Go Tell the Spartans*, a bleak look at the early days of American "advisors" in Vietnam that suggests the seeds of American defeat were planted early in the struggle. The same year, Michael Cimino's *The Deer Hunter* won the Best Picture Oscar for its story of three friends whose service in Vietnam changes them in markedly different ways. A year later, Francis Ford Coppola's *Apocalypse Now* premiered, a near-epic film injected with a heavy dose of surrealism. Surrealism also permeates the second half of Stanley Kubrick's 1987 film *Full Metal Jacket*, which follows a group of young men from the brutality of Marine Corps boot camp to the terrors of their deployment in Vietnam. Two other important films, Oliver Stone's *Platoon* (1986) and John Irvin's *Hamburger Hill* (1987) take a more realistic approach, emphasizing the individual tragedies of young men's lives wasted in a war they do not understand.

In addition to the differing film depictions of the actual fighting in the Vietnam War, two sub-genres of Vietnam War films emerged. One focuses on the figure of the Vietnam veteran, made crazy by the war, who brings his deadly skills home and directs them against his countrymen. Though many cheap exploitation films were based on this premise, using it as an excuse to revel in blood and explosions, two more complex treatments appeared. Martin Scorsese's *Taxi Driver* (1976), in which Robert De Niro offers a compelling portrait of the psychologically disintegrating Travis Bickle, and Ted Kotcheff's *First Blood* (1982), in which a former Green Beret is pushed beyond endurance by a brutal police chief who pays a high price for his callousness, offer interesting insights into the lasting wounds war inflicts on soldiers.

The second sub-genre of Vietnam War films posited that some Americans remained prisoners in Vietnam after the end of the war and required rescue. The Rambo character so prominent in this sub-genre was first seen in *First Blood* with Sylvester Stallone's first portrayal of John Rambo. The first of these films, 1983's *Uncommon Valor*, stars Gene Hackman and downplays the exploitative aspects of its premise. But other films flaunted the same premise, most notably the Chuck Norris vehicle *Missing in Action* (1984) and its two sequels, *Missing in Action II: The Beginning* (1985) and *Braddock: Missing in Action III* (1988). The most lurid example of this sub-genre is Stallone's *Rambo: First Blood Part II* (1985). Stallone's crazed ex-Green Beret character is released from prison to undertake a rescue mission of Americans held prisoner in Vietnam. Despite being betrayed, captured, and tortured, he manages to free the captive

GIs and mow down scores of Vietnamese soldiers and their Russian "advisors," thus symbolically "winning" the Vietnam War for America.

In addition to films, television shows and made-for-TV movies about the struggle in Vietnam appeared in the postwar era. *The A-Team*, which premiered in 1983, was based on the notion that a group of Special Forces troopers (hence the "A-team" designation), while serving in Vietnam were framed for a bank robbery and sent to prison. They escaped en masse and became fugitives. In order to pay the bills while on the run, they hired themselves out as mercenaries—but only, of course, in a good cause. The show's scripts were generally as improbable as its premise, but George Peppard (who played the leader of the team, which included the impressively muscled but diction-challenged Mr. T as "B.A. Baracus") led his group of virtuous vigilantes through four seasons of mayhem before cancellation of the show in 1987.

As *The A-Team* left television, a more serious drama about an Army platoon in Vietnam during the late 1960s called *Tour of Duty* debuted. Although the show had an ensemble cast, its prominent character was Sergeant Zeke Anderson (Terence Knox), an experienced combat leader who often took up the slack left by the unit's "green" Lieutenant. Although sometimes prone to cliches, the show dealt with the Vietnam experience fairly realistically, given the limitations of TV drama. It lasted three seasons and was canceled in 1990. Another serious show about combat in Southeast Asia also began in 1987. *Vietnam War Story* was an anthology show, with a new cast of characters each week—not unlike the previous decade's programs *Police Story* and *Medical Story*. The plots were supposedly based upon real incidents and many of the scripts were penned by actual Vietnam veterans. However, despite these efforts at verisimilitude, the show lasted only one season.

China Beach (which aired from 1988 to 1991) may be the best television series about the Vietnam War produced by the end of the twentieth century. Its setting was a military hospital complex in Danang during the period 1967-69. The ensemble cast of characters was large, including doctors and nurses, soldiers and Marines, USO singers and prostitutes. But the show's main character and moral center was Army nurse Coleen McMurphy (Dana Delaney). McMurphy volunteered for both the Army and Vietnam, and, although horrified by the realities of combat casualties, did her best as both a nurse and a human being. Mixing comedy and drama, the show explored the relationships between the people of the China Beach facility, and showed how such relationships can be created, changed, or destroyed by a war.

A large number of made-for-TV movies have been made about various facets of the Vietnam War. A few of the more interesting productions include *The Forgotten Man* (1971), in which Dennis Weaver plays a Vietnam veteran, presumed dead for years but actually a prisoner of war (POW), who returns home to find his wife remarried, his job gone, and his old life irrevocably lost. *When Hell Was in Session* (1979) tells the harrowing true story of Commander Jeremiah Denton's seven-year imprisonment as a POW in Hanoi. A similar tale is told in *In Love and War* (1987), about the captivity of Commander James Stockdale and his wife's efforts to have him released. *Friendly Fire* (1979) tells the story of a couple whose son is killed in Vietnam under mysterious circumstances. Their efforts to determine how he died bring them up against a wall of bureaucratic indifference. *The Children of An Loc* (1980) tells the true story of an American actress (Ina Balin, who plays herself) struggling to evacuate 217 children from a Vietnamese orphanage during the fall of

Saigon in 1975. One of the most affecting efforts was the HBO production *Dear America: Letters Home from Vietnam* (1987), based on Bernard Edelman's book of the same name. It combines the reading of actual letters with news footage and music of the period to tell the tale of the Vietnam War from the perspective of the men and women who lived it.

—Justin Gustainis

FURTHER READING:

Anderegg, Michael, editor. *Inventing Vietnam: The War in Film and Television.* Philadelphia, Temple University Press, 1991.

Franklin, H. Bruce, editor. *The Vietnam War in American Stories, Songs, and Poems.* Boston, Bedford Books, 1996.

Lanning, Michael Lee. *Vietnam at the Movies.* New York, Fawcett Columbine, 1994.

Rowe, John Carlos, and Rick Berg, editors. *The Vietnam War and American Culture.* New York, Columbia University Press, 1991.

Villella, Edward (1936—)

A critically acclaimed principal dancer with the New York City Ballet company during the 1960s and 1970s, Edward Villella brought a virile athleticism to the classical ballet stage that challenged the stereotype of the effeminate male dancer and popularized ballet and its male stars among the general public. His passionate energy and exceptional technique inspired the great neo-classical choreographer George Balanchine to create many ballets and roles for Villella, including *Tarantella* (1964) and the "Rubies" section of *Jewels* (1967). Committed to increasing Americans' awareness of ballet, Villella also danced in Broadway musicals, performed at President John F. Kennedy's inauguration, and appeared frequently on television, in variety and arts programs and once, as himself, in an episode of the situation-comedy *The Odd Couple*. Injuries had forced Villella to stop performing by 1986 when he became founder and artistic director of the Miami City Ballet.

—Lisa Jo Sagolla

FURTHER READING:

Villella, Edward, with Larry Kaplan. *Prodigal Son: Dancing for Balanchine in a World of Pain and Magic.* New York, Simon and Schuster, 1992.

Vitamin B17

See Laetrile

Vitamins

Apart from their actual health benefits, vitamins have played an important role in the American consciousness as the arena for a struggle between competing systems of knowledge: the positivist

authority of "normal science" with its controlled experiments and research protocols versus the anecdotal evidence and personal experiences of ordinary consumers. Since antiquity, it has been commonly known that there is a connection between diet and health, but it was not until the early 1900s that specific vitamins were isolated and accepted by the public as essential to our well-being. What began as an exercise in public health became big business: by the end of the century, retail sales of vitamins in America exceeded $3.5 billion, with surveys showing more than 40 percent of Americans using vitamins on a regular basis. The story of vitamins demonstrates, in the words of social historian Rima Apple, that "Science is not above commerce or politics; it is a part of both."

The term "vitamins" (originally spelled "vitamines") was coined shortly before World War I by Casimir Funk, a Polish-American biochemist who was among the first to investigate the role of these substances in combatting deficiency diseases such as rickets. By the middle of the 1920s, three vitamins had been identified (vitamin A, vitamin C, and vitamin D), as had the vitamin B complex. Even then, manufacturers were quick to seize on the public's interest in vitamins as an angle for promoting their own products. Red Heart trumpeted the vitamin D content of its dog biscuits; Kitchen Craft declared that since its Waterless Cooker cooked foods in their own juices, none of the "vital mineral salts and vitamin elements . . . are washed out and poured away with the waste water." Particularly compelling were the appeals to "scientific mothering" in ads for such products as Squibb's cod-liver oil ("the X-RAY shows tiny bones and teeth developing imperfectly"), its competitor H. A. Metz's Oscodal tablets ("children need the vital element which scientists call vitamin D"), Cream of Wheat, Quaker Oats, and Hygeia Strained Vegetables. Pharmaceutical firms likewise targeted mothers in periodicals such as *Good Housekeeping* and *Parents'* magazine, with the publishers' blessings: "An advertiser's best friend is a mother; a mother's best friend is 'The Parents' Magazine,'" proclaimed its advertising department, while the director of the Good Housekeeping Bureau generously promised clients that all products advertised in the magazine, "whether or not they are within our testing scope, are guaranteed by us on the basis of the claims made for them."

Harry Steenbock, a researcher at the University of Wisconsin, discovered in 1924 that ultraviolet irradiation of certain foods boosted their vitamin D content, thus providing an alternative source to wholesome but distasteful cod-liver oil. The Wisconsin Alumni Research Foundation was created to protect his patents and to license his process to manufacturers. (Ironically, it would be Wisconsin's Senator William Proxmire who, exactly half a century later, would spearhead a congressional campaign which resulted in the Food and Drug Administration's reclassifying most vitamins as food rather than drugs.)

The scientific reasons advanced for taking a particular vitamin were often compelling. In the late 1700s, fresh fruit, rich in vitamin C, had been dramatically shown to be a preventive for scurvy, the cause of many shipboard deaths on long sea voyages: Captain James Cook added citrus to the diet of his crew on his three-year circumnavigation of the globe, during which only one of his seamen died. (Cook's limes, which became a staple of shipboard diet throughout the British navy, gave rise to the slang term "limeys" for Englishmen.) But widespread consumption of a vitamin for its original purpose sometimes created partisans for its benign effects in another area, as when Nobel laureate Linus Pauling advocated high dosages of vitamin C in the 1970s as a therapy for the common cold, and subsequently proposed that it could even play a role in curing cancer.

The appeal to scientific authority helped to legitimate vitamin consumption, but as vitamins became popular science and demand grew, other marketers became eager players, and from the 1930s on there was increasing competition between health professionals (physicians and pharmacists) on the one hand, and grocers on the other. Trade journals for the druggists repeatedly stressed the profitability in vitamins and the desirability of keeping consumers coming back to the drugstore for their supplies (and discouraging them from buying vitamins in the general marketplace). The grocers (and later the health food stores) and their public wanted to keep vitamins readily available and affordable. And there were skeptics as well, including the FDA, whose own claim to scientific legitimacy had the force of law, and which attempted to regulate vitamin marketing in order to prevent what it often saw as fraudulent claims and medical quackery.

Often, however, when the FDA frustrated the demand for dietary supplements with its regulatory impediments, it aroused an endemic populist distrust of big government and fierce resentment of a professional pharmaceutical and medical establishment seen as monolithic or even conspiratorial. In the late decades of the century, the public found a willing ally in Congress, which received no fewer than 100,000 phone calls during debate on the Hatch-Richardson ''Health Freedom'' proposal of 1994 (it reduced the FDA's ''significant scientific agreement'' standard to ''significant scientific evidence'' for labeling claims, so long as they were ''truthful and non-misleading,'' and shortened the lead time for putting new products on the market); with 65 cosponsors in the Senate and 249 in the House, the bill passed handily.

—Nick Humez

FURTHER READING:

American Entrepreneurs' Association. *Health Food/Vitamin Store.* Irvine, Entrepreneur Group, 1993.

Apple, Rima D. *Vitamania: Vitamins in American Culture.* New Brunswick, Rutgers University Press, 1996.

Funk, Casimir, and H. E. Dubin. *Vitamin and Mineral Therapy: Practical Manual.* New York, U.S. Vitamin Corp, 1936.

Harris, Florence LaGanke. *Victory Vitamin Cook Book for Wartime Meals.* New York, Wm. Penn Publishing Co., 1943.

Pauling, Linus. *Vitamin C and the Common Cold.* San Francisco, W. H. Freeman, 1970.

Richards, Evelleen. *Vitamin C and Cancer: Medicine or Politics?* New York, St. Martin's Press, 1991.

Takton, M. Daniel. *The Great Vitamin Hoax.* New York, Macmillan, 1968.

Vogue

The first illustrated fashion magazine grew out of a weekly society paper that began in 1892. *Vogue* magazine's inauspicious start as a failing journal did not preview the success that it would become. In 1909, a young publisher, Condé Nast, bought the paper and transformed it into a leading magazine that signaled a new approach to women's magazines. In 1910, the once small publication changed to a bi-monthly format, eventually blossoming into an international phenomenon with nine editions in nine countries: America, Australia, Brazil, Britain, France, Germany, Italy, Mexico, and Spain.

Following the vision of Condé Nast, *Vogue* has continued to present cultural information, portraits of artists, musicians, writers, and other influential people as well as the current fashion trends. Since its inception, the magazine has striven to portray the elite and serve as an example of proper etiquette, beauty, and composure. *Vogue* not only contributes to the acceptance of trends in the fashion and beauty industry, but additionally has become a record of the changes in cultural thinking, actions, and dress. Glancing through *Vogue* from years past documents the changing roles of women, as well as the influences of politics and cultural ideas throughout the twentieth century.

The power that *Vogue* has had over many generations of women has spawned a plethora of other women's magazines—such as *Cosmopolitan, Glamour,* and *Mademoiselle*—which have sought to claim part of the growing market of interest. Despite the abundance of women's magazines, no other publication has been able to achieve the lasting influence and success of *Vogue*.

By incorporating photography in 1913, and under the direction of Edna Woolman Chase (Editor-in-Chief from 1914 to 1951) and Art Director Dr. Mehemed Gehmy Agha, *Vogue* reinvented its image several times. With the occurrence of the Depression and later, World War II, readership soared. Readers looked to the magazine to escape from the reality of the hardships in their lives. In the midst of the Depression fashions reflected the glamour of Hollywood; then came movies with their enormous influence on the ideas of fashion and beauty. Photographers Edward Steichen, Cecil Beaton, and Baron de Meyer emphasized this glamour by presenting their models in elaborate settings. Additionally, *Vogue* began focusing on more affordable, ready-to-wear clothing collections. During the war, images of fashions within the magazine emulated the practicality of the era. Different, more durable and affordable fabrics, and simple designs became prominent. The magazine demonstrated that even in difficult circumstances, women still strove for the consistency of caring for everyday concerns regarding fashion and beauty. Balancing the lighter features, ex-*Vogue* model and photographer Lee Miller's images of the liberation of Europe also provided a somber and intellectual view of the war. This element of the magazine kept readers involved and informed of the realities of the war.

Under the supervision of Jessica Daves (Editor-in-Chief 1952-1962) and Russian émigré Alexander Liberman (Art Director 1943-December 1963, Editorial Director of Condé Nast Publications, Inc. 1963—), simplicity of design in *Vogue* prevailed after World War II. One main component of the re-formatting undertaken by Daves and Liberman was the hiring of photographer Irving Penn in 1943, who, along with Richard Avedon, modernized fashion photography by simplifying it. Penn used natural lighting and stripped out all superfluous elements; his images focused purely on the fashions. Penn and other photographers also contributed portraits of notable people, travel essays, and ethnographic features to the magazine. Thoughtful coverage on the issues of the day, in addition to the variety of these stories and supplementary columns—including ''People Are Talking About,'' an editorial consisting of news regarding art, film, theater, and celebrities' lives—counterbalanced the fashion spreads which showcased the seasonal couture collections. *Vogue* magazine became multi-faceted, appealing to readers across several economic and social stratus.

Diana Vreeland (Editor-in-Chief, 1963 to June 1971), with her theatrical style, brought to the magazine a cutting-edge, exciting quality. Vreeland, famous for coining the term ''Youthquake,'' focused on the changing ideas of fashion in the 1960s. Under her hand, *Vogue* became even more fashion oriented, with many more pages devoted to clothing and accessories. Imagination and fantasy were the ideals to portray within the pages of the magazine. Clothes were colorful, bright, revealing, and filled with geometric shapes that played with the elements of sex and fun. Additionally, during this era, models no longer became merely mannequins but personalities. The photographs depicted the models in action-filled poses, often outside of a studio setting. The women became identifiable; Suzy Parker, Penelope Tree, Twiggy, and Verushka became household names and paved the way for Cindy, Claudia, Christy, and Naomi, the supermodels of the 1980s and 1990s.

Collaborating with photographers such as Helmut Newton, Sarah Moon, and Deborah Tuberville, Grace Mirabella (Editor-in-Chief, July 1971 to October 1988) also brought a sensual quality to the magazine; the blatant sexualized images from the 1960s became more understated, although no less potent. Tinged with erotic and sometimes violent imagery, the fashion layouts featured clothing with less of an exhibitionist quality; apparel became more practical. Filling the fashion pages were blue denim garments and easy to wear attire. Mirabella, in keeping with this practicality, adapted the magazine to a monthly publication. At this time, *Vogue* also shrank in cut size to conform to postal codes. As a result, each page became packed with information; *Vogue* became a magazine formulated for a society filled with working women on the go.

The tradition of *Vogue* as a publication that covers all aspects of each generation continues. Under the guidance of Anna Wintour (Editor-in-Chief, November 1988—) the magazine has expanded beyond only reporting cultural and political issues and presenting fashion trends, and is now considered to validate new designs and designers. *Vogue* continually seeks out, presents, and promotes new ideas regarding clothing, accessories, and beauty products, and as a magazine entertains, educates, and guides millions of women.

—Jennifer Jankauskas

FURTHER READING:

Devlin, Polly, with an introduction by Alexander Liberman. *Vogue Book of Fashion Photography*. London, Thames and Hudson, 1979.

Kazajian, Dodie, and Calvin Tomkins. *Alex: The Life of Alexander Liberman*. New York, A.A. Knopf, 1993.

Lloyd, Valerie. *The Art of Vogue Photographic Covers: Fifty Years of Fashion and Design*. New York, Harmony Books, 1986.

Volkswagen Beetle

The phenomenal success of Volkswagen's diminutive two-door sedan in the American automobile market in the 1950s and 1960s was a classic example of conventional wisdom proven false. Detroit's car manufacturers and their advertising agencies marketed large, comfortable cars with futuristic styling and plenty of extra gadgets. Futuristic rocket fins were in, and the more headlights and tail lights, the better. ''Planned obsolescence'' was built in: the look and feel of each year's models were to be significantly different from those of the previous year. But throughout the 1950s, there was a persistent niche market in foreign cars, particularly among better-educated drivers

who thought that Detroit's cars looked vulgar and silly, and who were appalled by their low mileage. Most European imports got well over 20 miles per gallon to an American automobile's eight. The German manufacturers of the Volkswagen claimed that their ''people's car'' got 32 miles per gallon at 50 miles an hour. Moreover, it was virtually impossible to tell a 1957 VW from a 1956 one—or indeed, from the 1949 model, of which just two had been imported, by way of Holland. (The first ''Transporter'' microbus sold in America arrived in 1950.)

To be sure, VW's sedan looked odd—rather like a scarab, which is why it was soon dubbed the ''Beetle''—but it worked. Its rear-mounted, air-cooled, four-cylinder 1200-cc engine proved extremely durable, with some owners reporting life spans in the high hundreds of thousands of miles. The cars had been designed so that they could be maintained by the owner, and many of them were, particularly by young owners who bought them used. And the microbus, with the same engine as the Beetle and a body only slightly longer, could hold an entire rock band and its instruments and still climb mountains. (It became so closely associated with the hippie movement that when the leader of the Grateful Dead died, VW ran an ad showing a microbus with a tear falling from its headlight and the headline ''Jerry Garcia. 1942-1995.'')

Developed by Dr. Ferdinand Porsche, the car had been ordered by German citizens for the first time in 1938 under the name ''KdF-Wagen'' (KdF stood for ''Kraft durch Freude,'' ''strength through joy.''), but war had broken out the following year, and the factory at Wolfsburg switched over, for the duration, to making a military version, the Kübelwagen (''bucketmobile''), and its amphibious sibling, the Schwimmwagen, until Allied planes bombed operations to a standstill. After the war, VW rebuilt its factory and resumed production, first under the British occupying forces, and subsequently under Heinrich Nordhoff, VW's CEO until his death in 1969.

From their modest beginnings, sales of imported VWs in America grew steadily. In 1955, the company incorporated in the United States as Volkswagen of America. In 1959, it hired a sassy new advertising agency, DDB Needham, which had already raised eyebrows with its ''You Don't Have to Be Jewish to Love Levy's Jewish Rye'' campaign. DDB's first ad was three columns of dense type explaining the advantages of buying the VW sedan, broken up only by three photos—all of the car.

It soon became apparent that people already knew what the Beetle looked like, and had looked like for 10 years, that it got great mileage, and that it cost less than anything from Detroit ($1545 new in 1959, still only $2000 in 1964). What they needed was a reason to identify with a nonconformist automobile. So DDB switched to ads containing very little copy, a picture of the car, a very short, startling headline in sans-serif type, and a lot of white space. One DDB headline was ''Ugly is only skin-deep.'' Another simply read ''Lemon.'' A third, turning one of Madison Avenue's favorite catchphrases of the day on its head, said ''Think Small.'' Indeed, almost all of DDB's VW ads were the conspicuous antithesis of conventional auto advertising. ''Where are they now?'' showed 1949 models of six cars, five by companies which had gone out of business in the subsequent decade. In the 1960s, the focus of the campaign shifted to true stories of satisfied customers with unusual angles: the rural couple who bought a VW after the mule died, the priest whose North Dakota mission had a total of 30 Beetles, the Alabama police department which got a VW sedan for its meter patrol.

Although VW lost some of its market share in the 1970s once Detroit, spurred by the 1973 OPEC oil embargo, began concentrating

A Volkswagen Beetle.

on cars that were less ostentatious and got better mileage, the company continued to make Beetles until the end of the decade, when anti-pollution standards were passed which neither the sedan nor the microbus could meet. Although production of Beetles in Germany and the United States ceased in 1978, they still continued to be turned out elsewhere, notably in Mexico, where in 1983 VWs amounted to 30 percent of all motor vehicles made in that country. Meanwhile, restored Beetles in the United States continued to command prices up to $7,000 (still a bargain compared to $15,000 for the cheapest new cars from Detroit) in the early 1990s.

When VW introduced a ''concept car'' at the Detroit Motor Show looking suspiciously like the old Beetle, response was so enthusiastic that the company went ahead and put its ''Concept 1'' into production at the same Mexican plant as the VW Golf (and powered by the same water-cooled engine, now under the front hood). The first new Beetles arrived in the United States in 1998 to nostalgic advertising produced by Arnold Communications in Boston in a reprise of the DDB style, but with even less body copy: a picture of the sedan above headlines such as ''Roundest car in its class'' and ''Zero to sixty. Yes.'' One ad read simply ''Think small. Again.''

—Nick Humez

Further Reading:

Addams, Charles, et al. *Think Small.* New York, Golden Press, 1967.

Burnham, Colin. *Air-Cooled Volkswagens: Beetles, Karmann Ghias Types 2 & 3.* London, Osprey, 1987.

Darmon, Olivier. *30 ans de publicité Volkswagen.* Paris, Hoebeke, 1993.

Keller, Maryann. *Collision: GM, Toyota, Volkswagen and the Race to Own the 21st Century.* New York, Currency Doubleday, 1993.

Nelson, Walter Henry. *Small Wonder: The Amazing Story of the Volkswagen.* Boston, Little, Brown, 1965.

Sloniger, Jerry. *The VW Story.* Cambridge, P. Stephens, 1980.

von Sternberg, Josef (1894-1969)

Although there are other achievements for which to salute film director (and screenwriter, producer, and occasional cinematographer) Josef von Sternberg, his reputation has come to rest indissolubly on his most famous creation, Marlene Dietrich. After making *Underworld* (1927) and *The Docks of New York* (1928), two near-masterpieces of the late silent era, von Sternberg was invited to Berlin to film *The Blue Angel* (1930). There he found Dietrich and cast her as the predatory Lola-Lola. He brought her to Hollywood and turned her into an international screen goddess of mystical allure in six exotic romances, beginning with *Morocco* (1930) and ending with *The Devil Is a Woman* (1935). In this last and most baroque of Sternberg's films, his sensual imagery and atmospheric play of light and shadow on fabulous costumes and inventive sets found its fullest expression. Once parted from Paramount and his star he endured a slow decline, but at the height of his success this Viennese-born son of poor immigrant Jews (the ''von'' was acquired), who had served a ten-year apprenticeship as an editor, was acknowledged as Hollywood's outstanding visual stylist and undisputed master technician.

—Robyn Karney

Further Reading:

Bach, Steven. *Marlene Dietrich: Life and Legend.* New York, HarperCollins, 1992.

Finler, Joel W. *The Movie Directors Story.* New York, Crescent Books, 1986.

Sternberg, Josef von. *Fun in a Chinese Laundry.* New York, MacMillan, 1965.

Vonnegut, Kurt, Jr. (1922—)

Having come to prominence only with his sixth novel, *Slaughterhouse-Five* (1969), Kurt Vonnegut, Jr. is a rare example of an author who has been equally important to popular audiences and avant-garde critics. His fiction and public spokesmanship spans all five of the decades since World War II and engages most social, political, and philosophical issues of these times. It is Vonnegut's manner of expression that makes him both popular and perplexing, for his humorous approach to serious topics confounds critical expectations while delighting readers who themselves may be fed up with expert opinion.

November 11, 1922, is the date of Kurt Vonnegut's birth, a birthday he considers significant for its coincidence with Armistice Day celebrations noting the end of World War I. From his upbringing in Indianapolis, Indiana among a culturally prominent family descended from German immigrant Free-Thinkers of the 1850s, the young author-to-be developed attitudes that would see him through the coming century of radical change. Pacifism was one such attitude; another was civic responsibility; a third was the value of large extended families in meeting the needs of nurture for both children

Kurt Vonnegut, Jr.

and adults. The first test of these attitudes came in the 1930s, when during the Great Depression his father's work as an architect came to an end (for lack of commissions) and his mother's inherited wealth was depleted. These circumstances forced Kurt into the public school system, where, unlike his privately educated older brother and sister, he was able to form close childhood friendships with working-class students, an experience he says meant the world to him. Sent off to college with his father's instruction to ''learn something useful,'' Vonnegut joined what would have been the class of 1944 at Cornell University as a dual major in biology and chemistry with an eye toward becoming a biochemist. Most of his time, however, was spent writing for and eventually becoming a managing editor of the independent student owned daily newspaper, the *Cornell Sun.*

World War II interrupted Kurt Vonnegut's education, but for awhile it continued in different form. In 1943, he avoided the inevitable draft by enlisting in the United States Army's Advanced Specialist Training Program, which made him a member of the armed services but allowed him to study mechanical engineering at the Carnegie Technical Institute and the University of Tennessee. In 1944, this one-of-a-kind program was canceled when Allied Commander Dwight D. Eisenhower made an immediate request for 50,000 additional men. Prepared as a rear-echelon artillery engineer, Vonnegut was thrown into combat as an advanced infantry scout, and was promptly captured by the Germans during the Battle of the Bulge. Interned as a prisoner of war at Dresden, he was one of the few survivors of that city's firestorm destruction by British and American air forces on the night of February 13, 1945, the event that becomes the unspoken center of *Slaughterhouse-Five,* named after the underground meatlocker where the author took shelter. Following his repatriation in May of 1945, Kurt Vonnegut married Jane Cox and began graduate study in anthropology at the University of Chicago.

During these immediately postwar years he also worked as a reporter for the City News Bureau, a pool service for Chicago's four daily newspapers. Unable to have his thesis topics accepted and with his first child ready to be born, Vonnegut left Chicago without a degree and began work as a publicist for the General Electric (GE) Research Laboratory in Schenedtady, New York. Here, where his older brother Bernard was a distinguished atmospheric physicist, Kurt drew on his talents as a journalist and student of science in order to promote the exciting new world where, as GE's slogan put it, ''Progress Is Our Most Important Product.'' Yet this brave new world of technology rubbed the humanitarian in Vonnegut the wrong way, and soon he was writing dystopian satires of a bleakly comic future in which humankind's relentless desire to tinker with things makes life immensely worse. When enough of these short stories had been accepted by *Collier's* magazine so that he could bank a year's salary, Kurt Vonnegut quit GE. Moving to Cape Cod, Massachusetts, in 1950, he thenceforth survived as a full time fiction writer, taking only the occasional odd job to tide things over when sales to publishers were slow.

Throughout the 1950s and into the early 1960s, Vonnegut published 44 such stories in *Collier's, The Saturday Evening Post,* and other family-oriented magazines, sending material to the lower-paying science fiction markets only after mainstream journals had rejected it. Consistently denying that he is or ever was a science fiction writer, the author instead used science as one of many elements in common middle class American life of the times. When his most representative stories were collected in 1968 as *Welcome to the Monkey House,* it became apparent that Vonnegut was as interested in high school bandmasters and small town tradesman as he was in rocket scientists and inventors of cyberspace; indeed, in such stories as ''Epicac'' and ''Unready to Wear,'' the latter behave like the former, with the most familiar of human weaknesses overriding the brainiest of intellectual concerns.

Kurt Vonnegut's novelist career began as a sidelight to his short story work, low sales, and weak critical notice for these books, making them far less remunerative than placing stories in such high-paying venues as *Cosmopolitan* and the *Post*. It was only when television replaced the family weeklies as prime entertainment that he had to make novels, essays, lectures, and book reviews his primary source of income, and until 1969, these earnings were no better than any of Vonnegut's humdrum middle class characters could expect. When *Slaughterhouse-Five* became a bestseller, however, all this earlier work was available for reprinting, allowing Vonnegut's new publisher (Seymour Lawrence, who had an independent line with Dell Publishing) to mine this valuable resource and further extend this long-overlooked new writer's fame.

It is in his novels that Vonnegut makes his mark as a radical restylist of both culture and language. *Player Piano* (1952) rewrites General Electric's view of the future in pessimistic yet hilarious terms, in which a revolution against technology takes a similar form to that of the ill-fated Ghost Dance movement among Plains Indians at the nineteenth century's end (one of the author's interests as an anthropology scholar). *The Sirens of Titan* (1959) is a satire of space opera, its genius coming from the narrative's use of perspective—for example, the greatest monuments of human endeavor, such as the Great Wall of China and the Palace of the League of Nations, are shown to be nothing more than banal messages to a flying saucer pilot stranded on a moon of Saturn, whiling away the time as his own extraterrestrial culture works its determinations on earthy events. *Mother Night* (1961) inverts the form of a spy-thriller to indict all nations for their cruel manipulations of individual integrity, while *Cat's Cradle* (1963) forecasts the world's end not as a bang but as a grimly humorous practical joke played upon those who would be creators. *With God Bless You, Mr. Rosewater* (1965) Vonnegut projects his bleakest view of life, centered as the novel is on money and how even the most philanthropical attempts to do good with it do great harm.

By 1965, Kurt Vonnegut was out of money, and to replace his lost short story income and supplement his meager earnings from novels, he began writing feature journalism in earnest (collected in 1974 as *Wampeter* and *Foma & Granfalloons*) and speaking at university literature festivals, climaxing with a two-year appointment as a fiction instructor at the University of Iowa. Here, in the company of the famous Writers Workshop, he felt free to experiment, the result being (in an age renowned for its cultural experimentation) his first bestseller, *Slaughterhouse-Five*. Ostensibly the story of Billy Pilgrim, an American P.O.W. (Prisoner of War) survivor of the Dresden firebombing, the novel in fact fragments six decades of experience so that past, present, and future can appear all at once. Using the fictive excuse of ''time travel'' as practiced by the same outer space aliens who played havoc with human events in *The Sirens of Titan*, Vonnegut in fact recasts perception in multidimensional forms, his narrative skipping in various directions so that no consecutive accrual of information can build—instead, the reader's comprehension is held in suspension until the very end, when the totality of understanding coincides with the reality of this actual author finishing his book at a recognizable point in time (the day in June, 1968 when news of Robert Kennedy's death is broadcast to the world). *Slaughterhouse-Five* is thus less about the Dresden firebombing than it is a replication of the author's struggle to write about this unspeakable event and the reader's attempt to comprehend it.

The 1970s and 1980s saw Vonnegut persevere as a now famous author. His novels become less metaphorical and more given to direct spokesmanship, with protagonists more likely to be leaders than followers. *Breakfast of Champions* (1973) grants fame to a similarly unknown writer, Kilgore Trout, with the result that the mind of a reader (Dwayne Hoover) is undone. *Slapstick* (1976) envisions a new American society developed by a United States president who replaces government machinery with the structure of extended families. *Jailbird* (1979) tests economic idealism of the 1930s in the harsher climate of post-Watergate America, while *Deadeye Dick* (1982) reexamines the consequences of a lost childhood and the deterioration of the arts into aestheticism. Critics at the time noted an apparent decline in his work, attributable to the author's change in circumstance: whereas he had for the first two decades of his career written in welcome obscurity, his sudden fame as a spokesperson for countercultural notions of the late 1960s proved vexing, especially as Vonnegut himself felt that his beliefs were firmly rooted in American egalitarianism preceding the 1960s by several generations. *Galápagos* (1985) reverses the self-conscious trend by using the author's understanding of both biology and anthropology to propose an interesting reverse evolution of human intelligence into less threatening forms. *Bluebeard* (1997) and *Hocus Pocus* (1990) confirm this readjustment by celebrating protagonists like the abstract expressionist Rabo Karabekian and the Vietnam veteran instructor Gene Hartke who articulate America's artistic and socioeconomic heritage from a position of quiet anonymity.

That Kurt Vonnegut remains a great innovator in both subject matter and style is evident from his later, better developed essay collections, *Palm Sunday* (1981) and *Fates Worse Than Death* (1991), and his most radically inventive work so far, *Timequake* (1997), which salvages parts of an unsuccessful fictive work and combines them with discursive commentary to become a compellingly effective autobiography of a novel. His model in both novel writing and spokesmanship remains Mark Twain, whose vernacular style remains Vonnegut's own test of authenticity. As he says in *Palm Sunday*, ''I myself find that I trust my own writing most, and others seem to trust it most, too, when I sound like a person from Indianapolis, which is what I am.''

—Jerome Klinkowitz

FURTHER READING:

Allen, William Rodney. *Understanding Kurt Vonnegut.* Columbia, University of South Carolina Press, 1991.

Ambrose, Stephen E. *Citizen Soldiers.* New York, Simon and Schuster, 1997.

Broer, Lawrence R. *Sanity Plea: Schizophrenia in the Novels of Kurt Vonnegut.* Tuscaloosa, University of Alabama Press, 1994.

Klinkowitz, Jerome. *Vonnegut in Fact: The Public Spokesmanship of Personal Fiction.* Columbia, University of South Carolina Press, 1998.

Merrill, Robert, editor. *Critical Essays on Kurt Vonnegut.* Boston, G. K. Hall, 1990.

Mustazza, Leonard. *Forever Pursuing Genesis: The Myth of Eden in the Works of Kurt Vonnegut.* Lewisburg, Pennsylvania, Bucknell University Press, 1990.

Yarmolinsky, Jane Vonnegut. *Angels without Wings.* Boston, Houghton Mifflin, 1987.

W

Wagner, Honus (1874-1955)

In 1936, Honus Wagner, ''The Flying Dutchman,'' became one of the first five players to be inducted into the Baseball Hall of Fame. When the Pittsburgh Pirates' shortstop retired in 1917, he had accumulated more stolen bases, total bases, RBIs, hits, and runs than any player to that point. He also hit over .300 for seventeen consecutive seasons, while winning the National League batting title eight times. In 1910, Wagner, a nonsmoker, asked for his American Tobacco Company baseball card to be recalled because he objected to being associated with tobacco promotion; the recalled card sold for $451,000 during a 1991 auction. He died in Carnegie, Pennsylvania, at the age of 81.

—Nathan R. Meyer

FURTHER READING:

Hageman, William. *Honus: The Life and Times of a Baseball Hero.* Champaign, IL, Sagamore Publishers, 1996.

Hittner, Arthur D. *Honus Wagner: The Life of Baseball's ''Flying Dutchman.''* Jefferson, North Carolina, McFarland, 1996.

Wagon Train

One of television's most illustrious westerns, *Wagon Train* wedded the cowboy genre to the anthology show format. Premiering in 1957, when the western first conquered prime time, *Wagon Train* told a different story each week about travelers making the long journey from St. Joseph, Missouri, to California during the post-Civil War era. Such guest stars as Ernest Borgnine and Shelley Winters interacted with series regulars: the wagonmaster (first played by Ward Bond, then after his death, by John McIntire); the frontier scout (first Robert Horton, then Scott Miller and Robert Fuller); and the lead wagon driver (Frank McGrath). Inspired by John Ford's *The Wagonmaster,* the hour-long series (expanded to 90 minutes during the 1963-64 season) was shot on location in the San Fernando Valley and produced by MCA, giving the episodes a cinematic sheen. For three years *Wagon Train* placed a close second to *Bonanza* before becoming the most popular series in the nation during the 1961-62 season. The show left the air in 1965 after 284 episodes.

—Ron Simon

FURTHER READING:

Cawelti, John. *The Six-Gun Mystique.* Bowling Green, Ohio, Popular Press, 1984.

MacDonald, J. Fred. *Who Shot the Sheriff? The Rise and Fall of the Television Western.* New York, Praeger, 1967.

West, Richard. *Television Westerns: Major and Minor Series, 1946-1978.* Jefferson, North Carolina, McFarland, 1994.

Waits, Tom (1949—)

The music and lyrics of Tom Waits evinced nostalgic pathos for the archetypal neighborhood barfly at a time when much of America was listening to soft rock or gearing up for punk. Like a time-warped beatnik, Waits debuted in 1973 with *Closing Time* and followed with several acoustic jazz/folk albums throughout the 1970s. His gravelly, bygone, bittersweet voice became one of the most distinctive in popular music. Later Waits revved up his stage persona and electrified his music for a semiautobiographical stage cabaret, album, and feature-length video, *Big Time* (1988). Tom Waits is also a regular contributor to film soundtracks and has appeared in movies as well, typically playing a gruff, gin-soaked palooka as in *The Outsiders* (1983), *Down by Law* (1986), *Ironweed* (1987), and *Short Cuts* (1992).

—Tony Brewer

FURTHER READING:

Humphries, Patrick. *Small Change: A Life of Tom Waits.* New York, St. Martin's Press, 1990.

Walker, Aaron ''T-Bone'' (1910-1975)

Jazz and blues streams have flowed side by side with occasional cross currents in the evolution of black music. The musical crosscurrents of Aaron ''T-Bone'' Walker bridge these two streams; he was equally

Honus Wagner

T-Bone Walker

at home in both jazz and blues. He performed with jazz musicians such as Johnny Hodges, Lester Young, Dizzy Gillespie, and Count Basie, among others. Walker and Charlie Christian, in their teens, both contemporaneously developed the guitar in blues and jazz, respectively. Walker linked the older rural country blues—à la Blind Lemon Jefferson—and the so-called city classic blues singers such as Ida Cox and Bessie Smith of the 1920s, to the jazz-influenced urban blues of the 1940s; he also linked the older rural folk blues to the virtuoso blues. Walker has no antecedent or successor in blues—he was the father of electric blues and one of the first to record electric blues and to further define, refine, and provide the musical language employed by successive guitarists. His showmanship—playing the guitar behind his back or performing a sideway split while never missing a beat or note—influenced Elvis Presley's act. Walker clearly influenced scores of musicians such as Chuck Berry, Freddie & Albert King, Mike Bloomfield, and Johnny Winter. "In a very real sense the modern blues is largely his creation . . . among blues artists he is nonpareil: no one has contributed as much, as long, or as variously to the blues as he has," noted the late Pete Welding in a Blue Note reissue of his work.

Aaron Thibeaux Walker (T-Bone is a probable mispronunciation of Thibeaux) was born on May 10, 1910 in rural Linden, Texas, but his mother moved to Dallas in 1912. His musical apprenticeship was varied and provided rich opportunities that prepared him for his role as showman and consummate artist. Walker was a self-taught singer, songwriter, banjoist, guitarist, pianist, and dancer. His mother, Movelia, was a musician, and her place served as a hangout for itinerant musicians. Her second husband, Marco Washington, was a multi-instrumentalist who led a string band and provided young Walker the opportunity to lead the band in street parades while dancing and collecting tips. At the age of eight, Walker escorted the legendary Blind Lemon Jefferson around the streets of Dallas, and at the age of 14, he performed in Dr. Breeding's Big B Medicine show. He returned home only to leave again with city blues singer Ida Cox. While in school, Walker played banjo with the school's 16-piece band. In 1929, he won first prize in a talent show which provided the opportunity to travel for a week with Cab Calloway's band. But it was during his engagement with Count Bulaski's white band that Walker fortuitously met Chuck Richardson, a music teacher who tutored Walker and Charlie Christian. Walker began earnestly honing his guitar techniques, and at times, also jammed with Christian. Unfortunately, he could not escape the pitfalls of "street life" during his musical apprenticeship and began gambling and drinking; he would later become a womanizer. In his teens, he contracted stomach ulcers, which continually plagued him throughout his career.

Walker first recorded for Columbia Records in 1929 as Oak Cliff T-Bone. The two sides were entitled "Witchita Falls" and "Trinity River Blues." By 1934, Walker had met and married Vida Lee; they were together until his death. Walker and Vida Lee moved to Los Angeles, where Walker played several clubs as a singer, guitarist, dancer, and emcee. His enormous popularity quickly secured him a firm place in the Hollywood club scene. When he complained to the management that his black audience could not come to see him, the management integrated the club. His big break came with Les Hite's Band, with whom he recorded "T-Bone Blues" in 1939-1940 and appeared on both East and West coasts. Ironically, Walker was not playing guitar on this recording but only sang. From 1945 to 1960, he recorded for a number of labels and became one of the principal architects of the California Blues. Some of his songs that have become classics of the blues repertoire are "Call it Stormy Monday," "T-Bone Shuffle," "Bobby Sox Blues," "Long Skirt Baby Blues," and "Mean Old World."

Walker was a musician's musician; his musicality was impeccable. His phrasing, balance, melodic inventions, and improvisations carried the blues to a higher aesthetic level than had been attained before. He serenaded mostly women with his songs of unrequited love, and the lyrics often gave a clue to the paradox of his own existence, as evidenced in "Mean Old World": "I drink to keep from worrying and Mama I smile to keep from crying / That's to keep the public from knowing just what I have on my mind."

Because Walker's recordings were made prior to the coming of rock 'n' roll, he missed out on the blues revival that Joe Turner and other blues artists enjoyed. His records never crossed over into the popular market, and his audience was primarily African American. While the Allman Brothers recording of his song "Call It Stormy Monday" sold millions, his version was allowed to go out of print. From the mid-1950s to the early 1970s, the balance of his career was played out in small West Coast clubs as one-nighters. Although he did tour Europe in the 1960s and was a sensation in Paris, there were few opportunities to record. Walker suffered a stroke in 1974, and on March 16, 1975, he died. More than 1,000 mourners came out to grieve the loss of this great musician.

—Willie Collins

FURTHER READING:

Dance, Helen Oakley, and Stanley. *Stormy Monday: The T-Bone Walker Story.* Baton Rouge, Louisiana State University Press, 1987.

Walker, Aida Overton (1880-1914)

Aida Overton Walker dazzled early-twentieth-century theater audiences with her original dance routines, her enchanting singing voice, and her penchant for elegant costumes. One of the premiere African American women artists of the turn of the century, she popularized the cakewalk and introduced it to English society. In addition to her attractive stage persona and highly acclaimed performances, she won the hearts of black entertainers for numerous benefit performances near the end of her tragically short career and for her cultivation of younger women performers. She was, in the words of the *New York Age*'s Lester Walton, the exponent of "clean, refined artistic entertainment."

Born in 1880 in Richmond, Virginia, Aida Overton grew up in New York City, where her family moved when she was young and where she gained an education and considerable musical training. At the tender age of fifteen, she joined John Isham's Octoroons, one of the most influential black touring groups of the 1890s, and the following year she became a member of the Black Patti Troubadours. Although the show consisted of dozens of performers, Overton emerged as one of the most promising soubrettes of her day. In 1898, she joined the company of the famous comedy team Bert Williams and George Walker, and appeared in all of their shows—*The Policy Players* (1899), *The Sons of Ham* (1900), *In Dahomey* (1902), *Abyssinia* (1905), and *Bandanna Land* (1907). Within about a year of their meeting, George Walker and Overton married and before long became one of the most admired and elegant African American couples on stage.

While George Walker supplied most of the ideas for the musical comedies and Bert Williams enjoyed fame as the "funniest man in America," Aida quickly became an indispensable member of the Williams and Walker Company. In *The Sons of Ham,* for example, her rendition of *Hannah from Savannah* won praise for combining superb vocal control with acting skill that together presented a positive, strong image of black womanhood. Indeed, onstage Aida refused to comply with the plantation image of black women as plump mammies, happy to serve; like her husband, she viewed the representation of refined African American types on the stage as important political work. A talented dancer, Aida improvised original routines that her husband eagerly introduced in the shows; when *In Dahomey* was moved to England, Aida proved to be one of the strongest attractions. Society women invited her to their homes for private lessons in the exotic cakewalk that the Walkers had included in the show. After two seasons in England, the company returned to the United States in 1904, and it was Aida who was featured in a *New York Herald* interview about their tour. At times Walker asked his wife to interpret dances made famous by other performers—one example being the "Salome" dance that took Broadway by storm in the early 1900s— which she did with uneven success.

After a decade of nearly continuous success with the Williams and Walker Company, Aida's career took an unexpected turn when her husband collapsed on tour with *Bandanna Land.* Initially Walker

returned to his boyhood home of Lawrence, Kansas, where his mother took care of him. In his absence, Aida took over many of his songs and dances to keep the company together. In early 1909, however, *Bandanna Land* was forced to close, and Aida temporarily retired from stage work to care for her husband, now clearly seriously ill. No doubt recognizing that he likely would not recover and that she alone could support the family, she returned to the stage in Bob Cole and J. Rosamond Johnson's *Red Moon* in autumn 1909, and she joined the Smart Set Company in 1910. Aida also began touring the vaudeville circuit as a solo act. Less than two weeks after Walker's death in January 1911, Aida signed a two-year contract to appear as a co-star with S. H. Dudley in another all-black traveling show.

Although still a relatively young woman in the early 1910s, Aida began to develop medical problems that limited her capacity for constant touring and stage performance. As early as 1908, she had begun organizing benefits to aid such institutions as the Industrial Home for Colored Working Girls, and after her contract with S. H. Dudley expired, she devoted more of her energy to such projects, which allowed her to remain in New York. She also took an interest in developing the talents of younger women in the profession, hoping to pass along her vision of black performance as refined and elegant. She produced shows for two such female groups in 1913 and 1914—the Porto Rico Girls and the Happy Girls. She encouraged them to work up original dance numbers and insisted that they don stylish costumes on stage.

When Aida Overton Walker died suddenly of kidney failure on October 11, 1914, the African American entertainment community in New York went into deep mourning. The *New York Age* featured a lengthy obituary on its front page, and hundreds of shocked entertainers descended on her residence to confirm a story they hoped was untrue. Walker left behind a legacy of polished performance and model professionalism. Her demand for respect and her generosity made her a beloved figure in African American theater circles.

—Susan Curtis

FURTHER READING:

"Aida Overton Walker Is Dead." *New York Age.* October 15, 1914, 1.

Riis, Thomas L. *Just before Jazz: Black Musical Theater in New York, 1890-1915.* Washington, D.C., Smithsonian Institution Press, 1989.

Walker, Alice (1944—)

Alice Walker won the Pulitzer Prize and the American Book Award for her 1982 novel *The Color Purple.* By that time she was already a well-established and published writer, but it was the Pulitzer that catapulted her into international recognition. Her books have since been translated into more than two dozen languages, and it was Steven Spielberg's 1985 film adaptation of the novel that brought her to the widespread attention of mainstream audiences. Both the book and the film were controversial, and Walker's fame was accompanied by severe criticism. In *The Same River Twice: Honoring the Difficult* (1996), a book containing essays, journal entries, letters, and her original, never-used screenplay for the film, Walker addresses the criticism that the film was not true to her book: "Though *The Color*

Purple is not what many wished, it is more than many hoped, or had seen on a movie screen before.'' She acknowledges that most hurtful were the accusations that she hated black men and had portrayed them in stereotypical and demeaning ways. Although Walker openly advocates black sisterhood, she also openly and adamantly advocates the spiritual survival of all black people, men and women. It is this preoccupation, to use her own term, that properly describes her life and her life's work of writing and activism.

Writing became important to Walker at an early age as a survival mechanism. Born Alice Malsenior Walker on February 9, 1944, in Eatonton, Georgia, she was the eighth child of Willie Lee and Minnie Lou Grant, southern sharecroppers. Walker has described the houses in which her family lived while she was growing up as ''shabby'' and ''crowded,'' and she therefore spent a great deal of time out of doors; her writing is partly rooted in her need for space. When she was just eight years old, one of her brothers accidentally shot her in the eye with a BB gun, which blinded her in that eye and left her physically and emotionally scarred. She writes poignantly in ''Beauty: When the Other Dancer Is the Self,'' of how years later, her young daughter Rebecca helped her to see herself as ''beautiful, whole and free.'' She also describes how fear of losing sight in the other eye enabled her to imagine life with all its injustices and all its beauty. As she put it, she ''dashed about the world madly . . . storing up images against the fading light.''

The dual themes of beauty and injustice permeate Walker's work and can explain the interrelationship of her writing and activism, as well as her popularity. Although critics have focused on the homosexuality and violence in *The Color Purple,* Walker juxtaposes images of rape, incest, and other examples of physical and emotional abuse with love, loyalty, pleasurable and empowering sex, parental joy, and the communal bonding of men and women. It was the characters' stories of joy and sorrow, rather than the negative depictions of black men, that helped keep *The Color Purple* on the *New York Times* Bestseller List for over a year. Similarly, in *Possessing the Secret of Joy,* another of her bestselling novels, Walker attacks the practice of female genital mutilation as she simultaneously depicts the beauty of love and sex between the young African woman Tashi and her American husband, Adam, who both appeared in *The Color Purple.*

Although it largely explores the oppressions and triumphs of black women, her collection of essays *In Search of Our Mothers' Gardens* (1983) holds interest for anyone who, like Walker, thinks black women are ''fascinating creatures.'' Both black and white women have praised its significant contribution to their own feminist enterprises. With these essays, Walker articulates the silences of generations of women whose stories were told through their everyday work such as quilting, gardening, and cooking. At the outset, she defines the term ''womanish'' and suggests that it may be useful in helping black women talk about their feminism in culturally specific ways. Still, throughout the various essays she provides a space for white feminists to discover the commonalities of women's oppression by emphasizing her belief that we are all part of one larger life story. Her 1976 novel *Meridian* is another example of her determination to revise the zero image of black women. In it she explores the important roles they played in the civil-rights movement of the 1960s, the success of which has historically been attributed to men. It is also partly because of Walker's dedication to the spiritual survival of her people generally and black women specifically that the life and work of Zora Neale Hurston have been recovered. Hurston was a black woman writer and anthropologist who participated significantly in the Harlem Renaissance. In making a personal sojourn to Florida to find

and mark Hurston's grave site, Walker has also helped restore dignity to a woman whose contributions to African American literature and culture are manifold but who died in poverty and obscurity.

Walker continues to be a prolific writer. She has authored six novels, as well as numerous collections of poetry, essays, short stories, and several children's books. She also continues to write about controversial issues, regardless of criticism, and remains popular because the issues are most often those that affect everyday people—ranging from the Million Man March and O. J. Simpson to repressed female sexuality and the need for struggle. She has said that she writes about controversial issues out of love, not hate, a reflection of her belief, as she expresses it in the Preface to *The Same River Twice,* that ''Art is the mirror, perhaps the only one, in which we can see our true collective face. We must honor its sacred function. We must let art help us.''

—Jacquelyn Y. McLendon

FURTHER READING:

Gates, Henry Louis, Jr., and K. A. Appiah, editors. *Alice Walker: Critical Perspectives Past and Present.* New York, Amistad, 1993.

Walker, Alice. *In Search of Our Mothers' Gardens: Womanist Prose.* New York, Harcourt Brace, 1983.

———. *The Same River Twice: Honoring the Difficult.* New York, Scribner, 1996.

Walker, George (1873-1911)

George Walker won fame at the turn of the twentieth century as the comedy half of the African American team of Williams and Walker. Up-to-date costuming, quick urban wit, and the character of the strutting dandy became the trademarks of his onstage persona. Walker's collaboration with Bert Williams resulted in one of the most popular black comedy teams to appear in successful musical comedy productions in the early 1900s. Beyond his personal fame, Walker also devoted great energy to the professionalization of black theater and performance. He served as a model to younger performers, and his efforts to form black professional organizations helped establish and maintain artistic and ethical standards for those working on the stage. Moreover, Walker's ambitious productions demanded scores of singers and dancers who gained employment and valuable stage experience.

Walker's humble beginnings did not predict the central role he would play in the black acting fraternity of the early twentieth century. Born in Lawrence, Kansas, in 1873, Walker began his career as part of a medicine show using the moniker ''Nash'' Walker. The show made its way westward to San Francisco, where in 1893, Walker met and teamed up with Bert Williams. The two formed a vaudeville act, toured with a succession of minstrel troupes, medicine shows, and traveling vaudeville shows, and found themselves stranded and unemployed in Chicago in the mid-1890s.

By this time, the pair had polished an act in which Williams played the straight man and Walker supplied the comic punch lines, so they continued from Chicago on to New York. There they made a splash in a bit sketch in Victor Herbert's otherwise unsuccessful *Gold Bug* (1896) and attracted the attention of producers of other comedy revues. They joined prominent white acts like McIntyre & Heath and Helena Mora in the Hyde Show, but left it in 1897 to join an all-black company in Will Marion Cook's *Clorindy*. Although the show did not succeed, their experience convinced them to seek the services of a professional management team. After reaching an agreement with Hurtig & Seamon, Williams and Walker starred in a string of musical comedies that put them at the center of the New York entertainment scene.

Under Hurtig & Seamon's management, Walker and Williams appeared in a variety show, *A Lucky Coon,* and three musical comedies that featured fuller plots, opportunities to act as well as sing and dance, and double-edged comedy that appealed to black and white audiences alike. In 1899, Walker married a talented singer and dancer, Aida Overton, who had joined the company a year earlier. His wife became a featured player in all the subsequent Williams and Walker musical comedies. While *The Policy Players* (1899) and *The Sons of Ham* (1900) enjoyed considerable success, it was Williams and Walker's *In Dahomey* (1902) that brought them national and international fame. The opening of this show on February 18, 1903 marked the first time a full-length African American musical comedy in three acts appeared on a Broadway stage. Following a run of 53 performances, the show traveled to England, where it remained for two seasons. A successful command performance at Buckingham Palace assured the show's success in London. Upon returning to the United States, the Williams and Walker company took *In Dahomey* on tour in this country for the 1904-1905 season.

Disagreements with their managers led to a break, and the two comedians signed with Melville B. Raymond and organized the extravagant production, *Abyssinia,* in 1905. Although Bert Williams was a more popular and perhaps more talented performer, George Walker supplied the main ideas for this production, which featured avant garde lighting effects, elaborate props, and elegant costumes for the entire cast. In their final show, *Bandanna Land* (1907), George Walker fell ill and was forced to retire from show business in the middle of the 1908-1909 season. He died in 1911.

Shortly before his retirement, Walker helped found an organization for African American professional entertainers. Like the more famous white actor's social club, the Lambs, the Frogs intended to promote ''social intercourse between the representative members of the Negro theatrical profession.'' Under Walker's leadership, the Frogs maintained club rooms in Harlem, organized occasional events like the ''Frolic of the Frogs'' that featured prominent black acts, dining, and dancing, and represented a standard of excellence in stage work to which younger entertainers were encouraged to aspire. Having devoted the last years of his career to this organization, Walker was remembered at his death as a ''dominating force in the theatrical world more because of the service he rendered the colored members of the profession because of the opportunities he created than for the types he has originated.'' Although adored for his famous stage smile, his insistence on fashionable costuming, and his practiced—and oft-imitated—dandy strutting on stage, George Walker set his sights higher than personal fame in Jim Crow America of the early 1900s. His chief aim, according to his friend Lester Walton, was ''to elevate the colored theatrical profession, and the race as well . . .

to give as elaborate productions as the white shows and play in the best theatres.'' To an extent, he realized this dream, but his death also marked the beginning of the rapid decline of black musical comedy in pre-World War I America.

—Susan Curtis

FURTHER READING:

Curtis, Susan. *The First Black Actors on the Great White Way.* Columbia, University of Missouri Press, 1998.

Riis, Thomas L. *Just Before Jazz: Black Musical Theater in New York, 1890-1915.* Washington, D.C., Smithsonian Institution Press, 1989.

Walton, Lester A. ''Death of George W. Walker.'' *New York Age.* January 12, 1911, 6.

Junior Walker and the All-Stars

Junior Walker and the All-Stars were a rhythm-and-blues band that produced several smash hits for the Motown label in the 1960s with an untutored, earthy sound that went against type for Motown, but that provided the first of a new kind of hit for the recording industry giant.

The group's leader, Junior Walker, whose real name was Autry DeWalt II (1931-1995), was born in Blythesville, Arkansas. As a young man he lived around South Bend, Indiana, where he met guitarist Willie Woods. During the early 1950s the two performed in a group called the Jumping Jacks. Walker, only a fair singer, was soon regarded as one of the best saxophonists of his generation.

By the mid-1950s, Walker and Woods had moved to Battle Creek, Michigan, and linked up with organist Vic Thomas and drummer James Graves. Those four called themselves the All-Stars, supposedly after a fan yelled out that every player was a star in this band. There was considerable truth in that statement, both because all four men were consummate R&B musicians, and because their relaxed, jam-session approach gave each player a chance to show his stuff. Years later, Grateful Dead guitarist Jerry Garcia would specifically cite ''Cleo's Mood,'' the 1966 instrumental tune penned by Willie Woods, as an inspiration for the Dead's give-and-take jams.

The All-Stars became very popular in Michigan clubs around 1960. In 1962, while they were performing at El Grotto, they were discovered by Johnny Bristol, at that time a recording artist for Tri-Phi Records in Detroit. Bristol strongly suggested that the group meet Tri-Phi president Harvey Fuqua. Fuqua himself was a former R&B performer; as one of the Moonglows, he had released a number of hits during the 1950s for Chicago's Chess Records. By 1962 he was president of both the Tri-Phi and the Harvey labels in Detroit; his wife owned Anna Records, and his brother-in-law, Berry Gordy, was the head of Motown, among the very few black-owned record labels of any size in the country. Fuqua quickly signed Junior Walker and the All-Stars to his Harvey label. Over the next year the band released three singles (but no hits), including ''Twistlackawanna'' and ''Good

Junior Walker and the All-Stars

Rockin' Tonight,'' the latter a cover of Elvis Presley's 1954 Sun label single (itself a cover of the Wynonie Harris version from 1948).

Harvey Fuqua's money troubles led him to fold his two companies and become a producer and talent scout for Berry Gordy. Although Junior Walker and the All-Stars did not automatically receive a contract with Motown, they did soon afterwards thanks to Fuqua's recommendation. Gordy used the All-Stars to launch his new, more R&B-oriented label, Soul.

In 1964 the band released "Monkey Jim," a song that sank without a trace, but its March 1965 single, "Shotgun," exceeded everyone's expectations. "Shotgun" started off literally with a bang: a gunshot that got its listeners' full attention right away. The song was a classic R&B tune that quickly went to #1 on the R&B charts; more surprisingly, it also spent several weeks in the pop Top Ten, peaking at #4. This performance was never surpassed by later All-Star releases. Most of their fifteen hit records would do significantly better on the R&B charts, because that is what they were. Two of these fifteen hits went to #1, and nine more singles reached the Top Ten. Junior Walker and the All-Stars had a dozen hits on the *Billboard* pop

charts though only two ever made it to the Top Ten. Unlike the typical middle of the road Motown product, Junior Walker's singles were unabashedly rough and tough.

The All-Stars' strongest pop singles, after "Shotgun," were "(I'm a) Road-Runner," written and produced by Holland, Dozier, and Holland, the trio most responsible for the Supremes' hits; "How Sweet It Is (To Be Loved By You)," from the same team; and "What Does It Take (To Win Your Love)," a ballad produced and co-written by the band's old associates Johnny Bristol and Harvey Fuqua, by that time colleagues in Motown's production department. "What Does It Take" was a different sort of song for the All-Stars, slow and dreamy by comparison with their usual output, but it was their only record to equal "Shotgun" on the charts. "Shotgun" itself was written by Autry DeWalt II; when the All-Stars performed, he was Junior Walker, but when he copyrighted his creations, he kept his original DeWalt name.

The All-Stars had a reasonably successful career by Motown standards, releasing fifteen charted singles (and several albums) over a seven-year period but, also typically, not making much money for that label. The band had no further charted singles after 1971, but continued to tour on Motown-sponsored revues. Junior Walker moved to southern California about the time Motown relocated there in the 1970s, but moved back to the Battle Creek area after a few years. He remained active as a performer, playing with a variety of sidemen; in 1988 Walker appeared in the comedy film, *Tape Heads.* In the 1990s, his son Autry DeWalt III was a frequent drummer with the band.

Much of the All-Stars' music was underappreciated by the audiences of their day, and some of it was not heard at all. Among professional musicians, though, the band is held in higher esteem than many with greater popular reputations. Junior Walker died of cancer in Battle Creek on November 23, 1995, one of the great musicians of his generation.

—David Lonergan

FURTHER READING:

George, Nelson. *Where Did Our Love Go? The Rise and Fall of the Motown Sound.* New York, St. Martin's Press, 1985.

Nite, Norm N. *Rock On Almanac.* 2nd Ed. New York, Harper Collins, 1992.

Whitburn, Joel. *The Billboard Book of Top 40 Hits.* 6th Ed. New York, Billboard Books, 1996.

Walker, Madame C. J. (1867-1919)

In the field of black hair care, Madame C. J. Walker employed groundbreaking entrepreneurial, organizational, and marketing strategies to revolutionize the industry. At her death in 1919 Walker had amassed a fortune, making her the first African-American female millionaire.

Born Sarah Breedlove in 1867 in Delta, Louisiana, Walker moved to St. Louis twenty years later in search of better social and economic opportunities. Widowed, with a two-year-old daughter, she struggled financially but was determined not to spend her entire life as a domestic. After moving to Denver in 1905 Walker's hair began to fall out and she experimented with several formulas until she stopped her hair loss. This encouraged her to develop and market her own product, the "Walker hair-grower," to black women throughout the Denver area. "My hair was coming in faster that it had ever fallen out. I tried it on my friends; it helped them. I made up my mind that I would begin to sell it." After much success with the product in Denver, Walker and her new husband, Charles Joseph Walker, began to market the product throughout the United States, South America, and the Caribbean. She soon developed an entire array of black hair care products that became simply known as the "Walker System," which included a shampoo, the "hair-grower," and a hot iron. Her method turned coarse hair into a straight and silky European-like hair.

To sell her products Walker hired black women (known as "Walker agents,") who went door-to-door dressed in white blouses and black skirts. This canvassing was supplemented by an intense advertising campaign in black newspapers and magazines across the

Madame C. J. Walker

country. Readers could hardly miss her ads which, like her products, carried her portrait. Later she established beauty parlors and beauty schools to acquaint people with her products and she also built factories and laboratories that manufactured her goods. This business approach enabled her to become the first black female millionaire.

In spite of her superb business acumen Walker was often criticized in the black community for trying to make black women look like white females. But she insisted that her products were not "straighteners," but rather a formula for a healthy scalp and manageable hair. After opening a second headquarters in Pittsburgh, Walker moved her company to Indianapolis in 1910, and then to New York City four years later as her gross revenues began to exceed $1 million annually. With her fortune Walker lived extravagantly, with massive real-estate investments in and around New York City. In spite of this extravagance, Walker was consistent in supporting a large number of black philanthropic endeavors, including the NAACP.

Walker's significance lies in the fact that she revolutionized and pioneered the black hair care industry which would eventually become a multi-billion dollar business. Hair care companies that had ignored the African-American consumer now began to develop and market products akin to Walker's. Walker died at the age of 51 after a brief illness.

—Leonard N. Moore

FURTHER READING:

Bundles, A'Lelia Perry. *Madame C.J. Walker.* New York, Chelsea House, 1991.

Elliott, Joan Curl. "Madame C. J. Walker." In *Epic Lives: One Hundred Black Women Who Made a Difference.* New York, Visible Ink Press, 1993.

Walkman

The Walkman became one of the most successful audio products of the postwar period, and like the Victrola before it, any personal portable cassette player was called a "walkman," regardless of manufacturer. The portable personal stereo was the most important electronics product of the 1980s. Bought by millions of people worldwide, it dramatically changed the way people listened to music. Its convenience and small size dictated the shape and function of the next generation of digital technology. Manufacturer Sony's hunch was right: Americans did buy them in the millions, and the walkman became one of those products that everybody owned, like a television, radio, or VCR.

The introduction of the Phillips compact tape cassette in 1963 was an important technological step in the reduction of size of talking machines. The machines that played them used transistorized, solid-state amplifiers that took up far less room than vacuum tubes. The size of the cassette tape recorder was continually reduced in the 1960s to about the size of a paperback book. This was considered small enough for a portable unit.

Masuru Ibuka of Sony wanted an even smaller stereo unit for his personal use, one that he could put in his coat pocket. The company he cofounded had made a profitable practice of reducing the size of electronic consumer goods; starting with reel-to-reel tape recorders, radios, and then televisions, Sony had managed to find an unexpectedly large market for scaled down versions of appliances that most families already owned. Sony's engineers took the path of a battery-operated cassette player that used highly efficient earphones instead of a loudspeaker. All the parts of the player were improved and reduced in size. Ibuka and his partner Akio Morita were the leading proponents of the miniature tape player within Sony, where there was considerable resistance to the idea. Why would anyone want to own a tape player that was just slightly larger than the cassette tape it played? Ignoring the advice of their marketing department, the leaders of Sony took a chance with a product that the experts expected would never sell.

In 1979 Sony introduced its Soundabout cassette player, which was later called the Walkman. Although the innovative elements of the Soundabout system were praised, it was initially treated as something of a novelty in the audio industry. Priced at $200, it could not realistically be considered as a product for the mass market. Although it sold very well in Japan, where people were used to listening to music on headphones, sales in the United States were not encouraging. Sony's engineers reduced the size and cost of the machine and introduced the Walkman II in 1981. It was 25 percent smaller than the original version and had 50 percent fewer moving parts. Even more enticing to consumers was that its price dropped considerably. The Walkman opened up a huge market for tape players that nobody knew existed. Americans were enjoying a more active lifestyle and embraced the concept of portable music, even if they had to sacrifice sound quality for portability. But as Sony developed the product, especially the earphone speakers, its fidelity and stereo reproduction improved drastically. It took about two years for Sony's Japanese competitors, including Matsushita, Toshiba, and Aiwa, to bring out portable personal stereos. Sony remained ahead of the competition by constant innovation: Dolby noise reduction circuits were added in 1982, and a rechargeable battery feature was introduced in 1985. The machine grew smaller and smaller until it was hardly larger than the audio cassette it played.

In the ten years following the introduction of the Walkman, Sony sold 50 million units, including 25 million in the United States. Its competitors sold millions more. They were manufactured all over the Far East and came in a broad range of sizes and prices, with the cheapest model selling for around $20. By the 1990s the market for personal stereos in the United States was around 20 to 30 million units a year. Those who doubted the appeal of a personal tape recorder were silenced by the variety of uses that only a walkman could provide. Waterproofed walkmen were marketed to those who enjoyed watersports, and there were special durable models for tennis players and runners. While sitting in a crowded subway car or jogging through a park one could enjoy high fidelity recorded sound.

Although a tribute to the semiconductor and the ingenuity of Japanese engineering, the walkman is not purely significant in the way it works but also in what it represents. It is an evolutionary step in a process that began about a hundred years earlier when pioneers of recorded sound began to reduce the size and cost of their machines. It is a significant product of portability resulting from the demands of an on-the-move, industrial society. It established a one-on-one relationship between people and their machines that changed the way that we hear recorded sound, having a noticeable effect on the way that people listen to music. The sound from the headphones of a portable player is intimate and immediate compared to the sound coming from the loudspeaker of a home stereo. Recording studios even began to mix the balance of their master recordings to suit the reproduction characteristics of walkman headphones.

—Andre Millard

FURTHER READING:

Gould, William. *Sony.* New York, Contemporary Press, 1997.

Millard, Andre. *America on Record: A History of Recorded Sound.* New York, Cambridge University Press, 1995.

Morita, Akio, E. Reingold, and M. Shimomura, *Made in Japan: Akio Morita and Sony.* New York, Dutton, 1980.

Wall Drug

A rest stop at Wall Drug in South Dakota is a passport to a truly egalitarian social setting. It is a place that not only relieves highway

Wall Drug, South Dakota.

tedium but enables friendly interaction with other people from all walks of life, none of which could have been foreseen in its humble origins. For summer travelers driving endless hot hours across the Great Plains, an offer of free ice water cannot possibly be ignored. This simple but effective advertising gimmick was the savior of a small shop threatened with extinction by the hard times of the Depression. It was the brainchild of Ted and Dorothy Hustead, who had owned the establishment for five years without seeing much in the way of profit. In 1936, they put up some signs along the highway, and visitors started pouring in. They were still arriving in droves by the end of the twentieth century, and the tiny drug store located off Interstate-90 in downtown Wall, South Dakota, has expanded, evolving into several blocks of representational Wild West architecture, where shaded arcades of shops share space with motel and restaurant facilities. And yes, you can still get that free ice water.

—Robert Kuhlken

FURTHER READING:

Jennings, Dana. *Free Ice Water: The Story of the Wall Drug.* Aberdeen, South Dakota, North Plains Books & Art, 1975.

"Wall Drug." http://www.walldrug.com. April 1999.

The Wall Street Journal

Someone glancing at the front page of *The Wall Street Journal* for the first time might be deceived. Unlike other newspapers, the

Journal does not have, with one exception, multiple-column headlines or any photographs. It does not look like most newspapers. One might get the impression that the *Journal* is a conservative newspaper, and on one hand, the observer would be correct. The *Journal* became the United States' first national newspaper in the twentieth century and was a leader both in innovative writing styles as well as espousing politically conservative opinions. On top of that, it had the highest circulation of any daily newspaper in the United States. Clearly, it would be wrong to pigeonhole a publication that began as a handwritten sheet of business news and a century later was a three-section highly regarded newspaper that could claim more than thirty Pulitzer Prizes.

The newspaper that a twentieth-century president (Harry Truman) referred to as "the Republican bible" was founded in 1882 by Charles H. Dow and Edward D. Jones as part of Dow Jones & Company. In fact, for at least the first fifty years of its existence, the *Journal* played second fiddle to the company's profitable business news ticker. In that first half century, it was not uncommon for *Journal* reporters to trade in stocks they also wrote about, a conflict of interest that William Henry Grimes ended when he became the managing editor in 1934. Grimes, who would win the *Journal*'s first Pulitzer Prize in 1947, established the paper as independent of its sources rather than beholden to them, which enabled it to report more freely and confidently on business news and to be more trusted by readers.

The man who ultimately shaped the modern *Wall Street Journal* was Barney "Bernard" Kilgore, who replaced Grimes in 1941. At the time, the *Journal* published two editions, the second of which was called the Pacific Coast edition. It was Kilgore's goal to make the paper national, meaning a reader in Los Angeles would get the same paper as readers in Miami, St. Paul, Houston, and New York City.

Folding the Pacific Coast edition into the regular edition was one of Kilgore's first steps in that direction. Kilgore was ahead of his time as far as technology was concerned. Although one could argue that because it was not delivered on the same day nationally, the *Journal* was not technically a national newspaper, Kilgore's vision paid off when satellites eventually made it easier for the newspaper to be distributed to regional printing plants for home delivery around the United States. The use of satellite delivery from a central location to regional plants became a model that other newspapers such as *USA Today* and *The New York Times* later followed.

Many of Kilgore's changes remain part of the newspaper. He had a great impact on the paper's writing style, for example. He told reporters to write for the readers, not for bankers. He had been a highly regarded writer, and when reporters once complained to President Franklin Roosevelt that they could not understand the federal budget, FDR replied: "Read Kilgore in *The Wall Street Journal*; he understands it." Kilgore's axiom that reporters should write for the readers, not the people being written about, became conventional wisdom throughout the newspaper industry.

Kilgore also decreed that not all stories had to be written in the inverted pyramid style, that is with the most important information at the beginning of the story and the least important at the end. Instead, he not only encouraged reporters to produce in-depth stories that did not have a peg to yesterday's news, but also broadened the topics that reporters could write about. In his mind, just about any story could fit under the rubric of business and economics. Reporters produced not only company profiles but also stories on social trends and stories that some editors would view as whimsical or off the wall. It was Kilgore who ended the use of photographs on the front page and it was Kilgore who moved the *Journal* out from under the shadow of the Dow Jones news ticker. Under his watch, the *Journal* began building circulation and making money.

In reality, *The Wall Street Journal* is more than just one newspaper. It encompasses several other business-related newspapers and magazines, both in print and on line. Among them are *The Asian Wall Street Journal, The Asian Wall Street Journal Weekly Edition, National Business Employment Weekly, The Wall Street Journal Americas, The Wall Street Journal Europe, Barron's, Dow Jones Financial Publishing,* and *SmartMoney.* One offshoot not listed is the *National Observer,* which Kilgore created in 1962 and which lasted until 1977. It was, in effect, the *Journal*'s Sunday paper or weekly magazine and it was filled with analysis and features. It was such a different paper that among its early staff writers were non-traditionalists such as Tom Wolfe, later a force in the New Journalism movement, and Hunter S. Thompson, whose first major success was *Hell's Angels,* based on an article he had written about the infamous motorcycle gang. Perhaps if Kilgore had lived longer, the *National Observer* would have succeeded. But he died within five years of its founding, after working for the *Journal* for 38 years. While the *Observer* survived for another 10 years it was without its founder's guiding hand.

As the *Journal* began its second century, it became more known for its archly conservative editorials than for its news coverage. This is somewhat surprising, since the bulk of the paper's Pulitzer Prizes have been awarded for its reporting, not its editorials, although that dichotomy reveals much about the paper. The *Journal,* of course, has always been conservative on its editorial page, but the page gained

notoriety because of the perception that its voice had changed from conservative to ideologue and had lost its independence.

Politics aside, the *Journal* ranks as a pacesetter in journalism, not just business journalism. Its large circulation and national audience speak to the wisdom of men like William Grimes and Barney Kilgore.

—R. Thomas Berner

FURTHER READING:

Dealy, Francis X. *The Power and the Money: Inside the Wall Street Journal.* Secaucus, New Jersey, Carol Publishing Company, 1993.

Rosenberg, Jerry Martin. *Inside the Wall Street Journal: The History and the Power of Dow Jones and Company and America's Most Influential Newspaper.* New York, Macmillan, 1982.

Scharff, Edward E. *Worldly Power: The Making of The Wall Street Journal.* New York, New American Library, 1986.

Wendt, Lloyd. *The Wall Street Journal: The Story of Dow Jones and the Nation's Business Newspaper.* Chicago, Rand McNally, 1982.

Wallace, Sippie (1898-1986)

Born Beulah Thomas in Texas, Sippie Wallace began her professional singing career as a teenager. After moving to Chicago in 1923 with her husband and brothers (with whom she wrote and performed), she won a recording contract with OKeh Records. Known for her risqué lyrics ("I'm a Mighty Tight Woman"), black- and woman-centered subjects ("Women, Be Wise"), and rough phrasing, Wallace recorded much of her best music for OKeh between 1923 and 1927. Her music, like much of the blues of the 1920s and 1930s, articulated the experience of being female, black, and poor, offering not only entertainment but also understanding and recognition to black listeners (though, ironically, these differences were often exploited in marketing aimed at whites). She disappeared from the blues scene for nearly 40 years, but made a comeback during the 1960s blues revival, recording several new albums between 1966 and 1986. As one of the blues most stirring voices, Wallace helped to write, sing, and shape twentieth-century American popular culture. She especially influenced singer songwriter Bonnie Raitt, who has recorded many of Wallace's songs.

—Deborah M. Mix

FURTHER READING:

Davis, Angela Y. *Blues Legacies and Black Feminism.* New York, Pantheon Books, 1998.

Harrison, Daphne Duval. *Black Pearls: Blues Queens of the 1920s.* New Brunswick, Rutgers University Press, 1988.

Sippie—Sippie Wallace, Blues Singer and Song Writer (videotape), produced by Michelle Paymar and Roberta Grossman. N.p., Rhapsody Films, 1982.

Wallace, Sippie. *Complete Recorded Works, Vol. 1 (1923-25) and Vol. 2 (1925-45)* (recording). Document, 1995.

Wal-Mart

With nearly 2,500 stores spread across the land, Wal-Mart has become an instantly recognizable and ubiquitous component of American popular culture. There are few places in this country anymore that are beyond a short drive to a Wal-Mart. With upwards of 50,000 different items on the shelves and racks of a typical store, Wal-Mart has literally changed the way Americans shop.

The phenomenal success of Wal-Mart has been the direct result of the vision and energy of its late founder, Sam Walton. His motivation and charisma alone shaped a company which helped to establish discount merchandising as the major form of retail operation in this country. His highly personal management style and folksy, down-home demeanor were instrumental in assembling a fiercely loyal work force and maintaining high employee morale.

Samuel Moore Walton (1918-1992) was born near Kingfisher, Oklahoma, into a farm family. He grew up in Missouri and graduated in 1940 from the University of Missouri with a degree in economics. After a short stint making 85 dollars a month as a manager trainee for the J.C. Penney Company, Walton served in the Army during World War II and attained the rank of captain. He launched his illustrious career in retailing with the purchase of a Ben Franklin variety store franchise in Newport, Arkansas, where he began his practice of high-volume, discount merchandising. From there, he moved to bigger stores in several locations, calling his newly formed chain ''Walton's Five & Dime.'' He depended on regular newspaper advertising and special sales promotions, and began to experiment with self-service shopping, stationing clerks only at check-out counters. His stores became larger and more numerous, and with his brother ''Bud'' as a partner in the business, ''Walton's Family Centers'' by 1962 was the largest independently operated chain of variety stores in the country.

A key strategy in the rapid expansion of Walton's stores was one that would be repeated successfully throughout the later Wal-Mart boom: placing new stores in small towns, based on the realization that the consumer power, represented by relatively small but concentrated populations, was more than adequate to support a large variety store. Walton formed early his notion that a big store in a small town would be lucrative, and would intercept the flow of shoppers traveling to larger cities for major purchases. By establishing initial occupation of these smaller market niches, any threat of subsequent competition

A Wal-Mart store in Williston, Vermont.

would be stifled. Although ready and willing to actively test his idea, Walton failed to find interested investors or franchise affiliation, and so went heavily into debt to finance the establishment of the first Wal-Mart in Rogers, Arkansas, which opened on July 2, 1962. The business prospered during the 1960s, first with several new stores opening in other locations in Arkansas, and then further extension into neighboring states. By the end of the decade, however, the need for expansion capital coaxed Walton into incorporation and sale of public stock.

Walton set a course for rapid enlargement of his new Wal-Mart venture, fearing that if he did not crack the market offered by small towns, some other discount store would beat him to it. From 38 stores in 1971, the chain grew to 276 outlets by 1980, most within a 300 mile radius of the firm's Bentonville, Arkansas headquarters. But the greatest growth was yet to come. In the early 1980s, Walton acquired several other retail chains, and transforming these stores into Wal-Marts allowed for quick saturation of new territory, particularly in the Deep South. At mid-decade, there were nearly 1,000 Wal-Marts in 22 states. For new construction, the prevailing expansion plan never wavered from the proven small town location strategy, although a clever ploy of capturing an increasing market share of large cities came about by setting up stores in nearby suburban areas. Overall, the growth and expansion of Wal-Mart has occurred in three phases. Initially, up until the mid-1970s, stores were tightly clustered around the northwest Arkansas operational hub. The second phase, through 1980, witnessed regional expansion into neighboring states, while in the third phase, Wal-Marts seemed to be springing up everywhere.

Sam Walton once described his management style as "MBWA"—management by walking around. He maintained a rigorous schedule of unannounced store visits, which always included Sam's own cheerleading drill and time for chatting with employees at every level. He acknowledged that human resources were the key to Wal-Mart's success, and Walton maintained a people orientation from the beginning that never wavered or waned. Hard work was always rewarded, with bonuses given for good ideas, and stock options and profit-sharing incentives offered to all personnel. Walton himself worked 16-hour days and expected his corporate executives to do likewise. The egalitarian tone of upper management was legendary, and was symbolized by the lack of assigned parking at corporate headquarters, even for Sam's old pick-up truck. The company nurtured several programs aimed at giving back to the community. There were college scholarships for employees' children, as well as local high school students. With the stated purpose of stemming the tide of jobs leaving the country, there was the much touted "Buy American" campaign (though as critics pointed out, Wal-Mart purchased domestically only if that was the cheapest price available). His recipe for prosperity evidently worked, for by the late 1980s, *Forbes* magazine had placed Sam Walton at the top of their list of the richest people in America for three years running.

By 1987, Wal-Mart ranked fourth among general retail chains, trailing Sears, Kmart, and J.C. Penney's, and in that year alone, the company opened 121 new stores. Its board of directors included the then-first lady of Arkansas—Hilary Rodham Clinton. In 1988, Sam Walton stepped down as CEO (Chief Executive Officer), though he still maintained an active voice in corporate plans and operations. The company he built was now a national icon. As one account opined, "By the end of the 1980s, for its personnel and for the public it served,

the firm had evolved into more than just a job or a store. In the eyes of its growing legion of admirers, Wal-Mart had become a cultural phenomenon." The new decade promised continued success and further expansion, and on one day alone, January 30, 1991, Wal-Mart opened 36 new stores. Later that year, Wal-Mart passed both Sears and Kmart to become the nation's leading retailer. Sad news for the company soon followed, for on April 5, 1992, Sam Walton died. But the retailing spectacle he engineered remained firmly entrenched in American culture.

Wal-Mart instituted a number of important and far-reaching technical innovations that serve as exemplars of retail trade management techniques in this country. In 1977, a company-wide computer system was installed that has grown in sophistication and applications to where its database is second only to the federal government's. Wal-Mart pioneered the use of UPC bar code scanning, not only at the check-out counter, but also at the backroom receiving area, which allowed for quick and accurate inventory data analysis. A satellite-based network, which initially cost $20 million and has now become the largest privately owned system in the country, allows for regular and instantaneous communications among staff at all stores and management personnel at headquarters.

Another way that Wal-Mart gained an edge on competition was to vertically integrate the processes of wholesale purchasing and distribution of merchandise. Walton set up a series of centrally located distribution centers that received bulk shipments in very large quantities from vendors and suppliers, often by rail. Through a process known as "cross-docking," the goods were then loaded on a fleet of company-owned trucks bound for individual stores, usually the same day. These distribution centers, full of automatic conveyor belts and often as large as 25 acres in area, did not actually function as warehouses, but rather facilitated rapid transfer of products from a wholesale to a retail mode. They now serve the growing network of retail locations at an approximate ratio of one distribution center per 100 stores. The company also assumed control of all departments within stores, including the jewelry, pharmaceutical, and automobile service sections which previously had belonged to outside contractors leasing floor space.

The success of Wal-Mart has been emblematic of changing retail trends in the United States, and has paralleled the rise of discount merchandising. The economies of scale involved with bigger and more numerous stores, bulk purchasing directly from manufacturers, and high volume sales enabled rapid growth and soaring profits even as individual item mark-ups were reduced and the savings passed on to the customer. The public was quick to respond. As traditional department stores declined in consumer appeal, the large variety outlet promising low prices took over. The year Wal-Mart opened its first store—1962—was the same year Kmart, Woolco, and Target first opened stores. But it was Wal-Mart that most successfully negotiated the transition from shopping center and mall-based retailing to one-stop shopping. Sales and service were guided by a pair of slogans which were displayed prominently in every store—"We sell for Less" and "Satisfaction guaranteed." Not only does management strive to uphold those maxims, but a well-trained staff at all locations exudes helpfulness and attention to customers' needs. The "store greeter," often a senior citizen, is a fixture at the entrance to every store.

The amazing spread of Wal-Mart across the American landscape has not been without controversy. Several locations have actually welcomed the new neighbor, finding that their own business community has prospered from the increased consumer traffic. But much more commonly, local communities perceive the giant store on the edge of town as a threat to main street merchants unable to compete with the bulk purchasing power of a national chain that prides itself on passing its savings on to the consumer. Charges of unfair labor practices have not fazed the infamously non-union shop. For all its self-congratulatory stance on promoting ecology issues and being green, the company has also been criticized for its use of veiled threats and other heavy-handed tactics in dealing with local zoning laws and environmental regulations. On-going opposition by local communities to Wal-Mart's expansion plans will most likely continue. There may come a time when the company feels it has largely saturated the market for its discount retailing operation. Increasing popularity of electronic catalogs and Internet-based shopping may begin to dent the fortunes of this giant, but so far there appears no sign of slowing down, and for now anyway, that big Wal-Mart store is here to stay.

—Robert Kuhlken

FURTHER READING:

Graff, Thomas, and Dub Ashton. ''Spatial Diffusion of Wal-Mart: Contagious and Reverse Hierarchical Elements.'' *Professional Geographer.* Vol.46, No. 1, 1994, 19-29.

McInerney, Francis, and Sean White. *The Total Quality Corporation.* New York, Truman Talley Books, 1995.

Ortega, Bob. *In Sam We Trust: The Untold Story of Sam Walton and How Wal-Mart Is Devouring America.* Times Books, 1998.

Schneider, Mary Jo. ''The Wal-Mart Annual Meeting: From Small-town America to a Global Corporate Culture.'' *Human Organization.* Vol.57, No. 3, 1998, 292-299.

Trimble, Vance. *Sam Walton: The Inside Story of America's Richest Man.* New York, Dutton, 1990.

Vance, Sandra, and Roy Scott. *Wal-Mart: A History of Sam Walton's Retail Phenomenon.* New York, Twayne Publishers, 1994.

Walters, Barbara (1931—)

About her career as a television newswoman and interviewer, first lady of the news Barbara Walters has said, ''I was the kind nobody thought could make it. I had a funny Boston accent. I couldn't pronounce my Rs. I wasn't a beauty.'' Walters did make it, even in the often superficial, looks-obsessed world of network television. Partially as a result of attempting to make it at the right time in history—the feminist movement of the early 1970s was gaining strength—Walters not only made a place for herself in television news, but also changed the way the news was presented on television.

Barbara Walters was born, however unwillingly, into show business. Her father, Lou, was a nightclub owner who ran the Latin Quarter, a chain of popular clubs in New York, Boston, and Florida. Though celebrities were a part of her everyday life growing up, the

Barbara Walters

girl who was to become a nightly visitor in the homes of millions of Americans wanted nothing more than to be ''normal.'' But that was denied her when her father suddenly went bankrupt and suffered a heart attack. In her yearbook from Sarah Lawrence College, Walters is pictured in a cartoon as an ostrich with its head stuck in the sand, but she was forced to face the world early. To help her parents and developmentally disabled sister out of their financial troubles, she went to work, first as a secretary, then as a writer on such television shows as *Jack Paar* and *The Dick Van Dyke Show.* In 1961, she got a job as a writer/researcher for the *Today Show,* and in 1964 she moved in front of the camera when she was promoted to ''Today girl,'' a title reflecting the sexist atmosphere prevailing in television at the time. But sexism notwithstanding, Walters was on her way to being a serious television journalist. In 1972, when President Nixon changed U.S. policy and paid an official visit to the People's Republic of China for the first time since their revolution, Barbara Walters was the only woman to cover that trip.

She continued to make history and created a buzz of controversy in 1976 when ABC signed her to a five-year contract for $1 million per year. She was given the job of co-anchor on the nightly news, sitting at the desk with longtime television news man Harry Reasoner. The industry and the country were shocked at the idea of a woman receiving so much money—twice the salary of venerable CBS news legend Walter Cronkite. When Walters went to work as the first woman to anchor the evening news, she encountered ridicule, dismissive attitudes, and outright hostility. Reasoner himself was not happy to be working with her and let it show. *Time* magazine dubbed Walters the ''Most Appalling Argument for Feminism.'' Even when she proved her journalistic skills by hosting the first joint interview with President Anwar Sadat of Egypt and Prime Minister Menachem Begin of Israel, viewers just did not seem to respond to her. The flagging ABC news ratings did not rise, and Walters was removed from the news desk in 1979 and given a new job—correspondent on the news magazine show *20/20*.

Walters soon rose to co-host *20/20* with Hugh Downs, and the show expanded from Friday nights to air editions on Wednesday and Sunday nights as well. Sunday nights she co-hosted with Diane Sawyer, another pioneering woman television journalist. In an industry that is more likely to capitalize on competition among women for high-visibility positions, the pairing of the two female anchors was unusual and refreshing.

Though her credentials as a newswoman are impressive, it is as an interviewer that Walters will be remembered. She has created more than sixty ''Barbara Walters Specials'' and ''Most Fascinating People'' shows, which aired at prime audience-grabbing times, such as following the Academy Awards show and on New Year's Eve. In each special she interviews several celebrities and over the years has delved into the personal lives of political figures, timeless icons of entertainment, and ''flashes in the pan.'' Her interviews have become such a television standard that it is not clear whether Barbara Walters interviews those who have ''made it,'' or whether one has not really ''made it'' until one has been interviewed by Walters. The interviews are incisive and revealing. Bill Geddie, producer of the Walters specials, says of her, ''She has a way that has matured over the years of getting people to say things on the air that they never thought they were going to say.'' Walters herself attributes much of her success as an interviewer to her devotion to her disabled sister, Jacqueline. Growing up so close to the difficulties her sister faced gave her an empathy and compassion she was able to use throughout her career.

In 1997, Walters branched out into another television standard—the talk show. Following her introduction ''I've always wanted to do a show with women who have very different views. . . '' *The View* introduced a new format—the multi-host talk show. Co-hosts journalist Meredith Viera, lawyer Star Jones, comic Joy Behar, and model Debbie Matenopoulos are occasionally joined by Walters for the usual talk show fare: a few celebrities, a few writers of self-help books, and some lightweight chat about current newsmaking events. *The View* is advertised by Walters as ''Four women, lots of opinions, and me—Barbara Walters.'' Though one suspects that Walters's separation of herself from the ''four women'' is not accidental, on *The View* she is looser and more relaxed—called ''B.W.'' by her colleagues and allowing herself to be teased and, occasionally, put on the spot.

Walters's distinctive style has often been parodied with a ruthlessness that indicates what an icon she herself has become. Probably the most famous send-up was performed by the late Gilda Radner on the early *Saturday Night Live* show. With stiffly flipped hair and exaggerated lisp, Radner's ''Barbara Wawa'' became almost as familiar to viewers as Walters herself. Later *SNL* crews also have parodied Walters's *The View*. Though hurt by the mockery at first,

Walters soon learned that it was a measure of her own popularity, and she even invited the *SNL* cast to perform their parody on an April Fool's edition of *The View*.

While satire is a tribute on one hand, Walters does have her critics. She has been called aggressive and overbearing, common criticisms of women successful in male-dominated businesses, and some have questioned her tactics for getting interviews. Many have criticized her for confusing news and entertainment. A standing joke in the industry revolves around her ''touchy-feely'' interviewing style, falsely attributing to her the question ''If you were a tree, what kind of tree would you be?'' In 1981, during an interview with actress Katharine Hepburn, Hepburn herself stated that at that point in her life she felt like a tree. Following her thought, Walters asked, ''What kind of tree are you?'' Hepburn responded that she felt like an oak, and the question moved forever into the archive of jokes about Walters.

Barbara Walters will be remembered for many ''firsts'' and ''onlys.'' Her critics blame her for bringing too much entertainment into the news, but, for better or worse, she has been pivotal in creating the face of television news in the 1990s, a blend of fact, entertainment, and personality. There is no doubt that every woman in television news owes a debt to the girl whose college yearbook pictured her as an ostrich but who could not keep her head in the sand. Walters does not glamorize herself or her contributions, ''I was frustrated and tenacious,'' she says, ''and that's a powerful combination.''

—Tina Gianoulis

FURTHER READING:

Fox, Mary Virginia. *Barbara Walters: The News Her Way.* Minneapolis, Dillon Press, 1980.

Malone, Mary. *Barbara Walters: TV Superstar.* Hillside, New Jersey, Enslow Publishers, 1990.

Oppenheimer, Jerry. *Barbara Walters, An Unauthorized Biography.* New York, St. Martin's Press, 1990.

Remstein, Henna. *Barbara Walters.* Philadelphia, Chelsea House, 1999.

Walton, Bill (1952—)

Despite an injury-plagued career, in his brief peak Bill Walton was compared with some of the greatest centers in National Basketball Association (NBA) history. In addition to his on-court contributions, which include leading the Portland Trailblazers to an NBA Championship in 1977 and serving as a key reserve during the Boston Celtics' 1986 Championship season, Walton's outspoken political views and colorful personal life have kept him in the spotlight.

Walton began his career playing for the University of California at Los Angeles (UCLA) in the early 1970s, where he won three consecutive College Player of the Year Awards. In the 1973 National Collegiate Athletic Association (NCAA) Championship game against Memphis State, Walton hit an unbelievable 21 out of 22 shots. During

The Trailblazers' Bill Walton (right) drives against the Celtics' Dave Cowens.

league in rebounding and blocked shots. The Trailblazers reached the NBA Finals against Philadelphia that season, but lost the first two games of the best-of-seven series, a situation which only one team in NBA history had overcome. Largely due to Walton's spectacular play, however, the Blazers won the next four games, capturing the NBA Championship in six games. Walton was named the Most Valuable Player (MVP) of the series, setting NBA finals single-game records for defensive rebounds and blocked shots.

The following season, 1977-1978, Walton played even more impressively, earning the league's MVP award as the Blazers won 50 of their first 60 games. Injuries, however, kept him out of the final 24 regular season games. Walton attempted to come back in the playoffs, but it was discovered that the navicular bone in his left foot was broken. Without Walton, the Blazers lost in the playoffs to the Seattle Supersonics.

Walton was traded to the then-San Diego Clippers following the 1977-1978 season, after an extremely acrimonious parting with the Trailblazers, whom he accused of providing him with poor medical advice. Walton missed most of his first two seasons with the Clippers, drawing criticism from his teammates and fans, who felt the team had erred in signing Walton to a lucrative long-term contract. Although Walton's health improved and he was able to play fairly extensively in the 1983-1984 and 1984-1985 seasons, the Clippers never rose above mediocrity, and Walton never had the chance to repeat his playoff successes with Portland.

After his contract with the Clippers ran out, Walton contacted several of the League's top teams, seeking to find out if they needed a reserve center. Fortunately for Walton, the Boston Celtics, a championship contender, needed a quality big man of Walton's caliber to provide them with greater depth. Walton joined the team for the 1985-1986 season. The pickup paid incredible dividends for the Celtics, as Walton played in all but two of the team's 82 regular season games and every playoff game. While Walton's numbers were modest, he made a major contribution to the team's 67-15 record, as he provided scoring, rebounding, passing, defense, and high energy during his time on the court. Walton received the league's Sixth Man Award, given to the top reserve player in the league. The Celtics, with Walton backing up frontcourt legends Kevin McHale and Robert Parish, breezed through the playoffs that season, defeating the Houston Rockets in six games. The following season, however, injuries limited Walton to only 10 games, after which he retired.

Walton became a television announcer in 1991 for the National Broadcasting Network (NBC), and has served as an analyst for basketball, volleyball, and other sports. He was named to the Naismith Memorial Basketball Hall of Fame in 1993, and in 1996 was named one of the 50 greatest players in NBA history. Walton, who studied law at Stanford University during his breaks from basketball, lives with his four sons in San Diego.

—Jason George

Walton's career, UCLA won 86 of 90 games and two national championships, one in 1972 and another in 1973. For his career, Walton holds the record for highest field goal percentage in NCAA tournament play, having hit almost 69 percent of the shots he attempted between 1972 and 1974.

While his play on the court was outstanding during his college career, Walton also began to attract attention for his political views at UCLA. He was arrested during his junior year at an anti-Vietnam War rally, and issued a public statement criticizing President Richard Nixon and the Federal Bureau of Investigation. Walton was also an avid fan of the rock group the Grateful Dead, frequently attending their concerts.

Although Walton's long history of injuries had already reared its head during his high school and college careers—he suffered a broken ankle and leg and underwent knee surgery while playing at Helix High School in La Mesa, California—he was nonetheless chosen as the first player in the 1974 NBA draft by the Portland Trailblazers. While Walton played impressively during his first two seasons, injuries limited him to approximately half of the possible games he could have played in during that time.

It was during the 1976-1977 season, however, that Walton really came into his own, scoring nearly 19 points per game and leading the

FURTHER READING:

Halberstam, David. *The Breaks of the Game.* New York, Alfred A. Knopf, 1981.

"NBA History: Bill Walton." http://www.nba.com/history/waltonbio.html. June 1999.

"NBA on NBC Broadcasters: Bill Walton." http://www.nba.com/ontheair/00421666.html. June 1999.

The Waltons

From 1972 to 1981, the Depression Era returned to America through the popular television series, *The Waltons.* For nearly a decade, American viewers embraced *The Waltons* into popular culture as a symbol of past family values that were largely absent in American television programs.

Earl Hamner, Jr., creator of *The Waltons,* grew up an aspiring writer in the Blue Ridge Mountains of Schuyler, Virginia. His early novel, *The Homecoming,* was a literary recollection of his own Depression Era childhood, of which he speaks fondly: "We were in a depression, but we weren't depressed. We were poor, but nobody ever bothered to tell us that. To a skinny, awkward, red headed kid who secretly yearned to be a writer . . . each of those days seemed filled with wonder." In 1970, Lorimar Productions approached Hamner to create a one-hour television special based on *The Homecoming,* and hence, the Walton family made its television debut. Against the advice of reviewers and network executives who had little faith in the appeal of family programming, CBS took a chance and placed *The Waltons* in a Thursday night prime-time slot. To the surprise of many, the series not only held its own, but maintained a number eight position in the ratings for years to follow.

(Left to right) Ralph Waite, Richard Thomas, and Michael Learned.

For viewers concerned with the growing number of television shows whose content often included violence or sexually oriented themes, the Walton family offered a refreshing option. Representative of Hamner's own family, members of the large Walton clan were richly endowed with a common thread of love, pride, and responsibility, yet each uniquely contributed to the depiction of rural America from the Depression era to World War II. This ideal family was headed by proud patriarch and millwright John Sr. (Ralph Waite), his wife, Olivia, a loving and devout Christian mother (Michael Learned), and the prolific writer and boy-next-door, John-Boy (Richard Thomas). There was Mary-Ellen, the headstrong nurse (Judy Norton), the musically talented Ben (Jon Walmsley), the lovely Erin (Mary McDonough), and Ben, the budding entrepreneur (Eric Scott). Along with these eight were aspiring aviator Jim Bob (David W. Harper), Elizabeth (Kami Cotler), the youngest Walton, and the grandparents—Grandpa Zeb, the beloved woodsman (Will Geer), and tenacious Grandma Ester (Ellen Corby). Added to this numerous collection of distinctive individuals was a large cast of vibrantly colorful and richly developed supporting characters.

While critics of *The Waltons* have accused the show of being "sugarcoated" and unrealistic, a glance at some of the thematic content might prove otherwise. Among the issues and events that were dealt with in the series were rural poverty, bigotry, the *Hindenburg* disaster, the bombing of Pearl Harbor, the death of a family member, draft evasion and, of course, the human cost of war. Richard Thomas, reflecting on this popular misconception in a 1995 interview said, "One of the common errors in describing the show is that it was all so nice, everyone was nice. It's just not true. Everyone in the show could be foolish, everyone was hotheaded. John-Boy was always confronting people . . . It was not this very sweet little family."

The family's unifying force, however, and perhaps the focal point of the show's broad demographic appeal, was that family members always maintained a high level of respect for one other, finding genuine joy in living while nevertheless working out the internal and external conflicts that defined their daily lives on Walton's Mountain. Perhaps, too, *The Waltons* fulfilled a desire in post-1960s America to return to a simpler time when families still ate supper together at the kitchen table, the General Merchandise was the social and economic hub of a community, and, at the end of a hard but honest day, familiar voices in the darkness of a white clapboard farmhouse could be heard to say, "Good night, John-Boy."

—Nadine-Rae Leavell

FURTHER READING:

"The Waltons Home Page." http://www.the-waltons.com. April 1999.

Hamner, Earl Jr. *The Homecoming.* New York, Random House, 1970.

Keets, Heather. "Good Night, Waltons." *Entertainment Weekly.* August 20, 1993, 76.

War Bonds

War bonds are a method of financing war that reduces demand for goods and services by taking money out of circulation through modern American tax structure, which saw the tax base increase four-fold and introduced tax withholding. Through these measures, the government raised about fifty percent of its costs during the war. This was a considerable accomplishment compared to the thirty percent raised during World War I and twenty-three percent during the Civil War. During World War II, war bonds raised approximately $150 billion, or a quarter of the government's costs.

According to historian John Blum, the Secretary of the Treasury, Henry Morgenthau, said he wanted "to use bonds to sell the war, rather than vice versa." Morgenthau believed that there were quicker and easier ways for the government to raise money than through bond issues, but that it would increase people's stake in the war effort if they bought bonds. Many businesses promoted war bond purchases. Entertainment industry figures lent their celebrity to bond drives. Singer Kate Smith sold $40 million worth of bonds in a sixteen-hour radio session on September 21, 1943. Hollywood starlet Loretta Young sold bonds at a Kiwanis meeting and pin-up girl Betty Grable auctioned off her stockings. Comic book publishers DC and Marvel carried advertisements and columns urging their readers to tell their parents to buy bonds and to purchase 10-cent defense stamps themselves. Covers of Batman and Superman comics appealed to readers to buy war bonds to "Keep Those Bullets Flying" and "Slap a Jap."

War bonds were a relatively effective measure in reducing inflation and financing the war. Moreover they served as a means of popularizing the war by giving non-combatants a direct stake in its outcome. As sound fiscal policy, the measure of their worth can be judged by the inflationary pressures unleashed by President Lyndon Johnson's decision to finance the Vietnam War, which cost $150 billion, by printing more money rather than raising taxes or selling bonds.

—Ian Gordon

FURTHER READING:

Blum, John Morton. *V Was for Victory: Politics and American Culture During World War II.* New York, Harcourt Brace Jovanovich, 1976.

Perrett, Geoffrey. *Days of Sadness, Years of Triumph: The American People, 1939-1945.* Baltimore, Penguin, 1973.

Polenberg, Richard. *War and Society: The United States, 1941-1945.* New York, J. B. Lippincott, 1972.

A War Bonds poster.

investment in the bonds. This provides funds to underwrite the war. Modern warfare is an expensive business and must be financed carefully, else a government risks triggering inflation by increasing demand for goods. One method of avoiding this outcome is to raise taxes to finance the war, but such methods risk making a war unpopular. Through the more popular method of selling war bonds, citizens, in effect, invest in the war effort of their government just as they might invest in stocks. Selling war bonds lessens the need for tax increases.

During World War I, the U.S. government raised $5 billion through the sale of Liberty Bonds. Mass rallies to sell the bonds featured celebrities such as Douglas Fairbanks, Sr. Nonetheless, when most Americans talk about war bonds they are generally referring to the bonds sold during World War II. In part this is because the efforts of World War I involved a good deal of compulsion rather than persuasion. During that war school children were badgered, courts imposed illegal fines on those not owning bonds, and the houses of non-purchasers were painted yellow. But World War II bonds are probably better remembered simply because, by then, mass media had expanded considerably and the scale of the media campaign was greater.

War bonds were but one of the means at the government's disposal to regulate the wartime economy. During World War II, the cost of living in the United States increased by about thirty-three percent. Most of this increase occurred before 1943, when the government put strict price controls in place through the Office of Price Administration. The Revenue Act of 1942 established the

War Movies

As long as films have been made, war movies have been a significant genre, with thousands of documentaries, propaganda films, comedies, satires, or dramas reminding moviegoers of the deep human emotion and violence of the combat experience. Throughout the twentieth century, war movies have both reflected and manipulated changing popular attitudes toward war. Some of the films, especially those created during wartime, were created as propaganda, showing the patriotism and heroism of soldiers and the glory attained

Troops storm the beach in a scene from the film *The Longest Day*.

in battle. Still others take on the subject of war only to criticize it, usually via a graphic depiction of the cost of war in terms of human lives.

War has interested filmmakers from the first days of cinematic technology. J. Stuart Blackton's 1898 film, "Tearing Down the Spanish Flag," is considered not only the first fictional American war movie, but also the first propaganda film. Set on an anonymous rooftop in Cuba during the Spanish-American War, this short film depicts a uniformed American soldier (played by Blackton himself) removing the Spanish flag and replacing it with an American one, then cuts to a title card stating, "Remember the Maine." Blackton's film was quickly followed by reenactments of the sinking of the Maine and other battles of the Spanish-American War. Even though the film is only a few minutes long, it managed to capture the contemporary popular imagination and established the foundation for war movies in the twentieth century.

Most American films made during World War I consisted of propaganda films either encouraging or, after 1917, supporting American involvement in the European conflict. Most of these films

romanticized the war, showing enlistment as a glorious, patriotic duty and emphasizing the power and importance of male bonding. Early World War I films often dealt with American citizens volunteering for the French, British, or Canadian armies. Later films showed American troops as the deciding factor in the European victory.

D. W. Griffith directed many of the key World War I propaganda films. Film historians credit Griffith with inventing many modern film techniques, and his impact on the history of the war movie is even more direct. For example, in his 1915 Civil War epic *Birth of a Nation,* Griffith used cross-cutting techniques within battle scenes to shift from large-scale images of fighting to more intimate moments focusing on the film's main characters. Such techniques allowed future filmmakers to develop individual characters within a larger historical context of the war. Griffith's key World War I film was *Hearts of the World* (1918), shot partially under war conditions in France. In this polemical prowar film, Erich Von Stroheim was cast as an evil and lustful German officer (a role he would repeat in numerous later films) who attempts to rape and brutally beat Marie (Lillian Gish). The film's anti-German sentiment is so strong that Gish's boyfriend is willing to kill her in order save her from such a violation at the hands of the enemy. This depiction of Germans as unrepentantly evil would influence not only later World War I films, but World War II films as well.

Few war movies appeared in the years immediately following the 1918 armistice. The propaganda of the wartime films was no longer necessary, and the American public seemed inclined to focus on domestic affairs. However, three movies in the 1920s brought about a resurgence of interest in World War I. *The Big Parade* (King Vidor, 1925) is credited with reviving the war film genre as well as being the first to realistically depict the war experiences of American soldiers. The plot, which follows a group of men from their enlistment through the conflict, would become standard in the later World War II films.

The following year, the comedy drama *What Price Glory?* (Raoul Walsh, 1926), based on the Laurence Stallings and Maxwell Anderson stage play, follows two marines, Captain Flagg and Sergeant Quirt, as they engage in their own personal rivalry over the same woman while fighting in France. Though the film version does temper the antiwar sentiment of the original play, the film's comedy is sharply contrasted with its graphic and shocking depictions of battle scenes. Later war movies would often capitalize on what Jeanine Basinger in *The World War II Combat Film* would call the ''Quirt/ Flagg relationship'' by focusing on two adversarial characters serving in the same platoon.

Wings (William Wellman, 1927), which won the first Academy Award for Best Picture, introduced a new subgenre of war films: the air drama. Director Wellman used his war experiences as a pilot for the Lafayette Flying Corps and the Army Air Service to create realistic aerial scenes that were accomplished by mounting cameras on the fighting planes and by using cameramen in other aircraft, instead of using rear projection effects. The realism and excitement of these scenes would be surpassed later in *Hell's Angels* (Howard Hughes, 1930), a film that cost over $4 million and that took over three years to make some of the most spectacular flying scenes ever filmed. Unlike *The Big Parade,* these latter two films do not make a profound statement about the war, and their popularity was based primarily on sheer spectacle and excitement. John Monk Saunders, a veteran pilot and the original writer of *Wings,* would later write air dramas, such as *Ace of Aces* (J. Walter Ruben, 1933), *The Dawn Patrol* (Howard Hawks, 1930; remade by Edmund Goulding, 1938), and *The Eagle and the Hawk* (Stuart Walker, 1933), that openly criticized the senseless waste of the war and starkly represented the mental strain suffered by pilots, yet still remained true to the adventurous nature of the subgenre.

The strongest antiwar statement made following World War I came in Lewis Milestone's 1930 adaptation of Erich Maria Remarque's novel *All Quiet on the Western Front.* This film begins with young German men enthusiastically volunteering to fight for their country. However, they quickly learn that this war has nothing to do with honor and glory, and the mental breakdown and violent death of these soldiers is depicted in graphic detail. The realism of the battle scenes, including the image of two disembodied hands clutching a barbed wire, accounts for this film's continued status as one of the great war films of the century. The final shot of Paul Baumer (played by Lew Ayres) dying as he reaches for a butterfly just outside his trench remains one of the most haunting and effective images in any war film. Even after World War II, the Great War served as the setting for profound antiwar commentary, including Stanley Kubrick's *Paths of Glory* (1957) and Dalton Trumbo's *Johnny Got His Gun* (1971).

As America entered World War II, however, Hollywood needed to reverse this antiwar sentiment by creating films that demonstrated American heroism and success in the earlier war. In *Sergeant York* (Howard Hawks, 1941), Gary Cooper's Alvin York, who went from devout pacifist to America's greatest war hero, provides a counterimage to the one created in such films as *All Quiet on the Western Front.* The film also showed the potential for individual heroic achievement and served as significant propaganda for the American war effort.

World War II films have a clearly defined sense of good and evil. As in the previous war, the enemies were presented not as complex human beings but as two-dimensional caricatures, designed to generate hate and loathing in the audience. Most films created during the war years focused on the adventure and glory of warfare, as well as the strength of both the U. S. military and the American spirit. In addition, most World War II films had a romantic subplot. The female love interests were either sweethearts pining away at the homefront; nurses, AWACs, or reporters serving some military duty; or European, usually French, women whom the G.I.'s meet while on leave. Often, the films followed soldiers from enlistment or training to combat. These formulas were sometimes mixed in with several variables, such as military branches or European or Pacific locales, to create a variety of successful films.

Surprisingly, most of the early World War II combat films made in 1942 and 1943, such as *Wake Island* (John Farrow, 1942) and *Bataan* (Tay Garnett, 1943), focused more on catastrophic American defeats than on the victories. *Wake Island,* the first large-scale combat film of World War II, closely followed a group of soldiers until they were all killed in the ensuing battle. Both films received the support of the U.S. government, and despite showing terrible defeats, these films mobilized popular support for the war and proved to be useful propaganda tools.

Few figures are more synonymous with the war movie than John Wayne. Just as in his Westerns, John Wayne represented the ideal of American masculinity in a persona that exemplified the hard, determined, yet compassionate soldier. Such a persona is evident in such wartime films as *Flying Tigers* (1942), *The Fighting Seabees* (1944), *They Were Expendable* (1945), and *Back to Bataan* (1945), and in postwar films like *The Sands of Iwo Jima* (1949), *Flying Leathernecks* (1951), and *In Harm's Way* (1965). These films follow the basic formulas of World War II movies, and Wayne repeated the same basic character in each. Although Wayne was criticized in later years for such repetitive, formulaic performances, he created an iconic hero, and his films were tremendous successes and morale boosters.

As the Second World War came to a close, movies like *The Story of G. I. Joe* (William Wellman, 1945) and *A Walk in the Sun* (Lewis Milestone, 1946) moved away from the patriotism and heroics of films made in the previous years of the war and toward a more realistic depiction of American soldiers in battle that emphasized the human cost of war over the glory of victory. Wellman continued to demythologize warfare in the 1949 film *Battleground,* which received an Academy Award nomination for Best Picture. These three films follow similar episodic plots focusing on a group of American soldiers, many of whom are killed through the course of the film. In the opening of *A Walk in the Sun,* Burgess Meredith (who also stars as famed war correspondent Ernie Pyle in *The Story of G. I. Joe*) describes the ethnic, class, and cultural diversity of his platoon:

> There was Tyne, who never had much urge to travel. Providence, Rhode Island may not be much as cities go, but it was all he wanted, a one town man; Rivera, Italian American, likes opera and would like a wife and kid, plenty of kids; Friedman, lathe operator and amateur boxing champ, New York City; Windy, minister's son, Canton, Ohio, used to take long walks alone and just think; . . . Sergeant Ward, a farmer who knows his soil, a good farmer; McWilliams, first aid man, slow, Southern, dependable; Archenbeau, platoon scout and prophet, talks a lot but he's all right; Porter, Sergeant Porter, . . . he has a lot on his mind . . . ; Tranella speaks two languages: Italian and Brooklyn.

This conventional Hollywood platoon became a stereotype in the American war movie with an ensemble cast, but in these early examples, this broad demographic representation was used to emphasize the impact of the war on America as a whole.

Following the war, Hollywood war films began to examine the complexities of warfare, exposing the fallibility and brutality of military authority by addressing the mental strain inflicted on war's participants and by showing the enemy as complex, human, and sympathetic. Gregory Peck in *12 O'Clock High* (Henry King, 1949) is shown to be a vulnerable hero suffering a mental breakdown during the war. In *From Here to Eternity* (Fred Zinnemann, 1953), the enemy is not the Axis powers, but the bullying, violent, murderous military authorities such as Ernest Borgnine's Fatso. In *The Caine Mutiny* (Edward Dmytryk, 1954), Humphrey Bogart's emotionally unstable Captain Queeg proves to be more of a danger to his men than any enemy is. In *The Bridge on the River Kwai* (David Lean, 1957), the Japanese prison camp commander is portrayed as a man caught between his sense of duty and honor for his country and his sympathy and respect for the prisoners. This is not to say that the tradition of heroic war movies did not continue. Films like *To Hell and Back* (Jesse Hibbs, 1955), the story of Audie Murphy (played by himself), America's most decorated war hero, as well as *The Great Escape* (John Sturges, 1963) and *The Dirty Dozen* (Robert Aldrich, 1967), continued to show the more adventurous and exciting side of the conflict. But into the 1960s and 1970s, in films like *The Longest Day* (Ken Annakin, et al, 1962) and *Patton* (Franklin J. Schaffner, 1970), Hollywood filmmakers increasingly delved into a critical examination of American militarism, reflecting the general disillusion of Americans as the Vietnam conflict escalated.

In 1998, the release of two World War II movies, *Saving Private Ryan* and *The Thin Red Line* raised the level of realistic violence depicted in the war movie to a new level. Steven Spielberg's *Saving Private Ryan* follows a fairly standard plot of a small group of soldiers sent on a mission to find one man lost in France during the Normandy invasion. The first thirty minutes of the movie, showing the mass slaughter that occurred in the opening minutes of the invasion of Omaha Beach, contain the most graphically violent and disturbing combat scenes presented in a fictional film. Terence Malik's *The Thin Red Line* is equally violent, but this film about the invasion of

Guadalcanal focuses more on the contrast between combat and the introspective moments available to soldiers during the lulls in battle. Both films rely on new developments in special effects and camera technology that allow for even more graphic and realistic depictions of military violence.

Of the more than 50 films made about the Korean War between 1951 and 1963, most presented the enemy as one-sided villains, and few moved beyond the standard cliches of the Hollywood World War II films. Two exceptions appeared early in the war. Samuel Fuller's *Steel Helmet* and *Fixed Bayonets,* both released in 1951, take a harsh, uncompromising, and realistic look at the stress suffered by soldiers while keeping to the standard plot that follows a diverse platoon through the conflict. The characters in Fuller's films are often plagued with doubts and fears, and they are more concerned with the struggle to survive than with any potential acts of heroism.

The controversy surrounding the Vietnam conflict caused Hollywood to shy away from it as a subject for war films while the conflict was ongoing. The only exception is John Wayne's 1968 directorial debut, *The Green Berets.* This film largely consists of Cold War propaganda justifying America's presence in Vietnam. Wayne transferred his World War II movie persona to this film, a persona that was clearly the product of another time. While the film was a box office success, it stands out as an anomaly in the development of the Vietnam War movie, which, in the late 1970s and 1980s, would approach the war much more critically. *The Deer Hunter* (Michael Cimino, 1978) and *Apocalypse Now* (Francis Ford Coppola, 1979) were among the first films to criticize the Vietnam War from a combat perspective. Both films contain graphic images of the most horrifying, and often surreal, aspects of the war. The Russian roulette scenes in *The Deer Hunter* show the extremes of mental and physical torture suffered by American prisoners of war, and the scene in *Apocalypse Now* where Colonel Kilgore orders a helicopter raid on a Viet Cong village so his men can surf on a nearby beach illustrates the extreme level of absurdity in this war. The absurdity of the Vietnam War would be addressed later in Stanley Kubrick's *Full Metal Jacket* (1987), a film that ends with a platoon spontaneously singing the Mickey Mouse Club theme in unison.

One of the most successful Vietnam War films was Oliver Stone's 1986 Academy Award winner, *Platoon.* While this film does have a strong antiwar message, it follows a fairly standard war-movie plot, following the experiences of a naïve young volunteer (played by Charlie Sheen) as he becomes increasingly disillusioned by the fighting. The film also follows a clear good-vs.-evil binary, but instead of America representing good and the Viet Cong representing evil, these moral forces are represented by two American sergeants. Tom Berenger's Barnes brutally terrorizes a native village early in the film, while Willem Dafoe's Elias strongly resists this descent into barbarism and tries to maintain high moral standards in an immoral environment. The success of *Platoon* resulted in a spate of Vietnam War films in the late 1980s, but their numbers never reached the level and density that occurred during World War II and the Korean War. In addition, all Vietnam War films made after 1978 engage in some level of criticism of the war, and none present themselves as the straightforward adventures that appeared in films about the earlier wars.

In general, films made during wartime emphasize glory, honor, and patriotic values, and it is only in the years following the wars that these values are analyzed and criticized. As filmmaking technology has changed and improved throughout the century, American filmmakers have achieved greater levels of realism in war movies, and these films collectively have enhanced and influenced Americans' awareness of the conditions of war.

—Andrew J. Kunka

FURTHER READING:

Basinger, Jeanine. *The World War II Combat Film: Anatomy of a Genre.* New York, Columbia University Press, 1986.

Dick, Bernard F. *The Star-Spangled Screen: The American World War II Film.* Lexington, The University of Kentucky Press, 1985.

Dittmar, Linda and Gene Michaud, editors. *From Hanoi to Hollywood: The Vietnam War in American Film.* New Brunswick, Rutgers University Press, 1991.

Doherty, Thomas. *Projections of War: Hollywood, American Culture, and World War II.* New York, Columbia University Press, 1993.

Langman, Larry and Ed Borg. *Encyclopedia of American War Films.* New York, Garland, 1989.

Quirk, Lawrence J. *Great War Films.* New York, Citadel, 1994.

Rubin, Steven Jay. *Combat Films.* Jefferson, North Carolina, McFarland, 1981.

Suid, Lawrence H. *Guts and Glory: Great American War Movies.* Reading, Massachusetts, Addison-Wesley, 1978.

War of the Worlds

Broadcast on October 30, 1938, Orson Welles' Mercury Theatre radio dramatization of H.G. Wells' *War of the Worlds* engendered a mass panic in which millions of Americans believed they were being invaded by Martians; in so doing, the broadcast dramatically demonstrated the nascent power of mass media in American culture.

The Mercury Theatre group, headed by the 23-year-old Welles, had built a small national audience with its weekly radio adaptations of literary classics such as Joseph Conrad's *Heart of Darkness*. Welles, his partner John Houseman, and writer Howard Koch collaborated on the hour-long scripts. The trio nearly scrapped their *War of the Worlds* adaptation, as Koch's faithful approximation of the novel did not translate well in rehearsals. The group decided to stick with the project after re-working the script to mirror a news broadcast. Nevertheless, as group members and even Welles himself later recalled, the feeling in the studio on the day of the broadcast was that *War of the Worlds* would not be a successful production.

The show commenced at 8 p.m. that Halloween eve, following an introduction by a CBS announcer which presented Wells' novel as the subject of the forthcoming dramatization. In the first 10 minutes of the broadcast, Welles masterfully built dramatic tension by juxtaposing fireside chat-styled meditations on renewed American prosperity with increasingly frequent news bulletins on atmospheric disturbances detected by astronomers across the United States. Just as

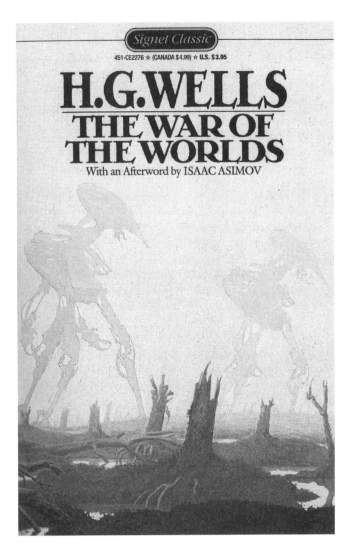

Cover of *The War of the Worlds,* by H.G. Wells.

thousands of listeners switched over from the more popular Charlie McCarthy show (a less-than-compelling singer had just been introduced), Welles' group delivered a frantic news report from the small town of Grovers Mill, New Jersey, where Martians had landed and wiped out an entire United States military force: "A humped shape is rising out of the pit. I can make out a small beam of light against a mirror. What's that? There's a jet of flame springing from that mirror, and it leaps right at the advancing men. It strikes them head on! Good Lord! They're turning into flame!" As the broadcast followed the progress of the Martians up the East Coast, the reports became even more dire. "People are falling like flies," Welles reported. "No more defense. Our army wiped out . . . artillery, air force, everything wiped out. This may be the last broadcast." An actor portraying the Secretary of the Interior informed listeners that President Franklin Delano Roosevelt had declared a national emergency.

As the dramatization continued, thousands of Americans panicked. In New York City, hundreds of people jammed railroad and bus stations to escape the menace. In Birmingham, Alabama, sorority women at a local college lined up at campus telephones to speak to parents and loved ones for the last time. In Pittsburgh, a man found his wife in the bathroom, clutching a poison bottle and yelling "I'd rather die this way than that.'' And, in a favorite story of Welles', actor John Barrymore, upon hearing the broadcast, drunkenly took to his backyard, where he unleashed his Great Danes from their doghouse with the admonition: ''Fend for yourselves!'' It has been estimated that 12 percent of the radio audience heard the broadcast and more than half that number took it seriously; by sociologist Hadley Cantril's account, which was published in a landmark contemporary study sponsored by the Rockefeller foundation, more than a million people were frightened by Welles' broadcast. Cantril's demographic survey placed the strongest currents of fear among less-educated people and poor Southern folk.

Welles concluded his broadcast with a re-statement of the fictionality of the presentation (''The Mercury Theatre's own radio version of dressing up in a sheet and saying 'Boo!''' as Welles put it), but the hysteria continued well into the night. CBS was inundated with calls; newspaper switchboards were jammed, and mobs continued to crowd the streets of New York and northern New Jersey. When the truth became apparent, public hysteria turned into ire directed at CBS. Hundreds threatened lawsuits against the network, not the least of which was from H.G. Wells himself; the Federal Communications Commission promised a full-fledged inquiry, and the New York City police, for a time, even contemplated arresting Welles. As calmer heads prevailed, the public furor died down, and Welles became an overnight sensation; many of his biographers claim that without the celebrity engendered by the *War of the Worlds* broadcast, Welles might never have been able to bring his craft to Hollywood, where he became a celebrated director with films such as *Citizen Kane* (1941) and *The Magnificent Ambersons* (1942).

The *War of the Worlds* episode highlighted the emerging power of mass media over the American public. It demonstrated the power of the media to form and shape opinion in American culture, and also the passive willingness on the part of the public to place its faith in the legitimacy of sound and image. Ironically, *War of the Worlds* represented one of radio's final assertions of power within the media sphere; by the 1950s, television had replaced radio as the dominant force in mass culture.

Scholars assert that Welles' broadcast was so widely believed because it struck a particular chord with Americans in the years before World War II. The show aired just after the Munich crisis, to which Welles alluded at the outset of the broadcast, and the recent international conflict may have influenced some to believe that the reported invasion was not extraterrestrial at all. Sociologists have also located the show's resonance in the latent anxiety of the general population, engendered by years of economic depression. ''On the surface, the broadcast was implausible and contradictory, but that didn't matter,'' asserts Joel Cooper. ''In that one instance, people had an immediate explanation for all the unease and disquiet they had been feeling. And suddenly, they could do something. They could gather their families. They could run.''

War of the Worlds remained a vibrant part of American popular culture in the second half of the twentieth century. In 1953, Byron Haskin produced a Hollywood film about the broadcast and, from 1988-1990, a television series inspired by Welles' take on *War of the Worlds* enjoyed a successful run. In 1988, the fiftieth anniversary of the broadcast, public radio stations across America aired an ambitious remake of *War of the Worlds* starring Jason Robards and featuring the Oscar-winning sound effects of Randy Thom; the citizens of Grovers

Mill commemorated their town's role in the historic broadcast with a four-day festival that culminated with the unveiling of a bronze statue of Welles at a microphone and a rapt family gathered around its radio.

Up until his death in 1985, Welles would never reveal whether he had anticipated the massive misinterpretation of his radio drama. Whether intended as a hoax or not, however, the landmark *War of the Worlds* broadcast demonstrated the American public's preference for reading media's sound—and later its images—as truth rather than fiction.

—Scott Tribble

FURTHER READING:

Baughman, James. *The Republic of Mass Culture: Journalism, Filmmaking, and Broadcasting in America Since 1941.* Baltimore and London, Johns Hopkins University Press, 1992.

Brown, Robert J. *Manipulating the Ether: The Power of Broadcast Radio in Thirties America.* Jefferson, McFarland & Co., 1998.

Cantril, Hadley. *The Invasion from Mars: A Study in the Psychology of Panic with the Complete Script of the Famous Orson Welles Broadcast.* Princeton, Princeton University Press, 1940.

Higham, Charles. *Orson Welles: The Rise and Fall of an American Genius.* New York, St. Martin's Press, 1985.

Thomson, David. *Rosebud: The Story of Orson Welles.* New York, Alfred A. Knopf, 1996.

Warhol, Andy (1928-1987)

Andy Warhol was the most renowned Pop artist in the 1960s and, more generally, one of the most important artists of the twentieth century. His boundless and apparently effortless creativity expressed itself in many forms. He was a commercial designer, painter, printmaker, filmmaker, and publisher.

Although Warhol was intentionally obscure about his background, he was born Andrew Warhola, the son of a Czech Roman Catholic emigrant miner, in remote Forest City, Pennsylvania. After his father's early death, Warhol enrolled in Pittsburgh's Carnegie Institute of Technology as an art student in 1946. At this time he worked as a window decorator in a Pittsburgh department store. By 1950 he had shortened his name to Andy Warhol, and had moved to New York where his reputation as a designer quickly blossomed. Besides doing graphic work for magazines such as *Vogue* and *Harper's Bazaar,* he won awards for his advertising designs, particularly those for I. Miller shoes. It is clear that had he never become a fine artist, he would nevertheless have been one of the most important designers in the postwar period. It was during these years Warhol dyed his hair the signature silver color that he would maintain for the rest of his life.

In 1960, the year Warhol began to paint, he made some of the earliest works that could be called Pop Art. His large paintings of Dick Tracy could be seen in Lord and Taylor's store windows on Fifth

Campbell's Soup I, **screenprint by Andy Warhol.**

Avenue. Warhol's position as the leading Pop artist was consolidated in 1962 at the seminal "New Realists" exhibition at the Sidney Janis Gallery in New York. After 1964, Warhol was represented by the New York dealer Leo Castelli, who also handled most of the other Pop artists.

Warhol quickly became notorious for his paintings of Campbell's Soup cans, which were first exhibited at Los Angeles' Ferus Gallery in 1962. These paintings were straightforward renderings of row upon row of soup cans. Not just publicity gambits, these were important avant-garde works, signaling a major change in the nature of art. They were a cool reaction to the passionate—and to the Pop artists' minds, excessive—art of the Abstract Expressionists, which then dominated the art scene. The soup cans were painted in the same spirit as Marcel Duchamp's "readymades" (objects designated as artworks merely by the artist's choice and recontextualization). Warhol was forced to defend the paintings as legitimate artworks when the Campbell Soup Company sued the him for copyright infringement. The corporation later decided that the paintings were good advertising. In 1963, inspired by the objects he had seen in supermarkets, Warhol precisely imitated Brillo soap-pad boxes. He had one-hundred wooden boxes constructed by a carpenter and stenciled the sides with exact imitations of the Brillo graphic. For sale at three hundred dollars each, these created great excitement when

they were exhibited at Manhattan's Stable Gallery the following year. When they were to be shown in a Toronto art gallery, their status as art was ignored. Warhol's dealer had to pay "merchandise duty" to have them delivered.

With works like these Warhol had abandoned painting by hand for other more anonymous techniques (such as photo-silkscreen). "I want to be a machine," he said in 1962, subverting the idea of the artist as an expressive medium who creates unique, handmade works. Warhol used Marilyn Monroe as a motif in several silk-screened works in the 1960s (as in *Gold Marilyn Monroe* [1962, The Museum of Modern Art, New York]). Rendered in the cheap-looking, off-register style of trashy reproduction, these artworks suggested that Marilyn's manufactured persona had overwhelmed her identity as a person. Celebrities became a major theme in Warhol's works. Throughout the next two decades he made images of athletes, politicians, and entertainers such as Elvis Presley, Troy Donahue, Jackie Kennedy Onassis, Elizabeth Taylor, and Chairman Mao. As in the Marilyn images, the colors were often garish and silk-screened off-register. A series from this period is entitled *Ten Portraits of Jews of the Twentieth Century.* Warhol's fascination with stars was reflected in the gossipy celebrity magazine he founded in 1969 entitled *Inter/View,* then *Andy Warhol's Interview,* and later simply *Interview.*

In response to the civic strife of the 1960s, Warhol created his *Disaster* series. Such works as *Car Crash, Race Riot,* and *Electric Chair* involve the stark appropriation of newspaper photographs saturated with color and often repeated within the same frame. Warhol suggested that in these works he wished to demonstrate how the callous repetition of the media's coverage of traumatic events creates a numbing apathy in viewers.

In 1964 Warhol established his "Factory," a rented attic that became a large mass-production studio in New York where assistants made works serially. It was responsible for turning out thousands of Warhol's works. Often, Warhol would clip photos from magazines and newspapers and have them silk-screened by his assistants. The very name "factory" challenged the notion of an artist's studio as a place of inspiration, a place where unique and precious pieces are made. In this spirit, Warhol once said that anybody "should be able to do all my paintings for me." The Factory became nearly as notorious for its denizens as the art that was produced there. Robert Hughes described its silver-papered walls as a place where "cultural space-debris, drifting fragments from a variety of Sixties subcultures (transvestite, drug, S & M, rock, Poor Little Rich, criminal, street, and all the permutations) orbiting in smeary ellipses around their unmoved mover." Shy and inhibited himself, Warhol became a voyeur of a subculture of his own creation. In his role as funky entrepreneur Warhol opened a nightclub with the thoroughly 1960s-sounding name "The Exploding Plastic Inevitable," whose house-band was The Velvet Underground. Its leader, Lou Reed, is now regarded as a soulful guru of heroine culture and musically a pioneer of Punk and New Wave.

In a decade racked by assassinations, Warhol himself was shot on June 3, 1968, by Valerie Solanis, a former Factory groupie turned militant feminist. The only member of S.C.U.M. ("The Society for Cutting Up Men"), Solanis later claimed that she did so because the artist "had too much control over her life." The scars of several bullet wounds to Warhol's chest are depicted in Alice Neel's well known portrait of the artist. Ominously, a woman had shot at one of Warhol's portraits of Marilyn Monroe four years earlier.

At the time of his first solo exhibition in 1965, at the Institute of Contemporary Art in Philadelphia, it was announced that Warhol had given up painting to concentrate on filmmaking. Throughout the 1960s the artist made several movies which have become classics of film history and of Minimalist cinema. Typically, they are outrageously boring and amateurish—qualities for which they are admired—and register the spontaneous exhibitionism of his Factory "actors." *Eat* (1964) showed artist Robert Indiana eating a mushroom. *Empire* (1964) was comprised of an eight-hour shot of one side of the Empire State Building in New York (the changing light is its only action). In 1964 *Film Culture* magazine awarded him their Independent Film Award. In all, Warhol collaborated on more than seventy-five films. His highly-regarded *The Chelsea Girls* (1966) was the first underground film to be shown at a conventional commercial theater. On a split screen viewers watched a quirky kind of documentary: the comings and goings of Warholian "superstars" in two different hotel rooms. *Four Stars* (1966-67) ran for more than twenty-four hours and was shown using three projectors simultaneously on one screen. The films *My Hustler* (1965), *Bike Boy,* and *Lonesome Cowboys* (both 1967) all dealt with homosexual themes. Paul Morrissey, a production assistant and occasional cameraman in the Factory, participated significantly in many of Warhol's films. He was enlisted to give them a greater sense of structure and professionalism, and to make them more appealing to a popular audience, as in *Andy Warhol's Frankenstein* (1974). Starting in 1980, Warhol was briefly interested in video; he worked to establish a private cable television station called "Andy Warhol TV."

As his works indicate, Warhol was genuinely obsessed with celebrity, and particularly Hollywood fame. In the 1970s and 1980s he seems to have given himself over to the popular media. He was often seen at Studio 54, and at nearly every opening and award ceremony. He appeared almost nightly on *Entertainment Tonight* escorting Brooke Shields, Bianca Jagger, Elizabeth Taylor, or the designer Halston. Not only attracted by the celebrity of entertainers, Warhol also courted rising young artists such as the graffiti artists Keith Haring (1958-1990) and Jean-Michel Basquiat (1960-1988). In the film *Basquiat* (directed by Julian Schnabel, 1997), rock star David Bowie plays a convincing Warhol in a vivid depiction of the 1980s New York art scene. In line with other artists of the 1980s who "appropriated" imagery from art history, Warhol made a series of paintings based on famous works by Botticelli and Leonardo da Vinci.

Like his films, Warhol's untimely death seemed anticlimactic, even banal. He died of complications after a fairly routine operation on February 22, 1987. The auction of his possessions, in itself a cultural event, revealed that Warhol had always been an impassioned collector. His extensive collection of folk art had been exhibited in 1977 at the Museum of Modern Art. His influence as an arbiter of taste continued even after his death. The sale of his possessions, including his collections of all manner of kitschy art and furnishings, influenced the retro styles of the late 1980s and 1990s. Today the Estate of Andy Warhol handles his artworks and their reproduction.

The meaning of Warhol's art has been endlessly debated and alternately seen to be tremendously deep or mind-numbingly superficial. The artist often mystified interviewers by affecting a profound detachment—often to the point of boredom. In one early interview the artist explained, "If you want to know all about Andy Warhol, just look at the surface of my paintings and films and me, and there I am.

There's nothing behind it." Warhol will always be associated with those aspects of 1960s popular culture that involve outrageous behavior, a sensationalist media, and the art world as glitzy big business. His most famous pronouncement, "in the future *everybody*, will be famous for fifteen minutes," seems an accurate observation about the media's insatiable appetite for creating quickly consumable media targets.

—Mark B. Pohlad

FURTHER READING:

Bockris, Victor. *Life and Death of Andy Warhol.* New York, Da Capo Press, 1997.

Cagle, Van M. *Reconstructing Pop/Subculture: Art, Rock, and Andy Warhol.* Thousand Oaks, California, Sage Publications, 1995.

Francis, Mark, and Margery King. *The Warhol Look: Glamour, Style, Fashion.* Boston, Little, Brown, 1997.

Hackett, Pat, editor. *The Andy Warhol Diaries.* New York, Warner Books, 1989.

Honnef, Klaus. *Andy Warhol, 1928-1987: Commerce into Art,* translated from the German by Carole Fahy and I. Burns. Cologne, Benedikt Taschen, 1993.

Koch, Stephan. *Stargazer: The Life, World and Films of Andy Warhol.* New York, Rizzoli, 1991.

Ratcliff, Carter. *Andy Warhol.* New York, Abbeville Press, 1983.

Shanes, Eric. *Warhol.* London, Studio Editions, 1993.

Tretiack, Philippe. *Andy Warhol.* New York, Universe Books, 1997.

Washington, Denzel (1954—)

A handsome, intelligent, and stylish actor, Denzel Washington is the natural heir, with a modern edge, to Sidney Poitier, the first film star to have demonstrated that an African American could become a heartthrob and a top box-office draw in the United States. Born in Mount Vernon, New York, Washington holds a B.A. in journalism from Fordham, studied acting at San Francisco's American Conservatory Theater, and worked on stage and in television (he was an ongoing character in the popular hospital series, *St. Elsewhere*) before Hollywood beckoned. He made his screen debut as white George Segal's black illegitimate son in *Carbon Copy* (1982). Five years later, his portrayal of South African political activist Steve Biko in *Cry Freedom* (1987) brought him stardom and an Oscar nomination for Best Supporting Actor. He won that award, and a Golden Globe, for his embittered but courageous runaway slave in *Glory* (1989). He has made several other films dealing with the issue of race; from the comedic (*Heart Condition,* 1990) through the romantic (*Mississippi Masala,* 1991) to the overtly political, as the title character in Spike Lee's *Malcolm X* (1993). He has, however, established his versatility in a broad range of work, notably including Shakespeare—on screen in Kenneth Branagh's *Much Ado About Nothing* (1993), and as *Richard III* on stage in New York's Central Park in 1990.

—Frances Gateward

Denzel Washington

FURTHER READING:

Brode, Douglas. *Denzel Washington: His Films and Career.* Secaucus, New Jersey, Carol Publishing Group, 1997.

Simmons, Alex. *Denzel Washington.* Austin, Texas, Raintree Steck-Vaughn, 1997.

Simon, Leslie. "Why Denzel Washington (not Tom Cruise) is the New Paul Newman." *Film Comment.* Vol. 34, March/April 1998, 72-75.

Washington Monument

The Washington Monument's tall, slender obelisk towers above the Mall in the nation's capitol, dominating the skyline. A grateful public constructed it in the nineteenth century to commemorate George Washington. Federal architect Robert Mills won a competition in 1845 with his proposal for a 600-foot obelisk and circular temple at the base. The monument was completed in 1884 without the temple and 45 feet shorter than Mills's design. Unlike the capitol's other presidential monuments, the Washington Monument is abstract, with no images or words; its power comes from the simple beauty of

its form. It has been largely uncontroversial, which is unique for a political monument. And unlike the nearby Lincoln Memorial, the Washington Monument has not been the site of any significant political events. Instead, it has stood for over 100 years in quiet solemnity as a proud testament to "the Father of our country."

—Dale Allen Gyure

FURTHER READING:

Liscombe, Rhodri Windsor. *Altogether American: Robert Mills, Architect and Engineer.* New York, Oxford University Press, 1994.

Scott, Pamela. *Temple of Liberty: Building the Capitol for a New Nation.* New York, Oxford University Press, 1995.

Scott, Pamela, and Antoinette J. Lee. *Buildings of the District of Columbia.* New York, Oxford University Press, 1993.

The Washington Post

The story of the *Washington Post* is really the story of three family members and one outsider who, over a period of four decades, took a somnolent and bankrupt newspaper in the capital of the United States and turned it into an icon of good journalism. The four people are Eugene Meyer, his son-in-law, Philip Graham, Meyer's daughter and Graham's wife, Katharine, and the man Katharine hired to be the executive editor, Ben Bradlee. It is also the tale of two Pulitzer Prizes, the yin and yang of the *Post*'s rise to fame.

The *Washington Post,* born in 1877, was undistinguished as a journalistic organ for a good part of its first century of life. Eugene Meyer bought the bankrupt paper in 1933 for $825,000 at an auction, a time when there were four other more substantial dailies in Washington and the premier paper was the *Star.* In fact, the *Post*'s early history under Meyer does not suggest that anything but disaster was in the cards because the paper continued to lose money, upwards of a million dollars a year. But Meyer, who was independently wealthy, stuck with the paper through thick and thin, saying: "In the pursuit of truth, the newspaper shall be prepared to make sacrifices of its material fortunes, if such course be necessary for the public good." His daughter one day would show the same resolve for the good of truth and to the paper's benefit.

The daughter, however, did not start out to become a newspaper publisher. When Katharine Meyer graduated from the University of Chicago in 1938, she went to work as a reporter for the San Francisco *Examiner.* But within a year, her father ordered her home to work at the *Post,* although not with the intention that she would be groomed as his successor. She eventually married Philip Graham, who became publisher in 1947; he was 31 and Katharine was 29. Katharine immediately took on the role of dutiful wife.

Her husband, in the meantime, following in his father-in-law's footsteps, got very involved in politics, and became something of a king maker, which creates complications for reporters who are trying to cover all sides of a story, not just the boss's side. Shortly after Graham took over, a young reporter named Ben Bradlee resigned

From left: Dustin Hoffman, Carl Bernstein and Bob Woodward of the *Washington Post*, and Robert Redford.

from the *Post* and joined the Washington bureau of *Newsweek.* The *Post* continued to prosper, and Meyer bought out and shut down another daily in Washington, reducing the number of dailies to three. In 1961, the *Post* purchased *Newsweek.*

Two years later, Philip Graham killed himself—he was a manic depressive—and Katharine Graham was thrust into the role of publisher of her late father's newspaper. She was a quick study. Realizing she needed to put her own team in place, she hired Bradlee and put him on the fast track to become executive editor. The *Post* was on its way.

The *Post* lived in the shadow of *The New York Times,* which had a much longer tradition of journalistic greatness. The *Times,* a paper that covered the federal government thoroughly, was a direct competitor for the *Post,* and it showed that one day in 1971 when it started to publish a series of stories about a top secret report that became popularly known as ''The Pentagon Papers,'' in effect, scooping the *Post* in it own backyard. The *Post* rose to the occasion, got its own copy of the papers, and published parts unavailable to the *Times,* thereby regaining its dignity, and also showing a measure of journalistic skill not seen before. When the federal government, through the courts, enjoined both papers from publishing, the papers united to fight in the Supreme Court for the right to publish and to maintain a sacred constitutional principle that the government does not have the right to censor. The newspapers won.

The *Post* reached national stature on its own a year later when it began almost exclusive coverage of a break-in at Democratic National Committee in a building called ''The Watergate.'' Essentially, it was a local cops beat story that took on added importance when the *Post* discovered that some of the Watergate burglars had worked for CREEP—the Committee to Re-Elect the President. Not only was it a great story, but the *Post*'s methodical unraveling of the machinations

of President Nixon's henchmen set high standards for reporting. Two young reporters, Bob Woodward and Carl Bernstein, sometimes aided by an unidentified source in the executive branch who became known as ''Deep Throat,'' dug through records and interviewed hundreds of people to produce a series of stories that helped lead to Richard Nixon's resignation as president and to the *Post*'s winning a Pulitzer Prize. The *Post* endured tremendous pressure to back off the story (its material fortunes were threatened), but Katharine Graham stood by her embattled newsroom and was eventually vindicated.

It has become part of the lore that Woodward and Bernstein brought down a president, but that overlooks all that was going on around President Nixon at the time. For example, one Watergate burglar, threatened by a judge with a long jail sentence, in effect, turned state's evidence on his friends. Then there was a Senate committee investigating what went on, and eventually, the House Judiciary Committee approved articles of impeachment. There was also the revelation that Nixon had taped many of his Oval Office conversations, and when the Supreme Court ruled that Nixon had to yield the tapes, he resigned. The *Post* did not single-handedly bring down the president, but if it had ignored the break-in story, the other facilitators might not have assumed their important roles.

As happens with so many on the way up, the *Post* became a victim of is own hubris when it published in 1981 a story about an 8-year-old boy named Jimmy, who supposedly used heroin. It was a dramatic story, written by a young reporter named Janet Cooke and published on the front page. The story created a controversy not because the *Post* had published it, but because it had not tried to help the boy; there was also churning inside the *Post* because the story had been published on the word of the reporter—no one asked for her sources and there was none of the double-checking that had made the Watergate reporting an exemplary effort. It was only after the reporter won a Pulitzer Prize that other journalists started to check her credentials and discovered that she had lied about her education and her degrees. And in her story, ''Jimmy'' was a fictional character, not a real person. The *Post* returned the Pulitzer, and Cooke resigned.

The *Post,* however, has continued to be a great newspaper. It made its mark with Watergate and stubbed its toe with Janet Cooke, but its owners and editors knew which way they wanted the paper to go and kept it on that track. Ironically, none of the newspapers that circulated in Washington when Eugene Meyer purchased the bankrupt *Post* survived beyond 1981. The *Post* had proved itself.

—R. Thomas Berner

FURTHER READING:

Bray, Howard. *The Pillars of the Post: The Making of a News Empire in Washington.* New York, W.W. Norton, 1980.

Graham, Katharine. *Personal History.* New York, Alfred A. Knopf, 1997.

Kelly, Tom. *The Imperial Post: The Meyers, the Grahams and the Paper That Rules Washington.* New York, William Morrow, 1983.

Roberts, Chalmers M. *The Washington Post: The First 100 Years.* Boston, Houghton Mifflin, 1977.

Ungar, Sanford J. *The Papers and the Papers.* New York, E.P. Dutton, 1972.

Watergate

On the evening of June 16, 1972, a security guard at the Watergate Hotel in Washington, D.C., discovered a piece of tape on the lock of the door that led to the National Democratic Headquarters and set off a chain of events that would, ultimately, bring down the presidency of Richard Milhous Nixon. Afterwards, Americans would wonder why Nixon and the Republican party risked so much on such a minor event when Nixon was leading in the election polls, and the Democratic party was in disarray. Indeed, Nixon would go on to win the presidency by a landslide, with 520 electoral votes. Only 270 electoral votes are needed to win the presidency.

The break-in at the Watergate was only part of a larger campaign designed by Nixon supporters to rattle Democratic candidates and tarnish the reputation of the whole party. This campaign included harassment of Democratic candidates, negative campaign ads, two separate break-ins at the National Democratic Headquarters, and an additional break-in at Daniel Ellsberg's psychiatrist's office. Ellsberg was the individual who offered up the ''Pentagon Papers'' for public consumption, detailing the strategy—or lack of it—for the United States' position in Vietnam.

Theodore H. White, chronicler of presidents from Dwight Eisenhower to Ronald Reagan, points out in *Breach of Faith* that the Watergate break-in was riddled with mistakes. G. Gordon Liddy, advisor to Richard Nixon, had been given $83,000 from Nixon's Committee to Re-Elect the President (CREEP) to provide the necessary equipment. When the tape was placed over the lock, it was placed

Richard Nixon leaving the White House after resigning the presidency following the Watergate scandal.

horizontally rather than vertically, which made it more noticeable. The tape had been spotted earlier in the day and removed by a security guard. It was replaced in the same position. Since only outside personnel were used for the break-in, they were easy to spot as not belonging in the Watergate. The electronic surveillance equipment purchased by Liddy was inferior and had no cut-off between those conducting the actual break-in and those listening in another hotel across the street. When the break-in was discovered, the police were led to Howard Hunt and Liddy in a hotel across the street. Furthermore, all participants had retained their own identification papers.

Instead of being honest with the American public and taking his advisors to task, Richard Nixon immediately became embroiled in a cover-up that would slowly unravel over the next two years—leading to Nixon's resignation in August 1974. As the facts surrounding the break-in were made known, it was revealed that the Nixon presidency had been involved in serious manipulation and abuse of power for years. It seemed that millions of dollars coming from Nixon supporters had been used to pay hush money in an ill-advised attempt to hide the truth from Congress and the American people. Richard Nixon, it was discovered, truly lived up to his nickname of ''Tricky Dick.''

During the investigation, the names of Richard Nixon's advisors would become as well known to the American people as those of Hollywood celebrities or sports heroes. Chief among these new celebrities were close friends of the President: John Ehrlichman and Bob Haldeman. Ehrlichman served as the President and Chief of the Domestic Council while Haldeman acted as Chief of Staff. Both would be fired in a desperate attempt to save the presidency. Another major player was John Dean, the young and ambitious Counsel to the President. John Mitchell, the Attorney General, and his wife Martha provided color for the developing story. Rosemary Woods, the president's personal secretary, stood loyally by as investigators kept demanding answers to two questions: "What did the president know?" and "When did he know it?" The answers to the two questions provided the crux of the investigation. If it had been proved that Nixon was the victim of over-enthusiastic supporters rather than a chief player in the entire scenario, his presidency would have survived. When Nixon learned of the break-in was integral to understanding his part, if any, in the subsequent cover-up.

An investigation revealed that Nixon knew about the break-in from the beginning and that he was involved in the cover-up as it progressed. When the Nixon presidency was over, James David Barber, political scientist and author of *The Presidential Character,* detailed its crimes: "Making secret war; Developing secret agreements to sell weapons to enemy nations; Supporting terroristic governments; Helping to overthrow progressive governments; Receiving bribes; Selling high political offices; Recruiting secret White House police force; Impounding sums of money appropriated by Congress; Subverting the electoral, judicial, legal, tax, and free speech systems; and Lying to just about everyone."

In the early days of the Watergate investigation, most forms of media reported the break-in as a minor story with little national significance. However, two aggressive young reporters who worked for *The Washington Post* began to dig deeper into the background surrounding the actual crime. Aided by an informant, who would be identified only as "Deep Throat," Carl Bernstein and Bob Woodward uncovered one of the major stories of the twentieth century and became instrumental in forcing the first presidential resignation in American history.

As Congress began to hold congressional hearings, Alexander Butterfield, a Nixon presidential aide, revealed that a complex taping system was in place, including in the Oval Office, Camp David, the Cabinet rooms, and Nixon's hideaway office. Nixon's distrust of others would prove to be his own undoing. He fought to maintain control over the tapes and went so far as to fire a number of White House officials in what became known as the "Saturday Night Massacre." The Supreme Court did not accept Nixon's argument that the tapes contained only private conversations between the president and his advisors and, as such, were protected by executive privilege. From the time in 1974 that the Court in *U.S. v. Nixon* ordered the president to release the tapes, it was widely accepted that Nixon had lost the presidency.

The tapes released in the 1970s contained 18 minutes of silence that have never been explained. In 1996 the lawsuit of historian Stanley I. Kutler and the advocacy group Public Citizen resulted in the release of over 200 additional hours of tape. In *Abuse of Power: The New Nixon Tapes,* Kutler writes that the new information reveals that Nixon was intimately involved both before and after Watergate in abuses of power. A taped conversation on June 23, 1972, proved that Nixon and Haldeman talked about using the CIA to thwart the FBI investigation into the cover-up. When the *New York Times* published the "Pentagon Papers," Nixon told his advisors: "We're up against an enemy conspiracy. They're using any means. We're going to use any means." This conversation goes a long way in illustrating

Nixon's paranoia and his adversarial relationship with the American citizenry. It also points out his belief in his own invincibility.

In mid-1974, after Nixon had been named an unindicted co-conspirator in the Watergate affair, the House of Representatives approved the following articles of impeachment: Article I: Obstruction of justice; Article II: Abuse of power; and Article III: Defiance of committee subpoena. These charges arose from months of listening to those involved in the Nixon presidency and the Watergate cover-up explain the machinations of the Nixon administration. In order to save themselves from serving time in prison, most Nixon cohorts were willing to implicate higher-ups. Ultimately, Howard Hunt, G. Gordon Liddy, James McCord, and four Cuban flunkies were convicted and served time in jail.

Until the final days of his presidency, Richard Nixon insisted that he would survive. When he recognized that it was over and that he had lost, he went into seclusion. Reportedly, Alexander Haig, his Chief of Staff, oversaw the dismantling of the presidency. On August 8, 1974, wearing a blue suit with a blue tie and a flag pin in his lapel, Richard Nixon announced to the world that he no longer had a political base strong enough to support his remaining time in office and resigned the presidency. The following day, Vice President Gerald Ford was sworn in as president of the United States.

Although it was a bitter and disillusioning time for the American people, Watergate proved that democracy continues to work—and that not even the president is above the law and the United States Constitution.

—Elizabeth Purdy

FURTHER READING:

Barber, James David. *The Presidential Character: Predicting Performance in the White House.* Englewood Cliffs, New Jersey, Prentice Hall, 1992.

Bernstein, Carl, and Bob Woodward. *All the President's Men.* New York, Touchstone Books, 1994.

Fremon, David K. *The Watergate Scandal in American History.* Springfield, New Jersey, Enslow Publishers, 1998.

Genovese, Michael A. *The Watergate Crisis.* Westport, Connecticut, Greenwood Press, 1999.

Kutler, Stanley I., editor. *Abuse of Power: The New Nixon Tapes.* New York, The Free Press, 1997.

Lukas, J. Anthony. *Nightmare: The Underside of the Nixon Years.* New York, Viking, 1976.

Schlesinger, Arthur M., Jr. *The Imperial Presidency.* New York, Popular Library, 1974.

Schudson, Michael. *Watergate in American Memory: How We Remember, Forget, and Reconstruct the Past.* New York, BasicBooks, 1992.

White, Theodore H. *Breach of Faith: The Fall of Richard Nixon.* New York, Atheneum Press, 1975.

Waters, Ethel (1900-1977)

Born in turn-of-the-century Chester, Pennsylvania, black singer-actor-entertainer Ethel Waters presided for nearly fifty years as one of

Ethel Waters

America's most celebrated performers. She began her career as a singer in 1917 at the Lincoln Theatre in Baltimore, Maryland. Billed as ''Sweet Mama Stringbean'' during her early years as a ''shimmy dancer'' and robust singer of heart-rending songs, her work traversed stage, movie screen, radio, and television. Her memorable credits include numerous Broadway reviews, the stage and screen versions of *Cabin the Sky* (1943) and *Member of the Wedding* (1952), the 1949 film classic *Pinky,* and the title role in the *Beulah* television series (1950-52).

—Pamala S. Deane

FURTHER READING:

Waters, Ethel, with Charles Samuels, *His Eye Is on the Sparrow: An Autobiography.* New York, Pyramid, 1967.

Knaack, Twila, *Ethel Waters: I Touched a Sparrow.* Waco, Texas, Word Books, 1978.

Young, William C. *Famous Actors and Actresses on the American Stage.* New York, R. R. Bowker, 1975.

Waters, John (1946—)

Director John Waters earned the title ''King of Bad Taste'' in 1972 for *Pink Flamingos,* a raunchy film that makes a laughing matter of most every type of perversion. The film ushered in a new era for popular culture, in which the shocking and bizarre would attract growing audiences and profits, penetrating every medium from mainstream newspapers to day-time television talk shows. Waters refined his obsession with ''good bad taste''—a term he coined—over several decades, creating a new movie genre of the bizarre, according to director David Lynch.

Waters identifies himself as a writer foremost, but he is an example of an entrepreneur who uses many channels effectively. His witty essays have been collected in two volumes, *Shock Value* (1981) and *Crackpot: The Obsessions of John Waters* (1983); collections of his screenplays and photographs also have been published. He has made a handful of cameo appearances in films and television programs, including the voice for a cartoon character in an Emmy-nominated episode of *The Simpsons.* In the 1990s, he mounted an traveling exhibit of movie stills. A charming talk-show guest, Waters is in demand as a speaker at college campuses, film schools, and festivals.

The director's opus may be grouped into two periods. Following *Pink Flamingos,* his movies *Female Trouble* (1975), *Desperate Living* (1977), and *Polyester* (1981) have been described as ''vulgar and cheerful nihilism,'' ''blasphemous,'' ''sophomoric,'' and ''whimsical.'' Foul language and scatological visual and verbal references made these works unappealing to middle America. Critics and audiences either hated his films or loved them, hailing him as an iconoclastic artist. His themes often presage cultural trends by decades. For example, in *Female Trouble,* the crazed heroine believes death in the electric chair for a life of crime is the equivalent of an Academy Award. Water's loopy characterization antedated by nearly 20 years Oliver Stone's controversial treatment of warped lovers who go on a killing rampage to achieve media notoriety in *Natural Born Killers* (1994).

In the 1990s, Waters graduated from cult and midnight-movie houses to suburban multiplexes with such films as *Hairspray* (1988), *Cry-Baby* (1990), *Serial Mom* (1994), and *Pecker* (1998). Waters' second period continues his biting satire of American culture but without reference to such perversions as incest, coprophagy, castration, necrophilia, and the gross visual images of the earlier films. A unifying theme of both periods is his focus on characters who are ''insane but believe they are sane,'' Waters told National Public Radio interviewer Terry Gross in 1998. His films turn normative American values upside-down and champion outsiders.

Raised in an upper middle class family in Baltimore, Waters, like many creative people, knew what he wanted to do early in life. He got his first subscription to *Variety* at age 12 and haunted the seedier movie theaters favoring horror films and B movies, especially admiring Russ Meyers. After he was dismissed from New York University's film school for smoking marijuana, he persuaded his father that financing a series of low-budget films would be cheaper than paying for his education. These early efforts include *Hag in a Black Leather Jacket* (1964); *The Diane Linkletter Story* (1966), a 10-minute exercise in bad taste about the LSD suicide of the daughter of a famous Hollywood entertainer; *Roman Candles* (1966), during which three short features are screened simultaneously on side-by-side screens; *Eat Your Make Up!* (1968), satirizing the modelling industry; *Mondo Trasho* (1969), a spoof of then-popular documentaries of the bizarre and pornographic around the world; and *Multiple Maniacs*

John Waters

(1971), which ends with the heroine being raped by a giant lobster. Most did not make it out of the church halls he rented for hometown showings.

Pink Flamingos brought Waters to the attention of the avant-garde artistic community. Andy Warhol—whose small budget films such as *Sleep* convinced Waters that he, too, could make movies on a shoestring—reportedly advised Federico Fellini to see *Pink Flamingos.* Waters' work has been compared to that of the Italian master. One critic suggested that Waters had created a "Theater of Nausea," comparable to Antonin Artaud's "Theater of Cruelty" and Charles Ludlam's "Theater of the Ridiculous." *New York* magazine hailed *Pink Flamingos* as an American version of the Luis Bunuel/Salvador Dali classic, *Andalusian Dogs. Pink Flamingos* was a commercial as well as an artistic success. Made for $12,000, it earned at least $2 million during the first few years after its release. His next movies were made with incrementally larger budgets and found growing audiences.

In the early films, Waters often took people on the margins of society and transformed them into "glamorous movie stars." He told the *Baltimore Sun* in 1978, "To me all those outrageous-looking people are beautiful. Because to me beauty is looks that you can never forget." It has been his life's work to ridicule the conventions of a society that ostracizes people who do not fit within its narrow

standards of perfection and to exploit the potential of film to bring them the fame and success which, in his eyes, they deserve.

The greatest of his on-screen creations was the metamorphosis of his friend Glenn Milstead into Divine, a 300-pound transvestite who vamped it up in the skin-tight gowns of Hollywood movie queens, with exaggerated make-up—including eyebrows that soared up his half-shaved head—and heavily bleached and teased blond hair. A charismatic performer, Divine took viewers by storm as the matriarch of a family of perverted criminals vying for the title of "Filthiest Family Alive" in *Pink Flamingos.* Mink Stole, a screen persona created for Waters' friend Nancy Stoll, played Divine's rival for the title, Connie Marble. Connie and her husband Raymond (the late David Lochary) kidnapped and impregnated young women, chaining them in the basement of their suburban house of horrors, then sold the babies to lesbian couples. In a scene that may never be topped for grossness, Divine eats dog feces from the pavement to secure the title.

Hairspray, with Divine in a supporting role, marked Waters' transition into shopping mall theaters. The only shocking thing left for him to do, Waters had concluded, was to make a mainstream film. *Hairspray* is a light-hearted musical treatment of a serious issue—integration. The story is based on Baltimore's *Buddy Deane Show,* a teen dance showcase that was driven off the air in 1964 by the NAACP for segregating African-American dancers to one program a month. In *Hairspray,* teenagers defeat their parents' resistance to integration, and everybody dances together in the film's happy ending. The story reflects the director's egalitarian sentiments. He praises Baltimore as the appropriate setting for his films because it is an "unholy mix" of old money and new immigrants, black and white poor, and a dirty industrial Eastern seaport with the Southern charm of the first city south of the Mason-Dixon line. When it comes to night life, Waters told Richard Gorelick, "I want to go somewhere where everyone is mixed—that's my ideal: rich, poor, black, white, gay, and straight, all together."

With the death of the irreplaceable Divine soon after the release of *Hairspray,* Waters' transition to the mainstream was virtually assured. *Cry-Baby,* an edgy *Bye-Bye Birdie* (1963), tells the story of a middle-class girl who longs to "go bad" and her romance with the leader of the "drapes," a rock-n-rolling, motorcycle riding, black-leather jacketed gang of juvenile delinquents. The freedom-loving "drapes" prevail against the repressed and repressive clean-cut clique of upper-middle-class suburban kids. "My movies are very moral," Waters told Pat Aufderheide. "The underdogs always win. The bitter people are punished, and people who are happy with themselves win. They're all about wars between two groups of people, usually involving fashion, which signifies morals. It's part of a lifelong campaign against people telling you what to do with your own business."

Johnny Depp as the title character with a tattooed tear-drop under one eye guaranteed the film's box office success. Waters turned to star power again in his next film, featuring Kathleen Turner as *Serial Mom,* a perfect suburban mother who just happens to be a serial killer. A prolific consumer of newspapers and magazines—he subscribes to over 80—Waters frequently pulls his inspiration from the headlines. *Pecker* pits the innocence of a young blue-collar Baltimore photographer who finds beauty everywhere against the exploitative glamour of the Manhattan art world. It features rising talents Edward Furlong, Lili Taylor, and Christina Ricci.

Waters' success owes much to his abilities as a promoter. Working from the trunk of his car in the early days, he persuaded East Coast theater owners to do midnight showings of *Pink Flamingos,* thus making money during hours when they normally would be closed. Through this stroke of marketing genius, he became an architect of the midnight cult movie showing.

Adapting his writing to yet another medium, Waters created a photography exhibit, ''Director's Cut,'' that toured galleries in the 1990s, using frames isolated from others' films to author original storyboards. This technique illustrates the cultural phenomenon that Europeans call ''bricolage,'' the art of recycling culture to create new works of art. Aufderheide sees the technique in Waters' films, commenting: ''John Waters is the bard of a culture that creates itself out of commercial trash; he's a visionary of sorts, someone who discovers the bizarre in the everyday and the everyday in the bizarre.''

It is the ultimate accolade to Waters' cultural influence that he helped make the unspeakable acceptable, by making people laugh about the strange and sometimes repulsive truths of everyday existence. People who were marginalized as ''freaks'' during the early 1970s now routinely appear as guests on television talk shows. Jokes about flatulence and other bodily functions were taken up in films by such well-known humorists as Carl Reiner and the Monty Python troupe. In an article entitled ''Mr. Bad Taste Goes Respectable,'' *U.S. News & World Report* noted that it was increasingly difficult for Waters to retain his title when comedian Jim Carrey told ''butt jokes'' during a televised presentation of the Academy Awards.

Waters, who still lives in Baltimore and sets all of his movies there, is a local hero because his success brought the city's picturesque locales to the attention of other film crews and made the city a site for East Coast film making. After such Hollywood luminaries as Alan Alda and Al Pacino arrived in town to make movies, the mayor established the city's Film Commission in 1980 to serve as a liaison for movie makers seeking Baltimore locations. During the late 1960s and early 1970s, the group of self-styled ''juvenile delinquents'' and eccentrics that Waters gathered around himself evolved into Dreamland Studio, an ensemble production company. Waters was still working with many of the same people in front of the camera and behind the scenes by the end of the 1990s. Reconciled with his family after years of rebellion, a proud home owner who holds backyard barbecues for the Dreamland survivors, Waters told Aufderheide, ''It's hilarious that in some ways I've become part of the establishment.''

To his credit, Waters has never tried to top the vulgarity of *Pink Flamingos,* instead honing his talent to mock social intolerance, transvalue society's standards, and take every bizarre reality to its extreme. Long before radio ''Shock Jock'' Howard Stern came along, John Waters was simultaneously offending people and making them laugh.

—E. M. I. Sefcovic

FURTHER READING:

Aufderheide, Pat. ''The Domestication of John Waters.'' *American Film.* Vol. 15, No. 7, April, 1990, 32-37.

Geier, Thom. ''Mr. Bad Taste Goes Respectable.'' *U. S. News & World Report.* April 28, 1997, 16.

Gorelick, Richard. ''John Waters' 'Pecker' Is His Gayest Film Ever, Mary.'' *Gay Life* (Baltimore). September 4, 1998, B6-B7.

Hirschey, Geri. ''Waters Breaks.'' *Vanity Fair.* March, 1990, 204-208, 245.

Hunter, Stephen. ''A Good Place to Raise a Movie.'' *Washington Post.* September 27, 1998, G1, G6.

Mandelbaum, Paul. ''Kink Meister.'' *New York Times Magazine.* April 7, 1991, 34-36, 52.

Sefcovic, Enid. ''Smutty Waters Just Keeps Rolling Along.'' *Extra.* April 20, 1975, 6, 10.

Waters, Muddy (1915-1983)

Muddy Waters' affirmation, in the title of his composition ''The Blues Had a Baby and They Called It Rock and Roll,'' is somewhat autobiographical, striking both at home and abroad. For rock 'n' roll, Waters was a mentor whose musical style was widely emulated, directly linking the blues to rock 'n' roll; he was the musical father of post-war Chicago blues.

Born McKinley Morganfield, the vocalist, guitarist, and songwriter played a major role in the evolution of rock 'n' roll, influencing scores of rock and blues musicians such as Mick Jagger, the Beatles, Mike Bloomfield, Paul Butterfield, Bob Dylan, James Cotton, and Johnny Winter. His 1950 composition, ''Rolling Stone,'' inspired the name for Jagger's rock group. In 1949, Waters transformed the ''down-home'' country Mississippi Delta style to an urbanized raw and uncompromising Chicago style blues. His band attracted some of the finest Chicago musicians, many of whom later formed their own bands. Waters' impact on the conventional blues aesthetic, Chicago blues, and rock 'n' roll music is unparalleled.

Muddy Waters

The basis for Waters' Chicago style was centered in the Mississippi Delta. He was born on April 4, 1915 in Rolling Fork, Mississippi. His father was a farmer and part-time musician. When his mother died, Waters moved to Clarksdale to live with his grandmother. His early musical experiences consisted of singing in the church choir and playing blues in juke joints and at suppers, picnics, and parties. When Waters was nine, his father taught him to play the harmonica and the guitar—he otherwise was largely self-taught. He earned the world-famous nickname Muddy Waters by often performing ''in the dirt'' in and around the Delta.

Black patrons' taste for the blues in the juke joints in the Mississippi Delta changed when they moved to Chicago. Likewise, when Waters decided to move to Chicago in 1943, he made changes in his music to appeal to this changing musical taste. The music became louder, with amplified instruments, more forceful rhythms, and the accompaniment now enhanced by five musicians. Before starting his own band, Waters was a sideman with John Lee ''Sonny Boy'' Williamson at the Plantation Club.

It was as a sideman for Sunnyland Slim that Waters got his first commercial recording break. Alan Lomax had initially recorded Waters in 1941 for the Library of Congress's archives on the Stovall plantation in Mississippi. In 1948, at the end of a recording session in the Aristocrat (later Chess) recording studio, some free time was allotted to Waters and he recorded his first single, ''Gypsy Woman.'' The record was successful enough to provide an opportunity for another recording session. Subsequent recordings of ''(I Feel Like) Going Home,'' ''Rollin' Stone,'' ''I Can't Be Satisfied,'' and ''Mannish Boy'' established the archetype for the post-war Chicago blues style.

While various musicians worked for him over the years, Waters in 1953 assembled one of the best-ever Chicago blues bands consisting of harmonica player Little Walter Jacobs, pianist Otis Spann, guitarist Jimmy Rodgers, and drummer Elgin Evans. With various personnel, Waters' band toured the South, the rest of the United States, and eventually Europe. Willie Dixon, a celebrated singer, bassist, and composer in his own right, wrote a number of songs specifically for Waters that were successful, including ''Hoochie Coochie Man'' and ''Same Thing.'' By 1958, Waters had scored 14 hits in the top ten rhythm and blues charts. In the same year, he toured with Otis Spann in the United Kingdom; reviews were mixed because the British audience's perception of the blues was misguided, having been accustomed to the acoustic performances of artists such as Big Bill Broonzy and Sonny Terry and Brownie McGhee.

Waters' vocal approach drew from the congregational song style of the black church. He often moaned (hummed) the ends of phrases. He also made extensive use of a recitative style, bending and sliding upward on syllables with shouts, vocal punches, and occasional use of the upper falsetto register. His guitar style made extensive use of the slide or bottleneck technique, the use of repetitive guitar phrases in response to his vocal line in typical call and response fashion, and an uncompromising rough musical texture.

As soul music gained favor among blacks in the 1960s, there was a decreasing interest in the blues. Waters' popularity among black patrons consequently began to wane. Fortunately, the blues revival was taking place in the United States and United Kingdom, and musicians were emulating American blues. As groups began to acknowledge Waters' influence, renewed attention to his music

occurred. This, along with his performance and recording at the 1960 Newport Jazz Festival, and Johnny Winter serving as producer for several successful collaborations with Waters in the 1970s, fueled a rediscovery of his music by a largely white audience. Waters was at the center of a revival of interest in the blues and the genre's influence on rock.

Waters continued to hit his artistic stride, gaining financial success. His band won the Downbeat Critics Poll for rhythm and blues group in 1968, and a Grammy for Best Ethnic/Traditional recording—*They Call Me Muddy Waters*—in 1971. In an interview, Waters defined the music he played as follows: ''I think it's about tellin' a beautiful story . . . something about the hard times you've had.'' Waters died quietly in his sleep at his home in the Chicago suburb of Westmont on April 30, 1983.

—Willie Collins

FURTHER READING:

Rooney, James. *Bossmen: Bill Monroe & Muddy Waters.* New York, Dial Press, 1971.

Watson, Tom (1949—)

Dominating golf in the late 1970s and early 1980s, Tom Watson is one of the greatest golfers of modern times. Watson is second only to Harry Vardon in British Open Championships with five wins. Performances overseas led to his immense popularity with citizens of the British Isles. His two Masters, along with his dramatic victory in the 1982 United States Open at Pebble Beach give him a total of 8 major championship victories. His fiery duels with Jack Nicklaus in the late 1970s made for excellent television, and in this, Watson contributed to the spread and popularity of golf. Watson was named Player of the Year for four consecutive years, and won the Vardon trophy for lowest scoring average three times.

—Jay Parrent

FURTHER READING:

Feinstein, John. *A Good Walk Spoiled.* Boston, Little, Brown and Company, 1995.

Peper, George, editor, with Robin McMillan and James A. Frank. *Golf in America: The First One Hundred Years.* New York, Harry N. Abrams, 1988.

The Wayans Family

Continuing to make strong contributions to the American comedy scene, the Wayans family has been one of the most successful and influential African-American families in show business. Of four actor/producer/comedian brothers, the eldest, Keenen Ivory Wayans, and his groundbreaking television show *In Living Color* got his siblings a start in show business. Damon has appeared on *Saturday Night Live* and a number of other television shows while maintaining a successful stand-up comedy career. Youngest brother Marlon appeared in a number of films in the late 1990s, and starred with brother Shawn on the television sitcom *The Wayans Brothers.* Sister Kim has appeared on *In Living Color* and many other television programs.

—Jay Parrent

FURTHER READING:

Graham, Judith, editor. *Current Biography Yearbook 1995.* New York, H.W. Wilson Co., 1995.

"Siblings Who Are Also Celebrities." *Jet.* January 19, 1998, 56-62.

Wayne, John (1907-1979)

To millions of people around the world, John Wayne has come to be more than just the single most recognizable screen actor in the history of film: John Wayne is America. From the late 1920s to the mid-1970s John Wayne played a cavalcade of heroes on screen. The characters Wayne usually played after his rise to stardom were not always likable. They were practically never what at the millennium has come to be known as "politically correct"; they rarely had any sensitivity for the plight of those who opposed them, and they were often characterized by an overt jingoism. Nevertheless, they uniformly had one thing in common: they were stereotypically American. As a result of this unifying trait, Wayne himself became, in the world's eye, synonymous with the mythical American values of rugged individualism, bravery, loyalty, integrity, and courage. However, even though he played a wide variety of characters, including soldiers, detectives, sailors, and football players, it is for his Western heroes that he is best remembered. As Garry Wills writes in *John Wayne's America,* "the strength of Wayne was that he embodied our deepest myth—that of the frontier."

John Wayne was born Marion Michael Morrison in Winterset, Iowa, on May 26, 1907. His mother, Mary (Molly) Brown Morrison, struggled to keep the family afloat in light of the shiftlessness of Wayne's father, Clyde Morrison. After a failed career as a druggist, Clyde made a decision that was ultimately good for Wayne, but very bad for himself: in 1913 he decided to migrate to California to be a farmer. In 1914 his wife and two sons joined him. In addition to his having had no previous experience as a farmer, Clyde made the misbegotten choice of Lancaster, which sits in the Antelope Valley, as his place of residence. The land's aridity, in addition to his inexperience, virtually assured Clyde's failure. It was here that most Wayne historians believe he first developed his ironic lifelong dislike of horses, which appears to have stemmed from his having to ride one daily from his father's farm to the school in Lancaster.

After Clyde's inevitable failure as a farmer, he once again began working in a pharmacy, this time in the Los Angeles suburb of Glendale, where the family moved in 1916. It was here that Wayne first began to blossom. His family life was relatively unstable—he lived in four different homes in his nine years in Glendale and his parents habitually fought, which resulted in their divorcing shortly after Wayne finished high school. Nevertheless, by most accounts Wayne enjoyed his time in Glendale, especially his four years (1921-1925) at Glendale High, where he was immensely popular with his peers. Wayne joined a number of social groups and was class vice president his sophomore and junior years, and class president his senior year. In addition, he wrote for the school paper, participated as an actor and stage hand in school productions, served on many social committees, and was a star guard on the football team. His football ability, in combination with his high grades, earned him a scholarship to play football at University of Southern California (USC) under legendary coach Howard Jones. In the fall of 1925, full of high hopes and promise, Wayne left Glendale for good, ostensibly headed towards a career as a football hero and then, after law school, a successful lawyer.

When Wayne first arrived at USC, things went well for him. To augment his scholarship, he worked in the fraternities for extra money. He loved fraternity life and pledged Sigma Chi. He earned his letter on the freshman team and was poised to join the varsity squad at the start of his sophomore year. It is at this point that things began to go awry. Wayne's size, six feet four inches, made him a formidable and intimidating high school football player. However, in the college game, sheer size and strength are not enough to secure a position on the team. Just as important is speed, of which Wayne possessed none. After his sophomore year of college Wayne lost his scholarship, thus ending his days at USC. In later years Wayne would claim it was injury that cut short a promising career. With his scholarship lost, Wayne began working at Fox studios in 1927. Although he occasionally appeared as an extra when needed and even had speaking roles in John Ford's *Salute* (1929) and *Men without Women* (1930), his main responsibilities consisted of using his enormous strength to move props and equipment from set to set. However, in 1929 Wayne was spotted doing manual labor by Raoul Walsh, who didn't notice a lack of speed so much as he did a grace and fluidity of motion. Walsh immediately decided to make Wayne a star; from these inauspicious circumstances began the most culturally influential career in screen acting history.

Walsh's first, and perhaps most important, suggestion to Wayne was that he change his name. With that suggestion, Marion Morrison became John "Duke" Wayne. Although Ford is generally credited with "discovering" John Wayne, he did not, nor was he initially responsible for Wayne's becoming a major star. Wayne did not become larger than life all at once, but cumulatively, after a long series of fits and starts. And more important perhaps than even *Stagecoach* (1939) was his long apprenticeship as a leading man in 1930s "B" Westerns, which began with his appearance in Walsh's epic *The Big Trail* in 1930. For *The Big Trail* Wayne underwent a Hollywood makeover that would pervade his on-screen persona for the remainder of his life. He was taught to communicate with Indians via hand signals, wear the garb of a cowboy, and, perhaps most importantly, to properly ride a horse; Walsh transformed Wayne into a Western hero. In the early 1990s the Museum of Modern Art restored *The Big Trail* to its original form, which resulted in contemporary critics raising it to its rightful place in the pantheon of Hollywood's Western classics. However, at the time of its release *The*

John Wayne on horseback in a scene from the film *The Searchers*.

Big Trail was a financial failure. This was disastrous for Fox Studios, which had gambled its survival on the film's anticipated box-office success. Fox went into receivership and Wayne was denied the studio buildup he otherwise would have received. Instead of becoming a major star, Wayne was forced to scramble to find work at seven different studios over the next eight years. Nevertheless, the film convinced Hollywood that Wayne had potential as a Western hero.

From 1930 to 1939 Wayne appeared as the hero in some 80 films, the vast majority of which were Westerns. Although he was

languishing financially, Wayne was nevertheless honing his craft, perfecting his famous walk, his economy of speech and movement, and learning, in his own words, to re-act rather than act—''How many times do I gotta tell you, I don't act at all, I *re*-act.'' Also important during this time was his relationship with Yakima Canutt, the famous Hollywood stunt man who profoundly influenced Wayne's career. Canutt was not only the toughest man on whatever set he happened to be working, he was also the most professional. Both traits rubbed off on Wayne. Many critics have poked fun at Wayne's sometimes stiff on-screen persona, especially during his later years when his work often seemed to unintentionally border on self-parody, but the fact of the matter is that under Canutt's influence in the 1930s Wayne became a consummate student of film, which he remained until the end of his life. Despite his off-screen ribaldry, on the set Wayne was always sober, prepared, intense, and by most accounts a generous actor. That Wayne survived the Depression as an actor is itself no small accomplishment, but he was nevertheless still a minor figure in the landscape of Hollywood cinema. And then came 1939 and John Ford's *Stagecoach,* the film that would begin to change John Wayne's career.

Although John Wayne was a firmly established ''B'' Western Movie star in 1939, literally hundreds of actors were better known than he. But *Stagecoach* changed all that. Walter Wanger, the film's producer, urged Ford to cast Gary Cooper and Marlene Dietrich as the Ringo Kid and Dallas, but according to Tag Gallagher, Ford, didn't want established stars and instead convinced Wanger that John Wayne and Claire Trevor were right for the parts. He did so because the casting of Cooper and Dietrich would have meant that audiences would automatically have brought preconceived notions to the film. They were not only stars, but ''personalities'' as well (especially Dietrich). In casting relative unknowns Ford was able to ensure that audiences would be enthralled with the story and not the visual presence of big stars. For Wayne it was the film that began his climb towards cultural immortality. However, even though *Stagecoach*'s success helped him in Hollywood, Wayne was still not quite the larger than life figure that he has since become. The final piece of that puzzle would not come until the release of Howard Hawks's *Red River* in 1948.

Howard Hawks saw in Wayne a man capable of better acting than had previously been required of him and cast him as Tom Dunson, a hard driving authoritarian cattleman who was an older, darker, and much less sympathetic character than Wayne had previously played. Wayne's performance was brilliant and other directors—the most important of whom was John Ford—took note. Once it was discovered that Wayne not only looked the part of a hero, but that he was a good actor as well, his career skyrocketed; John Wayne became a major Hollywood star at the age of forty. From this point on Wayne predominantly played the kinds of roles for which he is best remembered, what Garry Wills call ''the authority figure, the guide for younger men, the melancholy person weighed down with responsibility.'' Perhaps the blueprint for the iconic Wayne character is his Sergeant Stryker from *The Sands of Iwo Jima* (1949), who to this day is still an enduring symbol for right-wing America. Stryker's cry of ''Lock and Load'' has been used as a battle cry by many, including Oliver North, Pat Buchanan, and, more ironically, by Sergeant Barnes, the villain of Oliver Stone's anti-war film *Platoon* (1986).

John Wayne's on-screen persona became perhaps the only one in movie history that is hated or revered because of its perceived politics. A lot of people love John Wayne simply because they love his movies, but seemingly just as many either like or dislike his films on the basis of the right-wing politics with which they have become inextricably associated. Clearly, not all of Wayne's characters fit the right-wing stereotype with which they have been identified. However, beginning in the 1950s Wayne himself became increasingly political, which in turn affected the way people thought of his movies. Just as his on-screen persona came to be seen as representing American values, so too did he publicly begin to project the image of a super patriotic ultra-American defender of the Old Guard. During the height of the McCarthy era he helped form the Motion Picture

Alliance for the Preservation of American Ideals, over which he eventually presided as president. That he had this public persona apparently never struck Wayne as ironic, even though in his personal life he was both an active womanizer who married three times and a famously heavy drinker. In 1960 he directed and starred in *The Alamo,* which, despite some fine moments, is generally recognized as a mess. However, in the story of the siege of the Alamo, Wayne thought he saw a metaphor for all that was good in American character. Furthermore, Wayne was a fundamentalist hawk who made the Vietnam War a personal crusade, which ultimately resulted in his both starring in and co-directing the excruciatingly propagandistic *The Green Berets* (1969). In the face of the seemingly senseless deaths of so many American youths in Vietnam, this film rubbed many the wrong way, especially in light of the fact that the varied reasons the pro-military Wayne offered for his never having served in the armed forces himself were hazy at best.

Despite his success in other genres, Wayne was still the quintessential Western hero. After *Red River* the primary reason for the perpetuation of Wayne's work in Westerns was a renewed working relationship with John Ford, who saw in Wayne for perhaps the first time an actor capable of exuding the strength, confidence, and staunch independence typical of so many of Ford's heroes. Ford saw Wayne as emblematic of the kind of hero he wanted in his films, and he was also able to get better work out of Wayne than did any other director (with the notable exception of Hawks's *Red River* and Rio Bravo [1959]). But this is perhaps because in films after *Stagecoach* Ford cast Wayne in roles that were tailored to suit Wayne's particular talents. The result was a series of classic films, including the Cavalry Trilogy—*Fort Apache* (1948), *She Wore a Yellow Ribbon* (1949), and *Rio Grande* (1950)—and *The Quiet Man,* an Irish love story that is perhaps both Wayne and Ford's best-loved film. In Ford's later films, he cannily chipped away at the veneer of Wayne's Western hero image. In films such as *The Searchers* (1956) and *The Man Who Shot Liberty Valance* (1962), Ford played on Wayne's cinematic iconography and increasing chronological age to recreate him as a far more complex, embittered figure than he was in Ford's earlier work.

After his work as Tom Doniphon in Ford's last masterpiece, *The Man Who Shot Liberty Valance,* Wayne starred in films that capitalized on his iconic stature as the quintessential Western hero. He repeatedly played individualistic tough guys with a strong personal code of morality. Although films like *The Sons of Katy Elder* (1965), *Chisum* (1970), and *Big Jake* (1971) lacked the artistry of his earlier work with Ford and Hawks, they were nevertheless successful at the box-office. In 1969 Hollywood finally awarded Wayne a long overdue Oscar, which he received for his performance as Rooster Cogburn, *True Grit*'s hard drinking, eye-patch wearing, Western marshal. Off-screen, Wayne had survived cancer in 1963, at which time he had a lung removed. Wayne said he had ''Licked the Big C,'' but such was ultimately not the case.

In 1976 Wayne starred in *The Shootist,* the last of some 250 films and one which had haunting parallels with Wayne's real-life situation. In it Wayne plays J. B. Brooks, a reformed killer dying of cancer who is trying to live out his final days in peace. The film was not the celebratory cash cow that so much of his later work had been. Instead, it is a much more accurate depiction of the death of the West. It also contained an eerily prescient emotional resonance in its reflection of Wayne's off-screen battle with cancer. After its completion, Wayne underwent open-heart surgery in 1978. He then had his stomach removed in 1979. After a courageous battle, Wayne's cancer finally got the better of him. John Wayne died in Los Angeles on June 11, 1979. During his lifetime Wayne was Hollywood's biggest star, making the top ten in distributors' lists of stars with commercial appeal in all but one year from 1949 to 1974. Remarkably, death hasn't dimmed his stardom. In 1993 pollsters asked Americans "Who is your favorite star?" John Wayne came in second to Clint Eastwood, the same place he earned one year later when the poll was conducted again. In 1995, Wayne finished first. Even in death Wayne's cultural presence seems only to become more pervasive, continuing to flourish even in the late 1990s, an era in which most movie stars' time on top seems to be more accurately measured in minutes than in years. Why does Wayne's popularity continue to grow? Perhaps Joan Didion said it best when she wrote that John Wayne "determined forever the shape of certain of our dreams."

Early on in *Stagecoach* there is a moment in which the stage encounters the Ringo Kid (John Wayne), standing on the roadside, looking magnificent with his saddle slung over his left shoulder, and his rifle, which he spins with graceful aplomb, in his right hand. As contemporary viewers we can't help but think of Wayne, regardless of the particular character he is playing, as "The Duke." As historian Anne Butler writes, "more than any other medium, film is responsible for the image of the West as a place locked in the nineteenth century and defined by stark encounters between whites and Indians, law and disorder. Although social trends have altered the content of Western films, the strong, silent man of action—epitomized by John Wayne—remains the central figure." John Wayne has come to stand for a particular kind of American, one who takes no guff and fights for what he knows is right, which often appears to be what is best for America as well, for no other reason than we cannot imagine John Wayne, who in his personal life was far from an angel, as leading us down the wrong path. For better or worse, the perception of John Wayne as the defining human symbol of America has become firmly ensconced in the collective global psyche.

—Robert C. Sickels

FURTHER READING:

Butler, Anne M. "Selling the Popular Myth." *The Oxford History of the American West.* Edited by Clyde A. Milner, Carol A. O'Connor, and Martha A. Sandweiss. New York, Oxford University Press, 1994, 771-801.

Cameron, Ian, and Douglas Pye, eds. *The Book of Westerns.* New York, Continuum, 1996.

Davis, Ronald L. *Duke: The Life and Image of John Wayne.* Norman, University of Oklahoma Press, 1998.

Didion, Joan. "John Wayne, A Love Song." *Slouching Towards Bethlehem.* New York, Farar, Straus & Giroux, 1968.

Levy, Emanuel. *John Wayne: Prophet of the American Way of Life.* New Jersey, Scarecrow Press, 1988.

Riggin, Judith M. *John Wayne: A Bio-Bibliography.* New York, Greenwood Press, 1992.

Slotkin, Richard. *Gunfighter Nation: The Myth of the Frontier in Twentieth-Century America.* New York, Macmillan International, 1992.

Wills, Garry. *John Wayne's America: The Politics of Celebrity.* New York, Simon & Schuster, 1997.

Wayne's World

The release of *Wayne's World* in 1992 marked the dawn of a new era of deliberately "dumb" comedies, and insured the production, if not the success, of a slew of other movies based on popular characters from the television show *Saturday Night Live. Wayne's World* was significant not only for its surprising popularity—it grossed over $180 million worldwide—but also because its witty, self-conscious script and deliberately ludicrous jargon set a new standard for comedies aimed at a youth market in the 1990s.

Wayne's World was the first skit to be expanded from *Saturday Night Live* into a full-length feature since the very successful cult film *Blues Brothers* was released in 1980, and became something of a cult film itself. Like *Blues Brothers,* the chemistry in *Wayne's World* lay in the rapport between two characters, Wayne Campbell and Garth Algar, played by *Saturday Night Live* alumni Mike Myers and Dana Carvey. Myers developed the original characters, and shared writing credits with Bonnie Turner for the final movie script, with *Saturday Night Live* producer Lorne Michaels retaining his duties for the film. A less likely member of the production team was director Penelope Spheeris who, although well-respected, had built her reputation via a rather different take on youth culture with underground hits such as the dark *Suburbia* (1983) and *The Decline of Western Civilization Part II: The Metal Years* (1988), a documentary on the rise of heavy metal bands in the early 1980s.

Beyond the good-natured simplicity of its plot, *Wayne's World* influenced the marketing strategies of future comedies. The promotional team took the unprecedented step of pouring the majority of their relatively small budget into buying advertising time on the youth-oriented cable music channel, MTV, including sponsorship of an hour-long special on the film, and the bet paid off with huge box-office sales to the targeted youth audience. Cannily, the films had recognized that teenagers in the 1990s were increasingly cynical about exactly such marketing, and the plot of the film depicted a naive Wayne and Garth tempted by an unscrupulous television producer to include key products in their popular public access TV show. In a memorable scene, Wayne and Garth balk at the suggestion that they "sell out"; standing in front of a loaded buffet table, the producer (played by Rob Lowe) tells them they have no choice. With a grin that lets audiences in on the spoof, Wayne responds by picking up a Pepsi and replying that, in fact, he does have a choice—and it is "the choice of a New Generation," Pepsi's current tag-line. Similar overt references to other products are found throughout the movie, including spoofs on the campaigns for Doritos and Grey Poupon mustard.

In an ironic gesture befitting the movie, *Wayne's World* spun off a galaxy of commercial tie-ins, including a VCR board game, a Nintendo game, a book (*Wayne's World: Extreme Close Up*) co-written by Myers and his then-girlfriend, actress Robin Ruzan, as well as the usual coffee mugs, t-shirts, and action figures. Perhaps the most unusual tie-in was a planned *Wayne's World*-themed amusement park, to be opened in April of 1994 at Paramount King's Dominion in Virginia, where patrons could ride "The Hurler" rollercoaster and pose next to Garth's "Mirthmobile," a powder blue Pacer. The popularity of *Wayne's World* guaranteed a sequel, *Wayne's World II,* released in 1993. Although both Myers and Carvey returned and the film was a commercial success, it received mediocre reviews. Regardless, the *Wayne's World* movies are widely credited for leading the way for a new wave of comedy features starring television comics,

Mike Myers (left) and Dana Carvey in a scene from the film *Wayne's World*.

such as Jim Carrey's *Ace Ventura: Pet Detective* (1993), Adam Sandler's *Billy Madison* (1994), and Chris Farley's *Tommy Boy* (1995).

—Deborah Broderson

FURTHER READING:

Myers, Mike, and Robin Ruzan. *Wayne's World: Extreme Close Up.* New York, Cader Books, 1992.

The Postmodern Presence: Readings on Postmodernism. Walnut Creek, California, Altamira Press, 1998.

The Weathermen

Their avowed goal to bring about a violent Communist revolution in the United States, perhaps the Weathermen's greatest significance lay in their exploitation by the Nixon administration, which characterized them as typical protestors. These few hundred extremists were used to represent the thousands comprising the antiwar movement, a strategy that allowed President Nixon to offer the

"silent majority" a clear choice: either his plan of gradual disengagement from the war (called "Vietnamization") or the violent revolution supposedly espoused by all of the war's opponents.

The Weathermen arose from the ashes of the Students for a Democratic Society (SDS), which self-destructed at its 1969 convention in a power struggle between the Progressive Labor Coalition, whose adherents were older, socialist, and principally interested in organizing workers to bring about social change, and the Radical Youth Movement, younger, Communist-oriented revolutionaries who saw armed struggle as the only viable political option. RYM's manifesto, distributed at the conference, was titled after a Bob Dylan lyric: "You don't need a weatherman to know which way the wind blows." The crisis came when Bernadine Dohrn, a leader of RYM and one of SDS's three national secretaries, gave a blistering speech which ended with her announcing the expulsion of PL from SDS. Many other members, adherents of neither faction, quit in disgust, leaving behind only the most radicalized element, RYM, which initially retained SDS's name but soon became known as Weatherman, the Weather Underground, or, more commonly, the Weathermen.

The new organization was small, so recruitment was deemed necessary before meaningful political activity could take place. The Weathermen believed that working-class white youths offered the best prospects for new members—these young people were already alienated from the system, it was reasoned, and would thus be eager recruits for the revolution. The effort was not a success. Some Weathermen tried to impress urban street kids with their toughness by challenging them to fight. Brawls were easy to find, recruits less so. Other members invaded high schools in working-class areas, shouting "Jailbreak!" and disrupting classes, but most students were uninterested in the Weathermen's call to rise up against their teachers and the state.

More dramatic action to garner attention and interest seemed called for, and the Weathermen's solution was the Days of Rage, a planned four-day series of demonstrations in Chicago in November 1969. The Weathermen chose Chicago partly in the hope of exacting revenge on the city's police, who had brutalized demonstrators during the 1968 Democratic National Convention, and partly because the leaders of those demonstrations, the so-called Chicago 7, were facing trial on conspiracy charges there. The Weathermen wanted to protest the trial and also take advantage of the presence of the national news media, which would be covering the proceedings. Although the organizers of the Days of Rage predicted the attendance of thousands of protesters, only about seven hundred showed up. Over three days they demonstrated, rampaged through affluent downtown areas, and fought with the police. Many were arrested, with both police and protesters suffering injuries of varying severity. On balance, the Days of Rage were a failure. Chicago's working-class youth did not rally to the Weathermen's cause. Further, other organizations in the antiwar movement denounced the Weathermen's actions as counterproductive and cut off all ties with them. Even the Black Panthers, a militant group known for its defiant confrontations with authority, were critical of the Days of Rage.

The leaders of the Weathermen decided on a change of strategy. The most committed among them would drop out of public view, "go underground" in small groups, and strike out at the state with a coordinated program of bombings. The bombing went on for the next eleven months. The targets chosen were all politically symbolic, and the bombs were usually planted in retaliation for some action that the Weathermen perceived as oppressive: a bomb was set at the home of a New York City judge who was presiding over a trial of some Black Panthers; another went off in a Pentagon lavatory after President Nixon ordered increased bombing of North Vietnam; still another bomb exploded at the office of the New York State Department of Corrections after the brutal suppression of the Attica prison riot. Despite their reputation, as well as their violent-sounding rhetoric, the Weathermen were always careful to call in a bomb threat at least an hour before their bombs were timed to detonate. This allowed the target buildings to be evacuated, so no people were hurt in the blasts. The only fatalities due to the Weathermen's bombs were three of their own members. On March 8, 1970, a townhouse in New York's Greenwich Village blew up. The owner, James Wilkerson, was away; he had allowed his daughter Kathy to stay there, little suspecting that she had joined the Weathermen, or that the place would be used as a bomb factory. Diana Oughten, Ted Gold, and Terry Robbins were killed in the blast.

The deaths of their comrades sobered the surviving Weathermen. They called off the bombing campaign and began to adopt more mainstream methods of persuasion. While still underground, they put out a number of publications espousing their political views and also gave interviews to counterculture publications such as *The Berkeley Tribe*. The Weathermen leaders, including Bernadine Dohrn, even cooperated with director Emile DeAntonio in the making of a documentary called *Underground*.

But by 1975, the Communist victory in Vietnam made the Weathermen passe. Internal squabbling soon put a finish to the organization, and its leaders eventually abandoned their fugitive lifestyle and rejoined the society they had claimed to so despise.

—Justin Gustainis

FURTHER READING:

Collier, Peter, and David Horowitz. *Destructive Generation.* New York, Summit Books, 1990.

Jacobs, Harold, editor. *Weatherman.* New York, Ramparts Press, 1970.

Jacobs, Ron. *The Way the Wind Blew: A History of the Weather Underground.* London and New York, Verso, 1997.

Weaver, Sigourney (1949—)

Sigourney Weaver achieved fame battling bug-like monsters as Ellen Ripley in *Alien* (1979), a role she reprised in *Aliens* (1986), *Alien 3* (1992), and *Alien Resurrection* (1997). In these action films, Weaver impressed audiences and critics by demonstrating that a woman can be a fierce warrior without sacrificing her femininity. In her other work, Weaver has proven herself in genres ranging from comedies such as *Ghostbusters* (1984) and *Working Girl* (1988) to intensely dramatic roles such as *Gorillas in the Mist* (1988) and *Death and the Maiden* (1994).

—Christian L. Pyle

FURTHER READING:

Maguffee, T. D. *Sigourney Weaver.* New York, St. Martin's Press, 1989.

The Weavers

Formed in 1948 by folksinger and banjoist Pete Seeger, the Weavers were considered the quintessential U.S. folk music group of its era, popularizing such classic tunes as "On Top of Old Smokey" and "Goodnight Irene" before falling under the shadow of McCarthyism in the 1950s. When they began performing, the four members of the group had collectively amassed a repertoire exceeding 700 traditional ballads and folk songs; before disbanding in 1963, the Weavers had recorded many of these on popular albums, successfully bringing American folk music to the attention of a mass audience. Though their smooth, polished sound ruffled the feathers of a few folk-music purists, the Weavers have been credited for fueling the careers of the numerous young performers who followed them, prompting the formation of the Newport Folk Festival series in the late 1950s and what would later be known as the American Folk Revival.

Unlike most popular folk-music performers of the mid-twentieth century, which included the Kingston Trio, Peter, Paul & Mary, Bob Dylan, Joan Baez, the Clancy Brothers & Tommy Makem, and Canada's husband-and-wife team Ian & Sylvia, the members of the

The Weavers at their 25ᵗʰ Anniversary Reunion Concert: (from left) Pete Seeger, Lee Hays, Ronnie Gilbert, and Fred Hellerman.

Weavers were significantly older than their fans (Seeger was born in 1919). Rather than their youth, it was their enthusiasm and their folk-music credentials that earned the Weavers their legions of fans. Seeger, in particular, had ties to many folk performers of earlier decades, including the legendary Woody Guthrie, with whom he had performed as part of the Almanac Singers during the early 1940s.

The Weavers—Seeger, Lee Hays, Fred Hellerman, and female vocalist Ronnie Gilbert—debuted at New York City's Village Vanguard folk club in 1948. The Manhattan-born Seeger had abandoned a promising Harvard education to learn to play the long-necked banjo and to hitchhike across the United States for the purpose of collecting the nation's folk songs. His growing expertise later earned him a position as folk archivist for the Library of Congress. By contrast, Hays, with his deep, rumbling voice, had begun his career singing in the rural churches of his native Arkansas. The two younger members of the group, guitarist Hellerman and vocalist Gilbert, had become friends upon recognizing their common interest in folk music while working as summer-camp counselors in New Jersey.

The four musicians met during folk-music hootenannies in Greenwich Village during the mid-1940s, and quickly decided that their combined vocals, backed by Seeger's banjo and recorder and Hellerman's acoustic guitar, made for a good mix. Sponsored by the Socialist-leaning People's Songs, the foursome also received encouragement from folk-music fans wherever they performed. A six-month gig at the Village Vanguard, where such folkies as Burl Ives and Richard Dyer-Bennett had gotten their starts, earned the group $100 a week for its musical mix of everything from work-gang songs from the Old South to Indonesian lullabies.

Eventually the Weavers sparked the interest of Decca Records, which recorded two of the group's favorite songs: ''Goodnight, Irene,'' by bluesman Leadbelly, and the Israeli hora ''Tzena, Tzena.'' Both tunes were timely: Leadbelly had died only a year before, while the nation of Israel had only just come into being. Within a year, both songs made the hit parade, with record sales to the college crowd cresting the million mark. The Weavers moved to Manhattan's Blue Angel nightclub, and from there to Broadway's Strand Theater, where its take-home pay rose to $2,250 a week. The group was soon on its way to national prominence, with offers for bookings from venues in 30 U.S. cities.

The Weavers' meteoric rise to national prominence abruptly ended in 1952, when Seeger's leftist leanings caused the group to fall under the shadow of the ''Red Scare'' that was fueled by Senator

The Chick Webb Band with Ella Fitzgerald on vocals.

Joseph McCarthy and by the House Un-American Activities Committee (HUAC). Included among those entertainers suspected of pro-communist sentiments, the group was blacklisted by theatre owners and radio and television stations. Forced to return to the smaller folk clubs and coffeehouses where they had got their start, the Weavers continued their career in the folk community for another ten years before finally disbanding in 1963. During this period, the Weavers recorded several albums for both Decca and Vanguard, among them *Weavers Almanac, Weavers on Tour* (1958), *Travelling with the Weavers* (1958), and *The Weavers at Carnegie Hall* (1955), the last considered the group's finest album. Many of their songs continue to be available on album reissues.

While Seeger's political convictions may have ultimately ended the career of the Weavers—he was cited for contempt of Congress in 1961, although his conviction was ultimately overturned—he eventually emerged undaunted, and has continued to entertain generations of Americans with songs that have become modern-day folk classics, as well as composing "If I Had a Hammer" and "We Shall Overcome," both of which became anthems of the civil rights movement of the 1960s.

—Pamela L. Shelton

FURTHER READING:

Cantwell, Robert. *When We Were Good: The Folk Revival.* Cambridge, Harvard University Press, 1966.

Lawless, Ray M. *Folksingers and Folksongs in America: A Handbook.* New York, Duell, Sloan & Pearce, 1965.

"Out of the Corner." *Time.* September 25, 1950.

Willens, Doris. *Lonesome Traveller: The Life of Lee Hayes.* New York, Norton, 1988.

Webb, Chick (1902-1939)

With precise ensemble playing rather than standout soloists, drummer Chick Webb's orchestra regularly won big band jazz contests in the mid-1930s. Born in Baltimore, Webb moved to New York City, and in 1926 started a band that included star sax men Benny Carter and Johnny Hodges. Despite his diminutive stature, aggravated by a curved spine, Webb was a virtuoso drummer, anchoring his band's beat with impeccable taste. From 1933, Edgar Sampson arranged such landmark numbers as "Stompin' at the Savoy." When Webb discovered the teenaged Ella Fitzgerald in 1935, her singing led the band to new heights, with hit records for Decca and regular appearances at the Savoy Ballroom in Harlem broadcast nationally. After Webb died of spinal tuberculosis in 1939, Fitzgerald led the band for two years.

—Benjamin Griffith

FURTHER READING:

Atkins, Ronald, ed. *All That Jazz.* New York, Carlton Books, 1996.

Balliett, Whitney. *American Musicians.* New York, Oxford Press, 1986.

Simon, George T. *The Big Bands.* New York, MacMillan, 1974.

Webb, Jack (1920-1982)

Jack Webb's most famous public persona, Sgt. Joe Friday of the Los Angeles Police Department, seemed to be a man with virtually no personality. Yet, paradoxically, this amazingly versatile actor-director-writer-producer-editor-executive was one of the most influential personalities to work in television during the 1950s and 1960s—the heyday of the Big Three networks and the formative period of the Media Age. He did so by speaking directly to the hitherto unexploited American appetite for unemotional professionalism. He was, as Norman Mailer said of the astronaut Neil Armstrong, "apparently in communion with some string in the universe others did not think to play." His not-so-secret weapon was an intense and exclusive focus on surface reality, a focus summed up in the most famous (and endlessly lampooned) line from his television series, *Dragnet*: "Just the facts, ma'am."

Born April 2, 1920, in Santa Monica, California, Jack Webb was educated at Belmont High School and served in the Army Air Force during World War II (1942-1945). After his discharge, he joined the broadcast industry as a radio announcer in San Francisco. By the time he made his debut as a film actor—playing, significantly, a police detective in the superb film noir thriller, *He Walked by Night* (1948)—Webb was well-established lead in the radio dramas *Pat Novak for Hire* (1946) and *Johnny Modero, Pier 23* (1947). In 1949, he created the police series, *Dragnet.* Although continuing to produce the radio version until 1955, he took the series to television in 1951, where it became the most highly rated police drama in broadcast history. He continued to act in other people's motion pictures though 1951, most memorably in Billy Wilder's *Sunset Boulevard* and in Fred Zinneman's *The Men,* both in 1950. After 1951, he only acted in movies he directed: *Dragnet* (1954), *Pete Kelly's Blues* (1955), *The D.I.* (1957), *-30-* (1959), and *The Last Time I Saw Archie* (1961). As a filmmaker, Webb was a genuine auteur, his directing style an extension of his television techniques.

Although Webb's movies rarely enjoyed much critical or popular success, they were nevertheless individually quite enjoyable—especially *Pete Kelly's Blues,* with its meticulous reconstruction of 1920s New Orleans and its shining performance by the jazz singer Peggy Lee; *The D.I.,* about an unyielding Drill Instructor at the Marine Corps's Paris Island; and *-30-,* an exciting melodrama of a big city newspaper. Judging his work by the exaggerated standards of Hollywood, the critic Andrew Sarris said that Webb's "style was too controlled for the little he had to say"—a clever formulation, and accurate enough to be worth repeating, but too dismissive. Nevertheless, Jack Webb's impact on the American cinema was negligible, except that his 1954 film of *Dragnet* was one of the first motion pictures based on a television series.

His impact on television is another matter. New episodes of *Dragnet* were produced from December 16, 1951 to September 6, 1959 and again from January 12, 1967 through September 10, 1970. By the time it finally went into syndication, *Dragnet* had become a significant presence in modern American folklore. Particularly striking were Walter Schumann's title theme; Webb's laconic, understated narration ("This is the city. Los Angeles, California. I work here. I'm a cop."); the epilogue detailing the punishments imposed upon the evening's criminals ("Arthur Schnitzler was tried on fifteen counts of indecent exposure in the Superior Court of Los Angeles County. . . ."); the sweaty, muscular forearms which chiseled the logo "Mark VII" (Webb's production company) into granite at the end of the program; and, of course, the quick, staccato, emotionless dialogue—an effect Webb sought deliberately, and achieved by having his actors read their lines cold, from cue cards. Webb not only starred as Joe Friday, but also produced all the episodes, wrote and directed

Jack Webb

most of them, and provided the voice-over narration. Before each script of *Dragnet* was filmed, it was submitted to the Los Angeles Police Department for approval and possible changes.

Beginning in 1968, Webb created several other series, the most notable being *Adam 12* (1968-1970), about two LAPD officers in a patrol car, and *Emergency!* (1971-1975), which concerned the adventures of a mobile rescue unit. Though he did not appear in any of his other projects, each bore Webb's trademarks: they were about the lives of public service professionals, and the exclusive emphasis was on the characters' professional—not private—lives. Furthermore, the stories were told in Webb's patented low-key, obsessively factual, style—as if he were an engineer and making a television program was a dirty job but somebody had to do it.

Although he would undoubtedly have been horrified at the suggestion, Webb's laconic style was a kind of cool, which is why it worked so well on the "cool" medium of television. He understood instinctively that histrionics and violent spectacle did not go over very well on television and could even be off-putting. What did go over well were close-ups of people talking to each other, and a scrupulous, admiring record of people doing their jobs. His tremendous success was based upon his sure knowledge that, at any given moment in history, the squares outnumber the hipsters by about 500,000 to 1. Joe Friday was an archetypal stiff, and proud of it; his moral code was as simple and clear-cut as his conception of his job as a cop: things were either right or wrong, as an act was either legal or illegal. It should not surprise anyone that Americans found this appealing—that Webb was able to reintroduce *Dragnet* at the height of the chaotic 1960s and to keep it on the air, highly rated, through four complete seasons. Indeed, the people who welcomed *Dragnet* back on television in 1967 were the same people who elected Richard Nixon as president in 1968.

—Gerald Carpenter

FURTHER READING:

Anderson, Christopher. *Hollywood TV.* Austin, University of Texas Press, 1994.

Meyers, Richard. *TV Detectives.* San Diego, Barnes, 1981.

Newcomb, Horace, editor. *Encyclopedia of Television.* Chicago, Fitzroy Dearborn Publishers, 1997.

Reed, Robert M. *The Encyclopedia of Television, Cable, and Video.* New York, Van Nostrand Reinhold, 1992.

Sarris, Andrew. *The American Cinema: Directors and Directions, 1929-1968.* New York, E. P. Dutton, 1968.

Terrace, Vincent. *Encyclopedia of Television: Series, Pilots, and Specials.* New York, New York Zoetrope, 1985-1986.

Varni, Charles A. *Images of Police Work and Mass Media Propaganda: The Case of ''Dragnet.''* Ph.D. dissertation. Pullman, Washington State University, 1974.

Wedding Dress

The wedding dress is a costume or single-purpose article of clothing worn by a bride during the marriage ceremony. From antiquity, weddings have been highly regarded occasions. The clothing worn by the bride for her wedding has usually been distinguished from that of her daily wear. Symbolism may be attached to the dress, such as white for purity, and may be attached to items worn with the dress, such as something blue for luck. The symbolism associated with the wedding dress may have cultural, traditional, or personal significance.

Colonial immigrants kept the marriage traditions of their homelands. Brides in the English Jamestown settlement likely wore the costumes of young country brides of the mid-Elizabethan period. Although records of the first American weddings do not describe clothing, it is known that English brides of this era wore dresses of russet, a woolen fabric of natural wool color or dyed a reddish brown with tree bark. They wore simple, fitted white caps on the head. Dresses and caps made for weddings were usually adorned with fine embroidery.

American wedding dresses evolved into more festive or elaborate versions of the usual dress worn by women of each subsequent era. The dress was considered a best dress to be worn for special occasions after the wedding. The dress was usually new, although laces and trimmings might be old and handed down from a family member. Beginning in the mid-1800s, wearing a mother's wedding dress became an acceptable sentimental option.

As America prospered, brides marked the occasion of their wedding by bedecking themselves in the finest and most becoming dresses of their day. They were influenced by the styles of Europe and news of royal marriages. Although white had been worn for Roman weddings, all colors were used for early American wedding attire. Though other colors were occasionally seen, white settled into vogue as the preferred choice of color after the immensely popular Queen Victoria of England wed in 1840 clad in white satin.

A typical wedding dress.

Since the Victorian era's hooped creations, the wedding dress has known countless variations on the style of the day. While some early dresses displayed a slight trail of fabric behind, the wedding dress with train came into vogue in the mid-1870s, as did the use of the flowing veil.

Elaborate fabrics, embroideries, laces, braids, and trimmings were used whenever possible. The laces Aloncon, Venice, Honitan, and Chantilly were commonplace for wedding trims. The evolution of styles included the tubular skirts of the 1870s, the corset waists of the 1880s, the leg-o-mutton sleeves of the 1890s, the bustles of the early 1900s, the ankle-length Gibson girl silhouette of the 1910s, and the short-skirted flapper look with accompanying long, full veil of the 1920s.

In the 1930s the wedding dress became known as the wedding gown, as the term gown denoted a luxurious dress worn in Depression-era America. Over the years hemlines varied in the daily style of dress, but beginning in the 1930s, the majority of wedding dresses were designed floor length.

The 1940s war years' wedding gowns show an absence of elaborate laces and trims, but an attention to tailoring detail with padded shoulders and belted waistlines. The prosperous 1950s ushered in a new era of extravagant wedding gowns with yards of gathered skirting, laces, sweetheart and off-the-shoulder necklines, and peter pan collars. Since it had become traditional for the groom to present his bride a gift of a single strand of pearls, much emphasis was placed on the neckline design to show off this gift.

During the 1960s, the prominence of traditional styles of wedding dresses decreased in favor of contemporary dress styles. Many brides wore floor length flowered print dresses that were not significantly more elaborate than their usual mode of dress. By the late 1960s and early 1970s, the hippie bride marrying in a meadow gave way to the miniskirted bride repeating vows before a justice of the peace.

As the 1970s progressed, the traditional wedding gowns enjoyed a resurgence. Early baby-boomers found meaning in unpacking, refitting, and wearing their mother's gowns of the 1940s and 1950s. For those not fortunate enough to have a gown from these periods, the bridal apparel industry was ready with fresh designs in polyester fabrics. Elaborate gowns of finer materials were still produced, and by the 1980s it had become customary for at least the dress bodice to be covered in beading and laces.

The 1990s wedding dress and its symbolism was a matter of individual taste. While many wedding dresses resurrected styles of the past, other styles continued evolving, such as the mermaid dress, a creation form-fitted to the knees with a flared skirt. Dresses were designed with a skirted train, a detachable train, or a veil trailing beyond the hem of the dress simulating a train. Examples of wedding dresses with fine construction and beadwork continued to be made and preserved for wear by the next generation of brides. The majority of wedding dresses not designed for repeat wear might have had beading and trims glued to the dress instead of hand-sewn. These dresses were often boxed and kept for sentimental reasons. The practical bride may choose to rent a wedding dress.

The modern wedding dress is steeped in tradition and history. The elaborateness of the design and the association of any cultural significance or traditional symbolism to the dress or to items worn with the dress is the choice of the bride.

—Taylor Shaw

FURTHER READING:

Haines, Frank and Elizabeth. *Early American Brides. A Study of Costume and Tradition, 1594-1820.* Cumberland, Maryland, Hobby House Press, 1982.

Khalje, Susan. *Bridal Couture. Fine Sewing Techniques for Wedding Gowns and Evening Wear.* Iola, Wisconsin, Krause Publications, 1997.

Murphy, Brian. *The World of Weddings, An Illustrated Celebration.* New York, Paddington Press, 1978.

Tasman, Alice Lea Mast. *Wedding Album. Customs and Lore Through the Ages.* New York, Walker and Company, 1982.

Weekend

In contemporary American culture, the weekend generally signifies the end of the traditional work week, or the period from Friday night to Monday morning, a popular time for organized or unorganized leisure activities and for religious observances. Historically, the weekend was synonymous with the Sabbath which, among European cultures, was marked on Sunday by Christians and on Saturday by Jews. To understand the weekend, some background on the origin of the week itself is helpful. Human time was first measured by nature's cycles, seasonal for longer units, and celestial for shorter ones (i.e., the rising and setting of the sun, and the phases of the moon). Today this influence persists in that the names of the days are derived from the ancient astrological seven-day planetary week: ''Monday,'' a corruption of the word ''Moonday,'' which in turn evolved from European derivations of the Latin word for moon, and ''Sunday,'' the day long considered the first of the week until gradually being perceived as the last day of the weekend. The first calendar was devised by the Egyptians, who bequeathed it to ensuing civilizations. Egypt divided the years into three seasons, based on the cycles of the river Nile, and twelve months. The Egyptians' 24-hour days were also grouped into week-like ten-day periods (called ''decades''). The Mesopotamian calendar was similar, but its months were divided by a special day, *shabattu,* perhaps the first manifestation of recurring intervals of time regularly punctuated by a special day devoted to leisure or celebration. The Roman calendar also established special days within its 30 or 31-day months, such as the Kalends, the Nones, and the Ides. The Ides fell on the thirteenth or the fifteenth day of the month, and became part of the English language via Shakespeare's famous warning in *Julius Caesar*: ''Beware the Ides of March.''

In addition to the ancient Jewish Sabbath (and the Christian Sunday that evolved out of it), a later precursor of the modern weekend was the eighteenth-century European custom of Saint Monday, a weekly day of leisure. Saint Monday was gradually replaced by the Saturday holiday, first observed in Europe in the 1870s. In Britain and Ireland, shops often closed at midday on Wednesday, a custom observed in some American small towns until the 1950s. The custom of working half a day on Saturday took hold in the U.S. in the 1920s, with a full two-day ''weekend off'' soon following. During the earlier era of the six-day work week, conflict had frequently arisen between the Jewish Sabbath and the Christian Sunday, especially with the shifts in European immigration patterns in the early 1900s, and the five-day work week offered a convenient solution. In 1926 Henry Ford closed his factories all day on Saturdays, and in 1929 the Amalgamated Clothing Workers of America, composed primarily of Jewish employees, became the first union to propose a five-day week. While initially denounced in some quarters as both bad economics and worse religion, the five-day Monday through Friday workweek soon became standard.

As the structure of the week/weekend cycle solidified over the years, new cultural and capitalistic venues evolved with it. With the concept of personal leisure came a new ''business of leisure,'' boosted by new advertising venues, that soon began to promote leisure and the weekend not only as a pleasurable pastime, but as an integral element of a thriving capitalistic society. The first ''Sunday paper,'' the *London Observer,* appeared in 1791; while a Sunday edition first appeared in Baltimore in 1796, the American Sunday paper did not really catch on until the Civil War era. The prototype U.S. Sunday newspaper was established by Joseph Pulitzer, whose *Sunday World* pioneered leisure-oriented articles geared to every member of the family: book and entertainment reviews, travel essays, women's and children's pages, and color comics and supplements. Prolific department store advertising helped make the *World* a money-making success as well, and voluminous ad inserts remain a major part of most Sunday editions. In addition to Sunday papers, the magazine, a product designed specifically for pleasure, first appeared in Georgian England, where the more substantial and time-consuming novel was also introduced in the 1740s.

The first use of the term ''week-end'' appeared in England in an 1879 issue of the magazine, *Notes and Queries.* British practice also laid the groundwork for most of the public leisure pursuits that would grow into the entertainment industries of today. Among these was commercial theater, with its playhouses for both affluent and general audiences. While most of today's modern theaters perform throughout the week, weekends remain peak box-office periods that sometimes command higher ticket prices, and community theaters often perform only on weekends. Public concerts were given in London as early as 1672, and commercial musical venues developed in tandem with theater. Sports ran parallel in popularity, and hand in hand with betting. Thus, with only a few innovations, public entertainments born in eighteenth-century England flourished into the twentieth century. The music-hall, a popular Saturday night diversion in England, found its American counterpart in the vaudeville circuits that spread across the United States in the late 1800s.

The emergence of the cheap nickelodeon in turn-of-the-century America soon established ''going to the movies'' as the preeminent American pastime—one that soon spread to Europe and beyond. The first storefront nickelodeons appeared in the major metropolitan areas of the East coast and evolved into the movie palaces of the 1920s where patrons could see a feature film, a variety of short subjects, and a spectacular live stage show with an orchestra or some other form of live music. Movies and the weekend developed independently, but were soon reinforcing each other. Filmgoing became a major form of national recreation, and Saturday night soon became a favorite time for an excursion to the movies—Saturday afternoon matinees were generally reserved for the children. ''Going out on the town'' for dancing or partying also became a popular Saturday night ritual that, with ironic connotations, was graphically explored in the popular 1977 film, *Saturday Night Fever,* which also produced one of the bestselling soundtrack albums of the hedonistic disco scene in the 1970s. Even household routines had a particular weekend flavor: in the earlier part of the century, New Englanders traditionally sat down to a supper of baked beans on Saturday night. For others, especially in areas where water supplies were limited, the ''Saturday night bath'' became a familiar routine.

Sunday was long considered a ''day of rest'' in Western Europe and America, after the account of creation in Genesis in which God rested on the seventh day. In Catholic Europe, church law prohibited ''servile work'' on Sunday, unless the work was necessary to the glory of God, as a priest celebrating Mass, or the relief of one's neighbor, as in tending to the sick. In the British Isles, Scotland especially, Sunday was a day of solemnity and restraint in which families were expected to be at church morning and evening, and to engage in edifying pursuits during the day, like Bible reading, hymn singing, or innocent pastimes like music or word games. In some rural areas during the nineteenth century, zealous Sabbath observers tried to pass legislation prohibiting steam trains from operating on Sunday because they brought secularized passengers from the cities to disturb the holiness of the day with holiday frivolities. In some of the American colonies, especially Puritan New England and Pennsylvania, strict ''blue laws'' prohibited engaging in trade, dancing, playing games, or drinking on Sunday, laws that still survive in a number of places. It was not until the early 1970s, for example, that New York City boutiques and department stores were permitted to open on Sunday; many smaller jurisdictions still had old laws on the books that prohibited shopping on the Sabbath, except for small items like essential groceries, newspapers, or toiletries.

School schedules in the industrialized world followed this same Monday-to-Friday regimen. As Eviatar Zerubavel noted: ''Much of the attractiveness of the weekend can be attributed to the suspension of work-related—or, for the young, school-related obligations.'' While clearly not a part of the actual weekend—after all, it is still a day on which one still goes to work or school—Friday is nevertheless considered by many their favorite day of the week, because it promises the anticipation of the weekend, leading to the popular expression, ''T.G.I.F.,'' for ''Thank goodness (or God) it's Friday.''

Transportation innovations also revolutionized weekend possibilities. Prior to the introduction of railroads in the 1830s methods of travel had been essentially unchanged since ancient times. The time, as well as the expense involved, made travel a luxury reserved for the moneyed classes. Cheap rail excursions began around the 1840s in England, and soon achieved mass acceptance, especially among the working classes who for the first time in history could avail themselves of quick and inexpensive travel. In the twentieth century, the automobile and recreational vehicle would do the same thing, but even on a broader scale. Weekend excursions to the seashore, the mountains, or to new leisure and gambling boomtowns like Las Vegas and Atlantic City, soon revolutionized the tourist industry.

Post-World War II affluence brought significant changes to the structure and content of the American weekend. Zerubavel added that ''while the dominant motif of the weekdays is production, that of the weekend is, in a complementary fashion, consumption. Middle-class Protestant youngsters of the late 1940s and early 1950s could (with the family) attend a movie on Friday evening and fall asleep blissfully secure in the knowledge that two full days of freedom and media-supplied diversion lay ahead. Saturday morning might be spent with a radio, where traditional shows such as *No School Today* or *Let's Pretend,* were followed by such futuristic 1950s innovations as *Space Patrol.*''

A movie matinee might be on the agenda after lunch, and if this happened to be at a first-run downtown theater, the afternoon might also be taken up with exploring nearby five-and-dime and department stores, where treasures such as comic books and movie magazines could be had for as little as a dime or fifteen cents. Saturday evening might have found the family again attending a movie, probably at one of the less expensive second-run neighborhood houses, or at one of the popular new ''drive-in'' theaters. Sunday continued with the same ''special occasion'' mood, but with a euphoria now tempered by the bittersweet awareness that this period of freedom was predestined to come to an end that evening. After religious obligations were honored on Sunday morning—observant Jews of course attended synagogue or temple on Friday evening or Saturday morning—many families indulged in a special midday Sunday dinner, either at home or at a restaurant (perhaps a Howard Johnson's with its famous twenty-eight flavors of ice cream). Afternoons might be taken up with a Sunday drive or excursion, to the country or an amusement park, or to nowhere in particular. Radio could also occupy much of the afternoon and evening, and a light evening meal was sometimes enjoyed in the living room around the family radio. From the 1950s, when the concept of the frozen ''TV dinner'' entered the American culinary consciousness, television reserved its key programming for Sunday evenings.

As malls, suburbs, and automobiles became pervasive facts of American life in the 1950s and beyond, the status of the American ''downtown'' began to decline as a focus of weekend activities. The weekly Friday evening excursion on foot to the modest neighborhood grocery store, brief enough to be followed by a trip to the movies, was now replaced with an automobile excursion for a full evening at the shopping center or mall. Eventually movie theaters were added to the mall mix, hastening the decay of ''downtown'' as a space for social interaction. The combination of television and antitrust suits in the 1950s caused movie chains to close their downtown outlets for good, further changing the American experience of the weekend as a time for leisure activity ''downtown.'' Still, by the 1990s, weekend box-office takes for films had escalated to record highs. Likewise, professional sports events have become more important to the American weekend, and January's ''Superbowl Weekend'' has mushroomed into an event of national social and economic significance.

Analyzing the modern concept of the weekend, Witold Rybczynski wrote: ''. . . the weekend has imposed a rigid schedule on our free time. The weekly rush to the cottage is hardly leisurely, nor is the compression of various recreational activities into the two-day break. The freedom to do something has become the obligation to do something.'' He concludes that ''every culture chooses a different structure for its work and leisure, and in doing so makes a profound statement about itself.'' The weekend ''reflects the many unresolved contradictions in modern attitudes towards leisure. We want the freedom to be leisurely, but we want it regularly, every week, like clockwork. There is something mechanical about this oscillation, which creates a sense of obligation that interferes with leisure. Do we work for leisure, or the other way around? Unsure of the answer we have decided to keep the two separate.''

An interesting comment on the American view of weekend escape can be found in one of Walt Disney's Goofy cartoons, *Father's Weekend* (1953). After an exhausting weekend of battling crowded beaches and harrowing amusement parks, coping with screaming, tireless offspring, and fighting massive traffic gridlock at the end of it all, Goofy is finally seen blissfully setting off for work on Monday morning as voiceover narration declares, with obvious irony, that the harried Everyman may now finally relax again and rest up for another strenuous weekend of leisure.

—Ross Care

FURTHER READING:

Cross, Gary. *A Social History of Leisure since 1600.* State College, Pennsylvania, Venture Publishing, 1990.

———. *Time and Money: The Making of Consumer Culture.* London and New York, Routledge, 1993.

Grover, Kathryn, editor. *Hard at Play: Leisure in America, 1840-1940.* Amherst, University of Massachusetts Press, 1992.

Rybczynski, Witold. *Waiting for the Weekend.* New York, Viking, 1991.

Zelinski, Ernie J. *The Joy of Not Working.* Berkeley, California, Ten Speed Press, 1997.

Zerubavel, Eviatar. *The Seven Day Circle—The History and Meaning of the Week.* New York, The Free Press, 1985.

Weird Tales

J. C. Henneberger founded the American pulp magazine to cover the field of ''Poe-Machen Shudders'' in 1923. It followed the success of titles by Rural Publications, which appeared in a variety of genres, notably *College Humour* and *Magazine of Fun*. *Weird Tales* was in publication until 1954 and was most successful during the 1930s under the editorship of Farnsworth Wright. During this period it published fiction by influential fantasy and horror writers, H. P. Lovecraft, Robert Howard, Clark Ashton Smith, C. L. Moore, Edmond Hamilton, Robert Bloch, Manly Wade Wellman, and August Derleth.

Henneberger identified that there were quality writers who were unable to place their stories in the mixed-genre magazines of the early 1920s and presumed that there was an audience for stories that were weird and macabre. He established the character of the magazine through a policy of reprinting "weird" classics, such as Bulwer Lytton's "The Haunted and the Haunters," Edgar Allan Poe's "The Murders in the Rue Morgue," and a later series of Mary Shelley's *Frankenstein*.

Weird Tales did not immediately attract a regular readership. In its first year Henneberger employed Harry Houdini as a writer, which resulted in the column ''Ask Houdini'' and the publication of stories (ghost-written by H. P. Lovecraft) about supposed occurrences in Houdini's life. These adventures further established a fascination with Egypt, magic, and the supernatural. The oriental tales by Frank Owen and Seabury Quinn's long-running psychic detective series ''Jules de Grandin'' even furthered the magazine's popularity. Although it is notable that right from the first issue some of the bizarre events of the horror stories were explained in a rational scientific manner, the magazine achieved notoriety early on in its publishing history as it was allegedly banned from bookstalls in 1924 because it carried C. M. Eddy's ''The Loved Dead'' with its overtones of necrophilia.

After Farnsworth Wright and the Popular Fiction Publishing Co. took over from Henneberger in 1924, the magazine offered stories in the range of weird scientific, horror, sword and sorcery, exotic adventure, and fantasy, and it maintained an audience even during the Great Depression. The magazine was especially congenial for new writers. Robert E. Howard published his first story in *Weird Tales* in 1925 and went on to publish the ''Conan the Barbarian'' series between 1932 and 1936. H. P. Lovecraft first appeared in the readers' letters column, ''The Eyrie,'' commenting on stories from previous issues. He published most of his major works, especially those developing the Cthulhu Mythos, in *Weird Tales*. Other writers who were particularly influenced by Lovecraft also wrote for the magazine. These included Robert Bloch, who would go on to write *Psycho* in 1959; Henry Kuttner, who with his wife C. L. Moore would become prominent fantasy writers in the 1940s; and August Derleth, who, as well as being a writer, became an influential anthologist and founded the publishing company Arkham House.

Some of the fiction published in *Weird Tales* was known for its relatively sophisticated sexual themes. C. L. Moore's first short story, ''Shambleau,'' is a good example. She also published a fantasy series with the heroine ''Jirel of Joiry'' with the magazine. Along with Clark Ashton Smith, Moore contributed to the magazine's fascination with a medieval setting and sword and sorcery theme, as well as its acceptance of interplanetary locations.

The magazine's horror fiction tended to portray science as being out of control and subject to various representations of the mad scientist. It provided a niche for developing science fiction writers such as Edmond Hamilton, who was influential in the development of ''space opera.'' His series ''Interstellar Patrol'' was published in *Weird Tales* from 1928 to 1930.

In the late 1930s the magazine changed its overall style with the deaths of Howard (1936) and Lovecraft (1937), the retirement of Ashton Smith in 1936, and Farnsworth's relinquishment of the editorship in 1939 (he had been struggling with Parkinson's disease since 1921). The editorship was then taken over by Dorothy McIlwriath, an established magazine editor who stayed with *Weird Tales* until the publishing company went bankrupt in September 1954. Her editorial policy focused on supernatural fiction, especially occult detection such as Manly Wade Wellman's ''Judge Pursuivant'' series published between 1938 and 1941. She also featured the work of Ray Bradury and Fritz Leiber, but during this time *Weird Tales* was competing with a larger number of available outlets for fantasy writing. However, the pulp magazine's 31 years in publication and 279 issues were very significant in supporting the careers of many initially underrated popular fiction writers.

—Nickianne Moody

FURTHER READING:

Ashley, M., editor. *A History of the Science Fiction Magazine.* London, NEL, 1974.

Joshi, S. T. *H.P. Lovecraft: A Life.* Rhode Island, Necronomicon Press, 1996.

Weinberg, R. E., editor. *The Weird Tales Story.* West Linn, Oregon, Starmont House, 1977.

Weissmuller, Johnny (1904?-1984)

Although he first achieved fame as a free-style swimmer who won five Olympic gold medals and set 67 world records, Johnny Weissmuller is best known for his film role as Tarzan, King of the Jungle, who had been abandoned in the African wild as an orphaned infant and raised by apes. Weissmuller starred in twelve *Tarzan* films between 1932 and 1948.

The *Tarzan* series, written by Edgar Rice Burroughs, became widely popular from the first book, *Tarzan of the Apes* (1914). More than 25 million copies of Burroughs' books sold worldwide as the public embraced the stories of an English nobleman's son who grew up to be the King of the Jungle. Weissmuller added to the popularity—and added to his own wealth—when his first Tarzan movie, *Tarzan of the Apes,* was released, leading to spinoffs such as Tarzan radio programs and comic strips. The films co-starred Maureen O'Sullivan as Jane and featured a combination of naive love interest with plenty of action, interspersed with the comic relief supplied by Cheetah the chimp.

The facts concerning Weissmuller's birth are the subject of some dispute. Official Olympics sources say he was born in Windber, Pennsylvania, on June 2, 1904, but there is credible evidence that he was born at Freidorf, near Timisoara, Romania, and emigrated with his parents to the United States as a young child. It is believed by biographer David Fury and others that Weissmuller's parents later switched his identity with that of his American-born brother in order to qualify him for the U.S. Olympic team. He attended school in Chicago through the eighth grade. His ability as an athlete led to his being trained in swimming as a teenager by the Illinois Athletic Club in Chicago. In the 1920s Weissmuller participated as a member of several of the club's championship teams in relay and water polo events. He won 26 national championships in individual freestyle swimming in the 1920s in various events, including the 100 meters,

Johnny Weissmuller as Tarzan.

200 meters, 400 meters, and 800 meters, where he demonstrated his speed as well as stamina. At the 1924 Olympic Games in Paris he broke three world records while winning three gold medals in the 100-meter and 400-meter freestyle and in the 800-meter relay. In the Olympic Games in Amsterdam in 1928 he added two more gold medals for the 100-meter freestyle and the 800-meter relay. When he turned professional in 1929, Weissmuller was unchallenged as the world's finest swimmer. His sports fame led to the production of several short films showing his aquatic prowess, bringing him to the attention of MGM, the studio that offered him the Tarzan role.

More than a dozen actors had played the part of Tarzan in silent films as well as talkies, including Buster Crabbe, Glen Morris, Lex Barker, Gordon Scott, and Jock Mahoney, but the public considered them mere pretenders. No one else possessed the athleticism to skim through the alligator-filled rivers doing the Australian Crawl or swing on a vine through the trees yelling his high-pitched, chest-thumping call. Of the twelve *Tarzan* films Weissmuller starred in, the most popular were the ones that included Maureen O'Sullivan as Jane. After making a hit in *Tarzan of the Apes* (1932), the couple continued to win fans in *Tarzan and His Mate* (1934), considered by many to be the best of the series; *Tarzan Escapes* (1936); *Tarzan Finds a Son* (1939); *Tarzan's Secret Treasure* (1941); and *Tarzan's New York Adventure* (1942).

In the late 1940s and 1950s Weissmuller moved over to Columbia Pictures for a series of movies with African settings in which he played Jungle Jim. These films were shot with low budgets as the lesser ends of double features. A British film critic, writing in *The Monthly Film Bulletin* about the film *Jungle Moon Men,* was incensed: "This is a preposterous and in some respects a rather distasteful film, which insults the intelligence of the most tolerant spectator."

Weissmuller was married and divorced five times. His third wife (from 1933 to 1938) was Lupe Velez, a star of silent films who played in "B" movies and in early talkies as a tempestuous character known as "the Mexican Spitfire." After his retirement from his swimming and film careers, Weissmuller returned to Chicago, where he opened a swimming pool company. He moved to Florida in the 1960s, serving as the curator of the Swimming Pool Hall of Fame in Fort Lauderdale. In 1973, he became a "greeter" for Caesar's Palace Hotel in Las Vegas; a few years later he was hospitalized due to a stroke and died in 1984.

—Benjamin Griffith

FURTHER READING:

Behlmer, Rudy. "Johnny Weissmuller: Olympics to Tarzan." *Films in Review.* July/August 1996, 20-33.

Fury, David. *Kings of the Jungle: An Illustrated Reference to Tarzan on Screen and Television.* Jefferson, North Carolina, McFarland and Company, 1994.

Halliwell, Leslie. *The Filmgoer's Companion.* New York, Hill and Wang, 1967.

Platt, Frank C., editor. *Great Stars of Hollywood's Golden Age.* New York, New American Library, 1966.

Shipman, David. *The Great Movie Stars: The Golden Years.* New York, Crown, 1970.

Welcome Back, Kotter

A popular ABC-TV sitcom from 1975 to 1979, *Welcome Back, Kotter* featured Gabriel Kaplan in the title role of Gabriel Kotter, a teacher who returns to his alma mater, Brooklyn's fictional James Buchanan High School, to instruct a bunch of remedial students known as the Sweathogs. Kaplan, who created the show with Alan Sacks, based *Welcome Back, Kotter* on his own real-life experiences in the Bensonhurst section of Brooklyn, where he had himself been branded an "unteachable" student until inspired by a teacher named Miss Shepherd. Comedienne Janeane Garofalo once expressed relief that *Welcome Back, Kotter* was the fashion arbiter in her youth instead of *Beverly Hills 90210* with its designer duds, because it was easier to live up to *Kotter*'s image of frizzy-haired students dressed in flared jeans and army jackets.

The Sweathogs were tough and streetwise, although their worst insult amounted to "Up your nose with a rubber hose!" Kotter was hip to all of their tricks, having pulled them all himself a decade earlier. Yet, he was also still a rebel, flouting conventions and using humor in order to get his struggling students to learn something. Kaplan, a standup comedian with a bushy mustache and a perpetual smirk, incorporated some of his material, sometimes awkwardly, into the beginning and end of the episodes, but seemed a little less at ease as an actor carrying a sitcom. Luckily the Sweathogs picked up the slack.

The four main Sweathogs were Freddie "Boom Boom" Washington (Lawrence Hilton-Jacobs), a smooth African American who

John Travolta listens to Gabe Kaplan in a scene from *Welcome Back, Kotter.*

called his teacher "Mr. Kot-TAIR"; Juan Epstein (Robert Hegyes), a Puerto Rican Jew who was always bringing in fake excuse notes from home and signing them "Epstein's mother," and whose delivery resembled that of Chico Marx; Arnold Horshack (Ron Palillo), a braying geek who screamed "Oh! Oh Oh!" when he raised his hand and snorted when he laughed; and Vinnie Barbarino (John Travolta), the hunky dim-witted leader of the group. Other regulars included Kotter's wife Julie (Marcia Strassman), who had twins Robin and Rachel in 1977, and Kotter's nemesis, snotty vice-principal Mr. Woodman (John Sylvester White).

A typical plot from early in the series: Washington, whose signature phrase was an ultra-slick "Hi there," makes the varsity basketball team and decides he doesn't need to study anymore. Mr. Kotter confronts the class and the basketball coach, and threatens to fail Washington. In the end, Kotter teaches everyone about the importance of balancing education and sports.

Vinnie Barbarino proved the breakout role for Travolta, who soon launched his film career with *Saturday Night Fever,* in 1977 and *Grease* in 1978. By that year, he was rarely seen on *Kotter,* and was billed as a "special guest star." The year 1979 marked the final season for *Welcome Back, Kotter.* That year, Kaplan chose to sit out many of the episodes due to creative differences with ABC, and he was rarely seen on television after that. The fact that Travolta was also making fewer appearances prompted the network to move the show around to less desirable time slots, and to promote the show less vigorously. A slick southerner, Beau De Labarre, played by Stephen Shortridge, was brought in to replace the hunk void left by Travolta. Other character changes included the arrival—and quick departure— of Angie, the first female Sweathog, and the promotion of Kotter to vice principal and Woodman to principal.

Welcome Back, Kotter was used as a launching pad for other performers besides Travolta, though he is the only one for whom it really worked. A spinoff was attempted for the Horshack character and his family, but was soon aborted. There was also the short-lived *Mr. T. & Tina,* based on another original *Kotter* character, which starred Pat Morita as a madcap Japanese inventor who moves his family from Tokyo to Chicago.

The show's hit theme song, "Welcome Back," was composed and performed by John Sebastian, late performer of the Lovin' Spoonful. An FM radio staple in the 1970s, the song was later used to sell cold cuts and fast food. *Welcome Back, Kotter* enjoyed a revival on *Nick at Nite* in the mid-1990s.

—Karen Lurie

Further Reading:

Brooks, Tim and Earle Marsh. *The Complete Directory to Prime Time Network and Cable TV Shows 1946-present.* New York, Ballantine Books, 1995.

McNeil, Alex. *Total Television.* New York, Penguin, 1996.

Tucker, Ken. "Welcome Back, Kotter." *Entertainment Weekly.* 30 June 1995, 88.

Welk, Lawrence (1903-1992)

For three decades, Saturday night belonged to Lawrence Welk. The bandleader's program debuted on ABC in 1955 and quickly became an even more wholesome alternative to *The Ed Sullivan Show.* Despite breaking little artistic ground, *The Lawrence Welk Show* remained on the air for 27 years, making it the longest-running prime-time music program in television history. Welk's program highlighted conservative American values and was decidedly anti-hip, but retained a following into the 1990s, when reruns of the show made it one of PBS's most popular programs.

Though he would one day become the country's second most wealthy performer behind Bob Hope, Welk never forgot his poor beginnings in North Dakota as one of Ludwig and Christina Welk's eight children. His family's pre-Depression struggles were always with him and were partly responsible for his fierce loyalty to his band. His refusal to tip at restaurants could also be traced to his early struggles; instead of leaving money Welk would hand out penknives inscribed with his name. Work is what Welk knew, dropping out of school by the fourth grade to put time in on the family farm.

He learned to play music, starting on violin and graduating to his father's accordion. At 21, Welk left home to make his way in the music business. He had a brush with jazz history when, on an early recording session, he worked in the studio being shared by Louis Armstrong. But Welk never recorded hot jazz or the innovative big band style of Duke Ellington or Count Basie. He stumbled through much of the 1930s. One night in Dallas, South Dakota, his band even walked out on him, believing Welk would never make it as a leader. But by 1951, TV KTLA Channel 5 in Santa Monica began to broadcast Welk's band. Four years later, not long after his 52nd birthday, ABC added the show to its lineup. Welk's signature phrases—"ah-one and ah-two" and "wunnerful, wunnerful"— took hold.

Welk's successful formula called for short, tight musical and dance numbers and for songs people knew. Welk insisted that his show would "Keep it simple, so the audience can feel like they can do it too." In addition to Welk's band and the regular singers and dancers, *The Lawrence Welk Show* had many headliners: the Lennon Sisters, Joe Feeney, Norma Zimmer. But no star was bigger than the bandleader, whose Eastern European accent and humble nature endeared him to millions. Even though he had recorded for years, Welk rarely played on the show. Instead, his band featured a better accordionist, Myren Floren.

Welk's program maintained the clean-cut stability of the Eisenhower era even as the popularity of rock 'n' roll ruined many big bands in the 1950s and the country churned with the turmoil of the 1960s. As musical styles and tastes changed, Welk remained loyal to soft standards, or champagne jazz. He justified his decision by noting that "Champagne music puts the girl back in the boy's arms—where she belongs." Welk also refused to incorporate the new styles associated with the beatnik poets or play any jazz or rock 'n' roll, even when the network and his band members made suggestions. Welk didn't apologize for his tastes or opinions. He didn't like rock 'n' roll and didn't relate to the hippie culture. "It was always hard for me, for example, to understand the fad for patched-up jeans," he wrote in *Ah-One, Ah-Two.* "When I was a boy I had to wear them, much to my shame and embarrassment, and one of my earliest ambitions was to own a brand-new suit of clothes all my own." Because of Welk's clear vision of his show, *The Lawrence Welk Show* remained a snapshot of a happy, booming Middle America, frozen in a waltz and a smile.

Welk positioned himself as the conservative patriarch of his musical family. Women of all ages were his "girls," the players his "kids." Welk could be unforgiving when it came to his "kids." In 1959, at a time when Hugh Hefner's *Playboy* magazine was bringing sex into the forefront of mainstream culture, Welk fired Alice Lon, one of the popular Champagne ladies, when she flashed too much skin on camera. A few years later, in response to letters of protest, Welk gave the Lennon Sisters an earful after they wore one-piece bathing suits for a scene taped by a swimming pool and forbade the girls from wearing such things again on camera. For the band members, Welk's familial philosophy worked both ways. Welk felt he couldn't let his band down and retire when, at 68, ABC canceled his show; but he didn't believe his crew should be paid any more than minimum union scale, though they were able to participate in his profit-sharing plan.

The Lawrence Welk Show was popular through the 1960s, but in 1971, ABC dropped it, concerned that a program sponsored by Geritol and Sominex couldn't appeal to the young, advertiser-friendly audience craved by marketing executives. Nearing 70, Welk took the news hard, as if he had failed his first audition. "I felt just about as bad as a man can feel," he noted in 1974's *Ah-One, Ah-Two!* Initially deciding to put away his baton, Welk reconsidered when letters of

A musical moment from the *Lawrence Welk Show*.

support poured into his office, more than a million in the end, enough to convince Welk to syndicate the show himself. Eventually more than 250 stations picked up the show, giving the program air-time on more channels than during its ABC years. When Welk brought his show back to the air, he did it his way. In the first show back, Welk made it clear that the bad experience wouldn't effect his style; he wasn't about to pander to that younger audience. The broadcast featured "No, No, Nanette," "Tea for Two," and a group tap dance.

Welk retired in 1982 and last played with his band in 1989, three years before his death. By that time, he had amassed a business empire: a music library which includes all of Jerome Kern's work, resorts in Escondido, California, and Branson, Missouri, and the Welk Group, which includes several record labels. But for all his financial successes, Welk's greatest pleasure seemed to be pleasing an audience. In a 1978 interview with *The Los Angeles Times,* Welk talked of playing an impromptu show at a school in Macksville, Kansas. "That was the biggest applaud I ever had," he said. "I stayed for a half an hour and played the accordion. That was the highlight of my life."

During the 1990s, the lounge movement embraced everything square: martinis, hipster lingo, and the cocktail jazz of Les Baxter, Juan Garcia Esquivel, and Henry Mancini. The revival didn't include

Welk, however. Unlike these other figures, who were trapped in a particular time and embraced for irony's sake, Welk didn't need to make a comeback. Lawrence Welk never left.

—Geoff Edgers

FURTHER READING:

Sanders, Coyne Steven, and Ginny Weissman. *Champagne Music: The Lawrence Welk Show.* New York, St. Martins, 1985.

Schwienher, William K. *Lawrence Welk, an American Institution.* Chicago, Nelson-Hall, 1980.

Welk, Lawrence with Bernice McGeehan. *Ah-One, Ah-Two!: Life with My Musical Family.* Boston, Massachusetts, G.K. Hall, 1974.

———. *Lawrence Welk's Musical Family Album.* Englewood Cliffs, New Jersey, Prentice-Hall, 1977.

———. *My America, Your America.* Englewood Cliffs, New Jersey, Prentice-Hall, 1976.

———. *This I Believe.* Englewood Cliffs, New Jersey, Prentice-Hall, 1979.

———. *You're Never Too Young.* New Jersey, Prentice Hall, 1981.

Welles, Orson (1915-1985)

Considered by many to be the most influential and innovative filmmaker of the twentieth century, Orson Welles made movies that were ambitious, original, and epic. This alone would qualify him as a popular culture icon. But add to his genius his notorious life history, and Welles becomes a singular legend. Child prodigy at seven, Broadway's boy wonder at 22, radio's enfant terrible at 23, Hollywood's hottest director at 25, husband of sex symbol Rita Hayworth, Hollywood failure at 30, and 40 more years of attempted comebacks, obesity, and maverick films, the life of Orson Welles uniquely embodied the modern era.

Born on May 6, 1915, George Orson Welles, the second son of a successful inventor and his pianist wife, spent his first six years in provincial Kenosha, Wisconsin, before moving to Chicago. Shortly thereafter, his parents separated and Orson's older brother, Richard, was sent to boarding school, leaving Orson alone with his mother Beatrice, who soon commanded one of the city's most popular artistic and literary salons. Surrounded by actors, artists, and musicians and taken to the theatre, symphony, and opera, the boy responded to this cultural deluge by becoming a child prodigy. He learned Shakespeare soliloquies at seven, studied classical piano, and by eight had begun to write plays. But when his mother died shortly after his ninth birthday, Welles' life drastically changed.

Welles spent two difficult years living with his alcoholic father, who in turn exposed his son to his working-class artist and journalist friends. It was a relief when the 11-year-old was sent to the Todd School for Boys, a rigorous college preparatory academy. There his precocious talents flourished. Welles wrote, directed, and starred in school theatricals and studied painting. During Welles' summer vacations, father and son often traveled together, once taking a steamship as far as Shanghai. But when Dick Welles died suddenly a few months before Orson's 16th birthday, the boy was both distraught and relieved to no longer have to take care of his alcoholic parent.

Six months after his father's death, the gifted 16-year-old graduated from Todd and left for Ireland, planning to study painting. But after drifting around the country for a few months, he arrived in Dublin, where he began to haunt the local theatres. On his first visit to the experimental Gate Theatre, Welles decided to audition, touting himself as one of America's top young actors. Not surprisingly, the young self-promoter was hired and spent the next year learning his craft in the company of some of Ireland's cutting-edge actors and directors.

When he returned to America in 1932, Welles hoped to take Broadway by storm. But New York was singularly unimpressed, and

Orson Welles (center) in the title role of his film *Citizen Kane*.

the 17-year-old sheepishly returned to Chicago. Over the course of the next year and a half, Welles wrote plays, traveled to North Africa, and directed small productions before being hired by theatrical legends Katherine Cornell and Guthrie McClintic to join their Broadway company.

Welles made his Broadway debut at 18, playing Shakespeare and Shaw. A year later, he met the man who would orchestrate his stardom, 33-year-old director/producer John Houseman. Driven by the same high-flown theatrical goals, Houseman and Welles took part in the government-sponsored WPA (Work Projects Administration) Federal Theatre Project, where Welles directed an all-black, voodoo *Macbeth* to rave reviews. The two men soon formed their own repertory company, the Mercury Theatre, and, in 1937, they took Broadway by storm with their production of *Julius Caesar* set in fascist Italy. By age 22, Orson Welles was world famous as Broadway's boy wonder.

The Mercury Theatre soon branched out into hour-long radio broadcasts, the most notorious of which was certainly Welles' 1938 Halloween broadcast of H.G. Wells' *War of the Worlds*, which terrified a nation into truly believing that New Jersey was being invaded by Martians. Hollywood soon came to call. Hoping to exploit the hype around the brilliant enfant terrible, RKO offered Welles $225,000 to produce, direct, write, and act in two films. With total creative freedom and a percentage of the profits built into the contract, it was an offer Welles could not refuse.

Welles came out to Hollywood with the idea of filming Joseph Conrad's *Heart of Darkness,* but difficulties arose and he decided to work with veteran screenwriter Herman J. Mankiewicz. Together they wrote a brilliant screenplay about an aging media tycoon dying in his Florida mansion. A thinly disguised biography of newspaper magnate William Randolph Hearst, *Citizen Kane* depicted Kane/Hearst as a tyrant who has alienated everyone who loved him. The film tells Kane's story from five different points of view. With 25-year-old Welles directing, producing, and starring in the title role, *Citizen Kane* broke new cinematic ground. As described in Baseline's *Encyclopedia of Film,* its innovations included, ''1. composition in depth: the use of extreme deep focus cinematography to connect distant figures in space; 2. complex mise-en-scène, in which the frame overflowed with action and detail; 3. low angle shots that revealed ceilings and made characters, especially Kane, seem simultaneously dominant and trapped; 4. long takes; 5. a fluid, moving camera that expanded the action beyond the frame and increased the importance of off-screen space; and 6. the creative use of sound as a transition device . . . and to create visual metaphors.'' The film featured a superb cast, which included Joseph Cotten and George Coulouris from the Mercury Theatre as well as Agnes Moorehead, Ruth Warrick, and Everett Sloane.

Citizen Kane was lauded by the critics, but ran into trouble at the box office when Hearst refused to carry advertisements for the film in his newspapers and launched a smear campaign. Nominated for nine Academy Awards, Welles' masterpiece was snubbed by the Academy and only won one Oscar—Best Screenplay, shared by Mankiewicz and Welles. *Citizen Kane* has nonetheless come to be regarded as the greatest film ever made, ranking number one on the American Film Institute list of the top 100 movies of all time.

Welles' next film was an adaptation of the Booth Tarkington novel, *The Magnificent Ambersons.* A somewhat more conventional film than *Citizen Kane, The Magnificent Ambersons* utilized many of the same experimental techniques to depict turn-of-the-twentieth-century America, but when Welles left the country, RKO edited more

than 40 minutes out of the film. The film proved another commercial failure, losing more than half a million dollars, and Welles would never again be regarded as a bankable director.

Welles married World War II cinematic sex symbol, Rita Hayworth, but despite harnessing her star power to his marvelous 1948 film noir, *The Lady from Shanghai,* his directorial career was on the decline. When his experimental movie of Shakespeare's *Macbeth* failed at the box office a year later, the nails were all but in Welles' Hollywood coffin. He left Hollywood for a self-imposed 10-year exile, returning in 1958 to direct and act in the classic *Touch of Evil* with his frequent co-star Joseph Cotten.

Monica Sullivan has written, ''Orson Welles' early years were so spectacular that movie cultists might have preferred that he'd lived fast, died young and left a good-looking corpse.'' Indeed, although Welles returned to direct a few cinematic gems, it can only be said that his film career was uneven. As he grew older, he also gained weight, becoming a very obese man. Although he appeared on wine commercials and the occasional talk show, Welles became a somewhat tragic figure even as his status as filmmaking legend grew. His final film, *The Other Side of the Wind,* a quasi-autobiographical tale of a famous filmmaker struggling to get his picture financed, remained unfinished. As noted in Baseline's *Encyclopedia of Film,* ''As an unseen fragment, it was a sad an ironic end for a filmmaking maverick who set the standards for the modern narrative film and the man who was, in the words of Martin Scorcese, 'responsible for inspiring more people to be film directors than anyone else in the history of the cinema'.'' Troubled though the life of Orson Welles may have been—his potential as a director perhaps unfulfilled—his place in the pantheon of popular culture is assured.

—Victoria Price

FURTHER READING:

Brady, Frank. *Citizen Welles.* New York, Charles Scribner's Sons, 1989.

Callow, Simon. *Orson Welles: The Road to Xanadu.* New York, Viking Press, 1995.

Higham, Charles. *Orson Welles: The Rise and Fall of An American Genius.* New York, St. Martin's Press, 1985.

Kael, Pauline. *5001 Nights at the Movies.* New York, Henry Holt, 1991.

Leaming, Barbara. *Orson Welles: A Biography.* New York, Viking Press, 1985.

Microsoft Corporation. *Cinemania 96: The Best-Selling Interactive Guide to Movies and the Moviemakers.* Microsoft Corporation, 1996.

Monaco, James, and the Editors of Baseline. *Encyclopedia of Film.* New York, Perigee, 1991.

Sullivan, Monica. ''Orson Welles.'' *Movie Magazine International.* http://www.shoestring.org/mmirevs/welles-birthday.html. October 13, 1998.

Wells, Kitty (1919—)

Kitty Wells was a demure housewife with three children when she recorded ''It Wasn't God Who Made Honky-Tonk Angels,'' the

Kitty Wells

first in a series of records she released during the 1950s that made her country music's first female superstar. Her success demonstrated to the conservative country establishment that women could profitably perform honky-tonk songs about controversial subjects such as infidelity and divorce. Wells became known as "the Queen of Country Music," and the songs she popularized gave listeners a woman's perspective on classic country themes. Her sharp nasal twang blazed a trail that would be followed by other "girl singers," as female country artists were known, including Patsy Cline and Loretta Lynn.

A native of Nashville, Tennessee, Wells was born Muriel Ellen Deason on August 30, 1919, into a family of singers and musicians. As a child, she learned to play the guitar and sang gospel hymns with the church choir. While in her teens, she and her cousin performed on Nashville's WSIX as the Deason Sisters. Wells remembers that the song they chose for their radio debut, "Jealous Hearted Me" by the Carter Family, contained a line that made the station's managers uncomfortable: "It takes the man I love to satisfy my soul." Fearing that the audience might be offended, the girls were cut off in midsong. Listeners complained, however, and the Deason Sisters were given a short early-morning program.

In 1937, Wells married Johnnie Wright, a cabinetmaker and musician. With Wright's sister Louise, the newlyweds performed on WSIX as Johnnie Wright and the Harmony Girls. By 1939, Wright and his friend Jack Anglin had a new act, Johnnie and Jack and the Tennessee Mountain Boys, while Wells occupied herself with the care of their first child. She made occasional appearances with her husband's group, using a stage name he gave her that came from an old folk song titled "Kitty Wells." World War II dissolved the band,

interrupting their progress for a few years, but by 1947, Johnnie and Jack had reunited and appeared for a brief time on WSM's *Grand Ole Opry.* The following year, they joined a new hillbilly program, *Louisiana Hayride,* on Shreveport's KWKH. By this time, Wells was a permanent part of their show, the girl singer who performed gospel and sentimental folk songs.

Wells had the opportunity to record some of these songs for RCA Victor in 1949, after the label signed Johnnie and Jack. While their records made it onto the *Billboard* charts, with some reaching the Top Ten, hers were barely noticed. Wells remarked, "I think the record distributors were leery of taking them and trying to do anything with them." RCA let her go, and she withdrew from the music industry to focus attention on her family. In the spring of 1952, Paul Cohen of Decca Records suggested she record an answer song—one that responds to or continues the story of a previously released hit record—inspired by Hank Thompson's recent single "The Wild Side of Life." Wells was unenthusiastic about the song, but she agreed to return to the studio. Two months later, "It Wasn't God Who Made Honky-Tonk Angels" was heading for the top of the country charts, and Kitty Wells was poised for stardom.

While "The Wild Side of Life" attacks "honky-tonk angels," implying that women are solely responsible for leading men astray, Wells's song proclaims, "It's a shame that all the blame is on us women," noting that "married men [who] think they're still single" are also at fault. Though written by a man, the song offers a woman's point of view on "cheatin'," a common topic for country songwriters that had heretofore been strictly male territory. Initially, the song's controversial subject matter caused it to be banned by NBC radio and the Opry for being "suggestive." However, fans embraced the record, and it remained on the charts for four months.

Wells's Decca debut was followed by other popular answer songs, as well as songs that became country classics, such as "Release Me" (1954) and "Makin' Believe" (1955). According to Mary A. Bufwack and Robert K. Oermann, authors of *Finding Her Voice: The Saga of Women in Country Music,* Wells's body of work from the 1950s "essentially defin[ed] the postwar female style" in country music. After she achieved success, Wells continued to work package tours with her husband, who was told by Opry veteran Roy Acuff, "Don't ever headline a show with a woman. It won't ever work, because people just don't go for women." Most group shows during this era featured a single female performer, since promoters assumed that audiences would not tolerate more. Despite the prevalence of such prejudice throughout the music industry, Wright broke the rules and gave his wife top billing when they toured together. He also played an important role in her career, serving as her business manager, writing or choosing songs for her to record, and finding musicians for her recording sessions.

Two years after Wells's breakthrough single, the governor of Tennessee paid tribute to her music and her homemaking, calling her "an outstanding wife and mother, in keeping with the finest traditions of Southern womanhood." Although she married Wright shortly after she began her career, she was commonly introduced as "Miss Kitty Wells." As she sang of heartache and sin in a restrained voice, she put forth the public image of a devoted, well-behaved wife in gingham. Wells's popularity may have been largely due to the fact that she personally conformed to the mores of the 1950s, allowing her to dramatize unwholesome situations in her songs.

Wells won numerous awards during the first two decades of her career, and she continued recording into the 1970s. In the early 1980s, she and her husband began operating their own museum outside Nashville, and they continued performing into the late 1990s. Wells is a member of the Country Music Hall of Fame, and she received a Grammy for Lifetime Achievement in 1991.

—Anna Hunt Graves

FURTHER READING:

Bufwack, Mary A., and Robert K. Oermann. *Finding Her Voice: The Saga of Women in Country Music.* New York, Crown, 1993.

Kingsbury, Paul, and Alan Axelrod, editors. *Country: The Music and the Musicians.* New York, Abbeville Press, 1988, 314-341.

Wolfe, Charles. *The Queen of Country Music* (CD liner notes). Germany, Bear Family Records, 1993.

Wells, Mary (1943-1992)

Known as the "First Lady of Motown," singer and songwriter Mary Wells launched Motown into the black with a succession of hits. As a teenager, Wells was the first Motown artist to have a Top Ten and Number One single for the label. She was teamed with songwriter/producer Smokey Robinson, and their synergy produced the right combination of material and approach to show off Wells's talent to the fullest. During Wells's tenure with Motown, she had nine hit songs in the R&B category and six more in the pop category.

Mary Esther Wells was born on May 13, 1943 in Detroit and grew up singing gospel music at her uncle's Baptist church with aspirations to become a songwriter. While in high school, she penned the gospel-inspired "Bye Bye Baby" with singer Jackie Wilson in mind. Songwriter Berry Gordy had written several hits for Wilson and Wells sought out Gordy to listen to her new song. After hearing it, Gordy was convinced that the song wasn't for Wilson but instead for Wells herself. Gordy signed the seventeen-year-old Wells to his fledgling Motown label. "Bye Bye Baby" climbed to number eight on the *Billboard* R&B chart. Following another hit single, "I Don't Want to Take a Chance," Motown placed Wells in the artistic care of Smokey Robinson. Robinson and Wells represented Motown's first successful teaming of a songwriter/producer with an artist. Robinson encouraged Wells to veer away from the blues- and gospel-inspired songs in favor of the sweet girlish pop style, a natural for her innocent, sincere, and convincing voice.

"You Beat Me to the Punch," released in September of 1962, quickly climbed to number one on *Billboard*'s R&B chart and crossed over to number nine on the pop chart. Wells was destined to ride the R&B as well as pop charts, and after several more hits including "The One Who Really Loves You" and "Two Lovers," she recorded "My Guy." This, her greatest hit, shot to number one on the pop chart. It also was her last big pop hit. She also recorded the duet "What's the Matter with You Baby" with Marvin Gaye.

When Wells reached twenty-one, she was unsuccessful in renegotiating her contract with Motown and sued the company.

Reportedly, Motown had manipulated her contract so that she received the full percentage of royalties from neither her performances nor her songwriting. Prodded by her husband, former Motown artist Herman Griffin, Wells left Motown and succeeded in getting her contract declared null and void. This proved to be a disastrous move for her career, since she never was able to regain the success she had enjoyed with Motown and songwriter/producer Robinson. Wells signed with 20th Century-Fox Records, which was a profitable arrangement, then with Atlantic/Atco, Jubilee, Reprise, and Epic.

Wells's professional career as well as her personal life seemed to slowly disintegrate. Her marriage to Griffin ended in divorce and she married Cecil Womack, a relationship that also ended in divorce. Wells then shocked many by marrying Cecil's brother Curtis. She continued to perform her old hits until she was diagnosed with throat cancer in 1991. With no medical insurance, evicted from her residence, and placed in a charity ward, Wells was destitute. The Rhythm and Blues Foundation came to her assistance by setting up a Mary Wells Fund. Several well-known artists contributed to the fund, including Bruce Springsteen, Rod Stewart, Mary Wilson, as well as Motown entrepreneur Berry Gordy. Wells had a choice to have a laryngectomy or radiation. She chose the latter, but the treatment was unsuccessful. Wells died on July 26, 1992.

—Willie Collins

FURTHER READING:

Whital, Susan. *Women of Motown: An Oral History.* New York, Avon Books, 1998.

Wertham, Fredric (1895-1981)

Although Fredric Wertham is remembered primarily as the author of *Seduction of the Innocent* (1954), an incisive, blistering attack on the violence and horror purveyed by the comic book industry, his research took him through this era of crime comics to the culture that violent movies and television created. In 1966 Wertham wrote: "Television represents one of the greatest technological advances and is an entirely new, potent method of communication. Unfortunately as it is presently used, it does have something in common with crime comic books: the devotion to violence. In the School for Violence, television represents the classic course." The climate of violence developing since this observation has, if anything, increased with the emergence of new technologies, like the Internet and videos, and become more noxious in the late 1990s. Competition for audience share, demand for advertising revenue, and misguided applications of constitutional rights have all encouraged aggressive displays of violent behavior to be broadcast. Though originally derided, Wertham's observations that the grammar of violence and its impact on the culture constitutes a public health issue have been sustained by the research of Leonard Eron, George Gerbner, and Albert Bandura. Nevertheless, Wertham was not a Luddite, opposed to technological advances, but a physician of wide and deeply humane interests, an advocate of social reform, and a defender of civil liberties.

Born 20 March 1895 in Nuremberg, Germany, Fredric Wertham was one of five children of Sigmund and Mathilde Wertheimer, non-religious, assimilated middle-class Jews. As a young man on the eve of the World War I, Wertham spent several summers in England where he found the environment there open and relaxed, a stark contrast to the rigid, disciplined, and intellectually pedantic German culture at home. During this period he explored Fabian socialism, the writings of Karl Marx, and, more importantly, became an avid reader of Charles Dickens' writings on social reform. When war broke out in 1914, Wertham, pursuing medical studies at King's College, London University, found himself stranded in England and, as a German national, was for a short time interned in a prison camp near Wakefield, then paroled. An admirer of British society, Wertham remained in England during the war, reading medicine and literature. After the war he continued his studies at the Universities of Erlangen and Munich, obtaining his M.D. degree from the University of Wurzburg in 1921. Paris and Vienna were additional venues of postgraduate study before he joined Emile Kraepelin's clinic in Munich.

Wertham left Germany in 1922 to work with Kraepelin's protege Alfred Meyer at the Phipps Psychiatric Clinic at Johns Hopkins in Baltimore. During his years at Johns Hopkins, Wertham established a friendship with H. L. Mencken and worked with Clarence Darrow, becoming one of the first psychiatrists willing to testify on behalf of indigent black defendants. It was also during this period that he met and married Florence Hesketh, an artist doing biological research as a Charleton Fellow in Medicine at Johns Hopkins. Hesketh drew all the cell plate illustrations for *The Brain as an Organ: Its Postmortem Study and Interpretation* (1934), for which Wertham received the first psychiatric grant made by the National Research Council. In addition, Wertham published the first study on the effects of mescaline and did pioneer work on insulin use in psychotherapy. He developed the mosaic test in which a patient manipulated small multicolored pieces of wood into a freely chosen design, which was evaluated for what it revealed about the patient's ego. Wertham's diagnostic technique was often used in conjunction with paintings by patients, such as the watercolors done by Zelda Fitzgerald when she was under treatment at the Phipps Clinic.

During the 1930s Wertham's expertise as a forensic psychiatrist became known to the general public. His involvement in a number of spectacular murder cases, which he discussed in *Dark Legend: A Study in Murder* (1941) and *The Show of Violence* (1948), led him to advocate the duty of a psychiatrist to bring the psychiatric background of murder into the relationship with the law and the society it represents. Wertham's support for an intelligent use of the McNaughton's rule determining legal insanity, his understanding of how environmental forces shape individual responses, and his argument that violence and murder are diseases of society all persuaded him that violence is not innate, and so could be prevented.

Dark Legend investigates the story of Gino, a seventeen-year-old Italian-American who, commanded by the ghost of his dead father, murdered his promiscuous mother. Wertham's compelling narrative of his patient draws upon the myth of Orestes and the legend of Hamlet to explore matricide. The incisive analysis of matricide set out in *Dark Legend* prompted Ernest Jones to remark, "Freud and I both underestimated the importance of the mother problem in Hamlet. You have made a real contribution." *Dark Legend* is significant because it ties an actual murder case to important psychological types

in literature and supports a shift in an understanding of matriarchy among American psychiatrists.

In *The Show of Violence* Wertham explains for the layman his theory of the Catathymic Crisis, where "a violent act—against another person or against oneself—provides the only solution to profound emotional conflict whose real nature remains below the threshold of the consciousness of the patient." He discusses his own role in several celebrated murder cases, including the pathetic Madeline, a young mother who killed her two children and then failed in her suicide attempt; the notorious child-murderer Albert Fish; the "mad sculptor" Robert Irwin; and the professional gunman Martin Lavin. In each case Wertham probes the social background, the medical history, the political implications, and the legal response to uncover the effect societal forces had in the creation of the impulse to murder.

In 1932 Wertham moved to New York City where he became a senior psychiatrist at Bellevue and organized for the Court of General Sessions the nation's first clinic providing a psychiatric screening for every convicted felon. Wertham became director of psychiatric services at Queens Hospital Center in 1940 and pioneered a clinic for sex offenders, The Quaker Emergency Service Readjustment Center, in 1947. With the encouragement of Earl Brown, Paul Robeson, Richard Wright, and Ralph Ellison, Wertham enlisted a multi-racial, volunteer staff to establish in Harlem in 1946 a clinic dedicated to alleviating the "free-floating hostility" afflicting many in that community, and to understanding the realities of black life in America. Named in memory of Karl Marx's son-in-law, Dr. Paul Lefargue, the Lafargue Clinic became one of the most noteworthy institutions to serve poor Americans and to promote the cause of civil rights.

In order to prepare for discrimination cases in Delaware, attorneys Louis Redding, Jack Greenberg, and Thurgood Marshall needed medical testimony on the harm segregation caused children. Wertham's studies showed that the practice of racial separation "creates a mental health problem in many Negro children with a resulting impediment in their educational progress." Wertham's testimony was significant because his research was the first to examine both black and white children attending segregated schools. The evidence revealed the possibly that white children, too, may be harmed by school segregation. The Delaware cases became part of the legal argument used in the landmark school desegregation case, *Brown v. Board of Education of Topeka* (1954).

In addition to bringing psychotherapy to a neglected community, Wertham's work at the Lafargue Clinic led to the developments of his later ideas on the contribution horror and crime comic books made to a climate of juvenile violence. In 1948 Wertham organized the first symposium dealing with media violence at the New York Academy of Medicine. Not only did Wertham identify media-induced violence as a public health issue, but he also challenged "psychotherapy to overcome its own claustrophilia and take an interest in the social forces that bear on an individual." This research attracted widespread national attention, opening additional *fora* for Wertham to publicize his studies on the enigma of preventable violence. The quest to understand and prevent violence—the core of Wertham's psychiatric practice—shaped his thinking on how the mass media create a climate that both encourages and legitimizes violent anti-social acts.

In the 1950s America faced two primary fears: communism and juvenile delinquency. The axis on which these two met found Wertham, whose studies probed the social dynamics that permitted the development of these fears and the underlying violence that inflamed their intensity. Attorney Emanuel Bloch believed that Wertham might be willing to appear for the defense in the espionage trial of Ethel Rosenberg and her husband Julius. Convicted as members of a conspiracy to send stolen atomic-bomb secrets to Russia, the Rosenbergs nevertheless maintained their innocence and averred that they were victims of a United States government frame-up. Political passions, fears of the ''Red Menace,'' and charges of treason and betrayal swirled at the time against a backdrop the Korean War and Soviet activity in Eastern Europe. Such circumstances persuaded many prominent individuals to keep a low profile in order not to be tainted by helping the Rosenbergs.

Although the court absolutely refused to allow Wertham direct access to Ethel Rosenberg, it gave him permission to testify in federal court under oath about her mental condition. Not only did this order deny Rosenberg due process, it created the paradoxical situation of permitting Wertham to testify about the mental condition of a patient whom he was not allowed to examine. Using Bloch as an intermediary and relying on second-hand information, Wertham not only accepted these limitations, but also braved a vicious and often improper cross-examination. Nevertheless, his understanding of the condition ''prison psychosis'' and his humanitarian concern for Rosenberg's health made his testimony compelling. Within a few days Washington reversed itself and moved Julius Rosenberg to Sing Sing where husband and wife would be allowed to visit each other regularly. Moreover, Wertham was brought in to deal with the Rosenberg children, Michael and Robert, whom he advised and whose adoption by the Meeropol family he helped to make successful.

It was precisely Wertham's reputation for fearlessness and integrity that encouraged Senator Estes Kefauver to appoint him sole psychiatric consultant to the Senate Subcommittee for the Study of Organized Crime (1950). Not only did Wertham bring his expertise as a forensic psychiatrist to Kefauver's committee, but his experience in dealing with New York crime and governmental institutions made his observations particularly trenchant. The role organized crime played in American society was one that engendered fear, revulsion, cynicism, respect, and even admiration, especially for the way in which violent crime could be of service to politics. These televised hearings drew national attention, revealing the influence television had in shaping public opinion, and set the stage for the Senate Subcommittee to Investigate Juvenile Delinquency (1953-1956), which explored how juvenile delinquency led to adult crime.

A major theme of the investigation into juvenile delinquency was the impact the mass media exerted on youth and on a separate emerging youth culture. Wertham, who had published a series of articles and given lectures describing his research on the unhealthful effects of mass media violence, decided his work merited a book-length study aimed at the general public. In *Seduction of the Innocent* (1954) Wertham sets out his argument on the connection between the rise of juvenile delinquency and the role of crime comic books in promoting violent activity. The brutal and sadistic activity in these comics created a culture of violence and a coarsening of society. Such comic books routinely featured mutilation, gore, branding, blinding—so prominent as to receive its own classification of ''eye-motif''—racism, bigotry, and especially, crude, sexual exploitation of women. Wertham testified that these comics, so attractive and easily available to children, exploited them and harmed their development; he concluded that access to violent comics for children under

fourteen years of age must be controlled. Although Wertham was maligned as a censor—a charge he vigorously denied—his work did stimulate the comic book industry to adopt a code labeling the suitability of each comic book published (The Code of the Comics Magazine Association of America, October 26, 1954).

Wertham's studies on juvenile delinquency led him to probe deeper into the role various media play in creating, perpetuating, and distorting the social problems of teenagers. Not only comic books but also mass news publications, television, and the movies influenced behavior and distorted perceptions of teenagers and different ethnic groups. In *The Circle of Guilt* (1956) Wertham discovers the truth behind the death of ''model boy'' Billy Blankenship, murdered allegedly without provocation by Puerto Rican ''hoodlum'' Frank Santana in a New York City street fight. The paradigm of fear, racism, distrust, and prejudice many New Yorkers held conveniently fit Santana. Wertham, whose intuition told him that the case presented by the press reflected cultural prejudice rather than an understanding of the violent circumstances, agreed to investigate. He discovered that Blankenship was active in teenage gang activities and that Santana had an undeveloped personality, one lacking in hostility, anger, or resentment. Despite Wertham's testimony, the court handed down a harsh sentence of 25 years to life for second degree murder. His outrage at this sentence and at the prevailing climate of violence and prejudice compelled Wertham to write *The Circle of Guilt,* which exposes both failure and hypocrisy on the part of the legal system in complicity with the social service establishment. More importantly, this book reflects the violence afflicting society and the refusal to confront its own insidious cultural stereotyping.

In 1966 Wertham published his major study on human violence, *A Sign for Cain: An Exploration of Human Violence.* To answer the paradoxical question: ''Can we abolish violence without violence?'' Wertham probed ''why violence is becoming more entrenched in our society'' than many believe, and argued that if we are willing, it is within our capacity ''to conquer and to abolish it.'' Essentially a sociological history of violence in Western culture, *A Sign for Cain* focuses on the effects of mass media exposure on the virulence of political tyrannies in this century, on the emergence of the legal and medical legitimization of violence, and on the willing acceptance of the value of violence.

Wertham's thinking on the nature of violence provokes controversy among social theorists who interpret scientific data in ways to explain away anti-social behavior. Although such theorists admit the existence of cultural shaping, they argue that an instinctive drive for aggression is present at birth. The widespread acceptance of this idea of ''an inborn biologically fixed instinct of violence in man,'' Wertham argues is ''a theory that creates an entirely false and nihilistic destructive image of man.'' Violence may be the result of ''negative factors in the personality and in the social medium where the growth of personality takes place.'' Indeed, Wertham avers that ''the primary natural tendency [of man is] to maintain and care for the intactness and integrity of others. Man does not have an 'instinct' of violence; he has the *capacity* and the physiological apparatus for violence.'' To Wertham, man has survived as a species not because of an instinct for violence but because people value cooperation.

His interest in youth and how communication by the young shapes the culture led Wertham to publish his last book, *The World of Fanzines: A Special Form of Communication* (1973). Arguing that fanzines—magazines created by fans of fantasy and science fiction—are a revealing form of communication because they are ''free from outside interference, without control or manipulation from above, without *censorship,* visible or invisible,'' Wertham sees them as not just a product of our society but a reaction to it. Fanzines show the capacity of the individual fan to reshape violent material in a socially useful way. The paraculture that is the world of fanzines contains patterns of fantasy, art, and literature manifesting healthy creativity, independence, and social responsibility. The fan-produced magazine expresses a genuine voice wanting to be heard, defying the overpowering roar of the mass media. Since fanzine artists and writers stress the role of heroes who have ''cleared their minds of cant,'' Wertham sees in the integrity of heroes and super-heroes ''a message for our unheroic age.''

The last years of Fredric Wertham's life were spent at his beloved Blue Hills, a former Pennsylvania Dutch farm near the Hawk Mountain Bird Sanctuary at Kempton. He died November 18, 1981.

—James E. Reibman

FURTHER READING:

Barker, Martin. ''Fredric Wertham—The Sad Case of the Unhappy Humanist.'' In *Pulp Demons: International Dimensions of the Postwar Anti-Comics Campaign,* edited by John A. Lent. Cranbury, New Jersey, Associated University Presses, 1999, 215-233.

———. *A Haunt of Fears: The Strange History of the British Horror Comics Campaign.* London, Pluto Press, 1984.

Gilbert, James. *A Cycle of Violence: America's Reaction to the Juvenile Delinquent in the 1950s.* New York, Oxford University Press, 1986.

Kluger, Richard. *Simple Justice: The History of Brown v. Board of Education and Black America's Struggle for Equality.* New York, Vintage Books, A Division of Random House, 1975, 1977.

Reibman, James E. ''Fredric Wertham: A Social Psychiatrist Characterizes Crime Comic Books and Media Violence as Public Health Issues.'' In *Pulp Demons: International Dimensions of the Postwar Anti-Comics Campaign,* edited by John A. Lent. Cranbury, New Jersey, Associated University Presses, Inc., 1999, 234-268.

———. ''The Life of Dr. Fredric Wertham.'' *The Fredric Wertham Collection: Gift of His Wife Hesketh.* Cambridge, Busch-Reisinger Museum, Harvard University, 1990, 11-22.

———. *My Brother's Keeper: The Life of Fredric Wertham, M. D.* Forthcoming.

Reibman, James E. and N. C. Christopher Couch, editors. *A Fredric Wertham Reader.* Seattle, Fantagraphics Press, 2000.

West, Jerry (1938—)

One of the greatest guards ever to play in the National Basketball Association, Jerry West (''Mr. Clutch'') was an All-Star player during his NBA career in the 1960s and early 1970s and later served as head coach and general manager of the Los Angeles Lakers, one of

Jerry West, in mid-air.

the predominant cage teams of the 1980s. West's likeness has since become an icon to basketball fans and the general public as the silhouetted figure in the NBA's logo.

West might be described as an atypical basketball player. He weighed 185 pounds, and his 39-inch arms prompted some observers to comment on his ostrich-like appearance, but his competitive intensity and knack for sinking the last-second shot helped him overcome these deficiencies, earning for him his lifelong nickname, Mr. Clutch. A two-time All-American at the University of West Virginia, West later won a gold medal with the 1960 U.S. Olympic basketball team. He joined the Los Angeles Lakers the same year that another dynamic guard, Oscar Robertson, entered the NBA with the Milwaukee Bucks. During the 1960s the two men would emerge as the best shooters in basketball.

West averaged 27 points per game and made the All-Star team every year he played. Four times he averaged more than 30 points a season. He saved his best work for the post-season, averaging 29.1 points in 153 playoff contests and winning or tying numerous games with critical buzzer-beating baskets. Yet, the man who came to symbolize his sport spent much of his career beating back a reputation as a hard-luck player. Six times, West led the Lakers to the NBA finals, only to lose to the Boston Celtics. Finally, in 1972, the team broke through, defeating the New York Knicks in the championship round. ''The albatross around my neck,'' as West called the title drought, was lifted.

A pulled stomach muscle forced West to cut short his playing career in 1974. After a brief and unhappy retirement, he returned to the arena as Lakers head coach from 1976 to 1979. Despite some success, he clashed repeatedly with team owner Jack Kent Cooke and stepped out from behind the bench forever. New owner Jerry Buss convinced him to assume the post of general manager in 1982.

At the time, the Lakers were one of the NBA's premier teams. Star players Earvin "Magic" Johnson and Kareem Abdul-Jabbar led a potent offense, and head coach Pat Riley lent a Hollywood sheen to the proceedings with his slicked-back hair and expensive suits. Celebrities and swells flocked to the $350 courtside seats at the Lakers' home gym, dubbed "The Fabulous Forum." As general manager, West developed a reputation as the league's most astute evaluator of talent. On numerous occasions, he selected unheralded prospects from obscure colleges who quickly blossomed into productive NBA players. As one longtime friend of West's observed, "He's the only guy I know who went into oil for a tax loss and struck a gusher."

Under West, the Lakers grew into an NBA powerhouse. They won championships for him in 1982, 1985, 1987, and 1988, and challenged for league supremacy every other year in the decade. The team's up-tempo style of play, dubbed "Showtime," proved an enormously popular marketing angle for the NBA worldwide. While the rivalry between the Boston Celtics' Larry Bird and the Lakers' own Magic Johnson has been widely credited with reviving public interest in professional basketball, it would be no exaggeration to say that Jerry West's careful nurturing of the Laker dynasty also contributed to that resurgence.

—Robert E. Schnakenberg

FURTHER READING:

Deegan, Paul. *Jerry West.* Mankato, Minnesota, Children's Press, 1974.

West, Jerry, with Bill Libby. *Mr. Clutch: The Jerry West Story.* Englewood Cliffs, New Jersey, Prentice-Hall, 1969.

West, Mae (1893-1980)

Writer, stage performer, screen actress, and nightclub entertainer Mae West emerged, a ray of light during the Great Depression, as a uniquely independent, outspoken, flamboyant, and humorously erotic woman. She achieved legendary status in American show business folklore and won a wide international following. Rarely has a show business personality left so indelible a mark on American popular culture, influencing the laws of film censorship, and bequeathing a series of outrageous ripostes and innuendoes to the language—most famously, "Come up and see me sometime"—that were still used at the end of the twentieth century. During World War II, allied troops honored her hourglass figure by calling their inflatable life jackets "Mae Wests." Learning of this new meaning to her name, she commented: "I've been in Who's Who, and I know what's what, but it's the first time I've been in a Dictionary."

She began her stage career early, making her debut with Hal Clarendon's theatrical company in her home town of Brooklyn in 1901. There she played such well-known juvenile roles as Little Eva, Little Willie, and even Little Lord Fauntleroy. By 1907, at the age of

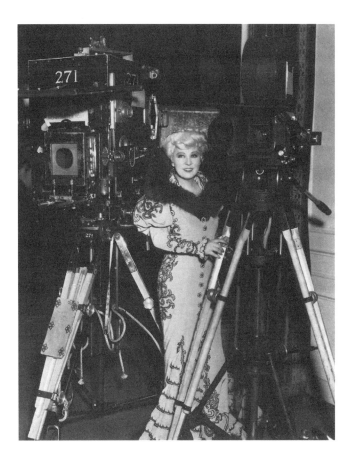

Mae West

14, she was a performer on the national vaudeville circuits with Frank Wallace, and in 1911 appeared as an acrobatic dancer and singer in the Broadway revue *A la Broadway and Hello, Paris.* She then began writing, producing, directing, and starring in her own plays on Broadway. Her first play, *Sex* (1926), starred Mae as Margie La Monte, a golden-hearted prostitute who wanders the wharves. The play ran for 37 performances and ended when Mae was jailed for ten days for obscenity and corruption of public morals. The publicity made her a national figure and added to the box-office success of her later plays, *Diamond Lil* (1928) and *The Constant Sinner* (1931).

A buxom blonde with a feline purr, imported to Hollywood from Broadway, Mae's film career flourished from 1932 to 1940. She wrote the screenplays for all but the first of her nine films during this period, and delivered her suggestive, sex-parodying lines to a variety of leading men from Cary Grant to W.C. Fields. Paramount offered her the unheard-of sum of $5,000 for a minor role in her debut film, *Night After Night* (1932), and Mae, with her vampy posturing and sexual innuendo, stole the show. The film's star, George Raft, said later, "In this picture, Mae West stole everything but the camera." Her entrance in this first of her films featured one of her most oft-repeated witticisms: when a hat-check girl, admiring Mae's bejeweled splendor, gushes, "Goodness, what beautiful diamonds!" the star responds with "Goodness had nothing to do with it, dearie." The joke was, of course, her own.

Paramount offered her a contract, and she agreed on condition that her next picture was a film version of *Diamond Lil.* That film, released as *She Done Him Wrong* (1933) and co-starring Cary Grant, unveiled her trademark line, "Come up and see me sometime." The film broke attendance records all over the world, and producer William Le Baron told exhibitors that "*She Done Him Wrong* must be credited with having saved Paramount when that studio was considering selling out to MGM, and when Paramount theaters—1700 of them—thought of closing their doors and converting into office buildings." She made *I'm No Angel,* again with Grant, the same year, by the end of which she was ranked as the eighth biggest box-office draw of 1933. By 1935, her combination of glamour, vulgarity, and self-parody had made Mae West the highest paid woman in the United States.

Her success, however, based as it was on the risqué, brought a strong reaction from the puritanical wing. The Hays Office, charged with keeping movies wholesome in the wake of a succession of Hollywood sex scandals, was forced to bring in their new production code—the Hays Code—in 1934, expressly to deal with the Mae West problem. Her next film had the working title of *It Ain't No Sin,* but the Hays Office decreed that it be designated less provocatively as *Belle of the Nineties* (1934). Mae reached the peak of her popularity as a Salvation Army worker in *Klondike Annie* (1936), co-starring Victor McLaglen. Posters for the movie announced, "She made the Frozen North Red Hot!" Another slogan used to publicize her movies was "Here's Mae West. When she's good, she's very good. When she's bad, she's better."

She co-starred with W.C. Fields in 1940 in the comic Western *My Little Chickadee,* each of them writing their own lines, but with disappointing results. When she failed to persuade Paramount to let her play Catherine the Great, she took her script about the controversial Russian empress to Broadway in the mid-1940s, where it was staged as a revue called *Catherine Was Great.* Her success led to a tour of England with her play *Diamond Lil* in 1947-48, and she took the play on a long tour of the United States for the next four years. With her film career over, she appeared in nightclubs and on television in an act with a group of young muscle men. During the 1960s, one of her few public appearances was in the 1964 TV series *Mister Ed,* but she made two last, disastrous screen appearances in the 1970s. She made a comeback as a Hollywood agent in the grotesque film version of Gore Vidal's sex-change comedy, *Myra Breckinridge* (1970), but despite the opprobrium heaped on the film (which starred Raquel Welch), Mae got most of the publicity, $350,000 for ten days' work and her own dialogue, and a tumultuous reception at the premiere from a new generation of fans. Then, aged 86, the indomitable Mae starred in the lascivious and highly embarrassing *Sextette* (1978), adapted from her own play. Surrounded by a bevy of men, who included old-timers George Raft, Walter Pidgeon, Tony Curtis, George Hamilton, and Ringo Starr, it was an ignominious exit, but the legend lives on.

—Benjamin Griffith

FURTHER READING:

Curry, Ramona. *Too Much of a Good Thing: Mae West as Cultural Icon.* Minneapolis, University of Minnesota Press, 1996.

Hamilton, Marybeth. *When I'm Bad I'm Better: Mae West, Sex, and American Entertainment.* New York, Harper Collins, 1995.

Leonard, Maurice. *Empress of Sex.* New York, Birch Lane Press, 1991.

West Side Story

When the curtain rose for the Broadway opening of the musical *West Side Story* on September 26, 1957, audiences were stunned and shaken by something new in American theater. Using a dynamic combination of classical theme and modern vernacular in script, music, and dance, the creators of *West Side Story* presented 1950s audiences with a disturbing, funny, and tragic look at what was happening in American society. Borrowing its plot from Shakespeare's *Romeo and Juliet, West Side Story* replaces the rival families with rival street gangs and augments the theme of love defeated by a conflict-torn environment. The play ran for 732 performances on Broadway, and, in 1961, was made into an award-winning film.

The plot of *West Side Story* is simple and familiar. Maria, newly arrived in New York from Puerto Rico, is expected to marry Chino, a nice Puerto Rican boy, but instead meets Polish-American Tony at a dance and they fall in love at first sight. But other forces are at work to keep them apart. Tony is one of the founders of the Jets, a street gang of white boys, and though he has drifted away from the gang and even gotten a job, he is still loyal to his "brothers" in the Jets. A new gang of Puerto Rican boys, the Sharks, led by Maria's brother Bernardo, is threatening the Jets supremacy on the streets, and the Jets are determined to hold on to their territory at all costs. The Sharks are equally determined to carve out a place for themselves in their new city, and the gangs scuffle regularly. Finally, Tony ends up involved in a rumble where his best friend is knifed, and in the ensuing melee, Tony accidentally kills Bernardo. Though grief-stricken, Maria forgives him and they plan to leave the city and run together to somewhere peaceful and safe. Before they can escape, however, Maria's spurned boyfriend Chino finds Tony and kills him. Devastated, Maria accuses both the Sharks and Jets of killing Bernardo and Tony and, united for a moment at least, the rival gang members carry Tony's body away.

West Side Story was the brainchild of theatrical great Jerome Robbins. Robbins, often considered one of the greatest American choreographers as well as a producer and director, got the idea for the musical when a friend was cast to play Romeo in a production of the Shakespeare play. While trying to help his friend get a grasp on Romeo's character, Robbins began to envision Romeo in modern times, dealing with modern issues. The idea stuck with him, and he eventually gathered a distinguished group of artists to help him create a modern day *Romeo and Juliet* that would speak to the dilemmas of 1950s America. Famed composer Leonard Bernstein was recruited to write the score, with then-newcomer Stephen Sondheim for the lyrics. The book was to be written by Arthur Laurents. Robbins' original name for the piece was "East Side Story," and the star-crossed lovers were to be a Jew and a Catholic from New York's lower east side. Robins, however, was looking for a new perspective and he felt the conflict between Jews and Catholics had been documented in theater in plays such as *Abie's Irish Rose.* Taking note of the increased numbers of Puerto Rican immigrants to New York following World War II, he moved his play to the upper west side of Manhattan and staged his conflict between a gang of Puerto Rican boys and a gang of "American" boys, the sons of less recent immigrants.

While critics were somewhat bemused by the comic-tragic darkness of *West Side Story,* audiences were captivated. To a society

Natalie Wood and Richard Beymer in a scene from the film *West Side Story*.

striving to be "normal" while seething with angry undercurrents, *West Side Story* spoke with a hip, rebellious authority. The morality play plot fits well within an accepted 1950s genre that included films like *Rebel without a Cause,* but what made *West Side Story* different was its marriage of the classical and the hip. Bernstein's almost operatic score accentuates the incisive hard edged lyrics of Sondheim, and Robbin's balletic choreography stretches tautly over the angry grace of youth with nothing to lose. With words like "juvenile delinquent" and "street gang" beginning to pop up in the news media, *West Side Story* gave the delinquent a voice, a cool, powerful archetype of a voice.

Some have criticized the play for glamorizing gangs, and others have called its portrayal of Puerto Ricans racist. Indeed, both the Broadway play and movie were flawed by a lack of authentic Latin casting. Of the major cast members, only Chita Rivera in the play and Rita Moreno in the movie (both, coincidentally, playing Bernardo's girlfriend Anita) were Latina. In spite of these weak points, it remains one of the strongest popular statements about troubled youth and the devastating effects of poverty and racism. In the song "Gee, Officer Krupke!," the Jets stage a mock scenario where a delinquent is shunted from police to judge to psychiatrist to social worker, coming to the dismal conclusion that juvenile delinquency is an ailment of society and, "No one wants a fella with a social disease!" The song is

as explicit as a sociological treatise about the causes of many of the problems of urban youth, and its acute goofiness easily transcends decades of at-risk teenagers.

The Shark's counterpoint to "Officer Krupke" is the song "America," sung by the Puerto Ricans about their new homeland. It is a bitter condemnation of the lie behind the "land of opportunity" couched in a rousing Latin rhythm and framed as an argument (in the play it is a debate among the girls; in the movie it is between the boys and the girls). "Here you are free and you have pride!" one side crows. "As long as you stay on your own side," the other counters. "Free to do anything you choose." "Free to wait tables and shine shoes." The song is a lively dance, showing the triumph of the spirit over the obstacles often faced by immigrants.

In contrast to the jubilantly angry mood of songs like "Officer Krupke" and "America," the song "Cool," sung by the leader of the Jets, seems to be ushering in a new age. Displacing the hotheaded cocky swagger of the 1950s, "Cool" ("Boy, boy, crazy boy, stay cool boy / Take it slow cause, daddy-o, you can live it up and die in bed") seems to point the way to the beatnik era of the 1960s, where rebellion takes a more passively resistant form.

On the cusp of the 1960s, American society, still recovering from the enormous upheaval of World War II, was seeking stability and control. American youth, particularly poor urban youth, rebelled against the falseness of this new American dream. *West Side Story* gave complacent 1950s audiences a taste of the bitter life on the streets, where working class youth had little opportunity in their future, and "owning the streets," or controlling activity in their gang's territory, was their only way of claiming power. Since life for disadvantaged youth has changed little, the musical still speaks to audiences. Since its long Broadway run and its acclaimed film release, *West Side Story* has been widely revived as a play in theater companies across the United States and in many other countries. The soundtrack albums for both the play and movie rode the Billboard 200 chart for lengthy periods. There have been Japanese and Chinese versions of the Sharks and Jets. In the mid-1980s, a recording of the score was released featuring world renowned opera singers, and in the mid-1990s, one was released featuring current pop stars. Though *Romeo and Juliet* has been reprised many times, few productions have managed as well as *West Side Story* to so capture a moment in history, as well as the universality of the hopes of youth tangled in the violence of society.

—Tina Gianoulis

FURTHER READING:

Bernstein, Leonard. *West Side Story*. New York, Random House, 1958.

Garesian, Keith. *The Making of West Side Story*. Toronto, LPC/ Inbook, 1995.

The Western

Over the course of the twentieth century, the cultural significance of the Western has overwhelmed the borders of a simple film genre. The Western film's many incarnations remain the most obvious and popular frame for the mythos of the American frontier, but the Western itself is usefully conceptualized as a widely transitory aesthetic mode comprised of recognizable conventions and icons that have spread across the face of international culture. From early-nineteenth-century examples like wild west shows, wilderness paintings, and dime novels to the legions of celluloid cowboys and Indians that ruled American movie houses from the 1930s through the 1960s, the full scope and majesty of the Western also made substantial contributions to radio dramas, television series, comic books, advertisements, rodeos, musicals, and novels. As the Western's various forms continue to coat our cultural landscape, its apparently simple images have acquired a prolific range of meanings. Today, the Western constitutes a truly international entity, but its visual and ideological roots retain a distinctly American sense of rugged individualism and entrepreneurship. At the heart of its mythology of cowboys, Indians, horses, and six-guns, the Western can be read as a potent allegory for American society. All the hopes, triumphs, failures, and anxieties of American cultural identity are subtly written into the Western's landscape.

The primary colors of the Western palette are simple but bold. First, the Western can never be Eastern; its aesthetic foundations are consistently grounded in the South, West, or Northwest portion of the American continents. Some Westerns like *The Treasure of the Sierra*

Madre (1948) or *Butch Cassidy and the Sundance Kid* (1969) migrate as far as South America. The Lone Ranger enjoyed a brief sojourn fighting pirates on the Barbary Coast, and *Midnight Cowboy*'s (1969) Texan Hustler, Joe Buck, even emigrates to New York City. In every case, the Westerner always operates in a distinctly obvious fashion that effectively brings the West into foreign and exotic locales. Jim Kitses and Edward Buscombe suggest that the Western mode is essentially a fusion of American history, myth, and art into

> a series of structuring tensions: between the individual and the community, between nature and culture, freedom and restriction, agrarianism and industrialism. All are physically separated by the frontier between the West and the East. These differences may be manifested in conflicts between gunfighters and townspeople, between ranchers and farmers, Indians and settlers, outlaws and sheriffs. But such are the complexities and richness of the material that the precise placing of any group or individual within these oppositions can never be pre-determined. Indians may well signify savagery; but sometimes they stand for what is positive in the idea of "nature." Outlaws may be hostile to civilization; but Jesse James often represents the struggle of agrarian values against encroaching industrialization.

A man with a gun is usually at the center of these continually shifting situations and conflicts. In any medium, from advertising to radio, the Western drama is rarely resolved without some use of, or reference to, masculine violence. The Western's "game" of binary conflicts also relies on an easily recognized hierarchy of standardized pawns. These "stock" characters comprise a profoundly limited cast of expressive icons headed by principal Westerners like the cowboy, the gunslinger, the sheriff, the cavalry man, the outlaw, the rancher, and the farmer. These are often accompanied by feminine companions and minor bourgeois players like the frontier wife, the saloon tart, the town drunk, the doctor, the mayor, the merchant, the gambler, the barber, the prospector, and the undertaker. Minorities like Mexicans, Indians, and half-breeds tend to exist on the periphery as obvious antagonists, "faithful companions," or ambiguous alien influences. Whatever their arrangement, this specialized cast populates a decidedly wild, moral universe that codifies the ethical complexities of a century that seeks order and peace through nostalgic backward glances at the untamed west. The form's continual preoccupation with the ghosts of the Civil War, the threat of Indian miscegenation, and the disappearance of the open plains all emphasize our wish to simplify or assuage a problem in American society through Western pageantry. Phil Hardy carefully delineates the cultural significance of the Western's therapeutic charms:

> In short, at a time when frustratingly complex issues like the Bomb, the Cold War, the House Un-American Activities Committee and Suez, were being raised, the Western remained a simple, unchanging, clear cut world in which notions of Good and Evil could be balanced against each other in an easily recognizable fashion.

This is not to say that Good always triumphs or that Good ever appears as constant and clear cut as the authors of Westerns might

John Wayne (left) with Montgomery Clift in a scene from the film *Red River*.

have wished. On the contrary, the evolution of the Western exhibits a tendency towards both pious optimism and depressed cynicism. For all the vibrant Americana celebrated in John Ford's *My Darling Clementine* (1946), Westerns like William Wellman's *Ox-Bow Incident* (1943), Sam Fuller's *Run of the Arrow* (1957), and Robert Altman's *McCabe and Mrs. Miller* (1971) depict a decidedly pessimistic American milieu that turns on ruthless physical, racial, and economic violence like lynching, massacres, and prostitution.

The majority of Western art obsesses over the stature of the ''Westerner,'' the white male hero in arms. Often expressed through the pedagogic interactions of men and children in films like *Red River* (1948), *Shane* (1953), and *High Noon* (1952), boys, sons, and orphans idealize the resolute father figures that teach them how to think, work, and fight. In radio drama, most Western heroes had young apprentices like the Lone Ranger's Dan Reed and Red Ryder's Little Beaver. Some Westerns like *Duel in the Sun* (1946), *The Searchers* (1956), *Broken Lance* (1954), and *The Shootist* (1979) would complicate this patriarchal formula with Oedipal and fraternal rebellions, but these conflicts usually result in an improvement or re-evaluation of the original pedagogical perpetuation of male control.

Although women and minorities often play crucial roles in the development of white western identity, these groups are consistently relegated to marginal status. Forward, sensual Western women like *My Darling Clementine*'s Chihuahua, *Duel in the Sun*'s Pearl, and *Destry Rides Again*'s (1939) Frenchy usually pay a deadly price for their sexual candor. A sexualized female only finds comfort in a Western scenario when humble heroes like *Stagecoach*'s (1939) Ringo Kid decide to ignore the tainted past of painted women like Dallas or when Ransom Stoddard shuttles the illiterate Hallie back East in *The Man Who Shot Liberty Valance* (1962). Jane Russell's infamous portrayal of Rio in *The Outlaw* (1943) remains one of the more celebrated exceptions to this otherwise deadly standard. The tough but modest frontier wives like *Shane*'s Marion Starrett and *High Noon*'s Quaker bride, Amy Kane, refrain from blatant action until their husbands require such activity. Male and female Mexicans and mulattos walk a grotesque line between hapless clowns à la *Stagecoach* and *The Magnificent Seven* (1960) or monstrous despots like the Rojos of *A Fistful of Dollars* (1964) and General Mapache in *The Wild Bunch* (1969). Native Americans generally signify the ethnic foil to white male order. This contrast can manifest itself as ravaging hordes in *Stagecoach* and *The Searchers*, as predictable savages in *Red River* and *The Naked Spur* (1953), or as noble alternatives to white hegemony in the Lone Ranger's Tonto, *Cheyenne Autumn* (1964), and *Dances with Wolves* (1990). Some revisionist Westerns like *Soldier Blue* (1970), *Little Big Man* (1970), and *A Man Called Horse* (1970) exhibit a morbid fascination with the cultural conflicts between white and "red" men, but the majority of Western art continues to produce a very ambiguous mystification of Native American culture.

Founded on a mixture of nineteenth-century American history, the melodramatic frontier fiction of James Fenimore Cooper and James Oliver Curwood, and the Western visions of Frederic Remington, Charles Russell, and Jules Tavernier, the Hollywood Western film has become the most prevalent of all modern wild west shows. In many ways, the Western and the movies have grown up together. Some of the earliest silent films like *Kit Carson* and *The Great Train Robbery* (1903) or *The Squaw Man* (1907) clearly echo Western themes, although they were probably likened to contemporary crime thrillers at the time of their production. As silent film matured into an art form in the 1910s and 1920s, early cowboy heroes like Broncho Billy Anderson, William S. Hart, Hoot Gibson, Harry Carey, Tom Mix, Buck Jones, and Tim McCoy initiated various flavors of Western entertainment. While Anderson, Hart, and McCoy created what Buscombe calls the realistic "good badman" whose natural roughness also includes a heart of gold, Tom Mix and others opted to formulate a more fantastic Jazz Age cowboy whose rope tricks, fancy duds, and horseback stunts revived the Wild West Carnival aesthetics of Buffalo Bill Cody and Annie Oakley. Later Western stars like John Wayne and Gary Cooper would epitomize the rough benevolence of the good badman, until Clint Eastwood's cool "Man with No Name" popularized the professional gunfighter in the mid-1960s. In later films like *The Magnificent Seven, The Wild Bunch,* and *The Long Riders* (1980), the gunfighter and the outlaw face a moral war between killing as a vocation and settling down on the frontier. Such films detail a world of lonely, desperate mercenaries and criminals whose worst enemy is the double-edged sword of their own profession.

Almost from the beginning, studios began to distinguish between prestigious "A" Westerns and the run-of-the-mill "B"-grade horse opera. Early studios like Biograph and Bison churned out silent serial Westerns whose standardized melodramas became the basis for the sub-genre of "B"-grade cowboy movies that would remain relatively unaltered well into the 1950s. By the mid-1930s, these series Westerns, produced predominantly by Herbert Yates' amalgamated Republic Pictures, had become an easily appreciated prefab package:

> There would be a fist fight within the first few minutes, a chase soon after, and, inevitably, a shoot-out at the end. Plots were usually motivated by some straightforward villainy which could be exposed and decisively defeated by the hero ... it was also common for footage to be reused. Costly scenes of Indian attacks or stampedes would re-appear, more or less happily satisfying the demands of continuity in subsequent productions.

For all their apparent poverty and simplicity, these assembly line dramas prepared both the talent and the audience that would eventually propel the "A" Western into its own. Some prestige epics like *The Big Trail* (1930), *The Covered Wagon* (1923), and the Oscar-winning best picture of 1930, *Cimarron*, clearly invoked Western forms, but Westerns for the most part were considered second-tier kiddy shows until the unprecedented success of John Ford's *Stagecoach* in 1939. *Stagecoach*'s microcosm of American society—complete with a

hypocritical banker, an arrogant debutante, a Southern gentleman, and the fiery youth of a suddenly famous John Wayne—proved that Western scenarios could yield serious entertainment. Soon after, Hollywood's production of Westerns rose rapidly as both "A" and "B" Westerns thrived in the hands of the most talented Hollywood actors and auteurs. Reaching its zenith in 1950, when 34 percent of all Hollywood films involved a Western scenario, the genre had developed a new energy and scope surrounding "A"- and "B"-level personalities like John Wayne, Henry Fonda, James Stewart, Audie Murphy, Roy Rogers, Gary Cooper, Randolph Scott, Ward Bond, and Joel McCrea. Amid the host of Western formula pictures, Phil Hardy notes the exciting innovations of Western auteur directors like Boetticher, Ford, Mann, Daves, Dwan, Fuller, Hawks, Lang, Penn, Ray, Sturges, Tourneur, and Walsh, who produced individual masterpieces through their manipulation of popular narrative forms.

Throughout the 1940s and 1950s, cinema remained the dominant showcase for Western drama, but other lesser Western media were also inundating American culture. While horses galloped across the silver screen, the roar of six guns also glutted the air waves as radio and TV shows brought the West into countless American living rooms. Between 1952 and 1970 no less than 11 Western TV series were on the air in any single year. The Lone Ranger, Matt Dillon, Hopalong Cassidy and their lesser known associates like Straight Arrow, the Six-Shooter (played by Jimmy Stewart), and Curly Burly, the Singing Marshall offered a generation of children almost daily doses of Western idealism. Often, these heroes became highly merchandised icons, moving from pulp magazines into commercial radio, matinee serials, TV series, and comic books. Thus, *Gunsmoke*'s Matt Dillon and *Have Gun, Will Travel*'s Paladin became product-driven Cowboy myths. Every TV series like *Rawhide, Gunsmoke, Bonanza, Maverick, The Big Valley,* and *The Wild, Wild West* had its own tie-in comic book that lingered in young hands during the many hours between broadcasts. The Lone Ranger himself appeared in over 10 different comic series, the last appearing as late as 1994. The 10-cent comic market could even bear separate series for Western Sidekicks like Tonto and Little Beaver. For almost eight years, Dell comics exclusively devoted an entire series to the Lone Ranger's faithful stallion, Silver. Major Western stars like John Wayne, Tim Holt, Gabby Hayes, Andy Devine, Roy Rogers, Dale Evans, and Hopalong Cassidy also bolstered their popularity through four-color dime comics, accentuating their already firm star image through the mass market pantheon of Western characters like the Ghost Rider, the Rawhide Kid, and Jonah Hex.

From the 1940s through the 1960s, while Anthony Mann twisted the genre with cynical stories of desperate and introspective Westerners and John Ford began a series of bitter re-examinations of his earlier frontier optimism, another form of self-conscious aestheticized Western had emerged—the musical. Clearly indebted to early singing cowboys like Gene Autry and Roy Rogers, the new singing Western fused song and dance spectacle with honky-tonk themes and images. Songs like Cole Porter's "Don't Fence Me In" and Livingston and Evans' Oscar-winning "Buttons and Bows" allowed popular vocalists a chance to dress up in silk bandanas, cow hide vests, and sequined Stetsons. Groups like the Sons of the Pioneers and the Riders of the Purple Sage celebrated trendy Cowboy fashions while Hollywood's *Oklahoma!* (1955), *Red Garters* (1954), *Annie Get Your Gun* (1950), *Paint Your Wagon* (1969), and *Seven Brides for Seven*

Brothers (1954) promoted melodious western set pieces. Even the down-to-earth satirist Will Rogers' rope-tricking, cowboy persona lent a humble quality to his jibes between numbers in the Ziegfeld Follies. Comedies and parodies also proliferated. Early Western clowning included Charles Laughton in *Ruggles of Red Gap* (1935) and Bob Hope in the *Paleface* films of 1948 and 1952. Among the most important later moments in Western comedy are Lee Marvin's Oscar-winning self-parody of a drunken gunfighter in *Cat Ballou* (1965), James Garner's send-up of *My Darling Clementine* in *Support Your Local Sheriff* (1969), and Mel Brooks's hugely successful black cowboy feature, *Blazing Saddles* (1973).

In the 1960s and 1970s, the traditionally conservative ideology of Western films fell prey to several new influences. The "International Western" reconfigured traditionally American material with an exaggerated European accent. The Italian-produced "Spaghetti Westerns" of Sergio Leone starring Clint Eastwood as the shrewd, silent nameless mercenary rejuvenated a genre that had become fairly exhausted in American hands. Leone revised tired gun fight scenarios through slow tension-building showdowns comprised of excruciatingly tight close-ups and split-second gun battles. Ennio Morricone's now famous parodic scores also lent Leone's gory duels and forbidding scenery a fascinating, surreal atmosphere. Leone's psychedelically violent images played alongside the American revisionist Westerns of Sam Peckinpah, Robert Altman, and Arthur Penn. As *Pat Garrett and Billy the Kid* (1973), *Buffalo Bill and the Indians* (1976), *McCabe and Mrs. Miller* (1971), and *Little Big Man* (1970) deconstructed long-established Western hierarchies, Dennis Hopper's *Easy Rider* (1969) subtly defiled the Cowboy image as his Buffalo Billy sold drugs, dropped acid, and toured America on a Harley. During the cultural upheaval of the 1960s, this trend towards the deconstruction of Western myths signified a popular cultural need to interrogate and explode previously accepted signs and images. For all their gratuitous revision, however the grim tales of drunks, swindlers, and psychopaths that dominate late 1960s and 1970s Westerns contributed a much-needed update to the general credibility and appreciation of Western forms. Of all these self-conscious filmmakers, only Clint Eastwood continued as a popular Western actor and director; his *Outlaw Josey Wales* (1976), *Pale Rider* (1985), and *Unforgiven* (1992) represent intense eulogies to older visions of the American West.

The postmodern Western of the eighties and nineties has sprouted into several fairly distinct branches. On the one hand, films like *Silverado* (1985), *The Quick and The Dead* (1995), *Maverick* (1994), *The Wild Wild West* (1999), *Young Guns* (1988), *Bad Girls* (1994), *Tombstone* (1993), and *Posse* (1993) utilize Western aesthetics as appropriated dramatic frames that emphasize their stars. More obviously expensive Western epics like *Dances with Wolves, Wyatt Earp* (1994), and *Lonesome Dove* (1989) attempt to recreate the spectacle of the great open plains. Along with these comprehensive Westerns, a noticeable Cowboy strain has leaked into blockbuster franchises like *Back to the Future III* (1990), unpopular "punk" odysseys like *Straight to Hell* (1987) and *Dudes* (1987), Neo-Noir Westerns like *Flesh and Bone* (1993) and *Red Rock West* (1993), and pastiche "cult" odysseys like *Buckaroo Banzai in the Eighth Dimension* (1984). Even the *The Muppet Movie* (1979) appropriates an old fashioned Western showdown. The 1990s have also seen a revival of the contemporary Western. Art house films like *Western* (1998), *The Hi-Lo Country* (1999), *Lone Star* (1996), and *The Last Picture Show*

(1971) find their roots in the well-named Hollywood epic, *Giant* (1956), and its quieter companions like *Hud* (1963), *The Lusty Men* (1952), *Bronco Billy* (1980), and *The Electric Horseman* (1979). These films are more concerned with describing the life of the modern west and the plight of the twentieth-century Westerner than in revising the myths of the old frontier. At same time however, each film offers sharp insight into how completely the Western and its heroes have shaped the popular appreciation of America's past.

—Daniel Yezbick

FURTHER READING:

Bazin, Andre. *What is Cinema? Volume II*. Berkeley, University of California Press, 1971.

Buscombe, Edward, editor. *The BFI Companion to the Western*. New York, Da Capo, 1988.

Cameron, Ian, and Douglas Pyle, editors. *The Book of Westerns*. New York, Continuum, 1996.

Frayling, Christopher. *Spaghetti Westerns*. London, Routledge, 1981.

Hardy, Phil, editor. *The Overlook Film Encyclopedia: The Western*. New York, Penguin, 1995.

Kitses, Jim. *Horizons West*. Bloomington, Indiana University Press, 1970.

MacDonald, J. Fred. *Don't Touch that Dial!: Radio Programming in American Life from 1920 to 1960*. Chicago, Nelson-Hall, 1996.

Mitchell, Lee Clark. *Westerns*. Chicago, University of Chicago Press, 1996.

Nachbar, Jack, editor. *Focus on the Western*. Englewood Cliffs, New Jersey, Prentice-Hall, 1974.

Newman, Kim. *Wild West Movies*. London, Bloomsbury, 1990.

Wharton, Edith (1862-1937)

Edith Wharton, one of the most successful American novelists of her time, wrote twenty-five novels and novellas as well as eighty-six short stories. Her *Age of Innocence* (1920), about Old New York society, won a Pulitzer prize, and she was the first woman to receive either the honorary Doctor of Letters from Yale University or the Gold Medal of the National Institute of Arts and Letters. Though critics have often over-emphasized Henry James's influence upon her, she has impacted American narrative in many ways, perhaps most notably in her treatment of gender issues and the supernatural.

—Joe Sutliff Sanders

FURTHER READING:

Roillard, Douglas, editor. *American Supernatural Fiction: From Edith Wharton to the Weird Tales Writers*. New York, Garland Publishing, 1996.

Singley, Carol J. *Edith Wharton: Matters of Mind and Spirit*. New York, Cambridge University Press, 1995.

What Would Jesus Do?

See WWJD? (What Would Jesus Do?)

What's My Line?

The television panel game *What's My Line?* became an American favorite in the course of its 17-year-long run. Aired on CBS from February 2, 1950 through September 3, 1967, it remains the longest-running show of its type in prime-time television history, having seduced viewers with a premise both rudimentary and clever. Contestants with uncommon occupations first signed their names on a blackboard, and then whispered their "lines," or professions, to master of ceremonies John Daly and the viewers at home. Next, four panelists queried the contestants in order to ascertain their professions. Questions could be answered only with a simple "yes" or "no." For each "no" response, a contestant earned $5; after ten negatives, the game ended with the contestant pocketing $50. One participant each week was a "mystery guest," an easily identifiable celebrity. Here, out of necessity, the panelists donned masks, with the contestants responding to questions in distorted voices.

The show, a Mark Goodson-Bill Todman production, exuded a civilized, urbane Park Avenue/Fifth Avenue Manhattan air. John Daly, the likable moderator, whose background was in journalism,

What's My Line moderator John Daly (center) is surrounded by regular panelists (from left) Arlene Francis, Bennet Cerf, and Dorothy Kilgallen.

established this ambience throughout its 17 years on the air until syndication. He bowed out on the syndicated version, produced between 1968 and 1975 and hosted by Wally Bruner and Larry Blyden. In the early years of the show, Daly concurrently enjoyed a high profile at rival networks, anchoring the ABC evening news between 1953 and 1960, while hosting *What's My Line?* for CBS.

The panelists on the debut broadcast were syndicated gossip columnist Dorothy Kilgallen (who stayed until her death in 1965), poet-critic Louis Untermeyer, former New Jersey governor Harold Hoffman, and Dr. Richard Hoffman, a psychiatrist. The following week, actress Arlene Francis came on board, and remained for the show's duration. Other regular panelists during the 1950s were television personality Steve Allen, comedian Fred Allen, and joke writer Hal Block. By the end of the decade, the group most often consisted of the set trio of Francis, Kilgallen, and writer, raconteur and co-founder of Random House publishers, Bennett Cerf, who joined the panel in 1951 and remained until the show went off the air. These three were supplemented with a celebrity guest panelist.

While watching *What's My Line?* and hearing the amusing and sophisticated banter of its panelists, one might have been eavesdropping on a chic and exclusive party whose guests included New York's wittiest intellectuals, peppered with celebrities from the world of entertainment, sports, and politics. The panelists in fact were personalities who exuded New York Upper East Side style, and donned their masks as if preparing for a society costume ball.

The contestants on *What's My Line?* were awesome in their variety. Over the years they included oddball inventors, tugboat captains, pet cemetery grave diggers, pitters of prunes and dates, thumbtack makers, pigeon trainers, female baseball stitchers, gas station attendants, and even a purveyor of fried chicken, who turned out to be none other than Colonel Harlan Sanders. As for the "mystery guests," writer/show business habitué Max Wilk has noted that, "it would be far more simple to list the names of the celebrities who have *not* appeared on the show over all these years than it would be to list those who did." Among them were athletes (Phil Rizzuto, who was the first *What's My Line?* mystery guest, and Ty Cobb), poets (Carl Sandburg), politicians (Eleanor Roosevelt, Estes Kefauver, Everett Dirksen), and numerous movie and television personalities from Gracie Allen to Warren Beatty, Ed Wynn, Ed McMahon, Harold Lloyd, and Howdy Doody.

The panelists on the final network telecast of *What's My Line?* were Arlene Francis, her actor husband Martin Gabel, Bennett Cerf, and Steve Allen. The mystery guest, appropriately enough, was John Daly!

—Rob Edelman

Further Reading:

Fates, Gilbert. *What's My Line? The Inside History of TV's Most Famous Panel Show,* Englewood Cliffs, New Jersey, Prentice-Hall, 1978.

Wheel of Fortune

In 1998, America's most popular television game show, *Wheel of Fortune,* celebrated its fifteenth year in syndication by broadcasting for the 3000th time. In the ubiquitous game created by executive producer Merv Griffin, popular co-hosts Pat Sajak and Vanna White have awarded contestants over $98 million in cash and prizes for guessing the blank letters of mystery phrases, with the winning amounts determined by spins of a giant wheel. While the wheel spins, it is traditional for contestants to scream "Big money!" and join Vanna in clapping hands. In fact, Miss White is listed in the *Guinness Book of World Records* as television's most frequent hand-clapper, averaging 720 claps per show and 28,000 per season.

The original *Wheel of Fortune* aired on NBC as a daytime game show on January 6, 1975, with hosts Chuck Woolery and Susan Stafford. Pat Sajak made his debut on the show in December 1981, with Stafford continuing as co-host. Vanna replaced Stafford in December 1982, and the show moved from the network to syndication in 1983, placing it in prime-time slots and greatly increasing the audience.

Pat Sajak likes to say, "I must have been born with broadcasting genes." He remembers sneaking out of bed at age eleven to watch Jack Paar host *The Tonight Show.* Even then he aspired to host his own television show some day. Sajak attended Columbia College in his native Chicago, majoring in broadcasting, before landing his first professional job as a newscaster on radio station WDDC in his hometown. The Vietnam War interrupted his career in 1968, and the 21-year-old Sajak was assigned as morning disc jockey with Armed Forces Radio in Saigon. During his eighteen months in that post, Sajak opened his show as Robin Williams did in the movie *Good Morning, Vietnam,* with the words, "Gooood morrrning, Vietnaaam!"

After his army discharge in 1972, Sajak worked briefly as a radio disc jockey in Kentucky and Washington, D.C., before landing his first television job as local weatherman on WSM-TV in Nashville, Tennessee. His relaxed style and sharp wit brought him additional assignments as host of a public affairs program as well as a talk show. In 1977 he was brought to Los Angeles to host KNBC's weekend public affairs program and to serve as their local weatherman. Four years later he was selected by Merv Griffin to host *Wheel of Fortune,* a match made in television heaven. He went on to star in many network and syndicated specials, briefly hosted a late night talk show in 1989, and appeared as a guest star on dozens of comedy, drama, and talk shows. He has won two Emmy Awards, a People's Choice Award, and a star on the Hollywood Walk of Fame. He lives in Los Angeles with his wife, Lesly, and their two children.

Vanna White, born in North Myrtle Beach, South Carolina, in 1957, attended the Atlanta School of Fashion design and became a top model in that area before moving to Los Angeles to pursue an acting career. In 1982, she auditioned for the job as Sajak's co-host on America's favorite game show and was selected from a field of more than 400 letter-turning hopefuls. Although she has been called the Wheel's "silent star," her weekly fan mail numbers in the thousands, and she is a frequent guest on talk shows. Her autobiography, *Vanna Speaks,* was a national bestseller. Her fans enjoy her habit of making a different fashion statement for every show and, at last count in 1998, she had worn 5,750 outfits in her career. Vanna is also seen in commercials, a nutritional video, and as the star of an NBC made for television movie, *Goddess of Love,* as well as cameos in various Hollywood movies. She lives in Beverly Hills with her husband, George, and two children, Nicholas and Giovanna.

One of the secrets of the ongoing success of *Wheel of Fortune* has been adding new features to the show's familiar format. High technology has been employed to update Vanna's puzzle board. Instead of turning letters, she activates the touch-sensitive membrane switches on a bank of 52 high-resolution Sony monitors. Interest in the show is heightened by special weeks in which the contestants are soap opera stars, best friends, celebrities and their moms, college students, and professional football players. The show has been renewed with a long-term contract through 2002.

—Benjamin Griffith

FURTHER READING:

Inman, David. *The TV Encyclopedia.* New York, Perigee Books, 1991.

White, Vanna. *Vanna Speaks.* New York, Warner, 1989.

Whisky a Go Go

Infused with the neon energy of the Sunset Strip, the Whisky a Go Go stands as Los Angeles's (L.A.) richest repository of rock 'n' roll history. With the affluence of Beverly Hills and Malibu to its west, the fantasy of Hollywood to its east, West Hollywood's gay and lesbian influence directly south, and "the hills," home to the world's rich and famous, above it, the Whisky finds itself at the heart of a city in which anything can happen—and often does. As its decades at the corner of Clark Drive and the famed Sunset Boulevard have proven, the Whisky's roster of rock performers chronicles the evolution of L.A.'s highly influential music industry and its impact on popular culture at large.

Older than neighboring rock 'n' roll haunts such as the Roxy and the Rainbow, the Whisky emerged onto L.A.'s music scene in January of 1964. Owners Elmer Valentine and Mario Maglieri transformed an old, three-story bank building into a Parisian-inspired discotheque complete with female DJs (Disc Jockeys) dancing in cages suspended above the stage. Hence, the term go-go girl was born.

The Whisky quickly became a breeding ground for the most influential musical talent of the mid-to-late 1960s. Opening night featured Johnny Rivers, whose blues-inspired pop album titled *Johnny Rivers at the Whisky a Go Go* took him to the top of the charts. Johnny Carson, Rita Hayworth, Lana Turner, and Steve McQueen were just a few of the personalities who turned out to revel in Rivers's performance.

As the turbulent socio-political energy of the late 1960s gained momentum, so too did the influence of the Whisky. Bands such as The Doors and Buffalo Springfield brought revolutionary sounds to the music world, and attracted the likes of John Belushi and Charles Manson to the venue. Guitar legend Jimi Hendrix dropped in on several occasions to jam with the Whisky's house bands, and rock's raspy leading lady, Janis Joplin, downed her last bottle of Southern Comfort at the Whisky before her death in 1970.

While the Whisky name is associated with some of the most significant performers of every rock era since the club's opening, it is the explosive decadence of the late 1960s that has most decisively defined the Whisky's place in the popular imagination. In his vivid film evocation of the period, *The Doors* (1991), Oliver Stone used simulated live footage of one of The Doors' early performances on the

Dancers at the Whisky a Go Go.

Whisky stage to recreate the spirit of that era's radical, drug-fueled excess. The film, and other similar representations of the 1960s, affirm the Whisky's status as a potent emblem of the rebellious energy of a particular moment in music and pop culture history.

Despite its indisputable ''hot spot'' status during the 1960s, the Whisky's popularity waned in the early 1970s as a softer, more folk-inspired sound penetrated live music in Los Angeles. The Whisky nearly burned to the ground in 1971, and the club was forced to close for several months before re-opening as a discotheque. With the buzz of its formative decade behind it, the club's producers sought out more economical performance ideas for the space, and operating a dance club appeared to be a cheaper, less troublesome, alternative to the live music format. The venue also hosted minor theatrical performances such as *The Rocky Horror Picture Show* during this period, but no attempt to transform the Whisky attracted the kind of talent or intensity that the club had cultivated during the 1960s.

The rebirth of the Whisky as a rock club occurred in the late 1970s, when the embers of a punk scene in L.A. began to smolder. The influence of punk bands from both London (the Sex Pistols, the Damned) and New York (Patti Smith, the Ramones) inspired L.A. groups like the Runaways and the Quick to bring a brash, do-it-yourself approach to music and to the Whisky. Kim Fowley, son of actor Douglas Fowley, hosted a ''New Wave Rock 'N' Roll Weekend'' at the Whisky in 1977 and introduced the likes of the Germs and the Weirdos to the Sunset Strip scene. Shortly thereafter, the legendary Elvis Costello played his first L.A. gig at the club.

By the early 1980s, rock once again ruled the L.A. music scene—and the Whisky—although this time in a much less lucrative fashion. No longer did the Whisky pay its bands for an evening's performance. Rather, upon reopening as a live venue—around the time that music mogul Lou Adler bought into the club—the musical acts themselves paid the Whisky for the opportunity to perform on its coveted stage. This new ''pay to play'' approach not only demonstrated how valuable the Whisky's reputation had become to up-and-coming talent, but also confirmed the fact that the music business itself was changing. The tremendous popularity of rock music yielded a surplus of bands, which shifted the market in favor of clubs and promoters. Groups had to compete for stage space and ultimately finance (or hope that a record company would pay for) their own publicity.

Against this new economic backdrop, a number of hard rock and metal bands—including mega-stars Van Halen, Guns N'Roses, and Metallica—rose to prominence in the 1980s. While these glam bad boys went on to fill tens of thousands of seats in arenas all over the world, they could all point to the Whisky's stage as the site of some of their earliest live performances.

In the early 1990s, the Whisky hosted a number of Seattle-based musicians who would later be dubbed "the godfathers of grunge." Bands such as Soundgarden, Nirvana, Mudhoney, The Melvins, and 7 Year Bitch brought their guitar-laden, punk-loyal sound to Los Angeles in a very large, very loud way. Grunge maintained an anti-aesthetic which scoffed at the glam-rock past of the 1980s, and seemed, if only briefly, to speak to the fears of a generation of teenagers ravaged by divorce and a distinctly postmodern sort of uncertainty. Throughout this time, the Whisky continued to act as a touchstone for local and indie bands and as a familiar haunt for the occasional celebrity rocker. Though the club's influence as a ground zero for cutting edge trends in the music industry—and youth culture in general—has diminished considerably since its heyday, the Whisky remains an important L.A. landmark and offers a revealing window into some of the most crucial figures and movement's of rock's relatively brief history.

—Jennifer Murray

FURTHER READING:

Huskyns, Barney. *Waiting For The Sun*. The Penguin Group, 1996.

Whistler's Mother

James Abbott McNeill Whistler's 1871 portrait of his mother, Anna Matilda McNeill, has crossed over from the realm of fine art to that of popular culture. Whistler (1834-1903), an expatriate American painter active in London and Paris, was one of a number of late nineteenth-century artists who downplayed subject matter and emphasized abstract values. People often refer to the painting as "Whistler's mother," but Whistler himself preferred to call it *Arrangement in Gray and Black*. Ironically, the painting is famous largely because of its subject. Recognized as a universal symbol of motherhood, Whistler's mother was featured, in 1934, on a United States postage stamp honoring Mother's Day. However, she has not always been treated so reverently. The somber, seated figure, a familiar reference point in many countries, has been widely lampooned in the popular performing, as well as visual, arts.

—Laural Weintraub

FURTHER READING:

Anderson, Ronald. *James McNeill Whistler: Beyond the Myth*. London, J. Murray, 1994.

Spencer, Robin. *Whistler*. Rev. ed. London, Studio Editions, 1993.

Barry White

White, Barry (1944—)

Barry White's immediately recognizable husky bass-inflected voice that obsessed over making love was a staple on black radio during the 1970s. Songs such as "Your Sweetness Is My Weakness," "Can't Get Enough of Your Love, Babe," and the appropriately titled "Love Makin' Music" made this heavy-set man a sex symbol, and were probably responsible for conceiving quite a few babies as well. And while his star did not shine as brightly through the 1980s and 1990s, White evolved into a oft-referred-to popular culture icon—appearing as himself on television shows like *The Simpsons* singing parodies of his own songs (which were already almost self-parodies).

Born in Galveston, Texas, White would work primarily out of Los Angeles and New York as an adult. White began his career in the music business at age 11, when he played piano on Jesse Belvin's hit single "Goodnight My Love." He recorded as a vocalist for a number of different labels in the early to mid-1960s, then went on to work as an A&R man for a small record label named Mustang. In 1969, White formed both a female trio called Love Unlimited, and a 40-piece instrumental group dubbed Love Unlimited Orchestra, the latter of which produced a number one Pop single in 1973, "Love's Theme."

The period of 1973-1974 was his commercial highpoint, with White performing on or producing a number of albums and singles

James Abbott McNeill Whistler's *"No. 1: Portrait of the Artist's Mother."*

that grossed a total of $16 million. Among his top ten Pop singles were: ''I'm Gonna Love You Just a Little More Baby,'' ''Never, Never Gonna Give Ya Up,'' ''You're the First, The Last, My Everything,'' ''What Am I Gonna Do With You,'' and the number one 1974 smash, ''Can't Get Enough of Your Love, Babe,'' as well as a handful of hits by Love Unlimited and Love Unlimited Orchestra.

While all of his up-tempo dance numbers and down-tempo slow jams tend to blend together, White was neither generic nor unoriginal. He had his own distinct style that can best be summed up lyrically in the following few lines from his song ''Love Serenade'': ''Take it off / Baby, take it aaaaalllllllllll off / I want you the way you came into the world / I don't wanna feel no clothes / I don't wanna see no panties / Take off that brassiere, my dear.'' White's spoken word delivery arguably influenced future rappers, and the drum breaks on songs like

''I'm Gonna Love You Just Little More Baby'' were sampled often by Hip-Hop artists.

Throughout the 1980s and 1990s, Barry White's chart presence almost seemed contingent on collaborating with other artists. For instance, his 1990 hit ''The Secret Garden'' (Sweet Seduction Suite) featured Al B. Sure!, James Ingram, Quincy Jones, and El DeBarge, and he also appeared on Big Daddy Kane's 1991 rhythm and blues hit ''All of Me,'' Lisa Stansfield's cover of ''Never, Never Gonna Give You Up,'' and Edie Brickell's ''Good Times'' (one of the strangest pairings of the 1990s). White also enjoyed some exposure from the sitcom *Ally McBeal,* in which the character John Cage sings and dances to White's ''You're the First, the Last, My Everything'' to prepare himself for a date.

—Kembrew McLeod

FURTHER READING:

Vincent, Rickey. *Funk: The Music, the People and the Rhythm of the One.* New York, St. Martin's Griffin, 1996.

White, Betty (1922—)

Betty White was one of the first women to form her own television production company, and she also became one of TV's best-loved performers, whether her character was sweetly innocent or a harridan. Her early roles ranged from girl-next-door (*Life with Elizabeth*, 1952-1955) to screwball wife (*Date with the Angels*, (1957-1958), but it was as a man-crazy schemer on *The Mary Tyler Moore Show* from 1973 to 1977 that White won her first major popularity. For her portrayal of the predatory Sue Ann Nivens, White won back-to-back best supporting actress Emmys (1975/1976), even though she appeared in less than half the episodes in any given season. After *The Mary Tyler Moore Show* ended, White briefly hosted a game show called *Just Men!* and became the only female to win an Emmy as best game-show host (1983). Two years later White returned to episodic television in the phenomenal hit *The Golden Girls* (1985-1992), in which she portrayed naive Rose Nyland, who never quite had the same conversation as those to whom she was talking and who often added seemingly unrelated comments dealing with life in her rural hometown, St. Olaf. A comedy that often placed the women in outlandish situations, the series showed that older women could have active lives, and it helped to weaken the ''ageism'' that had been a hallmark of American culture. In 1994 White became the tenth woman to be inducted into the Television Hall of Fame.

—Denise Lowe

FURTHER READING:

O'Dell, Cary. *Women Pioneers in Television.* Jefferson, North Carolina, McFarland & Company, 1997.

White, Betty. *Here We Go Again: My Life in Television.* New York, Scribner, 1995.

White Castle

White Castle was the world's original fast-food restaurant chain. From humble beginnings in Wichita, Kansas, White Castle grew into a large-scale multi-state operation that was copied by innumerable competitors. It all began when Walter Anderson, a short-order cook, developed a process in 1916 for making the lowly regarded hamburger more palatable to a distrusting public. He soon had a growing business of three shops. In 1921, Anderson took on a partner, Edward Ingram, a real estate and insurance salesman. Ingram coined the name and image of ''White Castle,'' based on the theory that '''White' signifies purity and 'Castle' represents strength, permanence and stability.'' By 1931 there were 115 standardized outlets in ten states. Previously, only grocery or variety stores had used the chain system. By providing inexpensive food in a clean environment at uniform

locations over a wide territory, White Castle helped shape the fast-food industry that would dominate the lives and landscape of America at the end of the twentieth century.

—Dale Allen Gyure

FURTHER READING:

Hogan, David Gerald. *Selling 'em by the Sack: White Castle and the Creation of American Food.* New York, New York University Press, 1998.

Ingram, E.W., Sr. *All This from a 5-cent Hamburger!* New York, Newcomen Society in North America, 1975.

Langdon, Philip. *Orange Roofs, Golden Arches: The Architecture of America's Chain Restaurants.* New York, Alfred A. Knopf, 1986.

White, E. B. (1899-1985)

Charlotte's Web author E. B. White has delighted people of all ages with his essays, poems, and classic children's stories since the 1920s. He was one of the early *New Yorker* writers and helped set the tone that established it as the magazine of elegant writing that it continued to be for decades.

Elwyn Brooks White graduated from Cornell University, where he was the editor of the *Cornell Sun.* He worked as a journalist and a copywriter in an advertising agency before joining the infant *New Yorker* in 1926. (Katharine Angell, who hired him, later became his wife.) From 1938-43, White contributed the monthly column ''One Man's Meat'' to *Harper's* magazine.

White's elegant yet informal, humorous, and humanitarian writing covered diverse subjects. Following the premature death of a pig in 1947 at the Whites' rural home in Maine, White said he wrote an essay ''in grief, as a man who failed to raise his pig.'' This same writing style is apparent in White's three classic children's books: *Stuart Little* (1945), about a mouse born to a human family and his adventures while searching for his best friend, a beautiful bird; *Charlotte's Web* (1952), in which a spider named Charlotte cleverly saves Wilbur the pig from death; and *The Trumpet of the Swan* (1970), in which a mute trumpeter swan tries to win the affection of the beautiful swan Serena.

In 1957 White published an essay praising his former Cornell English professor, William Strunk Jr., for his forty-three-page handbook on grammar—''the little book.'' White praised Strunk's attempt ''to cut the vast tangle of English rhetoric down to size and write its rules and principles on the head of a pin.'' A publisher coaxed the ever-modest White into reviving and revising *The Elements of Style* (1959), known among its users as ''Strunk and White,'' which has remained a fundamental text. White bolstered the original with an essay titled ''An Approach to Style,'' which remains a timeless reflection of the virtues of good writing.

—R. Thomas Berner

FURTHER READING:

Elledge, Scott. *E. B. White: A Biography.* New York, W. W. Norton, 1984.

Guth, Dorothy Lobrano, ed. *Letters of E. B. White.* New York, Harper & Row, 1976.

Hall, Katherine Romans. *E. B. White: A Bibliographic Catalogue of Printed Materials in the Department of Rare Books, Cornell University Library.* New York, Garland Publishing, 1979.

Root, Robert L. Jr., editor. *Critical Essays on E. B. White.* New York, G. K. Hall, 1994.

Russell, Isabel. *Katharine and E. B. White: An Affectionate Memoir.* New York, W. W. Norton, 1988.

Strunk, William Jr., and E. B. White. *The Elements of Style.* New York, Macmillan, 1959.

White, E. B. *Essays of E. B. White.* New York, Harper & Row, 1977.

———. *One Man's Meat.* New York, Harper & Row, 1942.

White Flight

White flight refers to the residential movement of whites to avoid self-determined, unacceptable levels of racial integration. Scholars disagree on how much race acts as a singular factor in white migratory decisions, many preferring a natural process called "ecological succession" in which older and less desirable housing stock filters down to lower status classes. The great episodes of neighborhood turnover in the United States after World War II, however, prompted social scientists to focus specifically on race as a "tipping point" that stimulated white exodus to suburbs and newer suburban areas.

White flight was principally a twentieth-century urban phenomenon. Before 1900, ninety percent of African Americans lived in the South. The few black populations in northern cities were small and highly centralized. Occasionally, upper-class blacks intermingled with whites and other ethnic groups. Deteriorating social and economic conditions in the South, including lynchings, led to a mass exodus of African Americans to northern cities starting around the time of World War I. These migrations increased the populations of African Americans in cities such as Chicago from as little as 2 percent in 1910 to more than 30 percent by 1970.

At first, newer ethnic groups were the most affected. Jewish residents felt compelled to move from Chicago's Maxwell Street neighborhood and New York's Harlem area by increasing numbers of blacks around 1920. The latter process contributed directly to the Harlem arts and cultural renaissance. Threatened by the social and cultural disruptions portended by African American mobility with time, native-born whites responded as well. They lobbied politicians, bankers, and real estate agents to restrict blacks informally to designated black neighborhoods, usually comprised of older housing stock. The Baltimore city council enacted an ordinance forbidding any black person from moving into a block where a majority of the residents were white in 1910, and a dozen other cities followed suit, even though the United States Supreme Court declared residential segregation unconstitutional in 1917. The all-white apartment house of Ralph and Alice Kramden as portrayed in the 1950s television series *The Honeymooners* personified inner-city racial exclusion. When legal or extra-legal exclusionary tactics failed, whites resorted to out-migration, turning over a neighborhood to their former adversaries. Residential homogeneity could be based on factors such as class, religion, or ethnicity, but white flight came to be the term for relocation related to racial differences.

Housing demand, restricted by the Depression and the exigencies of World War II, exploded in the decades following the war. New developments appeared almost overnight in outer-city and suburban areas, yet existing social standards continued to dictate settlement patterns based on racial considerations. The attractions of new suburbs, available only to middle and upper class whites, and the growing housing needs of African Americans produced an era of unprecedented racial turnover in cities as neighborhoods, sometimes triggered by blockbusting—the intentional placing of an African American in a previously all-white neighborhood to create panic selling for profit—changed their racial characteristics in short periods of time. Legal challenges to the status quo, judicial and legislative, contributed to the out-migration of whites from older urban areas. Although the white flight expanded areas for African Americans, it preserved traditional patterns of racial segregation. All-white suburbs were personified in television programs such as *Ozzie and Harriet, Leave It to Beaver,* and *The Dick Van Dyke Show.*

White flight became a particular problem in the wake of school desegregation decisions in the 1970s. Mandatory busing programs in cities such as Norfolk, Virginia, and Boston, Massachusetts, were given special examination, especially as to whether they were being counterproductive in achieving desegregation. While some used the trends to argue against forced busing, others maintained that metropolitan solutions were the only remedy for white flight. To a great extent, the debate over racial factors in changing school demographics mirrored the older debate about race and residence, with the same divergent results.

The last third of the twentieth century saw a replication of urban white settlement patterns as middle-class African Americans began to suburbanize. In part, the out-migration involved aging inner-ring suburbs which experienced the same type of ecological succession as inner-city neighborhoods did before and after World War II. But enhanced personal incomes and job expectations, improved infrastructure, and cheap gasoline prices allowed increasing numbers of blacks to become suburban home owners, a trend reflected in the 1980s television program *The Cosby Show.* In some cases, suburban white flight was matched by equally affluent blacks interested in the same personal safety, good schools, and aesthetics. Overall, the percentages of suburban blacks remained below urban averages, but African Americans became more of a factor in the suburbs than they ever had before.

Demographic studies in the 1990s have revealed a slower pace of racial turnover in metropolitan areas as some whites return to the cities in a process known as gentrification. The trends induced some observers to speculate that the radical racial changes of the postwar decades may have been temporary, especially in the older and larger northeastern and midwestern cities. Others theorize that small rural towns are benefitting from a new form of white flight as whites from large cities and their surrounding suburbs create a new rural renaissance. Los Angeles and New York City lost over one million domestic migrants (many replaced by foreign immigrants, not black) each in the 1990s while the greatest domestic migration gains during the decade occurred in predominately white, non-metropolitan areas such as the Mountain states, south Atlantic states, Texas, and the Ozarks. If the patterns continue, these scholars predict the traditional city-suburb model of white flight may have to be replaced by a urban-rural dichotomy. "The Ozzies and Harriets of the 1990s are bypassing the suburbs or big cities in favor of more livable, homogenous small towns and rural areas," according to University of Michigan demographer William H. Frey. Perhaps they aspire to another all-white 1960s television program, *The Andy Griffith Show*.

—Richard Digby-Junger

FURTHER READING:

Clark, Thomas A. *Blacks in Suburbs: A National Perspective*. New Brunswick, New Jersey, Rutgers University Center for Urban Policy Research, 1979.

Dennis, Sam Joseph. *African-American Exodus and White Migration, 1950-1970*. New York, Garland, 1989.

Frey, William H. ''The New White Flight.'' *American Demographics*. April 1994, 40-52.

Gordon, Danielle. ''White Flight Taking Off in Chicago Suburbs.'' *The Chicago Reporter*. December 1997, 5-9.

Orser, W. Edward. *Blockbusting in Baltimore: The Edmondson Village Story*. Lexington, University Press of Kentucky, 1994.

Rossell, Christine H. ''School Desegregation and White Flight.'' *Political Science Quarterly*. Vol. 90, No. 4, winter 1975-1976, 675-695.

Starobin, Paul. ''America in the '90s.'' *National Journal*. Vol. 23, No. 39, September 28, 1991, 2,337-2,342.

Teaford, Jon C. *The Twentieth-Century American City*. 2nd edition. Baltimore, Johns Hopkins University, 1993.

Thompson, Heather Ann. ''Rethinking the Politics of White Flight in the Postwar City: Detroit, 1945-1980.'' *Journal of Urban History*. Vol. 25, No. 2, January 1999, 163-198.

White, Stanford (1853-1906)

On July 25, 1906, Harry Thaw walked into the fashionable cabaret restaurant—the Roof Garden at Madison Square Garden—and shot and killed the architect Stanford White, who was dining with his lover, Mrs. Evelyn Nesbit Thaw. Thaw claimed that he had been driven to the murder by the knowledge that White had ''ruined'' his wife, a 22-year-old ''Floradora'' girl who had been involved in a sexual relationship with White since she was 16. After two sensational trials, Thaw (an heir to old Pittsburgh railroad money as well as a wife-beater) was acquitted by a jury who agreed that the cuckolded husband's murderous jealousy was justified. The sensational story of the fatal Nesbit/White/Thaw triangle was dramatized in a 1955 movie entitled *The Girl in the Red Velvet Swing*. White kept the infamous swing in his studio to use in his well-orchestrated and numerous seductions. According to his family, it was White who coined and popularized the sexual-innuendo-laden invitation ''come up and see my etchings.''

—Jackie Hatton

FURTHER READING:

Lessard, Suzannah. *The Architect of Desire: Beauty and Danger in the Stanford White Family*. New York, Dial Press, 1996.

Mooney, Michael Macdonald. *Evelyn Nesbit and Stanford White: Love and Death in the Gilded Age*. New York, William Morrow and Company, 1976.

White Supremacists

In a country of immigrants, white supremacy has been a curious and lasting preoccupation. Not just African Americans, but Catholics, Eastern Europeans, Italians, Jews, and all races not of Western European origin have been singled out as inferior at one time or another in United States history. But where did such behavior come from, and why do so many continue to cling to such a backward creed? The simplest answer is that racism and racist organizations provide a comprehensive world view in times of social turmoil, a way to interpret changes in social mores and often mystifying economic setbacks. But this is not enough. In virtually every country, bigotry exists, but in ostensibly classless, egalitarian America, it remains one of the most paradoxical features of our social landscape.

Until recently, white supremacy was very much the norm. At the turn of the twentieth century, most labor unions were overtly racist, as were many social activists of a radical stripe. The author Jack London was both a socialist and white supremacist, preaching the brotherhood of workers, provided they were lily white. It was London who first coined the term ''great white hope'' in articles beseeching a challenger to step forward against Jack Johnson, the black heavyweight boxing champion. In London's view—and he was regarded as a progressive—African Americans and Chinese ranked as hardly human. For the more conventional, the truth of racism was hardly given a second thought; it was self-evident.

Like religious mania or consumer habits, white supremacy is not a constant, but is inherently tied to historical conditions. It is a consolation in times of trouble, and a rationale in times of prosperity. In the 1920s, it was tied to the growing antipathy between city and country; during the Depression, it became inextricably linked to anti-Communism and opposition to Roosevelt's New Deal. Father Coughlin, a virulent anti-Communist radio personality, and William Pelley, leader of the fascist Silver Shirts, were both vocal enemies of the New Deal, and each embraced racist nationalism to explain the country's ills.

The world-wide Jewish conspiracy theory imported by Henry Ford in his *Dearborn Independent* had been integrated into supremacist beliefs during the 1920s. The next development was a theological justification for their beliefs. Soon after the conclusion of World War II, California preacher and Klansman Wesley Swift latched onto a racist Christian theology known as British Israelism. Swift renamed the theology Christian Identity. Exponents of British Israelism believe that the lost tribe of Israel immigrated to Britain; hence, Anglo Saxons were inherently superior, and were in fact God's chosen people. Christian Identity proved to be a popular idea, and under Swift's tutelage, the belief spread to Idaho, Michigan, and the South. Almost every supremacist group after World War II has in some way been influenced by Christian Identity, with Swift followers forming the Aryan Nation, Posse Comitatus, and the Minutemen, the most committed among the later waves of white supremacists.

By the 1960s, white supremacy was a vigorous movement. Lurking behind the Goldwater far right, white supremacists wielded enormous influence and political power. Frightened by a world that appeared out of control, many Americans found solace in the strident rhetoric of the American Nazi Party or the Minutemen. The publications of the Liberty Lobby and the John Birchers clearly explicated this dissatisfaction. The Ku Klux Klan mobilized visibly, and sometimes violently, against desegregation activists white and black alike; militia-like cells organized in the Midwest, and the John Birch Society, while professing no racist sentiment, actively supported the supremacist ideology through their political activities. As manifested in the 1964 presidential campaign of Arizona Senator Barry Goldwater, the openly racist platform of Governor George Wallace in his 1968 and 1972 primary campaigns, and Ronald Reagan's 1968 gubernatorial race, white supremacy was a force to be reckoned with.

Political positions and economic conditions go hand in hand, as any student of Hitler's rise to power will attest. In 1970s America, a rash of bank foreclosures and declining agricultural prices sent tremors of fear across the heartland. In many places thus stricken, groups like the Posse Comitatus, an organization vocally opposed to the Federal government, often organized to combat what was perceived as unfair bank practices by rigging auctions and seizing land and equipment, sometimes provoking gun battles between law enforcement and farmers. In the declining industrial areas, the loss of lucrative union jobs swelled the ranks of the unemployed, mobilizing soldiers in a new racial movement; they called it the Fifth Era. Groups like WAR (White Aryan Resistance) mobilized around white unrest, often reaping a tidy profit with marketing schemes and paraphernalia. Complete segregation was the goal most frequently advocated, and terrorism and paramilitary training the preferred method to attain it. Many groups published detailed maps that limited minorities to gerrymandered homelands. In Idaho, the quasi-military group The Order took a more direct approach, pulling off several profitable armed robberies (dispensing the proceeds among many supremacist groups) and murdering Denver talk-show host Alan Berg. The group was finally eradicated by the FBI, but not before they had distributed much of their illicit bounty, and there is evidence that their crimes have financed several campaigns and training camps.

Meanwhile, a new generation of disenchanted, working-class youth, having seen their parents lose a farm or well-paid factory job, had adopted the skinhead style and rhetoric of British youth, compensating for their helplessness with acts of racially motivated violence. For a time, skinhead gangs enjoyed a high visibility, and just as quickly, they learned the disadvantages of that conspicuity. Harassment by the police was a constant, and by the 1990s, skinhead leaders were urging their dome-headed minions to grow their hair and recede quietly.

It is easy to picture white supremacy as a marginal ideology. This would be a mistake. White supremacy is hydra-headed, springing up in unexpected places. Many supremacists, like David Duke, for example, have tempered their rhetoric sufficiently to win public office. Other groups cloak their agendas under neutral-sounding names like the League of Conservative Citizens, who made headlines in 1998 after Republican Senator Trent Lott addressed the group on several occasions and then was forced to disassociate from the group and their openly racist agenda. While the constant splintering off of the many organizations makes it difficult to ascertain how many active supremacists there are or how much political clout they wield, it can be safely asserted that White supremacy has become a permanent feature of the socio-political terrain.

—Michael Baers

FURTHER READING:

Bennet, David H. *The Party of Fear.* Chapel Hill, University of North Carolina Press, 1988.

Corcoran, James. *Gordon Kahl and the Posse Comitatus: Murder in the Heartland.* New York, Viking Penguin, 1990.

Flynn, Kevin, and Gary Gerhardt. *The Silent Brotherhood: Inside America's Racist Underground.* New York, Free Press, 1989.

Higham, Charles. *American Swastika.* New York, Doubleday, 1985.

Ridgeway, James. *Blood in the Face.* New York, Thunder's Mouth Press, 1990.

Wade, Wyn Craig. *The Fiery Cross: The Ku Klux Klan in America.* New York, Simon & Schuster, 1987.

Whiteman, Paul (1890-1967)

Denver-born bandleader Paul Whiteman is inseparable in American musical culture from George Gershwin's enduring classic, *Rhapsody in Blue,* which he famously commissioned, conducted at its sensational 1924 New York premiere, and recorded the same year. The most popular of all bandleaders prior to the Big Band era, Whiteman was called The King of Jazz, but this was not strictly accurate, despite the jazz-based *Rhapsody in Blue,* his association with several jazz musicians and vocalists, and his discovery and continued espousal of legendary trumpeter Bix Beiderbecke. Whiteman's disciplined arrangements left true jazz musicians little chance for improvisation and, as Wilder Hobson wrote, he "drew very little from the jazz language except for some of its simpler rhythmic patterns." A former violin and viola player with the Denver and San Francisco Symphony orchestras, Whiteman formed his band in 1919 with pianist/arranger Ferde Grofe and trumpeter Henry Busse, and over the next couple of decades unrolled a prodigious and unprecedented number of hits, well over 200 by 1936. The band appeared in Broadway shows and five films, of which the first, *King of Jazz* (1930), featuring *Rhapsody in Blue,* was a creative landmark in the early history of the Hollywood musical. He hosted several radio shows, including his own, during the 1930s, and a television series as late as the 1950s. By 1954, he was ranked second only to Bing Crosby (with whom he worked and recorded) as a best-selling recording artist. Eventually superseded by big band jazz artists such as Fletcher Henderson, Paul Whiteman's Beiderbecke compilations, along with his Gershwin and Crosby recordings, remain his lasting memorial.

—Benjamin Griffith

FURTHER READING:

DeLong, Thomas A. *Pops: Paul Whiteman, King of Jazz.* Piscataway, New Jersey, New Century Publisher, 1983.

Hobson, Wilder. *American Jazz Music.* New York, Norton, 1939.

Johnson, Carl. *A Paul Whiteman Chronology, 1890-1967.* Williamstown, Massachusetts, Whiteman Collection, Williams College, 1978.

Simon, George T. *The Big Bands.* New York, MacMillan, 1974.

Whiting, Margaret (1924—)

Margaret Whiting, born in 1924, was a child of show business twice over. Her father was songwriter Richard Whiting ("Too

Marvelous for Words," "On the Good Ship Lollipop"), and after Whiting died when Margaret was still a teenager, songwriter Johnny Mercer became her mentor. Signed to Mercer's Capitol label in the early 1940s, she had 12 gold records before the rock 'n' roll era, including Mercer's "My Ideal" and her signature song, "Moonlight in Vermont." One of the first singers to cross Nashville over into Tin Pan Alley, she hit Number One with "Slippin' Around," a duet with country star Jimmy Wakely.

A cabaret revival in the 1970s and 1980s gave Whiting a new career as one of New York's most beloved cabaret performers, on her own and as part of a revue, *4 Girls 4,* with Rosemary Clooney, Rose Marie, and Helen O'Connell. She also starred in a tribute to Johnny Mercer staged by her longtime companion, former gay porn star Jack Wrangler.

—Tad Richards

FURTHER READING:

Whiting, Margaret, and Will Holt. *It Might As Well Be Spring: A Musical Autobiography.* New York, William Morrow, 1987.

The Who

Still regarded in the late 1990s as one of the greatest rock bands of all time, the Who were bold innovators who changed the face of popular music forever. Having planted the seeds of heavy metal, art rock, punk, and electronica, the Who are almost without peer in their range of influence upon subsequent music. The Who boasted a dynamic singer and stage presence in Roger Daltrey, a powerful virtuoso bassist in John Entwistle, and one of the world's greatest drummers in the frenetic Keith Moon. But the guiding genius of the Who was guitarist and songwriter Pete Townshend, who wrote and arranged each song, and recorded the guitar, bass, drums, and vocals onto a demo before presenting it to the band to learn and perform.

Born in West London in 1945, Townshend attended Ealing Art school, where he learned about Pop Art and the merging realms of high and low culture. When he formed the Who, he found a suitable audience for this background among a youth subculture called the Mods, who wore Pop Art clothing and sought out stylish new music and amphetamine-driven dance styles. The Who's manager, Kit Lambert, encouraged the band to adopt the Mod look and write significant songs that would appeal to Mods. Their early hit, "Can't Explain" (1964) expressed adolescent frustration, followed by the angst-ridden "My Generation" (1965), one of the great rock anthems of the period.

The Who were most famous for outrageous stage performances. Townshend specialized in "windmill" power chords, in which he would swiftly swing his arm 360 degrees before striking a chord. The Who often smashed their instruments at the end of a show, with Townshend shoving his guitar through the amplifier and Moon smashing through the drumskins and kicking over the entire drum set. Despite their commercial success, the Who remained in debt until 1969 because of this expensive habit.

The Who released their first album, *The Who Sing My Generation* in 1965. Their next album, *A Quick One* (1967; renamed *Happy Jack* in America) featured a miniature "rock opera" on side two, a series of five songs narrating a tale of suburban infidelity. *The Who*

Sell Out (1968) satirized commercials, again revealing their interest in Pop Art. *Magic Bus* (1968) was the best album of their early period but offered no hint of the grandeur of their next project, a full-scale rock opera. The double album *Tommy* (1969) told the story of a deaf, dumb, and blind boy who, after a miracle cure, becomes a cult leader. The album was influenced by Townshend's involvement with his guru, Meher Baba. If spirituality was an unexpected theme from the author of teen frustration and masturbation, the music was an equally bold advance, establishing Townshend as a versatile guitarist and ambitious composer. Nevertheless, responses to *Tommy* were mixed, partly due to the difficulty of following the story. Charges of pretentiousness were frequent. The artistic audacity of *Tommy* left the Who with a formidable dilemma—where do you go from here?

The Who followed up the rock opera with the raunchy, visceral *Live at Leeds* (1970), but soon Townshend grew ambitious again, formulating another opera, *Lifehouse*. Eventually the concept was abandoned, and the better half of the songs written for the project were released as *Who's Next* (1971), which many regard as the greatest rock album ever made. Among its highlights are "Behind Blue Eyes," "Teenage Wasteland," and one of the greatest rock songs of all time, "Won't Get Fooled Again," a masterpiece of overwhelming power, featuring incredible performances by each band member. *Who's Next* made innovative use of synthesizers and sequencers, anticipating electronic music, and it established the Who as a major creative power in rock. The following year, Townshend released a solo album, *Who Came First,* devoted to Meher Baba.

Townshend then embarked upon yet another opera, based on the raw passions of youth rather than philosophical ideas. *Quadrophenia* (1973) told the story of the Mods and their rival subculture, the Rockers. The story was simpler than *Tommy* but still rather confusing. However, the Who had grown musically since their first opera. Townshend was a more sophisticated arranger and made greater use of piano (played by himself) and horns (played by Entwistle). *Quadrophenia* was regarded as Townshend's masterpiece, the definitive expression of adolescent angst, combining the ambitions of *Tommy* with the virtuosity and emotional power of *Who's Next.* Both *Tommy* and *Quadrophenia* were made into movies, the former an awkward musical starring Daltrey, the latter a gritty drama which helps to explain the album's plotline, as well as the cultural milieu in which the Who developed. For most Americans, the movie version of *Quadrophenia* is a prerequisite for understanding the album.

The triumph of *Quadrophenia* left the Who in the same quandary that *Tommy* had: where do you go from here? They avoided the question with *Odds & Sods* (1974), a mixture of singles, B-sides, and leftovers from the *Lifehouse* project. For a hodgepodge, it was a fine album. *The Who by Numbers* (1975) was quieter, with thoughtful, introspective lyrics. *Who Are You* (1978) found the Who delivering up-tempo rock again. The lengthy title song was a worthy follow-up to "Won't Get Fooled Again." The entire album was reminiscent of *Who's Next,* packed with powerful songs, and again featuring innovative use of synthesizers. Unfortunately, Keith Moon died shortly afterwards from an overdose of anti-alcoholic medication.

Following this tragedy, Townshend withdrew to record the fascinating *Empty Glass* (1981), his finest solo album. Moon was replaced by Kenny Jones of the Small Faces, and the Who recorded two albums, *Face Dances* (1981) and *It's Hard* (1982), before breaking up. Then came countless collections of rarities, outtakes, B-sides, demo tapes, etc., testifying to the Who's enduring popularity, although respect for the group was compromised by the weakness of

Members of the Who (l-r) John Entwistle, Roger Daltry, Pete Townshend, and Keith Moon

the post-Moon albums and by various anticlimactic reunions in the 1980s and 1990s. Townshend remained prolific as a solo artist but tended to rely overmuch on concept albums. He published a book of short stories, *Horse's Neck,* in 1985.

—Douglas Cooke

FURTHER READING:

Barnes, Richard. *The Who: Maximum R & B.* London, Eel Pie, 1982.

The Whole Earth Catalogue

First published in 1968 by Stewart Brand, *The Whole Earth Catalogue* introduced Americans to green consumerism and quickly became the unofficial handbook of the 1960s counter-culture. Winner of the National Book Award and a national best-seller, *TWEC* contained philosophical ideas based in science, holistic living, and metaphysics as well as listings of products that functioned within these confines. As many Americans sought to turn their backs on America's culture of consumption, *TWEC* offered an alternative paradigm based in values extending across the counterculture.

TWEC combined the best qualities of the *Farmer's Almanac* and a Sears catalog, merging wisdom and consumption with environmental activism and expression. The first page declared that "the establishment" had failed and that *TWEC* aimed to supply tools to help an individual "conduct his own education, find his own inspiration, shape his own environment, and share his adventure with whoever is interested." The text offered advice about organic gardening, massage, meditation, or do-it-yourself burial: "Human bodies are an organic part of the whole earth and at death must return to the ongoing stream of life." Many Americans found the resources and rationale within *TWEC* to live as rebels against the American establishment.

Interestingly, Brand did not urge readers to reject consumption altogether. *TWEC* helped to create the consumptive niche known as green consumerism, which seeks to resist products contributing to or deriving from waste or abuse of resources, applications of intrusive technologies, or use of non-natural raw materials. *TWEC* sought to appeal to this niche by offering products such as recycled paper and the rationale for its use. As the trend-setting publication of green consumption, *TWEC* is viewed by many Americans as having started the movement toward whole grains, healthy living, and the environmentally friendly products that continue to make up a significant portion of all consumer goods. Entire national chains have based themselves around the sale of such goods.

Even though green culture has infiltrated society, Whole Earth continues in the late 1990s as a network of experts who gather information and tools in order to live a better life and, for some, to construct ''practical utopias.'' *The Millennium Whole Earth Catalog,* for instance, claims to integrate the best ideas of the past twenty-five years with the best for the next, based on *TWEC* standards such as environmental restoration, community-building, whole systems thinking, and medical self-care.

—Brian Black

FURTHER READING:

Anderson, Terry H. *The Movement and the Sixties.* New York, Oxford University Press, 1995.

The Millennium Whole Earth Catalog. San Francisco, Harper, 1998.

Wide World of Sports

''The thrill of victory and the agony of defeat'' became one of the most familiar slogans on television for the American Broadcast Company (ABC) sports show that lived up to its title. Beginning as a summer replacement in 1961, *Wide World of Sports* endured into the 1990s, making a household name of original host Jim McKay and launching the domination of ABC in sports and the rise of future ABC Sports and News president Roone Arledge.

Arledge came up with the concept of packaging various sports under this umbrella title and sent Jim McKay to anchor live coverage of two venerable track meets—the Drake Relays from Des Moines, Iowa, and the Penn Relays from Philadelphia—for the inaugural broadcast of the program, on April 29, 1961. *Wide World of Sports* survived its initial 13 weeks and returned every year as a 90-minute program on Saturday afternoons beginning in January, and often expanding to Sundays as well. The opening narration became famous: ''Spanning the world to give you the constant variety of sports. The thrill of victory and the agony of defeat, the human drama of athletic competition. This is ABC's Wide World of Sports.''

Early on, *Wide World of Sports* covered many sports that later became separate live broadcast institutions—tennis's Wimbledon, golf's British Open, soccer's World Cup. But *Wide World* made its name with ''nontraditional'' sports, such as auto racing, boxing, swimming, diving, track and field, gymnastics, and figure skating. The particularly daring and unusual sports drew the most fans: surfing, bodybuilding, World's Strongest Man competitions, lumberjack contests, cliff divers from Acapulco, the Calgary Stampede rodeo, and most notably, stunt motorcyclist Evel Knievel. Knievel dominated shows of the early 1970s jumping barrels, cars, and busses and nearly making it across the Snake River Canyon on his motorcycle (and by rocket), breaking numerous bones in the process.

The program provided ABC Sports with sports coverage experience that it utilized to cover the Olympics. *Wide World* truly traveled the globe, covering events in Europe and Asia, even Cuba and China. Many of the events were carried live via satellite. The program also developed the style that made Americans sit still and watch unfamiliar sports and foreign performers such as Russian gymnast Olga Korbut, Brazilian soccer star Pele, or Russian weightlifter Vasily Alekseev. The ''up close and personal'' features emphasizing the life stories of the athletes grew out *Wide World of Sports* and revolutionized sports coverage. After *Wide World,* sports coverage became storytelling rather than simply showing games and scores. The success of the Olympics propelled ABC out of its low ratings status into a respectable television network and Roone Arledge into a position as the head of ABC Sports and ABC News.

During the 1970s, *Wide World of Sports* became a brand name, and its most famous image was set: the ''agony of defeat.'' While the ''thrill of victory'' changed almost every year, ''the agony of defeat'' was forever symbolized by hapless Yugoslavian ski jumper, Vinko Bogataj, whose spectacular wipeout was taped in 1970.

By the end of the 1980s, *Wide World of Sports* lost its prominence, as cable network ESPN became a superior ratings grabber as the ultimate sports show—24 hours a day of the type of sports coverage that *Wide World* pioneered. ESPN's rise was ironic, as it was partly owned by ABC.

In the 1990s, McKay left the role of studio host to a succession of other ABC Sports personalities including Al Michaels and Julie Moran. On January 3, 1998, McKay declared that *Wide World of Sports* was canceled; the hour-and-a-half of all sorts of sports was replaced by a studio host introducing single event broadcasts such as the Indy 500, horse racing's Triple Crown, and the national and world championships in figure skating.

—Michele Lellouche

FURTHER READING:

The Best of ABC's Wide World of Sports (three volumes). CBS/Fox Video, 1990.

McKay, Jim. with Jim McPhee. *The Real McKay: My Wide World of Sports.* New York, Dutton, 1998.

Sugar, Bert Randolph. *Thrill of Victory: The Inside Story of ABC Sports.* New York, Hawthorn Books, 1978.

The Wild Bunch

The Wild Bunch (1969) was the definitive film, and only true epic, by one of Hollywood's greatest directors, Sam Peckinpah; and when it came to movie violence, it set the bar higher than it had ever been set before. Earlier Westerns had good guys and bad guys as clearly demarcated as the sides in World War II, but *The Wild Bunch* came out during the Vietnam War, and it better reflected that war in both its complexity and carnage. Arthur Penn's *Bonnie and Clyde* (1967), which ended with its two protagonists being riddled by bullets, was the first major Hollywood film to show graphic violence—to suggest that shooting someone had consequences, that it was messy and painful—but nothing could have prepared 1960s audiences for the hundreds of deaths, the wave after wave of unrelenting carnage—shown in slow motion and freeze-frame sequences—that climaxed *The Wild Bunch.* Seven years before the film premiered, Peckinpah was deer hunting when he shot a buck and was struck by the fact that the bullet going in was the size of a dime, yet the blood on the snow was the size of a bowling ball. He concluded that was the way violence and death were, and that was what he wanted to put on film. During filming, Peckinpah had the technicians lay thin slices of raw steak across the bags of stage blood, so when they exploded it looked like the bullets were ripping out of bodies mixed with blood and chunks of flesh. ''Listen,'' Peckinpah said, ''killing is no fun. I was trying to show what the hell it's like to get shot.'' He believed people would shun violence if he showed what violence was really like.

But violence in movies without flesh-and-blood characters (see almost any slasher film) is meaningless. Fortunately, Peckinpah had great characters, played by superb actors, in a strong story, acted out before beautiful vistas gorgeously photographed. As the movie opens, the audience sees a tiny band of soldiers riding into a small town, then walking into the local railroad office, as scruffy, armed men flit back and forth on the rooftops overhead. It looks as though the bad guys are about to ambush the good guys, though the reverse is true. The railroad office manager asks the lead soldier, Bishop Pike (William Holden), ''May I help you?'' and Pike grabs the manager, pulls him out of his chair, shoves him and another against the wall, and tells the other soldiers, ''If they move . . . kill 'em!'' These aren't really soldiers at all, but the Wild Bunch in disguise, and the men on the roof are bounty hunters, there to ambush the outlaws and collect the prices

on their heads. Leading the bounty hunters is former Wild Bunch member Deke Thornton (Robert Ryan)—whose feud with Pike stems from the time they were busted by Pinkerton agents, with Thornton being shot and captured and Pike running away. Realizing they're about to be ambushed, the Wild Bunch times its departure to coincide with the passing of a parade of temperance marchers, and the resulting carnage is fairly intense.

The gang escapes to Mexico with the bounty hunters in hot pursuit. In the town of Agua Verde they cross paths with Mapache, a ruthless general at war with revolutionary Pancho Villa who has been oppressing the local natives, even murdering the father and stealing the fiancée of the Wild Bunch's one Mexican member, Angel. The gang agrees to rob a military supply train loaded with munitions for Mapache in exchange for gold, and the robbery itself is a slickly done caper, a Western *Topkapi!* Worried about helping Mapache get more guns, Angel agrees to participate if, instead of gold, he can take one case of guns for the revolutionaries. But Mapache finds out, and when the gang returns to Agua Verde to trade the arms for the gold, Mapache keeps Angel. At the end, the remaining outlaws decide to rescue Angel, and their fight against the soldiers provides the climactic bloodshed.

A scene from the film *The Wild Bunch*, with (l to r) Ben Johnson, Warren Oates, William Holden, and Ernest Borgnine.

More complex than it first appears, *The Wild Bunch* is ultimately about redemption. Early in the film, Pike tells a gang member who wants to kill another, "We're gonna stick together, just like it used to be. When you side with a man you stay with him, and if you can't do that you're like some animal, you're finished!—we're finished!—all of us!" Yet Pike betrays this code again and again. During the original railroad office job, when Crazy Lee (Bo Hopkins) tells Pike he'll hold the hostages until Pike says different, Pike just leaves him behind to die. This is brought home when Pike's oldest friend, Sykes (Edmund O'Brien), tells Pike that Crazy Lee is his grandson. When another gang member is wounded and might slow them down, Pike shoots him; even Sykes himself is expendable when he becomes wounded. At first, Angel is abandoned to Mapache and his men, but Pike has finally had enough, and, against impossible odds, he and the rest of the Wild Bunch decide to redeem themselves. They go down in a blaze of glory—and, joining the revolutionaries, the one remaining gang member and the one remaining bounty hunter ride off to fight the good fight.

—Bob Sullivan

FURTHER READING:

Bliss, Michael. *Justified Lives: Morality and Narrative in the Films of Sam Peckinpah.* Carbondale, Ill., Southern Illinois University Press, 1993.

Fine, Marshall. *Bloody Sam: The Life and Films of Sam Peckinpah.* New York, Donald I. Fine, 1991.

Seydor, Paul. *Peckinpah: The Western Films: A Reconsideration.* Chicago, University of Illinois Press, 1997.

Weddle, David. *If They Move . . . Kill 'Em!: The Life and Times of Sam Peckinpah.* New York, Grove Press, 1994.

Wild Kingdom

The first television program to help Americans visualize distant life and consider ways they might help, *Wild Kingdom* became a crucial tool in the formation of America's environmental consciousness and particularly in the movement's shift toward global concerns. Mutual of Omaha's *Wild Kingdom* has served as Americans' window to the exotic species of the natural world since the 1960s. In the tradition of *National Geographic,* host Marlon Perkins traveled throughout the world sending back images of danger and intrigue. Perkins's pursuit of animals in their natural surroundings contributed to the interest in "eco tourism" in which the very wealthy now travel to various portions of the world not to shoot big game but only to view it. *Wild Kingdom* continues production and has spawned an entire genre of television, particularly for young viewers.

—Brian Black

The Wild One

The camera looks down a stretch of straight country highway, then in bold, white letters appears the following: "This is a shocking story. It could never take place in most American towns—but it did in

Marlon Brando in *The Wild One*.

this one. It is a public challenge not to let it happen again." The words fade away to be replaced by Marlon Brando's voice speaking in a southern drawl. "It begins for me on this road," he says. "How the whole mess happened I don't know, but I know it couldn't happen again in a million years. Maybe I coulda stopped it early, but once the trouble was on its way, I was just going with it." A crowd of leather-clad motorcyclists roar past the camera, and with the confident declaration that what follows is an aberration, Stanley Kramer launched *The Wild One* in 1954. The truth of the matter is somewhat more complicated, for not only did the film incite a rash of copy-cat behavior, but may have had an affect on the Hell's Angels' delectations a decade later.

The Wild One derives from a real riot, following a large motorcycle rally in the Northern California town of Hollister. According to witnesses, six to eight thousand participants drag-raced up and down the streets of Hollister; fist-fights, lewd behavior, and vandalism were the norm, but the event was eventually dispatched by 29 policemen and it ended without a single loss of life. The coverage in the July 1947 issue of *Life* magazine was sufficiently lurid and alarmist, and it inspired Frank Rooney to turn the incident into a short story, "The Cyclists' Raid." Rooney told the story from the point of view of Joel Bleeker, a hotel manager (and significantly, a World War II veteran) who witnesses his daughter's death at the hands of the cyclists. Bleeker views the motorcyclists as inhuman quasi-fascists, but in its transition from story to film, sympathies were switched. The hero became Johnny (Marlon Brando), leader of the Black Rebels Motorcycle Club, who is sullen and incommunicative, but also reserved and possessing a degree of chivalry lacking in his compatriots.

The rioting itself is transformed in typical Hollywood fashion into a Manichean contest between Johnny and his dissipated rival, Chino (Lee Marvin), who, to make matters perfectly clear, wears a horizontal striped sweatshirt closely resembling prison garb. After gratuitously interfering in a local motorcycle race, the bikers proceed to the nearby town of Carbondale where they cause all manner of havoc, prompted in part by the local saloon owner, who all but rubs his hands in excitement at the prospect of a bar full of hard-drinking motorcyclists. The tension between locals and bikers, already tense after a notoriously bad driver hits one of the bikers, is further exacerbated by the arrival of Chino and his cohorts. As the motorcyclists begin to run genuinely amuck, the town's craven police officer cowers in his office while his daughter, Kathy, is accosted by the bikers, rescued by Johnny who drives off with her, and is thus absent from the ensuing carnage. Nonetheless, as the leader he is blamed by the townspeople, locked up, and when he escapes, knocked off his motorcycle as he flees, accidentally killing an elderly man, and then is unjustly accused of the killing.

Despite the rather thin story line—the *New Yorker* magazine called it "a picture that tries to grasp an idea even though the reach falls short"—*The Wild One* was an instant hit with young audiences. Theater owners throughout the country reported that teenage boys had taken to dressing in leather jackets and boots like Marlon Brando and accosting passersby. The pioneering members of the Hell's Angels (most of the group that later came to notoriety were children at the time) identified deeply with Brando. "Whatta ya got?" was Brando's insouciant reply to the famous question, "Hey Johnny, what are you rebelling against?" and it echoed in the real-life outlaws inchoate dissatisfaction. "We went up to the Fox Theater on Market Street," a founding member told journalist Hunter S. Thompson. "There were about fifty of us, with jugs of wine and our black leather jackets . . . We sat up there in the balcony and smoked cigars and drank wine and cheered like bastards. We could all see ourselves right there on the screen. We were all Marlon Brando."

Much of the lasting allure of *The Wild One* stems from Brando's lionization by not only the Hell's Angels, but by countless teenagers. In "The Cyclists' Raid," Rooney had written: "They were all alike. They were standardized figurines, seeking in each other a willful loss of identity, dividing themselves equally among one another until there was only a single mythical figure, unspeakably sterile and furnishing the norm for hundreds of others." In light of the Hell's Angels' response to *The Wild One* as quoted above, and considering the way Marlon Brando's image was disseminated on posters, in books, and turned into an archetype, it is no wonder many blamed *The Wild One* for the Hell's Angels' excesses a decade later. Hollywood gossip columnist Hedda Hopper blamed Kramer entirely for the whole outlaw phenomenon, and Frank Rooney might well have identified Marlon Brando as that "single mythical figure furnishing the norm for hundreds of others."

It would be simplistic to blame the filmmaker and leading man for a real life contagion, but the suspicion remains to this day. Perhaps Hunter S. Thompson put it best when he wrote that the film "told a story that was only beginning to happen and which was inevitably influenced by the film. It gave the outlaws a lasting, romance-glazed image of themselves, a coherent reflection that only a very few had been able to find in a mirror, and it quickly became the bike-rider's answer to *The Sun Also Rises*."

—Michael Baers

FURTHER READING:

Carey, Gary. *Marlon Brando: The Only Contender.* New York, St. Martin's Press, 1985.

Lewis, Jon. *The Road to Romance and Ruin: Teen Films and Youth Culture.* New York, Routledge, 1992.

Pettigrew, Terence. *Raising Hell: The Rebel in the Movies.* New York, St. Martin's Press, 1986.

Rooney, Frank. "The Cyclists' Raid." *Stories Into Film.* Edited by William Kittredge and Steven M. Krauzer. New York, Harper & Row, 1979.

Shaw, Sam. *Brando in the Camera Eye.* New York, Exeter Books, 1979.

Spoto, Donald. *Stanley Kramer, Filmmaker.* New York, G.P. Putnam's Sons, 1978.

Thomas, Tony. *The Films of Marlon Brando.* Secaucus, New Jersey, Citadel Press, 1973.

Thompson, Hunter S. *Hell's Angels, A Strange and Terrible Saga.* New York, Ballantine Book, 1966.

Wilder, Billy (1906—)

Born Samuel Wilder in an Austrian village, this six-time Academy Award winning director, screenwriter, and producer was dubbed Billy after Buffalo Bill of the 1880s traveling western show. That American nickname apparently foretold, in the wake of the Nazi rise to power, his 1934 emigration to Hollywood where he joined fellow European exiles, learned English, and cultivated a legendary career that indelibly marked American movie history. With partner Charles Brackett, he co-wrote acclaimed comedies like *Ball of Fire* (1941), then scripted, directed, and produced a string of hugely popular films, including the quintessential film noir *Double Indemnity* (1944), and *The Lost Weekend* (1945). Their alliance culminated with the savage portrayal of Hollywood in *Sunset Boulevard* (1950). With I.A.L. Diamond, Wilder created *Some Like it Hot* (1959) and *The Apartment* (1960). His self-produced works more flagrantly expressed his cynicism and penchant for vulgarity with *Ace in the Hole* (1951), betraying a jaded sensibility ahead of its times.

—Elizabeth Haas

FURTHER READING:

Lally, Kevin. *Wilder Times: The Life of Billy Wilder.* New York, Henry Holt, 1996.

Sikov, Ed. *On Sunset Boulevard: The Life and Times of Billy Wilder.* New York, Hyperion, 1998.

Zolotow, Maurice. *Billy Wilder in Hollywood.* New York, Putnam, 1977.

Wilder, Laura Ingalls (1867-1957)

One of the best-known children's authors, Laura Ingalls Wilder wrote the popular, autobiographical "Little House" novels about her late-nineteenth-century childhood on the American frontier. Published in the 1930s and 1940s, these eight books were considered classics of children's literature by the 1950s and have appealed to every succeeding generation of readers who thirsted for nostalgia.

The second of four daughters of Charles and Caroline Ingalls, a post-Civil War American pioneering family, Wilder began writing in childhood. Laura and her sisters penned poetry and compositions in the many homes the Ingalls family built in the wilderness. Her writing permitted her to have a voice, public and private, denied to many nineteenth-century women and provided a way to release her frustrations, disappointments, and enthusiasms during her life as pioneer, teacher, wife, mother, farmer, businesswoman, and author. Wilder continued her writing after she married her husband Almanzo in 1885. Keeping a travel diary of their 1894 trip to Mansfield, Missouri, Wilder submitted it for publication to the *De Smet News,* where both of her younger sisters worked as journalists. Distracted by farm duties and volunteer work in her community, Wilder did not write seriously until 1911 when she began preparing essays about farm life for the *Missouri Ruralist.*

The fictional Laura was adventurous and inquisitive yet compliant to the culture she lived in, obediently silencing herself and being still to please her Pa. She was predictable, providing steadiness to her readers. The real Laura craved such stability. Accustomed to economic and physical hardships, Wilder persevered despite her son's death, her husband's disability from disease, conflicts with her strong-willed daughter, crop failures and debt, and the misogyny and anti-intellectualism of her patriarchal community. Ambitious and intelligent, she ensured that the couple's farm, Rocky Ridge, survived while asserting her individuality. Known as Bessie to her family, she became Laura Ingalls Wilder only in the last part of her life. This pen name represented a professional woman whom few people actually knew. The author Laura Ingalls Wilder answered fan mail, received awards, and signed books, while Bessie Wilder was an ordinary woman who performed her daily chores, read her Bible, attended club meetings, supported the local library, visited with friends, and cared for her ailing husband.

Wilder's daughter, Rose, an accomplished writer, encouraged her to write about her family's adventures on the frontier. Wilder completed her first attempt, *Pioneer Girl,* in 1930. In this novel, Laura narrated her story from childhood to marriage, but no publisher was interested. With Rose's help, Wilder rewrote her manuscript to meet literary expectations, dividing the novel into eight stories and presenting it in third person. Her publisher suggested that she make her characters two years older than they really were to appeal to adolescent readers. Although the books were presented as what Laura remembered, the early stories about events during her infancy were actually her parents' memories. Originally titled *When Grandma Was a Little Girl,* Wilder's first book, *Little House in the Big Woods,* was published in 1932 and was followed by *Farmer Boy* (1933), *Little House on the Prairie* (1935), *On the Banks of Plum Creek* (1937), *By the Shores of Silver Lake* (1939), *The Long Winter* (1940), *Little Town on the Prairie* (1941), and *These Happy Golden Years* (1943). (A manuscript for a story of Wilder's early years of marriage was found after her death. Edited by Roger Lea MacBride, *The First Four Years* was published in 1971.) Critics and readers immediately accepted her books, and the volumes sold well despite the Depression. The values of home, love, and personal courage formed an image of rural serenity

that fulfilled readers' need for comfort and a connection to a past that they believed was simpler and happier than contemporary times.

Scholars noted the books' archetypes: Pa was the dreamer and provider, while Ma was the civilizer and stabilizer. Laura was a blend of her parents. The Ingalls were praised for being spiritual, hard working, and resourceful, enduring tragedy while constantly moving in their covered wagon and homesteading virgin land. Aspects of nineteenth-century American culture were provided through the songs Pa sang, the items they purchased in stores, and the books and magazines the women read. Scholars have criticized the patriarchal, domestic, and materialistic messages of Wilder's books and denounced the characters' racism toward Native Americans and minorities. The women were often isolated and confined to homes, while men were active participants with the outside world. Laura faced conflicts between her need for individual freedom and expression, and self-sacrifice and obedience for the good of her family.

Wilder stressed that she wrote her stories to provide history lessons for new generations of children who no longer could experience the frontier and disappearing prairie that metaphorically offered hope, prosperity, and renewal. In so doing, she sparked a cultural phenomenon. Fans have dressed as Little House characters, collected memorabilia, and visited Laura Ingalls Wilder heritage sites. The Laura Ingalls Wilder-Rose Wilder Lane Home and Museum in Mansfield, Missouri, houses many items, such as Pa's fiddle, which are featured in the books. Bookstores sell adaptations of Wilder's stories, including series about Ma's and Roses's childhoods. The commercialization of Laura Ingalls Wilder has meant that fans can buy Little House dolls, T-shirts, cookbooks, videos, diaries, and calendars. Wilder's books never have been out of print, and edited versions of her periodical writing and letters are also available. Foreign readers have also identified with Wilder's universal themes; her books have been published in 40 languages, and Internet sites connect Wilder fans around the globe.

The American Library Association initiated the Laura Ingalls Wilder Medal for accomplishments in children's literature in 1954. A television series, *Little House on the Prairie* (1974-1983), unrealistically portrayed Wilder's life but was popular during an era when the Bicentennial and Alex Haley's book *Roots* revived Americans' interest in the past. A Broadway musical, *Prairie,* ran in 1982, and a Little House movie was in production in 1998.

—Elizabeth D. Schafer

FURTHER READING:

Anderson, William T. *Laura Ingalls Wilder: A Biography.* New York, HarperTrophy, 1995.

Miller, John E. *Becoming Laura Ingalls Wilder: The Woman behind the Legend.* Columbia and London, University of Missouri Press, 1998.

———. *Laura Ingalls Wilder's Little Town: Where History and Literature Meet.* Lawrence, University Press of Kansas, 1994.

Romines, Ann. *Constructing the Little House: Gender, Culture, and Laura Ingalls Wilder.* Amherst, University of Massachusetts Press, 1997.

Trosky, Susan M. and Donna Olendorf, editors. *Contemporary Authors.* Vol. 137. Detroit, Gale Research, 1992.

Wilder, Thornton (1897-1975)

Thornton Wilder, with an enthusiasm for experimentation and keen observation of human experience, enlivened the American literary scene in the middle years of the twentieth century. He received numerous awards, including the first Presidential Medal of Freedom, and two Pulitzer Prizes for drama—*Our Town* (1938) and *The Skin of Our Teeth* (1943). In 1927 he received his first Pulitzer Prize for his novel, *The Bridge of San Luis Rey* (1923), which established his reputation as a leading novelist. One of his most popular plays—*The Matchmaker* (1956)—became the mega-musical *Hello, Dolly*, an international box office success. Gertrude Stein became a close friend and influence during his last 12 years of major work. In 1997, one hundred years after his birth, cultural festivals throughout America celebrated the enormous talent of a man whose command of the classics was so great he was nicknamed, ''The Library.''

—Joan Gajadhar

FURTHER READING:

Burns, Edward, and Ulla Dydo. *The Letters of Gertrude Stein and Thornton Wilder.* Edited by William Rice. New Haven, Yale University Press, 1996.

Cunliffe, Marcus, *The Literature of the United States.* New York, Viking Penguin, 1986.

George F. Will

Will, George F. (1941—)

Political commentator, columnist, and amateur baseball historian, George F. Will is known for the way he imparts a conservative spin to his opinions about the intersection of American culture and politics in the closing years of the twentieth century. Best known for his syndicated column in the *Washington Post* and for his regular contributions to *Newsweek,* Will is also a frequent panelist on televised political commentary programs, such as ABC's *This Week with David Brinkley.* As R. Emmett Tyrell Jr. wrote in his review of *The Leveling Wind: Politics, the Culture, and Other News, 1990-1994,* ''George F. Will has always been a sober, civilized man with serious political principles buttressed by wise historical thoughts.''

Born in Champaign, Illinois, in 1941, George F. Will was educated at Trinity College (B.A. 1962), Magdalene College of Oxford University (B.A. 1964), and Princeton University (M.A., Ph.D. 1967). Several collections of Will's newspaper and magazine columns have been published including: *Suddenly: The American Idea Abroad and at Home, 1986-1990*; *The Morning After: American Successes and Excesses, 1981-1986*; *The Pursuit of Virtue and Other Tory Notions*; and *The Pursuit of Happiness, and Other Sobering Thoughts.* One of Will's biggest crusades has been against big government, notably as a supporter for term limitations for U.S. Senators and Representatives. Reflective of public frustration with the American political system during the 1980s and 1990s, Will consistently pushed for term limits believing, as Peter Knupfer notes

in the *Journal of American History,* these limits will ''restore democratic institutions to deliberative processes and to leadership by public-spirited amateurs'' who are more interested in the public good than in political careers. Will's writings on term limits are found in numerous columns and in one book, *Restoration: Congress, Term Limits, and the Recovery of Deliberative Democracy.*

Although he generally adopts a conservative position, he is by no means a typical Republican looking to either weaken government or weaken the Democratic Party. As a self-styled conservative, Will reshaped the way people viewed the spectrum of American political thought by insisting that conservatives move away from narrow self-interest toward an interest in the public good. Will's thought urges conservatives to reconsider their assumptions and adopt ideas steeped in the ''tradition of U.S. socio-political thought: the relation of individuals to the larger community, the ways of nurturing a dynamic democracy and the proper role of government,'' in the words of Marilyn Thie in *America.* From this position, Will wrote many columns on what he saw as wasteful government spending, government inefficiency, and political gridlock. Will came to believe one of the biggest problems for American culture was the public's heavy reliance on—and demands on—its government. If the government is misfiring in itself, then its ability to serve the public is highly problematic, Will believed.

Beyond his primary focus on politics and American culture, Will also wrote on a range of subjects that included pornography, journalistic ethics, advertising, the environment, and especially the game of baseball. Relating the myths of American life, such as the American dream and the great American pastime, to the realities of contemporary American life remains one of Will's contributions to cultural discourse. Besides several columns for a variety of periodicals, his book publications on the myths of American baseball include *Bunts: Curt Flood, Camden Yards, Pete Rose, and Other Reflections on Baseball* (1998) and *Men at Work: The Craft of Baseball* (1990).

—Randall McClure

FURTHER READING:

Chappell, Larry W. *George F. Will.* New York, Twayne Publishers, 1997.

Knupfer, Peter. ''Review—*Restoration: Congress, Term Limits, and the Recovery of Deliberative Democracy* by George F. Will.'' *Journal of American History.* June 1994, 325.

Thie, Marilyn. ''Suddenly: The American Idea Abroad and at Home, 1986-1990 by George F. Will.'' *America.* June 8, 1991, 628-630.

Tyrell, R. Emmett, Jr. ''Alone Again, Naturally—*The Leveling Wind* by George F. Will.'' *National Review.* January 23, 1995, 64.

Will, George F. *Bunts: Curt Flood, Camden Yards, Pete Rose, and Other Reflections on Baseball.* New York, Scribner, 1998.

———. *The Leveling Wind: Politics, the Culture, and Other News, 1990-1994.* New York, Viking, 1994.

———. *Men at Work: The Craft of Baseball.* New York, Macmillan, 1990.

———. *The Morning After: American Successes and Excesses, 1981-1986.* New York, Free Press, 1986.

———. *The Pursuit of Happiness, and Other Sobering Thoughts.* New York, Harper & Row, 1978.

———. *The Pursuit of Virtue and Other Tory Notions.* New York, Simon and Schuster, 1982.

———. *Restoration: Congress, Term Limits, and the Recovery of Deliberative Democracy.* New York, Free Press, 1992.

———. *Statecraft as Soulcraft: What Government Does.* New York, Simon and Schuster, 1983.

———. *Suddenly: The American Idea Abroad and at Home, 1986-1990.* New York, Free Press, 1990.

———. *The Woven Figure: Conservatism and America's Fabric, 1994-1997.* New York, Scribner, 1997.

Williams, Andy (1930—)

One of the great middle-of-the-road singers of the mid-twentieth century, Andy Williams is among the very few whose popularity survived the onset of rock 'n' roll in the 1950s. Howard Andrew Williams was born in the small town of Wall Lake, Iowa, the last of a set of four brothers. The Williams Brothers formed a singing group while Andy was still a child, and were regularly employed on radio from 1938. The family relocated several times to facilitate the Williams Brothers' obtaining new radio contracts. At various times they lived in Des Moines, Chicago, Cincinnati, and southern California. The two older brothers were drafted in the last days of World War Two, and Andy Williams spent a comparatively calm period finishing high school in Los Angeles.

In 1947 the foursome regrouped, joining with a new partner, Kay Thompson. They played a wide variety of clubs over the next several years, including a tour of Europe, before disbanding in 1953; the brothers went their separate ways professionally. Andy Williams landed a regular job on Steve Allen's *Tonight Show* from 1954 to 1957, singing and taking part in Allen's manic clowning, five nights a week. The year 1957 saw Williams hosting a summer replacement television program on NBC; he also had summer shows on ABC in 1958 and on CBS the following year. From 1962 to 1967, and again from 1969 to 1971, Williams had his own highly successful series on NBC. At various times his supporting cast included Dick Van Dyke, Jonathan Winters, Ray Stevens, and the Osmond Brothers. His program was noteworthy in that Williams was always willing to have competing singers—major personalities such as Bobby Darin or Robert Goulet—make guest appearances on his show.

Williams' recording career, benefitting from his national exposure on the *Tonight Show*, was a hit from the start. He recorded for the Cadence label until 1962, when he switched to the larger Columbia Records. His recording career had actually started much earlier, however, in 1944, when he was picked to sing ''Swingin' on a Star'' with Bing Crosby. Williams had several million-selling singles in the 1950s, including ''The Village of St. Bernadette,'' ''Canadian Sunset,'' and ''The Hawaiian Wedding Song.'' His version of ''Butterfly'' was the number-one record in America for three weeks in the spring of 1957.

The song most closely identified with Williams, 1961's ''Moon River,'' was never a hit for him. However, it so perfectly suited his smooth voice and mellow delivery that it became his signature song, and served as his television theme from 1962 onwards. His popularization of the Henry Mancini-written ''Moon River'' (from *Breakfast at Tiffany's*) was not lost on the composer; Andy Williams was invited to sing the theme for the 1963 film *Days of Wine and Roses,* another important Mancini work. Williams' LP of the same name was one of the six top-selling albums of 1963. Major hits were rare for Williams after that year, his last being the theme from *Love Story* in 1971. His albums, television work, and live concerts all remained quite successful.

Williams became a noted collector of art in the late 1950s. He has built a well-regarded private collection of Impressionist and modern paintings, located in his Manhattan home. In 1961 he married a nineteen-year-old Folies-Bergère showgirl, Claudine Longet, whom he met during her show's stay in Las Vegas. Longet unsuccessfully pursued careers in music and acting for years. The two separated in 1970, divorcing in 1975. The following year she fatally shot her long-time lover, professional skier Spider Sabich, in their Colorado home. Williams, who remained close to his ex-wife after the breakup of their marriage, was publicly supportive of Longet throughout her trial and the attendant media circus.

In addition to his highly rated variety program, which he ended in 1971, Williams is known for hosting numerous seasonal television specials. He is an avid golfer, and the host of the annual Andy Williams Open golf tournament. In 1992 he opened his own theater in Branson, Missouri, considered the second city of country music after Nashville. Andy Williams' Moon River Theatre there is one of the

Andy Williams and Ann Sothern (foreground) dancing during a rehersal for the *Andy Williams Show*.

more popular attractions, providing live music shows for many of the millions of tourists who visit Branson each year.

—David Lonergan

FURTHER READING:

Brooks, Tim, and Earle Marsh. *The Complete Directory to Prime Time Network TV Shows*. 5th Edition. New York, Ballantine, 1992.

Contemporary Musicians. Volume 2. Detroit, Gale Research, 1990.

Whitburn, Joel. *The Billboard Book of Top 40 Hits*. 6th Edition. New York, Billboard Books, 1996.

Williams, Bert (1874-1922)

Known during his lifetime as "the funniest man in America," Egbert Austin "Bert" Williams enjoyed fame as the straight man and ballad singer of the African American comedy team of Williams and Walker. Williams met his partner, George Walker, in San Francisco in 1893, when he began performing in order to finance his studies at Stanford University. They worked their way to New York, where in 1896 they appeared in Victor Herbert's *Gold Bug*. The two performed in such musical comedy hits as *The Sons of Ham* (1900), *In Dahomey* (1902), *Abyssinia* (1905), and *Bandanna Land* (1907). When Walker retired, Williams starred in *Mr. Lode of Koal* (1909) then performed with Florenz Ziegfeld's *Follies* from 1910 to 1919. In 1920 Williams joined Eddie Cantor in *Broadway Brevities*. Williams was admired for impeccable comedic timing and pantomimes. He died in 1922 after opening in *Under the Bamboo Tree*.

—Susan Curtis

FURTHER READING:

Charters, Ann. *Nobody: The Story of Bert Williams*. New York, Macmillan, 1970.

Riis, Thomas L. *Just Before Jazz: Black Musical Theater in New York, 1890-1915*. Washington, D.C., Smithsonian Institution Press, 1989.

Smith, Eric Lidell. *Bert Williams: A Biography of the Pioneer Black Comedian.* Jefferson, North Carolina, McFarland, 1992.

Williams, Hank, Jr. (1949—)

Perhaps no one has ever been simultaneously such a major star and so much in the shadow of his father as Hank Williams, Jr. As an eight-year-old, Williams began his career as an imitator of his deceased father, then still the biggest name in country music. Ultimately trading on the fact that his name made it impossible for the country establishment to reject him, he was to become perhaps the most significant force in bringing rock music into country.

In an industry that has never been ashamed of exploitation, young Williams was shamelessly exploited. Between the ages of eight and fourteen, he played fifty shows a year, singing his father's songs. By the time he was in his mid-teens, he was signed to MGM Records, his father's old label, and he was recording overdubbed duets with his father; he even overdubbed the singing for George Hamilton in *Your Cheatin' Heart,* a movie biography of Hank, Sr.

By the time he was in his late teens, Williams was drinking heavily; he felt utterly trapped inside a musical world that was making less and less sense to him. He was listening to the rock and roll of his generation—Chuck Berry, Fats Domino, and Elvis Presley—and thinking about the kind of music he really wanted to play. At 23, with his first marriage breaking up, Williams attempted suicide.

Hank Williams, Jr.

As part of his recovery, he left Nashville and moved to Alabama. He began to work seriously on developing his own music. In August 1975, after finishing work on what was to be a landmark country rock album, *Hank Williams, Jr. and Friends,* he took a vacation in Montana, and suffered a devastating accident: a near-fatal fall down a mountain virtually tore his face off.

After extensive physical therapy and plastic surgery to reconstruct his face, Williams returned to music with an absolute determination to create his own, rock-oriented kind of sound. A new country audience—one that had opened up to the "outlaw" sounds of Willie Nelson and Waylon Jennings—was ready for him. After a few modest successes, the highest-charting being his cover version of Bobby Fuller's "I Fought the Law," he reached his stride in 1979 with a song that looked back at the past at the same time it snarled with the beat and attitude of rock. The song was "Family Tradition," and it was highly autobiographical. In it Williams was asked, "Why do you drink, and why do you roll smoke, and why do you live out the songs that Hank wrote?" Williams responded that he was simply carrying on a family tradition.

This proved to be a winning formula for Williams. Many of his subsequent hits were autobiographical. In one, he asks an operator to put him through to Cloud Number Nine so he can talk to his father. In "All My Rowdy Friends Have Settled Down," he remembers the wildness of Nashville in the 1970s. Established as a major star in his own right by the mid-1980s, he was able to use his preoccupation with his father and his family history to successful record Hank Williams, Sr., hits like "Honky Tonkin'." In 1987, he even performed a duet with his father on a newly discovered, never released recording of a song called "There's a Tear in My Beer." Williams also released a video duet, in which his image is inserted into an old kinescope of his father. Since Williams, Sr. had never performed "There's a Tear in My Beer" for the cameras, a film was used in which he sings "Hey, Good Lookin'" with his mouth electronically doctored to lip-synch the words of the other song.

At the same time, Williams continued to be a major force in bringing rock into country, and making it an important part of the new country sound. In his semi-anthemic 1988 hit, "Young Country," he reminds his listeners that "We [the new generation of country performers] like old Waylon, and we like Van Halen." At the time, this was still a significant statement, and one that it took a child of traditional country like Williams to make. A few years later, the rockers themselves had become the country music establishment, with megastars like Garth Brooks modeling himself on arena rockers like Journey.

As Williams himself settled into the role of middle-aged country establishment figure in the 1990s, he remained solidly in the public eye with his theme song for *Monday Night Football.*

—Tad Richards

FURTHER READING:

Williams, Hank, Jr., with Michael Bane. *Living Proof: An Autobiography.* New York, G.P. Putnam's Sons, 1979.

Williams, Hank, Sr. (1923-1953)

Widely acknowledged as the father of contemporary country music, Hank Williams, Sr., was a superstar at the age of 25 and dead at

Hank Williams, Sr.

29. Like Jimmie Rodgers, Williams had a short but highly influential career in country music. Though he never learned to read or write music, during his years of greatest commercial success, Williams wrote and recorded over 100 polished, unique, and lasting songs, releasing at least half a dozen hit records every year from 1949 until 1953. His direct, sincere, and emotional lyrics (''Your cheatin' heart / Will make you weep / You'll cry and cry / And try to sleep'') set the stage for much of the country music that followed, and many of his songs, including ''Cold, Cold Heart'' and ''Your Cheatin' Heart,'' have become classics.

His ability to transfix his audiences is the stuff of legend. Chet Hagan's *Grand Ole Opry* offers the following assessments: Little Jimmy Dickens said that ''You could hear a pin drop when Hank was working. He just seemed to hypnotize those people. It was simplicity I guess. He brought his people with him. He put himself on their level.'' Minnie Pearl said, ''He had a real animal magnetism. He destroyed the women in the audience. And he was just as authentic as rain.'' And according to Mitch Miller (a Columbia Records executive), ''He had a way of reaching your guts and your head at the same time.'' Williams had the unique ability to connect with his audiences, comprised primarily of poor, white Southerners like himself, and, particularly in the early days, fist-fights often broke out among his female fans.

Born and raised in Alabama, Williams got a guitar at the age of eight and learned to play and sing from a local blues street performer known as ''Tee Tot.'' This early exposure to African-American blues styles shaped his own musical character, forming a key element of Williams's trademark honky-tonk, country-blues sound. When he

was 12 years old, Williams won 15 dollars in a songwriting contest with his ''WPA Blues.'' At the age of 14, Williams had organized his own band and had begun playing locally for hoedowns, square dances, and the like. In 1941, Williams and his band, the Drifting Cowboys, began performing at a local radio station, most often covering the songs of other country artists, including Williams's hero, Roy Acuff. Despite attempts to make a name for himself and his band, Williams's musical career stayed in a holding pattern for several years.

In 1946, Williams went to Nashville with his wife and manager, Audrey, where a music publishing executive for Acuff-Rose Publishing set up a recording session for Williams with Sterling Records. The two singles he recorded then, ''Never Again'' (released in late 1946) and ''Honky Tonkin''' (released in early 1947) were quite successful, rising to the top of the country music charts and breaking Williams's career out of its holding pattern. Williams signed the first exclusive songwriter's contract issued by Acuff-Rose Publishing, and he began a long and productive songwriting partnership with Fred Rose, with Williams writing the songs and Rose editing them.

In 1947, Williams won a contract with Metro Goldwyn Mayer (MGM) Records. ''Move It On Over,'' Williams's first MGM single, was a big hit, and Williams and the Drifting Cowboys began appearing regularly on KWKH Louisiana Hayride, a popular radio program. Several other releases followed, and Williams became a huge country music star. Already earning a reputation as a hard-drinking, womanizing man, he had trouble being accepted by the country music establishment, and Ernest Tubb's attempts to get the Grand Ole Opry to sign him on were initially rebuffed for fear that he would be too much trouble. He was finally asked to join the Opry in 1949, and earned an unprecedented six encores after singing the old country-blues standard ''Lovesick Blues'' at a 1949 Opry performance. Strings of hit singles in 1949 and 1950 (including ''Lovesick Blues,'' ''Mind Your Own Business,'' and ''Wedding Bells'' in 1949, and ''Long Gone Lonesome Blues,'' ''Moaning the Blues,'' and ''Why Don't You Love Me'' in 1950) led to sell-out shows for Williams and the reorganized Drifting Cowboys, earning Williams and the band over $1,000 per performance. From 1949 through 1953, Williams scored 27 top ten hits. During this period, Williams began recording religious material (both music and recitations) under the name Luke the Drifter, and he managed to keep his drinking and womanizing in check.

In 1951, Tony Bennett had a hit single with a cover of Williams' ''Cold, Cold Heart,'' and other singers began recording (and having hits) with Williams's songs: Jo Stafford recorded ''Jambalaya,'' Rosemary Clooney sang ''Half As Much,'' and both Frankie Laine and Jo Stafford covered ''Hey Good Lookin'.'' As a result, Williams began to enjoy crossover success on the popular music charts, appearing on the Perry Como television show, and touring as part of a package group that included Bob Hope, Jack Benny, and Minnie Pearl. Though not all of his hit records were his own compositions, many of his best known works are ones he wrote, and many of them seem to have an autobiographical bent.

Williams's professional success, however, began to take a toll on his private life. His long-time tendency to drink to excess became full-blown alcoholism. Williams began showing up at concerts drunk and abusive. As a result, he was fired from the Grand Ole Opry and told to return when he was sober. Rather than taking the Opry's action as a wake-up call, Williams drank even more heavily. An accident reinflamed an old back injury, and Williams began abusing the morphine he was prescribed to deal with back pain. His marriage fell apart, in part due to his drinking and drug abuse, and in part due to his increasingly frequent dalliances with other women. In 1952, after divorcing his first wife, Audrey, he quickly married a 19-year-old divorcee named Billie Jean, selling tickets to what was billed as a matinee ''wedding rehearsal'' and ''actual wedding'' that evening (both were frauds; Billie Jean and Williams had been legally married the previous day). Williams also came under the spell of a man calling himself ''Doctor'' Toby Marshall (actually a paroled forger), who often supplied him with prescriptions and shots for the sedative chloral hydrate, which Marshall claimed was a pain reliever.

In December of 1952, Williams suffered a heart attack brought on by ''alcoholic cardiomyopathy'' (heart disease due to excessive drinking); found in the back seat of his car, he was rushed to the hospital but was pronounced dead on January 1, 1953. His funeral, held at a city auditorium in Montgomery, Alabama, was attended by over 25,000 weeping fans. After his death, his record company continued to issue a number of singles he had previously recorded, including what is probably his most famous song, ''Your Cheatin' Heart.'' These singles earned a great deal of money for his record company and his estate, and artists as diverse as Johnny Cash and Elvis Costello have made their own recordings of Williams' songs in recent years. Many of those associated with Williams attempted to trade on his reputation after his death. Both of his wives went on tour, performing as ''Mrs. Hank Williams.'' A supposedly biographical film, *Your Cheatin' Heart,* also exploited Williams' fame and untimely death. Williams' children, Jett and Hank, Jr., went into country music and have enjoyed some success (particularly Hank ''Bocephus'' Williams, Jr.). But it is Hank, Sr., who left his mark on country music. Along with Jimmie Rodgers and Fred Rose, he was one of the first inductees into Nashville's Country Music Hall of Fame, elected in 1961.

—Deborah M. Mix

Robin Williams

FURTHER READING:

Hagan, Chet. *Grand Ole Opry: The Complete Story of a Great American Institution and Its Stars.* New York, Holt, 1989.

Williams, Hank, Sr. *The Complete Hank Williams.* Polygram Records, 1998.

Williams, Roger M. *Sing a Sad Song: The Life of Hank Williams.* Urbana, University of Illinois Press, 1981.

Williams, Robin (1952—)

With his manic versatility, comedic genius Robin Williams has defined comedy for the last three decades of the twentieth century. Whether expressing himself as a stand-up comic or an animated genie or a cross-dressing nanny, he is without equal in the field of American comedy. Much more than a comedian, however, some of his finest work has been in dramatic film roles to which he has brought humanity and warmth to a cast of characters ranging from a crazed widower in *The Fisher King* (1991) to a sad but optimistic psychiatrist in 1997's *Good Will Hunting,* which garnered an Academy Award for Best Supporting Actor.

Williams was born July 21, 1952, in Chicago, Illinois, to a father who was a Ford company executive and a mother who was a former model engaged in charity work. While both parents had sons by previous marriages, Williams essentially grew up as an only child. In interviews, he has described his childhood as lonely and himself as shy and chubby. His father was stern and distant, and his mother was charming and busy. While Williams was close to his mother, she was often absent, leaving him to roam their forty-room home for diversion. He turned to humor as a way to attract attention. His interest in comedy was aroused by hours spent in front of the television, and he was particularly enthralled by late-night shows where he discovered his idol, Jonathan Winters, another comic who consistently pushes the envelope.

In 1967 Williams's family moved to Tiburon, an affluent suburb of San Francisco. In the less inhibited atmosphere in California, Williams blossomed. When his father steered him toward a career in business, Williams rebelled. His innate comedic skills were honed in college, but he chose to leave two schools without finishing. He then entered the prestigious Juilliard School in New York on a scholarship, where he roomed with actor Christopher Reeve, who remains a close friend. While the other students found Williams's off-the-wall antics hilarious, his professors were unsure of how to handle such frenetic humor. Leaving Juilliard without graduating, Williams returned to California and appeared in comedy clubs such as the Improv and the Comedy Store.

By the mid-1970s, Williams had guest-starred on several television shows including *Saturday Night Live, Laugh-In,* and *The Richard Pryor Show.* In 1977, a guest appearance on *Happy Days* as the alien Mork from the planet Ork propelled him to stardom. Williams reportedly won the role of Mork by showing up at his audition in rainbow suspenders and standing on his head when asked to sit like an alien. The appearance was so successful that the character of Mork was given his own show, *Mork and Mindy* (1978-1982), which costarred Pam Dawber as the earthling who took in the stranded alien. In retrospect, it is inconceivable that anyone else could have played Mork with his zany innocence. Each week, the television audience discovered their own planet through Mork's reports to Ork leader Orson at show's end. Even though the characters of Mork and Mindy predictably fell in love and married, the birth of their first child was anything but predictable: Jonathan Winters as Mearth, who aged backward, was the surprising result of this intergalactic coupling. Even though Williams had so much control over the content of the show that it became known informally as ''The Robin Williams Show,'' he often felt stifled by the confines of network television as a medium. Williams said in a 1998 *TV Guide* interview that he found salvation in his HBO specials that aired without censorship, giving him freedom to expand as a comic and solidify his position as a top-notch performer.

In 1980 Williams lent his talent to the big screen with *Popeye*, based on the heavily muscled, spinach-eating sailor from the comic strip of the same name. It was a disappointing debut. His performance in *The World According to Garp* in 1982 was better received, but it was evident that Williams's vast talents were not being properly utilized outside of television. He managed to hit his stride with *Moscow on the Hudson* in 1984, playing a Russian defector. Perhaps the character who came closest to his own personality was that of an outrageous disc jockey in 1987's *Good Morning, Vietnam,* a role which earned him his first Academy Award nomination for Best Actor.

Drawing on his cross-generational appeal, Williams has appeared in a series of films aimed at family audiences, such as the role of Peter Pan in *Hook* in 1991. Although it was criticized by certain reviewers, the role allowed Williams to display his own split personality—that of the child who never quite grew up in the body of an adult burdened by the everyday cares of his world. Williams followed *Hook* with a delightful performance as the voice of Batty Koda in the animated environmental film *FernGully . . . The Last Rain Forest,* but nowhere was the enormity of Williams's comedic range more evident than in Disney's *Aladdin* in 1992. As Genie, he managed to steal the show. Refusing to be confined by his large-chested blue blob of a body, Williams's Genie metamorphosed by turns into a Scotsman, a dog, Arnold Schwarzenegger, Ed Sullivan, Groucho Marx, a waiter, a rabbit, a dinosaur, William F. Buckley Jr., Robert De Niro, a stewardess, a sheep, Pinocchio, Sebastian from *The Little Mermaid,* Arsenio Hall, Walter Brennan, Ethel Merman, Rodney Dangerfield, Jack Nicholson, and a one-man band. There was talk of an unheard-of Academy Award nomination for Best Actor for the portrayal of an animated character. Williams did, in fact, win a special Golden Globe award for his vocal work in *Aladdin.*

Even though *Toys* (1992) received little attention, Williams followed it up with the blockbuster *Mrs. Doubtfire,* in which he played the estranged husband of Sally Field and cross-dressed as a nanny in order to remain close to his three children. *Jumanji* (1995), a saga of characters trapped inside a board game, demonstrated a darker side to Williams. He finally came to terms with Disney and reprised the role of the genie in the straight-to-video *Aladdin and the King of Thieves* in 1996. Williams's zany side was again much in evidence in 1997's *Flubber,* a remake of the Disney classic *The Absent Minded Professor.* Before *Flubber,* Williams had returned to adult comedy with his uproarious portrayal of a gay father whose son is about to be married in *The Birdcage* (1996).

While comedy is the milieu in which Williams excels, his dramatic abilities have also won critical acclaim. He was nominated

for an Academy Award for his portrayal of John Keating, a teacher at a conservative prep school who attempts to open the eyes of his students to the world of poetry and dreams in *Dead Poet's Society* in 1989. The role of Parry in *The Fisher King* (1991) introduced a side to Williams that stunned audiences and critics alike. After Parry's wife is murdered in a random shooting at a restaurant, he descends into insanity from which he only occasionally emerges to search for his personal holy grail with the help of co-star Jeff Bridges. The role of Dr. Malcolm Sayer, a dedicated physician who temporarily restores life to catatonic patients, in *Awakenings* again demonstrated Williams's enormous versatility. In 1997, Williams won his Academy Award for Best Supporting Actor in the Matt Damon/Ben Affleck film *Good Will Hunting,* leading Damon's Will Hunting to awkward acceptance of his own reality and mathematical genius. Williams followed that success with back-to-back roles in *What Dreams May Come* and *Patch Adams* in 1998. Afterward, he expressed a desire to modify his busy schedule and perhaps return to a weekly series.

Personally, Williams has had highs and lows. As a young performer, he was well-known for his heavy consumption of drugs and alcohol. He was forced to reexamine his life when his friend and fellow comic John Belushi died after spending an evening with Williams in the pursuit of nirvana. Another setback occurred when his first marriage fell apart amid tabloid reports that he had left his wife for his son Zachery's nanny. Williams insisted that the marriage was over before he became involved with Marsha Gracos, whom he subsequently married. Their wedding rings are engraved with wolves to signify their intention to mate for life; they have two children: Zelda and Cody. Along with friends Billy Crystal and Whoopi Goldberg, Williams has labored diligently for ''Comic Relief,'' an annual benefit for the homeless.

—Elizabeth Purdy

FURTHER READING:

Corliss, Richard. ''Aladdin's Magic.'' *Time.* November 9, 1992, 74.

David, Jay. *The Life and Humor of Robin Williams: A Biography.* New York, William Morrow, 1999.

Dougan, Andy Y. *Robin Williams.* New York, Thunder's Mouth Press, 1998.

Weeks, Janet. ''Face to Face with Robin Williams.'' *TV Guide.* November 14-20, 1998.

Williams, Ted (1918—)

Ted Williams, ''The Splendid Splinter,'' was one of the best hitters of all time and is the last baseball player to hit over .400. His scientific view of hitting changed the dynamics of the game forever. But he was also probably the least celebrated modern-day baseball hero. While he had the makings of stardom, he was unable to cultivate the followings enjoyed by less talented but more amiable players, such as his contemporary Joe DiMaggio.

On August 30, 1918, Theodore Samuel Williams was born in San Diego, California, into a lower-middle class family. His parents

Ted Williams

worked constantly, leaving him plenty of time to play baseball. When he was seventeen he signed with the hometown San Diego Padres. But after only one year, he was sold to the Boston Red Sox.

Ted Williams proved himself immediately when he started for the Red Sox in 1939. He led the league with 143 RBIs, the first rookie to do so. In 1941, his batting average topped .400. Going into the last day of the season, Williams' average had been .39955, which in baseball terms is a .400 batting average. Manager Joe Cronin gave his star the option to sit out of the doubleheader, but he decided to play and went six-for-eight, raising his batting average to an incredible .406. His 1942 campaign earned him his first Triple Crown by hitting .356, 137 RBIs, and 36 home runs. But even though he won the Triple Crown, Williams did not win the MVP.

Williams interrupted his baseball career in 1943 to join World War II, and he spent the next three years stateside as a pilot. When he returned to baseball in 1946, the Red Sox had a talented postwar team and Williams had another outstanding season, winning his first MVP.

Baseball also encountered ''The Williams Shift'' in 1946. Cleveland manager Lou Boudreau pushed the infielders to the right side of the field, trying to force the left-handed Williams to hit the ball the opposite way, which he refused to do. That year Williams also led Boston to their only World Series during his career, but the Red Sox lost and Williams' hitting was criticized by the media.

Williams' relationship with the media, always tumultuous, turned ugly after the 1946 season. The Boston press and many fans often felt disenchanted with the temperamental superstar. Williams often went public with his anger, liked to spit, never tipped his cap to the fans or came out for curtain calls after home runs, and was candid about his dislike of the Boston sports writers, who in turn criticized him in print.

Williams rebounded after the World Series, and in 1947 he won his second Triple Crown but lost the MVP to Joe DiMaggio. He closed the decade by winning the batting title in 1948 and winning his second MVP in 1949, while leading the league in runs, walks, RBIs, and hitting.

The 1950s were less kind to Williams. In 1950, he missed half the season with a broken arm. In 1952 Williams was recalled to fight in the Korean War, in which he survived a fiery plane crash. He came back to baseball in 1954 and received two more batting titles in 1957 and in 1958, making him the oldest player in baseball history to do so. A pinched nerve in his neck caused Williams to hit a career low .254 in 1959 and made fans and Red Sox owner Tom Yawkey push for his retirement. But Williams came back to finish his career in 1960, hitting .316 with 29 home runs, including one in his final at-bat.

Williams finished his baseball career with a .344 lifetime batting average, the highest on-base percentage in history at .483, 521 home runs, and the second highest slugging average at .634. *The Sporting*

News named Ted Williams its "Player of the Decade" for the 1950s. He was inducted into the Baseball Hall of Fame in 1966.

Ted Williams had the stuff heroes were made of, even though his contemporaries believed otherwise. He served his country in two wars and was the most prolific hitter of his era. Williams changed the face of baseball with his scientific approach to hitting and forcing opposing managers to move their fielders. And today when any player chases .400, Williams is the man to beat. In his autobiography, *My Turn at Bat,* Williams states that when he walked down the street he dreamed people would say, "There goes Ted Williams, the greatest hitter who ever lived." While a case could be made for such a claim, Williams is less remembered than other more charismatic players. But he did receive some belated recognition when the Ted Williams Museum and Hitters Hall of Fame opened in Hernando, Florida, in 1994.

—Nathan R. Meyer

FURTHER READING:

Linn, Edward. *Hitter: The Life and Turmoils of Ted Williams.* San Diego, Harcourt Brace, 1994.

Williams, Ted, with John Underwood. *My Turn at Bat: The Story of My Life.* New York, Simon and Schuster, 1988.

Williams, Ted, with John Underwood. *The Science of Hitting.* New York, Simon and Schuster, 1986.

Wolff, Rick. *Ted Williams.* New York, Chelsea House, 1993.

Tennessee Williams

Williams, Tennessee (1911-1983)

An American playwright and screenwriter, Tennessee Williams was regarded in his literary prime with an equal measure of esteem and notoriety. After Eugene O'Neill, Williams was the first playwright to gain international respect for the emerging American dramatic genre. Williams excelled at creating richly realized characters peppered with humor and poignancy. The ever-shifting autobiography of Williams is equally renowned—always casual with fact, the playwright shone in an era that adored celebrity and encouraged excess.

Tennessee Williams was born Thomas Lanier Williams on March 26, 1911 in Columbus, Mississippi. His father, Cornelius Coffin Williams, was a rough man with a fine Southern pedigree. Absent for long periods of time, Cornelius moved his family from town to town throughout Williams' childhood. His mother, Edwina Dakin Williams, imagined herself to be a Southern belle in her youth; born in Ohio, Edwina insisted that her sickly young son focus on Shakespeare over sports, and a writer was born.

The plays of Tennessee Williams deeply resonated with the performing arts community of the 1940s. The complex characterization and difficult subject matter of young Williams' plays appealed to a new generation of actors. The 1949 Broadway production of *A Streetcar Named Desire* featured then-unknown actors Marlon Brando, Jessica Tandy, and Karl Malden, trained in "Method Acting," a new model of acting experientially to project character psychology. Actors trained in the Method technique quickly discovered Williams was writing plays that stripped bare an American culture of repression and denial. A close-knit circle of performers, directors, and writers immediately surrounded the temperamental Southern playwright. Williams preferred certain personalities to be involved with his projects, including actors Montgomery Clift and Maureen Stapleton, directors Elia Kazan and Stella Adler, and a cheerfully competitive group of writers including Truman Capote, Gore Vidal, and William Inge.

The 1950 film version of *A Streetcar Named Desire* brought Williams and the actors instant fame. Lines from the film have entered into the popular lexicon, from Blanche's pitiful ironies ("I have always depended on the kindness of strangers") to Stanley's scream in the New Orleans night ("Stella!"). More than any other of Williams' screenplays, *A Streetcar Named Desire*'s lines resurface today in the most unlikely places, from advertisements to television sitcoms; the public often recognizes these phrases without having seen the production at all.

Pairing misfortune and loneliness with gracefully lyrical speech, Williams wrestles in his works with a repressed culture emerging from Victorian mores. Social commentary is present in most works, but the focus for Williams is the poetry of human interaction, with its composite failings, hopes, and eccentricities. Early works were bluntly political in nature, as in *Me, Vashya!,* whose villain is a tyrannical munitions maker. After *The Glass Menagerie,* however, Williams found he had a talent for creating real, vivid characters. Often, figures in his plays struggle for identity and an awakened sense of sensuality with little to show for the effort. Roles of victim and victimizer are exchanged between intertwined couples, as with Alexandra and Chance in *Sweet Bird of Youth.* The paralyzing fear of mortality, so often an issue for his characters, plagues Mrs. Goforth of *The Milk Train Doesn't Stop here Anymore.* Most significantly, perhaps, characters like Shannon of *The Night of the Iguana,* one of

Williams' late plays, sometimes find peace of spirit after they can lose little else. Arthur Miller once declared Williams' most enduring theme to be ''the romance of the lost yet sacred misfits, who exist in order to remind us of our trampled instincts, our forsaken tenderness, the holiness of the spirit of man.''

The relationship between Williams' work and popular culture is long and varied. Many of his plays—*The Glass Menagerie, A Streetcar Named Desire, Cat on a Hot Tin Roof, Sweet Bird of Youth,* and *Night of the Iguana*—became major films of the 1950s and 1960s. Williams' films were immediately popular with mainstream audiences despite their focus on the darker elements of American society, including pedophilia, venereal disease, domestic violence, and rape. Williams was one of the first American dramatists to introduce problematic and challenging content on a broad level. Some of the playwright's subplots border on sensationalism, with scenes of implied cannibalism and castration. Consequently, Tennessee Williams had the curious distinction of being one of the most-censored writers of the 1960s; *Baby Doll, Suddenly Last Summer,* and other films were thoroughly revised by producers before general release. The modern paradigm of film studios, celebrating fame while editing content, can be seen in the choices made with Williams' work, as Metro Goldwyn Mayer produced his films and at the same time feared his subject matter to be too provocative for audiences.

Tennessee Williams nurtured a public persona that gradually shifted from shy to flamboyantly homosexual in an era reluctant to accept gay men. Williams' fears of audience backlash against his personal life gradually proved groundless. Even late in life, however, Williams was reluctant to assume the political agenda of others. *Gay Sunshine* magazine declared in 1976 that the playwright had never dealt openly with the politics of gay liberation, and Williams—always adept with the press—immediately responded: ''People so wish to latch onto something didactic; I do not deal with the didactic, ever . . . I wish to have a broad audience because the major thrust of my work is not sexual orientation, it's social. I'm not about to limit myself to writing about gay people.'' As is so often the case with Williams, the statement is both true and untrue—his great, mid-career plays focus upon relationships rather than politics, but the figure of the gay male appears in characters explicit (Charlus in *Camino Real*) and implicit (Brick in *Cat on a Hot Tin Roof*) throughout his works.

As is noted in *American Writers,* Williams took a casual approach toward the hard facts of his life. In the early period of his fame, Williams intrigued audiences by implying that characters like Tom (read Thomas Lanier) in *The Glass Menagerie* represented his own experiences. Elia Kazan, a director whose success was often linked to Williams, promoted the Williams myth once by declaring that ''everything in [Williams'] life is in his plays, and everything in his plays is in his life.'' Tennessee Williams' connection with the outside world was often one of gentrified deceit, beginning early as the Williams family sought to hide his sister's schizophrenia and eventual lobotomy. In the closest blend of reality and art, the playwright's attachment to his sister, Rose Williams, has been well documented by Lyle Leverich and others. The connection between Rose and Tennessee Williams was profound, and images of her mental illness and sexual abuse often surface in Williams' most poignant characters. The rose rises as a complex symbol in his plays, a flower indicative alternately of strength, passion, and fragility.

The 1970s saw a gradual decline in Tennessee Williams' artistic skill, but he continued to tinker with the older plays and write new works until his death. Williams was highly prolific, crafting over 40 plays, 30 screenplay adaptations of his work, eight collections of

fiction, and various books of poetry and essays. He won the Pulitzer Prize twice, once in 1948 for *A Streetcar Named Desire,* and again in 1955 for *Cat on a Hot Tin Roof.* His work continues to command considerable social relevance—in 1998, a play on prison abuses, *Not About Nightingales,* was staged in London for the first time.

—Ryan R. Sloan

FURTHER READING:

Leithauser, Brad. ''The Grand Dissembler: Sorting out the Life, and Myth, of Tennessee Williams.'' *Time Magazine.* Vol. 146, No. 22, November 27, 1995.

Leverich, Lyle. *Tom: The Unknown Tennessee Williams.* 2 Vols. New York, Crown, 1997.

Murphy, Brenda. *Tennessee Williams and Elia Kazan: A Collaboration in the Theatre.* New York, Cambridge University Press, 1992.

Phillips, Gene D. *The Films of Tennessee Williams.* Philadelphia, Art Alliance Press, 1980.

Savran, David. *Communists, Cowboys and Queers: The Politics of Masculinity in the Work of Arthur Miller and Tennessee Williams.* Minneapolis, University of Minnesota Press, 1992.

Spoto, Donald. *The Kindness of Strangers: The Life of Tennessee Williams.* Boston, Little, Brown, 1985.

Unger, Leonard, editor. *American Writers: A Collection of Literary Biographies.* 4 Vols. New York, Charles Scribner's and Sons, 1960, 1974, 378-398.

Willis, Bruce (1955—)

Bruce Willis first came to prominence as David Addison in the mid-1980s television show *Moonlighting.* With its appealingly eccentric mix of throwaway detective plots and screwball romantic comedy, the show was an ideal showcase for Willis's often bemused and often in control, wise-cracking action man. It seemed with his first two films, *Blind Date* (1987) and *Sunset* (1988), both directed by Blake Edwards, that Willis was going to follow the comedy route, but after *Die Hard* (1988) Willis became instead one of the leading action stars of the 1990s. Early attempts to break free of the John McClane character and action man image met with failure and it is only since *Pulp Fiction* (1994), perhaps, that Willis has been able to extend his range, now alternating action with the occasional touch of character. It is, however, easy to see why the *Die Hard* films succeeded, and how Willis's image was established through them.

Expertly directed by John McTiernan, the first *Die Hard* gave a new boost to action films, the rough and ready American hero fighting international terrorists in a disaster movie scenario leading to two sequels, numerous imitations, and bringing stylish action and violence to the genre. And for his part, Willis seemed to embody a new sort of action hero; in contrast to Rambo and the Terminator, John McClane was a vulnerable family man. Up against high-tech criminals with nothing but his wits and a gun, he is brutally beaten and his spirit is wearing thin. Of course, McClane wins the day, dispatching the terrorist mastermind with his cowboy catchphrase, ''Yippy kay yay, mother fucker,'' but he still has a few problems to face. The skyscraper dynamics that recalled the film *Towering Inferno* were followed up by the brutal airport action of *Die Hard 2: Die Harder*

Bruce Willis

(1990). Another dose of realism is added to *Die Hard with a Vengeance* (1995) in which McClane is divorced, alcoholic, and out of shape.

An attempt in the early 1990s to extend his range in such films as the Vietnam elegy, *In Country* (1989), did not altogether meet with favorable reviews—in particular, playing the "English journalist" in Brian De Palma's misguided adaptation of Thomas Wolfe's *The Bonfire of the Vanities* (1990), then starring in his own expensive box-office flop, *Hudson Hawk* (1991). Tony Scott's *The Last Boy Scout* (1991) only returned Willis to a more violent cop role; Robert Zemeckis's *Death Becomes Her* (1992) was an unfunny special effects comedy; and *Striking Distance* (1993) was a minor action film. In order to focus more attention on his acting rather than his movie star status, Willis took on some quite interesting cameo roles: as Dustin Hoffman's gangster rival in *Billy Bathgate* (1991); alongside his wife Demi Moore in *Mortal Thoughts* (1991); admirably sending up his action man image in Robert Altman's *The Player* (1992); starring alongside Paul Newman in *Nobody's Fool* (1994); and acting as a comedy bunny in Rob Reiner's otherwise uninteresting family film, *North* (1994).

By all accounts, the so-called erotic thriller, *Color of Night* (1994), is Willis's worst film, but in the same year he was to launch a more mature phase in his career as the boxer, Butch, in Quentin

Tarantino's *Pulp Fiction*. Taking his place amongst an ensemble cast and latching onto Tarantino's hip dialogue, Willis pared down his usual smirks and steely stares, resulting in a notably different performance that was all internal rage and insecurity. Terry Gilliam managed to get an even more vulnerable performance out of Willis as the confused time traveller in *12 Monkeys* (1995); Walter Hill's *Last Man Standing* (1996) showcased Willis's pared-down brutality, and for their part *The Fifth Element* (1996) and *Armageddon* (1998) ranged from glossy *Die Hard* action in the former to Willis saving the world from pre-millennial excess in the latter. In between his big action projects, however, Willis still managed to choose roles in such small and unsatisfactory action films as *The Jackal* (1997) and *Mercury Rising* (1998). Of the three owners of the Planet Hollywood restaurant chain, however, Willis has clearly managed to become the most accessible action hero of the 1990s, taking over from the previous might of Sylvester Stallone and Arnold Schwarzenegger and cultivating an altogether more easygoing screen appeal.

—Stephen Keane

FURTHER READING:

Parker, John. *Bruce Willis: An Unauthorised Biography*. London, Virgin, 1997.

Quinlan, David. *Quinlan's Illustrated Directory of Film Stars*. London, Batsford, 1996.

Bob Wills and his Texas Playboys

Bob Wills pioneered "western swing," an upbeat style of country music that had a lasting impact on the industry. Wills, who grew up in the cotton fields of northern Texas during the World War I era, combined the blues of black sharecroppers with southern "hill-billy" music. In the mid-1930s, Wills formed the Texas Playboys, a band using experienced swing and Dixieland jazz musicians, who toured throughout the southwest to packed houses. Western swing became a national phenomenon after their 1940 hit "New San Antonio Rose," and Wills was inducted into the Country Music Hall of Fame in 1968.

—Jeffrey W. Coker

FURTHER READING:

Knowles, Ruth Sheldon. *Bob Wills: Hubbin' It*. Nashville, Country Music Foundation Press, 1995.

Malone, Bill C. *Country Music USA*. Revised edition. Austin, University of Texas Press, 1985.

Townsend, Charles R. *San Antonio Rose: The Life and Music of Bob Wills*. Urbana, University of Illinois Press, 1986.

Wilson, Flip (1933-1998)

In the early 1970s, comedian Flip Wilson secured a place in television history as the first African American to headline a successful network variety series. Previous attempts by other black performers, such as Nat "King" Cole, Leslie Uggams, and Sammy Davis, Jr.,

Flip Wilson (left) with Richard Pryor on *The Flip Wilson Show*.

had all been ratings failures. From 1970 to 1974 *The Flip Wilson Show* presented comedy skits, musical performances, and top Hollywood guest stars. The main attraction, however, was always Wilson himself. He possessed a sharp and non-confrontational sense of humor that appealed to a diverse audience. During its first two seasons, his show was the second most popular program on television, second only to *All in the Family* in the ratings. The most popular aspect of the show was the large stable of stock characters portrayed by Wilson each week. His most famous creation was the sassy and liberated Geraldine Jones, who introduced the catch phrase "What you see is what you get" into the American lexicon. Flip Wilson proved that the mainstream American television audience could accept a performer of color.

Clerow Wilson was born on December 8, 1933, in Jersey City, New Jersey, and raised in extreme poverty as one of 18 children. He grew up in a series of foster homes and left school at 16. During a four-year hitch in the Air Force he traveled around the Pacific and entertained his fellow enlisted men. Wilson acquired the nickname "Flip" from the troops, who appreciated his flippant sense of humor. Upon being discharged from the service in 1954, he spent the next decade touring across America, honing his act in small nightclubs. His big break came during a 1965 appearance on *The Tonight Show Starring Johnny Carson,* which led to frequent guest spots on *The Ed Sullivan Show, Laugh-In,* and *Love, American Style.* In 1969, NBC signed the comedian to host an hour-long variety show.

The debut episode of *The Flip Wilson Show* premiered on September 17, 1970. Unlike other programs of the variety genre, it did not feature chorus girls and large production numbers, but rather was presented in a nightclub-like setting on a round stage surrounded by an audience. Wilson welcomed established entertainment stars such as John Wayne, Bing Crosby, Dean Martin, and Lucille Ball to the show and introduced audiences to musical guests like Issac Hayes, James Brown, and the Temptations. He continued the variety format tradition of portraying several recurring characters on the program. Among his most noteworthy personas were: Freddy the Playboy, Sonny the White House janitor, Reverend LeRoy of the Church of What's Happening Now, and, of course, Geraldine Jones. Geraldine, whom Wilson played in drag, became a national sensation as she made wisecracks about her unseen, and very jealous, boyfriend named "Killer." Wilson commented on the miniskirted character's popularity, "The secret of my success with Geraldine is that she's not a putdown of women. She's smart, she's trustful, she's loyal, she's sassy. Most drag impersonations are a drag. But women can like Geraldine, men can like Geraldine, everyone can like Geraldine." Along with Geraldine's trademark line "What you see is what you get," Wilson popularized the phrases "The devil made me do it!" and "When you're hot, you're hot (and when you're not, you're not!)." Although Wilson based many of his routines on ethnic humor and black stereotypes, his humor was rarely overtly political. In 1971, *The Flip Wilson Show* won Emmy Awards for Best Variety Series and Best Writing for a Variety Series. The show was canceled in 1974 due to strong competition from the CBS Depression-era drama *The Waltons.*

The second half of Wilson's career was marked by a much reduced public profile. He appeared in a few films, including *Uptown Saturday Night* and *The Fish That Saved Pittsburgh,* and made several television guest appearances. In the mid-1980s he returned to television with two short-lived series: *People Are Funny* (1984), a quiz show; and *Charlie & Company* (1985), a pale sitcom imitation of *The Cosby Show,* in which singer Gladys Knight played his wife. Wilson then retired from show business to raise his family. By the late 1990s, Wilson had again resurfaced due to the reruns of his 1970s series on the TVLand cable network. Flip Wilson died on November 25, 1998, of liver cancer.

Like Bill Cosby on the television drama *I Spy* and Diahann Carroll on the situation comedy *Julia,* Flip Wilson is regarded as a breakthrough performer who helped destroy the color line on network television in the late 1960s and early 1970s. He proved that white audiences would accept a black comedian and embrace his humor. His ability to employ racial humor without demeaning its targets gave him the opportunity to reach the masses and provide network television with a too-rare black perspective. In a *TV Guide* tribute shortly after the comic's death, Jay Leno wrote, "Flip was hip, but he made sure everybody could understand him and laugh. That's the sign of a great performer."

—Charles Coletta

FURTHER READING:

Anderson, Christopher. *The New Book of People.* New York, G. P. Putnam's Sons, 1986.

Brooks, Tim. *The Complete Directory to Prime Time TV Stars.* New York, Random House, 1987.

Leno, Jay. "Flip Wilson." *TV Guide.* December 26, 1998, 9.

"Flip Wilson - What You Saw Was What You Got." CNN Interactive. http://www.CNN.com. November 26, 1998.

Wimbledon

The world-renowned British tennis tournament, Wimbledon, has become more than tradition, according to British journalist and author John Barrett: more than ''just the world's most important and historic tennis tournament,'' having come to symbolize ''all that is best about sport, royal patronage, and social occasion that the British do so well, a subtle blend that the rest of the world finds irresistible.'' Held in late June and early July, Wimbledon is the only one of four Grand Slam tennis events still played on natural grass.

The event started in 1877 as an amateur tournament called the Lawn Tennis Championships hosted at the England Croquet and Lawn Tennis Club (later renamed the All England Lawn Tennis Club). The only event was men's singles. Twenty-two players participated, and Spencer Gore won the final match, which spectators paid one shilling to watch. The women's singles event was instituted in 1884. Maud Watson claimed victory over a field of thirteen. Previously played at Oxford, the men's doubles event was brought to Wimbledon in 1883. Over the years, Wimbledon's popularity continued to grow steadily. By the mid-1880s, permanent stands were in place for the crowds who were part of what Wimbledon historians refer to as the ''Renshaw Rush,'' coming to see the British twins Ernest and William Renshaw win 13 titles between them in both singles and doubles between 1881 and 1889.

By the turn of the century, Wimbledon had become an international tournament. American May Sutton won the women's singles title in 1905 to become Wimbledon's first overseas champion. About this time, the royal family began its long association with Wimbledon when the Prince of Wales and Princess Mary attended the 1907 tournament, and the Prince was named president of the club. In 1969, the Duke of Kent assumed the duty of presenting the winning trophy.

Play at Wimbledon was suspended during World War I, but the club survived on private donations. Tournament play resumed in 1919, with Suzanne Lenglen winning the women's and Gerald Patterson the men's titles. In 1920, the club purchased property on Church Road and built a 14,000-capacity stadium, which Wimbledon historians credit with playing a critical role in popularizing the event. World War II suspended play again, but the club remained open to serve various war-related functions such as a decontamination unit and fire and ambulance services. In 1940, a bomb struck Centre Court, demolishing 1,200 seats. Although the tournament's grounds were not fully restored until 1949, play resumed in 1946, producing men's champion Yvon Petra and women's champion Pauline Betz.

The expansion of air travel in the 1950s brought even more international players to Wimbledon. This period also saw the domination of American players at the tournament, with such champions as Jack Kramer, Ted Schroeder, Tony Trabert, Louise Brough, Maureen Connolly, and Althea Gibson (the first African-American winner). Australian players Lew Hoad, Neale Fraser, Rod Laver, Roy Emerson, and John Newcombe then dominated the men's singles title from 1956 through the early 1970s.

In 1959, the club began considering a change in its amateur-only policy in light of the increasing number of players receiving financial assistance in excess of the limits set by the International Tennis Federation. It was not until 1967, however, that the Lawn Tennis Association voted to officially open the championship to both professionals and amateurs. At the first open tournament in 1968, Rod Laver and Billie Jean King won the men's and women's singles titles, respectively.

In 1977, Wimbledon celebrated its centenary anniversary. In honor of the occasion, the Wimbledon Lawn Tennis Museum was opened at Wimbledon. 1984 marked the centenary of the women's singles event. The tournament now has five main events: men's and women's singles, men's and women's doubles, and mixed doubles. It also sponsors four events for juniors (18 and under) and invitation events for former players. Each of the five main championships has a special trophy. The women's singles trophy, first presented by the All England Club in 1886, is a silver parcel gilt tray made by Elkington and Company in 1864. The men's singles trophy is a silver gilt cup and cover inscribed ''The All England Lawn Tennis Club Single Handed Champion of the World,'' and was first presented by the All England Club in 1887. The men's doubles trophy is a silver challenge cup, first presented in 1884. The women's doubles trophy is a silver cup and cover, known as ''The Duchess of Kent Challenge Cup,'' and was first presented in 1949 by Her Royal Highness the Princess Marina, then president of the All England Club.

Roughly 500 players currently compete at Wimbledon. To participate, players have to submit an entry six weeks prior to the tournament. A Committee of Management and a referee rank the entries and place players into three categories: accepted, need to qualify, and rejected. The committee then decides which ''wild cards'' to include in the draw. Wild cards are players who do not have a high enough international ranking to make the draw, but are included by the committee on the basis of past performance at Wimbledon or popularity with British spectators. A qualifying tournament takes place a week before the championships at the Bank of England Sports Club in Roehampton, and the winners in the finals of this tournament qualify to play at Wimbledon. An exception is players who, although they lose in the final round of the qualifying tournament, are still selected to play. Dubbed the ''lucky losers'' by tournament organizers, these players are chosen in order of their international ranking to fill any vacancies that occur after the first round of the draw.

To date, the youngest-ever male champion is Boris Becker of Germany. In 1985, the 17-year-old won the men's singles championship. In 1996, Swedish player Martina Hingis became the youngest ever female champion at age 15. Other notable records include American Martina Navratilova's unprecedented six-year reign on Centre Court as women's singles champion, and her overall all-time record of nine singles titles. Two men have won the men's singles tournament five consecutive times, although a century apart: Bjorn Borg of Sweden (1976-1980), and William Renshaw (1881-1886) of Britain.

—Courtney Bennett

FURTHER READING:

Little, A. ''The History of the Championships.'' http://www.wimbledon.com/news.nsf/allstatichtml/history.html. December 1998.

Medlycott, James. *100 Years of the Wimbledon Tennis Championships.* London and New York, Hamlyn, 1977.

Robertson, Max. *Wimbledon, Centre Court of the Game.* London, British Broadcasting Corporation, 1981.

Wade, Virginia, with Jean Rafferty. *Ladies of the Court: A Century of Women at Wimbledon.* New York, Atheneum, 1984.

Winchell, Walter (1897-1972)

For almost 40 years during the mid-twentieth century, Walter Winchell was thought to be the most powerful man in America. A Jewish former vaudevillian, Winchell's power came not from money, family connections, or politics—Winchell was a gossip columnist. Indeed, it has even been said that Winchell invented gossip. Although this is clearly hyperbolic—gossip has always existed in some form—certainly Winchell was the first member of the modern media to both understand its power and know how to wield it. At the height of his influence, more than 50 million Americans, or two thirds of the adult population of the country, either read his daily column or listened to his weekly radio program. His grasp of the potent uses to which gossip could be put changed the face of American culture, and ultimately led to the overweening power held by the media at the turn of the millennium.

The future Walter Winchell was born Walter Winschel on April 7, 1897, in Harlem, New York City. His grandfather was a Russian émigré who had come to America hoping for literary fame. His son, Walter's father, was similarly a man of high expectations and low achievement—a silk salesman who devoted much of his time to his mistresses. Because Walter received little attention at home, he sought it across the street at a local movie theater where he and two other boys, one of whom was George Jessel, sang songs between movies for money. When they were spotted by a vaudeville talent scout, 13-year-old Walter left home to join the troupe, saying, "I knew what I didn't want . . . I didn't want to be hungry, homeless, or anonymous."

Walter spent his teenage years in vaudeville and when he outgrew the boys act, he joined forces with another young vaudevillian, Rita Greene, with whom he had fallen in love. Winchell (as he now called himself) and Greene continued to travel the country, performing their vaudeville act to surprising success. Booked to a two-year contract, in his free time Walter Winchell began producing a vaudeville newsletter and sending in articles to *Billboard*. But after marrying Rita Greene, Winchell realized that his wife wanted to get out of show business, and so the couple moved back to New York City, where Winchell landed a job writing for *The Vaudeville News*. As Neal Gabler writes, "The twenty-three-year-old Winchell was columnist, office boy, deputy editor, part-time photographer, salesman, and general factotum. And he loved it, throwing himself into the job with desperate energy. Days he spent racing down Broadway, mingling, glad-handing, joking, collecting items for the column, making himself known. Nights he spent at the National Vaudeville Association Club on Forty-sixth Street, working the grill-room, campaigning for himself as a Broadway figure."

Walter Winchell

Although Winchell's breakneck pace ultimately led to the dissolution of his marriage, it earned him a reputation as Broadway's man-about-town. And so, in 1924, when the young columnist heard that a new tabloid newspaper was being launched, he easily won the position of Broadway columnist and drama critic on the New York *Evening Graphic*.

Winchell's column in the *Evening Graphic* was composed of Broadway news, jokes, and puns, and it was written in a catchy slang of Winchell's own invention. His unique linguistic twists captured the public's attention, but it was his brazen use of rumor, gossip, and innuendo in his column that made him famous. He saw himself as a maverick, who had broken the cardinal rule of journalism by using unverified sources. He looked behind closed doors and reported what he saw—affairs, abortions, children out of wedlock; nothing was taboo to Winchell.

The public loved it, sensing that the formerly impenetrable walls between the powerful and the common man were being torn down by one of their own. Walter Winchell, born into a lower-middle class Jewish family, was daring to put the private lives of the rich and famous in print. And the rich and famous were duly shocked and alarmed. As Gabler has observed, "Winchell understood that gossip was a weapon that empowered his readers. Invading the lives of the famous and revealing their secrets brought them to heel, humanized them, and in humanizing them demonstrated that they were no better than we and in many cases worse."

By 1928, Walter Winchell's column was syndicated throughout the country and the 31-year-old was already one of the most influential public figures in America. By the early 1930s, when he began his weekly radio broadcast, he wielded as much power with his pen as most politicians and public figures did with money and political clout. As Winchell himself put it, "Democracy is where everybody can kick everybody else's ass, but you can't kick Winchell's."

Throughout the 1930s, Winchell's power continued to grow, extending beyond show business to politics and big business. Gabler writes, "When Depression America was venting its own anger against economic royalists, Winchell was not only revealing the transgressions of the elites but needling industrialists and exposing bureaucratic cruelties so much that he became, in the words of one paper, a 'people's champion'." Recognizing the extent of Winchell's influence, President Franklin D. Roosevelt invited the columnist to the White House not long after his first inauguration, thus initiating a relationship that would prove mutually beneficial to both men.

As Adolf Hitler's power grew in Germany during the mid-1930s, Winchell turned his attention to the international front, becoming one of the Führer's most ardent and outspoken foes in America. In this task he had the full support of the Roosevelt administration, which grew to rely on Winchell's influence in encouraging the United States to enter the war. For Winchell, this foray into international politics was intoxicating. The former vaudevillian became a dedicated patriot, and once the United States entered the war, he devoted himself to supporting Roosevelt's wartime policies and keeping up the spirits of our boys overseas.

Winchell was at the height of his power. As Gabler writes, "If Winchell's career had ended then, he might have been regarded as the greatest journalistic phenomenon of the age: a colossus who straddled newspapers and radio, show business and politics. He almost certainly would have been remembered as a prime force in the public relations battle to boost America's home-front morale during World War II and as a defender of press freedom." Following the war, however, Winchell's infatuation with politics led him to become

involved in the McCarthy witch hunt, as Communism became the new target of his ire. The intellectual elites, who had tolerated Winchell as long as he was espousing liberal causes, were enraged and they sought to bring him down. When the columnist became involved in a scandal involving African American singer Josephine Baker, who was not served at Winchell's favorite watering hole—the Stork Club—while the famed columnist was in attendance, the left turned on Winchell, accusing him of racism.

In the ensuing battle between the liberal media and the now right-wing Winchell, the gossipmonger ultimately lost. Over the course of the next two decades, Walter Winchell would fall from his position as one of the most powerful men on the planet and become a relic of a distant era. As television became the main conduit for media, the man whom Winchell had once helped find a job, Ed Sullivan, would become an icon, while Walter Winchell would fade into obscurity, eventually dying in Arizona in 1972.

Although it is perhaps now difficult to imagine the power once wielded by this man who gave rise to contemporary celebrity culture, Walter Winchell was indeed once among the most influential men on the planet. But although his authority ultimately languished, he left the world a vastly changed place. By legitimizing the use of gossip in the mainstream media, Winchell both paved the way for the extreme power now held by the media at the millennium, as well as laid the foundation for contemporary celebrity society.

—Victoria Price

FURTHER READING:

Brodkey, Harold. "The Last Word on Winchell." *The New Yorker*. Vol. 70, No. 47, January 30, 1995, 71-81.

Gabler, Neal. "Walter Winchell." *American Heritage*. Vol. 45, No. 7, November 1994, 96-105.

———. *Winchell: Gossip, Power, and the Culture of Celebrity*. New York, Alfred A. Knopf, 1994.

Klurfeld, Herman. *Winchell: His Life and Times*. New York, Praeger, 1976.

Weinraub, Bernard. "He Turned Gossip Into Power." *The New York Times*. November 18, 1998, E1.

The Windy City

One of Chicago's most enduring nicknames, "The Windy City" originally had nothing to do with the Illinois city's sometimes formidable atmospheric conditions, but was coined by a nineteenth-century New Yorker to describe the city's loud, "windy" boosterism. For chilled Chicago Bears football fans at lakefront Soldier Field, or holiday shoppers on Michigan Avenue's famed Magnificent Mile, however, the nickname has had little to do with political opportunism.

Also know as the "Second City" because of its historical status as America's second largest city behind New York, throughout much of the nineteenth century Chicago business promoters roamed up and down the East Coast loudly praising the city's cosmopolitan character and excellent investment opportunities in an effort to lure capital needed for growth and expansion. Trying to debunk the popular image of their city as a cultural backwater and a "cow-town," the boosters painted a picture of a Midwestern mecca where there was boundless money to be made. Detractors claimed that these boosters were full of hot air, and tension between backers of various cities came to its zenith in the race to obtain the 1893 World's Columbian Exposition in celebration of the four-hundredth anniversary of Columbus's landing (one year late). Having arisen from a swamp in just more than 60 years, reversed the flow of the Chicago River, and made a stunning rebound from the Great Fire of 1871, city leaders in the early 1890s felt Chicago to be an obvious choice to demonstrate American enterprise and ingenuity to the rest of the world, not to mention establishing Chicago's status as a world-class city. They therefore organized a company to generate the necessary funds to underwrite the exposition. However, when Illinois Senator Shelby M. Cullom introduced a bill into the United States Congress in favor of federal support for the exposition, he neglected to specify that Chicago would play host. Immediately, a vicious contest arose to obtain the event, with Chicago, New York, Washington, D.C., and St. Louis (which would host a similar affair only 10 years later) emerging as the major players. Charles A. Dana, editor of the *New York Sun,* wrote an editorial in his paper snobbishly discounting the ''nonsensical claims of that windy city. Its people could not build a world's fair even if they won it.'' According to most accounts, it is this editorial that popularized the ''Windy City'' nickname on a national basis.

After New York was able to match Chicago's original five-million-dollar bid, Chicago doubled it, and in April of 1890, President Benjamin Harrison announced that the blustering and confident Midwestern city had won the exposition lottery. Three years later, the famous ''white city'' opened its gates, and, according to a contemporary city booster, ''The Columbian Exposition was the most stupendous, interesting and significant show ever spread out for the public.'' With its imperial architecture, famous ''midway,'' giant Ferris wheel, and exhibits of technology and science, the exposition continues to be remembered as one of the great defining moments in Chicago's history.

Though the Dana quotation was soon forgotten, the nickname stuck, having struck a nerve deeper than the rhetoric of boosterism. Over the course of the early twentieth century, the ''windy city'' appellation came more and more to refer to Chicago's often severe weather. Chicago ranks fourteenth for wind velocity among United States cities, and breezes coming off the lake can sometimes make it feel a lot cooler than the reported temperature. This is especially the case in late autumn and winter. Local weather reporters often talk of the ''lake effect'' in regard to conditions near Lake Michigan, where the water temperature and wind tone down summer's extremes and intensify winter chills. With 29 miles of shoreline, and with many of the city's business, cultural, and residential centers located along the coast, the lake effect truly can influence the city as a whole. Moreover, Chicago's downtown ''Loop'' streets long have been known as wind-swept corridors nestled among some of the world's oldest and tallest skyscrapers. It is this wind ''having no regard for living things,'' not the blustering political rhetoric of nineteenth-century boosters, which Edgar Lee Masters credited in 1933 with giving the name of the Windy City to Chicago in the first pages of his city portrait. Technically, consensus opinion holds Masters to be incorrect, but his error does demonstrate that by the third decade of the twentieth century at least, the original and the contemporary meaning of the nickname had diverged. As originally noted by Masters, winter winds coming off of Lake Michigan are blocked by Michigan Avenue's wall of buildings, ''swirl down from the towers of the great city,'' and are diverted down the Loop's long, straight thoroughfares, making the second city a very windy city indeed.

—Steve Burnett

FURTHER READING:

Cronon, William. *Nature's Metropolis: Chicago and the Great West.* New York, W. W. Norton, 1991.

Dedmon, Emmett. *Fabulous Chicago.* New York, Random House, 1953.

Hayes, Dorsha B. *Chicago: Crossroads of American Enterprise.* New York, Julian Messner, 1944.

Heise, Kenan, and Mark Frazel. *Hands on Chicago: Getting Hold of the City.* Chicago, Bonus, 1987.

Masters, Edgar Lee. *The Tale of Chicago.* New York, Putnam's, 1933.

Miller, Donald, L. *City of the Century: The Epic of Chicago and the Making of America.* New York, Simon and Schuster, 1996.

Winfrey, Oprah (1954—)

Oprah Winfrey, who began her career as a Midwest talk show host in 1985, wielded such clout in the entertainment field at the end

Oprah Winfrey

of the twentieth century that her participation in a project guaranteed its success. Her strong identification with her audience could be witnessed again and again; when she did something as simple as starting a diet, or as complex as taking a stand against social injustice, millions of people across the United States followed suit. Yet, her considerable influence was neither happenstance nor opportunism. Her social and political views came from a lifetime of struggle that has imbued her with a missionary zeal to get her message across.

The television persona of "Oprah" is virtually inseparable from the person herself. She was born into poverty in 1954 in rural Mississippi and then spent many of her formative years living in a Milwaukee ghetto with her divorced mother. As a teenager, her life began a downward spiral marked by sexual abuse and early signs of delinquency that were only interrupted by the reappearance of her father, a Nashville barber. He took custody of her, brought her to Tennessee and placed her in a local high school where she developed an interest in oratory. This experience led her to a student internship at a black radio station that sparked her interest in a career in journalism.

After graduation, she matriculated at Tennessee State University where she garnered more experience in broadcast journalism but also competed for and won the "Miss Black Nashville" and "Miss Black Tennessee" titles. Despite her later, pro-feminist stands on various issues, she harbored no regrets for cashing in on her physical beauty saying that she won on "poise and talent." "I was raised to believe that the lighter your skin, the better you were," she later admitted. "I wasn't light skinned, so I decided to be the best and the smartest." Her experience and poise also positioned her for a job as a "street reporter" at the CBS-TV affiliate in Nashville.

She then parlayed this job into a co-anchor position at Baltimore's ABC outlet where she ran into her first setback as a broadcaster. Her journalistic skills were undermined by her tendency to become emotional when hosting unpleasant stories and questions were raised about her professional objectivity. ABC management thus decided to try her out on a morning talk program where her emotionalism and penchant for becoming personally involved with her subject matter actually became a bonus.

After six years in Baltimore, Winfrey was hired in January 1984 to take over a faltering morning program on WLS-TV's *AM Chicago* which had employed a succession of hosts only to finish dead last among the competition for the 9 a.m. ratings slot. Not the least of the show's problems was the fact that it was scheduled opposite *The Phil Donahue Show* (1970-1996), hosted by Chicago's favorite son and national ratings champ. Yet, in Winfrey, WLS-TV found an engaging personable host who had a "common touch" not possessed by the somewhat patrician-appearing Donahue. Her formula was simple: working with a studio audience and a number of guests in a classic town meeting format, she rose above the traditional moderator role by injecting both her persona and her life experiences into debates on failed relationships, sexual abuse, and weight loss plans. Although her manner of interjecting her audience into the discussions by walking quickly through the crowd and jabbing the microphone into someone's face to get their point into play did not differ terribly much from Donahue's, she allowed herself to almost become part of her own audience in a way that her male counterpart did not.

By 1985, the show had displaced *The Phil Donahue Show* at the top of the Chicago ratings, prompting the station management to extend the show to one hour and to take advantage of Winfrey's growing stardom by renaming it *The Oprah Winfrey Show* in 1986. But when film composer Quincy Jones happened to turn on the show while on a visit to Chicago, he was so impressed that he mentioned

Winfrey to director Steven Spielberg, who was beginning to cast roles for his film *The Color Purple*. Her performance as Sophia earned her an Academy Award nomination for "Best Supporting Actress" and transformed her into a household name. Within 18 months, Winfrey had become a star in one medium and was standing on the threshold in another.

In 1986, WLS-TV began to syndicate the show nationally through King World, making Winfrey the first black woman to host her own show and become a millionaire by the age of 32. At the same time, she formed her own production company, Harpo (her name spelled backwards), and began to take a more active role in the creation of the show. Within its first five months, the show ranked number one among talk shows in 192 cities, forcing competitor Phil Donahue to move his home base from Chicago to New York in an attempt to stay competitive.

When her contract expired in 1988, she threatened to leave in order to pursue other opportunities in film and television. This forced ABC, King World, and WLS-TV to guarantee her complete control of the show in return for her promise to stay on until 1993. Industry estimates at that time figured that Winfrey's company would garner more than $50 million for the 1988-89 season alone. This assured her position as the richest and most powerful woman on television and also freed her to pursue her own agenda without network interference.

Under her guidance, Harpo became a major player in prime-time dramatic programming with a miniseries *The Women of Brewster Place* in 1989 and a spin-off sitcom *Brewster Place,* the following year. The company was also active in the TV documentary field during the early 1990s with a number of special programs on social issues particularly dealing with the topics of abused children and women's issues.

By the time Oprah reached her 40th birthday in 1994, *The Oprah Winfrey Show* was available in 54 countries and was reaching 15 million viewers a day in the United States alone, becoming the highest rated show in syndication history and enhancing its host's personal fortune to $250 million dollars. In 1996, Winfrey realized one of her long held goals "to get America reading" by founding a book club segment on her show. Beginning with first-time novelist Jacquelyn Mitchard's *The Deep End of the Ocean,* considered by many to be strictly a woman's romance, Winfrey got it discussed in a serious vein on her show and generated enough sales to make it the number one national bestseller within four months of its publication, with sales of more than 850,000 hardcover copies. The phenomenon continued with the talk show host's next selection Toni Morrison's 16-year-old *Song of Solomon,* which was being re-released in paperback. Between October 1996 and January 1997, the publisher reported more than 830,000 copies sold due to Winfrey's influence alone.

The key to Winfrey's selection of projects, whether books or television, is the personal impact that the source material has made on her. If she likes a book, she will champion it; if she sees audience potential in it she will produce it as a television program or a feature film. Under the banner *Oprah Winfrey Presents,* Harpo Productions has produced three television movies *The Wedding,* based on a book by Dorothy West; *David and Lisa* (a remake of the 1962 film), which portrayed two teens in a mental home; and *Before Women Had Wings,* which addressed the tragedy of domestic violence and child abuse. Winfrey also made a return to acting in 1998 with a film version of Toni Morrison's *Beloved,* which while it didn't do terribly well at the box-office spoke to several of her deeply held feelings about racism, slavery, and the power of a mother's love. "I look for projects that show individuals being responsible for themselves," she says. "It's all about seeing human beings as active creators of their lives rather than as passive victims.''

She carries this philosophy over to her personal life, as well. In 1997, she launched *The Angel Network,* an ongoing campaign to spur her viewers into doing good works such as helping to build new houses for needy families. She also organized ''Better Chance,'' a Boston-based organization that helps minority students receive a better education as well as a number of individual scholarships at various institutions including her alma mater Tennessee State University and Morehouse College.

Yet, it is the continuing success of *The Oprah Winfrey Show* that makes all of these endeavors possible. In 1997, *Variety* reported that the show had also supplanted *Saturday Night Live* as the best spot on television to generate music sales. The show thus became the first stop for mainstream artists to promote their latest releases. Performers such as Madonna, Rod Stewart, and Whitney Houston saw their albums experience significant sales gains following an appearance on *The Oprah Winfrey Show.* Stewart, for example, watched as his CD *If We Fall in Love Tonight* jumped 25 places on the sales charts within two days of his appearance with sales of 40,000 units. This achievement extended Winfrey's clout to virtually all forms of media.

The far-reaching impact of the show was also demonstrated the same year when Winfrey expressed her personal opinion on eating beef in a discussion of England's ''Mad Cow Disease.'' Predictably, beef sales fell off a bit and a cattleman's association in Texas hauled her into court for defamation. After a two-month trial, she was vindicated but no one would ever again doubt the pervasive influence of her show.

The show has earned 32 Emmy awards, including seven for its star. But the awards have not made Winfrey complacent; she has continued to incorporate new items of interest into her show. In September, 1998, for example, Winfrey took singing lessons and began to sing the theme song herself. She also created a segment called ''Change Your Life TV,'' which assists viewers in taking steps to reorder their bankbooks, their family life, and the clutter of their lives. After one show, she told her viewers, ''The opportunity to have a voice and speak to the world every day is a gift.'' She then sang a few bars from an old spiritual that summed up her outlook on life. ''I believe I'll run on, see what the end will be. I believe I'll work on, see what the end will be.'' Yet, for Winfrey, there appears to be no end in sight, just new horizons and new worlds to conquer.

—Sandra Garcia-Myers

FURTHER READING:

Berthed, Joan. ''Here Comes Oprah! From *The Color Purple* to TV Talk Queen.'' *MS.* August, 1986.

Glimpse, Marcia Ann. ''Winfrey Takes All.'' *MS.* November, 1988.

Kindles, Bridgett. ''The Oprah Effect.'' *Publishers Weekly.* January 20, 1997.

Marie, George. *Oprah Winfrey: The Real Story.* Secaucus, New Jersey, Carol, 1994.

Mascariotte, Gloria-Jean. ''C'mon Girl'': Oprah Winfrey and the Discourse of Feminine Talk.'' *Genders.* Fall, 1991.

''Oprah Winfrey Reveals the Real Reason Why She Stayed on TV.'' *Jet.* November 24, 1997.

Randolph, Laura B. ''Oprah Opens Up.'' *Ebony.* October 1993.

Sandler, Adam. ''Warblers Warm Up at Oprah's House.'' *Variety.* December 26-January 5, 1997.

Stodgill, Ron. ''Daring to Go There.'' *Time.* October 5, 1998.

White, Mimi. *Tele-Advising: Therapeutic Discourse in American Television.* Chapel Hill, University of North Carolina Press, 1992.

Winnie-the-Pooh

From learning videos to silk boxer shorts, from hatboxes to wristwatches, Winnie-the-Pooh has become as synonymous with Disney as Mickey Mouse. The Bear of Very Little Brain enjoyed a renaissance in popularity in the 1990s, and has parlayed his endearing befuddlement into a multi-million dollar franchise. ''Pooh'' and his companions from the Hundred Acre Wood are icons of a gentler, simpler childhood, a childhood without games like Mortal Kombat and Duke Nukem.

Alan Alexander Milne found inspiration for the Winnie-the-Pooh characters while watching his son Christopher Robin Milne at play; Pooh is based on a stuffed bear that Christopher received on his first birthday. Originally named Edward Bear, he was soon christened Winnie-the-Pooh. Winnie-the-Pooh is derived from Christopher's favorite bear in the London Zoo (named either Winnifred or Winni-peg, depending on the source) and a swan named Pooh. The stuffed menagerie grew to include a stuffed tiger, pig, and donkey. Milne introduced us to Pooh, Rabbit, Piglet, Eeyore, Owl, Tigger, Kanga, and Roo in his 1924 collection of verses *When We Were Very Young.* *Winnie-the-Pooh* was published in 1926, followed by *Now We Are Six* in 1927, and *The House at Pooh Corner* in 1928. All four volumes were enchantingly illustrated by Ernest H. Shepard.

The Pooh stories enjoyed early success on both sides of the Atlantic (and have since been translated into over 25 languages). Winnie-the-Pooh became a favorite of Walt Disney's daughters, and he decided to bring Pooh to the American movie screens. Originally conceived as a feature length film, Disney felt that featurettes would slowly introduce the beloved bear and establish Pooh's recognition with American audiences. The first of the three featurettes, *Winnie-the-Pooh and the Honey Tree,* was released in 1966. The three shorts were connected and reissued as *The Many Adventures of Winnie-the-Pooh,* Disney's twenty-second feature length film, in 1977. It was re-released in 1996 to celebrate the thirtieth anniversary of the original Pooh release. In 1997, *Pooh's Grand Adventure* resumed where the first film left off.

Thanks to renewed popularity based on video sales and rentals of the re-released movies, Disney found someone to rival Mickey Mouse as the face of Disney. Pooh and friends can be found on an animated cartoon series on ABC, interactive stories and learning games for computers, and learning videos, not to mention products such as pewter earrings and assorted neckties, which are targeted toward adult consumers.

Demand for Pooh merchandise stops just short of mania. When Disney stores released a limited edition Beanie Pooh on November 27, 1998, merchants found customers lining up as early as four o'clock in the morning in order to improve their chances of purchasing the bear. These limited edition bears were sold out nationally in a matter of hours. What makes Pooh marketing such a cultural phenomenon is Pooh's broad appeal to all ages. Specifically, marketing is directed at two of the largest segments of society: the Baby Boomers and their children, Generation X.

These two distinct markets have created a split in Pooh's persona. For the comparatively more affluent Boomers, there is a merchandising renaissance of the original Pooh as illustrated by Shepard. The Gund company markets stuffed versions modeled on the original ink and watercolor pictures found in the books; but these stuffed animals are not priced as items you would let a one-year-old drool on and play with. Shepard-inspired products also include decorative lamps, bookends, hatboxes, and charms—all valuable and collectible. These products are often found in larger, more upscale department stores, such as Dillards and Macy's. In contrast, Generation X is targeted with the "Disney-fied" Pooh. It is the round, yellow bear that is found on everything from watches and nightshirts to neckties and boxer shorts. While many such products are available only at Disney Stores, far more are readily available (and affordable) at stores like Target and Wal-Mart. These products include many items directed at children: books, puzzles, games, educational toys, and durable stuffed animals. Pooh's appearance, and significance, is in the eye of the beholder.

For both Gen Xers and their parents, Pooh represents a childhood sense of safety and comfort. Pooh muddles through a world inevitably made more complex than necessary by his good friends Rabbit and Owl. Eventually, the bear whose head is "stuffed with fluff" figures out a simpler, and often gentler, way of solving the various problems of the Hundred Acre Wood. Not only does Pooh's gentleness of spirit triumph, but his other endearing attribute is the special bond of love and constancy between himself and Christopher Robin. In a world of high-tech, high-speed, and high-violence, Pooh and company provide a haven from the breakneck lunacy of everyday life. Pooh wonders where he will find his next smackeral of honey, not whether his 401K will roll over. Pooh does not stab anyone's back while climbing the honey tree—honey trees are not corporate ladders. Pooh does not abandon Piglet who, as a Small and Timid Animal, fails to be an adequate partner for material success. In the Hundred Acre Wood, the concerns of daily life are no longer the priority issues; instead, love, loyalty, curiosity, generosity, companionship, and the celebration of the human spirit are Really Important Things.

—Julie L. Peterson

FURTHER READING:

Hoff, Benjamin. *The Tao of Pooh*. New York, E. P. Dutton, 1982.

———. *The Te of Piglet*. New York, E. P. Dutton, 1992.

Swan, T.B. *A. A. Milne*. New York, Twayne Publishers, Inc., 1971.

Thwaite, Ann. *The Brilliant Career of Winnie-the-Pooh: The Definitive History of the Best Bear in the World*. London, Methuen, 1992.

Williams, John Tyerman. *Pooh and the Millennium: In Which the Bear of Very Little Brain Explores the Ancient Mysteries at the Turn of the Century*. New York, Dutton, 1999.

———. *Pooh and the Philosophers*. London, Methuen, 1995.

Winnie Winkle the Breadwinner

The comic strip *Winnie Winkle the Breadwinner* first appeared in newspapers on September 21, 1920. Created by former vaudevillian Martin Branner (1888-1970), it was the first of a genre of working girl strips that later inspired imitators such as *Tillie the Toiler* (1921-1959). A "new woman" of the 1920s, Winnie worked in an office

and provided for her parents and adopted brother Perry. As the strip evolved Branner focussed on Winnie's search for a husband, the strip's central running theme until she married William Wright in 1937. By 1955—with Mr. Wright killed in a mine accident in 1950 after several near mishaps during World War II—Winnie became the chief executive of a fashion house. Branner's strip criticized the feminization of culture through the consumption of goods and services and the use of celebrity endorsements, and lamented the passing of vaudeville and its replacement by Hollywood movies. The last episode appeared July 28, 1956.

—Ian Gordon

FURTHER READING:

Gordon, Ian. *Comic Strips and Consumer Culture, 1890-1945*. Washington, D.C., Smithsonian Institution Press, 1998.

Winston, George (1949—)

One of the parents of a new style of instrumental pop music called "new age," George Winston is known for his passion for the traditional and the ability to synthesize the elements of very different types of American music into his own style of "rural folk piano." Though some might sneer at his music as "easy listening," many welcome it as a deeply felt musical reminder of a simpler time, when life was led to the primal rhythm of the seasons.

George Winston

As a child growing up in Montana, Mississippi, and Florida, Winston spent hours listening to pop music on the radio. He especially loved the instrumentals and made sure to tune in each hour for the short piece of instrumental music that preceded the news. The bands he heard in those formative pop music years of the 1950s and 1960s, the Ventures, Booker T. and the MGs, the Mar-Keys, Floyd Cramer, and the like, were his first musical inspirations. Winston began playing music himself after he graduated from high school in 1967. He began with the electric piano and organ, but by 1971 he was listening to the swing piano of such musicians as Fats Waller and Teddy Wilson, and Winston switched to the acoustic piano, where he has remained at home ever since, with occasional forays into guitar and harmonica.

Also in the early 1970s, Winston met another musician who became one of his mentors, guitarist John Fahey. Fahey was responsible for developing the "American primitive" style of guitar, and he and Winston shared a passion for nurturing and evolving traditional styles of music. In 1972, Winston released his first album, *Ballads and Blues,* on Fahey's Takoma label, but the album did not sell well, and Winston went back to doing odd jobs for his living.

In 1979, Winston was introduced to the music of 1940s and 1950s progenitors of rhythm and blues such as Professor Longhair and James Booker. This music, especially Professor Longhair's "Rock 'n Roll Gumbo," inspired Winston anew. Able to find the common thread of earthy emotion in rural and urban traditional music, folk, jazz, and rhythm and blues, Winston created his own style: crystal clear, rhythmic, and sincere. In the materialistic atmosphere of the 1980s there arose a subculture seeking spirituality and a return to roots, and with these seekers Winston's mellow music struck a chord. Those who sought more peaceful and traditional alternatives to a high-tech, fast-paced, hedonistic lifestyle turned to Eastern and other indigenous spiritual traditions for inspiration. They called their movement "new age," and they welcomed Winston's spare, gentle music as a part of its soundtrack.

Winston began to record again on Dancing Cat Records and became one of the anchors of William Ackerman's budding new age label, Windham Hill. This time there was no question of going back to odd jobs. Fans loved Winston's seasonal meditations with names such as *Autumn* (1980), *December* (1982), and *Winter into Spring* (1982). He also wrote and performed soundtracks for several animated children's videos, notably *The Velveteen Rabbit* (1984) and *This is America, Charlie Brown* (1988). Winston maintains an intensive concert schedule, playing more than 110 live concerts a year. Most are in the United States, though he is beginning to gain an international following as well and is especially popular in Japan and Korea.

Winston has continued to seek inspiration in traditional and vintage music, and he has never ceased his attempts to bring those kinds of music to the public attention. In his 1996 work *Linus and Lucy: The Music of Vince Guaraldi,* he highlights the music of the little-known composer of such famous pieces as 1960's classic "Cast Your Fate to the Wind" and many of the *Peanuts* television specials. Most recently, he has worked to bring attention to the traditional Hawaiian slack key guitar, a folk guitar style which originated in Hawaii in the early 1800s and inspired modern steel guitar. An accomplished steel guitar player himself, Winston has devoted much energy to recording the masters of the Hawaiian guitar in an effort to preserve the quickly dying traditional art.

—Tina Gianoulis

FURTHER READING:

Loder, Kurt. "Windham Hill's Left-Field Success." *Rolling Stone.* March 17, 1983, 41.

Milkowski, Bill. "George Winston: Mood Maker, Closet Rocker." *Down Beat.* Vol. 50, March 1983, 22.

Winters, Jonathan (1925—)

An improvisational comedian who brought a new kind of comedy to American television and films, Jonathan Winters challenged his audiences by allowing humor to happen spontaneously. He created such characters as Maude Frickert, Chester Honeyhugger, and Elwood P. Suggins, placing them in hilarious situations suggested by impromptu cues. The unpredictable comic appeared often on NBC's *Tonight Show,* starring Jack Paar, who gave Winters free rein to extemporize and called him "pound for pound the funniest man on earth." His genius for mimicry allowed him to assume the character of anyone from a small lisping child to a large, wisecracking grandmother.

Born in Dayton, Ohio, to an affluent family, Jonathan demonstrated early his talent for imitating sounds as he played with his toy automobiles and stuffed animals. When he was seven, his parents divorced and his paternal grandfather—owner of the Winters National Bank—became the dominant male figure in his life. According to

Jonathan Winters

Winters, his grandfather was an irrepressible extrovert whose behavior was a strong influence on his grandson's comic talents.

In school he majored in being the class clown and told an interviewer, "I used to drive some of my teachers crazy." At 17 he quit school and joined the U.S. Marine Corps, serving in combat in the Pacific during World War II. In his spare time he entertained his buddies with sidesplitting imitations of the officers. After the war he returned to finish high school and then drift around the country, taking odd jobs picking apricots or working in factories, always adding to his store of interesting material that would find its way into comic routines. He decided on a career as a cartoonist and studied at the Dayton Art Institute for two and a half years, which he credits for increasing his power of observation as he later focused his wit on humorous characters and situations.

His future wife, a fellow art student, was entranced by Winter's talents as a comic improviser and encouraged him to enter a local contest for amateur entertainers, which he won. A Dayton radio station, impressed with his talents, hired him as an early-morning disc jockey. As Jonathan told interviewer Alan Gill, "I couldn't entice one guest on the program that whole year. So I made up characters myself, drawing from the characters I'd observed over the years—the hip rubes, the Babbits, the pseudointellectuals, the little politicians." In 1950 he moved to a larger radio station in Columbus, Ohio, honing his talents there until 1953, when he left for New York City.

Arriving in Manhattan with $55.46, Winters began performing at the Blue Angel nightclub, where he met and impressed television personalities Arthur Godfrey, Jack Paar, and Mike Wallace. All three found spots for him on their shows, and his career was launched. Particularly enthusiastic was Jack Paar, who gave him a network audience on *The Morning Show,* which Paar emceed for CBS at that time. In the late 1950s Winters was a frequent guest on Paar's *The Tonight Show* (renamed *The Jack Paar Show* in 1958). He also filled in for the star, drawing rave reviews in newspapers all over the United States.

The comedian suffered a mental breakdown in May of 1959, bursting into tears onstage in a San Francisco nightclub; a few days later, policemen took him in custody for climbing the rigging of an old sailing ship docked at Fisherman's Wharf. His wife transferred him to a private sanatarium, and after a month in analysis, Winters modified his work habits and life style. He explained to Joe Hymans in an interview in the New York *Herald Tribune,* "I had a compulsion to entertain. Now I've found the button. I can push it, sit back, and let people come to me instead of going to them, as do most clowns like me who are victims of hypertension."

In the early 1960s Winters worked almost exclusively in television, playing dramatic roles on Shirley Temple's children's programs and comedy on variety shows hosted by Garry Moore and Paar. In May of 1964 he signed an exclusive long-term contract with NBC calling for six television specials a season. He was already scheduled for a special with Art Carney called *A Wild Winter's Night* early in 1964, and the show disappointed both his fans and the critics, who found it too rigid in format for the freewheeling comedian. When Jonathan made an attempt to correct this problem in his six specials called *The Jonathan Winters Show,* critics found the shows too loose. Dennis Braithwaite of the *Toronto Globe and Mail* believed he was better as an intruder on other people's shows as "a mocking corporeal wraith who comes ambling out of nowhere to delight and shock us awake and then retires to his tree." After one ill-fated season of the specials, Winters's appearances on NBC were limited sporadic guest

appearances. In the 1980s, he performed with Robin Williams as the baby in the *Mork and Mindy* series.

One of Winters's major goals in the 1960s was to work in motion pictures. The most important films he appeared in were *It's a Mad, Mad, Mad, Mad World, The Loved One,* and *The Russians Are Coming.* He also starred in another medium: audio albums for Verve-MGM, including *The Wonderful World of Jonathan Winters, Down to Earth with Jonathan Winters,* and *Whistle-Stopping with Jonathan Winters,* a satire on politicians of all stripes. Making use of his artistic talents, he created both the drawings and captions in the book *Mouth Breath, Conformity, and Other Social Ills,* published by Bobbs-Merrill in 1965.

Winters is an entertainer with a rare and bountiful combination of talents. Director Stanley Kramer, who directed Winters in *It's a Mad, Mad, Mad, Mad World,* called him "the only genius I know."

—Benjamin Griffith

FURTHER READING:

Aylesworth, Thomas G. *The World Almanac Who's Who of Film.* New York, World Almanac, 1987.

Braithwaite, Dennis. *Toronto Globe and Mail.* February 19, 1964.

Gill, Alan. Interview in *TV Guide.* February 8, 1964.

Hymans, Joe. *New York Herald Tribune.* March 5, 1961.

Inman, David. *The TV Encyclopedia: The Most Comprehensive Guide to Everybody Who Is Anybody in Television.* New York, Putnam, 1991.

Lackmann, Ron. *Remember Television.* New York, Putnam, 1971.

Wire Services

At the end of the twentieth century, news was readily available from a variety of competing sources: newspapers and magazines, radio, television, and the Internet. Yet a given story, no matter where it ran, often would contain much of the same material, word for word, owing to the heavy dependence of all news media on wire services, which collected reporters' stories and pictures, edited them to a standard style, and distributed them to individual broadcast stations and print media.

Organizations such as the Associated Press and Reuters are called *wire* services because of their early connection with the telegraph. In fact, Reuters was originally a bird service: In 1849 Paul Julius Reuter, a former bookseller, saw an opportunity to exploit a gap in the telegraph lines between Aachen and Brussels and used carrier pigeons to transmit stock quotes until the telegraph finally connected the two cities in 1850. Reuter then moved the company to London, where it opened in 1851 and used the new Dover-Calais cable to communicate between the British and French stock markets. Reuters later expanded its content to include general news as well, and scooped other news bureaus with the first European reports of Abraham Lincoln's assassination in 1865.

New York had had a news agency, the Association of Morning Newspapers, since as early as 1820, its main purpose being to coordinate the reporting of incoming news from Europe; and there were other small local agencies as well. The Associated Press was formed in 1848, largely in response to the new technology of the telegraph, by a group of ten newspaper editors who had come to realize that pooling news-gathering made more sense than competing for transmittal over wires already crowded with messages (multiplexing would not be invented—by General George Owen Squier, founder of Muzak—for another six decades). Included in the original consortium were the *Journal of Commerce* and New York's biggest dailies, the *Sun, Herald,* and *Tribune.* The first major story to be covered and distributed through AP was the 1848 presidential election (Zachary Taylor won on the Whig ticket).

When Reuters and AP were first started, any exchange of news between Europe and America was dependent on dispatches carried by ships. One of the first joint ventures by the AP newspapers was a small, fast steamboat based in Halifax, Nova Scotia, whose crew would race out to meet passing vessels en route to the major East Coast seaports, then speed back to harbor and telegraph whatever news reports they carried, often beating by a day or more the reporters accustomed to waiting on the piers of Boston or New York for the transatlantic ships to arrive in port. On the other side of the ocean, as a boat from the United States came in sight of the British Isles, at Crookhaven on the Irish coast, a Reuters launch came out to retrieve a hermetically sealed container thrown from the larger ship as it sailed past; once back ashore, the wire service crew opened the box, retrieved the dispatches inside, and cabled their contents to London eight hours before the ship from America would dock.

This system remained in effect until the transatlantic cable came into permanent operation in 1865—for though the first cable had been laid in 1857, it soon snapped, probably as a result of undersea earthquakes. (It had, however, functioned long enough to bring the United States a report of the suppression of the Sepoy uprising in India. The telegram's succinct 42 words summarized five separate stories from the British press).

The expense and time of telegraphic transmission tended to force brevity on reporters, but the wire services in their earliest days did not necessarily sacrifice accuracy to terseness: AP correspondent Joseph L. Gilbert's on-the-spot transcription of Lincoln's Gettysburg address almost immediately was accepted as authoritative, and other reporters' variants soon forgotten. "My business is to communicate facts," wrote another veteran AP newsman, Lawrence A. Gobright; but readers had to plunge 200 words—about five column-inches—into his front-page story on the Lincoln assassination before reaching the statement that the president had been shot. It was not until the 1880s that AP mandated the so-called "inverted pyramid" structure for news stories familiar today, with the most important facts at the top and successive layers of elaboration down at the bottom.

The effect of standardized newspaper style on popular culture has been subtle but far-reaching. Apart from the business correspondence and departmental memos encountered on the job, newspapers are often the most-read news sources in the course of the average day, and it is not uncommon for people to consume an hour or more of leisure time reading the Sunday edition of their local daily. Moreover, many writers whose later works have attained the status of canonical literature (four from the turn of the twentieth century, for example, were Stephen Crane, Mark Twain, Jack London, and Ambrose Bierce) served their apprenticeship in journalism.

Wire-service style manuals continue to play an important role in shaping other types of writing. AP's libel guidelines—a prominent section of their stylebook as a whole—also serve as the standard reference by which American journalists stay on the right side of the law, or at least flout the rules at their peril. Ian Macdowall, a 33-year Reuters veteran, summed up the goal of news copywriting in the

introduction to that company's manual as "simple, direct language which can be assimilated quickly, which goes straight to the heart of the matter, and in which, as a general rule, facts are marshalled in logical sequence according to their relative importance." This ideal fairly matched the aspirations of many twentieth-century writers in English—journalists, historians, novelists, essayists, even scientists—who wanted their words to be bought and their ideas assimilated by the ordinary reader. Such authors in turn helped to mold the public's taste towards expectation of clarity, brevity, and pertinence in the popular press.

Another way in which the wire services have made a lasting contribution to mass consciousness is in photographs. Starting with AP's first photos in 1927 (wirephotos would be introduced in 1935, at the then astronomical research-and-development cost of $5 million), on-the-scene photographers have captured news events with images that have become cultural icons in their own right, integral elements of the American collective visual consciousness: the raising of Old Glory atop Mount Suribachi on Iwo Jima, caught on film by Joe Rosenthal in 1945, when American troops stormed the Pacific island in the final days of World War II and won it from its Japanese occupiers; a little girl, Phan Thi Kim Phuc, running naked, scorched, and screaming in terror towards photographer Huynh Cong ("Nick") Ut with the smoke of her burning village behind her, during the height of the Vietnam War in 1972; Murray Becker's stark and terrible photo of the dirigible airship *Hindenberg* burning after it exploded while landing in New Jersey in 1937; Harry Truman snapped by Byron Rollins on election night in 1948 as the newly reelected president gleefully held aloft a newspaper with the premature and erroneous headline "Dewey Defeats Truman."

Rarely has so great a mistake as the Truman headline had so lasting a place in the public mind, but the need to make deadlines, however fragmentary the information available by press time, has sometimes led to educated guesses by editors who were proven horribly wrong by subsequent information. Initial reports of the sinking of the *Titanic* in 1909 reported that most if not all passengers had been rescued; only later was it learned that many passengers had in fact been lost, and it was several days before the full extent of the catastrophe was known and printed. But though accuracy and speed of publication often work at cross purposes, the wire services have attempted to reconcile the conflict throughout their history by enthusiastically embracing new technology, from Marconi's "wireless telegraphy" introduced in 1899 (its inventor held for a time a monopoly on radio news service to Europe), the teletype (1915), and the tape-fed teletypewriter machine (late 1940s) to communications satellites and computerized typesetting (1960s), computer-driven presses (late 1970s), fiber-optic cable networks (1980s), and reporters with laptop computers filing stories by modem (1990s).

In wartime, at least, a second problem with accuracy in reporting has been military censorship, compounded by the need for the wire services to maintain a credible arm's-length relationship with government while remaining on friendly enough terms with officialdom to get the news at all. At the beginning of World War II the head of Reuters, Sir Roderick Jones, received an ominously enigmatic letter directing that the company and its officers "will at all times bear in mind any suggestion made to them on behalf of His Majesty's government as to the development or orientation of their news service or as to the topics or events which from time to time may require particular attention," a directive sufficiently vague that the wire service spent the duration of the war interpreting it as creatively as it dared.

During the Vietnam War, on the other hand, the American military simply lied, with the Johnson cabinet's connivance, pulling the wool over the eyes of Congress and press alike (the Gulf of Tonkin resolution; the falsified count of enemy troops in the field which allowed U.S. forces to be blindsided by the Tet offensive of 1968). Though the wire services for a time dutifully printed what they were given, the gap grew between official reports and the observations of reporters in the field, who began compiling reports that were increasingly skeptical. An additional spur may have been the small upstart Liberation News Service, run by young leftists in America and feeding to a burgeoning alternative press—the LNS story on the 1967 protest march and police action at the Pentagon was carried by 100 such newspapers—with information often more accurate than anything in a government press release. The American government fought back by attempting to discredit the press; AP's Peter Arnett, reporting from South Vietnam's capital, Saigon, was subjected to a smear campaign by the Federal Bureau of Investigation. But in the end the public sided with the wire services, whose photographs, film clips, and live reports flowing from the southeast Asia war zone home to newspaper readers and television viewers in the United States played a crucial role in turning American popular sentiment against the war.

Although wire services have sometimes been criticized as exploiters of human suffering, especially when it comes to war coverage, such news is vital to investors and fascinating to most ordinary readers, as when the Reuters report of Napoleon III's speech in February of 1859 ran in the London *Times,* giving Britons clear warning of France's impending entry into the Austro-Prussian war. On such occasions an effective monopoly on news seems a blessing to subscribers, if a bane to the competition. In fact, three years earlier, in 1856, Reuters had signed a contract to share stock price news with Germany's Continental Telegraphien Compagnie (also known as the Wolff agency, it had been founded in 1849, the same year Reuter's pigeons took wing) and the news company of Charles-Louis Havas in France (founded in 1835, later called Agence France-Presse, and still a key player in world news at the end of the twentieth century). In 1870, the three companies followed up with an agreement to carve up the world into exclusive news territories for each, in much the same manner as the spheres-of-influence diplomacy then fashionable among the major imperial powers; as a result Reuters, Havas, and Wolff dominated international news-gathering up until the first World War.

Ironically, it was World War I that brought the first serious competition in the Western Hemisphere to bear on the Associated Press, at that time available only to its members and subscribers, who typically blocked rival dailies in their circulation areas from joining. In fact, AP had managed to coerce even its subscriber newspapers not to do business with rival news bureaus, until a court decision put a stop to the practice in 1915. In response to such tactics, several powerful newspaper companies formed their own agencies, such as William Randolph Hearst's International News Service and the Scripps Howard chain's United Press Association (whose name was later changed to United Press International when INS merged with it in 1958.) When World War I broke out, newspapers in Argentina, frustrated in their attempts to reach an agreement with either AP or Havas, turned to UPI, which soon came to dominate the South American news market as a result, an edge it held for most of the century.

Unfortunately for UPI, an anti-trust suit was successfully brought in the 1940s to force AP to let anyone subscribe who paid the fee. This did not have much effect on UPI's domestic market share at the time, since many newspapers in the postwar boom years subscribed to more than one wire service. But a generation later, several factors combined to weaken UPI's position: the phenomenal growth of television news, whose evening programs provided stiff competition for afternoon dailies, forcing them to close or to be transformed into morning editions, plus the creation of news services by some of the larger chains such as Knight-Ridder, Hearst, and, ironically, UPI's former owners, Scripps Howard, which had prudently divested itself of the wire service in 1982. These new bureaus offered well-written supplemental news stories to fill in the gaps around AP's coverage, and did so at much cheaper rates than UPI could offer. A series of bad managers also helped to cripple UPI and it ceased to be a significant player by 1990, leaving AP much as it had been at the beginning of the century: the dominant source for print news in America, and one of a handful of major players across the globe.

Even as UPI was failing, Reuters was enjoying unprecedented prosperity: In 1989, when UPI's staff had dwindled to 650 reporters and 30 photographers, for the first time more major dailies in America were now carrying Reuters than UPI. Reuters had never lost sight of its roots in the stock market, and although it had also prudently diversified into television in 1985 by acquiring an international TV agency, Visnews (renamed Reuters Television), and had successfully broken into the Internet by supplying news to nearly 200 web sites by the end of the 1990s, it remained a robust source of financial news, obtaining quotes from over 250 stock and commodities exchanges, disseminating financial data via a large cable network and its own synchronous-orbit communications satellites, and employing a staff of over 16,000.

Still, for most Americans, AP remained the quintessential wire service. In *Flash! The Associated Press Covers the World,* an anthology of its photographers' work published in 1998, Peter Arnett proudly wrote that AP copy that year comprised as much as 65 percent of the news content of some American newspapers, that 99 percent of American dailies and 6,000 broadcasters carried AP stories, that the wire service employed over 3,500 people in 236 bureaus, turning out millions of words of copy every day and hundreds of pictures, that its employees had won 43 Pulitzer prizes—and on a more somber note, that nearly two dozen AP correspondents and photographers had died in the line of duty in the century and a half since the organization was founded, ranging from reporter Mark Kellogg, who perished while covering Custer's Last Stand at the Little Bighorn River in June of 1876, to photographer Huynh Thanh My, killed by the Viet Cong in October of 1965. Wire service reporters, Arnett argued, are ubiquitous; that's their job. Thus when Mahatma Gandhi was discharged by the British viceregal government in India after serving one of numerous jail terms for civil disobedience in the 1930s, he was driven to a remote village and let go—and came face to face with AP reporter Jim Mills, who had gotten wind of where the illustrious prisoner was to be released and wanted to be on the spot to interview him. With wry amusement Gandhi declared, ''I suppose when I go to the Hereafter and stand at the Golden Gate, the first person I shall meet will be a representative of the Associated Press!''

—Nick Humez

FURTHER READING:

Adams, Sam. *War of Numbers: An Intelligence Memoir.* South Royalton, Steerforth Press, 1994.

Alabaiso, Vincent, Kelly Smith Tunney, and Chuck Zoeller, editors. *Flash! The Associated Press Covers the World.* New York, Associated Press and Harry N. Abrams, 1998.

Associated Press. *Charter and By-Laws of the Associated Press, Incorporated in New York, December 1, 1901.* New York, Associated Press, 1901.

———. *Member Editorials on the Monopoly Complaint Filed by the Government Against the Associated Press on August 28, 1942.* New York, Associated Press, 1942.

Collins, Henry M. *From Pigeon Post to Wireless.* London, Hodder and Stoughton, 1925.

Diehl, Charles Sanford. *The Staff Correspondent.* San Antonio, Clegg Company, 1931.

Goldstein, Norman, editor. *The Associated Press Stylebook and Libel Manual.* Reading, Addison-Wesley, 1996.

Gordon, Gregory, and Ronald E. Cohen. *Down to the Wire: UPI's Fight for Survival.* New York, McGraw Hill, 1990.

MacDowall, Ian, compiler. *Reuters Handbook for Journalists.* Boston, Butterworth-Heinemann, 1992.

Mungo, Raymond. *Famous Long Ago: My Life and Hard Times with the Liberation News Service.* Boston, Beacon Press, 1970.

Read, Donald. *The Power of News: The History of Reuters.* New York, Oxford University Press, 1992.

United Nations Educational, Scientific, and Cultural Organization (UNESCO). *News Agencies, Their Structure and Operation.* New York, UNESCO, 1969.

Wister, Owen (1860-1938)

Owen Wister was one of a long line of lawyer-writers in American literary history. This Pennsylvania-born, Harvard-educated patrician became one of America's first and most prominent writers of the Western genre. Popular in his own time, Wister developed his reputation as a short story writer. He began to publish his Western stories in 1895 and was acclaimed by many, including Rudyard Kipling. In 1902 he wrote his most famous novel, one that is said by many to define the Western genre: *The Virginian: A Horseman of the Plains.* Loren D. Estleman wrote in the *Dictionary of Literary Biography* that: "Most if not all of the staples associated with the western genre—fast-draw contests, the Arthurian code, and such immortal lines as "This town ain't big enough for both of us" and "When you call me that—smile!"—first appeared in this groundbreaking novel about one man's championship of justice in the wilderness. Wister's interpretation of the West as a place where few of the civilized concepts of social conduct apply separated his stories from the sensational accounts then popular."

Wister was the only child of Sarah Butler and Owen Jones Wister. His father was an intellectual, his mother the daughter of a 19th-century actress, Fanny Kemble. Her family had many literary and musical connections in Europe. Wister, known as "Dan" to friends and family, went to a private school near his home and then to Harvard. There he continued a literary bent shown in earlier years by writing for the college paper, the *Crimson,* and dabbling in light opera. Although his mother encouraged his musical talents, she never

seemed happy with his writing work. A review of Wister's correspondence reveals that neither parent ever seemed fully pleased with this capable, well-rounded Harvard Phi Beta Kappa.

After his 1882 graduation, Wister studied music in Europe and his piano virtuosity was touted by no less than Franz Lizst. His father opposed the young man's love of music and pushed his own desire to see him established in a business career in Boston. Ever the obedient son, he returned to the United States. While the talented young Wister languished in his position at the Union Safe Deposit Vaults of Boston, he wrote a novel with a cousin but did not submit it for publication.

Although Wister formed many literary-minded friendships and enjoyed the men's clubs in Boston, his health began to deteriorate. Following the orders of his doctor, in 1885 Wister summered in Wyoming. The clean air revived his physical powers and ignited a love of the West that would guide his future career. It was on the frontier that he found his métier, both creatively and spiritually. Wister once wrote: "One must come to the West to realize what one may have most probably believed all one's life long—that it is a very much bigger place than the East and the future of America is just bubbling and seething in bare legs and pinafores here—I don't wonder a man never comes back (East) after he has been here a few years."

According to biographer Darwin Payne, "Wister's deep sense of the antithesis between the civilized East and the untamed West was constant." He did return East to study and then practice law, but ever after he regularly vacationed in the West. Law school gave Wister a chance to renew old Harvard friendships: he corresponded with Robert Louis Stevenson and became close friends with Oliver Wendell Holmes. But none of his letters from that period seem to indicate any real interest in law, even after he began his practice as member of the Pennsylvania bar in Philadelphia in 1890. The law seemed only something to do in between trips to the West.

In 1891, after an evening with friends lamenting that the American West was known in the East only through rough "dime" novels, Wister said that he regretted the lack of an American Rudyard Kipling to chronicle what he called "our sagebrush country." As they spoke Wister suddenly decided to take action himself and become that sage. He completed his first story that very night. Soon after he sent "How Lin McLean Went West" and "Hank's Woman" to *Harper's* magazine. "Hank's Woman" is the story of an Austrian servant girl who, fired in a visit to Yellowstone Park, marries a worthless man and is then driven to murder. The story of McLean describes a cowboy's return to Massachusetts, where his mean-spirited brother finds him an embarrassment. Both were published and found instant popular and critical acclaim.

These tales used the same style and formula that would characterize all of his Western works. The stories were based on anecdotes he had heard, used vernacular language in dialogue-based actual speech (which Wister painstakingly recorded in his own notebooks), and were full of descriptions of the West. Others had already written Western tales but it was Wister who defined the heroic, Arthurian character of the Western hero and gave him substance.

Wister's popularity and Western topics brought him into collaboration with Frederick Remington. The two worked together on a story for an 1895 issue of *Harper's,* about the evolution of the cow puncher. Their friendship and collaboration was a "natural," since many critics both past and present felt that Remington expressed in bronze and with paint the same feeling about the West that Wister evoked with words. Harvard chum Theodore Roosevelt labeled Wister an "American Kipling" and arranged for him to meet Kipling, then a Vermont resident, in the spring of 1895. Upon meeting Wister, Kipling blurted out, "I approve of you thoroughly!" His approbation was great balm for Wister, who suffered much of his life without the approval of his parents—despite the fact that he now had a national reputation.

Not long after his father's death in 1896, Wister began to date a second cousin, Mary Channing "Molly" Wister. A practical young woman, Molly had a career in education underway when they married on April 28, 1898, the same day the United States declared war on Spain. For their honeymoon the Wisters toured the United States, making a long visit to Charleston, South Carolina, where Wister's grandfather had signed the U.S. Constitution, and trekking to the state of Washington so that Molly could see her "Dan" in his beloved West. Molly was supportive of his writing and he supported her activities in education. Wister's writing flourished and their family grew—they had three boys and three girls.

Wister soon decided to write a longer work and he began to study the art of the novel. In 1902, Wister published *The Virginian*, with its nameless hero, his schoolteacher sweetheart Molly, and the villain, Trampas. Payne reports that the *New York Times Saturday Review of Books,* in its review of *The Virginian* claimed: "Owen Wister has come pretty near to writing the American Novel." Henry James wrote enthusiastically about the novel, which Wister had dedicated to his friend, Theodore Roosevelt. *The Virginian* was a financial, critical, and popular success. Wister himself turned it into play and it continued to be popular long after his death. According to Estleman, "If the importance of a work is evaluated by the number of people it reaches, *The Virginian* stands among the three or four important books this century has produced. By 1952, fifty years after its first publication, eighteen million copies had been sold, and it had been read by more Americans than any other book."

Four movies were made of the book during the century, in 1914 (with a screenplay by D. W. Griffith), 1923, 1929, and 1946. Of the four movie versions, the best known was the 1929 version starring Gary Cooper in the title role and directed by Victor Fleming. Cooper seemed best to capture the near-mythic nature of Wister's hero. The nameless Virginian is an American knight—a soft-spoken gentleman who is ready and able to survive and even tame the travails and splendid chaos of the West. Wister's novel defined our mythic Western hero as a quiet but volcanic strong man who plays by the rules. The story was also adapted for the small screen in a television series that ran from 1962 to 1966. *The Virginian* was thus one of the few stories that shaped Americans' understanding of the American West and of the place of individuals within it.

Most of his later fiction deals with the conflict between the good and the bad within the West. According to Jane Tompkins in *West of Everything,* his work is realistic in setting, situation, and characters—more so than rival fiction of the period—but still tending toward the sentimental and melodramatic. Wister tried to expand his writing style by writing his own "novel of manners," modeled on Flaubert's *Madame Bovary* but set in genteel Charleston, South Carolina. The novel, *Lady Baltimore,* was not critically acclaimed and had moderate sales in its time. In 1913, his wife died and he no longer wrote fiction. He began several projects and then took the path of political and non-fiction writing in the era just before World War I.

His major post-*Virginian* achievement was a biography of his old friend, Theodore Roosevelt, and many articles about his past acquaintances and friendships. At the end of his life Wister was no longer remembered as a great literary figure. He died on July 21, 1938, just seven days after his 78th birthday. His reputation was

resuscitated late in the century by the Western Writers of America, which named a major award after Wister, and by an increasing number of scholars willing to take his work seriously.

—Joan Leotta

FURTHER READING:

Cobbs, John L. *Owen Wister.* Boston, Twayne, 1984.

Estleman, Loren D. *The Wister Trace: Classic Novels of the American Frontier.* Ottawa, Illinois, Jameson Books, 1987.

Folsom, James K., editor. *The Western: A Collection of Critical Essays,* Englewood Cliffs, New Jersey, Prentice Hall, 1979.

Payne, Darwyn. *Owen Wister: Chronicler of the West, Gentleman of the East.* Dallas, Texas, Southern Methodist University Press, 1985.

Tompkins, Jane. *West of Everything.* New York, Oxford University Press, 1992.

White, G. Edward. *The Eastern Establishment and the Western Experience: The West of Frederick Remington, Theodore Roosevelt, and Owen Wister.* Austin, University of Texas Press, 1989.

Wister, Owen. *Owen Wister's West: Selected Articles,* edited by Robert Murray Davis. Albuquerque, University of New Mexico Press, 1987.

———. *The Virginian: A Horseman of the Plains.* New York, Macmillan, 1902.

The Wizard of Oz

The 1939 Metro Goldwyn Mayer (MGM) film *The Wizard of Oz,* based on L. Frank Baum's 1900 book was hugely influential. Its simple message—that there is no place like home, and that you have the power to achieve what you most desire—had a general appeal to the American public. Starting in 1956, a new generation of American children was annually entranced by the television showing of Dorothy's journey down the Yellow Brick Road.

In the film, after a cyclone carries her to Oz, Dorothy meets the Scarecrow, the Tin Woodman, and the Cowardly Lion, and they set off together for the Emerald City in search of what they most desire: for Dorothy, a home; for the Scarecrow, a brain; for the Tin Woodman, a heart; and for the Cowardly Lion, courage. When they kill the Wicked Witch of the West and go to the Wizard for their promised reward, they discover he is nothing but a humbug. Nevertheless, he supplies them with the symbols of what they already possess—a degree for the Scarecrow, a ticking heart-shaped clock for the Tin Woodman, and a medal for the Cowardly Lion. Glinda the Good Witch helps Dorothy use the magic in the ruby slippers she has been wearing all along to whisk her back to Kansas.

The film was made during the heyday of the studio system and the golden era of MGM. Directed by Victor Fleming (among others), it starred Judy Garland, Ray Bolger, Jack Haley, Bert Lahr, Frank Morgan, and Margaret Hamilton. From the beginning, it was a production beset by trouble: cast changes, director changes, injuries, and script rewrites kept cast and crew busy for 23 weeks, the longest shoot in MGM history.

The opening and closing Kansas scenes were filmed in black-and-white, while the Oz scenes were done in sumptuous (and expensive) Technicolor. Dorothy's amazement at entering the world of

A scene from the film *The Wizard of Oz*, with Judy Garland as Dorothy.

color mirrored audiences' feelings about the new technology. The importance of wonder did not stop there: Jack Haley (the Tin Woodman) created the breathless, slightly stilted way he and Ray Bolger (as the Scarecrow) would speak to Dorothy. Haley told Victor Fleming, "I want to talk the way I talk when I'm telling a story to my five-year-old son," and Bolger agreed, saying later "I tried to get a sound in my voice that was complete wonderment." Haley, Bolger, and Lahr (the Cowardly Lion) came out of the vaudeville tradition and filled the movie with the kind of jokes and physical humor with which stage audiences were already familiar.

Frank Morgan, as the Wizard, perfectly embodied the harmless-trickster aspects of his character. Margaret Hamilton, as the Wicked Witch of the West, scared many youngsters with her bright green skin and high-pitched cackle. L. Frank Baum, the original author of the story, had wanted to create a fairy tale that eliminated "all the horrible and blood-curdling incidents" of fairy tales, one that "aspires to being a modernized fairy tale, in which the wonderment and joy are retained and the heart-aches and nightmares are left out." The Wicked Witch, however, terrorized children in the audience—the scene where Dorothy watches Aunt Em in the crystal ball dissolve into the Witch has been interpreted by psychologists to symbolize the unpleasant fusion of good and bad mother figures.

The film was released in 1939 to receptive audiences, but was overshadowed by the epic *Gone with the Wind* and did not start to turn a real profit until CBS bought it for television in 1956. From then on, it was shown annually, and by the year 2000 held seven of the places in a list of the top 25 highest-rated movies on network television (no other film held more than one spot.) The aggregate audience from 1956 until the year 2000 was more than one billion people. In 1998, *The Wizard of Oz* was re-released on the big-screen.

The songs, by Harold Arlen and E.Y. Harburg, were hugely popular from the start. "Somewhere Over the Rainbow"—Judy Garland's plaintive song of a place where "the dreams that you dare to dream really do come true"—became a jazz standard in the United States and an anthem of hope in England during World War II. Garland's version remains the most famous, but pop artists as diverse as Willie Nelson, Tori Amos, and Stevie Ray Vaughan recorded covers. After gay icon Garland's death, the rainbow in her song became a gay coat-of-arms.

The Wizard of Oz spawned numerous remakes and sequels, including animated cartoons, a Broadway show, "Oz on Ice," and *The Wiz*, an all-black, urban revision of the original film, starring Diana Ross as Dorothy and Michael Jackson as the Scarecrow. Many films, including *Star Wars,* David Lynch's *Wild at Heart,* and John Boorman's *Zardoz,* contain major allusions to *The Wizard of Oz*—minor references to it are pervasive in American movies. In literature, dark revisionist fantasies, including Geoff Ryman's *Was,* a bleak Oz story that incorporates AIDS (Acquired Immune Deficiency Syndrome), child abuse, and Judy Garland's childhood, and Gregory Maguire's *Wicked,* an Oz prequel written from the witch's point of view, owe great debts to the film. It was also influential in popular music—Elton John titled an album *Goodbye Yellow Brick Road,* Ozzie Osbourne titled one *Blizzard of Oz,* and Electric Light Orchestra's *Eldorado* album cover showed a pair of green hands reaching for Dorothy's ruby slippers, with no explanation required.

The Wizard of Oz film seeped into the everyday life of Americans in countless ways. Dunkin' Donuts named its donut-hole creations "Munchkins" after the little-people inhabitants of Munchkinland, where Dorothy's house lands in Oz. Quotes from the movie—"Toto, I've a feeling we're not in Kansas anymore"; "Lions, and tigers, and

bears, oh my''; "Pay no attention to that man behind the curtain"—were emblazoned on t-shirts. A 25-cent postage stamp depicting Dorothy and Toto was released in 1989 as part of the United States Postal Service "Classic Films" series. References to the film showed up in political cartoons, advertisements, and greeting cards. There was an Oz theme park, an Oz fan club, and a series of Oz conventions. During the Watergate scandal, Nixon was compared more than once to the humbug Wizard. The plot of the first episode of the 1970s television program *H.R. Pufnstuf* was unmistakably borrowed from *The Wizard of Oz*. And in the 1980s and 1990s, self-help gurus used the Yellow Brick Road as a metaphor for the quest for self-knowledge.

Popular myths also sprung up about the film, such as its supposed synchronicity with Pink Floyd's *Dark Side of the Moon* album, and exaggerated stories of the Munchkin actors' bad behavior on the set. A myth about a Munchkin suicide visible in the back of one scene persists despite being debunked numerous times.

When the film was originally released, with the tagline "The Greatest Picture in the History of Entertainment," MGM launched an aggressive merchandising campaign; objects from this campaign now fetch high prices as collectors' items. Memorabilia from the film is also extremely valuable: one pair of Judy Garland's ruby slippers is on permanent display at the Smithsonian Institution in Washington, D.C., at the National Museum of American History; another pair was auctioned at Christie's for $165,000 in 1988.

Film critic Roger Ebert attempts to explain the movie's popularity, saying: "The Wizard of Oz fills such a large space in our imagination. It somehow seems real and important in a way most movies don't. Is that because we see it first when we're young? Or simply because it is a wonderful movie? Or because it sounds some buried universal note, some archetype or deeply felt myth?" Ebert leans toward the last possibility, and indeed, Baum deliberately set out in 1900 to create a uniquely American fairy tale, one with timeless appeal to all the "young in heart." The film—and all that followed—made his dream come true.

—Jessy Randall

FURTHER READING:

Baum, Frank Joslyn, and Russell P. Macfall. *To Please a Child: A Biography of L. Frank Baum, Royal Historian of Oz.* Chicago, Reilly & Lee, 1961.

Fricke, John, Jay Scarfone, and William Stillman. *The Wizard of Oz: The Official 50th Anniversary Pictorial History.* New York, Warner Books, 1989.

Harmetz, Aljean. *The Making of "The Wizard of Oz."* New York, Delta, 1989.

Hearn, Michael Patrick. *The Annotated Wizard of Oz.* New York, Clarkson Potter, 1973.

Shipman, David. *Judy Garland: The Secret Life of an American Legend.* New York, Hyperion, 1993.

Vare, Ethlie Ann, editor. *Rainbow: A Star-Studded Tribute to Judy Garland.* New York, Boulevard Books, 1998.

WKRP in Cincinnati

The sitcom *WKRP in Cincinnati* mirrored late-1970s American culture through the lives and antics of the employees of a small AM radio station. In its four-year run on CBS from 1978 to 1982, *WKRP* developed one of the best ensemble casts on television and produced some of the more memorable scenes from the period. The show's ability to build contemporary issues into many of the stories makes it a time capsule for the period, as it dealt with issues such as alcoholism, urban renewal, drugs, infidelity, crime, guns, gangs, elections, and even other television shows. In a classic episode about a Thanksgiving promotion gone bad, Les Nesman's report—a dead-on take from the Hindenburg disaster—and Arthur Carlson's trailing words—''As God is my witness I thought turkeys could fly''—crackle with the show's characteristic intelligence and humor.

—Frank E. Clark

FURTHER READING:

Brooks, Tim, and Earle Marsh. *The Complete Directory to Prime Time Network TV Shows*. 5th Edition. New York, Ballantine, 1992.

Kassel, Michael. *America's Favorite Radio Station: WKRP in Cincinnati*. Bowling Green, Popular Press, 1993.

McNeil, Alex. *Total Television: A Comprehensive Guide to Programming from 1948 to the Present*. 3rd edition. New York, Penguin Books, 1991.

Wobblies

A radical labor union committed to empowering all workers, especially the nonskilled laborers excluded from the American Federation of Labor (AFL), the so-called Wobblies, members of the Industrial Workers of the World (IWW), played a pivotal role in America's labor history. Believing that the nation's most exploited and poorest workers deserved a voice, the Wobblies called for ''One Big Union'' that would challenge the capitalist system first in the United States and later worldwide.

In 1905 a group of two hundred radical labor activists met in Chicago and formed the IWW. The group was overwhelmingly leftist and called for the ultimate overthrow of capitalism worldwide. Immediately feared by most and despised by AFL leader Samuel Gompers, the Wobblies challenged the status quo and fought for the rights of America's working poor. The Wobblies planned to do what no union had tried before: unite blacks, immigrants, and assembly-line workers into one powerful force.

IWW leaders included some of the most famous names in American labor history, such as Big Bill Haywood, head of the Western Federation of Miners; Mary ''Mother'' Jones; and Eugene Debs, the leader of the Socialist Party. Initially, the ranks of the IWW were filled with western miners under Haywood's control. These individuals became increasingly militant as they were marginalized by the AFL. Traveling hobo-like by train, IWW organizers fanned out across the nation. Wobbly songwriters like Joe Hill immortalized the union through humorous folk songs. The simple call for an inclusive union representing all workers took hold. At its peak, 1912-1917, IWW membership approached 150,000, although only 5,000 to 10,000 were full-time members.

Long before the rise of the Bolsheviks in Russia, the courageous and militant Wobblies were calling for a socialist revolution and began organizing strikes around the nation as a prelude to a general worldwide strike among the working class. The strikes often turned bloody, but the Wobblies continued to fight. They were attacked by the newspapers, the courts, the police, and goon squads formed to protect the interests of corporations. The IWW led important strikes at Lawrence, Massachusetts (1912); Paterson, New Jersey (1913); and Akron, Ohio (1913). As the Wobblies battled for free speech and higher wages across the nation, a legendary folklore developed regarding the union because of the violence and mayhem that seemed to follow them everywhere. The Wobblies became the scourge of middle-class America, especially in the highly charged atmosphere of World War I and the postwar Red Scare. The IWW, according to labor historian Melvyn Dubofsky in *We Shall Be All,* became ''romanticized and mythologized.'' The reality was that the Wobblies mixed Marxism and Darwinism with American ideals to produce a unique brand of radicalism.

As the Wobbly ''menace'' became more influential, American leaders took action to limit the union's power. World War I provided the diversion the government needed to crush the IWW once and for all. Anti-labor forces labeled the IWW subversive allies of both Germany and Bolshevik Russia; one senator called the group ''Imperial Wilhelm's Warriors.'' President Woodrow Wilson and his attorney general believed the Wobblies should be suppressed. On September 5, 1917, justice department agents raided every IWW headquarters in the country, seizing five tons of written material. By the end of September nearly two hundred Wobbly leaders had been arrested on sedition and espionage charges. In April 1918, 101 IWW activists went on trial, which lasted five months and was the nation's longest criminal trial to date. All the defendants were found guilty, and fifteen were sentenced to twenty years in prison, including Haywood, who jumped bail and fled to the Soviet Union where he died a decade later.

The lasting importance of the IWW was bringing unskilled workers into labor's mainstream. After the demise of the Wobblies, the AFL gradually became more inclusive and political. The Congress of Industrial Organizations, founded in 1935 by another mining leader, John L. Lewis, successfully organized unskilled workers. In 1955 the AFL and CIO merged to form the AFL-CIO, America's leading trade union throughout the second half of the century.

The heyday of the IWW lasted less than twenty years, but in that short span it took hold of the nation's conscience. Nearly forgotten today, the Wobbly spirit still can be found in novels by John Dos Passos and Wallace Stegner, as well as numerous plays and movies. By the 1950s and 1960s, IWW songs, collected in the famous *Little Red Song Book,* were rediscovered by a new generation of activists fighting for civil rights and an end to the Vietnam War.

—Bob Batchelor

FURTHER READING:

Carlson, Peter. *Roughneck: The Life and Times of Big Bill Haywood*. New York, W. W. Norton, 1983.

Conlin, Joseph R., editor. *At the Point of Production: The Local History of the IWW*. Westport, Connecticut, Greenwood Press, 1981.

Dubofsky, Melvyn. *We Shall Be All: A History of the Industrial Workers of the World*. Chicago, University of Illinois Press, 1988.

Montgomery, David. *The Fall of the House of Labor: The Workplace, the State, and American Labor Activism, 1865-1925*. New York, Oxford University Press, 1987.

Wodehouse, P. G. (1881-1975)

P. G. Wodehouse's best known creations are upper-class incompetent Bertie Wooster, and his capable servant, Jeeves, who first appeared in the story ''Extricating Young Gussie'' in 1917. His satirical view of the Jazz Age is both affectionate and incisive; he pokes fun at such emblems of the inter-war period as flappers, gangsters, the fascist ''Black Shirts,'' and the dreaded moralizing aunt. Born Pelham Grenville Wodehouse in Guildford, Surrey, and educated at Dulwich College in London, he took United States citizenship in 1955, having lived there from 1909. A journalist and writer of over ninety books, Wodehouse also worked as a lyricist and writer with such luminaries as Jerome Kern and George Gershwin. Aged ninety-three, newly knighted, and with a waxwork of himself in Madame Tussaud's in London, he declared himself satisfied. He died the same year.

—Chris Routledge

FURTHER READING:

Green, B. *P. G. Wodehouse: A Literary Biography.* London, Pavilion Books, 1981.

Wodehouse, P. G. *Over Seventy: An Autobiography with Digressions.* London, Jenkins, 1957.

Wolfe, Nero
See Stout, Rex

Wolfe, Tom (1931—)

Since the 1960s, American journalist Tom Wolfe has been one of the chief chroniclers of the times. Known for analyzing trends and exposing inherent cultural absurdities, Wolfe has coined terminology such as ''radical chic'' and ''the Me decade.'' He has the knack for pinpointing an age, wrapping it up in vivid and readable prose, and presenting it back to society as a kind of mirror. Wolfe was one of the first in a cadre of writers—among them, Jimmy Breslin, Truman Capote, Hunter Thompson, and Gay Talese—to adopt a style called the New Journalism, the practice of writing nonfiction with many of the traditional storytelling elements of fiction. In addition, Wolfe distinguished himself by his frequent use of unorthodox punctuation and spelling and by peppering his text with interjections and onomatopoeia. Some of his most famous works include *The Kandy-Kolored Tangerine-Flake Streamlined Baby* (1965), *The Electric Kool-Aid Acid Test* (1968), and *Radical Chic and Mau-Mauing the Flak Catchers* (1970). He was also applauded for his 1979 portrait of the early era of the American space program, *The Right Stuff,* and for his first, and so far only, novel, 1987's social satire *Bonfire of the Vanities.* Over a decade later, in late 1998, Wolfe again won warm critical reception with his second novel, *A Man in Full,* which shot to the top of the best-seller lists.

Thomas Kennerly Wolfe, Jr. was born on March 2, 1931, in Richmond, Virginia. In high school, Wolfe was the editor of his student newspaper, and he went on to serve as sports editor of the campus paper at Washington and Lee University in Lexington, Virginia, where he also cofounded the literary quarterly *Shenandoah.* He received his bachelor's degree in English in 1951. After that, he went on to obtain a doctoral degree in American studies at Yale University in 1957. Meanwhile, eager to begin a professional writing career, he sent out one hundred letters to publications, but received just three responses—two of them negative. He thus went to work at the *Springfield Union* in Massachusetts from 1956 to 1959, then moved to the *Washington Post* in June of 1959, where he won awards for reporting and humor.

In 1962 Wolfe began working at the New York *Herald Tribune.* There, he had the opportunity to contribute to its Sunday supplement, *New York,* which later became an independent magazine. During a newspaper strike, Wolfe landed an assignment for *Esquire* writing about the custom car craze in California. Though he was enamored of his subject matter—the chrome-laden, supercharged vehicles and their young enthusiasts—Wolfe told his editor that he could not manage to construct a story. He was told to type up his notes and send them in so that another writer could do the job. The editor was so struck with Wolfe's lengthy stream-of-consciousness descriptions and musings that he ran it unaltered. This became ''There Goes (Varoom! Varoom!) That Kandy-Kolored Tangerine-Flake Streamline Baby,'' which Wolfe later included in his 1965 collection of essays, *The Kandy-Kolored Tangerine-Flake Streamlined Baby.* The article's fertile detail, hip language, and unusual punctuation became Wolfe's trademarks.

Early on, Wolfe's style was characterized as gimmicky, but also applauded as the best way to approach some of the wacky topics he covered for his pieces. How better to record the rise in LSD and growth of the hippies than to use the language of the people about whom he wrote? Indeed, Wolfe eloquently outlined the 1960s drug era in *The Electric Kool-Aid Acid Test* in documenting the antics of novelist Ken Kesey and his ''Merry Pranksters,'' a group of LSD users on the West Coast who personified hippie culture. Subsequently, Wolfe delighted some and angered others in *Radical Chic and Mau-Mauing the Flak Catchers,* actually two separate long essays. *Radical Chic* was his bitingly humorous depiction of a fundraising party given by the white bourgeois in support of the Black Panthers. His satiric observations cut too close to the bone for some white liberals and black activists; still others were appalled by his seemingly cruel mimicry. However, many critics praised his sharp eye and sociological approach.

Wolfe toned down his style somewhat to pen *The Right Stuff* in 1979, a best-seller explaining the rise of NASA and the birth of the program to send an American into space. Much of the book's focus was on the people involved, from Chuck Yeager, the Air Force pilot who first broke the sound barrier, to the Apollo Seven astronauts and their families. It gave a personal, behind-the-scenes look at the lives affected by the space program, painting the men not only as heroes with the requisite ''stuff'' needed to fulfill such a duty, but as regular humans with failings and feelings as well. Wolfe's nonfiction throughout his career was as gripping as fiction due to his use of the genre's devices: dialogue, a shifting point-of-view, character development, and intensive descriptions of setting and other physical qualities in a scene. He finally tried his hand at a novel in 1987, publishing the widely praised *Bonfire of the Vanities,* a keen and darkly witty profile of 1980s Americana, from the bottom social strata to the top. His second novel, *A Man in Full* (1998), dealt with similar themes of race and class in late-twentieth-century America, but took place in the up-and-coming metropolis of Atlanta, Georgia. *A Man in Full* was trademark Wolfe, featuring encylopedic knowledge of a variety of subcultures and incisive observations about each. It, too, was a popular and critical success.

Being one of the most visible purveyors of the art known as New Journalism, Wolfe co-edited and contributed to an anthology titled *The New Journalism* in 1973. A staple in some college journalism courses, the volume expertly collects some of the finest examples of the practice from top names in the field and explained the constructs involved. Wolfe has also served as a contributing editor of *Esquire* magazine since 1977. Though his novel was considered a fine achievement, his contribution to the field of literature generally rests on his nonfiction sociocultural examinations.

—Geri Speace

FURTHER READING:

Lounsberry, Barbara, ''Tom Wolfe.'' *Dictionary of Literary Biography, Volume 152: American Novelists Since World War II, Fourth Series.* James Giles and Wanda Giles, editors. Detroit, Gale Research, 1995.

McKeen, William. *Tom Wolfe.* New York, Twayne, 1995.

Salamon, Julie. *The Devil's Candy: The Bonfire of the Vanities Goes to Hollywood.* Boston, Houghton Mifflin, 1991.

Scura, Dorothy M., editor. *Conversations with Tom Wolfe.* Jackson, University of Mississippi Press, 1990.

Shomette, Doug, editor. *The Critical Response to Tom Wolfe.* Westport, Connecticut, Greenwood Press, 1992.

Wolfe, Tom, and E.W. Johnson, editors. *The New Journalism.* New York, Harper, 1973.

The Wolfman

The Wolfman—a bipedal, cinematic version of the werewolf archetype—dramatically embodies the Jekyll/Hyde (superego/id) dichotomy present in us all. The Wolfman first took center stage in Universal's *Werewolf of London* (1935), starring Henry Hull in a role reprised decades later by Jack Nicholson (*Wolf,* 1994). Soon after, Curt Siodmak (*Donovan's Brain*) finished the screenplay for Universal's latest horror classic, *The Wolf Man* (1941), directed by George Waggner. Lon Chaney, Jr. starred as Lawrence Talbot, an American-educated Welshman who wants nothing more than to be cured of his irrepressible lycanthropy. Make-up king Jack Pierce devised an elaborate yak-hair costume for Chaney that would come to serve as the template for countless Halloween masks. Siodmak's story differed from previous werewolf tales in emphasizing the repressed sexual energy symbolically motivating Talbot's full-moon transformations. Four more Chaney-driven Wolfman films came out in the 1940s; numerous imitators, updates, and spoofs have since followed.

—Steven Schneider

FURTHER READING:

Skal, David. '''I Used to Know Your Daddy': The Horrors of War, Part Two.'' *The Monster Show: A Cultural History of Horror.* New York, W.W. Norton, 1993, 211-227.

Lon Chaney Jr. in character in the film *Frankenstein Meets the Wolfman.*

Twitchell, James B. ''Dr. Jekyll and Mr. Werewolf.'' *Dreadful Pleasures: An Anatomy of Modern Horror.* New York, Oxford University Press, 1985, 204-257.

Wolfman Jack (1938-1995)

With his trademark gravelly voice and howl, disc jockey Wolfman Jack became a cultural icon over the airwaves during the 1960s and was integral in popularizing rock music. The first radio personality to introduce rhythm-and-blues music to a mainstream audience, he opened the doors for African American artists to reach widespread success in the music world. The Wolfman did more than announce songs over the radio; his unique personality lent a context to the sound of a new generation and made him the undisputed voice of rock and roll.

Wolfman Jack was born Robert Weston Smith in Brooklyn, New York, on January 21, 1938 and grew up in a middle-class environment. Always fond of music, as a teenager he would pretend he was a disc jockey using his own stereo equipment. After some odd jobs selling encyclopedias and Fuller brushes, Wolfman Jack attended the National Academy of Broadcasting in Washington, D.C. He got his professional start in 1960 at WYOU in Newport News, Virginia, a station that catered to a mostly black audience. There, the Wolfman began experimenting with on-air characters, and off the air, hosted dance parties. In 1962, he crossed the border to begin airing a show on

Wolfman Jack

Mexican radio's XERF, which held an extremely powerful 250,000-watt signal that reached across much of the continent. At this job, Bob Smith developed his Wolfman Jack persona.

Wolfman Jack's raspy voice and on-air howls and commands to "get nekkid" caught the attention of young music fans across the country. Unfortunately, the Federal Trade Commission was interested in his advertisements for an array of products over his show, including drug paraphernalia and sugar pills that supposedly helped with sexual arousal, which led to the demise of the station's profits. Meanwhile, however, the Wolfman became known for playing a range of black artists such as Ray Charles, Wilson Pickett, Clarence Carter, and more, leading to the crossover of African American artists into white culture. Though record company executives were pleased to see their markets broadening, not everyone was thrilled with the development, since integration was still a new concept. Later, when Wolfman Jack moved back to Louisiana and hosted racially mixed dances, the Ku Klux Klan burned crosses on his lawn. Subsequently, Bob Smith kept Wolfman Jack within the confines of the studio to avoid hostility.

Later, Wolfman Jack moved to Minneapolis, Minnesota, where he ran a small local station and sent taped shows down to XERF. Wishing to resume live on-air performances, in 1966 he and a partner opened their own station on Sunset Strip in Los Angeles, which flourished until 1971. After that folded, Wolfman Jack accepted a humble salary at KDAY and also began hosting the television show *Midnight Special* on NBC, airing from 1972 to 1981. He appeared in most of the episodes. He also had a part as himself in the hit George Lucas film *American Graffiti*, a nostalgia movie about a group of teenagers in the early 1960s. The appearance finally put a face to the name for fans, who were reassured to discover that the Wolfman looked every bit the part, with bulging eyes and a bushy beard, sideburns, and hairstyle. Wolfman Jack used this publicity to land jobs on commercials and appearing at concerts and conventions. He was also a guest on *Hollywood Squares,* and began working on WNBC in New York City hosting a radio show. In addition, he lent his voice to the rock song "Clap for the Wolfman" by the Guess Who.

In the early 1990s, Wolfman Jack flew from his home in North Carolina to Washington, D.C. each Friday to host the syndicated radio oldies program *Live from Planet Hollywood* on WXTR-FM. In 1995, he published his autobiography, which related the ups and downs of his career, from hobnobbing with other celebrities to his battle with a cocaine addiction. Shortly after completing a 20-day tour to promote the book, he died of a heart attack at his home in Belvidere, North Carolina, on July 1, 1995. He was survived by his wife of 34 years, Elizabeth ''Lou'' Lamb Smith, and his two children, Todd Weston Smith and Joy Renee Smith.

—Geri Speace

FURTHER READING:

Stark, Phyllis. ''Wolfman Dies on Cusp of Greatness.'' *Billboard.* July 15, 1995, 4.

Wolfman Jack with Byron Lauren. *Have Mercy! Confessions of the Original Rock 'n' Roll Animal.* New York, Warner Books, 1995.

Woman's Day

Begun during the 1930s depression, *Woman's Day* magazine ''like the supermarket. . . helped to change the habits of the American family,'' according to Helen Woodward in *The Lady Persuaders. Woman's Day* began as a giveaway menu leaflet, the ''A&P Menu Sheet,'' published and distributed to its customers by the Great Atlantic & Pacific Tea Company. The sheet ''told the housewife how to get the most for her food dollar, then how to use the food purchased to provide her family with appetizing and nourishing meals,'' James Playsted Wood reported in *Magazines in the Twentieth Century.* It included suggested menus for families with adequate as well as for those with meager and less-than-meager budgets. The first issue in 1934 offered menus for a family of four ranging from eleven to thirteen dollars a week to five to six dollars a week. The April 30, 1934, sheet contained ''menus especially adapted to the needs of children.''

The menu sheet was so successful and so expensive to produce that two A&P executives, Frank Wheeler and Donald P. Hanson, developed plans to make a women's service magazine of it. A subsidiary was founded, and in October 1937 the first 815,000 copies of *Woman's Day* were ready for sale for three cents in A&P grocery stores. Six of the 32 pages were devoted to recipes and menus. Other pages included advertising for products chiefly found in the A&P, an article that told ''What to Do about Worry,'' and another that asked, ''Is Football Worthwhile?'' From its beginning, the magazine contained how-to-do-it articles, expanded in 1947 to a complete how-to section, ''How to Make It—How to Do It—How to Fix It.'' By 1940 the magazine was able to guarantee advertisers a circulation of 1.5 million.

In 1943, Mabel Hill Souvaine began her fifteen-year tenure as editor, and under her management the magazine grew in circulation to nearly five million. By 1952, *Woman's Day* was distributed in 4,500 A&P stores and, like its arch rival, *Family Circle,* was, as reported in *Business Week,* ''hard on the heels of the big women's service magazines.'' In the 1950s, *Woman's Day* told stores which dress patterns it would feature and then told readers which stores stocked fabrics appropriate for those patterns. In 1958, after a federal judge dismissed a suit brought by several food companies that alleged the magazine engaged in discriminatory practices that guaranteed it advertising revenues, A&P sold *Woman's Day* to the Fawcett Company.

Of the many store-distributed magazines founded in the 1930s, *Woman's Day* and *Family Circle* emerged as the hardiest and most prosperous. With a readership of nearly 20 million in the late 1980s, *Woman's Day* was a close competitor to the ''world's largest women's magazine,'' *Family Circle,* which boasted a readership of more than 21 million. By the 1990s, *Woman's Day* continued to be one of the most popular sources of information designed specifically for women and their daily life.

—Erwin V. Johanningmeier

FURTHER READING:

''Food-Store Magazines Hit the Big Time.'' *Business Week.* No. 1171, February 9, 1952.

Taft, William H. *American Magazines for the 1980s.* New York, Hasting House Publishers, 1982.

Wood, James Playsted. *Magazines in the United States.* New York, Ronald Press, 1956.

Woodward, Helen. *The Lady Persuaders.* New York, Ivan Obolensky, 1960.

Wonder, Stevie (1950—)

In the 1970s, as pop music fractured into a thousand competing subgenres, Stevie Wonder blended pop, jazz, soul, rock, funk, and reggae without trivializing or pastiching. As he grew from child prodigy to music's foremost ambassador, he topped the charts while winning three consecutive Album of the Year Grammy awards. A producer, arranger, composer, singer, and master of numerous instruments, Wonder also did more than anyone to tame the synthesizer, transforming it from special effect to musical instrument. Lyrically, he addressed everything from social inequity to romance and heartbreak, from Plant Rights to the birth of his daughter; and topped it all off with unrelenting good humor.

Born prematurely on May 13, 1950, Stevland Judkins (later Stevland Morris) lost his sight while in a hospital incubator. From his earliest years he demonstrated an aptitude for music, banging on anything he could get his hands near until his family managed, despite their poverty, to acquire some instruments for him to play. When he was ten years old, a family friend introduced the boy to Motown founder Berry Gordy, who promptly signed the youth he soon renamed ''Little Stevie Wonder.'' In addition to performing and recording, Wonder also took music lessons from Motown's legendary studio band, the Funk Brothers. Though two early singles flopped, the boy's exuberance and showmanship came through on a 1963 live recording, ''Fingertips Part Two,'' that soon became a number one single; the album, *Recorded Live—The Twelve Year Old Genius,* also rose to number one, a first for Motown.

A couple of lean years followed before Wonder displayed an ability to write his own songs: his 1965 composition ''Uptight'' became a major hit and Gordy, who usually discouraged artists from writing their own material, assigned songwriters to help the budding genius. Over the next few years, hits included ''For Once in My Life,'' ''I Was Made to Love Her,'' and a cover of Bob Dylan's ''Blowin' in the Wind'' which marked Wonder's (and Motown's) first take on social themes. Wonder's ''My Cherie Amour'' was recorded in 1966 but only saw release in 1969 as a ''B'' side; it proved

Stevie Wonder

Motown's Quality Control department wrong when it soared up the charts. As he grew, Wonder became increasingly disenchanted with Motown's assembly line approach to hit-making, though he had more freedom than most of the label's artists. He was allowed to start producing some of his own music starting in 1968, and in 1970 won a Best R&B (rhythm and blues) Producer Grammy for *Signed, Sealed & Delivered.*

But in 1971, when he reached the age of majority and received a ten-year backlog of royalties, he did not re-sign with the company. Instead, he invested much of his fortune in new synthesizers and devoted himself to recording at Electric Lady Studios, designed by fellow sonic explorer Jimi Hendrix. Shocked that Wonder would consider abandoning the Motown family, Gordy negotiated a new contract that gave the artist unprecedented artistic freedom, including his own music publishing company. Wonder responded with a run of the most innovative, popular, and critically praised albums in Motown history, starting with two albums in 1972: *Music of My Mind* and *Talking Book,* which spawned two number one singles, the ballad "You Are the Sunshine of My Life" and the funk tune "Superstition." The astonishing diversity of the material and the ear-opening range of synthesized sounds (programmed by associate producers

Robert Margouleff and Malcolm Cecil) were to become trademarks of Wonder's adult career. The following three albums, *Innervisions, Fulfillingness' First Finale,* and the double album *Songs in the Key of Life* each won Album of the Year Grammies, and contained hit singles like "Livin' for the City," "You Haven't Done Nothin'," "I Wish," and "Sir Duke." The combination of trenchant political lyrics set to breathtaking melodies, unorthodox harmonies, and satisfying rhythms set a high-water mark for pop music; his positive, engaging manner kept the material from dragging the listener down.

Wonder was the foremost contributor to a trend in 1970s soul music (also upheld by Earth, Wind & Fire, the Isley Brothers, and War, among others) that shined a bright light on social problems but always with spirituality, a constructive attitude, and musical innovation. His do-it-yourself approach inspired a generation of artists who wrote and produced their own material (Prince being the most prominent example), and his unwillingness to take the easy way out has resulted in a book of compositions frequently played and recorded by top jazz musicians. Wonder's easy good cheer refuted the stereotype of the troubled, harassed superstar.

After *Songs,* however, his fame began to fade. A 1979 soundtrack to the film version of the bestselling non-fiction book *The Secret Life* of Plants, received mixed reviews from critics and record buyers alike, and Wonder rushed out *Hotter Than July* in 1980 to reassure confused fans that he had not lost his mind. The new album focused on more traditional political issues, with ''Happy Birthday'' kicking off Wonder's ultimately successful campaign to make Martin Luther King Jr.'s birthday a national holiday. While his next album was in the works, a duet written by and performed with Paul McCartney, ''Ebony and Ivory,'' kept Wonder in the public eye. Then in 1984, ''I Just Called to Say I Love You'' (from the movie *The Woman in Red*) became Wonder's bestselling single ever, but had lasting negative consequences: the syrupy tune alienated many music critics and Wonder became pigeonholed as a sappy balladeer. That opinion was bolstered by *In Square Circle* (1985) and its hit ''Part Time Lover,'' which marked an end to Wonder's dominance of the pop charts. The 1987 follow-up, *Characters,* which sold relatively poorly, led off with the single ''Skeletons,'' a hard funk groove with lyrics obliquely addressing the Iran-contra affair. Despite the feel-good fundraising of mid-1980s events like ''We Are the World'' and ''That's What Friends Are For'' (Wonder participated in both), social criticism with any sharpness had fallen out of favor in pop music. The 1991 soundtrack to Spike Lee's *Jungle Fever* also sank without an impact, though it contained some fine work.

But even as styles changed, Wonder's influence could still be heard all over the airwaves, as his distinctive vocal style inspired New Jack Swing and soul artists like Boyz II Men, Mint Condition, and Jodeci. Later, in the mid-1990s, British retro outfit Jamiroquai rose to multiplatinum success by directly copying Wonder's landmark 1970s sound. In 1996, Wonder won a Lifetime Achievement Award and two Grammies for the new album *Conversation Peace;* he seems secure in his role as a living legend whose best work may be behind him, but who can still, on occasion, work his melodic magic.

—David B. Wilson

FURTHER READING:

Horn, Martin E. *Stevie Wonder: Career of a Rock Legend.* New York, Barclay House, 1999.

Taylor, Rick. *Stevie Wonder: The Illustrated Disco/Biography.* London, Omnibus Press, 1985.

Wonder Woman

As America prepared to enter World War II and American women prepared to take on the roles of men at home, Wonder Woman became the first female superhero in the male-dominated world of comic books. Wonder Woman originally appeared in a nine-page spread in the December 1941 issue of DC Comics' popular *All Star Comics.* Her story was so well received that she was given a spot in DC's *Sensation Comics* in January 1942 and her own self-titled series that debuted in the summer. Strong, agile, intelligent, and brave, Wonder Woman challenged gender stereotypes, demonstrating that women, too, could rescue people from imminent danger and fight for justice. Wonder Woman, however, differed from her male counterparts in an important aspect: when she pursued her enemies—who were typically villains threatening America or seeking to subvert peace—she did so with an eye for reform rather than vengeance.

Equipped with her golden lasso, bullet-deflecting bracelets, and Amazonian agility, rather than guns or a propensity for violence, Wonder Woman was made into a role model for young women, encouraging them to compete and win in a man's world without ever surrendering their femininity.

Dreamed up by William Moulton Marston, who wrote under the pen name Charles Moulton, Wonder Woman was created to fill a void in the comic book market. Marston, then employed as an educational consultant for Detective Comics, Inc. (now DC Comics), was the first to notice that the world of superheroes ignored an important demographic: girls. While young boys could pretend to be Batman, Superman, or the Green Lantern, young girls had to swap genders in order to participate in the role-playing, a practice Marston perceived as damaging to their self-esteem. So, with the go ahead from Max Gaines, then head of DC Comics, Marston began work on the female superhero who was to become an American icon.

Marston's Wonder Woman was a kinder, gentler superhero than those who had come before her. Originally known as Princess Diana, she was raised as part of a hidden colony of Amazons who had fled Greece and Rome to escape male domination. From infancy, all of the Amazons had been trained in Grecian contests of agility, dexterity, speed, and strength, enabling them to attain greater speed than Mercury and greater strength than Hercules. In addition, each possessed the wisdom of Athena and Aphrodite's ability to inspire love. The Amazons inhabited the tiny Paradise Island, located in the Bermuda Triangle and surrounded by magnetic thought fields that prevented its detection. But when Major Steve Trevor of American Intelligence crash-landed his plane there, the Amazons' lives changed. Diana found him and stayed by his side until he was well, falling in love with him in the process. When Major Trevor was well enough to be returned to the United States, Diana won permission to follow him and aid him in his battle for truth, justice, and the American way. Thus, Wonder Woman was born.

From the beginning, Wonder Woman's mission was one of peace, justice, and equality. While she did set out to capture criminals, she was never violent, nor did she use excessive force unless necessary. She did not carry a weapon, but instead relied upon her intelligence and agility to outwit and outmaneuver her opponents. Frequently, she encircled villains in her magic lasso, forcing them to reveal all of their evil secrets, and then delivered them to Transformation Island, a rehabilitation facility created by the Amazons of her native land. Many of her early foes were successfully reformed in this manner.

In addition to being a peaceful superhero, it is also notable that Wonder Woman was a self-made one. Although changes made to the series in the 1950s and 1960s described Wonder Woman's powers as a gift from the Gods, the original storyline attributed her superhero qualities to years of rigorous training and self-discipline. This concept, which was finally restored to the series in the late 1980s, suggested that young readers who worked hard enough could also achieve greatness. Or, as Wonder Woman herself said in one of her early comic strips in the 1940s, ''Girls who realize woman's true powers can do greater things than I have done.'' In a time when millions of men were about to become heroes in World War II, Wonder Woman provided an ideal to which young girls could aspire, and a vehicle through which they could find their own strength.

While her comic continued to appeal to readers into the 1990s, Wonder Woman is also remembered for her television program. Between 1975 and 1979, Wonder Woman, played by Lynda Carter, charmed audiences in one season on ABC in a show set in the 1940s and faithful to the comic book of that time, and then for two more seasons on CBS in a show set in modern times.

—Belinda S. Ray

FURTHER READING:

Handy, Amy, Gloria Steinem, and Steven Korte, eds. *Wonder Woman: Featuring over Five Decades of Great Covers (A Tiny Folio).* New York, Abbeville Press, 1995.

Marston, William Moulton. *Wonder Woman Archives Volume I.* New York, DC Comics, 1998.

Wong, Anna May (1905-1961)

Anna May Wong was the first Asian American actress to achieve Hollywood film star status and an early outspoken critic of Hollywood's racist attitudes. Born Wong Liu Tsong in Los Angeles, she was third-generation Chinese-American. Her first role was as an extra in *The Red Lantern* (1919), and her first lead was in the first Technicolor film, *Toll of The Sea* (1922). Her most memorable part was in *Shanghai Express* (1932), which starred Marlene Dietrich. Although she won critical acclaim for her acting in *The Thief of Bagdad* (1924), Wong grew tired of stereotyped casting and emigrated to Europe, where her stage and film work were well received. A gifted linguist, she played roles in several languages. After she returned to the United States, she declined, on principle, to consider playing the role of the concubine in *The Good Earth.* In the early 1950s, she starred in a short-lived television series. Her last film was *Portrait in Black* (1960).

—Yolanda Retter

FURTHER READING:

Parish, James Robert, and William T. Leonard, editors. *Hollywood Players: The Thirties.* New Rochelle, New York, Arlington House, 1976.

Zia, Helen, and Susan B. Gall, editors. *Notable Asian Americans.* Detroit, Gale Research, 1995.

Wood, Ed (1924-1978)

The director of some of filmdom's campiest flicks during the Tarnished Age of the ''B'' movie, the cross-dressing Edward D. Wood, Jr. is remembered by a loyal cult following as the ''worst director of all time'' for such unforgettable creations as the transvestite epic *Glen or Glenda* (1953) and the mock-serious science-fiction drama *Plan 9 from Outer Space* (1958). Replete with bad dialogue, moralistic narration, infamously cheap special effects, and starring an eclectic group of Hollywood outcasts, including an aging Bela Lugosi, Wood's films rank among the most dreadful spectacles in cinematic history. His films mouldered in relative obscurity for decades, known only to ''B'' film buffs, until the 1994 biographical comedy *Ed Wood* triggered a resurgence of interest in his work. This film showed how, in the words of *Boston Herald* film critic James Verniere, sometimes ''a dream can take you further than talent.''

Born in 1924, Wood spent his formative years in New Jersey, cultivating his love of both Hollywood and angora sweaters. Although he was always a heterosexual, he admitted finding comfort in women's clothing. As a marine in World War II, Wood feared being injured in battle lest medics discover the bra and panties underneath his combat fatigues. In 1946, fresh from the service, Wood arrived in Hollywood with nothing but his unbreakable optimism and a change of lingerie. He spent a few years on the backest of back lots, paying his dues, producing some short films, and planning his first major feature. The opportunity finally came in 1953 when Wood released *Glen or Glenda,* in which he himself starred as a cross-dressing businessman also known as Danal Davis. It was during the filming that Wood met Lugosi, at that time an aging, drug-addicted actor desperate for the dignity of regular work. Enamoured to have crossed paths with the star of *Dracula,* the 1931 horror classic, and desperate for publicity, Wood immediately invented a part for Lugosi. In the final scene of *Glen or Glenda,* when Wood's character divulges his obvious secret to his girlfriend, and she dramatically hands him her prized angora sweater, Lugosi appears as an obviously out-of-place supreme being, inexplicably chanting ''pull the string.''

Over the next few years, Wood refined his unique style of moviemaking by working on several short films, including the high-camp horror flick *Bride of the Monster* (1956). With neither studio connections nor talented talent, Wood was forced to work entirely outside the Hollywood system, accepting financial backing from any willing sponsor and collecting old stock footage to fill screen time. He also assembled his own unusual Hollywood ''family,'' including future wife Loretta King, the morphine-addicted Lugosi, Criswell, a fake television psychic who once predicted an outbreak of cannibalism, Bunny Breckenridge, a drag queen, and Tor Johnson, a 300-pound Swedish wrestler turned actor. Despite the lack of production values, experienced actors or quality scripts, Wood truly believed his pictures could make a difference, often relying on blatant narration to illustrate his point. Ever the optimist, Wood never once did a second take, because in each instance, he truly believed the first take was perfect.

In 1955, Wood released his most renowned film, *Plan 9 from Outer Space,* about aliens who transform the dead into killer zombies to teach the warmongers of Earth a lesson. Originally entitled *Grave Robbers from Outer Space,* Wood was forced to rename the film after his unlikely sponsors, the First Baptist Church of Beverly Hills, opposed the original title for religious reasons. Lugosi died shortly after filming began, but rather than remove the only remotely marketable name from the marquee, Wood substituted his wife's chiropractor—who was a full foot taller—for Lugosi in the rest of the scenes. Ed Wood ''fans'' have practically made an industry of ridiculing *Plan 9 from Outer Space* for the cheap sets, simplistic dialogue, and especially the laughable special effects, like the UFOs, which were nothing more than spinning hubcaps dangling from very visible strings. The film is Wood's true ''masterpiece,'' a perpetual candidate for the worst film of all time.

Wood went on to direct several more movies, including *Violent Years* (1956), a tale of the ''untamed girls of the pack gang'' which nonetheless preaches a return to family values, and *Night of the Ghouls* (1959), a film that announced that it was ''so astounding that some of you might faint.'' As low-budget as they were, Wood's films rarely made a cent. By the late 1960s, Wood was broke and resorted to making soft-core pornography films and writing a few ''adult books'' including *Death of a Transvestite.* Wood himself descended into alcoholism and died in 1978 at the age of 54.

A few months after his death, Wood was chosen the ''worst director of all-time'' by the Golden Turkey Awards. Over the next decade, his films appeared in ''B'' movie festivals around the world and gained a small cult following, which included director Tim Burton. In 1994, Burton released *Ed Wood,* a comedic tribute in which Johnny Depp was cast as the starry-eyed Wood. The film details Wood's life between 1952 and 1955, focusing on his relationship with Bela Lugosi. Although it did not last long in theatres, the film drew considerable critical acclaim, making many critics' top-ten lists for 1994. Rather than patronizing the obviously untalented director, Burton presents Wood as a naive and charismatic man with true affection for Lugosi and the rest of his coterie of ''misfits and dope fiends.'' Martin Landau won the Oscar for Best Supporting Actor for his mesmerizing portrayal of the drug-addicted Lugosi, bitter at the Hollywood world that had cast him aside. In the words of film critic Phillip Wuntch of the *Dallas Morning News,* Ed Wood ''succeeds as a salute to filmmaking and, on a personal level, as a valentine to the uncrushed human spirit.''

Thanks to the 1994 film, the public gained some respect for the ''worst director of all-time.'' Many of his films became available on video, and Wood has become the center of a small but devoted cult following.

—Simon Donner

FURTHER READING:

Alexander, Scott, and Larry Koraszewski. *Ed Wood.* Boston, Faber and Faber, 1995.

Cross, Robin. *The Big Book of B-movies.* New York, St. Martin's Press, 1981.

Grey, Rudolph. *Nightmare of Ecstasy: The Life and Art of Edward D. Wood, Jr.* New York, Feral House, 1994

Wood, Natalie (1938-1981)

Natalie Wood will always be remembered as the beautiful, sad little girl who learned to believe in Santa Claus in *The Miracle on 34th Street* (1947). In that movie, she was flanked by such outstanding talents as Edmund Gwenn and Maureen O'Hara, yet she held held her own. Later, Wood proved her talents as an adult, starring in such notable films as *Rebel without a Cause, West Side Story,* and *Splendor in the Grass.*

Born Natasha Virapaeff on July 20, 1938, to poor Russian immigrants, Wood was destined to become a star. Her mother was a classic stage mother, aggressive, obstinate, insistent, and convinced that others should recognize her daughter's beauty and talent. Although five-year-old Natalie failed to impress at her first screen test, her mother nevertheless convinced producer Irving Pichel to give her a part in his 1943 film *Happy Land.* In 1946 she had a small part in *Tomorrow Is Forever,* with veteran stars Claudette Colbert, Orson Welles, and George Brent, and one year later she starred in *Miracle on 34th Street,* launching her legendary career.

Quickly becoming a seasoned performer, Wood made several films each year throughout her childhood. With *Rebel without a Cause,* she showed audiences that she was also capable of more complex roles in an Academy Award-nominated performance, and

Natalie Wood

this promise was borne out in *Splendor in the Grass* (1961) in which she played a young woman whose parents' attempts to suppress her burgeoning sexuality result in her madness. It was also in 1961 that she starred in the hugely successful *West Side Story,* completing her transition from child star to hardworking adult actress. Critics consider her performance in *Love with the Proper Stranger* (1963) her finest.

Although her career was successful, Wood's personal life was frequently troubled. She married Wagner for the first time in 1957, but the couple divorced only five years later. In her search for love and stability, she engaged in a number of high-profile romances with such stars as James Dean, Elvis Presley, Dennis Hopper, and most notably, Warren Beatty. Her title role in the movie *Inside Daisy Clover* (1965) is considered to be somewhat autobiographical, with its portrayal of a young girl pushed so hard by her mother into becoming a singer that she loses control and blows up her own house. Daisy Clover's attempt at suicide is comical, but Natalie Wood's was not. After a failed marriage and a number of failed romances, she decided to end her life. Fortunately, her attempt failed.

Wood continued working, but her career after 1963 was less distinguished. She tried her hand at comedy, most notably in the 1969 sex farce *Bob and Carol and Ted and Alice,* and later worked in television. In 1972, she remarried Wagner, and as the decade progressed, the couple came to symbolize that rare phenomenon, a truly successful Hollywood marriage. One of the many tragedies of the entertainment industry is that Natalie Wood died so soon after finding the stability and love for which she had searched her whole life. On Thanksgiving weekend 1981, Wood was killed while sailing with her husband and actor Christopher Walken, with whom she was making a film. The boat had been purchased after the remarriage and named the *Splendour* to commemorate their love and happiness. The coroner's report states that she was accidentally drowned while attempting to either enter a dinghy tied to the boat or to stop the dinghy from banging against the bigger boat. She was dressed in a nightgown, a down jacket, and slippers. Reports indicated that Wood, Wagner, and Walken had been drinking, as had the boat's skipper, but the actual circumstances surrounding the event remain unclear.

—Elizabeth Purdy

FURTHER READING:

Harris, Warren G. *Natalie Wood and R.J.: Hollywood's Star-Crossed Lovers.* New York, Doubleday, 1988.

Wood, Lana. *Natalie: A Memoir by Her Sister.* New York, Portway, 1986.

John Wooden

Wooden, John (1910—)

John Wooden coached the UCLA Bruins basketball team for 23 years, ten of those years ending with the NCAA championship. Wooden won his first title in 1964, then again in 1965. After a year out of the winner's circle, Wooden's team achieved seven consecutive national titles (1967-73). In 1975, "The Wizard of Westwood" (a nickname Wooden despised) won his last title.

Wooden finished his 23-year career with a .804 winning percentage, fourth all-time behind Jerry Tarkanian, Clair Bee, and Adolph Rupp. Included among his many accomplishments are an 88-game winning streak, 38 straight NCAA Tournament wins, and 19 conference championships. As a coach, as Curry Kirkpatrick noted in a 1998 *Sport* article, he was considered "the best who ever coached, any time, any sport."

Wooden coached some of the best college players of their time, including Lew Alcindor (who later would be known as Kareem Abdul-Jabbar), Bill Walton, Sidney Wicks, and Walt Hazzard, as well as *Hill Street Blues* star Mike Warren.

Wooden's life started in the Midwest, in Martinsville, Indiana. It was there he met his beloved wife, Nellie, who died in 1985 after 53 years of marriage, leaving John Wooden despondent for quite a while. He dedicated *They Call Me Coach* to her, writing, "Her love, faith, and loyalty through all our years together are primarily responsible for what I am." Later in the book, reminiscing about Nellie again, he called her death "the ultimate tragedy."

Wooden was considered one of the greatest Indiana schoolboy players in history, quite an accomplishment considering the long history of great high school basketball in the Hoosier state. He had a brilliant athletic career as a guard at Purdue University, and he has been called at times the "Michael Jordan of his day" because of his accomplishments as a Boilermaker.

Wooden decided to retire after 1975 upon recognizing that his professional responsibilities in addition to coaching, such as acting as

liaison with athletic boosters, began to wear on him. He noted in his first book, *They Call Me Coach,* "As the years passed, . . . the pressure of the crowds at our regular season games and especially at our championship tournaments began to disturb me greatly. I found myself getting very uncomfortable and anxious to get away from it all."

His name has not been forgotten after his retirement. An annual event entitled the John Wooden Classic was established to ensure that Wooden's legacy would not be forgotten as time passed and that he would "not become a footnote in American sports history." The strength of his talent in basketball was recognized again when he became the first man elected to the Basketball Hall of Fame as a player and as a coach. In addition, each year since 1977 the top college basketball player has been presented the John R. Wooden award by the U.S. Basketball Writers Association. (One critical factor that Wooden demanded before he agreed to attach his name to the award was that the recipient be a good student, stressing that the primary reason athletes are in school is to earn an education.)

By the end of 1990s, Wooden remained active in basketball camps, which he has enjoyed since his retirement in 1975. He took particular pleasure in teaching kids the fundamentals of basketball. In *They Call Me Coach,* Wooden noted that during his camps scrimmages are "the least important part of what we teach." Instead, they emphasize complete attention to the fundamentals of the game. In Wooden's second book, *Wooden: A Lifetime of Observations On and Off the Court,* former UCLA player and assistant coach and current Louisville basketball coach Denny Crum commented, "Coach Wooden was first of all a teacher. I believe he takes more pleasure from teaching than from all the recognition he amassed during his illustrious career."

Wooden's simple style and unique expressions have become well known in the sports world. Some "Woodenisms" include, as listed in *Wooden:* "What is right is more important than who is right;" "Don't let making a living prevent you from making a life;"

''Much can be accomplished by teamwork when no one is concerned about who gets credit;'' ''It is what you learn after you know it all that counts;'' and ''Discipline yourself and others won't need to.''

—D. Byron Painter

FURTHER READING:

Kirkpatrick, Curry. ''Same as He Ever Was.'' *Sport.* January 1998, 70-76.

Wooden, John, with Jack Tobin. *They Call Me Coach.* Lincolnwood, Illinois, Contemporary Books, 1988.

Wooden, John, with Steve Jamison. *Wooden: A Lifetime of Observations On and Off the Court.* Lincolnwood, Illinois, Contemporary Books, 1997.

Woods, Tiger (1975—)

Prepared by his father for golf stardom from an early age, Eldrick ''Tiger'' Woods is off to a solid start in reaching his father's goals. Even before he turned professional in 1996 after two years at Stanford University, Woods (the ''Eldrick'' officially disappeared when he was 21) became the first amateur ever to win three consecutive U.S. amateur titles. By the end of 1998, Woods had won one major tournament, the 1997 Masters (becoming the first person of color to do so), and several other tournaments, while racking up

Tiger Woods

millions of dollars both on the course as well as from advertisers such as Titleist, Nike, and American Express. In 1997, he won the PGA Tour money title by winning just more than two million dollars.

For many years, golf was mostly a white man's sport (through 1961, the PGA of America constitution actually contained a ''Caucasian clause''), mostly elitist in nature. In addition to his solid play on the course, many people believe that Woods's success has opened up the game of golf to minorities, with many blacks specifically picking up golf because of him. Woods himself has grappled with his race, however. With his mother a Thailand native, Woods considers himself Cablinasian—Caucasian, black, Indian, and Asian—because of his racially diverse background. Throughout his short career, he has at times shunned the African-American label, though he does not deny his father's African-American roots. When Woods turned professional, discussing whether or not he would be a role model for minorities, he said in a 1996 *Newsweek* article, ''I don't see myself as the Great Black Hope. I'm just a golfer who happens to be black and Asian. It doesn't matter whether they're white, black, brown or green. All that matters is I touch kids the way I can through clinics and they benefit from them.''

Earl Woods started teaching his only child the finer points of golf almost from the beginning. Tiger watched his father take practice swings when he was only six months old, and he was mesmerized watching his father swing the club. Four months later, Woods took swings of his own before he even took his first steps, and he also was on the practice green before his first birthday. When Woods was five years old, he appeared on the television show *That's Incredible!* and was featured in *Golf Digest.* Often, Woods's punishment would result in no golf, a good way to encourage him to stay out of trouble. He also could not practice golf until his homework was complete. Not only did Earl and Kultida encourage their son toward the golf course, but they also ingrained in him trust and respect. During Woods's preteen and teen years, his father used his military training to help toughen up his son for the rigors of golf. For example, Earl would intentionally distract his son when he was preparing a shot.

At age 15, Woods was the youngest golfer ever to win the U.S. Junior Amateur title, the first of three consecutive titles at that level. He went on to win three consecutive U.S. Men's Amateur titles, the only player in U.S. history to have won both the Junior and Amateur titles. In 1996, he became the NCAA champion. However, Woods became bored with the college game, looking toward the day he would turn professional and start playing for money.

Shortly after that third amateur title, Woods did turn professional. Playing at the Greater Milwaukee Open in September 1996, he finished a respectable sixteenth place, with a seven-under-par score. He won $2,544 for his efforts. A few weeks later, Woods won his first tournament in Las Vegas, which assured him of a spot on the PGA Tour for 1997, when he led the tour in prize money. In only eight tournaments, Woods earned almost eight hundred thousand dollars. After his fantastic start, *Sports Illustrated* named him ''Sportsman of the Year.''

Woods's biggest accomplishment, however, came in April 1997 when he shattered the Masters record for largest margin of victory. After nine holes on Thursday, Woods found himself four over par. According to Earl, his son made a subtle adjustment to his swing. On the next 63 holes, Woods put on a show the likes of which the famed Augusta National Golf Club had never seen. He eventually finished at 18 under par, winning by 12 strokes, both of which were new records. In total, Woods broke 20 records with his performance and tied six others. Woods became the youngest Masters champ in history (at 21, he was two years younger than 1980 champ Severiano Ballesteros). Unfortunately, Woods's smashing win was somewhat overshadowed by some racially insensitive comments made by fellow golfer Fuzzy Zoeller. Zoeller immediately apologized for his remarks, but the story did not die as soon as it might have. Some people blamed Woods for that fact, because he was less than forgiving toward Zoeller—not returning Zoeller's repeated phone calls. Woods won the tournament almost 50 years to the day after Jackie Robinson broke baseball's color barrier.

After his Masters win, Woods had trouble fulfilling the extremely high expectations of his fans. In the three following majors, he finished no better than seventeenth. Part of his problem may have been his extremely strenuous schedule, which included several overseas trips and also lengthy commercial shoots. In 1999, however, Woods came out on top again with a 22-under-par win at the Buick Invitational in February and a 15-under-par win at the Deutsche Bank Open in May.

—D. Byron Painter

FURTHER READING:

Abrahams, Jonathan. "Golden Child or Spoiled Brat." *Golf Magazine.* April 1998, 56-65.

"Black America and Tiger's Dilemma; National Leaders Praise Golfer's Accomplishments and Debate Controversial 'Mixed Race' Issue." *Ebony.* July 1997, 28-33.

Feinstein, John. *The First Coming: Tiger Woods, Master or Martyr.* New York, Ballantine Publishing Group, 1998.

———. "Tiger by the Tail." *Newsweek.* September 9, 1996, 58-61.

McCormick, John, and Sharon Begley. "How to Raise a Tiger." *Newsweek.* December 9, 1996, 52-57.

Strege, John. *Tiger: A Biography of Tiger Woods.* New York, Broadway Books, 1997.

Woods, Earl. *Playing Through: Straight Talk on Hard Work, Big Dreams, and Adventures with Tiger.* New York, HarperCollins, 1998.

———. *Training a Tiger: A Father's Guide to Raising a Winner in Both Golf and Life.* New York, HarperCollins, 1997.

Woodstock

In the 1960s, the small town of Woodstock, New York, 40 miles north of New York City, nourished a small but growing community of folk musicians including Bob Dylan, the Band, Tim Hardin, and John Sebastian. In 1969, Michael Lang, a young entrepreneur who had promoted the Miami Pop Festival the previous year, decided to open a recording studio for the burgeoning music community of Woodstock, which would double as a woodland retreat for recording artists from New York City. Lang pitched his idea to Artie Kornfeld, a young executive at Capitol Records, and Joel Rosenman and John Roberts, two young entrepreneurs interested in unconventional business propositions. Together they formed a corporation, Woodstock Ventures, to create the studio/retreat. They also decided to organize a Woodstock Music and Arts Fair to promote the opening of the studio.

As their festival plans grew in ambition, they realized that the small town of Woodstock could not accommodate such a festival, and

a site in Wallkill, in the neighboring county, was chosen for the three-day weekend event. Throughout the summer of 1969 the project snowballed as more and more artists were signed to perform. It was decided that day one would feature folk-rock artists, day two would spotlight the burgeoning San Francisco scene, and day three would be saved for the hottest acts. By the time Jimi Hendrix was signed for $50,000, most of the major American bands were involved in Woodstock, as well as major British groups like the Who and Ten Years After. The music soon eclipsed all other aspects of the festival, such as the arts fair (which is almost forgotten) and the recording studio (which never materialized).

Woodstock Ventures spared no expense to cultivate a hip, counterculture image for their three days of peace and music. They advertised the event through the underground press—which was rapidly mushrooming into a national network of anti-establishment groups—to put the word out on the street that this was the happening event of the summer. The Wallkill site was chosen for its rustic scenery and laid-back atmosphere, but the name Woodstock was retained to convey the bucolic theme of the event. A pastoral craze of "getting back to nature" had been growing in 1968 and 1969, reflected in the country-rock movement spearheaded by Bob Dylan, the Band, and others. The lure of nature was celebrated in films like *Easy Rider* (1968), which depicted hippies cruising across the country, living off the land (more or less), and visiting communes. Woodstock Ventures hired the Hog Farm, a New Mexico hippie commune, to prepare the festival campgrounds and maintain a free kitchen for those who could not afford to buy food. The Hog Farm also set up a bad trip shelter called the Big Pink for the inevitable freakouts that were expected. A group of Indian artists were flown in from Arizona to sell handicrafts. An impromptu organization called Food for Love was hired to run concession booths. Wes Pomeroy was enlisted as Security Chief. Pomeroy was renowned for his enlightened attitude towards youth and crowd control. He had witnessed the riots of the 1968 Chicago Democratic Convention, and had developed theories about peaceful crowd control. For Woodstock he organized a non-aggressive, non-uniformed, unarmed security team, the "Peace Service Corps," to unobtrusively dissuade undesirable behavior such as riots, vandalism, and theft, while overlooking non-violent activities such as drugs, sex, and nudity. New York City police officers were recruited, and had to undergo intensive screening to demonstrate their ability to understand and peacefully cope with young, hedonistic, anti-authoritarian crowds. Unfortunately, almost all these groups eventually betrayed Woodstock Ventures. The town of Wallkill voted to drive out the festival a month before the scheduled weekend, and a new site was found in Bethel, New York (although some townsfolk offered resistance there, too). The Hog Farm turned out to be opportunistic and irresponsible, stealing watches and wallets from the Woodstock staff and clashing with anyone whom they perceived as establishmentarian, including the medical staff. The radical activist and showman Abbie Hoffman, a self-styled "cultural revolutionary" who was charged with inciting riots at the Chicago Democratic Convention, threatened to sabotage the festival with his influence over the underground press if Woodstock Ventures did not pay him $50,000. He claimed that the promoters were growing rich off the people, and he felt that Woodstock should return the money to "the people" by financing his own political mission, including his mounting legal debts from the Chicago Seven Trial. Hoffman also threatened to put acid in the water. The Woodstock promoters knew that Hoffman had the audacity and the influence to arouse anti-establishment animosity toward the festival, and they paid him $10,000 to appease him. But such was the reactionary nature of the times that many radical papers nevertheless portrayed Woodstock as a capitalist venture promoted by ''straights'' trying to profit from ''the people.''

Betrayals grew more frequent as the festival grew nearer. The day before the festival, the New York City Police Commissioner refused his officers permission to work at Woodstock. The officers then offered their services anonymously under their own conditions, and for extortionary wages. Food for Love threatened to quit during the festival, reneging on their prepaid $75,000 contract. A rumor soon arose that Woodstock Ventures was bankrupt, and during the festival many bands demanded that they be paid in cash before performing. Even the Grateful Dead, the most anti-commercial band on the scene, made this demand (two years earlier they had played for free outside the Monterey Pop Festival). In the end even Mother Nature reneged her clemency, and assailed her hippie worshippers with two rainstorms, steeping the throng of 500,000 in mud.

Many remember Woodstock primarily as a disaster, as it was officially pronounced, a monument to faulty planning, a testament to the limitations and hypocrisies of hippie idealism, a nightmare of absurdities, ironies, and incongruities. Over a million tickets were sold, but since the gates weren't built in time, droves of kids began streaming in days before the show, and by Friday the promoters, having no way to collect tickets, had to declare Woodstock a free

concert. Acres of land that had been rented for parking remained empty as cars, vans, delivery vehicles, and an estimated one million kids clogged several miles of the New York State Thruway. State troopers arrested hippies on their way to the show, then danced naked on their patrol cars after drinking water laced with acid. Tons of supplies, and even some musicians, were stuck in the traffic jam and never made it to the site. At the festival itself, a 40-foot trailer full of hot dogs rotted when refrigeration fuel ran out, and thousands of people endured the stench of rancid food while they went hungry. The revolving stage, designed to eliminate intermissions between acts, was the biggest and most expensive ever built, but once the equipment was loaded onto it, it wouldn't revolve (the only time it budged was when the mudslide moved it six inches). Out in the campgrounds, a ''pharmacy district'' developed in the middle of the woods, where one could shop for sundry drugs. Bethel residents witnessed outrageous acts of bohemianism. One neighbor awoke to find a shirtless girl riding his cow. Another found a couple having sex on his front porch. Meanwhile, thousands of disoriented hippies showed up in the quiet town of Woodstock, New York, looking for the Festival which was a county away.

Bad press, bad weather, bad trips, technical problems, human error, divine intervention—none of these pressures was enough to snuff the spirit of the crowd that had assembled for three days of peace

A crowd shot at Woodstock, 1969.

and music. The most common feeling among all parties—producers, musicians, audience, town, and nation—was the sense of history in the making. It was the largest group of young people ever gathered, and the greatest roster of musicians ever assembled, and it became the defining moment of a generation. Initial media response tended toward panic, reporting the disastrous aspects of the event. But when riots failed to flare up, the media recanted, reporting that Woodstock was a peaceful event, a mass epiphany of good will and communal sharing. On Sunday, Max Yasgur, the dairy farmer who rented his 600 acres to the festival, took the stage and complimented the crowd, observing how the festival proved that ''half a million kids can get together and have three days of fun and music, and have nothing BUT fun and music.'' Of course, most of these kids were having a lot more than that, but the conspicuous absence Yasgur alluded to was violence. Rock festivals had become increasingly frequent since Monterey Pop in 1967, and each one was bigger and more riotous than the last. The assassinations of Martin Luther King, Jr. and Robert Kennedy also added a feeling of dread to any large gathering. When Woodstock promised nothing but disaster, then passed without a single act of violence, the relief that swept over the watching nation was almost intoxicating; it seemed like a miracle. The relief among the public and the evanescent bliss of the kids led to fanatical pronouncements of the dawning of the Age of Aquarius.

However, many commentators have since claimed that peace and good will arose not in spite of disaster but because of it. The hunger, rain, mud, and unserviced toilets conspired to create an adversity against which people could unite and bond. In ''The Woodstock Wars,'' Hal Aspen observed that the communal spirit of Woodstock was typical of the group psychology of disasters: ''What takes hold at the time is a humbling sense of togetherness . . . with those who shared the experience. What takes hold later is a privileged sense of apartness . . . from those who didn't.'' Aspen explained that the memory of Woodstock led a generation to arrogate ''an epic and heroic youth culture'' that subsequent generations could not match. Those who were once simply called baby boomers now dubbed themselves ''Woodstock Nation,'' an independent and enlightened subculture. Abbie Hoffman wrote a book of editorials called *Woodstock Nation* immediately after the event, contrasting the newly united masses with the ''Pig Nation'' of mainstream America. He even contrasted Woodstock with the moon landing of July 20, less than a month before the festival, calling Woodstock ''the first attempt to land a man on the earth.'' The closeness of the two milestone events in one summer invited such ironic comparisons. Ayn Rand used Nietzsche's dichotomy of Apollo and Dionysus to contrast the two events. She observed that the moon landing represented the culmination of the Apollonian, or civilized, aspect of man, which is governed by reason, while Woodstock expressed the Dionysian, or primeval, aspect of man, which is ruled by hedonism. The name of the moonlanding mission, Apollo, made this interpretation all the more compelling. But such was the sheer physical magnitude of the Woodstock Festival that it afforded enough complexity to accommodate many interpretations. The moonwalk analogies tended to view Woodstock as a moment of separation from the establishment, but it was also possible to view it as reconciliation. It wasn't just the audience of hippies who bonded together in the face of disaster. Community and nation also rushed to their aid. The Red Cross, Girl Scouts, and Boy Scouts all donated food and supplies to the starving hoards. Even local townspeople pardoned the havoc wrought upon their town and made sandwiches for the infiltrators. The youths who had fled from their parents in pursuit of utopian visions ended up welcoming assistance from the very establishment that Woodstock symbolically rejected. They were led to appreciate that these groups had maintained efficiency to get them out of their jam. Someone, they realized, had to stay sober. Many Bethel residents, for their part, commented with surprise on the hippies' politeness and peaceful behavior. Mainstream America saw Max Yasgur's observation born out, that rock and violence were not inseparable, and that perhaps the peace the hippies advocated wasn't such a pipedream after all. In 1972 Woodstock Nation repaid the compliment by nominating Yasgur for president.

When the initial euphoria wore off it became common to view Woodstock not as the beginning of a new era but as an ending, the high-water mark of the 1960s, when hippie freakdom reached critical mass and dissipated into mainstream, and the establishment coopted the diluted attitudes and fashions into a commodity. Much of the pride and idealism of Woodstock Nation crumbled as the following years brought devastating casualties to their culture. Someone was stabbed at the Rolling Stones' free concert at Altamont in December of 1969; 1970 brought the student massacres at Kent Sate University, the breakup of the Beatles, and the deaths of Jimi Hendrix and Janis Joplin later that year. The following year, 1971, brought the death of Jim Morrison, the closing of the Fillmore Concert Halls, and the reelection of Nixon. Such defeats hastened the trend toward escapism, exemplified by rock's detour into country music and apolitical singer/songwriters, sinking into the quagmire of narcissistic spiritual odysseys in the ''Me Decade.''

In the wake of disillusion many claimed that the music was the most significant aspect of Woodstock, the only legacy successfully preserved. The documentary, *Woodstock: Three Days of Peace and Music* (1970), provided vicarious excitement for the millions who couldn't be there, and was enormously popular. It made innovative use of split-screen techniques to simulate the excitement of a live-performance, and won an Oscar for Best Documentary. The three-album soundtrack, *Woodstock: Music from the Original Soundtrack and More,* also awoke nostalgia for the swiftly vanishing epoch. However, the arrangement was jumbled, and many performers were omitted. A two-album sequel, *Woodstock Two,* provided more songs by the artists already favored, but there were still notable absences. For some people, the albums proved what they felt all along, that the music was only a minor part of what was really a spiritual event that couldn't be captured on vinyl. Janis Joplin and the Grateful Dead, who seemed to epitomize the youth culture that had sprouted in San Francisco, reportedly delivered lackluster performances, while then-unknown acts such as Santana and Joe Cocker proved to be among the highlights of the festival. A privileged few recall Joan Baez's performance at the free stage as the highlight. The free stage had been built outside the festival fence so that those who did not have tickets could be entertained by amateur bands and open mic. But even after the festival was declared free and the fence was torn down, the ever-valiant Joan Baez, surveying the crowd of a half-million people, perceived that the free stage would still be useful for entertaining those who could not get close to the main stage, and she played to a fringe audience for 40 minutes until her manager summoned her to her scheduled gig at the main stage. This touching moment was not captured on film or record.

The 25th anniversary of Woodstock in 1994 brought a 4-CD box set which represented most of the performers and preserved the chronological order (although many performers, such as Ravi Shankar and the Incredible String Band, have yet to appear on any Woodstock recording). The documentary was rereleased on video as a "Director's Cut" package offering 40 minutes of additional footage of Hendrix, Joplin, and Jefferson Airplane. A CD-ROM was also released, boasting music, film clips, lyrics, hypertext biographies, and other features.

The most spectacular product of the 25th anniversary was the Woodstock Two festival in Saugerties, New York. As early as 1970 there were plans for sequels, but the original producers were in such legal and emotional disarray that it was impossible. For the tenth anniversary there had been an unspectacular sequel in New York City in 1979 with many of the original players, but nostalgia for 1960s flower-power was at low ebb at that time. But by the late 1980s and 1990s, nostalgia became almost clockwork, and in 1994 the sons and daughters of Woodstock Nation were ready to prove that they could party like their parents. Woodstock Two was a three-day concert with a ticket price of $135 (the original Woodstock tickets had been $18). It, too, generated a movie and soundtrack, and was broadcast on pay-per-view television. Woodstock Two featured mostly popular 1990s bands such as the Cranberries and Green Day, but also included older bands like Aerosmith, while Bob Dylan, the Woodstock, New York, resident who had missed the original festival, finally performed. Original Woodstock alumni included Joe Cocker and Crosby, Stills, and Nash. However, CSN's presence did little to add enhance the sequel's image. In 1969 CSN epitomized the 1960s spirit of togetherness with their angelic harmonies and intricate interplay of guitars. By 1994, they had sold "Teach Your Children" to a diaper commercial and consequently sold their respect. Woodstock Two also mixed rock and advertising, charging corporations a million dollars per billboard space. Pearl Jam, Neil Young, and others refused to participate for this reason. On the other hand, the promoters refused to accept alcohol and tobacco sponsors—a far cry from the pharmaceutical anarchy of the original Woodstock. The advertising slogan for the pay-per-view option was one of the worst ever conceived: "All you have to do to change the world is change the channel." The slogan alluded to John Lennon's line, "We all want to change the world," from the Beatles song, "Revolution" (1968), which was very typical of the political preoccupations of late 1960s music. The idiotic Woodstock Two slogan reflected the apathy and passive consumption often associated with Generation X.

However, one cannot blame the youth for the ineptly chosen phrase, nor assume that it reflected their attitude. The status of women, blacks, and gays was infinitely better in the 1990s than it had been in the 1960s. Beyond a few protest songs, Woodstock was a largely apolitical event. When Abbie Hoffman attempted to make a speech about marijuana reform, Pete Townsend swatted him off the stage. Many forget that the original Woodstock was quite commercial, as Hoffman and others had observed at the time. A common myth is that Woodstock was always a free concert, though it was only declared free by necessity. Hal Aspen notes that Woodstock is nostalgically eulogized as anti-commercial when in fact it was simply unsuccessfully commercial. Many of the innovations of Woodstock Two, such as the pay-per-view option, merely reflect improved technology and better planning rather than greater capitalism.

What really caused the Woodstock promoters to lose their credibility was their lawsuit against a simultaneous festival called Bethel '94 which was planned at the original Woodstock site in Bethel. The event was scheduled to include such veterans as Melanie, Country Joe McDonald, and Richie Havens. Woodstock Ventures, who had been thwarted and sued by many during the first Woodstock,

launched an $80 million law suit to prevent Bethel '94 from happening. But 12,000 attended anyway, and Arlo Guthrie and others gave free impromptu performances. The litigation against Bethel '94 robbed Woodstock Two of any vestige of counterculture coolness.

Woodstock Ventures retained its exclusive rights, but the memory of Woodstock Nation belongs to the world; it is irrevocably imbedded in American culture. One of the most fertile legacies of Woodstock is the anecdotes, stories, and legends which recall the color and humor of that absurd decade. One elusive legend reports that a child was born, though no one seems to know whatever became of the child. The question usually comes up at anniversaries of the event, but remains a mystery. It is possible that the child born at Woodstock is simply a myth providing counterpoint to the deaths (there were three deaths at Woodstock: a youth died Saturday morning when a tractor ran over him as he slept in his sleeping bag; another died of a heroin overdose, and a third died of appendicitis). Besides the dozens of histories and memoirs, Woodstock has also inspired novels, stories, and songs. Its most famous anthem is Crosby, Stills, Nash, and Young's version of "Woodstock" from their album *Déjà Vu* (1970). The song was penned by Joni Mitchell and also appears on her album, *Ladies of the Canyon* (1970). Written in the style of a folk ballad, her song beautifully conveys the spirit—as well as the ironies—of Woodstock Nation, with its theme of pastoral escape, the rally of "half a million strong," the haunting subtext of Vietnam, and the poignantly passive dream of peace.

—Douglas Cooke

FURTHER READING:

Espen, Hal. "The Woodstock Wars." *New Yorker.* August 15, 1994, 70-74.

Hoffman, Abbie. *Woodstock Nation.* New York, Random House, 1969.

Makower, Joel. *Woodstock: The Oral History.* New York, Doubleday, 1989.

Spitz, Bob. *Barefoot in Babylon: The Creation of the Woodstock Music Festival.* New edition. New York, Norton, 1989.

Works Progress Administration (WPA) Murals

In the mid-1930s, in the midst of the Great Depression, the U.S. federal government initiated a series of programs that were meant to provide economic relief to unemployed visual artists. The first such program was the Public Works of Art Project (PWAP), a Treasury Department initiative under the direction of Edward Bruce. Launched in December 1933 and terminated the following spring, the PWAP was short-lived; even so, several hundred murals were completed under its auspices. In October 1934 the Treasury Department launched a second program, initially called the Section of Painting and Sculpture. Unlike the PWAP, which hired artists and paid them weekly wages, the new program sponsored competitions and awarded commissions to selected artists. Over 1000 post office murals were commissioned by the Treasury Section between 1934 and 1943, the year of the program's demise. The Federal Art Project (FAP) of the Works Progress Administration (WPA) was established in May 1935 and also survived until 1943. In addition to employing painters, sculptors,

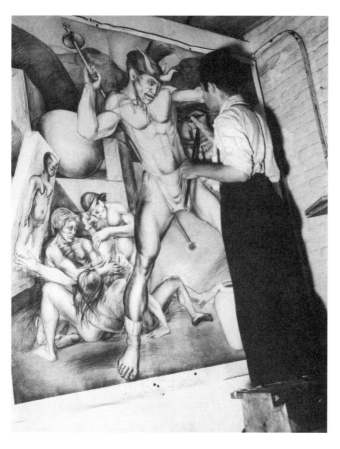

WPA artist Isidore Lipshitz, working on a sketch for the portable mural "Primitive and Modern Medicine."

and graphic artists, the FAP provided funding for community art centers and exhibitions, operated a design laboratory, and supported indexing and bibliographic projects. Artists employed in the Mural Division were assigned projects in schools, hospitals, prisons, airports, public housing, and recreational facilities, and altogether produced over 2500 murals. Under a fourth program, the Treasury Relief Art Project (TRAP), in existence from July 1935 until June 1939, fewer than 100 murals were created.

As a popular art form, mural painting was in its ascendancy in North America in the 1920s and 1930s. In the early 1920s, the Mexican government began to subsidize the painting of murals celebrating Mexican history and the ideals of the Mexican Revolution. Artists such as Diego Rivera and Jose Clemente Orozco participated in this effort and later were privately commissioned to paint murals in the United States. Rivera, in particular, gained notoriety in the United States when, in 1933, he chose to include a portrait of Nikolai Lenin in a mural he had been invited to paint in the new Rockefeller Center in New York. John D. Rockefeller, Jr., who had commissioned the mural, ordered the portrait removed. Rivera refused, and the mural was subsequently destroyed. The Rivera debacle, according to Karal Ann Marling, forced painters, critics, and ordinary citizens "to weigh the principle of freedom of expression against the countervailing rights of a majority that did not share Rivera's communistic faith." Issues surrounding the mural artist's responsibility to the public versus his or her right to creative autonomy would surface frequently in discussions of government-sponsored mural painting in the 1930s and 1940s.

The government did not officially dictate the style of the murals it sponsored; however, it did encourage its artists to paint with the public in mind. An artist commissioned to paint a post office mural by the Treasury Section, in particular, was expected to spend time in the community for which the mural was destined and to solicit suggestions for themes from community members. Most of the government-sponsored murals were realistic in style. Several abstract murals were, however, sponsored by the FAP, including *Aviation: Evolution of Forms under Aerodynamic Limitations* by Arshile Gorky (1904-1948), which was installed at Newark Airport, in New Jersey, in 1937. A typical mural reflected the influence of American Scene painting, a development in American art that emerged in the late 1920s as a reaction against European modern art and gained impetus in the 1930s. The most influential American Scene painter was Thomas Hart Benton (1889-1975), who painted four sets of murals between 1930 and 1936—including *America Today* for the New School of Social Research in New York City, and *The Social History of the State of Missouri* for the State Capitol Building in Jefferson City—but never worked on any federally sponsored projects. American Scene paintings often depicted regional landscapes, local customs, and ordinary, hard-working people. This was exactly the sort of subject matter deemed appropriate by agency officials for government-sponsored murals. In the murals produced, the settings were both contemporary and historical, but the values reflected in either case were traditional. Across the country, murals depicting Abraham Lincoln, the frontiersman Daniel Boone, the poet Carl Sandburg, the explorers Lewis and Clark, and the social reformer Jane Addams were produced. Often the subject chosen had local significance, as in the *Jane Addams Memorial* painted by Mitchell Siporin (1910-1976) for the Illinois FAP. This was also true of *The Role of the Immigrant in the Industrial Development of America* by Edward Laning (1906-1981), done under the auspices of the FAP for the Dining Room of Ellis Island. Subjects related to the processing and delivery of mail, in the present and in the past, were frequently represented in post office murals: Philip Guston (1913-1980), for example, painted *Early Mail Service and the Construction of the Railroad* for the post office in Commerce, Georgia.

Although conservative opposition to the federal art projects had existed from the start, it increased throughout the 1930s, and by the start of World War II, the nation's priorities began to shift. By 1943 the federal government had essentially ended its patronage of art. In slightly less than a decade it had sponsored some 4000 murals, a large and diverse body of work that contributes to our enduring awareness of the value of public art.

—Laural Weintraub

FURTHER READING:

Baigell, Matthew. *The American Scene: American Painting of the 1930s.* New York, Praeger, 1974.

Bustard, Bruce I. *A New Deal for the Arts.* Washington, D.C., National Archives and Records Administration in association with University of Washington Press, Seattle, 1997.

Harris, Jonathan. *Federal Art and National Culture: The Politics of Identity in New Deal America.* New York, Cambridge University Press, 1995.

Marling, Karal Ann. *Wall-to-Wall America: A Cultural History of Post-Office Murals in the Great Depression.* Minneapolis, University of Minnesota Press, 1982.

McKinzie, Richard D. *The New Deal for Artists.* Princeton, New Jersey, Princeton University Press, 1973.

O'Connor, Francis V., editor. *Art for the Millions: Essays from the 1930s by Artists and Administrators of the WPA Federal Art Project.* Greenwich, Connecticut, New York Graphic Society, 1973.

Park, Marlene, and Gerald E. Markowitz. *Democratic Vistas: Post Offices and Public Art in the New Deal.* Philadelphia, Temple University Press, 1984.

World Cup

The World Cup of football, or soccer as the game is called in the United States, is the most popular sporting event in the world. For two years, teams representing virtually every country in the world compete for the right to play in the summer tournament, which has been staged in different countries every four years since 1930. In front of a worldwide television audience, the winners claim the title of the best soccer team in the world. Although the U.S. team reached the semifinals of the tournament in its inaugural year, the World Cup and soccer have had little impact on American popular culture.

In the late nineteenth century soccer became a leading spectator sport in many major countries. Rules of the game were systematized, clubs were formed, and leagues were established. In 1900, the Olympic Games introduced soccer as one of its sports. In 1904, Frenchman Jules Rimet assumed the presidency of the newly created world governing body of soccer, the Federation Internationale de Football Associations (FIFA), with the intention of creating an international soccer tournament. However, the competition did not materialize for more than twenty years because of conflict among national federations over whether to allow only amateur players to compete, as in the Olympic Games, or to accept professional players, who were becoming more prevalent in Europe. Finally, FIFA agreed to include professional players and to hold the tournament every four years, alternating with the Olympic Games.

Members of the U.S. National Team Alexi Lalas (right) and Cobi Jones (foreground) play for the World Cup.

FIFA selected Uruguay to host the first ever World Cup finals in 1930. Uruguay was chosen partly based on the country's dominance in capturing gold medals in the 1924 and 1928 Olympic Games and partly because no other viable candidate came forward. Only thirteen teams, including the USA, competed in the very first World Cup tournament. Belgium, France, Romania, and Yugoslavia were the only Europeans to enter because of the three weeks it took to get to Uruguay by boat. The hosts beat Argentina 4-2 in the final in Montevideo to become the first winners of the FIFA world championship.

Although the USA has never won the tournament, between 1930 and 1998 it qualified six times, and its best finish was the semi-final in 1930. Soccer has, however, always played a shadowy existence in American popular culture. In the late nineteenth century, immigrants from Europe formed soccer clubs and organized into local leagues, but as soccer flourished in Europe, U.S. political and business elites sought to create their own national identity in a land of immigrants by promoting American sports like baseball. Soccer received no state support and was played in few U.S. colleges or schools. As Americanization movements increased at the turn of the century, more pressure was put on foreigners to assimilate by adopting American games such as baseball or gridiron football. Thus, the U.S. teams that competed in the World Cups of 1930, 1934, and 1950 consisted largely of immigrant players.

After World War II, soccer became the most popular sport on the planet. The sport produced international stars of the caliber of the Brazilian Pele and great teams like Brazil—which won the World Cup four times between 1958 and 1994—Argentina, Germany, and Italy. FIFA increased the number of teams competing in the World Cup from its original thirteen participants in 1930 to sixteen in 1958 and to twenty-four in 1982. Because of Cold War nationalism and the increase in television coverage of U.S. sports, however, the American public remained uninterested in soccer. In the 1950s baseball was still supreme, American football began its rise to prominence, and in the 1960s ice hockey and basketball captured a national television audience. Soccer, with its continuous forty-five minutes of play, was less suitable for commercial television and held little interest for the major television networks. Between 1950 and 1990, the USA never qualified for the World Cup finals. In the 1970s the North American Soccer League operated, but this effort soon collapsed.

After the 1970s, however, the World Cup and soccer in general gained popularity with some sections of the American population. Relying more on skill than size or strength, soccer became a popular participatory sport amongst many American women and youth. In 1991 the USA women's team won the first ever FIFA Women's World Cup in China with a 2-1 win over Norway. At the same time, FIFA, commercial sponsors, and television networks saw America as the last major market to be conquered by soccer. As a result, FIFA selected the United States to stage the World Cup finals for the first time in 1994. The tournament was a great success as it gained national television coverage and was played in packed stadiums, including 95,000 for the final in Los Angeles between Italy and the eventual winners, Brazil. Subsequently, Major League Soccer was formed in America and began its first season in 1996. It remains to be seen whether this new soccer league can gain the attention of the American public and whether the United States can produce a team talented enough to mount a serious challenge for the World Cup.

—John F. Lyons

FURTHER READING:

Granville, Brian. *The History of the World Cup.* London, Faber and Faber, 1980.

Murray, Bill. *Football: A History of the World Game.* London, Scolar Press, 1994.

Robinson, John. *The FIFA World Cup 1930-1986.* Grimsby, Marksman, 1986.

World Series

Throughout much of the twentieth century, the annual World Series baseball championship has consistently set standards for well-staged national sporting scenarios, earning its reputation as the "Fall Classic." There have been heroes, villains, fools, and unknowns who have stolen the spotlight from "superstars."

The term "World Series" was first coined for a nine-game series between the Boston Pilgrims and the Pittsburgh Pirates, an informal outgrowth of a 1903 "peace treaty" signed between the two competing "major" baseball leagues, the 27-year-old National League (N.L.) and the upstart 2-year-old American League (A.L.). The A.L. champion Pilgrims (later called the Red Sox) won, five games to three, to surprisingly good crowds and gate receipts. Yet the following year, manager John McGraw and owner John Brush of the runaway National League champion New York Giants refused to face the repeating Boston club, stating publicly that such a meeting was beneath the quality of their team, which showcased future Hall of Fame pitcher, Christy Mathewson. A less publicized reason, however, was that they had objected to the growing popularity of the new A.L. franchise in New York City, the Highlanders (soon to be known as the Yankees).

Public and press outcry was so great against the Giants that Brush relented in 1905 and proposed a seven-game World Series as a mandatory annual event. The Giants won easily that year (with Mathewson pitching the first three of his still-standing record four Series shutouts), but would not prove to be as transcendent as Brush and McGraw believed, for they failed to win another Series until 1921. A worse fate awaited the Chicago Cubs, another early dominating N.L. team. After winning Series in 1907 and 1908, they never won again, and never even reached another Series after 1945. Starting in 1910, A.L. teams won eight out of the next ten Series, establishing an edge over the N.L. that they have yet to relinquish.

The World Series soon gained formal acceptance, with President Woodrow Wilson attending the second game of the 1915 Boston Red Sox-Philadelphia Phillies Series. The year 1915 also marked the Series debut of Boston pitcher George Herman "Babe" Ruth. Ruth set a Series record of 29 2/3 scoreless innings pitched, spanning Red Sox Series Championships in 1916 and 1918. The next year, after converting Ruth into an outfielder and watching him shatter all previous home run (and league attendance) records, Red Sox owner Harry Frazee sold the Babe to the New York Yankees for $100,000 and a $350,000 loan to cover one of his Broadway shows. For Boston fans, thus was cast the "Curse of the Bambino"—after winning four Series in the decade, the Red Sox, like the Cubs, never won a Series again. The Yankees would be another story.

In 1919, the World Series endured its worst scandal. Many players had long felt the owners were denying them their fair share of

Frankie Frisch of the New York Giants in action during the 1922 World Series.

club profits, and in no more obvious instance than in the World Series, where the triumphant owners were taking in record receipts and were rumored to have sold tickets to scalpers to make even more. The owners countered with rumors of their own, to the effect that players were being bribed to throw games by professional gamblers. Tensions had even precipitated a brief player's strike before the fifth game of the Red Sox-Cubs Series in 1918, but the worst was yet to come. Questionable betting patterns on the 1919 Series, in which the Cincinnati Reds upset the Chicago White Sox, prompted a grand jury investigation. In 1920 eight White Sox players were indicted for taking bribes. Among them was "Shoeless Joe" Jackson, the star who was confronted on the courtroom steps by a young fan with the soon-to-be-famous line, "Say it ain't so, Joe!" The eight players were ultimately acquitted in court, but as a result of what was now known as the "Black Sox" scandal, were subsequently banned from baseball for life in 1921. The rather draconian measure was enacted by the Baseball Commissioner, a post newly created by the owners in order to quickly restore baseball's image as well as maintain their own authority over the players.

The World Series not only bounced back in the 1920s, but came to form the centerpiece of a new era of popularity and stability for baseball. Key factors were the rise of the New York Yankees and the coinciding development of radio as a mass medium. John McGraw's Giants had returned to the World Series in 1921 to find they were in the first of 13 "Subway Series," facing their co-tenants at the Polo Grounds, the Yankees, who now had the biggest star in sports, Babe Ruth. In the first of their 29 Series appearances over the next 44 years, the Yankees bowed to McGraw's veteran club. McGraw's pitchers kept throwing low curve balls to Ruth in 1922 as well, allowing the Giants to sweep the first World Series to be broadcast by radio (the announcer was Grantland Rice) and the last Series triumph for their manager.

In 1923, Yankee Stadium was completed across the Harlem River in the Bronx, to be christened "the house that Ruth built" as all previous league attendance records were smashed. Ruth hit three homers in that year's rematch with the Giants, bringing the Yankees their first of 20 Series victories. By their 1927 sweep, which was also the first Series broadcast coast-to-coast, they had become America's team, setting a standard of excellence that McGraw and his Giants had never quite achieved, and they maintained a stranglehold on money and talent that most of the teams in the rest of the country could only admire from afar. All knew, however, that a victory over the Yankees in the Series would assure their place in the annals of baseball. Such was the case when grizzled pitcher Grover Cleveland Alexander braved the Yankees "Murderer's Row" to preserve a 1926 Series victory for the St. Louis Cardinals, a feat later to be immortalized on film (with Ronald Reagan playing Alexander).

On through the Great Depression and World War II, radio provided the yearly vignettes about players both rough-edged ("Pepper" Martin) and refined (Joe DiMaggio) that would cheer millions of Americans. However, one episode stood out particularly during this period. In the 1932 Cubs-Yankees series, the faltering Babe Ruth, brushing off ancestral slurs from the Cub bench and the hostile crowd at Chicago's Wrigley Field, paused to point to the centerfield bleachers. He soon followed with his 15th and last World Series home run. The Yankees went on to sweep the Series, but the "called shot" is what is still remembered and discussed today.

The climax of World War II brought with it the appearance of television and the breaking of the unofficial color line in baseball with Brooklyn Dodger star Jackie Robinson. The postwar years also marked the period of greatest dominance for the Yankees, who appeared in 15 of 18 Series through 1964, winning 10 (including 5 in a row between 1949 and 1953) mostly with manager Casey Stengel and new stars Mickey Mantle, Yogi Berra, and Whitey Ford. The phrase "wait 'til next year" was made famous by Brooklyn fans as their "Bums" lost five Series to the Yankees before winning in 1955, their only Series championship before they relocated with the Giants three years later to California. Also in 1955, the Most Valuable Player Award was initiated, won first by Johnny Podres of the Dodgers. Many call this baseball's and the Series' "golden era." The many highlights from this period include Willie Mays' incredible over-the-shoulder catch in his Giants' sweep of the Cleveland Indians in 1954, Yankee Don Larsen's perfect game over the Dodgers in 1956, and Pittsburgh Pirate Bill Mazeroski's Series-winning home run in 1960.

A revamping of baseball's amateur draft rules, the sharing of network broadcast revenues among all franchises, and internal turmoil eventually restored mortality to the Yankees, and after 1964 they failed to appear in the post-season for 12 years. Apart from the flamboyant, mustachioed "Swinging" Oakland A's of 1972 to 1974, no team would again win more than two Series in a row. The advent of free agency allowed the players to get even (financially) with the owners, and exploding player salaries and bidding wars from the mid 1970s onward added some of the roster unpredictability of the early days to the game. As television ratings came to be regarded as a measure of success, the Series encountered increasingly stiff competition from the National Basketball Association championship, football's Super Bowl, and even its own playoff system, created in 1969. Yet the Series has persevered, adding more classic moments for each generation: Carleton Fisk waving his homer fair in the sixth game of the 1975 Red Sox-Reds Series; Reggie Jackson hitting three homers on three pitches off three different pitchers in the sixth game of the 1977 Yankees-Dodgers Series, the New York crowd chanting "Reggie!"; The Curse of the Bambino willing New York Met Mookie Wilson's grounder through Red Sox first baseman Bill Buckner's legs in 1986; pinch-hitter Kirk Gibson homering off "closer" Dennis Eckersley to win the first game of the 1988 Dodgers-A's Series.

Continuing animosity between the owners and players' union in 1994 caused what even two World Wars could not: the cancellation of the World Series, as the result of a strike. Through the efforts of many, including President Bill Clinton, the two sides declared a truce and the season and Series were resumed in 1995. Well played (and watched) seven-game Series in 1996 and 1997 at least temporarily silenced the doomsayers predicting the coming end of the World Series as a "marquee event." For day-to-day sustained interest, capping a six-month-long season's endeavors, it is still hard to imagine any other event in sports ever surpassing the intensity of World Series competitive drama.

—C. Kenyon Silvey

FURTHER READING:

Schoor, Gene. *The History of the World Series.* New York, William Morrow & Co., 1990.

Devaney, John, and Burt Goldblatt. *The World Series: The Complete Pictorial History.* New York, Rand McNally & Co., 1972.

Boswell, Thomas. *How Life Imitates the World Series.* New York, Doubleday & Co., 1982.

Schiffer, Don, editor. *World Series Encyclopedia.* New York, Thomas Nelson & Sons, 1961.

World Trade Center

The two massive buildings of the World Trade Center are the tallest structures on Manhattan Island. The twin towers designed by Minoru Yamasaki and Associates in the early 1970s stand 1,350 feet, surpassing the Empire State Building by 100 feet, but the World Trade Center's faceless Modernist aesthetic lacks the character that has made its predecessor an enduring urban landmark. After a run of initial publicity, and a prominent appearance in the 1976 remake of the film *King Kong,* the World Trade Center began to fade into the urban fabric, failing to become the symbol of New York City that its developers had hoped. It has, however, become an icon of corporate America to some discontented groups. In February, 1993, one of the towers was bombed by Islamic terrorists attempting to strike a blow at the heart of American society. Amazingly, the building survived with no structural damage.

—Dale Allen Gyure

FURTHER READING:

Douglas, George H. *Skyscrapers: A Social History of the Very Tall Building in America.* Jefferson, North Carolina, and London, McFarland & Company, Inc., 1996.

Goldberger, Paul. *The Skyscraper.* New York, Alfred A. Knopf, 1992.

World War I

The Great War (World War I), fought between 1914 and 1918, was one of the most decisive events of the twentieth century. The political and economic catastrophes in its wake led to another, even greater conflict from 1939 to 1945, leading some historians to view the two World Wars as aspects of the same struggle, separated by an uneasy truce in the 1920s and 1930s. Some of the ethnic and national-identity conflicts left unresolved at the Versailles peace conference of 1919 are still sources of tension and open hostility in the Balkans. It was in that fractious region of eastern Europe that World War I began when Serbian nationalists assassinated the heir to the throne of Austria-Hungary in the city of Sarajevo. As a total war, World War I required the unlimited commitment of all the resources of each warring society. Governments were forced to allocate human and natural resources, set economic priorities, and take measures to ensure the full cooperation of their citizens. Some societies cracked under the pressure. Monarchies collapsed in Russia, Germany, and Austria-Hungary. Even the victors, especially France and Belgium, were deeply scarred. The human sacrifices were appalling; the economic cost was overwhelming. World War I marked the decisive end of the old order in Europe, which, except for the Crimean War and the Franco-Prussian War and a few minor skirmishes, seemed to have weathered a century of relative peace after the Napoleonic wars that had ended exactly 100 years earlier.

The outbreak of the war had at first been greeted with jingoistic enthusiasm. It was not until the combatants experienced a tremendous loss of life in the trenches on the western front that this view was shattered. By the end of the war, pessimism and disillusion were endemic. For many in the West, the war denied the notion of progress. The same science and technology that had dazzled the nineteenth

Soldiers in a foxhole during World War I.

century with advances in medicine, communication, and transportation had produced poison gas, machine guns, and terror weapons. The Great War's legacy would include a deep pessimism, expressed in many forms, including antiwar literature that would be translated to the screen in the form of popular film.

World War I began when Serbian nationalists assassinated Archduke Francis Ferdinand, the heir to the throne of Austria-Hungary. Austria's attack upon Serbia on July 28 led to war with her protector, Russia. Prewar alliances assured that Germany would declare war on Russia. When the French announced their intention to honor their commitments to Russia, Germany declared war on France. As the German armies passed through neutral Belgium to get at France, Britain declared war on Germany. Within a week of Austria's attack upon Serbia, the other four great European powers had gone to war over issues that few truly understood, or indeed, cared about. They seemed to have been swept along by their alliances in an inevitable cascade of falling dominos over which humans had little control.

On the Western front, the German armies smashed through Belgium and into France, where they were halted 25 miles north of Paris. Both armies tried to get around the other in a ''race to the sea.''

When they failed, the exhausted armies dug defensive positions. Two lines of trenches, six to eight feet deep, zigzagged across northern France, from the Swiss border to the English Channel. The distance between the Allied trenches and those of the Germans depended upon the terrain, and ranged from 150 yards in Flanders to 500 yards at Cambrai. The great irony of warfare in the industrial age was that modern weapons forced the armies to live below ground and use periscopes to observe the other side. Steps in the sides of the trenches were used as platforms for firing at the enemy. The trench soldiers slept in sleeping holes dug into the sides of the trenches, where they suffered from rain, cold, poor sanitary facilities, lice, flies, trench foot, and a constant stench. Rats as big as small dogs fed on the dead. Of the casualties on the Western front, 50 percent were directly attributable to conditions in the trenches.

In 1916, the major efforts to break the stalemate came at Verdun, and on the Somme river. The Germans decided to attack Verdun, an historic city they knew the French would defend at all costs. The two sides fired more than 40 million artillery shells into a narrow front of less than 10 miles. When the firing ceased after 302 days, each side had suffered half a million casualties, with more than one hundred thousand dead. To relieve Verdun, the British opened an offensive on the Somme. An artillery bombardment of a million and a half shells was supposed to decimate the German positions. When the British army went "over the top" on July 1, however, they were cut down by German machine guns. On the first day of battle on the Somme, the British suffered 60,000 casualties, including 20,000 dead. After gaining five miles of territory, at the cost of 420,000 casualties, the British halted the offensive on November 13.

When the war began, the common assumption was that it would be over within six months. In the prewar years, many seemingly perceptive writers had written that modern economies were too integrated to accept a long war. There was also a general ignorance about what war in the industrial age would be like. There had not been a general European war since the defeat of Napoleon at Waterloo in 1815. Bourgeois middle class life seemed boring and lacking in adventure. When World War I began, the armies marched to war with enthusiastic support. Intellectuals signed manifestos supporting the war. Sigmund Freud offered "all his libido to Austria-Hungary." Young men literally raced to the recruiting centers to sign up so they could be sure of getting into combat before the war was over. Fired by patriotism, and martial values of honor and glory, they were the first to be mowed down. In "From 1914," Rupert Brooke, the English poet, expressed his belief that his death in battle would sanctify a "foreign field" as "for ever England." The most popular poem of the war, John McCrae's "In Flanders Fields" appeared anonymously in *Punch* in December 1915. The poem may describe how "the poppies blow, Between the crosses, row on row," but as Paul Fussell writes, the poem ends with "recruiting-poster rhetoric" demanding that others pick up the torch and not "break faith with us who die." These viewpoints changed with the reality of mass death and stalemate. Fussell observes that Edmund Blunden, Robert Graves, and Siegfried Sassoon came to an image of the war as lasting forever. Trench warfare, in which neither side could gain the advantage, regardless of their courage, honor, and valor, suggested that humans had lost control of their history. Indeed, what did courage, honor and valor have to do with modern war? In 1924, the German expressionist painter Otto Dix wrote thus of his trench experiences: "Lice, rats, barbed wire, fleas, shells, bombs, underground caves, corpses, blood, liquor, mice, cats, artillery, filth, bullets, mortars, fire, steel; that is what war is. It is the work of the devil."

To raise the large armies needed to continue the struggle, governments turned to the use of posters. The British Parliamentary Recruitment Committee commissioned a poster featuring Lord Kitchener's head and finger pointing at the viewer. The caption read "Your Country Wants You." As enlistments declined, the emphasis shifted to shaming those healthy young men still in Britain. The message was blunt in the poster "Women of Britain say, GO." A more subtle, but perhaps as effective, message was expressed in the British poster showing a little girl sitting on her father's knee, with an open book in her lap. The writing at the bottom of the poster asked the question, "Daddy, what did You do in the Great War?" At the father's feet was a little boy playing with a toy army and about to place a new soldier in the ranks. The Committee would eventually commission 100 different posters, some of which were published in lots of 40,000. It is estimated that these posters generated one-quarter of all British enlistments. While most conscientious objectors accepted noncombatant alternatives, a hard core of 1500 refused to accept any position that indirectly supported the war. They were sent to prison where they suffered brutal treatment—70 of them died there. Poster art certainly contributed to this view that in time of war, a man's place was in uniform.

The failure of the armies to achieve success led each side to seek new allies, open new fronts, resort to new military technologies, and engage in new forms of warfare. In 1915, Italy joined the Allies, and new fronts against the Austrians were opened in the Swiss Alps and on the Izonzo River. In the same year, the British opened a new front at Gallipoli, but, after nearly a year of being pinned down on the beaches by Turkish guns, were forced to withdraw. The Germans introduced gas warfare in 1915; the British introduced the tank in 1916. The romantic nature of air combat yielded to a more deadly form as machine guns were added to fighter aircraft. Germans bombed British cities; the British bombed German cities. The British mined German harbors and blockaded German ports; Germany responded with unrestricted submarine warfare. In the face of American protests, following the sinking of the *Lusitania,* the Germans suspended their attacks in 1915.

In Germany, general rationing went into effect in 1916. The winter of 1916-1917, known as the "turnip winter," was particularly difficult. Bread riots, wage strikes, and a burgeoning black market that separated rich and poor threatened support for the war. There were also demands for political reform as a condition for continued support. In January 1917, the German government made the fateful decision to return to unrestricted submarine warfare with the full knowledge this could lead to war with the United States. The German decision was predicated upon the belief that Britain could be starved out of the war before the United States could train a large army and send it to Europe.

Up to this point, the United States had been officially neutral during the war, keeping with its long tradition of avoiding "foreign entanglements." By 1917, however, its sympathies and economic interests had shifted to the allied side. British propaganda had been highly effective in accusing Germans of atrocities in Belgium. President Woodrow Wilson resisted going to war because he feared what it would do to the progressive reforms of his administration, and that war would release ugly patriotic excesses that would be difficult to control. His hand was forced by the sinking of American merchant ships and the Zimmerman telegram suggesting that in return for a successful alliance, Germany would aid Mexico in its reacquisition of Arizona, Texas, and New Mexico. Finally, Congress declared war on Germany on April 6, 1917, a move that Wilson promised would "make the world safe for democracy."

To raise a mighty army to fight in Europe, the American government was forced to resort to locally supervised conscription. Unfortunately, these local boards often lacked objectivity. Not only was preference on exemptions given to family and friends, but African Americans were drafted in disproportionate numbers, and conscientious objectors without religious affiliations were either drafted or sent to prison. The government sought to encourage enlistments and discourage draft resisters by using British posters as a model. The Kitchener poster was deemed to be so effective that Americans substituted Uncle Sam's head, and included the same caption "I Want You." The power of shame was also evident in the American poster that featured a young women dressed in sailor's uniform with the caption, "Gee, I Wish I Were a Man, I'd Join the Navy."

By 1917, all of the major belligerents had begun to regulate their industries and agriculture, borrow money to finance the war, ration food, and employ women in areas of the economy where they had not before worked. They also shaped consent for their policies and discouraged dissent. The War Industries Board, headed by Bernard Baruch, regulated American industries and set priorities. The Fuel

Administration increased coal production by one-third and campaigned for heatless Mondays and gasless Sundays. The American Food Administration's appeal for food conservation included wheatless Mondays and Wednesdays, meatless Tuesdays, and porkless Thursdays and Saturdays. This voluntary conservation worked to such an extent that America was able to feed her armies, and increase food exports to allies by one third without having to resort to rationing. Before radio and television, with film still in its infancy, the poster was a highly effective method of generating support. Posters were used to inspire industrial effort, urge citizens to conserve needed materials, and in general, to support the war effort. Posters were also used extensively to gain support for the purchase of war bonds. While all the nations did this, none matched the American effort in this regard. For the third Liberty Loan drive, nine million posters were produced.

While voluntary sacrifices and poster art made everyone feel they were part of the war effort, they tended to generate emotional patriotic fervor. In America, this reached heights of absurdity. High schools stopped teaching German, frankfurters became hot dogs, and orchestras stopped playing Brahms, Bach, and Beethoven. None of this was humorous to German Americans, who were attacked verbally and physically. These attacks seemed to have the support of the American government. The Committee of Public Information, directed by George Creel, not only kept the public informed about war news through films and pamphlets, but sent out 75,000 speakers to churches, schools, and movie theatres, where they lectured on war aims and German atrocities. The Post Office denied mail delivery to "radical," "socialist," and foreign language newspapers and periodicals. The May 1918 Sedition Act made it a crime to speak or publish anything disloyal. This could be and was used against those questioning American participation in the war, the nation's war aims, and how it managed the war effort. Robert Goldstein, a Hollywood producer, was sentenced to 10 years in prison because his film *The Spirit of '76* was not supportive of our British ally. The film, set in the period of the American Revolution, had shown British soldiers bayoneting civilians. Particularly vulnerable were Socialists such as Eugene Debs, who was sentenced to 10 years, and leaders of the International Workers of the World (I.W.W.), who were given 20-year sentences. Their offenses stemmed more from their opposition to capitalism than to the war itself. The U.S. Justice Department brought charges of opposition to the war against 2200 people, of whom 1055 were convicted.

World War I brought forth great songs that would be sung long after the war was over. Many of these originated in London music halls, French cabarets, and on Broadway. Some of America's greatest songwriters, Jerome Kern, Irving Berlin, George M. Cohan, and George Gershwin, participated in this creative explosion. The most famous of these songs were the French "Madelon"; the British "Your King and Country Want You," "There's a Long, Long, Trail," "Roses of Picardy," and "It's a Long Way to Tipperary"; and the American "Pack Up Your Troubles in an Old Kit Bag," "Over There," "Keep the Home Fires Burning," "Goodbye Broadway, Hello France," "Mademoiselle from Armentieres," and "How Ya Gonna Keep 'em Down on the Farm?" These songs were sung at bond rallies, but were also taught to the troops by official army song leaders. Most of the songs were comic, sentimental, and innocent. They were offered as a means to lift morale and provide a human respite for soldiers in an inhumane existence. Only the unofficial French song, "La Chanson de Craonne," which declared soldiers

doomed and victims of a wretched war, reflected the reality of the front.

What was most remarkable about the conflict until the end of 1916 was the willingness of European soldiers and civilians to accept the hardships the war demanded. Millions of soldiers had left home to face the horrors of modern war and endure life in the trenches of the Western front. This support collapsed in 1917. The German resumption of unrestricted submarine warfare reflected this change of mood. Most significant were the riots and insurrection in Petrograd, Russia which led directly to the abdication of the Romanovs in March 1917. War weariness, the failure of Russian offensives in the summer of 1917, and the desertion of two million soldiers finally led to the October Bolshevik revolution and Russia's withdrawal from the war. In 1917, whole units of the French army refused to go to the front; those that did went chanting "ba ba ba"—the bleating of sheep being led to the slaughter. The British army's morale was close to the breaking point after the 1917 Flanders offensive resulted in 400,000 casualties for five captured miles of mud in which thousands of soldiers had literally drowned. At Caporetto, the Italian army reached its breaking point, and over 275,000 Italian soldiers surrendered in a single day.

British and French generals desperately wanted American soldiers who would be merged into their own units. Wilson and his commander John Pershing were totally opposed to this. They wanted the United States to field her own independent army, with its own commanders, support forces, and separate sector of operations. Both recognized that unless a U.S. army fought as an independent entity, the United States would not be able to shape the peace. The United States would fight neither for the imperialistic aims of the great powers, nor to restore the balance of power, but "to make the world safe for democracy" by advocating self-determination, democratic government, the abolition of war, freedom of the seas, and an international organization to protect the peace. These lofty ideals were expressed in January 1918 in Wilson's Fourteen Points speech.

With Russia out of the war, Germany transferred its troops from the eastern front to the western front, and launched its great offensive in the spring of 1918. As in 1914, the Germans were halted on the Marne river. American units put into battle at key places in the Allied lines fought well under French overall command. This time, the German army did not settle into a trench line, but was forced into a continuous retreat under the pressure of Allied armies. While the Germans were exhausted from four years of war, fresh American soldiers were arriving at the rate of 300,000 per month, and fighting as an independent army at Saint Mihiel and in the Argonne Forest. In other sectors, the Central Powers collapsed. Turkey and Bulgaria were out of the war by October 1918. Austria-Hungary disintegrated, as the Hungarians sought a separate peace, and Slavs sought their own nations. Within Germany, there were demonstrations at military bases, and in Berlin. When the Kaiser abdicated, the Germans asked for a peace based upon what they had previously scorned, the Fourteen Points. The Germans signed the armistice, and at 11:00 a.m. on November 11, 1918, the guns went silent.

Four years of war had resulted in nine million deaths, one million of which were civilian. Many more millions of soldiers who lived through the war were crippled mentally or physically. So many soldiers were facially disfigured that a new branch of medicine, plastic surgery, was developed. A great influenza pandemic resulted in thousands of civilian deaths in Europe and the United States. A deep pessimism settled over Europe. Arnold Toynbee declared that the news from the front led him to believe that Western Civilization was following the same pattern that Classical Civilization had followed in its breakdown. His 12-volume *A Study of History* would argue that World War I was to the West what the Punic Wars had been to the ancient world. Oswald Spengler's *Decline of the West* was even more pessimistic. W. B. Yeats's 1919 ''Second Coming'' saw anarchy ''loosed upon the World'' and the coming of another Dark Age. T. S. Eliot's ''The Waste Land'' expressed the despair and hopelessness felt by many. Sigmund Freud admitted in *Civilization and Its Discontents* that it was the events of the war that led him to seek a second basic force at the core of human nature: the death instinct, in constant struggle against the life instinct. Vera Britton's autobiographical *Testament of Youth* described the shattering impact of the war on her personal life. This pessimism shared the same viewpoint that was expressed by the war poets such as Siegfried Sassoon and Wilfred Owen, who wrote their poetry and letters while at the front. David Kennedy has observed that he had not found this pessimism amongst American soldiers. Whereas the pessimism of the European writers came from the destructive impact of the war itself, American disillusionment came from the belief that America's entrance into the war had failed to create the new world of Wilson's vision. In addition, progressivism and protection of individual rights at home seemed to have been reversed, and the nation retreated into isolationism rather than follow Wilson's lead into the new League of Nations.

While the European and American reactions to the war were different, there is one area of popular culture where they seem to have coalesced. Within a decade of the war, outstanding antiwar books and films were written and produced both in Europe and the United States. The German film *Westfront 1918* (1930) depicted French and German soldiers dying without victory. Jean Renoir's *Grand Illusion* (1937) was another antiwar attack upon the European aristocracy that brought forth the horrors of World War I. Ludwig Renn wrote a critically acclaimed novel, *Krieg (War)*, that was an impressive piece of literature but never achieved the popularity of Erich Maria Remarque's antiwar novel *All Quiet on the Western Front* (1929), which described the experiences of German youth who had gone to war as enthusiastic soldiers. The film by the same title, released in 1930, was so relentlessly antiwar that Remarque had to leave Germany. In 1930, the film received an Academy Award for best picture. Another antiwar book made into a film was Ernest Hemingway's *A Farewell to Arms* (1932), which describes the fate of an American ambulance driver who deserts the madness of the Italian retreat at Caporetto. Two of the most powerful antiwar films done in the post-World War II period also dealt with specific events of World War I. Stanley Kubrick's *Paths of Glory* (1957) was based upon the mutinies in the French army. The film starred Kirk Douglas, but it is Adolph Menjou's depiction of a French general demanding the random selection and execution of three soldiers to cover his own failures that is the picture's most powerful image. Finally, Paramount's film *Gallipoli* (1981), appropriately starring the Australian actor Mel Gibson, faithfully describes what happened to those idealistic young Australian soldiers who went to war with enthusiasm and in search of adventure, only to be slaughtered like so many of their comrades on other fronts.

—Thomas W. Judd

FURTHER READING:

Chambers, John. *To Raise an Army: The Draft Comes to Modern America.* New York, The Free Press, 1987.

Ellis, John. *Eye-Deep in Hell: Trench Warfare in World War I.* Baltimore, Johns Hopkins Press, 1976.

Fussell, Paul. *The Great War and Modern Memory.* New York, Oxford University Press, 1975.

Gilbert, Martin. *The First World War: A Complete History.* New York, Henry Holt, 1994.

Goldman, Dorothy. *Woman Writers and the Great War.* New York, Twayne Publishers, 1995.

Hardach, Gerd. *The First World War, 1914-1918.* Berkeley, University of California Press, 1977.

Harries, Meiron, and Susie Harries. *The Last Days of Innocence: America At War, 1917-1918.* New York, Random House, 1997.

Kennedy, David. *Over Here: The First World War and American Society.* New York, Oxford University Press, 1980.

Lyons, Michael. *World War I: A Short History.* Englewood Cliffs, New Jersey, Prentice Hall, 1994.

Rochester, Stuart I. *American Liberal Disillusionment in the Wake of World War I.* University Park, Pennsylvania, Pennsylvania State University, 1977.

Roth, Jack J. *World War I: A Turning Point.* New York, Alfred A. Knopf, 1967.

Silkin, Jon, editor. *First World War Poetry.* London, Penguin Books, 1979.

Stromberg, Roland. *Redemption by War: The Intellectuals and 1914.* Lawrence, Kansas, Regents Press, 1982.

Timmers, Margaret. *The Power of the Poster.* London, V & A Publications, 1998.

Trask, David. *The AEF & Coalition Warmaking, 1917-1918.* Lawrence, Kansas, University of Kansas Press, 1993.

Winter, Jay, and Blaine Baggett. *The Great War and the Shaping of the 20th Century.* London, Penguin Books, 1996.

World War II

Despite the Japanese invasion of China in 1937, most historians date the start of the Second World War as September 1, 1939, the day that German forces attacked Poland. Although Polish resistance was quickly overcome, treaty obligations brought Britain and France into the fray, and the war for Europe began in earnest.

Strong isolationist sentiments among much of its populace kept the United States out of the conflict until the Japanese bombed American naval forces anchored at Pearl Harbor in Hawaii. The surprise attack, which inflicted devastating losses on the U.S. fleet, occurred on December 7, 1941. The next day, President Franklin Roosevelt asked for, and received, a Senate declaration of war on Japan. Two days later, Germany and Italy, which were bound to Japan

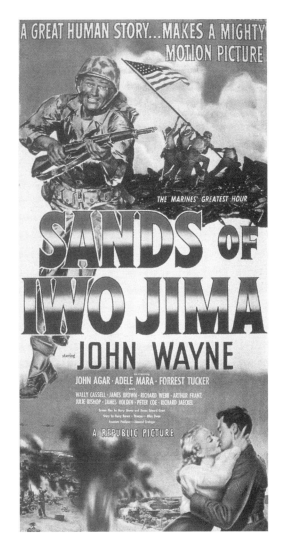

Poster from the 1949 WWII film epic *Sands of Iwo Jima*.

Bunny joined the war effort, poking fun at the Nazis in *Confessions of a Nutsy Spy*. Bugs' cartoon colleague at Warner Brothers, Daffy Duck, also mocked the Third Reich in *Daffy the Commando.* Superman, America's favorite comic book hero, took to the screen to thwart evil Japanese agents in *The Japateurs,* while another cartoon, *Tokyo Jokie-o,* made sport of the Japanese war effort by using blatantly racist stereotypes.

Then came the feature film. It might be a documentary, perhaps one of Frank Capra's *Why We Fight* series (1942-45). Capra, already famous as a director, had been drafted out of Hollywood, put in a major's uniform, and given the task of making films for new military recruits that would motivate them to fight in a war that many understood dimly, if at all. Relying mostly on seized Axis propaganda footage, Capra put together seven inspirational films covering different aspects of the global conflict. After a screening of the first, *Prelude to War,* President Roosevelt declared, ''Every man, woman and child in America must see this film!'' All seven were eventually shown in theatres, as well as in the boot camps for which they had originally been intended.

Other notable Hollywood directors also made documentary films in support of the war effort. William Wyler directed *Memphis Belle,* (1943) the saga of the last combat mission flown by an American bomber crew over Europe; John Huston helmed *The Battle of San Pietro* (1945), focusing on the bloody assault by American troops to capture an Italian town from the Germans; and John Ford lent his talents to *The Battle of Midway* (1942), which chronicled the first major American naval victory over the Japanese.

But most films playing in neighborhood theatres during the war told fictional stories, although about one-third of these dealt with the war in one way or another. There were combat films, often based on actual battles fought earlier in the war. The first of these was *Wake Island* (1942), and it would be followed by many others, including *Flying Tigers* (1942), *Bataan* (1943), *Destination Tokyo* (1943),

in a mutual-defense treaty, declared war on the United States. The fighting continued until August, 1945, when Japan (the last Axis belligerent left) surrendered, following the destruction of two Japanese cities by American atomic bombs.

The war affected every aspect of American life, including popular culture in all its forms. Some of this influence was the result of deliberate government propaganda, but much of it was simply the nation's response to the exigencies of life in wartime.

American moviegoers during the war were frequently exposed to a triple dose of war-related messages. First, a newsreel would showcase stories of recent developments in the theatres of combat, along with a healthy dose of pleasant feature stories unrelated to the conflict. An average newsreel ran about ten minutes, and was changed twice each week. Although the typical moviegoer might not know it, wartime newsreels were subject to indirect government censorship (since all film footage from overseas passed first through the government's hands), as well as ''guidance'' as to content from the Office of War Information, the government's propaganda bureau.

The newsreel was usually followed by one or more animated cartoons. Although many of the wartime versions were as innocuous as ever, quite a few leavened their laughs with propaganda. Bugs

The Iwo Jima Monument.

Gung Ho! (1943), *Thirty Seconds over Tokyo* (1944), and *Objective Burma!* (1945).

Other films offered intrigue, focusing on the shadowy war of spies, assassins, and double agents. These included *Sherlock Holmes and the Voice of Terror* (1942), *Nazi Agent* (1942), *Saboteur* (1942), and *They Came to Blow Up America* (1943). Still other productions glorified the heroic struggle of the citizens of occupied countries who fought against their Axis oppressors; *Hangmen Also Die* (1943), *Till We Meet Again* (1944), and *The Seventh Cross* (1944) are representative of the genre.

But fully two-thirds of Hollywood films released during the war never mentioned the conflict at all. If such films had a subtext, it was that America was a place worth fighting for—a message conveyed subtly in such sentimental films as *Going My Way* (1943), *Meet Me in St. Louis* (1944), *Since You Went Away* (1942), and *An American Romance* (1943).

Film was certainly not the only communications medium to portray the war. It was prominent in all media—including posters, which could be found everywhere. Prominent artists and illustrators such as James Montgomery Flagg, Ben Shahn, Everett Henry, Stevan Dohanos, and John Atherton all created posters to encourage American citizens' support of the war effort. Posters called men to military service, urged women to can food at home and consider getting a "war job," and extolled everyone to hate the nation's ruthless, bestial foes, the Axis powers. Further, although Axis espionage never amounted to a serious threat to the United States, homefront Americans were nonetheless given a sense that they were helping to safeguard the nation when posters warned them not to discuss war information in public. The most famous of these admonitions appeared in a poster published by the Seagram Distillery Company. Below an illustration of a half-submerged freighter was the slogan "Loose lips might sink ships!" Even Norman Rockwell lent his distinctive vision of Americana to the war effort, with a series of four illustrations collectively entitled "The Four Freedoms."

Radio was the principal entertainment medium for Americans during World War II. Although many no doubt listened to the radio to escape from the war and its cares, it was difficult to avoid the conflict for very long. President Roosevelt continued to give his "fireside chats," the tradition of informal-sounding speeches that he had begun during the 1930s. But, whereas the early addresses usually concerned the Depression and FDR's efforts to alleviate it, the wartime broadcasts reflected the nation's principal preoccupation, which was the war itself. Roosevelt used these speeches to reassure his audience that the war was going well and that eventual victory was assured—and history shows that he did so even early in the war, when such optimism was not shared by his advisors or justified by the military situation.

The government also used radio for propaganda in less obvious ways. William B. Lewis, head of the Office of War Information's Domestic Radio Division, understood that people wanted entertainment from their radios, not heavy-handed propaganda. Lewis, a former vice president of CBS, worked out a rotation system (called the Network Allocation Plan) wherein the existing radio dramas and comedies would voluntarily take turns integrating government propaganda into their scripts, thus guaranteeing a large audience for OWI's messages while preserving radio's money-making programs. As a result, the popular comedy *Fibber McGee and Molly* justified the new gas rationing program by letting the character of Fibber (already established as a buffoon) complain about it, only to be set straight through the humor of the other characters. On another evening, *The*

Jack Benny Show featured America's most lovable tightwad finally getting rid of his ancient automobile—by donating it to the War Salvage Drive. Benny's character had to be persuaded of the need for such a contribution, but then declared afterwards that it had been the right thing to do, indirectly encouraging his listeners to do likewise.

Radio also brought the news into American homes, and much of that information came courtesy of a new kind of reporter: the on-air correspondent who would broadcast live from the site of the story he was covering. Some World War II radio correspondents, like William L. Shirer, Charles Collingwood, and Eric Severeid, would earn impressive reputations as journalists, but the dean of them all was Edward R. Murrow. Whether reporting from a London rooftop in the middle of an air raid or broadcasting a description of the Buchenwald concentration camp on the day it was liberated by the Allies, Murrow combined superb journalistic skills with a sonorous voice and a gift for near-poetic language to produce a series of radio programs that are still considered classics.

Music has always been one of the mainstays of radio, and many of the songs that Americans listened to during the war were reflections of the era. The rousing "We Did It Before (And We Can Do It Again)" was penned by Charles Tobias and Cliff Friend immediately following the Japanese bombing of Pearl Harbor. It compared the current struggle with World War One, and predicted the same outcome for the Allies. Irving Berlin's tune "Any Bonds Today?" was used by the government in a series of bond drives designed to raise money for the war effort. "I'll Walk Alone" by Sammy Cahn and Jule Styne was a promise to every serviceman stationed overseas that his wife or girlfriend would still be waiting when he returned home. Louis Jordan, Antonio Casey, and Collenane Clark composed "Ration Blues" in 1943 as a good-natured lament over war-related shortages of material goods. One of the most popular patriotic songs of the war was Kate Smith's rendering of "God Bless America." Although written by Irving Berlin near the end of World War One, the song went unrecorded and forgotten until the next war. It became Smith's trademark, and she sang it frequently, especially at a series of hugely successful war bond rallies.

The "funnies" (broadly defined) also pitched in to help the war effort. Many cartoons, comic books, and newspaper comic strips had their characters participating in the conflict. Bill Mauldin was the most famous of the war's cartoonists, although much of his work was initially drawn and published for a military audience (principally in *Yank*, the armed forces newspaper). Mauldin's characters Willie and Joe, who could find grim humor in being wet, filthy, tired, and scared, constituted a gritty and realistic portrayal of the average front-line "grunt's" existence. Virgil Partch II, who signed his cartoons "VIP," was a master of the grotesque and the absurd, and his work showed that the war contained no shortage of either one.

Comic books were an immensely popular entertainment medium in America during the 1940s. By the war's end, more than 20 million comics were sold every month. During the war years, dozens of comic book characters participated in the struggle against fascism and militarism. A year before Pearl Harbor, the team of Joe Simon and Jack Kirby created Captain America, the first comic book superhero to fight the Nazis. Another Captain, Midnight by name, began his career as the hero of a radio drama in the 1930s, but branched out into comic books after America entered the war. Alan Armstrong, better known as Spy Smasher, foiled Axis plots both at home and abroad. Wonder Woman, virtually the only female superhero of the era, was an Amazon warrior princess who possessed magic bracelets and a hatred of evil. Superman, the first popular comic superhero, spent the war at home in America, but he found no shortage of Axis villains to defeat with his super powers.

The heroes of newspaper comic strips were also active in the war. According to a study conducted by the Office of War Information, more than fifty regularly appearing strips were using the war as part of their story lines. The first to ''join up'' was Joe Palooka, a clean-cut professional boxer who was shown enlisting in the army in 1940. Milton Caniff's character Terry Lee (of *Terry and the Pirates*) first appeared in 1933 but joined the Army after Pearl Harbor and spent the war flying missions against the Japanese. Little Orphan Annie's contributions to the war effort were mostly nonviolent, although she did on one occasion help to blow up a German submarine. Other popular comic strip characters, such as Captain Easy, Smilin' Jack, Tillie the Toiler, and Snuffy Smith also did their part to make the world again safe for democracy.

Although the fighting ended in August, 1945, the war did not disappear from American popular culture. Although many non-fiction books about the war had sold well while the conflict raged, there seemed to be little market for novels about it (an exception was John Hershey's *A Bell for Adano,* the 1944 story of U.S. soldiers occupying a Sicilian town, which won the 1945 Pulitzer Prize). But the war's end signaled the beginning of a flood of literary efforts, several of which proved to be of enduring significance.

In 1948, Norman Mailer published *The Naked and the Dead,* which uses the motif of an American effort to take a Japanese-held Pacific island to discuss issues such as fascism, personal freedom, and individual vs. group responsibility. The same year saw the release of Irwin Shaw's *The Young Lions,* a sweeping saga that examines the lives of three soldiers (two American and one German) against the backdrop of the European war's most momentous events.

Leon Uris's *Battle Cry* is one of the best novels about the U.S. Marines in the Pacific war. It follows a group of young men through basic training and into combat at Guadalcanal and, later, Tarawa. Although James Jones's celebrated novel *From Here to Eternity* (1951) is not really a war story (the Japanese attack on Pearl Harbor, where the novel is set, provides the climax), his next, *The Thin Red Line* (1962) surely is. The grimly realistic story of a group of Marines fighting to take Guadalcanal from the Japanese, the novel emphasizes the ugly, capricious and, ultimately pointless nature of war. The absurdity of war is also the theme of Joseph Heller's 1961 classic *Catch-22.* The protagonist, Yossarian, is an Army Air Force bombardier based in Italy who knows that his chances of survival decrease with every mission he flies. There is a limit on the number of missions that a bomber crew can be sent on, but Yossarian's superiors keep raising the number. This darkly comic novel centers on Yossarian's efforts to stay alive in the midst of a system that seems determined to kill him.

Absurdity edges into surrealism in Kurt Vonnegut's *Slaughterhouse-Five* (1969), which mixes realism, science fiction, black comedy, and existentialism in the story of Billy Pilgrim, a man who ''comes unstuck in time.'' He starts experiencing his life out of chronological sequence, and some of these temporal glitches take him back to his World War II experience, when, as a prisoner of the Germans, he experienced the terrible Allied firebombing of Dresden.

Comic book publishers seemed to be almost as interested in the war after it was over as they had been while the struggle was in progress. Several long-running comic series, most of which had begun during the war, outlasted the conflict and continued to provide drama and adventure through the perspective of fictional American heroes. The most popular of these included *Gunner and Sarge*

(Marines fighting in the Pacific), *The Haunted Tank* (commanded by Lt. Jeb Stuart and protected by the ghost of the original Jeb Stuart of Confederate cavalry fame), and the most famous of all, Sgt. Rock of Easy Company. Unlike most of his fellow comic warriors, Rock was not created until 1959, when he made his first appearance in a DC comic entitled *Our Army at War.* Although most of the other World War II comics faded away in the 1960s, Sgt. Rock and his men marched on until 1988.

Hollywood's interest in portraying World War II also continued long after the end of the fighting; indeed no other war in history has been the subject of as many films. The postwar movies dealing with the conflict can be discussed in terms of three broad categories: combat films, historic recreations, and comedies.

Combat films constituted a popular genre during the war itself, and they continued to be the most common type of war film made after 1945. One of the first was the John Wayne film *Sands of Iwo Jima* (1949), which deftly integrated documentary footage of the actual landing with the recreated elements filmed later. Marines are also the focus of 1955's *Battle Cry,* based on the popular novel. Norman Mailer's book *The Naked and the Dead* was filmed in 1958, but it disappointed critics by leaving out most of the philosophical issues raised by the novel. *The Guns of Navarone* (1961), based on Alistair McLean's novel, chronicles a commando raid to disable German cannons that control a strait vital to the Allies. *The Dirty Dozen* (1967) focuses on the efforts of a tough Army Major (Lee Marvin) as he struggles to turn a squad of condemned U.S. prisoners into a commando unit for a secret mission on the eve of D-Day. *Castle Keep* (1969) is the surreal story of a group of Army misfits relegated to duty in a Belgian castle that suddenly assumes strategic importance in the Battle of the Bulge. Samuel Fuller's *The Big Red One* (1979) follows a squad of soldiers of the First Infantry Division as they fight their way across Europe. Although the combat film languished throughout most of the 1980s and 1990s, two powerful examples were released near the end of the latter decade. Steven Spielberg's *Saving Private Ryan* (1998) starred Tom Hanks and is notable for the most realistically gruesome battle footage ever shown in a mainstream motion picture. *The Thin Red Line* (1999) is the second filmed version of James Jones' classic novel and devotes as much time to moral issues as it does to combat.

A sub-genre of the combat film involves stories focusing on prisoners of war, a category that includes some of the best films made about the war. *Stalag 17,* based on a popular play, is a comedy-drama about American prisoners held by the Germans. The *Bridge on the River Kwai* (1957), which won innumerable awards, tells the story of a group of British POWs in Burma who are forced to build a railroad bridge by their Japanese captors. *The Great Escape* (1963), based loosely on a true story, involves a German ''escape-proof'' prison camp and the Allied prisoners who escape from it. *Von Ryan's Express* (1965) stars Frank Sinatra as an American Colonel who masterminds the hijacking of a German train by the Allied POWs it is transporting.

Films that chronicle actual battles, campaigns, or leaders include 1965's *Battle of the Bulge* and 1968's *The Bridge at Remagen. Patton* (1970) is George C. Scott's brilliant portrait of the General known to his troops as ''Old Blood and Guts.'' *The Longest Day* (1972) is a sprawling, epic account of the D-Day invasion, while 1977s *A Bridge Too Far* tells the story of a disastrous Allied plan to outflank the Germans that almost, but not quite, succeeded in ending the war a year early.

Comedies about World War II have been attempted over the years, with varying success. *Mister Roberts* (1955) focuses on sailors fighting boredom while stationed far from the combat. Cary Grant starred in *Operation Petticoat* (1959) as the commander of a submarine that must take on a bevy of beautiful nurses as passengers. Grant also stars in 1964's *Father Goose*, as a coastwatcher who reluctantly helps a group of children escape internment by the Japanese. *What Did You Do in the War, Daddy?* (1966) stars James Coburn as the reluctant commander of a squad occupying an Italian village, and director Steven Spielberg had one of his few cinematic flops with the inane farce *1941* (1979).

The war was also a fruitful subject for television programs well into the 1960s. One of the earliest TV shows was the documentary series *Battle Report*, which ran from 1950-1952. Host Robert McCormick introduced a new "battle" each week, with film footage and interviews with surviving participants used to elucidate what had happened and why.

Fictional programs began to appear in 1956 with the premiere of *Combat Sergeant*, which offered drama against the backdrop of the battle for North Africa. The program lasted only a year, as did *O.S.S.*, which debuted in 1957 and featured the espionage adventures of Frank Hawthorne, operating behind enemy lines on behalf of the Office of Strategic Services. It would be several years before the networks tried another World War II show, but *The Gallant Men* appeared in 1962. The story of an infantry unit fighting its way through Italy, it also was cancelled after its first season.

But 1962 also saw the debut of what many regard as the best television drama about World War II ever aired. *Combat* focused on a U.S. infantry platoon in France (and, later, Germany) during the last two years of the war. The ensemble cast included Rick Jason as Lieutenant Hanley and Vic Morrow as Sergeant Saunders. The show had good writing and able directing, and never used action as a substitute for human drama—all of which probably contributed to its long run, which lasted until 1967.

In 1966, *The Rat Patrol* premiered, starring Christopher George as the leader of a four-man mechanized commando unit fighting the Germans in North Africa. The show lasted two seasons, which was one season longer than *Garrison's Gorillas*, which was a blatant attempt to cash in on the popularity of the film *The Dirty Dozen*; this "criminals behind the lines" saga ran from 1967-68.

World War II dramas largely disappeared from the airwaves until the arrival of *Baa Baa Black Sheep* (retitled *Black Sheep Squadron* for its second, and last, season) in 1976. Loosely based on a real Marine aviation unit, the show starred Robert Conrad as Greg "Pappy" Boyington, who led a group of misfit fighter pilots into aerial combat against the Japanese.

There were several television comedies based on the war, some of which proved surprisingly popular. One was *McHale's Navy*, which made its debut in 1962. Ernest Borgnine played Lt. Commander McHale, a seagoing Sgt. Bilko simultaneously conning his superiors, ripping off the navy, and striving to avoid combat with the Japanese. He was aided and abetted during the four years of the show's run by Ensign Parker, played by Tim Conway.

The success of *McHale's Navy* may have inspired another maritime war comedy, *The Wackiest Ship in the Army*, which was launched in 1965 and sunk at season's end. Jack Warden and Gary Collins played the officers commanding a mixed squad of soldiers and sailors that roamed the South Pacific in an old wooden sailboat, attempting to gather intelligence about the Japanese forces in the area.

Perhaps the unlikeliest hit of the group was *Hogan's Heroes*, a comedy set in a German POW camp for Allied prisoners. Premiering in 1965, the show derived its humor from the abilities of the prisoners, led by Colonel Hogan (Bob Crane) to outsmart their German captors. So incompetent was the camp commander, Colonel Klink (Werner Klemperer) and his ranking noncom, Sergeant Schultz (John Banner), that the prisoners were able to run an espionage ring out of the camp, help downed Allied airmen return to England, and construct an elaborate underground complex directly under the camp itself. Despite the implausibility of both the premise and most of the show's scripts, it lasted for 168 episodes before cancellation in 1971.

—Justin Gustainis

FURTHER READING:

Blum, John Morton. *V was for Victory: Politics and American Culture during World War II.* New York, Harcourt, Brace, Jovanovich, 1976.

Braverman, Jordan. *To Hasten the Homecoming: How Americans Fought World War II through the Media.* Lanham, Maryland, Madison Books, 1996.

Dick, Bernard F. *The Star-Spangled Screen: The American World War II Film.* Lexington, University Press of Kentucky, 1985.

Waldmeir, Joseph J. *American Novels of the Second World War.* The Hague, Mouton Publishers, 1971.

World Wrestling Federation

While the World Wrestling Federation claims to have been the leader in "sports entertainment for over fifty years," the WWF really was formed in the early 1980s when Vince McMahon Jr. took over his ailing father's regional wrestling promotion and transformed it into an international marketing success story. McMahon Jr. is credited with taking professional wrestling out of the "smoke-filled arenas" and putting it on the map as family entertainment.

McMahon's father started the WWF (then called the WWWF) in 1963, breaking away from the National Wrestling Alliance over disagreements about the booking of the World Champion. McMahon Sr.'s home base was New York's Madison Square Garden, and he ran shows all along the East Coast. Playing to the heavy ethnic composition of his customers, he installed Italian strongman Bruno Sammartino as his World Champion, and the promotion was off and running. McMahon Sr. pioneered the big event card, holding two successful shows at Shea Stadium, both headlined by Sammartino. By the early 1980s, McMahon Jr., who had been working for his father as an announcer but was posed for something bigger for the business, had taken over the promotion. (McMahon told *New York* magazine that he "fell in love with it from the first contact.") Eventually buying out his father's stock in the parent company, Capital Sports, he changed the name to Titan Sports and proceeded to revolutionize wrestling.

McMahon broke all the rules: he "stole" other promoter's talent, bought out their television time, signed exclusive agreements with their arenas, and scheduled shows opposite theirs. Soon the traditional wrestling territories started drying up. McMahon's new company, headlined by Hulk Hogan as lead babyface and Roddy Piper as lead heel, used the emerging cable television industry to

World Wrestling Federation wrestlers compete in a match in Kowloon, Hong Kong.

market his promotion across the country. Shows such as *WWF Superstars* and McMahon's faux talk show *Tuesday Night Titans* were the top rated shows on all cable. He also set up syndicated shows that became the highest rated in syndication. Attracting mainstream press, using celebrities like Liberace and Cindy Lauper, merchandising wrestlers as characters (the WWF would copyright and own each wrestler's gimmick), having wrestlers use entrance music, and, finally, making wrestling a true ''show'' thrust the WWF into the national consciousness.

After 1985's Wrestlemania I, a live event at Madison Square Garden covered by hundreds of media outlets but also shown across the country via closed-circuit TV, McMahon expanded his empire. He signed agreements for a cartoon show on CBS and inked a series of license agreements to create all sorts of products, from lunch boxes to trading cards, featuring the likenesses of his wrestlers. Rather than appealing to adults, McMahon aimed his product at the family market. The WWF scored a coup in landing a monthly spot on network TV with *Saturday Night's Main Event* premiering on NBC in 1985 in the 11:30 p.m. time slot. Forays into prime time began in 1988. Success followed success as the WWF dominated in the United States with events like 1987's Wrestlemania III drawing more than 90,000 to the Pontiac Silverdome in Michigan, while wrestling became the cash cow of the early pay-per-view industry. The WWF

even ''exposed'' the wrestling industry in a hearing in New Jersey to rid itself of being taxed as a sport. A WWF official testified that wrestling was indeed ''fake,'' a headline which ended up in the *New York Times*. McMahon didn't even attempt to put up the façade any longer, telling *New York* magazine, ''We're storytellers—this is a soap opera, performed by the greatest actors and athletes in the world. I'd like to say that it's the highest form of entertainment.''

The WWF subsequently expanded to more than 1,000 events a year. The wrestlers were divided up into the three ''teams,'' the big stars headlining in the major markets and new talent headlining in small towns. Already successful in Canada, in the late 1980s the WWF started running TV all over the world and promoting live events in England, Germany, and Italy as well as in the Middle East. In 1991, more than 60,000 fans jammed into Wembley Stadium in England for the ''Summer Slam'' show, while events in other countries sold out both tickets and merchandise.

While the success of the WWF was built on many factors, one of its main selling points was always the physique of its wrestlers. Champion Hulk Hogan bragged about having the ''largest arms in the world,'' and performers like the Ultimate Warrior were touted not because of their ring talent, but because of their bodybuilder physiques. McMahon marketed bodybuilders by developing the World Bodybuilding Federation in 1991, a huge, and expensive, failure.

More bad times followed for the WWF with the arrest of a WWF-affiliated doctor for trafficking in steroids. McMahon and the company itself were taken to court for distributing steroids in 1994 after a very public three-year investigation. About the same time the steroid scandal broke, former WWF wrestlers and announcers were coming forth with stories of sex scandals involving WWF officials. *Jerry Springer, Geraldo,* and other daytime talk shows covered the story, as did the *New York Post.* McMahon was on the ropes. The negative publicity from the scandals, coupled with the shrinking nature of the top wrestlers' physiques and the departure of top stars like Hulk Hogan caused a downturn in business. The WWF tried its old tricks of involving celebrities like Chuck Norris, Jenny McCarthy, Burt Reynolds, Pam Anderson, and even getting NFL Hall of Famer Lawrence Taylor to wrestle in a Wrestlemania main event, but fan interest was waning.

After dominating wrestling for more than a decade, the WWF faced its first serious competition in 1995 when Ted Turner's World Championship Wrestling challenged the WWF directly by scheduling a show called *Monday Nitro* opposite the WWF's long-standing *Monday Night Raw.* Losing talent, advertisers, and viewers, the WWF was clearly the number-two promotion. The turning point came when the WWF decided to abandon its family-friendly approach. It adopted a new hardcore edge and marketing campaign, ''WWF attitude,'' while building the promotion around trash-talking Steve Austin rather than dependable champion Bret Hart. When Hart decided to leave the promotion in the fall of 1997, McMahon took a bold gamble. During a championship match, which McMahon and Hart had agreed would end in Hart NOT losing the WWF title, McMahon had the timekeeper ring the bell and declare Hart's opponent, Shawn Michaels, the winner and new champ. The controversy and interest in the finish, the emergence of Austin as the most popular wrestler in the country as well as a mainstream celebrity (showing up on awards shows, voicing MTV's *Celebrity Death Match,* being profiled in *Rolling Stone* and *People*), and lots of innovative promotion and matchmaking found the WWF back on top and once again ''the leader in sports entertainment.''

—Patrick Jones

FURTHER READING:

Kerr, Peter. ''Now It Can Be Told: Wrestling Is All Fun.'' *New York Times.* January 5, 1990, A1.

Morton, Gerald, and George M. O'Brien. *Wrestling to Rasslin': Ancient Sport to American Spectacle.* Bowling Green, Ohio, Bowling Green State University Press, 1985.

Sales, Nancy Jo. ''Beyond Fake.'' *New York.* October 26, 1998, 10-15.

World's Fairs

World's fairs are modern events of the nineteenth and twentieth centuries. Whereas medieval fairs were concerned with the selling of goods, modern world's fairs were involved in the selling of industrial technology and industrial society; they fostered the idea that industrial development was to be equated with social progress. World's fairs not only furnished a place where the latest technological achievements could be presented to an international public, but they provided an orientation to people confronting the vast and rapid changes of industrialism. They offered a photograph of the present, a story of past progress, and a vision of the future. But by the middle of the twentieth century, world's fairs had lost much of their importance and charm.

The first world's fair was held in London in 1851. Prince Albert, husband of Queen Victoria and president of the Royal Society of the Arts, wanted to go beyond the national industrial exhibitions that France had made famous and Britain was ready to duplicate. After much discussion, a building of glass and iron/wood beams was constructed in Hyde Park. The Crystal Palace held all of the exhibits. Since it was built with prefabricated interchangeable parts, the building was constructed and taken down quickly, with little damage to the Park. In fact, the building was actually constructed over 10 large elm trees. During the 141 days it was open, over six million attended. The Crystal Palace Exhibition's success inspired other nations to hold international exhibitions.

World's fairs are remembered by the products they introduced to the public. Americans did very well at the Crystal Palace Exhibition. Cyrus McCormick's reaper, Samuel Morse's telegraph, and Charles Goodyear's vulcanized rubber products were well received. Colt revolvers and Robbins-Lawrence rifles made with interchangeable parts were recognized as having revolutionized the making of firearms. Elisa Otis demonstrated his safety elevator at the New York World's Fair in 1853. At the Philadelphia Exposition of 1876, Alexander Graham Bell introduced the telephone, and Thomas Edison gave his first public demonstration of the phonograph in Paris in 1889. Sound-synchronized movies, x-rays, and wireless telegraphy marked the 1900 Paris fair. The St. Louis World's Fair of 1904 introduced the safety razor, the ice cream cone, iced tea, and rayon. President Franklin Roosevelt's televised opening of the 1939 New York World's Fair began regular television broadcasting in the United States. IBM's (International Business Machine) computer demonstrations educated visitors to the New York World's Fair of 1964-1965.

More important than the inventions were the industrial systems that the fairs exhibited to the public. The Philadelphia Exposition of 1876 celebrated the age of steam. In Machinery Hall, the giant Corliss steam engine, 40-feet high and 2,520 horsepowers strong, powered all the machinery in the hall. There were also steam fire engines, steam locomotives, and steam pumps. By 1893, the Chicago World's Fair was celebrating the age of electricity. At night, the fair was lighted by thousands of incandescent light bulbs. In the Electrical building were Edison and Westinghouse dynamos and electric motors that powered other machines. Transportation, however, was the theme in St. Louis in 1904. Trains, streetcars, and over 160 motorcars were displayed. A major feature of the fair was the dirigible contest, where a large cash prize awaited anyone who could pilot his airship over a prescribed route.

While world's fairs were held to celebrate historic milestones, contemporary concerns were often in the minds of fair planners. The 1876 Philadelphia Exposition recognized the centennial of the signing of the Declaration of Independence. The fair was also viewed as a means to remind Americans of their common ideals, and thus heal the wounds of the Civil War. Paris' 1889 World's Fair celebrated the centennial of the French Revolution. Chicago's Exposition of 1893 recognized the 400th year anniversary of Columbus' discovery; and the St. Louis World's Fair of 1904 commemorated the centennial of the Louisiana Purchase. Both fairs were also seen as demonstrating the importance of the midwest to the nation. The centennial of the founding of the city of Chicago was the reason given for holding a world's fair in 1933. New York's World's Fair in 1939 celebrated the

150th year anniversary of George Washington's inauguration. The "Building the World of Tomorrow" theme had the high purpose of showing how a well planned democratic society would survive the world's turmoil. The outbreak of World War II in September resulted in the new theme of "Peace and Freedom" for the 1940 opening.

The outside world had a way of impinging upon world's fairs. At the New York World's Fair of 1853, Susan B. Anthony led a demonstration for women's rights. For the Philadelphia Exposition in 1876, a women's building housed a display of inventions by women, and photographs showing women working in a variety of occupations. Of particular note was Emma Allison, who operated a steam engine that ran five looms and a printing press. When a man asked her if the work was too demanding for someone of her sex, she replied "It's easier than teaching, and the pay is better." At the Chicago World's Fair of 1893, the women's building displayed a great collection of works by women. These included a library of 5,000 books, paintings, and sculptures, and mechanical devices invented by women. A careful selection of statistics from around the world showed the extent to which women were a part of the world economy. Susan B. Anthony believed the women's building did more to raise the consciousness of women than all the demonstrations of the nineteenth century.

At the Philadelphia Exposition of 1876, vendors and amusements were located outside the fairgrounds. The 1893 Chicago planners recognized that a profit could be realized by bringing the amusements and vendors into the fair itself. One of the most popular of the Midway exhibits was the "streets of Cairo" featuring the belly dancer "Little Egypt." She also appeared at the 1904 St. Louis World's Fair, but was outdrawn by "Jim Key," the talking horse. The 1933 Chicago World's Fair had Midget Town and the fan dancer, Sally Rand. The New York World's Fair of 1939 featured the synchronized swimming of "Aqua girls" in Billy Rose's Aquacade. The world's fairs would be remembered for their outstanding amusements. The Eiffel Tower was a huge success at the 1889 Paris fair. For a generation that had not yet flown in an airplane, seeing the world from 985 feet was unlike anything they had ever experienced. The 1893 Chicago fair offered Charles Ferris' great wheel: 40 cars, each carrying 36 passengers, rode to a height of 270 feet. Forty years later, Chicago offered a 200-foot high Sky Ride across the second longest suspension span in the United States. The parachute jump at the 1939 New York World's Fair attracted thrill seekers and onlookers.

Since world's fairs were international events, international organizations held their meetings at the fairs. At the 1900 Paris World's Fair, 127 international organizations met. Paris in 1900 and St. Louis in 1904 hosted the second and third Olympic games. Featured at the fairs were villages of natives from around the world. Dressed in their native costumes, these villages were publicized as serving an educational function. The subtle message, however, was an ethnocentric view that celebrated Western progress by comparing Western achievements at the fair with the backwardness of these native cultures. Following the Olympics, the St. Louis fair held three days of "Anthropology games." Native peoples at the fair were enticed to demonstrate their skills. Sioux Indians participated in archery contests, African natives threw javelins, and seven-foot Patagonians tried the shot put. Their inability to match Western records not only confirmed the value of training, but again suggested the superiority of Western civilization.

Those who went to the fairs had their faith in Western industrial progress confirmed. At the height of the Depression, Chicago's 1933 Century of Progress assured visitors that science guaranteed a better future. The science building had a giant statue gently guiding a trembling man and woman into the future. The official guidebook to the fair stated, "Science Finds, Industry Applies, Man Conforms." By 1939, Fascism and Nazism were on the move in Europe. Visitors to the New York fair were given a powerful message of hope. The symbols of the fair, the Trylon and Perisphere, suggested that soaring human aspirations could be realized on this earth. Inside the sphere was a giant model city known as Democracity. This utopian city had Centerton as its business and cultural center, Millvilles of light industry, and Pleasantvilles, which were exclusively residential. Democracity, with its defined zones and rational streets, carried the message that well-planned livable cities were possible through democratic forms of government. Futurama, the General Motors exhibit, the most popular at the fair, presented a vision of America united by a 14 lane national highway in which radio-controlled autos moved at 100 miles per hour. With its green suburbs, industrial parks, productive farms, and high rise urban centers, this vision of America in 1960 offered an inspirational alternative to the chaos that the world was experiencing.

World's fairs have lost their importance because technical fairs and television are a more effective means of presenting new technological developments to specialists and to the general public. Television can bring foreign cultures to our homes, and air travel can bring us to foreign cultures. Today, international organizations are connected with permanent agencies of the United Nations. Theme Parks such as Disney World and Epcot Center provide the amusements and thrills that were once found at world's fairs. Finally, the expense of holding a world's fair required corporate sponsorship. The resulting commercialization of the 1964-1965 New York World's Fair suggested that fairs were now oriented toward selling products. The fair's ferris wheel, for example, was a giant tire with the name of the tire company in huge letters on the sides of the tires. Our view of technology has also changed. We no longer accept the idea that because we can do something technologically, we ought to do it, and that we will do it. General Motors' 1964-1965 exhibit demonstrated how humans could explore and colonize the oceans, the deserts, and the polar ice caps. Few were inspired by this vision.

—Thomas W. Judd

FURTHER READING:

Allwood, John. *The Great Exhibitions*. New York, Studio Vista, 1978.

Badger, Reid. *The Great American Fair: The World's Columbian Exposition and American Culture*. Chicago, Nelson-Hall, 1979.

Briggs, Asa. *Iron Bridge to Crystal Palace: Impact and Images of the Industrial Revolution*. London, Thames and Hudson, 1979.

Burg, David. *Chicago's White City of 1893*. Lexington, University of Kentucky Press, 1976.

Findling, John E. *Chicago's Great World's Fairs*. Manchester, Manchester University Press, 1994.

Harrison, Helen. *Dawn of A New Day: The New York World's Fair, 1939/40*. New York, New York University Press, 1980.

Luckhurst, Kenneth. *The Story of Exhibitions*. London, Studio Publications, 1951.

Mandell, Richard. *Paris, 1900: The Great World's Fair*. Toronto, University of Toronto Press, 1967.

Weimann, Jeanne. *The Fair Women: The Story of the Women's Building, World's Columbian Exposition, Chicago, 1893.* Chicago, Academy Press, 1981.

Wrangler Jeans

Wrangler jeans became the pant de rigueur for late-twentieth-century country and western fashion. Popular with mid-century rodeo riders after their introduction in 1947 because of their snug fit and boot-cut pant leg, Wranglers have come to symbolize the free spirit and individualism embodied in the myths of the American frontier West. While other brands, especially Levi's, became connected with urban chic, Wrangler focused its marketing almost exclusively on associations with rural authenticity and Western roots. As the jeans of choice for almost any star in the growing country music industry of the late 1980s and 1990s, Wranglers benefitted from the resurgence of country music and the heavy advertising tie-ins associated with the music's rural and Western image. Wrangler became culturally connected, and often financially intertwined, with rodeos, country music, competitive fishing, and pick-up truck sales.

—Dan Moos

FURTHER READING:

Gordon, Beverly. "American Denim: Blue Jeans and Their Multiple Layers of Meaning." *Dress and Popular Culture,* edited by Patricia A. Cunningham and Susan Voso Lab. Bowling Green, Ohio, Bowling Green State University Popular Press, 1991.

Wray, Fay (1907—)

Despite a long, versatile career, Canadian-born actress Fay Wray is indelibly etched on the public mind as the shrieking heroine in the grasp of a giant ape climbing the Empire State Building in the film *King Kong* (1933). For 40 years she acted in 78 motion pictures as well as on the Broadway stage and television. She also co-authored a play with Nobel Prize winner Sinclair Lewis. Although she proved her acting ability in such films as *The Affairs of Cellini* (1934), opposite Frederic March, she was doomed to be typecast as the champion screamer and bedeviled heroine. In the 1950s she played in the television series *Pride of the Family* as the wife of Paul Hartman and mother of Natalie Wood. "When I'm in New York," she once said with a laugh, "I look at the Empire State Building and feel that it belongs to me—or vice versa."

—Benjamin Griffith

FURTHER READING:

Parish, James Robert, and William T. Leonard. *Hollywood Players: The Thirties.* New Rochelle, New York, Arlington House, 1976.

Ragan, David. *Movie Stars of the '30s: A Complete Reference Guide for the Film Historian or Trivia Buff.* Englewood Cliffs, New Jersey, Prentice-Hall, 1985.

Wright, Richard (1908-1960)

Once at the center of African-American culture—chosen by the Schomburg Collection poll as one of the "twelve distinguished Negroes" of 1939, recipient of the Spingarn Medal in 1941 (then the highest award given by the NAACP), and mentor to young black writers such as James Baldwin, Gwendolyn Brooks, and Ralph Ellison—Richard Wright became an unpalatable novelist to readers and critics of his own race in the 1980s and 1990s.

Born on a plantation in Roxie, near Natchez, Mississippi, Wright spent his childhood traveling intermittently from one relative to the next because of his father's desertion and his mother's bad health. In 1927, Wright moved to the South Side of Chicago where he worked as a postal clerk and insurance policy vendor. In Chicago, Wright joined first the John Reed Club and then the Communist Party and started to publish essays and poetry in leftist reviews such as *Midland Left, New Masses,* and *International Literature.* By 1936, Wright had become one of the principal organizers of the Communist Party, but his relationship with the party would always be difficult until his definite break in 1942.

In 1936, Wright's short story "Big Boy Leaves Home" appeared in the anthology *The New Caravan* and received critical praise in mainstream newspapers and magazines, marking a decisive step for his career as a writer. The following year Wright moved to New York where, with Dorothy West, he launched the magazine *New Challenge* (which, lacking Communist support, was short-lived). In *New Challenge,* Wright published the influential essay "Blueprint for Negro Writing" (1937) where he urged black writers to adopt a Marxist approach as a starting point in their analysis of society. In the same essay, with a move which is considered problematic by contemporary black critics, Wright encouraged black writers to consider as their heritage Eliot, Stein, Joyce, Proust, Hemingway, Anderson, Barbusse, Nexo, and Jack London "no less than the folklore of the Negro himself."

Wright's first novel, *Native Son,* based on a true story, describes the progressive entrapment and final execution of Bigger Thomas, a young African-American chauffeur living in the Chicago slums who involuntarily killed his boss's daughter. Published in 1940 by Harper, the novel sold 215,000 copies in its first three weeks and became a Book-of-the-Month Club selection, thus marking, as Paul Gilroy has pointed out, an important change in the political economy of publishing black writers. The following year Orson Welles directed a successful stage version of *Native Son.* Two movie versions have been realized so far: the first in 1951 by Pierre Chenal starring Wright himself, the second one in 1995 by Jerrold Freedman starring Victor Love, Matt Dillon, and Oprah Winfrey. *Native Son* has had a great impact on successive generations of African-American writers who have either followed its pattern of "protest novel," as in the case of Anne Petry, Chester Himes, and William Gardner Smith (sometimes significantly grouped together as "the Wright school"), or reacted to it very critically as James Baldwin did in his famous essay "Everybody's Protest Novel" (1949), stating: "The failure of the protest novel lies in its rejection of life, the human being, the denial of his beauty, dread, power, in its insistence that it is his categorization alone which is real and which cannot be transcended."

After the success of *Native Son,* Wright published with equal success and critical acclaim the folk history *12 Million Black Voices* (1941) and the first part of his autobiography, *Black Boy* (1945, the second part was published posthumously as *American Hunger* in

1977), which became another Book-of-the-Month Club selection. In 1945 Wright wrote the introduction to *Black Metropolis,* St. Claire Drake and Horace Cayton's classic sociological study of the black ghetto in Chicago. Thanks to *Native Son* and *Black Boy,* which were translated into several languages, Richard Wright was the first black writer to enjoy a global readership. However, *Black Boy* has attracted much criticism by contemporary African-American scholars for Wright's depiction of black life in America as, to quote his own words, ''bleak'' and ''barren.'' Henry Louis Gates, for example, finds that ''Wright's humanity is achieved only at the expense of his fellow blacks . . . who surround and suffocate him'' which makes Wright's autobiographical persona ''a noble black savage, in the ironic tradition of Oroonoko and film characters played by Sidney Poitier—the exception, not the rule.'' Paul Gilroy has suggested a less disparaging, and ultimately more useful, perspective, describing Wright's work as fascinating precisely because ''the tension of racial particularity on one side and the appeal of those modern universals that appear to transcend race on the other arises in the sharpest possible way.''

In 1946, the French cultural attaché in Washington and famous anthropologist Claude Lévi-Strauss sent Wright an official invitation from the French government to visit Paris, where Wright was welcomed by prominent intellectuals such as Gertrude Stein, Simone de Beauvoir, Jean-Paul Sartre and André Gide. The following year Wright decided to settle down in Paris permanently where he started to work on his existentialist novel *The Outsider* (1953) and where he had an active role in several organizations such as Sartre's Rassemblement Democratique Révolutionnaire, Léopold Sédar Senghor and Aimé Césaire's Présence Africaine, and the Société Africaine de Culture. Wright's other books of this late period include a report on his travels in Africa (*Black Power,* 1954); an account, introduced by Gunnar Myrdal, of the conference of non-aligned nations in Bandung, Indonesia (*The Color Curtain,* 1956); a collection of essays (*White Man, Listen!,* 1957); and two novels (*Savage Holiday,* 1954, and *The Long Dream,* 1958).

Wright's last years were plagued by his progressive alienation from the African-American community in Paris, which suspected Wright of being an agent for the FBI (in fact, evidence shows that the FBI monitored Wright's activities all his life), and by his increasing financial problems. Paradoxically and sadly for a writer who had to fight against white racism all his life and whose books were not allowed during his lifetime on the library shelves of several American towns, Richard Wright is now being held in contempt by influential black critics who are disturbed by his unaffirmative portrayal of the African-American community, by his controversial relationship with black culture, and by what many consider a stereotypical depiction of black women. It is hoped that critics and readers will find new and more inclusive strategies to recenter Richard Wright within the American and African-American literary tradition.

—Luca Prono

FURTHER READING:

Baldwin, James. *Notes of a Native Son.* Boston, Beacon Press, 1955.

Bloom, Harold, editor. *Richard Wright.* New York, Chelsea House Publishers, 1987.

Cappetti, Carla. *Writing Chicago: Modernism, Ethnography and the Novel.* New York, Columbia University Press, 1993.

Richard Wright

Fabre, Michel. *The Unfinished Quest of Richard Wright.* Translated from the French by Isabel Barzun. New York, William Morrow & Company, 1973.

Gates, Henry Louis, Jr. *The Signifying Monkey: A Theory of African-American Literary Criticism.* New York, Oxford University Press, 1988.

Gilroy, Paul. *The Black Atlantic: Modernity and Double Consciousness.* London, Verso, 1993.

Sollors, Werner. ''Modernization as Adultery: Richard Wright, Zora Neale Hurston and American Culture of the 1930s and 1940s.'' *Hebrew University Studies in Literature and the Arts.* Vol. 18. 1990, 109-155.

Wrigley Field

At 1060 West Addison Street in Chicago sits Wrigley Field, the venerable home of the Chicago Cubs baseball team of the National League. Wrigley Field has played host to some of the most memorable and bizarre incidents in the history of professional baseball. Opposing teams dread playing within ''The Friendly Confines'' due to the vicious winds blowing in from nearby Lake Michigan as well as the raucous, loyal fans who turn out in droves to cheer on their beloved and ''Cubbies,'' one of the least successful teams in baseball history.

Wrigley Field came into existence in March of 1914 as the home of the Chicago Whales, taking the name Weegham Park, after Whales owner Charles Weegham. In 1916, Weegham bought the Cubs and moved them to Weegham Park. The name changed shortly thereafter to Cubs Park when the Wrigley family (of chewing-gum fame) bought the Cubs in 1920, changing its name yet one more time in 1926 to Wrigley Field. Despite many changes throughout the years, Wrigley Field still preserves a touch of old-time baseball with its downtown stadium surrounding a domeless field with real grass, plus 1930s-vintage amenities like a hand-operated scoreboard, a beautiful ivy-covered outfield wall with no advertising placards, and an infamous bleacher section often packed with "Bleacher Bums." Wrigley Field and the Cubs also maintain a longstanding commitment to afternoon baseball games.

Among the more-famous incidents in the history of Wrigley Field include Babe Ruth's "called shot" and the 1969 "black cat." The legend of Ruth's "called shot" in Game Three of the 1932 World Series, in which he purportedly predicted the trajectory of one of his home runs, has achieved almost mythical status, despite evidence suggesting the story was probably apocryphal. In the midst of the dramatic, disastrous 1969 season, a black cat wandered into the Cubs dugout, supposedly contributing to the bad-luck season that found the Cubs relinquishing a huge lead to New York's "Miracle Mets."

In the late 1990s, Wrigley Field remains the only major-league baseball park to prohibit advertising on any of the walls or scoreboards surrounding the playing field. The Tribune Company, publishers of the *Chicago Tribune,* bought the Cubs in 1985 and made one concession to the modern age by installing lights for night-baseball games, though the first night game at Wrigley Field (August 8, 1988 vs. the Philadelphia Phillies) was rained out after three and a half innings. The Cubs completed its first official night game the next evening, defeating the New York Mets 6-4.

With a seating capacity of 38,902, Wrigley Field is one of the smallest parks in major-league baseball, which only adds to the intimacy of watching an old-fashioned baseball game within the stadium's "Friendly Confines."

—Jason McEntee

FURTHER READING:

Golenbock, Peter. *Wrigleyville: A Magical History Tour of the Chicago Cubs.* New York, St. Martin's Press, 1996.

The Chicago Cubs Media Guide. Chicago, Chicago National League Ball Club, published annually.

"The Official Web Site of the Chicago Cubs." http://www.cubs.com/index2.frm. June 1999.

Wuthering Heights

Emily Brontë's 1847 Gothic novel about the brooding Heathcliff's passion for Cathy has become one of cinema's most enduring love stories. Director A. V. Bramble, in a British silent production (1920), first brought *Wuthering Heights* to the screen; but Samuel Goldwyn's 1939 version, directed by William Wyler and starring Laurence Olivier and Merle Oberon, is considered the film classic (and a source

of much Hollywood lore, such as Goldwyn's post-production decision to add a new "happy" ending, the now famous scene of the lovers walking together on the crag filmed with unknown actors.) Subsequent refilmings and adaptations—by director Luis Buñuel, as *Abismos de Pasion* (1954); by Robert Fuest (1970), starring Timothy Dalton; by the BBC (in 1948, 1953, 1962, 1967, and, most notably, by Peter Hammond in 1978); by Jacques Rivette, as *Hurlevent* (1985); and by Peter Kosminsky, as *Emily Brontë's Wuthering Heights* (1992), with Ralph Fiennes and Juliette Binoche; and by David Skynner, again as *Emily Brontë's Wuthering Heights* (1998)—confirm the popularity of Brontë's tale and filmmakers' ongoing fascination with it.

—Barbara Tepa Lupack

WWJD? (What Would Jesus Do?)

The twentieth century has seen no phrase so consistently popular with Protestant America as "What Would Jesus Do?" What began as a series of evening story-sermons delivered by a Kansas preacher in 1896 became by the end of the century a billion dollar industry as millions of Americans purchased bracelets, t-shirts, coffee mugs, and other paraphernalia with the acronym "WWJD?" inscribed upon them. For some the remarkable sales which the phrase engendered bespoke a hunger for the Christian gospel in the American public sphere, but to others it showcased the ability of market-savvy capitalists to turn even the deepest religious impulses into profit-making ventures.

Charles M. Sheldon (1857-1946), a social gospel minister at the Central Congregational Church in Topeka, Kansas, landed on the idea of the story-sermon as a cure for chronically poor attendance at Sunday evening services. These serial messages would then be printed in the private weekly magazine *The Advance* and later compiled and released in book form. In 1896 the series he composed was entitled "In His Steps," recounting the experiences of Rev. Henry Maxwell as he and his congregation discovered spiritual awakening and moral regeneration when they asked themselves "What would Jesus do?" in every situation they faced and sought to act accordingly.

The *Advance* series proved so popular that Sheldon decided to reissue the material as a book. But when he applied for copyright protection, it was discovered that the original magazine series had not itself been copyrighted and so the story was in public domain. Thus as the book began to sell, many firms other than the Advance Publishing Company rushed to meet the demand. By mid-century 41 companies had published the book in the United States, 15 in Great Britain, and the original text had been translated into 26 languages. The results of all this activity were mixed for Sheldon. He was catapulted to international fame, with his book selling no fewer than 8 million copies and perhaps as many as 30 million, but Sheldon himself received very little in the way of royalties on the sales. Thus was born a mythology about *In His Steps*, the book which outsold all others save the Bible but whose author received not a penny in royalties.

In His Steps has been continually in print since 1896, usually in more than one edition. But the end of the twentieth century saw an astonishing revival in its popularity. In 1989 Janie Tinklenberg, youth leader at the Calvary Reformed Church in Holland, Michigan, read

Sheldon's book and discussed it with her youth group. Noticing that many of her kids were making ''friendship bracelets'' for one another, she hit upon the idea of creating a bracelet which would remind her charges to ask themselves what Jesus would do in a given situation. She contacted the Lesco Corporation, based in Lansing, Michigan, and had them make two hundred bracelets with the acronym ''WWJD?'' stitched into them. Many of the students in her group began explaining the message of Jesus Christ to their class-mates, who would often themselves ask for a bracelet. The original supply was quickly depleted and the phenomenon began to spread across the country. During the first seven years of marketing, Lesco Corp. sold 300,000 bracelets. But in the spring of 1997 Paul Harvey mentioned them on his syndicated radio show and sales skyrocketed. Fifteen million bracelets were sold by Lesco in 1997, and dozens of other corporations rushed to capitalize on the market craze.

Lesco quickly expanded its merchandising beyond the bracelets to include baseball caps, coffee mugs, key chains, jewelry, sweaters, and t-shirts, all sold by Christian bookstores around the country. An Indiana-based web site (http://www.whatwouldjesusdo.com) was sell-ing 300,000 bracelets a month by 1998. 1998 also witnessed several Christian publishing companies compiling youth curriculum materi-als and offering inspirational publications using the moniker. Fore-Front Records released a WWJD? compact disc showcasing some of the most popular artists in Contemporary Christian Music, and publishing giant Zondervan issued the WWJD Interactive Devotional Bible. Most releases sold quite well. Some, like Beverly Courrege's *Answers to WWJD?,* became bestsellers.

By 1998 the fad had caught the attention of mainstream media outlets such that WWJD? materials could be purchased from high-profile stores like Kmart, Wal-Mart, Hallmark, Barnes and Noble, and Borders Books and Music. The Christian press was astir with debate over whether Jesus Himself would smile upon such vigorous marketing of His message, and controversy emerged over copyrights on the phrase itself. Fuel was added to the flames of controversy when it was found that some of the pewter jewelry bearing the WWJD inscription contained such high quantities of lead that children were contracting lead poisoning.

Despite such difficulties, it was clear that the message Charles Sheldon had preached first to his congregation and then to millions of readers around the world at the beginning of the twentieth century was still being heeded and put into practice over one hundred years later in a characteristically American blend of religious zeal and the entrepreneurial spirit.

—Milton Gaither

FURTHER READING:

Miller, Timothy. *Following in His Steps: A Biography of Charles M. Sheldon.* Knoxville, University of Tennessee Press, 1987.

Sheldon, Charles M. *In His Steps; ''What Would Jesus Do?.''* Chicago, Advance Publishing Co., 1899.

Singleton III, William C. ''W.W.J.D. Fad or Faith?'' *Homelife.* August, 1998.

Smith, Michael R. ''What Would Jesus Do? The Jesus Bracelet Fad: Is It Merchandising or Ministry?'' *World Magazine.* January 10, 1998.

''WWJD? What Would Jesus Do?'' http:\www.whatwouldjesusdo.com. February 1999.

Wyeth, Andrew (1917—)

The Realist painter Andrew Wyeth was born the youngest of five children to the successful artist/illustrator, N.C. Wyeth, in Chadds Ford, Pennsylvania in 1917. He learned to paint with the keen observation and the drafting skills that his father passed on to him. His subjects, mainly nostalgic images of unpainted houses, austere New Englanders, and landscapes from his surroundings, have been enor-mously popular since his first sold out one-man show in New York in 1937. Like his father, he was offered the opportunity to paint covers for *The Saturday Evening Post,* but unlike his father, he declined, preferring to pursue a free interpretative course in his art. Ironically, because of his ability to capture on canvas the American sense of courage and its triumph over the struggles and trials of life, Andrew Wyeth was the first artist to be featured on the cover of *Time* magazine.

Nearly all of Wyeth's paintings are either executed in drybrush, watercolor, or egg tempera, a technique that allows for extreme precision. His subdued earth-colors palette, realistic style, and subject matter have remained the same throughout his career, often featuring a neighbor's farm in Chadds Ford and landscape scenes from his summers in Cushing, Maine. In the 1960s, he began to paint portraits of his sister, Carolyn, which encouraged him eventually to embark on a series of nudes of Helga Testorf, one of his Chadds Ford neighbors. An early Wyeth model, Christina Olson, was the subject of several of his portraits and one of his most famous paintings, *Christina's World* (1948). The painting shows the crippled woman gazing back towards her house from a windswept, grassy pasture. As an egg tempera work painted shortly after his father's tragic railway accident, it emphasizes the somber introspection and sense of struggle for which Wyeth gained a great deal of notoriety. The Olson House, featured in *Christina's World,* is the first house listed in the National Historic Register of Places to become famous through being featured in a painting, thus attesting to the popularity of the artist's work.

During the years 1972-1986, Wyeth painted his popular ''Helga'' studies. These pictures were painted in secret and comprise 247 images of the artist's most mature works, featuring the same model in numerous environments and moods. A sense of moral dignity and courage is characteristic of the portraits in this series of paintings, which were exhibited at the National Gallery of Art in 1987 and were the first works by a living artist to be shown there. This came after Wyeth's 1976 honor of having been the first living American artist to be given a retrospective at the New York Metropolitan Muse-um of Art.

Imbuing his art with a sense of visual poetry, mysterious in its evocation of emotion, Andrew Wyeth's craft has developed indepen-dently of the modern and contemporary *avant garde* movements. His apolitical, somewhat sentimental nature and keen sense of tenacity in subjects, appeals to those who find beauty in the tangibly representa-tional rather than the abstract. Wyeth, however, finds that there is a kind of abstract discipline in utilitarian subjects that he is able to capture in paint, rendering image in a realistic style that appears to reveal the truth to his viewers. In the late 1970s he said, with obvious affection for his Maine subjects, ''[Maine] is to me almost like going to the surface of the moon. I feel things are just hanging on the surface and that it's all going to blow away.'' Andrew Wyeth became popular because he depicts traditional values and grassroots images. His

Dodge's Ridge by Andrew Wyeth.

exhibitions draw record-breaking crowds and command some of the highest prices paid for the works of living American artists.

—Cheryl McGrath

FURTHER READING:

Duff, I.H., and others. *An American Vision: Three Generations of Wyeth Art* (exhibition catalog). Chadds Ford, Pennsylvania, Brandywine River Museum, 1987.

Canaday, J. *Works by Andrew Wyeth from the Holly and Arthur Magill Collection.* Greenville, South Carolina, 1979.

Whittet, G. S. "Wyeth, Andrew." In *Contemporary Artists.* Chicago, St. James Press, 1989.

Wilmerding, John. *Andrew Wyeth: The Helga Pictures.* New York, H.N. Abrams, 1987.

Wyeth, N. C. (1882-1945)

Indisputably one of the world's greatest illustrators, Newell Convers Wyeth is best known for adding a new and unforgettable dimension to dozens of classic adventure books—*Treasure Island* (1911), *The Boy's King Arthur* (1917), and *Robinson Crusoe* (1920) among them—in the early decades of the twentieth century. Combining skilled draftsmanship and a genius for light and color with the ability dictated by his teacher Howard Pyle to project himself into each painting, Wyeth succeeded brilliantly at evoking movement, mood, and the range of human emotions. His prolific output, in addition to easel paintings and murals, included illustrations for hundreds of stories in periodicals from *McCall's* to the *Saturday Evening Post,* popular prints, posters, calendars, and advertisements. His early portrayals of the Old West reveal the influence of Frederic Remington, while much of his later work clearly made a strong impression on the art of his son Andrew, like his father one of America's most admired painters.

—Craig Bunch

FURTHER READING:

Allen, Douglas, and Douglas Allen, Jr. *N. C. Wyeth: The Collected Paintings, Illustrations and Murals.* New York, Bonanza Books, 1984.

Michaelis, David. *N. C. Wyeth: A Biography.* New York, Alfred A. Knopf, 1998.

Wynette, Tammy (1942-1998)

Often criticized for her conservative, traditional values, country vocalist Tammy Wynette became famous in the late 1960s for "Stand by Your Man," a hit single that made her an unintentional spokesperson for antifeminists. While she was known for her "doormat" songs, in which men treat women subserviently, much of her material offered valuable insights into the lives of working-class housewives and mothers. Her songs often exhibited an optimistic perseverance in a never-ending quest for love and happiness. Wynette expressed this attitude with a heartfelt sincerity, for even after she became a country superstar, her life was not easy. Sometimes referred to as the "Heroine of Heartbreak," she suffered from marital difficulties, drug addiction, financial troubles, and countless severe health problems. Although she was portrayed as an unhappy victim, Wynette was stronger than she appeared to be. As a woman in the male-dominated music industry of the 1960s, she held her own as a performer. During her 30-year career she sold more than 30 million records, had 39 Top Ten country hits, and received three Country Music Association awards.

Born in Itawamba County, Mississippi, on May 5, 1942, Virginia Wynette Pugh was raised by her grandparents after her father died not long after she was born and her mother found work at a Memphis defense plant. As a child, she picked cotton on their farm, and this arduous and exhausting work made her determined to create a better life for herself. She learned to play the piano and the guitar, and she started singing in church. Accompanied by a female friend, she performed on local radio programs and in area talent competitions. In her autobiography, *Stand by Your Man,* she recalled, "during my adolescence I daydreamed a lot about singing professionally." However, in the spring of 1959, 17-year-old Wynette married Euple Byrd, and in 1961, their first child was born. Two years later, after the birth of a second child, she was training to become a licensed beautician. The family lived in Memphis briefly, where she worked as a barmaid, occasionally singing songs requested by the customers. Unhappy in her marriage, Wynette asked Byrd for a divorce; he responded by attempting to have her committed to an institution. In 1965, pregnant with their third child, she and her two daughters moved to Birmingham, Alabama. Born prematurely, her third daughter was diagnosed with spinal meningitis. Wynette managed to support her family by working as a hairdresser full-time and singing on a local early morning television show. She maintained her dream of being a professional country singer, and after attending a disc jockey convention in Nashville, she decided to move there and focus her efforts on landing a record deal.

Wynette auditioned unsuccessfully for several labels located in the part of Nashville known as Music Row. Executives and producers repeatedly turned her down, saying that they were looking for a "girl singer" who sounded like a particular established male country artist, or that they simply did not need any more female artists. After a series of rejections, she approached Billy Sherrill, a producer/songwriter with Epic Records. Recognizing her tremendous vocal capability, he agreed to record her. Within a few weeks, he suggested that she call herself Tammy Wynette, and he chose "Apartment #9" as her first single. By December of 1966, Wynette's debut release was on the country charts; less than a year later, her first album, *Your Good Girl's Gonna Go Bad,* reached the Top Ten. Despite this success, Wynette

Tammy Wynette

encountered further difficulties as she searched for a booking agency. According to her autobiography, one agent she approached expressed the opinion that women were "not worth the trouble" because of conflicting obligations to their families and their careers. She managed to find an agent lacking this prejudice and began performing regularly as her next three singles became number-one hits. She married songwriter Don Chapel, but their marriage dissolved as she became involved with singer George Jones. By the time she married Jones in 1969, she was a full-fledged star known for the anthems "D-I-V-O-R-C-E" and "Stand by Your Man," which became one of the best-selling country songs ever recorded by a female artist.

As Jones's wife, Wynette was known as "The First Lady of Country Music," and together they performed and recorded duets that often reflected problems existing in their own relationship. Jones's legendary substance abuse and his tendency toward violence caused Wynette to seek a divorce in 1975. A year later, her fourth marriage lasted less than two months. Her fifth and final marriage took place in 1978 to George Richey, a songwriter she had known for several years. During the 1970s, she began to be plagued by a variety of medical problems, many requiring operations, that continued up until her death. Her house in Nashville was broken into on 15 separate occasions and mysteriously set on fire. In 1978, she was the victim of a bizarre kidnapping incident. By the late 1980s, she had been treated for addiction to painkillers and had filed for bankruptcy. As a writer for *People* noted after her death, ''in Tammy Wynette's world, something always seemed to go wrong.''

As Wynette's career continued into the 1990s, so did her image as the devoted, subordinate wife. In 1992, after Hillary Clinton made a condescending reference to Wynette on *60 Minutes,* she quickly apologized at Wynette's insistence. That same year, Wynette collaborated with the dance group KLF on ''Justified and Ancient,'' which became a British club hit. An album she released in 1994 featured duets with Elton John, Smokey Robinson, and Sting, among others, and the following year, she and George Jones were reunited on a new album, which would be her last. While the country industry essentially abandoned older artists like Wynette, the fans remained faithful. In spite of increasingly serious health problems, she persisted in performing up until a month before she died on April 6, 1998. Months later, artists from various musical genres recorded a tribute album of her songs entitled *Tammy Wynette Remembered.*

—Anna Hunt Graves

FURTHER READING:

Bufwack, Mary A., and Robert Oermann. *Finding Her Voice: The Saga of Women in Country Music.* New York, Crown, 1993.

Dew, Joan. *Singers and Sweethearts: The Women of Country Music.* Garden City, New York, Doubleday and Company, 1977.

Gliatto, Tom. ''Heroine of Hardship.'' *People.* April 20, 1998, 54-61.

Wynette, Tammy, with Joan Dew. *Stand by Your Man.* New York, Simon and Schuster, 1979.

X

X Games

The annual Summer and Winter X Games bring together "extreme" athletes who compete in such sporting events as skateboarding, in-line skating, snowboarding, sky-surfing, sport-climbing, stunt bicycling, street luge, and barefoot water-ski jumping. The cable TV sports network ESPN developed the X Games and first broadcast them in the summer of 1995; the Winter X Games debuted in 1998. Touted as an alternative Olympics, the X Games cater to youth culture (the name is a convenient play on Generation X) and popularize athletic risk-taking. The X Games also commercialize and organize characteristically marginal and disorderly activities like skateboarding and skydiving, calling into question whether these increasingly mainstreamed sports can still be considered "extreme."

"Extreme" sports are those largely individualistic athletic activities that require people to push themselves "to the extreme," often by defying both gravity and society's standards for reasonable risk. Typically, extreme athletes also project an image that counters that of the "normal" athlete in terms of appearance, attitude, and training regimen. The emerging popularity of extreme sports in the 1990s reflected a shift in American fitness trends. The fitness craze of the 1980s inspired many otherwise inactive, non-athletic individuals to take up activities like jogging and aerobics. Memberships at health clubs boomed. While health and fitness remained a big business into the 1990s, both advertisers and young adult consumers transformed fitness into a *lifestyle* rather than just a periodic visit to the health club. A cult of "adrenaline addiction" infiltrated the rhetoric of youth culture and influenced the marketing strategies aimed at these new consumers of the "extreme" image. Sales of mountain bikes, in-line skates, and snowboards increased dramatically, as did the popularity of bungee jumping and skydiving. ESPN's X Games capitalized on this emerging fitness and consumer trend.

The X Games codify activities that typically have no rules. By applying measurable performance criteria to such recreational pursuits as in-line skating, rock climbing, and snowboarding, ESPN is able to order and control potentially chaotic sports. Because of their inherent physical dangers, extreme sports have generally garnered society's disapproval, thus amplifying their popularity in youth culture. However, in the wake of the X Games, which have assimilated extreme sports into an organized brand of Olympic-like games, such activities have become more respectable and organized. As a result, "extreme" has an increasingly slippery connotation—extreme sports are a popular pleasure because of their marginality and perceived threat to the mainstream, but events like the X Games render extreme sports *less* marginal and subsequently alter their popular culture meanings.

Ultimately, the X Games represent far more than just a sports competition. Mass marketing and media strategies tie in music, fashion, and manifold product endorsements aimed at ESPN's mostly male, 12 to 34-year-old viewing audience. Sponsors include caffeinated colas, athletic shoes, fast-food restaurants, and an "official" pain-killing aspirin. Additionally, the competition annually promotes related alternative music soundtracks and videos. ESPN also launches a road show prior to the Games, and the touring sports extravaganza spotlights the various events. The featured sports even have their own unique language; ESPN offers a glossary of "X Speak" on its World Wide Web X Games homepage.

—Adam Golub

FURTHER READING:

Youngblut, Shelly, editor. *Way Inside ESPN's X Games.* New York, Hyperion, 1998.

Xena, Warrior Princess

A 1996 *Ms.* magazine cover story lauded *Xena, Warrior Princess* as a feminist and progressive retelling of Greek myth, as television that is notable for "breaking new ground in its treatment of sex." Debuting in syndication in 1995, the series chronicles the adventures of a sword-wielding princess seeking to atone for her violent past. Accompanied by her sidekick, Gabrielle (Reneé O'Connor), Xena (Lucy Lawless) battles fickle gods, tyrants, slave traders, barbaric tribes, and other nemeses in a magical land that evokes ancient Greece and Rome. Filmed in New Zealand and produced by Renaissance Pictures in conjunction with MCA TV, the series is a postmodern pastiche of classical mythology, characterized by hyperbolic violence and slapstick. At the same time, it manages to explore sexuality and ethical issues without losing its mass audience. Xena's sexually-charged relationship with Gabrielle has made the series popular with lesbian audiences, in particular.

—Neal Baker

FURTHER READING:

Minkowitz, Donna. "Xena: She's Big, Tall, Strong—and Popular." *Ms.* July/August, 1996, 74-77.

Weisbrot, Robert. *Xena, Warrior Princess: The Official Guide to the Xenaverse.* New York, Doubleday, 1998.

The X-Files

When *The X-Files* premiered on the Fox network in the fall of 1993, no one predicted the degree of success that the show would eventually enjoy. After all, dramas in the fantasy and science fiction genres had not done well on TV for a decade (the *Star Trek* spin-offs excepted). But there was considerable interest in UFO phenomena in America, as evidenced by news accounts of alleged alien abductions, speculations about "crop circles," and sightings of supposed alien

David Duchovny (right) and Gillian Anderson as they appear in *The X-Files*.

spacecraft streaking across the skies. For some Americans, belief in UFO visitations dovetailed with their mistrust of the U.S. government, which has consistently denied any knowledge of alien encounters. Thus when the show premiered, tales of visitors from space and government conspiracies to cover up those visits might find a ready audience—and *The X-Files* did. It finished its first season with respectable ratings, and the second season began with an even larger audience. The show was clearly a hit, one of the few Fox programs to compete successfully with the major networks. Soon there were Golden Globe awards for the show, then Emmy awards, a successful full-length film released in the summer of 1998, and talk of a second film to follow.

The show's premise is that the FBI occasionally encounters cases that seem inexplicable in terms of science and logic—which are, in short, paranormal. Such investigations, designated "X-files," are referred to the show's two protagonists: Special Agent Fox Mulder (David Duchovny) and Special Agent Dana Scully (Gillian Anderson). Mulder tends readily to accept paranormal explanations for the cases that he and his partner investigate—partly due to the fact that he believes that his sister Samantha, who disappeared when they

were children, was a victim of alien abduction. Scully, who earned a medical degree before joining the FBI, is usually a skeptic, positing rational explanations for phenomena that appear to defy reason. The two agents are supervised by FBI Assistant Director Walter Skinner (Mitch Pileggi). In the show's early years, Skinner tended to be suspicious, and sometimes hostile, toward Mulder and Scully. By the fourth season, however, he appeared to have become their ally.

From the beginning, the show has had a recurring theme involving alien visitation, alien abductions, and the efforts of certain powerful groups to conceal or deny these sinister activities. The show's writers and producers refer to this story arc as "the mythology," although some fans call it "the conspiracy." The character most closely identified with the effort to cover up the alien presence is known only as "Cigarette Smoking Man" (William Davis), a ruthless covert operator who has cold-bloodedly ordered the deaths of several people who came too close to the truth - including Mulder's father. When asked by an associate why he did not have the troublesome Fox Mulder killed, the CSM replied, in effect, "Alive, Mulder is merely a nuisance; dead, he's a martyr."

But the mythology is not the sum total of the series. In a typical season of *The X-Files*, about half the episodes deal with the ongoing struggle over the aliens, while the other shows find agents Mulder and Scully investigating other sorts of paranormal phenomena. Over the course of several seasons, the agents have dealt with zombies, werewolves, ghosts, vampires, demons, and witches, not to mention astral projection, precognition, reincarnation, and the transmigration of souls. A few of their cases have had no paranormal aspects at all, involving instead relatively mundane subjects such as serial murder, psychological obsession, and genetic mutation.

In some of their cases involving the mythology, Mulder and Scully receive assistance from a group called "The Lone Gunmen"—an ironic reference to the Warren Commission's much-disbelieved conclusion that President John F. Kennedy was assassinated by a "lone gunman." These three men, identified only by their last names of Byers (Bruce Harwood), Langly (Dean Haglund) and Frohike (Tom Braidwood) are self-styled "conspiracy freaks" who once told Mulder that they help him because "You're more paranoid than we are."

Chris Carter is the series' creator, producer, and principal writer. After some time spent writing for *Surfing* magazine, Carter married a television writer and soon began to turn out scripts of his own. He wrote for several TV series, which gave him the contacts that allowed him to sell *The X-Files* to the Fox network. Carter says that his idea for the show is derived from his memories of a short-lived TV series (lasting only the 1974-75 season) called *Kolchak: The Night Stalker*. The show was, in turn, based on two successful made-for-TV movies: *The Night Stalker* and *The Night Strangler*. The premise for the movies and the series was the same: hard-bitten newspaper reporter Karl Kolchak (Darren McGavin), while covering the story of one or more bizarre crimes, comes to the conclusion that some supernatural creature is involved. Kolchak then researches the phenomenon (vampire, werewolf, witch, or whatever), learns how to kill the creature, and does so.

The 1998 feature film based on Carter's series, entitled *X-Files: Fight the Future*, may be unique in one respect. Although it was not uncommon during the 1990s to see theatrical films based on popular TV shows, such films were invariably produced after the TV series that inspired them had gone off the air. The X-Files movie may be the only one to date to be based on a TV show still on the air with first-run episodes when the film was released. Indeed, *X-Files: Fight the Future* was tied into the last episode of the 1997-98 season, its plot resolving several issues raised by the show's season-ending cliffhanger.

The popularity of *The X-Files* has been manifested through several aspects of popular culture beyond the series itself. Animated versions of Mulder and Scully (voiced by Duchovny and Anderson) appeared in an episode of the popular Fox cartoon *The Simpsons.* David Duchovny guest-hosted *Saturday Night Live* several times, which led to skits parodying his series. *The X-Files* was also satirized on Fox's comedy show *Mad TV,* in a skit about porn films called "The XXX Files." More respectful treatment has come from comic books and novels based on the series, fan clubs (many of whose members communicate with each other via Internet discussion groups), WWW sites, and Fox-sponsored X-Files conventions. The show has also generated the usual ephemera of anything in popular culture with a devoted following—hats, t-shirts, posters, PC screen-savers, and coffee mugs. In addition, episodes from the show are available on video about a year after airing.

Although the first five seasons of *The X-Files* were shot in Vancouver, British Columbia (to save production costs), the show moved to Los Angeles beginning with the 1998-99 season. The change was in response to a demand from David Duchovny, who wanted to be nearer to his Los Angeles-based wife, actress Tea Leoni. That the Fox network was willing to undergo the expense and inconvenience involved in the move was testimony to the popularity of the show and the network's high expectations for its future success.

—Justin Gustainis

FURTHER READING:

Farrand, Phil. *The Nit-Picker's Guide for X-Philes.* New York, Dell, 1997.

Genge, N.E. *The Unofficial X-Files Companion.* New York, Crown, 1995.

Lavery, David and Angela Hague, editors. *"Deny All Knowledge": Reading the X-Files.* Syracuse, New York, Syracuse University Press, 1996.

Lowry, Brian. *The Truth Is Out There: The Official Guide to The X-Files.* New York, HarperCollins, 1995.

The X-Men

The X-Men is the most popular team of superheroes in comic books in the 1990s. Featuring an often changing lineup of young mutant superheroes and unusually complex story lines, the X-Men have found a consistently large and loyal audience of comic-book readers. Since 1980 only Spider-Man and Batman have rivaled them in popularity and sales. The X-Men's market clout has helped publisher Marvel Comics remain the undisputed industry leader, and the series' formula has been widely imitated throughout the superhero

genre. Few other comic-book series of recent decades have been as influential.

Marvel first published *The X-Men* in 1963. The concept devised by Stan Lee and Jack Kirby was an extension of the Marvel formula already realized in such characters as Spider-Man and the Fantastic Four. The X-Men were teenaged costumed superheroes who used their powers in the service of humanity, even though the society at large misunderstood and feared them. Unlike their superhero peers, however, the X-Men had never even been human. As mutants, they were born with their special powers—usually as a consequence of parents exposed to radioactivity. This distinction left the X-Men especially alienated from human society and made them special victims of misplaced human anxieties. Lee and later writers would often use this premise to conceive stories critical of bigotry and racial persecution.

The first X-Men lineup consisted of Cyclops, with the power to project devastating "optic blasts"; the Beast, with the agility and strength of his namesake; the Angel, who could fly with the aid of natural wings; Iceman, with power over cold and ice; and Marvel Girl, with the mental ability to move objects. Their leader was the enigmatic Professor Xavier, who, though confined to a wheelchair, possessed an impressive variety of telepathic powers. Xavier recruited the teenage mutants to enroll in his private School for Gifted Youngsters, which was a front for the X-Men's training facility. The X-Men defended humanity against an array of evil mutants, the most formidable of whom was Magneto—"the master of magnetism." The heroes also had to fight in their own defense against the Sentinels—a series of mutant-hunting robots engineered by bigoted humans determined to resolve the "mutant question."

A modest-selling title, *The X-Men* did not achieve the spectacular commercial success enjoyed by most other Marvel comic books in the 1960s. By the early 1970s the series consisted of only reprinted stories and seemed doomed for cancellation. But in 1975 Marvel revamped the series, keeping only Cyclops and Professor Xavier in the group and introducing a new lineup of international mutants. Created by writer Len Wein and artist Dave Cockrum, the new X-Men included Nightcrawler, a German with superhuman agility, the power of teleportation, and a horrifying demonic appearance; Colossus, a Russian—one of the first to be a hero in comic books—with extraordinary physical strength; Storm, an African princess with the ability to summon and control weather and the elements; and Wolverine, a hot-tempered Canadian armed with indestructible steel claws and the ferocious fighting tendencies of his namesake.

Between 1977 and 1981 writer Chris Claremont and writer/artist John Byrne transformed *The X-Men* from a second-tier title to the top-selling comic book on the market. As the lineup of the X-Men continued to evolve, the story lines became increasingly intricate and absorbing. There was something about the series for most fans to enjoy. The interplay among the distinctive characters was exceptionally well-developed and believable by comic-book standards. Wolverine's ethos of righteous morality backed up by violence made him one of the most popular superheroes of the Reagan/Rambo era. Strong and complex female characters like Storm, Phoenix, and Rogue helped to make the X-Men one of the few superhero titles to win a significant following among teenage girls.

The X-Men's fantastic commercial success predictably spawned a host of comic-book crossovers, spin-offs, and rip-offs. Throughout the 1980s and 1990s, they multiplied. There were titles devoted to adult mutants (*Excalibur, X-Factor*), adolescent mutants (*The New Mutants, Generation-X*), and even pre-pubescent mutants (*Power Pack*). The concept of the 1980s Teenage Mutant Ninja Turtles originated in part as a satire of the X-Men's overexposure (before graduating itself to overexposure). The first issue of a new X-Men title launched in 1991 set an industry record by selling more than eight million copies. An array of licensed products highlighted by the Fox network's successful *X-Men* animated series broadened the X-Men's market even further. The consequences of this ''X-treme'' mutant proliferation became a matter of some controversy among comic-book fans. While many fans welcomed the varieties of X-Men spin-offs and crossovers, others criticized them for being poorly conceived and confusing, and some fan critics charged Marvel with exploiting brand loyalty at the expense of good storytelling. To a large extent, the overexposure of the X-Men epitomized the problem of a saturated and shrinking market that plagued the comic-book industry as a whole in the mid-1990s.

Still, the X-Men remain at or near the top of the best-selling comic-book titles. Among the more fully realized comic-book expressions of modern adolescent fantasies, Marvel's team of misunderstood mutants fully deserve their status as the preferred superheroes of Generation X.

—Bradford Wright

FURTHER READING:

Daniels, Les. *Marvel: Five Fabulous Decades of the World's Greatest Comic Book Heroes*. New York, Harry N. Abrams, 1991.

Lee, Stan. *Son of Origins of Marvel Comics*. New York, Simon and Schuster, 1975.

The Uncanny X-Men. New York, Marvel Comics, 1984.

Y

Y2K

The expression Y2K, shorthand for the year 2000 (Y=year; 2=two; K=the symbol for 1,000), helped define the closing days of the twentieth century by spotlighting some pitfalls of the computer age. Y2K represented a major problem—some called it a crisis of global proportions—caused mainly by older computers whose programmers and software designers failed to foresee what could happen in the year 2000. Often called ''the Y2K bug,'' this problem came about because early computer designers used only a two-digit year—uniformly dropping the ''19'' that stands at the beginning of every year from 1900 to 1999. What the designers failed to take into consideration was the problem posed by the year 2000. Computer logic meant the machines would translate the numbers 00 not as the year 2000 but as 1900. In the closing days of the century, the world was put on notice that computers using the two-digit formulation could malfunction because of this inability to distinguish years belonging to different centuries.

Because computers had become intertwined with almost every facet of life in America and virtually the rest of the world, some doomsayers predicted that banks would fail, military systems would become paralyzed, planes would fall out of the sky, elevators would stop, stock exchanges would collapse, and life in general would be dramatically disrupted.

Although the problem had been known about for years, governments and businesses waited until the last few years of the twentieth century to tackle the potential crisis. For example, it was not until September 1997 that the Securities and Exchange Commission (SEC), the U.S. government watchdog over the stock exchange markets, issued a notice to investors to pressure investment companies to make their computers ''Y2K compliant''—a phrase meaning that computers had been checked and fixed, if necessary, to avoid any year 2000 problems when the clock struck midnight on December 31, 1999. The SEC also urged investors to press publicly traded companies to take steps to avoid a Y2K disaster, including assessing the cost of fixing their computers and making sure their officers and board members took out personal liability insurance for what could be an avalanche of lawsuits.

With great fanfare, U.S. President Bill Clinton announced in December 1998 that the Social Security Administration, which then handled some 40 million checks each month for pensioners, disabled people, and widows, was Y2K compliant. Nevertheless, some Republicans took issue with the Democratic president's claims that checks would go out on time, noting that some banks that receive checks for recipients and are vital to the system might be noncompliant.

Later, the Agriculture Secretary, Dan Glickman, announced at a Senate hearing on the Y2K problem that there would not be widespread food shortages in the United States because of the millennium bug. ''There are some fear-mongers there,'' Glickman said, as he urged people to avoid stockpiling or hoarding food as the year 2000 approached. Glickman conceded, however, that although he did not see major food shortages, ''there will be some glitches'' and disruptions in the marketplace.

While American businesses and local, state, and federal governments were spending millions of dollars to correct the problem with computers, some developing countries lagged. The World Bank reported that some areas, notably sub-Sahara Africa, could run into major problems with electricity, food, and health care. In early 1999, with less than a year to go before the 2000 bug might hit, the Bank found in a survey of 139 countries that only 21 had taken major steps to solve the problem, although 54 had some kind of national policy to deal with the bug.

By the end of 1999, observers hoped that the steps taken by companies and governments would prevent Y2K from causing any major disasters. The fear of Y2K ebbed and swelled in different areas across the globe, depending on whether the most important computer systems had become Y2K compliant. But certainly, Y2K had done more than create a global panic; it deflated the esteem some held for the early designers of software machinery, who had been looked upon as geniuses and had become millionaires and billionaires virtually overnight. Their use of the two-digit code saved steps in millions of computer applications, but at the same time lobbed a gigantic, ticking time bomb into the next century.

—Michael Posner

FURTHER READING:

De Jaeger, Peter, and Richard Bergeon and Robin Guenier. *Countdown Y2K: Business Survival Planning for the Year 2000.* New York, John Wiley and Sons, 1998.

Yankee Doodle Dandy

In 1942, James Cagney starred in the Hollywood film *Yankee Doodle Dandy*—the story of the life of George M. Cohan. The title refers to Cohan's famous song, ''I'm a Yankee Doodle Dandy,'' written for the Broadway play, *Little Johnny Jones*, in 1904. In this musical, Cohan sang the lyrics that would live through the century: ''I'm a Yankee Doodle Dandy, / A Yankee Doodle, do or die; / A real live nephew of my Uncle Sam's / Born on the Fourth of July.'' It is one of several Cohan tunes that have been passed from generation to generation in celebration of the American spirit. Released shortly after the Japanese attack on Pearl Harbor, *Yankee Doodle Dandy* was warmly received by American wartime audiences, who were particularly receptive to the patriotic songs in the film. Cagney won an Oscar for his performance, and the movie won Academy Awards for Best Sound Recording and Best Scoring of a Musical Picture. On July 4, 1985, the Cagney film was rereleased as the first computer-colorized production by Ted Turner.

—Sharon Brown

FURTHER READING:

Buckner, Robert, and Patrick McGilligan. *Yankee Doodle Dandy.* Madison, University of Wisconsin Press, 1981.

James Cagney in a scene from the film *Yankee Doodle Dandy*.

Yankee Stadium

Yankee Stadium, one of the oldest stadiums in the United States is a shrine to baseball fans. Some of the game's most dramatic and historic moments have occurred there. But this most hallowed of ballparks, haunted by the ghosts of baseball past, is also one of the sport's grittiest, most plebeian arenas, famed around the major leagues for its rowdy, roughhouse Bronx crowd.

The Yankee Stadium area covers approximately 11.6 acres in the South Bronx, with the playing field itself spanning 3.5 acres. Construction began on the new park, designed as a permanent home for New York's American League baseball team, on May 5, 1922. On April 18 of the following year, Yankee Stadium opened to the public. Yankee right fielder Babe Ruth promptly delivered the edifice's first home run. Soon the park was renowned for its 296-foot "short porch" in right field, conducive to home runs by left-handed hitters. Righties were commensurately daunted by "Death Valley," a 457-foot expanse in left-center where sure home runs miraculously turned into fly ball outs. With the advent of night baseball in 1946, a combination of 800 multi-vapor and incandescent lamps were installed to illuminate the field.

In 1932, the Yankees began to honor their greatest legends with the erection of monuments and plaques in the outfield section of the stadium. The first monument was dedicated to the memory of Miller Huggins, the manager who led the team to three world championships in the 1920s. Subsequent plaques and monuments have honored team captains Lou Gehrig and Thurman Munson, both of whom died tragically, as well as Hall of Fame players like Ruth, Joe DiMaggio, and Mickey Mantle. Originally located on the playing field itself, the monuments posed a curious obstacle for outfielders, who often had to dodge the memorials to retrieve fly balls. Relocated in 1976 to a new area dubbed "Monument Park," the monuments are now safely behind the outfield fences and available for viewing by the public.

In 1973, as the Yankees completed their fiftieth anniversary season in what was now known as "The House That Ruth Built," Yankee Stadium was remodeled and renovated. While the two-year project was under way, the team played its home dates at nearby Shea Stadium. The new Yankee Stadium opened on April 15, 1976, to mostly positive reviews. The building's distinctive art deco facade was retained in part and relocated to the centerfield bleachers.

In both its incarnations, Yankee Stadium has played host to some of baseball's most historic moments. On September 27, 1927, Babe Ruth clouted his record sixtieth home run there off Washington Senators pitcher Tom Zachary. Thirty-four years later, Yankee outfielder Roger Maris eclipsed Ruth's record with his sixty-first homer off the Boston Red Sox Tracy Stallard, a mark which stood until St.

Louis Cardinal Mark McGwire shattered it in 1998. The old stadium also provided the setting for some emotional farewells, from a dying Lou Gehrig's inspiring valedictory in 1939, when he told the world he was "the luckiest man on the face of the earth," to a cancer-ravaged Babe Ruth's last salute in 1948. In 1977, the Yankees celebrated their return to championship status after a 15-year drought in the Bronx ballpark after a clinching game that saw slugging outfielder Reggie Jackson club three home runs off three different Los Angeles Dodger pitchers. The following April, jubilant fans showered the field with "Reggie Bars," a chocolate and peanut confection named for the hot-dogging star after he vowed he would become so famous "they'll name a candy bar after me."

Candy bars have not been the only objects to come flying out of the Yankee Stadium stands over the years. At various times, golf balls, shot glasses, batteries, assorted coins, and torrents of beer have been flung onto the field by jubilant, angry, or just plain inebriated fans looking to terrorize Yankee opponents. The prevailing air of rowdiness has occasionally taken a more endearing form, as when ten-year-old Jeffrey Maier snatched a fly ball away from Baltimore Oriole right fielder Tony Tarasco during the 1996 American League Championship series, resulting in a game-tying Yankee home run. Around the major leagues, Yankee Stadium is known as an exhilarating, if intimidating, place to play, in part due to its fans.

In the 1990s, baseball's pre-eminent shrine suffered the ironic fate of becoming something of a political football, when Yankee owner George Steinbrenner loudly threatened to move the team when its lease expired if he could not get a new stadium constructed with municipal assistance. New York politicians responded with recrimination and posturing. Several civic leaders called for a referendum aimed at keeping the team in the Bronx. Baseball purists and fans of the old building largely sided with them. The fact that the team's crosstown rivals—the New York Mets—play in Shea Stadium, a drab cookie cutter facility, has contributed to the glorification of "the Stadium" as one of baseball's high holy places. Even as the Yankees won their twenty-fourth World Series in 1998, Steinbrenner continued to threaten to move the team if a new stadium is not built. Despite the stadium's hallowed status, Steinbrenner's wish may become a reality. When a beam fell from the roof during the 1997-1998 season (luckily when the stadium was empty) the future of Yankee Stadium seemed more uncertain than ever.

—Robert E. Schnakenberg

FURTHER READING:

Gershman, Michael. *Diamonds: The Evolution of the Ballpark*. New York, Houghton Mifflin, 1995.

Lowry, Phillip J. *Green Cathedrals: The Ultimate Celebrations of All 273 Major League and Negro League Ballparks Past and Present*. Cooperstown, Society for American Baseball Research, 1986.

Robinson, Ray, and Christopher Jennison. *Yankee Stadium: 75 Years of Drama, Glamor, and Glory*. New York, Penguin Studio, 1998.

Yankovic, "Weird Al" (1959—)

Rock 'n' roll's top jester goes by the name "Weird Al" Yankovic. He specializes in creating amusing lyrics for popular rock tunes as well as writing humorous ditties in generic song styles. Yankovic has appeared on albums, starred in his own television show, and appeared in several films.

Yankovic was born Alfred Matthew Yankovic on October 23, 1959 in the Los Angeles suburb of Lynwood. He first took up the accordion when a salesman came around to solicit business for a music school. His parents, Nick and Mary Yankovic, decided on the accordion because of polka king Frankie Yankovic (no relation). As a child and young teen, Al watched a lot of TV, and TV provided the inspiration for much of his later work (most of his songs center around either food or television shows). He also became a fan of such musician/comedians as Allan Sherman (who also specialized in creating song parodies) and Spike Jones. Yankovic became acquainted with these musicians through the Dr. Demento radio show, which would later become a great source of publicity for his talents. In fact, Yankovic played his first song to be heard on the air, "Belvedere Cruising," on the Dr. Demento show in 1976.

After an extraordinary career at Lynwood High School, where he graduated as valedictorian, Yankovic attended the California Technical Institute in San Luis Obispo to study architecture, a field he chose because it was listed first in the catalogue. It was at California Polytechnic Institute that Yankovic had a radio show and earned the nickname "Weird Al." In 1979 Yankovic recorded his first real hit, a parody of the popular "My Sharona" by The Knack called "My Bologna." (The Knack liked the song so much they convinced their label to release the song as a single.) After the astounding success of that song, forever to be known as the "bathroom recording" as it was recorded in the acoustically perfect men's room, Al launched into a phenomenal career that has spanned 17 albums, movies, videos, and edible underwear.

Yankovic reached wide public attention in 1984 with his song "Eat It," a parody of Michael Jackson's popular hit "Beat It." Yankovic's video of the song amusingly parodied the visuals of the Jackson video, earning it a good deal of play on MTV. "Eat It" earned Yankovic his first Grammy Award, and the album, *"Weird Al" Yankovic in 3-D*, reached the top 15. On the album, Yankovic also recreated the set of the original *Jeopardy* TV series for his parody "I Lost on Jeopardy," which was based on a tune by the Greg Kihn Band.

Yankovic was tapped to provide songs for films, including "This Is the Life" for *Johnny Dangerously* (1984) and "Dare to Be Stupid" for *Transformers: The Movie* (1986). He starred in his own film, *UHF* (1989), as George Newman, head of a beleaguered, small-time cable station, as well as appearing in all three *Naked Gun* movies (1988, 1991, 1994), *Tapeheads* (1988), *Nothing Sacred* (1997), and *Desperation Boulevard* (1998). Yankovic was given his own Saturday morning TV show, *The "Weird Al" Show*, that ran during 1997-98 season and was compared to *Pee-wee's Playhouse*. In it, Al starred as himself opposite his best friend "Harvey the Wonder Hamster" (a daredevil hamster in his own habitrail), with a collection of friends and regulars (including Stan Freberg) who dropped by to discuss that week's moral problem. Also included in the show were a series of "Fatman" animated cartoons (for which Yankovic supplied the voice) based on the overweight character from the video "Fat" done up as a superhero.

His 1992 video "Smells Like Nirvana" pushed the pretentious original Nirvana video a step too far while lampooning the unintelligibility of its lyrics, and earned a place on *Rolling Stone*'s top 100 videos of all-time. Nirvana members commented that they knew they had made it when Yankovic parodied their song. Yankovic's

"Weird Al" Yankovic

videos are some of the best in the business and have been compiled on two collections, first the *Compleat Al* (1985), and updated as the *Al Yankovic: The Videos* (1996). Yankovic had his biggest success to date with his album *Bad Hair Day* (1996), which featured a parody of Coolio's "Gangsta Paradise" as "Amish Paradise." (Though Coolio granted permission for the video, he later condemned Al's version).

Yankovic has also tried his hand at directing, creating a parody of Maurice Binder's James Bond opening titles for the film *Spy Hard* (1996), with Yankovic singing "Theme from *Spy Hard*" while silhouettes of overweight women swim by. Yankovic's stage shows are often described as some of the funniest and most entertaining around. At the end of the century, Yankovic reigned as the king of musical parody, a singular phenomenon in American musical history.

—Dennis Fischer

FURTHER READING:

Insana, Tino, and Al Yankovic. *The Authorized Al.* Chicago, Contemporary Books, 1985.

"The Official Weird Al Web Site." http://www.weirdal.com. May 1999.

Yanni (1954—)

Along with Slim Whitman, Ray Stevens, and Kenny G, New Age artist Yanni is one of those inexplicable music curiosities who rode to the top of the charts on a sea of critical incredulity. Dismissed by one reviewer as a "musical Fabio," Yanni is known not so much for the music he makes as the sensation he creates. His albums and videos have sold multiple millions worldwide, and he has personally saved more than a few public television stations with his prodigious pledge-drive potency.

Born Yanni Chryssomallis in Kalamata, Greece, the future New Age superstar was a national swimming champion in his teens. After immigrating to the United States in 1972, he passed up a career in clinical psychology to pursue his creative muse full time. A self-taught musician, Yanni began composing in his head, relying on collaborators to put his orchestrations down on paper. He released his first full-length album, *Keys to Imagination,* in 1986.

The "Yanni sound" changed very little over the next several years. Gauzy strains of synthesizer continued to waft insidiously down upon the listener, as vaguely Mediterranean-sounding hooks are stated and restated by various instruments. The music incorporated elements of classical, New Age, and world beat into a sonic melange that one unfavorable reviewer called "aural wallpaper." Even Yanni himself often referred to the plastic arts when describing it. "Music is like creating an emotional painting," he explained. "The sounds are colors." Colors derived from an irritatingly narrow spectrum, according to some critics, who found Yanni's repetition of musical themes numbingly aggravating. Despite these brickbats, however, the Greek tycoon's record sales climbed throughout the 1980s.

Yanni's live appearances became major moneymakers as well, as the mustachioed and classically handsome composer developed a large and devoted fan following. For concerts, Yanni assembled a multi-piece orchestra with instrumentation culled from virtually every continent, over which he would preside beatifically from behind a stack of keyboards. Yanni often staged his appearances at major international landmarks, like the Taj Mahal and China's Forbidden City. These lavishly mounted productions generated enormous viewership for public television stations across America and were aired repeatedly during pledge weeks. On one Saturday night in 1994, his concert documentary at Greece's Acropolis helped one PBS affiliate raise over $50,000 in pledges. A number of PBS stations even canceled a previously scheduled Andy Williams special to rebroadcast Yanni's performance.

Befitting his superstar status, Yanni cultivated a personal life designed to keep him in the crosshairs of the paparazzi. In 1989, the then little-known Yanni began dating Linda Evans, star of TV's *Dynasty.* The flaxen-haired beauty reportedly was won over by the sinewy Greek's command of the music of the spheres. They would remain a couple until 1998, when conflicts over the directions of their respective careers compelled them to end the relationship.

Indeed, much of Yanni's success has been attributed to his appeal to women. But the New Age superstar has bristled at the suggestion that his cover-of-a-romance-novel appearance drove his record sales. He claimed the bulk of his fan mail comes not from sex-starved housewives but from the homebound and the infirm, who find his music soothing. Some have even ascribed healing powers to Yanni's compositions, a claim the composer modestly deflected away.

"I don't see myself as a peacemaker at all or anything like that," he told the *Orange County Register* in 1998, "I'm merely standing in one place saying it's possible for us to do this, for people of the world to share in my music. If I can play even a minute role in something like that in my lifetime, then I will have accomplished something special."

Yanni's earthly mission continued to draw adherents throughout the 1990s. In early 1999, he sold out ten dates at New York's Radio City Music Hall. Other performers have even followed his path to success, the critics be damned. The composer and former *Entertainment Tonight* host John Tesh appeared to have schooled on Yanni's PBS-driven marketing plan, replete with extravagantly produced performances at such notable sites as Red Rocks, Nevada.

—Robert E. Schnakenberg

FURTHER READING:

Ferguson, Andrew. "PBS: The Yanni State." *National Review.* May 2, 1994.

Wener, Ben. "Yanni, The World's Most Loved and Loathed Music Figure, Is Back." *The Orange County Register.* March 4, 1998.

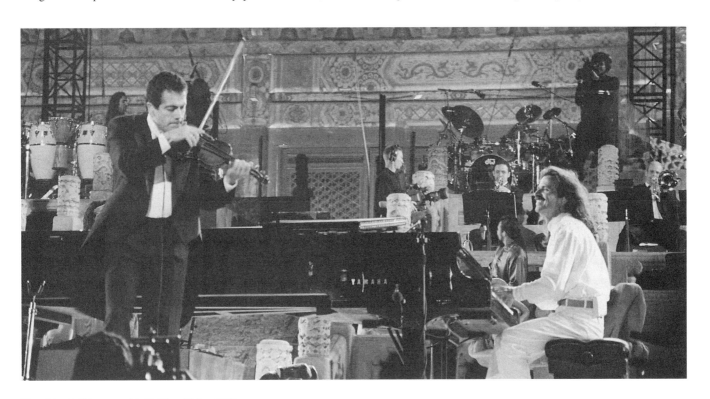

Yanni (seated) in concert in Beijing, China, 1997.

The Yardbirds

The backbone of the rock band The Yardbirds consisted of vocalist Keith Relf, rhythm guitarist Chris Dreja, bassist Paul Samwell-Smith, and drummer Jim McCarty. However, they were most famous for their succession of luminary lead guitarists, Eric Clapton, Jeff Beck, and Jimmy Page. Under Clapton the Yardbirds played high-energy R&B with long improvisations called "rave-ups" in which they would alter tempo and volume, building to a climax before returning to the song. Although the recording technology is poor by today's standards, *Five Live Yardbirds* (1965) reveals a tight unit of talented musicians. Inspired by the phenomenal success of the Beatles, the Yardbirds then recorded the pop song, "For Your Love," written by Graham Gouldman, and this became their first hit. The song featured a harpsichord and bongos, but very little Clapton. Uncomfortable with the band's commercial direction, Clapton left to pursue pure blues in John Mayall's Bluesbreakers.

Guitar wizard Jeff Beck then joined the band and transformed the Yardbirds into trailblazing musical pioneers. Innovating with fuzztone, feedback, and harmonic sustain within the medium of Gouldman-penned pop songs, they produced classics such as "Evil Hearted You" and "Heart Full of Soul." Their first original studio album, *The Yardbirds* (1966, renamed *Over, Under, Sideways, Down* in the U.S., but commonly known as *Roger the Engineer* in either country) is a *tour de force* on Beck's part. When Samwell-Smith left the band, session musician Jimmy Page was recruited as bassist until Dreja could learn the bass, then Page moved up as second lead guitarist alongside Beck. The Beck-Page lineup recorded only four songs, one of them being "Stroll On" (a version of "Train Kept A-Rollin'"), which they performed in Michelangelo Antonioni's 1966 film *Blow-Up*, a cult classic of the Swingin' London scene.

When Beck left the group, Page introduced his own musical visions and recorded *Little Games* (1967). An odd mixture of pop songs and virtuoso guitar playing, this album is most intriguing as a document of Page's early development, displaying many riffs and effects which were later redeveloped in Led Zeppelin. Especially noteworthy is the instrumental "White Summer," later reworked as "Black Mountain Side" and the introduction of "Over the Hills and Far Away." When the remaining members left, Page recruited vocalist Robert Plant, bassist John Paul Jones, and drummer John Bonham, and debuted the band as the New Yardbirds, later renamed Led Zeppelin.

In 1984, ex-Yardbirds Samwell-Smith, Dreja, and McCarty formed the band Box of Frogs (Relf had died in 1976, electrocuted by a guitar). Although some tracks from *Box of Frogs* (1984) and *Strange Land* (1986) featured guest guitarists Page and Beck, these heavy-metal offerings made little impact.

The Yardbirds are aptly called "legendary," for although their recordings have lapsed into obscurity, their influence on guitar-driven rock is enduring and pervasive. Clapton, Beck, and Page gave rise to the "guitar hero," displacing the singer as the focal point of the rock and roll band, and a legion of 1970s guitarists cited the Yardbirds as a major influence. In spite of their uneven recording history, the Yardbirds' small, experimental body of work places them just behind the Beatles, the Stones, and the Who as a major band of the British Invasion.

—Douglas Cooke

FURTHER READING:

Mackay, Richard. *Yardbirds World.* Mackay/Ober, 1989.

Platt, John A. *The Yardbirds.* London, Sidgwick & Jackson, 1983.

Russo, Greg. *Yardbirds: The Ultimate Rave-Up.* Floral Park, New York, Crossfire Publishers, 1997.

Yastrzemski, Carl (1939—)

Better known as "Yaz," Carl Michael Yastrzemski of the Boston Red Sox epitomized the spirit of hard work and determination that made baseball players American heroes in the twentieth century. As left-fielder, Yaz mastered the art of playing hits off Fenway Park's infamous "Green Monster," earning seven Gold Gloves during the course of his career. He also was a consistently dangerous batter with a flair for getting crucial hits in big games. Yaz achieved the coveted Triple Crown for highest batting average (.326), most runs batted in (121), and most home runs (44) in 1967 on the way to Boston's first pennant in three decades. By the time he retired, he had amassed more than three thousand hits and four hundred homers, a mark met by no other player in the American League. He was inducted into the Hall of Fame in 1989.

—Susan Curtis

FURTHER READING:

Yastrzemski, Carl, and Al Hirshberg. *YAZ: The Autobiography of Carl Yastrzemski.* New York, Viking Press, 1968.

The Yellow Kid

The Yellow Kid by Richard Felton Outcault (1863-1928) is generally held to be the character that gave birth to American comic strips. The Kid, later named Mickey Dugan by Outcault, was a smallish figure dressed in a nightshirt who roamed the streets of New York in company with other urchins. The Yellow Kid was not a comic strip, rather he appeared as a character in a series of large single panel color comic illustrations in the *New York World* with the more or less continuous running title *Hogan's Alley*. The *World* published the first of these illustrations, *At the Circus in Hogan's Alley*, on May 5, 1895. The newspaper's readers, it seems, singled out the Kid as a distinctive character and his popularity led other artists to create similar characters. In short succession these actions gave rise to the comic strip.

Outcault was born in Lancaster, Ohio and studied design in Cincinnati before joining the laboratories of Thomas Edison as an illustrator in 1888. By 1890 Outcault combined employment as an illustrator on the *Electrical World,* a trade journal, with freelance cartoon work for illustrated humor journals such as *Puck, Judge, Life,* and *Truth*. The Kid's genesis lay in the genre of city urchin cartoons made popular by these journals. In particular Outcault drew inspiration from Michael Angelo Woolf's work.

A prototype Yellow Kid appeared in Outcault's "Feudal Pride in Hogan's Alley" published in *Truth* June 2, 1894. This small figure in a nightshirt cropped up in several other Outcault cartoons before blossoming into a larger more familiar, but as yet unnamed, Kid in Outcault's "Fourth Ward Brownies" published in *Truth* February 9,

1895 and reprinted in the *World* February 17, 1895. The Kid appeared again in Outcault's ''The Fate of the Glutton'' in the *World* March 10, 1895. In these two appearances the Kid's nightshirt had an ink smudged handprint a distinctive feature of the later *World* panels. After the May 5 episode the *World* published ten more ''Hogan's Alley'' panels in 1895. The Kid appeared in them all. On January 5, 1896 the Kid was center stage in a yellow nightshirt and thereafter became the focus of each panel.

The Yellow Kid became the mainstay of the *World's* comic supplement during 1896, but in mid October Outcault moved his strip from the *World* to William Randolph Hearst's *New York Journal.* Hearst had infamously bought the talent of the *World* to staff the *Journal* and naturally enough poached Outcault for the launch of the comic supplement on October 18, 1896. Thereafter the Kid appeared in tabloid page size illustration under the running title ''McFadden's Row of Flats'' before departing on a world tour in 1897. Beginning October 25, 1896 the Kid also began to appear in an occasional comic strip like series of panels under the running title of ''The Yellow Kid,'' which was Outcault's first use of that name in a comic supplement. Outcault stayed with Hearst's *Journal* for a little over a year. The last Yellow Kid comic feature appeared in the *Journal* January 23, 1898. Outcault then returned to the *World,* producing a series of ''Hogan's Alley''–like panels featuring an African-American character.

Outcault's shift of the Yellow Kid from the *World* to the *Journal* raised issues of copyright. The *World* continued to publish a version of the Kid drawn by George Luks. Prior to leaving the *World* Outcault had sought copyright protection for his creation in a letter to the Library of Congress on September 7, 1896. He had also attached the label ''Do Not Be Deceived None Genuine Without This Signature'' above his signature in the *World's* September 6, 1896 episode of ''Hogan's Alley.'' Later advice from W. B. Howell of the Treasury Department, which policed copyright laws at that time, advised Outcault that he had failed to secure protection on the image of the Kid because he had only included one illustration instead of two in his application. Outcault did however secure protection for the title ''The Yellow Kid.''

Two minor controversies have marked the history of the Yellow Kid. Until the late 1980s accounts of the origins of comic strips generally accepted that the Yellow Kid's nightshirt was colored yellow as a test of the ability of yellow ink to bond to newsprint. But Richard Marschall argues in his *America's Great Comic Strip Artists* that this could not have been the case since yellow ink had been used earlier. Likewise Bill Blackbeard gives a detailed account of the *World's* use of color in his introduction to *The Yellow Kid: A Centennial Celebration* that makes clear the testing yellow ink theory is incorrect. The Yellow Kid is often cited as the origin of the term ''yellow journalism.'' However, the historian Mark D. Winchester has demonstrated that the term yellow journalism came into use during the Spanish-American War in 1898 to describe the war hysteria whipped up by Hearst and Pulitzer. The Yellow Kid was transformed into a symbol of yellow journalism during this campaign rather than giving his name to it. The distinction is subtle but crucial.

—Ian Gordon

FURTHER READING:

Blackbeard, Bill and Martin Williams. *The Smithsonian Collection of Newspaper Comics.* Washington, D.C., Smithsonian Institution Press, 1977.

Gordon, Ian. *Comic Strips and Consumer Culture, 1890-1945.* Washington, D.C., Smithsonian Institution Press, 1998.

Harvey, Robert. *The Art of the Funnies: An Aesthetic History.* Jackson, University Press of Mississippi, 1994.

Howell, W. B., ''Assistant Secretary, Treasury Department to W.Y. Connor, *New York Journal,* April 15, 1897,'' reprinted in, *Decisions of the United States Courts Involving Copyright and Literary Property, 1789-1909.* Bulletin 15, Washington, D.C., Library of Congress, 1980, 3187-3188.

Marschall, Richard. *America's Great Comic Strip Artists.* New York, Abbeville Press, 1989.

Outcault, Richard. *The Yellow Kid: A Centennial Celebration of the Kid Who Started the Comics.* Northampton, Massachusetts, Kitchen Sink Press, 1995.

Winchester, Mark D. ''Hully Gee, It's a War!!! The Yellow Kid and the Coining of 'Yellow Journalism.''' *Inks,* Vol. 2, No. 3, 1995, 22-37.

Yellowstone National Park

Comprising 2.2 million acres of northwest Wyoming, with slight incursions into Montana and Idaho, Yellowstone is the oldest national park in the United States. The park's unique sights originally inspired a nation that had not even fully conceived of what the term ''national park'' entailed. The park has evolved to stand as the preeminent symbol of the national park idea, whether inspiring the designation of other locations or revealing systematic flaws. Today, Yellowstone serves as an active battleground as Americans strive to define the meaning of preservation and wilderness.

From the outset, Yellowstone's unique attraction derived from its natural oddities. The region was the stuff of rumors; the return of explorers from the northern Rockies in 1810 had piqued the public's attention with stories of odd natural occurrences: thermal phenomena, a beautiful mountain lake, and a magnificent canyon entered into the unconfirmed reports. ''Could such a place exist?'' Americans asked upon hearing descriptions of ''Earth's bubbling cauldron.'' In 1870, other expeditions set out to explore the sights. In 1871 the Hayden Survey explored Yellowstone. Overwhelmed by the majesty and oddity that they beheld, they were at once overcome by its attraction and potential development. Such economic development, though, could exploit and ruin all that made the site peculiar. During this era of development and the massive harvesting of natural resources, these attributes were not sufficient to warrant preservation; the site also needed to be of no worth otherwise. Hayden repeatedly assured Congress that the entire area was worthless for anything but tourism. Lurking behind such plans were railroad companies eager to find tourist attractions in the West.

The establishment of the park by President Ulysses S. Grant on March 1, 1872, rings hollow by the standards of modern environmentalism. However, such designation, albeit under the jurisdiction of the U.S. Army until 1916, kept the area free of development during some of the region's boom years. As an example, Yellowstone's herd of North American bison is given credit for the species' endurance. While hunters decimated the larger herd by 1880, the park offered sanctuary to at least a few bison. Today, the Yellowstone herd is considered an anchor for the entire species. The present herd, ironically, has also led to controversy as it creeps past park borders.

The geyser named Old Faithful in the Yellowstone National Park.

In 1916, President Woodrow Wilson signed the National Park Act, creating the National Park Service and initiating the search for the meaning of such designation. Tourism rose steadily through the war years, and Park Service Director Stephen T. Mather largely developed and linked the park system. With the Wilderness Act of 1964, the shared cause of the park system became the effort to preserve areas as unspoiled "wilderness." While it had originally been set aside due to geological oddities, Yellowstone became a primary illustration of one of the most unique and secure ecosystems in the United States.

Yellowstone has proven to be an attraction of enduring proportions. Tourist visitation to the park has increased throughout the twentieth century, with the park becoming an international attraction. Massive visitation rates, however, have taken a toll on the remaining wilderness within the park. Many environmentalists call over-visitation Yellowstone's major threat. In addition, fires have repeatedly torn through the park, forcing administrators to consistently revisit their mandate. Proponents of wilderness argue that naturally occurring fires must be allowed to burn, whether or not they endanger tourists or damage park service property; administrators who see their responsibility to visitors argue for fire suppression. Such issues force

Americans to consider what a national park seeks to accomplish and reidentify Yellowstone's position as the symbolic leader of the American system of national parks.

—Brian Black

FURTHER READING:

Runte, Alfred. *National Parks: The American Experience.* Lincoln, University of Nebraska Press, 1987.

Yes

Yes's combination of technical proficiency, enigmatic lyrics, and large egos captured the essence of the progressive rock movement. Formed in 1968, the British art-rock band achieved international success with *The Yes Album* in 1971. Further success came with *Fragile* (1972) and its hit single "Roundabout," and *Close to the Edge* (1972), which is considered by many to be the band's masterpiece.

The band excelled in live shows and is known for its long-jamming songs, some of which are more than twenty minutes long. Lavish crystalline stage sets designed by artist Roger Dean (who also drew the band's album covers) helped make for hugely successful live shows; in the late 1970s, Yes set a record for selling out New York's Madison Square Garden 16 times. In 1983 Yes released *90125* which became their biggest selling album, carried by their only American number one hit "Owner of a Lonely Heart."

Even though the members of the band have changed incessantly over the years, Yes has continued to tour and release new material through the 1980s and 1990s. Their exuberant, complex music and fusion of celestial, spiritual, and pastoral themes have influenced such bands as Genesis, King Crimson, and Rush and has made Yes an all-time favorite for art-rock fans worldwide.

—Dave Goldweber

FURTHER READING:

Martin, Bill. *Music of Yes: Structure and Vision in Progressive Rock.* Chicago, Open Court, 1996.

Morse, Tim, editor. *Yesstories: Yes in Their Own Words.* New York, St. Martin's, 1996.

Stump, Paul. *The Music's All That Matters: A History of Progressive Rock.* London, Quartet, 1998.

Yippies

One of the more outlandish and short-lived groups of the 1960s American counterculture, Yippies were members of the Youth International Party, which was officially formed in January of 1968 by founding members Abbie Hoffman and Jerry Rubin in Washington, D.C. The group was essentially defunct as an activist organization within three years. During their brief life span, the Yippies were an influential presence at some of the later New Left's key protests, notably the mass demonstration at the Chicago Democratic Convention in August 1968, and the March on the Pentagon in October 1967, a demonstration which Rubin claimed as the birth of Yippie politics. Frequently reviled by other New Left activist groupings for the countercultural spirit and the carnival ethic which infused their activism, the Yippies were renowned for a surreal style of political dissent whose principle weapon was the public (and publicity-driven) mockery of institutional authority of any kind. The Yippies' departure from an earlier generation of 1960s radicalism which had been seen through the Civil Rights Act of 1964, and the first mass demonstration against the Vietnam War the following year, is one way into the story of what happened to the American New Left. Yippie activism captured perfectly the chaotic final years of the ''movement,'' as the New Left subsided into a factionalism and confusion over political objectives which replaced the relatively focused thinking of the first generation of 1960s radicals.

The politics which Hoffman and Rubin brought to Yippie activism had its roots in the broad coalition of dissent which grew out of the Civil Rights struggles of the early 1960s, and which, outside of the southern states, grouped itself initially around Students for a Democratic Society (SDS). Hoffman had worked for a northern support group of the civil rights organization Student Nonviolent Coordinating Committee (SNCC) before the group abandoned its integrationist stance in 1966 and purged the organization of white members. Rubin had enjoyed a high profile in the Free Speech Movement (FSM) founded at Berkeley in 1964. But the presence of poets (Allen Ginsberg) and musicians (Country Joe and the Fish, Phil Ochs, the Fugs) in the founding ranks of the party is one way of highlighting how far Yippie politics had travelled from the relatively orthodox activist strategies of the first generation New Left. In the place of politics, as such, Yippie activism preached the political dimension of culture, stressing the subversive potential inherent in spontaneous acts of individual dissent exercised through the free play of imagination and the integration of an erotic theatricality into daily life. SDS itself may never have adhered to a coherent political agenda, but with Rubin and Hoffman, any attempt at sustaining a structured theoretical programme was abandoned altogether. Separating itself abruptly from the early New Left emphasis on community organizing and relatively directed acts of protest, whilst retaining the New Left's pursuit of individual liberation, Yippie politics thus arrived as an untheorised synthesis of 1950s ''Beat'' thinking, Dadaism, and various positions taken within Marxist criticism from the 1930s onwards (notably the thinking of Bertolt Brecht and Herbert Marcuse).

Summarized by Ochs as ''merely an attack of mental disobedience on an obediently insane society,'' the ''cultural politics'' of Yippie took American state capitalism, the Vietnam War, and the University as its principal targets, with Rubin and Hoffman staging a range of theatrical street events in which the moral bankruptcy of ''the system'' was exposed, or (ideally) was forced into exposing itself. As early as 1965, Rubin could be found rehearsing the Yippie ethos following his subpoena to appear before the House Un-American Activities Committee (HUAC). Summoned before the Committee alongside a group of radicals drawn mainly from the Maoist Progressive Labor Party (PL), Rubin arrived in full American Revolutionary War costume and stood stoned, blowing giant gum bubbles, while his co-witnesses taunted the committee with Nazi salutes. In 1967, Hoffman was among a group who scattered dollar bills from the balcony of the New York stock exchange, whilst newspaper photographers captured the ensuing scramble for banknotes among the stockbrokers on the floor below. In October of the same year, Hoffman led a mass ''exorcism of demons'' during the March on the Pentagon.

But it was in Chicago, during the Democratic Convention of August 1968, that Yippie tactics were to find their defining moment. With the war in Vietnam dragging on, and frustration mounting among the various different groupings of the New Left, a series of mass demonstrations were planned to coincide with the Convention. From the very beginning, the lack of a coordinating voice or coherent agenda threatened to collapse the demonstration from within and bring violence to the streets of Chicago. All of the significant dissenting groups apart from SDS agreed on the need for a large scale protest of some kind, but each grouping had its own agenda. Dave Dellinger of National Mobilization to end the War in Vietnam (MOBE) argued for a combination of routine speeches, marches, and picketing against the War, while the old guard of SDS made plans of their own, independently of the reluctant SDS leadership. While representatives of PL, the Black Panther Party (BBP), and New York anarchist group the Motherfuckers also planned to attend in some capacity, young Democrats sought to tie a more restrained demonstration to the proceedings of the Convention itself.

The confusion was compounded by local Chicago residents, who turned out to stage a Poor People's March, and by a late change of heart by SDS who urged its members to attend. Against this backdrop, Mayor Daley announced that he would turn Chicago into an armed camp, and laid plans to call in the National Guard and the United States Army. It was the perfect scenario for the Yippies' own brand of chaotic theatrical dissent. With Hoffman and Rubin at the Yippie helm, the group embarked on a campaign of maximum publicity and misinformation, first announcing that it would leave town for $200,000, and then spreading the word that the City's water supply was to be contaminated with LSD. In Lincoln Park, the Yippies staged a free-wheeling carnival, a ''Festival of Life'' in opposition to the Convention's ''Festival of Death,'' the high point of which saw the nomination of a 150 pound pig named ''Pigasus'' as the Yippie's own presidential candidate (a direct reference to the International Dada Fair of 1920, in which the figure of ''Pigasus'' had made its first appearance). As had always seemed likely, the ''Festival of Life'' was broken up by violent police action which escalated over the following two days into a full blown riot, many officers notoriously removing their identification badges before wading into the crowds. Hoffmann and Rubin were arrested and charged with conspiracy to commit violence, alongside representatives from SDS, MOBE, and the BPP.

Before being given prison terms, Hoffman and Rubin used their bail conditions to good effect, hounding the judge from table to table while he lunched at a private members club, and then introduced Yippie politics to the judicial process itself, appearing in court dressed in judge's clothes and the white shirt of a Chicago policeman. Having summoned Ginsberg to appear before the court, the prosecution again drew attention to the cultural dimension of Yippie politics by cross-examining the poet on the seditious (meaning homosexual) content of his writings. The Yippies achieved massive press coverage during and after the trial, and by the time that Hoffman and Rubin were jailed in 1970, the pair had become international celebrities. Rubin's book *Do It!*, and Hoffman's *Revolution for the Hell of It* subsequently became international bestsellers. Although an organization calling itself the Yippies continued to publish protest literature into the 1980s, the party was more or less finished as an activist political movement soon after the trial.

—David Holloway

FURTHER READING:

Albert, Judith Clavir, and Stewart Edward Albert. *The Sixties Papers: Documents of a Rebellious Decade.* New York, Praeger, 1984.

Caute, David. *Sixty-Eight: The Year of the Barricades.* London, Paladin, 1988.

Hayden, Tom. *Trial.* London, Jonathan Cape, 1971.

Hoffman, Abbie. *Revolution for the Hell of It.* New York, Dial Press, 1968.

Rubin, Jerry. *Do It!.* New York, Simon and Schuster, 1970.

Steigerwald, David. *The Sixties and the End of Modern America.* New York, St Martin's Press, 1995.

Yoakam, Dwight (1956—)

In 1986, Dwight Yoakam helped revitalize country music with his twangy debut album *Guitars, Cadillacs, Etc., Etc.* Recorded in Los Angeles, the album mixed classic country covers with Yoakam's own compositions. Born in Kentucky, Yoakam grew up in Ohio, where he attended college before moving to southern California in the late 1970s. There he met his guitarist/producer Pete Anderson and developed an electric honky-tonk style derived from the early recordings of country legend Buck Owens. Unable to break into Nashville's music scene, Yoakam found a niche playing to rock audiences in California. He recorded an EP that caught the attention of record executives and launched his career. By the early 1990s, he was creating his own unconventional country style and scoring hits with songs like "A Thousand Miles from Nowhere." During the late 1990s, Yoakam also demonstrated his acting talent in films such as *Sling Blade* and *The Newton Boys.*

—Anna Hunt Graves

FURTHER READING:

Bego, Mark. *Country Hunks.* Chicago, Contemporary Books, 1994.

Kingsbury, Paul, Alan Axelrod, and Susan Costello, editors. *Country: The Music and the Musicians from the Beginnings to the '90s.* New York, Abbeville Press, 1994.

McCall, Michael, Dave Hoekstra, and Janet Williams. *Country Music Stars: The Legends and the New Breed.* Lincolnwood, Illinois, Publications International, 1992.

The Young and the Restless

When *The Young and the Restless* premiered on March 26, 1973, it revolutionized the entire concept of the "soap opera." Historically, the format reflected its roots in radio and, despite its jump to television, was still an aural medium with its primary emphasis on dialogue and story content. *The Young and the Restless,* however, placed a premium on shadowy, sensuous lighting, intriguing camera angles, and production values that provided a lavish romanticism that appealed to female viewers and, by eroticizing the genre, changed forever the way that "soaps" were photographed. But the series did not rely on style alone. Building from the typical soap opera structure of two intertwining families—one rich (The Brooks, who owned the

city newspaper) and one poor (the Fosters)—the show featured the inevitable star-crossed romance. But the show ventured into new areas, providing the first soap opera treatment of an extended rape sequence and the aftermath of a trial. It also dealt with such issues as euthanasia, drugs, obesity, eating disorders, mental illness, and problems of the handicapped.

In the 1980s, the show once again revolutionized the genre by shifting its focus away from its original core families to an entirely new set of younger characters. During the 1990s it continued to introduce mysterious new characters while maintaining the consistency of its vision and of its storylines, a remarkable feat for the genre, which allowed it to keep pace with its traditional competitors and the new programs that debuted during the decade.

—Sandra Garcia-Myers

FURTHER READING:

La Guardia, Robert. *Soap World.* New York, Arbor House, 1983.

Schemening, Christopher. *The Soap Opera Encyclopedia.* New York, Ballantine Books, 1985.

Young, Cy (1867-1955)

"Y is for Young/The magnificent Cy/People batted against him/ But I never knew why." So wrote Ogden Nash about the man who

Pitcher Cy Young of the Cleveland Naps.

won more Major League Baseball games than anyone else—Denton True ''Cy'' Young. Young's 511 recorded victories number nearly 100 more than the nearest challenger. And though baseball historians have insisted that Walter Johnson, Lefty Grove, and Roger Clemens may have been better on the mound, they are confident that Young's lifetime totals of 7,356 innings pitched and 750 complete games will never be broken.

Young was born in Gilmore, Ohio, on March 29, 1867. He began his organized baseball career in nearby Canton, where he soon earned his nickname. Some claim the name Cy is short for cyclone, referring to his fastball, while others claim that Cy, like Rube, was a common nickname of the age for a naive, small town ballplayer. Young began his major league career in 1890 for the Cleveland Spiders of the National League, where in his rookie season he had an unprepossessing 9-7 win-loss record. Two seasons later, however, he went 36-12 for the Spiders. Young was so dominant that, before the 1893 season, the major leagues moved the pitcher's mound—from 50 feet from home plate to its current distance of 60 feet, 6 inches—to give batters a fighting chance. Yet even with the 10 extra feet, Young won 34 games in 1893, and 35 games in 1895.

After the 1898 season Young was traded to the St. Louis Cardinals, where he won 45 games in two seasons. Young then jumped to the Boston Somersets (later Red Sox) of the brand-new American League. Now in his mid-30s and in a new environment, Young proceeded to win 193 games for Boston during eight years. In 1903 Young won 28 games and pitched Boston into the first modern World Series, where he led his team to an upset victory over Honus Wagner's Pittsburgh Pirates, winning two games for his club.

Young was the first major league pitcher to throw three no-hitters during his career—a feat later equaled by Bob Feller and surpassed by Sandy Koufax and Nolan Ryan. In May 1904 against the Philadelphia Athletics, Young pitched the first perfect game of the twentieth century—a game in which he did not allow an Athletic batter to reach base.

In 1909 Young was traded to the American League's Cleveland Naps (now Indians), where he won his 500th game in 1910. However, his efficiency was declining with the onset of age and an expanding waistline. Young admitted that, as he grew heavier, he was unable to field bunts, and at the end of his career batters were taking advantage of this. In 1911 he ended his career with the Boston Braves of the National League. In his final start in September 1911, he lost a 1-0 game to Grover Cleveland Alexander, the rookie sensation for the Phillies who would go on to win 373 games in his lifetime.

Young returned to farming in Ohio, and became a regular celebrity at major league old-timer's games. When the Baseball Hall of Fame held its first election in 1936, Young narrowly missed being inducted in the first group of immortals; voters had to select from a pool of nineteenth-century players and a pool of twentieth-century players, and Young's career covered both eras. He was elected in 1937, and attended the inaugural induction ceremony in Cooperstown, New York, in 1939, where he posed for photographs with Honus Wagner, Babe Ruth, and Connie Mack.

Young died on November 4, 1955 in Newcomerstown, Ohio, at the age of 88. In his honor, the following year Major League Baseball initiated an annual award named after him: The Cy Young Award is presented to the best pitcher in each league. In the modern era, Roger Clemens has won five Cy Young Awards in the American League, while Greg Maddux has won four National League Cy Youngs.

—Andrew Milner

FURTHER READING:

James, Bill. *The Bill James Historical Baseball Abstract.* New York, Villard, 1986.

———. *Whatever Happened to the Hall of Fame?: Baseball, Cooperstown and the Politics of Glory.* New York, Fireside, 1995.

Okrent, Daniel, and Harris Lewine. *The Ultimate Baseball Book.* New York, Houghton Mifflin, 1991.

Thorn, John, and Pete Palmer. *Total Baseball.* New York, Total Sports, 1999.

Young, Loretta (1913—)

In a career that lasted from the silent films to the 1980s, Loretta Young embodied the image of the eternal lady. She appeared as a child extra in early films before she received her first major film role in *Laugh Clown Laugh* (1928). Thereafter she was invariably cast in roles as a young innocent. After winning an Academy Award for the film *The Farmer's Daughter* (1947), Young turned to television. Her anthology series, *The Loretta Young Show* (1953-60), won her several Emmy Awards although it was most notable for the fabulous costumes she wore. After Young's television show went off the air she continued to act on rare occasions, most notably in *Christmas Eve,* a television movie telecast in 1986.

—Jill A. Gregg

FURTHER READING:

Lewis, Judy. *Uncommon Knowledge.* New York, Simon & Schuster, 1994.

Morella, Joe. *Loretta Young: An Extraordinary Life.* New York, Delacorte Press, 1986.

Young, Neil (1945—)

A modest commercial success in the late 1970s, Neil Young's heavy-rocking music had a profound impact on young musicians who started a new movement of grunge rock in the 1990s, leading many to dub him the ''godfather of grunge.'' From his beginnings in the mid-1960s rock band Buffalo Springfield, to his intermittent stints as a 1970s acoustic singer-songwriter and hard-rocker, on through his 1990s incarnation as grunge's guru, Neil Young has spent his career ducking audience expectations. This US-based Canadian expatriate's idiosyncratic and sometimes perverse approach to music-making has allowed him to be perhaps the only member of his generation to maintain critical respect years after most of his peers began artistically treading water.

On his varied and numerous albums Neil Young has worn many hats, including those of folk-rocker, acoustic singer-songwriter, rockabilly artist, hard-rocker, punk-rocker, techno-dance artist, and blues guitarist. His body of work, which is matched in its depth and breadth only by Bob Dylan, is characterized by a sense of restlessness and experimentalism. More often than not it is the contrasting acoustic Neil Young and distorted-guitar-meltdown Neil Young that are most prominent.

Neil Young

confused and lost much of his audience, but with the release of 1989's *Freedom* he began to regain the critical and commercial clout that had dissipated in the 1980s.

Another key to Young's career rejuvenation (that had little to do with his then-current output) was the changing musical climate during the late-1980s and early-1990s: the rise of alternative guitar rock. One marker that signaled Young's reincarnation as the "godfather of grunge" was the release of the Neil Young tribute album *The Bridge* in 1989. This compilation album featured contributions by the likes of Soul Asylum, Flaming Lips, The Pixies, Sonic Youth, and Dinosaur Jr.—all of whom became minor or major mainstream successes. By the early 1990s, Young was named by the likes of Nirvana and Pearl Jam (who later played with Young) as a main influence. Young cultivated this fandom by playing the most rocking, noisy music of his career and by taking guitar experimentalists Sonic Youth and grunge kings Pearl Jam on the road with him.

Young's influence over young grunge musicians took a sad turn when Nirvana's Kurt Cobain referenced a well-known Neil Young lyric in his suicide note, stating "it's better to burn out than it is to rust," a line from "Hey Hey, My My." Young reacted to this by recording *Sleeps with Angels,* a mournful low-key album filled with meditations on death and depression that served as a eulogy for Cobain. Throughout the rest of the 1990s, Young continued to release a series of solid but stylistically similar live and studio albums, primarily with his longtime band Crazy Horse.

—Kembrew McLeod

FURTHER READING:

Williams, Paul. *Neil Young: Love to Burn: Thirty Years of Speaking Out, 1966-1996.* New York, Omnibus, 1997.

Young, Neil, and J. McDonough. *Neil Young.* New York, Random House, 1998.

Young, Robert (1907-1998)

Robert Young is best remembered for his two successful television shows, *Father Knows Best* (1954-60) and *Marcus Welby, M.D.* (1969-75), which together earned him three Emmy awards. He began his career in motion pictures of the 1930s and 1940s, invariably playing the amiable, dependable guy who loses the girl. Young made his film debut opposite Helen Hayes in *The Sin of Madelon Claudet* (1931) and appeared in classics such as *Secret Agent* (1936) and *The Enchanted Cottage* (1944) before turning to television. He was married to wife Betty from 1933 until her death in 1994 and together they had four daughters. Young left an indelible impression on American culture of the early television era as everyone's favorite father figure.

—Jill A. Gregg

FURTHER READING:

Parish, James Robert. *The Hollywood Reliables.* Connecticut, Arlington House, 1980.

———. *The MGM Stock Company: The Golden Era.* Connecticut, Arlington House, 1973.

After leaving Buffalo Springfield he released two solo albums in 1969 that would set a pattern for the rest of his career. His self-titled debut album featured country and folk-styled songs, utilizing acoustic guitars buffeted by lush string sections and tasteful female backing vocals. His second album, released a few months later, was a collaboration with an unknown garage band called Crazy Horse, a group Young would use throughout the rest of his career. The Crazy Horse collaboration, *Everybody Knows This is Nowhere,* showed off Young's other half—the hard rocking, noisy side.

Most of his 1970s albums would follow this pattern, with *Harvest* and *Comes a Time* filling his acoustic singer-songwriter shoes and *Tonight's the Night* and *Zuma* satisfying his craving for molten-hot guitar distortion. Young's artistic and commercial success reached its zenith with 1979's *Rust Never Sleeps,* which incorporated both musical tendencies into one album split into a quiet side and a loud side.

During the 1980s, Young's career began to falter as he released a series of wildly varying albums that incorporated rockabilly, garage rock, electronic dance, folk, country, and blues. His records weren't selling, and his new label Geffen sued him for releasing non-commercial, non-Neil Young-like albums. From 1983 to 1988 Young

Youngman, Henny (1906-1998)

Perhaps no comedian better understood the great truism among comedians that, regardless of the time devoted to working on an act and the energy put into a stage performance, a comic's material is the key to success or failure, than the "King of the One-Liners," Henny Youngman. For more than 70 years he entertained audiences as the quintessential Catskills comedian. His rapid-fire delivery, in which he could tell a half dozen wisecracks in 60 seconds, was filled with timeless bits that drew as many groans as laughs. Youngman's theory of comedy was to keep his jokes simple and compact. Beginning in the mid-1920s and extending into the 1990s, he repeated countless gags that could be immediately understood by everyone. Among his most famous lines are such comic gems as: "I just got back from a pleasure trip. I drove my mother-in-law to the airport," "The food at this restaurant is fit for a king. Here, King! Here, King!" and "A man goes to a psychiatrist. 'Nobody listens to me!' The doctor says, 'Next!'" In 1991, Youngman commented on his act's enduring popularity when he wrote, "Fads come and go in comedy. But the one-liner always remains sacred. People laughed at these jokes when I told them at Legs Diamond's Hotsy Totsy Club sixty years ago—and they're still laughing at these same one-liners at joints I play today."

Henny Youngman

Born on March 16, 1906, in England to Russian Jewish immigrants who later settled in New York, Henry Youngman harbored dreams of entering show business from an early age. His first taste of success came as a bandleader for a quartet known as Henny Youngman and the Swanee Syncopaters. By the mid-1920s, the group became a regular presence in the "Borscht Belt"—an area in the Catskill Mountains filled with private summer resorts that catered to a predominantly Jewish clientele. At the Swan Lake Inn, Youngman played with his musical group, while between sets he acted as the hotel's "tummler," a job that consisted of walking around the resort to make sure all the guests were having a good time. The tummler would often schmooze the male guests, dance with any unattached female guests, and even serve as an unofficial matchmaker. To keep the guests amused, a tummler had to have many jokes for practically any situation at his fingertips. Youngman recalled his days in the Catskills and their influence on his comedic style when he stated, "I'm quite sure my love of one-liners came from this mountain laboratory. You had to be able to rat-a-tat-tat them out, on all subjects, to all kinds of people, every hour, day or night."

Youngman abandoned the Swanee Syncopaters for the life of a standup comedian when a nightclub owner asked him to fill in for an act that failed to show. His comedy routine, honed from his days as a tummler, was a great hit. He soon came to the attention of a rising comedy headliner named Milton Berle, who was impressed with Youngman's delivery and helped him get standup gigs at small clubs and bar mitzvahs. By the 1940s, the former tummler had become the featured comedian on radio's *The Kate Smith Show*. For two years he had a regular six-minute spot during which he told his one-liners and played the violin. It was in this period that Youngman acquired his signature joke: When his wife Sadie arrived at the show with several friends the nervous comedian wanted her to sit in the audience so he could prepare. He grabbed an usher and told him, "Take my wife, please." The comic incorporated the humorous ad-lib into his act and continued to use the line even after his wife died in 1987.

Youngman spent the greatest portion of his career touring throughout the world with his unvarying act. He was proud to say he had performed before both Queen Elizabeth II and the gangster Dutch Schultz. No matter the audience or setting, he would take to the stage with his prop violin and still-humorous lines. Jokes such as "My doctor told me I was dying. I asked for a second opinion. He said you're ugly, too." were repeated for years to audiences long familiar with Youngman's routine. He also frequently appeared on television talk and variety shows into his eighties. However, his attempts to become a regular TV performer were less successful. The summer of 1955 saw the failure of *The Henny and Rocky Show*, which paired him with ex-middleweight boxing champion Rocky Graziano. In 1990, he made a brief appearance as the emcee at the Copacabana in Martin Scorsese's mobster epic *Goodfellas*. He died in New York on February 23, 1998.

Audiences laughed at Henny Youngman's nearly endless supply of one-liners because they were instantly funny and recognizable to almost everyone. He did not offer long comic monologues, controversial humor, or provocative social satire, but rather provided funny gags for anyone who has ever had to deal with life's more mundane occurrences, such as bad drivers, unhelpful doctors, drunken husbands, and mothers-in-law. Furthermore, his longevity allowed younger audiences to experience a still vital performer with roots in vaudeville. He proved that even the most well worn jokes, like "One fellow comes up to me and says he hasn't eaten in three days. I say, 'Force yourself!''' are still funny.

—Charles Coletta

FURTHER READING:

Youngman, Henny. *Take This Book, Please.* New York, Gramercy Publishing, 1984.

Youngman, Henny, and Neal Karlen. *Take My Life, Please!* New York, William Morrow, 1991.

Your Hit Parade

A landmark musical variety series on both radio (1935-1953) and television (1950-1959, 1974), *Your Hit Parade* was one of the first and most important manifestations of the musical countdown or survey. Unlike later variations on this format, however, on *Your Hit Parade* the songs were performed live by a regular cast of singers, some of them famous (Frank Sinatra, Doris Day, Dinah Shore). The TV version of *Your Hit Parade* has been cited, somewhat implausibly, as a forerunner of music video and MTV.

The radio series *Lucky Strike Hit Parade* debuted on the NBC Red network on April 20, 1935. During the next two years, both NBC and CBS carried the program from time to time, until in 1937 it found its "home" in the Saturday evening schedule on CBS, where it

Jill Corey rehearsing for an appearance on *Your Hit Parade*.

remained until 1947, when it moved back to NBC. The TV version premiered in 1950 as a simulcast of the radio series. This arrangement lasted until 1953, at which point the radio series was canceled. *Your Hit Parade* continued on NBC until 1958, then moved back to CBS and was canceled in 1959. A revival on CBS in 1974 lasted less than a year and is notable mainly for employing future *Love Connection* host Chuck Woolery as a singer. The cast of singers and orchestra leaders changed frequently, especially during the show's radio years. The TV cast was more stable and included singers Dorothy Collins, Snooky Lanson, Gisele MacKenzie, and Russell Arms, bandleader (and future electronic music pioneer) Raymond Scott, and announcer Andre Baruch. The most memorable feature of the series is probably its opening, which consists of the sound of a tobacco auctioneer; in the TV version there were also pictures of animated, dancing cigarettes. As Philip Eberly points out, *Your Hit Parade* was one of a multitude of musical programs sponsored by tobacco companies during the Golden Age of American radio.

The idea behind *Your Hit Parade* was simple yet novel for the 1930s. Each week, the program's house orchestra and featured singers performed the week's most popular songs. The length of the show ranged from 30 to 60 minutes during the program's history, and the number of songs in the "hit parade" varied from seven to fifteen. The American Tobacco Company owned and sponsored the program, and the company's "dictatorial" president, George Washington Hill, "personally controlled every facet of the program," according to Arnold Shaw's account in *Let's Dance*. The ranking of songs was determined by a secret methodology administered by the company's advertising agency—at first, Lord and Thomas; later, Batten, Barton, Durstine & Osborne. The hit parade placed songs in competition with each other, and the unveiling of each week's number one song became an eagerly awaited event.

The TV program's opening announcement asserted that the hit parade was an "accurate, authentic tabulation of America's taste in popular music," based on sheet-music sales, record sales, broadcast airplay, and coin-machine play. The most important factor, at least until the mid-1950s, was radio airplay—and, as Shaw points out in *Let's Dance, Your Hit Parade* itself helped to establish radio as the major venue for American popular music. Radio's dominance came at the expense of vaudeville. Nevertheless, *Your Hit Parade* remained rooted in Tin Pan Alley—the slang term for the music publishing district in 1890s Manhattan, and the name that eventually came to symbolize the (white) mainstream in American popular music. Tin Pan Alley stood for the primacy of songs (as opposed to records) and for a highly conventionalized song structure and performance style (usually a verse-chorus structure, romantic or novelty lyrics, smooth singing or "crooning," and orchestration). The prevalence of songs over records allowed *Your Hit Parade* to showcase its own performers along with the week's hits. A song would often remain on the survey for several weeks, so, for variety's sake, the song would be handed off from one singer to another from week to week.

The advent of the TV series prompted an additional attempt at variety—each week, the song would receive a new "visualization." Rather than delivering a straight performance into the camera, singers were placed in a fictional and dramatic context ostensibly inspired by the title or lyrics of the song. For example, in a 1952 episode, Snooky Lanson portrayed a customer singing "Slow Poke" to the back of a female customer at a diner. In this case, as in most others, the visualization had only a tenuous and forced connection with the text of the song—a "slow poke" sandwich appeared on the diner's menu, and the female customer kept Lanson waiting for a seat while he sang lyrics that complained about "you" (presumably his lover) keeping him waiting. As unremarkable as the song itself was, the visualization managed to trivialize it by converting it from a love song into an imaginary monologue about Snooky Lanson's lunch.

Contrary to Michael Shore's contention that "*Your Hit Parade* was a pathfinder in the conceptualization of music video," the program in fact was a clumsy attempt to import the dramatic premise and visual splendor of musical films into the more frantic production context of live TV. Most music videos, even if they have a dramatic premise, use a prerecorded soundtrack and show the singer lip-synching directly into the camera. Thus the typical music video is quite different from the standard visualization on *Your Hit Parade*. This is one reason why the TV series, when viewed today, seems unique and old-fashioned.

The reason for the show's demise, however, has as much to do with sound as with image. As the 1950s progressed, Tin Pan Alley gradually lost ground to rock and roll, and records became the predominant medium in the music industry. Radio lost much of its audience to television and soon discovered the Top Forty format as one of the best ways to stay in business. Top Forty, of course, is much like a hit parade but ranks records (as performed by a specific singer) rather than songs (as performed by anybody). Snooky Lanson performed "Heartbreak Hotel" on *Your Hit Parade* in 1956, but the song was so definitively associated with Elvis Presley that the version by crooner Lanson lacked credibility. This sort of incongruity became more and more common on *Your Hit Parade* as the decade wore on, and the program's contrived and corny "visualizations" only underscored the series's irrelevance.

Despite belated attempts to make the program more contemporary, *Your Hit Parade* could not survive the ascendance of rock and roll and the triumph, in both radio and TV, of recording over live performance. The look of the future in musical TV programs was *American Bandstand,* which rose just as *Your Hit Parade* was falling, and which remained dominant in its field until MTV supplanted it in the 1980s.

—Gary Burns

FURTHER READING:

Brooks, Tim, and Earle Marsh. *The Complete Directory to Prime Time Network TV Shows, 1946-Present.* New York, Ballantine Books, 1979.

Burns, Gary. "Visualising 1950s Hits on *Your Hit Parade.*" *Popular Music.* Vol. 17, No. 2, 1998, 139-152.

Eberly, Philip K. *Music in the Air: America's Changing Tastes in Popular Music, 1920-1980.* New York, Hastings House, 1982.

Elrod, Bruce C., compiler. *Your Hit Parade.* Columbia, South Carolina, Colonial Printing Co., 1977.

Sanjek, Russell. *American Popular Music and Its Business, the First Four Hundred Years: III, From 1900 to 1984.* New York, Oxford University Press, 1988.

Shaw, Arnold. *Let's Dance: Popular Music in the 1930s.* Edited by Bill Willard. New York, Oxford University Press, 1998.

———. *The Rockin' '50s: The Decade That Transformed the Pop Music Scene.* New York, Hawthorn Books, 1974.

Shore, Michael. *The Rolling Stone Book of Rock Video.* New York, Quill, 1984.

Syng, Dan. "Electric Babyland." *Mojo.* December 1998, 24-25.

Wolfe, Arnold S. "Pop on Video: Narrative Modes in the Visualisation of Popular Music on Your 'Hit Parade' and 'Solid Gold.'" *Popular Music Perspectives 2.* Edited by David Horn. Göteborg, Sweden, International Association for the Study of Popular Music (IASPM), 1985, 428-441.

Your Show of Shows

A 1950s variety program, *Your Show of Shows* (1950-1954) distinguished itself with its artful satire and parody performed by an ensemble led by Sid Caesar. Caesar was blessed with a stable of young writers that included, at one time or another, Neil Simon, Woody Allen, Mel Brooks, Carl Reiner, and Larry Gelbart.

The program took advantage of television's ability to be topical. It was live television at its best, and Caesar and his partner, Imogene Coca, could parody recent films—including foreign films—at will; because of the dangers of McCarthyism, however, they could not parody politics. Because there were no retakes in live television, the ability of its performers to ad lib was essential to its success, and soon became a secret to the show's popularity.

Caesar was born in Yonkers, New York, in 1922. He entered show business as a Juilliard trained saxophonist and enjoyed success in a number of famous big bands. During his Army service, Max Leibemann, who became his producer on *Your Show of Shows,* noticed his ability to make his fellow band members laugh. He decided to feature Caesar as a comedian in future productions. In 1949, after appearing in nightclubs and on Broadway, Caesar began his television career in the forerunner of *Your Show of Shows.*

The program took six days to put on, from writing to performing. In an interview for *The Saturday Evening Post,* Caesar noted the difference between *Your Show of Shows* and television in the late twentieth century: "I didn't come in and have a script handed to me. Never happened. The show took six long days to write, and I was there on Monday morning, working with the writers, putting in the blank sheet of paper. See, the show had to be written by Wednesday. Thursday we put it up on its feet. Friday we went over it with the technicians and Saturday was the show—live."

The program ran for 90 minutes and was number one for four years. NBC soon began plans for two programs that would be highly rated, and *Caesar's Hour* and *The Imogene Coca Show* were born. *Caesar's Hour* was highly rated for a time, but Caesar's descent into alcoholism and pill-taking finally took its toll, and its fourth season was its last.

Although Caesar eventually had a number of female partners on his various shows, Imogene Coca is the one best remembered by fans. She began acting at the age of 11 and had a long career before joining Caesar on *Your Show of Shows.* Leonard Sillman drafted Coca and Henry Fonda into doing comedy bits for scene changes for his Broadway production, *New Faces.* Until then, she had been noted for her singing, dancing, and acting. Eventually, she so impressed the critics that she became hailed as the next great comedienne. In 1949,

Your Show of Shows **stars Sid Caesar (left) and Imogene Coca (right) pose with the show's producer Max Liebman.**

she joined Caesar in the "Admiral Revue," the forerunner of *Your Show of Shows.* Coca left to do her own television program after the 1954 season. The program, however, failed, and so did her reunion with Caesar in 1958.

Your Show of Shows paved the way for *Saturday Night Live,* and other similar live revues like "Second City." It has remained popular on PBS (Public Broadcasting Station) and in the sale of videos. The movie *Ten from Your Show of Shows,* featuring 10 of its classic skits, also did well commercially and is still available on video.

—Frank A. Salamone

FURTHER READING:

Gold, Todd. "Sid Caesar's New Grasp on Life." *Saturday Evening Post.* Vol. 238, January/February, 1986, 64-66.

Oder, Norman. "Caesar's Writers: A Reunion of Writers from 'Your Show of Shows' and 'Caesar's Hour'." *Library Journal.* Vol. 121, No. 16, October 1, 1998, 146.

Youth International Party

See Yippies

The Youth's Companion

For just over a century, from 1827 to 1929, a monthly periodical called *The Youth's Companion* dispensed moral education, information, and fiction to generations of young people. By 1885, the periodical was claiming 385,000 copies were printed each week, making it the most widely circulated journal of its day, largely due to the premiums and prizes it offered for new subscriptions. *The Youth's Companion* was founded in Boston in 1827 by Nathaniel Willis and Asa Rand as a Sunday-School organ in the tradition of Boston Congregationalism, one that would "warn against the ways of transgression, error and ruin, and allure to those of virtue and piety." The classic children's bedtime prayer "Now I Lay Me Down to Sleep" appeared in its first issue. Rand left the venture after three years and Willis remained as editor until he sold the paper in 1857 to John W. Olmstead and Daniel Sharp Ford. Ford, who was known to his readers as "Perry Mason," after the name he gave to his business, remained as editor until his death in 1899. During his editorship, he completely revamped its content and format, making *The Youth's Companion* into a well-respected publication of high literary merit. By publishing serial and scientific articles and puzzles, by soliciting articles from readers, and by including contributions from notable writers such as Harriett Beecher Stowe, Rudyard Kipling, Thomas

Hardy, and Jack London, Ford was able to increase the circulation tenfold within a decade, and to nearly half a million by 1899. The magazine survived until it finally folded at the onset of the Great Depression, when it merged with *American Boy*, a victim of financial woes and changing tastes.

—Edward Moran

FURTHER READING:

Tebbel, John. *The American Magazine: A Compact History.* New York, Hawthorn Books, 1969.

Tebbel, John, and Mary Ellen Zuckerman. *The Magazine in America: 1741-1990.* New York, Oxford University Press, 1991.

Yo-Yo

A Filipino immigrant, Pedro Flores, introduced a Philippine hunting weapon named Yo-Yo, translated in English as "come back," to the United States in the 1920s. Donald Duncan bought the rights to the name and the toy in 1929. He created the Duncan Imperial and the well-known Butterfly Yo-Yo. Tricks done with the toy include "Walk the Dog" and "Around the World." Used in tournaments from the beginning in the United States, the Yo-Yo became a fad again during the 1960s and surged in popularity in 1962. Yo-Yo Tournaments have enjoyed popularity throughout the 1990s.

—S. Naomi Finkelstein

FURTHER READING:

Duncan Toy Company, *The Duncan Trick Book,* MiddleField, Duncan Toy Company.

Former Yo-Yo champ John Farmer performs a trick.

Skolnik, Peter. *Fads: America's Crazes, Fevers and Fancies,* New York, Crowell, 1978.

Yuppies

Following the social upheaval and counterculture ideals that received popular attention the 1970s, the 1980s ushered in a backlash, at least in the middle and upper middle classes. A number of former college students, protesters, and hippies who came from these classes left the counterculture behind and took high-paying white collar jobs. Because many of them postponed marriage and children, they found themselves with large disposable incomes and few responsibilities. These Young Urban Professionals were soon dubbed "yuppies" by the press.

Tired of the moral and political seriousness of the activist 1960s and 1970s, the yuppies began to spend their money on themselves, often going into debt to purchase high-priced status symbols and expensive adult playthings. Rolex watches, designer fashions, trendy gourmet foods, and BMW cars came to represent the self-indulgent lifestyle of the wealthy young professionals. Snob appeal became the measuring stick for purchases. Drug use was associated with yuppies, but not the bohemian marijuana of the hippies. Rather, it was cocaine, the expensive drug of the jet set. "Whoever dies with the most toys, wins," and "Who says you can't have it all?" became the catch phrases of the day.

The yuppies soon came to symbolize everything the media found to criticize in the 1980s. Calling the 1980s the "me" generation and the "greed decade," media pundits lambasted the yuppie swingers as they had their hippie counterparts. Books like Jay McInerney's *Bright Lights, Big City* and Tom Wolfe's *The Bonfire of the Vanities* chronicled the self-aggrandizing decadence of the yuppie life. In reality, the economic boom of the early 1980s contributed to rising consumption throughout middle class America, and the well-educated young elite were merely particularly well-positioned to take advantage of it. They had been raised with a sense of their own importance and entitlement, and they had been given jobs with salaries that reinforced that sense. Their lifestyle values were the opposite of those of their parents, the conservative children of the Great Depression. Professional life seemed merely like a step beyond college parties, and the fun was less limited. Profitably employed married couples without children were given the name dinks (double income no kids) by the press, which showed a liking for catchy acronyms. Dinks had unprecedented disposable income, and in an increasingly consumer society, it was easy to spend.

Those young professionals who did have families tried as best they could to fit them into the yuppie status symbol mold. Two career households necessitated nannies and housekeepers. Young couples began to search for the "right" schools while their children were still babies. Along with the expensive party lifestyle came pressure to keep up appearances and to keep making money. As Stan Schultz, a cultural historian at the University of Wisconsin described it, "We are terribly busy souls, doing things that no one else can do." Internal conflicts began to emerge, as the yuppies' liberal ideologies started to conflict with their economic conservatism. The 1980s was the Reagan era in United States politics, and new advantages were being doled out to the rich and the corporations at the expense of social services. The yuppies found themselves on an uncomfortable side of this dichotomy. Jerry Rubin, once a leader of the famous radical group the Yippies, was one of those who traded in his revolutionary politics for economic security—"Money in my pockets mellowed out my radicalism," he said.

Of course, frenzied spending has its price, and the yuppies soon found themselves in deep debt. As long as high-salaried jobs were available, the debt was not a problem, but toward the late 1980s, the economic boom began to end. In 1987, the stock market crashed, and its effects were felt in every societal stratum. Many of the previously secure young professional found themselves "downsized," laid off from jobs or forced to take great cuts in salary. So many defaulted on credit card payments that bankers coined the term "yuppie bill syndrome" to describe them. New "yuppie pawnshops" sprang up, not the sad dark hock shops of the inner-city, but upscale shops with bright lighting in middle class shopping areas, so that the yuppies could cash in some of their costly toys to help cover more necessary expenses. "Downscale chic" was the term used to describe the return to simpler consumption—jeans and T-shirts instead of designer clothes.

Receiving less attention in the media than the maligned yuppies were the working class and poor, whose circumstances were less improved by the 1980s boom. Working class people, too, often had two income families which did not create a pool of disposable income, but instead barely covered their bills. They had little sympathy with the overextended yuppies, who in fact became a convenient scapegoat, exemplifying as they did the waste and irresponsibility of the upper classes.

Just as the yuppies themselves had been part of a backlash, they caused their own backlash. Redefining the word yuppie to mean "young unhappy professionals," some young professionals began to look for a new way of life. Some were dubbed domo's for "downwardly mobile professionals," and dropped out of the fast-paced life of the urban professional, choosing a simpler life, perhaps moving to the country. One exodus took many former yuppies to Montana, seeking a bucolic freedom from stress in the mountains. Other yuppies did not drop out, but rather changed their focus to making money by doing work they could believe in, such as environmental protection work or fighting cancer. *The Artist's Way* by Julia Cameron and *Getting a Life* by Jacqueline Blix describe the joys of trading the consumer rat race for a more fulfilling life by making a dramatic lifestyle change.

The term "yuppie" has been widely used—many say overused—by the media to describe a certain privileged segment of the baby boom generation at a particular time in their lives. As the upper middle class professionals of that generation began to reach middle age, the press began to announce the "death of the yuppie." While conspicuous consumption will never go entirely out of style for the rich, the set of circumstances that created the yuppie mindset is unlikely to recur. Rebelling both against the economic stodginess of their parents' generation and the unwelcome demands of their own youthful ideals, the young professional elite that the press called "yuppies" went on a wild spending spree. When the bills came due, their lives and values changed. In the 1980s, they were sneered at; no one admitted to being a yuppie. They were other people who spent and consumed too much and too richly. In the early 1990s, Michael Thomas of the *New York Observer* said, "I think that's one of the big stories now—denial of the 1980s."

—Tina Gianoulis

FURTHER READING:

Adler, Jerry. "The Rise of the Overclass." *Newsweek.* Vol. 126, No. 5, July 31, 1995, 32.

Shapiro, Walter. "The Birth and—Maybe—Death of Yuppiedom: After 22,000 Articles, is This Truly the End?" *Time.* Vol. 137, No. 14, April 8, 1991, 65.

Yuppies and Baby Boomers: A Benchmark Study from Market Facts, Inc. Chicago, Market Facts, 1985.

Z

Zanuck, Darryl F. (1902-1979)

Darryl F. Zanuck ranks as one of the most famous, long-lived of Hollywood's movie moguls. He oversaw scores of films and created many film stars. Many of these films and their stars were tremendously popular at the time and remain so today. He revived and created Twentieth Century-Fox, functioning as its chief of production from the mid-1930s through the mid-1950s. Three of the films he produced received academy awards: *How Green Was My Valley,* 1941; *Gentlemen's Agreement,* 1947; and *All About Eve,* 1950. Zanuck created several stars; child star Shirley Temple and Betty Grable (World War II's "pin-up girl") made his Twentieth Century-Fox into a true powerhouse. After the war, Zanuck produced a series of films that dealt with social issues including racism and mental hospitals. These post-war films, *Gentlemen's Agreement, Pinky,* and *The Snake Pit,* proved tremendously popular money-makers for the studio. Upon returning to Fox in the early 1960s, Zanuck worked with his son Richard and produced one major hit, *The Sound of Music.* Zanuck was a brilliant producer who possessed the unequaled ability to detect potential in screenplays and screen actors.

—Liza Black

FURTHER READING:

Behlmer, Rudy, editor. *Memo from Darryl F. Zanuck: The Golden Years at Twentieth Century-Fox.* New York, Grove Press, 1993.

Custen, George. *Twentieth Century's Fox: Darryl F. Zanuck and the Culture of Hollywood.* New York, Basic Books, 1997.

Zap Comix

Considered by pop-culture critics to be the quintessential underground comic book of the 1960s, *Zap Comix* can trace its genealogy to the publication of Jack Jaxon's *God Nose* in 1963. By 1999, there were estimated to be more than two million copies of the countercultural *Zap Comix* in print, including such classics as the sexually explicit "Fritz the Cat" series and the trippy "Mr. Natural" books. Three men, working out of the San Francisco Bay area, were chiefly responsible for the *Zap Comix* phenomenon: Don Donahue and Charles Plymell were instrumental in securing the money and arranging the distribution of the early issues, while visionary cartoonist Robert Crumb assumed editorial control. Crumb, a Philadelphia native with no formal art training, was to become one of underground comics' most influential creators.

A one-time illustrator for the American Greeting Card Company, Crumb began doing freelance work for *Help* magazine in the mid-1960s, a publication by *Mad* magazine's co-creator Harvey Kurtzmann. Crumb's experimentation with LSD and other drugs inspired him to create ever more bizarre situations and characters, with "Fritz the Cat" and "Mr. Natural" emerging from his pen during this acid-soaked period. Crum's best early work was published in the pages of

underground newspapers like New York's *East Village Other,* and in 1966, he moved to San Francisco, where he hooked up with a community of artists and writers who shared his countercultural sensibility. Donahue and Plymell soon enlisted him to take the reins of *Zap* as a vehicle for his unique talents. The first issue of *Zap,* numbered zero, hit the streets in February of 1967. Dubbed "the comic that plugs you in," the cover featured a Crumb drawing of an embryonic figure with its umbilical cord plugged into an electrical socket. The comic quickly became a forum for some of the most prominent underground cartoonists of the time, many of them influenced by the early *Mad* magazine. Illustrators whose work appeared in *Zap* included S. Clay Wilson, Spain Rodriguez, and Gilbert Shelton.

Zap's content ranged widely, from instructions on how to smoke a joint to quasi-pornographic features like "Wonder Wart Hog," in which the eponymous swine overcomes his impotence by using his snout. The pages of *Zap Comix* offered readers an explicit panorama of the sex, drugs, and revolution ethos of the 1960s, subjects never before seen in comic books. *Zap Comix* were often sold in head shops, sharing counter space with bongs and roach clips, making them the unofficial bibles of the tuned-in, turned-on generation of hippies and other countercultural folk. With the success of *Zap,* Robert Crumb became an icon of the underground. The hip cachet of his comics allowed him to triumph over his own sexual frustration. As he explained later in an autobiographical cartoon story, "I made up for all those years of deprivation by lunging maniacally at women I was attracted to . . . squeezing faces and humping legs . . . I usually got away with it . . . famous eccentric artist, you know." Occasionally, however, Crumb's commitment to exploring his own personal sexual obsessions got him and the comics in hot water. In 1969, Crumb's incest-themed story "Joe Blow" in *Zap* #4 sparked obscenity busts at several bookstores.

The daring style and content of *Zap Comix* paved the way for a generation of cartoonists, both mainstream and underground, who felt comfortable tackling previously taboo, adult-themed subjects. "[T]o say [*Zap*] made a deep impression is an understatement," commented Alan Moore, a comics writer who created the popular title *Watchmen* in the 1980s. Author Trina Robbins likened reading *Zap* for the first time to "discovering Jesus [by] a born-again Christian."

—Robert E. Schnakenberg

FURTHER READING:

Crumb, Robert. *The Complete Crumb Comics.* Seattle, Fantagraphics, 1988.

Sabin, Roger. *Adult Comics: An Introduction.* London, Routledge, 1993.

Zappa, Frank (1940-1993)

Few rock and roll icons can match the originality, innovation, and prolific output of Frank Zappa. His synthesis of blues, rock, jazz, doo-wop, classical, and avant-garde, combined with irreverent lyrics and politically-oriented stage theatrics expanded the range of popular

Frank Zappa

music. From his work with seminal 1960s freak band the Mothers of Invention to his final, posthumously-released studio project called *Civilization: Phaze III* (1994), Zappa made music by his own rules, rewriting the rules of the music industry in the process.

Frank Vincent Zappa was born December 21, 1940 in Baltimore, Maryland. The Zappa family moved often, his father following wartime civil service employment until 1956 when they settled in Lancaster, California, north of Los Angeles. Frank's main interests during his formative years were chemistry (specifically explosives), drums, and the dissonant music of Edgard Varèse, a modern composer who worked with sound effects, electronics, and large percussion sections. This was an important influence on young Zappa as it introduced him to unconventional musical forms before the advent of rock and roll.

Bored with high school, Frank taught himself to read and write 12-tone symphonic music, and began composing his own. After graduation he worked as a rhythm guitarist in various lounge cover bands, when it became clear that merely composing wouldn't pay the bills. In 1963, however, at age 22, he scored the soundtrack for a low-budget film, and acquired a homemade recording studio in downtown Cucamonga, California. Unfortunately, Studio Z had a brief life.

Trouble with the locals culminating in a ten-day jail sentence and impending urban development forced Frank to move to Los Angeles where he found gigs for his proto-rock-and-roll band, The Mothers.

After "perfecting" their artsy, improvisational live show, the Mothers recorded *Freak Out!* (1966), the first rock double album. Out of necessity, though, the band became the Mothers of Invention, as record executives objected to the original name. *Freak Out!* was a landmark in musique concrète as pop music, and was a bracing satire on the hippie culture oozing into Southern California. The follow-up album *Absolutely Free* (1968) intensified these themes, laying the groundwork for much of Zappa's future lyrical and compositional endeavors. Later, he created the cult film *200 Motels* (1971), named for the estimated number of dives the band had stayed in during its five-year life span. Dissonant and self-consciously weird, *200 Motels* foreshadowed the music video even as it lampooned life inside a touring rock and roll band, incorporating ballet, opera, and Zappa's dizzying orchestrations to make its acidic point. As freaky as Zappa was, though, he was an adamant teetotaler which caused tension among fellow musicians. This, combined with low pay and bad reviews, ultimately led to the breakup of the Mothers of Invention. Zappa, however, was just getting started.

Throughout the 1970s, Zappa's reputation grew, especially in Eastern Europe where he provided the soundtrack for revolution. Frank also became known for his prowess with a guitar while his lyrics became more surreal and confrontational. His attempts at ''serious'' music, however, were thwarted, beginning with contractual disputes stemming from the *200 Motels* sessions with the Royal Philharmonic, and continuing every time he tried to hire an orchestra. Frank still considered himself primarily a composer, though; an odd vocation for a subversive rock musician, but as he remarked, ''Apart from the political stuff, which I enjoy writing, the rest of my lyrics wouldn't exist at all if it weren't for the fact that we live in a society where instrumental music is irrelevant.''

In 1977 Frank became embroiled in lawsuits involving ownership of his early albums. During this litigious period (and in an effort to fulfill remaining contracts) he released as many as four albums a year and toured relentlessly, while another self-referential work called *Joe's Garage* (1979) achieved mainstream popularity with its Orwellian plot and scatological humor. Eventually Zappa became the owner of his entire back catalog and an eponymous record label, as well as a new recording studio in the basement of his Los Angeles home.

The establishment began to recognize Frank Zappa in the 1980s, and his first Billboard-charting single ''Valley Girl'' (1982) was a fluffy parody of Southern California teen pop culture featuring the voice of his daughter Moon. In 1985, Zappa testified before a Senate committee and denounced legislation calling for explicit-content warning labels on albums. He later became close friends with then president of Czechoslovakia, Vàclav Havel, and was nearly appointed ambassador of trade and culture to that country. Frank also received a Best Instrumental Album Grammy Award in 1986 for *Jazz From Hell* which was conceived on the Synclavier, an electronic device allowing him to play his most difficult compositions note for note.

In 1990 Frank Zappa was diagnosed with prostate cancer. Between debilitating treatments he produced a live program of his orchestral works called *The Yellow Shark* (1993), which was performed by ardent fans, the renowned German Ensemble Modern. He also set up the Zappa Family Trust, placing total creative and financial control of his successful niche-market mail-order business in the hands of his partner/wife Gail. He died on December 4, 1993, and was inducted into the Rock and Roll Hall of Fame in 1995.

The legacy of Frank Zappa lives on in every outspoken, self-made rock star, in every do-it-yourself basement recording and autobiographical music video montage. He rescued the stodgy reputation of the serious orchestral composer by marrying it to the lifestyle of a hard-touring rock band, creating some of the most challenging and defiant music of the twentieth century. He also pioneered recording technologies, stretching the boundaries of what popular music could be. Frank Zappa is known worldwide for his irreverent attitude and masterful musicianship, proving that, as he often quoted Edgard Varèse, ''The present day composer refuses to die!''

—Tony Brewer

FURTHER READING:

Walley, David. *No Commercial Potential: The Sage of Frank Zappa,* updated edition. New York, De Capo Press, 1996.

Watson, Ben. *Zappa: The Negative Dialectics of Poodle Play.* New York, St. Martin's Press, 1995.

Zappa, Frank. *Them or Us.* Los Angeles, Barfko-Swill, 1984.

————, with Peter Occhiogrosso. *The Real Frank Zappa Book.* New York, Poseidon Press, 1989.

The Ziegfeld Follies

Brainchild of Broadway impresario Florenz Ziegfeld and his first wife, European singer Anna Held, *The Ziegfeld Follies* dominated the American theatrical revue scene from 1907 until the late 1920s and early 1930s when the popularity of vaudeville began to diminish. Featuring scores of women in elaborate costumes and boasting the debut of some of the country's most popular songs like ''Shine on Harvest Moon,'' *The Follies* started as an American version of satiric French cabaret acts whose sophistication Ziegfeld hoped to evoke in order to appeal to a high-hat audience. Ziegfeld's attempt at continental appeal, however, could not match the flamboyance and over-the-top glitz his own personal flair lended to his works. Thus *The Ziegfeld Follies* offered a hybrid: high-brow artistic endeavor reflected, for example, in the Art Nouveau sets designed by artist Nathan Urban and near vulgarity evidenced by skimpy, even gaudy, costuming. Though *The Passing Show* originating in 1894 constitutes the very first American revue, Ziegfeld's combination of dance routines, still tableaux, stand-up comedy, political satire, one-act plays, and optical illusions became the most well known, an emblem of its era and the quintessential revue. The spectacle was what critic Marjorie Farnsworth calls, ''a feast of desire'' and it reflected what F. Scott Fitzgerald

Bob Hope surrounded by women in the *Ziegfeld Follies of 1936*.

called the Jazz Age and its celebration of economic prosperity and hedonism.

The key to *The Ziegfeld Follies'* extraordinary popularity and influence lay in Ziegfeld's appreciation for the revue staple, the chorus girl. Where other revue shows at the time typically used around twenty chorus girls and perhaps two or three costume-changes a show, Ziegfeld arrayed 120 girls before his audiences. He dressed them in imported fabrics of tremendous extravagance and his own outrageous design, giving them five or six wardrobe changes an evening. He famously handpicked not only his fabrics but his chorus line as well, selecting only those he considered the most beautiful women of the day. Based on his connoisseurship of women and his helping to launch the Broadway musical called *Glorifying the American Girl*, Ziegfeld became known as "the Glorifier." He adored women and had numerous affairs with his employees, but he also viewed them as art objects to sculpt and perfect. He wrote newspaper columns outlining his specifications for the perfect female figure. In the mid-1920s he declared the tall statuesque look "out" and the shorter, more vivacious figure "in." His aim was to create a fantasy world of radiant women with perfect figures whose beauty and allure transcended anything any spectator could have ever before witnessed. *The Follies* offered outlandish dance numbers, including one in which the chorines dressed as taxicabs and moved across a darkened stage, their headlamps the only light. Ziegfeld also billed optical illusions that played off the encroaching movie industry. In one, he displayed a film of a featured performer running down a path. At the end of the path there suddenly appeared the actress herself, the screen apparently disappearing behind her. In another famous routine, "Laceland," the dancers wore glow-in-the-dark painted costumes and dressed as milliner objects—scissors, thimble, needle, etc.—and danced around a woman tatting lace. As early as 1909 Ziegfeld rigged his theatre ceiling to "fly" performer Lillian Lorraine above audience's heads while she sang, "Up, Up, Up in My Airship." Ziegfeld is also credited with the idea of a chorine or featured female performer entering the stage by descending a staircase. This image was later picked up and magnified by musical choreographer, Busby Berkeley in movies like his *Gold Digger* series, all of which were influenced by *The Ziegfeld Follies.*

The Follies chorus became known as "Ziegfeld Girls." Discussed in gossip columns as public personalities, Ziegfeld Girls were precursors to movie stars, both figuratively and literally. Before them, chorus girls were anonymous, everyday women. After Ziegfeld promoted them, they became celebrities, and many of them then went on to become famous film stars. That list includes Barbara Stanwyck, Paulette Goddard, and Ziegfeld's last wife, Billie Burke.

The Ziegfeld Follies launched a number of other famous personalities. Among the male comedians to take their first bow on Ziegfeld's stage were Bert Lahr, Eddy Cantor, and the well-loved humorist, Will Rogers, who began his career with Ziegfeld by making fun of politicians and satirizing news of the day. His style was folksy but his humor had a contemporary edge. The comedienne Fanny Brice also made her name as a long-running performer in *The Ziegfeld Follies* as did legendary songwriters, Irving Berlin, Jerome Kern, and Oscar Hammerstein.

The Ziegfeld Follies' vaunted showgirl lives on in the nightclub acts of Las Vegas and Atlantic City but she's lost the lavish, individualized attention Florenz Ziegfeld bestowed upon her. His own legend survives in films based on his career and the dizzying, singular history of *The Follies*. These include 1941's *Ziegfeld Girl,* directed by Busby Berkeley and featuring James Stewart and Lana

Turner and the 1946 Academy Award-winning *Ziegfeld Follies* directed by Vincent Minnelli and starring William Powell as Ziegfeld. Fanny Brice's life and career became the subject of the 1964 play, *Funny Girl,* made into a film in 1968 and for which actress and singer Barbra Streisand won an Academy Award. A follow-up film also based on Brice and featuring Streisand appeared in 1975 titled, *Funny Lady.* In the mid-1990s, Broadway staged *The Will Rogers Follies,* a Tony Award-winning musical billed as "paying tribute to two American legends—Will Rogers and *The Ziegfeld Follies.*"

—Elizabeth Haas

FURTHER READING:

Cantor, Eddie. *The Great Glorifier.* New York, A. H. King, 1934.

Carter, Randolph. *The World of Flo Ziegfeld.* New York, Praeger, 1974.

Farnsworth, Marjorie. *The Ziegfeld Follies.* New York, Bonanza Books, 1956.

Higham, Charles. *Ziegfeld.* Chicago, Regnery, 1972.

Zines

Zines are nonprofessional, anti-commercial, small-circulation magazines their creators produce, publish, and distribute themselves. Typed up and laid out on home computers, zines are reproduced on photocopy machines, assembled on kitchen tables, and sold or swapped through the mail or found at small book or music stores. Today, somewhere between 10,000 and 20,000 different zines circulate throughout the United States and the world. With names like *Dishwasher, Temp Slave, Pathetic Life, Practical Anarchy, Punk Planet,* and *Slug & Lettuce,* their subject matter ranges from the sublime to the ridiculous, making a detour through the unfathomable. What binds all these publications together is a prime directive: D.I.Y.—Do-It-Yourself. Stop shopping for culture and go out and create your own.

While shaped by the long history of alternative presses in the United States—zine editor Gene Mahoney calls Thomas Paine's revolutionary pamphlet *Common Sense* "the zine heard 'round the world"— zines as a distinct medium were born in the 1930s. It was then that fans of science fiction, often through the clubs they founded, began producing what they called "fanzines" as a way of sharing SF stories and commentary. Although it's difficult to be certain of anything about a cultural form as ephemeral as zines, it is generally accepted that the first fanzine was *The Comet,* published by the Science Correspondence Club in May 1930. Nearly half a century later, in the mid-1970s, the other defining influence on modern-day zines began as fans of punk rock music, ignored by and critical of the mainstream music press, started printing fanzines about their music and cultural scene. The first punk zine, appropriately named *Punk,* appeared in New York City in January 1976.

Central to the story of zines is *Factsheet Five* and its creator Mike Gunderloy. Part accidental offspring of the same letter sent to a dozen friends, and part conscious plan to "connect up the various people who were exercising their First Amendment rights in a small, non-profit scale [so] . . . they could learn from each other . . . and help generate a larger alternative community," Gunderloy began *Factsheet Five* in May 1982 by printing reviews and contact addresses for any and all zines sent to him. The result was a consolidation and cross-fertilization of the two major zine tributaries of SF and punk, joined by smaller streams of publications created by fans of other cultural genres, disgruntled self-publishers, and the remnants of printed political dissent from the 1960s. A genuine subculture of zines developed over the next decade as the ''fan'' was by and large dropped off ''zine,'' and their number increased exponentially. Three editors and over sixty issues later, *Factsheet Five* continued to function in 1999 as the nodal point for the geographically dispersed zine world.

Zines are, first and foremost, about the individuals who create them. Zinesters use their zines to unleash an existential howl: ''I exist, and here's what I think.'' While their subject matter varies from punk music to Pez candy dispensers to anarchist politics, it is the authors and their own personal perspective on the topic that defines the editorial ''rants,'' essays, comics, illustrations, poems, and reviews that make up the standard fare of zines. Consider the prominent sub-genre of ''perzines,'' that is, personal zines that read like the intimate diaries usually kept hidden safely in the back of a drawer. Here personal revelation outweighs rhetoric, and polished literary style takes a back seat to honesty. Unlike most personal diaries, however, these intimate thoughts, philosophical musings, or merely events of the day retold are written for an outside audience.

The audience for zines is, by and large, other zine editors. While the practice is changing, and selling zines is becoming commonplace, it is traditional practice to trade zine for zine. Those individuals doing the selling and trading in the 1980s and 1990s are predominantly young, white, and middle-class. Raised in a relatively privileged position within the dominant society, zinesters have since embarked on careers of deviance that have moved them to the margins: embracing downwardly mobile career aspirations, unpopular musical and artistic tastes, transgressive ideas about sexuality, and a politics resolutely outside the status quo (more often to the left but sometimes to the right). In short, they are what used to be called bohemians. But there is no Paris anymore, instead there are small subcultural scenes in cities scattered across the country, and bohemians living isolated lives in small towns and suburbs. Zines are a way to share, define, and hold together a culture of discontent: a virtual bohemia. ''Let's all be alienated together in a newspaper,'' zine editor John Klima of *Day and Age* describes only half in jest.

One of the things that keeps these alienated individuals together is a shared ethic and practice that they call: Do-It-Yourself. Zines are a response to a society where consuming culture and entertainment that others have produced for you is the norm. By writing about the often commercial music, sports, literature, etc. that is so central to their lives, fans use their zines to forge a personal connection with what is essentially a mass produced product. Zines also constitute another type of reaction to living in a consumer society: Publishing a zine is an act of creating ones' own culture. As such, zine writers consider what they do as a small step toward reversing their traditional role from cultural consumer to cultural producer. Deliberately low-tech, the message of the medium is that anyone can do-it-themselves. ''The scruffier the better,'' argues Michael Carr, one of the editors of the punk zine *Ben is Dead,* because ''they look as if no corporation, big business or advertisers had anything to do with them.'' The amateur ethos of the zine world is so strong that writers who dare to move their project across the line into profitability—or at times even popularity—are reigned in with the accusation of ''selling out.''

Sell out to whom? For over 50 years zines were unknown outside their small circle. But this changed in the last years of the 1980s and the first few of 1990s when a lost generation was found, and young people born in the 1960s and 1970s were tagged with, among other names, ''Generation X.'' This discovery of white, alternative youth culture was fueled in part by the phenomenal success of the post-punk ''grunge'' band Nirvana in 1991, but it was stoked by nervous apprehension on the part of business that a 125-billion-dollar market was passing them by. In December 1992 *Business Week* voiced these fears—and attendant desires—in a cover story: ''Grunge, anger, cultural dislocation, a secret yearning to belong: they add up to a daunting cultural anthropology that marketers have to confront if they want to reach twentysomethings. But it's worth it. Busters do buy stuff.'' As the underground press of this generation, zines were ''discovered'' as well. *Time, Newsweek, New York Times, Washington Post,* and *USA Today* all ran features on zines. Looking to connect with the youth market, marketers began to borrow the aesthetic look of the zines and lingo of the zine culture. Some went as far as to produce faux fanzines themselves: the Alternative Marketing division of Warner Records produced a ''zine'' called *Dirt,* Nike created *U Don't Stop,* and the chain store Urban Outfitters printed up *Slant*—including a ''punk rock'' issue.

As zines became more popular the walls of the old bohemian ghetto crumbled. New life and new ideas made their way inside and the norms and mores of the zine world were challenged. For some, the disdain for commercial and professional culture was supplanted by the realization that zines could be a stepping stone into the main-stream publishing world. For others the reaction was the opposite: the call was to raise the drawbridge and keep the barbarians at the gate. Writers searched for more and more obscure topics, and thicker layers of irony, to separate themselves from the mainstream. Accusations of ''sell out'' became as commonplace in zines as bad poetry.

The attention span of the culture industry is fleeting, but what motivates individuals to write and share that writing endures. And so zines will endure as well. The medium of zines, however, may be changing. With the rise of the Internet, and the lowering of financial and technical barriers to its entry, zines have been migrating steadily to the World Wide Web. But there will always be a place for traditional paper zines. After all, the telegraph, telephone, radio and television never did away with the newspaper. It also doesn't really matter, for zines are less about a material form and more about a persistent creative and communicative desire: to do-it-yourself.

—Stephen Duncombe

FURTHER READING:

Duncombe, Stephen. *Notes from Underground: Zines and the Politics of Underground Culture.* New York and London, Verso, 1997.

Friedman, R. Seth. *The Factsheet Five Reader.* New York, Crown, 1997.

Gunderloy, Mike, and Cari Goldberg Janice. *The World of Zines: A Guide to the Independent Magazine Revolution.* New York and London, Penguin, 1992.

Rowe, Chip. *The Book of Zines.* New York, Henry Holt, 1997.

Taormino, Tristan, and Karen Green. *A Girl's Guide to Taking Over The World: Writings from the Girl Zine Revolution.* New York, St. Martins, 1997.

Vale, V. *Zines!* San Francisco, V/SEARCH, 1996.

Wertham, Fredric. *The World of Fanzines.* Carbondale, Southern Illinois Press, 1973.

Zippy the Pinhead

Known for its non-linear style, quirky dialogue, experimental graphics, and social satire, the *Zippy the Pinhead* comic strip has entertained and interested a loyal following of readers since its inception in 1970. Created by Bill Griffith, the strip revolves around the non-sequitur spouting microcephalic and his small circle of friends. These include Griffy, the creator's alter-ego; Shelf-Life, the manic observer of marketing trends; Claude Funston, the trailer-inhabiting good old boy; and Mr. Toad, whose violent impulses create an occasional bit of suspense within the strip. Collectively, the exploits of this fivesome have cultivated the loyalty of an intensely specified audience who continue to identify with the strip's counter-culture world view.

To appreciate Zippy, and to understand his value as an agent of satire, one must know a bit about the world of Bill Griffith. Zippy was in part shaped by several meetings that Griffith had in the early 1970's with microcephalics, in whose disconnected impulses and childlike personalities he found appropriate material for a comic strip. Zippy's first appearance was in a "really weird love story" published in October 1970, in an underground comic book called *Real Pulp*. Soon, he had enough of a following to appear in his own comic venue, *Yow! Comics,* and attained a measure of mainstream status when the strip became a nationally syndicated comic in 1976. It then appeared regularly in both weekly and later daily newspapers in cities like Boston, Detroit, Washington, Los Angeles, and Phoenix, appealing to a vocal circle of followers who would protest any efforts to remove it.

Because of its non-linear narrative structure and quirky, non-sequitur dialogue, the strip has been criticized by detractors who don't "get" its humor. What its fans do admire is the astute social commentary that Zippy offers through his childlike perspective on current fads and issues, and he illustrates to viewers just how strange modern culture can be. The style of *Zippy*'s social commentary has its origins in the absurdity of crass consumerism, and its real roots are perhaps best located in Griffith's suburban origins in Levittown, NY, which he describes in a 1997 *Boston Globe* interview as a "surreal space." Griffith's sense of absurdism is attributable to many childhood influences, but two that are addressed regularly in the strip are the comic strip *Nancy* by Ernie Bushmiller, and the TV show *Sgt. Bilko.* The conception of *Zippy* began to take shape during Griffith's tenure at a Brooklyn art college in 1962-4, where he took an interest in the sideshow microcephalics, or "pinheads," portrayed in the 1932 movie *Freaks.* A connection with a famous Barnum and Bailey pinhead, "Zip the What-Is-It," solidified the character. "Zip's" real name, William H. Jackson (1842-1926), is also the name of Griffith's great-grandfather. And Griffith's own name, not coincidentally, is William H. Jackson Griffith, a fact he described in a 1981 interview as "a bit unnerving."

True to its absurdist roots, the strip chooses not to locate its main character in any set origins. In one series, Zippy's parents, Eb and Flo, are introduced. His depressed brother Lippy, dressed in trademark black suit, makes an occasional visit. And his family, including wife Zerbina and children Fuelrod and Meltdown, appear occasionally as well. Zippy is a regular in laundromats, where the machinations of the washing machine unfailingly fascinate him. He is intensely loyal to donut shops, and even more so to Hostess products, which he is drawn to because of the many preservatives they contain, particularly polysorbate 80. Ultimately, Zippy's commentary on consumerism mirrors Griffith's own immersion in it; in the same 1981 interview,

Griffith claimed that he has "absorbed the characters and plotlines of 10,000 sitcoms, B-movies, and talk shows. Doing comics gives me a way to re-channel some of this nuttiness so it doesn't back up on me like clogged plumbing."

What Zippy is best known for, however, is his famous question, "Are We Having Fun Yet?" The strip's unofficial slogan, it has worked its way into Bartlett's Quotations and also into national consciousness as a cliché to describe any surreal moment that one might encounter in a post-modern, consumption-driven world. While many claim to be the first to pose this question, Griffith explained in a National Public Radio interview in 1995 that Zippy first posed it on the cover of a comic book in 1976 or 1977; in the context of that particular scene, Grifffith noted, "it just seemed like the right existential thought at the moment . . . if you have to ask it, I guess you aren't, or maybe you are. Or are you questioning the very nature of fun? It seemed like the right question to ask. And his devotees believe that the microcephalic social critic is just the one to ask it."

—Warren Tormey

FURTHER READING:

McIntyre, Tom. "Zippy's Roots in . . . Levittown? Community Was Both 'Wonderland' and Dullsville, Artist Griffith Says." *The Bioston Globe,* 5 October 1997, p. E3.

"NPR Interview with Bill Griffith." *Zippy the Pinhead Pages.* 1995. http:\www.cs.unc.edu~culverzippyorigin.html. 9 November 1998.

"An Interview with Bill Griffith," *Zippy Stories.* 4th ed. San Francisco, Last Gasp, Inc., 1986, pp. 6-8.

Zoos

Collecting and displaying live animals, often from exotic locales and faraway continents, has been part of human life for at least 4,500 years. Originally featured in royal or imperial parks and pleasure gardens, upon the rise of bourgeois culture such animal collections opened to the public and became known as zoological gardens, or zoos, where visitors could contemplate "the wild" and its relationship to human civilization. By the end of the twentieth century a zoo visit had become one of the rituals of modern life, particularly during childhood; according to a study by the American Association of Zoological Parks and Aquariums, 98 percent of all American and Canadian adults had been to a zoo by 1987, and one-third of them had paid a visit in the last year. Around the same time, the legitimacy of collecting and displaying animals became hotly debated, with some people arguing that putting animals in any kind of cage or enclosure was inhumane, and others pointing out that zoos and captive breeding programs offered many species their only hope of survival. In any event, by the turn of the millennium modern zoos seemed to be focusing on animal welfare and conservation, combined with human education, rather than on entertaining visitors at the expense of inmates.

Zoos have traditionally been dispersal points for information about the relationship between humanity and nature—information deliberately shaped by the owners and/or caretakers of the animals, whose decisions have in turn been guided (at least in the twentieth century) by what research shows the zoogoers want to see. In any collection, the animals have been essentially packaged, made into

The Hippoquarium at the Toledo Zoo, Ohio.

products filtered by human minds and placed in surroundings that say something about the beauty of Creation, the dominance of humankind over nature, or the need for environmental economy and sensitivity. Whether enclosed in cages or moated ''environments,'' they usually seem to do no work, earning their keep simply by *being* and being looked at—only passively conveying their controllers' subliminal messages to viewers.

For most of the zoo's history, this perceived limited utilitarian function resulted in cramped quarters, poor diets, depression, and early death for the animals. In an era when animals' value was measured by the physical work they did or the food they produced, perhaps it was reasoned that if the animals served a merely decorative function—as most zoo owners and visitors seemed to have felt they did—they were not entitled to comfortable environments and interesting daily activities. In the twentieth century, studies proved again and again that for most animals a caged life was a short and unhappy one. To begin with, for many species (including *Homo sapiens*), a stare is received as a threat. Bored and depressed animals might fill the hours with repetitive behaviors known as stereotypy: masturbating to a

danger point, pacing their paws raw, or—like many chained elephants—swaying endlessly from side to side. Some chimpanzees developed bulimia, and scientists documented psychosis in a baboon kept on Cyprus. While some people were concerned about these conditions over the years, few took it upon themselves to do much more than decry them; the zoos were not there for the animals.

Over the years, animal collections and their subliminal significance evolved from the huge local-antelope assemblages in Sakkarah, Egypt, through signs of imperial power in ancient China and Rome, to the living museums of the late twentieth century. In ancient times, a large collection of exotics made a fine testament to royal or imperial power, demonstrating a warrior's ability to bring natural (and, by extension, human) populations under control. Egyptian, Greek, and Persian rulers were avid collectors, and the Hebrew Bible attributes a substantial menagerie to King Solomon in the tenth century b.c.e. In the early Common Era, Roman emperors kept lions, tigers, crocodiles, elephants, and other impressive animals; the public could view these exotics in between triumphal imperial processions and spectacular gladiatorial exhibitions in which the animals were, by and large, massacred—occasionally by the thousand. Medieval European nobles and monarchs assembled private menageries that then testified to the owners' social position; exotic animals were often exchanged as gifts and potent tokens of esteem. Lions and leopards were considered particularly valuable; indeed, from the Middle Ages to the nineteenth century, Europeans were more interested in the animals of Africa and the Far East than in those of the New World. Meanwhile, European voyagers were discovering the same passion for exotic animals in other cultures: In the thirteenth century, Marco Polo marveled at Chinese emperor Kublai Khan's extensive menagerie, including leopards, tigers, elephants, and hunting birds, while in 1519 Hernando Cortés reported that Aztec emperor Montezuma employed hundreds of gardeners and animal keepers for his collections (three hundred worked in the aviaries alone).

Zoos became increasingly attractive and important to the public as cities developed; humankind was moving away from daily contact with nature, and even locally occurring animals were exoticized by urban living. Commoners—most of whom had no opportunity to travel to distant locales—were just as interested in exotic collections as their rulers were. Ancient Greeks could pay to see certain bird collections, and starting in 1252 the subjects of Henry III of England could visit his menagerie in the Tower of London for a small fee. In the Renaissance, some enterprising men toured menageries around smaller towns and villages. With the Industrial Revolution and its attendant notions of educating and "re-creating" the worker, zoos (like other large urban parks) became truly widespread and available to the masses. A stroll through a zoological garden, it was believed, was an opportunity for relaxation, play (visitors were usually encouraged to feed the animals), and useful contemplation of the wild and exotic.

Zoos were never more popular than in the late nineteenth and early twentieth centuries. The Philadelphia Zoo, the first to be founded (though not the first to be opened) in the U.S., welcomed its first visitors in 1874; that year 200,000 people paid 10 or 25 cents, depending on age, to see 282 exotics. In an era when a bear cub could cost only $10, the Central Park and Lincoln Park Zoos weren't far behind; the National Zoo opened in 1889, closely associated with the Smithsonian Museum of Natural History. In fact, although there was some emphasis on educating and enriching the common mind, such a relationship between live- and dead-animal museums was not rare; many zoos were founded as a response to taxidermists' and scientists' clamoring for live models. In the early 1800s, the nascent Zoological Society of London declared its intention to bring together animals "from every part of the globe, to be applied either to some useful purpose, or as objects of scientific research, not of vulgar admiration." Yet vulgar admiration could be said to have carried the day; trained by television and amusement parks, the majority of twentieth-century zoogoers went for cotton candy and sea lion stunt shows, elephant feedings and monorail rides. Education—about habitat destruction, the human value of the rainforest, the life cycle of the koala bear—was largely incidental, though it did become the administrators' battle cry.

Late in the 1900s, to visit a typical modern zoological garden was to step into an exotic realm, from the African village-style gateway to the far reaches of the polar bear environment and the ubiquitous jungle-themed trading posts and snack bars. But immersion in an exotic environment was not always part of the experience. Until well into the century, stacks of cages and gloomy indoor display areas (some of them located in the upper stories of warehouses) were considered acceptable; after all, the public was coming to see the

animals, not how the animals lived. The London Zoo, for example, was famous for housing its collection in buildings that would be considered stylish for human inhabitants—but those buildings were not necessarily the most healthful or comfortable for the exotic species. Plants were not part of a typical exhibit until France's Louis XIV established what is considered the first real zoological *garden,* at Versailles. His design was revolutionary in that it displayed animals (222 species) and plants together (rather than animals in cages and plants outside). In 1907, German maverick Carl Hagenbeck opened the first barless zoo, whose enclosures incorporated plant life along with animals. Yet, until the end of the twentieth century, indoor barracks and outdoor cages were the norm, and an effort toward naturalism might mean someone had painted an iceberg on the wall of the polar bear exhibit. To avoid harmful drafts, animals were often denied any form of fresh air; historian Emily Hahn has written that in 1902, the cats, monkeys, and parrots in London's Regent's Park zoo were kept from oxygen. To keep an animal alive under these conditions was nearly miraculous—and, again, made a neat statement about the powers of its possessor.

In 1993 Stephen St. C. Bostock, author of a book on zoos and animal rights, pointed out that zoo animals weren't really prisoners, largely because they showed no consciousness of imprisonment; but nonetheless their status was hotly debated in the late twentieth century, with the result that many of the conditions in which they lived underwent radical change. The newly documented stereotypy led zookeepers to try sometimes radical treatments. A few animals were given the antidepressant Prozac, with surprisingly positive results; however, the cost of dosing a multi-ton elephant was prohibitive, and in any case drugs were usually a last resort. It was generally considered more desirable to enrich animals' lives through stimulating activities, such as searching for food, and more naturalistic environments. Landscape architects and contractors with truckloads of faux rock moved in and remade one zoo after another with cinematic realism. The more dangerous and exotic an animal was perceived to be, the more popular it was, and hence the more money and attention was lavished on its environment; lions, tigers, giant pandas, koala bears, and gorillas were among the first to benefit from new-generation treatment. In the 1980s, according to a *Newsweek* estimate, 143 American zoos spent a billion dollars on enriching their animals' lives. Much of that sum went toward creating new naturalistic environments with record-setting price tags, such as Zoo Atlanta's $4.5 million rainforest and the Bronx Zoo's $9.5 million Jungleworld. Most spending was on a more modest scale, but administrators discovered that the animals tended to be happier in their new environments—or at least, the animal lovers were happier with them.

Even these attempts at creating natural environments might disappoint their inhabitants; a heap of gunite boulders probably doesn't feel like the real thing to a lion-tailed macaque. Moreover, only the parts of an exhibit visible to viewers were likely to be redesigned; the night cages, where the animals slept, generally didn't change. One administrator declared an intention to "mold an exhibit that would provide zoo guests with an experience as natural as possible"; accordingly, most redesigns still kept the zoogoer, rather than the inhabitant, in mind. Studies did in fact show that zoogoers (all TV-trained by this point) tended to think animals displayed in natural environments were more active and attractive, those in cages more passive and less interesting. But all that planning and work was, in the end, lavished on a fleeting experience: The 1987 AAZPA study found that most visitors stayed at an exhibit for only one to three minutes.

Hand in hand with redesign came an interest in conservation, most of it dependent on highly developed technologies. In fact, zoos already had a long history as breeding-grounds for scientific discovery and research: In the eighteenth century, visits to the Swedish royal menagerie inspired Carl von Linné (Linnaeus) to develop the latinate system of binomial nomenclature by which animals and plants have been classified ever since, and post-Industrial Revolution zoos were considered valuable resources for natural historians and taxidermists. In the mid-twentieth century, as human concern for the environment mounted, zoo animals took on a new function, as agents of global salvation. By means of captive breeding programs, including cryogenically frozen eggs and sperm, zoos set out to become latter-day arks, saving species from what many people saw as inevitable extinction due to expanding industrialism and consequent environmental catastrophe. There was also a concern with preserving not just an animal's body, but its natural behaviors (including mating, predation, foraging, and leisure activities) as well. These new interests, like the surge in redesign, were perhaps the indirect result of the technology used in TV's nature programs and cinema's special effects: Zoos had to become more ''authentic,'' too.

This emphasis on conservation was seen by some as ironic, given the depredations that had taken place as industrial-era zoos were first stocked. Until the Endangered Species Act was passed in 1973, famous animal suppliers such as Frank Buck regularly ventured into the wild to slaughter adult animals and bring the babies back alive. But by the end of the millennium there seemed to be little doubt that preservation of individuals and conservation of species, as well as enrichment of captive lives, were high priorities. Accredited zoos joined a worldwide breeding network; under the SSPs, or Species Survival Plans, sperm and eggs were frozen, live animals shipped from one end of the globe to the other in order to mate. Some embryos of rare animals, such as zebras, were gestated inside more common species, such as domestic horses. Yet even with their best efforts and most sophisticated technology, zoos estimated that they could save only about 900 of the 2,000 vertebrate species expected to go extinct by the year 2000.

With the cryogenic zoo, humankind became more than ever the race that had mastered all others. Even as most zoological gardens attempted to educate visitors about the beauty and importance of wild animals and plants, other workers behind the scenes were manipulating nature with their test tubes and psychotropic medications; zoos were thus a combination of television-era entertainment, lite news, and science fiction. It must be emphasized that most of those scientists and keepers—and many fee-paying visitors—were indeed motivated by high ideals such as respect for other species, rather than the appetite for self-aggrandizement that marked older zoos. But the desire to rescue those species nonetheless may be said to stem from the old impulse to control nature and make use of it as something both antithetical and complementary to human civilization. In *New Worlds, New Animals,* Michael H. Robinson, onetime director of the Smithsonian Institution's National Zoological Park, placed the drive to collect living things and ''alter [. . .] them for our benefit'' at the origin of civilization. The twentieth-century zoo, like its predecessors, was a living (though increasingly cryogenic) embodiment of that drive.

—Susann Cokal

FURTHER READING:

Bartlett, A. D. *Wild Animals in Captivity.* London, Chapman and Hall, 1899.

Bostock, Stephen St. C. *Zoos and Animal Rights: The Ethics of Keeping Animals.* New York, Routledge, 1993.

Croke, Vicki. *The Modern Ark.* New York, Avon, 1997.

Hahn, Emily. *Animal Gardens.* New York, Doubleday, 1967.

Hoage, R. J., and William A. Deiss, editors. *New Worlds, New Animals.* Baltimore, Johns Hopkins, 1996.

Livingston, Bernard. *Zoo Animals, People, Places.* New York, Arbor House, 1974.

Lord Zuckerman, editor. *Great Zoos of the World: Their Origins and Significance.* Boulder, Colorado, Westview Press, 1980.

Zoot Suit

The zoot suit was a style of clothing popularized by young male African Americans, Filipino Americans, and Mexican Americans during the 1930s and 1940s. A zoot suit consisted of very baggy high-waisted pants, pegged around the ankles, worn with a long jacket that came to below the knee. The jacket had high, wide shoulder pads that jetted out from the shoulder, giving the wearer a broad look. A long

A zoot suit.

chain dangled from the belt, and the outfit was trimmed with thick-soled shoes and a wide-brimmed hat. It was the style of very hip cats. It is believed the style was created in the African-American community, and there are several stories as to where it actually originated.

In the urban jazz culture of Harlem, the word "zoot" meant something exaggerated, either in style, sound, or performance. The style of dress was an extravagant style, out of proportion to the norm, and it later came to be known as the zoot suit, which consisted of "a killer-diller coat with a drape-shape, reat-pleats and shoulders padded like a lunatic's cell." The suit was for having fun, with the baggy pants made for dancing the jitterbug, and the long coat and the wide-brimmed hat giving the wearer a grown-up look. Many famous black entertainers and musicians wore the zoot suit. Duke Ellington performed at the Orpheum Theatre in Los Angeles in 1941 with a musical number called "Jump for Joy," and all his performers wore zoot suits. Cab Calloway wore a zoot suit in the 1943 film *Stormy Weather.*

One theory of the origins of the zoot suit was that it was imitated from the suit worn by Clark Cable in the movie *Gone with the Wind.* In fact, some people called them "Gone with the Wind suits." Others say that a big band leader and clothier, Harold C. Fox from Chicago, designed the first zoot suit. He said he copied the fashions of ghetto-dwelling teenagers, and in 1941 made such suits for musicians who wanted an "eye-poppin' style." When Fox died in 1996 at the age of 86, he was buried in a lavender zoot suit. The most believed story is one published in the *New York Times* in 1943 during the zoot suit riots taking place in Los Angeles, stating that a young African-American busboy from Gainesville, Georgia, placed an order with a tailor for what would be the "first zoot suit on record." Clyde Duncan ordered a suit with a 37-inch-long coat and with pants 26 inches at the knees and 14 inches at the ankle. Once the suit was made, the tailor took his picture and sent it to *Men's Apparel Reporter,* where the photo was printed.

On the West Coast, the suit came to be identified with young Mexican Americans, known as Pachucos. They were mostly second-generation Mexicans, the sons of working-class immigrants, who settled in Los Angeles. Pachucos created a subculture with a mysterious argot that incorporated archaic Spanish, modern Spanish, and English slang words. They dressed in zoot suits, creating a distinct style that identified them as neither Mexican nor American, but that emphasized their social detachment and isolation. Because there was a war going on, and there was conservation of fabric, wearing the zoot suit was considered an unpatriotic act. In the summer of 1943, while the whole country watched, gangs of sailors and zoot-suiters fought in the streets of Los Angeles. Outraged at the zoot suit style, sailors chased the zoot suiters through the streets and unclothed them. It is unclear if this was a race riot or a riot of patriotism by the sailors who attacked, beat, and stripped young Mexican Americans whom they perceived to be disloyal immigrants.

The zoot suit received wide attention and recognition in the 1970s with the production of the play *Zoot Suit,* written and produced by Luis Valdez. It was performed in Los Angeles and New York. A film of the play, with the same name, was released in 1981 with performances by actors Daniel Valdez and Edward James Olmos.

In the late 1990s, the zoot suit has had a rebirth with the revival of swing music—with imitations of Cab Calloway, the zoot suit, and the jump dance steps. From Chicago to San Francisco, twenty-somethings were dancing to big bands with names like Mighty Blue Kings, The Big Six, Bag Bad Voodoo Daddy, and Indigo Swing, who played swing music from the 1930s and 1940s. Part of the fun of this music was dancing at the big clubs and wearing the clothes to match.

A 1996 article in the *Los Angeles Times* claimed that fashion designers such as Bill Blass and Ralph Lauren were picking up the zoot suit look in their fall designs, including wide jacket lapels and hip-chains, but not the big shoulders. In 1999, numerous suppliers of zoot suits and swing-style clothing were listed on the Internet.

—Rafaela Castro

FURTHER READING:

Cosgrove, Stuart. "The Zoot Suit and Style Warfare." In *Zoot Suits and Second-Hand Dresses: An Anthology of Fashion and Music,* edited by Angela McRobbie. London, Macmillan, 1989, 3-22.

Eig, Jonathan. "Swing Kids." *Down Beat.* Vol. 64, No. 12, December 1997, 56-62.

———. "'Zoot Suit' Fox Dead at Age 86." *Down Beat.* Vol. 63, No. 11, November 1996, 16-18.

Rourke, Mary. "A Suitable Enterprise for the Counterculture: Reflections on the Zoot Suit." *Los Angeles Times.* Vol. 115, August 5, 1996, E1.

Sanchez, Thomas. *Zoot-suit Murders: A Novel.* New York, Dutton, 1978.

Tyler, Bruce. "Zoot-Suit Culture and the Black Press." *Journal of American Culture.* Vol. 17, No. 2, 1994, 21-33.

White, Shane, and Graham White. *Stylin': African American Expressive Culture from Its Beginnings to the Zoot Suit.* Ithaca, New York, Cornell University Press, 1998.

Zorro

Zorro, the sword-wielding, black-clad avenger, is one of the most influential fictional characters of twentieth century literature. By day he was Don Diego, a respected nobleman of nineteenth century California. By night, however, he cut a much more dashing figure as "The Fox," El Zorro. Dressed completely in black with a mask and wide-brimmed hat to conceal his identity, Zorro battled evildoers with the aid of his whip and sword, and made fast getaways on his black steed, Tornado. He was a superbly talented fencer—only Cyrano de Bergerac, D'Artagnan, and the Three Musketeers can challenge him for the title of fiction's most popular swordsman. No matter where he went, he always signed his work with a distinctive Z, often cut into the clothing or skin of his enemies.

Zorro's adventures have been chronicled in many different media. Created by writer Johnston McCulley in 1919 for "The Curse of Capistrano," which was serialized in the pulp magazine *All-Story Weekly,* Zorro is the oldest of the modern superheroes. McCulley would write a total of 65 adventures of the black-clad avenger over the next 39 years. Since Zorro's introduction, countless characters have been created using the same basic theme: a normally law-abiding individual who is faced with great injustice and takes up a mask and secret identity to right wrongs and protect the innocent. Moreover, Zorro's devil-may-care attitude, mastery with the sword, daring escapes, and tendency to laugh in the face of authority have become common traits of swashbuckling heroes.

Though he began as a pulp magazine character, Zorro soared to popularity as a movie character. In all, Zorro has been featured in 37 movies, plus a number of Republic serialized adventures. Zorro's first foray onto the big screen came when popular actor Douglas Fairbanks, on his honeymoon with Mary Pickford, read ''The Curse of Capistrano.'' He and Pickford chose that story to kick off their new film studio, United Artists, and in 1920 released it as *The Mark of Zorro*. Zorro remained a popular film character in the decades that followed. Tyrone Power took up the sword and mask in 1940's *The Mark of Zorro*. Zorro starred in 10 screen adventures, most of them in serial form, from Republic starting in 1937.

A 1950s Disney television show, *Zorro*, starred Guy Williams in the title role. *Zorro* was, at the time, the highest-budgeted Western on television. According to the Official Zorro Web Site, the Zorro merchandising mania that resulted is still well known among toy and comics collectors. Many more movie and television adaptations of Zorro's adventures were made in the 1960s, 1970s, and 1980s. Included among these were films from Europe and an animated series, *The New Adventures of Zorro*, which ran from 1981 to 1983.

Zorro experienced another resurgence in popularity in the 1990s with another live-action television series that ran for 88 episodes. A new animated series debuted in 1992, and a 1995 stage musical opened to critical acclaim. The year 1998 saw the release of *The Mask of Zorro*, starring Antonio Banderas as the protege of Anthony Hopkins' Don Diego. The film was a great success, collecting $95 million at the box office, the highest total for any Zorro film. Yet another animated series was unveiled around the same time, along with a new line of Zorro toys.

Zorro has also seen his share of caricature. In the early 1980s the television series *Zorro and Son* took a comedic approach towards his adventures, and the 1981 film *Zorro, the Gay Blade* featured George Hamilton as an effeminate relative of Zorro who fought injustice in a pink leather costume, complete with Zorro's trusty whip.

Zorro was one of the earliest of many successful twentieth-century characters that tapped into the frustration of readers. People were afraid: afraid of crime, afraid of war, afraid of oppressive governments. El Zorro and his dashing adventures allowed them to imagine a world where wrongs could be righted, not through a system that was often slow and corrupt, but swiftly and surely. His sword and whip attacked villains justice could not touch; sometimes the villains were themselves the supposed guardians of justice.

Zorro is also the consummate romantic, a combination of Latin lover, gentleman bandit, and charming rogue. Even as enemy forces closed in from all sides, he often found the time to give his leading lady a passionate kiss before he executed another daring escape.

Another important component of Zorro's appeal lies in his near-supernatural ability to defy the odds. No matter how great the challenge or powerful the enemy, Zorro always came out on top and set things right. He was the underdog who could even the odds with a stroke of his blade, taking down the powerful and arrogant by several notches. Whenever a screen swashbuckler defies a sputtering tyrant or a grim, black-clad comic book vigilante stalks the night seeking criminal prey, both are following in the footsteps of El Zorro and the ideals that made him popular through four generations of fans.

—Paul F.P. Pogue

FURTHER READING:

Curtis, Sandra R. *Zorro Unmasked: The Official History*. New York, Hyperion, 1998.

Hutchison, Don. *The Great Pulp Heroes*. Buffalo, New York, Mosaic Press, 1996.

McCulley, Johnston. *The Mark of Zorro*. New York, American Reprint Co., 1924, 1976.

Toth, Alex. *Zorro: The Complete Classic Adventures*. Forestville, California, Eclipse Books, 1988.

''Zorro.'' http:\www.zorro.com. March 1999.

Zydeco

Zydeco is a unique blend of Afro-American and Afro-French musical traditions which developed amid the prairie landscapes of southwest Louisiana. Born out of close interaction between the Cajun (white) and Creole (black) French-speaking cultures, zydeco's current popularity as an infectious dance music is directly tied to the past when house dances were the primary form of entertainment and interaction for the rural Creole population. The music played for these gatherings was called ''la-la'' and was the immediate precursor to modern zydeco. From this hearth area the music has spread to other regions, at first associated with the out-migration patterns of Creoles to East Texas and southern California. The availability of this music in recorded form has enabled people everywhere to listen to the sounds of southwest Louisiana. Following zydeco's commercial success many groups have toured extensively, both nationally and internationally, and zydeco has now become very popular in other parts of the world.

The origin of the term ''zydeco'' is most often attributed to the folk expression ''les haricots sont pas sales'' (the beans are not salted), a saying that reflected those hard times when people could not even afford to put salt pork in their pot of beans. The name found its way into popular culture when folk music field recording anthologist Mack McCormick spelled out the word for the first time in the 1950s. The proper pronunciation is with the accent on the first syllable. Early forms of zydeco utilized the same instruments as Cajun music. The fiddle, which came to Louisiana from Canada after 1755 by way of the Acadian migration, was the standard lead instrument. During the mid 1800s the accordion was adopted and soon replaced the fiddle as the lead; the typical configuration was a diatonic accordion with a single or double row of buttons. A unique rhythm instrument—the ''frottoir,'' or rubboard—is the signature instrument of zydeco, and no band is deemed complete without one. Its antecedents most likely are the rasped or notched gourds common to African and Afro-Caribbean traditions. The modern instrument, made out of corrugated sheet metal, is worn over the shoulders like a breastplate and played with a pair of spoons or old-style bottle openers. Zydeco pioneer Clifton Chenier was fond of telling the story of how he first traced out the design for the contemporary frottoir in the sand of an oil refinery yard.

During the first several decades of the twentieth century, when social events were still strictly segregated in Louisiana, the most influential Creole musician was Amédé Ardoin, who was a much sought after performer at both white and black dances. The effect of his accordion playing and plaintive singing on audiences is the stuff of legend. A grimmer remembrance concerns the career-ending incident where he was brutally assaulted while walking home after a dance for allegedly accepting a white woman's handkerchief to wipe off his sweaty brow. As with other aspects of popular culture in America, the zydeco landscape experienced rapid changes after World War II. The house dances faded away, to be replaced by the dance halls and clubs which hosted a variety of music in vogue with black audiences, although zydeco bands still formed a major component of the bookings. Despite a more commercial, adult-oriented setting, many of the clubs retained something of a family, or at least a familiar atmosphere. Instrumentation responded to the popularity of other musical forms and the newer, more spacious venues, becoming a fuller sound with the addition of drums, electric guitars, and even saxophones. As the music became influenced by an urbanized blues and other commercially recorded styles of the 1940s and 1950s, the piano accordion replaced the Cajun button accordion within zydeco. The emerging genre was best personified by the undisputed King of Zydeco, the late Clifton Chenier, who was born in 1925 near Opelousas, in the very heart of Louisiana's Creole country. In 1947 he moved to Lake Charles, then to Port Arthur, Texas and in 1958 to Houston, where his playing became influenced heavily by the urban blues scene. It was Chenier who popularized the term "zydeco" and specifically linked it to his music, which ranged from blues sung in either French or English and backed by a full ensemble, to more traditional Afro-French songs accompanied only by an accordian and frottoir.

Other prominent musicians have helped to guide the development of zydeco and to place it in a more accessible position within the wider arena of popular culture. Another early pioneer, Boozoo Chavis, after cutting a few records during the 1950s, actually stopped playing music publicly for more than twenty years. In 1984 he emerged from relative obscurity in a joyous comeback, and has since become the favorite zydeco performer for many devoted fans; Boozoo still prefers the older button accordion with its raw energy and more traditional sound. Queen Ida Guillory, originally from Lake Charles, but living for many years in the San Francisco Bay Area, began playing for the displaced Louisiana Creoles who had migrated out West and were holding traditional house dances in their basements or at the Catholic church halls. As her music gained fans among the general population, she began touring, and was the first zydeco artist to play in Japan. In 1983 she also became the first zydeco musician to receive a Grammy Award, for her album *Queen Ida on Tour*. Other notable musicians of corresponding vintage include several who have passed away: Alton "Rockin' Dopsie" Rubin, Sr., and John Delafose. Certain performers have deliberately sought a wider audience for zydeco, either by touring extensively or by blending more rock and soul influences into their sound; these include Terrance Simien and Stanley "Buckwheat Zydeco" Dural.

A newer generation has emerged in Louisiana to carry the tradition into the future. Dubbed "zydekids" by some, they play a "nouveau zydeco" which in many ways draws on the earlier French "la-la" music rather than any of the more recent attempts at crossover appeal. Foremost among the newer zydeco artists, Beau Jocque only began playing accordion after a painful industrial accident in 1987 temporarily left him paralyzed. In 1981 he made his first public appearance and now is widely acclaimed as the leader of the new zydeco sound: simplified accordion chords, a deeper, more powerful bass, and from the drums a catchy dance rhythm known as "double clutching." Among others pursuing a revitalized zydeco are Keith Frank, Jo Jo Reed, and a pair of traditionalist women accordion players: Ann Goodly and Rosie Ledet.

Perhaps the most effective carrier for diffusion of this music to other places has been the commercial recording and widespread distribution of the music on records, tapes, and, most recently, compact digital discs (CDs). Early zydeco recordings by Douglas Bellard, Amédé Ardoin, and others were strictly for regional release. Beaumont musician Clarence Garlow had a few minor hits in the early 1950s, paving the way for two back-to-back releases that began the commercial success of recorded zydeco: "Paper in My Shoe" by Boozoo Chavis in 1954, followed by Chenier's "Ay-Tete-Fee" in 1955. Before national record labels began capitalizing on the growing popularity of this music, the commercial recording and distribution of most zydeco records were shepherded by two independent labels: Chris Strachwitz's Arhoolie Records in El Cerrito, California, and Floyd Soileau's Maison de Soul in Ville Platte, Louisiana. In 1982, Rockin' Sidney Simien's hit single "My Toot-Toot" became an international sensation, and with over a million copies sold it is still the biggest selling record in zydeco history.

Zydeco clubs remain active throughout the Lafayette-to-Houston corridor, and heartily welcome people of all races who want to hear the music in its original setting. Since 1982 the tiny crossroads community of Plaisance each year plays host to the Southwest Louisiana Zydeco Festival. This event showcases the leading zydeco musicians in the world, and consists of a full roster of entertainment, with bands taking the stage one after another in a twelve-hour long continuous celebration. Although still identified with Creole culture in its home territory, zydeco has become a popular style of dance music in many other places around the world.

—Robert Kuhlken

FURTHER READING:

Ancelet, Barry. "Zydeco/Zarico: Beans, Blues, and Beyond." *Black Music Research Journal* Vol. 8, 1988, 33-49.

Broven, John. *South to Louisiana: The Music of the Cajun Bayous.* Gretna, Louisiana, Pelican Publishing Co., 1983.

Gould, Philip and Barry Jean Ancelet. *Cajun Music and Zydeco.* Baton Rouge, Louisiana State University Press, 1992.

Kuhlken, Robert, and Rocky Sexton. "The Geography of Zydeco Music." *The Sounds of People and Places: A Geography of American Folk and Popular Music.* Ed. G. Carney, 3rd edition, Lanham, Maryland, Rowman & Littlefield, 1994, 63-76.

Nyhan, Patricia, and Brian Rollins, David Babb, Michael Doucet. *Let the Good Times Roll! A Guide to Cajun & Zydeco Music.* Portland, Maine, Upbeat Books, 1997.

Tisserand, Michael. *The Kingdom of Zydeco.* New York, Arcade Publishing, 1998.

ZZ Top

From respected roots rockers to bearded music video age icons, this Texas band maintained a consistently successful career throughout the 1970s and 1980s, embracing many new trends that crossed its path. While not as active in the late 1990s as they were in their prime, ZZ Top's three members (Billy Gibbons, Dusty Hill, and Frank Beard on guitar, bass, and drums, respectively) remain one of the few groups

ZZ Top in concert.

to have its original members intact after 25 years. Existing throughout the 1970s as a critically acclaimed, popular Texas blues-boogie band, the band updated its sound to include propulsive synthesizer rhythms. Further, ZZ Top was one of the first pre-music-video rock bands to immediately take advantage of the advent of MTV.

In the late 1960s, Billy Gibbons played in the Texas psych-punk band The Moving Sidewalks, and Dusty Hill and Frank Beard were the rhythm section for American Blues. Future ZZ Top manager Bill Ham brought the three together in 1970 and, due to Ham's plan of constant recording and ceaseless touring, by the decade's end the group had carved out a sizable niche as a popular blues-boogie band. In 1970, ZZ Top released *ZZ Top's First Album*, and by its third album it struck gold with its first major hit and concert staple, "La Grange," a tribute to an infamous whorehouse. "La Grange" (whose signature riff was based on the John Lee Hooker song, "Boogie Chillen") set the fire that would culminate in one the 1970s most successful tours, the year and a half long "Worldwide Texas Tour."

While their string of hits never abated through the end of the 1970s and into the early 1980s, it was the group's 1983 *Eliminator*

album that propelled ZZ Top to superstardom. That the group adopted synthesizers and drum machines to augment their sound didn't hurt, but what perhaps helped most was their videos. With sunglasses and long beards, ZZ Top had a perfect made-for-music-video image, and they filled their videos with scantily clad, sexy women—a perfect formula for early MTV success. *Eliminator* contained a number of hit singles and videos, including "Legs," "Sharp Dressed Man," and "Gimmie All Your Lovin'." Choosing not to disrupt their successful formula, the group made their 1985 *Afterburner* in the image of their multi-platinum predecessor, and the album spawned the hits "Sleeping Bag," "Velcro Fly," "Rough Boy," and "Stages." Predictably, the group applied its "if it ain't broke don't fix it" philosophy to *Afterburner*'s videos as well.

ZZ Top never climbed the commercial peaks of its mid-1980s period, but they continued to be a big concert draw, and their albums continued to sell respectably. The 1996 release of *Rhythmeen*, a back-to-basics album, cleared the table of the high production sheen and synthesizers that characterized their *Afterburner* and *Eliminator* period. The album was critically acclaimed and demonstrated that

Billy Gibbons was certainly one of the most talented white blues guitarists this side of Stevie Ray Vaughan.

—Kembrew McLeod

FURTHER READING:

Blayney, David. *Sharp Dressed Men: ZZ Top behind the Scenes from Blues to Boogie to Beards.* New York, Hyperion, 1994.

Sinclair, David. *The Story of ZZ Top: Tres Hombre.* London, Virgin, 1986.

READING LIST

The following reading list is meant as a supplement to the bibliographies that accompany the subject specific essays in this collection. We have selected two types of works for this list: those works that explain the long-term, historical development of popular culture in the United States; and those works that discuss the academic study of popular culture. Among the latter are both theoretical explications and reference works. This reading list is not intended to be exhaustive.

Barthes, Roland. *Mythologies.* Translated by Annette Lavers. 1957. Reprint, New York, The Noonday Press, 1972.

Bigsby, C. W. E., editor. *Approaches to Popular Culture.* Bowling Green, Ohio, Bowling Green State University Popular Press, 1976.

Bluestein, Gene. *Poplore: Folk and Pop in American Culture.* Amherst, University of Massachusetts Press, 1994.

Bode, Carl. *The Anatomy of American Popular Culture, 1840-1861.* Berkeley, University of California Press, 1960.

Browne, Ray B. *Popular Culture and the Expanding Consciousness.* New York, Wiley, 1973.

Browne, Ray B., and David Madden. *The Popular Culture Explosion.* Dubuque, Iowa, W. C. Brown Co., 1972.

Browne, Ray B., and Marshall W. Fishwick, editors. *Preview 2001+: Popular Culture Studies in the Future.* Bowling Green, Ohio, Bowling Green State University Popular Press, 1995.

———, editors. *Symbiosis: Popular Culture and Other Fields.* Bowling Green, Ohio, Bowling Green State University Popular Press, 1988.

Browne, Ray B., and Michael T. Marsden, editors. *Pioneers in Popular Culture Studies.* Bowling Green, Ohio, Bowling Green State University Popular Press, 1999.

Browne, Ray B., and Ronald J. Ambrosetti, editors. *Continuities in Popular Culture: The Present in the Past and the Past in the Present and Future.* Bowling Green, Ohio, Bowling Green State University Popular Press, 1993.

Browne, Ray B., Marshall W. Fishwick, and Kevin O. Browne, editors. *Dominant Symbols in Popular Culture.* Bowling Green, Ohio, Bowling Green State University Popular Press, 1990.

Buhle, Paul, editor. *Popular Culture in America.* Minneapolis, University of Minnesota Press, 1987.

Cantor, Norman F., and Michael S. Werthman, editors. *The History of Popular Culture.* Volume 1: *To 1815,* Volume 2: *Since 1815.* New York, Macmillan, 1968.

Carter, Steven. *Leopards in the Temple: Studies in American Popular Culture.* San Francisco, International Scholars Publications, 1997.

Cullen, Jim. *The Art of Democracy: A Concise History of Popular Culture in the United States.* New York, Monthly Review Press, 1996.

Denney, Reuel. *The Astonished Muse.* 1957. Reprint, Chicago, University of Chicago Press, 1974.

Denning, Michael. *The Cultural Front: The Laboring of American Culture in the Twentieth Century.* New York, Verso, 1998.

Fishwick, Marshall W. *Common Culture and the Great Tradition: The Case for Renewal.* Westport, Connecticut, Greenwood Press, 1982.

———. *Parameters of Popular Culture.* Bowling Green, Ohio, Bowling Green State University Popular Press, 1974.

Fiske, John. *Understanding Popular Culture.* Boston, Unwin/Hyman, 1989.

Flaherty, David H., and Frank E. Manning, editors. *The Beaver Bites Back?: American Popular Culture in Canada.* Montreal and Buffalo, McGill-Queen's University Press, 1993.

Gans, Herbert J. *Popular Culture and High Culture: An Analysis and Evaluation of Taste.* New York, Basic Books, 1974.

Geist, Christopher D., and Jack Nachbar, editors. *The Popular Culture Reader.* Bowling Green, Ohio, Bowling Green State University Popular Press, 1983.

Geist, Christopher D., Ray B. Browne, Michael T. Marsden, and Carole Palmer, editors. *The Directory of Popular Culture Collections.* Phoenix, Arizona, Oryx Press, 1989.

Gibian, Peter, editor. *Mass Culture and Everyday Life.* New York, Routledge, 1997.

Giroux, Henry A. *Disturbing Pleasures: Learning Popular Culture.* New York, Routledge, 1994.

Gordon, Mark, and Jack Nachbar, compilers and editors. *Currents of Warm Life: Popular Culture in American Higher Education.* Bowling Green, Ohio, Bowling Green University Popular Press, 1980.

Hall, Stuart, and Paddy Whannel. *The Popular Arts.* New York, Pantheon, 1965.

Hoffmann, Frank W. *American Popular Culture: A Guide to the Reference Literature.* Englewood, Colorado, Libraries Unlimited, 1995.

Inge, M. Thomas, editor. *Concise Histories of American Popular Culture.* Westport, Connecticut, Greenwood Press, 1982.

———, editor. *Handbook of American Popular Culture.* 2nd edition. Westport, Connecticut, Greenwood Press, 1989.

———, editor. *Handbook of American Popular Literature.* Westport, Connecticut, Greenwood Press, 1988.

Laforse, Martin W., and James A. Drake. *Popular Culture and American Life: Selected Topics in the Study of American Popular Culture.* Chicago, Nelson-Hall, 1981.

Landrum, Larry N. *American Popular Culture: A Guide to Information Sources.* Detroit, Gale Research, 1982.

Levine, Lawrence W. *Highbrow/Lowbrow: The Emergence of Cultural Hierarchy in America.* Cambridge, Harvard University Press, 1988.

———. *The Opening of the American Mind: Canons, Culture, and History.* Boston, Beacon Press, 1996.

———. *The Unpredictable Past: Explorations in American Cultural History.* New York, Oxford University Press, 1993.

Lipsitz, George. *Time Passages: Collective Memory and American Popular Culture.* Minneapolis, University of Minnesota Press, 1990.

Lowenthal, Leo. *Literature, Popular Culture, and Society.* Englewood Cliffs, New Jersey, Prentice-Hall, 1961.

Lynes, Russell. *The Tastemakers.* New York, Harper, 1954.

MacDonald, Dwight. *Against the American Grain.* New York, Random House, 1962.

Maltby, Richard, editor. *The Passing Parade: A History of Popular Culture in the Twentieth Century.* New York, Oxford University Press, 1989.

Motz, Marilyn F., et al. *Eye on the Future: Popular Culture Scholarship into the Twenty-First Century in Honor of Ray B. Browne.* Bowling Green, Ohio, Bowling Green State University Popular Press, 1994.

Mukerji, Chandra, and Michael Schudson, editors. *Rethinking Popular Culture: Contemporary Perspectives in Cultural Studies.* Berkeley, University of California Press, 1991.

Nachbar, Jack, and Kevin Lause, editors. *Popular Culture: An Introductory Text.* Bowling Green, Ohio, Bowling Green State University Popular Press, 1992.

Norton, Anne. *Republic of Signs: Liberal Theory and American Popular Culture.* Chicago, University of Chicago Press, 1993.

Nye, Russel B. *The Unembarrassed Muse: The Popular Arts in America.* New York, Dial Press, 1970.

———, editor. *New Dimensions in Popular Culture.* Bowling Green, Ohio, Bowling Green State University Popular Press, 1972.

Radway, Janice. *Reading the Romance: Women, Patriarchy, and Popular Literature.* Chapel Hill, University of North Carolina Press, 1984.

Root, Robert L. *The Rhetorics of Popular Culture: Advertising, Advocacy, and Entertainment.* Westport, Connecticut, Greenwood Press, 1987.

Ross, Andrew. *No Respect: Intellectuals and Popular Culture.* New York, Routledge, 1989.

Schroeder, Fred E. H., editor. *Twentieth-Century Popular Culture in Museums and Libraries.* Bowling Green, Ohio, Bowling Green State University Popular Press, 1981.

Seldes, Gilbert. *The Seven Lively Arts.* New York and London, Harper and Brothers, 1924.

Smith, Henry Nash. *Virgin Land: The American West as Symbol and Myth.* 1950. Reprint, New York, Vintage, 1957.

Stanton, Frank Nicholas. *Mass Media and Mass Culture.* New York, Columbia Broadcasting System, 1962.

Storey, John. *An Introductory Guide to Cultural Theory and Popular Culture.* Athens, University of Georgia Press, 1993.

Susman, Warren. *Culture as History: The Transformation of American Society in the Twentieth Century.* New York, Pantheon, 1984.

Toll, Robert C. *The Entertainment Machine: American Show Business in the Twentieth Century.* New York, Oxford University Press, 1989.

Ulanov, Barry. *The Two Worlds of American Art: The Private and the Popular.* New York, Macmillan, 1965.

Warshow, Robert. *The Immediate Experience: Movies, Comics, Theatre, and Other Aspects of Popular Culture.* Garden City, New York, Doubleday, 1964.

Wertheim, Arthur Frank, editor. *American Popular Culture: A Historical Bibliography.* Santa Barbara, California, ABC-Clio Information Services, 1984.

White, David Manning, and John Pendleton, editors. *Popular Culture: Mirror of American Life.* Del Mar, California, Publisher's Inc., 1977.

Whiting, Cecile. *A Taste for Pop: Pop Art, Gender, and Consumer Culture.* Cambridge and New York, Cambridge University Press, 1997.

Williams, Martin T. *Hidden in Plain Sight: An Examination of the American Arts.* New York, Oxford University Press, 1992.

Williams, Raymond. *Culture and Society, 1780-1950.* London, Chatto and Windus, 1960.

Wilmeth, Don B. *American and English Popular Entertainment: A Guide to Information Sources.* Detroit, Gale Research, 1980.

ACKNOWLEDGMENTS

The editors wish to thank the copyright holders of the photographs included in this volume and the permissions managers of many book and magazine publishing companies for assisting us in securing reproduction rights. We are also grateful to the staffs of the Detroit Public Library, the Library of Congress, the University of Detroit Mercy Library, Wayne State University Purdy/Kresge Library Complex, and the University of Michigan Libraries for making their resources available to us. Every effort has been made to trace copyright, but if omissions have been made, please bring them to the attention of the editors. The following is a list of the copyright holders who have granted us permission to reproduce material in the *St. James Encyclopedia of Popular Culture* as well as from where said resources were received:

Al Pearce. Richard Petty.

American Automobile Association. Cadillac; Corvette; Edsel; Model T.

Andy Warhol Foundation, Inc./Art Resource, New York. Andy Warhol.

Apple Paperbacks. R. L. Stine/Apple Paperbacks is a registered trademark of Scholastic Inc. Goosebumps is a registered trademark of Parachute Press, Inc. All rights reserved.

AP/Wide World Photos. Hank Aaron; Academy Awards; *The Adventures of Ozzie and Harriet*; Advertising; Aerobics; Alabama; Marv Albert; Alan Alda; Muhammad Ali; *Alice*; *All in the Family*; Steve Allen; Luther Allison; Robert Altman; Morey Amsterdam; *The Amos 'n' Andy Show*; Amtrak; Marian Anderson; *The Andy Griffith Show*; Anita Hill-Clarence Thomas Senate Hearings; Henry Armstrong; Louis Armstrong; Bea Arthur; Arthur Ashe; Fred Astaire and Ginger Rogers; Chet Atkins; Frankie Avalon; *Back to the Future*; *The Bad News Bears*; Josephine Baker; Jim Bakker and Tammy Faye; James Baldwin; Hank Ballard; Ballet; Barbie; Batman; Beanie Babies; The Beastie Boys; Candice Bergen; Ingrid Bergman; Sandra Bernhard; Leonard Bernstein; Yogi Berra; The Big Apple; Larry Bird; Black Panthers; Black Sabbath; *Blade Runner*; Ruben Blades; Mel Blanc; Blaxploitation Films; Judy Blume; Body Decoration; *Bonnie and Clyde*; Victor Borge; Boston Marathon/Winslow Townson; Boston Strangler; Boxing/Nick Ut; Brat Pack; Tom Brokaw; Mel Brooks; Jim Brown; Jimmy Buffet; Ted Bundy; Burlesque; Ken Burns; William S. Burroughs; *Butch Cassidy and the Sundance Kid*; Cabbage Patch Kids; Cab Calloway; *Candid Camera*; Eddie Cantor; Dale Carnegie; The Cars; Dick Cavett; Celebrity Caricature; Celebrity Caricature; Wilt Chamberlain; *Charlie's Angels*; Cheech and Chong; The Chicago Seven; Child Stars; *Chinatown*; Christo; Chrysler Building; *City Lights*/United Artists; Civil Rights Movement; Dick Clark; Montgomery Clift; Rosemary Clooney; Ty Cobb; Coca-Cola; Communes; Perry Como; Condoms; Coney Island; Jimmy Connors; Sam Cooke; James J. Corbett; The Cosby Show; Cindy Crawford; Jim Croce; Bing Crosby; Crosby, Stills, and Nash; Bill Dana; Charlie Daniels; *Death of a Salesman*; *The Deer Hunter*; Ellen DeGeneres; Cecil B. DeMille; Department Stores; Devo; Bo Diddley; Babe Didrickson; Marlene Dietrich; Joe DiMaggio; Diners; Disc Jockeys; Disney (Walt Disney Company); Divine; E. L. Doctorow; Fats Domino; Phil Donahue; Donovan; The Doors; *Double Indemnity*; Drag Racing; Dr. Seuss; *Dr. Strangelove or: How I Learned to Stop Worrying and Love the Bomb*; Drag; Dream Team; Isadora Duncan; Bob Dylan; *Dynasty*; *Ebony*; Ralph Edwards; Emmy Awards; *ER*; Julius ''Dr. J'' Erving; ESPN; *E.T. The Extra-Terrestrial*; The Everly Brothers; *Fantasy Island*; Farm Aid; Farrah Fawcett; José Feliciano; Feminism; Stepin Fetchit; *Fiddler on the Roof*; Sally Field; W. C. Fields; Eddie Fisher; Peggy Fleming; Flipper; Henry Fonda; Tennessee Ernie Ford; George Foreman; Jodie Foster; Frankenstein; *Frazier*; Freedom Rides; Nancy Friday; *Friends*; Annette Funicello; *The Fugitive*; Gambling; Ava Gardner; Marvin Gaye; *Gentlemen Prefer Blondes*; Richard Gere; Ghettos; Althea Gibson; Bob Gibson; Mel Gibson; *Gilligan's Island*; Allen Ginsberg; Arthur Godfrey; Rube Goldberg; Whoopi Goldberg; Berry Gordy; John Gotti; Betty Grable; Bill Graham; Martha Graham; Amy Grant; Cary Grant; Zane Grey; Merv Griffin; Matt Groening; Grunge; Gulf War; Merle Haggard; Haight-Ashbury; *Hair*; Hairstyles; Hairstyles (b); W. C. Handy; Howard Hawks; Rita Hayworth; *Hee Haw*; *Hello, Dolly!*; Hell's Angels; Hippies; Abbie Hoffman; Dustin Hoffman; Hulk Hogan; *Hogan's Heroes*; William Holden; Edward Hopper; Hot Rods; L. Ron Hubbard; Rock Hudson; Helen Hunt; *Hustler*; John Huston; *I Dream of Jeanie*; *I Love Lucy;* Ice-T; Indianapolis 500; Iran Contra; Ironman Triathlon; The Jackson Five; Jesse Jackson; Mahalia Jackson; Michael Jackson; Reggie Jackson; James Bond Films; Jefferson Airplane/Starship; *The Jeffersons*; Earvin ''Magic'' Johnson; Bobby Jones; Tom Jones; Michael Jordan; Florence Griffith Joyner; Raúl Juliá; Boris Karloff; Casey Kasem; Garrison Keillor; Harvey Keitel; Gene Kelly; Key West; Albert King; Billie Jean King; Carol King; Rodney King; Stephen King; The Kingston Trio; Evel Knievel; *Kojak*; David Koresh and the Branch Davidians; Sandy Koufax; Alan Ladd; Ricki Lake; Veronica Lake; Louis L'Amour; k.d. lang; *The Larry Sanders Show*; Tommy Lasorda; Lassie; *Laugh-In*; Ralph Lauren; Leadbelly; Norman Lear; Timothy Leary; Led Zeppelin; Spike Lee; Tom Lehrer; Sugar Ray Leonard; Sergio Leone; Leopold and Loeb; *Les Miserables*; Carl Lewis; Jerry Lee Lewis; Roy Lichtenstein; Little League; Little Richard; Lollapalooza; The Lone Ranger; Joe Louis; Lucky Luciano; Loretta Lynn; Moms Mabley; Fred MacMurray; Mafia/Organized Crime; Malcolm X; Mall of America; Malls; The Mamas and the Papas; Manhattan Transfer; Charlie Manson; Mariachi Music; Dean Martin; Steve Martin; Martini; *Mary Hartman, Mary Hartman*; *M*A*S*H*; *Maude*; Willie Mays; McCarthyism; John McEnroe; Reba McEntire; John Mellencamp; *Miami Vice*; *The Mickey Mouse Club*; Microsoft; Bette Midler; Militias; Harvey Milk; Miss America Pageant; *Mister Ed*; Joni Mitchell; *Modern Times*; *Monday Night Football*; Earl ''The Pearl'' Monroe; Marilyn Monroe; Joe Montana; Demi Moore; Rita Moreno; Alanis Morissette; *Mr. Smith Goes to Washington*; Anne Murray; Arthur Murray; Muscle Cars; Joe Namath; New Age Music; The New Kids on the Block; *Nightline*; 1968 Mexico City Summer Olympic Games; Rudolph Nureyev; Georgia O'Keefe; *Oklahoma!*; Laurence Olivier; *On the Waterfront*; Shaquille O'Neal; Roy Orbison; Rosa Parks; *Patton*; Walter Payton; Minnie Pearl; Peep Shows; *Perry Mason*; Michelle Pfeiffer; *The Phantom of the Opera*; The Pittsburgh Steelers; The Pointer Sisters; Iggy Pop; Pornography; Cole Porter; Promise Keepers; Richard Pryor; Tito Puente; Punk/Wide World Photos; *Queen for a Day*; Queen Latifah; Gertrude ''Ma'' Rainey; The Ramones; Ronald Reagan; Robert Redford; R.E.M.; Burt Reynolds; *Ripley's Believe It Or Not*; Geraldo Rivera; Joan Rivers; Julia Roberts; Paul Robeson; Jackie Robinson; Smokey Robinson; Sugar Ray Robinson; Gene Roddenberry; Dennis Rodman; Kenny Rogers; Roy Rogers; Esther Rolle; The Rolling Stones; Romance Novels; *Roots*; Julius and Ethel Rosenberg; Diana Ross and the Supremes; Route 66; Run-DMC; RuPaul; Babe Ruth; Meg Ryan; Safe Sex; *Sanford and Son*; *Saturday Night Live*; *Schindler's List*; Dr. Laura Schlessinger; Julian Schnabel; Pete Seeger; Serial Killers; *Sesame Street*; Sex Scandals; *Shaft*; Tupac Shakur; Bugsy Siegel; Simon and Garfunkel; Neil Simon; O. J. Simpson; Simpson Trial; Frank Sinatra; Sinbad; Siskel and

Ebert; *60 Minutes*; Skateboarding; Skating; Kate Smith; Jimmy Smits; The Smothers Brothers; Snoop Doggy Dogg; Sonny and Cher; Soul Music; John Philip Sousa; Mark Spitz; Jerry Springer; Sputnik; Sylvester Stallone; *Star Wars*; Roger Staubach; George Steinbrenner; Howard Stern; George Strait; Meryl Streep; *A Streetcar Named Desire*; Barbra Streisand; Strip Joints/Striptease; Marty Stuart; Oliver Stone; Studio 54; Suburbia; Donna Summer; Superman; Supermodels; Jimmy Swaggart; Talk Radio; Teen Idols; Tennis; *This Is Your Life*; Danny Thomas; The Three Stooges; *To Tell the Truth*; *Today*; Tokyo Rose; The Tonight Show; Spencer Tracy; Ted Turner; Mike Tyson; Johnny Unitas; Van Halen; Vivian Vance; The Velvet Underground; Victoria's Secret; Wal-Mart; Barbara Walters; Denzel Washington; Watergate; Ethel Waters; Muddy Waters; The Weavers; Jack Webb; Lawrence Welk; Orson Welles; *What's My Line?*; Whiskey A Go Go; Barry White; George F. Will; Andy Williams; Hank Williams; Robin Williams; Flip Wilson; Oprah Winfrey; Stevie Wonder; Tiger Woods; Woodstock; World Series; World War I; World War II; Yanni; ''Weird Al'' Yankovic; *Your Hit Parade*; *Your Show of Shows*; Frank Zappa; ZZ Top.

Archive Photos, Inc. Cannonball Adderley/Frank Driggs Collection; Altamont/William L. Rukeyser; *American Bandstand*; Amusement Parks; Mario Andretti; *Annie Hall*; *Apocalypse Now*; Fatty Arbuckle; Ed Asner; Dan Aykroyd/NBC; George Balanchine; The Band; *Barney Miller*; The Beatles; Warren Beatty; Bellbottoms; Milton Berle; John Belushi/NBC; Busby Berkely/Popperfoto; *The Beverly Hillbillies*; *Beverly Hills 90210*/ Fotos International; *Bewitched*; *The Blackboard Jungle*; *The Blob*; Blackface Minstrelsy; *Blue Velvet*; Blues/Frank Driggs Collection; The Blues Brothers; Board Games/Lamber; Bowling; Boy Scouts; Terry Bradshaw/Sporting News; *Breakfast at Tiffany's*; *Bringing Up Baby*; David Brinkley; Lenny Bruce; Buffalo Springfield; Dick Butkus/Sporting News; Butterfly McQueen; *Cagney & Lacey,* photograph by Cliff Lipson/ Fotos International; Camping/Lamber; Steve Carlton/Photo File; Hoagy Carmichael; Carnegie Hall; The Carpenters; Carter Family/Frank Driggs Collection; Cassette Tape/Douglas or Connie Corry; David Cassidy/Peter Borsari; Century 21 Exposition; Central Park/Gerald Israel; Chevy Chase/NBC; Chubby Checker; Cheerleading; *Cheers*; Clifton Chenier/Joseph A. Rosen; Patsy Cline; College Fads; The Commodores; Joan Crawford; Creedence Clearwater Revival; Robert Crumb; *Davy Crockett*; *Dallas*; Doris Day; Daytona 500; Jack Dempsey/American Stock; John Denver, photograph by Deborah Feingold; Diana, Princess of Wales/Newsphotos/Press Association; *Diff'rent Strokes*/NBC; Dime Store; Dixieland Music; Larry Doby/Photo File; Tommy and Jimmy Dorsey/American Stock; Leo Durocher; Wayne Dyer, photograph by Frank Capri/ SHGG; Electric Appliances/Photo File; Electric Guitar; Cory Everson/Agron; Fabian; *Family Matters*/Foto International; *Fantasia*; William Faulkner, photograph by Neil Boenzi/*New York Times*; Firearms; *A Fistful of Dollars*; Ella Fitzgerald/Frank Driggs Collection; *The Flying Nun*; Connie Francis, photograph by Ken Settle; *Forrest Gump*/Fotos International; *42nd Street*; *Freaks*; *Friday the 13th*; Lou Gehrig; Gibson Girl/ American Stock; Girl Groups/Frank Driggs Collection; Jackie Gleason; Samuel Goldwyn; Benny Goodman; *Good Times*; *GoodFellas*; Gossip Columns; *The Graduate*; The Grateful Dead; Harry Greb/American Stock; Graham Greene; John Grisham/Capri/Saga; Gymnastics; Dorothy Hamill; *Happy Days*/ABC Television; Hare Krishna; Harley-Davidson/Crady von Pawlak; *Hawaii Five-O*; John Havlichek; Hugh Heffner/ McNeely; Jimi Hendrix; *Hercules: The Legendary Journeys*; Ernest Hemingway; *High Noon*; *Hill Street Blues*/American Stock; Alfred Hitchcock; Billie Holiday; Buddy Holly; Hollywood, photograph by Michael Guthrie/Michael Guthrie; *Hollywood Squares*; *The Honeymooners*; Hopalong Cassidy; Hot Dogs/Lamber; *The Howdy Doody Show*; Hot Pants, photograph by McNeely/McNeely; Howlin' Wolf/McNeely; Howard Hughes; Tab Hunter; Ice Cream Cone, photograph by Dan Coleman/Dan Coleman; Iron Maiden/McNeely; Ivy League/McNeely; *Jaws*; *The Jazz Singer*; *Jesus Christ Superstar*; *JFK*; Blind Willie Johnson/Frank Driggs Collection; Janis Joplin; Scott Joplin; Louis Jordan; Andy Kaufman; Buster Keaton; Grace Kelly; *Keystone Kops*/American Stock; Larry King/Lee; Kitsch/Ace or Adrian Bradshaw; *Knots Landing*; Gene Krupa; Jake LaMotta/Popperfoto; Burt Lancaster; Cyndi Lauper/Popperfoto; *Leave It to Beaver*; Bruce Lee; Gypsy Rose Lee; Peggy Lee; Jay Leno/ Hammond; Elmore Leonard; Liberace; Sonny Liston; Andrew Lloyd-Webber; Guy Lombardo; Bela Lugosi; Jimmie Lunceford/Frank Driggs Collection; Lynching; Lynyrd Skynyrd; *The Maltese Falcon*; *The Man Who Shot Liberty Valance*; Jayne Mansfield; Mickey Mantle; Mardi Gras; Marijuana, photograph by Joan Slatkin/Joan Slatkin; Bob Marley/Express Newspapers; Marshall McLuhan, photograph by Bernard Gotfryd; Johnny Mathis; *Meet Me in St. Louis*; *Midnight Cowboy*; Glenn Miller/Frank Driggs; Roger Miller; *Mission: Impossible*; *Mister Rogers' Neighborhood*/Family Communications, Inc.; Mod; The Monkees/Frank Driggs Collection; Bill Monroe/Frank Driggs Collection; *Mork & Mindy*; Motown; *Murder, She Wrote*; Eddie Murphy/NBC; Bill Murray; Edward R. Murrow; *Mutiny on the Bounty*/American Stock; *My So Called Life*; The New York Yankees; *North by Northwest*; Kim Novak/Express Newspapers; *The Odd Couple*; Rosie O'Donnell; *The Outer Limits*; Buck Owens; Al Pacino/Grant; William S. Paley; Charlie Parker; Les Paul/Les Paul; Pearl Jam; Pepsi-Cola; Ross Perot; Peyton Place/ABC Television; Plastic; Polyester, photograph by Lambert/Lamber; Popsicles; *The Postman Always Rings Twice*; Prince; Psychedelia/Blank Archives; Gilda Radner/NBC; Raggedy Ann and Raggedy Andy; Rambo; *Rear Window*; Steve Reeves; Charlie Rich/Fotos International; Cal Ripken, Jr.; Frank Robinson; The Rockettes; Knute Rockne; Roller Coasters; Pete Rose; *Roseanne*; Nolan Ryan/Photo File; Saks Fifth Avenue; *Saturday Night Fever*; Savoy Ballroom; Martin Scorcese; Sedona, Arizona; Selena; Rod Serling; The Shirelles/Fotos International; *The Silence of the Lambs*/Ken Regan/Fotos International; Paul Simon; *The Six Million Dollar Man*; Skyscrapers/Lamber; Sly and the Family Stone; *Some Like It Hot*; Spice Girls/Popperfoto; *Starsky and Hutch*/Frank Edwards/Fotos International; Steven Spielberg; Bruce Springsteen/Popperfoto; Bart Starr/Sporting News; State Fairs; Gloria Steinem; Ray Stevens; Jimmy Stewart; Streaking/Russell Reif; Ed Sullivan; Lynn Swann/Sporting News; Swimming Pools; Swing Dancing; *Taxi*; Teddy Bears/Express Newspapers; Shirley Temple/Popperfoto; The Temptations; Tennis Shoes/Sneakers/Ed Carlin; *The Terminator*; Bobby Thompson/Photo File; Hunter S. Thompson, photograph by Darlene Hammond; *Three's Company*; The Titanic; Lily Tomlin; *Tootsie*; *Tora! Tora! Tora!*; Mel Torme; Tramps; John Travolta; *The Treasure of the Sierra Madre*/Blank Archives; Twiggy/Popperfoto; 2 Live Crew/SAGA; Tupperware; Ike and Tina Turner, photograph by Frank Driggs/McNeely; TV Dinners; Dick Van Dyke; Vanilla Ice, photograph by Bob Scott; Video Games; Vietnam; Volkswagen Beetle; Aaron ''T-Bone'' Walker/Frank Driggs Collection; Junior Walker and the All Stars/Frank Driggs; *The Waltons*; *The Washington Post*; John Waters, Nancy Rica Schiff/SAGA; *Wayne's World*/Suzanne Tenner/Fotos International; Chic Webb/Frank Driggs Collection; Wedding Dress/Lamber; *Welcome Back, Kotter*; Kitty Wells/Frank Driggs Collection; The Who; *The Wild One*; Hank Williams, Sr.; Bruce Willis; *The Wolfman*; Wolfman Jack; World War II; Richard Wright; Cy Young/Photo File; *Ziegfeld Follies*.

Arte Publico Press Archives, University of Houston. Freddie Prinze.

ASUCLA Photography. John Wooden.

Buckeye Invitational. Barbershop Quartets, photograph by Clark Hanmer.

Byron Preiss Multimedia Company, Inc. *Spider-Man*/Byron Preiss Multimedia Company, Inc., 1995. TM & (c) 1999 Marvel Characters, Inc. All rights reserved. Reproduced by permission of Marvel Entertainment Group, Inc.

Carroll & Graf Publishers, Inc. Philip K. Dick, c. 1987.

CORBIS. Edward Abbey/Jonathan Blair; Kareem Abdul-Jabbar/Bettmann; *American Gothic*/Bettmann Association, Inc. for Grant Wood, reproduced by permission of the Visual Artists and Galleries; Andy Hardy/Bettmann; *Annie Get Your Gun*/Bettmann; Apple Computer/Bettmann; Aunt Jemima; Bruce Barton; Baseball Cards/Lake County Museum; Rex Beach, photograph by Harris; Beer, photograph by Thomas A. Kelly and Gail Moon/Karl Kowall; Betty Boop, photograph by Joseph Sohm/Joseph Sohm, ChromoSohm Inc.; Billboards, photograph by Arthur Rothstein; *Blondie* (comic strip); Bob and Ray/Bettmann; Bodybuilding; Bra/Bettmann; Broadway/Bettmann; The Brooklyn Dodgers/Bettmann; Paul Brown/Bettmann; Budweiser, photograph by Tony Arruza/Tony Arruza; Bumper Stickers, photograph by Joseph Sohm/Joseph Sohm, ChromoSohm Inc.; Héctor ''Macho'' Camacho, photograph by Michael Brennan/Michael Brennan; Century of Progress (Chicago, 1933)/Lake County Museum; Christmas; Civil War Reenactors, photograph by Kevin Fleming/Kevin Fleming; CNN, photograph by Mark Gibson/Mark Gibson; Coffee, photograph by Stuart Westmorland/Stuart Westmorland; Coors, photograph by Joseph Sohm/Joseph Sohm, ChromoSohm Inc.; Norman Corwin/Bettmann-UPI; Bill Cosby/Bettmann; *Cosmopolitan*, photograph by Stephanie Maze/Stephanie Maze; The Cotton Club/Bettmann; Jeffrey Dahmer, photograph by Allen Fredrickson Stringer/Reuters; The Dallas Cowboys, photograph by Sergio Carmona/S. Carmona; *The Day the Earth Stood Still*; *Days of Our Lives*; The Dead Kennedys, photograph by Roger Ressmeyer/Roger Ressmeyer; Debutantes/Seattle Post-Intelligencer Collection Museum of History & Industry; Dime Novels/Ted Streshinsky; Doc Savage/Bettmann; Roberto Duran/Bettmann; Ebbets Field/Bettmann; Erector Sets; Chris Evert/Bettmann; FBI/Bettmann; Flea Markets, photograph by Gail Mooney/Gail Mooney; Folk Music/Bettmann; French Fries, photograph by Lois Ellen Frank/Lois Ellen Frank; Kinky Friedman/Will Van Overbeek; Gangs, photograph by Daniel Lainé/Daniel Lainé; *General Hospital*/Bettmann; GI Joe, photograph by Michael Reed/M. M. H. Reed; Golden Gate Bridge/Kevin Schafer; Graceland, photograph by Kevin Fleming/Kevin Fleming; Graffiti, photograph by David Robinson/David Robinson; Greenpeace, photograph by Martial Dosdane/AFB; Greyhound Buses/Bettmann; Marvelous Marvin Hagler/Bettmann; Hamburger, photograph by Philip Gould/Philip Gould; Hanna-Barbera/Bettmann; Harlem Globetrotters, photograph by Charles Harris/Pittsburgh Courier Photographics; Dennis Hopper, photograph by Catherine Karnow/Catherine Karnow; Horror Movies/Bettmann; Ina Ray Hutton; *It Happened One Night*/John Springer; Jet Skis, photograph by Todd Gipstein/Todd Gipstein; Juke Boxes/Bettmann; Kewpie Dolls/Underwood & Underwood; Bobby Knight, photograph by Sue Ogrocki/Bettmann-UPI; Stan Lee; Benny Leonard/Bettmann; Levi's/Carl Corey; Rush Limbaugh/Bettmann Archive; Vince Lombardi/Bettmann; Louisiana Purchase Exposition (St. Louis, 1904), photograph by Keystone View Company; Low Riders, photograph by Macduff Everton/Macduff Everton; Macy's/Karl Kowall; *MAD Magazine*, photograph by Jacques M. Chenet/Jacques M. Chenet; John Madden/Bettman-UPI; Winsor McCay/Bettmann-UPI; McDonald's/Bettmann; Rachel McLish/Neal Preston; Minstrel Shows; *The Mod Squad*/Bettmann; Mother's Day/Hulton-Deutsch Collection; Movie Palaces/Bettmann; MTV, photograph by Jan Butchofsky-Houser/Jan Butchofsky-Houser; Neckties, photograph by David Tullis/Bettmann-UPI; *The New York Times*/Bettmann; Olympics, photograph by Wally McNamee/Wally McNamee; Jacqueline Kennedy Onassis/Bettmann; *One Day at a Time*/Bettmann; Ouija Boards/Bettmann; Pants for Women/Bettmann; Pantyhose/Bettmann; *Pee-wee's Playhouse*/Neal Preston; Phonograph/Bettmann; *Playboy*/Bettmann; Elvis Presley/Bettmann; Prom/Bettmann; Public Enemy/Bettmann; Dan Rather/Bettmann; *Rebel without a Cause*/Bettmann; Otis Redding/Bettmann; Reggae, photograph by Henry Diltz/Henry Diltz; Ringling Bros., Barnum & Bailey Circus, photograph by Sheldan Collins/Sheldan Collins; Rockefeller Family/Bettmann; Chi Chi Rodriguez/Bettmann; Bill Russel/Bettmann; Barry Sanders, photograph by John G. Mabanglo/AFP; Eugen Sandow/Bettmann; *The Saturday Evening Post*, photograph by Lewis W. Hine; Science Fiction Publishing/Bettmann; Sears Roebuck Catalogue/Bettmann; Frank Shorter/Bettmann; Slinky/Bettmann; *Soul Train*/Neal Preston; Mickey Spillane/Bettmann; Stadium Concerts/Neal Preston; Amos Alonzo Stagg; Stand-up Comedy/David Turnley; Stetson Hat, photograph by Marc Garanger/Marc Garanger; Tanning/Nik Wheeler; Tarzan/Bettmann; Televangelism, photograph by Philip Gould/Bettmann; Trailer Parks/Jonathan Blair; Al Unser/Bettmann; Fernando Valenzuela, photograph by Neal Preston/Neal Preston; Vampires/Bettmann; Vaudeville/Underwood & Underwood; Madame C. J. Walker/Underwood & Underwood; *Whistler's Mother*/Bettmann; George Winston/Bettmann-UPI; Works Progress Administration (WPA) Murals; World Cup, photograph by Neal Preston/Neal Preston; World Wrestling Federation, photograph by Earl Kowall/Karl Kowall; Yellowstone National Park/John Noble.

Del Valle Gallery. *Dracula*.

Dona Ann McAdams. Performance Artists.

E. R. Burroughs, Inc. Edgar Rice Burroughs.

Fisk University Library. Harry Belafonte; Satchel Paige.

Fortean Picture Library. *Baywatch*; *The Bionic Woman*; *Close Encounters of the Third Kind*; Cowboy Look; *Easy Rider*; *Married . . . with Children*; *The Mary Tyler Moore Show*; *The Love Boat*; UFOs.

Gale Group. Stock-Car Racing, photograph by Dennis Winn.

Girl Scouts of the USA. Girls Scouts.

Greater Toledo Convention & Visitors Bureau. Zoos.

HarperBusiness. *Dilbert*/1996, reproduced by permission of HarperCollins Publishers, Copyright (c) 1996 by United Feature Syndicate, Inc., all rights reserved.

Houghton Mifflin Company. Curious George.

IBM. IBM.

Jack Vartoogian. Beach Boys; Robert Cray; Vic Damone; Miles Davis; Buddy Guy; Herbie Hancock; John Lee Hooker; Jazz; B. B. King; Curtis Mayfield; Reggae; Ricky Skaggs.

Jane Addams Memorial Collection, Special Collections, University Library, University of Illinois at Chicago. Jane Addams.

Jerry Bauer. Michael Crichton, photograph by Jerry Bauer.

Ken Regan. Bobby Hull, photograph by Ken Regan.

Ken Settle. AC/DC; Joan Baez; Tony Bennet; Clint Black; Bon Jovi; Garth Brooks, photograph by Ken Settle; Jackson Browne; Alice Cooper; Nanci Griffith; Waylon Jennings; Elton John; George Jones; Judas Priest; KISS; Los Lobos; Courtney Love; Madonna; Martha and the Vandellas; Mötley Crüe; Willie Nelson; Ozzy Osbourne; Dolly Parton; Lou Reed; Salt-n-Pepa; Patti Smith; Sun Records; Stevie Ray Vaughan; Tammy Wynette; Neil Young.

Kmart Corporation. Kmart.

Kobal Collection *Alien*; *American Graffiti*; *Ben Hur*; *The Big Sleep*; *The Birth of a Nation*; Humphrey Bogart; *The Brady Bunch*; *The Bridge on the River Kwai*; Charles Bronson; James Cagney; *Catch-22*; *Citizen Kane*; *A Clockwork Orange*; Gary Cooper; Kevin Costner; Tom Cruise, photograph by Murray Close; Bo Diddley; *Disaster Movie*; Clint Eastwood; *The Exorcist*; Douglas Fairbanks Jr.; Douglas Fairbanks, Sr.; *Field of Dreams*; Errol Flynn; Harrison Ford; Frankenstein; *The French Connection*; *From Here to Eternity*; Lillian Gish; Godzilla; *Gone with the Wind*; *The Good, the Bad and the Ugly*, Produzioni Europee Associate; *The Grapes of Wrath*; *Greed*; Buddy Hackett; *Halloween*; Tom Hanks, photograph by David James; *How the West Was Won*; *I Love Lucy*; *It Happened One Night*; *It's a Wonderful Life*; Peter Jennings; *King Kong*; Hedy Lamarr; National Lampoon; *Lawrence of Arabia*; Jerry Lewis; *The Magnificent Seven*; The Marx Brothers; Steve McQueen; Bob Newhart; *Night of the Living Dead*; *One Flew Over the Cukoo's Nest*; Gregory Peck; *The Philadelphia Story*, photograph by James Stewart; *Planet of the Apes*; *Platoon*; *Psycho*; *Pulp Fiction*, photograph by Linda R. Chen; *Raging Bull*; *Raiders of the Lost Ark*; *Rocky*; *Rocky Horror Picture Show*; Arnold Schwarzenegger; George C. Scott; Randolph Scott; *Scream*, photograph by David M. Moir, Miramax; *Seinfeld*; *Shane*; *Showboat*; Red Skelton; *The Sound of Music*; *South Pacific*; *Spartacus*; *Stagecoach*; *Star Trek*; *Taxi Driver*; *The Ten Commandments*; *The Thing*; *To Kill a Mockingbird*; Lana Turner; *2001: A Space Odyssey*; *Unforgiven*; Rudolph Valentino; *Vertigo*; War Movies; John Wayne; Mae West; *West Side Story*; *The Wild Bunch*; The Western; *The Wizard of Oz*; *Yankee Doodle Dandy*; *The X-Files*.

Library of Congress. Advice Columns; Alvin Ailey; Ashcan School; Isaac Asimov; Charles Atlas; Automobile; Lucille Ball; Mikail Baryshnikov; Baseball; Count Basie; Jack Benny; Irving Berlin; Chuck Berry; Clara Bow; Marlon Brando; Dr. Joyce Brothers; James Brown; Brownie Cameras (Kodak); Paul "Bear" Bryant; Al Capone; Truman Capote; George Carlin; Johnny Carson; Enrico Caruso; Johnny Cash; Charlie Chaplin; Ray Charles; Agatha Christie; Buffalo Bill Cody and His Wild West Show; Nat "King" Cole; John Coltrane; Convertibles; Howard Cosell; Father Charles E. Coughlin; James Dean; John Dillinger; W. E. B. DuBois; Albert Einstein; Duke Ellington, photographed by Gordon Parks; Empire State Building; Evangelism; Father Divine; Flapper Girl, photograph by C. W. Turner; Jane Fonda; Bob Fosse; Sigmund Freud; Robert Frost; Clark Gable; Judy Garland; Gas Stations; Billy Graham; Great Depression; Green Bay Packers; Dick Gregory; D.W. Griffith; Woody Guthrie; Bill Haley/NYWTS; Hallmark Hall of Fame; Dashiell Hammett; William Randolph Hearst; Audrey Hepburn; Woody Herman; Highway System; Alger Hiss; J. Edgar Hoover; Lena Horne; Harry Houdini; Gordie Howe; Lee Iacocca; The Indian; George Jessel; Jack Johnson; Al Jolson; Dr. Alfred Kinsey; Ku Klux Klan; John Lennon; Charles Lindbergh; Walter Lippman; Jack London; Huey Long; Henry Luce; Aimee Semple Macpherson; Rocky Marciano; Paul McCartney; Hattie McDaniel; Bernarr McFadden, photograph by F. W. Guerin; H. L. Mencken; Arthur Miller; Margaret Mitchell; Tom Mix; Mr. Dooley; Ralph Nader; Jack Nicklaus; Eugene O'Neill; Bobby Orr; Jesse Owens/NYWTS; Norman Vincent Peale; Mary Pickford; Sidney Poitier; Jackson Pollock/Reproduced by permission of Artists Rights Society, Inc.; Pop Art; Dan Quayle; Radio; Norman Rockwell, photograph by Underwood & Underwood; Carl Sagan; Charles Schultz; Scopes Monkey Trial; Peter Sellers; *Sex and the Single Girl*; Stephen Sondheim; Dr. Benjamin Spock; State Fairs; Leopold Stokowski; John L. Sullivan, photograph by J. M. Mora; Billy Sunday; Booth Tarkington; Elizabeth Taylor; Television Anchors; J. R. R. Tolkien; Tennessee Williams.

Louisville and Jefferson County Convention & Visitors Bureau. Kentucky Derby.

Mary E. Yeomans/IBMA. Bluegrass, photograph by Mary E. Yeomans.

Mayor's Office of Special Events, City of Chicago. Country Music, reproduced by permission of RS Entertainment for Ricky Skaggs.

Michael Ochs Archives Ltd. Steppenwolf.

Miller Brewing Company. Miller Beer.

Museum of the City of New York, Archive Photos. Musical.

Nancy Ann Lee. Dizzy Gillespie.

National Archives and Records Administration. Roberto Clemente; Prohibition; Lee Trevino; War Bonds.

National Museum of American Art/Art Resource, New York. Andrew Wyeth.

Nevada Commission on Tourism. Hoover Dam.

Nightfall, Inc. *War of the Worlds*/Copyright (c) 1986 by Nightfall, Inc., afterword, used by permission of Dutton Signet, a division of Penguin Putnam Inc.

NYS Department of Economic Development. Niagra Falls.

NYWTS/The Library of Congress. Cigarettes, photograph by Fred Palumbo; Sarah Vaughan, photograph by James J. Kriegsmann.

Oklahoma Tourism. Will Rogers, sculpture by Electra A. Waggoner, Claremore, Oklahoma, Fred Marvel.

Otto Penzler. Black Mask.

Photo Researchers, Inc. Gay Liberation Movement.

Pocket Books, a division of Simon & Schuster, Inc. Nancy Drew/Copyright 1930, renewed (c) 1957 by Simon & Schuster Inc. All rights reserved. Reproduced by permission of Pocket Books, a Division of Simon & Schuster, Inc.

Rapid City Convention & Visitors Bureau. Mount Rushmore.

Rene Dahinden/Fortean Picture Library. Bigfoot, photograph by Patterson and Gimlin/Rene Dahinden 1967, reproduced by permission of Rene Dahinden.

Reuters. Abortion/Bruce Young/Archive Photos, Inc.; David Bowie/Jeff Christensen/Archive Photos, Inc.; *Cats*/Mike Segar/Archive Photos, Inc.; Chicago Bulls/Steve Wilson/Archive Photos, Inc.; John Elway/Mike Blake/Archive Photos, Inc.; Michael Johnson/Archive Photos; *Jurassic Park*/(c) Archive Photos, 530 West 25th St., New York, New York 10001; Tom Landry/Eggitt/Archive Photos, Inc.; Las Vegas/Corbis-Bettmann; Legos/Michael Crabtree/Archive Photos, Inc.; Monica Lewinsky/Ho/Archive Photos, Inc.; Marlboro Man/Robb Wright/Archive Photos, Inc.; Nirvana, photograph by Lee Celano/(c) Archive Photos, 530 West 25th St., New York, New York 10001; Edward James Olmos/Steve Grayson/Archive Photos, Inc.; The Pope/Luciano Mellace/Archive Photos, Inc.; Pat Robertson, photograph by Steve Jaffe/(c) Archive Photos, 530 West 25th St., New York, New York 10001; Roswell Incident/Andrew Hay/Archive Photos, Inc.; Starbucks/Andrew Wong/Archive Photos, Inc.; Kenneth Starr/Jeff Mitchell/Archive Photos, Inc.; Jesse ''The Body'' Ventura/Eric Miller/Archive Photos, Inc.

Rink Foto. AIDS.

Ken Settle. Heavy Metal.

Swedish Information Service. Greta Garbo.

Taco Bell Corp. Fast Food.

Thomas Victor. Ray Bradbury, photograph by Thomas Victor, 1986, all rights reserved, reproduced by permission of the estate of Thomas Victor.

United Artists. Woody Allen; *The Manchurian Candidate*/Archive Photos, Inc.

United Press International. Harry Caray/Corbis-Bettman; Emile Coué; Ford Motor Company/Corbis-Bettman; A. J. Foyt/Corbis-Bettman; Greenwich Village/Corbis-Bettman; Wayne Gretzky; Hockey; Jogging/Corbis-Bettman; John Jakes/Corbis-Bettman; Jonestown/Corbis-Bettman; Hans von Kaltenborn/Corbis-Bettman; Jack LaLanne/Corbis-Bettman; David Letterman/Bettmann; Levittown/Corbis-Bettman; C. S. Lewis/Corbis-Bettman; Barry Manilow/Corbis-Bettman; Masters and Johnson/Corbis-Bettman; Negro Leagues/Corbis-Bettman; 1980 U.S. Olympic Hockey Team; Pet Rocks/Corbis-Bettman; Diego Rivera/Corbis-Bettman; Spring Break/Corbis-Bettman; Teenagers/Corbis-Bettman; *Variety*/Corbis-Bettman; Bill Walton/Corbis-Bettman; Yo-Yo/Corbis-Bettman; Zoot Suit/Corbis-Bettman.

University of Cincinnati. Oscar Robertson.

U.S. National Aeronautics and Space Administration. Telephone.

Vintage Books. Raymond Chandler/c. 1976, reproduced by permission of Random House, Inc.

Wall Drug. Wall Drug.

Warner Brothers, Inc. *Casablanca*; *Natural Born Killers*/Reuters/Archive Photos, Inc.

West Virginia University. Jerry West.

Wyoming Division of Tourism. Rodeo.

Yorking Publications. George Burns and Gracie Allen.

NOTES ON ADVISORS AND CONTRIBUTORS

ABRAMS, Nathan. Independent scholar, London; editor, "Containing America: Cultural Production and Consumption" in *Fifties America* (Birmingham University Press, 1999).

ALDAMA, Frederick Luis. Freelance writer; graduate student, University of California, Berkeley.

ALVAREZ, Roberto. Freelance writer; student, University of California, Los Angeles; writes about English literature and Latin America.

ANDERSON, Byron. Associate professor and head of reference, University Libraries, Northern Illinois University, DeKalb, Illinois; compiler and editor, *Alternative Publishers of Books in North America,* 4th ed. (Crises Press, 1999).

ANDREWS, Carly. Freelance writer; student, University of California, Los Angeles.

APARICIO, Frances R. Professor of Spanish and American culture/ Latino studies, University of Michigan, Ann Arbor; author, *Listening to Salsa: Gender, Latin Popular Music, and Puerto Rican Cultures* (1998) and co-editor of *Tropicalizations: Transcultural Representations of Latinidad* (1997).

APPEL, Jacob M. Freelance writer; Ph.D. candidate in history, Columbia University; M.A., Brown University, studied popular celebrities of the 1920s.

ARNOLD, Tim. Member of English department, University of Kentucky.

ASHDOWN, Paul. Professor of journalism, University of Tennessee, Knoxville; editor, *James Agee: Selected Journalism* (University of Tennessee Press, 1985); contributor of articles to scholarly journals.

ATTIAS, Bernardo Alexander. Assistant professor of communication studies, College of Arts, Media, and Communication, California State University, Northridge.

AUGUSTYN, Frederick J., Jr. Cataloger, Library of Congress; Ph.D. in American history, University of Maryland—College Park.

BADIKIAN, Beatriz. Lecturer in English, Roosevelt University, Chicago, Illinois; author of several essays on popular culture, including film and travel literature.

BAERS, Michael. Freelance writer, Los Angeles, California; contributor to *LA Weekly, Glue Magazine,* and other publications.

BAKER, Neal. Information technologies and reference librarian, Earlham College, Richmond, Indiana.

BANE, S. K. Assistant professor of history and director of Honors Program, Arkansas Tech University; editor, *American Personalities* (1997).

BARBAS, Samantha. Freelance writer; Ph.D. candidate in history, University of California at Berkeley; writing a dissertation on movie fandom; has been published in *The San Francisco Chronicle* and *Film History.*

BARKSDALE, Allen. Freelance writer.

BARTEL, Pauline. Author of *Amazing Animal Actors* (Taylor Publishing Company, 1997), *Reel Elvis* (Taylor Publishing Company, 1994), and *The Complete GONE WITH THE WIND Trivia Book* (Taylor Publishing Company, 1989).

BATCHELOR, Bob. Contributing editor, *Inside Business Magazine*; author, *American Culture through History: 1900s* (Greenwood Press, forthcoming).

BELL, Vance. Freelance art, film, and new media critic; editor-in-chief, *Other Voices: The Journal of Cultural Criticism* at the University of Pennsylvania.

BELLMAN, Samuel I. Professor emeritus of English, California State Polytechnic University, Pomona; author of two biographies in the G.K. Hall/Twayne United States Authors Series: *Marjorie Kinnan Rawlings* (1974) and *Constance Mayfield Rourke* (1981); editor of *The College Experience* (1951) and *Survey and Forecast* (1966); author of numerous poems, short stories, reviews, and articles in journals and reference books.

BELPEDIO, James R. Professor of history, government, and humanities, Becker College, Worcester, Massachusetts; Ph.D., University of North Dakota; master's degree, Eastern Michigan University.

BENNETT, Courtney. Freelance writer; Ph.D. candidate, Annenberg School for Communication, University of Pennsylvania; and contributor of articles to scholarly journals.

BERG, Timothy. Visiting lecturer, Department of American Thought and Language, Michigan State University, East Lansing, Michigan; Ph.D., Purdue University, 1999.

BERGERON-DUNCAN, Lisa. Instructor of psychology and sociology, Ouachita Technical College, Malvern, Arkansas.

BERNARDI, Daniel. Assistant professor, New Media, University of Arizona. Author of *Star Trek and History: Race-Ing toward a White Future* (Rutgers University Press, 1998); editor of *Classic Whiteness: Race and the Emergence of U.S. Cinema* (Rutgers University Press, 1996) and *Classic Whiteness: Race and the Hollywood Style* (University of Minnesota Press, forthcoming).

BERNER, R. Thomas. Professor of journalism and American studies, Pennsylvania State University; author of *The Literature of Journalism: Text and Context*; Fulbright lecturer in China in 1994.

BEVIS, Charlie. Member of Society for American Baseball Research; author, *Mickey Cochrane: The Life of a Baseball Hall of Fame Catcher* (McFarland & Company Publishers, 1998).

BICKELL, Lara. Freelance writer; graduate student in history, Claremont Graduate University; contributor, *The American West.*

BINKLEY, Sam. Freelance writer; Ph.D. candidate, New School University, New York; writing dissertation on the production and commodification of countercultural cuisine in post war America.

BLACK, Brian. Landscape and environmental history specialist and teacher, American Studies, Skidmore College, New York; author, *Petrolia: The Landscape of the First Oil Boom* (Johns Hopkins University Press, 2000).

BLACK, Liza. Member of visiting faculty, Theatre Arts, Cornell University, Ithaca, New York; author of an unpublished work titled *Movie Indians, 1941-1960.*

BLANKENSHIP, Bethany. Freelance writer; Ph.D. candidate, Washington State University, Pullman, Washington; author of "Visualizing Voice: Popular Songs in the Composition Course," *Washington English Journal* (1998).

BLUSTEIN, Rebecca. Freelance writer; student, University of California, Los Angeles.

BODROGHKOZY, Aniko. Assistant professor of film and media studies, University of Alberta; author of *Groove Tube: Sixties Television and Youth Rebellion* (Duke University Press, forthcoming).

BOND, Gregory. Freelance writer; Ph.D. candidate, Department of History, University of Wisconsin—Madison.

BONE, Martyn. Freelance writer; Ph.D. candidate, University of Nottingham, England; writing dissertation on "sense of place" in contemporary Southern literature.

BOOTH, Austin. Humanities specialist, State University of New York at Buffalo.

BOWLER, Gerry. Social historian, Canada; fellow, Centre for the Study of Christianity and Contemporary Culture.

BOYD, Anne. Assistant professor of American literature, University of New Orleans; Ph.D. in American studies, Purdue University; dissertation on nineteenth-century American women writers.

BREMSETH, Marlena E. Adjunct professor, Black Studies Program, The College of William & Mary, Williamsburg, Virginia; Ph.D. candidate in American studies.

BRENNAN, Carol. Freelance writer, Detroit, Michigan.

BREWER, Tony. B.A. in English, Indiana University; producer and director of the audio horror series *Hayward Sanitarium,* National Public Radio's NPR Playhouse, 1994; actor, script writer, lyricist, musician, and sound effects artist; has performed live radio theatre as well as music and spoken-word presentations, and published numerous articles, essays, stories, and poems.

BRODERSON, Deborah. Freelance writer; Ph.D. candidate, Department of Art History, Duke University; writing dissertation on the history of playgrounds in the twentieth century.

BRODY, Michael. Freelance writer.

BROESKE, Pat H. Co-author, *Howard Hughes: The Untold Story* (Dutton, 1996) and *Down at the End of Lonely Street: The Life and Death of Elvis Presley* (Dutton, 1997).

BROWN, Robert J. Freelance writer; Ph.D. candidate in history, Syracuse University; author of *Manipulating the Ether: The Power of Broadcast Radio in Thirties America* (McFarland & Company, 1998); and of numerous articles on the history of broadcasting.

BROWN, Sharon. Instructor in American literature, State University of New York at Stony Brook; author of *American Travel Narratives as a Literary Genre from 1542-1832: The Art of a Perpetual Journey* (Edwin Mellen, 1993).

BUHLE, Paul. Visiting associate professor, American Civilization Department, Brown University; written or edited twenty-one books, including *Popular Culture in America* (University of Minnesota, 1987), *Encyclopedia of the American Left* (Garland/Oxford, 1990), and *Tender Comrades: A Backstory of the Hollywood Blacklist* (St. Martin's, 1997); frequent contributor to *Journal of American History, Village Voice,* and the *Nation.*

BUNCH, Craig. Librarian, Coldspring-Oakhurst C.I.S.D. (Texas); review editor, *Popular Culture in Libraries* (1991-96).

BURNETT, Stephen. Freelance writer; doctoral student, Department of History, Carnegie Mellon University.

BURNS, Gary. Professor of communication, Northern Illinois University; co-editor of *Making Television* (Praeger, 1990), and editor of journal, *Popular Music and Society.*

BURNS, Margaret. Freelance writer, Bloomington, Indiana.

CABRERA, Manuel V., Jr. Freelance writer; student, University of California, Los Angeles.

CARE, Ross B. Freelance composer and author; writes music for theater and films; contributor, *Scarlet Street, Sight and Sound, Film Quarterly,* and *Performing Arts: Motion Pictures* (Library of Congress, 1998).

CARNEY, George O. Regents Professor of Geography, Oklahoma State University, Stillwater; author of *The Sounds of People and Places: A Geography of American Folk and Popular Music* (Rowman & Littlefield, 1994), *Fast Food, Stock Cars, and Rock 'n' Roll: Place and Space in American Pop Culture* (Rowman & Littlefield, 1995), and *Baseball, Barns, and Bluegrass: A Geography of American Folklife* (Rowman & Littlefield, 1998); contributor of articles to *Journal of Cultural Geography, Journal of Geography,* and *Material Culture.*

CARPENTER, Gerald. Contributing editor, *Santa Barbara Independent*; lifestyle editor, *Goleta Valley Voice*; Ph.D., French History, University of California.

CAST, Anthony. Instructor of rhetoric, University of Illinois, Urbana-Champaign.

CASTRO, Rafaela. Humanities/social sciences librarian, Shields Library, University of California, Davis; author of "Latino Literature" in *What Do I Read Next?: Multicultural Literature* (Gale, 1997), and *Dictionary of Chicano Folklore* (ABC-Clio, 2000).

CHAMBERS, Jason. Freelance writer; Ph.D. candidate in history, The Ohio State University.

CHANDLER, Chris. Award-winning broadcast journalist; broadcast historian and collector.

CHAPMAN, Michael K. Freelance writer; graduate student, History, University of Nebraska at Omaha.

CHAPMAN, Roger. Freelance writer; doctoral candidate, Bowling Green State University.

CHIASSON, Lloyd, Jr. Professor, Department of Mass Communications, Nicholls State University; co-author of *Reporter's Notebook,* a journalism interactive computer textbook; editor and co-author of

The Press in Times of Crisis, The Press on Trial, and *Three Centuries of American Media.*

CIASULLO, Ann M. Freelance writer; Ph.D. candidate, English, University of Kentucky, Lexington; writing dissertation on twentieth-century popular culture interpretations of nineteenth-century American literary narratives.

CLARK, Dylan. Freelance writer; Ph.D. candidate in anthropology, University of Washington, Seattle; specialist in American ethnography, urban culture, youth subcultures, and culture studies.

CLARK, Frank. Freelance writer; graduate work in history at University of Maine; co-author of *Around Somersworth*; contributor to newspapers and magazines; presenter at Northeast Popular Culture Association meetings; technical writer (software, 1996-99).

CLARK, Randy. Freelance writer.

COBANE, Craig T. Assistant professor, Political Science, Culver-Stockton College, Canton, Missouri; contributor, "PS: Political Science and Politics," *International Journal, Journal of Criminal Justice Education.*

COFFEY, Dan. Reference librarian, Lockwood Memorial Library, State University of New York at Buffalo; music critic, *City Newspaper* (Rochester, N.Y.).

COHEN, Adam Max. Member of Department of English, University of Virginia; author of "The Nature of Genius: Blake, Einstein, and Theories of Relativity," *The Wordworth Circle* (1999).

COHEN, Toby I. Graduate of The Ohio State University and Harvard Graduate School of Education; retired teacher; writes about the movies and stars of the golden age of Hollywood; author of an unpublished biography on Claude Rains.

COKAL, Susann. Freelance writer; Ph.D. candidate, University of California—Berkeley; writing dissertation on incest and narrative design.

COKER, Jeffrey W. Freelance writer; graduate student, Department of History, Ohio University, Athens.

COLETTA, Charles A., Jr. Freelance writer; doctoral candidate, American Culture Studies Program, Bowling Green State University.

COLLINGS, Michael R. Professor of English, director of creative writing, and poet-in-residence at Seaver College, Pepperdine University; author of multiple volumes of scholarship, criticism, bibliography, and poetry.

COLLINS, Willie. Ph.D. Cultural specialist and CEO of the Consortium for California Cultural Conservation, Oakland, California; author of "California Rhythm and Blues Recordings, 1942-1972: A Diversity of Styles" in *California Soul: Music of African Americans in the West* (University of California Press, 1998); contributor of articles on African-American music and culture to scholarly journals.

CONSALVO, Mia L. Graduate instructor, School of Journalism and Mass Communication, University of Iowa; author of "Hegemony, Domestic Violence and Cops: A Critique of Concordance," *Journal of Popular Film & Television* (Vol. 26, No. 2, Summer 1998).

COOKE, Douglas. Freelance writer, Buffalo, New York; B.A. (English), M.A. (classics), M.L.S.

COOPER, B. Lee. Provost and vice president for Academic Affairs, University of Great Falls, Montana. Author of twelve books, including *Images of American Society in Popular Music* (Nelson-Hall, 1982), *A Resource Guide to Themes in Contemporary Song Lyrics, 1950-1985* (Greenwood Press, 1986), *Popular Music Perspectives* (Popular Press, 1991), and *Rock Music in American Popular Culture,* 3 volumes (Haworth Press, 1995, 1997, 1999); contributor of articles and reviews to *Popular Music and Society, Journal of American Culture, Rock and Blues News,* and other scholarly journals and music magazines.

CORONADO, ViBrina. Clothing designer and researcher, most recently in beauty contests and Native American and Latina/o performance; M.A. in performance studies, New York University; Ph.D. candidate, Theater, with emphasis on costume and popular entertainments.

COTTRELL, Robert C. Professor of history and American studies, California State University, Chico; author of *Izzy: A Biography of I.F. Stone* (Rutgers University Press, 1992) and *The Social Gospel of E. Nicholas Comfort: Founder of the Oklahoma School of Religion* (University of Oklahoma Press, 1997).

CREEKMUR, Corey K. Assistant professor of English, University of Iowa; co-editor, *Out in Culture: Gay, Lesbian, and Queer Essays on Popular Culture* (Duke University Press, 1995); author of essays and reviews in *The Road Movie Book* (Routledge, 1998), *Oscar Micheaux and His Circle* (Smithsonian Institution Press, 1999), *Film Quarterly, Wide Angle, The Hitchcock Annual, Discourse,* and elsewhere.

CREPEAU, Richard C. Professor of history, University of Central Florida; specializes in Sport in America.

CULLEN, Jim. Preceptor in expository writing, Harvard University; author of *The Civil War in Popular Culture: A Reusable Past* (Smithsonian Institution Press, 1995); *The Art of Democracy: A Concise History of Popular Culture in the United States* (Monthly Review Press, 1996); and *Born in the U.S.A.: Bruce Springsteen and the American Tradition* (HarperCollins, 1997).

CURTIS, Susan. Professor of history and director of the American Studies Program, Purdue University, West Lafayette, Indiana; author of *A Consuming Faith: the Social Gospel and Modern American Culture* (Johns Hopkins University Press, 1991), *Dancing to a Black Man's Tune: A Life of Scott Joplin* (University of Missouri Press, 1994), and *The First Black Actors on the Great White Way* (University of Missouri Press, 1998).

DAVIS, Glyn. Lecturer in media and cultural studies, College of Ripon and York St. John; Ph.D. candidate, University of Sussex; papers published on lesbian and gay film, and contemporary Hollywood cinema.

DAVIS, Janet M. Assistant professor of American studies, University of Texas at Austin; author of an unpublished work titled *The Human Menagerie: The Circus and American Culture at the Turn of the Century.*

DEANE, Pamala S. M.A.; independent writer and scholar, Lanham, Maryland.

DECHERT, S. Renee. Assistant professor of English, Northwest College; author of *Larry McMurtry and the Western: The Rhetoric of Novelization* (1997).

DEITRICK, John. Freelance writer.

DIEM, Gordon Neal, D.A. Primary associate, Advance Education and Development Institute, and assistant professor of political science, North Carolina Central University.

DIGBY-JUNGER, Richard. Professor of English, Western Michigan University; author of *The Journalist as Reformer: Henry Demarest Lloyd and Wealth Against Commonwealth* (Greenwood Press, 1996).

DiMAURO, Laurie. Writer and editor specializing in biographical and literary reference, Saline, Michigan.

DOHERTY, John J. Librarian and freelance writer, Flagstaff, Arizona.

DOMINA, Thurston. Freelance writer, New York, New York.

DONLON, Jon Griffin. Director and coordinator, Center for the Study of Controversial Leisure, University of Southwestern Louisiana; Ph.D., Leisure Studies Department, University of Illinois in Urbana-Champaign; fellow of the *Royal Geographic Society*; research on such contested areas as gaming, cock fighting, sport hunting, risky travel and related controversial pastimes.

DONNER, Simon. Freelance writer and environmental scientist, Canada.

DUNCAN, Randy. Professor of communication, Henderson State University, Arkadelphia, Arkansas; co-founder of the Comic Arts Conference.

DUNCOMBE, Stephen. Assistant professor of American studies, State University of New York, College at Old Westbury; author of *Notes from Underground: Zines and the Politics of Alternative Culture* (Verso, 1997).

DuPELL, Eugenia Griffith. Freelance writer; master's degree student, information and library science, State University of New York at Buffalo.

DYER, Stephanie. Freelance writer; Ph.D. candidate in history, University of Pennsylvania.

EDELMAN, Rob. Film journalist and historian; contributing editor, *Leonard Maltin's Movie & Video Guide*; author, *Great Baseball Films* (Citadel Press), *Baseball on the Web* (MIS: Press), *Angela Lansbury: A Life on Stage and Screen* (Birch Lane Press; co-author), and *Meet the Mertzes* (Renaissance Books; co-author).

EDGERS, Geoff. Staff writer for the *News & Observer,* Raleigh, North Carolina; author of *The Midnight Hour: Bright Ideas for After Dark* (Penguin, 1987); contributor to *Details, Spin, The New York Times Sunday Magazine, Salon,* and the *Boston Phoenix.*

EMBRY, Jessie L. Assistant director, Charles Redd Center for Western Studies, and instructor in history, Brigham Young University; author of articles on aviation in the West with Roger D. Launius.

ESCOFFIER, Jeffrey. Author, *American Homo:Community and Perversity* (University of California Press).

EVANS, Cindy Peters. Manager of retail education, TruServ Corporation; Ph.D. in anthropology; author of training programs in customer satisfaction, personnel selection, and orientation.

EVANS, Sean. Collection documenter, Cline Library, Northern Arizona University; M.A. in American history; avid Route 66 traveler and researcher.

EVERETT, William A. Assistant professor of music history, Conservatory of Music, University of Missouri, Kansas City; contributor of articles on musical theater and other topics to various journals and other publications.

FALWELL, Alyssa. Public relations consultant; M.A., Georgetown University.

FEINBERG, Richard. Professor, Department of Consumer Sciences and Retailing; director, Center for Customer-Driven Quality, Purdue University; seminar presenter, consultant, and expert witness; co-author of *Customer Relationship Management* and of numerous research and trade articles.

FINCHUM, G. Allen. Assistant professor of geography, Oklahoma State University; editor, *Sport Place: An International Journal of Sports Geography.*

FINKELSTEIN, S. Naomi. Anti-poverty activist, writer and radical historian; contributor, *Bridges, Sinister Wisdom,* and *Gay Community News.*

FISCHER, Dennis. Author of *Horror Film Directors* and *Science Fiction Film Directors*; contributor, *American Film, Movieline, Cinefantastique, Starlog, The Aliens Story, The Kung Fu Book, Bela Lugosi, Backstory II* and *Backstory III.*

FREIND, Bill. Instructor, Department of English, University of Washington, Seattle. Contributor of articles to scholarly journals.

FREIRE-MEDEIROS, Bianca. Freelance writer; Ph.D. candidate, Binghamton University, State University of New York; writing dissertation titled "For Your Eyes Only: Images of Rio de Janeiro on North American Films and Travel Writing (1930-1990)."

FRENTNER, Shaun. Freelance writer.

FRIEDMAN, James. Manager UCLA Film and Television Archive Research and Study Center. Editor of *Really Squared: Televisual Discourse on the Real* (Rutgers University Press, forthcoming). Ph.D. candidate, University of California, Los Angeles; completing dissertation on the relationship between forms of live television, viewer engagement, and the public sphere.

FURNESS, Adrienne. Freelance writer and reference librarian, Lockport Public Library, Lockport, New York.

GAFFNEY, Paul. Freelance writer; Ph.D. candidate, University of Virginia, Charlottesville; reviewer, *Virginia Quarterly Review.*

GAITHER, Milton. Freelance writer; doctoral candidate in history of American education, Indiana University.

GAJADHAR, Joan. Communications lecturer, Open Polytechnic of New Zealand; author (with Jim Sinclair) of "A Modern Detective

Fiction'' in *Encyclopedia of British Culture* (Routledge), and ''Plagiarism and The Internet'' in *Ultibase* (November 1999), an online journal for tertiary education.

GALLEY, Catherine C. Architect D.P.L.G, E.N.S.A.D. and urban designer M.A.U.D.; doctoral student, Department of Urban Planning and Policy Development, Rutgers University.

GAMSON, Joshua. Associate professor of sociology, Yale University, New Haven, Connecticut; author of *Claims to Fame: Celebrity in Contemporary America* (University of California Press, 1994), *Freaks Talk Back: Tabloid Talk Shows and Sexual Nonconformity* (University of Chicago Press, 1998), and numerous scholarly and nonscholarly articles on media, social movements, popular culture, and sexuality.

GANNON, Caitlin L. Freelance writer and teacher of communications and software; owner/editor of Javelina Books, a women's press in Tucson, Arizona.

GARCIA-MYERS, Sandra. Associate director, Cinema-Television Library and Archives of the Performing Arts, University of Southern California, Los Angeles; humanities/social science librarian, Southern Oregon University.

GARMAN, Bryan. Ph.D. in American studies, Emory University; author of *A Race of Singers: Making an American Working Class Hero* (University of North Carolina Press, forthcoming).

GARROUTTE, Eva Marie. Assistant professor of sociology, Boston College, Chestnut Hill, Massachusetts; author, *Real Indians: Identity and the Survival of Native America* (University of California, forthcoming), and contributor of articles to scholarly journals.

GATEWARD, Frances. Media scholar and independent film and video artist; has taught at American University, Indiana University, and the University of Illinois Urbana-Champaign; essays published in journals and the anthologies *Still Lifting Still Climbing* and *Ladies and Gentlemen, Boys and Girls: Gender and Media.*

GEORGE, Jason. Freelance writer; Ph.D. candidate, Ohio University.

GIANOULIS, Tina. Freelance writer and lesbian activist, Bainbridge Island, Washington.

GILES, James R. Professor of English, Northern Illinois University; author of several books including *Understanding Hubert Selby, Jr.* (1998) and *The Naturalistic Inner-City Novel in America* (1995).

GOLDIN, Milton. Fund raising counsel and writer, Tarrytown, New York; author, *The Music Merchants* (Macmillan, 1969) and *Why They Give* (Macmillan, 1976); member, National Coalition of Independent Scholars (NCIS).

GOLDMAN, Ilene. Independent film scholar, Chicago, Illinois. Contributor of articles and reviews to *JumpCut, Journal of Film and Video, Latin American Research Review, The Chicago Tribune,* and *Spectator,* as well as essays on contemporary Latin American cinema in *The Ethnic Eye: Latino Media Arts* and *Framing Latin American Cinema: Contemporary Critical Perspectives.*

GOLDSTEIN, Matthew Mulligan. Freelance writer, Oakland, California.

GOLDWEBER, Dave. Adjunct professor of English, San Francisco area; contributor of articles to scholarly journals.

GORDON, Ian. Professor of American studies, National University of Singapore; Ph.D. in American history, University of Rochester; has held fellowships from the Smithsonian Institution and the Swann Foundation; author of *Comic Strips and Consumer Culture, 1890-1945* (Smithsonian Institution Press, 1998).

GORDON, W. Terrence. Professor of French, Italian, and linguistics, Dalhousie University, Halifax, Canada; author of *McLuhan for Beginners* (Writers & Readers Publishing, 1997) and *Marshall McLuhan: Escape into Understanding. A Biography* (Harper Collins, 1997).

GOULART, Ron. Freelance writer, Weston, Connecticut; author, *The Funnies* (Adams, 1995), and *Groucho Marx, Private Eye* (St. Martin's Press, 1999).

GRAINGE, Paul. Freelance writer; doctoral student, University of Nottingham, England; writing on cultural nostalgia.

GRANGER, Brian. Author-composer, *Deirdre,* a musical (1999); member and composer for a national performing a cappella group.

GRAVES, Anna Hunt. B.A., American studies, Yale University; author of *Folk* (Friedman/Fairfax Publishers, 1994).

GRAVES, Steve. Assistant professor of geography, Louisiana Tech University.

GREGG, Jill A. M.L.S.; reference librarian, Toledo Lucas County Public Library, Toledo, Ohio.

GRIFFITH, Benjamin. Emeritus professor of English and dean of the Graduate School, State University of West Georgia, Carrollton, Georgia; author of twelve books on language and literature, and contributor of articles to scholarly journals.

GROSSMAN, Perry. Freelance writer; Ph.D. candidate in sociology, New York University; dissertation on ''Globalization and the Linkage of Trade and Environmental Politics''; author of ''Identity Crisis: The Dialectics of Punk, Rock, and Grunge,'' in *Berkeley Journal of Sociology.*

GUSTAINIS, Justin. Professor of communication, State University of New York at Plattsburgh; author of *American Rhetoric and the Vietnam War* (Praeger, 1993).

GYURE, Dale Allen. Freelance writer; Ph.D. candidate, Architectural History, University of Virginia; co-author of ''Architecture'' in Dennis R. Hall and M. Thomas Inge, eds., *Handbook of American Popular Culture,* 3rd. ed. (Greenwood Press, 1999).

HA, Kristine J. Freelance writer; student, University of California, Los Angeles.

HAAS, Elizabeth. Freelance writer, Ann Arbor, Michigan.

HABERSKI, Ray, Jr. Freelance writer; Ph.D. candidate in history, Ohio University; completing a dissertation entitled, ''Movies into Art: From Amusement to Auteur.''

HALL, Jeanne Lynn. Associate professor of communications, Pennsylvania State; author of numerous essays on film history and criticism; co-author, ''Beat the Press'' (monthly column), *Voices.*

HANSON, Steve. Director, Cinema-Television Library and Archives of Performing Arts, University of Southern California, Los

Angeles; humanities biographer, University of Southern California, Los Angeles; co-author, *Lights, Camera, Action: A History of the Movies in the Twentieth Century* (1991), *Sourcebook for the Performing Arts* (1988), *Film Review Index 1950-1985* (1987), *Film Review Index (1882-1949)* (1986); film reviewer, *Screen International (1987-1990)*; feature writer for *Stills (1983-1986)*; associate editor, *Magill's Survey of Cinema, Series I, II, III, 1979-81, Magill's Bibliography of Literary Criticism, 1979.*

HATTON, Jacqueline Anne. Ph.D., Cornell University, M.A., University of Melbourne, Australia; author, *True Story Magazine,* (University of North Carolina Press, forthcoming).

HAVEN, Chris. Freelance writer; Ph.D. candidate in creative writing, University of Houston; author of several stories and articles; teaches a literature class titled "Crime and Punishment."

HAY, Ethan. M.A., Educational specialist, Sausalito, California; freelance writer, illustrator, editor; contributing writer/illustrator for *The Learn 2 Guide: How to Do Almost Anything* (Villard Press, 1999) and *Birth of a Notion* (New Mexico State Legislature, 1998).

HEER, Jeet. Freelance writer; Ph.D. candidate, York University, Toronto, Canada; writing dissertation on Little Orphan Annie and its audience.

HEINZE, Andrew R. Associate professor of history, University of San Francisco; author of *Adapting to Abundance: Jewish Immigrants, Mass Consumption and the Search for American Identity* (Columbia University Press, 1990).

HESS, Mary. Reviewer, *Magill's Cinema Annual*; graduate student in American history, Michigan State University.

HIRSCH, Joshua. Freelance writer; doctoral candidate, film and television, University of California, Los Angeles; writing dissertation on film and the Holocaust.

HIXSON, David L. Research assistant, The Center for the Study of Popular Television; Ph.D. student, S.I. Newhouse School of Public Communications, Syracuse University, Syracuse, New York.

HOFFMAN, Scott W. Bachelor of science, radio-television-film, University of Texas at Austin; master of arts, liturgical studies, St. John's School of Theology, Collegeville, Minnesota; author of "How Do You Solve a Problem Like Maria? St. Maria Goretti in the Post-Countercultural World," *The Critic* (fall 1995) and of the forthcoming "Holy Martin: The Overlooked Canonization of Dr. Martin Luther King."

HOLCOMB, Briavel. Professor of urban studies and geography, Rutgers University; co-author of *Revitalizing Cities* (AAG, 1981) and of *The United States: A Contemporary Human Geography* (Wiley, 1988).

HOLLORAN, Peter C. Assistant professor of history, Bentley College, Waltham, Massachusetts; executive secretary, Northeast Popular Culture/American Culture Association.

HOLLOWAY, David. Lecturer in American studies, University of Derby (England); author of a number of articles on American novelist Cormac McCarthy.

HOVDE, Karen. Reference librarian, Northern Illinois University Libraries.

HOWLEY, Kevin. Assistant professor, Communication Studies, Northeastern University; Ph.D., Indiana University.

HUMEZ, Nick. Silversmith; co-author of books on romance philology and its cultural corollaries, including *Latin for People/Latina pro Populo* (Little, Brown, 1976); former principal music reviewer for the *Maine Sunday Telegram* and its associated daily, the Portland *Press Herald.*

ISAKSEN, Judy L. Visiting assistant professor of rhetoric, Eckerd College, St. Petersburg, Florida; Ph.D. candidate, Rhetoric and Composition, University of South Florida, Tampa; author of several articles in composition journals.

JANKAUSKAS, Jennifer. Freelance writer.

JOHANNINGMEIER, E. V. Freelance writer.

JONES, Patrick. Librarian, Houston, Texas; author, *What's So Scary About R.L. Stine?* (Scarecrow Press, 1998).

JONES, Patrick. Freelance writer; Ph.D. candidate, University of Wisconsin-Madison; writing a dissertation on civil rights insurgency in Milwaukee, Wisconsin, 1963-72.

JONES, Preston Neal. Writer and film historian; contributor, *Cinefantastique Magazine, American Art Review,* and *The Library of Congress Performing Arts Annual.*

JOSEPH, Mark. President of MJM Entertainment Group, Los Angeles, California; author of *Out Of This World: Why People of Faith Abandoned Rock and Roll, Why They're Coming Back* (Broadman & Holman, 1999).

JUDD, Thomas. Freelance writer.

KALLINEY, Peter. Freelance writer; graduate student, English language and literature, University of Michigan; writing dissertation entitled "Cities of Affluence and Anger: Urbanism and Literature in Postwar Britain."

KANELLOS, Nicolás. Brown Professor of Hispanic literature, University of Houston, and author of various reference books and histories of Hispanic culture.

KARNEY, Robyn. Editor and writer specializing in film subjects; co-author of *The Foreign Film Guide*; editor, *Crown Series of Hollywood Studio Histories;* editor-in-chief, *The Chronicle of the Cinema*; author of biographies of Audrey Hepburn and Burt Lancaster.

KEANE, Stephen. Lecturer in English, Bretton Hall College, University of Leeds, United Kingdom; teaching and research interests include modernism, postmodernism, critical theory, and popular culture.

KEELINE, James D. Freelance writer and independent scholar; author of *Stratemeyer Syndicate Ghostwriters* (self published, 1999), an unpublished work titled *Series Book Encyclopedia,* and numerous articles for scholarly and genre periodicals; area chair, Popular Culture Association section on Dime Novels, Pulps, and Series Books.

KELLERMAN, Max. Freelance writer.

KEMPCKE, Ken. Reference librarian, Montana State University—Bozeman.

KENNY, Stephen C. Freelance writer; Ph.D. candidate, forthcoming dissertation on ''Slavery and Medicine in Antebellum South Carolina''; author of an essay, ''Southern Landscapes: Heaven, Hell and Hospital,'' included in N. Moody and J. Hallam, eds., *Medical Fictions* (John Moores University Press, 1998).

KERCHER, Stephen. Freelance writer; Ph.D. candidate, Departments of History and American Studies, Indiana University; dissertation on 1950s and early-1960s American satire.

KERR, Matt. Freelance writer; doctoral student, Ohio University, specializing in Modern German and European History.

KIBLER, M. Alison. Visiting scholar in the history program at the Research School of Social Sciences at the Australian National University (Canberra); author of *Rank Ladies: Gender and Cultural Hierarchy in American Vaudeville* (University of North Carolina Press, 1999).

KIDD, Kimberley H. Adjunct instructor of English, King College, Bristol, Tennessee, and East Tennessee State University, Johnson City.

KILLMEIER, Matthew A. Freelance writer; doctoral student, School of Journalism and Mass Communication, University of Iowa; co-author of ''Wireless Pleasure: Locating Radio in the American Home,'' in Hanno Hardt, editor, *In the Company of Media: Cultural Constructions of Communication 1920s-1930s* (Westview Press, forthcoming).

KING, Jason. Playwright; doctoral candidate, performance studies, New York University.

KLINKOWITZ, Jerome. Professor of English and university distinguished scholar at the University of Northern Iowa; author of forty books on modern and contemporary culture, including *Literary Disruptions, Listen: Gerry Mulligan,* and *Writing Baseball.*

KLINKOWITZ, Jon. Journalist, *Iowa City Press-Citizen*; professional blues guitar player.

KONICKI, Leah. Historic preservation officer, City of Covington, Kentucky; author of various articles on Sears and catalog houses.

KOTOK, Steven. Publisher, DDM Press, New York, New York.

KUHLKEN, Robert. Cultural geographer on the faculty of Central Washington University in Ellensburg; numerous published journal articles on subjects ranging from agricultural history to zydeco music.

KUNKA, Andrew J. Freelance writer; doctoral candidate, Purdue University.

KUPFERBERG, Audrey. Film and video archivist and appraiser; teaches film history at the State University of New York at Albany; co-author, *Angela Lansbury: A Life on Stage and Screen* (Birch Lane Press) and *Meet the Mertzes* (Renaissance Books).

KUPPERS, Petra. Freelance writer.

LAMBERT, Emma. Teaching assistant, modern American and African American history, University of Birmingham, England; Ph.D. candidate, University of Birmingham, England; writing thesis on Time Inc. and the Cold War under Eisenhower.

LANE, Christina. Freelance writer.

LAUSE, Kevin. Freelance writer; master's degree candidate, American culture studies, Bowling Green State University; co-author, *Popular Culture: An Introductory Text* (Popular Press, 1992).

LEAVELL, Nadine-Rae. M.L.S. research coordinator and information specialist, Roswell Park Cancer Institute, Buffalo, New York.

LEE, Christopher A. Freelance writer; doctoral student, University of California, Los Angeles; contributor, *An Encyclopedia of American Literature of the Sea and the Great Lakes* and the *Publications of the Arkansas Philological Association.*

LELLOUCHE, Michele. Attorney, Corbel & Co.; contributor, *History of the Modern Olympic Movement* (Greenwood Press, 1996).

LENT, Robin. Associate professor and head of collection development, University of New Hampshire Library.

LEOTTA, Joan. Freelance journalist, Burke, Virginia; specializing in business, history, education, and travel.

LEVINE, Richard. Freelance writer; graduate student, University of Maryland, Department of American Studies; currently finishing a thesis on bumper stickers, T-shirts, pin-back buttons and other forms of ''personal graffiti.''

LIMSKY, Drew. Adjunct professor, Brooklyn College; cultural criticism and fiction contributor, *Washington Post, The Los Angeles Times, Genre, His 2* (Faber & Faber), and *His 3* (Farrar, Straus & Giroux).

LINDLEY, Daniel. Freelance writer and editor, Eugene, Oregon; author, *Ambrose Bierce Takes on the Railroad* (Praeger, 1999).

LINEHAN, Joyce. Manager of recording artists Mike Ireland, Holler, and the Pernice Brothers, and producer Michael Deming; M.A. candidate, American studies, University of Massachusetts, Boston.

LITTON, Margaret. Master's degree, University of Kentucky, Lexington; thesis ''The Southerner's Other Problem'' on poor whites in Depression-era fiction.

LLOYD, James H. Director of libraries, Cincinnati Bible College & Seminary; minister.

LONERGAN, David. Reference librarian, Northern Illinois University; research interests in the popular music of the last fifty years, especially rock and roll.

LONGLEY, Eric. Writer, Durham, North Carolina.

LOTT, Rick. Teaches in the English Department at Arkansas State University; articles published in *Journal of Popular Culture University of Mississippi Studies in English,* and *Clues: a Journal of Detection*; poems widely published in magazines.

LOVETT-GRAFF, Bennett. Ph.D. Multimedia editor, Primary Source Media; independent scholar.

LOWE, Denise. Academic conference and seminar presenter throughout the U.S.; M.A., American studies, California State University at Fullerton; thesis on ''The Depiction of Single Career Women in Network Situation Comedies, 1950-1994'' (1994); author of the tentatively titled reference volume, ''Women and American Television'' (ABC-CLIO, 1999).

LUCAS, Debra M. Research and technical consultant; freelance writer and contributor to newspapers, newsletters, books, Buffalo, New York.

LUPACK, Barbara Tepa. Editor and publisher, Round Table Publications; author of numerous books on American literature and culture, including *Critical Essays on Jerzy Kosinski* (G. K. Hall, 1998), *King Arthur in America* (Boydell and Brewer, 1999), *Arthurian Literature by Women* (Garland, 1999), and *Nineteenth-Century Women at the Movies* (Bowling Green State University/Popular Press, 1999).

LURIE, Karen. Author of *TV Chefs: The Dish on the Stars of Your Favorite Cooking Shows*; extensive writings about television and popular culture, including four other books.

LUTES, Michael A. Reference and government documents librarian, University of Notre Dame; contributor, *Encyclopedia of AIDS* (1998), *Gay and Lesbian Biography* (1998), *Gay and Lesbian Literature Vols. I and II* (1994/1998), *Gay and Lesbian Literary Companion* (1995); reviewer for *Library Journal* and *Choice*.

LYONS, James. Freelance writer; Ph.D. candidate, University of Nottingham, England; writing dissertation on representations of Seattle in contemporary culture.

LYONS, John F. Freelance writer; Ph.D. candidate, University of Illinois at Chicago; thesis on the Chicago Teachers' Union.

MACEK, Steve. Freelance writer; Ph.D. candidate, Department of Cultural Studies and Comparative Literature, University of Minnesota, Twin Cities.

MACOR, Alison. Film critic for the Austin American-Statesman, Austin, Texas; Ph.D. candidate, University of Texas at Austin; writing dissertation about cult film and television fan communities.

MARC, David. Visiting professor and Steven H. Scheuer Scholar in Television Studies, S.I. Newhouse School of Public Communications at Syracuse University; author of *Comic Visions* (Blackwell, 1989; 2nd ed. 1997), a history of American television comedy.

MARKOWITZ, Robin. Ph.D. lecturer in sociology, California State University, Long Beach; editor and founder, *Cultural Studies Central* http://www.culturalstudies.net/, an electronic clearinghouse of cultural studies resources and original analysis.

MARSH, Tilney L. Freelance writer; Ph.D. candidate, English literature, University of Wisconsin—Madison; M.A., University of Wisconsin—Madison; B.A., University of Michigan, Ann Arbor.

MARTIN, Richard. Curator, The Costume Institute, The Metropolitan Museum of Art, New York City; adjunct professor of art history and archaeology, Columbia University, and adjunct professor art, New York University; author of *Fashion and Surrealism* (Rizzoli, 1987), *Cubism and Fashion* (1998), and *The Ceaseless Century: Three Hundred Years of Eighteenth-Century Costume* (Metropolitan Museum of Art, 1998); also author of hundreds of essays and dozens of exhibition catalogues.

MARTIN, Sara. Senior assistant teacher, Universitat Autonoma de Barcelona, Spain; co-founder of S.I.N.P.L.I. (Spanish Association for the Study of Popular Texts in English).

MARTINDALE, Linda A. Administrative assistant, Humanities Division, Elon College, North Carolina; author of ''Some Positive Images of Alternative Lifestyles on Television in the Nineties,'' in Anne Cassebaum and Rosemary Haskell's *American Culture and the Media: Reading, Writing, and Thinking* (Houghton Mifflin Company, 1997); presenter at popular culture conferences.

MATTSON, Kevin. Research director, Walt Whitman Center for the Culture and Politics of Democracy, Rutgers University, and independent scholar; author of *Creating a Democratic Public: The Struggle for Urban Participatory Democracy during the Progressive Era* (Pennsylvania State University Press, 1998); also author of numerous essays and reviews.

McCLURE, Randall. Member of the Department of English, Bowling Green State University.

McCRACKEN, Allison. Freelance writer; Ph.D. candidate, Program in American Studies, University of Iowa.

McDAID, Jennifer Davis. Assistant editor, *Virginia Cavalcade*, Library of Virginia.

McENTEE, Jason. Freelance writer; Ph.D. candidate in film, composition/rhetoric, and 20th century American literature, University of Kentucky, Lexington; M.A., English: language studies and rhetoric, South Dakota State University (May 1998).

McGRATH, Cheryl S. Independent art historian, graphic designer, and art curator; has taught Survey of Art classes at Texas A&M University—Corpus Christi.

McKEAND, Daryna. Freelance writer; Ph.D. candidate, English Literature, New York University; writing dissertation on alcoholism in Victorian novels.

McLENDON, Jacquelyn Y. Associate professor of English and director of black studies, College of William and Mary; author, *The Politics of Color in the Fiction of Jessie Fauset and Nella Larsen* (The University Press of Virginia, 1995).

McLEOD, Kembrew. Freelance writer; Ph.D. candidate, Department of Communication, University of Massachusetts—Amherst; contributor, *The Village Voice*, *Raygun* and *SonicNet;* author, ''Authenticity Within Hip-Hop and Other Cultures Threatened With Assimilation,'' *Journal of Communication* (1999).

McQUAIL, Josephine A. Associate professor of English, Tennessee Technological University; author of an unpublished book of Grateful Dead lyrics.

MEDEIROS, Alex. Programming consultant, Walt Disney Television International; M.S. candidate, television/radio/film, Syracuse University, Syracuse, New York.

MELTON, Brad. Editorial assistant, *Arizona Highways*; assistant editor, *Documentary Editing*; graduate history student, Arizona State University.

MENDIBLE, Myra. Ph.D. Associate professor, contemporary literary and cultural studies, Florida Gulf Coast University; contributor of articles to scholarly journals and academic conferences.

MERRON, Jeff. Assistant professor of communications, State University of West Georgia, and senior editor, SportsJones.com.

MERTZ, Thomas J. Freelance writer; doctoral student, United States History, University of Wisconsin-Madison.

MEYER, Nathan R. Secondary educator and historical researcher, Eureka, Illinois.

MIDDLEBROOK, Jonathan. Professor of English, San Francisco State University; author, *Mailer and the Times of His Time* (1976) and various articles, scholarly and popular.

MILLARD, Andre. Professor of history and director of American studies, University of Alabama at Birmingham; author, *America on Record: A History of Recorded Sound* (Cambridge, 1995); contributor, *National Academy of Recording Arts and Sciences Journal*.

MILLER, Jeffrey S. Assistant professor of English and journalism, Augustana College, Sioux Falls, South Dakota; author, *Something Completely Different: British Television and American Culture* (University of Minnesota, 1999).

MILLER, Karen. Freelance writer; graduate student and freelance writer, Detroit, Michigan.

MILLER, P. Andrew. Lecturer in creative writing at Northern Kentucky University; member, Science Fiction Writer's of America; publishes short fiction.

MILLS, Dorothy Jane. Freelance author and editor; author of *The Sceptre* (Xlibris, 1999).

MILNER, Andrew. Critic, Philadelphia *City Paper*; contributor, *Spy Magazine* and *Stephen Sondheim: A Casebook* (Garland Press, 1997).

MINTZ, Lawrence E. Associate professor, American studies, University of Maryland; director, Art Gliner Center for Humor Studies; editor of *Humor: International Journal of Humor Research*; author of numerous articles, book chapters, reviews, and conference papers on popular culture, particularly American humor.

MIX, Deborah M. Teacher, Department of American Thought and Language, Michigan State University.

MOODY, Nickianne. Principal lecturer, Media and Cultural Studies, Liverpool, John Moores University; convenor, Association for Research in Popular Fictions.

MOODY, Richard L. Professor of film studies, Utah Valley State College and Salt Lake Community College, Utah; author of *Introduction to Media Art* and contributor of articles to scholarly journals.

MOORE, Charles F. Member of staff, Center for Appalachian Studies and Services, East Tennessee State University; editor, *Asunaro: Living in the Mountains of Japan* (Center for Appalachian Studies & Services, 1998).

MOORE, Leonard N. Assistant professor of history, Louisiana State University; specializes in African-American and urban history.

MOOS, Dan. Freelance writer; graduate student in English, State University of New York—Buffalo.

MORACE, Robert A. Professor of English, Daemen College; author, *The Dialogic Novels of Malcolm Bradbury and David Lodge* (Southern Illinois University Press, 1989); contributor to journals and collections, including *The Chippewa Landscape of Louise Erdrich*.

MORAN, Edward. Writes about American cultural and literary history of the twentieth century; associate editor, *Random House Dictionary of the English Language* and for H.W. Wilson's *World Authors* and *World Musicians* reference series.

MORRIS, Barry. Associate professor of speech communication, Pace University, New York; contributor of articles on rhetoric, politics, and culture to *The Quarterly Journal of Speech* and other publications.

MURPHY, Michael J. Freelance writer; doctoral candidate, Department of Art History and Archaeology, Washington University, St. Louis.

MURRAY, Jennifer A. Freelance writer; student, University of California, Los Angeles.

MURRAY, Susan. Assistant professor of television and radio, City University of New York—Brooklyn College.

MVUYEKURE, Pierre-Damien. Assistant professor of English and African American Literature, University of Northern Iowa, Cedar Falls; contributor of articles to critical sourcebooks (Greenwood Press).

NAJJAR, Michael. Founding artistic director, Riverside Repertory Theatre; free-lance writer, Albuquerque, New Mexico.

NASH, Ilana. Freelance writer; doctoral student in American culture studies, Bowling Green State University; co-author, *Series Books and the Media* (SynSine Press, 1996); contributor to scholarly and popular journals on the history of series books.

NEMANIC, Mary Lou. Assistant professor of mass media, Western State College, Gunnison, Colorado; Ph.D. in American studies; co-director of Tamarack Documentary; contributor, *Biographical Encyclopedia of Indoor Sports* (1987); co-director of a hockey culture documentary and of a documentary project of the Minnesota Iron Range.

NEWMAN, Scott. Freelance writer; Ph.D. candidate, Loyola University, Chicago; writing dissertation on middle-class leisure in early twentieth-century Chicago.

NICKS, Joan. Associate professor of film studies and popular culture, Brock University, St. Catharines, Ontario, Canada; chapters in *Documenting the Documentary* (Wayne State University Press, 1998), *Gendering the Nation: Canadian Women's Cinema* (University of Toronto Press, 1999), and contributor of articles to scholarly journals.

NORDEN, Martin F. Professor of communication, University of Massachusetts—Amherst; author of *The Cinema of Isolation: A History of Physical Disability in the Movies* (Rutgers University Press, 1994) and *John Barrymore: A Bio-Bibliography* (Greenwood Press, 1995).

NORDSTROM, Justin. Freelance writer; Ph.D. candidate in American ethnic and religious history; M.A., U.S. history, Indiana University—Bloomington.

NOTARO, Anna. Research fellow in visual culture, working on the research project "Literary and Visual Representations of Three American Cities (New York, Chicago, Los Angeles) 1870s-1930s," University of Nottingham, United Kingdom.

O'CONNOR, William F. Professor, School of Liberal Arts, Asia University, Tokyo, Japan; co-editor, *The Kenkyusha Dictionary of English Collocations* (Kenkyusha, 1995).

O'HARA, Paul. Freelance writer; Ph.D. student, Indiana University—Bloomington.

O'NEAL, Angela. Freelance writer; graduate student, Miami University of Ohio; thesis titled "The McGuffey Readers: Agents of Americanization."

O'SHEA, Christopher D. Freelance writer; Ph.D. program, University of Guelph; specializing in Canadian and United States history, class, gender, and social construction.

OCKERSTROM, Lolly. Freelance writer, American Friends Service Committee, Washington; Ph.D., English, Northeastern University; has taught writing and women's literature at Northeastern and Virginia Commonwealth University.

OWENS, Kerry. Assistant professor, Northeast Louisiana University.

OXOBY, Marc. Freelance writer; Ph.D. candidate, University of Nevada, Reno.

PAINO, Troy. Assistant professor of history, Winona State University, Winona, Minnesota; contributor of articles and book reviews on subjects related to sports in American culture.

PAINTER, D. Byron. Freelance writer; master's student in history, University of Illinois at Springfield; political science and history degree, Eureka College, Eureka, Illinois.

PALLADINO, Grace. Co-director, The Samuel Gompers Papers, University of Maryland, College Park; author, *Teenagers: An American History* (Basic Books, 1996) and books on working-class history.

PARATTE, Henri-Dominique. Freelance writer and professor, Acadia University; specializes in translation, cultural studies, Acadian studies; author of 10 books and numerous articles in journals, magazines, and newspapers in Canada, Europe, and the United States.

PARIS, Leslie. Freelance writer; doctoral candidate, program in American culture, University of Michigan; dissertation on interwar summer camps.

PARRENT, Jay. Freelance writer and historic preservation consultant, Owensboro, Kentucky.

PAXTON, Felicity. Freelance writer; Ph.D. candidate, University of Pennsylvania, Philadelphia, writing dissertation on the high school prom.

PENDERGAST, Sara. President, Full Circle Editorial, Inc.; editor, *Contemporary Designers,* 3rd edition (1997); co-editor, *Gay and Lesbian Literature,* Vol. 2 (1998), *St. James Guide to Children's Writers,* 5th edition (1999), and *St. James Guide to Young Adult Writers,* 2nd edition (1999).

PENDERGAST, Tom. Principal, Full Circle Editorial, Inc.; Ph.D. in American studies, Purdue University; author, *Consuming Men: Masculinity, Race, and American Magazines, 1900-1950* (University of Missouri Press, forthcoming); co-editor, *Gay and Lesbian Literature,* Vol. 2 (1998), *St. James Guide to Children's Writers,* 5th edition (1999), and *St. James Guide to Young Adult Writers,* 2nd edition (1999).

PENDRAGON, Jana. Writer, teacher, and critic; masters degree in history; author of a published thesis entitled "The Use of King Arthur as an Icon in Popular American Culture"; documents traditional country and western music; teaches classes to adults on the culture and history of Native Americans, country & western music, cowboys, and King Arthur.

PETERSON, Geoff. Assistant professor of political science, Southwestern Oklahoma State University; research on the media and politics, voting behavior, conspiracy theory and the X-Files, and Native American politics.

PETERSON, Kurt W. Assistant professor of history, Judson College; Ph.D. candidate in history, University of Notre Dame.

PETTIGREW, Emily. Freelance writer, Lakewood, Ohio. M.A. in American culture studies, Bowling Green State University, 1997; thesis, "Sounds Like the End of the World: How the Postmodernism of Generation X Is Given Voice Through Industrial Rock."

PHILIPPON, Daniel J. Assistant professor of rhetoric, University of Minnesota, Twin Cities; editor, *The Height of Our Mountains: Nature Writing from Virginia's Blue Ridge Mountains and Shenandoah Valley* (Johns Hopkins, 1998); editor, *The Friendship of Nature: A New England Chronicle of Birds and Flowers,* by Mabel Osgood Wright (Johns Hopkins, 1999).

PHILO, S. J. Lecturer in American studies, University of Derby (United Kingdom); published chapters and articles on *The Simpsons,* MTV, American youth television, and the literature of the Vietnam War.

PHY-OLSEN, Allene. Professor of English and director of honors program, Austin Peay State University, Clarksville, Tennessee.

PIACENTINO, Ed. Professor of English, High Point University; author of *T. S. Stribling: Pioneer Realist in Modern Southern Literature* (University Press of America, 1988); contributor of numerous articles and reviews on American literature and culture to scholarly journals and reference books.

PIETERS, Jürgen. Teacher, literary theory, University of Ghent, Belgium; doctoral candidate, dissertation on the New Historicism of Stephen Greenblatt; several published articles in the fields of literary theory, literature, and theatre.

POGUE, Paul F. P. Freelance writer and photographer, Muncie, Indiana; former editor-in-chief, *Ball State Daily News.*

POHLAD, Mark B. Assistant professor, Department of Art and Art History, DePaul University, Chicago; teaches and publishes in American art and in the history of photography.

PORTA, Fernando. Ph.D., English literature, Reading, United Kingdom; M.A. in critical theory, Sheffield, United Kingdom; B.A. in modern languages, Salerno, Italy; author of *La scienza come favola* (1995), and of scholarly articles.

POSNER, Michael L. Retired correspondent for Reuters and United Press International.

PRICE, John A. Freelance writer; Ph.D. candidate, The University of Texas at Dallas; M.F.A. in actor training/directing, Boston University.

PRICE, Victoria. Writer, A&E's *Biography* series; author of a biography of Vincent Price (St. Martin's Press, forthcoming); doctoral candidate, American studies, Santa Fe, New Mexico.

PRONO, Luca. Freelance writer; Ph.D. candidate, University of Nottingham, United Kingdom; studying literary, cinematic and sociological representations of Chicago in the twentieth century; graduated cum laude from the University of Venice, Italy.

PURDY, Elizabeth. Ph.D. Assistant professor of political science, Georgia Baptist College of Nursing, Atlanta, Georgia; contributor to various scholarly works on political science and women's issues.

PYLE, Christian L. Freelance writer, Lexington, Kentucky.

RABINOVITZ, Lauren. Professor of American studies and film studies, University of Iowa, Iowa City; author, *Points of Resistance: Women, Power and Politics in the New York Avant-Garde Cinema, 1943-1971* (University Illinois Press, 1991) and *For the Love of Pleasure: Women, Movies, and Culture in Turn-of-the-Century Chicago* (Rutgers University Press, 1998); co-author, *The Rebecca Project* (Rutgers University Press, 1995); co-editor, *Seeing through the Media: The Persian Gulf War* (Rutgers University Press, 1994) and *Television, History, and American Culture: Feminist Critical Essays* (Duke University Press, forthcoming).

RANDALL, Jessy. Curator of women's history collection, Library Company of Philadelphia, Pennsylvania.

RAVID, Taly. Freelance writer; student, University of California, Los Angeles.

RAY, Belinda S. At-home mother; Women's History Guide, The Mining Company; columnist, ''Portland Woman,'' Portland, Maine; author, *Sweet Valley High #138* (Bantam/Doubleday/Dell, 1997) and *Sweet Valley High: Senior Year #5* (Bantam/Doubleday/Dell, 1999).

RAYKOFF, Ivan. Pianist and musicologist; Ph.D., University of California—San Diego.

REAVES, Wendy Wick. Freelance writer.

REED, T. V. Associate professor of English and director of American studies, Washington State University, Pullman; author of *Fifteen Jugglers, Five Believers: Literary Politics and the Poetics of American Social Movements* (University of California Press, 1992).

REIBMAN, James E. Lafayette College, Easton, Pennsylvannia; author, *My Brother's Keeper: The Life of Fredric Wertham, M.D.*; annotated Wertham's *Seduction of the Innocent*; co-editor, *A Fredric Wertham Reader*; author of numerous articles and book chapters on legal writers of the Scottish Enlightenment; Samuel Johnson and his circle; law and literature, and popular culture.

RETTER, Yolanda. M.L.S. librarian, International Gay and Lesbian Archives, Los Angeles; manager, Lesbian History Project web site; contributor to various anthologies and reference works. Ph.D. in American studies expected in 1999.

REVELS, Tracy J. Associate professor of history, Wofford College, Spartanburg, South Carolina.

RHOLETTER, Wylene. Instructor, Department of English, Auburn University; author of poems published in *Caesura, Chattahoochee Review,* and other literary magazines and of papers delivered at SAMLA, NCTE, and other conferences.

RICHARDS, Tad. Author of *The New Country Music Encyclopedia* (Simon & Schuster, 1993, with Melvin B. Shestack) and *My Night with the Language Thieves: Collected Poems* (Ye Olde Font Shoppe, 1998).

RIDINGER, Robert B. Full professor, University Libraries, Northern Illinois University; author of *The Gay and Lesbian Movement; References and Resources* (G.K. Hall, 1998) and contributor to *St. James Gay and Lesbian Almanac* and *Gay and Lesbian Biography.*

RITTER, Jeff. Assistant professor of communication design, La Roche College, Pittsburgh; producer and writer in a variety of media including video, radio, and the Internet.

ROBERTSON, Thomas. Freelance writer; Ph.D. candidate, University of Wisconsin—Madison.

ROBINSON, Arthur. Adjunct professor of American culture, Diablo Valley College, Pleasant Hill, California, and Santa Rosa Junior College, Santa Rosa, California; teaches English, literature, history, and technical writing; author of "Teaching About Social Unrest: The 1992 L.A. Uprising as a Text in the Critical Thinking Classroom," *Inside English,* Winter 1999.

ROSA, Todd Anthony. Teaching fellow, The George Washington University; extensive writings on American cultural, political, and diplomatic history.

ROSE, Ava. Social worker specializing in working with trauma survivors; has taught college courses, published, and presented conference papers on film and television theory, culture studies, feminism, and psychoanalysis; master's degree in social welfare, University of California—Los Angeles; master's degree in cinema studies, New York University; B.A. in women's studies, Barnard College/Columbia University.

ROUTLEDGE, Chris. Freelance writer and lecturer, Kent, England.

ROY, Abhijit. Freelance writer; doctoral candidate, marketing, Boston University; author of articles in *Journal of Consumer Marketing, Journal of Direct Marketing, Journal of Product and Brand Management,* and *Journal of Services Marketing.*

RUSSELL, Adrienne. Freelance writer; Ph.D. candidate, Indiana University, Bloomington; writing dissertation about social movements on the Internet.

RUSSELL, Dennis. Associate professor, Walter Cronkite School of Journalism and Telecommunication, Arizona State University; author of articles published in *Studies in Popular Culture, Popular Culture Review,* and *Southwestern Mass Communication Journal.*

SAGOLLA, Lisa Jo. Ed.D. Dance instructor, Columbia University; adjunct professor, Marymount Manhattan College; dance critic, *Back Stage.*

SALAMONE, Frank A. Chair, Department of Sociology, Iona College, New Rochelle, New York; authored many books on Africa,

Religion, and Missions as well as a number of articles on jazz and popular culture.

SANDERS, Joe Sutliff. Freelance writer; Ph.D. candidate, University of Kentucky; author of various speculative fiction short stories as well as theoretical studies of Tolkien and King.

SARGENT, Andrew. Teaching associate, Department of English, University of California, Los Angeles; writes on film, popular culture, and American literature.

SCELFO, Julie. Instructor in Communication studies, New York University; assistant editor, *Brill's Content.*

SCHAFER, Elizabeth D. Independent scholar. Ph.D., American history, Auburn University; graduate study, children's literature, Hollins University; co-author of *Women Who Made A Difference in Alabama* (League of Women Voters, 1995), and "'I'm Gonna Glory in Learnin': Academic Aspirations of African-American Characters in Children's Literature," *African American Review* 32 (spring 1998).

SCHEEDER, Louis. Director of the Classical Studio, New York University.

SCHIFF, James. Adjunct assistant professor, University of Cincinnati; author of *Updike's Version: Rewriting "The Scarlet Letter"* (University of Missouri Press, 1992), *Understanding Reynolds Price* (University of South Carolina Press, 1996), *John Updike Revisited* (Twayne, 1998); editor, *Critical Essays on Reynolds Price* (G.K. Hall, 1998).

SCHNAKENBERG, Robert E. Freelance writer; author of *The Encyclopedia Shatnerica* (Renaissance Books, 1998).

SCHNEIDER, Steven. Freelance writer; Ph.D. student in philosophy, Harvard University; author of articles in *Paradoxa: Studies in World Literary Genres* and *Other Voices: A Journal of Critical Thought.*

SCHRUM, Kelly. Freelance writer; doctoral student in history, Johns Hopkins University; emphases in twentieth-century United States social and cultural history, consumer culture, youth, and gender; author of "Teena Means Business: Teenage Girls' Culture and Seventeen Magazine, 1944-1950" in *Delinquents and Debutantes: Twentieth-Century American Girls' Cultures,* edited by Sherrie A. Inness (NYU Press, 1998); writing dissertation, "Some Wore Bobby Sox: The Development of Teenage Girls' Cultures in the United States, 1930-1960."

SCHURK, William L. Professor/sound recordings archivist, Bowling Green State University, Bowling Green, Ohio; co-author, *Tarnished Gold* (Transaction, 1986); associate editor of *Popular Music and Society,* and on the editorial boards of *Journal of Popular Culture, Journal of American Culture,* and *Popular Culture and Libraries.*

SCODARI, Christine. Associate professor of communication, Florida Atlantic University; author of an unpublished work titled *Serial Monogamy: Soap Opera Lifespan, and the Gendered Politics of Fantasy,* and numerous scholarly articles relating to popular culture.

SCOTT, Alison M. Head librarian and associate professor, Popular Culture Library, Bowling Green State University, Bowling Green, Ohio; co-editor, *The Atomic Age Opens: American Culture Confronts the Atomic Bomb* (University Press of America, 1997) and author of articles on popular culture in libraries and the history of the book.

SCOTT, Randall W. Original catalog librarian and comic art bibliographer, Special Collections Division, Michigan State University Libraries, East Lansing; author, *A Subject Index to Comic Books and Related Material* (Michigan State University Libraries, 1975), *Comic Books and Strips, an Information Sourcebook* (Oryx Press, 1988), *Comics Librarianship, a Handbook* (McFarland Press, 1990), and *The Comic Art Collection Catalog* (Greenwood Press, 1993).

SEARS, Ann. Professor of music, Wheaton College, Norton, Massachusetts; review editor for the College Music Society Journal Symposium; contributor of articles to scholarly journals.

SEFCOVIC, E. M. I. Assistant professor of journalism and media studies, Florida Atlantic University; 20 years as a reporter and editor for Hearst, Globe, and Cox newspapers (using byline Enid Sefcovic); academic publications and conference papers in the areas of labor rhetoric and culture, and women's aging and health issues.

SEGAL, Eric J. Freelance writer; doctoral candidate, Department of Art History, University of California, Los Angeles.

SENF, Carol A. Associate professor, School of Literature, Communication, and Culture, The Georgia Institute of Technology; author of *Dracula: Between Tradition and Modernism* (Twayne, 1998), *The Critical Response to Bram Stoker* (Greenwood, 1994), and *The Vampire in Nineteenth-Century British Fiction* (The Popular Press, 1988).

SEUL, Tim. Assistant professor of government, Adams State College, Alamosa, Colorado.

SHASHKO, Alexander. Freelance writer; doctoral candidate, American History, University of Michigan.

SHAUF, Michele S. Associate professor, School of Literature, Communication, and Culture, Georgia Institute of Technology; editor, *Computers, Ethics, and Society* (Oxford University Press, 1997).

SHAW, Taylor. Freelance writer.

SHEEHAN, Anne. Freelance writer; graduate student, Department of English, University of California, Los Angeles; writes on nineteenth century American literature and culture.

SHEEHAN, Steven T. Freelance writer; Ph.D. candidate, Indiana University, Bloomington; writing dissertation on consumerism and masculinity in American culture.

SHELTON, Pamela. Freelance writer and editor, Avon, Connecticut.

SHERMAN, Sandra. Freelance writer; student, University of California, Los Angeles.

SHINDO, Charles J. Associate professor of history, Louisiana State University; author of *Dust Bowl Migrants in the American Imagination* (University Press of Kansas, 1997).

SHUPP, Mike. Former aerospace engineer; graduate student, Anthropology Department, California State University, Northridge; author of *With Fate Conspire, Morning of Creation, Soldier of Another Fortune, Death's Gray Land,* and *The Last Reckoning* (Del Rey Books, 1986-91).

SICKELS, Robert C. Lecturer, American film and literature, University of Nevada, Reno.

SILVEY, C. Kenyon. University of California at Berkeley graduate; contributor, *SF Weekly, Penthouse, High Times* and *Lounge.*

SIMON, Ron. Curator, The Museum of Television & Radio; adjunct associate professor, Columbia University; author and curator of *Jack Benny: The Radio and Television Work* (HarperPerennial, 1991), *Witness to History* (The Museum of Television & Radio, 1991), and *World's Without End: The Art and History of the Soap Opera* (Abrams, 1997).

SIMPSON, Philip. Assistant professor, communications and humanities, Brevard Community College, Palm Bay, Florida; has published numerous essays on contemporary film and literature; Area Chair in the Popular Culture Association.

SKAINE, Rosemarie. Author of *Power and Gender: Issues in Sexual Dominance and Harassment* (McFarland Publishers, 1996) and *Women at War: Gender Issues of Americans in Combat* (McFarland Publishers, 1998).

SLOANE, Ryan R. Freelance writer; graduate student, University of California, Los Angeles.

SLONIOWSKI, Jeannette. Chair, Department of Communications, Popular Culture and Film, Brock University; co-editor, *Documenting the Documentary: Close Readings of Documentary Film and Video,* and *Canadian Communications: Current Issues in Media and Culture.*

SMITH, Cheryl A. Associate director of publications, Denver Seminary; author of *The Falcon and the Serpent* (Crossway Books, 1990) and numerous articles on popular culture.

SMITH, Erin. Assistant professor of American studies, literature and gender studies, University of Texas at Dallas; author, *Reading Pulp Fiction: Hard-Boiled Writing Culture and Working-Class Life* (Temple University Press, forthcoming 2000), and contributor of articles to scholarly journals.

SMITH, Kyle. Freelance writer; Ph.D. candidate, Department of American and Canadian Studies, University of Birmingham, United Kingdom; studying Thomas Pynchon and pre-Cold War British spy fiction.

SMOLENSKI, John. Freelance writer; Ph.D. candidate, University of Pennsylvania; dissertation entitled: ''Friends and Strangers: Religion, Diversity and the Ordering of Public Life in Colonial Pennsylvania, 1681-1765.''

SOCHEN, June. Professor of history, Northeastern Illinois University, Chicago.

SOLOMON, Irvin D. History program director, Florida Gulf Coast University; author of *Feminism and Black Activism in Contemporary America: An Ideological Assessment,* 2nd ed. (Greenwood, 1993).

SPEACE, Geri. Professional writer and editor; proprietor of Expert Editorial Services; M.A. in communications, Wayne State University.

SPIELDENNER, Andrew. Contributor, *Queer P.A.P.I. Porn* (Cleis Press, 1998), *Names We Call Home: Autobiography on Racial*

Identity (Routledge, 1995), *Voices of Identity, Rage and Empowerment* (No Press Collective, 1994), and the Vietnamese magazine *Doi Dien.*

stabin, tova. Freelance writer, editor, poet, researcher, and photographer; contributor to many journals, magazines, and anthologies; editor, *Bridges: A Journal for Jewish Feminists and Our Friends.*

STABLER, Scott. Former coach, teacher, and professional baseball umpire; graduate student in history, University of Houston.

STERNGRASS, Jon. Freelance writer.

STUMP, Roger W. Associate professor of geography and planning, and religious studies, University at Albany, S.U.N.Y.; author of *Boundaries of Faith: Geographical Perspectives on Religious Fundamentalism* (Rowman and Littlefield, forthcoming).

SULLIVAN, Bob. Freelance writer; attended U.S.C. film school; wrote the award-winning Peter Graves sci-fi "B" movie classic *Clonus.*

SUPANCE, Lauren Ann. Freelance writer; student, University of California, Los Angeles.

SYKES, Marc R. Freelance writer; Ph.D. candidate, Rutgers University; author of an unpublished work titled *Risque Rhythms: Sex and the Blues Tradition in America.*

TAKAGI, Midori. Associate professor of history, Fairhaven College, Western Washington University, Bellingham, Washington; author, *Rearing Wolves to Our Own Destruction: Slavery in Richmond, Virginia, 1782-1865* (University Press of Virginia, 1999).

TAYLOR, Candida. Freelance writer; Ph.D. student and part-time lecturer in hispanic studies; author of ''Zoot Suit: Parading UnAmericanism'' in *Containing America: Cultural Production and Consumption in Fifties America,* edited by Julie Hughes and Nathan Abrams (Birmingham Press, forthcoming).

THILL, Scott. Freelance writer.

THOMPSON, Robert. Director, Center for the Study of Popular Television, Syracuse University.

THOMPSON, Stephen L. Reference/collection development librarian (humanities), John D. Rockefeller, Jr. Library, Brown University, Providence, Rhode Island.

THOMSON, Rosemarie Garland. Associate professor of English, Howard University; author of *Extraordinary Bodies: Figuring Physical Disability in American Literature and Culture* (Columbia University Press, 1997); editor of *Freakery: Cultural Spectacles of the Extraordinary Body* (New York University Press, 1996).

TODD, Jan. Assistant professor, Department of Kinesiology and Health Education, University of Texas at Austin; co-editor of *Iron Game History: The Journal of Physical Culture;* curator, the Todd-McLean Physical Culture Collection; author of *Physical Culture and the Body Beautiful: Purposive Exercise in the Lives of American Women.*

TODD, Terry. Senior lecturer, Department of Kinesiology and Health Education, University of Texas at Austin; co-editor of *Iron Game History: The Journal of Physical Culture;* director, the Todd-McLean Physical Culture Collection.

TOMASIC, John. Freelance writer; Ph.D. candidate, Indiana University, Bloomington; writing a dissertation on emigre artists working in Paris during the 1920s and the 1950s.

TORMEY, Warren. Professor, Department of English, Middle Tennessee State University, Murfreesboro.

TRACEY, Grant. Assistant professor, University of Northern Iowa; teaches film theory, popular culture, and creative writing; editor, *Literary Magazine Review.*

TREVINO, David. Professor of history, Ohio Northern University.

TREVINO, Marcella Bush. Instructor of history, Texas A&M University, Kingsville; Ph.D. in American culture studies, Bowling Green State University, Bowling Green, Ohio.

TRIBBLE, Scott. Freelance writer, Boston, Massachusetts; master's degree in American civilization, Brown University, Providence, Rhode Island.

TRINCHERA, Tom. Reference librarian, Dutchess Community College, Poughkeepsie, New York.

TURSE, Nicholas A. Master of arts in history, Rutgers University—Newark; thesis: ''Prometheus Bound: The Technology of Bodybuilding in the Nervous Age.''

UBELHOR, Anthony. Freelance writer; M.A. student in literature, University of Kentucky; editor of *Pulsar: Science Fiction and Fantasy* (1985-1991).

UMBERGER, Daryl. Freelance writer, Harrisburg, Pennsylvania; M.A. in American studies, Pennsylvania State University, Harrisburg.

VAN KRANENBURG, Rob. Cultural studies researcher, University of Gent.

VanWYNSBERGHE, Robert. Professor of sociology, University of British Columbia, Vancouver, British Columbia, Canada; articles published in the areas of sport, leisure, social movements and native environmental justice

VARGAS, Colby. U.S. history and popular culture teacher, New Trier High School, Winnetka, Illinois.

WALKER, Sue. Chair and professor of English, University of South Alabama, Mobile; editor/publisher of *Negative Capability*, a literary journal; poet and contributor of articles to scholarly journals.

WALTERS, Lori C. Ph.D., Florida State University; specializing in Post World War II American popular culture, United States Space Program and Florida.

WANG, Nancy Lan-Jy. Freelance writer; student, University of California, Los Angeles; winner of the 1997 Ina Coolbrith Memorial Poetry Contest; contributor of poetry, *The Los Angeles Times.*

WATHEN, Adam. Assistant professor, reference librarian, Montana State University, Bozeman.

WEINTRAUB, Laural. Art historian, New York, New York.

WEISBERGER, Jon. Freelance writer, Kenton County, Kentucky.

WELKY, David B. Freelance writer; Ph.D. candidate, History, Purdue University; contributor, *Journal of Sport History* and *Culture, Sport, Society.*

WELLS, Christopher W. Freelance writer; Ph.D. student, University of Wisconsin—Madison; forthcoming dissertation on the automobile in American culture.

WHITE, Celia. Freelance writer.

WILSON, Christopher S. Visiting instructor, Faculty of Fine Arts, Design and Architecture, Bilkent University, Ankara, Turkey.

WILSON, David B. Computer programmer; associate editor, *Weekly News Update on the Americas;* has published articles on Latin America and cross-cultural relations in other magazines and periodicals; online music reviewer; author of *Dirty Clothes.*

WILSON, Kristi M. Lecturer, Literature Department, University of California, San Diego.

WILTSE, Jeff. Freelance writer.

WOLOSON, Wendy. Ph.D. in American civilization, University of Pennsylvania; dissertation on sugar and consumers in nineteenth-century America.

WOODWARD, David E. Ph.D. in history, University of Minnesota, 1996; contributor, *Civil War History, Transactions of the Illinois State Historical Society, Gulf Coast Historical Review, American National Biography,* and *Teaching History: A Journal of Methods*; has taught university American history and international relations.

WRIGHT, Bradford W. Ph.D. Instructor in history, University of Maryland University College in Europe; published articles on comic books and American history.

YABLON, Sharon. Produced playwright and director, and published writer, Los Angeles, California.

YEZBICK, Daniel Francis. Instructor in film, popular culture, and business communication, University of Illinois at Urbana—Champaign.

YOUNGKIN, Stephen D. Freelance writer and archivist, Utah State Historical Society; co-author, *The Films of Peter Lorre* (Citadel, 1982), *Peter Lorre: Portrait des Schauspielers auf der Flucht* (Belleville, 1998), author, *The Lost One: A Biography of Peter Lorre* (University of California Press, forthcoming).

ZOOK, Kristal Brent. Visiting assistant professor, African American and cultural studies, California State University, Northridge; author of *Color by Fox: The Fox Network and the Revolution in Black Television* (Oxford University Press, 1999).

TIME-FRAME INDEX

1900-1909

Addams, Jane, I 17
Advertising, I 23
Advice Columns, I 26
African American Press, I 32
Agents, I 34
Air Travel, I 38
Alaska-Yukon Exposition (Seattle, 1909), I 40
American Museum of Natural History, I 72
Amusement Parks, I 77
Argosy, I 109
Arrow Collar Man, I 118
Arthurian Legend, I 120
Ashcan School, I 122
Astrology, I 129
AT&T, I 130
Atlantic City, I 133
Atlas, Charles, I 135
Aunt Jemima, I 137
Avon, I 146
Bagels, I 158
Baker, Ray Stannard, I 159
Barbecue, I 168
Barrymore, John, I 178
Baseball, I 180
Baseball Cards, I 183
Basketball, I 186
Baum, L. Frank, I 191
Beach, Rex, I 197
Beauty Queens, I 207
Beer, I 210
Berlin, Irving, I 230
Bestsellers, I 236
Bicycling, I 245
Big Apple, I 246
Bigfoot, I 251
Billboards, I 253
Birthing Practices, I 260
Blackface Minstrelsy, I 270
Board Games, I 297
Bobbsey Twins, I 300
Bodybuilding, I 305
Bok, Edward, I 310
Borscht Belt, I 321
Boston Marathon, I 323
Boston Symphony Orchestra, I 325
Bowling, I 328
Boxing, I 330
Boy Scouts of America, I 333
Bridge, I 349
Broadway, I 356
Brooklyn Dodgers, I 362
Brownie Cameras, I 371
Budweiser, I 380
Bungalow, I 387
Burlesque, I 388
Buster Brown, I 398
Cadillac, I 406
Cahan, Abraham, I 411
Cakewalks, I 411
Camping, I 417
Cancer, I 418
Capital Punishment, I 424
Carnegie Hall, I 439
Caruso, Enrico, I 446
Castle, Vernon and Irene, I 454
Catalog Houses, I 455
Cather, Willa, I 459
Cemeteries, I 467
Central Park, I 468
Chautauqua Institution, I 481
Cheerleading, I 486
Chicago Cubs, I 493
Child Stars, I 498
Christmas, I 503
Church Socials, I 509
Cigarettes, I 510
Circus, I 512
Cobb, Ty, I 538
Coca-Cola, I 540
Cocaine/Crack, I 542

Cody, Buffalo Bill, and his Wild West Show, I 545
Coffee, I 546
Cohan, George M., I 548
College Football, I 555
Comics, I 562
Condoms, I 578
Coney Island, I 580
Consumerism, I 589
Corbett, James J., I 601
Cosmopolitan, I 610
Coué, Emile, I 615
Cowboy Look, I 622
Creationism, I 627
Darrow, Clarence, I 660
Debs, Eugene V., I 679
Debutantes, I 680
Department Stores, I 688
Detective Fiction, I 693
Detroit Tigers, I 695
Dime Novels, I 716
Dime Stores/Woolworth's, I 717
Disability, I 721
Doyle, Arthur Conan, I 755
Dr. Jekyll and Mr. Hyde, I 756
Drag, I 762
Du Bois, W. E. B., I 771
Duncan, Isadora, I 773
Eddy, Mary Baker, II 11
Edison, Thomas Alva, II 13
Einstein, Albert, II 16
Electric Trains, II 22
Environmentalism, II 29
Etiquette Columns, II 44
Evangelism, II 46
Factor, Max, II 54
Family Reunions, II 63
Feminism, II 84
Field and Stream, II 92
Flea Markets, II 114
Florida Vacations, II 119
Folk Music, II 123
Ford, Henry, II 132
Ford Motor Company, II 135
Fourth of July Celebrations, II 146
Freak Shows, II 158
French Fries, II 165
Freud, Sigmund, II 166
Gambling, II 188
Gangs, II 195
Gay Men, II 215
Gernsback, Hugo, II 225
Gibson Girl, II 233
Good Housekeeping, II 265
Gospel Music, II 274
Graffiti, II 281
Great Train Robbery, II 297
Greenwich Village, II 304
Greeting Cards, II 306
Grey, Zane, II 309
Grits, II 319
Hairstyles, II 340
Handy, W. C., II 352
Harley-Davidson, II 368
Harper's, II 372
Hearst, William Randolph, II 379
Higginson, Major Henry Lee, II 400
Hiking, II 405
Hockey, II 417
Hollywood, II 431
Hopalong Cassidy, II 444
Hopscotch, II 449
Hot Dogs, II 454
Houdini, Harry, II 456
Ice Cream Cone, II 483
Indian, II 487
Industrial Design, II 491
Jackson, "Shoeless" Joe, II 521
Jeans, II 532
Jell-O, II 537
Johnson, Jack, II 554
Johnson, James Weldon, II 555

Jolson, Al, II 559
Joplin, Scott, II 566
Kentucky Derby, III 19
Kewpie Dolls, III 22
Kitsch, III 43
Kodak, III 51
Ku Klux Klan, III 64
Labor Unions, III 72
Leisure Time, III 128
Lesbianism, III 140
Levi's, III 146
Liberty, III 157
Life, III 160
Lionel Trains, III 170
Lipstick, III 171
London, Jack, III 187
Louisiana Purchase Exposition, III 201
Louisville Slugger, III 201
Lynching, III 217
Macfadden, Bernarr, III 226
Marching Bands, III 267
Mardi Gras, III 269
Martini, III 282
Mass Market Magazine Revolution, III 299
Masses, III 302
McCall's Magazine, III 313
McCay, Winsor, III 317
McClure's, III 318
Medicine Shows, III 339
Metropolitan Museum of Art, III 347
Milton Bradley, III 369
Minstrel Shows, III 371
Model T, III 386
Modern Dance, III 388
Modernism, III 390
Morton, Jelly Roll, III 416
Mother's Day, III 417
Mr. Dooley, III 430
Muckraking, III 438
Munsey's Magazine, III 442
Muscular Christianity, III 456
Musical, III 458
Mutt & Jeff, III 462
Naismith, James, III 470
Nation, III 476
National Collegiate Athletic Association (NCAA), III 479
National Geographic, III 484
National Parks, III 489
Neckties, III 495
New York Times, III 518
Niagara Falls, III 528
Nickelodeons, III 530
Norris, Frank, III 540
Olympics, III 558
Ouija Boards, III 576
Pants for Women, IV 7
Parades, IV 12
Parrish, Maxfield, IV 16
Peep Shows, IV 30
Pepsi-Cola, IV 36
Pets, IV 44
Phonograph, IV 52
Picasso, Pablo, IV 54
Pizza, IV 62
Plastic, IV 64
Pope, IV 86
Popular Mechanics, IV 89
Popular Psychology, IV 90
Pornography, IV 92
Postcards, IV 96
Prang, Louis, IV 104
Professional Football, IV 116
Protest Groups, IV 124
PTA/PTO (Parent Teacher Association/ Organization), IV 130
Public Libraries, IV 133
Race Riots, IV 156
Rainey, Gertrude "Ma", IV 168
Redbook, IV 189
Ringling Bros., Barnum & Bailey Circus, IV 212
Rockefeller Family, IV 239

Rodeo, IV 252
Rogers, Will, IV 263
Roller Coasters, IV 265
Romance Novels, IV 270
Rose Bowl, IV 275
Saks Fifth Avenue, IV 302
Sandow, Eugen, IV 309
Saratoga Springs, IV 312
Saturday Evening Post, IV 315
Scientific American, IV 334
Scribner's, IV 344
Sennett, Mack, IV 357
Sex Scandals, IV 367
Silent Movies, IV 393
Sinclair, Upton, IV 414
Slang, IV 434
Soccer, IV 449
Social Dancing, IV 450
Soda Fountains, IV 452
Sousa, John Philip, IV 463
Spalding, Albert G., IV 468
Sporting News, IV 483
St. Denis, Ruth, IV 494
Stagg, Amos Alonzo, IV 499
Stand-up Comedy, IV 504
State Fairs, IV 518
Steffens, Lincoln, IV 521
Stereoscopes, IV 528
Stetson Hat, IV 532
Stickball, IV 534
Stratemeyer, Edward, IV 548
Stratton-Porter, Gene, IV 550
Street and Smith, IV 553
Strip Joints/Striptease, IV 557
Studio System, IV 565
Sullivan, John L., IV 572
Summer Camp, IV 573
Sunday, Billy, IV 578
Swimming Pools, IV 590
Tabloids, IV 597
Tap Dancing, IV 605
Tarbell, Ida, IV 606
Tarkington, Booth, IV 607
Teddy Bears, IV 616
Telephone, IV 623
Tennis, IV 635
Tennis Shoes/Sneakers, IV 637
Thanksgiving, IV 640
Thorpe, Jim, IV 649
Tiffany & Company, IV 655
Times Square, IV 659
Tour de France, IV 684
Town Meetings, IV 684
Toys, IV 685
Tramps, IV 691
Traveling Carnivals, IV 692
Valentine's Day, V 16
Vampires, V 22
Vardon, Harry, V 30
Variety, V 31
Vaudeville, V 33
Vogue, V 53
Walker, Aida Overton, V 61
Walker, George, V 62
Walker, Madame C. J., V 65
Wall Street Journal, V 67
Washington Monument, V 83
Washington Post, V 83
Wedding Dress, V 100
Western, V 118
Wharton, Edith, V 121
Whistler's Mother, V 125
White, Stanford, V 129
Williams, Bert, V 140
Wimbledon, V 150
Wire Services, V 158
Wister, Owen, V 161
Wobblies, V 165
World Series, V 182
World's Fairs, V 194
WWJD? (What Would Jesus Do?), V 198
Yankee Doodle Dandy, V 207

Yellow Kid, V 212
Yellowstone National Park, V 213
Young, Cy, V 216
Youth's Companion, V 222
Ziegfeld Follies, V 227
Zoos, V 230

1910-1919
Addams, Jane, I 17
Advertising, I 23
Advice Columns, I 26
African American Press, I 32
Agents, I 34
Air Travel, I 38
American Museum of Natural History, I 72
Amusement Parks, I 77
Anderson, Sherwood, I 83
Arbuckle, Fatty, I 107
Arden, Elizabeth, I 109
Argosy, I 109
Armory Show, I 112
Armstrong, Louis, I 114
Arrow Collar Man, I 118
Arthurian Legend, I 120
Ashcan School, I 122
Astrology, I 129
AT&T, I 130
Atlantic City, I 133
Atlas, Charles, I 135
Aunt Jemima, I 137
Automobile, I 137
Bagels, I 158
Baker, Ray Stannard, I 159
Bara, Theda, I 168
Barbecue, I 168
Barbershop Quartets, I 169
Barrymore, John, I 178
Barton, Bruce, I 179
Baseball, I 180
Baseball Cards, I 183
Basketball, I 186
Baum, L. Frank, I 191
Beach, Rex, I 197
Beauty Queens, I 207
Beer, I 210
Ben-Hur, I 219
Berlin, Irving, I 230
Bestsellers, I 236
Bicycling, I 245
Big Apple, I 246
Bigfoot, I 251
Billboards, I 253
Birth of a Nation, I 258
Birthing Practices, I 260
Black Sox Scandal, I 266
Blackface Minstrelsy, I 270
Blockbusters, I 280
Board Games, I 297
Bobbsey Twins, I 300
Bodybuilding, I 305
Bok, Edward, I 310
Borscht Belt, I 321
Boston Marathon, I 323
Bowling, I 328
Boy Scouts of America, I 333
Bra, I 335
Brice, Fanny, I 348
Bridge, I 349
Broadway, I 356
Brooklyn Dodgers, I 362
Brownie Cameras, I 371
Bungalow, I 387
Burlesque, I 388
Burroughs, Edgar Rice, I 396
Buster Brown, I 398
Butterbeans and Susie, I 400
Camping, I 417
Cancer, I 418
Cantor, Eddie, I 423
Capital Punishment, I 424
Carnegie Hall, I 439
Caruso, Enrico, I 446
Castle, Vernon and Irene, I 454

Catalog Houses, I 455
Cather, Willa, I 459
Celebrity Caricature, I 465
Cemeteries, I 467
Central Park, I 468
Chaplin, Charlie, I 475
Chautauqua Institution, I 481
Cheerleading, I 486
Child Stars, I 498
Christmas, I 503
Church Socials, I 509
Cigarettes, I 510
Circus, I 512
City of Angels, I 516
Cobb, Ty, I 538
Coca-Cola, I 540
Cocaine/Crack, I 542
Cody, Buffalo Bill, and his Wild West
   Show, I 545
Coffee, I 546
Cohan, George M., I 548
College Football, I 555
Comics, I 562
Communism, I 569
Community Media, I 570
Community Theatre, I 573
Condé Nast, I 577
Condoms, I 578
Coney Island, I 580
Confession Magazines, I 581
Consumerism, I 589
Corbett, James J., I 601
Cosmopolitan, I 610
Coué, Emile, I 615
Country Music, I 617
Cowboy Look, I 622
Creationism, I 627
Crisis, I 633
Crossword Puzzles, I 641
Currier and Ives, I 650
Darrow, Clarence, I 660
Debs, Eugene V., I 679
Debutantes, I 680
DeMille, Cecil B., I 683
Dempsey, Jack, I 685
Denishawn, I 686
Department Stores, I 688
Detective Fiction, I 693
Detroit Tigers, I 695
Dime Novels, I 716
Dime Stores/Woolworth's, I 717
Disability, I 721
Dixieland, I 734
Doyle, Arthur Conan, I 755
Dr. Jekyll and Mr. Hyde, I 756
Draft, I 761
Drag, I 762
Dreiser, Theodore, I 768
Drug War, I 771
Du Bois, W. E. B., I 771
Duncan, Isadora, I 773
Ebbets Field, II 5
Eddy, Mary Baker, II 11
Edison, Thomas Alva, II 13
Einstein, Albert, II 16
Electric Trains, II 22
Environmentalism, II 29
Erector Sets, II 34
Etiquette Columns, II 44
Evangelism, II 46
Factor, Max, II 54
Fairbanks, Douglas, Sr., II 57
Fan Magazines, II 64
Father's Day, II 76
Fauset, Jessie Redmon, II 78
FBI (Federal Bureau of Investigation), II 80
Felix the Cat, II 83
Feminism, II 84
Fenway Park, II 87
Field and Stream, II 92
Firearms, II 101
Flea Markets, II 114

Florida Vacations, II 119
Folk Music, II 123
Ford, Henry, II 132
Ford, John, II 133
Ford Motor Company, II 135
Fourth of July Celebrations, II 146
Freak Shows, II 158
Freud, Sigmund, II 166
Frost, Robert, II 177
Fu Manchu, II 179
Gambling, II 188
Gangs, II 195
Gas Stations, II 206
Gay Men, II 215
Gernsback, Hugo, II 225
Gertie the Dinosaur, II 226
Ghettos, II 227
Gibson Girl, II 233
Girl Scouts, II 242
Gish, Dorothy, II 243
Gish, Lillian, II 244
Goldberg, Rube, II 256
Good Housekeeping, II 265
Gospel Music, II 274
Graffiti, II 281
Graham, Martha, II 285
Greenwich Village, II 304
Greeting Cards, II 306
Grey, Zane, II 309
Greyhound Buses, II 312
Griffith, D. W., II 313
Grits, II 319
Hairstyles, II 340
Handy, W. C., II 352
Harlem Renaissance, II 365
Harley-Davidson, II 368
Harper's, II 372
Hearst, William Randolph, II 379
Highway System, II 402
Hiking, II 405
Hockey, II 417
Hollywood, II 431
Hopalong Cassidy, II 444
Hopscotch, II 449
Horror Movies, II 450
Hot Dogs, II 454
Houdini, Harry, II 456
IBM (International Business Machines), II 481
Ice Shows, II 484
Indian, II 487
Indianapolis 500, II 490
Industrial Design, II 491
Intolerance, II 498
Jackson, "Shoeless" Joe, II 521
Jeans, II 532
Jell-O, II 537
Jessel, George, II 542
Johnson, Jack, II 554
Johnson, James Weldon, II 555
Jolson, Al, II 559
Joplin, Scott, II 566
Juvenile Delinquency, II 583
Karloff, Boris, III 4
Katzenjammer Kids, III 7
Keaton, Buster, III 10
Kentucky Derby, III 19
Kewpie Dolls, III 22
Keystone Kops, III 24
Kitsch, III 43
Kiwanis, III 46
Kodak, III 51
Krazy Kat, III 62
Ku Klux Klan, III 64
Labor Unions, III 72
Lardner, Ring, III 90
Leadbelly, III 108
Leisure Time, III 128
Lesbianism, III 140
Levi's, III 146
Life, III 160
Lionel Trains, III 170
Lipstick, III 171

Little Black Dress, III 173
L.L. Bean, Inc., III 180
London, Jack, III 187
Loos, Anita, III 194
Louisville Slugger, III 201
Lubitsch, Ernst, III 209
Lynching, III 217
Macfadden, Bernarr, III 226
Marching Bands, III 267
Mardi Gras, III 269
Martini, III 282
Marx Brothers, III 287
Mass Market Magazine Revolution, III 299
Masses, III 302
Mayer, Louis B., III 309
McCall's Magazine, III 313
McCay, Winsor, III 317
McClure's, III 318
Medicine Shows, III 339
Metropolitan Museum of Art, III 347
Militias, III 359
Millay, Edna St. Vincent, III 363
Milton Bradley, III 369
Mix, Tom, III 383
Model T, III 386
Modern Dance, III 388
Modernism, III 390
Morton, Jelly Roll, III 416
Mother's Day, III 417
Movie Palaces, III 426
Movie Stars, III 428
Mr. Dooley, III 430
Muckraking, III 438
Munsey's Magazine, III 442
Muscular Christianity, III 456
Musical, III 458
Mutt & Jeff, III 462
Naismith, James, III 470
Nation, III 476
National Collegiate Athletic Association
    (NCAA), III 479
National Hockey League (NHL), III 485
National Parks, III 489
Neckties, III 495
Negro Leagues, III 497
New Republic, III 514
New York Times, III 518
New York Yankees, III 520
Niagara Falls, III 528
Nickelodeons, III 530
O'Keeffe, Georgia, III 552
Olympics, III 558
Original Dixieland Jass (Jazz) Band, III 573
Ouija Boards, III 576
Outline of History, III 581
Pants for Women, IV 7
Parades, IV 12
Parrish, Maxfield, IV 16
Peep Shows, IV 30
Pets, IV 44
Phonograph, IV 52
Photoplay, IV 53
Picasso, Pablo, IV 54
Pickford, Mary, IV 55
Pizza, IV 62
Plastic, IV 64
Plastic Surgery, IV 67
Political Bosses, IV 77
Pop Music, IV 83
Pope, IV 86
Popular Psychology, IV 90
Postcards, IV 96
Professional Football, IV 116
Prohibition, IV 119
Protest Groups, IV 124
PTA/PTO (Parent Teacher Association/
    Organization), IV 130
Public Libraries, IV 133
Race Riots, IV 156
Raggedy Ann and Raggedy Andy, IV 163
Rainey, Gertrude "Ma", IV 168
Rains, Claude, IV 168

Red Scare, IV 188
Ringling Bros., Barnum & Bailey Circus, IV 212
Rockefeller Family, IV 239
Rockne, Knute, IV 243
Rockwell, Norman, IV 244
Rodeo, IV 252
Rogers, Will, IV 263
Roller Coasters, IV 265
Romance Novels, IV 270
Rose Bowl, IV 275
Ruth, Babe, IV 293
RV, IV 295
Saks Fifth Avenue, IV 302
Sandburg, Carl, IV 306
Sandow, Eugen, IV 309
Saratoga Springs, IV 312
Sarnoff, David, IV 312
Saturday Evening Post, IV 315
Scientific American, IV 334
Scribner's, IV 344
Sears Roebuck Catalogue, IV 346
Sennett, Mack, IV 357
Sex Scandals, IV 367
Sex Symbol, IV 369
Shawn, Ted, IV 381
Silent Movies, IV 393
Slang, IV 434
Soccer, IV 449
Social Dancing, IV 450
Soda Fountains, IV 452
Soldier Field, IV 453
Sousa, John Philip, IV 463
Sporting News, IV 483
St. Denis, Ruth, IV 494
Stagg, Amos Alonzo, IV 499
Standardized Testing, IV 502
Stand-up Comedy, IV 504
State Fairs, IV 518
Steffens, Lincoln, IV 521
Stereoscopes, IV 528
Stetson Hat, IV 532
Stickball, IV 534
Stokowski, Leopold, IV 541
Stratemeyer, Edward, IV 548
Stratton-Porter, Gene, IV 550
Street and Smith, IV 553
Strip Joints/Striptease, IV 557
Studio System, IV 565
Summer Camp, IV 573
Sunday, Billy, IV 578
Sunday Driving, IV 578
Swimming Pools, IV 590
Tabloids, IV 597
Tap Dancing, IV 605
Tarbell, Ida, IV 606
Tarkington, Booth, IV 607
Tarzan, IV 608
Teddy Bears, IV 616
Telephone, IV 623
Tennis, IV 635
Tennis Shoes/Sneakers, IV 637
Thanksgiving, IV 640
Thorpe, Jim, IV 649
Tiffany & Company, IV 655
Times Square, IV 659
Titanic, IV 661
Tom Swift Series, IV 674
Town Meetings, IV 684
Toys, IV 685
Tramps, IV 691
Traveling Carnivals, IV 692
United Artists, V 8
Valentine's Day, V 16
Valentino, Rudolph, V 17
Vampires, V 22
Vanity Fair, V 28
Vardon, Harry, V 30
Vaudeville, V 33
Vogue, V 53
Wagner, Honus, V 59
Walker, Aida Overton, V 61
Walker, Madame C. J., V 65

Wall Street Journal, V 67
War Bonds, V 74
War Movies, V 75
Washington Post, V 83
Waters, Ethel, V 86
Wedding Dress, V 100
Western, V 118
Wharton, Edith, V 121
White Castle, V 127
White Flight, V 128
White Supremacists, V 129
Williams, Bert, V 140
Wimbledon, V 150
Wire Services, V 158
Wister, Owen, V 161
Wobblies, V 165
Wong, Anna May, V 172
World Series, V 182
World War I, V 184
World's Fairs, V 194
Wrigley Field, V 197
WWJD? (What Would Jesus Do?), V 198
Wyeth, N. C., V 200
Yellowstone National Park, V 213
Young, Cy, V 216
Youth's Companion, V 222
Ziegfeld Follies, V 227
Zoos, V 230
Zorro, V 234

1920-1929

A&R Men/Women, I 1
Abbott and Costello, I 5
Academy Awards, I 12
Adams, Ansel, I 17
Addams, Jane, I 17
Adidas, I 20
Advertising, I 23
Advice Columns, I 26
African American Press, I 32
Agents, I 34
Air Travel, I 38
Amazing Stories, I 64
American Mercury, I 72
American Museum of Natural History, I 72
Amos 'n' Andy Show, I 72
Amsterdam, Morey, I 74
Amusement Parks, I 77
Anderson, Marian, I 81
Anderson, Sherwood, I 83
Arbuckle, Fatty, I 107
Arden, Elizabeth, I 109
Argosy, I 109
Arizona Highways, I 110
Armstrong, Henry, I 113
Armstrong, Louis, I 114
Arrow Collar Man, I 118
Arthurian Legend, I 120
Ashcan School, I 122
Astrology, I 129
Atlantic City, I 133
Atlantic Monthly, I 134
Atlas, Charles, I 135
Aunt Jemima, I 137
Automobile, I 137
Autry, Gene, I 142
Bagels, I 158
Baker, Josephine, I 158
Barbecue, I 168
Barbershop Quartets, I 169
Barrymore, John, I 178
Barton, Bruce, I 179
Baseball, I 180
Baseball Cards, I 183
Basie, Count, I 184
Basketball, I 186
Baum, L. Frank, I 191
Beach, Rex, I 197
Beau Geste, I 207
Beauty Queens, I 207
Beer, I 210
Beiderbecke, Bix, I 214
Benchley, Robert, I 219

Ben-Hur, I 219
Benny, Jack, I 222
Berle, Milton, I 228
Berlin, Irving, I 230
Bestsellers, I 236
Better Homes and Gardens, I 238
Betty Crocker, I 241
Bicycling, I 245
Big Apple, I 246
Bigfoot, I 251
Billboards, I 253
Birthing Practices, I 260
Black Mask, I 263
Black Sox Scandal, I 266
Blackface Minstrelsy, I 270
Blanc, Mel, I 276
Blues, I 290
Board Games, I 297
Bodybuilding, I 305
Bogart, Humphrey, I 308
Book-of-the-Month Club, I 318
Borscht Belt, I 321
Boston Garden, I 323
Boston Marathon, I 323
Bow, Clara, I 326
Bowling, I 328
Boy Scouts of America, I 333
Bra, I 335
Brice, Fanny, I 348
Bridge, I 349
Brill Building, I 351
Broadway, I 356
Brooklyn Dodgers, I 362
Brooks, Louise, I 365
Brownie Cameras, I 371
Buck Rogers, I 377
Bungalow, I 387
Burlesque, I 388
Burma-Shave, I 390
Burroughs, Edgar Rice, I 396
Buster Brown, I 398
Butterbeans and Susie, I 400
Cadillac, I 406
Camping, I 417
Cancer, I 418
Cantor, Eddie, I 423
Capital Punishment, I 424
Capone, Al, I 425
Capra, Frank, I 428
Carnegie Hall, I 439
Carr, John Dickson, I 442
Carter Family, I 445
Caruso, Enrico, I 446
Caspar Milquetoast, I 450
Catalog Houses, I 455
Cather, Willa, I 459
Celebrity, I 463
Celebrity Caricature, I 465
Cemeteries, I 467
Central Park, I 468
Chanel, Coco, I 475
Chaplin, Charlie, I 475
Charlie Chan, I 478
Charlie McCarthy, I 478
Chautauqua Institution, I 481
Cheerleading, I 486
Chicago Bears, I 492
Chicago Jazz, I 493
Child Stars, I 498
Christie, Agatha, I 502
Christmas, I 503
Chrysler Building, I 507
Church Socials, I 509
Cigarettes, I 510
Circus, I 512
City of Angels, I 516
Civil War Reenactors, I 521
Cobb, Ty, I 538
Coca-Cola, I 540
Cocaine/Crack, I 542
Coffee, I 546
Cohan, George M., I 548

College Fads, I 553
College Football, I 555
Columbo, Russ, I 560
Comics, I 562
Communism, I 569
Community Media, I 570
Community Theatre, I 573
Condé Nast, I 577
Condoms, I 578
Confession Magazines, I 581
Consumerism, I 589
Cooper, Gary, I 597
Copland, Aaron, I 600
Cosmopolitan, I 610
Cotton Club, I 614
Coué, Emile, I 615
Country Music, I 617
Cowboy Look, I 622
Cox, Ida, I 624
Crawford, Joan, I 625
Creationism, I 627
Crisis, I 633
Crossword Puzzles, I 641
Cullen, Countee, I 643
Darrow, Clarence, I 660
Debs, Eugene V., I 679
Debutantes, I 680
DeMille, Cecil B., I 683
Dempsey, Jack, I 685
Denishawn, I 686
Department Stores, I 688
Derleth, August, I 692
Detective Fiction, I 693
Detroit Tigers, I 695
Dieting, I 706
Dime Stores/Woolworth's, I 717
Disability, I 721
Disney (Walt Disney Company), I 728
Dixieland, I 734
Dorsey, Jimmy, I 750
Douglas, Melvyn, I 753
Doyle, Arthur Conan, I 755
Dr. Jekyll and Mr. Hyde, I 756
Dr. Seuss, I 757
Drag, I 762
Dreiser, Theodore, I 768
Drug War, I 771
Du Bois, W. E. B., I 771
Duncan, Isadora, I 773
Durocher, Leo, I 777
Ebbets Field, II 5
Edison, Thomas Alva, II 13
Einstein, Albert, II 16
Electric Appliances, II 20
Electric Trains, II 22
Environmentalism, II 29
Equal Rights Amendment, II 32
Erector Sets, II 34
Escher, M. C., II 37
Etiquette Columns, II 44
Evangelism, II 46
Factor, Max, II 54
Fairbanks, Douglas, Jr., II 55
Fairbanks, Douglas, Sr., II 57
Fan Magazines, II 64
Fast Food, II 71
Father's Day, II 76
Faulkner, William, II 77
Fauset, Jessie Redmon, II 78
FBI (Federal Bureau of Investigation), II 80
Felix the Cat, II 83
Feminism, II 84
Fenway Park, II 87
Fetchit, Stepin, II 88
Fibber McGee and Molly, II 89
Field and Stream, II 92
Fields, W. C., II 95
Firearms, II 101
Fitzgerald, F. Scott, II 109
Flagpole Sitting, II 111
Flappers, II 112
Flea Markets, II 114

Florida Vacations, II 119
Folk Music, II 123
Ford, Henry, II 132
Ford, John, II 133
Ford Motor Company, II 135
Fourth of July Celebrations, II 146
Freak Shows, II 158
Freud, Sigmund, II 166
Frost, Robert, II 177
Fu Manchu, II 179
Fundamentalism, II 181
Gambling, II 188
Game Shows, II 191
Gangs, II 195
Garbo, Greta, II 199
Garvey, Marcus, II 205
Gas Stations, II 206
Gay and Lesbian Press, II 210
Gay Men, II 215
Gehrig, Lou, II 217
General, II 218
Gentlemen Prefer Blondes, II 223
Gernsback, Hugo, II 225
Ghettos, II 227
Girl Scouts, II 242
Gish, Dorothy, II 243
Gish, Lillian, II 244
Gold, Mike, II 255
Goldberg, Rube, II 256
Goldwyn, Samuel, II 260
Golf, II 261
Good Housekeeping, II 265
Goodman, Benny, II 270
Gospel Music, II 274
Gossip Columns, II 275
Graffiti, II 281
Graham, Martha, II 285
Grand Ole Opry, II 286
Grant, Cary, II 288
Greb, Harry, II 297
Greed, II 298
Green Bay Packers, II 300
Greenwich Village, II 304
Greeting Cards, II 306
Grey, Zane, II 309
Greyhound Buses, II 312
Grits, II 319
Hairstyles, II 340
Handy, W. C., II 352
Happy Hour, II 359
Hard-Boiled Detective Fiction, II 359
Hardy Boys, II 360
Harlem Globetrotters, II 364
Harlem Renaissance, II 365
Harley-Davidson, II 368
Harmonica Bands, II 370
Harper's, II 372
Hawkins, Coleman, II 376
Hearst, William Randolph, II 379
Hemingway, Ernest, II 386
Henderson, Fletcher, II 390
Hiking, II 405
Hirschfeld, Albert, II 412
Hitchcock, Alfred, II 414
Hockey, II 417
Hollywood, II 431
Hoover, J. Edgar, II 443
Hopalong Cassidy, II 444
Hopper, Edward, II 448
Hopscotch, II 449
Horror Movies, II 450
Hot Dogs, II 454
Houdini, Harry, II 456
Hughes, Howard, II 464
Hughes, Langston, II 465
IBM (International Business Machines), II 481
Ice Cream Cone, II 483
Indian, II 487
Indianapolis 500, II 490
Industrial Design, II 491
J. Walter Thompson, II 511
Jackson, "Shoeless" Joe, II 521

James, Elmore, II 525
Jazz, II 529
Jazz Singer, II 531
Jeans, II 532
Jell-O, II 537
Jessel, George, II 542
Johnson, Blind Willie, II 552
Johnson, Jack, II 554
Jolson, Al, II 559
Jones, Bobby, II 560
Judge, II 577
Juke Boxes, II 579
Juvenile Delinquency, II 583
Kaltenborn, Hans von, III 1
Kansas City Jazz, III 2
Kantor, MacKinlay, III 3
Karloff, Boris, III 4
Katzenjammer Kids, III 7
Keaton, Buster, III 10
Kentucky Derby, III 19
Kern, Jerome, III 21
Kewpie Dolls, III 22
Kitsch, III 43
Kiwanis, III 46
Kodak, III 51
Krazy Kat, III 62
Ku Klux Klan, III 64
Labor Unions, III 72
Laetrile, III 76
Lahr, Bert, III 76
Lang, Fritz, III 87
Lansky, Meyer, III 90
Lardner, Ring, III 90
Latin Jazz, III 97
Laurel and Hardy, III 100
La-Z-Boy Loungers, III 106
Leadbelly, III 108
Leisure Time, III 128
Leonard, Benny, III 133
Leopold and Loeb, III 138
Lesbianism, III 140
Lewis, Sinclair, III 155
Liberty, III 157
Life, III 160
Lindbergh, Charles, III 166
Lionel Trains, III 170
Lippmann, Walter, III 170
Lipstick, III 171
Little Black Dress, III 173
Little Blue Books, III 173
Little Orphan Annie, III 177
Locke, Alain, III 182
Lombardo, Guy, III 187
Long, Huey, III 191
Loos, Anita, III 194
Louisville Slugger, III 201
Lovecraft, H. P., III 205
Lubitsch, Ernst, III 209
Luce, Henry, III 210
Luciano, Lucky, III 212
Lugosi, Bela, III 213
Lynching, III 217
Mabley, Moms, III 223
Macfadden, Bernarr, III 226
Macon, Uncle Dave, III 229
Macy's, III 229
Mafia/Organized Crime, III 237
Mall, III 247
Maltese Falcon, III 249
Marching Bands, III 267
Mardi Gras, III 269
Marie, Rose, III 272
Marijuana, III 272
Marlboro Man, III 274
Martini, III 282
Marx Brothers, III 287
Marx, Groucho, III 288
Mass Market Magazine Revolution, III 299
Masses, III 302
Mayer, Louis B., III 309
McCall's Magazine, III 313
McCay, Winsor, III 317

McClure's, III 318
McCrea, Joel, III 319
McKay, Claude, III 327
McPherson, Aimee Semple, III 331
Medicine Shows, III 339
Mencken, H. L., III 342
Metropolis, III 347
Metropolitan Museum of Art, III 347
MGM (Metro-Goldwyn-Mayer), III 347
Middletown, III 355
Millay, Edna St. Vincent, III 363
Milton Bradley, III 369
Miss America Pageant, III 374
Mix, Tom, III 383
Model T, III 386
Modern Dance, III 388
Modernism, III 390
Morton, Jelly Roll, III 416
Mother's Day, III 417
Mount Rushmore, III 423
Movie Palaces, III 426
Movie Stars, III 428
Mr. Dooley, III 430
Munsey's Magazine, III 442
Muscular Christianity, III 456
Musical, III 458
Mutt & Jeff, III 462
Naismith, James, III 470
Nancy Drew, III 473
Nation, III 476
National Collegiate Athletic Association
   (NCAA), III 479
National Enquirer, III 480
National Football League (NFL), III 482
National Hockey League (NHL), III 485
National Parks, III 489
Neckties, III 495
Negro Leagues, III 497
Networks, III 503
New Republic, III 514
New York Times, III 518
New York Yankees, III 520
New Yorker, III 522
Niagara Falls, III 528
Noloesca, La Chata, III 540
O'Keeffe, Georgia, III 552
Olivier, Laurence, III 556
Olympics, III 558
O'Neill, Eugene, III 569
Opportunity, III 570
Original Dixieland Jass (Jazz) Band, III 573
Ouija Boards, III 576
Our Gang, III 576
Outline of History, III 581
Oxford Bags, III 584
Paley, William S., IV 6
Pants for Women, IV 7
Parades, IV 12
Parker, Dorothy, IV 14
Parrish, Maxfield, IV 16
Peep Shows, IV 30
Pets, IV 44
Phonograph, IV 52
Photoplay, IV 53
Picasso, Pablo, IV 54
Pickford, Mary, IV 55
Pin-Up, IV 58
Pizza, IV 62
Plastic, IV 64
Political Bosses, IV 77
Pop Music, IV 83
Pope, IV 86
Popeye, IV 87
Popsicles, IV 88
Popular Psychology, IV 90
Pornography, IV 92
Porter, Cole, IV 95
Postcards, IV 96
Professional Football, IV 116
Prohibition, IV 119
Prom, IV 120
Protest Groups, IV 124

Public Libraries, IV 133
Queen, Ellery, IV 148
Race Music, IV 155
Race Riots, IV 156
Radio, IV 157
Radio Drama, IV 160
Raggedy Ann and Raggedy Andy, IV 163
Rainey, Gertrude "Ma", IV 168
Rains, Claude, IV 168
Reader's Digest, IV 177
Red Scare, IV 188
Religious Right, IV 197
Renoir, Jean, IV 204
Ringling Bros., Barnum & Bailey Circus, IV 212
Ripley's Believe It Or Not, IV 215
Rivera, Diego, IV 216
Robeson, Paul, IV 227
Rockne, Knute, IV 243
Rockwell, Norman, IV 244
Rodeo, IV 252
Rodgers and Hart, IV 256
Rodgers, Jimmie, IV 258
Rogers, Will, IV 263
Roller Coasters, IV 265
Romance Novels, IV 270
Rose Bowl, IV 275
Route 66, IV 284
Runyon, Damon, IV 289
Ruth, Babe, IV 293
RV, IV 295
Saks Fifth Avenue, IV 302
Sandburg, Carl, IV 306
Sandow, Eugen, IV 309
Saratoga Springs, IV 312
Sarnoff, David, IV 312
Saturday Evening Post, IV 315
Savoy Ballroom, IV 322
Scientific American, IV 334
Scopes Monkey Trial, IV 335
Scribner's, IV 344
Sears Roebuck Catalogue, IV 346
Selznick, David O., IV 356
Sennett, Mack, IV 357
Sex Scandals, IV 367
Sex Symbol, IV 369
Shawn, Ted, IV 381
Show Boat, IV 389
Silent Movies, IV 393
Skating, IV 429
Skyscrapers, IV 432
Slang, IV 434
Smith, Bessie, IV 439
Soccer, IV 449
Social Dancing, IV 450
Soda Fountains, IV 452
Soldier Field, IV 453
Sousa, John Philip, IV 463
Sporting News, IV 483
Sports Hero, IV 484
St. Denis, Ruth, IV 494
Stagg, Amos Alonzo, IV 499
Standardized Testing, IV 502
Stand-up Comedy, IV 504
Star System, IV 507
State Fairs, IV 518
Steamboat Willie, IV 521
Steffens, Lincoln, IV 521
Stengel, Casey, IV 526
Stereoscopes, IV 528
Stetson Hat, IV 532
Stickball, IV 534
Stock Market Crashes, IV 539
Stokowski, Leopold, IV 541
Stratemeyer, Edward, IV 548
Stratton-Porter, Gene, IV 550
Street and Smith, IV 553
Strip Joints/Striptease, IV 557
Studio System, IV 565
Sturges, Preston, IV 566
Suicide, IV 569
Summer Camp, IV 573
Sunday, Billy, IV 578

Sunday Driving, IV 578
Swimming Pools, IV 590
Tabloids, IV 597
Tanning, IV 603
Tap Dancing, IV 605
Tarbell, Ida, IV 606
Tarkington, Booth, IV 607
Tarzan, IV 608
Teddy Bears, IV 616
Telephone, IV 623
Ten Commandments, IV 634
Tennis, IV 635
Tennis Shoes/Sneakers, IV 637
Thalberg, Irving G., IV 640
Thanksgiving, IV 640
Thorpe, Jim, IV 649
Thurber, James, IV 654
Tiffany & Company, IV 655
Tijuana Bibles, IV 656
Time, IV 657
Times Square, IV 659
Toga Parties, IV 669
Tolkien, J. R. R., IV 671
Tormé, Mel, IV 683
Town Meetings, IV 684
Toys, IV 685
Tramps, IV 691
Traveling Carnivals, IV 692
True Detective, IV 699
True Story Magazine, IV 699
Twenties, IV 710
23 Skidoo, IV 712
United Artists, V 8
U.S. One, V 11
Valentine's Day, V 16
Valentino, Rudolph, V 17
Vallee, Rudy, V 21
Vampires, V 22
Van Dine, S. S., V 24
Van Vechten, Carl, V 26
Vanity Fair, V 28
Vardon, Harry, V 30
Variety, V 31
Vaudeville, V 33
Velveeta Cheese, V 39
Vidor, King, V 48
Vitamins, V 52
Vogue, V 53
Walker, Aaron "T-Bone", V 59
Wall Street Journal, V 67
Wallace, Sippie, V 68
War Movies, V 75
Washington Post, V 83
Waters, Ethel, V 86
Wayne, John, V 91
Wedding Dress, V 100
Weird Tales, V 103
Weissmuller, Johnny, V 104
Western, V 118
Wharton, Edith, V 121
White Castle, V 127
White, E. B., V 127
White Flight, V 128
White Supremacists, V 129
Whiteman, Paul, V 130
Wilder, Thornton, V 138
Williams, Bert, V 140
Wimbledon, V 150
Winchell, Walter, V 151
Winnie-the-Pooh, V 155
Winnie Winkle the Breadwinner, V 156
Wire Services, V 158
Wister, Owen, V 161
Wodehouse, P. G., V 166
Wong, Anna May, V 172
World Series, V 182
World's Fairs, V 194
Wrigley Field, V 197
Wuthering Heights, V 198
WWJD? (What Would Jesus Do?), V 198
Wyeth, N. C., V 200
Yankee Stadium, V 208

Yellowstone National Park, V 213
Young, Cy, V 216
Young, Loretta, V 217
Youngman, Henny, V 219
Youth's Companion, V 222
Yo-Yo, V 223
Ziegfeld Follies, V 227
Zoos, V 230
Zorro, V 234

1930-1939
A&R Men/Women, I 1
Abbott and Costello, I 5
Abstract Expressionism, I 11
Academy Awards, I 12
Adams, Ansel, I 17
Addams Family, I 18
Addams, Jane, I 17
Adidas, I 20
Advertising, I 23
Advice Columns, I 26
African American Press, I 32
Agents, I 34
Air Travel, I 38
Alka Seltzer, I 49
All Quiet on the Western Front, I 52
Amazing Stories, I 64
American Gothic, I 69
American Mercury, I 72
American Museum of Natural History, I 72
Amos 'n' Andy Show, I 72
Amsterdam, Morey, I 74
Amusement Parks, I 77
Anderson, Marian, I 81
Andrews Sisters, I 84
Androgyny, I 85
Andy Hardy, I 87
Animated Films, I 90
Apollo Theatre, I 104
Arbuckle, Fatty, I 107
Arden, Elizabeth, I 109
Argosy, I 109
Arizona Highways, I 110
Armstrong, Henry, I 113
Armstrong, Louis, I 114
Arthurian Legend, I 120
Asimov, Isaac, I 125
Astaire, Fred, and Ginger Rogers, I 127
Astounding Science Fiction, I 129
Astrology, I 129
AT&T, I 130
Atkins, Chet, I 132
Atlantic City, I 133
Atlas, Charles, I 135
Aunt Jemima, I 137
Automobile, I 137
Autry, Gene, I 142
Avery, Tex, I 145
"B" movies, I 149
Babar, I 151
Baker, Josephine, I 158
Balanchine, George, I 161
Ballet, I 165
Barbecue, I 168
Barber, Red, I 169
Barbershop Quartets, I 169
Barrymore, John, I 178
Barton, Bruce, I 179
Baseball, I 180
Baseball Cards, I 183
Basie, Count, I 184
Basketball, I 186
Baum, L. Frank, I 191
Beach, Rex, I 197
Beau Geste, I 207
Beauty Queens, I 207
Beer, I 210
Benchley, Robert, I 219
Ben-Hur, I 219
Benny, Jack, I 222
Bergen, Edgar, I 225
Bergman, Ingmar, I 225
Bergman, Ingrid, I 226

Berkeley, Busby, I 227
Berle, Milton, I 228
Berlin, Irving, I 230
Bestsellers, I 236
Better Homes and Gardens, I 238
Betty Boop, I 239
Bicycling, I 245
Big Apple, I 246
Big Bands, I 247
Big Little Books, I 249
Big Sleep, I 250
Bigfoot, I 251
Billboards, I 253
Birthing Practices, I 260
Black Mask, I 263
Blackface Minstrelsy, I 270
Blanc, Mel, I 276
Blockbusters, I 280
Blondie (comic strip), I 283
Bluegrass, I 287
Blues, I 290
Board Games, I 297
Bobbsey Twins, I 300
Bobby Socks, I 301
Bodybuilding, I 305
Bogart, Humphrey, I 308
Bonnie and Clyde, I 316
Book-of-the-Month Club, I 318
Borge, Victor, I 320
Borscht Belt, I 321
Boston Garden, I 323
Boston Marathon, I 323
Bow, Clara, I 326
Bowling, I 328
Boxing, I 330
Boy Scouts of America, I 333
Bra, I 335
Bradbury, Ray, I 337
Bridge, I 349
Brill Building, I 351
Bringing Up Baby, I 352
Broadway, I 356
Brooklyn Dodgers, I 362
Brown, Les, I 370
Brownie Cameras, I 371
Bryant, Paul ''Bear'', I 374
Buck, Pearl S., I 375
Buck Rogers, I 377
Budweiser, I 380
Burlesque, I 388
Burma-Shave, I 390
Burns, George, and Gracie Allen, I 392
Burroughs, Edgar Rice, I 396
Butterbeans and Susie, I 400
Cagney, James, I 409
Caldwell, Erskine, I 412
Calloway, Cab, I 412
Camping, I 417
Cancer, I 418
Caniff, Milton, I 421
Canova, Judy, I 421
Cantor, Eddie, I 423
Capital Punishment, I 424
Capra, Frank, I 428
Carmichael, Hoagy, I 436
Carnegie, Dale, I 437
Carnegie Hall, I 439
Carr, John Dickson, I 442
Carter Family, I 445
Catalog Houses, I 455
Cather, Willa, I 459
Celebrity, I 463
Celebrity Caricature, I 465
Cemeteries, I 467
Central Park, I 468
Century of Progress International Exposition
   (Chicago, 1933), I 471
Chandler, Raymond, I 473
Chandu the Magician, I 475
Chanel, Coco, I 475
Chaplin, Charlie, I 475
Charlie Chan, I 478

Charlie McCarthy, I 478
Charm Bracelets, I 480
Cheerleading, I 486
Chicago Bears, I 492
Child Stars, I 498
Christie, Agatha, I 502
Christmas, I 503
Chrysler Building, I 507
Church Socials, I 509
Cigarettes, I 510
Circus, I 512
City Lights, I 515
City of Angels, I 516
Civil War Reenactors, I 521
Clairol Hair Coloring, I 523
Cobb, Ty, I 538
Coca-Cola, I 540
Cocaine/Crack, I 542
Coffee, I 546
Colbert, Claudette, I 548
College Fads, I 553
College Football, I 555
Columbo, Russ, I 560
Comic Books, I 560
Comics, I 562
Communism, I 569
Community Media, I 570
Community Theatre, I 573
Condé Nast, I 577
Condoms, I 578
Confession Magazines, I 581
Coniff, Ray, I 583
Consumer Reports, I 587
Consumerism, I 589
Cooper, Gary, I 597
Cooperstown, New York, I 598
Copland, Aaron, I 600
Cosmopolitan, I 610
Cotton Club, I 614
Coughlin, Father Charles E., I 616
Country Music, I 617
Cowboy Look, I 622
Cox, Ida, I 624
Crawford, Joan, I 625
Creationism, I 627
Crisis, I 633
Crosby, Bing, I 638
Crossword Puzzles, I 641
Cukor, George, I 643
Cult Films, I 643
Darrow, Clarence, I 660
Davis, Bette, I 661
DC Comics, I 671
Debutantes, I 680
Del Río, Dolores, I 683
DeMille, Cecil B., I 683
Dempsey, Jack, I 685
Denishawn, I 686
Department Stores, I 688
Derleth, August, I 692
Detective Fiction, I 693
Detroit Tigers, I 695
Dick and Jane Readers, I 700
Dick Tracy, I 702
Didrikson, Babe, I 704
Dieting, I 706
Dietrich, Marlene, I 708
Dillinger, John, I 713
DiMaggio, Joe, I 715
Dime Stores/Woolworth's, I 717
Diners, I 719
Dionne Quintuplets, I 720
Disability, I 721
Disney (Walt Disney Company), I 728
Doc Savage, I 738
Do-It-Yourself Improvement, I 742
Dorsey, Jimmy, I 750
Dorsey, Tommy, I 751
Double Indemnity, I 751
Douglas, Melvyn, I 753
Downs, Hugh, I 754
Dr. Jekyll and Mr. Hyde, I 756

Dr. Kildare, I 756
Dr. Seuss, I 757
Dracula, I 760
Drag, I 762
Dragon Lady, I 767
Drive-In Theater, I 769
Drug War, I 771
Du Bois, W. E. B., I 771
Duck Soup, I 773
Dunne, Irene, I 776
Durbin, Deanna, I 776
Durocher, Leo, I 777
Ebbets Field, II 5
Eckstine, Billy, II 10
Eddy, Nelson, II 13
Einstein, Albert, II 16
Eisner, Will, II 18
Electric Appliances, II 20
Electric Trains, II 22
Ellington, Duke, II 23
Empire State Building, II 28
Environmentalism, II 29
Erector Sets, II 34
Escher, M. C., II 37
Esquire, II 40
Etiquette Columns, II 44
Factor, Max, II 54
Fadiman, Clifton, II 55
Fairbanks, Douglas, Jr., II 55
Fairbanks, Douglas, Sr., II 57
Family Circle, II 59
Fan Magazines, II 64
Fast Food, II 71
Father Divine, II 74
Father's Day, II 76
Faulkner, William, II 77
Fauset, Jessie Redmon, II 78
FBI (Federal Bureau of Investigation), II 80
Felix the Cat, II 83
Feminism, II 84
Fenway Park, II 87
Fetchit, Stepin, II 88
Fibber McGee and Molly, II 89
Field and Stream, II 92
Fields, W. C., II 95
Firearms, II 101
Fisher-Price Toys, II 106
Fitzgerald, Ella, II 107
Fitzgerald, F. Scott, II 109
Flash Gordon, II 113
Flea Markets, II 114
Florida Vacations, II 119
Flynn, Errol, II 121
Folk Music, II 123
Fonda, Henry, II 127
Ford, John, II 133
Ford Motor Company, II 135
Fortune, II 142
42nd Street, II 142
Fourth of July Celebrations, II 146
Frankenstein, II 152
Freak Shows, II 158
Freaks, II 159
Freud, Sigmund, II 166
Frost, Robert, II 177
Frozen Entrées, II 178
Fu Manchu, II 179
Fuller, Buckminster, II 180
Fundamentalism, II 181
Gable, Clark, II 187
Gambling, II 188
Game Shows, II 191
Gangs, II 195
Garbo, Greta, II 199
Garfield, John, II 201
Garland, Judy, II 202
Garvey, Marcus, II 205
Gas Stations, II 206
Gay and Lesbian Press, II 210
Gay Men, II 215
Gehrig, Lou, II 217
General Motors, II 220

Gernsback, Hugo, II 225
Ghettos, II 227
Gillespie, Dizzy, II 236
Girl Scouts, II 242
Gish, Dorothy, II 243
Gish, Lillian, II 244
Gold, Mike, II 255
Goldberg, Rube, II 256
Golden Gate Bridge, II 259
Goldwyn, Samuel, II 260
Golf, II 261
Gone with the Wind, II 263
Good Housekeeping, II 265
Goodman, Benny, II 270
Gospel Music, II 274
Gossip Columns, II 275
Graffiti, II 281
Graham, Martha, II 285
Grand Ole Opry, II 286
Grant, Cary, II 288
Grapes of Wrath, II 290
Great Depression, II 295
Green Bay Packers, II 300
Greenberg, Hank, II 302
Greenwich Village, II 304
Greeting Cards, II 306
Grey, Zane, II 309
Greyhound Buses, II 312
Grimek, John, II 316
Grits, II 319
Guiding Light, II 323
Guthrie, Woody, II 328
Hairstyles, II 340
Halas, George "Papa Bear", II 342
Hammett, Dashiell, II 349
Handy, W. C., II 352
Hanna-Barbera, II 355
Hard-Boiled Detective Fiction, II 359
Hardy Boys, II 360
Harlem Globetrotters, II 364
Harley-Davidson, II 368
Harlow, Jean, II 370
Harmonica Bands, II 370
Harper's, II 372
Hawkins, Coleman, II 376
Hawks, Howard, II 376
Hayworth, Rita, II 377
Hearst, William Randolph, II 379
Hellman, Lillian, II 384
Hemingway, Ernest, II 386
Hemlines, II 390
Henderson, Fletcher, II 390
Henry Aldrich, II 392
Hep Cats, II 393
Hepburn, Katharine, II 394
Herman, Woody, II 398
Highway System, II 402
Hiking, II 405
Hindenburg, II 409
Hirschfeld, Albert, II 412
Hiss, Alger, II 413
Hitchcock, Alfred, II 414
Hockey, II 417
Holden, William, II 426
Holiday, Billie, II 427
Holliday, Judy, II 429
Hollywood, II 431
Hoover Dam, II 442
Hoover, J. Edgar, II 443
Hopalong Cassidy, II 444
Hope, Bob, II 446
Hopper, Edward, II 448
Hopscotch, II 449
Horne, Lena, II 449
Horror Movies, II 450
Hot Dogs, II 454
Hughes, Howard, II 464
Hughes, Langston, II 465
Hurston, Zora Neale, II 469
Hutton, Ina Ray, II 472
I Love a Mystery, II 476
IBM (International Business Machines), II 481

Ice Cream Cone, II 483
Indian, II 487
Indianapolis 500, II 490
Industrial Design, II 491
It Happened One Night, II 504
Ivy League, II 509
J. Walter Thompson, II 511
Jack Armstrong, II 512
Jackson, Mahalia, II 515
James, Elmore, II 525
James, Harry, II 525
Jazz, II 529
Jeans, II 532
Jell-O, II 537
Jessel, George, II 542
Johnson, Blind Willie, II 552
Johnson, Robert, II 557
Jolson, Al, II 559
Jones, Bobby, II 560
Joy of Cooking, II 572
Judge, II 577
Judson, Arthur, II 578
Judy Bolton, II 578
Juke Boxes, II 579
Juvenile Delinquency, II 583
Kaltenborn, Hans von, III 1
Kansas City Jazz, III 2
Kantor, MacKinlay, III 3
Karloff, Boris, III 4
Katzenjammer Kids, III 7
Keaton, Buster, III 10
Kentucky Derby, III 19
Kern, Jerome, III 21
Kewpie Dolls, III 22
Key West, III 22
King Kong, III 30
Kitsch, III 43
Kiwanis, III 46
Kodak, III 51
Krazy Kat, III 62
Ku Klux Klan, III 64
Labor Unions, III 72
Ladd, Alan, III 75
Lahr, Bert, III 76
Lake, Veronica, III 79
Lamarr, Hedy, III 82
Lamour, Dorothy, III 83
Lang, Fritz, III 87
Lansky, Meyer, III 90
Las Vegas, III 92
Lassie, III 95
Latin Jazz, III 97
Laurel and Hardy, III 100
La-Z-Boy Loungers, III 106
Leadbelly, III 108
Lee, Gypsy Rose, III 119
Legos, III 125
Leisure Time, III 128
Lesbianism, III 140
Let Us Now Praise Famous Men, III 142
Let's Pretend, III 143
Levin, Meyer, III 145
Liberty, III 157
Life, III 160
Li'l Abner, III 163
Lincoln Center for the Performing Arts, III 165
Lindbergh, Charles, III 166
Linkletter, Art, III 168
Lionel Trains, III 170
Lippmann, Walter, III 170
Lipstick, III 171
Little Blue Books, III 173
Little League, III 174
Little Magazines, III 176
Little Orphan Annie, III 177
Loafers, III 182
Locke, Alain, III 182
Lombard, Carole, III 184
Lombardo, Guy, III 187
Lone Ranger, III 189
Long, Huey, III 191
Loos, Anita, III 194

Lorre, Peter, III 195
Louis, Joe, III 200
Louisville Slugger, III 201
Lovecraft, H. P., III 205
Loy, Myrna, III 207
LSD, III 207
Lubitsch, Ernst, III 209
Luce, Henry, III 210
Luciano, Lucky, III 212
Lugosi, Bela, III 213
Lynching, III 217
Ma Perkins, III 223
Mabley, Moms, III 223
MacDonald, Jeanette, III 224
Macfadden, Bernarr, III 226
MacMurray, Fred, III 228
Macon, Uncle Dave, III 229
Mafia/Organized Crime, III 237
Mah-Jongg, III 242
Mall, III 247
Maltese Falcon, III 249
Marching Bands, III 267
Mardi Gras, III 269
Marie, Rose, III 272
Marijuana, III 272
Marlboro Man, III 274
Martin, Freddy, III 281
Martini, III 282
Marvel Comics, III 285
Marx Brothers, III 287
Marx, Groucho, III 288
Mary Poppins, III 291
Mary Worth, III 294
Mass Market Magazine Revolution, III 299
Masses, III 302
Masters Golf Tournament, III 305
Mayer, Louis B., III 309
McCall's Magazine, III 313
McCay, Winsor, III 317
McCoy, Horace, III 319
McCrea, Joel, III 319
McDaniel, Hattie, III 320
McKay, Claude, III 327
McPherson, Aimee Semple, III 331
McQueen, Butterfly, III 332
Media Feeding Frenzies, III 337
Medicine Shows, III 339
Mencken, H. L., III 342
Mendoza, Lydia, III 344
Metropolitan Museum of Art, III 347
MGM (Metro-Goldwyn-Mayer), III 347
Middletown, III 355
Miller, Arthur, III 363
Miller, Glenn, III 364
Miller, Henry, III 367
Milton Bradley, III 369
Miss America Pageant, III 374
Mitchell, Margaret, III 380
Mix, Tom, III 383
Modern Dance, III 388
Modern Times, III 389
Modernism, III 390
Monopoly, III 396
Montana, Patsy, III 403
Morton, Jelly Roll, III 416
Mother's Day, III 417
Mount Rushmore, III 423
Movie Palaces, III 426
Movie Stars, III 428
Mr. Dooley, III 430
Mr. Smith Goes to Washington, III 432
Mummy, III 441
Muni, Paul, III 442
Murray, Arthur, III 448
Murrow, Edward R., III 451
Muscle Beach, III 453
Muscular Christianity, III 456
Musical, III 458
Mutiny on the Bounty, III 461
Mutt & Jeff, III 462
Muzak, III 463
Naismith, James, III 470

Nancy Drew, III 473
Nation, III 476
National Collegiate Athletic Association
    (NCAA), III 479
National Enquirer, III 480
National Football League (NFL), III 482
National Hockey League (NHL), III 485
National Parks, III 489
Neckties, III 495
Negro Leagues, III 497
Networks, III 503
New Deal, III 508
New Republic, III 514
New York Times, III 518
New York Yankees, III 520
New Yorker, III 522
Newsweek, III 527
Niagara Falls, III 528
Noloesca, La Chata, III 540
Nylon, III 544
O'Keeffe, Georgia, III 552
Olivier, Laurence, III 556
Olsen, Tillie, III 558
Olympics, III 558
One Man's Family, III 567
O'Neill, Eugene, III 569
Opportunity, III 570
Ouija Boards, III 576
Our Gang, III 576
Outline of History, III 581
Owens, Jesse, III 583
Oxford Bags, III 584
Paige, Satchel, IV 5
Paley, William S., IV 6
Pants for Women, IV 7
Paperbacks, IV 9
Parades, IV 12
Parker Brothers, IV 13
Parker, Dorothy, IV 14
Parrish, Maxfield, IV 16
Paul, Les, IV 20
Peep Shows, IV 30
Pepsi-Cola, IV 36
Perry Mason, IV 41
Pets, IV 44
Phillips, Irna, IV 51
Phonograph, IV 52
Photoplay, IV 53
Picasso, Pablo, IV 54
Pin-Up, IV 58
Pittsburgh Steelers, IV 61
Pizza, IV 62
Plastic, IV 64
Polio, IV 76
Political Bosses, IV 77
Pop Music, IV 83
Pope, IV 86
Popeye, IV 87
Popsicles, IV 88
Popular Mechanics, IV 89
Popular Psychology, IV 90
Pornography, IV 92
Porter, Cole, IV 95
Postcards, IV 96
Postman Always Rings Twice, IV 97
Powell, Dick, IV 102
Powell, William, IV 102
Professional Football, IV 116
Prohibition, IV 119
Prom, IV 120
Protest Groups, IV 124
Public Libraries, IV 133
Pulp Magazines, IV 139
Queen, Ellery, IV 148
Race Music, IV 155
Radio, IV 157
Radio Drama, IV 160
Raft, George, IV 162
Raggedy Ann and Raggedy Andy, IV 163
Rainey, Gertrude "Ma", IV 168
Rains, Claude, IV 168
Rand, Sally, IV 173

Reader's Digest, IV 177
Reagan, Ronald, IV 179
Religious Right, IV 197
Renoir, Jean, IV 204
Rice, Grantland, IV 209
Riggs, Bobby, IV 211
Ripley's Believe It Or Not, IV 215
Rivera, Diego, IV 216
Robeson, Kenneth, IV 227
Robeson, Paul, IV 227
Robinson, Edward G., IV 229
Rockettes, IV 241
Rockne, Knute, IV 243
Rockwell, Norman, IV 244
Rodeo, IV 252
Rodgers and Hart, IV 256
Rodgers, Jimmie, IV 258
Rogers, Roy, IV 262
Rogers, Will, IV 263
Roller Coasters, IV 265
Roller Derby, IV 266
Romance Novels, IV 270
Romero, Cesar, IV 273
Rose Bowl, IV 275
Route 66, IV 284
Rudolph the Red-Nosed Reindeer, IV 287
Runyon, Damon, IV 289
Russell, Rosalind, IV 293
Ruth, Babe, IV 293
RV, IV 295
Saks Fifth Avenue, IV 302
Sandburg, Carl, IV 306
Saratoga Springs, IV 312
Sarnoff, David, IV 312
Sarong, IV 313
Saturday Evening Post, IV 315
Savoy Ballroom, IV 322
Science Fiction Publishing, IV 330
Scientific American, IV 334
Scott, Randolph, IV 339
Screwball Comedies, IV 342
Scribner's, IV 344
Sears Roebuck Catalogue, IV 346
Selznick, David O., IV 356
Sennett, Mack, IV 357
Sex Scandals, IV 367
Sex Symbol, IV 369
Shadow, IV 375
Shaw, Artie, IV 381
Shawn, Ted, IV 381
Shirer, William L., IV 384
Shock Radio, IV 386
Show Boat, IV 389
Sinatra, Frank, IV 409
Sinclair, Upton, IV 414
Singer, Isaac Bashevis, IV 414
Skating, IV 429
Skelton, Red, IV 431
Skyscrapers, IV 432
Slang, IV 434
Smith, Bessie, IV 439
Smith, Kate, IV 439
Snow White and the Seven Dwarfs, IV 445
Soap Operas, IV 446
Soccer, IV 449
Social Dancing, IV 450
Soda Fountains, IV 452
Sousa, John Philip, IV 463
Sporting News, IV 483
Sports Hero, IV 484
St. Denis, Ruth, IV 494
Stagecoach, IV 497
Stagg, Amos Alonzo, IV 499
Standardized Testing, IV 502
Stand-up Comedy, IV 504
Stanwyck, Barbara, IV 506
Star System, IV 507
State Fairs, IV 518
Steamboat Willie, IV 521
Steinbeck, John, IV 522
Stengel, Casey, IV 526
Stetson Hat, IV 532

Stewart, Jimmy, IV 532
Stickball, IV 534
Stock-Car Racing, IV 537
Stock Market Crashes, IV 539
Stokowski, Leopold, IV 541
Stone, Irving, IV 542
Stout, Rex, IV 546
Stratemeyer, Edward, IV 548
Street and Smith, IV 553
Strip Joints/Striptease, IV 557
Studio System, IV 565
Sturges, Preston, IV 566
Suicide, IV 569
Summer Camp, IV 573
Sunday, Billy, IV 578
Superman, IV 581
Swimming Pools, IV 590
Swing Dancing, IV 592
Tabloids, IV 597
Tanning, IV 603
Tap Dancing, IV 605
Tarbell, Ida, IV 606
Tarkington, Booth, IV 607
Tarzan, IV 608
Taylor, Robert, IV 615
Teddy Bears, IV 616
Teen Idols, IV 617
Tejano Music, IV 623
Telephone, IV 623
Television, IV 626
Temple, Shirley, IV 631
Tennis, IV 635
Tennis Shoes/Sneakers, IV 637
Terry and the Pirates, IV 640
Thalberg, Irving G., IV 640
Thanksgiving, IV 640
Thomas, Lowell, IV 645
Thorpe, Jim, IV 649
Three Stooges, IV 651
Thurber, James, IV 654
Tiffany & Company, IV 655
Tijuana Bibles, IV 656
Time, IV 657
Times Square, IV 659
To Kill a Mockingbird, IV 663
Toga Parties, IV 669
Tolkien, J. R. R., IV 671
Tone, Franchot, IV 676
Tormé, Mel, IV 683
Town Meetings, IV 684
Toys, IV 685
Tracy, Spencer, IV 687
Tramps, IV 691
Traveling Carnivals, IV 692
Trevor, Claire, IV 697
Trout, Robert, IV 698
True Detective, IV 699
Tupperware, IV 700
TV Dinners, IV 706
Twelve-Step Programs, IV 708
United Artists, V 8
U.S. One, V 11
Valentine's Day, V 16
Vallee, Rudy, V 21
Vampires, V 22
Van Dine, S. S., V 24
Van Vechten, Carl, V 26
Vanity Fair, V 28
Varga Girl, V 30
Variety, V 31
Velez, Lupe, V 39
Velveeta Cheese, V 39
Vidor, King, V 48
Vitamins, V 52
Vogue, V 53
Von Sternberg, Josef, V 55
Wagner, Honus, V 59
Walker, Aaron "T-Bone", V 59
Wall Drug, V 66
Wall Street Journal, V 67
Wallace, Sippie, V 68
War Movies, V 75

War of the Worlds, V 79
Washington Post, V 83
Waters, Ethel, V 86
Wayne, John, V 91
Webb, Chick, V 98
Wedding Dress, V 100
Weekend, V 101
Weird Tales, V 103
Weissmuller, Johnny, V 104
Welles, Orson, V 108
Wertham, Fredric, V 111
West, Mae, V 115
Western, V 118
Wharton, Edith, V 121
White Castle, V 127
White, E. B., V 127
White Flight, V 128
White Supremacists, V 129
Whiteman, Paul, V 130
Wilder, Billy, V 136
Wilder, Laura Ingalls, V 136
Wilder, Thornton, V 138
Wills, Bob, and His Texas Playboys, V 148
Wimbledon, V 150
Winchell, Walter, V 151
Windy City, V 152
Winnie-the-Pooh, V 155
Winnie Winkle the Breadwinner, V 156
Wire Services, V 158
Wizard of Oz, V 162
Wodehouse, P. G., V 166
Wolfman, V 167
Woman's Day, V 169
Wong, Anna May, V 172
Works Progress Administration (WPA)
    Murals, V 179
World Cup, V 181
World Series, V 182
World's Fairs, V 194
Wray, Fay, V 196
Wright, Richard, V 196
Wrigley Field, V 197
Wuthering Heights, V 198
WWJD? (What Would Jesus Do?), V 198
Wyeth, Andrew, V 199
Wyeth, N. C., V 200
Yankee Stadium, V 208
Yellowstone National Park, V 213
Young, Cy, V 216
Young, Loretta, V 217
Young, Robert, V 218
Youngman, Henny, V 219
Your Hit Parade, V 220
Ziegfeld Follies, V 227
Zines, V 228
Zoos, V 230
Zoot Suit, V 233
Zorro, V 234

1940-1949

A&R Men/Women, I 1
AARP (American Association for Retired
    Persons), I 3
Abbott and Costello, I 5
Abortion, I 9
Abstract Expressionism, I 11
Academy Awards, I 12
Ace, Johnny, I 15
Adams, Ansel, I 17
Adderley, Cannonball, I 18
Adventures of Ozzie and Harriet, I 21
Advertising, I 23
Advice Columns, I 26
African American Press, I 32
African Queen, I 33
Agents, I 34
Air Travel, I 38
Alka Seltzer, I 49
Amazing Stories, I 64
American Museum of Natural History, I 72
Amos 'n' Andy Show, I 72
Amsterdam, Morey, I 74
Amusement Parks, I 77

Anderson, Marian, I 81
Andrews Sisters, I 84
Andy Hardy, I 87
Animated Films, I 90
Anne Frank: The Diary of a Young Girl, I 95
Annie Get Your Gun, I 96
Apollo Theatre, I 104
Archie Comics, I 108
Arden, Elizabeth, I 109
Argosy, I 109
Arizona Highways, I 110
Armed Forces Radio Service, I 112
Armstrong, Henry, I 113
Armstrong, Louis, I 114
Arnaz, Desi, I 116
Arthurian Legend, I 120
Asimov, Isaac, I 125
Astaire, Fred, and Ginger Rogers, I 127
Astounding Science Fiction, I 129
Astrology, I 129
AT&T, I 130
Athletic Model Guild, I 132
Atkins, Chet, I 132
Atlantic City, I 133
Atlantic Monthly, I 134
Atlantic Records, I 135
Atlas, Charles, I 135
Aunt Jemima, I 137
Automobile, I 137
Autry, Gene, I 142
Avedon, Richard, I 144
Avery, Tex, I 145
''B'' movies, I 149
Babar, I 151
Baby Boomers, I 151
Baker, Josephine, I 158
Balanchine, George, I 161
Ballet, I 165
Barbecue, I 168
Barber, Red, I 169
Barbershop Quartets, I 169
Barrymore, John, I 178
Baseball, I 180
Baseball Cards, I 183
Basie, Count, I 184
Basketball, I 186
Batman, I 189
Beat Generation, I 201
Beauty Queens, I 207
Beer, I 210
Bell Telephone Hour, I 216
Benny, Jack, I 222
Bergen, Edgar, I 225
Bergman, Ingmar, I 225
Bergman, Ingrid, I 226
Berkeley, Busby, I 227
Berle, Milton, I 228
Berlin, Irving, I 230
Bernstein, Leonard, I 233
Berra, Yogi, I 233
Best Years of Our Lives, I 236
Bestsellers, I 236
Better Homes and Gardens, I 238
Betty Crocker, I 241
Bicycling, I 245
Big Apple, I 246
Big Bands, I 247
Big Little Books, I 249
Big Sleep, I 250
Bigfoot, I 251
Billboards, I 253
Birthing Practices, I 260
Black Mask, I 263
Blackface Minstrelsy, I 270
Blacklisting, I 272
Blanc, Mel, I 276
Blondie (comic strip), I 283
Bluegrass, I 287
Blues, I 290
Board Games, I 297
Bob and Ray, I 299
Bobby Socks, I 301

Bodybuilding, I 305
Bogart, Humphrey, I 308
Bomb, I 311
Book-of-the-Month Club, I 318
Borge, Victor, I 320
Borscht Belt, I 321
Boston Celtics, I 322
Boston Garden, I 323
Boston Marathon, I 323
Boston Symphony Orchestra, I 325
Bowling, I 328
Boxing, I 330
Boy Scouts of America, I 333
Bra, I 335
Bradbury, Ray, I 337
Brenda Starr, I 348
Bridge, I 349
Brill Building, I 351
Broadway, I 356
Brooklyn Dodgers, I 362
Brooks, Gwendolyn, I 365
Brown, Les, I 370
Brown, Paul, I 370
Brownie Cameras, I 371
Bruce, Lenny, I 372
Buck, Pearl S., I 375
Buck Rogers, I 377
Bugs Bunny, I 383
Bumper Stickers, I 384
Burlesque, I 388
Burma-Shave, I 390
Burns, George, and Gracie Allen, I 392
Burr, Raymond, I 394
Burroughs, Edgar Rice, I 396
Butterbeans and Susie, I 400
Buttons, Red, I 401
Cagney, James, I 409
Caldwell, Erskine, I 412
Calloway, Cab, I 412
Camping, I 417
Cancer, I 418
Candid Camera, I 420
Caniff, Milton, I 421
Canova, Judy, I 421
Capital Punishment, I 424
Capote, Truman, I 426
Capra, Frank, I 428
Captain America, I 429
Captain Marvel, I 432
Caray, Harry, I 433
Carmichael, Hoagy, I 436
Carnegie, Dale, I 437
Carnegie Hall, I 439
Carr, John Dickson, I 442
Carson, Johnny, I 444
Carter Family, I 445
Casablanca, I 447
Catalog Houses, I 455
Catch-22, I 457
Cather, Willa, I 459
CB Radio, I 462
Celebrity, I 463
Celebrity Caricature, I 465
Cemeteries, I 467
Central Park, I 468
Chandler, Raymond, I 473
Chandu the Magician, I 475
Chaplin, Charlie, I 475
Charlie McCarthy, I 478
Cheerleading, I 486
Cherry Ames, I 491
Chessman, Caryl, I 492
Chicago Bears, I 492
Chicago Cubs, I 493
Child Stars, I 498
Christie, Agatha, I 502
Christmas, I 503
Chun King, I 509
Church Socials, I 509
Cigarettes, I 510
Circus, I 512
Citizen Kane, I 514

City of Angels, I 516
Civil Disobedience, I 517
Clairol Hair Coloring, I 523
Clift, Montgomery, I 529
Cline, Patsy, I 530
Cobb, Ty, I 538
Coca-Cola, I 540
Coffee, I 546
Colbert, Claudette, I 548
Cold War, I 549
Cole, Nat ''King'', I 552
College Football, I 555
Coltrane, John, I 557
Comic Books, I 560
Comics, I 562
Communism, I 569
Community Media, I 570
Community Theatre, I 573
Como, Perry, I 574
Condé Nast, I 577
Condoms, I 578
Confession Magazines, I 581
Coniff, Ray, I 583
Consumer Reports, I 587
Consumerism, I 589
Cooper, Gary, I 597
Cooperstown, New York, I 598
Coors, I 599
Copland, Aaron, I 600
Corwin, Norman, I 604
Cosmopolitan, I 610
Cotten, Joseph, I 613
Country Music, I 617
Cowboy Look, I 622
Cox, Ida, I 624
Crawford, Joan, I 625
Creationism, I 627
Crime Does Not Pay, I 632
Crisis, I 633
Crosby, Bing, I 638
Crossword Puzzles, I 641
Cukor, George, I 643
Curious George, I 649
Dance Halls, I 657
Davis, Bette, I 661
Davis, Miles, I 661
Day, Doris, I 664
Daytime Talk Shows, I 667
DC Comics, I 671
Death of a Salesman, I 678
Debutantes, I 680
Del Río, Dolores, I 683
DeMille, Cecil B., I 683
Denishawn, I 686
Department Stores, I 688
Derleth, August, I 692
Detective Fiction, I 693
Detroit Tigers, I 695
Dick and Jane Readers, I 700
Didrikson, Babe, I 704
Dieting, I 706
DiMaggio, Joe, I 715
Dime Stores/Woolworth's, I 717
Diners, I 719
Dionne Quintuplets, I 720
Dirty Dozen, I 721
Disability, I 721
Disc Jockeys, I 725
Disney (Walt Disney Company), I 728
Dixieland, I 734
Doby, Larry, I 736
Doc Martens, I 737
Doc Savage, I 738
Do-It-Yourself Improvement, I 742
Domino, Fats, I 743
Dorsey, Jimmy, I 750
Dorsey, Tommy, I 751
Double Indemnity, I 751
Douglas, Lloyd C., I 753
Douglas, Melvyn, I 753
Downs, Hugh, I 754
Dr. Jekyll and Mr. Hyde, I 756

Dr. Kildare, I 756
Dr. Seuss, I 757
Dracula, I 760
Draft, I 761
Drag, I 762
Dragnet, I 766
Dragon Lady, I 767
Drive-In Theater, I 769
Drug War, I 771
Du Bois, W. E. B., I 771
Dunkin' Donuts, I 775
Dunne, Irene, I 776
Durbin, Deanna, I 776
Durocher, Leo, I 777
Eames, Charles and Ray, II 1
Ebbets Field, II 5
Ebony, II 7
Eckstine, Billy, II 10
Eddy, Nelson, II 13
Edwards, James, II 14
Edwards, Ralph, II 16
Einstein, Albert, II 16
Eisner, Will, II 18
Electric Appliances, II 20
Electric Guitar, II 21
Electric Trains, II 22
Ellington, Duke, II 23
Ellison, Harlan, II 25
Emmy Awards, II 27
Empire State Building, II 28
Environmentalism, II 29
Erector Sets, II 34
Ertegun, Ahmet, II 35
Escher, M. C., II 37
Esquire, II 40
Etiquette Columns, II 44
Existentialism, II 50
Factor, Max, II 54
Fadiman, Clifton, II 55
Fairbanks, Douglas, Jr., II 55
Fallout Shelters, II 58
Family Circle, II 59
Fan Magazines, II 64
Fantasia, II 65
Fast Food, II 71
Father Divine, II 74
Father's Day, II 76
Faulkner, William, II 77
FBI (Federal Bureau of Investigation), II 80
Felix the Cat, II 83
Feminism, II 84
Fenway Park, II 87
Fetchit, Stepin, II 88
Fibber McGee and Molly, II 89
Field and Stream, II 92
Fields, W. C., II 95
Film Noir, II 99
Firearms, II 101
Fisher, Eddie, II 104
Fisher-Price Toys, II 106
Fitzgerald, Ella, II 107
Flash Gordon, II 113
Flatt, Lester, II 113
Flea Markets, II 114
Florida Vacations, II 119
Flynn, Errol, II 121
Foggy Mountain Boys, II 122
Folk Music, II 123
Folkways Records, II 126
Fonda, Henry, II 127
Fonteyn, Margot, II 130
Ford, Glenn, II 131
Ford, John, II 133
Ford Motor Company, II 135
Fortune, II 142
Fourth of July Celebrations, II 146
Francis the Talking Mule, II 152
Frankenstein, II 152
Freak Shows, II 158
Frederick's of Hollywood, II 159
French Fries, II 165
Frost, Robert, II 177

Frozen Entrées, II 178
Fu Manchu, II 179
Fuller, Buckminster, II 180
Fundamentalism, II 181
Gable, Clark, II 187
Gambling, II 188
Game Shows, II 191
Gangs, II 195
Garbo, Greta, II 199
Gardner, Ava, II 200
Garfield, John, II 201
Garland, Judy, II 202
Gas Stations, II 206
Gay and Lesbian Press, II 210
Gay Men, II 215
Gehrig, Lou, II 217
General Motors, II 220
Gentlemen Prefer Blondes, II 223
Ghettos, II 227
Gibson, Althea, II 230
Gillespie, Dizzy, II 236
Girl Scouts, II 242
Gish, Lillian, II 244
Glass Menagerie, II 245
Gleason, Jackie, II 245
Godfrey, Arthur, II 251
Gold, Mike, II 255
Goldberg, Rube, II 256
Golden Books, II 258
Golden Gate Bridge, II 259
Goldwyn, Samuel, II 260
Golf, II 261
Good Housekeeping, II 265
Goodman, Benny, II 270
Goodson, Mark, II 271
Gospel Music, II 274
Gossip Columns, II 275
Grable, Betty, II 277
Graffiti, II 281
Graham, Billy, II 284
Graham, Martha, II 285
Grand Ole Opry, II 286
Grant, Cary, II 288
Grapes of Wrath, II 290
Green Bay Packers, II 300
Green Lantern, II 302
Greenberg, Hank, II 302
Greenwich Village, II 304
Greeting Cards, II 306
Greyhound Buses, II 312
Grimek, John, II 316
Grits, II 319
Gucci, II 323
Guiding Light, II 323
Guthrie, Woody, II 328
Hackett, Buddy, II 333
Hairstyles, II 340
Halas, George ''Papa Bear'', II 342
Hammett, Dashiell, II 349
Hanna-Barbera, II 355
Hardy Boys, II 360
Harlem Globetrotters, II 364
Harley-Davidson, II 368
Harmonica Bands, II 370
Harper's, II 372
Hawkins, Coleman, II 376
Hawks, Howard, II 376
Hayward, Susan, II 377
Hayworth, Rita, II 377
Hearst, William Randolph, II 379
Hellman, Lillian, II 384
Hell's Angels, II 384
Hemingway, Ernest, II 386
Hemlines, II 390
Henderson, Fletcher, II 390
Henry Aldrich, II 392
Hep Cats, II 393
Hepburn, Katharine, II 394
Herman, Woody, II 398
Hersey, John, II 399
Highway System, II 402
Hiking, II 405

Hirschfeld, Albert, II 412
Hiss, Alger, II 413
Hitchcock, Alfred, II 414
Hockey, II 417
Hogan, Ben, II 421
Holden, William, II 426
Holiday, Billie, II 427
Holliday, Judy, II 429
Hollywood, II 431
Hollywood Ten, II 434
Hooker, John Lee, II 440
Hoover, J. Edgar, II 443
Hopalong Cassidy, II 444
Hope, Bob, II 446
Hopkins, Sam ''Lightnin','' II 447
Hopper, Edward, II 448
Hopscotch, II 449
Horne, Lena, II 449
Horror Movies, II 450
Hot Dogs, II 454
Hot Rods, II 455
Howdy Doody Show, II 459
Howe, Gordie, II 460
Hughes, Howard, II 464
Hughes, Langston, II 465
Hurston, Zora Neale, II 469
Huston, John, II 471
Hutton, Ina Ray, II 472
I Love a Mystery, II 476
IBM (International Business Machines), II 481
Ice Cream Cone, II 483
Indian, II 487
Indianapolis 500, II 490
Industrial Design, II 491
Ink Spots, II 493
Inner Sanctum Mysteries, II 493
It's a Wonderful Life, II 506
Ives, Burl, II 508
J. Walter Thompson, II 511
Jack Armstrong, II 512
Jackson, Mahalia, II 515
Jackson, Shirley, II 520
James, Elmore, II 525
James, Harry, II 525
Japanese American Internment Camps, II 525
Jazz, II 529
Jeans, II 532
Jeep, II 533
Jell-O, II 537
Jessel, George, II 542
Jolson, Al, II 559
Jones, Jennifer, II 562
Jordan, Louis, II 568
Joy of Cooking, II 572
Judson, Arthur, II 578
Judy Bolton, II 578
Juke Boxes, II 579
Juvenile Delinquency, II 583
Kaltenborn, Hans von, III 1
Kansas City Jazz, III 2
Kantor, MacKinlay, III 3
Karloff, Boris, III 4
Kaye, Danny, III 9
Kelly, Gene, III 14
Kentucky Derby, III 19
Kern, Jerome, III 21
Key West, III 22
King, B. B., III 26
Kinsey, Dr. Alfred C., III 40
Kirby, Jack, III 42
Kitsch, III 43
Kiwanis, III 46
Kodak, III 51
Kraft Television Theatre, III 60
Krazy Kat, III 62
Krupa, Gene, III 63
Ku Klux Klan, III 64
Kukla, Fran, and Ollie, III 68
Labor Unions, III 72
Ladd, Alan, III 75
Lahr, Bert, III 76
Lake, Veronica, III 79

Lamarr, Hedy, III 82
LaMotta, Jake, III 83
Lamour, Dorothy, III 83
L'Amour, Louis, III 84
Lancaster, Burt, III 85
Landry, Tom, III 87
Lang, Fritz, III 87
Lansky, Meyer, III 90
Las Vegas, III 92
Lassie, III 95
Latin Jazz, III 97
Laura, III 100
Laurel and Hardy, III 100
La-Z-Boy Loungers, III 106
Leadbelly, III 108
League of Their Own, III 110
Lee, Gypsy Rose, III 119
Lee, Peggy, III 121
Lee, Stan, III 124
Legos, III 125
Leisure Time, III 128
Leopold and Loeb, III 138
Lesbianism, III 140
Let Us Now Praise Famous Men, III 142
Let's Pretend, III 143
Levin, Meyer, III 145
Levi's, III 146
Levittown, III 147
Lewis, Jerry, III 152
Liberace, III 155
Liberty, III 157
Life, III 160
Li'l Abner, III 163
Lincoln Center for the Performing Arts, III 165
Lindbergh, Charles, III 166
Linkletter, Art, III 168
Lionel Trains, III 170
Lippmann, Walter, III 170
Lipstick, III 171
Little League, III 174
Little Magazines, III 176
Little Orphan Annie, III 177
Loafers, III 182
Lombard, Carole, III 184
Lombardo, Guy, III 187
Lone Ranger, III 189
Long-Playing Record, III 192
Loos, Anita, III 194
Lorre, Peter, III 195
Los Angeles Lakers, III 196
Lost Weekend, III 199
Louis, Joe, III 200
Louisville Slugger, III 201
Loy, Myrna, III 207
LSD, III 207
Lubitsch, Ernst, III 209
Luce, Henry, III 210
Luciano, Lucky, III 212
Lugosi, Bela, III 213
Lunceford, Jimmie, III 214
Lupino, Ida, III 215
Lynching, III 217
Ma Perkins, III 223
Mabley, Moms, III 223
MacDonald, Jeanette, III 224
Macfadden, Bernarr, III 226
MacMurray, Fred, III 228
Macon, Uncle Dave, III 229
Mafia/Organized Crime, III 237
Mah-Jongg, III 242
Mailer, Norman, III 242
Mall, III 247
Maltese Falcon, III 249
Mancini, Henry, III 256
March On Washington, III 266
Marching Bands, III 267
Mardi Gras, III 269
Marie, Rose, III 272
Marlboro Man, III 274
Martin, Dean, III 280
Martin, Freddy, III 281
Martini, III 282

Marvel Comics, III 285
Marx Brothers, III 287
Marx, Groucho, III 288
Mary Worth, III 294
Masses, III 302
Masters Golf Tournament, III 305
Mayer, Louis B., III 309
Mayfield, Percy, III 310
McCall's Magazine, III 313
McCoy, Horace, III 319
McCrea, Joel, III 319
McDaniel, Hattie, III 320
McDonald's, III 321
McKay, Claude, III 327
McPherson, Aimee Semple, III 331
McQueen, Butterfly, III 332
Media Feeding Frenzies, III 337
Medicine Shows, III 339
Meet Me in St. Louis, III 339
Mencken, H. L., III 342
Mendoza, Lydia, III 344
Merton, Thomas, III 345
Metropolitan Museum of Art, III 347
MGM (Metro-Goldwyn-Mayer), III 347
Michener, James, III 351
Mildred Pierce, III 359
Miller, Arthur, III 363
Miller, Glenn, III 364
Miller, Henry, III 367
Milton Bradley, III 369
Minnelli, Vincente, III 370
Minoso, Minnie, III 371
Miranda, Carmen, III 373
Miss America Pageant, III 374
Mitchell, Margaret, III 380
Mitchum, Robert, III 381
Mix, Tom, III 383
Modern Dance, III 388
Monopoly, III 396
Monroe, Bill, III 396
Monroe, Marilyn, III 399
Montalbán, Ricardo, III 401
Montana, Patsy, III 403
Morse, Carlton E., III 415
Motely, Willard, III 419
Mother's Day, III 417
Mount Rushmore, III 423
Movie Stars, III 428
Mummy, III 441
Muni, Paul, III 442
Murray, Arthur, III 448
Murrow, Edward R., III 451
Muscle Beach, III 453
Muscular Christianity, III 456
Musical, III 458
Mutt & Jeff, III 462
Muzak, III 463
My Darling Clementine, III 464
Nancy Drew, III 473
Nation, III 476
National Basketball Association (NBA), III 477
National Collegiate Athletic Association
   (NCAA), III 479
National Enquirer, III 480
National Football League (NFL), III 482
National Hockey League (NHL), III 485
National Parks, III 489
Neckties, III 495
Negro Leagues, III 497
Networks, III 503
New Look, III 512
New Orleans Rhythm and Blues, III 513
New Republic, III 514
New York Knickerbockers, III 517
New York Times, III 518
New York Yankees, III 520
New Yorker, III 522
Newsweek, III 527
Niagara Falls, III 528
Noloesca, La Chata, III 540
Nylon, III 544
Objectivism/Ayn Rand, III 547

O'Keeffe, Georgia, III 552
Oklahoma!, III 553
Olivier, Laurence, III 556
Olsen, Tillie, III 558
Olympics, III 558
Onassis, Jacqueline Lee Bouvier Kennedy,
    III 564
One Man's Family, III 567
O'Neill, Eugene, III 569
Opportunity, III 570
Ouija Boards, III 576
Our Gang, III 576
Outline of History, III 581
Owens, Jesse, III 583
Pachucos, IV 2
Paige, Satchel, IV 5
Paley, William S., IV 6
Pants for Women, IV 7
Paperbacks, IV 9
Parades, IV 12
Parker Brothers, IV 13
Parker, Charlie, IV 13
Parrish, Maxfield, IV 16
Paul, Les, IV 20
Pearl, Minnie, IV 28
Peck, Gregory, IV 29
Penn, Irving, IV 33
Perry Mason, IV 41
Pets, IV 44
Philadelphia Story, IV 50
Philco Television Playhouse, IV 50
Phillips, Irna, IV 51
Phonograph, IV 52
Photoplay, IV 53
Picasso, Pablo, IV 54
Pin-Up, IV 58
Pittsburgh Steelers, IV 61
Pizza, IV 62
Plastic, IV 64
Pogo, IV 73
Poitier, Sidney, IV 75
Polio, IV 76
Political Bosses, IV 77
Pollock, Jackson, IV 79
Pop Music, IV 83
Pope, IV 86
Popeye, IV 87
Popsicles, IV 88
Popular Mechanics, IV 89
Popular Psychology, IV 90
Porter, Cole, IV 95
Postcards, IV 96
Postman Always Rings Twice, IV 97
Powell, Dick, IV 102
Powell, William, IV 102
Price, Vincent, IV 110
Prince, Hal, IV 114
Professional Football, IV 116
Prom, IV 120
Protest Groups, IV 124
Public Libraries, IV 133
Puente, Tito, IV 137
Pulp Magazines, IV 139
Queen, Ellery, IV 148
Queen for a Day, IV 149
Race Music, IV 155
Race Riots, IV 156
Radio, IV 157
Radio Drama, IV 160
Raft, George, IV 162
Rains, Claude, IV 168
Ranch House, IV 173
Rand, Sally, IV 173
Reader's Digest, IV 177
Reagan, Ronald, IV 179
Reed, Donna, IV 191
Reese, Pee Wee, IV 193
Reeves, Steve, IV 193
Reno, Don, IV 204
Renoir, Jean, IV 204
Rhythm and Blues, IV 206
Riggs, Bobby, IV 211

Ringling Bros., Barnum & Bailey Circus, IV 212
Ripley's Believe It Or Not, IV 215
Rizzuto, Phil, IV 220
Road Runner and Wile E. Coyote, IV 222
Robeson, Kenneth, IV 227
Robeson, Paul, IV 227
Robinson, Edward G., IV 229
Robinson, Jackie, IV 231
Robinson, Sugar Ray, IV 234
Rockettes, IV 241
Rockwell, Norman, IV 244
Rodeo, IV 252
Rodgers and Hammerstein, IV 254
Rodgers and Hart, IV 256
Rodgers, Jimmie, IV 258
Rogers, Roy, IV 262
Roller Coasters, IV 265
Roller Derby, IV 266
Romance Novels, IV 270
Romero, Cesar, IV 273
Rose Bowl, IV 275
Roswell Incident, IV 282
Route 66, IV 284
Rudolph the Red-Nosed Reindeer, IV 287
Rupp, Adolph, IV 290
Russell, Rosalind, IV 293
Ruth, Babe, IV 293
RV, IV 295
Saks Fifth Avenue, IV 302
Sandburg, Carl, IV 306
Saratoga Springs, IV 312
Sarnoff, David, IV 312
Sarong, IV 313
Saturday Evening Post, IV 315
Savoy Ballroom, IV 322
Science Fiction Publishing, IV 330
Scientific American, IV 334
Scott, Randolph, IV 339
Screwball Comedies, IV 342
Scribner's, IV 344
Scruggs, Earl, IV 345
Sears Roebuck Catalogue, IV 346
Seduction of the Innocent, IV 350
Seeger, Pete, IV 351
Sellers, Peter, IV 355
Selznick, David O., IV 356
Seventeen, IV 364
Sex Scandals, IV 367
Sex Symbol, IV 369
Shadow, IV 375
Shane, IV 378
Shaw, Artie, IV 381
Shawn, Ted, IV 381
She Wore a Yellow Ribbon, IV 381
Sheldon, Sidney, IV 381
Shirer, William L., IV 384
Shore, Dinah, IV 387
Show Boat, IV 389
Shulman, Max, IV 391
Siegel, Bugsy, IV 392
Sinatra, Frank, IV 409
Sinclair, Upton, IV 414
Singer, Isaac Bashevis, IV 414
Sitcom, IV 418
Skating, IV 429
Skelton, Red, IV 431
Slang, IV 434
Slinky, IV 436
Smith, Kate, IV 439
Soap Operas, IV 446
Soccer, IV 449
Social Dancing, IV 450
Soda Fountains, IV 452
South Pacific, IV 465
Spillane, Mickey, IV 477
Spock, Dr. Benjamin, IV 480
Sport Utility Vehicles (SUVs), IV 482
Sporting News, IV 483
Sports Hero, IV 484
St. Denis, Ruth, IV 494
Stagg, Amos Alonzo, IV 499
Standardized Testing, IV 502

Stand-up Comedy, IV 504
Stanley Brothers, IV 506
Stanwyck, Barbara, IV 506
Star System, IV 507
State Fairs, IV 518
Steinbeck, John, IV 522
Steinberg, Saul, IV 523
Stengel, Casey, IV 526
Stetson Hat, IV 532
Stewart, Jimmy, IV 532
Stickball, IV 534
Stock-Car Racing, IV 537
Stock Market Crashes, IV 539
Stockton, "Pudgy", IV 541
Stone, Irving, IV 542
Stout, Rex, IV 546
Street and Smith, IV 553
Streetcar Named Desire, IV 554
Strip Joints/Striptease, IV 557
Studio One, IV 563
Studio System, IV 565
Sturges, Preston, IV 566
Suicide, IV 569
Sullivan, Ed, IV 570
Summer Camp, IV 573
Superman, IV 581
Surf Music, IV 585
Swimming Pools, IV 590
Swing Dancing, IV 592
Tabloids, IV 597
Tanning, IV 603
Tap Dancing, IV 605
Tarbell, Ida, IV 606
Tarkington, Booth, IV 607
Tarzan, IV 608
Taylor, Elizabeth, IV 612
Taylor, Robert, IV 615
Teddy Bears, IV 616
Teen Idols, IV 617
Teenagers, IV 620
Tejano Music, IV 623
Telephone, IV 623
Television, IV 626
Temple, Shirley, IV 631
Tennis, IV 635
Tennis Shoes/Sneakers, IV 637
Terry and the Pirates, IV 640
Thanksgiving, IV 640
Third Man, IV 643
This Is Your Life, IV 643
Thomas, Lowell, IV 645
Thomson, Bobby, IV 647
Three Caballeros, IV 650
Three Stooges, IV 651
Thurber, James, IV 654
Tierney, Gene, IV 655
Tiffany & Company, IV 655
Tijuana Bibles, IV 656
Time, IV 657
Times Square, IV 659
Tokyo Rose, IV 669
Tolkien, J. R. R., IV 671
Tom Swift Series, IV 674
Tone, Franchot, IV 676
Top 40, IV 679
Tormé, Mel, IV 683
Town Meetings, IV 684
Toys, IV 685
Tracy, Spencer, IV 687
Tramps, IV 691
Traveling Carnivals, IV 692
Treasure of the Sierra Madre, IV 695
Trevor, Claire, IV 697
Trixie Belden, IV 698
Trout, Robert, IV 698
T-Shirts, IV 700
Tupperware, IV 700
Turner, Lana, IV 703
TV Dinners, IV 706
Tweety Pie and Sylvester, IV 707
Twelve-Step Programs, IV 708
UFOs (Unidentified Flying Objects), V 1

United Artists, V 8
U.S. One, V 11
Valentine's Day, V 16
Vallee, Rudy, V 21
Vampires, V 22
Van Vechten, Carl, V 26
Varga Girl, V 30
Vaughan, Sarah, V 36
Velez, Lupe, V 39
Velveeta Cheese, V 39
Vidal, Gore, V 45
Vidor, King, V 48
Vitamins, V 52
Vogue, V 53
Walker, Aaron "T-Bone", V 59
Wall Drug, V 66
Wall Street Journal, V 67
War Bonds, V 74
War Movies, V 75
Washington Post, V 83
Waters, Ethel, V 86
Waters, Muddy, V 89
Wayne, John, V 91
Weavers, V 96
Wedding Dress, V 100
Weekend, V 101
Weird Tales, V 103
Weissmuller, Johnny, V 104
Welles, Orson, V 108
Wertham, Fredric, V 111
West, Mae, V 115
Western, V 118
White Castle, V 127
White, E. B., V 127
White Flight, V 128
Whiteman, Paul, V 130
Whiting, Margaret, V 130
Wilder, Billy, V 136
Wilder, Laura Ingalls, V 136
Wilder, Thornton, V 138
Williams, Hank, Sr., V 141
Williams, Ted, V 144
Williams, Tennessee, V 146
Wills, Bob, and His Texas Playboys, V 148
Wimbledon, V 150
Winchell, Walter, V 151
Windy City, V 152
Winnie-the-Pooh, V 155
Winnie Winkle the Breadwinner, V 156
Wire Services, V 158
Wister, Owen, V 161
Wodehouse, P. G., V 166
Wolfman, V 167
Woman's Day, V 169
Wong, Anna May, V 172
Wood, Natalie, V 173
Works Progress Administration (WPA)
    Murals, V 179
World Series, V 182
World War II, V 188
World's Fairs, V 194
Wrangler Jeans, V 196
Wray, Fay, V 196
Wright, Richard, V 196
Wuthering Heights, V 198
WWJD? (What Would Jesus Do?), V 198
Wyeth, Andrew, V 199
Yankee Doodle Dandy, V 207
Yankee Stadium, V 208
Yellowstone National Park, V 213
Young, Loretta, V 217
Young, Robert, V 218
Youngman, Henny, V 219
Your Hit Parade, V 220
Zanuck, Darryl F., V 225
Zines, V 228
Zoos, V 230
Zoot Suit, V 233
Zorro, V 234

1950-1959
A&R Men/Women, I 1
Aaron, Hank, I 2

AARP (American Association for Retired
    Persons), I 3
Abbott and Costello, I 5
Abstract Expressionism, I 11
Academy Awards, I 12
Ace, Johnny, I 15
Adams, Ansel, I 17
Adderley, Cannonball, I 18
Adventures of Ozzie and Harriet, I 21
Advertising, I 23
Advice Columns, I 26
African American Press, I 32
African Queen, I 33
Agents, I 34
Air Travel, I 38
Alka Seltzer, I 49
All About Eve, I 50
Allen, Steve, I 52
Allison, Luther, I 54
Alternative Press, I 60
Altman, Robert, I 63
Amazing Stories, I 64
American Bandstand, I 65
American International Pictures, I 71
American Museum of Natural History, I 72
Amos 'n' Andy Show, I 72
Amsterdam, Morey, I 74
Amusement Parks, I 77
Amway, I 80
Anderson, Marian, I 81
Andretti, Mario, I 84
Androgyny, I 85
Andy Griffith Show, I 86
Animated Films, I 90
Anka, Paul, I 95
Anne Frank: The Diary of a Young Girl, I 95
Annie Get Your Gun, I 96
Aparicio, Luis, I 101
Apollo Theatre, I 104
Archie Comics, I 108
Arden, Elizabeth, I 109
Argosy, I 109
Arizona Highways, I 110
Armed Forces Radio Service, I 112
Armstrong, Louis, I 114
Army-McCarthy Hearings, I 116
Arnaz, Desi, I 116
Arthur, Bea, I 118
Arthurian Legend, I 120
As the World Turns, I 121
Ashe, Arthur, I 123
Asimov, Isaac, I 125
Asner, Edward, I 126
Astounding Science Fiction, I 129
Astrology, I 129
AT&T, I 130
Athletic Model Guild, I 132
Atkins, Chet, I 132
Atlantic Records, I 135
Atlas, Charles, I 135
Auerbach, Red, I 136
Aunt Jemima, I 137
Automobile, I 137
Autry, Gene, I 142
Avalon, Frankie, I 143
Avedon, Richard, I 144
Avery, Tex, I 145
"B" movies, I 149
Babar, I 151
Baby Boomers, I 151
Bacall, Lauren, I 154
Balanchine, George, I 161
Baldwin, James, I 161
Ball, Lucille, I 163
Ballard, Hank, I 164
Ballet, I 165
Barbecue, I 168
Barber, Red, I 169
Barbershop Quartets, I 169
Barbie, I 171
Baseball, I 180
Baseball Cards, I 183

Basie, Count, I 184
Basketball, I 186
Batman, I 189
Baum, L. Frank, I 191
Bay, Mel, I 191
Beat Generation, I 201
Beauty Queens, I 207
Beer, I 210
Belafonte, Harry, I 214
Bell Telephone Hour, I 216
Ben-Hur, I 219
Bennett, Tony, I 221
Benny Hill Show, I 222
Benny, Jack, I 222
Bergman, Ingmar, I 225
Bergman, Ingrid, I 226
Berle, Milton, I 228
Berlin, Irving, I 230
Bernstein, Leonard, I 233
Berra, Yogi, I 233
Berry, Chuck, I 234
Bestsellers, I 236
Better Homes and Gardens, I 238
Betty Crocker, I 241
Beulah, I 241
Bicycling, I 245
Big Apple, I 246
Big Bopper, I 249
Bigfoot, I 251
Billboards, I 253
Birthing Practices, I 260
Blackboard Jungle, I 268
Blackface Minstrelsy, I 270
Blacklisting, I 272
Blanc, Mel, I 276
Bland, Bobby Blue, I 278
Blob, I 280
Blockbusters, I 280
Blondie (comic strip), I 283
Bluegrass, I 287
Blues, I 290
Board Games, I 297
Bob and Ray, I 299
Bobbsey Twins, I 300
Bodybuilding, I 305
Bogart, Humphrey, I 308
Bomb, I 311
Bonanza, I 316
Book-of-the-Month Club, I 318
Boone, Pat, I 319
Borge, Victor, I 320
Borscht Belt, I 321
Boston Celtics, I 322
Boston Garden, I 323
Boston Marathon, I 323
Bowling, I 328
Boxing, I 330
Boy Scouts of America, I 333
Bra, I 335
Bradbury, Ray, I 337
Brando, Marlon, I 342
Brenda Starr, I 348
Bridge, I 349
Bridge on the River Kwai, I 349
Brill Building, I 351
Broadway, I 356
Bronson, Charles, I 360
Brooklyn Dodgers, I 362
Brooks, Gwendolyn, I 365
Brooks, Mel, I 365
Brothers, Dr. Joyce, I 367
Brown, James, I 367
Brown, Les, I 370
Brown, Paul, I 370
Brubeck, Dave, I 372
Bruce, Lenny, I 372
Brynner, Yul, I 375
Buck, Pearl S., I 375
Buck Rogers, I 377
Budweiser, I 380
Bugs Bunny, I 383
Bumper Stickers, I 384

Burger King, I 387
Burlesque, I 388
Burma-Shave, I 390
Burnett, Carol, I 391
Burns, George, and Gracie Allen, I 392
Burr, Raymond, I 394
Burroughs, Edgar Rice, I 396
Burroughs, William S., I 397
Butterbeans and Susie, I 400
Buttons, Red, I 401
Cadillac, I 406
Caesar, Sid, I 408
Cagney, James, I 409
Cahan, Abraham, I 411
Calloway, Cab, I 412
Camp, I 415
Camping, I 417
Cancer, I 418
Candid Camera, I 420
Caniff, Milton, I 421
Canova, Judy, I 421
Capital Punishment, I 424
Capote, Truman, I 426
Capra, Frank, I 428
Captain America, I 429
Captain Kangaroo, I 430
Car Coats, I 433
Caray, Harry, I 433
Carmichael, Hoagy, I 436
Carnegie, Dale, I 437
Carnegie Hall, I 439
Carr, John Dickson, I 442
Carson, Johnny, I 444
Carter Family, I 445
Cash, Johnny, I 449
Catcher in the Rye, I 458
CB Radio, I 462
Celebrity, I 463
Cemeteries, I 467
Central Park, I 468
Chamberlain, Wilt, I 472
Chandler, Raymond, I 473
Chaplin, Charlie, I 475
Charles, Ray, I 477
Charlie McCarthy, I 478
Charm Bracelets, I 480
Chavis, Boozoo, I 483
Chayefsky, Paddy, I 484
Checker, Chubby, I 484
Cheerleading, I 486
Chemise, I 490
Chenier, Clifton, I 490
Cherry Ames, I 491
Chessman, Caryl, I 492
Chicago Bears, I 492
Child Stars, I 498
Chipmunks, I 501
Christie, Agatha, I 502
Christmas, I 503
Church Socials, I 509
Cigarettes, I 510
Circus, I 512
City of Angels, I 516
Civil Rights Movement, I 519
Clairol Hair Coloring, I 523
Clark, Dick, I 525
Clarke, Arthur C., I 527
Clemente, Roberto, I 528
Clift, Montgomery, I 529
Cline, Patsy, I 530
Clooney, Rosemary, I 533
Closet, I 536
Cobb, Ty, I 538
Coca, Imogene, I 540
Coca-Cola, I 540
Cocktail Parties, I 544
Coffee, I 546
Colbert, Claudette, I 548
Cold War, I 549
Cole, Nat ''King'', I 552
College Fads, I 553
College Football, I 555

Coltrane, John, I 557
Comic Books, I 560
Comics, I 562
Comics Code Authority, I 565
Communism, I 569
Community Media, I 570
Community Theatre, I 573
Como, Perry, I 574
Condé Nast, I 577
Condoms, I 578
Confession Magazines, I 581
Coniff, Ray, I 583
Conspiracy Theories, I 586
Consumer Reports, I 587
Consumerism, I 589
Conway, Tim, I 594
Cooke, Sam, I 594
Cooper, Gary, I 597
Cooperstown, New York, I 598
Corman, Roger, I 603
Corvette, I 603
Cosmopolitan, I 610
Cotten, Joseph, I 613
Country Music, I 617
Cousteau, Jacques, I 621
Cowboy Look, I 622
Crawford, Joan, I 625
Creationism, I 627
Credit Cards, I 628
Crime Does Not Pay, I 632
Crinolines, I 633
Crisis, I 633
Cronkite, Walter, I 635
Crosby, Bing, I 638
Crossword Puzzles, I 641
Cukor, George, I 643
Cult Films, I 643
Cults, I 646
Cunningham, Merce, I 648
Curious George, I 649
Dana, Bill, I 656
Dance Halls, I 657
Dandridge, Dorothy, I 658
Davis, Bette, I 661
Davis, Miles, I 661
Davy Crockett, I 663
Day, Doris, I 664
Day the Earth Stood Still, I 665
Daytime Talk Shows, I 667
Daytona 500, I 670
DC Comics, I 671
Dean, James, I 676
Death of a Salesman, I 678
Debutantes, I 680
Del Río, Dolores, I 683
DeMille, Cecil B., I 683
Denishawn, I 686
Department Stores, I 688
Depression, I 690
Derleth, August, I 692
Detective Fiction, I 693
Detroit Tigers, I 695
Dick and Jane Readers, I 700
Dick, Philip K., I 701
Diddley, Bo, I 703
Dieting, I 706
Dietrich, Marlene, I 708
Diller, Phyllis, I 712
DiMaggio, Joe, I 715
Dime Stores/Woolworth's, I 717
Diners, I 719
Disability, I 721
Disaster Movies, I 723
Disc Jockeys, I 725
Disney (Walt Disney Company), I 728
Dixieland, I 734
Dobie Gillis, I 735
Doby, Larry, I 736
Doc Martens, I 737
Doctor Zhivago, I 740
Do-It-Yourself Improvement, I 742
Domino, Fats, I 743

Doo-wop Music, I 750
Dorsey, Jimmy, I 750
Dorsey, Tommy, I 751
Douglas, Lloyd C., I 753
Douglas, Melvyn, I 753
Downs, Hugh, I 754
Dr. Jekyll and Mr. Hyde, I 756
Dr. Kildare, I 756
Dr. Seuss, I 757
Dracula, I 760
Draft, I 761
Drag, I 762
Drag Racing, I 764
Dragnet, I 766
Drifters, I 769
Drive-In Theater, I 769
Drug War, I 771
Dunkin' Donuts, I 775
Durocher, Leo, I 777
Eames, Charles and Ray, II 1
Eastwood, Clint, II 2
Ebbets Field, II 5
Ebony, II 7
EC Comics, II 9
Eckstine, Billy, II 10
Eddy, Duane, II 11
Edge of Night, II 13
Edsel, II 14
Edwards, James, II 14
Edwards, Ralph, II 16
Einstein, Albert, II 16
Eisner, Will, II 18
Electric Appliances, II 20
Electric Guitar, II 21
Electric Trains, II 22
Ellington, Duke, II 23
Ellison, Harlan, II 25
Emmy Awards, II 27
Empire State Building, II 28
Environmentalism, II 29
Erector Sets, II 34
Ertegun, Ahmet, II 35
Escher, M. C., II 37
Esquire, II 40
Etiquette Columns, II 44
Evangelism, II 46
Everly Brothers, II 47
Existentialism, II 50
Fabares, Shelley, II 53
Facelifts, II 54
Factor, Max, II 54
Fadiman, Clifton, II 55
Fallout Shelters, II 58
Family Circle, II 59
Fan Magazines, II 64
Fantasia, II 65
Farr, Jamie, II 71
Fast Food, II 71
Father Knows Best, II 75
Father's Day, II 76
Faulkner, William, II 77
FBI (Federal Bureau of Investigation), II 80
Felix the Cat, II 83
Fellini, Federico, II 84
Feminism, II 84
Fenway Park, II 87
Fibber McGee and Molly, II 89
Field and Stream, II 92
Fifties, II 96
Film Noir, II 99
Firearms, II 101
Fisher, Eddie, II 104
Fisher-Price Toys, II 106
Fitzgerald, Ella, II 107
Flash Gordon, II 113
Flatt, Lester, II 113
Flea Markets, II 114
Fleming, Ian, II 116
Florida Vacations, II 119
Flynn, Errol, II 121
Foggy Mountain Boys, II 122
Folk Music, II 123

Folkways Records, II 126
Fonda, Henry, II 127
Fonteyn, Margot, II 130
Ford, Glenn, II 131
Ford, John, II 133
Ford Motor Company, II 135
Ford, Tennessee Ernie, II 138
Ford, Whitey, II 138
Fortune, II 142
Fosse, Bob, II 143
Fourth of July Celebrations, II 146
Foxx, Redd, II 148
Foyt, A. J., II 148
Francis, Arlene, II 150
Francis, Connie, II 151
Francis the Talking Mule, II 152
Frankenstein, II 152
Franklin, Aretha, II 154
Frawley, William, II 157
Frederick's of Hollywood, II 159
Freed, Alan ''Moondog'', II 162
French Fries, II 165
Frisbee, II 174
Frizzell, Lefty, II 175
From Here to Eternity, II 175
Frost, Robert, II 177
Frosty the Snowman, II 178
Frozen Entrées, II 178
Fu Manchu, II 179
Fuller, Buckminster, II 180
Fundamentalism, II 181
Funicello, Annette, II 183
Gable, Clark, II 187
Gambling, II 188
Game Shows, II 191
Gangs, II 195
Gardner, Ava, II 200
Garfield, John, II 201
Garland, Judy, II 202
Garner, James, II 204
Gas Stations, II 206
Gay and Lesbian Press, II 210
Gay Men, II 215
General Motors, II 220
Gentlemen Prefer Blondes, II 223
Ghettos, II 227
Giant, II 230
Gibson, Althea, II 230
Gifford, Frank, II 236
Gillespie, Dizzy, II 236
Ginny Dolls, II 239
Ginsberg, Allen, II 239
Girl Scouts, II 242
Gish, Lillian, II 244
Gleason, Jackie, II 245
Gnagy, Jon, II 249
Godfrey, Arthur, II 251
Godzilla, II 252
Gold, Mike, II 255
Golden Books, II 258
Golden Gate Bridge, II 259
Goldwyn, Samuel, II 260
Golf, II 261
Good Housekeeping, II 265
Goodbye, Columbus, II 268
Goodman, Benny, II 270
Goodson, Mark, II 271
Gordy, Berry, II 272
Gospel Music, II 274
Gossip Columns, II 275
Graffiti, II 281
Graham, Billy, II 284
Graham, Martha, II 285
Grand Ole Opry, II 286
Grant, Cary, II 288
Greeley, Andrew, II 298
Green Bay Packers, II 300
Greenwich Village, II 304
Greeting Cards, II 306
Gregory, Dick, II 307
Greyhound Buses, II 312
Grits, II 319

Guaraldi, Vince, II 323
Guiding Light, II 323
Gunsmoke, II 326
Guthrie, Woody, II 328
Guy, Buddy, II 329
Hackett, Buddy, II 333
Haight-Ashbury, II 336
Hairstyles, II 340
Halas, George ''Papa Bear'', II 342
Haley, Bill, II 343
Hallmark Hall of Fame, II 345
Hamburger, II 347
Hanna-Barbera, II 355
Hansberry, Lorraine, II 356
Hardy Boys, II 360
Harlem Globetrotters, II 364
Harley-Davidson, II 368
Harmonica Bands, II 370
Harper's, II 372
Havlicek, John, II 374
Hawks, Howard, II 376
Hayward, Susan, II 377
Hayworth, Rita, II 377
Hearst, William Randolph, II 379
Hefner, Hugh, II 383
Hellman, Lillian, II 384
Hell's Angels, II 384
Hemingway, Ernest, II 386
Hemlines, II 390
Henderson, Fletcher, II 390
Henry Aldrich, II 392
Hep Cats, II 393
Hepburn, Audrey, II 394
Hepburn, Katharine, II 394
Herman, Woody, II 398
Heston, Charlton, II 399
High Noon, II 400
Highway System, II 402
Hiking, II 405
Himes, Chester, II 408
Hirschfeld, Albert, II 412
Hiss, Alger, II 413
Hitchcock, Alfred, II 414
Hockey, II 417
Hogan, Ben, II 421
Holbrook, Hal, II 424
Holden, William, II 426
Holiday, Billie, II 427
Holiday Inns, II 428
Holliday, Judy, II 429
Holly, Buddy, II 429
Hollywood Ten, II 434
Honeymooners, II 439
Hooker, John Lee, II 440
Hoover, J. Edgar, II 443
Hopalong Cassidy, II 444
Hope, Bob, II 446
Hopkins, Sam ''Lightnin','' II 447
Hopper, Dennis, II 447
Hopper, Edward, II 448
Hopscotch, II 449
Horne, Lena, II 449
Horror Movies, II 450
Hot Dogs, II 454
Hot Rods, II 455
Howdy Doody Show, II 459
Howe, Gordie, II 460
Howlin' Wolf, II 461
Hubbard, L. Ron, II 461
Hudson, Rock, II 462
Hughes, Howard, II 464
Hughes, Langston, II 465
Hula Hoop, II 466
Hull, Bobby, II 467
Hunter, Tab, II 468
Huntley, Chet, II 469
Hurston, Zora Neale, II 469
Huston, John, II 471
Hutton, Ina Ray, II 472
I Love a Mystery, II 476
I Love Lucy, II 477
I Was a Teenage Werewolf, II 480

IBM (International Business Machines), II 481
Indian, II 487
Indianapolis 500, II 490
Industrial Design, II 491
Ink Spots, II 493
Inner Sanctum Mysteries, II 493
Invisible Man, II 498
It's a Wonderful Life, II 506
Ives, Burl, II 508
J. Walter Thompson, II 511
Jack Armstrong, II 512
Jackson, Mahalia, II 515
Jackson, Shirley, II 520
James, Elmore, II 525
James, Harry, II 525
Jazz, II 529
Jeans, II 532
Jeep, II 533
Jell-O, II 537
Jennings, Waylon, II 540
Jessel, George, II 542
Jet, II 544
John Birch Society, II 549
Johns, Jasper, II 551
Jones, George, II 561
Jordan, Louis, II 568
Joy of Cooking, II 572
Judy Bolton, II 578
Juke Boxes, II 579
Juvenile Delinquency, II 583
Kaltenborn, Hans von, III 1
Kantor, MacKinlay, III 3
Karloff, Boris, III 4
Kasem, Casey, III 6
Kaye, Danny, III 9
Keaton, Buster, III 10
Kelly Bag, III 14
Kelly, Gene, III 14
Kelly, Grace, III 15
Kentucky Derby, III 19
Kentucky Fried Chicken, III 20
Kershaw, Doug, III 21
King, B. B., III 26
King, Martin Luther, Jr., III 33
Kingston Trio, III 39
Kinsey, Dr. Alfred C., III 40
Kirby, Jack, III 42
Kitsch, III 43
Kiwanis, III 46
Kodak, III 51
Korman, Harvey, III 56
Kovacs, Ernie, III 58
Kraft Television Theatre, III 60
Krupa, Gene, III 63
Ku Klux Klan, III 64
Kubrick, Stanley, III 66
Kukla, Fran, and Ollie, III 68
''La Bamba'', III 71
Labor Unions, III 72
Ladd, Alan, III 75
Laetrile, III 76
Lahr, Bert, III 76
LaLanne, Jack, III 80
Lamarr, Hedy, III 82
LaMotta, Jake, III 83
Lamour, Dorothy, III 83
L'Amour, Louis, III 84
Lancaster, Burt, III 85
Landon, Michael, III 86
Landry, Tom, III 87
Lang, Fritz, III 87
Lansky, Meyer, III 90
Las Vegas, III 92
Lasorda, Tommy, III 93
Lassie, III 95
Latin Jazz, III 97
La-Z-Boy Loungers, III 106
Leachman, Cloris, III 108
League of Their Own, III 110
Lear, Norman, III 111
Leary, Timothy, III 112
Leave It to Beaver, III 115

Lee, Bruce, III 117
Lee, Gypsy Rose, III 119
Lee, Peggy, III 121
Lee, Stan, III 124
Legos, III 125
Lehrer, Tom, III 126
Leisure Time, III 128
Leopold and Loeb, III 138
Lesbianism, III 140
Let's Pretend, III 143
Levi's, III 146
Levittown, III 147
Lewis, C. S., III 150
Lewis, Jerry, III 152
Lewis, Jerry Lee, III 153
Liberace, III 155
Life, III 160
Life of Riley, III 162
Li'l Abner, III 163
Lincoln Center for the Performing Arts, III 165
Lindbergh, Anne Morrow, III 166
Lindbergh, Charles, III 166
Linkletter, Art, III 168
Lionel Trains, III 170
Lippmann, Walter, III 170
Lipstick, III 171
Little League, III 174
Little Magazines, III 176
Little Orphan Annie, III 177
Little Richard, III 178
Live Television, III 178
Loafers, III 182
Lolita, III 183
Lombardi, Vince, III 185
Lombardo, Guy, III 187
Lone Ranger, III 189
Long-Playing Record, III 192
Loos, Anita, III 194
Lorre, Peter, III 195
Los Angeles Lakers, III 196
Louis, Joe, III 200
Louisville Slugger, III 201
Low Riders, III 206
LSD, III 207
Luce, Henry, III 210
Ludlum, Robert, III 213
Lugosi, Bela, III 213
Lynching, III 217
Ma Perkins, III 223
Mabley, Moms, III 223
MacDonald, Jeanette, III 224
MacDonald, John D., III 226
MacMurray, Fred, III 228
Macon, Uncle Dave, III 229
MAD Magazine, III 230
Mafia/Organized Crime, III 237
Mah-Jongg, III 242
Mailer, Norman, III 242
Malcolm X, III 243
Mall, III 247
Manchurian Candidate, III 254
Mancini, Henry, III 256
Mansfield, Jayne, III 259
Mantle, Mickey, III 262
March On Washington, III 266
Marching Bands, III 267
Marciano, Rocky, III 268
Mardi Gras, III 269
Mariachi Music, III 270
Marie, Rose, III 272
Maris, Roger, III 274
Marlboro Man, III 274
Marley, Bob, III 274
Martin, Dean, III 280
Martini, III 282
Marvel Comics, III 285
Marx Brothers, III 287
Marx, Groucho, III 288
Mary Worth, III 294
Masses, III 302
Masters Golf Tournament, III 305
Mathis, Johnny, III 305

Mayfield, Curtis, III 310
Mayfield, Percy, III 310
Mays, Willie, III 311
McBain, Ed, III 312
McCall's Magazine, III 313
McCarthyism, III 314
McCartney, Paul, III 316
McCoy, Horace, III 319
McCrea, Joel, III 319
McDonald's, III 321
McKuen, Rod, III 328
McQueen, Butterfly, III 332
Meadows, Audrey, III 336
Media Feeding Frenzies, III 337
Medicine Shows, III 339
Mencken, H. L., III 342
Mendoza, Lydia, III 344
Merton, Thomas, III 345
Metalious, Grace, III 346
Metropolitan Museum of Art, III 347
MGM (Metro-Goldwyn-Mayer), III 347
Michener, James, III 351
Mickey Mouse Club, III 351
Miller, Arthur, III 363
Miller, Henry, III 367
Miller, Roger, III 367
Milton Bradley, III 369
Minnelli, Vincente, III 370
Minoso, Minnie, III 371
Miss America Pageant, III 374
Mitchum, Robert, III 381
Mix, Tom, III 383
Modern Dance, III 388
Modern Maturity, III 388
Monopoly, III 396
Monroe, Bill, III 396
Monroe, Marilyn, III 399
Montalbán, Ricardo, III 401
Montana, Patsy, III 403
Moreno, Rita, III 410
Morse, Carlton E., III 415
Mother's Day, III 417
Mount Rushmore, III 423
Mouseketeers, III 425
Movie Stars, III 428
Mr. Wizard, III 433
Mummy, III 441
Murray, Arthur, III 448
Murrow, Edward R., III 451
Muscle Beach, III 453
Muscle Cars, III 455
Muscular Christianity, III 456
Musical, III 458
Mutt & Jeff, III 462
Muzak, III 463
My Fair Lady, III 464
Nancy Drew, III 473
NASA, III 475
Nation, III 476
National Basketball Association (NBA), III 477
National Collegiate Athletic Association
    (NCAA), III 479
National Enquirer, III 480
National Football League (NFL), III 482
National Hockey League (NHL), III 485
National Parks, III 489
Natural, III 492
Neckties, III 495
Nelson, Ricky, III 499
Nelson, Willie, III 501
Nerd Look, III 502
Networks, III 503
New Look, III 512
New Orleans Rhythm and Blues, III 513
New Republic, III 514
New York Knickerbockers, III 517
New York Times, III 518
New York Yankees, III 520
New Yorker, III 522
Newhart, Bob, III 524
Newport Jazz and Folk Festivals, III 526
Newsweek, III 527

Niagara Falls, III 528
Nichols, Mike, and Elaine May, III 529
Nicklaus, Jack, III 531
Nixon, Agnes, III 539
North by Northwest, III 541
Novak, Kim, III 543
Nylon, III 544
O'Connor, Flannery, III 549
Objectivism/Ayn Rand, III 547
O'Keeffe, Georgia, III 552
Oklahoma!, III 553
Olivier, Laurence, III 556
Olsen, Tillie, III 558
Olympics, III 558
Omnibus, III 561
On the Road, III 561
On the Waterfront, III 562
Onassis, Jacqueline Lee Bouvier Kennedy,
    III 564
One Man's Family, III 567
O'Neill, Eugene, III 569
Op Art, III 569
Orbison, Roy, III 571
Organization Man, III 572
Ouija Boards, III 576
Outing, III 580
Owens, Buck, III 582
Owens, Jesse, III 583
Paar, Jack, IV 1
Pachucos, IV 2
Paige, Satchel, IV 5
Paley, William S., IV 6
Palmer, Arnold, IV 7
Pants for Women, IV 7
Paperbacks, IV 9
Parades, IV 12
Parker Brothers, IV 13
Parker, Charlie, IV 13
Parks, Rosa, IV 15
Parrish, Maxfield, IV 16
Paul, Les, IV 20
Peale, Norman Vincent, IV 23
Peanuts, IV 25
Pearl, Minnie, IV 28
Peck, Gregory, IV 29
Pelé, IV 33
Penn, Irving, IV 33
Perry Mason, IV 41
Pets, IV 44
Petting, IV 45
Petty, Richard, IV 46
Peyton Place, IV 47
Philco Television Playhouse, IV 50
Phillips, Irna, IV 51
Phonograph, IV 52
Picasso, Pablo, IV 54
Pin-Up, IV 58
Pittsburgh Steelers, IV 61
Pizza, IV 62
Place in the Sun, IV 63
Plastic, IV 64
Plath, Sylvia, IV 68
Playboy, IV 70
Playhouse 90, IV 73
Pogo, IV 73
Poitier, Sidney, IV 75
Polio, IV 76
Political Bosses, IV 77
Pollock, Jackson, IV 79
Pop Music, IV 83
Pope, IV 86
Popeye, IV 87
Popsicles, IV 88
Popular Mechanics, IV 89
Popular Psychology, IV 90
Pornography, IV 92
Porter, Cole, IV 95
Postcards, IV 96
Powell, Dick, IV 102
Powell, William, IV 102
Preminger, Otto, IV 104
Presley, Elvis, IV 105

Price Is Right, IV 108
Price, Vincent, IV 110
Prince, Hal, IV 114
Professional Football, IV 116
Prom, IV 120
Protest Groups, IV 124
Public Libraries, IV 133
Public Television (PBS), IV 135
Puente, Tito, IV 137
Pulp Magazines, IV 139
Pynchon, Thomas, IV 145
Queen, Ellery, IV 148
Queen for a Day, IV 149
Quiz Show Scandals, IV 151
Race Riots, IV 156
Radio, IV 157
Raft, George, IV 162
Rains, Claude, IV 168
Ranch House, IV 173
Rand, Sally, IV 173
Reader's Digest, IV 177
Reagan, Ronald, IV 179
Rear Window, IV 184
Rebel without a Cause, IV 185
Redbook, IV 189
Redding, Otis, IV 189
Reed, Donna, IV 191
Reese, Pee Wee, IV 193
Reeves, Steve, IV 193
Reiner, Carl, IV 196
Reno, Don, IV 204
Renoir, Jean, IV 204
Rhythm and Blues, IV 206
Riggs, Bobby, IV 211
Ripley's Believe It Or Not, IV 215
Rivera, Chita, IV 216
Rizzuto, Phil, IV 220
Road Runner and Wile E. Coyote, IV 222
Robeson, Paul, IV 227
Robinson, Edward G., IV 229
Robinson, Frank, IV 230
Robinson, Jackie, IV 231
Robinson, Sugar Ray, IV 234
Rock and Roll, IV 235
Rockefeller Family, IV 239
Rockettes, IV 241
Rockwell, Norman, IV 244
Rocky and Bullwinkle, IV 248
Rodeo, IV 252
Rodgers and Hammerstein, IV 254
Rodgers, Jimmie, IV 258
Rogers, Kenny, IV 261
Rogers, Roy, IV 262
Roller Coasters, IV 265
Roller Derby, IV 266
Romance Novels, IV 270
Romero, Cesar, IV 273
Rose Bowl, IV 275
Rosenberg, Julius and Ethel, IV 279
Route 66, IV 284
Rudolph the Red-Nosed Reindeer, IV 287
Rupp, Adolph, IV 290
Russell, Bill, IV 290
Russell, Jane, IV 292
Russell, Nipsey, IV 293
RV, IV 295
Rydell, Bobby, IV 298
Sahl, Mort, IV 301
Saks Fifth Avenue, IV 302
Sales, Soupy, IV 303
Sandburg, Carl, IV 306
Saratoga Springs, IV 312
Sarnoff, David, IV 312
Satellites, IV 314
Saturday Evening Post, IV 315
Saturday Morning Cartoons, IV 317
Savoy Ballroom, IV 322
Science Fiction Publishing, IV 330
Scientific American, IV 334
Scott, George C., IV 338
Scott, Randolph, IV 339
Scruggs, Earl, IV 345

Scully, Vin, IV 345
Search for Tomorrow, IV 346
Searchers, IV 346
Sears Roebuck Catalogue, IV 346
Second City, IV 348
Seduction of the Innocent, IV 350
Seeger, Pete, IV 351
Sellers, Peter, IV 355
Serling, Rod, IV 361
Seven Year Itch, IV 364
Seventeen, IV 364
Sex Scandals, IV 367
Sex Symbol, IV 369
Sexual Revolution, IV 373
Shane, IV 378
Shaw, Artie, IV 381
Shawn, Ted, IV 381
She Wore a Yellow Ribbon, IV 381
Sheldon, Sidney, IV 381
Shirer, William L., IV 384
Shore, Dinah, IV 387
Show Boat, IV 389
Shulman, Max, IV 391
Sinatra, Frank, IV 409
Singer, Isaac Bashevis, IV 414
Singin' in the Rain, IV 415
Sirk, Douglas, IV 416
Sitcom, IV 418
$64,000 Question, IV 427
Skateboarding, IV 428
Skelton, Red, IV 431
Skyscrapers, IV 432
Slang, IV 434
Slinky, IV 436
Smith, Kate, IV 439
Soap Operas, IV 446
Soccer, IV 449
Social Dancing, IV 450
Soda Fountains, IV 452
Some Like It Hot, IV 453
.Sondheim, Stephen, IV 454
Soul Music, IV 458
South Pacific, IV 465
Spartacus, IV 468
Spector, Phil, IV 471
Spelling, Aaron, IV 472
Spillane, Mickey, IV 477
Spock, Dr. Benjamin, IV 480
Sport Utility Vehicles (SUVs), IV 482
Sporting News, IV 483
Sports Hero, IV 484
Sports Illustrated, IV 487
Spring Break, IV 488
Sputnik, IV 493
St. Denis, Ruth, IV 494
Stagg, Amos Alonzo, IV 499
Standardized Testing, IV 502
Stand-up Comedy, IV 504
Stanley Brothers, IV 506
Star System, IV 507
Starr, Bart, IV 515
State Fairs, IV 518
Steinbeck, John, IV 522
Steinberg, Saul, IV 523
Stengel, Casey, IV 526
Stetson Hat, IV 532
Stewart, Jimmy, IV 532
Stickball, IV 534
Stiller and Meara, IV 535
Stock-Car Racing, IV 537
Stock Market Crashes, IV 539
Stockton, ''Pudgy'', IV 541
Stone, Irving, IV 542
Street and Smith, IV 553
Streetcar Named Desire, IV 554
Strip Joints/Striptease, IV 557
Stuckey's, IV 560
Studio One, IV 563
Studio System, IV 565
Suburbia, IV 567
Suicide, IV 569
Sullivan, Ed, IV 570

Summer Camp, IV 573
Sun Records, IV 576
Sunset Boulevard, IV 579
Superman, IV 581
Surf Music, IV 585
Susskind, David, IV 587
Swimming Pools, IV 590
Swing Dancing, IV 592
Syndication, IV 595
Tabloids, IV 597
Tales from the Crypt, IV 600
Talk Radio, IV 600
Tang, IV 603
Tanning, IV 603
Tap Dancing, IV 605
Tarzan, IV 608
Taylor, Elizabeth, IV 612
Taylor, Robert, IV 615
Teddy Bears, IV 616
Teen Idols, IV 617
Teenagers, IV 620
Telephone, IV 623
Televangelism, IV 625
Television, IV 626
Television Anchors, IV 629
Ten Commandments, IV 634
Tennis, IV 635
Tennis Shoes/Sneakers, IV 637
Terry and the Pirates, IV 640
Thanksgiving, IV 640
Them!, IV 641
Thing, IV 642
This Is Your Life, IV 643
Thomas, Danny, IV 644
Thomas, Lowell, IV 645
Thomson, Bobby, IV 647
Three Stooges, IV 651
Tierney, Gene, IV 655
Tiffany & Company, IV 655
Tijuana Bibles, IV 656
Time, IV 657
Times Square, IV 659
Timex Watches, IV 661
Titanic, IV 661
To Kill a Mockingbird, IV 663
To Tell the Truth, IV 664
Today, IV 666
Tokyo Rose, IV 669
Tolkien, J. R. R., IV 671
Tom of Finland, IV 673
Tom Swift Series, IV 674
Tone, Franchot, IV 676
Tonight Show, IV 677
Top 40, IV 679
Tormé, Mel, IV 683
Town Meetings, IV 684
Toys, IV 685
Tracy, Spencer, IV 687
Trading Stamps, IV 688
Trailer Parks, IV 689
Tramps, IV 691
Traveling Carnivals, IV 692
Trevor, Claire, IV 697
Trixie Belden, IV 698
Trout, Robert, IV 698
T-Shirts, IV 700
Tupperware, IV 700
Turner, Ike and Tina, IV 702
Turner, Lana, IV 703
TV Dinners, IV 706
TV Guide, IV 706
Tweety Pie and Sylvester, IV 707
Twelve-Step Programs, IV 708
Twilight Zone, IV 713
Uecker, Bob, V 1
UFOs (Unidentified Flying Objects), V 1
Unitas, Johnny, V 6
United Artists, V 8
Unser, Al, V 8
U.S. One, V 11
Valens, Ritchie, V 16
Valentine's Day, V 16

Vallee, Rudy, V 21
Vampires, V 22
Van Dyke, Dick, V 24
Vance, Vivian, V 27
Varga Girl, V 30
Vaughan, Sarah, V 36
Velveeta Cheese, V 39
Vertigo, V 42
Vidal, Gore, V 45
Videos, V 47
Vidor, King, V 48
Vietnam, V 49
Vitamins, V 52
Vogue, V 53
Volkswagen Beetle, V 54
Vonnegut, Kurt, Jr., V 56
Wagon Train, V 59
Walker, Aaron ''T-Bone'', V 59
Walker, Junior, and the All-Stars, V 63
Wall Drug, V 66
Wall Street Journal, V 67
War Movies, V 75
Warhol, Andy, V 80
Washington Post, V 83
Waters, Ethel, V 86
Waters, Muddy, V 89
Wayne, John, V 91
Weavers, V 96
Webb, Jack, V 98
Wedding Dress, V 100
Weekend, V 101
Weird Tales, V 103
Weissmuller, Johnny, V 104
Welk, Lawrence, V 106
Welles, Orson, V 108
Wells, Kitty, V 109
Wertham, Fredric, V 111
West, Mae, V 115
West Side Story, V 116
Western, V 118
What's My Line?, V 122
White, Betty, V 127
White Castle, V 127
White, E. B., V 127
White Flight, V 128
White, Stanford, V 129
Whiteman, Paul, V 130
Whiting, Margaret, V 130
Wild One, V 135
Wilder, Billy, V 136
Wilder, Laura Ingalls, V 136
Wilder, Thornton, V 138
Williams, Andy, V 139
Williams, Hank, Jr., V 141
Williams, Hank, Sr., V 141
Williams, Ted, V 144
Williams, Tennessee, V 146
Wimbledon, V 150
Winchell, Walter, V 151
Windy City, V 152
Winnie-the-Pooh, V 155
Winnie Winkle the Breadwinner, V 156
Winters, Jonathan, V 157
Wire Services, V 158
Wizard of Oz, V 162
Wobblies, V 165
Wodehouse, P. G., V 166
Wolfman, V 167
Woman's Day, V 169
Wong, Anna May, V 172
Wood, Ed, V 172
Wood, Natalie, V 173
World Series, V 182
World War II, V 188
World's Fairs, V 194
Wrangler Jeans, V 196
Wray, Fay, V 196
Wright, Richard, V 196
Wuthering Heights, V 198
WWJD? (What Would Jesus Do?), V 198
Wyeth, Andrew, V 199
Yankee Stadium, V 208

Yellowstone National Park, V 213
Young, Loretta, V 217
Young, Robert, V 218
Youngman, Henny, V 219
Your Hit Parade, V 220
Your Show of Shows, V 221
Zanuck, Darryl F., V 225
Zines, V 228
Zoos, V 230
Zorro, V 234
Zydeco, V 235

1960-1969
A&R Men/Women, I 1
Aaron, Hank, I 2
AARP (American Association for Retired
    Persons), I 3
Abbey, Edward, I 4
Abbott and Costello, I 5
Abstract Expressionism, I 11
Academy Awards, I 12
Adams, Ansel, I 17
Addams Family, I 18
Adderley, Cannonball, I 18
Adidas, I 20
Adventures of Ozzie and Harriet, I 21
Advertising, I 23
Advice Columns, I 26
Advocate, I 29
Aerobics, I 30
African American Press, I 32
Agents, I 34
Ailey, Alvin, I 37
Air Travel, I 38
Album-Oriented Rock, I 41
Alda, Alan, I 42
Ali, Muhammad, I 44
Alka Seltzer, I 49
Allen, Steve, I 52
Allen, Woody, I 53
Allison, Luther, I 54
Allman Brothers Band, I 56
Alpert, Herb, and the Tijuana Brass, I 57
Altamont, I 57
Alternative Country Music, I 59
Alternative Press, I 60
Altman, Robert, I 63
Amazing Stories, I 64
American Bandstand, I 65
American International Pictures, I 71
American Museum of Natural History, I 72
Amos 'n' Andy Show, I 72
Amsterdam, Morey, I 74
Amusement Parks, I 77
Amway, I 80
Andretti, Mario, I 84
Androgyny, I 85
Andy Griffith Show, I 86
Angell, Roger, I 88
Animal House, I 89
Animated Films, I 90
Anka, Paul, I 95
Annie Get Your Gun, I 96
Another World, I 99
Anthony, Piers, I 100
Aparicio, Luis, I 101
Apollo Missions, I 102
Apollo Theatre, I 104
Archie Comics, I 108
Argosy, I 109
Arizona Highways, I 110
Arledge, Roone, I 111
Armed Forces Radio Service, I 112
Armstrong, Louis, I 114
Arnaz, Desi, I 116
Arthurian Legend, I 120
As the World Turns, I 121
Ashe, Arthur, I 123
Asimov, Isaac, I 125
Asner, Edward, I 126
Astounding Science Fiction, I 129
Astrology, I 129
AT&T, I 130

Athletic Model Guild, I 132
Atlantic Monthly, I 134
Atlantic Records, I 135
Atlas, Charles, I 135
Auerbach, Red, I 136
Aunt Jemima, I 137
Automobile, I 137
Avalon, Frankie, I 143
Avedon, Richard, I 144
Avengers, I 144
''B'' movies, I 149
Babar, I 151
Baby Boomers, I 151
Bacall, Lauren, I 154
Bach, Richard, I 155
Baez, Joan, I 156
Bagels, I 158
Bakker, Jim, and Tammy Faye, I 160
Balanchine, George, I 161
Baldwin, James, I 161
Ball, Lucille, I 163
Ballard, Hank, I 164
Ballet, I 165
Band, I 167
Baraka, Amiri, I 168
Barbecue, I 168
Barber, Red, I 169
Barbershop Quartets, I 169
Barbie, I 171
Baseball, I 180
Baseball Cards, I 183
Basketball, I 186
Batman, I 189
Bay, Mel, I 191
Bay of Pigs Invasion, I 192
Beach Boys, I 195
Beatles, I 203
Beatty, Warren, I 206
Beauty Queens, I 207
Beer, I 210
Belafonte, Harry, I 214
Bell Telephone Hour, I 216
Bellbottoms, I 216
Ben Casey, I 218
Bennett, Tony, I 221
Benny Hill Show, I 222
Benny, Jack, I 222
Bergman, Ingmar, I 225
Bergman, Ingrid, I 226
Berle, Milton, I 228
Berlin, Irving, I 230
Bernstein, Leonard, I 233
Berra, Yogi, I 233
Berry, Chuck, I 234
Bestsellers, I 236
Better Homes and Gardens, I 238
Beverly Hillbillies, I 241
Bewitched, I 243
Bicycling, I 245
Big Apple, I 246
Bigfoot, I 251
Bilingual Education, I 252
Billboards, I 253
Birkenstocks, I 257
Birthing Practices, I 260
Black Panthers, I 264
Black Sabbath, I 265
Blacklisting, I 272
Blanc, Mel, I 276
Bland, Bobby Blue, I 278
Blass, Bill, I 278
Blockbusters, I 280
Blount, Roy, Jr., I 285
Bluegrass, I 287
Blues, I 290
Bly, Robert, I 296
Board Games, I 297
Bob and Ray, I 299
Bobbsey Twins, I 300
Bodybuilding, I 305
Bogart, Humphrey, I 308
Bomb, I 311

Bombeck, Erma, I 314
Bonanza, I 316
Bonnie and Clyde, I 316
Booker T. and the MG's, I 318
Book-of-the-Month Club, I 318
Borge, Victor, I 320
Borscht Belt, I 321
Boston Celtics, I 322
Boston Garden, I 323
Boston Marathon, I 323
Boston Strangler, I 324
Bouton, Jim, I 326
Bowie, David, I 328
Bowling, I 328
Boxing, I 330
Boy Scouts of America, I 333
Bra, I 335
Bradbury, Ray, I 337
Bradley, Bill, I 338
Brando, Marlon, I 342
Brautigan, Richard, I 345
Breakfast at Tiffany's, I 346
Breast Implants, I 347
Brenda Starr, I 348
Brice, Fanny, I 348
Bridge, I 349
Brill Building, I 351
British Invasion, I 354
Broadway, I 356
Bronson, Charles, I 360
Brooks, Gwendolyn, I 365
Brooks, Mel, I 365
Brothers, Dr. Joyce, I 367
Brown, James, I 367
Brown, Jim, I 369
Brown, Paul, I 370
Brubeck, Dave, I 372
Bruce, Lenny, I 372
Bryant, Paul "Bear", I 374
Brynner, Yul, I 375
Bubblegum Rock, I 375
Buck, Pearl S., I 375
Buckley, William F., Jr., I 379
Budweiser, I 380
Buffalo Springfield, I 381
Bugs Bunny, I 383
Bumper Stickers, I 384
Burger King, I 387
Burma-Shave, I 390
Burnett, Carol, I 391
Burr, Raymond, I 394
Burroughs, William S., I 397
Butch Cassidy and the Sundance Kid, I 398
Butkus, Dick, I 399
Buttons, Red, I 401
Byrds, I 402
Cadillac, I 406
Cagney, James, I 409
Cahan, Abraham, I 411
Calloway, Cab, I 412
Camelot, I 414
Camp, I 415
Campbell, Glen, I 416
Camping, I 417
Cancer, I 418
Candid Camera, I 420
Caniff, Milton, I 421
Canova, Judy, I 421
Capital Punishment, I 424
Capote, Truman, I 426
Captain America, I 429
Captain Kangaroo, I 430
Car 54, Where Are You?, I 432
Car Coats, I 433
Caray, Harry, I 433
Carlin, George, I 434
Carlton, Steve, I 435
Carmichael, Hoagy, I 436
Carnegie, Dale, I 437
Carnegie Hall, I 439
Carr, John Dickson, I 442
Carson, Johnny, I 444

Carter Family, I 445
Cash, Johnny, I 449
Cassette Tape, I 451
Cassidy, David, I 452
Castaneda, Carlos, I 453
Castro, I 454
Catch-22, I 457
Cavett, Dick, I 460
CB Radio, I 462
Celebrity, I 463
Cemeteries, I 467
Central Park, I 468
Century 21 Exposition (Seattle, 1962), I 470
Chamberlain, Wilt, I 472
Charles, Ray, I 477
Chavez, Cesar, I 482
Chayefsky, Paddy, I 484
Checker, Chubby, I 484
Cheerleading, I 486
Chenier, Clifton, I 490
Cherry Ames, I 491
Chessman, Caryl, I 492
Chicago Bears, I 492
Chicago Bulls, I 493
Chicago Cubs, I 493
Chicago Seven, I 495
Child, Julia, I 496
Child Stars, I 498
Chipmunks, I 501
Christie, Agatha, I 502
Christmas, I 503
Christo, I 505
Chun King, I 509
Church Socials, I 509
Cigarettes, I 510
Circus, I 512
City of Angels, I 516
Civil Disobedience, I 517
Civil Rights Movement, I 519
Civil War Reenactors, I 521
Clairol Hair Coloring, I 523
Clapton, Eric, I 525
Clark, Dick, I 525
Clarke, Arthur C., I 527
Clemente, Roberto, I 528
Cleopatra, I 529
Clift, Montgomery, I 529
Cline, Patsy, I 530
Clinton, George, I 532
A Clockwork Orange, I 532
Clooney, Rosemary, I 533
Closet, I 536
Coca-Cola, I 540
Cocktail Parties, I 544
Coffee, I 546
Colbert, Claudette, I 548
Cold War, I 549
Cole, Nat "King", I 552
College Fads, I 553
College Football, I 555
Collins, Albert, I 557
Coltrane, John, I 557
Comic Books, I 560
Comics, I 562
Comics Code Authority, I 565
Coming Out, I 566
Communes, I 568
Communism, I 569
Community Media, I 570
Community Theatre, I 573
Como, Perry, I 574
Concept Album, I 576
Conceptual Art, I 577
Condé Nast, I 577
Condoms, I 578
Confession Magazines, I 581
Coniff, Ray, I 583
Consciousness Raising Groups, I 585
Conspiracy Theories, I 586
Consumer Reports, I 587
Consumerism, I 589
Convertible, I 593

Conway, Tim, I 594
Cooke, Sam, I 594
Cooper, Alice, I 595
Cooperstown, New York, I 598
Coors, I 599
Corman, Roger, I 603
Corvette, I 603
Cosby, Bill, I 606
Cosell, Howard, I 608
Cosmopolitan, I 610
Cotten, Joseph, I 613
Country Gentlemen, I 617
Country Music, I 617
Cousteau, Jacques, I 621
Cowboy Look, I 622
Crawford, Joan, I 625
Creationism, I 627
Credit Cards, I 628
Creedence Clearwater Revival, I 630
Crichton, Michael, I 631
Crisis, I 633
Cronkite, Walter, I 635
Crosby, Bing, I 638
Crosby, Stills, and Nash, I 639
Crossword Puzzles, I 641
Crumb, Robert, I 641
Cukor, George, I 643
Cult Films, I 643
Cults, I 646
Cunningham, Merce, I 648
Curious George, I 649
Dallas Cowboys, I 654
Dana, Bill, I 656
Dance Halls, I 657
Dandridge, Dorothy, I 658
Daredevil, the Man Without Fear, I 659
Dark Shadows, I 659
Davis, Bette, I 661
Davis, Miles, I 661
Day, Doris, I 664
Day the Earth Stood Still, I 665
Days of Our Lives, I 666
Daytime Talk Shows, I 667
Daytona 500, I 670
DC Comics, I 671
Death of a Salesman, I 678
Debutantes, I 680
Denishawn, I 686
Department Stores, I 688
Depression, I 690
Derleth, August, I 692
Detective Fiction, I 693
Detroit Tigers, I 695
Diamond, Neil, I 698
Dick and Jane Readers, I 700
Dick, Philip K., I 701
Dickinson, Angie, I 703
Diddley, Bo, I 703
Dieting, I 706
Dietrich, Marlene, I 708
Diller, Phyllis, I 712
Dime Stores/Woolworth's, I 717
Diners, I 719
Dirty Dozen, I 721
Disability, I 721
Disc Jockeys, I 725
Disney (Walt Disney Company), I 728
Ditka, Mike, I 731
Divine, I 731
Divorce, I 732
Dobie Gillis, I 735
Doby, Larry, I 736
Doc Martens, I 737
Doc Savage, I 738
Doctor Who, I 739
Doctor Zhivago, I 740
Doctorow, E. L., I 740
Do-It-Yourself Improvement, I 742
Domino, Fats, I 743
Donahue, Phil, I 744
Donovan, I 745
Doors, I 748

Doo-wop Music, I 750
Douglas, Melvyn, I 753
Douglas, Mike, I 754
Downs, Hugh, I 754
Dr. Jekyll and Mr. Hyde, I 756
Dr. Kildare, I 756
Dr. Seuss, I 757
Dr. Strangelove or: How I Learned How to Stop Worrying and Love the Bomb, I 759
Dracula, I 760
Drag, I 762
Drag Racing, I 764
Drifters, I 769
Drive-In Theater, I 769
Drug War, I 771
Dunkin' Donuts, I 775
Durocher, Leo, I 777
Dylan, Bob, I 780
Eames, Charles and Ray, II 1
Eastwood, Clint, II 2
Easy Rider, II 4
Ebony, II 7
Eddy, Duane, II 11
Edge of Night, II 13
Edwards, James, II 14
Edwards, Ralph, II 16
Eight-track Tape, II 16
Eisner, Will, II 18
El Teatro Campesino, II 18
Electric Guitar, II 21
Electric Trains, II 22
Elizondo, Hector, II 22
Ellison, Harlan, II 25
E-mail, II 26
Emmy Awards, II 27
Empire State Building, II 28
Environmentalism, II 29
Erector Sets, II 34
Ertegun, Ahmet, II 35
Escher, M. C., II 37
Esquire, II 40
Etiquette Columns, II 44
Everly Brothers, II 47
Existentialism, II 50
Fabares, Shelley, II 53
Fabian, II 53
Facelifts, II 54
Factor, Max, II 54
Fail-Safe, II 55
Fallout Shelters, II 58
Family Circle, II 59
Family Circus, II 61
Family Reunions, II 63
Fan Magazines, II 64
Fantasia, II 65
Fantastic Four, II 67
Farr, Jamie, II 71
Fast Food, II 71
Father Knows Best, II 75
Father's Day, II 76
Faulkner, William, II 77
FBI (Federal Bureau of Investigation), II 80
Feliciano, José, II 82
Felix the Cat, II 83
Fellini, Federico, II 84
Feminism, II 84
Fenway Park, II 87
Ferrante and Teicher, II 88
Fiddler on the Roof, II 90
Field and Stream, II 92
Field, Sally, II 94
Firearms, II 101
Firesign Theatre, II 103
Fisher, Eddie, II 104
Fisher-Price Toys, II 106
Fistful of Dollars, II 107
Fitzgerald, Ella, II 107
Flag Clothing, II 111
Flatt, Lester, II 113
Flea Markets, II 114
Fleetwood Mac, II 114
Fleming, Ian, II 116

Fleming, Peggy, II 116
Flintstones, II 118
Flipper, II 118
Florida Vacations, II 119
Flying Nun, II 120
Foggy Mountain Boys, II 122
Folk Music, II 123
Folkways Records, II 126
Fonda, Henry, II 127
Fonda, Jane, II 129
Fonteyn, Margot, II 130
Ford, Glenn, II 131
Ford, John, II 133
Ford Motor Company, II 135
Ford, Tennessee Ernie, II 138
Ford, Whitey, II 138
Foreman, George, II 138
Fortune, II 142
Fosse, Bob, II 143
Fourth of July Celebrations, II 146
Foxx, Redd, II 148
Foyt, A. J., II 148
Francis, Arlene, II 150
Francis, Connie, II 151
Frankenstein, II 152
Franklin, Aretha, II 154
Frawley, William, II 157
Frazier, Joe, II 157
Frazier, Walt "Clyde", II 158
Frederick's of Hollywood, II 159
Free Speech Movement, II 161
Freed, Alan "Moondog", II 162
Freedom Rides, II 163
French Fries, II 165
Frisbee, II 174
Frizzell, Lefty, II 175
Frost, Robert, II 177
Frosty the Snowman, II 178
Frozen Entrées, II 178
Fugitive, II 179
Fuller, Buckminster, II 180
Fundamentalism, II 181
Funicello, Annette, II 183
Funk, II 184
Gable, Clark, II 187
Gambling, II 188
Game Shows, II 191
Gangs, II 195
Gardner, Ava, II 200
Garland, Judy, II 202
Garner, James, II 204
Gas Stations, II 206
Gay and Lesbian Press, II 210
Gay Liberation Movement, II 211
Gay Men, II 215
Gaye, Marvin, II 216
General Hospital, II 218
General Motors, II 220
Get Smart, II 227
Ghettos, II 227
GI Joe, II 229
Gibson, Bob, II 231
Gifford, Frank, II 236
Gillespie, Dizzy, II 236
Gilligan's Island, II 238
Ginsberg, Allen, II 239
Girl Groups, II 240
Girl Scouts, II 242
Gish, Lillian, II 244
Gleason, Jackie, II 245
Godzilla, II 252
Golden Books, II 258
Golden Gate Bridge, II 259
Golf, II 261
Good Housekeeping, II 265
Good, the Bad, and the Ugly, II 266
Goodman, Benny, II 270
Goodson, Mark, II 271
Gordy, Berry, II 272
Gospel Music, II 274
Gossip Columns, II 275
Graduate, II 279

Graffiti, II 281
Graham, Bill, II 282
Graham, Billy, II 284
Graham, Martha, II 285
Grand Ole Opry, II 286
Grant, Cary, II 288
Grateful Dead, II 291
Greeley, Andrew, II 298
Green, Al, II 300
Green Bay Packers, II 300
Greenwich Village, II 304
Greeting Cards, II 306
Gregory, Dick, II 307
Greyhound Buses, II 312
Grier, Pam, II 312
Griffin, Merv, II 313
Grits, II 319
Grusin, Dave, II 322
Guaraldi, Vince, II 323
Guiding Light, II 323
Gunsmoke, II 326
Guthrie, Arlo, II 328
Guthrie, Woody, II 328
Guy, Buddy, II 329
Hackett, Buddy, II 333
Hackman, Gene, II 334
Haggard, Merle, II 334
Haight-Ashbury, II 336
Hair, II 338
Hairstyles, II 340
Halas, George "Papa Bear", II 342
Haley, Alex, II 343
Haley, Bill, II 343
Hallmark Hall of Fame, II 345
Halston, II 346
Hamburger, II 347
Hancock, Herbie, II 350
Hanna-Barbera, II 355
Hansberry, Lorraine, II 356
Happy Hour, II 359
Hardy Boys, II 360
Hare Krishna, II 362
Harlem Globetrotters, II 364
Harley-Davidson, II 368
Harmonica Bands, II 370
Harper's, II 372
Hate Crimes, II 373
Havlicek, John, II 374
Hawaii Five-O, II 375
Hayward, Susan, II 377
Heavy Metal, II 380
Hee Haw, II 381
Hefner, Hugh, II 383
Hellman, Lillian, II 384
Hello, Dolly!, II 384
Hell's Angels, II 384
Hemingway, Ernest, II 386
Hemlines, II 390
Hendrix, Jimi, II 391
Henson, Jim, II 393
Hepburn, Audrey, II 394
Hepburn, Katharine, II 394
Herbert, Frank, II 395
Herman, Woody, II 398
Heston, Charlton, II 399
Highway System, II 402
Hiking, II 405
Hippies, II 410
Hirschfeld, Albert, II 412
Hiss, Alger, II 413
Hitchcock, Alfred, II 414
Hockey, II 417
Hoffman, Abbie, II 419
Hoffman, Dustin, II 420
Hogan's Heroes, II 424
Holbrook, Hal, II 424
Holden, William, II 426
Holiday Inns, II 428
Hollywood, II 431
Hollywood Squares, II 434
Honeymooners, II 439
Hooker, John Lee, II 440

Hoover, J. Edgar, II 443
Hope, Bob, II 446
Hopkins, Sam ''Lightnin','' II 447
Hopper, Dennis, II 447
Hopper, Edward, II 448
Hopscotch, II 449
Horne, Lena, II 449
Horror Movies, II 450
Hot Dogs, II 454
Hot Rods, II 455
How the West Was Won, II 458
Howe, Gordie, II 460
Howlin' Wolf, II 461
Hubbard, L. Ron, II 461
Hudson, Rock, II 462
Hughes, Howard, II 464
Hughes, Langston, II 465
Hula Hoop, II 466
Hull, Bobby, II 467
Huntley, Chet, II 469
Huston, John, II 471
I Dream of Jeannie, II 475
I Love Lucy, II 477
I Spy, II 479
Iacocca, Lee, II 480
IBM (International Business Machines), II 481
Ice Shows, II 484
Incredible Hulk, II 486
Indian, II 487
Indianapolis 500, II 490
Industrial Design, II 491
Ink Spots, II 493
It's a Wonderful Life, II 506
Ives, Burl, II 508
J. Walter Thompson, II 511
Jackson Five, II 513
Jackson, Jesse, II 514
Jackson, Mahalia, II 515
Jackson, Michael, II 517
Jackson, Reggie, II 519
Jackson, Shirley, II 520
Jakes, John, II 522
James Bond Films, II 523
James, Elmore, II 525
Jazz, II 529
Jeans, II 532
Jeep, II 533
Jefferson Airplane/Starship, II 534
Jell-O, II 537
Jennings, Peter, II 538
Jennings, Waylon, II 540
Jeopardy!, II 541
Jessel, George, II 542
Jet, II 544
Jewish Defense League, II 545
JFK (The Movie), II 545
John Birch Society, II 549
Johns, Jasper, II 551
Jones, George, II 561
Jones, Tom, II 563
Joplin, Janis, II 565
Jordan, Louis, II 568
Joy of Cooking, II 572
Judy Bolton, II 578
Juke Boxes, II 579
Julia, II 580
Juliá, Raúl, II 581
Juvenile Delinquency, II 583
Kaltenborn, Hans von, III 1
Kantor, MacKinlay, III 3
Karloff, Boris, III 4
Kasem, Casey, III 6
Katzenjammer Kids, III 7
Kaye, Danny, III 9
Keaton, Buster, III 10
Keillor, Garrison, III 11
Kelly Bag, III 14
Kelly Girls, III 14
Kelly, Grace, III 15
Kennedy Assassination, III 16
Kent State Massacre, III 17
Kentucky Derby, III 19

Kentucky Fried Chicken, III 20
Kershaw, Doug, III 21
Kesey, Ken, III 22
Key West, III 22
King, Albert, III 25
King, B. B., III 26
King, Billie Jean, III 28
King, Freddie, III 30
King, Larry, III 32
King, Martin Luther, Jr., III 33
Kingston Trio, III 39
Kirby, Jack, III 42
Kitsch, III 43
Kiwanis, III 46
Kmart, III 47
Knievel, Evel, III 48
Knight, Bobby, III 49
Kodak, III 51
Koontz, Dean R., III 53
Korman, Harvey, III 56
Kosinski, Jerzy, III 56
Koufax, Sandy, III 57
Kovacs, Ernie, III 58
Krassner, Paul, III 61
Ku Klux Klan, III 64
Kubrick, Stanley, III 66
Kuhn, Bowie, III 68
Labor Unions, III 72
Ladd, Alan, III 75
Laetrile, III 76
Lahr, Bert, III 76
LaLanne, Jack, III 80
L'Amour, Louis, III 84
Lancaster, Burt, III 85
Landon, Michael, III 86
Landry, Tom, III 87
Lansky, Meyer, III 90
Las Vegas, III 92
Lasorda, Tommy, III 93
Lassie, III 95
Latin Jazz, III 97
Laugh-In, III 98
Lauren, Ralph, III 102
Laver, Rod, III 103
Lawrence of Arabia, III 104
Lawrence, Vicki, III 106
La-Z-Boy Loungers, III 106
Le Carré, John, III 106
Le Guin, Ursula K., III 107
Leachman, Cloris, III 108
Lear, Norman, III 111
Leary, Timothy, III 112
Leave It to Beaver, III 115
Led Zeppelin, III 116
Lee, Bruce, III 117
Lee, Gypsy Rose, III 119
Lee, Peggy, III 121
Lee, Stan, III 124
Legos, III 125
Lehrer, Tom, III 126
Leisure Time, III 128
L'Engle, Madeleine, III 131
Lennon, John, III 131
Leonard, Elmore, III 134
Leone, Sergio, III 136
Lesbianism, III 140
Levi's, III 146
Lewis, C. S., III 150
Lewis, Jerry, III 152
Lewis, Jerry Lee, III 153
Liberace, III 155
Lichtenstein, Roy, III 158
Life, III 160
Li'l Abner, III 163
Lincoln Center for the Performing Arts, III 165
Lindbergh, Anne Morrow, III 166
Lindbergh, Charles, III 166
Linkletter, Art, III 168
Lionel Trains, III 170
Lippmann, Walter, III 170
Lipstick, III 171
Liston, Sonny, III 171

Little League, III 174
Little Magazines, III 176
Little Orphan Annie, III 177
Live Television, III 178
Loafers, III 182
Lolita, III 183
Lombardi, Vince, III 185
Lombardo, Guy, III 187
Long-Playing Record, III 192
Loos, Anita, III 194
Lorre, Peter, III 195
Los Angeles Lakers, III 196
Lottery, III 199
Louisville Slugger, III 201
Low Riders, III 206
LSD, III 207
Luce, Henry, III 210
Ludlum, Robert, III 213
Lynching, III 217
Lynn, Loretta, III 218
Ma Perkins, III 223
Mabley, Moms, III 223
MacDonald, John D., III 226
MacMurray, Fred, III 228
MAD Magazine, III 230
Madden, John, III 232
Made-for-Television Movies, III 233
Mafia/Organized Crime, III 237
Magnificent Seven, III 240
Mah-Jongg, III 242
Mailer, Norman, III 242
Malcolm X, III 243
Mall, III 247
Mamas and the Papas, III 251
Man from U.N.C.L.E., III 253
Man Who Shot Liberty Valance, III 253
Manchurian Candidate, III 254
Mancini, Henry, III 256
Mansfield, Jayne, III 259
Manson, Charles, III 261
Mantle, Mickey, III 262
March On Washington, III 266
Marching Bands, III 267
Marcus Welby, M.D., III 269
Mardi Gras, III 269
Mariachi Music, III 270
Marichal, Juan, III 272
Marie, Rose, III 272
Marijuana, III 272
Maris, Roger, III 274
Marlboro Man, III 274
Marley, Bob, III 274
Marshall, Garry, III 278
Martha and the Vandellas, III 279
Martin, Dean, III 280
Martin, Quinn, III 282
Martini, III 282
Marvel Comics, III 285
Marx Brothers, III 287
Marx, Groucho, III 288
Mary Kay Cosmetics, III 290
Mary Poppins, III 291
Mary Worth, III 294
Mason, Jackie, III 298
Masters and Johnson, III 303
Masters Golf Tournament, III 305
Mathis, Johnny, III 305
Max, Peter, III 308
Mayfield, Curtis, III 310
Mayfield, Percy, III 310
Mays, Willie, III 311
McBain, Ed, III 312
McCaffrey, Anne, III 313
McCall's Magazine, III 313
McCartney, Paul, III 316
McCoy, Horace, III 319
McCrea, Joel, III 319
McDonald's, III 321
McHale's Navy, III 327
McKuen, Rod, III 328
McLuhan, Marshall, III 329
McMurtry, Larry, III 330

McQueen, Steve, III 333
Meadows, Audrey, III 336
Media Feeding Frenzies, III 337
Medicine Shows, III 339
Mendoza, Lydia, III 344
Merton, Thomas, III 345
Metalious, Grace, III 346
Metropolitan Museum of Art, III 347
MGM (Metro-Goldwyn-Mayer), III 347
Michener, James, III 351
Midler, Bette, III 356
Midnight Cowboy, III 357
Militias, III 359
Miller, Arthur, III 363
Miller Beer, III 364
Miller, Henry, III 367
Miller, Roger, III 367
Milton Bradley, III 369
Minimalism, III 369
Minivans, III 370
Minoso, Minnie, III 371
*Miranda*Warning, III 373
Miss America Pageant, III 374
Mission: Impossible, III 375
Mister Ed, III 376
Mister Rogers' Neighborhood, III 378
Mitchell, Joni, III 379
Mitchum, Robert, III 381
Mod, III 384
Mod Squad, III 385
Modern Dance, III 388
Modern Maturity, III 388
Momaday, N. Scott, III 392
Monkees, III 394
Monopoly, III 396
Monroe, Bill, III 396
Monroe, Earl ''The Pearl'', III 397
Monroe, Marilyn, III 399
Montalbán, Ricardo, III 401
Montana, Patsy, III 403
Monty Python's Flying Circus, III 403
Moreno, Rita, III 410
Morrison, Van, III 415
Mother's Day, III 417
Motown, III 420
Mount Rushmore, III 423
Mountain Biking, III 424
Mouseketeers, III 425
Movie Stars, III 428
Mr. Wizard, III 433
Multiculturalism, III 439
Mummy, III 441
Muppets, III 444
Murray, Arthur, III 448
Murrow, Edward R., III 451
Muscle Cars, III 455
Muscular Christianity, III 456
Musical, III 458
Mutiny on the Bounty, III 461
Mutt & Jeff, III 462
Muzak, III 463
My Fair Lady, III 464
My Lai Massacre, III 465
My Three Sons, III 467
Nader, Ralph, III 469
Namath, Joe, III 471
Nancy Drew, III 473
NASA, III 475
Nation, III 476
National Basketball Association (NBA), III 477
National Collegiate Athletic Association
    (NCAA), III 479
National Enquirer, III 480
National Football League (NFL), III 482
National Hockey League (NHL), III 485
National Organization for Women
    (N.O.W.), III 489
National Parks, III 489
Neckties, III 495
Neighborhood Watch, III 499
Nelson, Ricky, III 499
Nelson, Willie, III 501

Nerd Look, III 502
Networks, III 503
New Age Spirituality, III 507
New Left, III 511
New Orleans Rhythm and Blues, III 513
New Republic, III 514
New York Knickerbockers, III 517
New York Mets, III 517
New York Times, III 518
New York Yankees, III 520
New Yorker, III 522
Newhart, Bob, III 524
Newlywed Game, III 526
Newport Jazz and Folk Festivals, III 526
Newsweek, III 527
Niagara Falls, III 528
Nichols, Mike, and Elaine May, III 529
Nicklaus, Jack, III 531
Night of the Living Dead, III 532
Nike, III 535
1968 Mexico City Summer Olympic
    Games, III 537
Nixon, Agnes, III 539
Novak, Kim, III 543
Nureyev, Rudolf, III 544
Nylon, III 544
O'Connor, Flannery, III 549
Oakland Raiders, III 547
Oates, Joyce Carol, III 547
Objectivism/Ayn Rand, III 547
Ochs, Phil, III 549
Odd Couple, III 550
O'Keeffe, Georgia, III 552
Oklahoma!, III 553
Oliphant, Pat, III 555
Olivier, Laurence, III 556
Olsen, Tillie, III 558
Olympics, III 558
Omnibus, III 561
Onassis, Jacqueline Lee Bouvier Kennedy,
    III 564
One Flew Over the Cuckoo's Nest, III 566
Op Art, III 569
Orbison, Roy, III 571
O'Rourke, P. J., III 573
Orr, Bobby, III 574
Osborne Brothers, III 575
Ouija Boards, III 576
Outer Limits, III 579
Outing, III 580
Owens, Buck, III 582
Paar, Jack, IV 1
Pachucos, IV 2
Pacino, Al, IV 3
Paige, Satchel, IV 5
Paley, Grace, IV 6
Paley, William S., IV 6
Palmer, Arnold, IV 7
Palmer, Jim, IV 7
Pants for Women, IV 7
Pantyhose, IV 9
Paperbacks, IV 9
Parades, IV 12
Parker Brothers, IV 13
Parks, Rosa, IV 15
Parrish, Maxfield, IV 16
Parton, Dolly, IV 17
Paulsen, Pat, IV 22
Peale, Norman Vincent, IV 23
Peanuts, IV 25
Pearl, Minnie, IV 28
Peck, Gregory, IV 29
Peep Shows, IV 30
Pelé, IV 33
Penn, Irving, IV 33
Penthouse, IV 34
Peppermint Lounge, IV 36
Pepsi-Cola, IV 36
Perry Mason, IV 41
Peter, Paul, and Mary, IV 42
Pets, IV 44
Petting, IV 45

Petty, Richard, IV 46
Peyton Place, IV 47
Phillips, Irna, IV 51
Phonograph, IV 52
Picasso, Pablo, IV 54
Pill, IV 57
Pink Floyd, IV 58
Pin-Up, IV 58
Pittsburgh Steelers, IV 61
Pizza, IV 62
Planet of the Apes, IV 63
Plastic, IV 64
Plastic Surgery, IV 67
Plath, Sylvia, IV 68
Platoon, IV 69
Playboy, IV 70
Playhouse 90, IV 73
Pogo, IV 73
Poitier, Sidney, IV 75
Polio, IV 76
Political Bosses, IV 77
Polyester, IV 80
Pop Art, IV 81
Pop, Iggy, IV 82
Pop Music, IV 83
Pope, IV 86
Popeye, IV 87
Popsicles, IV 88
Popular Mechanics, IV 89
Popular Psychology, IV 90
Pornography, IV 92
Postcards, IV 96
Potter, Dennis, IV 102
Preminger, Otto, IV 104
Presley, Elvis, IV 105
Price Is Right, IV 108
Price, Reynolds, IV 110
Price, Vincent, IV 110
Pride, Charley, IV 111
Prince, Hal, IV 114
Prisoner, IV 116
Professional Football, IV 116
Prom, IV 120
Protest Groups, IV 124
Pryor, Richard, IV 126
Psychedelia, IV 128
Psychics, IV 129
Psycho, IV 130
Public Libraries, IV 133
Public Television (PBS), IV 135
Puente, Tito, IV 137
Pynchon, Thomas, IV 145
Queen for a Day, IV 149
Race Riots, IV 156
Radio, IV 157
Ragni, Gerome and James Rado, IV 166
Rains, Claude, IV 168
Rand, Sally, IV 173
Rather, Dan, IV 176
Reader's Digest, IV 177
Reagan, Ronald, IV 179
Redding, Otis, IV 189
Redford, Robert, IV 190
Reed, Donna, IV 191
Reed, Ishmael, IV 191
Reed, Lou, IV 192
Reeves, Steve, IV 193
Reggae, IV 194
Reiner, Carl, IV 196
Reno, Don, IV 204
Renoir, Jean, IV 204
Retro Fashion, IV 205
Reynolds, Burt, IV 205
Rhythm and Blues, IV 206
Rich, Charlie, IV 209
Rigby, Cathy, IV 210
Riggs, Bobby, IV 211
Ringling Bros., Barnum & Bailey Circus, IV 212
Ripley's Believe It Or Not, IV 215
Rivera, Chita, IV 216
Rivers, Joan, IV 219
Rizzuto, Phil, IV 220

Road Runner and Wile E. Coyote, IV 222
Robertson, Oscar, IV 225
Robertson, Pat, IV 225
Robeson, Kenneth, IV 227
Robeson, Paul, IV 227
Robinson, Edward G., IV 229
Robinson, Frank, IV 230
Robinson, Smokey, IV 233
Robinson, Sugar Ray, IV 234
Rock and Roll, IV 235
Rockefeller Family, IV 239
Rockettes, IV 241
Rockwell, Norman, IV 244
Rocky and Bullwinkle, IV 248
Roddenberry, Gene, IV 251
Rodeo, IV 252
Rodríguez, Chi Chi, IV 259
Rogers, Kenny, IV 261
Rogers, Roy, IV 262
Roller Coasters, IV 265
Roller Derby, IV 266
Rolling Stone, IV 267
Rolling Stones, IV 269
Romance Novels, IV 270
Romero, Cesar, IV 273
Rose Bowl, IV 275
Rose, Pete, IV 276
Rosemary's Baby, IV 279
Ross, Diana, and the Supremes, IV 280
Route 66, IV 284
Royko, Mike, IV 285
Rudolph the Red-Nosed Reindeer, IV 287
Russell, Bill, IV 290
Russell, Jane, IV 292
Russell, Nipsey, IV 293
RV, IV 295
Ryan, Nolan, IV 297
Rydell, Bobby, IV 298
Sagan, Carl, IV 300
Saks Fifth Avenue, IV 302
Sales, Soupy, IV 303
Salsa Music, IV 303
Sandburg, Carl, IV 306
Santana, IV 311
Saratoga Springs, IV 312
Sarnoff, David, IV 312
Sassoon, Vidal, IV 313
Satellites, IV 314
Saturday Evening Post, IV 315
Saturday Morning Cartoons, IV 317
Schlatter, George, IV 325
Science Fiction Publishing, IV 330
Scientific American, IV 334
Scorsese, Martin, IV 337
Scott, George C., IV 338
Scott, Randolph, IV 339
Scruggs, Earl, IV 345
Scully, Vin, IV 345
Sea World, IV 345
Seals, Son, IV 345
Search for Tomorrow, IV 346
Sears Roebuck Catalogue, IV 346
Second City, IV 348
Seeger, Pete, IV 351
Sellers, Peter, IV 355
Serling, Rod, IV 361
Sesame Street, IV 362
Seven Days in May, IV 364
Seventeen, IV 364
Sex and the Single Girl, IV 366
Sex Scandals, IV 367
Sex Symbol, IV 369
Sexual Revolution, IV 373
Sheldon, Sidney, IV 381
Shepard, Sam, IV 382
Shirelles, IV 384
Shirer, William L., IV 384
Shock Radio, IV 386
Shore, Dinah, IV 387
Show Boat, IV 389
Shula, Don, IV 391
Shulman, Max, IV 391

SIDS (Sudden Infant Death Syndrome), IV 391
Silver Surfer, IV 399
Simon and Garfunkel, IV 399
Simon, Neil, IV 401
Simon, Paul, IV 403
Simpson, O. J., IV 404
Sinatra, Frank, IV 409
Singer, Isaac Bashevis, IV 414
Sitcom, IV 418
60 Minutes, IV 425
Skateboarding, IV 428
Skating, IV 429
Skelton, Red, IV 431
Slang, IV 434
Slasher Movies, IV 435
Slinky, IV 436
Sly and the Family Stone, IV 437
Smith, Dean, IV 439
Smith, Kate, IV 439
Smothers Brothers, IV 442
Soap Operas, IV 446
Soccer, IV 449
Social Dancing, IV 450
Sondheim, Stephen, IV 454
Sonny and Cher, IV 456
Soul Music, IV 458
Sound of Music, IV 462
South Pacific, IV 465
Southern, Terry, IV 466
Spaghetti Westerns, IV 467
Spartacus, IV 468
Special Olympics, IV 470
Spector, Phil, IV 471
Spelling, Aaron, IV 472
Spider-Man, IV 474
Spielberg, Steven, IV 476
Spillane, Mickey, IV 477
Spitz, Mark, IV 479
Spock, Dr. Benjamin, IV 480
Sport Utility Vehicles (SUVs), IV 482
Sporting News, IV 483
Sports Hero, IV 484
Sports Illustrated, IV 487
Spring Break, IV 488
St. Denis, Ruth, IV 494
Stagg, Amos Alonzo, IV 499
Standardized Testing, IV 502
Stand-up Comedy, IV 504
Stanley Brothers, IV 506
Star Trek, IV 508
Starr, Bart, IV 515
State Fairs, IV 518
Staubach, Roger, IV 520
Steinbeck, John, IV 522
Steinberg, Saul, IV 523
Steinem, Gloria, IV 524
Stengel, Casey, IV 526
Steppenwolf, IV 527
Stetson Hat, IV 532
Stevens, Ray, IV 532
Stewart, Jimmy, IV 532
Stickball, IV 534
Stiller and Meara, IV 535
Stock-Car Racing, IV 537
Stone, Irving, IV 542
Stonewall Rebellion, IV 544
Street and Smith, IV 553
Streisand, Barbra, IV 556
Strip Joints/Striptease, IV 557
Stuckey's, IV 560
Student Demonstrations, IV 560
Students for a Democratic Society (SDS), IV 563
Styron, William, IV 567
Suburbia, IV 567
Suicide, IV 569
Sullivan, Ed, IV 570
Summer Camp, IV 573
Sun Records, IV 576
Super Bowl, IV 579
Superman, IV 581
Surf Music, IV 585
Susann, Jacqueline, IV 586

Susskind, David, IV 587
Swimming Pools, IV 590
Swing Dancing, IV 592
Syndication, IV 595
Tabloids, IV 597
Talk Radio, IV 600
Tang, IV 603
Tanning, IV 603
Tap Dancing, IV 605
Tarzan, IV 608
Taylor, Elizabeth, IV 612
Taylor, Robert, IV 615
Teddy Bears, IV 616
Teen Idols, IV 617
Teenagers, IV 620
Tejano Music, IV 623
Telephone, IV 623
Televangelism, IV 625
Television, IV 626
Television Anchors, IV 629
Temple, Shirley, IV 631
Temptations, IV 632
Tennis, IV 635
Tennis Shoes/Sneakers, IV 637
Terry and the Pirates, IV 640
Thanksgiving, IV 640
Tharp, Twyla, IV 641
This Is Your Life, IV 643
Thomas, Danny, IV 644
Thomas, Lowell, IV 645
Thomas, Marlo, IV 645
Thompson, Hunter S., IV 646
Thomson, Bobby, IV 647
Three Investigators Series, IV 651
Three Stooges, IV 651
Thurber, James, IV 654
Tiffany & Company, IV 655
Time, IV 657
Times Square, IV 659
Timex Watches, IV 661
Tiny Tim, IV 661
To Tell the Truth, IV 664
Today, IV 666
Toffler, Alvin, IV 668
Tokyo Rose, IV 669
Tolkien, J. R. R., IV 671
Tom of Finland, IV 673
Tone, Franchot, IV 676
Tonight Show, IV 677
Top 40, IV 679
Tormé, Mel, IV 683
Town Meetings, IV 684
Toys, IV 685
Tracy, Spencer, IV 687
Trading Stamps, IV 688
Trailer Parks, IV 689
Tramps, IV 691
Traveling Carnivals, IV 692
Treviño, Lee, IV 696
Trevor, Claire, IV 697
Trillin, Calvin, IV 697
Trixie Belden, IV 698
Trout, Robert, IV 698
T-Shirts, IV 700
Tupperware, IV 700
Turner, Ike and Tina, IV 702
TV Dinners, IV 706
TV Guide, IV 706
Tweety Pie and Sylvester, IV 707
Twelve-Step Programs, IV 708
Twiggy, IV 713
Twilight Zone, IV 713
Twister, IV 715
2001: A Space Odyssey, IV 717
Uecker, Bob, V 1
UFOs (Unidentified Flying Objects), V 1
Underground Comics, V 4
Unitas, Johnny, V 6
United Artists, V 8
Unser, Al, V 8
Unser, Bobby, V 10
Updike, John, V 10

U.S. One, V 11
Valdez, Luis, V 15
Valentine's Day, V 16
Valium, V 20
Vallee, Rudy, V 21
Vampires, V 22
Van Dyke, Dick, V 24
Vaughan, Sarah, V 36
Velveeta Cheese, V 39
Velvet Underground, V 39
Vidal, Gore, V 45
Videos, V 47
Vietnam, V 49
Villella, Edward, V 52
Vitamins, V 52
Vogue, V 53
Volkswagen Beetle, V 54
Vonnegut, Kurt, Jr., V 56
Wagon Train, V 59
Walker, Aaron ''T-Bone'', V 59
Walker, Junior, and the All-Stars, V 63
Wall Drug, V 66
Wall Street Journal, V 67
Wallace, Sippie, V 68
Wal-Mart, V 69
Walters, Barbara, V 71
War Movies, V 75
Warhol, Andy, V 80
Washington Post, V 83
Waters, Muddy, V 89
Wayne, John, V 91
Weathermen, V 95
Weavers, V 96
Webb, Jack, V 98
Wedding Dress, V 100
Welk, Lawrence, V 106
Welles, Orson, V 108
Wells, Mary, V 111
Wertham, Fredric, V 111
West, Jerry, V 114
West, Mae, V 115
West Side Story, V 116
Western, V 118
What's My Line?, V 122
Whisky A Go Go, V 123
White, Betty, V 127
White Castle, V 127
White Flight, V 128
White Supremacists, V 129
Whiting, Margaret, V 130
Who, V 131
Whole Earth Catalogue, V 132
Wild Bunch, V 133
Wild Kingdom, V 135
Wilder, Billy, V 136
Wilder, Laura Ingalls, V 136
Wilder, Thornton, V 138
Williams, Andy, V 139
Williams, Hank, Jr., V 141
Williams, Tennessee, V 146
Wilson, Flip, V 148
Wimbledon, V 150
Windy City, V 152
Winnie-the-Pooh, V 155
Winters, Jonathan, V 157
Wire Services, V 158
Wizard of Oz, V 162
Wobblies, V 165
Wolfe, Tom, V 166
Wolfman, V 167
Wolfman Jack, V 167
Woman's Day, V 169
Wonder, Stevie, V 169
Wonder Woman, V 171
Wong, Anna May, V 172
Wood, Ed, V 172
Wood, Natalie, V 173
Wooden, John, V 174
Woodstock, V 176
World Series, V 182
World War II, V 188
World's Fairs, V 194

Wrangler Jeans, V 196
Wrigley Field, V 197
Wuthering Heights, V 198
WWJD? (What Would Jesus Do?), V 198
Wyeth, Andrew, V 199
Wynette, Tammy, V 201
Yankee Stadium, V 208
Yardbirds, V 212
Yastrzemski, Carl, V 212
Yellowstone National Park, V 213
Yippies, V 214
Young, Loretta, V 217
Young, Neil, V 217
Young, Robert, V 218
Youngman, Henny, V 219
Yo-Yo, V 223
Zanuck, Darryl F., V 225
Zap Comix, V 225
Zappa, Frank, V 225
Zines, V 228
Zoos, V 230
Zorro, V 234
Zydeco, V 235

1970-1979
A&R Men/Women, I 1
Aaron, Hank, I 2
AARP (American Association for Retired Persons), I 3
ABBA, I 4
Abbey, Edward, I 4
Abbott and Costello, I 5
Abortion, I 9
Abdul-Jabbar, Kareem, I 7
Academy Awards, I 12
AC/DC, I 14
Acker, Kathy, I 16
Acupuncture, I 16
Adams, Ansel, I 17
Adderley, Cannonball, I 18
Adidas, I 20
Adler, Renata, I 21
Advertising, I 23
Advice Columns, I 26
Advocate, I 29
Aerobics, I 30
Aerosmith, I 31
African American Press, I 32
Agents, I 34
Air Travel, I 38
Airplane!, I 38
Albert, Marv, I 40
Album-Oriented Rock, I 41
Alda, Alan, I 42
Ali, Muhammad, I 44
Alice, I 47
Alien, I 48
Alka Seltzer, I 49
All in the Family, I 50
All My Children, I 51
Allen, Steve, I 52
Allen, Woody, I 53
Allison, Luther, I 54
Allman Brothers Band, I 56
Alternative Country Music, I 59
Alternative Press, I 60
Altman, Robert, I 63
Amazing Stories, I 64
American Bandstand, I 65
American Graffiti, I 69
American International Pictures, I 71
American Museum of Natural History, I 72
Amsterdam, Morey, I 74
Amtrak, I 75
Amusement Parks, I 77
Amway, I 80
Andretti, Mario, I 84
Androgyny, I 85
Angell, Roger, I 88
Angelou, Maya, I 89
Animal House, I 89
Animated Films, I 90
Annie, I 96

Annie Get Your Gun, I 96
Annie Hall, I 98
Another World, I 99
Anthony, Piers, I 100
Aparicio, Luis, I 101
Apocalypse Now, I 101
Apollo Missions, I 102
Apollo Theatre, I 104
Apple Computer, I 106
Archie Comics, I 108
Argosy, I 109
Arizona Highways, I 110
Arledge, Roone, I 111
Armani, Giorgio, I 111
Armstrong, Louis, I 114
Arthur, Bea, I 118
Arthurian Legend, I 120
As the World Turns, I 121
Ashe, Arthur, I 123
Asimov, Isaac, I 125
Asner, Edward, I 126
Astounding Science Fiction, I 129
Astrology, I 129
AT&T, I 130
Athletic Model Guild, I 132
Atlantic City, I 133
Atlas, Charles, I 135
Aunt Jemima, I 137
Automobile, I 137
Avalon, Frankie, I 143
Avedon, Richard, I 144
Avengers, I 144
Avon, I 146
Aykroyd, Dan, I 147
''B'' movies, I 149
Babar, I 151
Baby Boomers, I 151
Bacall, Lauren, I 154
Bach, Richard, I 155
Bad News Bears, I 155
Baez, Joan, I 156
Bagels, I 158
Bakker, Jim, and Tammy Faye, I 160
Balanchine, George, I 161
Baldwin, James, I 161
Ballet, I 165
Bambaataa, Afrika, I 166
Band, I 167
Baraka, Amiri, I 168
Barbecue, I 168
Barber, Red, I 169
Barbershop Quartets, I 169
Barbie, I 171
Barney Miller, I 176
Barry, Dave, I 177
Baryshnikov, Mikhail, I 180
Baseball, I 180
Baseball Cards, I 183
Basketball, I 186
Bathhouses, I 188
Batman, I 189
Bay, Mel, I 191
Beach Boys, I 195
Beatles, I 203
Beatty, Warren, I 206
Beauty Queens, I 207
Beer, I 210
Belafonte, Harry, I 214
Bellbottoms, I 216
Belushi, John, I 216
Bench, Johnny, I 219
Ben-Hur, I 219
Benny Hill Show, I 222
Bergman, Ingmar, I 225
Bergman, Ingrid, I 226
Berlin, Irving, I 230
Bernstein, Leonard, I 233
Berra, Yogi, I 233
Bestsellers, I 236
Better Homes and Gardens, I 238
Beverly Hillbillies, I 241
Bewitched, I 243

Bicycling, I 245
Big Apple, I 246
Big Sleep, I 250
Bigfoot, I 251
Bilingual Education, I 252
Billboards, I 253
Bionic Woman, I 255
Birkenstocks, I 257
Birthing Practices, I 260
Black Sabbath, I 265
Blades, Ruben, I 275
Blanc, Mel, I 276
Blass, Bill, I 278
Blockbusters, I 280
Blondie (rock band), I 284
Blount, Roy, Jr., I 285
Blueboy, I 287
Bluegrass, I 287
Blues, I 290
Blume, Judy, I 294
Bly, Robert, I 296
Board Games, I 297
Boat People, I 298
Bob and Ray, I 299
Bochco, Steven, I 302
Bodybuilding, I 305
Bomb, I 311
Bombeck, Erma, I 314
Bonanza, I 316
Book-of-the-Month Club, I 318
Borge, Victor, I 320
Borscht Belt, I 321
Boston Celtics, I 322
Boston Garden, I 323
Boston Marathon, I 323
Bouton, Jim, I 326
Bowie, David, I 328
Bowling, I 328
Boy Scouts of America, I 333
Bra, I 335
Bradbury, Ray, I 337
Bradley, Bill, I 338
Bradshaw, Terry, I 339
Brady Bunch, I 339
Brando, Marlon, I 342
Brautigan, Richard, I 345
Breast Implants, I 347
Brenda Starr, I 348
Brice, Fanny, I 348
Bridge, I 349
Brill Building, I 351
Broadway, I 356
Brokaw, Tom, I 359
Bronson, Charles, I 360
Brooks, Gwendolyn, I 365
Brooks, James L., I 365
Brooks, Louise, I 365
Brooks, Mel, I 365
Brothers, Dr. Joyce, I 367
Brown, James, I 367
Brown, Jim, I 369
Brown, Paul, I 370
Browne, Jackson, I 371
Bryant, Paul ''Bear'', I 374
Brynner, Yul, I 375
Bubblegum Rock, I 375
Buckley, William F., Jr., I 379
Buckwheat Zydeco, I 380
Budweiser, I 380
Buffett, Jimmy, I 382
Bugs Bunny, I 383
Bumper Stickers, I 384
Bundy, Ted, I 384
Burger King, I 387
Burnett, Carol, I 391
Burr, Raymond, I 394
Burroughs, William S., I 397
Butch Cassidy and the Sundance Kid, I 398
Butkus, Dick, I 399
Butler, Octavia E. (1947--), I 400
Buttons, Red, I 401
Byrds, I 402

Cable TV, I 403
Cadillac, I 406
Cagney, James, I 409
Calloway, Cab, I 412
Camp, I 415
Campbell, Glen, I 416
Camping, I 417
Cancer, I 418
Candid Camera, I 420
Caniff, Milton, I 421
Capital Punishment, I 424
Capote, Truman, I 426
Captain America, I 429
Captain Kangaroo, I 430
Captain Marvel, I 432
Caray, Harry, I 433
Carlin, George, I 434
Carlton, Steve, I 435
Carmichael, Hoagy, I 436
Carnegie, Dale, I 437
Carnegie Hall, I 439
Carpenters, I 440
Carr, John Dickson, I 442
Cars, I 442
Carson, Johnny, I 444
Carter Family, I 445
Carver, Raymond, I 447
Cassette Tape, I 451
Cassidy, David, I 452
Castro, I 454
Catch-22, I 457
Cathy, I 460
Cavett, Dick, I 460
CB Radio, I 462
CBS Radio Mystery Theater, I 463
Celebrity, I 463
Cemeteries, I 467
Central Park, I 468
Chamberlain, Wilt, I 472
Charles, Ray, I 477
Charlie's Angels, I 479
Chase, Chevy, I 480
Chavez, Cesar, I 482
Chayefsky, Paddy, I 484
Cheech and Chong, I 485
Cheerleading, I 486
Chenier, Clifton, I 490
Chicago Bears, I 492
Chicago Bulls, I 493
Chicago Seven, I 495
Child, Julia, I 496
Child Stars, I 498
China Syndrome, I 500
Chinatown, I 500
Chipmunks, I 501
Choose-Your-Own-Ending Books, I 502
Christie, Agatha, I 502
Christmas, I 503
Christo, I 505
Church Socials, I 509
Cigarettes, I 510
Circus, I 512
City of Angels, I 516
Civil Disobedience, I 517
Civil War Reenactors, I 521
Claiborne, Liz, I 523
Clairol Hair Coloring, I 523
Clapton, Eric, I 525
Clark, Dick, I 525
Clarke, Arthur C., I 527
Clemente, Roberto, I 528
Clinton, George, I 532
Clockwork Orange, I 532
Clooney, Rosemary, I 533
Close Encounters of the Third Kind, I 534
Closet, I 536
Coca-Cola, I 540
Cocaine/Crack, I 542
Cocktail Parties, I 544
Coffee, I 546
Colbert, Claudette, I 548
Cold War, I 549

College Fads, I 553
College Football, I 555
Columbo, I 559
Comic Books, I 560
Comics, I 562
Comics Code Authority, I 565
Coming Out, I 566
Commodores, I 566
Communes, I 568
Communism, I 569
Community Media, I 570
Community Theatre, I 573
Como, Perry, I 574
Concept Album, I 576
Condé Nast, I 577
Condoms, I 578
Confession Magazines, I 581
Coniff, Ray, I 583
Connors, Jimmy, I 584
Consciousness Raising Groups, I 585
Conspiracy Theories, I 586
Consumer Reports, I 587
Consumerism, I 589
Contemporary Christian Music, I 591
Conway, Tim, I 594
Cooper, Alice, I 595
Cooperstown, New York, I 598
Coors, I 599
Corvette, I 603
Cosby, Bill, I 606
Cosell, Howard, I 608
Cosmopolitan, I 610
Costello, Elvis, I 612
Cotten, Joseph, I 613
Country Gentlemen, I 617
Country Music, I 617
Cowboy Look, I 622
Creationism, I 627
Credit Cards, I 628
Creedence Clearwater Revival, I 630
Crichton, Michael, I 631
Crisis, I 633
Croce, Jim, I 634
Cronkite, Walter, I 635
Crosby, Bing, I 638
Crosby, Stills, and Nash, I 639
Crossword Puzzles, I 641
Crumb, Robert, I 641
Cukor, George, I 643
Cult Films, I 643
Cults, I 646
Cunningham, Merce, I 648
Curious George, I 649
Dallas, I 652
Dallas Cowboys, I 654
Daly, Tyne, I 655
Dana, Bill, I 656
Dance Halls, I 657
Daniels, Charlie, I 658
Daredevil, the Man Without Fear, I 659
Dark Shadows, I 659
Davis, Bette, I 661
Davis, Miles, I 661
Day, Doris, I 664
Day the Earth Stood Still, I 665
Days of Our Lives, I 666
Daytime Talk Shows, I 667
Daytona 500, I 670
DC Comics, I 671
De Niro, Robert, I 673
Death of a Salesman, I 678
Debutantes, I 680
Deer Hunter, I 681
Denishawn, I 686
Denver, John, I 686
Department Stores, I 688
Depression, I 690
Detective Fiction, I 693
Detroit Tigers, I 695
Devo, I 696
Diamond, Neil, I 698
Dick and Jane Readers, I 700

Dick, Philip K., I 701
Dickinson, Angie, I 703
Diddley, Bo, I 703
Didion, Joan, I 704
Dieting, I 706
Diff'rent Strokes, I 709
Dillard, Annie, I 711
Diller, Phyllis, I 712
Dime Stores/Woolworth's, I 717
Diners, I 719
Disability, I 721
Disaster Movies, I 723
Disc Jockeys, I 725
Disco, I 726
Disney (Walt Disney Company), I 728
Ditka, Mike, I 731
Divine, I 731
Divorce, I 732
Dobie Gillis, I 735
Doby, Larry, I 736
Doc Martens, I 737
Doc Savage, I 738
Doctor Who, I 739
Doctorow, E. L., I 740
Docudrama, I 741
Do-It-Yourself Improvement, I 742
Domino, Fats, I 743
Donahue, Phil, I 744
Donovan, I 745
Doobie Brothers, I 747
Doonesbury, I 747
Douglas, Melvyn, I 753
Douglas, Mike, I 754
Downs, Hugh, I 754
Dr. Jekyll and Mr. Hyde, I 756
Dr. Kildare, I 756
Dr. Seuss, I 757
Dracula, I 760
Draft, I 761
Drag, I 762
Drag Racing, I 764
Drive-In Theater, I 769
Drug War, I 771
Dukes of Hazzard, I 773
Dungeons and Dragons, I 774
Dunkin' Donuts, I 775
Durán, Roberto, I 776
Durocher, Leo, I 777
Duvall, Robert, I 778
Dyer, Wayne, I 779
Dylan, Bob, I 780
Eames, Charles and Ray, II 1
Earth Day, II 1
Earth Shoes, II 2
Eastwood, Clint, II 2
Ebony, II 7
Eco-Terrorism, II 10
Edge of Night, II 13
Edwards, James, II 14
Edwards, Ralph, II 16
Eight-track Tape, II 16
Eisner, Will, II 18
El Teatro Campesino, II 18
Electric Guitar, II 21
Electric Trains, II 22
Elizondo, Hector, II 22
Ellis, Perry, II 25
Ellison, Harlan, II 25
E-mail, II 26
Emmy Awards, II 27
Empire State Building, II 28
Environmentalism, II 29
Equal Rights Amendment, II 32
Ertegun, Ahmet, II 35
Erving, Julius "Dr. J", II 36
ESPN, II 38
Esquire, II 40
Est, II 42
Etiquette Columns, II 44
Evangelism, II 46
Everly Brothers, II 47
Evert, Chris, II 48

Existentialism, II 50
Exorcist, II 50
Fabares, Shelley, II 53
Facelifts, II 54
Factor, Max, II 54
Fallout Shelters, II 58
Family Circle, II 59
Family Circus, II 61
Family Reunions, II 63
Fan Magazines, II 64
Fantasia, II 65
Fantastic Four, II 67
Fantasy Island, II 68
Farr, Jamie, II 71
Fast Food, II 71
Father's Day, II 76
Fawcett, Farrah, II 79
Fawlty Towers, II 80
FBI (Federal Bureau of Investigation), II 80
Feliciano, José, II 82
Fellini, Federico, II 84
Feminism, II 84
Fenway Park, II 87
Fetchit, Stepin, II 88
Fidrych, Mark "Bird", II 92
Field and Stream, II 92
Field, Sally, II 94
Film Noir, II 99
Firearms, II 101
Firesign Theatre, II 103
Fischer, Bobby, II 104
Fisher-Price Toys, II 106
Fisk, Carlton, II 106
Fitzgerald, Ella, II 107
Flack, Roberta, II 111
Flatt, Lester, II 113
Flea Markets, II 114
Fleetwood Mac, II 114
Fleming, Peggy, II 116
Flintstones, II 118
Florida Vacations, II 119
Flying Nun, II 120
Folk Music, II 123
Folkways Records, II 126
Follett, Ken, II 127
Fonda, Henry, II 127
Fonda, Jane, II 129
Fonteyn, Margot, II 130
Ford, Harrison, II 131
Ford Motor Company, II 135
Foreman, George, II 138
Forsyth, Frederick, II 141
Fortune, II 142
Fosse, Bob, II 143
Foster, Jodie, II 145
Fourth of July Celebrations, II 146
Foxx, Redd, II 148
Foyt, A. J., II 148
Francis, Arlene, II 150
Frankenstein, II 152
Franklin, Aretha, II 154
Franklin, Bonnie, II 156
Frazier, Joe, II 157
Frazier, Walt "Clyde", II 158
Frederick's of Hollywood, II 159
French Connection, II 164
French Fries, II 165
Friday, Nancy, II 169
Friedman, Kinky, II 171
Frisbee, II 174
Frizzell, Lefty, II 175
Frosty the Snowman, II 178
Frozen Entrées, II 178
Fuller, Buckminster, II 180
Fundamentalism, II 181
Funk, II 184
Gambling, II 188
Game Shows, II 191
Gangs, II 195
Gangsta Rap, II 198
Gap, II 198
Gardner, Ava, II 200

Garner, James, II 204
Garvey, Steve, II 206
Gas Stations, II 206
Gay and Lesbian Marriage, II 208
Gay and Lesbian Press, II 210
Gay Liberation Movement, II 211
Gay Men, II 215
Gaye, Marvin, II 216
General Hospital, II 218
General Motors, II 220
Gentlemen Prefer Blondes, II 223
Gere, Richard, II 224
Get Smart, II 227
Ghettos, II 227
GI Joe, II 229
Gibson, Bob, II 231
Gibson, Mel, II 234
Gillespie, Dizzy, II 236
Gilligan's Island, II 238
Ginsberg, Allen, II 239
Girl Groups, II 240
Girl Scouts, II 242
Gish, Lillian, II 244
Gleason, Jackie, II 245
Glitter Rock, II 247
Godfather, II 250
Godzilla, II 252
Golden Books, II 258
Golden Gate Bridge, II 259
Golf, II 261
Good Housekeeping, II 265
Good Times, II 267
Goodman, Benny, II 270
Goodson, Mark, II 271
Gordy, Berry, II 272
Gospel Music, II 274
Gossip Columns, II 275
Graffiti, II 281
Graham, Bill, II 282
Graham, Billy, II 284
Graham, Martha, II 285
Grand Ole Opry, II 286
Grant, Cary, II 288
Grateful Dead, II 291
Gray Panthers, II 294
Greeley, Andrew, II 298
Green, Al, II 300
Green Bay Packers, II 300
Green Lantern, II 302
Greenpeace, II 303
Greenwich Village, II 304
Greeting Cards, II 306
Gregory, Dick, II 307
Gretzky, Wayne, II 308
Greyhound Buses, II 312
Grier, Pam, II 312
Griffin, Merv, II 313
Griffith, Nanci, II 315
Grits, II 319
Grusin, Dave, II 322
Guaraldi, Vince, II 323
Guardian Angels, II 323
Gucci, II 323
Guiding Light, II 323
Gunsmoke, II 326
Guthrie, Arlo, II 328
Guy, Buddy, II 329
Gymnastics, II 331
Hackett, Buddy, II 333
Hackman, Gene, II 334
Haggard, Merle, II 334
Hagler, Marvelous Marvin, II 335
Haight-Ashbury, II 336
Hairstyles, II 340
Halas, George "Papa Bear", II 342
Haley, Alex, II 343
Haley, Bill, II 343
Hall and Oates, II 345
Hallmark Hall of Fame, II 345
Halloween, II 346
Halston, II 346
Hamburger, II 347

Hamill, Dorothy, II 348
Hancock, Herbie, II 350
Hanna-Barbera, II 355
Hansberry, Lorraine, II 356
Happy Days, II 357
Happy Hour, II 359
Hardy Boys, II 360
Hare Krishna, II 362
Harlem Globetrotters, II 364
Harlequin Romances, II 367
Harley-Davidson, II 368
Harmonica Bands, II 370
Harper, Valerie, II 371
Harper's, II 372
Hate Crimes, II 373
Havlicek, John, II 374
Hawaii Five-O, II 375
Hayworth, Rita, II 377
Hearst, Patty, II 378
Heavy Metal, II 380
Hee Haw, II 381
Hefner, Hugh, II 383
Hellman, Lillian, II 384
Hell's Angels, II 384
Hemlines, II 390
Henson, Jim, II 393
Hepburn, Katharine, II 394
Herbert, Frank, II 395
Herman, Woody, II 398
Heston, Charlton, II 399
Hiking, II 405
Hillerman, Tony, II 407
Hippies, II 410
Hirschfeld, Albert, II 412
Hiss, Alger, II 413
Hitchcock, Alfred, II 414
Hite, Shere, II 416
Hockey, II 417
Hoffman, Abbie, II 419
Hoffman, Dustin, II 420
Holbrook, Hal, II 424
Holiday Inns, II 428
Hollywood, II 431
Hollywood Squares, II 434
Holocaust, II 436
Home Shopping Network/QVC, II 438
Honeymooners, II 439
Hooker, John Lee, II 440
Hoover, J. Edgar, II 443
Hope, Bob, II 446
Hopkins, Sam ''Lightnin','' II 447
Hopper, Dennis, II 447
Hopscotch, II 449
Horror Movies, II 450
Hot Dogs, II 454
Hot Pants, II 454
Howe, Gordie, II 460
Howlin' Wolf, II 461
Hubbard, L. Ron, II 461
Hudson, Rock, II 462
Hughes, Howard, II 464
Hughes, Langston, II 465
Hull, Bobby, II 467
Hunt, Helen, II 468
Huntley, Chet, II 469
Hustler, II 470
Huston, John, II 471
I Dream of Jeannie, II 475
I Love Lucy, II 477
Iacocca, Lee, II 480
IBM (International Business Machines), II 481
Ice Shows, II 484
Incredible Hulk, II 486
Indian, II 487
Indianapolis 500, II 490
Industrial Design, II 491
Ink Spots, II 493
International Male Catalog, II 494
Internet, II 495
Ironman Triathlon, II 503
Irving, John, II 504
It's a Wonderful Life, II 506

Ives, Burl, II 508
Ivy League, II 509
J. Walter Thompson, II 511
Jackson Five, II 513
Jackson, Jesse, II 514
Jackson, Michael, II 517
Jackson, Reggie, II 519
Jakes, John, II 522
James Bond Films, II 523
Jaws, II 526
Jazz, II 529
Jeans, II 532
Jeep, II 533
Jefferson Airplane/Starship, II 534
Jeffersons, II 536
Jell-O, II 537
Jennings, Peter, II 538
Jennings, Waylon, II 540
Jeopardy!, II 541
Jessel, George, II 542
Jesus Christ Superstar, II 543
Jet, II 544
Jet Skis, II 545
Jewish Defense League, II 545
Jogging, II 547
John Birch Society, II 549
John, Elton, II 550
Johns, Jasper, II 551
Jones, George, II 561
Jones, Tom, II 563
Jonestown, II 563
Jong, Erica, II 564
Joplin, Janis, II 565
Jordan, Louis, II 568
Joy of Cooking, II 572
Joy of Sex, II 573
Judas Priest, II 577
Juke Boxes, II 579
Julia, II 580
Juliá, Raúl, II 581
Juvenile Delinquency, II 583
Kahn, Roger, III 1
Kantor, MacKinlay, III 3
Kasem, Casey, III 6
Kaufman, Andy, III 7
Kaye, Danny, III 9
Keillor, Garrison, III 11
Keitel, Harvey, III 12
Kelly Bag, III 14
Kelly Girls, III 14
Kelly, Grace, III 15
Kennedy Assassination, III 16
Kent State Massacre, III 17
Kentucky Derby, III 19
Kentucky Fried Chicken, III 20
Kesey, Ken, III 22
King, Albert, III 25
King, B. B., III 26
King, Billie Jean, III 28
King, Carole, III 29
King, Freddie, III 30
King, Larry, III 32
King, Stephen, III 36
Kingston, Maxine Hong, III 39
KISS, III 42
Kitsch, III 43
Kiwanis, III 46
Klein, Robert, III 47
Kmart, III 47
Knievel, Evel, III 48
Knight, Bobby, III 49
Knots Landing, III 50
Kodak, III 51
Kojak, III 52
Koontz, Dean R., III 53
Korman, Harvey, III 56
Kosinski, Jerzy, III 56
Kotzwinkle, William, III 56
Krantz, Judith, III 60
Krassner, Paul, III 61
Ku Klux Klan, III 64
Kubrick, Stanley, III 66

Kuhn, Bowie, III 68
Kung Fu, III 68
Labor Unions, III 72
Laetrile, III 76
LaLanne, Jack, III 80
L'Amour, Louis, III 84
Lancaster, Burt, III 85
Landon, Michael, III 86
Landry, Tom, III 87
Lansky, Meyer, III 90
LaRussa, Tony, III 92
Las Vegas, III 92
Lasorda, Tommy, III 93
Lassie, III 95
Late Great Planet Earth, III 96
Latin Jazz, III 97
Laugh-In, III 98
Lauren, Ralph, III 102
Laverne and Shirley, III 103
Lavin, Linda, III 103
Lawrence, Vicki, III 106
La-Z-Boy Loungers, III 106
Le Carré, John, III 106
Le Guin, Ursula K., III 107
Leachman, Cloris, III 108
Lear, Norman, III 111
Leary, Timothy, III 112
Led Zeppelin, III 116
Lee, Bruce, III 117
Lee, Peggy, III 121
Lee, Stan, III 124
Legos, III 125
Lehrer, Tom, III 126
Leisure Suit, III 127
Leisure Time, III 128
L'Engle, Madeleine, III 131
Lennon, John, III 131
Leno, Jay, III 132
Leonard, Elmore, III 134
Leonard, Sugar Ray, III 136
Leone, Sergio, III 136
Lesbianism, III 140
Lewis, C. S., III 150
Lewis, Jerry, III 152
Lewis, Jerry Lee, III 153
Liberace, III 155
Liebovitz, Annie, III 159
Life, III 160
Li'l Abner, III 163
Lindbergh, Anne Morrow, III 166
Lindbergh, Charles, III 166
Linkletter, Art, III 168
Lionel Trains, III 170
Lippmann, Walter, III 170
Lipstick, III 171
Little League, III 174
Little Magazines, III 176
Little Orphan Annie, III 177
Live Television, III 178
Lloyd Webber, Andrew, III 181
Loafers, III 182
Long-Playing Record, III 192
Loos, Anita, III 194
López, Nancy, III 194
Los Angeles Lakers, III 196
Los Lobos, III 197
Lottery, III 199
Louisville Slugger, III 201
Love Boat, III 203
Low Riders, III 206
Lucas, George, III 209
Ludlum, Robert, III 213
LuPone, Patti, III 216
Lynch, David, III 216
Lynching, III 217
Lynn, Loretta, III 218
Lynyrd Skynyrd, III 220
Mabley, Moms, III 223
MacDonald, John D., III 226
MacMurray, Fred, III 228
MAD Magazine, III 230
Madden, John, III 232

Made-for-Television Movies, III 233
Mafia/Organized Crime, III 237
Mailer, Norman, III 242
Mall, III 247
Mancini, Henry, III 256
Manhattan Transfer, III 257
Manilow, Barry, III 258
Manson, Charles, III 261
Manufactured Homes, III 263
Mapplethorpe, Robert, III 265
Marching Bands, III 267
Marcus Welby, M.D., III 269
Mardi Gras, III 269
Mariachi Music, III 270
Marie, Rose, III 272
Marijuana, III 272
Marlboro Man, III 274
Marley, Bob, III 274
Marshall, Garry, III 278
Martin, Dean, III 280
Martin, Quinn, III 282
Martin, Steve, III 282
Martini, III 282
Marvel Comics, III 285
Marx Brothers, III 287
Mary Hartman, Mary Hartman, III 289
Mary Kay Cosmetics, III 290
Mary Tyler Moore Show, III 292
Mary Worth, III 294
M*A*S*H, III 295
Masterpiece Theatre, III 302
Masters and Johnson, III 303
Masters Golf Tournament, III 305
Mathis, Johnny, III 305
Maude, III 306
Maupin, Armistead, III 307
Max, Peter, III 308
Mayfield, Curtis, III 310
Mayfield, Percy, III 310
Mays, Willie, III 311
McBain, Ed, III 312
McCaffrey, Anne, III 313
McCall's Magazine, III 313
McCartney, Paul, III 316
McDonald's, III 321
McEnroe, John, III 324
McEntire, Reba, III 325
McKuen, Rod, III 328
McLuhan, Marshall, III 329
McMurtry, Larry, III 330
McQueen, Butterfly, III 332
McQueen, Steve, III 333
Me Decade, III 335
Meadows, Audrey, III 336
Mean Streets, III 336
Media Feeding Frenzies, III 337
Mellencamp, John Cougar, III 341
Men's Movement, III 344
Metropolitan Museum of Art, III 347
MGM (Metro-Goldwyn-Mayer), III 347
Michener, James, III 351
Mickey Mouse Club, III 351
Microsoft, III 353
Midler, Bette, III 356
Milk, Harvey, III 361
Miller, Arthur, III 363
Miller Beer, III 364
Miller, Roger, III 367
Milton Bradley, III 369
Minimalism, III 369
Minoso, Minnie, III 371
MirandaWarning, III 373
Miss America Pageant, III 374
Mission: Impossible, III 375
Mister Rogers' Neighborhood, III 378
Mitchell, Joni, III 379
Mitchum, Robert, III 381
Mod, III 384
Mod Squad, III 385
Modern Dance, III 388
Modern Maturity, III 388
Monday Night Football, III 393

Monkees, III 394
Monopoly, III 396
Monroe, Bill, III 396
Monroe, Earl ''The Pearl'', III 397
Montalbán, Ricardo, III 401
Montana, Joe, III 402
Montana, Patsy, III 403
Monty Python's Flying Circus, III 403
Moonies/Reverend Sun Myung Moon, III 405
Moral Majority, III 409
Moreno, Rita, III 410
Mork & Mindy, III 411
Morris, Mark, III 413
Morrison, Toni, III 414
Morrison, Van, III 415
Mother's Day, III 417
Motown, III 420
Mount Rushmore, III 423
Mountain Biking, III 424
Mouseketeers, III 425
Movie Stars, III 428
Mr. Wizard, III 433
Ms., III 434
Multiculturalism, III 439
Mummy, III 441
Muppets, III 444
Murray, Anne, III 447
Murray, Arthur, III 448
Murray, Bill, III 450
Muscle Cars, III 455
Muscular Christianity, III 456
Musical, III 458
Mutt & Jeff, III 462
Muzak, III 463
My Three Sons, III 467
Nader, Ralph, III 469
Nagel, Patrick, III 470
Namath, Joe, III 471
Nancy Drew, III 473
NASA, III 475
Nation, III 476
National Basketball Association (NBA), III 477
National Collegiate Athletic Association
      (NCAA), III 479
National Enquirer, III 480
National Football League (NFL), III 482
National Geographic, III 484
National Hockey League (NHL), III 485
National Lampoon, III 487
National Organization for Women
      (N.O.W.), III 489
National Parks, III 489
Navratilova, Martina, III 495
Neckties, III 495
Neighborhood Watch, III 499
Nelson, Ricky, III 499
Nelson, Willie, III 501
Nerd Look, III 502
Network, III 503
Networks, III 503
New Age Music, III 506
New Age Spirituality, III 507
New Left, III 511
New Republic, III 514
New Wave Music, III 515
New York Knickerbockers, III 517
New York Mets, III 517
New York Times, III 518
New York Yankees, III 520
New Yorker, III 522
Newhart, Bob, III 524
Newlywed Game, III 526
Newport Jazz and Folk Festivals, III 526
Newsweek, III 527
Newton, Helmut, III 528
Niagara Falls, III 528
Nicklaus, Jack, III 531
Night of the Living Dead, III 532
Nightline, III 533
Nike, III 535
Nixon, Agnes, III 539
Novak, Kim, III 543

Nureyev, Rudolf, III 544
Nylon, III 544
Oakland Raiders, III 547
Oates, Joyce Carol, III 547
Objectivism/Ayn Rand, III 547
O'Brien, Tim, III 548
Ochs, Phil, III 549
Odd Couple, III 550
O'Keeffe, Georgia, III 552
Oklahoma!, III 553
Oliphant, Pat, III 555
Olivier, Laurence, III 556
Olmos, Edward James, III 557
Olsen, Tillie, III 558
Olympics, III 558
Onassis, Jacqueline Lee Bouvier Kennedy,
      III 564
One Day at a Time, III 565
One Flew Over the Cuckoo's Nest, III 566
Op Art, III 569
Orbison, Roy, III 571
O'Rourke, P. J., III 573
Orr, Bobby, III 574
Osborne Brothers, III 575
Osbourne, Ozzy, III 575
Ouija Boards, III 576
Outing, III 580
Owens, Buck, III 582
Pacino, Al, IV 3
Paige, Satchel, IV 5
Paley, Grace, IV 6
Paley, William S., IV 6
Palmer, Jim, IV 7
Pants for Women, IV 7
Pantyhose, IV 9
Paperbacks, IV 9
Parades, IV 12
Parker Brothers, IV 13
Parks, Rosa, IV 15
Parton, Dolly, IV 17
Partridge Family, IV 18
Patinkin, Mandy, IV 19
Patton, IV 19
Paulsen, Pat, IV 22
Payton, Walter, IV 23
Peale, Norman Vincent, IV 23
Peanuts, IV 25
Pearl, Minnie, IV 28
Peck, Gregory, IV 29
Pelé, IV 33
Penn, Irving, IV 33
Penthouse, IV 34
People, IV 35
Pepsi-Cola, IV 36
Performance Art, IV 37
Pet Rocks, IV 42
Peter, Paul, and Mary, IV 42
Pets, IV 44
Petty, Richard, IV 46
Pfeiffer, Michelle, IV 48
Phonograph, IV 52
Picasso, Pablo, IV 54
Pill, IV 57
Pink Floyd, IV 58
Piper, ''Rowdy'' Roddy, IV 60
Pittsburgh Steelers, IV 61
Pizza, IV 62
Planet of the Apes, IV 63
Plastic, IV 64
Plastic Surgery, IV 67
Plath, Sylvia, IV 68
Playboy, IV 70
Playgirl, IV 72
Pogo, IV 73
Pointer Sisters, IV 74
Poitier, Sidney, IV 75
Polyester, IV 80
Pop, Iggy, IV 82
Pop Music, IV 83
Pope, IV 86
Popeye, IV 87
Popsicles, IV 88

Popular Mechanics, IV 89
Popular Psychology, IV 90
Pornography, IV 92
Postcards, IV 96
Postmodernism, IV 98
Potter, Dennis, IV 102
Preminger, Otto, IV 104
Preppy, IV 105
Presley, Elvis, IV 105
Price Is Right, IV 108
Price, Reynolds, IV 110
Price, Vincent, IV 110
Pride, Charley, IV 111
Prince, IV 112
Prince, Hal, IV 114
Prinze, Freddie, IV 115
Professional Football, IV 116
Prom, IV 120
Protest Groups, IV 124
Pryor, Richard, IV 126
Psychedelia, IV 128
Public Libraries, IV 133
Public Television (PBS), IV 135
Puente, Tito, IV 137
Punisher, IV 142
Punk, IV 142
Pynchon, Thomas, IV 145
Queen, Ellery, IV 148
Radio, IV 157
Radner, Gilda, IV 162
Raitt, Bonnie, IV 170
Ramones, IV 171
Rand, Sally, IV 173
Rap/Hip-Hop, IV 174
Rather, Dan, IV 176
Reader's Digest, IV 177
Reagan, Ronald, IV 179
Recycling, IV 187
Redbook, IV 189
Redford, Robert, IV 190
Reed, Donna, IV 191
Reed, Ishmael, IV 191
Reed, Lou, IV 192
Reggae, IV 194
Reiner, Carl, IV 196
Religious Right, IV 197
Replacements, IV 204
Reynolds, Burt, IV 205
Rich, Charlie, IV 209
Rigby, Cathy, IV 210
Riggs, Bobby, IV 211
Ringling Bros., Barnum & Bailey Circus, IV 212
Ripley's Believe It Or Not, IV 215
Rivera, Chita, IV 216
Rivera, Geraldo, IV 218
Rivers, Joan, IV 219
Rizzuto, Phil, IV 220
Road Runner and Wile E. Coyote, IV 222
Robbins, Tom, IV 223
Roberts, Jake ''The Snake'', IV 223
Robertson, Oscar, IV 225
Robertson, Pat, IV 225
Robeson, Kenneth, IV 227
Robeson, Paul, IV 227
Robinson, Edward G., IV 229
Robinson, Frank, IV 230
Robinson, Smokey, IV 233
Rock and Roll, IV 235
Rockefeller Family, IV 239
Rockettes, IV 241
Rockwell, Norman, IV 244
Rocky, IV 246
Rocky Horror Picture Show, IV 248
Roddenberry, Gene, IV 251
Rodeo, IV 252
Rodríguez, Chi Chi, IV 259
Roe v. Wade, IV 260
Rogers, Kenny, IV 261
Rolle, Esther, IV 265
Roller Coasters, IV 265
Roller Derby, IV 266
Rolling Stone, IV 267

Rolling Stones, IV 269
Romance Novels, IV 270
Romero, Cesar, IV 273
Roots, IV 273
Rose Bowl, IV 275
Rose, Pete, IV 276
Ross, Diana, and the Supremes, IV 280
Roswell Incident, IV 282
Roundtree, Richard, IV 282
Rouse Company, IV 283
Royko, Mike, IV 285
Rubik's Cube, IV 286
Rudolph the Red-Nosed Reindeer, IV 287
Russell, Bill, IV 290
Russell, Jane, IV 292
Russell, Nipsey, IV 293
RV, IV 295
Ryan, Nolan, IV 297
Rydell, Bobby, IV 298
Sagan, Carl, IV 300
Saks Fifth Avenue, IV 302
Sales, Soupy, IV 303
Salsa Music, IV 303
Sanford and Son, IV 310
Santana, IV 311
Sarandon, Susan, IV 312
Saratoga Springs, IV 312
Saturday Morning Cartoons, IV 317
Saturday Night Fever, IV 319
Saturday Night Live, IV 320
Schlatter, George, IV 325
Schoolhouse Rock, IV 328
Schwarzenegger, Arnold, IV 329
Science Fiction Publishing, IV 330
Scientific American, IV 334
Scorsese, Martin, IV 337
Scott, George C., IV 338
Scully, Vin, IV 345
Sea World, IV 345
Seals, Son, IV 345
Search for Tomorrow, IV 346
Sears Roebuck Catalogue, IV 346
Sears Tower, IV 347
Second City, IV 348
Seeger, Pete, IV 351
Selena, IV 354
Sellers, Peter, IV 355
Serial Killers, IV 358
Sesame Street, IV 362
Seventeen, IV 364
Sex Scandals, IV 367
Sex Symbol, IV 369
Sexual Revolution, IV 373
Shaft, IV 376
Sheldon, Sidney, IV 381
Shepard, Sam, IV 382
Sherman, Cindy, IV 383
Shirer, William L., IV 384
Shock Radio, IV 386
Shore, Dinah, IV 387
Shorter, Frank, IV 388
Show Boat, IV 389
Shula, Don, IV 391
Shulman, Max, IV 391
SIDS (Sudden Infant Death Syndrome), IV 391
Simon and Garfunkel, IV 399
Simon, Neil, IV 401
Simon, Paul, IV 403
Simpson, O. J., IV 404
Sinatra, Frank, IV 409
Singer, Isaac Bashevis, IV 414
Singles Bars, IV 415
Siskel and Ebert, IV 417
Sitcom, IV 418
Six Million Dollar Man, IV 424
60 Minutes, IV 425
Skaggs, Ricky, IV 427
Skateboarding, IV 428
Skating, IV 429
Skelton, Red, IV 431
Skyscrapers, IV 432
Slang, IV 434

Slasher Movies, IV 435
Slinky, IV 436
Sly and the Family Stone, IV 437
Smith, Dean, IV 439
Smith, Kate, IV 439
Smith, Patti, IV 440
Smithsonian Institution, IV 441
Smothers Brothers, IV 442
Soap Operas, IV 446
Soccer, IV 449
Social Dancing, IV 450
Soldier Field, IV 453
Sondheim, Stephen, IV 454
Sonny and Cher, IV 456
Soul Music, IV 458
Soul Train, IV 461
Southern, Terry, IV 466
Spacek, Sissy, IV 467
Spaghetti Westerns, IV 467
Special Olympics, IV 470
Spelling, Aaron, IV 472
Spielberg, Steven, IV 476
Spillane, Mickey, IV 477
Spitz, Mark, IV 479
Spock, Dr. Benjamin, IV 480
Sport Utility Vehicles (SUVs), IV 482
Sporting News, IV 483
Sports Hero, IV 484
Sports Illustrated, IV 487
Spring Break, IV 488
Springer, Jerry, IV 490
Springsteen, Bruce, IV 491
Sprinkle, Annie, IV 493
Stadium Concerts, IV 496
Stallone, Sylvester, IV 500
Standardized Testing, IV 502
Stand-up Comedy, IV 504
Stanley Brothers, IV 506
Star Trek, IV 508
Star Wars, IV 511
Starbucks, IV 514
Starr, Bart, IV 515
Starsky and Hutch, IV 517
State Fairs, IV 518
Staubach, Roger, IV 520
Steel Curtain, IV 521
Steinberg, Saul, IV 523
Steinbrenner, George, IV 523
Steinem, Gloria, IV 524
Steppenwolf, IV 527
Stern, Howard, IV 530
Stetson Hat, IV 532
Stevens, Ray, IV 532
Stewart, Jimmy, IV 532
Stickball, IV 534
Stiller and Meara, IV 535
Stock-Car Racing, IV 537
Stock Market Crashes, IV 539
Stone, Irving, IV 542
Stone, Oliver, IV 543
Strait, George, IV 547
Streaking, IV 551
Streep, Meryl, IV 552
Street and Smith, IV 553
Streisand, Barbra, IV 556
Strip Joints/Striptease, IV 557
Stuart, Marty, IV 558
Studio 54, IV 563
Styron, William, IV 567
Suburbia, IV 567
Suicide, IV 569
Sullivan, Ed, IV 570
Summer Camp, IV 573
Summer, Donna, IV 575
Sun Records, IV 576
Super Bowl, IV 579
Superman, IV 581
Susann, Jacqueline, IV 586
Susskind, David, IV 587
Swaggart, Jimmy, IV 587
Swann, Lynn, IV 588
Swimming Pools, IV 590

Swinging, IV 593
Sylvia, IV 594
Syndication, IV 595
Tabloids, IV 597
Talk Radio, IV 600
Talking Heads, IV 602
Tang, IV 603
Tanning, IV 603
Tap Dancing, IV 605
Tarkanian, Jerry, IV 606
Tarzan, IV 608
Taxi, IV 610
Taxi Driver, IV 611
Taylor, Elizabeth, IV 612
Taylor, James, IV 615
Teddy Bears, IV 616
Teen Idols, IV 617
Teenagers, IV 620
Tejano Music, IV 623
Telephone, IV 623
Televangelism, IV 625
Television, IV 626
Television Anchors, IV 629
Temple, Shirley, IV 631
Temptations, IV 632
Tennis, IV 635
Tennis Shoes/Sneakers, IV 637
Terry and the Pirates, IV 640
Thanksgiving, IV 640
Tharp, Twyla, IV 641
Thing, IV 642
This Is Your Life, IV 643
Thomas, Danny, IV 644
Thomas, Lowell, IV 645
Thomas, Marlo, IV 645
Thompson, Hunter S., IV 646
Thompson, John, IV 647
Thorogood, George, IV 648
Three Investigators Series, IV 651
Three Stooges, IV 651
Three's Company, IV 653
Tiffany & Company, IV 655
Time, IV 657
Times Square, IV 659
Timex Watches, IV 661
Tiny Tim, IV 661
To Tell the Truth, IV 664
Today, IV 666
Toffler, Alvin, IV 668
Toga Parties, IV 669
Tokyo Rose, IV 669
Tom of Finland, IV 673
Tomlin, Lily, IV 675
Tonight Show, IV 677
Top 40, IV 679
Tora! Tora! Tora!, IV 681
Tormé, Mel, IV 683
Town Meetings, IV 684
Toys, IV 685
Trailer Parks, IV 689
Tramps, IV 691
Traveling Carnivals, IV 692
Travolta, John, IV 694
Treviño, Lee, IV 696
Trevor, Claire, IV 697
Trillin, Calvin, IV 697
Trixie Belden, IV 698
Trout, Robert, IV 698
T-Shirts, IV 700
Tupperware, IV 700
Turner, Ike and Tina, IV 702
Turner, Ted, IV 704
TV Dinners, IV 706
TV Guide, IV 706
Tweety Pie and Sylvester, IV 707
Twelve-Step Programs, IV 708
20/20, IV 712
Twilight Zone, IV 713
Twister, IV 715
2001: A Space Odyssey, IV 717
Uecker, Bob, V 1
UFOs (Unidentified Flying Objects), V 1

Ulcers, V 3
Underground Comics, V 4
Unitas, Johnny, V 6
United Artists, V 8
Unser, Al, V 8
Unser, Bobby, V 10
Updike, John, V 10
Upstairs, Downstairs, V 11
U.S. One, V 11
Valdez, Luis, V 15
Valentine's Day, V 16
Valium, V 20
Vampires, V 22
Van Dyke, Dick, V 24
Van Halen, V 26
Varga Girl, V 30
Vaughan, Sarah, V 36
Velveeta Cheese, V 39
Velvet Underground, V 39
Versace, Gianni, V 41
Vidal, Gore, V 45
Video Games, V 45
Videos, V 47
Vietnam, V 49
Villella, Edward, V 52
Vitamins, V 52
Vogue, V 53
Volkswagen Beetle, V 54
Vonnegut, Kurt, Jr., V 56
Waits, Tom, V 59
Walker, Aaron "T-Bone", V 59
Walker, Alice, V 61
Wall Drug, V 66
Wall Street Journal, V 67
Wallace, Sippie, V 68
Wal-Mart, V 69
Walters, Barbara, V 71
Walton, Bill, V 72
Waltons, V 74
War Movies, V 75
Warhol, Andy, V 80
Washington Post, V 83
Waters, John, V 87
Waters, Muddy, V 89
Watson, Tom, V 90
Wayne, John, V 91
Weathermen, V 95
Weaver, Sigourney, V 96
Webb, Jack, V 98
Wedding Dress, V 100
Weekend, V 101
Welcome Back, Kotter, V 105
Welk, Lawrence, V 106
Welles, Orson, V 108
Wells, Mary, V 111
Wertham, Fredric, V 111
West, Jerry, V 114
West, Mae, V 115
Western, V 118
What's My Line?, V 122
Wheel of Fortune, V 122
Whisky A Go Go, V 123
White, Barry, V 125
White, Betty, V 127
White Castle, V 127
White Flight, V 128
White Supremacists, V 129
Whiting, Margaret, V 130
Who, V 131
Whole Earth Catalogue, V 132
Wide World of Sports, V 133
Wilder, Laura Ingalls, V 136
Williams, Andy, V 139
Williams, Hank, Jr., V 141
Williams, Robin, V 143
Williams, Tennessee, V 146
Wilson, Flip, V 148
Wimbledon, V 150
Windy City, V 152
Winnie-the-Pooh, V 155
Winters, Jonathan, V 157
Wire Services, V 158

Wizard of Oz, V 162
WKRP in Cincinnati, V 164
Wolfe, Tom, V 166
Wolfman, V 167
Wolfman Jack, V 167
Woman's Day, V 169
Wonder, Stevie, V 169
Wonder Woman, V 171
Wood, Ed, V 172
Wood, Natalie, V 173
Wooden, John, V 174
World Series, V 182
World Trade Center, V 184
World War II, V 188
Wrangler Jeans, V 196
Wuthering Heights, V 198
WWJD? (What Would Jesus Do?), V 198
Wyeth, Andrew, V 199
Wynette, Tammy, V 201
Yankee Stadium, V 208
Yankovic, "Weird Al", V 209
Yardbirds, V 212
Yastrzemski, Carl, V 212
Yellowstone National Park, V 213
Yes, V 214
Yippies, V 214
Young and the Restless, V 216
Young, Loretta, V 217
Young, Neil, V 217
Young, Robert, V 218
Youngman, Henny, V 219
Zappa, Frank, V 225
Zines, V 228
Zippy the Pinhead, V 230
Zoos, V 230
Zoot Suit, V 233
Zorro, V 234
Zydeco, V 235
ZZ Top, V 236

1980-1989
A&R Men/Women, I 1
AARP (American Association for Retired
    Persons), I 3
ABBA, I 4
Abbey, Edward, I 4
Abdul-Jabbar, Kareem, I 7
Abortion, I 9
Academy Awards, I 12
AC/DC, I 14
Acker, Kathy, I 16
Acupuncture, I 16
Adams, Ansel, I 17
Adidas, I 20
Adler, Renata, I 21
Advertising, I 23
Advice Columns, I 26
Advocate, I 29
Aerobics, I 30
Aerosmith, I 31
African American Press, I 32
Agassi, Andre, I 33
Agents, I 34
AIDS, I 35
Air Travel, I 38
Airplane!, I 38
Alabama, I 39
Albert, Marv, I 40
Album-Oriented Rock, I 41
Alda, Alan, I 42
Ali, Muhammad, I 44
Alice, I 47
Alien, I 48
Alka Seltzer, I 49
All My Children, I 51
Allen, Steve, I 52
Allen, Woody, I 53
Allison, Luther, I 54
Allman Brothers Band, I 56
Alternative Country Music, I 59
Alternative Press, I 60
Alternative Rock, I 62
Altman, Robert, I 63

Amazing Stories, I 64
American Bandstand, I 65
American Girls Series, I 67
American Museum of Natural History, I 72
Amtrak, I 75
Amusement Parks, I 77
Amway, I 80
Andretti, Mario, I 84
Androgyny, I 85
Angell, Roger, I 88
Animated Films, I 90
Annie, I 96
Annie Get Your Gun, I 96
Another World, I 99
Anthony, Piers, I 100
Apollo Theatre, I 104
Apple Computer, I 106
Archie Comics, I 108
Argosy, I 109
Arizona Highways, I 110
Arledge, Roone, I 111
Armani, Giorgio, I 111
Arthur, Bea, I 118
Arthurian Legend, I 120
As the World Turns, I 121
Ashe, Arthur, I 123
Asimov, Isaac, I 125
Asner, Edward, I 126
Astounding Science Fiction, I 129
Astrology, I 129
AT&T, I 130
A-Team, I 132
Athletic Model Guild, I 132
Atlantic City, I 133
Aunt Jemima, I 137
Automobile, I 137
Avalon, Frankie, I 143
Avedon, Richard, I 144
Avon, I 146
Aykroyd, Dan, I 147
"B" movies, I 149
Babar, I 151
Baby Boomers, I 151
Babyface, I 154
Bach, Richard, I 155
Back to the Future, I 155
Baez, Joan, I 156
Bagels, I 158
Bakker, Jim, and Tammy Faye, I 160
Balanchine, George, I 161
Ballard, Hank, I 164
Ballet, I 165
Bambaataa, Afrika, I 166
Band, I 167
Barbecue, I 168
Barber, Red, I 169
Barbershop Quartets, I 169
Barbie, I 171
Barker, Clive, I 174
Barkley, Charles, I 175
Barney Miller, I 176
Barry, Dave, I 177
Barry, Lynda, I 178
Baseball, I 180
Baseball Cards, I 183
Basketball, I 186
Bathhouses, I 188
Batman, I 189
Bay, Mel, I 191
Beach Boys, I 195
Beastie Boys, I 200
Beatty, Warren, I 206
Beauty Queens, I 207
Beer, I 210
Belafonte, Harry, I 214
Belushi, John, I 216
Bench, Johnny, I 219
Benneton, I 221
Bergen, Candice, I 224
Bergman, Ingmar, I 225
Bergman, Ingrid, I 226
Berlin, Irving, I 230

Bernhard, Sandra, I 231
Bernstein, Leonard, I 233
Berra, Yogi, I 233
Berry, Chuck, I 234
Bestsellers, I 236
Better Homes and Gardens, I 238
Bewitched, I 243
Bicycling, I 245
Big Apple, I 246
Bigfoot, I 251
Bilingual Education, I 252
Billboards, I 253
Bionic Woman, I 255
Bird, Larry, I 255
Birkenstocks, I 257
Birthing Practices, I 260
Black, Clint, I 262
Black Sabbath, I 265
Blade Runner, I 273
Blades, Ruben, I 275
Blanc, Mel, I 276
Blass, Bill, I 278
Blockbusters, I 280
Blondie (rock band), I 284
Bloom County, I 284
Blount, Roy, Jr., I 285
Blue Velvet, I 286
Blueboy, I 287
Bluegrass, I 287
Blues, I 290
Blues Brothers, I 293
Blume, Judy, I 294
Bly, Robert, I 296
Board Games, I 297
Boat People, I 298
Bob and Ray, I 299
Bochco, Steven, I 302
Body Decoration, I 303
Bodybuilding, I 305
Bomb, I 311
Bon Jovi, I 315
Book-of-the-Month Club, I 318
Borge, Victor, I 320
Boston Celtics, I 322
Boston Garden, I 323
Boston Marathon, I 323
Bowie, David, I 328
Bowling, I 328
Boy Scouts of America, I 333
Bra, I 335
Bradbury, Ray, I 337
Bradley, Bill, I 338
Bradshaw, Terry, I 339
Brady Bunch, I 339
Brando, Marlon, I 342
Brat Pack, I 344
Brautigan, Richard, I 345
Breakfast Club, I 347
Breast Implants, I 347
Brenda Starr, I 348
Brideshead Revisited, I 348
Bridge, I 349
Broadway, I 356
Brokaw, Tom, I 359
Bronson, Charles, I 360
Brooks, Garth, I 364
Brooks, James L., I 365
Brooks, Mel, I 365
Brothers, Dr. Joyce, I 367
Brown, James, I 367
Browne, Jackson, I 371
Bubblegum Rock, I 375
Buckley, William F., Jr., I 379
Buckwheat Zydeco, I 380
Budweiser, I 380
Buffett, Jimmy, I 382
Bugs Bunny, I 383
Bumper Stickers, I 384
Bundy, Ted, I 384
Burger King, I 387
Burnett, Carol, I 391
Burns, Ken, I 394

Burr, Raymond, I 394
Burroughs, William S., I 397
Butler, Octavia E.(1947--), I 400
Buttons, Red, I 401
Cabbage Patch Kids, I 403
Cable TV, I 403
Cagney and Lacey, I 409
Calloway, Cab, I 412
Calvin and Hobbes, I 413
Camacho, Héctor "Macho", I 414
Camp, I 415
Campbell, Naomi, I 416
Camping, I 417
Cancer, I 418
Candid Camera, I 420
Caniff, Milton, I 421
Canseco, Jose, I 422
Capital Punishment, I 424
Captain Kangaroo, I 430
Captain Marvel, I 432
Caray, Harry, I 433
Carlin, George, I 434
Carlton, Steve, I 435
Carnegie, Dale, I 437
Carnegie Hall, I 439
Cars, I 442
Carson, Johnny, I 444
Carver, Raymond, I 447
Cassette Tape, I 451
Cassidy, David, I 452
Castro, I 454
Casual Friday, I 455
Cathy, I 460
Cats, I 460
Cavett, Dick, I 460
CB Radio, I 462
CBS Radio Mystery Theater, I 463
Celebrity, I 463
Cemeteries, I 467
Central Park, I 468
Challenger Disaster, I 472
Charles, Ray, I 477
Charlie's Angels, I 479
Charm Bracelets, I 480
Chase, Chevy, I 480
Chavis, Boozoo, I 483
Cheech and Chong, I 485
Cheerleading, I 486
Cheers, I 488
Chenier, Clifton, I 490
Chicago Bears, I 492
Chicago Bulls, I 493
Chicago Cubs, I 493
Child, Julia, I 496
Child Stars, I 498
China Syndrome, I 500
Chipmunks, I 501
Choose-Your-Own-Ending Books, I 502
Christie, Agatha, I 502
Christmas, I 503
Christo, I 505
Chuck D, I 508
Church Socials, I 509
Cigarettes, I 510
Circus, I 512
Cisneros, Sandra, I 513
City of Angels, I 516
Civil War Reenactors, I 521
Claiborne, Liz, I 523
Clairol Hair Coloring, I 523
Clancy, Tom, I 524
Clapton, Eric, I 525
Clark, Dick, I 525
Clarke, Arthur C., I 527
Cline, Patsy, I 530
Clinton, George, I 532
Clooney, Rosemary, I 533
Closet, I 536
CNN, I 537
Coca-Cola, I 540
Cocaine/Crack, I 542
Cocktail Parties, I 544

Coffee, I 546
Colbert, Claudette, I 548
Cold War, I 549
College Football, I 555
Collins, Albert, I 557
Columbo, I 559
Comic Books, I 560
Comics, I 562
Coming Out, I 566
Commodores, I 566
Communism, I 569
Community Media, I 570
Community Theatre, I 573
Compact Discs, I 575
Concept Album, I 576
Conceptual Art, I 577
Condé Nast, I 577
Condoms, I 578
Coniff, Ray, I 583
Connors, Jimmy, I 584
Conspiracy Theories, I 586
Consumer Reports, I 587
Consumerism, I 589
Contemporary Christian Music, I 591
Conway, Tim, I 594
Cooper, Alice, I 595
Cooperstown, New York, I 598
Coors, I 599
Corvette, I 603
Cosby, Bill, I 606
Cosby Show, I 607
Cosell, Howard, I 608
Cosmopolitan, I 610
Costas, Bob, I 612
Costello, Elvis, I 612
Costner, Kevin, I 612
Cotten, Joseph, I 613
Country Music, I 617
Covey, Stephen, I 621
Cowboy Look, I 622
Crawford, Cindy, I 624
Crawford, Joan, I 625
Cray, Robert, I 626
Creationism, I 627
Credit Cards, I 628
Crichton, Michael, I 631
Crisis, I 633
Crosby, Stills, and Nash, I 639
Crossword Puzzles, I 641
Cruise, Tom, I 641
Crumb, Robert, I 641
Crystal, Billy, I 643
Cult Films, I 643
Cults, I 646
Cunningham, Merce, I 648
Curious George, I 649
Dallas, I 652
Dallas Cowboys, I 654
Daly, Tyne, I 655
Dana, Bill, I 656
Dance Halls, I 657
Daniels, Charlie, I 658
Daredevil, the Man Without Fear, I 659
Davis, Bette, I 661
Davis, Miles, I 661
Day the Earth Stood Still, I 665
Days of Our Lives, I 666
Daytime Talk Shows, I 667
Daytona 500, I 670
DC Comics, I 671
De Niro, Robert, I 673
Dead Kennedys, I 675
Death of a Salesman, I 678
Debutantes, I 680
Denver, John, I 686
Department Stores, I 688
Depression, I 690
Detective Fiction, I 693
Detroit Tigers, I 695
Devers, Gail, I 696
Devo, I 696
Diamond, Neil, I 698

Diana, Princess of Wales, I 698
Dick, Philip K., I 701
Dickinson, Angie, I 703
Diddley, Bo, I 703
Didion, Joan, I 704
Dieting, I 706
Diff'rent Strokes, I 709
Dillard, Annie, I 711
Diller, Phyllis, I 712
Dime Stores/Woolworth's, I 717
Disability, I 721
Disaster Movies, I 723
Disc Jockeys, I 725
Disney (Walt Disney Company), I 728
Ditka, Mike, I 731
Divine, I 731
Divorce, I 732
Do the Right Thing, I 735
Dobie Gillis, I 735
Doc Martens, I 737
Doc Savage, I 738
Doctor Who, I 739
Doctorow, E. L., I 740
Docudrama, I 741
Do-It-Yourself Improvement, I 742
Domino, Fats, I 743
Donahue, Phil, I 744
Doonesbury, I 747
Douglas, Mike, I 754
Downs, Hugh, I 754
Dr. Jekyll and Mr. Hyde, I 756
Dr. Seuss, I 757
Dracula, I 760
Drag, I 762
Drag Racing, I 764
Drug War, I 771
Duck Soup, I 773
Dukes of Hazzard, I 773
Dungeons and Dragons, I 774
Dunkin' Donuts, I 775
Durán, Roberto, I 776
Duvall, Robert, I 778
Dyer, Wayne, I 779
Dykes to Watch Out For, I 780
Dylan, Bob, I 780
Dynasty, I 783
Earth Day, II 1
Eastwood, Clint, II 2
Ebony, II 7
Eco-Terrorism, II 10
Edge of Night, II 13
Edwards, Ralph, II 16
Eisner, Will, II 18
El Teatro Campesino, II 18
El Vez, II 19
Electric Guitar, II 21
Electric Trains, II 22
Elizondo, Hector, II 22
Elkins, Aaron, II 23
Ellis, Bret Easton, II 24
Ellis, Perry, II 25
Ellison, Harlan, II 25
Elway, John, II 25
E-mail, II 26
Emmy Awards, II 27
Empire State Building, II 28
Environmentalism, II 29
Equal Rights Amendment, II 32
Erdrich, Louise, II 34
Ertegun, Ahmet, II 35
Erving, Julius "Dr. J", II 36
ESPN, II 38
Esquire, II 40
Est, II 42
E.T. The Extra-Terrestrial, II 43
Etiquette Columns, II 44
Evangelism, II 46
Everson, Cory, II 48
Evert, Chris, II 48
Existentialism, II 50
Exorcist, II 50
Fabares, Shelley, II 53

Fabian, II 53
Fabio, II 53
Facelifts, II 54
Factor, Max, II 54
Fairbanks, Douglas, Jr., II 55
Fallout Shelters, II 58
Family Circle, II 59
Family Circus, II 61
Family Matters, II 62
Family Reunions, II 63
Family Ties, II 64
Fan Magazines, II 64
Fantasia, II 65
Fantastic Four, II 67
Fantasy Island, II 68
Far Side, II 69
Farm Aid, II 69
Farr, Jamie, II 71
Fast Food, II 71
Fatal Attraction, II 74
Father's Day, II 76
Fawcett, Farrah, II 79
FBI (Federal Bureau of Investigation), II 80
Feliciano, José, II 82
Felix the Cat, II 83
Fellini, Federico, II 84
Feminism, II 84
Fenway Park, II 87
Field and Stream, II 92
Field of Dreams, II 93
Field, Sally, II 94
Fierstein, Harvey, II 96
Film Noir, II 99
Firearms, II 101
Firesign Theatre, II 103
Fisher-Price Toys, II 106
Fisk, Carlton, II 106
Fitzgerald, Ella, II 107
Flack, Roberta, II 111
Flag Burning, II 111
Flashdance Style, II 113
Flea Markets, II 114
Fleetwood Mac, II 114
Fleming, Peggy, II 116
Flintstones, II 118
Florida Vacations, II 119
Folk Music, II 123
Folkways Records, II 126
Follett, Ken, II 127
Fonda, Henry, II 127
Fonda, Jane, II 129
Ford, Harrison, II 131
Ford Motor Company, II 135
Forsyth, Frederick, II 141
Fortune, II 142
Foster, Jodie, II 145
Fourth of July Celebrations, II 146
Foxx, Redd, II 148
Foyt, A. J., II 148
Francis, Arlene, II 150
Frankenstein, II 152
Franklin, Aretha, II 154
Franklin, Bonnie, II 156
Frederick's of Hollywood, II 159
Free Agency, II 160
French Fries, II 165
Friday, Nancy, II 169
Friday the 13th, II 170
Friedman, Kinky, II 171
Frisbee, II 174
Frosty the Snowman, II 178
Frozen Entrées, II 178
Fuller, Buckminster, II 180
Fundamentalism, II 181
Funicello, Annette, II 183
Funk, II 184
Gambling, II 188
Game Shows, II 191
Gammons, Peter, II 195
Gangs, II 195
Gangsta Rap, II 198
Gap, II 198

Gardner, Ava, II 200
Garner, James, II 204
Garvey, Steve, II 206
Gas Stations, II 206
Gated Communities, II 208
Gay and Lesbian Marriage, II 208
Gay and Lesbian Press, II 210
Gay Liberation Movement, II 211
Gay Men, II 215
Gaye, Marvin, II 216
General Hospital, II 218
General Motors, II 220
Generation X, II 221
Gentlemen Prefer Blondes, II 223
Gere, Richard, II 224
Ghettos, II 227
GI Joe, II 229
Gibson, Mel, II 234
Gibson, William, II 235
Gillespie, Dizzy, II 236
Gilligan's Island, II 238
Ginsberg, Allen, II 239
Girl Groups, II 240
Girl Scouts, II 242
Gish, Lillian, II 244
Gleason, Jackie, II 245
Godfather, II 250
Godzilla, II 252
Goldberg, Whoopi, II 257
Golden Books, II 258
Golden Gate Bridge, II 259
Golden Girls, II 260
Golf, II 261
Gone with the Wind, II 263
Good Housekeeping, II 265
Gooden, Dwight, II 268
Goodman, Benny, II 270
Goodson, Mark, II 271
Gordy, Berry, II 272
Gospel Music, II 274
Gossip Columns, II 275
Goth, II 277
Gotti, John, II 277
Graceland, II 278
Graffiti, II 281
Grafton, Sue, II 282
Graham, Bill, II 282
Graham, Billy, II 284
Grand Ole Opry, II 286
Grandmaster Flash, II 286
Grant, Amy, II 287
Grant, Cary, II 288
Grateful Dead, II 291
Gray Panthers, II 294
Greeley, Andrew, II 298
Green Bay Packers, II 300
Green Lantern, II 302
Greene, Graham, II 303
Greenpeace, II 303
Greenwich Village, II 304
Greeting Cards, II 306
Gregory, Dick, II 307
Gretzky, Wayne, II 308
Greyhound Buses, II 312
Griffin, Merv, II 313
Griffith, Nanci, II 315
Grisham, John, II 318
Grits, II 319
Grizzard, Lewis, II 319
Groening, Matt, II 319
Grunge, II 321
Grusin, Dave, II 322
Guardian Angels, II 323
Gucci, II 323
Guiding Light, II 323
Guthrie, Arlo, II 328
Guy, Buddy, II 329
Gymnastics, II 331
Hackett, Buddy, II 333
Hackman, Gene, II 334
Haggard, Merle, II 334
Hagler, Marvelous Marvin, II 335

Haight-Ashbury, II 336
Hairstyles, II 340
Halas, George "Papa Bear", II 342
Hall and Oates, II 345
Hallmark Hall of Fame, II 345
Hamburger, II 347
Hamill, Dorothy, II 348
Hancock, Herbie, II 350
Hanks, Tom, II 353
Hanna-Barbera, II 355
Happy Days, II 357
Happy Hour, II 359
Hardy Boys, II 360
Hare Krishna, II 362
Haring, Keith, II 363
Harlem Globetrotters, II 364
Harlequin Romances, II 367
Harley-Davidson, II 368
Harmonica Bands, II 370
Harper's, II 372
Hate Crimes, II 373
Havlicek, John, II 374
Hawaii Five-O, II 375
Heavy Metal, II 380
Hee Haw, II 381
Hefner, Hugh, II 383
Hellman, Lillian, II 384
Hell's Angels, II 384
Hemlines, II 390
Henson, Jim, II 393
Hepburn, Katharine, II 394
Herbert, Frank, II 395
Herman, Woody, II 398
Hess, Joan, II 399
Heston, Charlton, II 399
Hijuelos, Oscar, II 405
Hiking, II 405
Hill Street Blues, II 406
Hillerman, Tony, II 407
Himes, Chester, II 408
Hirschfeld, Albert, II 412
Hispanic Magazine, II 412
Hite, Shere, II 416
Hockey, II 417
Hoffman, Abbie, II 419
Hoffman, Dustin, II 420
Hogan, Hulk, II 423
Holbrook, Hal, II 424
Holiday Inns, II 428
Hollywood, II 431
Hollywood Squares, II 434
Home Shopping Network/QVC, II 438
Honeymooners, II 439
Hooker, John Lee, II 440
Hoosiers, II 442
Hope, Bob, II 446
Hopkins, Sam "Lightnin'," II 447
Hopper, Dennis, II 447
Hopscotch, II 449
Horne, Lena, II 449
Horror Movies, II 450
Hot Dogs, II 454
Houston, Whitney, II 458
Howe, Gordie, II 460
Hubbard, L. Ron, II 461
Hudson, Rock, II 462
Hughes, Langston, II 465
Hull, Bobby, II 467
Hunt, Helen, II 468
Hustler, II 470
Huston, John, II 471
I Dream of Jeannie, II 475
Iacocca, Lee, II 480
IBM (International Business Machines), II 481
Ice Cream Cone, II 483
Ice Shows, II 484
Ice-T, II 485
Incredible Hulk, II 486
Indian, II 487
Indianapolis 500, II 490
Industrial Design, II 491
Ink Spots, II 493

International Male Catalog, II 494
Internet, II 495
Iran Contra, II 499
Iron Maiden, II 501
Ironman Triathlon, II 503
Irving, John, II 504
It's a Wonderful Life, II 506
It's Garry Shandling's Show, II 507
Ives, Burl, II 508
Jackson Five, II 513
Jackson, Jesse, II 514
Jackson, Michael, II 517
Jackson, Reggie, II 519
Jakes, John, II 522
James Bond Films, II 523
Jazz, II 529
Jeans, II 532
Jeep, II 533
Jefferson Airplane/Starship, II 534
Jeffersons, II 536
Jell-O, II 537
Jennings, Peter, II 538
Jennings, Waylon, II 540
Jeopardy!, II 541
Jessel, George, II 542
Jet, II 544
Jet Skis, II 545
Jewish Defense League, II 545
Jogging, II 547
John Birch Society, II 549
John, Elton, II 550
Johns, Jasper, II 551
Johnson, Earvin "Magic", II 553
Johnson, Michael, II 556
Jones, George, II 561
Jones, Tom, II 563
Jong, Erica, II 564
Joplin, Janis, II 565
Jordan, Michael, II 570
Joy of Cooking, II 572
Joy of Sex, II 573
Joyner, Florence Griffith, II 574
Joyner-Kersee, Jackie, II 575
Judas Priest, II 577
Judy Bolton, II 578
Juliá, Raúl, II 581
Juvenile Delinquency, II 583
Kahn, Roger, III 1
Karan, Donna, III 4
Kasem, Casey, III 6
Kate & Allie, III 7
Kaufman, Andy, III 7
Kaye, Danny, III 9
Keillor, Garrison, III 11
Keitel, Harvey, III 12
Kelley, David E., III 13
Kelly Bag, III 14
Kelly Girls, III 14
Kelly, Grace, III 15
Kennedy Assassination, III 16
Kentucky Derby, III 19
Kentucky Fried Chicken, III 20
Kesey, Ken, III 22
King, Albert, III 25
King, B. B., III 26
King, Billie Jean, III 28
King, Carole, III 29
King, Larry, III 32
King, Stephen, III 36
Kingston, Maxine Hong, III 39
Kinison, Sam, III 40
KISS, III 42
Kitsch, III 43
Kiwanis, III 46
Klein, Calvin, III 46
Klein, Robert, III 47
Kmart, III 47
Knight, Bobby, III 49
Knots Landing, III 50
Kodak, III 51
Kojak, III 52
Koontz, Dean R., III 53

Korman, Harvey, III 56
Kosinski, Jerzy, III 56
Kotzwinkle, William, III 56
Krantz, Judith, III 60
Ku Klux Klan, III 64
Kudzu, III 66
Kuhn, Bowie, III 68
L. A. Law, III 71
L. L. Cool J., III 71
''La Bamba'', III 71
Labor Unions, III 72
Lacoste Shirts, III 75
Laetrile, III 76
Lake, Ricki, III 78
LaLanne, Jack, III 80
L'Amour, Louis, III 84
Lancaster, Burt, III 85
Landon, Michael, III 86
Landry, Tom, III 87
Lang, k.d., III 88
LaRussa, Tony, III 92
Las Vegas, III 92
Lasorda, Tommy, III 93
Latin Jazz, III 97
Lauper, Cyndi, III 99
Lauren, Ralph, III 102
Lawrence, Vicki, III 106
La-Z-Boy Loungers, III 106
Le Carré, John, III 106
Le Guin, Ursula K., III 107
Lear, Norman, III 111
Leary, Timothy, III 112
Least Heat Moon, William, III 114
Leave It to Beaver, III 115
Led Zeppelin, III 116
Lee, Peggy, III 121
Lee, Spike, III 122
Lee, Stan, III 124
Legos, III 125
Lehrer, Tom, III 126
Leisure Suit, III 127
Leisure Time, III 128
LeMond, Greg, III 130
L'Engle, Madeleine, III 131
Lennon, John, III 131
Leno, Jay, III 132
Leonard, Elmore, III 134
Leonard, Sugar Ray, III 136
Leone, Sergio, III 136
Les Miserables, III 139
Lesbianism, III 140
Letterman, David, III 144
Levi's, III 146
Lewis, C. S., III 150
Lewis, Carl, III 151
Lewis, Jerry, III 152
Lewis, Jerry Lee, III 153
Liberace, III 155
Liebovitz, Annie, III 159
Life, III 160
Linkletter, Art, III 168
Lionel Trains, III 170
Lipstick, III 171
Little Black Dress, III 173
Little League, III 174
Little Magazines, III 176
Little Orphan Annie, III 177
Live Television, III 178
L.L. Bean, Inc., III 180
Lloyd Webber, Andrew, III 181
Loafers, III 182
Lone Ranger, III 189
Long, Shelley, III 192
Long-Playing Record, III 192
López, Nancy, III 194
Los Angeles Lakers, III 196
Los Lobos, III 197
Lottery, III 199
Louisville Slugger, III 201
Love Boat, III 203
Love, Courtney, III 204
Lucas, George, III 209

Ludlum, Robert, III 213
LuPone, Patti, III 216
Lynch, David, III 216
Lynching, III 217
Lynn, Loretta, III 218
MacDonald, John D., III 226
MAD Magazine, III 230
Madden, John, III 232
Made-for-Television Movies, III 233
Madonna, III 235
Mafia/Organized Crime, III 237
Magnum, P.I., III 241
Mah-Jongg, III 242
Mailer, Norman, III 242
Mall, III 247
Mamet, David, III 252
Mancini, Henry, III 256
Manhattan Transfer, III 257
Manilow, Barry, III 258
Manufactured Homes, III 263
Mapplethorpe, Robert, III 265
Marching Bands, III 267
Mardi Gras, III 269
Mariachi Music, III 270
Marie, Rose, III 272
Marijuana, III 272
Marlboro Man, III 274
Marley, Bob, III 274
Married . . . with Children, III 277
Marshall, Garry, III 278
Martin, Dean, III 280
Martin, Steve, III 282
Martini, III 282
Marvel Comics, III 285
Mary Kay Cosmetics, III 290
Mary Worth, III 294
*M*A*S*H*, III 295
Mason, Jackie, III 298
Masterpiece Theatre, III 302
Masters Golf Tournament, III 305
Mathis, Johnny, III 305
Mattingly, Don, III 306
Maupin, Armistead, III 307
Maus, III 308
Max, Peter, III 308
Mayfield, Curtis, III 310
Mayfield, Percy, III 310
McBain, Ed, III 312
McCaffrey, Anne, III 313
McCall's Magazine, III 313
McCartney, Paul, III 316
McDonald's, III 321
McEnroe, John, III 324
McEntire, Reba, III 325
McGwire, Mark, III 326
McKuen, Rod, III 328
McLish, Rachel, III 328
McLuhan, Marshall, III 329
McMurtry, Larry, III 330
McQueen, Butterfly, III 332
McQueen, Steve, III 333
Meadows, Audrey, III 336
Media Feeding Frenzies, III 337
Mellencamp, John Cougar, III 341
Men's Movement, III 344
Metropolitan Museum of Art, III 347
MGM (Metro-Goldwyn-Mayer), III 347
Miami Vice, III 349
Michener, James, III 351
Mickey Mouse Club, III 351
Microsoft, III 353
Midler, Bette, III 356
Miller, Arthur, III 363
Miller Beer, III 364
Miller, Roger, III 367
Milli Vanilli, III 368
Milton Bradley, III 369
Minimalism, III 369
Minivans, III 370
Minoso, Minnie, III 371
*Miranda*Warning, III 373
Miss America Pageant, III 374

Mission: Impossible, III 375
Mister Rogers' Neighborhood, III 378
Mitchell, Joni, III 379
Mitchum, Robert, III 381
Mod, III 384
Modern Dance, III 388
Modern Maturity, III 388
Momaday, N. Scott, III 392
Monday Night Football, III 393
Monkees, III 394
Monopoly, III 396
Monroe, Bill, III 396
Montalbán, Ricardo, III 401
Montana, Joe, III 402
Montana, Patsy, III 403
Monty Python's Flying Circus, III 403
Moonies/Reverend Sun Myung Moon, III 405
Moonlighting, III 406
Moore, Demi, III 407
Moore, Michael, III 408
Moral Majority, III 409
Moreno, Rita, III 410
Mork & Mindy, III 411
Morris, Mark, III 413
Morrison, Toni, III 414
Morrison, Van, III 415
Mother's Day, III 417
Mötley Crüe, III 418
Motown, III 420
Mount Rushmore, III 423
Mountain Biking, III 424
Mouseketeers, III 425
Movie Stars, III 428
Mr. Wizard, III 433
Ms., III 434
MTV, III 435
Multiculturalism, III 439
Mummy, III 441
Muppets, III 444
Murder, She Wrote, III 445
Murphy Brown, III 446
Murphy, Eddie, III 447
Murray, Anne, III 447
Murray, Arthur, III 448
Murray, Bill, III 450
Muscular Christianity, III 456
Musical, III 458
Mutt & Jeff, III 462
Muzak, III 463
Nader, Ralph, III 469
Nagel, Patrick, III 470
Nancy Drew, III 473
NASA, III 475
Nation, III 476
National Basketball Association (NBA), III 477
National Collegiate Athletic Association (NCAA), III 479
National Enquirer, III 480
National Football League (NFL), III 482
National Geographic, III 484
National Hockey League (NHL), III 485
National Lampoon, III 487
National Organization for Women (N.O.W.), III 489
National Parks, III 489
Natural, III 492
Nava, Gregory, III 495
Navratilova, Martina, III 495
Naylor, Gloria, III 495
Neckties, III 495
Neighborhood Watch, III 499
Nelson, Ricky, III 499
Nelson, Willie, III 501
Nerd Look, III 502
Networks, III 503
New Age Music, III 506
New Age Spirituality, III 507
New Kids on the Block, III 510
New Republic, III 514
New Wave Music, III 515
New York Knickerbockers, III 517
New York Mets, III 517

New York Times, III 518
New York Yankees, III 520
New Yorker, III 522
Newhart, Bob, III 524
Newlywed Game, III 526
Newport Jazz and Folk Festivals, III 526
Newsweek, III 527
Newton, Helmut, III 528
Niagara Falls, III 528
Nicklaus, Jack, III 531
Night of the Living Dead, III 532
Nightline, III 533
1980 U.S. Olympic Hockey Team, III 536
Nirvana, III 538
Nixon, Agnes, III 539
Novak, Kim, III 543
Nureyev, Rudolf, III 544
Nylon, III 544
Oakland Raiders, III 547
Oates, Joyce Carol, III 547
O'Brien, Tim, III 548
Odd Couple, III 550
O'Donnell, Rosie, III 551
O'Keeffe, Georgia, III 552
Oklahoma!, III 553
Oliphant, Pat, III 555
Olivier, Laurence, III 556
Olmos, Edward James, III 557
Olympics, III 558
Omnibus, III 561
Onassis, Jacqueline Lee Bouvier Kennedy,
      III 564
One Day at a Time, III 565
Orbison, Roy, III 571
O'Rourke, P. J., III 573
Orr, Bobby, III 574
Osbourne, Ozzy, III 575
Ouija Boards, III 576
Outing, III 580
Owens, Buck, III 582
Pacino, Al, IV 3
Paley, Grace, IV 6
Paley, William S., IV 6
Palmer, Jim, IV 7
Pants for Women, IV 7
Pantyhose, IV 9
Paperbacks, IV 9
Parades, IV 12
Paretsky, Sara, IV 12
Parker Brothers, IV 13
Parks, Rosa, IV 15
Parton, Dolly, IV 17
Patinkin, Mandy, IV 19
Paulsen, Pat, IV 22
Payton, Walter, IV 23
Peanuts, IV 25
Pearl, Minnie, IV 28
Peck, Gregory, IV 29
Pee-wee's Playhouse, IV 32
Penn, Irving, IV 33
Penthouse, IV 34
People, IV 35
Pepsi-Cola, IV 36
Performance Art, IV 37
Perry Mason, IV 41
Peter, Paul, and Mary, IV 42
Peters, Bernadette, IV 44
Pets, IV 44
Petty, Richard, IV 46
Pfeiffer, Michelle, IV 48
Phantom of the Opera, IV 49
Phone Sex, IV 51
Phonograph, IV 52
Pill, IV 57
Pink Floyd, IV 58
Piper, "Rowdy" Roddy, IV 60
Pittsburgh Steelers, IV 61
Pizza, IV 62
Plastic, IV 64
Plastic Surgery, IV 67
Plath, Sylvia, IV 68
Platoon, IV 69

Playboy, IV 70
Playgirl, IV 72
Pogo, IV 73
Pointer Sisters, IV 74
Poitier, Sidney, IV 75
Political Correctness, IV 78
Polyester, IV 80
Pop, Iggy, IV 82
Pop Music, IV 83
Pope, IV 86
Popeye, IV 87
Popsicles, IV 88
Popular Mechanics, IV 89
Popular Psychology, IV 90
Pornography, IV 92
Postcards, IV 96
Postman Always Rings Twice, IV 97
Postmodernism, IV 98
Potter, Dennis, IV 102
Preppy, IV 105
Presley, Elvis, IV 105
Price Is Right, IV 108
Price, Reynolds, IV 110
Price, Vincent, IV 110
Pride, Charley, IV 111
Prince, IV 112
Prince, Hal, IV 114
Professional Football, IV 116
Prom, IV 120
Protest Groups, IV 124
Prozac, IV 125
Pryor, Richard, IV 126
Public Enemy, IV 132
Public Libraries, IV 133
Public Television (PBS), IV 135
Punisher, IV 142
Punk, IV 142
Pynchon, Thomas, IV 145
Quayle, Dan, IV 147
Queen Latifah, IV 150
Radio, IV 157
Radner, Gilda, IV 162
Raging Bull, IV 165
Raiders of the Lost Ark, IV 166
Raitt, Bonnie, IV 170
Rambo, IV 170
Ramones, IV 171
Rap/Hip-Hop, IV 174
Rather, Dan, IV 176
Reader's Digest, IV 177
Reagan, Ronald, IV 179
Reality Television, IV 181
Recycling, IV 187
Redford, Robert, IV 190
Reed, Donna, IV 191
Reed, Ishmael, IV 191
Reed, Lou, IV 192
Reggae, IV 194
Reiner, Carl, IV 196
Religious Right, IV 197
R.E.M., IV 201
Replacements, IV 204
Reynolds, Burt, IV 205
Rice, Jerry, IV 209
Rich, Charlie, IV 209
Rigby, Cathy, IV 210
Riley, Pat, IV 212
Ripken, Cal, Jr., IV 214
Ripley's Believe It Or Not, IV 215
Rivera, Chita, IV 216
Rivera, Geraldo, IV 218
Rivers, Joan, IV 219
Rizzuto, Phil, IV 220
Road Rage, IV 221
Road Runner and Wile E. Coyote, IV 222
Robbins, Tom, IV 223
Roberts, Jake "The Snake", IV 223
Roberts, Julia, IV 223
Roberts, Nora, IV 224
Robertson, Pat, IV 225
Robinson, Frank, IV 230
Robinson, Smokey, IV 233

Rock and Roll, IV 235
Rock Climbing, IV 238
Rockettes, IV 241
Rocky Horror Picture Show, IV 248
Roddenberry, Gene, IV 251
Rodeo, IV 252
Rodman, Dennis, IV 259
Rodríguez, Chi Chi, IV 259
Rogers, Kenny, IV 261
Roller Coasters, IV 265
Roller Derby, IV 266
Rolling Stone, IV 267
Rolling Stones, IV 269
Romance Novels, IV 270
Rose Bowl, IV 275
Rose, Pete, IV 276
Roseanne, IV 277
Ross, Diana, and the Supremes, IV 280
Roswell Incident, IV 282
Roundtree, Richard, IV 282
Rouse Company, IV 283
Route 66, IV 284
Royko, Mike, IV 285
Rubik's Cube, IV 286
Rudolph the Red-Nosed Reindeer, IV 287
Run-DMC, IV 287
RV, IV 295
Ryan, Meg, IV 297
Ryan, Nolan, IV 297
Rydell, Bobby, IV 298
Ryder, Winona, IV 298
Safe Sex, IV 299
Sagan, Carl, IV 300
Sahl, Mort, IV 301
Saks Fifth Avenue, IV 302
Sales, Soupy, IV 303
Salsa Music, IV 303
Salt-n-Pepa, IV 305
Sandman, IV 307
Santana, IV 311
Sarandon, Susan, IV 312
Saratoga Springs, IV 312
Sassy, IV 313
Saturday Morning Cartoons, IV 317
Saturday Night Live, IV 320
Savage, Randy "Macho Man", IV 322
Schnabel, Julian, IV 327
Schoolhouse Rock, IV 328
Schwarzenegger, Arnold, IV 329
Science Fiction Publishing, IV 330
Scientific American, IV 334
Scorsese, Martin, IV 337
Scott, George C., IV 338
Scully, Vin, IV 345
Sea World, IV 345
Seals, Son, IV 345
Search for Tomorrow, IV 346
Sears Roebuck Catalogue, IV 346
Second City, IV 348
Selena, IV 354
Seles, Monica, IV 355
Sellers, Peter, IV 355
Serial Killers, IV 358
Sesame Street, IV 362
Seventeen, IV 364
Sex Scandals, IV 367
Sex Symbol, IV 369
Sexual Harassment, IV 371
Sheldon, Sidney, IV 381
Shepard, Sam, IV 382
Sherman, Cindy, IV 383
Shirer, William L., IV 384
Shock Radio, IV 386
Shore, Dinah, IV 387
Show Boat, IV 389
Shula, Don, IV 391
SIDS (Sudden Infant Death Syndrome), IV 391
Silver Surfer, IV 399
Simon, Neil, IV 401
Simon, Paul, IV 403
Simpson, O. J., IV 404
Simpsons, IV 408

Sinatra, Frank, IV 409
Sinbad, IV 413
Singer, Isaac Bashevis, IV 414
Singles Bars, IV 415
Siskel and Ebert, IV 417
Sitcom, IV 418
Six Million Dollar Man, IV 424
60 Minutes, IV 425
Skaggs, Ricky, IV 427
Skateboarding, IV 428
Skating, IV 429
Skyscrapers, IV 432
Slaney, Mary Decker, IV 433
Slang, IV 434
Slasher Movies, IV 435
Slinky, IV 436
Smith, Dean, IV 439
Smits, Jimmy, IV 441
Smothers Brothers, IV 442
Soap Operas, IV 446
Soccer, IV 449
Social Dancing, IV 450
Sondheim, Stephen, IV 454
Sonny and Cher, IV 456
Soul Train, IV 461
South Pacific, IV 465
Spacek, Sissy, IV 467
Special Olympics, IV 470
Spelling, Aaron, IV 472
Spielberg, Steven, IV 476
Spillane, Mickey, IV 477
Spin, IV 478
Spitz, Mark, IV 479
Spock, Dr. Benjamin, IV 480
Sport Utility Vehicles (SUVs), IV 482
Sporting News, IV 483
Sports Hero, IV 484
Sports Illustrated, IV 487
Spring Break, IV 488
Springer, Jerry, IV 490
Springsteen, Bruce, IV 491
Sprinkle, Annie, IV 493
St. Elsewhere, IV 495
Stadium Concerts, IV 496
Stallone, Sylvester, IV 500
Stand and Deliver, IV 501
Standardized Testing, IV 502
Stand-up Comedy, IV 504
Stanley Brothers, IV 506
Star System, IV 507
Star Trek, IV 508
Star Wars, IV 511
Starbucks, IV 514
Starr, Bart, IV 515
State Fairs, IV 518
Steinberg, Saul, IV 523
Steinbrenner, George, IV 523
Steinem, Gloria, IV 524
Steppenwolf, IV 527
Stern, Howard, IV 530
Stetson Hat, IV 532
Stevens, Ray, IV 532
Stewart, Jimmy, IV 532
Stickball, IV 534
Stiller and Meara, IV 535
Stine, R. L., IV 535
Stock-Car Racing, IV 537
Stock Market Crashes, IV 539
Stone, Irving, IV 542
Stone, Oliver, IV 543
Strait, George, IV 547
Strawberry, Darryl, IV 551
Streep, Meryl, IV 552
Street and Smith, IV 553
Streetcar Named Desire, IV 554
Streisand, Barbra, IV 556
Strip Joints/Striptease, IV 557
Stuart, Marty, IV 558
Styron, William, IV 567
Suburbia, IV 567
Suicide, IV 569
Summer Camp, IV 573

Sun Records, IV 576
Sundance Film Festival, IV 576
Super Bowl, IV 579
Superman, IV 581
Supermodels, IV 583
Susskind, David, IV 587
Swaggart, Jimmy, IV 587
Swann, Lynn, IV 588
Swatch Watches, IV 589
Sweatshirt, IV 589
Swimming Pools, IV 590
Swinging, IV 593
Sylvia, IV 594
Syndication, IV 595
Tabloid Television, IV 597
Tabloids, IV 597
Talk Radio, IV 600
Talking Heads, IV 602
Tanning, IV 603
Tap Dancing, IV 605
Tarkanian, Jerry, IV 606
Tarzan, IV 608
Taxi, IV 610
Taylor, Elizabeth, IV 612
Taylor, James, IV 615
Teddy Bears, IV 616
Teen Idols, IV 617
Teenage Mutant Ninja Turtles, IV 620
Teenagers, IV 620
Tejano Music, IV 623
Telephone, IV 623
Televangelism, IV 625
Television, IV 626
Television Anchors, IV 629
Temple, Shirley, IV 631
Temptations, IV 632
Tennis, IV 635
Tennis Shoes/Sneakers, IV 637
10,000 Maniacs, IV 638
Tenuta, Judy, IV 638
Terminator, IV 639
Thanksgiving, IV 640
Thing, IV 642
This Is Your Life, IV 643
Thomas, Isiah, IV 645
Thomas, Marlo, IV 645
Thompson, Hunter S., IV 646
Thompson, John, IV 647
Thorogood, George, IV 648
Three Investigators Series, IV 651
Three Stooges, IV 651
Three's Company, IV 653
Tiffany & Company, IV 655
Time, IV 657
Times Square, IV 659
Timex Watches, IV 661
Tiny Tim, IV 661
Today, IV 666
Toffler, Alvin, IV 668
Tom of Finland, IV 673
Tom Swift Series, IV 674
Tomlin, Lily, IV 675
Tonight Show, IV 677
Tootsie, IV 678
Top 40, IV 679
Tormé, Mel, IV 683
Tour de France, IV 684
Town Meetings, IV 684
Toys, IV 685
Trailer Parks, IV 689
Tramps, IV 691
Traveling Carnivals, IV 692
Travolta, John, IV 694
Treviño, Lee, IV 696
Trevor, Claire, IV 697
Trillin, Calvin, IV 697
Trivial Pursuit, IV 698
Trixie Belden, IV 698
Trout, Robert, IV 698
T-Shirts, IV 700
Tupperware, IV 700
Turner, Ike and Tina, IV 702

Turner, Ted, IV 704
TV Dinners, IV 706
TV Guide, IV 706
Tweety Pie and Sylvester, IV 707
Twelve-Step Programs, IV 708
20/20, IV 712
Twilight Zone, IV 713
Twister, IV 715
2 Live Crew, IV 715
Tyler, Anne, IV 718
Tyson, Mike, IV 718
Uecker, Bob, V 1
UFOs (Unidentified Flying Objects), V 1
Ulcers, V 3
Underground Comics, V 4
United Artists, V 8
Unser, Al, V 8
Unser, Bobby, V 10
Updike, John, V 10
U.S. One, V 11
USA Today, V 11
Valdez, Luis, V 15
Valentine's Day, V 16
Valenzuela, Fernando, V 19
Valium, V 20
Vampires, V 22
Van Dyke, Dick, V 24
Van Halen, V 26
Vanity Fair, V 28
Variety, V 31
Vaughan, Sarah, V 36
Vaughan, Stevie Ray, V 37
Velveeta Cheese, V 39
Ventura, Jesse, V 41
Versace, Gianni, V 41
Vertigo, V 42
Victoria's Secret, V 43
Vidal, Gore, V 45
Video Games, V 45
Videos, V 47
Vietnam, V 49
Villella, Edward, V 52
Vitamins, V 52
Vogue, V 53
Vonnegut, Kurt, Jr., V 56
Waits, Tom, V 59
Walker, Alice, V 61
Walkman, V 66
Wall Drug, V 66
Wall Street Journal, V 67
Wallace, Sippie, V 68
Wal-Mart, V 69
Walters, Barbara, V 71
Walton, Bill, V 72
Waltons, V 74
War Movies, V 75
Warhol, Andy, V 80
Washington, Denzel, V 82
Washington Post, V 83
Waters, John, V 87
Watson, Tom, V 90
Wayans, V 90
Weaver, Sigourney, V 96
Wedding Dress, V 100
Welk, Lawrence, V 106
Welles, Orson, V 108
Wertham, Fredric, V 111
West, Jerry, V 114
Western, V 118
Wheel of Fortune, V 122
Whisky A Go Go, V 123
White, Barry, V 125
White, Betty, V 127
White Castle, V 127
White Flight, V 128
Whiting, Margaret, V 130
Whole Earth Catalogue, V 132
Wide World of Sports, V 133
Wilder, Laura Ingalls, V 136
Will, George F., V 138
Williams, Hank, Jr., V 141
Williams, Robin, V 143

Willis, Bruce, V 147
Wilson, Flip, V 148
Wimbledon, V 150
Windy City, V 152
Winfrey, Oprah, V 153
Winnie-the-Pooh, V 155
Winston, George, V 156
Winters, Jonathan, V 157
Wire Services, V 158
Wizard of Oz, V 162
WKRP in Cincinnati, V 164
Wolfe, Tom, V 166
Wolfman, V 167
Wolfman Jack, V 167
Woman's Day, V 169
Wonder, Stevie, V 169
Wonder Woman, V 171
Wood, Natalie, V 173
Wooden, John, V 174
World Series, V 182
World Trade Center, V 184
World War II, V 188
World Wrestling Federation, V 192
Wrangler Jeans, V 196
Wright, Richard, V 196
Wrigley Field, V 197
Wuthering Heights, V 198
WWJD? (What Would Jesus Do?), V 198
Wynette, Tammy, V 201
Y2K, V 207
Yankee Doodle Dandy, V 207
Yankee Stadium, V 208
Yankovic, ''Weird Al'', V 209
Yanni, V 210
Yastrzemski, Carl, V 212
Yellowstone National Park, V 213
Yes, V 214
Yoakam, Dwight, V 216
Young and the Restless, V 216
Young, Loretta, V 217
Young, Neil, V 217
Youngman, Henny, V 219
Yuppies, V 223
Zappa, Frank, V 225
Zines, V 228
Zippy the Pinhead, V 230
Zoos, V 230
Zoot Suit, V 233
Zorro, V 234
Zydeco, V 235
ZZ Top, V 236

1990-1999

A&R Men/Women, I 1
AARP (American Association for Retired
    Persons), I 3
Abortion, I 9
Abdul-Jabbar, Kareem, I 7
Academy Awards, I 12
Acker, Kathy, I 16
Acupuncture, I 16
Adams, Ansel, I 17
Addams Family, I 18
Adidas, I 20
Advertising, I 23
Advice Columns, I 26
Advocate, I 29
Aerobics, I 30
Aerosmith, I 31
African American Press, I 32
Agassi, Andre, I 33
Agents, I 34
AIDS, I 35
Air Travel, I 38
Albert, Marv, I 40
Alda, Alan, I 42
Alien, I 48
Alka Seltzer, I 49
All My Children, I 51
Allen, Steve, I 52
Allen, Woody, I 53
Allison, Luther, I 54
Allman Brothers Band, I 56

Ally McBeal, I 57
Alternative Country Music, I 59
Alternative Press, I 60
Alternative Rock, I 62
Altman, Robert, I 63
Amazing Stories, I 64
American Girls Series, I 67
American Museum of Natural History, I 72
Amsterdam, Morey, I 74
Amtrak, I 75
Amusement Parks, I 77
Amway, I 80
Andretti, Mario, I 84
Androgyny, I 85
Angell, Roger, I 88
Angelou, Maya, I 89
Animated Films, I 90
Anita Hill-Clarence Thomas Senate
    Hearings, I 93
Annie, I 96
Annie Get Your Gun, I 96
Another World, I 99
Anthony, Piers, I 100
Apocalypse Now, I 101
Apollo Theatre, I 104
Apple Computer, I 106
Archie Comics, I 108
Argosy, I 109
Arizona Highways, I 110
Arledge, Roone, I 111
Armani, Giorgio, I 111
Arthur, Bea, I 118
Arthurian Legend, I 120
As the World Turns, I 121
Ashe, Arthur, I 123
Asimov, Isaac, I 125
Asner, Edward, I 126
Astounding Science Fiction, I 129
Astrology, I 129
AT&T, I 130
Athletic Model Guild, I 132
Atlantic City, I 133
Atlantic Monthly, I 134
Aunt Jemima, I 137
Automobile, I 137
Avalon, Frankie, I 143
Avedon, Richard, I 144
Avengers, I 144
Avon, I 146
Aykroyd, Dan, I 147
''B'' movies, I 149
Babar, I 151
Baby Boomers, I 151
Babyface, I 154
Bach, Richard, I 155
Baez, Joan, I 156
Bagels, I 158
Ballard, Hank, I 164
Ballet, I 165
Barbecue, I 168
Barbershop Quartets, I 169
Barbie, I 171
Barker, Clive, I 174
Barkley, Charles, I 175
Barney and Friends, I 175
Barry, Dave, I 177
Barry, Lynda, I 178
Baseball, I 180
Baseball Cards, I 183
Basketball, I 186
Bathhouses, I 188
Batman, I 189
Bay, Mel, I 191
Baywatch, I 193
Beach Boys, I 195
Beanie Babies, I 198
Beastie Boys, I 200
Beatty, Warren, I 206
Beauty Queens, I 207
Beavis and Butthead, I 209
Beer, I 210
Belafonte, Harry, I 214

Bellbottoms, I 216
Bench, Johnny, I 219
Benneton, I 221
Bennett, Tony, I 221
Bergen, Candice, I 224
Bergman, Ingmar, I 225
Bernhard, Sandra, I 231
Bernstein, Leonard, I 233
Berra, Yogi, I 233
Bestsellers, I 236
Better Homes and Gardens, I 238
Betty Crocker, I 241
Beverly Hills 90210, I 242
Bewitched, I 243
Bicycling, I 245
Big Apple, I 246
Big Bands, I 247
Bigfoot, I 251
Bilingual Education, I 252
Billboards, I 253
Bird, Larry, I 255
Birkenstocks, I 257
Birthing Practices, I 260
Black, Clint, I 262
Black Sabbath, I 265
Blade Runner, I 273
Blades, Ruben, I 275
Blass, Bill, I 278
Blockbusters, I 280
Blount, Roy, Jr., I 285
Blueboy, I 287
Bluegrass, I 287
Blues, I 290
Blues Brothers, I 293
Blume, Judy, I 294
Bly, Robert, I 296
Board Games, I 297
Boat People, I 298
Bochco, Steven, I 302
Body Decoration, I 303
Bodybuilding, I 305
Bogart, Humphrey, I 308
Bomb, I 311
Bon Jovi, I 315
Book-of-the-Month Club, I 318
Borge, Victor, I 320
Borscht Belt, I 321
Boston Celtics, I 322
Boston Garden, I 323
Boston Marathon, I 323
Bowie, David, I 328
Bowling, I 328
Boxing, I 330
Boy Scouts of America, I 333
Bra, I 335
Bradbury, Ray, I 337
Bradley, Bill, I 338
Bradshaw, Terry, I 339
Brady Bunch, I 339
Brando, Marlon, I 342
Breast Implants, I 347
Brenda Starr, I 348
Brideshead Revisited, I 348
Bridge, I 349
Bridges of Madison County, I 350
Broadway, I 356
Brokaw, Tom, I 359
Bronson, Charles, I 360
Brooks, Garth, I 364
Brooks, James L., I 365
Brooks, Mel, I 365
Brothers, Dr. Joyce, I 367
Brown, James, I 367
Browne, Jackson, I 371
Bubblegum Rock, I 375
Buckley, William F., Jr., I 379
Buckwheat Zydeco, I 380
Budweiser, I 380
Buffett, Jimmy, I 382
Bugs Bunny, I 383
Bumper Stickers, I 384
Burger King, I 387

Burnett, Carol, I 391
Burns, Ken, I 394
Burr, Raymond, I 394
Butler, Octavia E.(1947--), I 400
Buttons, Red, I 401
Cable TV, I 403
Calloway, Cab, I 412
Calvin and Hobbes, I 413
Camacho, Héctor "Macho", I 414
Camp, I 415
Campbell, Naomi, I 416
Camping, I 417
Cancer, I 418
Candid Camera, I 420
Canseco, Jose, I 422
Capital Punishment, I 424
Captain Kangaroo, I 430
Captain Marvel, I 432
Carey, Mariah, I 434
Carlin, George, I 434
Carlton, Steve, I 435
Carnegie, Dale, I 437
Carnegie Hall, I 439
Carson, Johnny, I 444
Cash, Johnny, I 449
Cassidy, David, I 452
Castro, I 454
Casual Friday, I 455
Cathy, I 460
Cats, I 460
CB Radio, I 462
Celebrity, I 463
Cemeteries, I 467
Central Park, I 468
Charles, Ray, I 477
Chase, Chevy, I 480
Chautauqua Institution, I 481
Chavis, Boozoo, I 483
Checker, Chubby, I 484
Cheerleading, I 486
Cheers, I 488
Chicago Bears, I 492
Chicago Bulls, I 493
Chicago Cubs, I 493
Child, Julia, I 496
Child Stars, I 498
Choose-Your-Own-Ending Books, I 502
Christie, Agatha, I 502
Christmas, I 503
Christo, I 505
Chuck D, I 508
Chun King, I 509
Church Socials, I 509
Cigarettes, I 510
Circus, I 512
Cisneros, Sandra, I 513
City of Angels, I 516
Civil War Reenactors, I 521
Clairol Hair Coloring, I 523
Clancy, Tom, I 524
Clark, Dick, I 525
Clarke, Arthur C., I 527
Clooney, Rosemary, I 533
Closet, I 536
CNN, I 537
Coca-Cola, I 540
Cocaine/Crack, I 542
Cocktail Parties, I 544
Coffee, I 546
College Football, I 555
Collins, Albert, I 557
Columbo, I 559
Comic Books, I 560
Comics, I 562
Coming Out, I 566
Communism, I 569
Community Media, I 570
Community Theatre, I 573
Compact Discs, I 575
Concept Album, I 576
Conceptual Art, I 577
Condé Nast, I 577

Condoms, I 578
Coniff, Ray, I 583
Conspiracy Theories, I 586
Consumer Reports, I 587
Consumerism, I 589
Contemporary Christian Music, I 591
Cooper, Alice, I 595
Cooperstown, New York, I 598
Corvette, I 603
Cosby, Bill, I 606
Cosmopolitan, I 610
Costas, Bob, I 612
Costner, Kevin, I 612
Cotten, Joseph, I 613
Country Music, I 617
Covey, Stephen, I 621
Cowboy Look, I 622
Crawford, Cindy, I 624
Cray, Robert, I 626
Creationism, I 627
Credit Cards, I 628
Crichton, Michael, I 631
Crisis, I 633
Crosby, Stills, and Nash, I 639
Crossword Puzzles, I 641
Cruise, Tom, I 641
Crumb, Robert, I 641
Crystal, Billy, I 643
Cult Films, I 643
Cults, I 646
Cunningham, Merce, I 648
Curious George, I 649
Dahmer, Jeffrey, I 651
Dallas, I 652
Dallas Cowboys, I 654
Daly, Tyne, I 655
Dance Halls, I 657
Daredevil, the Man Without Fear, I 659
Davis, Miles, I 661
Day the Earth Stood Still, I 665
Days of Our Lives, I 666
Daytime Talk Shows, I 667
Daytona 500, I 670
DC Comics, I 671
De La Hoya, Oscar, I 673
De Niro, Robert, I 673
Death of a Salesman, I 678
Debutantes, I 680
DeGeneres, Ellen, I 682
Denver, John, I 686
Department Stores, I 688
Depression, I 690
Detective Fiction, I 693
Detroit Tigers, I 695
Devers, Gail, I 696
Devo, I 696
Diamond, Neil, I 698
Diana, Princess of Wales, I 698
DiCaprio, Leonardo, I 700
Dick Tracy, I 702
Diddley, Bo, I 703
Didion, Joan, I 704
Dieting, I 706
Dilbert, I 710
Dillard, Annie, I 711
Diller, Phyllis, I 712
Dime Stores/Woolworth's, I 717
Dionne Quintuplets, I 720
Disability, I 721
Disaster Movies, I 723
Disc Jockeys, I 725
Disney (Walt Disney Company), I 728
Ditka, Mike, I 731
Divorce, I 732
Doc Martens, I 737
Doc Savage, I 738
Doctor Who, I 739
Doctorow, E. L., I 740
Docudrama, I 741
Do-It-Yourself Improvement, I 742
Domino, Fats, I 743
Donahue, Phil, I 744

Donovan, I 745
Doonesbury, I 747
Douglas, Mike, I 754
Downs, Hugh, I 754
Dr. Jekyll and Mr. Hyde, I 756
Dr. Seuss, I 757
Dracula, I 760
Drag, I 762
Drag Racing, I 764
Dream Team, I 767
Drug War, I 771
Dungeons and Dragons, I 774
Dunkin' Donuts, I 775
Durán, Roberto, I 776
Duvall, Robert, I 778
Dyer, Wayne, I 779
Dykes to Watch Out For, I 780
Dylan, Bob, I 780
Earth Day, II 1
Eastwood, Clint, II 2
Ebony, II 7
Eco-Terrorism, II 10
Eisner, Will, II 18
El Teatro Campesino, II 18
El Vez, II 19
Electric Guitar, II 21
Electric Trains, II 22
Elizondo, Hector, II 22
Elkins, Aaron, II 23
Ellis, Bret Easton, II 24
Ellison, Harlan, II 25
Elway, John, II 25
E-mail, II 26
Emmy Awards, II 27
Empire State Building, II 28
Environmentalism, II 29
ER, II 33
Erdrich, Louise, II 34
Ertegun, Ahmet, II 35
ESPN, II 38
Esquire, II 40
Est, II 42
Etiquette Columns, II 44
Evangelism, II 46
Everson, Cory, II 48
Existentialism, II 50
Exorcist, II 50
Fabian, II 53
Fabio, II 53
Facelifts, II 54
Factor, Max, II 54
Fallout Shelters, II 58
Family Circle, II 59
Family Circus, II 61
Family Matters, II 62
Family Reunions, II 63
Fan Magazines, II 64
Fantasia, II 65
Fantastic Four, II 67
Far Side, II 69
Fargo, II 69
Farm Aid, II 69
Fast Food, II 71
Father Divine, II 74
Father's Day, II 76
Fawcett, Farrah, II 79
FBI (Federal Bureau of Investigation), II 80
Feliciano, José, II 82
Fellini, Federico, II 84
Feminism, II 84
Fenway Park, II 87
Field and Stream, II 92
Field of Dreams, II 93
Field, Sally, II 94
Fierstein, Harvey, II 96
Film Noir, II 99
Firearms, II 101
Firesign Theatre, II 103
Fischer, Bobby, II 104
Fisher-Price Toys, II 106
Flack, Roberta, II 111
Flag Burning, II 111

Flag Clothing, II 111
Flea Markets, II 114
Fleetwood Mac, II 114
Fleming, Peggy, II 116
Flintstones, II 118
Florida Vacations, II 119
Folk Music, II 123
Follett, Ken, II 127
Ford, Harrison, II 131
Ford Motor Company, II 135
Foreman, George, II 138
Forrest Gump, II 140
Forsyth, Frederick, II 141
Fortune, II 142
Foster, Jodie, II 145
Fourth of July Celebrations, II 146
Foyt, A. J., II 148
Frankenstein, II 152
Franklin, Aretha, II 154
Frasier, II 156
Frederick's of Hollywood, II 159
Free Agency, II 160
French Fries, II 165
Friday, Nancy, II 169
Friday the 13th, II 170
Friedman, Kinky, II 171
Friends, II 172
Frisbee, II 174
Frosty the Snowman, II 178
Frozen Entrées, II 178
Fu Manchu, II 179
Fugitive, II 179
Fundamentalism, II 181
Funk, II 184
Fusco, Coco, II 185
Gambling, II 188
Game Shows, II 191
Gammons, Peter, II 195
Gangs, II 195
Gangsta Rap, II 198
Gap, II 198
Garner, James, II 204
Gas Stations, II 206
Gated Communities, II 208
Gay and Lesbian Marriage, II 208
Gay and Lesbian Press, II 210
Gay Liberation Movement, II 211
Gay Men, II 215
General Hospital, II 218
General Motors, II 220
Generation X, II 221
Gentlemen Prefer Blondes, II 223
Gere, Richard, II 224
Ghettos, II 227
GI Joe, II 229
Gibson, Mel, II 234
Gibson, William, II 235
Gillespie, Dizzy, II 236
Gilligan's Island, II 238
Ginsberg, Allen, II 239
Girl Groups, II 240
Girl Scouts, II 242
Godfather, II 250
Godzilla, II 252
Goldberg, Whoopi, II 257
Golden Books, II 258
Golden Gate Bridge, II 259
Golden Girls, II 260
Golf, II 261
Gone with the Wind, II 263
Good Housekeeping, II 265
Gooden, Dwight, II 268
GoodFellas, II 269
Goodson, Mark, II 271
Gordy, Berry, II 272
Gospel Music, II 274
Gossip Columns, II 275
Goth, II 277
Gotti, John, II 277
Graceland, II 278
Graffiti, II 281
Grafton, Sue, II 282

Graham, Bill, II 282
Graham, Billy, II 284
Grand Ole Opry, II 286
Grandmaster Flash, II 286
Grant, Amy, II 287
Grateful Dead, II 291
Gray Panthers, II 294
Greeley, Andrew, II 298
Green Bay Packers, II 300
Green Lantern, II 302
Greene, Graham, II 303
Greenpeace, II 303
Greenwich Village, II 304
Greeting Cards, II 306
Gregory, Dick, II 307
Gretzky, Wayne, II 308
Greyhound Buses, II 312
Griffith, Nanci, II 315
Grisham, John, II 318
Grits, II 319
Grizzard, Lewis, II 319
Groening, Matt, II 319
Grunge, II 321
Grusin, Dave, II 322
Guardian Angels, II 323
Gucci, II 323
Guiding Light, II 323
Gulf War, II 325
Guthrie, Arlo, II 328
Guy, Buddy, II 329
Gymnastics, II 331
Hackett, Buddy, II 333
Hackman, Gene, II 334
Haggard, Merle, II 334
Haight-Ashbury, II 336
Hairstyles, II 340
Hallmark Hall of Fame, II 345
Hamburger, II 347
Hanks, Tom, II 353
Hanna-Barbera, II 355
Happy Hour, II 359
Harding, Tonya, II 360
Hardy Boys, II 360
Hare Krishna, II 362
Harlem Globetrotters, II 364
Harlequin Romances, II 367
Harley-Davidson, II 368
Harmonica Bands, II 370
Harper's, II 372
Hate Crimes, II 373
Havlicek, John, II 374
Hearst, Patty, II 378
Heavy Metal, II 380
Hee Haw, II 381
Hefner, Hugh, II 383
Hell's Angels, II 384
Hemlines, II 390
Hepburn, Katharine, II 394
Hercules: The Legendary Journeys, II 397
Hess, Joan, II 399
Heston, Charlton, II 399
Hijuelos, Oscar, II 405
Hiking, II 405
Hillerman, Tony, II 407
Hirschfeld, Albert, II 412
Hispanic Magazine, II 412
Hite, Shere, II 416
Hockey, II 417
Hoffman, Dustin, II 420
Hogan, Hulk, II 423
Holbrook, Hal, II 424
Holiday Inns, II 428
Hollywood, II 431
Hollywood Squares, II 434
Holyfield, Evander, II 436
Home Improvement, II 437
Home Shopping Network/QVC, II 438
Hooker, John Lee, II 440
Hope, Bob, II 446
Hopper, Dennis, II 447
Hopscotch, II 449
Horne, Lena, II 449

Horror Movies, II 450
Hot Dogs, II 454
Houston, Whitney, II 458
Hubbard, L. Ron, II 461
Hughes, Langston, II 465
Hunt, Helen, II 468
Hustler, II 470
I Dream of Jeannie, II 475
IBM (International Business Machines), II 481
Ice Shows, II 484
Ice-T, II 485
In Living Color, II 486
Incredible Hulk, II 486
Independence Day, II 486
Indian, II 487
Indianapolis 500, II 490
Industrial Design, II 491
Ink Spots, II 493
International Male Catalog, II 494
Internet, II 495
Iron Maiden, II 501
Ironman Triathlon, II 503
Irving, John, II 504
It's a Wonderful Life, II 506
It's Garry Shandling's Show, II 507
Ives, Burl, II 508
Ivy League, II 509
Jackson Five, II 513
Jackson, Jesse, II 514
Jackson, Michael, II 517
Jackson, Reggie, II 519
Jakes, John, II 522
James Bond Films, II 523
Jazz, II 529
Jeans, II 532
Jeep, II 533
Jefferson Airplane/Starship, II 534
Jell-O, II 537
Jennings, Peter, II 538
Jennings, Waylon, II 540
Jeopardy!, II 541
Jessel, George, II 542
Jesus Christ Superstar, II 543
Jet, II 544
Jet Skis, II 545
Jewish Defense League, II 545
JFK(The Movie), II 545
Jogging, II 547
John Birch Society, II 549
John, Elton, II 550
Johns, Jasper, II 551
Johnson, Earvin "Magic", II 553
Johnson, Michael, II 556
Jones, George, II 561
Jones, Tom, II 563
Jong, Erica, II 564
Joplin, Janis, II 565
Jordan, Michael, II 570
Joy of Cooking, II 572
Joy of Sex, II 573
Joyner, Florence Griffith, II 574
Joyner-Kersee, Jackie, II 575
Judas Priest, II 577
Judy Bolton, II 578
Juliá, Raúl, II 581
Jurassic Park, II 581
Juvenile Delinquency, II 583
Kahn, Roger, III 1
Karan, Donna, III 4
Kasem, Casey, III 6
Keillor, Garrison, III 11
Keitel, Harvey, III 12
Kelley, David E., III 13
Kelly Bag, III 14
Kelly Girls, III 14
Kennedy Assassination, III 16
Kentucky Derby, III 19
Kentucky Fried Chicken, III 20
Kerrigan, Nancy, III 21
Kesey, Ken, III 22
King, B. B., III 26
King, Billie Jean, III 28

King, Carole, III 29
King, Larry, III 32
King, Rodney, III 34
King, Stephen, III 36
Kingston Trio, III 39
Kinison, Sam, III 40
KISS, III 42
Kitsch, III 43
Kiwanis, III 46
Klein, Calvin, III 46
Klein, Robert, III 47
Kmart, III 47
Knight, Bobby, III 49
Knots Landing, III 50
Kodak, III 51
Koontz, Dean R., III 53
Koresh, David, and the Branch Davidians, III 54
Korman, Harvey, III 56
Kotzwinkle, William, III 56
Krantz, Judith, III 60
Ku Klux Klan, III 64
Kudzu, III 66
Kwan, Michelle, III 70
L. A. Law, III 71
L. L. Cool J., III 71
Labor Unions, III 72
Lacoste Shirts, III 75
Laetrile, III 76
Lake, Ricki, III 78
LaLanne, Jack, III 80
Landon, Michael, III 86
Lang, k.d., III 88
Larry Sanders Show, III 91
LaRussa, Tony, III 92
Las Vegas, III 92
Lasorda, Tommy, III 93
Latin Jazz, III 97
Lauper, Cyndi, III 99
Lauren, Ralph, III 102
Lawrence, Vicki, III 106
La-Z-Boy Loungers, III 106
Le Carré, John, III 106
Le Guin, Ursula K., III 107
League of Their Own, III 110
Leary, Timothy, III 112
Least Heat Moon, William, III 114
Leave It to Beaver, III 115
Led Zeppelin, III 116
Lee, Spike, III 122
Lee, Stan, III 124
Legos, III 125
Lehrer, Tom, III 126
Leisure Suit, III 127
Leisure Time, III 128
LeMond, Greg, III 130
L'Engle, Madeleine, III 131
Leno, Jay, III 132
Leonard, Elmore, III 134
Leopold and Loeb, III 138
Les Miserables, III 139
Lesbianism, III 140
Letterman, David, III 144
Levi's, III 146
Lewinsky, Monica, III 149
Lewis, C. S., III 150
Lewis, Carl, III 151
Lewis, Jerry, III 152
Lewis, Jerry Lee, III 153
Liebovitz, Annie, III 159
Life, III 160
Like Water for Chocolate, III 162
Limbaugh, Rush, III 163
Linkletter, Art, III 168
Lion King, III 169
Lionel Trains, III 170
Lipstick, III 171
Little League, III 174
Little Magazines, III 176
Little Orphan Annie, III 177
Live Television, III 178
Lloyd Webber, Andrew, III 181
Loafers, III 182

Lolita, III 183
Lollapalooza, III 184
Los Angeles Lakers, III 196
Los Lobos, III 197
Lottery, III 199
Louisville Slugger, III 201
Love, Courtney, III 204
Lucas, George, III 209
Ludlum, Robert, III 213
LuPone, Patti, III 216
Lynch, David, III 216
Lynching, III 217
Lynn, Loretta, III 218
Macy's, III 229
MAD Magazine, III 230
Madden, John, III 232
Made-for-Television Movies, III 233
Madonna, III 235
Mafia/Organized Crime, III 237
Mah-Jongg, III 242
Mailer, Norman, III 242
Malcolm X, III 243
Mall, III 247
Mall of America, III 245
Mamet, David, III 252
Mancini, Henry, III 256
Manhattan Transfer, III 257
Manilow, Barry, III 258
Mantle, Mickey, III 262
Manufactured Homes, III 263
Mapplethorpe, Robert, III 265
Marching Bands, III 267
Mardi Gras, III 269
Mariachi Music, III 270
Marichal, Juan, III 272
Marie, Rose, III 272
Marijuana, III 272
Marlboro Man, III 274
Married . . . with Children, III 277
Marshall, Garry, III 278
Martin, Dean, III 280
Martin, Steve, III 282
Martini, III 282
Marvel Comics, III 285
Mary Kay Cosmetics, III 290
Mary Worth, III 294
Mason, Jackie, III 298
Masterpiece Theatre, III 302
Masters Golf Tournament, III 305
Mathis, Johnny, III 305
Mattingly, Don, III 306
Maupin, Armistead, III 307
Max, Peter, III 308
Mayfield, Curtis, III 310
McBain, Ed, III 312
McCaffrey, Anne, III 313
McCall's Magazine, III 313
McCartney, Paul, III 316
McDonald's, III 321
McEnroe, John, III 324
McEntire, Reba, III 325
McGwire, Mark, III 326
McHale's Navy, III 327
McKuen, Rod, III 328
McMurtry, Larry, III 330
Media Feeding Frenzies, III 337
Mellencamp, John Cougar, III 341
Men's Movement, III 344
Metropolitan Museum of Art, III 347
MGM (Metro-Goldwyn-Mayer), III 347
Michener, James, III 351
Mickey Mouse Club, III 351
Microsoft, III 353
Midler, Bette, III 356
Midnight Cowboy, III 357
Militias, III 359
Miller, Arthur, III 363
Miller Beer, III 364
Milli Vanilli, III 368
Million Man March, III 368
Minimalism, III 369
Minivans, III 370

*Miranda*Warning, III 373
Miss America Pageant, III 374
Mission: Impossible, III 375
Mister Rogers' Neighborhood, III 378
Mitchell, Joni, III 379
Mitchum, Robert, III 381
Mod, III 384
Modern Dance, III 388
Modern Maturity, III 388
Monday Night Football, III 393
Monkees, III 394
Monopoly, III 396
Monroe, Bill, III 396
Montana, Joe, III 402
Montana, Patsy, III 403
Monty Python's Flying Circus, III 403
Moonies/Reverend Sun Myung Moon, III 405
Moore, Demi, III 407
Moore, Michael, III 408
Morissette, Alanis, III 413
Morris, Mark, III 413
Morrison, Toni, III 414
Morrison, Van, III 415
Mosley, Walter, III 416
Moss, Kate, III 417
Mother's Day, III 417
Mötley Crüe, III 418
Mount Rushmore, III 423
Mountain Biking, III 424
Movie Stars, III 428
Ms., III 434
MTV, III 435
Multiculturalism, III 439
Mummy, III 441
Muppets, III 444
Murder, She Wrote, III 445
Murphy Brown, III 446
Murphy, Eddie, III 447
Murray, Anne, III 447
Murray, Arthur, III 448
Murray, Bill, III 450
Murray, Lenda, III 451
Muscular Christianity, III 456
Musical, III 458
Muzak, III 463
My Family, Mi Familia, III 464
My So-Called Life, III 466
Nader, Ralph, III 469
Nancy Drew, III 473
NASA, III 475
Nation, III 476
National Basketball Association (NBA), III 477
National Collegiate Athletic Association (NCAA), III 479
National Enquirer, III 480
National Football League (NFL), III 482
National Geographic, III 484
National Hockey League (NHL), III 485
National Lampoon, III 487
National Organization for Women (N.O.W.), III 489
National Parks, III 489
Natural Born Killers, III 493
Nava, Gregory, III 495
Navratilova, Martina, III 495
Naylor, Gloria, III 495
Neckties, III 495
Neighborhood Watch, III 499
Nelson, Willie, III 501
Nerd Look, III 502
Networks, III 503
New Age Music, III 506
New Age Spirituality, III 507
New Kids on the Block, III 510
New Republic, III 514
New York Knickerbockers, III 517
New York Mets, III 517
New York Times, III 518
New York Yankees, III 520
New Yorker, III 522
Newport Jazz and Folk Festivals, III 526
Newsweek, III 527

Newton, Helmut, III 528
Niagara Falls, III 528
Nicklaus, Jack, III 531
Night of the Living Dead, III 532
Nightline, III 533
Nike, III 535
Nirvana, III 538
Northern Exposure, III 542
Novak, Kim, III 543
Nylon, III 544
NYPD Blue, III 545
Oakland Raiders, III 547
Oates, Joyce Carol, III 547
O'Brien, Tim, III 548
Odd Couple, III 550
O'Donnell, Rosie, III 551
Oklahoma!, III 553
Old Navy, III 555
Oliphant, Pat, III 555
Olmos, Edward James, III 557
Olympics, III 558
Onassis, Jacqueline Lee Bouvier Kennedy,
    III 564
O'Neal, Shaquille, III 568
O'Rourke, P. J., III 573
Osbourne, Ozzy, III 575
Ouija Boards, III 576
Outer Limits, III 579
Outing, III 580
Pachucos, IV 2
Pacino, Al, IV 3
Paglia, Camille, IV 4
Paley, Grace, IV 6
Pants for Women, IV 7
Pantyhose, IV 9
Paperbacks, IV 9
Parades, IV 12
Paretsky, Sara, IV 12
Parker Brothers, IV 13
Parks, Rosa, IV 15
Parton, Dolly, IV 17
Patinkin, Mandy, IV 19
Paulsen, Pat, IV 22
Peanuts, IV 25
Pearl Jam, IV 26
Pearl, Minnie, IV 28
Peck, Gregory, IV 29
Pee-wee's Playhouse, IV 32
Penn, Irving, IV 33
Penthouse, IV 34
People, IV 35
Pepsi-Cola, IV 36
Performance Art, IV 37
Perot, Ross, IV 39
Peter, Paul, and Mary, IV 42
Peters, Bernadette, IV 44
Pets, IV 44
Petty, Richard, IV 46
Pfeiffer, Michelle, IV 48
Phantom of the Opera, IV 49
Phone Sex, IV 51
Phonograph, IV 52
Pink Floyd, IV 58
Piper, ''Rowdy'' Roddy, IV 60
Pippen, Scottie, IV 61
Pittsburgh Steelers, IV 61
Pizza, IV 62
Plastic, IV 64
Plastic Surgery, IV 67
Plath, Sylvia, IV 68
Playboy, IV 70
Playgirl, IV 72
Pogo, IV 73
Pointer Sisters, IV 74
Poitier, Sidney, IV 75
Political Correctness, IV 78
Polyester, IV 80
Pop, Iggy, IV 82
Pop Music, IV 83
Pope, IV 86
Popeye, IV 87
Popsicles, IV 88

Popular Mechanics, IV 89
Popular Psychology, IV 90
Pornography, IV 92
Postcards, IV 96
Postman Always Rings Twice, IV 97
Postmodernism, IV 98
Potter, Dennis, IV 102
Preppy, IV 105
Presley, Elvis, IV 105
Price Is Right, IV 108
Price, Reynolds, IV 110
Pride, Charley, IV 111
Prince, IV 112
Prince, Hal, IV 114
Professional Football, IV 116
Prom, IV 120
Promise Keepers, IV 122
Protest Groups, IV 124
Prozac, IV 125
Pryor, Richard, IV 126
Psychics, IV 129
PTA/PTO (Parent Teacher Association/
    Organization), IV 130
Public Enemy, IV 132
Public Libraries, IV 133
Public Television (PBS), IV 135
Puente, Tito, IV 137
Pulp Fiction, IV 138
Punisher, IV 142
Punk, IV 142
Pynchon, Thomas, IV 145
Quayle, Dan, IV 147
Queen Latifah, IV 150
Queer Nation, IV 150
Quiz Show Scandals, IV 151
Race Riots, IV 156
Radio, IV 157
Raitt, Bonnie, IV 170
Ramones, IV 171
Rap/Hip-Hop, IV 174
Rather, Dan, IV 176
Reader's Digest, IV 177
Real World, IV 181
Reality Television, IV 181
Recycling, IV 187
Redbook, IV 189
Redford, Robert, IV 190
Reed, Ishmael, IV 191
Reed, Lou, IV 192
Reggae, IV 194
Reiner, Carl, IV 196
Religious Right, IV 197
R.E.M., IV 201
Replacements, IV 204
Retro Fashion, IV 205
Reynolds, Burt, IV 205
Rice, Jerry, IV 209
Rigby, Cathy, IV 210
Riley, Pat, IV 212
Ripken, Cal, Jr., IV 214
Ripley's Believe It Or Not, IV 215
Rivera, Chita, IV 216
Rivera, Geraldo, IV 218
Rivers, Joan, IV 219
Rizzuto, Phil, IV 220
Road Rage, IV 221
Road Runner and Wile E. Coyote, IV 222
Robbins, Tom, IV 223
Roberts, Jake ''The Snake'', IV 223
Roberts, Julia, IV 223
Roberts, Nora, IV 224
Robertson, Pat, IV 225
Robeson, Kenneth, IV 227
Robinson, Frank, IV 230
Robinson, Smokey, IV 233
Rock and Roll, IV 235
Rock, Chris, IV 238
Rock Climbing, IV 238
Rockefeller Family, IV 239
Rockettes, IV 241
Rocky and Bullwinkle, IV 248
Rocky Horror Picture Show, IV 248

Roddenberry, Gene, IV 251
Rodeo, IV 252
Rodman, Dennis, IV 259
Rodríguez, Chi Chi, IV 259
Rogers, Kenny, IV 261
Roller Coasters, IV 265
Roller Derby, IV 266
Rolling Stone, IV 267
Rolling Stones, IV 269
Romance Novels, IV 270
Rose Bowl, IV 275
Rose, Pete, IV 276
Roseanne, IV 277
Ross, Diana, and the Supremes, IV 280
Roswell Incident, IV 282
Roundtree, Richard, IV 282
Route 66, IV 284
Royko, Mike, IV 285
Rudolph the Red-Nosed Reindeer, IV 287
Run-DMC, IV 287
RuPaul, IV 289
RV, IV 295
Ryan, Meg, IV 297
Ryan, Nolan, IV 297
Rydell, Bobby, IV 298
Ryder, Winona, IV 298
Safe Sex, IV 299
Sagan, Carl, IV 300
Sahl, Mort, IV 301
Saks Fifth Avenue, IV 302
Sales, Soupy, IV 303
Salsa Music, IV 303
Salt-n-Pepa, IV 305
Sanders, Barry, IV 307
Sandman, IV 307
Santana, IV 311
Sarandon, Susan, IV 312
Saratoga Springs, IV 312
Sassy, IV 313
Saturday Morning Cartoons, IV 317
Saturday Night Live, IV 320
Savage, Randy ''Macho Man'', IV 322
Schindler's List, IV 324
Schlessinger, Dr. Laura, IV 326
Schnabel, Julian, IV 327
Schoolhouse Rock, IV 328
Schwarzenegger, Arnold, IV 329
Science Fiction Publishing, IV 330
Scientific American, IV 334
Scorsese, Martin, IV 337
Scott, George C., IV 338
Scream, IV 341
Scully, Vin, IV 345
Sea World, IV 345
Seals, Son, IV 345
Sears Roebuck Catalogue, IV 346
Second City, IV 348
Sedona, Arizona, IV 349
Seinfeld, IV 352
Selena, IV 354
Seles, Monica, IV 355
Sesame Street, IV 362
Seventeen, IV 364
Sex Scandals, IV 367
Sex Symbol, IV 369
Sexual Harassment, IV 371
Shakur, Tupac, IV 377
Sheldon, Sidney, IV 381
Shepard, Sam, IV 382
Sherman, Cindy, IV 383
Shirer, William L., IV 384
Shock Radio, IV 386
Shore, Dinah, IV 387
Show Boat, IV 389
Shula, Don, IV 391
SIDS (Sudden Infant Death Syndrome), IV 391
Silence of the Lambs, IV 393
Silver Surfer, IV 399
Simon, Neil, IV 401
Simon, Paul, IV 403
Simpson, O. J., IV 404
Simpson Trial, IV 405

Simpsons, IV 408
Sinatra, Frank, IV 409
Sinbad, IV 413
Singer, Isaac Bashevis, IV 414
Singles Bars, IV 415
Siskel and Ebert, IV 417
Sister Souljah, IV 418
Sitcom, IV 418
Six Million Dollar Man, IV 424
60 Minutes, IV 425
Skaggs, Ricky, IV 427
Skateboarding, IV 428
Skating, IV 429
Slaney, Mary Decker, IV 433
Slang, IV 434
Slasher Movies, IV 435
Slinky, IV 436
Smith, Dean, IV 439
Smith, Patti, IV 440
Smithsonian Institution, IV 441
Smits, Jimmy, IV 441
Smothers Brothers, IV 442
Snoop Doggy Dogg, IV 444
Soap Operas, IV 446
Soccer, IV 449
Social Dancing, IV 450
Sondheim, Stephen, IV 454
Sonny and Cher, IV 456
Sosa, Sammy, IV 458
Soul Train, IV 461
South Park, IV 466
Spacek, Sissy, IV 467
Spawn, IV 470
Special Olympics, IV 470
Spelling, Aaron, IV 472
Spice Girls, IV 473
Spider-Man, IV 474
Spielberg, Steven, IV 476
Spin, IV 478
Spitz, Mark, IV 479
Spock, Dr. Benjamin, IV 480
Sport Utility Vehicles (SUVs), IV 482
Sporting News, IV 483
Sports Hero, IV 484
Sports Illustrated, IV 487
Spring Break, IV 488
Springer, Jerry, IV 490
Springsteen, Bruce, IV 491
Sprinkle, Annie, IV 493
Stadium Concerts, IV 496
Stallone, Sylvester, IV 500
Standardized Testing, IV 502
Stand-up Comedy, IV 504
Stanley Brothers, IV 506
Star System, IV 507
Star Trek, IV 508
Star Wars, IV 511
Starbucks, IV 514
Starr, Kenneth, IV 516
State Fairs, IV 518
Steinberg, Saul, IV 523
Steinbrenner, George, IV 523
Steinem, Gloria, IV 524
Steppenwolf, IV 527
Stern, Howard, IV 530
Stetson Hat, IV 532
Stevens, Ray, IV 532
Stickball, IV 534
Stiller and Meara, IV 535
Stine, R. L., IV 535
Stock-Car Racing, IV 537
Stock Market Crashes, IV 539
Stone, Oliver, IV 543
Strait, George, IV 547
Strawberry, Darryl, IV 551
Streaking, IV 551
Streep, Meryl, IV 552
Street and Smith, IV 553
Streetcar Named Desire, IV 554
Streisand, Barbra, IV 556
Strip Joints/Striptease, IV 557
Stuart, Marty, IV 558

Styron, William, IV 567
Suburbia, IV 567
Suicide, IV 569
Summer Camp, IV 573
Sun Records, IV 576
Sundance Film Festival, IV 576
Super Bowl, IV 579
Superman, IV 581
Supermodels, IV 583
Surf Music, IV 585
Swatch Watches, IV 589
Sweatshirt, IV 589
Swimming Pools, IV 590
Swing Dancing, IV 592
Swinging, IV 593
Sylvia, IV 594
Syndication, IV 595
Tabloid Television, IV 597
Tabloids, IV 597
Talk Radio, IV 600
Talking Heads, IV 602
Tanning, IV 603
Tap Dancing, IV 605
Tarantino, Quentin, IV 606
Tarkanian, Jerry, IV 606
Tarzan, IV 608
Taylor, Elizabeth, IV 612
Taylor, James, IV 615
Teddy Bears, IV 616
Teen Idols, IV 617
Teenage Mutant Ninja Turtles, IV 620
Teenagers, IV 620
Tejano Music, IV 623
Telephone, IV 623
Televangelism, IV 625
Television, IV 626
Television Anchors, IV 629
Temptations, IV 632
Tennis, IV 635
Tennis Shoes/Sneakers, IV 637
10,000 Maniacs, IV 638
Tenuta, Judy, IV 638
Terminator, IV 639
Thanksgiving, IV 640
Thomas, Isiah, IV 645
Thompson, Hunter S., IV 646
Thompson, John, IV 647
Thorogood, George, IV 648
Three Stooges, IV 651
Tiffany & Company, IV 655
Time, IV 657
Times Square, IV 659
Timex Watches, IV 661
Titanic, IV 661
Today, IV 666
Toffler, Alvin, IV 668
Tom of Finland, IV 673
Tom Swift Series, IV 674
Tomlin, Lily, IV 675
Tonight Show, IV 677
Top 40, IV 679
Tormé, Mel, IV 683
Touched by an Angel, IV 684
Tour de France, IV 684
Town Meetings, IV 684
Toy Story, IV 685
Toys, IV 685
Trailer Parks, IV 689
Tramps, IV 691
Traveling Carnivals, IV 692
Travolta, John, IV 694
Trillin, Calvin, IV 697
Trivial Pursuit, IV 698
Tupperware, IV 700
Turner, Ted, IV 704
TV Dinners, IV 706
TV Guide, IV 706
Tweety Pie and Sylvester, IV 707
Twelve-Step Programs, IV 708
20/20, IV 712
Twilight Zone, IV 713
Twin Peaks, IV 715

Twister, IV 715
2 Live Crew, IV 715
2001: A Space Odyssey, IV 717
Tyler, Anne, IV 718
Tyson, Mike, IV 718
Uecker, Bob, V 1
UFOs (Unidentified Flying Objects), V 1
Ulcers, V 3
Underground Comics, V 4
Unforgiven, V 5
United Artists, V 8
Updike, John, V 10
U.S. One, V 11
USA Today, V 11
Valdez, Luis, V 15
Valentine's Day, V 16
Valenzuela, Fernando, V 19
Valium, V 20
Vampires, V 22
Van Dyke, Dick, V 24
Van Halen, V 26
Vanilla Ice, V 28
Vanity Fair, V 28
Variety, V 31
Velveeta Cheese, V 39
Velvet Underground, V 39
Ventura, Jesse, V 41
Versace, Gianni, V 41
Viagra, V 43
Victoria's Secret, V 43
Vidal, Gore, V 45
Video Games, V 45
Videos, V 47
Vitamins, V 52
Vogue, V 53
Volkswagen Beetle, V 54
Vonnegut, Kurt, Jr., V 56
Waits, Tom, V 59
Walker, Alice, V 61
Walkman, V 66
Wall Drug, V 66
Wall Street Journal, V 67
Wal-Mart, V 69
Walters, Barbara, V 71
Walton, Bill, V 72
War Movies, V 75
Washington, Denzel, V 82
Washington Post, V 83
Waters, John, V 87
Watson, Tom, V 90
Wayans, V 90
Wayne's World, V 94
Weaver, Sigourney, V 96
Wedding Dress, V 100
Weekend, V 101
Welk, Lawrence, V 106
Wells, Mary, V 111
Western, V 118
Wheel of Fortune, V 122
Whisky A Go Go, V 123
White, Barry, V 125
White, Betty, V 127
White Castle, V 127
White Flight, V 128
White Supremacists, V 129
Whole Earth Catalogue, V 132
Wide World of Sports, V 133
Wilder, Laura Ingalls, V 136
Will, George F., V 138
Williams, Hank, Jr., V 141
Williams, Robin, V 143
Willis, Bruce, V 147
Wimbledon, V 150
Windy City, V 152
Winfrey, Oprah, V 153
Winnie-the-Pooh, V 155
Winston, George, V 156
Winters, Jonathan, V 157
Wire Services, V 158
Wizard of Oz, V 162
Wolfe, Tom, V 166
Wolfman, V 167

Woman's Day, V 169
Wonder, Stevie, V 169
Wood, Ed, V 172
Wooden, John, V 174
Woods, Tiger, V 175
World Cup, V 181
World Series, V 182
World Trade Center, V 184
World War II, V 188
World Wrestling Federation, V 192
Wrangler Jeans, V 196
Wright, Richard, V 196
Wuthering Heights, V 198

WWJD? (What Would Jesus Do?), V 198
Wynette, Tammy, V 201
X Games, V 203
Xena, Warrior Princess, V 203
X-Files, V 203
X-Men, V 205
Y2K, V 207
Yankee Stadium, V 208
Yankovic, ''Weird Al'', V 209
Yanni, V 210
Yellowstone National Park, V 213
Yoakam, Dwight, V 216
Young and the Restless, V 216

Young, Neil, V 217
Youngman, Henny, V 219
Yo-Yo, V 223
Yuppies, V 223
Zappa, Frank, V 225
Zines, V 228
Zippy the Pinhead, V 230
Zoos, V 230
Zoot Suit, V 233
Zorro, V 234
Zydeco, V 235
ZZ Top, V 236

CATEGORY INDEX

Action/Adventure, Film
Alien, I 48
American International Pictures, I 71
Arthurian Legend, I 120
Batman, I 189
Beau Geste, I 207
Blockbusters, I 280
Bonnie and Clyde, I 316
Bronson, Charles, I 360
Brown, Jim, I 369
Clancy, Tom, I 524
Cult Films, I 643
Davy Crockett, I 663
Disaster Movies, I 723
Easy Rider, II 4
Fleming, Ian, II 116
Flipper, II 118
Ford, Harrison, II 131
Fu Manchu, II 179
Great Depression, II 295
Great Train Robbery, II 297
Heston, Charlton, II 399
Hitchcock, Alfred, II 414
Independence Day, II 486
James Bond Films, II 523
Jaws, II 526
Jurassic Park, II 581
King Kong, III 30
Leone, Sergio, III 136
Man from U.N.C.L.E., III 253
McQueen, Steve, III 333
Mutiny on the Bounty, III 461
North by Northwest, III 541
Novak, Kim, III 543
Platoon, IV 69
Raiders of the Lost Ark, IV 166
Rambo, IV 170
Reeves, Steve, IV 193
Rocky, IV 246
Silent Movies, IV 393
Spartacus, IV 468
Stallone, Sylvester, IV 500
Star Wars, IV 511
Tarzan, IV 608
Terminator, IV 639
Weissmuller, Johnny, V 104
Willis, Bruce, V 147
Zorro, V 234

Action/Adventure, Print
Batman, I 189
Beach, Rex, I 197
Beau Geste, I 207
Burroughs, Edgar Rice, I 396
Caniff, Milton, I 421
Captain Marvel, I 432
Clancy, Tom, I 524
Comics, I 562
Crichton, Michael, I 631
Crime Does Not Pay, I 632
Daredevil, the Man Without Fear, I 659
DC Comics, I 671
Dime Novels, I 716
Doc Savage, I 738
Douglas, Lloyd C., I 753
Fantastic Four, II 67
Fleming, Ian, II 116
Follett, Ken, II 127
Forsyth, Frederick, II 141
Fu Manchu, II 179
Green Lantern, II 302
Incredible Hulk, II 486
Jakes, John, II 522
Jurassic Park, II 581
London, Jack, III 187
Maus, III 308
Mutiny on the Bounty, III 461
Natural, III 492
On the Road, III 561
Pulp Magazines, IV 139
Silver Surfer, IV 399
Spillane, Mickey, IV 477
Superman, IV 581

Tales from the Crypt, IV 600
Tarzan, IV 608
Tom Swift Series, IV 674
Underground Comics, V 4
Wonder Woman, V 171
Zorro, V 234

Action/Adventure, Television
A-Team, I 132
Avengers, I 144
Batman, I 189
Bionic Woman, I 255
Davy Crockett, I 663
Flipper, II 118
Follett, Ken, II 127
General Hospital, II 218
Hercules: The Legendary Journeys, II 397
Jakes, John, II 522
Kung Fu, III 68
Made-for-Television Movies, III 233
Martin, Quinn, III 282
Olmos, Edward James, III 557
Piper, ''Rowdy'' Roddy, IV 60
Romero, Cesar, IV 273
Wild Kingdom, V 135
Wonder Woman, V 171
Xena, Warrior Princess, V 203
Zorro, V 234

Activists
AARP (American Association for Retired Persons), I 3
Abbey, Edward, I 4
Abdul-Jabbar, Kareem, I 7
Addams, Jane, I 17
Ashe, Arthur, I 123
Baldwin, James, I 161
Baraka, Amiri, I 168
Belafonte, Harry, I 214
Blades, Ruben, I 275
Bruce, Lenny, I 372
Buck, Pearl S., I 375
Chavez, Cesar, I 482
Chicago Seven, I 495
Civil Disobedience, I 517
Communism, I 569
Consciousness Raising Groups, I 585
Cousteau, Jacques, I 621
Crisis, I 633
Darrow, Clarence, I 660
Debs, Eugene V., I 679
Du Bois, W. E. B., I 771
Dylan, Bob, I 780
Eco-Terrorism, II 10
Eddy, Mary Baker, II 11
Einstein, Albert, II 16
Farm Aid, II 69
Fierstein, Harvey, II 96
Fleming, Peggy, II 116
Fonda, Jane, II 129
Free Speech Movement, II 161
Freedom Rides, II 163
Gere, Richard, II 224
Ginsberg, Allen, II 239
Gray Panthers, II 294
Greeley, Andrew, II 298
Heston, Charlton, II 399
Jackson, Jesse, II 514
Johnson, James Weldon, II 555
King, Billie Jean, III 28
King, Martin Luther, Jr., III 33
King, Rodney, III 34
Lancaster, Burt, III 85
Leary, Timothy, III 112
Lennon, John, III 131
Lindbergh, Anne Morrow, III 166
Malcolm X, III 243
Marley, Bob, III 274
Michener, James, III 351
Militias, III 359
Miller, Arthur, III 363
Nader, Ralph, III 469
Ochs, Phil, III 549

Pearl Jam, IV 26
Price Is Right, IV 108
Raitt, Bonnie, IV 170
Red Scare, IV 188
Robertson, Pat, IV 225
RuPaul, IV 289
Shakur, Tupac, IV 377
Sinatra, Frank, IV 409
Sinclair, Upton, IV 414
Springsteen, Bruce, IV 491
Steffens, Lincoln, IV 521
Stonewall Rebellion, IV 544
Streisand, Barbra, IV 556
Turner, Ted, IV 704
Twilight Zone, IV 713
Weathermen, V 95
Wobblies, V 165

Actors
Abbott and Costello, I 5
Abdul-Jabbar, Kareem, I 7
Alda, Alan, I 42
Allen, Steve, I 52
Allen, Woody, I 53
Amsterdam, Morey, I 74
Arbuckle, Fatty, I 107
Asner, Edward, I 126
Astaire, Fred, and Ginger Rogers, I 127
Barrymore, John, I 178
Beatty, Warren, I 206
Belafonte, Harry, I 214
Benchley, Robert, I 219
Benny, Jack, I 222
Bergen, Edgar, I 225
Blackboard Jungle, I 268
Blades, Ruben, I 275
Bob and Ray, I 299
Bon Jovi, I 315
Boone, Pat, I 319
Borge, Victor, I 320
Brando, Marlon, I 342
Brat Pack, I 344
Bronson, Charles, I 360
Brooks, Mel, I 365
Brynner, Yul, I 375
Burr, Raymond, I 394
Butterbeans and Susie, I 400
Buttons, Red, I 401
Caesar, Sid, I 408
Cagney, James, I 409
Cantor, Eddie, I 423
Carmichael, Hoagy, I 436
Caruso, Enrico, I 446
Cassidy, David, I 452
Chase, Chevy, I 480
Chayefsky, Paddy, I 484
Cheech and Chong, I 485
Child Stars, I 498
Clift, Montgomery, I 529
Cohan, George M., I 548
Cole, Nat ''King,'' I 552
Cooper, Gary, I 597
Costner, Kevin, I 612
Cotten, Joseph, I 613
Crosby, Bing, I 638
Cruise, Tom, I 641
Dana, Bill, I 656
De Niro, Robert, I 673
DeMille, Cecil B., I 683
Diamond, Neil, I 698
Disability, I 721
Divine, I 731
Douglas, Melvyn, I 753
Eastwood, Clint, II 2
Edwards, James, II 14
Elizondo, Hector, II 22
Fairbanks, Douglas, Jr., II 55
Fairbanks, Douglas, Sr., II 57
Farr, Jamie, II 71
Fetchit, Stepin, II 88
Fields, W. C., II 95
Fierstein, Harvey, II 96
Fisher, Eddie, II 104

Flynn, Errol, II 121
Ford, Glenn, II 131
Ford, Harrison, II 131
Forrest Gump, II 140
Foxx, Redd, II 148
Frawley, William, II 157
Gable, Clark, II 187
Garfield, John, II 201
Garner, James, II 204
Gere, Richard, II 224
Gibson, Mel, II 234
Gleason, Jackie, II 245
Grant, Cary, II 288
Greene, Graham, II 303
Hanks, Tom, II 353
Hepburn, Audrey, II 394
Heston, Charlton, II 399
Hoffman, Dustin, II 420
Holbrook, Hal, II 424
Holden, William, II 426
Hollywood, II 431
Hollywood Ten, II 434
Hopalong Cassidy, II 444
Hopper, Dennis, II 447
Hudson, Rock, II 462
Hunter, Tab, II 468
Huston, John, II 471
It Happened One Night, II 504
Ives, Burl, II 508
Jolson, Al, II 559
Juliá, Raúl, II 581
Karloff, Boris, III 4
Kaufman, Andy, III 7
Kaye, Danny, III 9
Keitel, Harvey, III 12
Klein, Robert, III 47
Kojak, III 52
Korman, Harvey, III 56
Kung Fu, III 68
Ladd, Alan, III 75
Lancaster, Burt, III 85
Landon, Michael, III 86
Lee, Bruce, III 117
Lee, Spike, III 122
Lewis, Jerry, III 152
Liebovitz, Annie, III 159
Lone Ranger, III 189
Lorre, Peter, III 195
Love, Courtney, III 204
Lubitsch, Ernst, III 209
MacMurray, Fred, III 228
Magnificent Seven, III 240
Marcus Welby, M.D., III 269
Marshall, Garry, III 278
Martin, Steve, III 282
Marx, Groucho, III 288
McCoy, Horace, III 319
McCrea, Joel, III 319
McKuen, Rod, III 328
McQueen, Steve, III 333
Mitchum, Robert, III 381
Mix, Tom, III 383
Montalbán, Ricardo, III 401
Moonlighting, III 406
Movie Stars, III 428
Muni, Paul, III 442
Murray, Bill, III 450
Musical, III 458
Nelson, Ricky, III 499
Olivier, Laurence, III 556
Olmos, Edward James, III 557
Our Gang, III 576
Paar, Jack, IV 1
Pacino, Al, IV 3
Patinkin, Mandy, IV 19
Peck, Gregory, IV 29
Piper, ''Rowdy'' Roddy, IV 60
Poitier, Sidney, IV 75
Powell, Dick, IV 102
Preminger, Otto, IV 104
Presley, Elvis, IV 105
Price, Vincent, IV 110

Pryor, Richard, IV 126
Raft, George, IV 162
Rains, Claude, IV 168
Reagan, Ronald, IV 179
Redford, Robert, IV 190
Reynolds, Burt, IV 205
Robeson, Paul, IV 227
Robinson, Edward G., IV 229
Rock, Chris, IV 238
Rodman, Dennis, IV 259
Rogers, Kenny, IV 261
Romero, Cesar, IV 273
Roundtree, Richard, IV 282
Russell, Nipsey, IV 293
Rydell, Bobby, IV 298
Sanford and Son, IV 310
Schwarzenegger, Arnold, IV 329
Scott, George C., IV 338
Scott, Randolph, IV 339
Sellers, Peter, IV 355
Sex Symbol, IV 369
Shakur, Tupac, IV 377
Shepard, Sam, IV 382
Simpson, O. J., IV 404
Sinbad, IV 413
Smits, Jimmy, IV 441
Sonny and Cher, IV 456
Stallone, Sylvester, IV 500
Stand and Deliver, IV 501
Star System, IV 507
Stewart, Jimmy, IV 532
Stiller and Meara, IV 535
Stone, Oliver, IV 543
Streetcar Named Desire, IV 554
Taylor, Robert, IV 615
Ten Commandments, IV 634
Thomas, Danny, IV 644
Tiny Tim, IV 661
Tone, Franchot, IV 676
Tormé, Mel, IV 683
Tracy, Spencer, IV 687
Travolta, John, IV 694
Uecker, Bob, V 1
Valdez, Luis, V 15
Valentino, Rudolph, V 17
Vallee, Rudy, V 21
Van Dyke, Dick, V 24
Ventura, Jesse, V 41
Walker, George, V 62
War Bonds, V 74
Wayans, V 90
Wayne, John, V 91
Webb, Jack, V 98
Weissmuller, Johnny, V 104
Welles, Orson, V 108
Wheel of Fortune, V 122
Whiting, Margaret, V 130
Williams, Robin, V 143
Willis, Bruce, V 147
Winters, Jonathan, V 157
Yoakam, Dwight, V 216
Young, Robert, V 218

Actresses

Andrews Sisters, I 84
Arthur, Bea, I 118
Astaire, Fred, and Ginger Rogers, I 127
Bara, Theda, I 168
Bergen, Candice, I 224
Bergman, Ingrid, I 226
Bernhard, Sandra, I 231
Beulah, I 241
Bow, Clara, I 326
Brat Pack, I 344
Butterbeans and Susie, I 400
Canova, Judy, I 421
Charlie's Angels, I 479
Child Stars, I 498
Clooney, Rosemary, I 533
Coca, Imogene, I 540
Colbert, Claudette, I 548
Crawford, Joan, I 625
Daly, Tyne, I 655

Dandridge, Dorothy, I 658
Davis, Bette, I 661
Day, Doris, I 664
Del Río, Dolores, I 683
Dickinson, Angie, I 703
Dietrich, Marlene, I 708
Diller, Phyllis, I 712
Disability, I 721
Dunne, Irene, I 776
Durbin, Deanna, I 776
Fabares, Shelley, II 53
Fawcett, Farrah, II 79
Field, Sally, II 94
Flying Nun, II 120
Fonda, Jane, II 129
Foster, Jodie, II 145
Francis, Arlene, II 150
Francis, Connie, II 151
Franklin, Bonnie, II 156
Funicello, Annette, II 183
Garbo, Greta, II 199
Gardner, Ava, II 200
Gish, Lillian, II 244
Goldberg, Whoopi, II 257
Grable, Betty, II 277
Grier, Pam, II 312
Harlow, Jean, II 370
Harper, Valerie, II 371
Hayward, Susan, II 377
Hayworth, Rita, II 377
Hemlines, II 390
Hepburn, Katharine, II 394
Holliday, Judy, II 429
Hollywood, II 431
Hollywood Ten, II 434
Horne, Lena, II 449
Houston, Whitney, II 458
It Happened One Night, II 504
Jones, Jennifer, II 562
Kate & Allie, III 7
Lake, Ricki, III 78
Lake, Veronica, III 79
Lamarr, Hedy, III 82
Lamour, Dorothy, III 83
Lang, k.d., III 88
Lauper, Cyndi, III 99
Lavin, Linda, III 103
Lawrence, Vicki, III 106
Leachman, Cloris, III 108
Lee, Gypsy Rose, III 119
Lee, Peggy, III 121
Liebovitz, Annie, III 159
Lombard, Carole, III 184
Long, Shelley, III 192
Loy, Myrna, III 207
Lupino, Ida, III 215
LuPone, Patti, III 216
Mansfield, Jayne, III 259
Marie, Rose, III 272
Mary Hartman, Mary Hartman, III 289
McDaniel, Hattie, III 320
McQueen, Butterfly, III 332
Meadows, Audrey, III 336
Midler, Bette, III 356
Miranda, Carmen, III 373
Monroe, Marilyn, III 399
Moonlighting, III 406
Moore, Demi, III 407
Moreno, Rita, III 410
Movie Stars, III 428
Musical, III 458
Novak, Kim, III 543
O'Donnell, Rosie, III 551
Parton, Dolly, IV 17
Peters, Bernadette, IV 44
Pfeiffer, Michelle, IV 48
Pickford, Mary, IV 55
Queen Latifah, IV 150
Radner, Gilda, IV 162
Reed, Donna, IV 191
Rigby, Cathy, IV 210
Rivera, Chita, IV 216

Rivers, Joan, IV 219
Roberts, Julia, IV 223
Rolle, Esther, IV 265
Russell, Jane, IV 292
Russell, Rosalind, IV 293
Ryan, Meg, IV 297
Sarandon, Susan, IV 312
Sex Symbol, IV 369
Shore, Dinah, IV 387
Sonny and Cher, IV 456
Spacek, Sissy, IV 467
Star System, IV 507
Stiller and Meara, IV 535
Streep, Meryl, IV 552
Streetcar Named Desire, IV 554
Streisand, Barbra, IV 556
Taylor, Elizabeth, IV 612
Temple, Shirley, IV 631
Ten Commandments, IV 634
Thomas, Marlo, IV 645
Tierney, Gene, IV 655
Trevor, Claire, IV 697
Turner, Lana, IV 703
Vance, Vivian, V 27
Velez, Lupe, V 39
Walker, Aida Overton, V 61
War Bonds, V 74
Wayans, V 90
West, Mae, V 115
Wheel of Fortune, V 122
White, Betty, V 127
Wong, Anna May, V 172
Wood, Natalie, V 173
Wray, Fay, V 196
Young, Loretta, V 217

Advertising
Advertising, I 23
Agassi, Andre, I 33
Alka Seltzer, I 49
Amtrak, I 75
Apple Computer, I 106
Arrow Collar Man, I 118
Automobile, I 137
Avedon, Richard, I 144
Avon, I 146
Barton, Bruce, I 179
Beer, I 210
Benneton, I 221
Bestsellers, I 236
Billboards, I 253
Board Games, I 297
Bra, I 335
Budweiser, I 380
Burma-Shave, I 390
Cable TV, I 403
Catalog Houses, I 455
Cigarettes, I 510
Clairol Hair Coloring, I 523
Coca-Cola, I 540
Condoms, I 578
Consumerism, I 589
Dr. Seuss, I 757
Family Circle, II 59
Fifties, II 96
Good Housekeeping, II 265
Hallmark Hall of Fame, II 345
Hamburger, II 347
Indian, II 487
J. Walter Thompson, II 511
Jaws, II 526
Klein, Calvin, III 46
Kraft Television Theatre, III 60
Lasorda, Tommy, III 93
Lewis, Carl, III 151
Liebovitz, Annie, III 159
Manilow, Barry, III 258
Marlboro Man, III 274
Miller Beer, III 364
Montalbán, Ricardo, III 401
Murray, Arthur, III 448
Parades, IV 12
Pepsi-Cola, IV 36

RuPaul, IV 289
Russell, Jane, IV 292
Safe Sex, IV 299
Sarnoff, David, IV 312
Schoolhouse Rock, IV 328
Soap Operas, IV 446
Spitz, Mark, IV 479
Stiller and Meara, IV 535
Super Bowl, IV 579
Supermodels, IV 583
Television, IV 626
Times Square, IV 659
Timex Watches, IV 661
Toys, IV 685
Twenties, IV 710
Vanity Fair, V 28
Victoria's Secret, V 43
Volkswagen Beetle, V 54
Wall Drug, V 66
War Bonds, V 74
X Games, V 203

Alcohol
Arbuckle, Fatty, I 107
Beer, I 210
Bowling, I 328
Budweiser, I 380
Caesar, Sid, I 408
Capone, Al, I 425
Cocktail Parties, I 544
Coors, I 599
Dahmer, Jeffrey, I 651
Flynn, Errol, II 121
Happy Hour, II 359
Jones, George, II 561
Lost Weekend, III 199
Mafia/Organized Crime, III 237
Mantle, Mickey, III 262
Martini, III 282
Miller Beer, III 364
Prohibition, IV 119
Singles Bars, IV 415
Spring Break, IV 488
Thompson, Hunter S., IV 646
Twelve-Step Programs, IV 708
Vaughan, Stevie Ray, V 37

Alternative Music
Alternative Country Music, I 59
Alternative Rock, I 62
Bowie, David, I 328
Cars, I 442
Clinton, George, I 532
Concept Album, I 576
Devo, I 696
Electric Guitar, II 21
Gospel Music, II 274
Goth, II 277
Graham, Bill, II 282
Grunge, II 321
Lollapalooza, III 184
Love, Courtney, III 204
Marley, Bob, III 274
Minimalism, III 369
Morissette, Alanis, III 413
Nirvana, III 538
Osbourne, Ozzy, III 575
Pearl Jam, IV 26
R.E.M., IV 201
Replacements, IV 204
10,000 Maniacs, IV 638
Whisky A Go Go, V 123
Young, Neil, V 217
Zappa, Frank, V 225

Animals
Chipmunks, I 501
Circus, I 512
Curious George, I 649
Felix the Cat, II 83
Flipper, II 118
Francis the Talking Mule, II 152
Kentucky Derby, III 19
Lassie, III 95

Lion King, III 169
Little Orphan Annie, III 177
Mister Ed, III 376
Muppets, III 444
Pogo, IV 73
Road Runner and Wile E. Coyote, IV 222
Sea World, IV 345
State Fairs, IV 518
Stratton-Porter, Gene, IV 550
Teddy Bears, IV 616
Wild Kingdom, V 135
Zoos, V 230

Architecture
Better Homes and Gardens, I 238
Bungalow, I 387
Catalog Houses, I 455
Century 21 Exposition (Seattle, 1962), I 470
Century of Progress International Exposition
    (Chicago, 1933), I 471
Chrysler Building, I 507
Coney Island, I 580
Diners, I 719
Eames, Charles and Ray, II 1
Empire State Building, II 28
Fuller, Buckminster, II 180
Golden Gate Bridge, II 259
Industrial Design, II 491
Lawn Care/Gardening, III 104
Lincoln Center for the Performing Arts, III 165
Mall of America, III 245
Metropolis, III 347
Minimalism, III 369
Movie Palaces, III 426
Ranch House, IV 173
Rouse Company, IV 283
Sears Tower, IV 347
Skyscrapers, IV 432
Times Square, IV 659
Trailer Parks, IV 689
Wall Drug, V 66
Washington Monument, V 83
Yankee Stadium, V 208

Art
Abstract Expressionism, I 11
Adams, Ansel, I 17
American Gothic, I 69
Armory Show, I 112
Ashcan School, I 122
Avedon, Richard, I 144
Balanchine, George, I 161
Ballet, I 165
Baraka, Amiri, I 168
Barker, Clive, I 174
Billboards, I 253
Celebrity Caricature, I 465
Christo, I 505
Conceptual Art, I 577
Crumb, Robert, I 641
Cunningham, Merce, I 648
Currier and Ives, I 650
Eames, Charles and Ray, II 1
Escher, M. C., II 37
Gibson Girl, II 233
Gnagy, Jon, II 249
Graffiti, II 281
Haring, Keith, II 363
Hirschfeld, Albert, II 412
Hopper, Edward, II 448
Industrial Design, II 491
Johns, Jasper, II 551
Kitsch, II 43
Lichtenstein, Roy, III 158
Mapplethorpe, Robert, III 265
Maus, III 308
Max, Peter, III 308
McCay, Winsor, III 317
Metropolitan Museum of Art, III 347
Minimalism, III 369
Modernism, III 390
Mount Rushmore, III 423
Nagel, Patrick, III 470

New Deal, III 508
O'Keeffe, Georgia, III 552
Oliphant, Pat, III 555
Op Art, III 569
Parrish, Maxfield, IV 16
Picasso, Pablo, IV 54
Pin-Up, IV 58
Pollock, Jackson, IV 79
Pop Art, IV 81
Prang, Louis, IV 104
Remington, Frederic, IV 203
Rivera, Diego, IV 216
Rockwell, Norman, IV 244
Schnabel, Julian, IV 327
Sherman, Cindy, IV 383
Steinberg, Saul, IV 523
Stratton-Porter, Gene, IV 550
Tom of Finland, IV 673
Vanity Fair, V 28
Varga Girl, V 30
Warhol, Andy, V 80
Whistler's Mother, V 125
Works Progress Administration (WPA)
   Murals, V 179
Wyeth, Andrew, V 199
Wyeth, N. C., V 200

Auto Racing
Andretti, Mario, I 84
Automobile, I 137
Drag Racing, I 764
Foyt, A. J., II 148
Hot Rods, II 455
Indianapolis 500, II 490
Petty, Richard, IV 46
Stock-Car Racing, IV 537
Unser, Al, V 8

Automobile
American Graffiti, I 69
Automobile, I 137
Cadillac, I 406
Camping, I 417
Chrysler Building, I 507
Convertible, I 593
Corvette, I 603
Daytona 500, I 670
Diners, I 719
Edsel, II 14
Fifties, II 96
Ford, Henry, II 132
Ford Motor Company, II 135
Gas Stations, II 206
General Motors, II 220
Highway System, II 402
Iacocca, Lee, II 480
Jeep, II 533
Low Riders, III 206
Minivans, III 370
Model T, III 386
Muscle Cars, III 455
On the Road, III 561
Route 66, IV 284
Sport Utility Vehicles (SUVs), IV 482
Twenties, IV 710
Unser, Bobby, V 10
U.S. One, V 11
Volkswagen Beetle, V 54

Awards, Music, Film, Theatre, and Television
Academy Awards, I 12
Albert, Marv, I 40
Alien, I 48
All About Eve, I 50
All Quiet on the Western Front, I 52
Allen, Woody, I 53
American Graffiti, I 69
Asner, Edward, I 126
Astaire, Fred, and Ginger Rogers, I 127
Beau Geste, I 207
Bergen, Candice, I 224
Bewitched, I 243
Blanc, Mel, I 276
Bochco, Steven, I 302

Brokaw, Tom, I 359
Bronson, Charles, I 360
Brooks, Gwendolyn, I 365
Brooks, James L., I 365
Brooks, Mel, I 365
Brynner, Yul, I 375
Buttons, Red, I 401
Cagney, James, I 409
Carmichael, Hoagy, I 436
Coca, Imogene, I 540
Cole, Nat "King," I 552
Cooper, Gary, I 597
Cousteau, Jacques, I 621
Crawford, Joan, I 625
Daniels, Charlie, I 658
Day, Doris, I 664
Deer Hunter, I 681
DeMille, Cecil B., I 683
Diddley, Bo, I 703
Edwards, James, II 14
El Teatro Campesino, II 18
Emmy Awards, II 27
Feliciano, José, II 82
Flynn, Errol, II 121
Forrest Gump, II 140
Garner, James, II 204
Glass Menagerie, II 245
Goldberg, Rube, II 256
Gospel Music, II 274
Grusin, Dave, II 322
Guaraldi, Vince, II 323
Hallmark Hall of Fame, II 345
Hansberry, Lorraine, II 356
Hayward, Susan, II 377
King, B. B., III 26
King, Larry, III 32
Korman, Harvey, III 56
Kovacs, Ernie, III 58
Lancaster, Burt, III 85
Laura, III 100
Lawrence of Arabia, III 104
Lost Weekend, III 199
Lynn, Loretta, III 218
Meet Me in St. Louis, III 339
Midnight Cowboy, III 357
Milli Vanilli, III 368
Mutiny on the Bounty, III 461
My Family, Mi Familia, III 464
One Flew Over the Cuckoo's Nest, III 566
Opportunity, III 570
Patton, IV 19
Peck, Gregory, IV 29
Peters, Bernadette, IV 44
Puente, Tito, IV 137
Raitt, Bonnie, IV 170
Rivera, Chita, IV 216
Rocky, IV 246
Sarandon, Susan, IV 312
Schlatter, George, IV 325
Skaggs, Ricky, IV 427
Sturges, Preston, IV 566
Taxi, IV 610
Ten Commandments, IV 634
Thalberg, Irving G., IV 640
Thomas, Marlo, IV 645
Turner, Ted, IV 704
United Artists, V 8
Valdez, Luis, V 15
Wilder, Billy, V 136
Wilder, Thornton, V 138
Wonder, Stevie, V 169

Baseball
Aaron, Hank, I 2
Angell, Roger, I 88
Aparicio, Luis, I 101
Bad News Bears, I 155
Barber, Red, I 169
Baseball, I 180
Baseball Cards, I 183
Bench, Johnny, I 219
Berra, Yogi, I 233
Black Sox Scandal, I 266

Bouton, Jim, I 326
Brooklyn Dodgers, I 362
Canseco, Jose, I 422
Caray, Harry, I 433
Carlton, Steve, I 435
Chicago Cubs, I 493
Clemente, Roberto, I 528
Cobb, Ty, I 538
Cooperstown, New York, I 598
Detroit Tigers, I 695
Didrikson, Babe, I 704
DiMaggio, Joe, I 715
Doby, Larry, I 736
Durocher, Leo, I 777
Ebbets Field, II 5
Fenway Park, II 87
Fidrych, Mark "Bird," II 92
Field of Dreams, II 93
Fisk, Carlton, II 106
Ford, Whitey, II 138
Free Agency, II 160
Gammons, Peter, II 195
Garvey, Steve, II 206
Gehrig, Lou, II 217
Gibson, Bob, II 231
Gooden, Dwight, II 268
Greenberg, Hank, II 302
Jackson, Reggie, II 519
Jackson, "Shoeless" Joe, II 521
Kahn, Roger, III 1
Koufax, Sandy, III 57
Kuhn, Bowie, III 68
LaRussa, Tony, III 92
Lasorda, Tommy, III 93
League of Their Own, III 110
Little League, III 174
Louisville Slugger, III 201
Mantle, Mickey, III 262
Marichal, Juan, III 272
Maris, Roger, III 274
Mattingly, Don, III 306
Mays, Willie, III 311
McGwire, Mark, III 326
Minoso, Minnie, III 371
Negro Leagues, III 497
New York Mets, III 517
New York Yankees, III 520
Paige, Satchel, IV 5
Palmer, Jim, IV 7
Reese, Pee Wee, IV 193
Ripken, Cal, Jr., IV 214
Rizzuto, Phil, IV 220
Robinson, Frank, IV 230
Robinson, Jackie, IV 231
Rose, Pete, IV 276
Ruth, Babe, IV 293
Ryan, Nolan, IV 297
Scully, Vin, IV 345
Sosa, Sammy, IV 458
Spalding, Albert G., IV 468
Sporting News, IV 483
Sports Hero, IV 484
Steinbrenner, George, IV 523
Stengel, Casey, IV 526
Stickball, IV 534
Strawberry, Darryl, IV 551
Sunday, Billy, IV 578
Thomson, Bobby, IV 647
Uecker, Bob, V 1
Valenzuela, Fernando, V 19
Wagner, Honus, V 59
Williams, Ted, V 144
World Series, V 182
Wrigley Field, V 197
Yankee Stadium, V 208
Yastrzemski, Carl, V 212
Young, Cy, V 216

Basketball
Abdul-Jabbar, Kareem, I 7
Albert, Marv, I 40
Auerbach, Red, I 136
Barkley, Charles, I 175

Basketball, I 186
Bird, Larry, I 255
Boston Celtics, I 322
Boston Garden, I 323
Bradley, Bill, I 338
Chamberlain, Wilt, I 472
Chicago Bulls, I 493
Didrikson, Babe, I 704
Dream Team, I 767
Erving, Julius "Dr. J," II 36
Frazier, Walt "Clyde," II 158
Free Agency, II 160
Harlem Globetrotters, II 364
Havlicek, John, II 374
Hoosiers, II 442
Johnson, Earvin "Magic," II 553
Jordan, Michael, II 570
Knight, Bobby, III 49
Los Angeles Lakers, III 196
Monroe, Earl "The Pearl," III 397
Naismith, James, III 470
National Basketball Association (NBA), III 477
National Collegiate Athletic Association
    (NCAA), III 479
New York Knickerbockers, III 517
O'Neal, Shaquille, III 568
Pippen, Scottie, IV 61
Riley, Pat, IV 212
Robertson, Oscar, IV 225
Rodman, Dennis, IV 259
Rupp, Adolph, IV 290
Russell, Bill, IV 290
Smith, Dean, IV 439
Sports Hero, IV 484
Tarkanian, Jerry, IV 606
Thomas, Isiah, IV 645
Thompson, John, IV 647
Walton, Bill, V 72
West, Jerry, V 114
Wooden, John, V 174

Big Band Music
Armstrong, Louis, I 114
Arnaz, Desi, I 116
Basie, Count, I 184
Big Bands, I 247
Brown, Les, I 370
Calloway, Cab, I 412
Cotton Club, I 614
Day, Doris, I 664
Dorsey, Jimmy, I 750
Dorsey, Tommy, I 751
Ellington, Duke, II 23
Goodman, Benny, II 270
Hawkins, Coleman, II 376
Henderson, Fletcher, II 390
Hutton, Ina Ray, II 472
James, Harry, II 525
Jazz, II 529
Kansas City Jazz, III 2
Krupa, Gene, III 63
Lee, Peggy, III 121
Lombardo, Guy, III 187
Lunceford, Jimmie, III 214
Mancini, Henry, III 256
Marching Bands, III 267
Martin, Dean, III 280
Martin, Freddy, III 281
Miller, Glenn, III 364
Savoy Ballroom, IV 322
Shore, Dinah, IV 387
Social Dancing, IV 450
Sousa, John Philip, IV 463
Tejano Music, IV 623
Vallee, Rudy, V 21
Webb, Chick, V 98
Welk, Lawrence, V 106
Whiteman, Paul, V 130

Black Comedy
Butterbeans and Susie, I 400
*Dr. Strangelove or: How I Learned How to Stop
    Worrying and Love the Bomb*, I 759

Inner Sanctum Mysteries, II 493
Mary Hartman, Mary Hartman, III 289
*M*A*S*H*, III 295
Network, III 503
Pulp Fiction, IV 138
Sunset Boulevard, IV 579

Bluegrass Music
Alternative Country Music, I 59
Bluegrass, I 287
Country Gentlemen, I 617
Flatt, Lester, II 113
Foggy Mountain Boys, II 122
Grand Ole Opry, II 286
Grateful Dead, II 291
Ives, Burl, II 508
Monroe, Bill, III 396
Osborne Brothers, III 575
Reno, Don, IV 204
Scruggs, Earl, IV 345
Stanley Brothers, IV 506

Blues Music
AC/DC, I 14
Ace, Johnny, I 15
Allison, Luther, I 54
Armstrong, Louis, I 114
Atlantic Records, I 135
Ballard, Hank, I 164
Basie, Count, I 184
Bland, Bobby Blue, I 278
Blues, I 290
Blues Brothers, I 293
British Invasion, I 354
Brown, James, I 367
Charles, Ray, I 477
Chavis, Boozoo, I 483
Chenier, Clifton, I 490
Clapton, Eric, I 525
Collins, Albert, I 557
Cox, Ida, I 624
Cray, Robert, I 626
Crumb, Robert, I 641
Diddley, Bo, I 703
Doors, I 748
Electric Guitar, II 21
Ertegun, Ahmet, II 35
Fleetwood Mac, II 114
Folkways Records, II 126
Gordy, Berry, II 272
Gospel Music, II 274
Grateful Dead, II 291
Guthrie, Arlo, II 328
Guy, Buddy, II 329
Handy, W. C., II 352
Heavy Metal, II 380
Herman, Woody, II 398
Holiday, Billie, II 427
Hooker, John Lee, II 440
Hopkins, Sam "Lightnin'," II 447
Horne, Lena, II 449
Howlin' Wolf, II 461
James, Elmore, II 525
Johnson, Blind Willie, II 552
Johnson, Robert, II 557
Joplin, Janis, II 565
Juke Boxes, II 579
Kansas City Jazz, III 2
King, Albert, III 25
King, B. B., III 26
King, Freddie, III 30
Leadbelly, III 108
Led Zeppelin, III 116
Lewis, Jerry Lee, III 153
Mayfield, Percy, III 310
Pop Music, IV 83
Race Music, IV 155
Rainey, Gertrude "Ma," IV 168
Raitt, Bonnie, IV 170
Rhythm and Blues, IV 206
Rock and Roll, IV 235
Rodgers, Jimmie, IV 258
Rolling Stones, IV 269

Seals, Son, IV 345
Skaggs, Ricky, IV 427
Smith, Bessie, IV 439
Sun Records, IV 576
Thorogood, George, IV 648
Vaughan, Stevie Ray, V 37
Walker, Aaron "T-Bone," V 59
Wallace, Sippie, V 68
Waters, Muddy, V 89
Williams, Hank, Sr., V 141
Zydeco, V 235
ZZ Top, V 236

Boxing
Ali, Muhammad, I 44
Armstrong, Henry, I 113
Boxing, I 330
Camacho, Héctor "Macho," I 414
Corbett, James J., I 601
De La Hoya, Oscar, I 673
Dempsey, Jack, I 685
Durán, Roberto, I 776
Foreman, George, II 138
Frazier, Joe, II 157
Greb, Harry, II 297
Hagler, Marvelous Marvin, II 335
Holyfield, Evander, II 436
Johnson, Jack, II 554
LaMotta, Jake, III 83
Leonard, Benny, III 133
Leonard, Sugar Ray, III 136
Liston, Sonny, III 171
Louis, Joe, III 200
Mafia/Organized Crime, III 237
Marciano, Rocky, III 268
Robinson, Sugar Ray, IV 234
Rocky, IV 246
Sullivan, John L., IV 572
Tyson, Mike, IV 718

Brands
Arden, Elizabeth, I 109
Aunt Jemima, I 137
Barbie, I 171
Beanie Babies, I 198
Betty Crocker, I 241
Blass, Bill, I 278
Burger King, I 387
Buster Brown, I 398
Cigarettes, I 510
Clairol Hair Coloring, I 523
Ellis, Perry, II 25
Factor, Max, II 54
Fisher-Price Toys, II 106
Gap, II 198
Gucci, II 323
Halston, II 346
Harley-Davidson, II 368
Jell-O, II 537
Karan, Donna, III 4
Klein, Calvin, III 46
Levi's, III 146
Marlboro Man, III 274
McDonald's, III 321
Pepsi-Cola, IV 36
Prozac, IV 125
Slinky, IV 436
Starbucks, IV 514
Toys, IV 685
Tupperware, IV 700
Victoria's Secret, V 43

Broadcasters
Adventures of Ozzie and Harriet, I 21
Albert, Marv, I 40
Barber, Red, I 169
Brinkley, David, I 352
Brokaw, Tom, I 359
Brothers, Dr. Joyce, I 367
Caray, Harry, I 433
Clark, Dick, I 525
Community Media, I 570
Corwin, Norman, I 604
Cosell, Howard, I 608

Costas, Bob, I 612
DiMaggio, Joe, I 715
Donahue, Phil, I 744
Douglas, Mike, I 754
Downs, Hugh, I 754
ESPN, II 38
Fleming, Peggy, II 116
Freed, Alan ''Moondog,'' II 162
Gammons, Peter, II 195
Godfrey, Arthur, II 251
Huntley, Chet, II 469
Jennings, Peter, II 538
Kaltenborn, Hans von, III 1
Kasem, Casey, III 6
Keillor, Garrison, III 11
King, Larry, III 32
Madden, John, III 232
McEnroe, John, III 324
McPherson, Aimee Semple, III 331
Monday Night Football, III 393
Murrow, Edward R., III 451
Radio, IV 157
Rather, Dan, IV 176
Religious Right, IV 197
Rizzuto, Phil, IV 220
Robertson, Pat, IV 225
Scully, Vin, IV 345
Shirer, William L., IV 384
Shock Radio, IV 386
60 Minutes, IV 425
Sullivan, Ed, IV 570
Swann, Lynn, IV 588
Talk Radio, IV 600
Television Anchors, IV 629
Thomas, Isiah, IV 645
Thomas, Lowell, IV 645
Tokyo Rose, IV 669
Trout, Robert, IV 698
Uecker, Bob, V 1
Vallee, Rudy, V 21

Cartoonists
Avery, Tex, I 145
Beavis and Butthead, I 209
Calvin and Hobbes, I 413
Caniff, Milton, I 421
Celebrity Caricature, I 465
Comics, I 562
Curious George, I 649
Dick Tracy, I 702
Dilbert, I 710
Disability, I 721
Doonesbury, I 747
Dr. Seuss, I 757
Family Circus, II 61
Far Side, II 69
Felix the Cat, II 83
Groening, Matt, II 319
Katzenjammer Kids, III 7
Krazy Kat, III 62
Li'l Abner, III 163
Little Orphan Annie, III 177
Oliphant, Pat, III 555
Pogo, IV 73
Popeye, IV 87
Saturday Morning Cartoons, IV 317
Simpsons, IV 408
Sylvia, IV 594
Teddy Bears, IV 616
Thurber, James, IV 654

Cartoons/Animation
Animated Films, I 90
Archie Comics, I 108
Beavis and Butthead, I 209
Betty Boop, I 239
Blanc, Mel, I 276
Bugs Bunny, I 383
Captain Kangaroo, I 430
Chipmunks, I 501
Dick Tracy, I 702
Disney (Walt Disney Company), I 728
Doonesbury, I 747

EC Comics, II 9
Fantasia, II 65
Felix the Cat, II 83
Flintstones, II 118
Gertie the Dinosaur, II 226
Groening, Matt, II 319
Hanna-Barbera, II 355
Judge, II 577
Katzenjammer Kids, III 7
Krazy Kat, III 62
Lion King, III 169
Little Orphan Annie, III 177
Mary Worth, III 294
McCay, Winsor, III 317
Mouseketeers, III 425
Peanuts, IV 25
Pogo, IV 73
Popeye, IV 87
Raggedy Ann and Raggedy Andy, IV 163
Road Runner and Wile E. Coyote, IV 222
Rocky and Bullwinkle, IV 248
Rudolph the Red-Nosed Reindeer, IV 287
Saturday Morning Cartoons, IV 317
Schoolhouse Rock, IV 328
Simpsons, IV 408
Snow White and the Seven Dwarfs, IV 445
South Park, IV 466
Spider-Man, IV 474
Steamboat Willie, IV 521
Tarkington, Booth, IV 607
Teenage Mutant Ninja Turtles, IV 620
Three Caballeros, IV 650
Toy Story, IV 685
Tweety Pie and Sylvester, IV 707
Winnie-the-Pooh, V 155
Zippy the Pinhead, V 230

Children's Films
Avery, Tex, I 145
Bad News Bears, I 155
Child Stars, I 498
Henson, Jim, II 393
Lassie, III 95
Lewis, C. S., III 150
Little Orphan Annie, III 177
Mary Poppins, III 291
Our Gang, III 576
Popeye, IV 87
Rudolph the Red-Nosed Reindeer, IV 287
Snow White and the Seven Dwarfs, IV 445
Teenage Mutant Ninja Turtles, IV 620
Three Caballeros, IV 650
Toy Story, IV 685
Winnie-the-Pooh, V 155
Wizard of Oz, V 162

Children's Print
American Girls Series, I 67
Babar, I 151
Baum, L. Frank, I 191
Blume, Judy, I 294
Bobbsey Twins, I 300
Choose-Your-Own-Ending Books, I 502
Crime Does Not Pay, I 632
Curious George, I 649
Derleth, August, I 692
Dick and JaneReaders, I 700
Dr. Seuss, I 757
Frosty the Snowman, II 178
Golden Books, II 258
Hardy Boys, II 360
Hughes, Langston, II 465
Judy Bolton, II 578
Kewpie Dolls, III 22
Kotzwinkle, William, III 56
L'Engle, Madeleine, III 131
Lewis, C. S., III 150
Little Orphan Annie, III 177
Mary Poppins, III 291
Mr. Wizard, III 433
Nancy Drew, III 473
Parrish, Maxfield, IV 16
Raggedy Ann and Raggedy Andy, IV 163

Singer, Isaac Bashevis, IV 414
Spillane, Mickey, IV 477
Stine, R. L., IV 535
Stratemeyer, Edward, IV 548
Stratton-Porter, Gene, IV 550
Tales from the Crypt, IV 600
Tarkington, Booth, IV 607
Teddy Bears, IV 616
Three Investigators Series, IV 651
Tom Swift Series, IV 674
White, E. B., V 127
Wilder, Laura Ingalls, V 136
Winnie-the-Pooh, V 155

Children's Television
Avery, Tex, I 145
Barney and Friends, I 175
Captain Kangaroo, I 430
Child Stars, I 498
Chipmunks, I 501
Cosby, Bill, I 606
Family Matters, II 62
Flintstones, II 118
Frosty the Snowman, II 178
Funicello, Annette, II 183
Gnagy, Jon, II 249
Hardy Boys, II 360
Henson, Jim, II 393
Howdy Doody Show, II 459
Ives, Burl, II 508
Kukla, Fran, and Ollie, III 68
Lassie, III 95
Linkletter, Art, III 168
Lone Ranger, III 189
Mickey Mouse Club, III 351
Mister Rogers' Neighborhood, III 378
Mouseketeers, III 425
Mr. Wizard, III 433
Muppets, III 444
O'Donnell, Rosie, III 551
Pee-wee's Playhouse, IV 32
Popeye, IV 87
Public Television (PBS), IV 135
Road Runner and Wile E. Coyote, IV 222
Saturday Morning Cartoons, IV 317
Schoolhouse Rock, IV 328
Sesame Street, IV 362
Stine, R. L., IV 535
Teenage Mutant Ninja Turtles, IV 620
Winnie-the-Pooh, V 155
Wizard of Oz, V 162

Classical Music
Anderson, Marian, I 81
Bernstein, Leonard, I 233
Borge, Victor, I 320
Boston Symphony Orchestra, I 325
Carnegie Hall, I 439
Copland, Aaron, I 600
Fantasia, II 65
Ferrante and Teicher, II 88
Higginson, Major Henry Lee, II 400
Joplin, Scott, II 566
Judson, Arthur, II 578
Liberace, III 155
Martin, Freddy, III 281
Patinkin, Mandy, IV 19
Stokowski, Leopold, IV 541
Yanni, V 210

Columnists
Advice Columns, I 26
Angell, Roger, I 88
Barry, Dave, I 177
Benchley, Robert, I 219
Blount, Roy, Jr., I 285
Brothers, Dr. Joyce, I 367
Capote, Truman, I 426
Etiquette Columns, II 44
Gammons, Peter, II 195
Gold, Mike, II 255
Grizzard, Lewis, II 319
Lardner, Ring, III 90
Lippmann, Walter, III 170

Mailer, Norman, III 242
Mencken, H. L., III 342
Mitchell, Margaret, III 380
Mr. Dooley, III 430
O'Rourke, P. J., III 573
Parker, Dorothy, IV 14
Siskel and Ebert, IV 417
Steffens, Lincoln, IV 521
Steinem, Gloria, IV 524
Stratton-Porter, Gene, IV 550
Thompson, Hunter S., IV 646
Trillin, Calvin, IV 697
Weird Tales, V 103
White, E. B., V 127
Will, George F., V 138
Winchell, Walter, V 151

Comedians

Adventures of Ozzie and Harriet, I 21
Allen, Steve, I 52
Amsterdam, Morey, I 74
Aykroyd, Dan, I 147
Benny, Jack, I 222
Berle, Milton, I 228
Beulah, I 241
Blues Brothers, I 293
Borscht Belt, I 321
Brice, Fanny, I 348
Brooks, Mel, I 365
Bruce, Lenny, I 372
Burns, George, and Gracie Allen, I 392
Buttons, Red, I 401
Caesar, Sid, I 408
Canova, Judy, I 421
Captain Marvel, I 432
Carlin, George, I 434
Carson, Johnny, I 444
Chase, Chevy, I 480
Cheech and Chong, I 485
Cosby, Bill, I 606
Crystal, Billy, I 643
DeGeneres, Ellen, I 682
Diller, Phyllis, I 712
Fetchit, Stepin, II 88
Fibber McGee and Molly, II 89
Fields, W. C., II 95
Foxx, Redd, II 148
Goldberg, Whoopi, II 257
Gregory, Dick, II 307
Hackett, Buddy, II 333
Hope, Bob, II 446
Jessel, George, II 542
Kaufman, Andy, III 7
Kaye, Danny, III 9
Keaton, Buster, III 10
Kinison, Sam, III 40
Korman, Harvey, III 56
Kovacs, Ernie, III 58
Larry Sanders Show, III 91
Lawrence, Vicki, III 106
Leno, Jay, III 132
Lewis, Jerry, III 152
Mabley, Moms, III 223
Marx Brothers, III 287
Marx, Groucho, III 288
Mason, Jackie, III 298
Murphy, Eddie, III 447
Networks, III 503
Newhart, Bob, III 524
O'Donnell, Rosie, III 551
Paar, Jack, IV 1
Paulsen, Pat, IV 22
Pearl, Minnie, IV 28
Prinze, Freddie, IV 115
Reiner, Carl, IV 196
Rivers, Joan, IV 219
Rock, Chris, IV 238
Russell, Nipsey, IV 293
Sales, Soupy, IV 303
Saturday Night Live, IV 320
Second City, IV 348
Sellers, Peter, IV 355
Sinbad, IV 413

Skelton, Red, IV 431
Smothers Brothers, IV 442
Stand-up Comedy, IV 504
Stiller and Meara, IV 535
Tenuta, Judy, IV 638
Thomas, Danny, IV 644
Three Stooges, IV 651
Tomlin, Lily, IV 675
Uecker, Bob, V 1
Walker, George, V 62
Williams, Robin, V 143
Wilson, Flip, V 148
Winters, Jonathan, V 157
Yankovic, "Weird Al," V 209
Youngman, Henny, V 219

Comedy

Allen, Woody, I 53
Androgyny, I 85
Avery, Tex, I 145
Barry, Dave, I 177
Bergen, Edgar, I 225
Blackface Minstrelsy, I 270
Blanc, Mel, I 276
Borge, Victor, I 320
Cavett, Dick, I 460
Cheers, I 488
Day, Doris, I 664
Firesign Theatre, II 103
Goodbye, Columbus, II 268
Klein, Robert, III 47
Lewis, Jerry, III 152
Mabley, Moms, III 223
Martin, Dean, III 280
Martin, Steve, III 282
Nichols, Mike, and Elaine May, III 529
One Flew Over the Cuckoo's Nest, III 566
Patinkin, Mandy, IV 19
Peter, Paul, and Mary, IV 42
Porter, Cole, IV 95
Radner, Gilda, IV 162
Reiner, Carl, IV 196
Rivers, Joan, IV 219
Rogers, Will, IV 263
Second City, IV 348
Stand-up Comedy, IV 504
Stevens, Ray, IV 532
Stiller and Meara, IV 535
Suburbia, IV 567
Williams, Robin, V 143
Wilson, Flip, V 148
Winnie Winkle the Breadwinner, V 156
Winters, Jonathan, V 157
Youngman, Henny, V 219

Comedy, Film

Abbott and Costello, I 5
Addams Family, I 18
Airplane!, I 38
All About Eve, I 50
American Graffiti, I 69
Amos 'n' Andy Show, I 72
Andy Hardy, I 87
Animal House, I 89
Annie Hall, I 98
Arbuckle, Fatty, I 107
Aykroyd, Dan, I 147
Back to the Future, I 155
Bad News Bears, I 155
Beavis and Butthead, I 209
Belushi, John, I 216
Benchley, Robert, I 219
Benny, Jack, I 222
Blondie (comic strip), I 283
Blues Brothers, I 293
Borge, Victor, I 320
Brice, Fanny, I 348
Bringing Up Baby, I 352
Brooks, Mel, I 365
Bugs Bunny, I 383
Burnett, Carol, I 391
Canova, Judy, I 421
Capra, Frank, I 428

Chaplin, Charlie, I 475
Chase, Chevy, I 480
Cheech and Chong, I 485
City Lights, I 515
Clooney, Rosemary, I 533
Colbert, Claudette, I 548
Conway, Tim, I 594
Disaster Movies, I 723
Divine, I 731
Douglas, Melvyn, I 753
Dr. Strangelove or: How I Learned How to Stop Worrying and Love the Bomb, I 759
Drag, I 762
Duck Soup, I 773
Dunne, Irene, I 776
Fargo, II 69
Field, Sally, II 94
Fields, W. C., II 95
Francis the Talking Mule, II 152
Gentlemen Prefer Blondes, II 223
Goodbye, Columbus, II 268
Graduate, II 279
Hanks, Tom, II 353
Hayworth, Rita, II 377
Henry Aldrich, II 392
Hoffman, Dustin, II 420
Holliday, Judy, II 429
Hope, Bob, II 446
Hudson, Rock, II 462
Hunter, Tab, II 468
Irving, John, II 504
It Happened One Night, II 504
Kaufman, Andy, III 7
Kaye, Danny, III 9
Keaton, Buster, III 10
Keystone Kops, III 24
Kovacs, Ernie, III 58
Lahr, Bert, III 76
Laurel and Hardy, III 100
Lee, Spike, III 122
Lewis, Jerry, III 152
Lombard, Carole, III 184
Long, Shelley, III 192
Mabley, Moms, III 223
Martin, Dean, III 280
Martin, Steve, III 282
Marx Brothers, III 287
Marx, Groucho, III 288
Modern Times, III 389
Muppets, III 444
Murphy, Eddie, III 447
National Lampoon, III 487
Nerd Look, III 502
Network, III 503
One Flew Over the Cuckoo's Nest, III 566
Our Gang, III 576
Parton, Dolly, IV 17
Philadelphia Story, IV 50
Powell, William, IV 102
Reiner, Carl, IV 196
Rivers, Joan, IV 219
Russell, Rosalind, IV 293
Sales, Soupy, IV 303
Screwball Comedies, IV 342
Sellers, Peter, IV 355
Sennett, Mack, IV 357
Seven Year Itch, IV 364
Shulman, Max, IV 391
Silent Movies, IV 393
Simon, Neil, IV 401
Skelton, Red, IV 431
Some Like It Hot, IV 453
Stanwyck, Barbara, IV 506
Stiller and Meara, IV 535
Temple, Shirley, IV 631
Three Stooges, IV 651
Tootsie, IV 678
Velez, Lupe, V 39
Waters, John, V 87
Wayne's World, V 94
Williams, Robin, V 143
Wilson, Flip, V 148

Winters, Jonathan, V 157

Comedy, Performance
Abbott and Costello, I 5
Ball, Lucille, I 163
Belushi, John, I 216
Bernhard, Sandra, I 231
Brice, Fanny, I 348
Burns, George, and Gracie Allen, I 392
Butterbeans and Susie, I 400
Caesar, Sid, I 408
Canova, Judy, I 421
Cantor, Eddie, I 423
Charlie McCarthy, I 478
Chase, Chevy, I 480
Cheech and Chong, I 485
Cohan, George M., I 548
Drag, I 762
Gleason, Jackie, II 245
Hackett, Buddy, II 333
Jessel, George, II 542
Klein, Robert, III 47
Letterman, David, III 144
Lewis, Jerry, III 152
Martin, Steve, III 282
Mason, Jackie, III 298
Minstrel Shows, III 371
Moore, Michael, III 408
Prinze, Freddie, IV 115
Pryor, Richard, IV 126
Rogers, Will, IV 263
Sahl, Mort, IV 301
Second City, IV 348
Sennett, Mack, IV 357
Sinbad, IV 413
Smothers Brothers, IV 442
Stand-up Comedy, IV 504
Stiller and Meara, IV 535
Tomlin, Lily, IV 675
Vaudeville, V 33
Walker, Aida Overton, V 61
Wayans, V 90
Williams, Bert, V 140
Williams, Robin, V 143
Winters, Jonathan, V 157

Comedy, Radio
Amos 'n' Andy Show, I 72
Benny, Jack, I 222
Beulah, I 241
Bob and Ray, I 299
Borge, Victor, I 320
Burns, George, and Gracie Allen, I 392
Canova, Judy, I 421
Cantor, Eddie, I 423
Charlie McCarthy, I 478
Father Knows Best, II 75
Fibber McGee and Molly, II 89
Firesign Theatre, II 103
Henry Aldrich, II 392
Inner Sanctum Mysteries, II 493
Marx Brothers, III 287
Radio Drama, IV 160
Sellers, Peter, IV 355
Skelton, Red, IV 431
Stand-up Comedy, IV 504
Yankovic, ''Weird Al,'' V 209

Comedy, Television
Addams Family, I 18
Adventures of Ozzie and Harriet, I 21
Alda, Alan, I 42
Alice, I 47
All in the Family, I 50
Ally McBeal, I 57
American Graffiti, I 69
Amos 'n' Andy Show, I 72
Amsterdam, Morey, I 74
Andy Griffith Show, I 86
Another World, I 99
Arnaz, Desi, I 116
Arthur, Bea, I 118
A-Team, I 132
Aykroyd, Dan, I 147

Ball, Lucille, I 163
Barney Miller, I 176
Barry, Dave, I 177
Beavis and Butthead, I 209
Belushi, John, I 216
Benny Hill Show, I 222
Benny, Jack, I 222
Bergen, Candice, I 224
Berle, Milton, I 228
Bernhard, Sandra, I 231
Beulah, I 241
Beverly Hillbillies, I 241
Bewitched, I 243
Blondie (comic strip), I 283
Blues Brothers, I 293
Bob and Ray, I 299
Borge, Victor, I 320
Brady Bunch, I 339
Burnett, Carol, I 391
Burns, George, and Gracie Allen, I 392
Buttons, Red, I 401
Caesar, Sid, I 408
Candid Camera, I 420
Cantor, Eddie, I 423
Car 54, Where Are You?, I 432
Carson, Johnny, I 444
Cassidy, David, I 452
Charlie McCarthy, I 478
Chase, Chevy, I 480
Cheers, I 488
Coca, Imogene, I 540
Conway, Tim, I 594
Cosby Show, I 607
Dana, Bill, I 656
DeGeneres, Ellen, I 682
Diff'rent Strokes, I 709
Dobie Gillis, I 735
Drag, I 762
Dukes of Hazzard, I 773
Family Matters, II 62
Family Ties, II 64
Farr, Jamie, II 71
Far Side, II 69
Father Knows Best, II 75
Fawlty Towers, II 80
Field, Sally, II 94
Flying Nun, II 120
Foxx, Redd, II 148
Franklin, Bonnie, II 156
Frasier, II 156
Frawley, William, II 157
Friends, II 172
Get Smart, II 227
Gilligan's Island, II 238
Gleason, Jackie, II 245
Golden Girls, II 260
Good Times, II 267
Hackett, Buddy, II 333
Hanna-Barbera, II 355
Happy Days, II 357
Harper, Valerie, II 371
Hee Haw, II 381
Henry Aldrich, II 392
Hogan's Heroes, II 424
Hollywood Squares, II 434
Home Improvement, II 437
Honeymooners, II 439
Hope, Bob, II 446
Hunt, Helen, II 468
I Dream of Jeannie, II 475
I Love Lucy, II 477
In Living Color, II 486
It's Garry Shandling's Show, II 507
Jeffersons, II 536
Julia, II 580
Kate & Allie, III 7
Kaufman, Andy, III 7
Kelley, David E., III 13
Korman, Harvey, III 56
Kovacs, Ernie, III 58
Larry Sanders Show, III 91
Laugh-In, III 98

Laverne and Shirley, III 103
Lavin, Linda, III 103
Lear, Norman, III 111
Leave It to Beaver, III 115
Life of Riley, III 162
Long, Shelley, III 192
Love Boat, III 203
Mabley, Moms, III 223
Made-for-Television Movies, III 233
Marie, Rose, III 272
Married . . . with Children, III 277
Marshall, Garry, III 278
Marx Brothers, III 287
Marx, Groucho, III 288
Mary Hartman, Mary Hartman, III 289
Mary Tyler Moore Show, III 292
M*A*S*H, III 295
Mason, Jackie, III 298
Maude, III 306
McHale's Navy, III 327
Meadows, Audrey, III 336
Mister Ed, III 376
Monkees, III 394
Monty Python's Flying Circus, III 403
Moonlighting, III 406
Moore, Michael, III 408
Mork & Mindy, III 411
Muppets, III 444
Murphy Brown, III 446
Murray, Bill, III 450
My Three Sons, III 467
Nelson, Ricky, III 499
Nerd Look, III 502
Network, III 503
Newhart, Bob, III 524
Northern Exposure, III 542
Odd Couple, III 550
One Day at a Time, III 565
O'Rourke, P. J., III 573
Owens, Buck, III 582
Parton, Dolly, IV 17
Partridge Family, IV 18
Paulsen, Pat, IV 22
Prinze, Freddie, IV 115
Reiner, Carl, IV 196
Rivers, Joan, IV 219
Roseanne, IV 277
Sales, Soupy, IV 303
Sanford and Son, IV 310
Saturday Night Live, IV 320
Schlatter, George, IV 325
Second City, IV 348
Seinfeld, IV 352
Sheldon, Sidney, IV 381
Simon, Neil, IV 401
Simpsons, IV 408
Sinbad, IV 413
Sitcom, IV 418
Skelton, Red, IV 431
Smothers Brothers, IV 442
Sonny and Cher, IV 456
South Park, IV 466
Stand-up Comedy, IV 504
Stiller and Meara, IV 535
Taxi, IV 610
Thomas, Danny, IV 644
Thomas, Marlo, IV 645
Three Stooges, IV 651
Three's Company, IV 653
Tomlin, Lily, IV 675
Tonight Show, IV 677
Van Dyke, Dick, V 24
Vance, Vivian, V 27
Wayans, V 90
Welcome Back, Kotter, V 105
White, Betty, V 127
Wilson, Flip, V 148
Winters, Jonathan, V 157
WKRP in Cincinnati, V 164
Your Show of Shows, V 221

Comics
Addams Family, I 18

Alternative Press, I 60
Annie, I 96
Archie Comics, I 108
Barry, Lynda, I 178
Batman, I 189
Bazooka Joe, I 194
Betty Boop, I 239
Blondie (comic strip), I 283
Bloom County, I 284
Bodybuilding, I 305
Brenda Starr, I 348
Buck Rogers, I 377
Buster Brown, I 398
Calvin and Hobbes, I 413
Caniff, Milton, I 421
Captain America, I 429
Caspar Milquetoast, I 450
Cathy, I 460
Comic Books, I 560
Comics, I 562
Comics Code Authority, I 565
Crime Does Not Pay, I 632
Crumb, Robert, I 641
Daredevil, the Man Without Fear, I 659
Dark Shadows, I 659
DC Comics, I 671
Dick Tracy, I 702
Dilbert, I 710
Doc Savage, I 738
Doctor Who, I 739
Dragon Lady, I 767
Dykes to Watch Out For, I 780
EC Comics, II 9
Eisner, Will, II 18
Family Circus, II 61
Fantastic Four, II 67
Far Side, II 69
Felix the Cat, II 83
Flash Gordon, II 113
Goldberg, Rube, II 256
Green Lantern, II 302
Groening, Matt, II 319
Hearst, William Randolph, II 379
Hopalong Cassidy, II 444
Incredible Hulk, II 486
Jack Armstrong, II 512
Kewpie Dolls, III 22
Kirby, Jack, III 42
Kudzu, III 66
Lee, Stan, III 124
Li'l Abner, III 163
MAD Magazine, III 230
Marvel Comics, III 285
Maus, III 308
McCay, Winsor, III 317
Mix, Tom, III 383
Mutt & Jeff, III 462
Peanuts, IV 25
Pogo, IV 73
Popeye, IV 87
Punisher, IV 142
Sahl, Mort, IV 301
Sandman, IV 307
Seduction of the Innocent, IV 350
Silver Surfer, IV 399
Spawn, IV 470
Spider-Man, IV 474
Superman, IV 581
Sylvia, IV 594
Tales from the Crypt, IV 600
Tarzan, IV 608
Teenage Mutant Ninja Turtles, IV 620
Terry and the Pirates, IV 640
Thompson, Hunter S., IV 646
Tijuana Bibles, IV 656
Underground Comics, V 4
War Bonds, V 74
Wertham, Fredric, V 111
Wonder Woman, V 171
X-Men, V 205
Yellow Kid, V 212
Zap Comix, V 225

Zippy the Pinhead, V 230
Zorro, V 234

Communications
AT&T, I 130
Cable TV, I 403
Carnegie, Dale, I 437
CB Radio, I 462
Community Media, I 570
E-mail, II 26
Field and Stream, II 92
Graffiti, II 281
Greeting Cards, II 306
IBM (International Business Machines), II 481
Internet, II 495
Microsoft, III 353
Phone Sex, IV 51
Phonograph, IV 52
Postcards, IV 96
Rolling Stone, IV 267
Sarnoff, David, IV 312
Satellites, IV 314
Shirer, William L., IV 384
Slang, IV 434
Spin, IV 478
Syndication, IV 595
Telephone, IV 623
Time, IV 657

Community
AARP (American Association for Retired
   Persons), I 3
Automobile, I 137
Baby Boomers, I 151
Barbecue, I 168
Better Homes and Gardens, I 238
Boat People, I 298
Boy Scouts of America, I 333
Brown, Jim, I 369
Castro, I 454
Catalog Houses, I 455
CB Radio, I 462
Church Socials, I 509
Closet, I 536
Communes, I 568
Community Media, I 570
Community Theatre, I 573
Detroit Tigers, I 695
Dime Stores/Woolworth's, I 717
Dionne Quintuplets, I 720
Ebbets Field, II 5
Family Reunions, II 63
Fourth of July Celebrations, II 146
Gated Communities, II 208
Ghettos, II 227
Green Bay Packers, II 300
Greenwich Village, II 304
Guardian Angels, II 323
Hoosiers, II 442
Juliá, Raúl, II 581
Kiwanis, III 46
Levittown, III 147
Lincoln Center for the Performing Arts, III 165
Live Television, III 178
Mall, III 247
Mass Market Magazine Revolution, III 299
Middletown, III 355
Militias, III 359
Million Man March, III 368
Minstrel Shows, III 371
Neighborhood Watch, III 499
New Deal, III 508
Organization Man, III 572
Parades, IV 12
Polio, IV 76
PTA/PTO (Parent Teacher Association/
   Organization), IV 130
Public Libraries, IV 133
Robertson, Oscar, IV 225
Rockwell, Norman, IV 244
Rouse Company, IV 283
Starbucks, IV 514
State Fairs, IV 518

Summer Camp, IV 573
Sunday Driving, IV 578
Telephone, IV 623
Times Square, IV 659
Town Meetings, IV 684
Trailer Parks, IV 689
Tupperware, IV 700
White Flight, V 128
Works Progress Administration (WPA)
   Murals, V 179

Consumption/Consumerism
Adidas, I 20
Advertising, I 23
Alaska-Yukon Exposition (Seattle, 1909), I 40
American Girls Series, I 67
Amway, I 80
Arden, Elizabeth, I 109
Astrology, I 129
Automobile, I 137
Bagels, I 158
Beavis and Butthead, I 209
Bestsellers, I 236
Big Little Books, I 249
Billboards, I 253
Birkenstocks, I 257
Black Sabbath, I 265
Board Games, I 297
Budweiser, I 380
Burma-Shave, I 390
Cabbage Patch Kids, I 403
Cable TV, I 403
Cadillac, I 406
Camp, I 415
Camping, I 417
Cassette Tape, I 451
Catalog Houses, I 455
Christmas, I 503
Comics, I 562
Condoms, I 578
Coney Island, I 580
Consumer Reports, I 587
Consumerism, I 589
Convertible, I 593
Coors, I 599
Credit Cards, I 628
Department Stores, I 688
Dime Stores/Woolworth's, I 717
Disability, I 721
Disco, I 726
Disney (Walt Disney Company), I 728
Do-It-Yourself Improvement, I 742
Dracula, I 760
Drive-In Theater, I 769
Eight-track Tape, II 16
Family Circle, II 59
Fifties, II 96
Flappers, II 112
Flea Markets, II 114
Ford Motor Company, II 135
Freak Shows, II 158
Gas Stations, II 206
General Motors, II 220
Great Depression, II 295
Hallmark Hall of Fame, II 345
Hamburger, II 347
Harlequin Romances, II 367
Hemlines, II 390
Home Shopping Network/QVC, II 438
Hot Dogs, II 454
IBM (International Business Machines), II 481
Ice Cream Cone, II 483
Industrial Design, II 491
J. Walter Thompson, II 511
Jack Armstrong, II 512
Jell-O, II 537
Juke Boxes, II 579
Kewpie Dolls, III 22
Kitsch, III 43
Kmart, III 47
Kodak, III 51
Leather Jacket, III 114
Lincoln Center for the Performing Arts, III 165

Lucas, George, III 209
Mall, III 247
Mall of America, III 245
Medicine Shows, III 339
Middletown, III 355
Miller Beer, III 364
Mod, III 384
Muscular Christianity, III 456
Muzak, III 463
Nader, Ralph, III 469
National Enquirer, III 480
Niagara Falls, III 528
Nike, III 535
O'Neal, Shaquille, III 568
Paperbacks, IV 9
Parker Brothers, IV 13
Penn, Irving, IV 33
Pepsi-Cola, IV 36
Phone Sex, IV 51
Picasso, Pablo, IV 54
Polyester, IV 80
Pop Art, IV 81
Postcards, IV 96
Presley, Elvis, IV 105
Price Is Right, IV 108
Prozac, IV 125
Recycling, IV 187
Rouse Company, IV 283
Saturday Morning Cartoons, IV 317
Sea World, IV 345
Sears Roebuck Catalogue, IV 346
Star Wars, IV 511
Starbucks, IV 514
Stock Market Crashes, IV 539
Studio One, IV 563
Supermodels, IV 583
Swatch Watches, IV 589
Teenagers, IV 620
Television, IV 626
Tennis Shoes/Sneakers, IV 637
Tiffany & Company, IV 655
Titanic, IV 661
Toys, IV 685
Trading Stamps, IV 688
Tupperware, IV 700
Twenties, IV 710
Valentine's Day, V 16
Victoria's Secret, V 43
Videos, V 47
Vitamins, V 52
Wall Drug, V 66
Wayne's World, V 94
Whole Earth Catalogue, V 132
Winnie Winkle the Breadwinner, V 156
World's Fairs, V 194
Yuppies, V 223
Zines, V 228

Contests/Pageants/Shows
Academy Awards, I 12
Beauty Queens, I 207
Century of Progress International Exposition
    (Chicago, 1933), I 471
Circus, I 512
Civil War Reenactors, I 521
Cody, Buffalo Bill, and his Wild West
    Show, I 545
Daytona 500, I 670
Fischer, Bobby, II 104
Flagpole Sitting, II 111
Freak Shows, II 158
Miss America Pageant, III 374
Parades, IV 12
Piper, ''Rowdy'' Roddy, IV 60
Ringling Bros., Barnum & Bailey Circus, IV 212
Rodeo, IV 252
State Fairs, IV 518
Vaudeville, V 33
World Cup, V 181

Country Music
Alabama, I 39
Allman Brothers Band, I 56

Alternative Country Music, I 59
Atkins, Chet, I 132
Autry, Gene, I 142
Ballard, Hank, I 164
Band, I 167
Black, Clint, I 262
Bluegrass, I 287
Brooks, Garth, I 364
Buffett, Jimmy, I 382
Byrds, I 402
Campbell, Glen, I 416
Carter Family, I 445
Cash, Johnny, I 449
Charles, Ray, I 477
Cline, Patsy, I 530
Concept Album, I 576
Country Gentlemen, I 617
Country Music, I 617
Daniels, Charlie, I 658
Denver, John, I 686
Electric Guitar, II 21
Everly Brothers, II 47
Ford, Tennessee Ernie, II 138
Friedman, Kinky, II 171
Frizzell, Lefty, II 175
Grand Ole Opry, II 286
Griffith, Nanci, II 315
Haggard, Merle, II 334
Hee Haw, II 381
Holly, Buddy, II 429
Jennings, Waylon, II 540
Jones, George, II 561
Kershaw, Doug, III 21
Lang, k.d., III 88
Lewis, Jerry Lee, III 153
Lynn, Loretta, III 218
Macon, Uncle Dave, III 229
McEntire, Reba, III 325
Miller, Roger, III 367
Monroe, Bill, III 396
Montana, Patsy, III 403
Murray, Anne, III 447
Nelson, Willie, III 501
Osborne Brothers, III 575
Owens, Buck, III 582
Parton, Dolly, IV 17
Paul, Les, IV 20
Pearl, Minnie, IV 28
Pop Music, IV 83
Pride, Charley, IV 111
Rich, Charlie, IV 209
Rodgers, Jimmie, IV 258
Rogers, Kenny, IV 261
Rogers, Roy, IV 262
Selena, IV 354
Skaggs, Ricky, IV 427
State Fairs, IV 518
Stevens, Ray, IV 532
Strait, George, IV 547
Stuart, Marty, IV 558
Wells, Kitty, V 109
Whiting, Margaret, V 130
Williams, Hank, Jr., V 141
Williams, Hank, Sr., V 141
Wills, Bob, and His Texas Playboys, V 148
Wynette, Tammy, V 201
Yoakam, Dwight, V 216

Cowboys
Autry, Gene, I 142
Cody, Buffalo Bill, and his Wild West
    Show, I 545
Friedman, Kinky, II 171
Hopalong Cassidy, II 444
Leone, Sergio, III 136
Magnificent Seven, III 240
Mix, Tom, III 383
Remington, Frederic, IV 203
Rodeo, IV 252
Rogers, Roy, IV 262
Searchers, IV 346
Wayne, John, V 91
Western, V 118

Crime/Criminals
Altamont, I 57
Arbuckle, Fatty, I 107
Bonnie and Clyde, I 316
Boston Strangler, I 324
Bundy, Ted, I 384
Butch Cassidy and the Sundance Kid, I 398
Capital Punishment, I 424
Capone, Al, I 425
Chessman, Caryl, I 492
Crime Does Not Pay, I 632
Dahmer, Jeffrey, I 651
Dick Tracy, I 702
Dillinger, John, I 713
FBI (Federal Bureau of Investigation), II 80
Firearms, II 101
Gangs, II 195
Gangsta Rap, II 198
Ghettos, II 227
Godfather, II 250
GoodFellas, II 269
Gotti, John, II 277
Grafton, Sue, II 282
Harding, Tonya, II 360
Harley-Davidson, II 368
Hate Crimes, II 373
Hawaii Five-O, II 375
Hearst, Patty, II 378
Himes, Chester, II 408
Hiss, Alger, II 413
Hoover, J. Edgar, II 443
Ice-T, II 485
Jewish Defense League, II 545
Juvenile Delinquency, II 583
Kennedy Assassination, III 16
Kerrigan, Nancy, III 21
King, Rodney, III 34
Ku Klux Klan, III 64
LaMotta, Jake, III 83
Lansky, Meyer, III 90
Las Vegas, III 92
Leary, Timothy, III 112
Lee, Spike, III 122
Leopold and Loeb, III 138
Liston, Sonny, III 171
Luciano, Lucky, III 212
Mafia/Organized Crime, III 237
Manson, Charles, III 261
*Miranda*Warning, III 373
Neighborhood Watch, III 499
Prohibition, IV 119
Reality Television, IV 181
Road Rage, IV 221
Robinson, Edward G., IV 229
Rosenberg, Julius and Ethel, IV 279
Seduction of the Innocent, IV 350
Serial Killers, IV 358
Siegel, Bugsy, IV 392
Simpson, O. J., IV 404
Simpson Trial, IV 405
Snoop Doggy Dogg, IV 444
Wertham, Fredric, V 111
White, Stanford, V 129

Critics
Adler, Renata, I 21
American Mercury, I 72
Barry, Dave, I 177
Benchley, Robert, I 219
Blues Brothers, I 293
Bly, Robert, I 296
Capote, Truman, I 426
Clancy, Tom, I 524
Crumb, Robert, I 641
Escher, M. C., II 37
Gold, Mike, II 255
Hurston, Zora Neale, II 469
Levin, Meyer, III 145
Lippmann, Walter, III 170
Lolita, III 183
Mencken, H. L., III 342
Parker, Dorothy, IV 14
Rolling Stone, IV 267

Siskel and Ebert, IV 417
Van Dine, S. S., V 24
Van Vechten, Carl, V 26
Will, George F., V 138
Wolfe, Tom, V 166
Zines, V 228

Cults
Communes, I 568
Cults, I 646
Est, II 42
Father Divine, II 74
Grateful Dead, II 291
Hubbard, L. Ron, II 461
Jonestown, II 563
Manson, Charles, III 261
Moonies/Reverend Sun Myung Moon, III 405
New Age Spirituality, III 507
Objectivism/Ayn Rand, III 547
Sedona, Arizona, IV 349
UFOs (Unidentified Flying Objects), V 1

Daily Life
Barry, Dave, I 177
Better Homes and Gardens, I 238
Blume, Judy, I 294
Bomb, I 311
Bombeck, Erma, I 314
Boy Scouts of America, I 333
Bungalow, I 387
Casual Friday, I 455
Central Park, I 468
Child, Julia, I 496
Civil Rights Movement, I 519
Closet, I 536
Family Circle, II 59
Fifties, II 96
Great Depression, II 295
Happy Hour, II 359
Lawn Care/Gardening, III 104
Leave It to Beaver, III 115
Leisure Time, III 128
Mary Hartman, Mary Hartman, III 289
Middletown, III 355
Model T, III 386
People, IV 35
Pets, IV 44
Polyester, IV 80
Postcards, IV 96
Reality Television, IV 181
Rockwell, Norman, IV 244
Soda Fountains, IV 452
Starbucks, IV 514
State Fairs, IV 518
Sunday Driving, IV 578
Tarkington, Booth, IV 607
Twenties, IV 710
Updike, John, V 10
Weekend, V 101

Dance
ABBA, I 4
Ailey, Alvin, I 37
American Bandstand, I 65
Astaire, Fred, and Ginger Rogers, I 127
Baker, Josephine, I 158
Balanchine, George, I 161
Ballet, I 165
Baryshnikov, Mikhail, I 180
Baum, L. Frank, I 191
Berkeley, Busby, I 227
Blackface Minstrelsy, I 270
Butterbeans and Susie, I 400
Cakewalks, I 411
Calloway, Cab, I 412
Castle, Vernon and Irene, I 454
Clark, Dick, I 525
Cohan, George M., I 548
Copland, Aaron, I 600
Crawford, Joan, I 625
Cunningham, Merce, I 648
Dance Halls, I 657
Denishawn, I 686
Dietrich, Marlene, I 708

Disco, I 726
Drifters, I 769
Duncan, Isadora, I 773
Fantasia, II 65
Fonteyn, Margot, II 130
42nd Street, II 142
Fosse, Bob, II 143
Graham, Martha, II 285
Kelly, Gene, III 14
Latin Jazz, III 97
Modern Dance, III 388
Morris, Mark, III 413
Murray, Arthur, III 448
Noloesca, La Chata, III 540
Nureyev, Rudolf, III 544
Oklahoma!, III 553
Peppermint Lounge, IV 36
Prom, IV 120
Raft, George, IV 162
Rand, Sally, IV 173
Rockettes, IV 241
Salsa Music, IV 303
Saturday Night Fever, IV 319
Savoy Ballroom, IV 322
Shawn, Ted, IV 381
Social Dancing, IV 450
Soul Train, IV 461
St. Denis, Ruth, IV 494
Strip Joints/Striptease, IV 557
Summer, Donna, IV 575
Swing Dancing, IV 592
Tap Dancing, IV 605
Tejano Music, IV 623
Tharp, Twyla, IV 641
Twenties, IV 710
Vaudeville, V 33
Villella, Edward, V 52
Walker, Aaron ''T-Bone,'' V 59
Walker, Aida Overton, V 61
Waters, Ethel, V 86
Zoot Suit, V 233

Detective/Mystery, Film
Big Sleep, I 250
Boston Strangler, I 324
Chandler, Raymond, I 473
Charlie Chan, I 478
Dick Tracy, I 702
Film Noir, II 99
French Connection, II 164
Hammett, Dashiell, II 349
Leonard, Elmore, III 134
Loy, Myrna, III 207
Maltese Falcon, III 249
North by Northwest, III 541
Perry Mason, IV 41
Powell, William, IV 102
Psycho, IV 130
Queen, Ellery, IV 148
Rear Window, IV 184
Shadow, IV 375
Shaft, IV 376
Vertigo, V 42

Detective/Mystery, Print
Argosy, I 109
Bestsellers, I 236
Big Sleep, I 250
Black Mask, I 263
Brand, Max, I 342
Carr, John Dickson, I 442
Chandler, Raymond, I 473
Cherry Ames, I 491
Christie, Agatha, I 502
DC Comics, I 671
Derleth, August, I 692
Detective Fiction, I 693
Dick Tracy, I 702
Dime Novels, I 716
Double Indemnity, I 751
Doyle, Arthur Conan, I 755
Elkins, Aaron, II 23
Follett, Ken, II 127

Friedman, Kinky, II 171
Grafton, Sue, II 282
Greeley, Andrew, II 298
Grisham, John, II 318
Hammett, Dashiell, II 349
Hard-Boiled Detective Fiction, II 359
Hardy Boys, II 360
Hess, Joan, II 399
Hillerman, Tony, II 407
Himes, Chester, II 408
Judy Bolton, II 578
Kantor, MacKinlay, III 3
Koontz, Dean R., III 53
Kotzwinkle, William, III 56
Le Carré, John, III 106
Leonard, Elmore, III 134
Ludlum, Robert, III 213
MacDonald, John D., III 226
Maltese Falcon, III 249
Manchurian Candidate, III 254
McBain, Ed, III 312
Mosley, Walter, III 416
Nancy Drew, III 473
Paperbacks, IV 9
Paretsky, Sara, IV 12
Perry Mason, IV 41
Postman Always Rings Twice, IV 97
Pulp Magazines, IV 139
Queen, Ellery, IV 148
Robeson, Kenneth, IV 227
Shadow, IV 375
Spillane, Mickey, IV 477
Stout, Rex, IV 546
Three Investigators Series, IV 651
Trixie Belden, IV 698
True Detective, IV 699
Van Dine, S. S., V 24
Weird Tales, V 103

Detective/Mystery, Television
Avengers, I 144
Cagney and Lacey, I 409
Charlie's Angels, I 479
Christie, Agatha, I 502
Columbo, I 559
Daly, Tyne, I 655
Dick Tracy, I 702
Fawcett, Farrah, II 79
Follett, Ken, II 127
Grafton, Sue, II 282
Hardy Boys, II 360
Hawaii Five-O, II 375
I Spy, II 479
Kojak, III 52
Lynch, David, III 216
Made-for-Television Movies, III 233
Magnum, P.I., III 241
Moonlighting, III 406
Murder, She Wrote, III 445
NYPD Blue, III 545
Perry Mason, IV 41
Prisoner, IV 116
Queen, Ellery, IV 148
Sheldon, Sidney, IV 381
Starsky and Hutch, IV 517
Webb, Jack, V 98

Disasters
Challenger Disaster, I 472
China Syndrome, I 500
Disaster Movies, I 723
Hindenburg, II 409
Independence Day, II 486
My Lai Massacre, III 465

Documentaries
Burns, Ken, I 394
Let Us Now Praise Famous Men, III 142
60 Minutes, IV 425

Drama, Film
African Queen, I 33
Alda, Alan, I 42
Altman, Robert, I 63

Bacall, Lauren, I 154
Benchley, Robert, I 219
Ben-Hur, I 219
Best Years of Our Lives, I 236
Birth of a Nation, I 258
Blockbusters, I 280
Blue Velvet, I 286
Bogart, Humphrey, I 308
Bonnie and Clyde, I 316
Brando, Marlon, I 342
Brat Pack, I 344
Breakfast Club, I 347
Brooks, Louise, I 365
Brynner, Yul, I 375
Burnett, Carol, I 391
Burr, Raymond, I 394
Cagney, James, I 409
Capra, Frank, I 428
Casablanca, I 447
Chaplin, Charlie, I 475
Chayefsky, Paddy, I 484
China Syndrome, I 500
Chinatown, I 500
Citizen Kane, I 514
Cleopatra, I 529
Clooney, Rosemary, I 533
Colbert, Claudette, I 548
Costner, Kevin, I 612
Crawford, Joan, I 625
Cukor, George, I 643
Dean, James, I 676
DiCaprio, Leonardo, I 700
Dirty Dozen, I 721
Disability, I 721
Do the Right Thing, I 735
Doctor Zhivago, I 740
Double Indemnity, I 751
Douglas, Melvyn, I 753
Dr. Jekyll and Mr. Hyde, I 756
Dr. Kildare, I 756
Eddy, Nelson, II 13
Fatal Attraction, II 74
Fellini, Federico, II 84
Field of Dreams, II 93
Field, Sally, II 94
Film Noir, II 99
Fonda, Henry, II 127
Ford, Harrison, II 131
Forrest Gump, II 140
Fugitive, II 179
Gable, Clark, II 187
Garland, Judy, II 202
General, II 218
Giant, II 230
Gish, Dorothy, II 243
Gish, Lillian, II 244
Gleason, Jackie, II 245
Godfather, II 250
Gone with the Wind, II 263
GoodFellas, II 269
Graduate, II 279
Grapes of Wrath, II 290
Greed, II 298
Grisham, John, II 318
Hanks, Tom, II 353
Hayward, Susan, II 377
Heston, Charlton, II 399
Hijuelos, Oscar, II 405
Hitchcock, Alfred, II 414
Hoffman, Dustin, II 420
Holliday, Judy, II 429
Hoosiers, II 442
Hudson, Rock, II 462
Ice-T, II 485
Independence Day, II 486
Intolerance, II 498
It's a Wonderful Life, II 506
James Bond Films, II 523
Jazz Singer, II 531
JFK(The Movie), II 545
Jones, Jennifer, II 562
Juliá, Raúl, II 581

Juvenile Delinquency, II 583
Kantor, MacKinlay, III 3
Keitel, Harvey, III 12
Kelly, Grace, III 15
Ku Klux Klan, III 64
Kubrick, Stanley, III 66
Lancaster, Burt, III 85
Laura, III 100
Lawrence of Arabia, III 104
Lee, Spike, III 122
Leonard, Elmore, III 134
Like Water for Chocolate, III 162
Lion King, III 169
Lolita, III 183
Lorre, Peter, III 195
Lost Weekend, III 199
Loy, Myrna, III 207
Lupino, Ida, III 215
Lynch, David, III 216
Man Who Shot Liberty Valance, III 253
Manchurian Candidate, III 254
Martin, Dean, III 280
McDaniel, Hattie, III 320
Mean Streets, III 336
Metalious, Grace, III 346
Midnight Cowboy, III 357
Minnelli, Vincente, III 370
Mr. Smith Goes to Washington, III 432
Muni, Paul, III 442
My Family, Mi Familia, III 464
Natural, III 492
Natural Born Killers, III 493
Novak, Kim, III 543
Objectivism/Ayn Rand, III 547
Olivier, Laurence, III 556
Olmos, Edward James, III 557
On the Waterfront, III 562
One Flew Over the Cuckoo's Nest, III 566
Parton, Dolly, IV 17
Patinkin, Mandy, IV 19
Peyton Place, IV 47
Place in the Sun, IV 63
Platoon, IV 69
Poitier, Sidney, IV 75
Postman Always Rings Twice, IV 97
Psycho, IV 130
Pulp Fiction, IV 138
Raging Bull, IV 165
Rebel without a Cause, IV 185
Redford, Robert, IV 190
Rivers, Joan, IV 219
Robeson, Paul, IV 227
Rocky, IV 246
Saturday Night Fever, IV 319
Schindler's List, IV 324
Scott, Randolph, IV 339
Seven Days in May, IV 364
Shaft, IV 376
Shepard, Sam, IV 382
Silence of the Lambs, IV 393
Silent Movies, IV 393
Sirk, Douglas, IV 416
Spacek, Sissy, IV 467
Spartacus, IV 468
Stand and Deliver, IV 501
Star Wars, IV 511
Steinbeck, John, IV 522
Stone, Irving, IV 542
Streetcar Named Desire, IV 554
Taxi Driver, IV 611
Taylor, Elizabeth, IV 612
Temple, Shirley, IV 631
Ten Commandments, IV 634
Third Man, IV 643
Titanic, IV 661
Trevor, Claire, IV 697
Turner, Lana, IV 703
Valdez, Luis, V 15
Valens, Ritchie, V 16
Vertigo, V 42
Wayne, John, V 91
West Side Story, V 116

White, Stanford, V 129
Wild One, V 135
Wood, Ed, V 172
Wuthering Heights, V 198
Yankee Doodle Dandy, V 207

Drama, Radio
Dragnet, I 766
Great Depression, II 295
Guiding Light, II 323
Gunsmoke, II 326
I Love a Mystery, II 476
Inner Sanctum Mysteries, II 493
One Man's Family, III 567
Radio Drama, IV 160
Shadow, IV 375
Soap Operas, IV 446
War of the Worlds, V 79

Drama, Television
Another World, I 99
Baywatch, I 193
Ben Casey, I 218
Beverly Hills 90210, I 242
Bochco, Steven, I 302
Bonanza, I 316
Brideshead Revisited, I 348
Brown, Jim, I 369
Burnett, Carol, I 391
Burr, Raymond, I 394
Colbert, Claudette, I 548
Crichton, Michael, I 631
Dallas, I 652
Dark Shadows, I 659
Days of Our Lives, I 666
Disability, I 721
Docudrama, I 741
Dr. Kildare, I 756
Dragnet, I 766
Dynasty, I 783
Edge of Night, II 13
ER, II 33
Fantasy Island, II 68
Fugitive, II 179
Guiding Light, II 323
Gunsmoke, II 326
Hill Street Blues, II 406
Holliday, Judy, II 429
Holocaust, II 436
Hudson, Rock, II 462
Kelley, David E., III 13
Knots Landing, III 50
Kraft Television Theatre, III 60
Ku Klux Klan, III 64
L. A. Law, III 71
Landon, Michael, III 86
Made-for-Television Movies, III 233
Marcus Welby, M.D., III 269
Martin, Quinn, III 282
Mary Hartman, Mary Hartman, III 289
*M*A*S*H*, III 295
Masterpiece Theatre, III 302
Metalious, Grace, III 346
Miami Vice, III 349
Mission: Impossible, III 375
Mod Squad, III 385
Murphy Brown, III 446
My So-Called Life, III 466
Northern Exposure, III 542
NYPD Blue, III 545
Olmos, Edward James, III 557
Omnibus, III 561
Patinkin, Mandy, IV 19
Peyton Place, IV 47
Philco Television Playhouse, IV 50
Playhouse 90, IV 73
Poitier, Sidney, IV 75
Potter, Dennis, IV 102
Public Television (PBS), IV 135
Real World, IV 181
Rivers, Joan, IV 219
Roots, IV 273
Serling, Rod, IV 361

Smits, Jimmy, IV 441
Soap Operas, IV 446
St. Elsewhere, IV 495
Studio One, IV 563
Susskind, David, IV 587
Taylor, Robert, IV 615
Titanic, IV 661
Touched by an Angel, IV 684
Trevor, Claire, IV 697
Twin Peaks, IV 715
Upstairs, Downstairs, V 11
Waltons, V 74

Drama, Theatre
Bacall, Lauren, I 154
Ben-Hur, I 219
Broadway, I 356
Burr, Raymond, I 394
Death of a Salesman, I 678
Glass Menagerie, II 245
Hoffman, Dustin, II 420
Holbrook, Hal, II 424
Hughes, Langston, II 465
Juliá, Raúl, II 581
Lupino, Ida, III 215
Mamet, David, III 252
Olivier, Laurence, III 556
Phantom of the Opera, IV 49
Robeson, Paul, IV 227
Shepard, Sam, IV 382
Steinbeck, John, IV 522
Streetcar Named Desire, IV 554
Valdez, Luis, V 15

Drugs/Drug Culture
Altamont, I 57
Alternative Press, I 60
Another World, I 99
Beach Boys, I 195
Beat Generation, I 201
Beatles, I 203
Belushi, John, I 216
Bodybuilding, I 305
Breakfast Club, I 347
Bruce, Lenny, I 372
Burroughs, William S., I 397
Castaneda, Carlos, I 453
Clapton, Eric, I 525
Cocaine/Crack, I 542
Coltrane, John, I 557
Communes, I 568
Dick, Philip K., I 701
Donovan, I 745
Doors, I 748
Drug War, I 771
Easy Rider, II 4
Everly Brothers, II 47
French Connection, II 164
Gangs, II 195
Ghettos, II 227
Gooden, Dwight, II 268
Grateful Dead, II 291
Haight-Ashbury, II 336
Heavy Metal, II 380
Hendrix, Jimi, II 391
Hep Cats, II 393
Himes, Chester, II 408
Hippies, II 410
Hoffman, Abbie, II 419
Holiday, Billie, II 427
Hopper, Dennis, II 447
Joplin, Janis, II 565
Kesey, Ken, III 22
Leary, Timothy, III 112
Lennon, John, III 131
Love, Courtney, III 204
LSD, III 207
Lugosi, Bela, III 213
Mafia/Organized Crime, III 237
Mamas and the Papas, III 251
Manson, Charles, III 261
Marijuana, III 272
Maupin, Armistead, III 307

Mötley Crüe, III 418
National Basketball Association (NBA), III 477
One Flew Over the Cuckoo's Nest, III 566
Op Art, III 569
Pachucos, IV 2
Parker, Charlie, IV 13
Pop, Iggy, IV 82
Pop Music, IV 83
Presley, Elvis, IV 105
Pryor, Richard, IV 126
Psychedelia, IV 128
Reed, Lou, IV 192
Robbins, Tom, IV 223
Rolling Stones, IV 269
Slang, IV 434
Strawberry, Darryl, IV 551
Suicide, IV 569
Thompson, Hunter S., IV 646
Twelve-Step Programs, IV 708
Underground Comics, V 4
Valium, V 20
Vaughan, Stevie Ray, V 37
Yuppies, V 223

Economy
Alaska-Yukon Exposition (Seattle, 1909), I 40
Amway, I 80
Automobile, I 137
Baby Boomers, I 151
Birkenstocks, I 257
Catalog Houses, I 455
Century 21 Exposition (Seattle, 1962), I 470
Consumerism, I 589
Credit Cards, I 628
Department Stores, I 688
Do-It-Yourself Improvement, I 742
Dunkin' Donuts, I 775
Electric Appliances, II 20
Fast Food, II 71
Fifties, II 96
Ford Motor Company, II 135
General Motors, II 220
Ghettos, II 227
Grapes of Wrath, II 290
Great Depression, II 295
Highway System, II 402
Home Shopping Network/QVC, II 438
IBM (International Business Machines), II 481
Internet, II 495
J. Walter Thompson, II 511
Kelly Girls, III 14
Kitsch, III 43
Labor Unions, III 72
Mall of America, III 245
Microsoft, III 353
Model T, III 386
Muscle Cars, III 455
New Deal, III 508
Nike, III 535
Old Navy, III 555
Opportunity, III 570
Prang, Louis, IV 104
Prom, IV 120
Rockefeller Family, IV 239
Starbucks, IV 514
Stock Market Crashes, IV 539
Trading Stamps, IV 688
Twenties, IV 710
Videos, V 47
Wall Drug, V 66
Wal-Mart, V 69
War Bonds, V 74
World's Fairs, V 194

Education
Blackboard Jungle, I 268
Blume, Judy, I 294
Boy Scouts of America, I 333
Captain Kangaroo, I 430
Carnegie, Dale, I 437
Chautauqua Institution, I 481
Child, Julia, I 496
Cosby, Bill, I 606

Creationism, I 627
Dick and Jane Readers, I 700
Dr. Seuss, I 757
Family Circle, II 59
Flipper, II 118
Free Speech Movement, II 161
Gnagy, Jon, II 249
Henson, Jim, II 393
Ivy League, II 509
Legos, III 125
Lincoln Center for the Performing Arts, III 165
Luce, Henry, III 210
Mickey Mouse Club, III 351
Mister Rogers' Neighborhood, III 378
Mouseketeers, III 425
National Parks, III 489
Political Correctness, IV 78
Postmodernism, IV 98
Prang, Louis, IV 104
PTA/PTO (Parent Teacher Association/
    Organization), IV 130
Public Enemy, IV 132
Public Libraries, IV 133
Public Television (PBS), IV 135
Sagan, Carl, IV 300
Schoolhouse Rock, IV 328
Scopes Monkey Trial, IV 335
Smithsonian Institution, IV 441
Sputnik, IV 493
Stand and Deliver, IV 501
Standardized Testing, IV 502
Twenties, IV 710

Environment
Abbey, Edward, I 4
Camping, I 417
Eco-Terrorism, II 10
Environmentalism, II 29
Ghettos, II 227
Greenpeace, II 303
Grey, Zane, II 309
Herbert, Frank, II 395
Lawn Care/Gardening, III 104
Lindbergh, Anne Morrow, III 166
Nader, Ralph, III 469
National Geographic, III 484
National Parks, III 489
New Age Spirituality, III 507
Recycling, IV 187
Whole Earth Catalogue, V 132

Essayists
Angell, Roger, I 88
Baldwin, James, I 161
Barry, Dave, I 177
Benchley, Robert, I 219
Blount, Roy, Jr., I 285
Didion, Joan, I 704
Ellison, Harlan, II 25
Erdrich, Louise, II 34
Fadiman, Clifton, II 55
Fitzgerald, F. Scott, II 109
Greeley, Andrew, II 298
Grizzard, Lewis, II 319
Hubbard, L. Ron, II 461
Invisible Man, II 498
Jong, Erica, II 564
Lardner, Ring, III 90
Le Guin, Ursula K., III 107
Lewis, C. S., III 150
Mailer, Norman, III 242
Mencken, H. L., III 342
Objectivism/Ayn Rand, III 547
O'Connor, Flannery, III 549
Price, Reynolds, IV 110
Reed, Ishmael, IV 191
Rolling Stone, IV 267
Royko, Mike, IV 285
Steinbeck, John, IV 522
Steinem, Gloria, IV 524
Tarkington, Booth, IV 607
Thurber, James, IV 654
Trillin, Calvin, IV 697

Vonnegut, Kurt, Jr., V 56
Walker, Alice, V 61
Waters, John, V 87
White, E. B., V 127
Will, George F., V 138
Williams, Tennessee, V 146

Exercise
Aerobics, I 30
Atlas, Charles, I 135
Bicycling, I 245
Bodybuilding, I 305
Boston Marathon, I 323
Fairbanks, Douglas, Sr., II 57
Grimek, John, II 316
Gymnastics, II 331
Hiking, II 405
Ironman Triathlon, II 503
Jogging, II 547
LaLanne, Jack, III 80
Macfadden, Bernarr, III 226
McLish, Rachel, III 328
Murray, Lenda, III 451
Muscle Beach, III 453
Sandow, Eugen, IV 309
Shorter, Frank, IV 388
Special Olympics, IV 470
Stockton, ''Pudgy,'' IV 541
Summer Camp, IV 573

Fads/Crazes
ABBA, I 4
American Bandstand, I 65
American Graffiti, I 69
Amway, I 80
Astrology, I 129
Bagels, I 158
Beach Boys, I 195
Beanie Babies, I 198
Beavis and Butthead, I 209
Birkenstocks, I 257
Bobby Socks, I 301
Body Decoration, I 303
Bridge, I 349
Buffett, Jimmy, I 382
Cabbage Patch Kids, I 403
CB Radio, I 462
Charm Bracelets, I 480
Chemise, I 490
College Fads, I 553
Coué, Emile, I 615
Crinolines, I 633
Cult Films, I 643
Dallas, I 652
Davy Crockett, I 663
Dieting, I 706
Dime Novels, I 716
Disco, I 726
Doc Martens, I 737
Doctor Who, I 739
Drag Racing, I 764
Drive-In Theater, I 769
Dungeons and Dragons, I 774
Eight-track Tape, II 16
Est, II 42
Fawcett, Farrah, II 79
Flagpole Sitting, II 111
Flappers, II 112
Freak Shows, II 158
Goth, II 277
Hairstyles, II 340
Hemlines, II 390
Hula Hoop, II 466
Kewpie Dolls, III 22
Latin Jazz, III 97
Leisure Suit, III 127
Martini, III 282
Medicine Shows, III 339
Mod, III 384
Muscle Cars, III 455
New Age Music, III 506
New Age Spirituality, III 507
New Look, III 512

Oxford Bags, III 584
Peppermint Lounge, IV 36
Pet Rocks, IV 42
Polyester, IV 80
Postmodernism, IV 98
Retro Fashion, IV 205
Rubik's Cube, IV 286
Shorter, Frank, IV 388
Singles Bars, IV 415
Skateboarding, IV 428
Slinky, IV 436
Starbucks, IV 514
Streaking, IV 551
Studio 54, IV 563
Swinging, IV 593
Toga Parties, IV 669
23 Skidoo, IV 712
Valentino, Rudolph, V 17
Varga Girl, V 30
Viagra, V 43
Walkman, V 66

Family/Home
Andy Hardy, I 87
Avon, I 146
Baby Boomers, I 151
Barbecue, I 168
Birthing Practices, I 260
Blume, Judy, I 294
Bobbsey Twins, I 300
Brady Bunch, I 339
Bungalow, I 387
Captain Kangaroo, I 430
Christmas, I 503
Circus, I 512
Cosby Show, I 607
Dionne Quintuplets, I 720
Divorce, I 732
Dobie Gillis, I 735
Etiquette Columns, II 44
Family Circle, II 59
Family Circus, II 61
Family Reunions, II 63
Family Ties, II 64
Father Knows Best, II 75
Father's Day, II 76
Frozen Entrées, II 178
Gated Communities, II 208
Good Housekeeping, II 265
Henry Aldrich, II 392
Home Improvement, II 437
Leave It to Beaver, III 115
Levittown, III 147
Manufactured Homes, III 263
Mary Tyler Moore Show, III 292
McCall's Magazine, III 313
Middletown, III 355
Mother's Day, III 417
Pets, IV 44
Promise Keepers, IV 122
Ranch House, IV 173
Rockwell, Norman, IV 244
Roots, IV 273
Schlessinger, Dr. Laura, IV 326
Spock, Dr. Benjamin, IV 480
State Fairs, IV 518
Stock Market Crashes, IV 539
Suburbia, IV 567
Swinging, IV 593
Thanksgiving, IV 640
Toys, IV 685
Trailer Parks, IV 689
Tyler, Anne, IV 718
Vance, Vivian, V 27
Woman's Day, V 169
Young, Robert, V 218
Yuppies, V 223

Fashion/Clothing
Academy Awards, I 12
Adidas, I 20
Annie Hall, I 98
Arden, Elizabeth, I 109

Armani, Giorgio, I 111
Avedon, Richard, I 144
Beauty Queens, I 207
Bellbottoms, I 216
Benneton, I 221
Birkenstocks, I 257
Blass, Bill, I 278
Bobby Socks, I 301
Body Decoration, I 303
Bomb, I 311
Bra, I 335
Breakfast at Tiffany's, I 346
Camp, I 415
Campbell, Naomi, I 416
Car Coats, I 433
Casual Friday, I 455
Chanel, Coco, I 475
Charlie's Angels, I 479
Charm Bracelets, I 480
Chemise, I 490
Claiborne, Liz, I 523
Clairol Hair Coloring, I 523
Cline, Patsy, I 530
Cosmopolitan, I 610
Cowboy Look, I 622
Crawford, Cindy, I 624
Crawford, Joan, I 625
Crinolines, I 633
Debutantes, I 680
Dieting, I 706
Dietrich, Marlene, I 708
Disco, I 726
Doc Martens, I 737
Earth Shoes, II 2
Ellis, Perry, II 25
Factor, Max, II 54
Flag Clothing, II 111
Flappers, II 112
Flashdance Style, II 113
Frederick's of Hollywood, II 159
Fu Manchu, II 179
Gap, II 198
Gibson Girl, II 233
Goth, II 277
Grunge, II 321
Gucci, II 323
Hairstyles, II 340
Halston, II 346
Hemlines, II 390
Hot Pants, II 454
Jeans, II 532
Karan, Donna, III 4
Kelly Bag, III 14
Klein, Calvin, III 46
Lacoste Shirts, III 75
Lauren, Ralph, III 102
Leather Jacket, III 114
Leisure Suit, III 127
Levi's, III 146
Lipstick, III 171
Little Black Dress, III 173
Loafers, III 182
Miami Vice, III 349
Mod, III 384
Moss, Kate, III 417
Neckties, III 495
Nerd Look, III 502
New Look, III 512
Newton, Helmut, III 528
Nirvana, III 538
Old Navy, III 555
Op Art, III 569
Oxford Bags, III 584
Pachucos, IV 2
Pants for Women, IV 7
Pantyhose, IV 9
Penn, Irving, IV 33
Polyester, IV 80
Preppy, IV 105
Retro Fashion, IV 205
RuPaul, IV 289
Sarong, IV 313

Sassoon, Vidal, IV 313
Sports Illustrated, IV 487
Stetson Hat, IV 532
Supermodels, IV 583
Sweatshirt, IV 589
Tanning, IV 603
Tennis Shoes/Sneakers, IV 637
Toga Parties, IV 669
T-Shirts, IV 700
Twiggy, IV 713
Vanity Fair, V 28
Versace, Gianni, V 41
Victoria's Secret, V 43
Vogue, V 53
Walker, Madame C. J., V 65
Wedding Dress, V 100
Wheel of Fortune, V 122
Wrangler Jeans, V 196
Zoot Suit, V 233

Film Directors
Alda, Alan, I 42
Allen, Woody, I 53
Altman, Robert, I 63
American Graffiti, I 69
Annie Hall, I 98
Arbuckle, Fatty, I 107
''B'' movies, I 149
Beatty, Warren, I 206
Ben-Hur, I 219
Bergman, Ingmar, I 225
Berkeley, Busby, I 227
Blackboard Jungle, I 268
Blade Runner, I 273
Brooks, James L., I 365
Brooks, Mel, I 365
Capra, Frank, I 428
Casablanca, I 447
Chaplin, Charlie, I 475
Citizen Kane, I 514
City Lights, I 515
Corman, Roger, I 603
Costner, Kevin, I 612
Crichton, Michael, I 631
Cukor, George, I 643
DeMille, Cecil B., I 683
Duvall, Robert, I 778
Fellini, Federico, II 84
Film Noir, II 99
Ford, John, II 133
Fosse, Bob, II 143
Foster, Jodie, II 145
Gibson, Mel, II 234
GoodFellas, II 269
Griffith, D. W., II 313
Hawks, Howard, II 376
Hitchcock, Alfred, II 414
Hollywood, II 431
Hollywood Ten, II 434
Hopper, Dennis, II 447
Hughes, Howard, II 464
Huston, John, II 471
Jaws, II 526
Kubrick, Stanley, III 66
Lee, Spike, III 122
Leone, Sergio, III 136
Lubitsch, Ernst, III 209
Lucas, George, III 209
Lupino, Ida, III 215
Marshall, Garry, III 278
Nava, Gregory, III 495
Platoon, IV 69
Preminger, Otto, IV 104
Psycho, IV 130
Raiders of the Lost Ark, IV 166
Rear Window, IV 184
Redford, Robert, IV 190
Reiner, Carl, IV 196
Renoir, Jean, IV 204
Scorsese, Martin, IV 337
Sennett, Mack, IV 357
Sirk, Douglas, IV 416
Spartacus, IV 468

Spielberg, Steven, IV 476
Stagecoach, IV 497
Stone, Oliver, IV 543
Streisand, Barbra, IV 556
Sturges, Preston, IV 566
Tarantino, Quentin, IV 606
Taxi Driver, IV 611
Ten Commandments, IV 634
Thalberg, Irving G., IV 640
Thing, IV 642
Treasure of the Sierra Madre, IV 695
Vertigo, V 42
Vidor, King, V 48
Von Sternberg, Josef, V 55
Waters, John, V 87
Webb, Jack, V 98
Welles, Orson, V 108
Wilder, Billy, V 136
Wood, Ed, V 172

Film Noir
Bara, Theda, I 168
Big Sleep, I 250
Blade Runner, I 273
Chandler, Raymond, I 473
Chinatown, I 500
Conspiracy Theories, I 586
Crawford, Joan, I 625
Day the Earth Stood Still, I 665
Dick Tracy, I 702
Dietrich, Marlene, I 708
Double Indemnity, I 751
Fargo, II 69
Film Noir, II 99
Ford, Glenn, II 131
Keitel, Harvey, III 12
Lancaster, Burt, III 85
Lang, Fritz, III 87
Laura, III 100
Maltese Falcon, III 249
Mildred Pierce, III 359
Perry Mason, IV 41
Preminger, Otto, IV 104
Robinson, Edward G., IV 229
Stanwyck, Barbara, IV 506
Sunset Boulevard, IV 579
Treasure of the Sierra Madre, IV 695
Webb, Jack, V 98

Film Production
Advertising, I 23
African Queen, I 33
Agents, I 34
Alien, I 48
All Quiet on the Western Front, I 52
Allen, Woody, I 53
Altman, Robert, I 63
American Graffiti, I 69
American International Pictures, I 71
Andy Hardy, I 87
Animated Films, I 90
Arbuckle, Fatty, I 107
''B'' movies, I 149
Beau Geste, I 207
Ben-Hur, I 219
Billboards, I 253
Blockbusters, I 280
Blue Velvet, I 286
Bogart, Humphrey, I 308
Capra, Frank, I 428
Casablanca, I 447
Chaplin, Charlie, I 475
Citizen Kane, I 514
City Lights, I 515
Civil Rights Movement, I 519
Cleopatra, I 529
Close Encounters of the Third Kind, I 534
Corman, Roger, I 603
Cousteau, Jacques, I 621
Day the Earth Stood Still, I 665
Devo, I 696
Disaster Movies, I 723
Disney (Walt Disney Company), I 728

Drive-In Theater, I 769
Duvall, Robert, I 778
E.T. The Extra-Terrestrial, II 43
Exorcist, II 50
Factor, Max, II 54
Fan Magazines, II 64
Film Noir, II 99
French Connection, II 164
From Here to Eternity, II 175
Gibson, Mel, II 234
Goldwyn, Samuel, II 260
Gordy, Berry, II 272
Great Train Robbery, II 297
Greed, II 298
Griffith, D. W., II 313
Halloween, II 346
Hanna-Barbera, II 355
Henson, Jim, II 393
Hollywood, II 431
How the West Was Won, II 458
Hughes, Howard, II 464
It Happened One Night, II 504
It's a Wonderful Life, II 506
Jaws, II 526
Jazz Singer, II 531
King Kong, III 30
Ladd, Alan, III 75
Lancaster, Burt, III 85
Lang, Fritz, III 87
Lee, Spike, III 122
Loos, Anita, III 194
Lucas, George, III 209
Made-for-Television Movies, III 233
Magnificent Seven, III 240
Mayer, Louis B., III 309
McCoy, Horace, III 319
Meet Me in St. Louis, III 339
Metropolis, III 347
MGM (Metro-Goldwyn-Mayer), III 347
Natural Born Killers, III 493
Nickelodeons, III 530
Olivier, Laurence, III 556
Peep Shows, IV 30
Photoplay, IV 53
Poitier, Sidney, IV 75
Potter, Dennis, IV 102
Psycho, IV 130
Raiders of the Lost Ark, IV 166
Redford, Robert, IV 190
Retro Fashion, IV 205
Schindler's List, IV 324
Schnabel, Julian, IV 327
Scream, IV 341
Selznick, David O., IV 356
Sennett, Mack, IV 357
Silent Movies, IV 393
Siskel and Ebert, IV 417
Snow White and the Seven Dwarfs, IV 445
Some Like It Hot, IV 453
Spaghetti Westerns, IV 467
Spartacus, IV 468
Spielberg, Steven, IV 476
Stagecoach, IV 497
Star System, IV 507
Star Wars, IV 511
Steamboat Willie, IV 521
Stone, Oliver, IV 543
Studio System, IV 565
Sundance Film Festival, IV 576
Taxi Driver, IV 611
Teenagers, IV 620
Ten Commandments, IV 634
Terminator, IV 639
Three Caballeros, IV 650
Toys, IV 685
Twenties, IV 710
United Artists, V 8
Variety, V 31
Vertigo, V 42
Warhol, Andy, V 80
Wild Bunch, V 133
Wilder, Billy, V 136

Wizard of Oz, V 162
Wood, Ed, V 172
Zanuck, Darryl F., V 225

Folk Music
Baez, Joan, I 156
Belafonte, Harry, I 214
Bluegrass, I 287
Byrds, I 402
Copland, Aaron, I 600
Country Gentlemen, I 617
Croce, Jim, I 634
Denver, John, I 686
Donovan, I 745
Dylan, Bob, I 780
Feliciano, José, II 82
Foggy Mountain Boys, II 122
Folk Music, II 123
Folkways Records, II 126
Griffith, Nanci, II 315
Guthrie, Arlo, II 328
Guthrie, Woody, II 328
Hopkins, Sam "Lightnin'," II 447
Ives, Burl, II 508
King, Carole, III 29
Kingston Trio, III 39
Macon, Uncle Dave, III 229
Mamas and the Papas, III 251
Mariachi Music, III 270
Mitchell, Joni, III 379
Monroe, Bill, III 396
Murray, Anne, III 447
Newport Jazz and Folk Festivals, III 526
Ochs, Phil, III 549
Peter, Paul, and Mary, IV 42
Rock and Roll, IV 235
Rodgers, Jimmie, IV 258
Seeger, Pete, IV 351
Selena, IV 354
Simon and Garfunkel, IV 399
Simon, Paul, IV 403
Springsteen, Bruce, IV 491
Taylor, James, IV 615
Tejano Music, IV 623
Weavers, V 96
Winston, George, V 156
Young, Neil, V 217

Foodways
Bagels, I 158
Barbecue, I 168
Bazooka Joe, I 194
Beer, I 210
Better Homes and Gardens, I 238
Betty Crocker, I 241
Burger King, I 387
Child, Julia, I 496
Chun King, I 509
Civil Rights Movement, I 519
Coca-Cola, I 540
Coffee, I 546
Dieting, I 706
Dime Stores/Woolworth's, I 717
Diners, I 719
Dunkin' Donuts, I 775
Fast Food, II 71
Foreman, George, II 138
French Fries, II 165
Frozen Entrées, II 178
Good Housekeeping, II 265
Grits, II 319
Hamburger, II 347
Hot Dogs, II 454
Ice Cream Cone, II 483
Jell-O, II 537
Joy of Cooking, II 572
Kentucky Fried Chicken, III 20
Laetrile, III 76
Macfadden, Bernarr, III 226
Madden, John, III 232
McDonald's, III 321
Pepsi-Cola, IV 36
Pizza, IV 62

Popsicles, IV 88
Soda Fountains, IV 452
State Fairs, IV 518
Stuckey's, IV 560
Tang, IV 603
Trillin, Calvin, IV 697
TV Dinners, IV 706
Velveeta Cheese, V 39
White Castle, V 127

Football
Albert, Marv, I 40
Bradshaw, Terry, I 339
Brown, Jim, I 369
Brown, Paul, I 370
Bryant, Paul "Bear," I 374
Butkus, Dick, I 399
Chicago Bears, I 492
College Football, I 555
Cosell, Howard, I 608
Dallas Cowboys, I 654
Didrikson, Babe, I 704
Ditka, Mike, I 731
Elway, John, II 25
Free Agency, II 160
Gifford, Frank, II 236
Green Bay Packers, II 300
Halas, George "Papa Bear," II 342
Landry, Tom, III 87
Lombardi, Vince, III 185
Monday Night Football, III 393
Montana, Joe, III 402
Naismith, James, III 470
Namath, Joe, III 471
National Collegiate Athletic Association
(NCAA), III 479
National Football League (NFL), III 482
Oakland Raiders, III 547
Payton, Walter, IV 23
Pittsburgh Steelers, IV 61
Professional Football, IV 116
Rice, Jerry, IV 209
Rockne, Knute, IV 243
Rose Bowl, IV 275
Sanders, Barry, IV 307
Shula, Don, IV 391
Simpson, O. J., IV 404
Soldier Field, IV 453
Sports Hero, IV 484
Stagg, Amos Alonzo, IV 499
Starr, Bart, IV 515
Staubach, Roger, IV 520
Steel Curtain, IV 521
Super Bowl, IV 579
Swann, Lynn, IV 588
Thorpe, Jim, IV 649
Unitas, Johnny, V 6
Williams, Hank, Jr., V 141
World Cup, V 181

Gambling
Atlantic City, I 133
Gambling, II 188
Kentucky Derby, III 19
Lansky, Meyer, III 90
Las Vegas, III 92
Lottery, III 199
Mafia/Organized Crime, III 237
Mah-Jongg, III 242
Siegel, Bugsy, IV 392
Super Bowl, IV 579

Gender Issues
Abortion, I 9
Acker, Kathy, I 16
Addams, Jane, I 17
Advice Columns, I 26
Alice, I 47
Alien, I 48
Ally McBeal, I 57
American Girls Series, I 67
Androgyny, I 85
Anita Hill-Clarence Thomas Senate
Hearings, I 93

Another World, I 99
Argosy, I 109
Baby Boomers, I 151
Barbie, I 171
Basketball, I 186
Bathhouses, I 188
Betty Boop, I 239
Bicycling, I 245
Birthing Practices, I 260
Blues, I 290
Blume, Judy, I 294
Bly, Robert, I 296
Bobby Socks, I 301
Boston Marathon, I 323
Bow, Clara, I 326
Bowie, David, I 328
Boy Scouts of America, I 333
Bra, I 335
Breast Implants, I 347
Cagney and Lacey, I 409
Camp, I 415
Camping, I 417
Castro, I 454
Cathy, I 460
Cheerleading, I 486
Child, Julia, I 496
Circus, I 512
Clairol Hair Coloring, I 523
Consciousness Raising Groups, I 585
Consumerism, I 589
Cosmopolitan, I 610
Crumb, Robert, I 641
Cukor, George, I 643
Debutantes, I 680
Deer Hunter, I 681
DeMille, Cecil B., I 683
Department Stores, I 688
Dieting, I 706
Dietrich, Marlene, I 708
Divine, I 731
Donahue, Phil, I 744
Dracula, I 760
Drag, I 762
Duncan, Isadora, I 773
Eddy, Mary Baker, II 11
Equal Rights Amendment, II 32
Esquire, II 40
Etiquette Columns, II 44
Family Circle, II 59
Fatal Attraction, II 74
Feminism, II 84
Field, Sally, II 94
Flappers, II 112
Flynn, Errol, II 121
Franklin, Bonnie, II 156
Freud, Sigmund, II 166
Friday, Nancy, II 169
Gay and Lesbian Marriage, II 208
Gay and Lesbian Press, II 210
Gentlemen Prefer Blondes, II 223
Gibson Girl, II 233
Girl Groups, II 240
Girl Scouts, II 242
Gish, Dorothy, II 243
Gish, Lillian, II 244
Glitter Rock, II 247
Golden Girls, II 260
Good Housekeeping, II 265
Great Depression, II 295
Grier, Pam, II 312
Halloween, II 346
Harlequin Romances, II 367
Hellman, Lillian, II 384
Hite, Shere, II 416
Home Improvement, II 437
Hurston, Zora Neale, II 469
Hustler, II 470
I Dream of Jeannie, II 475
James Bond Films, II 523
Judy Bolton, II 578
Kate & Allie, III 7
King, Billie Jean, III 28

Kingston, Maxine Hong, III 39
Kinsey, Dr. Alfred C., III 40
Krantz, Judith, III 60
Labor Unions, III 72
Lang, k.d., III 88
Lauper, Cyndi, III 99
Laverne and Shirley, III 103
Le Guin, Ursula K., III 107
League of Their Own, III 110
Lesbianism, III 140
López, Nancy, III 194
Loy, Myrna, III 207
Lynn, Loretta, III 218
Mabley, Moms, III 223
Madonna, III 235
Mapplethorpe, Robert, III 265
Mary Kay Cosmetics, III 290
Mary Tyler Moore Show, III 292
Maude, III 306
McCall's Magazine, III 313
McEntire, Reba, III 325
Men's Movement, III 344
Mildred Pierce, III 359
Millay, Edna St. Vincent, III 363
Miss America Pageant, III 374
Montana, Patsy, III 403
Morrison, Toni, III 414
Ms., III 434
Multiculturalism, III 439
Murphy Brown, III 446
Muscular Christianity, III 456
Nancy Drew, III 473
Nation, III 476
National Collegiate Athletic Association
    (NCAA), III 479
National Organization for Women
    (N.O.W.), III 489
Naylor, Gloria, III 495
New Look, III 512
Novak, Kim, III 543
O'Keeffe, Georgia, III 552
Olsen, Tillie, III 558
Olympics, III 558
Outing, III 580
Paglia, Camille, IV 4
Pants for Women, IV 7
Paretsky, Sara, IV 12
Phone Sex, IV 51
Pill, IV 57
Pin-Up, IV 58
Plath, Sylvia, IV 68
Playboy, IV 70
Playgirl, IV 72
Pointer Sisters, IV 74
Political Correctness, IV 78
Pornography, IV 92
Preminger, Otto, IV 104
Prince, IV 112
Prom, IV 120
Promise Keepers, IV 122
Protest Groups, IV 124
Queen Latifah, IV 150
Reed, Donna, IV 191
Riggs, Bobby, IV 211
Rodeo, IV 252
Rodman, Dennis, IV 259
Roe v. Wade, IV 260
Russell, Rosalind, IV 293
Salt-n-Pepa, IV 305
Sassy, IV 313
Schlessinger, Dr. Laura, IV 326
Seventeen, IV 364
Sex and the Single Girl, IV 366
Sexual Harassment, IV 371
Sexual Revolution, IV 373
Shaft, IV 376
Sherman, Cindy, IV 383
Shirelles, IV 384
Silent Movies, IV 393
Singles Bars, IV 415
Slaney, Mary Decker, IV 433
Slasher Movies, IV 435

Soap Operas, IV 446
Sports Illustrated, IV 487
Steinem, Gloria, IV 524
Student Demonstrations, IV 560
Tarbell, Ida, IV 606
Taxi Driver, IV 611
Tennis, IV 635
Tootsie, IV 678
Tupperware, IV 700
Twenties, IV 710
Underground Comics, V 4
Updike, John, V 10
Valium, V 20
Varga Girl, V 30
Vogue, V 53
Walker, Alice, V 61
Walker, Madame C. J., V 65
Wallace, Sippie, V 68
Wayne, John, V 91
Western, V 118
Wilson, Flip, V 148
Wonder Woman, V 171
World's Fairs, V 194
Xena, Warrior Princess, V 203

Health/Medicine
AARP (American Association for Retired
    Persons), I 3
Acupuncture, I 16
Aerobics, I 30
AIDS, I 35
Alka Seltzer, I 49
Atlas, Charles, I 135
Ben Casey, I 218
Birthing Practices, I 260
Bodybuilding, I 305
Bomb, I 311
Breast Implants, I 347
Cancer, I 418
Carpenters, I 440
Cigarettes, I 510
Cocaine/Crack, I 542
Condoms, I 578
Coué, Emile, I 615
Depression, I 690
Dieting, I 706
Eddy, Mary Baker, II 11
Ellis, Perry, II 25
Facelifts, II 54
Freud, Sigmund, II 166
Gray Panthers, II 294
Gregory, Dick, II 307
Grimek, John, II 316
Grizzard, Lewis, II 319
Gymnastics, II 331
Herpes, II 399
Indian, II 487
Laetrile, III 76
Lewis, Jerry, III 152
Lindbergh, Charles, III 166
London, Jack, III 187
Macfadden, Bernarr, III 226
Marcus Welby, M.D., III 269
Marlboro Man, III 274
Maupin, Armistead, III 307
Medicine Shows, III 339
Murray, Lenda, III 451
Muscle Beach, III 453
Pill, IV 57
Plastic Surgery, IV 67
Polio, IV 76
Popular Psychology, IV 90
Prozac, IV 125
Reeves, Steve, IV 193
Roe v. Wade, IV 260
Safe Sex, IV 299
Sandow, Eugen, IV 309
SIDS (Sudden Infant Death Syndrome), IV 391
Special Olympics, IV 470
Spock, Dr. Benjamin, IV 480
Stockton, ''Pudgy,'' IV 541
Tanning, IV 603
Twelve-Step Programs, IV 708

Ulcers, V 3
Valium, V 20
Viagra, V 43
Vitamins, V 52
Wertham, Fredric, V 111

Heavy Metal
AC/DC, I 14
Androgyny, I 85
Black Sabbath, I 265
Dead Kennedys, I 675
Electric Guitar, II 21
Grunge, II 321
Heavy Metal, II 380
Iron Maiden, II 501
Judas Priest, II 577
KISS, III 42
Led Zeppelin, III 116
Mötley Crüe, III 418
Nirvana, III 538
Osbourne, Ozzy, III 575
Pop Music, IV 83
Steppenwolf, IV 527
Van Halen, V 26
Whisky A Go Go, V 123

Heroes
Aaron, Hank, I 2
Ali, Muhammad, I 44
Arthurian Legend, I 120
Ashe, Arthur, I 123
Batman, I 189
Bionic Woman, I 255
Black Mask, I 263
Bryant, Paul ''Bear,'' I 374
Buck Rogers, I 377
Captain America, I 429
Captain Marvel, I 432
Comic Books, I 560
Comics, I 562
Dallas Cowboys, I 654
Daredevil, the Man Without Fear, I 659
Davy Crockett, I 663
Dempsey, Jack, I 685
Dick Tracy, I 702
DiMaggio, Joe, I 715
Doc Savage, I 738
Fantastic Four, II 67
Forrest Gump, II 140
Green Lantern, II 302
Greenberg, Hank, II 302
Hemingway, Ernest, II 386
Hercules: The Legendary Journeys, II 397
Heston, Charlton, II 399
Hughes, Howard, II 464
Iacocca, Lee, II 480
Incredible Hulk, II 486
Jackson, Reggie, II 519
King, Martin Luther, Jr., III 33
Lindbergh, Charles, III 166
Lone Ranger, III 189
Malcolm X, III 243
Mantle, Mickey, III 262
Marvel Comics, III 285
McGwire, Mark, III 326
Mix, Tom, III 383
NASA, III 475
Olympics, III 558
Punisher, IV 142
Rambo, IV 170
Rockne, Knute, IV 243
Ruth, Babe, IV 293
Searchers, IV 346
She Wore a Yellow Ribbon, IV 381
Silver Surfer, IV 399
Spider-Man, IV 474
Spitz, Mark, IV 479
Sports Hero, IV 484
Stone, Irving, IV 542
Superman, IV 581
Thomson, Bobby, IV 647
Unitas, Johnny, V 6
Wayne, John, V 91

Western, V 118
Wonder Woman, V 171
World Series, V 182
Yastrzemski, Carl, V 212
Zorro, V 234

High Culture
Abstract Expressionism, I 11
Academy Awards, I 12
Allen, Woody, I 53
Armory Show, I 112
Ashcan School, I 122
Atlantic Monthly, I 134
Balanchine, George, I 161
Ballet, I 165
Boston Symphony Orchestra, I 325
Brideshead Revisited, I 348
Bridge, I 349
Carnegie Hall, I 439
Caruso, Enrico, I 446
Celebrity Caricature, I 465
City of Angels, I 516
Duncan, Isadora, I 773
Existentialism, II 50
Fadiman, Clifton, II 55
Freud, Sigmund, II 166
Hemingway, Ernest, II 386
Higginson, Major Henry Lee, II 400
Kitsch, III 43
Lichtenstein, Roy, III 158
Lincoln Center for the Performing Arts, III 165
Little Magazines, III 176
Mass Market Magazine Revolution, III 299
Masterpiece Theatre, III 302
Minimalism, III 369
Modern Dance, III 388
Modernism, III 390
Multiculturalism, III 439
New Yorker, III 522
Objectivism/Ayn Rand, III 547
Olivier, Laurence, III 556
Onassis, Jacqueline Lee Bouvier Kennedy, III 564
Paglia, Camille, IV 4
Paperbacks, IV 9
Picasso, Pablo, IV 54
Plath, Sylvia, IV 68
Postmodernism, IV 98
Public Television (PBS), IV 135
Smithsonian Institution, IV 441
Studio One, IV 563
Times Square, IV 659
Vogue, V 53
Works Progress Administration (WPA) Murals, V 179

Hockey
Disney (Walt Disney Company), I 728
Free Agency, II 160
Gretzky, Wayne, II 308
Hockey, II 417
Howe, Gordie, II 460
Hull, Bobby, II 467
National Hockey League (NHL), III 485
1980 U.S. Olympic Hockey Team, III 536
Orr, Bobby, III 574

Holidays
Christmas, I 503
Church Socials, I 509
Father's Day, II 76
Fourth of July Celebrations, II 146
Frosty the Snowman, II 178
Greeting Cards, II 306
Halloween, II 346
Hope, Bob, II 446
It's a Wonderful Life, II 506
Mardi Gras, III 269
Mother's Day, III 417
Parades, IV 12
Rudolph the Red-Nosed Reindeer, IV 287
Thanksgiving, IV 640
Toys, IV 685
Valentine's Day, V 16

Homosexuality
ABBA, I 4
Addams, Jane, I 17
Advocate, I 29
AIDS, I 35
Androgyny, I 85
Another World, I 99
Athletic Model Guild, I 132
Baldwin, James, I 161
Bathhouses, I 188
Blueboy, I 287
Broadway, I 356
Camp, I 415
Capote, Truman, I 426
Castro, I 454
Cherry Ames, I 491
Clift, Montgomery, I 529
Closet, I 536
Coming Out, I 566
Condoms, I 578
Days of Our Lives, I 666
Dean, James, I 676
DeGeneres, Ellen, I 682
Dieting, I 706
Dietrich, Marlene, I 708
Disco, I 726
Dracula, I 760
Drag, I 762
Dykes to Watch Out For, I 780
El Teatro Campesino, II 18
Fierstein, Harvey, II 96
Garland, Judy, II 202
Gay and Lesbian Marriage, II 208
Gay and Lesbian Press, II 210
Gay Liberation Movement, II 211
Gay Men, II 215
Glitter Rock, II 247
Hair, II 338
Hate Crimes, II 373
Hoover, J. Edgar, II 443
Hudson, Rock, II 462
Hunter, Tab, II 468
In Living Color, II 486
International Male Catalog, II 494
John, Elton, II 550
Joy of Sex, II 573
King, Billie Jean, III 28
Lawrence of Arabia, III 104
Leone, Sergio, III 136
Leopold and Loeb, III 138
Lesbianism, III 140
Liberace, III 155
Mapplethorpe, Robert, III 265
Masters and Johnson, III 303
Maupin, Armistead, III 307
Midnight Cowboy, III 357
Milk, Harvey, III 361
Outing, III 580
Paperbacks, IV 9
Pin-Up, IV 58
Preminger, Otto, IV 104
Prom, IV 120
Queer Nation, IV 150
Rainey, Gertrude "Ma," IV 168
Rodeo, IV 252
RuPaul, IV 289
Seduction of the Innocent, IV 350
Sexual Revolution, IV 373
Spartacus, IV 468
Stonewall Rebellion, IV 544
Streisand, Barbra, IV 556
Summer, Donna, IV 575
Tom of Finland, IV 673
Vampires, V 22
Vidal, Gore, V 45
Williams, Tennessee, V 146

Horror, Film
Addams Family, I 18
American International Pictures, I 71
Barker, Clive, I 174
Benchley, Robert, I 219
Blob, I 280

Crawford, Joan, I 625
Cult Films, I 643
Dracula, I 760
Exorcist, II 50
Frankenstein, II 152
Freaks, II 159
Friday the 13th, II 170
Great Depression, II 295
Halloween, II 346
Hitchcock, Alfred, II 414
Horror Movies, II 450
I Was a Teenage Werewolf, II 480
Karloff, Boris, III 4
King, Stephen, III 36
Lorre, Peter, III 195
Lugosi, Bela, III 213
Mummy, III 441
Night of the Living Dead, III 532
Price, Vincent, IV 110
Psycho, IV 130
Rocky Horror Picture Show, IV 248
Rosemary's Baby, IV 279
Scream, IV 341
Slasher Movies, IV 435
Them!, IV 641
Thing, IV 642
Vampires, V 22
Wolfman, V 167
Wood, Ed, V 172

Horror, Print
Barker, Clive, I 174
Bestsellers, I 236
Comics, I 562
Dark Shadows, I 659
Derleth, August, I 692
Dracula, I 760
EC Comics, II 9
Frankenstein, II 152
Inner Sanctum Mysteries, II 493
Jackson, Shirley, II 520
King, Stephen, III 36
Koontz, Dean R., III 53
Lovecraft, H. P., III 205
Mummy, III 441
Pulp Magazines, IV 139
Stine, R. L., IV 535
Tales from the Crypt, IV 600
Vampires, V 22
Weird Tales, V 103

Horror, Television
Addams Family, I 18
Dark Shadows, I 659
Made-for-Television Movies, III 233
Vampires, V 22

Humor, Print
Angell, Roger, I 88
Barry, Dave, I 177
Benchley, Robert, I 219
Blount, Roy, Jr., I 285
Bombeck, Erma, I 314
Comics, I 562
Hirschfeld, Albert, II 412
Judge, II 577
Krassner, Paul, III 61
Linkletter, Art, III 168
Martin, Steve, III 282
Mr. Dooley, III 430
National Lampoon, III 487
Rogers, Will, IV 263
Shulman, Max, IV 391
Tijuana Bibles, IV 656
Vonnegut, Kurt, Jr., V 56
White, E. B., V 127
Winnie Winkle the Breadwinner, V 156

Jazz
Ace, Johnny, I 15
Adderley, Cannonball, I 18
Armstrong, Louis, I 114
Band, I 167
Basie, Count, I 184

Beiderbecke, Bix, I 214
Bennett, Tony, I 221
Big Bands, I 247
Bluegrass, I 287
Blues, I 290
Brubeck, Dave, I 372
Calloway, Cab, I 412
Carmichael, Hoagy, I 436
Castle, Vernon and Irene, I 454
Charles, Ray, I 477
Chicago Jazz, I 493
Cole, Nat ''King,'' I 552
Coltrane, John, I 557
Copland, Aaron, I 600
Cotton Club, I 614
Davis, Miles, I 661
Dixieland, I 734
Domino, Fats, I 743
Dorsey, Jimmy, I 750
Dorsey, Tommy, I 751
Eckstine, Billy, II 10
Ellington, Duke, II 23
Ertegun, Ahmet, II 35
Fitzgerald, Ella, II 107
Flappers, II 112
Funk, II 184
Gillespie, Dizzy, II 236
Goodman, Benny, II 270
Gospel Music, II 274
Grusin, Dave, II 322
Guaraldi, Vince, II 323
Hancock, Herbie, II 350
Hawkins, Coleman, II 376
Henderson, Fletcher, II 390
Hep Cats, II 393
Herman, Woody, II 398
Holiday, Billie, II 427
Horne, Lena, II 449
Hutton, Ina Ray, II 472
Jazz, II 529
Jazz Singer, II 531
Jolson, Al, II 559
Jordan, Louis, II 568
Juke Boxes, II 579
Kansas City Jazz, III 2
King, B. B., III 26
Krupa, Gene, III 63
Latin Jazz, III 97
Lee, Peggy, III 121
Mancini, Henry, III 256
Manhattan Transfer, III 257
Mathis, Johnny, III 305
Mitchell, Joni, III 379
Morton, Jelly Roll, III 416
Newport Jazz and Folk Festivals, III 526
Original Dixieland Jass (Jazz) Band, III 573
Parker, Charlie, IV 13
Paul, Les, IV 20
Pointer Sisters, IV 74
Puente, Tito, IV 137
Race Music, IV 155
Rhythm and Blues, IV 206
Savoy Ballroom, IV 322
Shaw, Artie, IV 381
Smith, Bessie, IV 439
Social Dancing, IV 450
Tap Dancing, IV 605
Twenties, IV 710
Vaughan, Sarah, V 36
Walker, Aaron ''T-Bone,'' V 59
Webb, Chick, V 98
Whiteman, Paul, V 130

Leading Ladies
Annie Hall, I 98
Astaire, Fred, and Ginger Rogers, I 127
Bacall, Lauren, I 154
Ball, Lucille, I 163
Bara, Theda, I 168
Bergen, Candice, I 224
Bergman, Ingrid, I 226
Bionic Woman, I 255
Bow, Clara, I 326

Celebrity, I 463
Cleopatra, I 529
Colbert, Claudette, I 548
Crawford, Joan, I 625
Davis, Bette, I 661
Day, Doris, I 664
Dickinson, Angie, I 703
Dietrich, Marlene, I 708
Dunne, Irene, I 776
Fawcett, Farrah, II 79
Field, Sally, II 94
Foster, Jodie, II 145
Garbo, Greta, II 199
Gardner, Ava, II 200
Garland, Judy, II 202
Gish, Lillian, II 244
Grable, Betty, II 277
Harlow, Jean, II 370
Hayward, Susan, II 377
Hayworth, Rita, II 377
Hello, Dolly!, II 384
Hepburn, Audrey, II 394
Hepburn, Katharine, II 394
Horne, Lena, II 449
Hunt, Helen, II 468
Jones, Jennifer, II 562
Kelly, Grace, III 15
Lamarr, Hedy, III 82
Lombard, Carole, III 184
LuPone, Patti, III 216
MacDonald, Jeanette, III 224
MGM (Metro-Goldwyn-Mayer), III 347
Miranda, Carmen, III 373
Monroe, Marilyn, III 399
Pickford, Mary, IV 55
Roberts, Julia, IV 223
Ryder, Winona, IV 298
Sex Symbol, IV 369
Stanwyck, Barbara, IV 506
Star System, IV 507
Streep, Meryl, IV 552
Streisand, Barbra, IV 556
Taylor, Elizabeth, IV 612
Thomas, Marlo, IV 645
Turner, Lana, IV 703
Walker, Aida Overton, V 61
Waters, Ethel, V 86
Weaver, Sigourney, V 96
West, Mae, V 115

Leading Men
Andy Hardy, I 87
Astaire, Fred, and Ginger Rogers, I 127
Barrymore, John, I 178
Beatty, Warren, I 206
Benny, Jack, I 222
Bogart, Humphrey, I 308
Brando, Marlon, I 342
Bronson, Charles, I 360
Brynner, Yul, I 375
Cagney, James, I 409
Celebrity, I 463
Cleopatra, I 529
Clift, Montgomery, I 529
Cooper, Gary, I 597
Cotten, Joseph, I 613
De Niro, Robert, I 673
Dean, James, I 676
DiCaprio, Leonardo, I 700
Duvall, Robert, I 778
Eddy, Nelson, II 13
Fairbanks, Douglas, Jr., II 55
Fairbanks, Douglas, Sr., II 57
Flynn, Errol, II 121
Fonda, Henry, II 127
Ford, Glenn, II 131
Ford, Harrison, II 131
Gable, Clark, II 187
Garfield, John, II 201
Gibson, Mel, II 234
Gone with the Wind, II 263
Grant, Cary, II 288
Hackman, Gene, II 334

Heston, Charlton, II 399
Holden, William, II 426
Hudson, Rock, II 462
Hunter, Tab, II 468
Ladd, Alan, III 75
Lancaster, Burt, III 85
MacMurray, Fred, III 228
Marcus Welby, M.D., III 269
Martin, Dean, III 280
McQueen, Steve, III 333
MGM (Metro-Goldwyn-Mayer), III 347
Mitchum, Robert, III 381
Mix, Tom, III 383
Pacino, Al, IV 3
Peck, Gregory, IV 29
Powell, William, IV 102
Presley, Elvis, IV 105
Price, Vincent, IV 110
Redford, Robert, IV 190
Reynolds, Burt, IV 205
Scott, George C., IV 338
Sex Symbol, IV 369
Stagecoach, IV 497
Stallone, Sylvester, IV 500
Star System, IV 507
Stewart, Jimmy, IV 532
Taylor, Robert, IV 615
Ten Commandments, IV 634
Tracy, Spencer, IV 687
Travolta, John, IV 694
Valentino, Rudolph, V 17
Van Dyke, Dick, V 24
Washington, Denzel, V 82
Wayne, John, V 91

Legends/Myths
Arthurian Legend, I 120
Bigfoot, I 251
Civil Rights Movement, I 519
Davy Crockett, I 663
Dr. Jekyll and Mr. Hyde, I 756
Frankenstein, II 152
Gunsmoke, II 326
Lansky, Meyer, III 90
Lovecraft, H. P., III 205
Ripley's Believe It Or Not, IV 215
Roswell Incident, IV 282
Spartacus, IV 468
UFOs (Unidentified Flying Objects), V 1
Weird Tales, V 103

Leisure
Aerobics, I 30
Amusement Parks, I 77
Atlantic City, I 133
Bathhouses, I 188
Book-of-the-Month Club, I 318
Borscht Belt, I 321
Bridge, I 349
Burma-Shave, I 390
Camping, I 417
Central Park, I 468
Church Socials, I 509
Circus, I 512
Coney Island, I 580
Consumerism, I 589
Cotton Club, I 614
Department Stores, I 688
Disney (Walt Disney Company), I 728
Do-It-Yourself Improvement, I 742
Drive-In Theater, I 769
Electric Trains, II 22
Field and Stream, II 92
Fifties, II 96
Fischer, Bobby, II 104
Florida Vacations, II 119
Freak Shows, II 158
Frisbee, II 174
Harley-Davidson, II 368
Hiking, II 405
Jet Skis, II 545
Juke Boxes, II 579
La-Z-Boy Loungers, III 106

Leisure Time, III 128
Low Riders, III 206
Mah-Jongg, III 242
Martini, III 282
Me Decade, III 335
Movie Palaces, III 426
Muscle Beach, III 453
National Parks, III 489
Nickelodeons, III 530
Phonograph, IV 52
Postcards, IV 96
Rodeo, IV 252
Roller Coasters, IV 265
RV, IV 295
Saratoga Springs, IV 312
Seduction of the Innocent, IV 350
Singles Bars, IV 415
Soccer, IV 449
Spring Break, IV 488
Stereoscopes, IV 528
Stock-Car Racing, IV 537
Studio 54, IV 563
Summer Camp, IV 573
Surf Music, IV 585
Swimming Pools, IV 590
Tanning, IV 603
Times Square, IV 659
Trailer Parks, IV 689
Vanity Fair, V 28
Walkman, V 66
Wall Drug, V 66
Weekend, V 101
Zoos, V 230

Magazines
Advertising, I 23
Advocate, I 29
African American Press, I 32
Amazing Stories, I 64
American Mercury, I 72
Argosy, I 109
Arizona Highways, I 110
Asimov, Isaac, I 125
Astounding Science Fiction, I 129
Athletic Model Guild, I 132
Atlantic Monthly, I 134
Baker, Ray Stannard, I 159
Black Mask, I 263
Blueboy, I 287
Bodybuilding, I 305
Bok, Edward, I 310
Buckley, William F., Jr., I 379
Celebrity Caricature, I 465
Condé Nast, I 577
Confession Magazines, I 581
Cosmopolitan, I 610
Crisis, I 633
Crumb, Robert, I 641
Doc Savage, I 738
Ebony, II 7
Esquire, II 40
Family Circle, II 59
Fan Magazines, II 64
Field and Stream, II 92
Fortune, II 142
Gay and Lesbian Press, II 210
Gernsback, Hugo, II 225
Gibson Girl, II 233
Good Housekeeping, II 265
Harper's, II 372
Hefner, Hugh, II 383
Hispanic Magazine, II 412
Hustler, II 470
Jet, II 544
Judge, II 577
Kewpie Dolls, III 22
Krassner, Paul, III 61
Liberty, III 157
Liebovitz, Annie, III 159
Life, III 160
Lippmann, Walter, III 170
Little Magazines, III 176
Luce, Henry, III 210

Macfadden, Bernarr, III 226
MAD Magazine, III 230
Mass Market Magazine Revolution, III 299
Masses, III 302
McCall's Magazine, III 313
McClure's, III 318
Modern Maturity, III 388
Modernism, III 390
Ms., III 434
Muckraking, III 438
Munsey's Magazine, III 442
Nation, III 476
National Geographic, III 484
National Lampoon, III 487
New Republic, III 514
New Yorker, III 522
Newsweek, III 527
Opportunity, III 570
Parrish, Maxfield, IV 16
Penthouse, IV 34
People, IV 35
Photoplay, IV 53
Playboy, IV 70
Playgirl, IV 72
Popular Mechanics, IV 89
Pornography, IV 92
Pulp Magazines, IV 139
Queen, Ellery, IV 148
Reader's Digest, IV 177
Redbook, IV 189
Rockwell, Norman, IV 244
Rolling Stone, IV 267
Sassy, IV 313
Saturday Evening Post, IV 315
Scientific American, IV 334
Scribner's, IV 344
Seventeen, IV 364
Smithsonian Institution, IV 441
Sporting News, IV 483
Sports Illustrated, IV 487
Steinem, Gloria, IV 524
Thompson, Hunter S., IV 646
Time, IV 657
True Detective, IV 699
True Story Magazine, IV 699
TV Guide, IV 706
Vanity Fair, V 28
Varga Girl, V 30
Variety, V 31
Vogue, V 53
Weird Tales, V 103
Woman's Day, V 169
Youth's Companion, V 222
Zines, V 228

Modernism
Anderson, Sherwood, I 83
Celebrity Caricature, I 465
Chrysler Building, I 507
Eames, Charles and Ray, II 1
Faulkner, William, II 77
Fitzgerald, F. Scott, II 109
Generation X, II 221
Industrial Design, II 491
Johns, Jasper, II 551
Krazy Kat, III 62
Lichtenstein, Roy, III 158
Minimalism, III 369
Minnelli, Vincente, III 370
Modern Times, III 389
Modernism, III 390
New Age Spirituality, III 507
O'Keeffe, Georgia, III 552
Picasso, Pablo, IV 54
Pollock, Jackson, IV 79
Postmodernism, IV 98
Schnabel, Julian, IV 327
Twenties, IV 710
Works Progress Administration (WPA)
    Murals, V 179
World Trade Center, V 184

Monsters
Addams Family, I 18
Alien, I 48
Bigfoot, I 251
Disaster Movies, I 723
Dracula, I 760
Frankenstein, II 152
Freak Shows, II 158
Halloween, II 346
Jurassic Park, II 581
King Kong, III 30
Mummy, III 441
Outer Limits, III 579
Thing, IV 642
Vampires, V 22
Weird Tales, V 103
Wolfman, V 167

Music Festivals
Allison, Luther, I 54
Altamont, I 57
Bluegrass, I 287
Crosby, Stills, and Nash, I 639
Donovan, I 745
Farm Aid, II 69
Graham, Bill, II 282
Hendrix, Jimi, II 391
Jazz, II 529
Jefferson Airplane/Starship, II 534
King, Albert, III 25
Lollapalooza, III 184
Newport Jazz and Folk Festivals, III 526
Vaudeville, V 33
Woodstock, V 176
Zydeco, V 235

Music Production
A&R Men/Women, I 1
Album-Oriented Rock, I 41
Allison, Luther, I 54
Alpert, Herb, and the Tijuana Brass, I 57
Anka, Paul, I 95
Atkins, Chet, I 132
Atlantic Records, I 135
Ballard, Hank, I 164
Bay, Mel, I 191
Berlin, Irving, I 230
Berry, Chuck, I 234
Big Bands, I 247
Blacklisting, I 272
Blues Brothers, I 293
Brill Building, I 351
Brown, James, I 367
Cars, I 442
Cline, Patsy, I 530
Compact Discs, I 575
Concept Album, I 576
Coniff, Ray, I 583
Contemporary Christian Music, I 591
Copland, Aaron, I 600
Devo, I 696
Disc Jockeys, I 725
Duvall, Robert, I 778
Eight-track Tape, II 16
Electric Guitar, II 21
Ertegun, Ahmet, II 35
Girl Groups, II 240
Goodman, Benny, II 270
Gordy, Berry, II 272
Graham, Bill, II 282
Grandmaster Flash, II 286
Grant, Amy, II 287
Grusin, Dave, II 322
Ice-T, II 485
Jennings, Waylon, II 540
Kansas City Jazz, III 2
Kern, Jerome, III 21
Latin Jazz, III 97
Lennon, John, III 131
Long-Playing Record, III 192
Los Lobos, III 197
Mancini, Henry, III 256
McEntire, Reba, III 325

Motown, III 420
MTV, III 435
New Kids on the Block, III 510
Osbourne, Ozzy, III 575
Paul, Les, IV 20
Phonograph, IV 52
Pop, Iggy, IV 82
Retro Fashion, IV 205
Robinson, Smokey, IV 233
Ross, Diana, and the Supremes, IV 280
Sly and the Family Stone, IV 437
Sondheim, Stephen, IV 454
Soul Music, IV 458
Sousa, John Philip, IV 463
Spector, Phil, IV 471
Sun Records, IV 576
Turner, Ike and Tina, IV 702
2 Live Crew, IV 715
Walker, Junior, and the All-Stars, V 63
Williams, Andy, V 139
Wonder, Stevie, V 169
Yanni, V 210

Musicals, Film
Annie, I 96
Annie Get Your Gun, I 96
Astaire, Fred, and Ginger Rogers, I 127
Baum, L. Frank, I 191
Berkeley, Busby, I 227
Crawford, Joan, I 625
Crosby, Bing, I 638
Day, Doris, I 664
Dunne, Irene, I 776
42nd Street, II 142
Fosse, Bob, II 143
Grable, Betty, II 277
Hayworth, Rita, II 377
Hello, Dolly!, II 384
Herman, Woody, II 398
Kelly, Gene, III 14
Lee, Gypsy Rose, III 119
Little Orphan Annie, III 177
Lloyd Webber, Andrew, III 181
MacDonald, Jeanette, III 224
Mancini, Henry, III 256
Martin, Dean, III 280
Meet Me in St. Louis, III 339
Miller, Roger, III 367
Minnelli, Vincente, III 370
Moreno, Rita, III 410
Musical, III 458
My Fair Lady, III 464
Patinkin, Mandy, IV 19
Peters, Bernadette, IV 44
Powell, Dick, IV 102
Presley, Elvis, IV 105
Rivera, Chita, IV 216
Rocky Horror Picture Show, IV 248
Rodgers and Hart, IV 256
Sheldon, Sidney, IV 381
Show Boat, IV 389
Singin' in the Rain, IV 415
Sound of Music, IV 462
South Pacific, IV 465
Talking Heads, IV 602
Temple, Shirley, IV 631
Vallee, Rudy, V 21
Waters, Ethel, V 86
Yankee Doodle Dandy, V 207

Musicals, Theatre
Annie, I 96
Annie Get Your Gun, I 96
Arthur, Bea, I 118
Astaire, Fred, and Ginger Rogers, I 127
Baryshnikov, Mikhail, I 180
Baum, L. Frank, I 191
Broadway, I 356
Camelot, I 414
Cantor, Eddie, I 423
Caruso, Enrico, I 446
Cats, I 460
Cohan, George M., I 548

Cole, Nat "King," I 552
Daly, Tyne, I 655
Fiddler on the Roof, II 90
42nd Street, II 142
Fosse, Bob, II 143
Grable, Betty, II 277
Hair, II 338
Hello, Dolly!, II 384
Horne, Lena, II 449
Hughes, Langston, II 465
Jesus Christ Superstar, II 543
Kern, Jerome, III 21
Lamour, Dorothy, III 83
Latin Jazz, III 97
Lee, Gypsy Rose, III 119
Les Miserables, III 139
Lewis, Jerry, III 152
Li'l Abner, III 163
Little Orphan Annie, III 177
LuPone, Patti, III 216
Mancini, Henry, III 256
Manilow, Barry, III 258
Marching Bands, III 267
Midler, Bette, III 356
Miller, Roger, III 367
Moreno, Rita, III 410
Musical, III 458
My Fair Lady, III 464
Noloesca, La Chata, III 540
Oklahoma!, III 553
Patinkin, Mandy, IV 19
Peanuts, IV 25
Peters, Bernadette, IV 44
Phantom of the Opera, IV 49
Prince, Hal, IV 114
Ragni, Gerome and James Rado, IV 166
Rigby, Cathy, IV 210
Rivera, Chita, IV 216
Rockettes, IV 241
Rocky Horror Picture Show, IV 248
Rodgers and Hammerstein, IV 254
Rodgers and Hart, IV 256
Runyon, Damon, IV 289
Show Boat, IV 389
Smith, Kate, IV 439
Sondheim, Stephen, IV 454
Sound of Music, IV 462
South Pacific, IV 465
Sunset Boulevard, IV 579
Talking Heads, IV 602
Tap Dancing, IV 605
Titanic, IV 661
Vallee, Rudy, V 21
Villella, Edward, V 52
Walker, George, V 62
Waters, Ethel, V 86
West Side Story, V 116
Ziegfeld Follies, V 227

New Wave Music
Cars, I 442
Devo, I 696
New Wave Music, III 515

News
Alternative Press, I 60
Arledge, Roone, I 111
Baker, Ray Stannard, I 159
Brinkley, David, I 352
Brokaw, Tom, I 359
CNN, I 537
Corwin, Norman, I 604
Cronkite, Walter, I 635
Diana, Princess of Wales, I 698
Freedom Rides, II 163
Great Depression, II 295
Gulf War, II 325
Jennings, Peter, II 538
Kaltenborn, Hans von, III 1
Ku Klux Klan, III 64
Lippmann, Walter, III 170
Live Television, III 178
Luce, Henry, III 210

Media Feeding Frenzies, III 337
My Lai Massacre, III 465
National Enquirer, III 480
Network, III 503
New York Times, III 518
Newsweek, III 527
Nightline, III 533
People, IV 35
Rather, Dan, IV 176
Rivera, Geraldo, IV 218
Shirer, William L., IV 384
60 Minutes, IV 425
Spin, IV 478
Tabloid Television, IV 597
Television, IV 626
Television Anchors, IV 629
Time, IV 657
Today, IV 666
Trout, Robert, IV 698
TV Guide, IV 706
20/20, IV 712
USA Today, V 11
Walters, Barbara, V 71
Washington Post, V 83
Wire Services, V 158

Newspapers
African American Press, I 32
Alternative Press, I 60
Cahan, Abraham, I 411
Comics, I 562
Doonesbury, I 747
Hearst, William Randolph, II 379
Kaltenborn, Hans von, III 1
Krazy Kat, III 62
Leopold and Loeb, III 138
Lippmann, Walter, III 170
London, Jack, III 187
Macfadden, Bernarr, III 226
Muckraking, III 438
Munsey's Magazine, III 442
National Enquirer, III 480
New York Times, III 518
Oliphant, Pat, III 555
Rice, Grantland, IV 209
Ripley's Believe It Or Not, IV 215
Royko, Mike, IV 285
Sporting News, IV 483
Steffens, Lincoln, IV 521
Tabloids, IV 597
Thompson, Hunter S., IV 646
USA Today, V 11
Variety, V 31
Wall Street Journal, V 67
Washington Post, V 83

Nonfiction Writers
Abbey, Edward, I 4
Anne Frank: The Diary of a Young Girl, I 95
Bach, Richard, I 155
Baker, Ray Stannard, I 159
Baldwin, James, I 161
Barry, Dave, I 177
Barton, Bruce, I 179
Bestsellers, I 236
Blume, Judy, I 294
Bly, Robert, I 296
Bouton, Jim, I 326
Bradley, Bill, I 338
Brokaw, Tom, I 359
Brothers, Dr. Joyce, I 367
Buckley, William F., Jr., I 379
Burroughs, William S., I 397
Capote, Truman, I 426
Clooney, Rosemary, I 533
Curious George, I 649
Darrow, Clarence, I 660
Derleth, August, I 692
Dillard, Annie, I 711
Disability, I 721
Doyle, Arthur Conan, I 755
Du Bois, W. E. B., I 771
Eddy, Mary Baker, II 11

Einstein, Albert, II 16
Friday, Nancy, II 169
GoodFellas, II 269
Greeley, Andrew, II 298
Hersey, John, II 399
Hite, Shere, II 416
Hubbard, L. Ron, II 461
Hughes, Langston, II 465
Kahn, Roger, III 1
King, Larry, III 32
Koontz, Dean R., III 53
Kosinski, Jerzy, III 56
Late Great Planet Earth, III 96
Least Heat Moon, William, III 114
Let Us Now Praise Famous Men, III 142
Lindbergh, Anne Morrow, III 166
Locke, Alain, III 182
London, Jack, III 187
Mailer, Norman, III 242
McKay, Claude, III 327
McLuhan, Marshall, III 329
Mencken, H. L., III 342
Merton, Thomas, III 345
Michener, James, III 351
Miller, Henry, III 367
Morrison, Toni, III 414
Objectivism/Ayn Rand, III 547
O'Rourke, P. J., III 573
Outline of History, III 581
Peale, Norman Vincent, IV 23
Reiner, Carl, IV 196
Roots, IV 273
Royko, Mike, IV 285
Sagan, Carl, IV 300
Sandburg, Carl, IV 306
Schlessinger, Dr. Laura, IV 326
Sex and the Single Girl, IV 366
Shirer, William L., IV 384
Steinbeck, John, IV 522
Steinem, Gloria, IV 524
Stratton-Porter, Gene, IV 550
Tarbell, Ida, IV 606
Thomas, Lowell, IV 645
Thompson, Hunter S., IV 646
Toffler, Alvin, IV 668
Trillin, Calvin, IV 697
Walker, Alice, V 61
Wolfe, Tom, V 166

Novelists
Abbey, Edward, I 4
Acker, Kathy, I 16
Adler, Renata, I 21
American Girls Series, I 67
Anderson, Sherwood, I 83
Anthony, Piers, I 100
Asimov, Isaac, I 125
Bach, Richard, I 155
Baldwin, James, I 161
Barker, Clive, I 174
Barry, Dave, I 177
Baum, L. Frank, I 191
Beach, Rex, I 197
Beat Generation, I 201
Benchley, Robert, I 219
Ben-Hur, I 219
Big Sleep, I 250
Black Mask, I 263
Blade Runner, I 273
Blume, Judy, I 294
Bobbsey Twins, I 300
Brand, Max, I 342
Brautigan, Richard, I 345
Buck, Pearl S., I 375
Buckley, William F., Jr., I 379
Burroughs, William S., I 397
Cahan, Abraham, I 411
Caldwell, Erskine, I 412
Capote, Truman, I 426
Catch-22, I 457
Catcher in the Rye, I 458
Cather, Willa, I 459
Chandler, Raymond, I 473

Chayefsky, Paddy, I 484
Christie, Agatha, I 502
Clarke, Arthur C., I 527
Crichton, Michael, I 631
Derleth, August, I 692
Dick, Philip K., I 701
Didion, Joan, I 704
Dillard, Annie, I 711
Doctorow, E. L., I 740
Doyle, Arthur Conan, I 755
Dreiser, Theodore, I 768
Du Bois, W. E. B., I 771
Eisner, Will, II 18
Elkins, Aaron, II 23
Ellis, Bret Easton, II 24
Erdrich, Louise, II 34
Faulkner, William, II 77
Fauset, Jessie Redmon, II 78
Fitzgerald, F. Scott, II 109
Fleming, Ian, II 116
Follett, Ken, II 127
Forsyth, Frederick, II 141
Friedman, Kinky, II 171
Gibson, William, II 235
Gold, Mike, II 255
Gone with the Wind, II 263
Goodbye, Columbus, II 268
Grapes of Wrath, II 290
Greeley, Andrew, II 298
Grey, Zane, II 309
Grisham, John, II 318
Hammett, Dashiell, II 349
Hellman, Lillian, II 384
Hemingway, Ernest, II 386
Hersey, John, II 399
Hess, Joan, II 399
Hijuelos, Oscar, II 405
Hillerman, Tony, II 407
Himes, Chester, II 408
Hite, Shere, II 416
Hubbard, L. Ron, II 461
Hughes, Langston, II 465
Hurston, Zora Neale, II 469
Invisible Man, II 498
Irving, John, II 504
Jackson, Shirley, II 520
Jakes, John, II 522
Jaws, II 526
Johnson, James Weldon, II 555
Kantor, MacKinlay, III 3
Keillor, Garrison, III 11
Kesey, Ken, III 22
Kingston, Maxine Hong, III 39
Koontz, Dean R., III 53
Kosinski, Jerzy, III 56
Kotzwinkle, William, III 56
Krantz, Judith, III 60
L'Amour, Louis, III 84
Le Carré, John, III 106
Le Guin, Ursula K., III 107
L'Engle, Madeleine, III 131
Leonard, Elmore, III 134
Levin, Meyer, III 145
Lewis, Sinclair, III 155
Lolita, III 183
London, Jack, III 187
Loos, Anita, III 194
Lovecraft, H. P., III 205
Ludlum, Robert, III 213
Mailer, Norman, III 242
Maus, III 308
McBain, Ed, III 312
McCoy, Horace, III 319
McKay, Claude, III 327
McMurtry, Larry, III 330
Metalious, Grace, III 346
Michener, James, III 351
Miller, Arthur, III 363
Mitchell, Margaret, III 380
Momaday, N. Scott, III 392
Morrison, Toni, III 414
Motely, Willard, III 419

Naylor, Gloria, III 495
Norris, Frank, III 540
Oates, Joyce Carol, III 547
Objectivism/Ayn Rand, III 547
O'Brien, Tim, III 548
O'Connor, Flannery, III 549
On the Road, III 561
Organization Man, III 572
Outline of History, III 581
Paley, Grace, IV 6
Paperbacks, IV 9
Paretsky, Sara, IV 12
Peyton Place, IV 47
Price, Reynolds, IV 110
Pynchon, Thomas, IV 145
Reed, Ishmael, IV 191
Robbins, Tom, IV 223
Robeson, Kenneth, IV 227
Science Fiction Publishing, IV 330
Sheldon, Sidney, IV 381
Shirer, William L., IV 384
Show Boat, IV 389
Shulman, Max, IV 391
Sinclair, Upton, IV 414
Singer, Isaac Bashevis, IV 414
Southern, Terry, IV 466
Spartacus, IV 468
Spillane, Mickey, IV 477
Steinbeck, John, IV 522
Stine, R. L., IV 535
Stone, Irving, IV 542
Stratton-Porter, Gene, IV 550
Styron, William, IV 567
Susann, Jacqueline, IV 586
Tarkington, Booth, IV 607
To Kill a Mockingbird, IV 663
Tolkien, J. R. R., IV 671
Trillin, Calvin, IV 697
Tyler, Anne, IV 718
Updike, John, V 10
Van Dine, S. S., V 24
Van Vechten, Carl, V 26
Vidal, Gore, V 45
Vonnegut, Kurt, Jr., V 56
Walker, Alice, V 61
Weird Tales, V 103
Wharton, Edith, V 121
Wilder, Laura Ingalls, V 136
Wilder, Thornton, V 138
Williams, Tennessee, V 146
Wister, Owen, V 161
Wodehouse, P. G., V 166
Wright, Richard, V 196

Performance Art
Androgyny, I 85
Baraka, Amiri, I 168
Blackface Minstrelsy, I 270
Butterbeans and Susie, I 400
Carnegie Hall, I 439
Condé Nast, I 577
El Vez, II 19
Fusco, Coco, II 185
Kaufman, Andy, III 7
Lang, k.d., III 88
Performance Art, IV 37
Sprinkle, Annie, IV 493
Ziegfeld Follies, V 227

Performance, Live
Farm Aid, II 69
Flagpole Sitting, II 111
Freak Shows, II 158
Houdini, Harry, II 456
Lee, Gypsy Rose, III 119
Osbourne, Ozzy, III 575
Ringling Bros., Barnum & Bailey Circus, IV 212
Sullivan, Ed, IV 570

Periodicals, Other
African American Press, I 32
Big Little Books, I 249
Comic Books, I 560
Consumer Reports, I 587

Etiquette Columns, II 44
Fan Magazines, II 64
Gay and Lesbian Press, II 210
Gossip Columns, II 275
Rolling Stone, IV 267
Shadow, IV 375
Sporting News, IV 483

Photography
Athletic Model Guild, I 132
Kodak, III 51
Let Us Now Praise Famous Men, III 142
Liebovitz, Annie, III 159
Life, III 160
Mapplethorpe, Robert, III 265
New Deal, III 508
Newton, Helmut, III 528
Penn, Irving, IV 33
Pin-Up, IV 58
Sherman, Cindy, IV 383
Stereoscopes, IV 528
Van Vechten, Carl, V 26

Places/Locations
Abstract Expressionism, I 11
Alaska-Yukon Exposition (Seattle, 1909), I 40
Altamont, I 57
American Museum of Natural History, I 72
Apollo Theatre, I 104
Atkins, Chet, I 132
Atlantic City, I 133
Beach Boys, I 195
Big Apple, I 246
Borscht Belt, I 321
Boston Garden, I 323
Buffett, Jimmy, I 382
Cadillac, I 406
Carnegie Hall, I 439
Castro, I 454
Cemeteries, I 467
Central Park, I 468
Century 21 Exposition (Seattle, 1962), I 470
Century of Progress International Exposition (Chicago, 1933), I 471
Chautauqua Institution, I 481
Chrysler Building, I 507
City of Angels, I 516
Communes, I 568
Coney Island, I 580
Consumerism, I 589
Cooperstown, New York, I 598
Coors, I 599
Cults, I 646
Department Stores, I 688
Ebbets Field, II 5
Eco-Terrorism, II 10
Empire State Building, II 28
Fallout Shelters, II 58
Faulkner, William, II 77
Fenway Park, II 87
Flea Markets, II 114
Frost, Robert, II 177
Gas Stations, II 206
Gated Communities, II 208
Golden Gate Bridge, II 259
Graceland, II 278
Greenwich Village, II 304
Grey, Zane, II 309
Haight-Ashbury, II 336
Harlem Renaissance, II 365
Jonestown, II 563
Key West, III 22
King, Rodney, III 34
Las Vegas, III 92
Latin Jazz, III 97
Lawn Care/Gardening, III 104
Least Heat Moon, William, III 114
Lincoln Center for the Performing Arts, III 165
L.L. Bean, Inc., III 180
Los Lobos, III 197
Magnum, P.I., III 241
Mall of America, III 245
Metalious, Grace, III 346

Metropolitan Museum of Art, III 347
Middletown, III 355
Mount Rushmore, III 423
Movie Palaces, III 426
Muscle Beach, III 453
My Lai Massacre, III 465
NASA, III 475
National Parks, III 489
Niagara Falls, III 528
Peppermint Lounge, IV 36
Public Libraries, IV 133
Rockettes, IV 241
Roller Coasters, IV 265
Saratoga Springs, IV 312
Savoy Ballroom, IV 322
Sea World, IV 345
Sears Tower, IV 347
Smithsonian Institution, IV 441
Soldier Field, IV 453
Stadium Concerts, IV 496
Starbucks, IV 514
State Fairs, IV 518
Stuckey's, IV 560
Studio 54, IV 563
Suburbia, IV 567
Times Square, IV 659
Trailer Parks, IV 689
U.S. One, V 11
Wall Drug, V 66
Washington Monument, V 83
Whisky A Go Go, V 123
Wimbledon, V 150
Windy City, V 152
Works Progress Administration (WPA) Murals, V 179
World Trade Center, V 184
World's Fairs, V 194
Wyeth, Andrew, V 199
Yellowstone National Park, V 213

Playwrights
Allen, Woody, I 53
Baldwin, James, I 161
Barker, Clive, I 174
Capote, Truman, I 426
Chayefsky, Paddy, I 484
Christie, Agatha, I 502
Cohan, George M., I 548
DeMille, Cecil B., I 683
Glass Menagerie, II 245
Hansberry, Lorraine, II 356
Hellman, Lillian, II 384
Lardner, Ring, III 90
L'Engle, Madeleine, III 131
Loos, Anita, III 194
Mamet, David, III 252
Millay, Edna St. Vincent, III 363
Miller, Arthur, III 363
O'Neill, Eugene, III 569
Porter, Cole, IV 95
Price, Reynolds, IV 110
Reed, Ishmael, IV 191
Serling, Rod, IV 361
Shepard, Sam, IV 382
Simon, Neil, IV 401
Steinbeck, John, IV 522
Stiller and Meara, IV 535
Streetcar Named Desire, IV 554
Sturges, Preston, IV 566
Tarkington, Booth, IV 607
Valdez, Luis, V 15
West, Mae, V 115
Wilder, Thornton, V 138
Williams, Tennessee, V 146

Poets
Baraka, Amiri, I 168
Beat Generation, I 201
Bly, Robert, I 296
Brautigan, Richard, I 345
Brooks, Gwendolyn, I 365
Cisneros, Sandra, I 513
Cullen, Countee, I 643

Dillard, Annie, I 711
Disability, I 721
Du Bois, W. E. B., I 771
Duncan, Isadora, I 773
Erdrich, Louise, II 34
Frost, Robert, II 177
Ginsberg, Allen, II 239
Hughes, Langston, II 465
Johnson, James Weldon, II 555
Le Guin, Ursula K., III 107
L'Engle, Madeleine, III 131
Mailer, Norman, III 242
McKay, Claude, III 327
McKuen, Rod, III 328
Merton, Thomas, III 345
Millay, Edna St. Vincent, III 363
Momaday, N. Scott, III 392
Oates, Joyce Carol, III 547
O'Keeffe, Georgia, III 552
Paley, Grace, IV 6
Plath, Sylvia, IV 68
Price, Reynolds, IV 110
Reed, Ishmael, IV 191
Sandburg, Carl, IV 306
Smith, Patti, IV 440
Stratton-Porter, Gene, IV 550
Updike, John, V 10
Valdez, Luis, V 15
White, E. B., V 127
Williams, Tennessee, V 146

Police/Law Enforcement
Barney Miller, I 176
Boston Strangler, I 324
Capone, Al, I 425
Chicago Seven, I 495
Darrow, Clarence, I 660
Dick Tracy, I 702
Dragnet, I 766
Eco-Terrorism, II 10
FBI (Federal Bureau of Investigation), II 80
Free Speech Movement, II 161
Freedom Rides, II 163
French Connection, II 164
Fugitive, II 179
Gangs, II 195
Guardian Angels, II 323
Hawaii Five-O, II 375
Hollywood Ten, II 434
Hoover, J. Edgar, II 443
King, Rodney, III 34
Koresh, David, and the Branch Davidians, III 54
Luciano, Lucky, III 212
Miranda Warning, III 373
Neighborhood Watch, III 499
NYPD Blue, III 545
Prohibition, IV 119
Serial Killers, IV 358
Simpson Trial, IV 405
2 Live Crew, IV 715
Webb, Jack, V 98

Political Activism
Abortion, I 9
Academy Awards, I 12
Addams, Jane, I 17
Altamont, I 57
Alternative Press, I 60
Angelou, Maya, I 89
Anita Hill-Clarence Thomas Senate Hearings, I 93
Ashe, Arthur, I 123
Asner, Edward, I 126
Baby Boomers, I 151
Baez, Joan, I 156
Baker, Ray Stannard, I 159
Baldwin, James, I 161
Baraka, Amiri, I 168
Black Panthers, I 264
Bly, Robert, I 296
Bra, I 335
Buck, Pearl S., I 375
Caldwell, Erskine, I 412

Chavez, Cesar, I 482
Chicago Seven, I 495
Chuck D, I 508
Civil Disobedience, I 517
Closet, I 536
Consciousness Raising Groups, I 585
Coughlin, Father Charles E., I 616
Dead Kennedys, I 675
Debs, Eugene V., I 679
Douglas, Melvyn I 753
Du Bois, W. E. B., I 771
Earth Day, II 1
El Teatro Campesino, II 18
El Vez, II 19
Environmentalism, II 29
Flag Burning, II 111
Fundamentalism, II 181
Gay Liberation Movement, II 211
Gold, Mike, II 255
Greenpeace, II 303
Gregory, Dick, II 307
Haight-Ashbury, II 336
Hellman, Lillian, II 384
Hoffman, Abbie, II 419
Huston, John, II 471
Jewish Defense League, II 545
John Birch Society, II 549
Kent State Massacre, III 17
King, Martin Luther, Jr., III 33
Krassner, Paul, III 61
Kudzu, III 66
Labor Unions, III 72
Lee, Spike, III 122
Lennon, John, III 131
Levin, Meyer, III 145
Mailer, Norman, III 242
Masses, III 302
McKay, Claude, III 327
Militias, III 359
Milk, Harvey, III 361
Million Man March, III 368
Mod Squad, III 385
Moral Majority, III 409
Nation, III 476
New Left, III 511
1968 Mexico City Summer Olympic
    Games, III 537
Olsen, Tillie, III 558
Outing, III 580
Pachucos, IV 2
Paley, Grace, IV 6
Parks, Rosa, IV 15
Peter, Paul, and Mary, IV 42
Promise Keepers, IV 122
Protest Groups, IV 124
Public Enemy, IV 132
Queer Nation, IV 150
Reagan, Ronald, IV 179
Recycling, IV 187
Red Scare, IV 188
Redford, Robert, IV 190
Reggae, IV 194
Religious Right, IV 197
Rivera, Diego, IV 216
Robertson, Pat, IV 225
Seeger, Pete, IV 351
Sinclair, Upton, IV 414
Smothers Brothers, IV 442
Steinbeck, John, IV 522
Steinem, Gloria, IV 524
Student Demonstrations, IV 560
Students for a Democratic Society (SDS), IV 563
Televangelism, IV 625
Valdez, Luis, V 15
Vidal, Gore, V 45
Vietnam, V 49
Walton, Bill, V 72
Weathermen, V 95
Weavers, V 96
Wobblies, V 165
Wonder, Stevie, V 169
Wright, Richard, V 196

Yippies, V 214

Politicians
Army-McCarthy Hearings, I 116
Bradley, Bill, I 338
Chicago Seven, I 495
Communism, I 569
Fundamentalism, II 181
Iran Contra, II 499
Jackson, Jesse, II 514
JFK(The Movie), II 545
Kennedy Assassination, III 16
King, Larry, III 32
Limbaugh, Rush, III 163
Lincoln Center for the Performing Arts, III 165
Lippmann, Walter, III 170
Long, Huey, III 191
March On Washington, III 266
McCarthyism, III 314
Milk, Harvey, III 361
Perot, Ross, IV 39
Quayle, Dan, IV 147
Reagan, Ronald, IV 179
Sonny and Cher, IV 456
Spin, IV 478
Starr, Kenneth, IV 516
Tarkington, Booth, IV 607
Temple, Shirley, IV 631
Ventura, Jesse, V 41
War Bonds, V 74
Washington Monument, V 83

Politics
Amway, I 80
Anita Hill-Clarence Thomas Senate
    Hearings, I 93
Anne Frank: The Diary of a Young Girl, I 95
Apollo Missions, I 102
Army-McCarthy Hearings, I 116
Baraka, Amiri, I 168
Bay of Pigs Invasion, I 192
Bilingual Education, I 252
Blacklisting, I 272
Boat People, I 298
Bomb, I 311
Buckley, William F., Jr., I 379
Bumper Stickers, I 384
Captain America, I 429
Chaplin, Charlie, I 475
Chicago Seven, I 495
Cigarettes, I 510
Cocaine/Crack, I 542
Comics Code Authority, I 565
Communism, I 569
Draft, I 761
Gay and Lesbian Marriage, II 208
Gulf War, II 325
Hearst, William Randolph, II 379
High Noon, II 400
Hiss, Alger, II 413
Hoover, J. Edgar, II 443
Iran Contra, II 499
JFK(The Movie), II 545
Kennedy Assassination, III 16
King, Carole, III 29
Koresh, David, and the Branch Davidians, III 54
Labor Unions, III 72
Le Carré, John, III 106
Lewinsky, Monica, III 149
Liberty, III 157
Limbaugh, Rush, III 163
Lincoln Center for the Performing Arts, III 165
Lippmann, Walter, III 170
Lombardi, Vince, III 185
London, Jack, III 187
Long, Huey, III 191
Lottery, III 199
Luce, Henry, III 210
Macfadden, Bernarr, III 226
Manchurian Candidate, III 254
March On Washington, III 266
Marijuana, III 272
McCarthyism, III 314

Metropolis, III 347
Militias, III 359
Mount Rushmore, III 423
Mr. Smith Goes to Washington, III 432
My Lai Massacre, III 465
Nation, III 476
Network, III 503
New Deal, III 508
New Left, III 511
New Republic, III 514
Nightline, III 533
Oliphant, Pat, III 555
Olympics, III 558
Onassis, Jacqueline Lee Bouvier Kennedy,
    III 564
O'Rourke, P. J., III 573
Outing, III 580
Owens, Jesse, III 583
Parades, IV 12
Paulsen, Pat, IV 22
Pogo, IV 73
Political Bosses, IV 77
Pope, IV 86
Protest Groups, IV 124
Public Television (PBS), IV 135
Quayle, Dan, IV 147
Reader's Digest, IV 177
Reagan, Ronald, IV 179
Red Scare, IV 188
Robertson, Pat, IV 225
Robeson, Paul, IV 227
Rosenberg, Julius and Ethel, IV 279
Roswell Incident, IV 282
Sex Scandals, IV 367
Sister Souljah, IV 418
Spin, IV 478
Starr, Kenneth, IV 516
Stock Market Crashes, IV 539
Toffler, Alvin, IV 668
Town Meetings, IV 684
Twenties, IV 710
2 Live Crew, IV 715
Underground Comics, V 4
Washington Post, V 83
Winchell, Walter, V 151
Works Progress Administration (WPA)
    Murals, V 179

Pop Music
A&R Men/Women, I 1
ABBA, I 4
Ace, Johnny, I 15
Alabama, I 39
Alpert, Herb, and the Tijuana Brass, I 57
American Bandstand, I 65
Andrews Sisters, I 84
Anka, Paul, I 95
Arnaz, Desi, I 116
Avalon, Frankie, I 143
Baby Boomers, I 151
Barbershop Quartets, I 169
Beatles, I 203
Belafonte, Harry, I 214
Bennett, Tony, I 221
Berlin, Irving, I 230
Berry, Chuck, I 234
Black, Clint, I 262
Bon Jovi, I 315
Booker T. and the MG's, I 318
Boone, Pat, I 319
Bowie, David, I 328
Brill Building, I 351
British Invasion, I 354
Brooks, Garth, I 364
Brown, Les, I 370
Browne, Jackson, I 371
Bubblegum Rock, I 375
Buffett, Jimmy, I 382
Campbell, Glen, I 416
Carey, Mariah, I 434
Carpenters, I 440
Cash, Johnny, I 449
Cassidy, David, I 452

Charles, Ray, I 477
Chipmunks, I 501
Civil Rights Movement, I 519
Cline, Patsy, I 530
Clooney, Rosemary, I 533
Cole, Nat ''King,'' I 552
Columbo, Russ, I 560
Como, Perry, I 574
Concept Album, I 576
Coniff, Ray, I 583
Contemporary Christian Music, I 591
Cooke, Sam, I 594
Costello, Elvis, I 612
Cray, Robert, I 626
Creedence Clearwater Revival, I 630
Croce, Jim, I 634
Crosby, Bing, I 638
Davis, Miles, I 661
Denver, John, I 686
Diamond, Neil, I 698
Dietrich, Marlene, I 708
Disability, I 721
Disco, I 726
Domino, Fats, I 743
Donovan, I 745
Doo-wop Music, I 750
Dorsey, Jimmy, I 750
Drifters, I 769
Eckstine, Billy, II 10
El Vez, II 19
Fabares, Shelley, II 53
Fabian, II 53
Feliciano, José, II 82
Ferrante and Teicher, II 88
Fisher, Eddie, II 104
Fitzgerald, Ella, II 107
Flack, Roberta, II 111
Fleetwood Mac, II 114
Ford, Tennessee Ernie, II 138
Francis, Connie, II 151
Franklin, Aretha, II 154
Funicello, Annette, II 183
Funk, II 184
Gaye, Marvin, II 216
Girl Groups, II 240
Gleason, Jackie, II 245
Glitter Rock, II 247
Gordy, Berry, II 272
Grant, Amy, II 287
Haley, Bill, II 343
Houston, Whitney, II 458
Ice-T, II 485
Ink Spots, II 493
Jackson Five, II 513
Jackson, Michael, II 517
James, Harry, II 525
Jesus Christ Superstar, II 543
John, Elton, II 550
Joplin, Janis, II 565
Juke Boxes, II 579
Kasem, Casey, III 6
Kern, Jerome, III 21
Kingston Trio, III 39
KISS, III 42
Lang, k.d., III 88
Latin Jazz, III 97
Lauper, Cyndi, III 99
Lennon, John, III 131
Lewis, Jerry Lee, III 153
Liberace, III 155
Lloyd Webber, Andrew, III 181
Lombardo, Guy, III 187
Los Lobos, III 197
Madonna, III 235
Mamas and the Papas, III 251
Manhattan Transfer, III 257
Manilow, Barry, III 258
Martha and the Vandellas, III 279
Martin, Dean, III 280
Martin, Freddy, III 281
Mathis, Johnny, III 305
McCartney, Paul, III 316

Mellencamp, John Cougar, III 341
Mendoza, Lydia, III 344
Midler, Bette, III 356
Milli Vanilli, III 368
Mitchell, Joni, III 379
Mod, III 384
Monkees, III 394
Morissette, Alanis, III 413
Motown, III 420
MTV, III 435
Murray, Anne, III 447
New Kids on the Block, III 510
New Wave Music, III 515
Orbison, Roy, III 571
Partridge Family, IV 18
Paul, Les, IV 20
Pearl Jam, IV 26
Pointer Sisters, IV 74
Ramones, IV 171
Redding, Otis, IV 189
Reed, Lou, IV 192
Robinson, Smokey, IV 233
Rogers, Kenny, IV 261
Ross, Diana, and the Supremes, IV 280
Run-DMC, IV 287
Salt-n-Pepa, IV 305
Sam and Dave, IV 306
Seeger, Pete, IV 351
Selena, IV 354
Shore, Dinah, IV 387
Simon and Garfunkel, IV 399
Simon, Paul, IV 403
Sinatra, Frank, IV 409
Sly and the Family Stone, IV 437
Sondheim, Stephen, IV 454
Sonny and Cher, IV 456
Soul Music, IV 458
Soul Train, IV 461
Spector, Phil, IV 471
Spice Girls, IV 473
Springsteen, Bruce, IV 491
Stadium Concerts, IV 496
Streisand, Barbra, IV 556
Summer, Donna, IV 575
Sun Records, IV 576
Surf Music, IV 585
Talking Heads, IV 602
Taylor, James, IV 615
Teen Idols, IV 617
Teenagers, IV 620
Temptations, IV 632
10,000 Maniacs, IV 638
Thorogood, George, IV 648
Tiny Tim, IV 661
Top 40, IV 679
Tormé, Mel, IV 683
Turner, Ike and Tina, IV 702
Valens, Ritchie, V 16
Vanilla Ice, V 28
Vaughan, Sarah, V 36
Waits, Tom, V 59
Walker, Junior, and the All-Stars, V 63
Wells, Mary, V 111
White, Barry, V 125
Williams, Andy, V 139
Winston, George, V 156
Wonder, Stevie, V 169
Yanni, V 210
Your Hit Parade, V 220
ZZ Top, V 236

Postmodernism
Another World, I 99
Avery, Tex, I 145
Blume, Judy, I 294
Camp, I 415
Castaneda, Carlos, I 453
City of Angels, I 516
Days of Our Lives, I 666
Dick, Philip K., I 701
Do the Right Thing, I 735
Doctorow, E. L., I 740
Generation X, II 221

Industrial Design, II 491
Kitsch, III 43
Kotzwinkle, William, III 56
Miami Vice, III 349
Multiculturalism, III 439
Postmodernism, IV 98
Pynchon, Thomas, IV 145
Rock and Roll, IV 235
Scream, IV 341
Warhol, Andy, V 80

Products
Alka Seltzer, I 49
American Girls Series, I 67
Amway, I 80
Arden, Elizabeth, I 109
Bagels, I 158
Barbie, I 171
Baseball Cards, I 183
Beer, I 210
Birkenstocks, I 257
Bra, I 335
Brownie Cameras, I 371
Camping, I 417
Cassette Tape, I 451
Chanel, Coco, I 475
Clairol Hair Coloring, I 523
Compact Discs, I 575
Condoms, I 578
Consumerism, I 589
Convertible, I 593
Crawford, Cindy, I 624
Crawford, Joan, I 625
Credit Cards, I 628
Currier and Ives, I 650
Department Stores, I 688
Dime Novels, I 716
Eight-track Tape, II 16
Electric Appliances, II 20
Electric Trains, II 22
Erector Sets, II 34
Fabio, II 53
Frederick's of Hollywood, II 159
General Motors, II 220
Greeting Cards, II 306
Hallmark Hall of Fame, II 345
Harlequin Romances, II 367
Industrial Design, II 491
International Male Catalog, II 494
Jell-O, II 537
Kewpie Dolls, III 22
Kodak, III 51
Leather Jacket, III 114
Levi's, III 146
Long-Playing Record, III 192
Manufactured Homes, III 263
Mary Kay Cosmetics, III 290
Nike, III 535
Nylon, III 544
O'Neal, Shaquille, III 568
Pantyhose, IV 9
Pet Rocks, IV 42
Phonograph, IV 52
Plastic, IV 64
Postcards, IV 96
Prozac, IV 125
Rubik's Cube, IV 286
Starbucks, IV 514
Swatch Watches, IV 589
Tennis Shoes/Sneakers, IV 637
Timex Watches, IV 661
Trading Stamps, IV 688
Tupperware, IV 700
TV Dinners, IV 706
Valium, V 20
Velveeta Cheese, V 39
Video Games, V 45
Videos, V 47
Vitamins, V 52
Walkman, V 66
Winnie-the-Pooh, V 155
World's Fairs, V 194

Publishers
   African American Press, I 32
   American Girls Series, I 67
   Argosy, I 109
   Bestsellers, I 236
   Black Mask, I 263
   Bobbsey Twins, I 300
   Book-of-the-Month Club, I 318
   Comics, I 562
   Comics Code Authority, I 565
   Family Circle, II 59
   Golden Books, II 258
   Hardy Boys, II 360
   Hefner, Hugh, II 383
   Joy of Cooking, II 572
   Little Blue Books, III 173
   Luce, Henry, III 210
   Macfadden, Bernarr, III 226
   Marvel Comics, III 285
   McCall's Magazine, III 313
   Mencken, H. L., III 342
   National Geographic, III 484
   Paperbacks, IV 9
   Playgirl, IV 72
   Prang, Louis, IV 104
   Redbook, IV 189
   Spawn, IV 470
   Sporting News, IV 483
   Stratemeyer, Edward, IV 548
   Street and Smith, IV 553
   Superman, IV 581
   Time, IV 657
   Tom Swift Series, IV 674
   Variety, V 31

Punk Rock
   Alternative Country Music, I 59
   Beastie Boys, I 200
   Blondie (rock band), I 284
   Camp, I 415
   Cash, Johnny, I 449
   Costello, Elvis, I 612
   Devo, I 696
   Glitter Rock, II 247
   Goth, II 277
   Grunge, II 321
   Hairstyles, II 340
   Heavy Metal, II 380
   Love, Courtney, III 204
   Mod, III 384
   Morissette, Alanis, III 413
   Nirvana, III 538
   Pop, Iggy, IV 82
   Prince, IV 112
   Punk, IV 142
   Ramones, IV 171
   Reed, Lou, IV 192
   Replacements, IV 204
   Rock and Roll, IV 235
   Smith, Patti, IV 440
   Talking Heads, IV 602
   Warhol, Andy, V 80
   Zines, V 228

Race/Ethnicity
   Aaron, Hank, I 2
   Abdul-Jabbar, Kareem, I 7
   Ace, Johnny, I 15
   African American Press, I 32
   Ailey, Alvin, I 37
   Alien, I 48
   American Girls Series, I 67
   Amos 'n' Andy Show, I 72
   Anderson, Marian, I 81
   Angelou, Maya, I 89
   Anita Hill-Clarence Thomas Senate
      Hearings, I 93
   Aparicio, Luis, I 101
   Apollo Theatre, I 104
   Arnaz, Desi, I 116
   Ashe, Arthur, I 123
   Aunt Jemima, I 137
   Baby Boomers, I 151

   Baldwin, James, I 161
   Baraka, Amiri, I 168
   Basketball, I 186
   Belafonte, Harry, I 214
   Beulah, I 241
   Bilingual Education, I 252
   Bird, Larry, I 255
   Black Panthers, I 264
   Blackface Minstrelsy, I 270
   Blades, Ruben, I 275
   Blues, I 290
   Blume, Judy, I 294
   Booker T. and the MG's, I 318
   Borscht Belt, I 321
   Boxing, I 330
   Broadway, I 356
   Brooklyn Dodgers, I 362
   Brooks, Gwendolyn, I 365
   Brown, James, I 367
   Butterbeans and Susie, I 400
   Cahan, Abraham, I 411
   Camacho, Héctor "Macho," I 414
   Car 54, Where Are You?, I 432
   Castle, Vernon and Irene, I 454
   Charles, Ray, I 477
   Charlie Chan, I 478
   Cheerleading, I 486
   Chuck D, I 508
   Circus, I 512
   Cisneros, Sandra, I 513
   Civil Rights Movement, I 519
   Clemente, Roberto, I 528
   Clinton, George, I 532
   Cocaine/Crack, I 542
   Cody, Buffalo Bill, and his Wild West
      Show, I 545
   Cole, Nat "King," I 552
   Cosby, Bill, I 606
   Cotton Club, I 614
   Crisis, I 633
   Cullen, Countee, I 643
   Dana, Bill, I 656
   Detroit Tigers, I 695
   Diff'rent Strokes, I 709
   Do the Right Thing, I 735
   Doby, Larry, I 736
   Domino, Fats, I 743
   Dragon Lady, I 767
   Drug War, I 771
   Du Bois, W. E. B., I 771
   Durán, Roberto, I 776
   Ebony, II 7
   Edwards, James, II 14
   El Teatro Campesino, II 18
   El Vez, II 19
   Erdrich, Louise, II 34
   Ertegun, Ahmet, II 35
   Family Matters, II 62
   Fauset, Jessie Redmon, II 78
   Feliciano, José, II 82
   Fetchit, Stepin, II 88
   Freedom Rides, II 163
   Fu Manchu, II 179
   Fusco, Coco, II 185
   Gangs, II 195
   Garvey, Marcus, II 205
   Ghettos, II 227
   Gibson, Althea, II 230
   Goldberg, Whoopi, II 257
   Good Times, II 267
   Goodbye, Columbus, II 268
   Gordy, Berry, II 272
   Gospel Music, II 274
   Greenberg, Hank, II 302
   Gregory, Dick, II 307
   Grier, Pam, II 312
   Guiding Light, II 323
   Hairstyles, II 340
   Hansberry, Lorraine, II 356
   Harlem Globetrotters, II 364
   Harlem Renaissance, II 365
   Hate Crimes, II 373

   Hijuelos, Oscar, II 405
   Hillerman, Tony, II 407
   Himes, Chester, II 408
   Hispanic Magazine, II 412
   Holocaust, II 436
   Hoover, J. Edgar, II 443
   Horne, Lena, II 449
   Hughes, Langston, II 465
   Hurston, Zora Neale, II 469
   I Spy, II 479
   Indian, II 487
   Invisible Man, II 498
   Jackson, Jesse, II 514
   Japanese American Internment Camps, II 525
   Jazz, II 529
   Jazz Singer, II 531
   Jeffersons, II 536
   Jet, II 544
   Jewish Defense League, II 545
   Johnson, Jack, II 554
   Johnson, James Weldon, II 555
   Johnson, Robert, II 557
   Jolson, Al, II 559
   Joplin, Scott, II 566
   Julia, II 580
   Juliá, Raúl, II 581
   King, B. B., III 26
   King, Martin Luther, Jr., III 33
   Kingston, Maxine Hong, III 39
   Ku Klux Klan, III 64
   Kung Fu, III 68
   Labor Unions, III 72
   Latin Jazz, III 97
   Lear, Norman, III 111
   Lee, Bruce, III 117
   Lee, Spike, III 122
   Life, III 160
   Lion King, III 169
   Locke, Alain, III 182
   López, Nancy, III 194
   Los Lobos, III 197
   Louis, Joe, III 200
   Lynching, III 217
   Mabley, Moms, III 223
   Mafia/Organized Crime, III 237
   Malcolm X, III 243
   Marichal, Juan, III 272
   Marley, Bob, III 274
   Maus, III 308
   McDaniel, Hattie, III 320
   McKay, Claude, III 327
   McQueen, Butterfly, III 332
   Michener, James, III 351
   Million Man March, III 368
   Minoso, Minnie, III 371
   Minstrel Shows, III 371
   Miranda, Carmen, III 373
   Momaday, N. Scott, III 392
   Monroe, Earl "The Pearl," III 397
   Montalbán, Ricardo, III 401
   Morrison, Toni, III 414
   Mosley, Walter, III 416
   Multiculturalism, III 439
   My Family, Mi Familia, III 464
   National Basketball Association (NBA), III 477
   Nava, Gregory, III 495
   Naylor, Gloria, III 495
   Negro Leagues, III 497
   Night of the Living Dead, III 532
   Noloesca, La Chata, III 540
   Olmos, Edward James, III 557
   Opportunity, III 570
   Our Gang, III 576
   Owens, Jesse, III 583
   Pachucos, IV 2
   Paige, Satchel, IV 5
   Parker, Charlie, IV 13
   Parks, Rosa, IV 15
   Poitier, Sidney, IV 75
   Pop Music, IV 83
   Pope, IV 86
   Pride, Charley, IV 111

Prince, IV 112
Prinze, Freddie, IV 115
Prom, IV 120
Promise Keepers, IV 122
Protest Groups, IV 124
Pryor, Richard, IV 126
Public Enemy, IV 132
Queen Latifah, IV 150
Race Music, IV 155
Race Riots, IV 156
Redding, Otis, IV 189
Reed, Ishmael, IV 191
Reese, Pee Wee, IV 193
Rivera, Diego, IV 216
Rivera, Geraldo, IV 218
Robeson, Paul, IV 227
Robinson, Frank, IV 230
Robinson, Jackie, IV 231
Rock and Roll, IV 235
Rockettes, IV 241
Rockwell, Norman, IV 244
Rodgers, Jimmie, IV 258
Rodríguez, Chi Chi, IV 259
Rolle, Esther, IV 265
Roller Derby, IV 266
Romero, Cesar, IV 273
Roots, IV 273
Rosenberg, Julius and Ethel, IV 279
Ross, Diana, and the Supremes, IV 280
Roundtree, Richard, IV 282
Salsa Music, IV 303
Sanford and Son, IV 310
Savoy Ballroom, IV 322
Schindler's List, IV 324
Searchers, IV 346
Sedona, Arizona, IV 349
Seinfeld, IV 352
Selena, IV 354
Shaft, IV 376
Shakur, Tupac, IV 377
Show Boat, IV 389
Silent Movies, IV 393
Simpson, O. J., IV 404
Sinbad, IV 413
Sirk, Douglas, IV 416
Sister Souljah, IV 418
Sly and the Family Stone, IV 437
Smits, Jimmy, IV 441
Social Dancing, IV 450
Soul Train, IV 461
Stand and Deliver, IV 501
Standardized Testing, IV 502
Student Demonstrations, IV 560
Styron, William, IV 567
Summer, Donna, IV 575
Swimming Pools, IV 590
Tap Dancing, IV 605
Tejano Music, IV 623
Thompson, John, IV 647
Thorpe, Jim, IV 649
Three Caballeros, IV 650
To Kill a Mockingbird, IV 663
Treviño, Lee, IV 696
Tyson, Mike, IV 718
Valdez, Luis, V 15
Valenzuela, Fernando, V 19
Van Vechten, Carl, V 26
Vanilla Ice, V 28
Walker, Aaron ''T-Bone,'' V 59
Walker, Aida Overton, V 61
Walker, Alice, V 61
Walker, George, V 62
Walker, Madame C. J., V 65
Wallace, Sippie, V 68
Washington, Denzel, V 82
Waters, Muddy, V 89
Wayans, V 90
Wertham, Fredric, V 111
West Side Story, V 116
Western, V 118
White, Barry, V 125
White Flight, V 128

White Supremacists, V 129
Wilson, Flip, V 148
Wolfman Jack, V 167
Wong, Anna May, V 172
Woods, Tiger, V 175
Wright, Richard, V 196

Radio
Abbott and Costello, I 5
Album-Oriented Rock, I 41
Amos 'n' Andy Show, I 72
Amsterdam, Morey, I 74
Armed Forces Radio Service, I 112
Autry, Gene, I 142
Barber, Red, I 169
Bell Telephone Hour, I 216
Bergen, Edgar, I 225
Blanc, Mel, I 276
Bob and Ray, I 299
Borge, Victor, I 320
Burns, George, and Gracie Allen, I 392
Burr, Raymond, I 394
Canova, Judy, I 421
Caray, Harry, I 433
Carlin, George, I 434
CBS Radio Mystery Theater, I 463
Chandu the Magician, I 475
Clooney, Rosemary, I 533
Community Media, I 570
Como, Perry, I 574
Corwin, Norman, I 604
Coughlin, Father Charles E., I 616
Crosby, Bing, I 638
Disc Jockeys, I 725
Disco, I 726
Dragon Lady, I 767
Edison, Thomas Alva, II 13
ESPN, II 38
Fadiman, Clifton, II 55
Fibber McGee and Molly, II 89
Freed, Alan ''Moondog,'' II 162
Game Shows, II 191
Godfrey, Arthur, II 251
Grand Ole Opry, II 286
Great Depression, II 295
Ives, Burl, II 508
Jack Armstrong, II 512
Kaltenborn, Hans von, III 1
Kasem, Casey, III 6
Keillor, Garrison, III 11
Ladd, Alan, III 75
Let's Pretend, III 143
Linkletter, Art, III 168
Lone Ranger, III 189
Long-Playing Record, III 192
Ma Perkins, III 223
Macon, Uncle Dave, III 229
Marie, Rose, III 272
Morse, Carlton E., III 415
Murrow, Edward R., III 451
Networks, III 503
Phillips, Irna, IV 51
Presley, Elvis, IV 105
Queen for a Day, IV 149
Radio, IV 157
Radio Drama, IV 160
Ripley's Believe It Or Not, IV 215
Rogers, Will, IV 263
RuPaul, IV 289
Sarnoff, David, IV 312
Schlessinger, Dr. Laura, IV 326
Shirer, William L., IV 384
Shock Radio, IV 386
Smith, Kate, IV 439
Stern, Howard, IV 530
Talk Radio, IV 600
This Is Your Life, IV 643
Tokyo Rose, IV 669
Top 40, IV 679
Trout, Robert, IV 698
Twenties, IV 710
Vallee, Rudy, V 21
Waters, Ethel, V 86

Winters, Jonathan, V 157
Wolfman Jack, V 167
World War II, V 188
Your Hit Parade, V 220

Rap/Hip-Hop
Bambaataa, Afrika, I 166
Beastie Boys, I 200
Brown, James, I 367
Chuck D, I 508
Clinton, George, I 532
Diddley, Bo, I 703
Electric Guitar, II 21
Funk, II 184
Gangsta Rap, II 198
Grandmaster Flash, II 286
Hancock, Herbie, II 350
Ice-T, II 485
King, Rodney, III 34
L. L. Cool J., III 71
Malcolm X, III 243
MTV, III 435
Pop Music, IV 83
Public Enemy, IV 132
Queen Latifah, IV 150
Rap/Hip-Hop, IV 174
Run-DMC, IV 287
Salt-n-Pepa, IV 305
Shakur, Tupac, IV 377
Sister Souljah, IV 418
Snoop Doggy Dogg, IV 444
Social Dancing, IV 450
Soul Train, IV 461
2 Live Crew, IV 715
Vanilla Ice, V 28

Religion/Spirituality
Astrology, I 129
Baby Boomers, I 151
Bach, Richard, I 155
Bakker, Jim, and Tammy Faye, I 160
Barton, Bruce, I 179
Ben-Hur, I 219
Blume, Judy, I 294
Boone, Pat, I 319
Cemeteries, I 467
Chautauqua Institution, I 481
Christmas, I 503
Church Socials, I 509
Civil Rights Movement, I 519
Communes, I 568
Contemporary Christian Music, I 591
Cooke, Sam, I 594
Coué, Emile, I 615
Coughlin, Father Charles E., I 616
Covey, Stephen, I 621
Creationism, I 627
Cults, I 646
Dillard, Annie, I 711
Douglas, Lloyd C., I 753
Dylan, Bob, I 780
Eddy, Mary Baker, II 11
Est, II 42
Evangelism, II 46
Exorcist, II 50
Father Divine, II 74
Franklin, Aretha, II 154
Fundamentalism, II 181
Goodbye, Columbus, II 268
Gospel Music, II 274
Graham, Billy, II 284
Grant, Amy, II 287
Greeley, Andrew, II 298
Green, Al, II 300
Grey, Zane, II 309
Hare Krishna, II 362
Hate Crimes, II 373
Holyfield, Evander, II 436
Hubbard, L. Ron, II 461
Indian, II 487
Jackson, Jesse, II 514
Jackson, Mahalia, II 515
Jewish Defense League, II 545

Jonestown, II 563
King, Martin Luther, Jr., III 33
Koresh, David, and the Branch Davidians, III 54
Late Great Planet Earth, III 96
L'Engle, Madeleine, III 131
Lewis, C. S., III 150
Malcolm X, III 243
Marley, Bob, III 274
McPherson, Aimee Semple, III 331
Merton, Thomas, III 345
Middletown, III 355
Million Man March, III 368
Moonies/Reverend Sun Myung Moon, III 405
Moral Majority, III 409
Muscular Christianity, III 456
New Age Music, III 506
New Age Spirituality, III 507
Ouija Boards, III 576
Parades, IV 12
Peale, Norman Vincent, IV 23
Pope, IV 86
Promise Keepers, IV 122
Reggae, IV 194
Religious Right, IV 197
Robertson, Pat, IV 225
Roe v. Wade, IV 260
Sam and Dave, IV 306
Schindler's List, IV 324
Schlessinger, Dr. Laura, IV 326
Scopes Monkey Trial, IV 335
Scribner's, IV 344
Sedona, Arizona, IV 349
Sunday, Billy, IV 578
Sunday Driving, IV 578
Swaggart, Jimmy, IV 587
Televangelism, IV 625
Touched by an Angel, IV 684
Twelve-Step Programs, IV 708
UFOs (Unidentified Flying Objects), V 1
WWJD? (What Would Jesus Do?), V 198

Retail
Alka Seltzer, I 49
Amway, I 80
Atlantic City, I 133
Bra, I 335
Burger King, I 387
Chanel, Coco, I 475
Claiborne, Liz, I 523
Compact Discs, I 575
Consumerism, I 589
Department Stores, I 688
Dime Stores/Woolworth's, I 717
Eight-track Tape, II 16
Electric Trains, II 22
Frederick's of Hollywood, II 159
Gap, II 198
Harlequin Romances, II 367
Home Shopping Network/QVC, II 438
Kewpie Dolls, III 22
L.L. Bean, Inc., III 180
Macy's, III 229
McDonald's, III 321
Old Navy, III 555
Pantyhose, IV 9
Paperbacks, IV 9
Parker Brothers, IV 13
Rouse Company, IV 283
Saks Fifth Avenue, IV 302
Sears Roebuck Catalogue, IV 346
Soda Fountains, IV 452
Starbucks, IV 514
Tennis Shoes/Sneakers, IV 637
Tiffany & Company, IV 655
Timex Watches, IV 661
Victoria's Secret, V 43
Videos, V 47
Wal-Mart, V 69
White Castle, V 127
World's Fairs, V 194

Rhythm and Blues
Ace, Johnny, I 15

Allison, Luther, I 54
Atlantic Records, I 135
Babyface, I 154
Ballard, Hank, I 164
Band, I 167
Blues Brothers, I 293
Brown, James, I 367
Charles, Ray, I 477
Chenier, Clifton, I 490
Cole, Nat ''King,'' I 552
Coltrane, John, I 557
Commodores, I 566
Cooke, Sam, I 594
Diddley, Bo, I 703
Domino, Fats, I 743
Doo-wop Music, I 750
Drifters, I 769
Ertegun, Ahmet, II 35
Franklin, Aretha, II 154
Freed, Alan ''Moondog,'' II 162
Funk, II 184
Gaye, Marvin, II 216
Gordy, Berry, II 272
Green, Al, II 300
Haley, Bill, II 343
Hendrix, Jimi, II 391
Hopkins, Sam ''Lightnin','' II 447
Houston, Whitney, II 458
Jackson Five, II 513
Jackson, Michael, II 517
James, Elmore, II 525
Jones, Tom, II 563
Jordan, Louis, II 568
King, Albert, III 25
Little Richard, III 178
Mayfield, Curtis, III 310
Mayfield, Percy, III 310
Morrison, Van, III 415
Motown, III 420
New Orleans Rhythm and Blues, III 513
Pointer Sisters, IV 74
Pop Music, IV 83
Prince, IV 112
Race Music, IV 155
Redding, Otis, IV 189
Rhythm and Blues, IV 206
Rock and Roll, IV 235
Salt-n-Pepa, IV 305
Santana, IV 311
Selena, IV 354
Shirelles, IV 384
Sly and the Family Stone, IV 437
Soul Music, IV 458
Soul Train, IV 461
Temptations, IV 632
Turner, Ike and Tina, IV 702
Walker, Junior, and the All-Stars, V 63
Waters, Muddy, V 89
Wells, Mary, V 111
Wolfman Jack, V 167
Wonder, Stevie, V 169
Zydeco, V 235

Riots/Civil Disturbances
Altamont, I 57
Alternative Press, I 60
Baldwin, James, I 161
Black Panthers, I 264
Chicago Seven, I 495
City of Angels, I 516
Civil Rights Movement, I 519
Detroit Tigers, I 695
Dime Stores/Woolworth's, I 717
Disco, I 726
Do the Right Thing, I 735
Eco-Terrorism, II 10
Firearms, II 101
Free Speech Movement, II 161
Ghettos, II 227
Hell's Angels, II 384
Hoffman, Abbie, II 419
Jefferson Airplane/Starship, II 534
Jet, II 544

Johnson, Jack, II 554
Kent State Massacre, III 17
King, Martin Luther, Jr., III 33
King, Rodney, III 34
Lee, Spike, III 122
Malcolm X, III 243
Milk, Harvey, III 361
New Left, III 511
Pachucos, IV 2
Race Riots, IV 156
Road Rage, IV 221
Spring Break, IV 488
Student Demonstrations, IV 560
Students for a Democratic Society (SDS), IV 563
Weathermen, V 95
Yippies, V 214
Zoot Suit, V 233

Rock 'n' Roll
A&R Men/Women, I 1
AC/DC, I 14
Adventures of Ozzie and Harriet, I 21
Aerosmith, I 31
Album-Oriented Rock, I 41
Allman Brothers Band, I 56
Altamont, I 57
Alternative Country Music, I 59
Alternative Press, I 60
Alternative Rock, I 62
American Bandstand, I 65
Atkins, Chet, I 132
Atlantic Records, I 135
Avalon, Frankie, I 143
Ballard, Hank, I 164
Band, I 167
Beach Boys, I 195
Beastie Boys, I 200
Beatles, I 203
Berry, Chuck, I 234
Big Bopper, I 249
Black, Clint, I 262
Blackboard Jungle, I 268
Blondie (rock band), I 284
Bluegrass, I 287
Blues, I 290
Bon Jovi, I 315
Bowie, David, I 328
Brill Building, I 351
British Invasion, I 354
Browne, Jackson, I 371
Bubblegum Rock, I 375
Buffalo Springfield, I 381
Byrds, I 402
Camp, I 415
Cash, Johnny, I 449
Clapton, Eric, I 525
Clark, Dick, I 525
Clinton, George, I 532
Concept Album, I 576
Contemporary Christian Music, I 591
Cooper, Alice, I 595
Creedence Clearwater Revival, I 630
Croce, Jim, I 634
Crosby, Stills, and Nash, I 639
Daniels, Charlie, I 658
Devo, I 696
Diddley, Bo, I 703
Disc Jockeys, I 725
Disco, I 726
Domino, Fats, I 743
Donovan, I 745
Doobie Brothers, I 747
Doors, I 748
Dylan, Bob, I 780
Easy Rider, II 4
Eddy, Duane, II 11
Electric Guitar, II 21
Ertegun, Ahmet, II 35
Everly Brothers, II 47
Feliciano, José, II 82
Fifties, II 96
Fleetwood Mac, II 114
Freed, Alan ''Moondog,'' II 162

Funk, II 184
Glitter Rock, II 247
Gordy, Berry, II 272
Graham, Bill, II 282
Grateful Dead, II 291
Green, Al, II 300
Grunge, II 321
Guy, Buddy, II 329
Hair, II 338
Haley, Bill, II 343
Hall and Oates, II 345
Heavy Metal, II 380
Hendrix, Jimi, II 391
Holly, Buddy, II 429
Hooker, John Lee, II 440
Houston, Whitney, II 458
Howlin' Wolf, II 461
Jackson, Michael, II 517
James, Elmore, II 525
Jazz, II 529
Jefferson Airplane/Starship, II 534
John, Elton, II 550
Johnson, Robert, II 557
Jones, George, II 561
Jones, Tom, II 563
Judas Priest, II 577
Juke Boxes, II 579
King, Albert, III 25
King, Carole, III 29
King, Freddie, III 30
KISS, III 42
"La Bamba," III 71
Lauper, Cyndi, III 99
Led Zeppelin, III 116
Lennon, John, III 131
Lewis, Jerry Lee, III 153
Little Richard, III 178
Lynyrd Skynyrd, III 220
Mamas and the Papas, III 251
Marley, Bob, III 274
McCartney, Paul, III 316
Mellencamp, John Cougar, III 341
Morissette, Alanis, III 413
Morrison, Van, III 415
Mötley Crüe, III 418
Motown, III 420
MTV, III 435
Nelson, Ricky, III 499
New Wave Music, III 515
Osbourne, Ozzy, III 575
Pearl Jam, IV 26
Peppermint Lounge, IV 36
Peter, Paul, and Mary, IV 42
Pink Floyd, IV 58
Pointer Sisters, IV 74
Pop, Iggy, IV 82
Pop Music, IV 83
Presley, Elvis, IV 105
Prince, IV 112
Psychedelia, IV 128
Punk, IV 142
Raitt, Bonnie, IV 170
Ramones, IV 171
Reed, Lou, IV 192
Rhythm and Blues, IV 206
Rock and Roll, IV 235
Rolling Stone, IV 267
Rolling Stones, IV 269
Rydell, Bobby, IV 298
Santana, IV 311
Selena, IV 354
Simon and Garfunkel, IV 399
Simon, Paul, IV 403
Sly and the Family Stone, IV 437
Smith, Patti, IV 440
Social Dancing, IV 450
Soul Train, IV 461
Springsteen, Bruce, IV 491
Stadium Concerts, IV 496
Steppenwolf, IV 527
Teen Idols, IV 617
Temptations, IV 632

10,000 Maniacs, IV 638
Thorogood, George, IV 648
Turner, Ike and Tina, IV 702
Valens, Ritchie, V 16
Van Halen, V 26
Vaughan, Stevie Ray, V 37
Velvet Underground, V 39
Waters, Muddy, V 89
Whisky A Go Go, V 123
Who, V 131
Williams, Hank, Jr., V 141
Wolfman Jack, V 167
Wonder, Stevie, V 169
Yankovic, "Weird Al," V 209
Yardbirds, V 212
Yes, V 214
Young, Neil, V 217
Your Hit Parade, V 220
Zappa, Frank, V 225
ZZ Top, V 236

Romance, Film
African Queen, I 33
Allen, Woody, I 53
American Graffiti, I 69
Astaire, Fred, and Ginger Rogers, I 127
Bogart, Humphrey, I 308
Breakfast at Tiffany's, I 346
Bridges of Madison County, I 350
City Lights, I 515
DiCaprio, Leonardo, I 700
Dunne, Irene, I 776
Flashdance Style, II 113
Ford, Harrison, II 131
Gish, Lillian, II 244
Gone with the Wind, II 263
Hunter, Tab, II 468
Meet Me in St. Louis, III 339
Wuthering Heights, V 198

Romance, Print
Bestsellers, I 236
Blume, Judy, I 294
Bridges of Madison County, I 350
Fabio, II 53
Fitzgerald, F. Scott, II 109
Gone with the Wind, II 263
Harlequin Romances, II 367
Jong, Erica, II 564
Paperbacks, IV 9
Roberts, Nora, IV 224
Romance Novels, IV 270
Stratton-Porter, Gene, IV 550

Romance, TV
Another World, I 99
Days of Our Lives, I 666
Fantasy Island, II 68
Guiding Light, II 323
I Dream of Jeannie, II 475
Made-for-Television Movies, III 233

Satirists
Acker, Kathy, I 16
Barry, Dave, I 177
Benchley, Robert, I 219
Berra, Yogi, I 233
Bloom County, I 284
Bob and Ray, I 299
Bruce, Lenny, I 372
Crumb, Robert, I 641
Doonesbury, I 747
Krassner, Paul, III 61
Lardner, Ring, III 90
Lehrer, Tom, III 126
Li'l Abner, III 163
MAD Magazine, III 230
Mencken, H. L., III 342
Moore, Michael, III 408
Mr. Dooley, III 430
Network, III 503
Nichols, Mike, and Elaine May, III 529
Oliphant, Pat, III 555
O'Rourke, P. J., III 573

Parker, Dorothy, IV 14
Pogo, IV 73
Radner, Gilda, IV 162
Reed, Ishmael, IV 191
Rocky and Bullwinkle, IV 248
Rogers, Will, IV 263
Saturday Night Live, IV 320
Smothers Brothers, IV 442
South Park, IV 466
Southern, Terry, IV 466
Stevens, Ray, IV 532
Thurber, James, IV 654
Underground Comics, V 4
Vonnegut, Kurt, Jr., V 56
Zines, V 228

Scandal
Arbuckle, Fatty, I 107
Army-McCarthy Hearings, I 116
Bakker, Jim, and Tammy Faye, I 160
Black Sox Scandal, I 266
Bouton, Jim, I 326
Bruce, Lenny, I 372
Chaplin, Charlie, I 475
Cocaine/Crack, I 542
Disc Jockeys, I 725
Doors, I 748
Fisher, Eddie, II 104
Flag Clothing, II 111
Greeley, Andrew, II 298
Harding, Tonya, II 360
Hiss, Alger, II 413
Hustler, II 470
Iran Contra, II 499
Jackson, Michael, II 517
Jackson, "Shoeless" Joe, II 521
Kerrigan, Nancy, III 21
Koresh, David, and the Branch Davidians, III 54
Lennon, John, III 131
Leopold and Loeb, III 138
Lewinsky, Monica, III 149
Lewis, Jerry Lee, III 153
Lolita, III 183
Love, Courtney, III 204
McCarthyism, III 314
Media Feeding Frenzies, III 337
Milli Vanilli, III 368
Mötley Crüe, III 418
Movie Stars, III 428
Murphy Brown, III 446
National Basketball Association (NBA), III 477
National Enquirer, III 480
Paperbacks, IV 9
Pee-wee's Playhouse, IV 32
Quiz Show Scandals, IV 151
Rose, Pete, IV 276
Sex Scandals, IV 367
Sexual Harassment, IV 371
Shock Radio, IV 386
Simpson Trial, IV 405
$64,000 Question, IV 427
Starr, Kenneth, IV 516
Swaggart, Jimmy, IV 587
Tabloids, IV 597
Tarkanian, Jerry, IV 606
Taylor, Elizabeth, IV 612
Televangelism, IV 625

Science
American Museum of Natural History, I 72
Apollo Missions, I 102
Asimov, Isaac, I 125
Challenger Disaster, I 472
China Syndrome, I 500
Clarke, Arthur C., I 527
Creationism, I 627
Einstein, Albert, II 16
Kinsey, Dr. Alfred C., III 40
Mr. Wizard, III 433
NASA, III 475
Nylon, III 544
Plastic, IV 64
Popular Mechanics, IV 89

Sagan, Carl, IV 300
Satellites, IV 314
Scientific American, IV 334
Scopes Monkey Trial, IV 335
Sputnik, IV 493
Stratton-Porter, Gene, IV 550
UFOs (Unidentified Flying Objects), V 1
Vitamins, V 52
World's Fairs, V 194

Science Fiction, Film
Alien, I 48
American International Pictures, I 71
Asimov, Isaac, I 125
Blade Runner, I 273
Clarke, Arthur C., I 527
Clockwork Orange, I 532
Close Encounters of the Third Kind, I 534
Conspiracy Theories, I 586
Crichton, Michael, I 631
Cult Films, I 643
Day the Earth Stood Still, I 665
Disaster Movies, I 723
Doctor Who, I 739
E.T. The Extra-Terrestrial, II 43
Godzilla, II 252
Herbert, Frank, II 395
Heston, Charlton, II 399
Independence Day, II 486
Jurassic Park, II 581
Lugosi, Bela, III 213
Lynch, David, III 216
Metropolis, III 347
Planet of the Apes, IV 63
Rocky Horror Picture Show, IV 248
Roddenberry, Gene, IV 251
Science Fiction Publishing, IV 330
Star Trek, IV 508
Terminator, IV 639
Thing, IV 642
2001: A Space Odyssey, IV 717
Wood, Ed, V 172

Science Fiction, Print
Amazing Stories, I 64
Anthony, Piers, I 100
Asimov, Isaac, I 125
Astounding Science Fiction, I 129
Barker, Clive, I 174
Blade Runner, I 273
Bradbury, Ray, I 337
Buck Rogers, I 377
Burroughs, Edgar Rice, I 396
Butler, Octavia E.(1947--), I 400
Clarke, Arthur C., I 527
Clockwork Orange, I 532
Comics, I 562
Crichton, Michael, I 631
Dick, Philip K., I 701
Dime Novels, I 716
Doctor Who, I 739
Ellison, Harlan, II 25
Gernsback, Hugo, II 225
Gibson, William, II 235
Herbert, Frank, II 395
Jurassic Park, II 581
Koontz, Dean R., III 53
Kotzwinkle, William, III 56
Le Guin, Ursula K., III 107
L'Engle, Madeleine, III 131
Lewis, C. S., III 150
Lovecraft, H. P., III 205
McCaffrey, Anne, III 313
Paperbacks, IV 9
Pulp Magazines, IV 139
Science Fiction Publishing, IV 330
Star Trek, IV 508
Superman, IV 581
Tolkien, J. R. R., IV 671
2001: A Space Odyssey, IV 717
Vonnegut, Kurt, Jr., V 56
Weird Tales, V 103
Zines, V 228

Science Fiction, Television
Conspiracy Theories, I 586
Doctor Who, I 739
Made-for-Television Movies, III 233
Outer Limits, III 579
Planet of the Apes, IV 63
Roddenberry, Gene, IV 251
Serling, Rod, IV 361
Six Million Dollar Man, IV 424
Star Trek, IV 508
Twilight Zone, IV 713
X-Files, V 203

Self-Help/Psychology
Advice Columns, I 26
Astrology, I 129
Barton, Bruce, I 179
Bly, Robert, I 296
Cabbage Patch Kids, I 403
Carnegie, Dale, I 437
Coué, Emile, I 615
Covey, Stephen, I 621
Dyer, Wayne, I 779
Friday, Nancy, II 169
Hubbard, L. Ron, II 461
Joy of Sex, II 573
Lake, Ricki, III 78
Leary, Timothy, III 112
Me Decade, III 335
Peale, Norman Vincent, IV 23
Prozac, IV 125
Psychics, IV 129
Schlessinger, Dr. Laura, IV 326
Sex and the Single Girl, IV 366

Sex Symbols
Arrow Collar Man, I 118
Bacall, Lauren, I 154
Baker, Josephine, I 158
Bara, Theda, I 168
Baywatch, I 193
Beach Boys, I 195
Beatty, Warren, I 206
Black, Clint, I 262
Bow, Clara, I 326
Carey, Mariah, I 434
Cassidy, David, I 452
Cooper, Gary, I 597
Crawford, Joan, I 625
Cruise, Tom, I 641
Dickinson, Angie, I 703
Dietrich, Marlene, I 708
Doors, I 748
Fawcett, Farrah, II 79
Funicello, Annette, II 183
Gable, Clark, II 187
Garbo, Greta, II 199
Gardner, Ava, II 200
Gere, Richard, II 224
Girl Groups, II 240
Grable, Betty, II 277
Harlow, Jean, II 370
Hayworth, Rita, II 377
Jones, Tom, II 563
Kelly, Grace, III 15
Klein, Calvin, III 46
Lee, Gypsy Rose, III 119
Mansfield, Jayne, III 259
Martin, Dean, III 280
Monroe, Marilyn, III 399
Movie Stars, III 428
Novak, Kim, III 543
Pfeiffer, Michelle, IV 48
Pin-Up, IV 58
Playboy, IV 70
Presley, Elvis, IV 105
Roberts, Julia, IV 223
Russell, Jane, IV 292
Sex Symbol, IV 369
Sports Illustrated, IV 487
Supermodels, IV 583
Taylor, Elizabeth, IV 612
Taylor, Robert, IV 615

Teen Idols, IV 617
Turner, Lana, IV 703
Twiggy, IV 713
Valentino, Rudolph, V 17
Varga Girl, V 30
West, Mae, V 115
White, Barry, V 125
Wonder Woman, V 171

Sexuality/The Body
Abortion, I 9
Advice Columns, I 26
AIDS, I 35
Albert, Marv, I 40
Androgyny, I 85
Anita Hill-Clarence Thomas Senate
    Hearings, I 93
Another World, I 99
Athletic Model Guild, I 132
Baywatch, I 193
Beavis and Butthead, I 209
Benny Hill Show, I 222
Blueboy, I 287
Blume, Judy, I 294
Bodybuilding, I 305
Bow, Clara, I 326
Bra, I 335
Bruce, Lenny, I 372
Bundy, Ted, I 384
Burlesque, I 388
Caldwell, Erskine, I 412
Campbell, Naomi, I 416
Charlie's Angels, I 479
Cheerleading, I 486
Communes, I 568
Condoms, I 578
Confession Magazines, I 581
Cosmopolitan, I 610
Days of Our Lives, I 666
Dietrich, Marlene, I 708
Disco, I 726
Divine, I 731
Dreiser, Theodore, I 768
Duncan, Isadora, I 773
Esquire, II 40
Everson, Cory, II 48
Facelifts, II 54
Feminism, II 84
Flappers, II 112
Freak Shows, II 158
Frederick's of Hollywood, II 159
Friday, Nancy, II 169
Girl Groups, II 240
Golden Girls, II 260
Grimek, John, II 316
Guiding Light, II 323
Hairstyles, II 340
Halloween, II 346
Harlequin Romances, II 367
Hefner, Hugh, II 383
Herpes, II 399
Hite, Shere, II 416
Hustler, II 470
Hutton, Ina Ray, II 472
Jong, Erica, II 564
Joy of Sex, II 573
Kinsey, Dr. Alfred C., III 40
Kotzwinkle, William, III 56
Lee, Gypsy Rose, III 119
Lesbianism, III 140
Lolita, III 183
Macfadden, Bernarr, III 226
Mapplethorpe, Robert, III 265
Masters and Johnson, III 303
Maupin, Armistead, III 307
Metalious, Grace, III 346
Midnight Cowboy, III 357
Miller, Henry, III 367
Moss, Kate, III 417
Navratilova, Martina, III 495
Newton, Helmut, III 528
NYPD Blue, III 545
Outing, III 580

Paglia, Camille, IV 4
Paperbacks, IV 9
Peep Shows, IV 30
Penthouse, IV 34
Petting, IV 45
Phone Sex, IV 51
Pill, IV 57
Pin-Up, IV 58
Playboy, IV 70
Playgirl, IV 72
Political Correctness, IV 78
Pornography, IV 92
Prince, IV 112
Rand, Sally, IV 173
Rocky Horror Picture Show, IV 248
Rolling Stones, IV 269
Safe Sex, IV 299
Sassy, IV 313
Seduction of the Innocent, IV 350
Sex and the Single Girl, IV 366
Sex Scandals, IV 367
Sexual Harassment, IV 371
Sexual Revolution, IV 373
Slasher Movies, IV 435
Spelling, Aaron, IV 472
Spice Girls, IV 473
Spring Break, IV 488
Sprinkle, Annie, IV 493
Stern, Howard, IV 530
Stockton, "Pudgy," IV 541
Strip Joints/Striptease, IV 557
Supermodels, IV 583
Susann, Jacqueline, IV 586
Swinging, IV 593
Teenagers, IV 620
Tijuana Bibles, IV 656
T-Shirts, IV 700
2 Live Crew, IV 715
Underground Comics, V 4
Updike, John, V 10
Viagra, V 43
Victoria's Secret, V 43
Waters, John, V 87
World Wrestling Federation, V 192

Short Story Writers
Barker, Clive, I 174
Beach, Rex, I 197
Benchley, Robert, I 219
Bradbury, Ray, I 337
Brand, Max, I 342
Brautigan, Richard, I 345
Caldwell, Erskine, I 412
Capote, Truman, I 426
Carver, Raymond, I 447
Cather, Willa, I 459
Christie, Agatha, I 502
Cisneros, Sandra, I 513
Derleth, August, I 692
Dick, Philip K., I 701
Du Bois, W. E. B., I 771
Ellis, Bret Easton, II 24
Ellison, Harlan, II 25
Erdrich, Louise, II 34
Fitzgerald, F. Scott, II 109
Fleming, Ian, II 116
Forsyth, Frederick, II 141
Gibson, William, II 235
Goodbye, Columbus, II 268
Hemingway, Ernest, II 386
Himes, Chester, II 408
Hubbard, L. Ron, II 461
Hughes, Langston, II 465
Invisible Man, II 498
Jackson, Shirley, II 520
Jakes, John, II 522
Kewpie Dolls, III 22
Koontz, Dean R., III 53
Kotzwinkle, William, III 56
Lardner, Ring, III 90
Lewis, Sinclair, III 155
Lovecraft, H. P., III 205
Mailer, Norman, III 242

Miller, Arthur, III 363
Norris, Frank, III 540
O'Brien, Tim, III 548
O'Connor, Flannery, III 549
Olsen, Tillie, III 558
Paley, Grace, IV 6
Paretsky, Sara, IV 12
Parker, Dorothy, IV 14
Price, Reynolds, IV 110
Pynchon, Thomas, IV 145
Runyon, Damon, IV 289
Singer, Isaac Bashevis, IV 414
Spillane, Mickey, IV 477
Steinbeck, John, IV 522
Stine, R. L., IV 535
Thurber, James, IV 654
Trillin, Calvin, IV 697
Updike, John, V 10
Vonnegut, Kurt, Jr., V 56

Soap Operas
All My Children, I 51
Another World, I 99
As the World Turns, I 121
Dallas, I 652
Dynasty, I 783
Edge of Night, II 13
General Hospital, II 218
Great Depression, II 295
Guiding Light, II 323
Ma Perkins, III 223
Mary Hartman, Mary Hartman, III 289
Nixon, Agnes, III 539
One Man's Family, III 567
Search for Tomorrow, IV 346
Soap Operas, IV 446
Young and the Restless, V 216

Social "Problems"
Abortion, I 9
Advice Columns, I 26
AIDS, I 35
Altamont, I 57
American Girls Series, I 67
Another World, I 99
Baldwin, James, I 161
Blackboard Jungle, I 268
Boat People, I 298
Butterbeans and Susie, I 400
Cancer, I 418
Capital Punishment, I 424
Chessman, Caryl, I 492
Chicago Seven, I 495
Cocaine/Crack, I 542
Conspiracy Theories, I 586
Dark Shadows, I 659
Days of Our Lives, I 666
Death of a Salesman, I 678
Divorce, I 732
Drug War, I 771
Du Bois, W. E. B., I 771
El Vez, II 19
Gangs, II 195
Ghettos, II 227
Graffiti, II 281
Gray Panthers, II 294
Happy Hour, II 359
Hate Crimes, II 373
Himes, Chester, II 408
Hippies, II 410
Juvenile Delinquency, II 583
L. A. Law, III 71
Lee, Spike, III 122
LSD, III 207
Lynching, III 217
*M*A*S*H*, III 295
McClure's, III 318
Minstrel Shows, III 371
Modern Times, III 389
Moore, Michael, III 408
Negro Leagues, III 497
New Deal, III 508
Opportunity, III 570

Phillips, Irna, IV 51
Pornography, IV 92
Protest Groups, IV 124
Road Rage, IV 221
Roseanne, IV 277
Saratoga Springs, IV 312
Sexual Harassment, IV 371
Shakur, Tupac, IV 377
Sinclair, Upton, IV 414
Stock Market Crashes, IV 539
Strip Joints/Striptease, IV 557
Suicide, IV 569
To Kill a Mockingbird, IV 663
Tramps, IV 691
Twelve-Step Programs, IV 708
White Supremacists, V 129

Social Events/Festivals
Century 21 Exposition (Seattle, 1962), I 470
Century of Progress International Exposition
    (Chicago, 1933), I 471
Cocktail Parties, I 544
Consciousness Raising Groups, I 585
Dance Halls, I 657
Debutantes, I 680
Hippies, II 410
Louisiana Purchase Exposition, III 201
Marching Bands, III 267
Traveling Carnivals, IV 692
World's Fairs, V 194

Social Groups (beatniks, hippies, boomers)
Altamont, I 57
Alternative Press, I 60
Baby Boomers, I 151
Baraka, Amiri, I 168
Beat Generation, I 201
Brautigan, Richard, I 345
British Invasion, I 354
Castaneda, Carlos, I 453
Castro, I 454
Chicago Seven, I 495
Communes, I 568
Crosby, Stills, and Nash, I 639
Donovan, I 745
Escher, M. C., II 37
Feminism, II 84
Fifties, II 96
Generation X, II 221
Ginsberg, Allen, II 239
Graham, Bill, II 282
Grateful Dead, II 291
Gray Panthers, II 294
Greenwich Village, II 304
Haight-Ashbury, II 336
Hair, II 338
Hare Krishna, II 362
Harley-Davidson, II 368
Hell's Angels, II 384
Hendrix, Jimi, II 391
Hep Cats, II 393
Hippies, II 410
Hoffman, Abbie, II 419
Home Improvement, II 437
Kesey, Ken, III 22
Koresh, David, and the Branch Davidians, III 54
Krassner, Paul, III 61
Lesbianism, III 140
Lombardi, Vince, III 185
Manson, Charles, III 261
Me Decade, III 335
Mod Squad, III 385
Modern Maturity, III 388
New Left, III 511
On the Road, III 561
Outing, III 580
Pachucos, IV 2
Pearl Jam, IV 26
Preppy, IV 105
Protest Groups, IV 124
Psychedelia, IV 128
Slang, IV 434
Student Demonstrations, IV 560

Students for a Democratic Society (SDS), IV 563
Surf Music, IV 585
Thompson, Hunter S., IV 646
Tramps, IV 691
Woodstock, V 176
Yippies, V 214
Yuppies, V 223
Zines, V 228

Social Movements
AARP (American Association for Retired
    Persons), I 3
Addams, Jane, I 17
Altamont, I 57
Baldwin, James, I 161
Bok, Edward, I 310
Castaneda, Carlos, I 453
Celebrity, I 463
Chicago Seven, I 495
China Syndrome, I 500
Civil Disobedience, I 517
Coming Out, I 566
Communism, I 569
Consciousness Raising Groups, I 585
Cults, I 646
Debs, Eugene V., I 679
Du Bois, W. E. B., I 771
Earth Day, II 1
Farm Aid, II 69
Feminism, II 84
Folk Music, II 123
Garvey, Marcus, II 205
Gay and Lesbian Press, II 210
Haight-Ashbury, II 336
Harlem Renaissance, II 365
Hite, Shere, II 416
Horne, Lena, II 449
Jackson, Jesse, II 514
John Birch Society, II 549
Johns, Jasper, II 551
Jonestown, II 563
Kent State Massacre, III 17
Kinsey, Dr. Alfred C., III 40
Kiwanis, III 46
Labor Unions, III 72
Lear, Norman, III 111
Leary, Timothy, III 112
Life, III 160
Lincoln Center for the Performing Arts, III 165
Little Magazines, III 176
Lynching, III 217
Malcolm X, III 243
March On Washington, III 266
Men's Movement, III 344
Militias, III 359
Million Man March, III 368
Mod, III 384
Moral Majority, III 409
Ms., III 434
Multiculturalism, III 439
Muscular Christianity, III 456
National Organization for Women
    (N.O.W.), III 489
New Age Music, III 506
New Age Spirituality, III 507
New Deal, III 508
New Left, III 511
Outing, III 580
Parks, Rosa, IV 15
Pearl Jam, IV 26
Political Correctness, IV 78
Pope, IV 86
Prohibition, IV 119
Promise Keepers, IV 122
Protest Groups, IV 124
PTA/PTO (Parent Teacher Association/
    Organization), IV 130
Recycling, IV 187
Red Scare, IV 188
Religious Right, IV 197
Robeson, Paul, IV 227
Ross, Diana, and the Supremes, IV 280
Seeger, Pete, IV 351

Sexual Revolution, IV 373
Steinem, Gloria, IV 524
Stonewall Rebellion, IV 544
Student Demonstrations, IV 560
Suburbia, IV 567
Thompson, Hunter S., IV 646
UFOs (Unidentified Flying Objects), V 1
Valdez, Luis, V 15
White Flight, V 128
Yippies, V 214
Yuppies, V 223

Sports Miscellaneous
Adidas, I 20
Advertising, I 23
Agents, I 34
Albert, Marv, I 40
Andretti, Mario, I 84
Arledge, Roone, I 111
Blount, Roy, Jr., I 285
Bodybuilding, I 305
Boston Marathon, I 323
Bowling, I 328
Bryant, Paul "Bear," I 374
Cheerleading, I 486
Cosell, Howard, I 608
Daytona 500, I 670
Devers, Gail, I 696
Didrikson, Babe, I 704
Disability, I 721
Disney (Walt Disney Company), I 728
ESPN, II 38
Everson, Cory, II 48
Field and Stream, II 92
Fleming, Peggy, II 116
Frisbee, II 174
Gibson, Althea, II 230
Golf, II 261
Grimek, John, II 316
Gymnastics, II 331
Hamill, Dorothy, II 348
Harding, Tonya, II 360
Hogan, Ben, II 421
Hogan, Hulk, II 423
Ice Shows, II 484
Indian, II 487
Ironman Triathlon, II 503
Jet Skis, II 545
Jogging, II 547
Johnson, Michael, II 556
Jones, Bobby, II 560
Joyner, Florence Griffith, II 574
Joyner-Kersee, Jackie, II 575
Kentucky Derby, III 19
Kerrigan, Nancy, III 21
Knievel, Evel, III 48
Kung Fu, III 68
Kwan, Michelle, III 70
LaLanne, Jack, III 80
Lee, Bruce, III 117
LeMond, Greg, III 130
Lewis, Carl, III 151
L.L. Bean, Inc., III 180
López, Nancy, III 194
Masters Golf Tournament, III 305
McLish, Rachel, III 328
Mountain Biking, III 424
Murray, Lenda, III 451
Muscle Beach, III 453
National Collegiate Athletic Association
    (NCAA), III 479
Nicklaus, Jack, III 531
Nike, III 535
1980 U.S. Olympic Hockey Team, III 536
1968 Mexico City Summer Olympic
    Games, III 537
Olympics, III 558
Owens, Jesse, III 583
Palmer, Arnold, IV 7
Pelé, IV 33
Piper, "Rowdy" Roddy, IV 60
Reeves, Steve, IV 193
Rice, Grantland, IV 209

Rigby, Cathy, IV 210
Roberts, Jake "The Snake," IV 223
Rock Climbing, IV 238
Rodeo, IV 252
Rodríguez, Chi Chi, IV 259
Roller Derby, IV 266
Sandow, Eugen, IV 309
Savage, Randy "Macho Man," IV 322
Schwarzenegger, Arnold, IV 329
Shorter, Frank, IV 388
Skateboarding, IV 428
Skating, IV 429
Slaney, Mary Decker, IV 433
Soccer, IV 449
Special Olympics, IV 470
Spitz, Mark, IV 479
Sporting News, IV 483
Sports Hero, IV 484
Sports Illustrated, IV 487
Stockton, "Pudgy," IV 541
Surf Music, IV 585
Thorpe, Jim, IV 649
Tour de France, IV 684
Treviño, Lee, IV 696
Unser, Bobby, V 10
Vardon, Harry, V 30
Ventura, Jesse, V 41
Watson, Tom, V 90
Weissmuller, Johnny, V 104
Wide World of Sports, V 133
Woods, Tiger, V 175
World Cup, V 181
World Wrestling Federation, V 192
X Games, V 203

Supporting Actors
Alien, I 48
Ball, Lucille, I 163
Bionic Woman, I 255
Buttons, Red, I 401
Calloway, Cab, I 412
Elizondo, Hector, II 22
Fabian, II 53
Fairbanks, Douglas, Jr., II 55
Frawley, William, II 157
Hackman, Gene, II 334
Hoffman, Dustin, II 420
Jones, Jennifer, II 562
Lahr, Bert, III 76
Loy, Myrna, III 207
McDaniel, Hattie, III 320
Ryder, Winona, IV 298
Ten Commandments, IV 634
Three Stooges, IV 651
Vance, Vivian, V 27

Tabloids/Sensational Journalism
Alternative Press, I 60
Ashe, Arthur, I 123
Cleopatra, I 529
Confession Magazines, I 581
Dionne Quintuplets, I 720
Gossip Columns, II 275
Hearst, William Randolph, II 379
Liberace, III 155
Liberty, III 157
Lindbergh, Charles, III 166
Media Feeding Frenzies, III 337
Muckraking, III 438
National Enquirer, III 480
Rivera, Geraldo, IV 218
Roswell Incident, IV 282
Sex Scandals, IV 367
Springer, Jerry, IV 490
Tabloid Television, IV 597
Tabloids, IV 597
True Story Magazine, IV 699
Winchell, Walter, V 151
Yellow Kid, V 212

Talk Shows, Radio
Bob and Ray, I 299
Daytime Talk Shows, I 667
Disability, I 721

Gossip Columns, II 275
Great Depression, II 295
King, Larry, III 32
Limbaugh, Rush, III 163
Linkletter, Art, III 168
Schlessinger, Dr. Laura, IV 326
Stern, Howard, IV 530
Talk Radio, IV 600
Winchell, Walter, V 151

Talk Shows, Television
Allen, Steve, I 52
Bakker, Jim, and Tammy Faye, I 160
Bob and Ray, I 299
Bradshaw, Terry, I 339
Brinkley, David, I 352
Carlin, George, I 434
Carson, Johnny, I 444
Crawford, Cindy, I 624
Daytime Talk Shows, I 667
Donahue, Phil, I 744
Douglas, Mike, I 754
Francis, Arlene, II 150
Griffin, Merv, II 313
Johnson, Earvin "Magic," II 553
King, Larry, III 32
Lake, Ricki, III 78
Lawrence, Vicki, III 106
Leno, Jay, III 132
Letterman, David, III 144
Linkletter, Art, III 168
Marx, Groucho, III 288
O'Donnell, Rosie, III 551
Paar, Jack, IV 1
Rivera, Geraldo, IV 218
Rivers, Joan, IV 219
Shore, Dinah, IV 387
Springer, Jerry, IV 490
Susskind, David, IV 587
Tonight Show, IV 677
Walters, Barbara, V 71
Winfrey, Oprah, V 153
Winters, Jonathan, V 157

Technology
Advertising, I 23
Apollo Missions, I 102
Apple Computer, I 106
Asimov, Isaac, I 125
AT&T, I 130
Billboards, I 253
Blade Runner, I 273
Bomb, I 311
Brownie Cameras, I 371
Cable TV, I 403
Cassette Tape, I 451
Catalog Houses, I 455
CB Radio, I 462
Century 21 Exposition (Seattle, 1962), I 470
Century of Progress International Exposition
   (Chicago, 1933), I 471
Challenger Disaster, I 472
Clarke, Arthur C., I 527
Community Media, I 570
Compact Discs, I 575
Coney Island, I 580
Dick Tracy, I 702
Disaster Movies, I 723
Drive-In Theater, I 769
Edison, Thomas Alva, II 13
Eight-track Tape, II 16
Electric Guitar, II 21
Electric Trains, II 22
E-mail, II 26
Ford Motor Company, II 135
Frozen Entrées, II 178
Fuller, Buckminster, II 180
Gernsback, Hugo, II 225
Great Depression, II 295
Gulf War, II 325
Home Shopping Network/QVC, II 438
Hoover Dam, II 442
Hughes, Howard, II 464

IBM (International Business Machines), II 481
Industrial Design, II 491
Internet, II 495
Juke Boxes, II 579
Kodak, III 51
Leisure Time, III 128
Lindbergh, Charles, III 166
Long-Playing Record, III 192
McLuhan, Marshall, III 329
Media Feeding Frenzies, III 337
Microsoft, III 353
Model T, III 386
NASA, III 475
Networks, III 503
Paul, Les, IV 20
Phonograph, IV 52
Plastic, IV 64
Plastic Surgery, IV 67
Popular Mechanics, IV 89
Postcards, IV 96
Public Libraries, IV 133
Roller Coasters, IV 265
Satellites, IV 314
Science Fiction Publishing, IV 330
Silent Movies, IV 393
Sputnik, IV 493
Stereoscopes, IV 528
Talk Radio, IV 600
Telephone, IV 623
Television, IV 626
Titanic, IV 661
Toffler, Alvin, IV 668
Twenties, IV 710
Video Games, V 45
Videos, V 47
World's Fairs, V 194
Y2K, V 207

Television Production
Advertising, I 23
Agents, I 34
All in the Family, I 50
American Bandstand, I 65
Another World, I 99
Arledge, Roone, I 111
Army-McCarthy Hearings, I 116
Bell Telephone Hour, I 216
Bestsellers, I 236
Bochco, Steven, I 302
Brooks, James L., I 365
Cable TV, I 403
Car 54, Where Are You?, I 432
Civil Rights Movement, I 519
Clark, Dick, I 525
CNN, I 537
Community Media, I 570
Consumerism, I 589
Cousteau, Jacques, I 621
Cronkite, Walter, I 635
Disney (Walt Disney Company), I 728
Emmy Awards, II 27
ER, II 33
ESPN, II 38
Game Shows, II 191
General Hospital, II 218
Gleason, Jackie, II 245
Good Times, II 267
Goodson, Mark, II 271
Gulf War, II 325
Hallmark Hall of Fame, II 345
Hanna-Barbera, II 355
Hawaii Five-O, II 375
Henson, Jim, II 393
Honeymooners, II 439
I Love Lucy, II 477
Jennings, Peter, II 538
Kelley, David E., III 13
Kovacs, Ernie, III 58
Kraft Television Theatre, III 60
LaLanne, Jack, III 80
Landon, Michael, III 86
Laugh-In, III 98
Lear, Norman, III 111

Liberace, III 155
Live Television, III 178
Made-for-Television Movies, III 233
Mantle, Mickey, III 262
Martin, Quinn, III 282
Masterpiece Theatre, III 302
Miami Vice, III 349
Mister Rogers' Neighborhood, III 378
Monday Night Football, III 393
MTV, III 435
Murrow, Edward R., III 451
My Three Sons, III 467
Networks, III 503
Nixon, Agnes, III 539
Omnibus, III 561
Paley, William S., IV 6
Philco Television Playhouse, IV 50
Phillips, Irna, IV 51
Potter, Dennis, IV 102
Public Television (PBS), IV 135
Quiz Show Scandals, IV 151
Reality Television, IV 181
Retro Fashion, IV 205
Roller Derby, IV 266
Sarnoff, David, IV 312
Satellites, IV 314
Saturday Night Live, IV 320
Schlatter, George, IV 325
Serling, Rod, IV 361
Sheldon, Sidney, IV 381
Shulman, Max, IV 391
Sitcom, IV 418
60 Minutes, IV 425
$64,000 Question, IV 427
Soul Train, IV 461
Spelling, Aaron, IV 472
Studio One, IV 563
Susskind, David, IV 587
Swaggart, Jimmy, IV 587
Syndication, IV 595
Tabloid Television, IV 597
Teenagers, IV 620
Television, IV 626
Television Anchors, IV 629
Thomas, Danny, IV 644
Thomas, Marlo, IV 645
Today, IV 666
Toys, IV 685
Turner, Ted, IV 704
20/20, IV 712
Videos, V 47
Webb, Jack, V 98
Welk, Lawrence, V 106
Wertham, Fredric, V 111
Wide World of Sports, V 133
World Wrestling Federation, V 192
Young and the Restless, V 216
Your Hit Parade, V 220

Tennis
Adidas, I 20
Agassi, Andre, I 33
Ashe, Arthur, I 123
Connors, Jimmy, I 584
Evert, Chris, II 48
King, Billie Jean, III 28
Laver, Rod, III 103
McEnroe, John, III 324
Navratilova, Martina, III 495
Riggs, Bobby, IV 211
Seles, Monica, IV 355
Tennis, IV 635
Wimbledon, V 150

Theatre
Allen, Woody, I 53
Apollo Theatre, I 104
Arbuckle, Fatty, I 107
Asner, Edward, I 126
Astaire, Fred, and Ginger Rogers, I 127
Baker, Josephine, I 158
Baldwin, James, I 161
Baraka, Amiri, I 168

Benchley, Robert, I 219
Blackface Minstrelsy, I 270
Bob and Ray, I 299
Borge, Victor, I 320
Brice, Fanny, I 348
Broadway, I 356
Brynner, Yul, I 375
Burlesque, I 388
Burr, Raymond, I 394
Buttons, Red, I 401
Camelot, I 414
Cats, I 460
Chayefsky, Paddy, I 484
Cohan, George M., I 548
Colbert, Claudette, I 548
Community Theatre, I 573
Dietrich, Marlene, I 708
Disney (Walt Disney Company), I 728
Divine, I 731
Edwards, James, II 14
El Teatro Campesino, II 18
Elizondo, Hector, II 22
Gish, Dorothy, II 243
Glass Menagerie, II 245
Graham, Bill, II 282
Hansberry, Lorraine, II 356
Holbrook, Hal, II 424
Ives, Burl, II 508
Jolson, Al, II 559
Karloff, Boris, III 4
Kaufman, Andy, III 7
Kaye, Danny, III 9
Lancaster, Burt, III 85
Lincoln Center for the Performing Arts, III 165
Lloyd Webber, Andrew, III 181
Lorre, Peter, III 195
Ludlum, Robert, III 213
Marie, Rose, III 272
McQueen, Steve, III 333
My Fair Lady, III 464
Nichols, Mike, and Elaine May, III 529
Odd Couple, III 550
Pearl, Minnie, IV 28
Peck, Gregory, IV 29
Poitier, Sidney, IV 75
Porter, Cole, IV 95
Prince, Hal, IV 114
Rains, Claude, IV 168
Rivers, Joan, IV 219
Robeson, Paul, IV 227
Rogers, Will, IV 263
Show Boat, IV 389
Shulman, Max, IV 391
Sondheim, Stephen, IV 454
Susskind, David, IV 587
Times Square, IV 659
23 Skidoo, IV 712
Valdez, Luis, V 15
Variety, V 31
War of the Worlds, V 79
Waters, Ethel, V 86
Welles, Orson, V 108
West, Mae, V 115
Williams, Tennessee, V 146
Ziegfeld Follies, V 227

Tourism
American Museum of Natural History, I 72
Atlantic City, I 133
Century 21 Exposition (Seattle, 1962), I 470
Century of Progress International Exposition
(Chicago, 1933), I 471
Coney Island, I 580
Cooperstown, New York, I 598
Empire State Building, II 28
Graceland, II 278
Holiday Inns, II 428
Hoover Dam, II 442
Las Vegas, III 92
Mall, III 247
Mall of America, III 245
Miami Vice, III 349
Mount Rushmore, III 423

New Deal, III 508
Niagara Falls, III 528
Postcards, IV 96
RV, IV 295
Sea World, IV 345
Sedona, Arizona, IV 349
Spring Break, IV 488
Stuckey's, IV 560
Times Square, IV 659
U.S. One, V 11
Yellowstone National Park, V 213

Toys/Games
American Girls Series, I 67
Barbie, I 171
Beanie Babies, I 198
Board Games, I 297
Bridge, I 349
Cabbage Patch Kids, I 403
Crossword Puzzles, I 641
Curious George, I 649
Dungeons and Dragons, I 774
Electric Trains, II 22
Erector Sets, II 34
Felix the Cat, II 83
Fischer, Bobby, II 104
Fisher-Price Toys, II 106
Frisbee, II 174
GI Joe, II 229
Ginny Dolls, II 239
Hopscotch, II 449
Hula Hoop, II 466
Kewpie Dolls, III 22
Legos, III 125
Lionel Trains, III 170
Madden, John, III 232
Mah-Jongg, III 242
Milton Bradley, III 369
Monopoly, III 396
Ouija Boards, III 576
Parker Brothers, IV 13
Popeye, IV 87
Raggedy Ann and Raggedy Andy, IV 163
Rambo, IV 170
Rubik's Cube, IV 286
Slinky, IV 436
Spawn, IV 470
Stickball, IV 534
Teddy Bears, IV 616
Toy Story, IV 685
Toys, IV 685
Trivial Pursuit, IV 698
Twister, IV 715
Video Games, V 45
Yo-Yo, V 223

Transportation
Air Travel, I 38
Amtrak, I 75
Automobile, I 137
Bicycling, I 245
Bumper Stickers, I 384
Camping, I 417
Electric Trains, II 22
Florida Vacations, II 119
Freedom Rides, II 163
Gas Stations, II 206
General Motors, II 220
Greyhound Buses, II 312
Harley-Davidson, II 368
Highway System, II 402
Hindenburg, II 409
Hughes, Howard, II 464
Lindbergh, Charles, III 166
Model T, III 386
NASA, III 475
On the Road, III 561
Road Rage, IV 221
Route 66, IV 284
RV, IV 295
Stuckey's, IV 560
Sunday Driving, IV 578
Titanic, IV 661

Trailer Parks, IV 689
U.S. One, V 11
Volkswagen Beetle, V 54
World's Fairs, V 194

Trials/Legal Events
Anita Hill-Clarence Thomas Senate
Hearings, I 93
Arbuckle, Fatty, I 107
Army-McCarthy Hearings, I 116
Black Sox Scandal, I 266
Boston Strangler, I 324
Bundy, Ted, I 384
Capital Punishment, I 424
Carlin, George, I 434
Chessman, Caryl, I 492
Civil Rights Movement, I 519
Dahmer, Jeffrey, I 651
Darrow, Clarence, I 660
Dead Kennedys, I 675
Equal Rights Amendment, II 32
Flag Burning, II 111
Free Agency, II 160
Fugitive, II 179
Gay and Lesbian Marriage, II 208
Gotti, John, II 277
Hate Crimes, II 373
Hiss, Alger, II 413
Hoffman, Abbie, II 419
Hollywood Ten, II 434
Hustler, II 470
Liberace, III 155
Lindbergh, Charles, III 166
Lynching, III 217
Macfadden, Bernarr, III 226
McCarthyism, III 314
Microsoft, III 353
Muzak, III 463
My Lai Massacre, III 465
Nader, Ralph, III 469
Parks, Rosa, IV 15
Penthouse, IV 34
Pornography, IV 92
Scopes Monkey Trial, IV 335
Selena, IV 354
Sexual Harassment, IV 371
Simpson, O. J., IV 404
Simpson Trial, IV 405
2 Live Crew, IV 715
Tyson, Mike, IV 718
Wertham, Fredric, V 111
White Flight, V 128
White, Stanford, V 129

Variety and Game Shows, Television
Allen, Steve, I 52
Amsterdam, Morey, I 74
Berle, Milton, I 228
Burnett, Carol, I 391
Caesar, Sid, I 408
Campbell, Glen, I 416
Cantor, Eddie, I 423
Cavett, Dick, I 460
Coca, Imogene, I 540
Como, Perry, I 574
Drag, I 762
Edwards, Ralph, II 16
Francis, Arlene, II 150
Game Shows, II 191
Godfrey, Arthur, II 251
Goodson, Mark, II 271
Hee Haw, II 381
Hollywood Squares, II 434
Hope, Bob, II 446
Hutton, Ina Ray, II 472
Jackson Five, II 513
Jeopardy!, II 541
Jones, Tom, II 563
Kasem, Casey, III 6
Laugh-In, III 98
Linkletter, Art, III 168
Martin, Dean, III 280
Miller, Roger, III 367

Muppets, III 444
Newlywed Game, III 526
Owens, Buck, III 582
Parton, Dolly, IV 17
Pearl, Minnie, IV 28
Price Is Right, IV 108
Queen for a Day, IV 149
Quiz Show Scandals, IV 151
Russell, Nipsey, IV 293
Shore, Dinah, IV 387
$64,000 Question, IV 427
Smith, Kate, IV 439
Sonny and Cher, IV 456
Sullivan, Ed, IV 570
This Is Your Life, IV 643
To Tell the Truth, IV 664
Welk, Lawrence, V 106
What's My Line?, V 122
Wheel of Fortune, V 122
Wilson, Flip, V 148
Winters, Jonathan, V 157
Your Show of Shows, V 221

Vaudeville
Abbott and Costello, I 5
Agents, I 34
Allen, Steve, I 52
Arbuckle, Fatty, I 107
Astaire, Fred, and Ginger Rogers, I 127
Benny, Jack, I 222
Bergen, Edgar, I 225
Berle, Milton, I 228
Blackface Minstrelsy, I 270
Brice, Fanny, I 348
Broadway, I 356
Burlesque, I 388
Burns, George, and Gracie Allen, I 392
Cantor, Eddie, I 423
Charlie McCarthy, I 478
Cohan, George M., I 548
Crosby, Bing, I 638
Didrikson, Babe, I 704
Drag, I 762
Holliday, Judy, II 429
Houdini, Harry, II 456
Jessel, George, II 542
Jolson, Al, II 559
Kaye, Danny, III 9
Keaton, Buster, III 10
Lahr, Bert, III 76
Laurel and Hardy, III 100
Lee, Gypsy Rose, III 119
Lewis, Jerry, III 152
Marx Brothers, III 287
McDaniel, Hattie, III 320
Minstrel Shows, III 371
Movie Palaces, III 426
Networks, III 503
Noloesca, La Chata, III 540
Radio Drama, IV 160
Rogers, Will, IV 263
Skelton, Red, IV 431
Smith, Kate, IV 439
St. Denis, Ruth, IV 494
Tap Dancing, IV 605
Three Stooges, IV 651
Traveling Carnivals, IV 692
Variety, V 31
Vaudeville, V 33
Walker, Aida Overton, V 61
Walker, George, V 62
West, Mae, V 115
Winchell, Walter, V 151
Youngman, Henny, V 219

Villains
Fu Manchu, II 179
Lorre, Peter, III 195
Lugosi, Bela, III 213
Price, Vincent, IV 110
Silence of the Lambs, IV 393
Slasher Movies, IV 435
Weird Tales, V 103

Western, V 118

War
Adidas, I 20
Alternative Press, I 60
Andrews Sisters, I 84
Anne Frank: The Diary of a Young Girl, I 95
Armed Forces Radio Service, I 112
Baby Boomers, I 151
Bay of Pigs Invasion, I 192
Board Games, I 297
Bomb, I 311
Capra, Frank, I 428
Catch-22, I 457
Chicago Seven, I 495
Civil War Reenactors, I 521
Clancy, Tom, I 524
Coca-Cola, I 540
Cold War, I 549
Communism, I 569
Coors, I 599
Corwin, Norman, I 604
Draft, I 761
Fallout Shelters, II 58
Firearms, II 101
Grable, Betty, II 277
Gulf War, II 325
Hersey, John, II 399
Japanese American Internment Camps, II 525
Kaltenborn, Hans von, III 1
Kantor, MacKinlay, III 3
Kent State Massacre, III 17
Lamarr, Hedy, III 82
League of Their Own, III 110
Life, III 160
Lindbergh, Charles, III 166
Luciano, Lucky, III 212
Marvel Comics, III 285
Militias, III 359
My Lai Massacre, III 465
Paperbacks, IV 9
Sandburg, Carl, IV 306
Seven Days in May, IV 364
Shirer, William L., IV 384
Smith, Kate, IV 439
Spin, IV 478
Stewart, Jimmy, IV 532
Students for a Democratic Society (SDS), IV 563
Tokyo Rose, IV 669
Trout, Robert, IV 698
Varga Girl, V 30
Vietnam, V 49
War Bonds, V 74
Works Progress Administration (WPA)
    Murals, V 179
World War I, V 184
World War II, V 188
Yankee Doodle Dandy, V 207

War, Film
All Quiet on the Western Front, I 52
Apocalypse Now, I 101
Best Years of Our Lives, I 236
Bridge on the River Kwai, I 349
Casablanca, I 447
Catch-22, I 457
Cold War, I 549
Deer Hunter, I 681
Dirty Dozen, I 721
Disability, I 721
Fail-Safe, II 55
From Here to Eternity, II 175
Gable, Clark, II 187
General, II 218
Gone with the Wind, II 263
Great Depression, II 295
Patton, IV 19
Platoon, IV 69
Rambo, IV 170
Schindler's List, IV 324
Silent Movies, IV 393
Spartacus, IV 468
Stallone, Sylvester, IV 500

Tora! Tora! Tora!, IV 681
Vietnam, V 49
War Movies, V 75
World War II, V 188

War, Print
Anne Frank: The Diary of a Young Girl, I 95
Bestsellers, I 236
Captain America, I 429
Catch-22, I 457
Cold War, I 549
Doctor Zhivago, I 740
From Here to Eternity, II 175
Gone with the Wind, II 263
Kantor, MacKinlay, III 3
Little Orphan Annie, III 177
Maus, III 308
O'Brien, Tim, III 548
Paperbacks, IV 9
Steinbeck, John, IV 522
Vietnam, V 49
World War II, V 188

War, TV
Alda, Alan, I 42
Cold War, I 549
Hogan's Heroes, II 424
Made-for-Television Movies, III 233
Magnum, P.I., III 241
*M*A*S*H*, III 295
McHale's Navy, III 327
World War II, V 188

Westerns, Film
Autry, Gene, I 142
Brand, Max, I 342
Butch Cassidy and the Sundance Kid, I 398
Cooper, Gary, I 597
Eastwood, Clint, II 2
Fistful of Dollars, II 107
Fonda, Henry, II 127
Ford, Glenn, II 131
Ford, John, II 133
Gable, Clark, II 187
Good, the Bad, and the Ugly, II 266
High Noon, II 400
Hopalong Cassidy, II 444
How the West Was Won, II 458
Ladd, Alan, III 75
L'Amour, Louis, III 84
Leone, Sergio, III 136
Lone Ranger, III 189
Magnificent Seven, III 240
Man Who Shot Liberty Valance, III 253
McCrea, Joel, III 319
Mix, Tom, III 383
My Darling Clementine, III 464
Redford, Robert, IV 190
Rogers, Roy, IV 262
Scott, Randolph, IV 339
Searchers, IV 346
Shane, IV 378
She Wore a Yellow Ribbon, IV 381
Silent Movies, IV 393
Spaghetti Westerns, IV 467
Stagecoach, IV 497
Unforgiven, V 5
Wayne, John, V 91
Western, V 118
Wild Bunch, V 133
Wister, Owen, V 161

Westerns, Print
Argosy, I 109
Arizona Highways, I 110
Bestsellers, I 236
Brand, Max, I 342
Cody, Buffalo Bill, and his Wild West
    Show, I 545
Grey, Zane, II 309
Hopalong Cassidy, II 444
Kantor, MacKinlay, III 3
L'Amour, Louis, III 84
Leonard, Elmore, III 134

Mix, Tom, III 383
My Darling Clementine, III 464
Paperbacks, IV 9
Pulp Magazines, IV 139
Shane, IV 378
Western, V 118
Wister, Owen, V 161

Westerns, Television
Bonanza, I 316
Gunsmoke, II 326
Hopalong Cassidy, II 444
Kung Fu, III 68
Lone Ranger, III 189
Mix, Tom, III 383
Wagon Train, V 59
Western, V 118

Work
Academy Awards, I 12
Agents, I 34
Amway, I 80
Avon, I 146
Baby Boomers, I 151
Carnegie, Dale, I 437
Casual Friday, I 455
Catalog Houses, I 455
Cathy, I 460
Chavez, Cesar, I 482
Covey, Stephen, I 621
Ford, Henry, II 132
Fuller, Buckminster, II 180
Grapes of Wrath, II 290
Happy Hour, II 359
Harlequin Romances, II 367
Iacocca, Lee, II 480
Industrial Design, II 491
Jeans, II 532
Kelly Girls, III 14
Kitsch, III 43
Labor Unions, III 72
Leisure Time, III 128
Modern Times, III 389
Muzak, III 463
New Deal, III 508
Organization Man, III 572
Pants for Women, IV 7
Red Scare, IV 188
Rock Climbing, IV 238
Sexual Harassment, IV 371
Sinclair, Upton, IV 414
Steinem, Gloria, IV 524
Suburbia, IV 567
Summer Camp, IV 573
Supermodels, IV 583
Tupperware, IV 700
Twenties, IV 710
Valdez, Luis, V 15
Wobblies, V 165
Yuppies, V 223

World Music/Reggae/Ska
Ally McBeal, I 57
Belafonte, Harry, I 214
Blades, Ruben, I 275
Puente, Tito, IV 137
Reggae, IV 194
Salsa Music, IV 303
Santana, IV 311
Simon, Paul, IV 403
Zydeco, V 235

Youth Culture
AC/DC, I 14
Altamont, I 57
Alternative Press, I 60
American Bandstand, I 65

American Graffiti, I 69
Anka, Paul, I 95
Archie Comics, I 108
Automobile, I 137
Baby Boomers, I 151
Batman, I 189
Beach Boys, I 195
Beanie Babies, I 198
Beat Generation, I 201
Beavis and Butthead, I 209
Bellbottoms, I 216
Beverly Hills 90210, I 242
Big Bands, I 247
Big Little Books, I 249
Black Sabbath, I 265
Blackboard Jungle, I 268
Blume, Judy, I 294
Bobby Socks, I 301
Body Decoration, I 303
Bon Jovi, I 315
Boy Scouts of America, I 333
Brady Bunch, I 339
Brat Pack, I 344
Breakfast Club, I 347
British Invasion, I 354
Buck Rogers, I 377
Burroughs, William S., I 397
Cassette Tape, I 451
Cassidy, David, I 452
Castaneda, Carlos, I 453
Catcher in the Rye, I 458
Charm Bracelets, I 480
Cherry Ames, I 491
Chicago Seven, I 495
Child Stars, I 498
Chuck D, I 508
Cigarettes, I 510
Clockwork Orange, I 532
Comic Books, I 560
Comics, I 562
Days of Our Lives, I 666
Dean, James, I 676
Devo, I 696
Dime Novels, I 716
Disco, I 726
Dobie Gillis, I 735
Donovan, I 745
Drive-In Theater, I 769
Dungeons and Dragons, I 774
Easy Rider, II 4
Electric Guitar, II 21
Environmentalism, II 29
Fabian, II 53
Facelifts, II 54
Family Circle, II 59
Flappers, II 112
Folk Music, II 123
Frisbee, II 174
Funicello, Annette, II 183
Gangs, II 195
Generation X, II 221
Girl Groups, II 240
Girl Scouts, II 242
Goth, II 277
Graffiti, II 281
Haight-Ashbury, II 336
Hair, II 338
Hairstyles, II 340
Haley, Bill, II 343
Heavy Metal, II 380
Hippies, II 410
Hot Rods, II 455
Hula Hoop, II 466
I Was a Teenage Werewolf, II 480
Judas Priest, II 577

Juvenile Delinquency, II 583
Kewpie Dolls, III 22
KISS, III 42
Klein, Calvin, III 46
Kukla, Fran, and Ollie, III 68
Lake, Ricki, III 78
Let's Pretend, III 143
Little League, III 174
Manson, Charles, III 261
Marvel Comics, III 285
Mickey Mouse Club, III 351
Midnight Cowboy, III 357
Mod, III 384
Mod Squad, III 385
Monkees, III 394
Moonies/Reverend Sun Myung Moon, III 405
Mötley Crüe, III 418
MTV, III 435
Muscle Cars, III 455
New Kids on the Block, III 510
Pachucos, IV 2
Pearl Jam, IV 26
Peppermint Lounge, IV 36
Pepsi-Cola, IV 36
Pop Music, IV 83
Presley, Elvis, IV 105
Prom, IV 120
Protest Groups, IV 124
Psychedelia, IV 128
Punk, IV 142
Rap/Hip-Hop, IV 174
Real World, IV 181
Rebel without a Cause, IV 185
Reggae, IV 194
Robbins, Tom, IV 223
Rock Climbing, IV 238
Rolling Stones, IV 269
Ryder, Winona, IV 298
Sassy, IV 313
Saturday Morning Cartoons, IV 317
Saturday Night Live, IV 320
Seduction of the Innocent, IV 350
Seventeen, IV 364
Skateboarding, IV 428
Slang, IV 434
Slasher Movies, IV 435
Soul Train, IV 461
Spice Girls, IV 473
Stadium Concerts, IV 496
State Fairs, IV 518
Student Demonstrations, IV 560
Surf Music, IV 585
Teen Idols, IV 617
Teenagers, IV 620
Tennis Shoes/Sneakers, IV 637
Toga Parties, IV 669
2 Live Crew, IV 715
23 Skidoo, IV 712
Trixie Belden, IV 698
Valens, Ritchie, V 16
Vampires, V 22
Video Games, V 45
Wayne's World, V 94
Wertham, Fredric, V 111
West Side Story, V 116
Who, V 131
X Games, V 203
X-Men, V 205
Young, Neil, V 217
Youth's Companion, V 222
Zap Comix, V 225
Zines, V 228

INDEX

A&M Records, I 57
A&P Bandwagon, The, IV 439
A&R, V 125
A & W Rootbeer, II 72
Abbey, Edward, II 11
Abbott and Costello Meet Frankenstein, III 214
Abbott, Bud, I 5
Abbott, George, IV 114
Abbott, Jack Henry, III 243
Abbott, Jim, I 722
Abby, I 279
ABC, I 111, 238, 353, 404, 683, II 219, III 269, 406,
    504, 579, IV 18, 424, 580
ABC Sports, I 111, V 133
Abdul, Paula, III 460
Abdul-Jabbar, Kareem, I 39, II 553, III 197, IV
    225, V 174
Abel, Bob, III 62
Abolitionists, I 124
Abominable Snowman, I 251
Abortion, II 85, III 307
Abrahams, Jim, I 39
Abrahamson, Herb, I 135, IV 208
Abramovic, Marina, IV 38
Abrams, Isaac, IV 128
Abramson, Herb, II 35
Abruzzese, Dave, IV 26
Absent-Minded Professor, III 229
Abstract Expressionism, II 551, IV 80, 81, V 81
Abyss, I 724
Academy Awards, I 641, II 44, 129, 133, 141, 303,
    401, 421, 429, 435, 487, III 4, 159, 320, 410, IV
    48, 76, 190, 230, 338, 358
Academy of Television Arts & Sciences, II 27
Acconci, Vito, IV 38
Ace, IV 11
Acheson, Lila, IV 177
Acker, Jean, V 17
Ackerman, Will, III 506
ACLU (American Civil Liberties Union), I 17
Action Comics, I 563, IV 582
Actors Equity Association, V 31
Actors Studio, I 342, 677, II 120, III 400, IV 3
Acuff, Roy, I 619, II 287, IV 29, V 142
Acuff-Rose Publishing, V 142
Adam 12, V 99
Adams, Ansel, II 405
Adams, Don, I 53
Adams, Edie, III 59
Adams, Franklin P., II 55
Adams, Harriet, II 361, III 474, IV 549
Adams, John, I 463
Adams, John G., I 116
Adams, Neal, I 190
Adams, Neile, III 334
Adams, Samuel, II 101
Adams, Scott, I 710
Adams, Scott. See *Dilbert*
Adams, "Uncle" Bill, III 143
Addams, Charles, I 18, III 523
Addams Family, II 153
Addams, Jane, I 310, II 583
Adidas, IV 637
Adios, Amigo, I 279
Adkins, David. See Sinbad
Adler, Larry, II 371
Adler, Lou, I 644, III 251
Adler, Stella, I 342
Adultery, V 10
Advance, V 198
Adventures of Huckleberry Finn, I 459
Adventures of Ozzie and Harriet, I 229, 607, III 500
Adventures of Robin Hood, II 121
Advise and Consent, IV 104, 676
Advocate, IV 545
Aerosmith, I 41, IV 288
Affirmative Action, I 253, IV 79
AFL-CIO, I 599
African Queen, II 471
Afro-Cuban Orchestra, III 97
Age of Innocence, IV 338
Agee, James, III 142

*Agony and the Ecstasy: A Novel of
    Michelangelo*, IV 542
Ahmal and the Night Visitors, II 345
AIDS, I 38, 99, 124, 359, 745, II 25, 209, 214, 215,
    463, 553, III 273, 581, IV 76, 299, 375, 391,
    416, 613, V 12
Aikman, Troy, I 654, IV 118
Ain't Misbehavin', III 459
"Ain't That a Shame," I 743
Airheads, I 119
Airplane, I 9
Airport, I 38, III 280
A.J. Croce, I 635
AK47 rifle, II 102
Alabama's Ghost, I 279
Aladdin, V 144
Aladdin Company, The, I 455
Alambrista!, III 558
Albatross, IV 10
Albertson, Jack, IV 116
Alcindor, Lew, V 174
Alcoholics Anonymous (AA), I 707, IV 708, 92
Alda, Alan, III 295
Alda, Robert, I 42
Aldon Music, I 351
Aldrich Family, IV 419
Aldrich, Robert, I 721
Aldrin, Buzz, I 104
Ale, I 210
Alexander, Ben, I 766
Alexander, E. Roy, III 211
Alexander, Grover Cleveland, V 183
Alexander, Jane, III 47
Alexander, Jason, IV 353
Alexander, Shana, IV 425
ALF, IV 535
Al-Fayed, Dodi, I 699
Alfred Hitchcock Presents, I 63, II 414
Alger, Horatio, Jr., I 109, III 177, 188, 442
Algonquin Circle, I 219
Algonquin Round Table, III 522, IV 14
Ali, Muhammad, I 20, 609, II 138, 157, III 136, 172,
    269, IV 234, 247, 487
Alice, III 103
Alice Adams, IV 607
Alice Doesn't Live Here Anymore, III 104, IV 337
Alice in Cartoonland, I 728
Alice in Chains, I 303
Alice's Restaurant Massacre, II 328
Alien, I 273, IV 436, V 96
Alien Resurrection, I 49
Alison, Joan, I 448
Alkon, Amy, I 28
All-American Football Conference, IV 117
All-American Girls Professional Baseball
    League, III 110
All Eyez On Me, IV 378
All Hail the Queen, IV 150
All in the Family, I 213, 656, II 148, 536, III 74, 103,
    111, 306, 505, IV 19, 278, 420, 441
All the King's Men, III 191, 192
All My Children, I 99, III 324, IV 540, 446
All the President's Men, IV 190
All Quiet on the Western Front, V 77, 188
All Stars, I 115
All-Story Magazine, IV 139
All That Jazz, II 144
Allan, Jed, III 96
Alland, William, I 514
Allen, Fred, V 22
Allen, Gracie, IV 504
Allen, Lewis, I 316
Allen, Mark, II 503
Allen, Paul, III 353
Allen, Phog, I 472
Allen, Steve, I 373, IV 1, 197, 677, V 139
Allen, Tim, II 437
Allen, Woody, I 43, 71, 98, II 50, III 47, 407, IV 505
Allied Artists, I 150
Allied Domecq PLC, I 775
Alligator Records, I 56
Allison, Fran, III 68

Allison, Jerry, II 430
Allman Brothers, III 220
Ally McBeal, I 25
Ally McBeal, II 390
Ally McBeal, III 13, 489
Almanac Singers, II 329, IV 351
Almo Sounds, I 57
Alpert, Herb, I 441
Alpert, Richard, IV 128
Also Sprach Zarathustra, I 527
Alsop, Joseph, I 116
Alston, Walter, III 94
Altamont, II 386, 535
Altamont speedway, IV 269
Alternative comics, V 4
Alternative Media Center (AMC), I 572
Alternative music, IV 85
Altman, Robert, I 316, III 295, V 119
Alton, John, I 99
Alvin and the Chipmunks, I 501
Alvin "Shipwreck" Kelly, II 111
Alvin Show, I 501
Amateur Athletic Union (AAU), I 306
Amazing Stories, I 125, 377, II 225, IV 141, 331
Amazon.com, II 497
Ameche, Don, II 512
Ameche, Jim, II 512
America Online (AOL), II 27, 497
American Association of Retired Persons
    (AARP), III 388
American Ballet Theater, I 180, IV 641
American Bandstand, I 165, 485, 525, III 352, 435,
    IV 461, 619
American Bandstand. See also Clark, Dick
American Baseball League, I 143
American Basketball Association (ABA), I 187, II
    36, III 478
American Basketball League (ABL), III 477
American Beauty, II 293
American Birth Control League, II 85
American Boy, V 223
American Broadcasting Company (ABC), III 504, IV
    48, 328, 712, V 133
American Camping Association, I 418
American Cancer Society, III 76
American Civil Liberties Union, II 209, IV 335
American Comedy Awards, IV 325
American Communist Party, III 314
American Derby, III 20
American Enterprise Institute, IV 125
American Express, I 628
American Family Association, IV 34
American Federation of Labor, V 165
American Federation of Musicians, I 326
American Federation of Television and Radio
    Artists, II 28
American Film Institute, II 66, 269, IV 75
American Film Institute Lifetime Achievement
    Award, II 135, 416
American Football Conference, IV 580
American Football League (AFL), III 232, 471, 483,
    IV 118, 580
American Gigolo, II 224
*American Girl*Magazine, I 68
American Graffiti, II 357, V 168
American Greetings, II 306
American Homes and Gardens, IV 335
American Hot Rod Association (AHRA), I 764
American Humane Association, II 119, IV 109
American Indian Movement, IV 581
American International Pictures, I 150, III 425
American Language, III 342, 343
American Legion, IV 671
American Library Association, IV 134
American Magazine, I 159
American Medical Association, I 16, III 226
American Mercury, III 342
American Motors, III 455
American Museum, II 158
American Music Awards, II 458
American Negro Theater, IV 75

American Professional Football Association, I 492
American Psycho, II 24
American Radio Company, III 11
American Railway Union, I 679
American Revolution, III 4
American Scene Magazine, II 247
American Scene painting, V 180
American Scientific Affiliation, I 627
American Telephone and Telegraph (AT&T), I 130, II 495, IV 314
American Top 40, III 6
American Tragedy, I 768, IV 63
American West, The, IV 529
American Women's Suffrage Association, II 85
American Writers Against the Vietnam War, I 296
America's Funniest Home Videos, IV 181
America's Most Wanted, IV 181
Ames, Leon, III 339
Ames, Teal, II 13
Amos, John, II 267
Amos 'n Andy Show, I 241, 271, II 536, 580, III 504, IV 160, 310, 419, 421, 711
Ampex Electric Corporation, V 47
Amphetamines, I 706
Amusement park, IV 266
Amyotrophic lateral sclerosis (ALS), II 218
Analog, I 129
Analog. See Astounding Science Fiction
Anchor Books, IV 11
Ancient Child, III 392
Anders, William, I 104
Andersen, Hans Christian, IV 430
Anderson, Broncho Billy, V 120
Anderson, Carl, II 544
Anderson, Eddie, I 223
Anderson, Gillian, V 204
Anderson, Harry, I 177
Anderson, Judith, II 415, IV 635
Anderson, Loni, IV 206
Anderson, Michael, I 280
Anderson, Pamela Lee, III 419, IV 34
Anderson, Pete, V 216
Anderson, Sherwood, I 570, II 387, IV 710
Anderson, Signe, II 535
Anderson, Sparky, I 696
Anderson, Stig, I 4
Anderson, Walt, II 72
Anderson, Walter, V 127
Andersonville, III 3
Andersson, Benny, I 4, III 460
Andress, Ursula, II 523
Andrews, Julie, I 414, III 292, 459, 464, IV 462
Andrews, Robert Hardy, II 512
Andrews Sisters, I 75, 84
Andromeda Strain, I 631
Andrus, Ethel Percy, I 3, III 388
Andy Griffith Show, IV 419, 645
Angel City, IV 383
Angel Street, IV 110
Angell, Katherine, III 523
Angell, Roger, III 523
Angels in America, I 36
Angels with Dirty Faces, I 411
Anger, Kenneth, III 262
Angola Prison Rodeo, IV 253
Angstrom, Harry, V 10
Anheuser-Busch, I 380, IV 580
Animal House, III 488, IV 669
Animal Man, I 672
Animals, The, I 355, II 391
Anime, I 92
Aniston, Jennifer, II 172
Anka, Paul, II 184
Annenberg, Moe, III 238
Annenberg, Walter H., IV 365, 706
Annie, III 177, 459
Annie Get Your Gun, IV 382, V 120
Annie Hall, I 54
Anniston, Alabama, II 163
Another Roadside Attraction, IV 223
Another Woman, I 54

Another World, II 324, IV 446
Anspaugh, David, II 442
Answer Man, II 192
Ant, Adam, I 86
Anthony, Marc, IV 304
Anthony, Michael, V 26
Anthony, Susan B., II 85, V 195
Anti-Semitism, I 321, II 521
Anything Goes, III 459, IV 96
Apartment, II 88
Apocalypse Now, IV 70, V 51, 78
Apodaca, Jerry, II 412
Apollo, I 164
Apollo 1, III 475
Apollo missions, I 527
Apollo Project, III 475
Apollo Theatre, I 248, II 108, III 154, 223
Appalachian Trail, III 491
Apple Computer, II 483, 496, III 354
Apple, Fiona, III 414
Apple Mary, III 294
Apple Records, IV 615
Applegate, Christina, III 278
Appleton, Victor, IV 674
Arau, Alfonso, III 162
Arbuckle, Roscoe "Fatty," I 108, II 64, 432, III 10, 24, IV 367, 397
Arby's, II 73
Arcade, III 308
Arcaro, Eddie, III 20
Arcel, Ray, I 776
Archerd, Army, V 32
Archie Bunker's Place, I 50, IV 535
Archie Comics, I 561
Archive of Folk Song, II 296, III 509
Arden, Jane, I 348
Ardoin, Amédé, V 235
Are You There God? It's Me, Margaret, I 294
Areu, Hermanos, III 540
Areu, José, III 540
Argosy, III 442, IV 139
Arista Records, III 368
Aristides, III 19
Arkham House, I 692
Arkin, Alan, I 458, IV 348
Arkoff, Samuel Z., I 71
Arkus-Duntov, Zora, I 603
Arledge, Roone, I 609, III 534, IV 712, V 133
Arlington Cemetery, I 585
Arm, Mark, II 321
Armijo, Antonio, III 92
Armory Show, I 123, III 391
Armstrong, Louis, I 214, 248, 494, 734, II 108, 353, 427, 525, 529, III 238, 435, 573, IV 168, 710
Armstrong, Neil, I 104, III 476
Army Mental Tests, IV 502
Arnaz, Desi, I 163, II 157, 477, III 97, IV 419
Arneson, Dave, I 775
Arness, James, II 327
Arno, Peter, III 523
Arnold, Eddy, III 368
Arnold, Tom, III 327
Around the World in 80 Days, I 280
ARPANET, II 26, 495
Arquette, Cliff, IV 1
Arrangement in Gray and Black, V 125
Arrowsmith, III 155
Art Deco, I 507
Art Nouveau, I 774
Art Rock, IV 602
Art Students League, IV 80
Arthur, Bea, II 91, 260, III 306
Arthur Godfrey and His Friends, II 251
Arthur Godfrey's Talent Scouts, II 251
Artist Formerly Known as Prince, The. See Prince
Arts and Crafts, I 387
Aryan Nation, V 129
Arzner, Dorothy, I 643, IV 396
As Nasty As They Wanna Be, IV 716
As the World Turns, I 99, 666, II 13, IV 446
Asch, Moses "Moe," II 126
Asch, Sholem, II 126

Ash, Mary Kay, III 290
Ashcan School, II 448
Ashe, Arthur, V 12
Asher, William, I 244
Ashford, Rosalind, III 279
Asimov, Isaac, I 129, III 107, IV 331
Askey, Gil, III 420
Asner, Ed, III 292, 294
Aspects of Love, III 182
Assassins, IV 456
Assembly line, II 137, III 387
Assembly of God Church, III 154
Associated Press, V 158
Association of Comics Magazine Publishers, IV 350
Association of Tennis Professionals, I 125
Astaire, Fred, II 203, III 14, IV 605
Astor, Mary, III 250, 339
Astounding Science Fiction, I 125
Astounding Stories, I 129, IV 141
Astounding Stories Magazine, III 108
Astounding Stories of Super-Science, IV 331
Astral Weeks, III 415
Astronomy, IV 300
AT&T Building, IV 433
Atanasoff, John V., II 495
Atari, V 45
A-Team, V 51
ATF (Bureau of Alcohol, Tobacco, and Firearms), III 54
Atherton, John, V 190
Athletic Model Guild, IV 59
Atkins, Chet, I 619, III 572, IV 111
Atkins, Cholly, III 420
Atkins, Robert, I 707
Atlanta Falcons, II 302
Atlantic City, New Jersey, III 86, 237, 396
Atlantic Records, I 352, 478, II 35, 155, III 117, IV 74, 208, 459
Atlas, Charles, I 306
Atlas Comics, III 42, 124
Atlas Shrugged, III 547
Atomic Cafe, I 313
Atomic Energy Commission, I 312
Atracciones Noloesca, III 540
Atwood, Margaret, IV 72
Aucoin, Bill, III 42
Auerbach, Red, I 322, IV 225
Auerbach-Levy, William, I 466
Auschwitz, I 95, II 436
Austen, Jane, IV 271
Auster, Paul, I 695, III 13
Austin, Phil, II 103
Austin, Steve, IV 424
Austin, Stone Cold Steve, IV 223
Autobiography of Malcolm X, II 343
Automobiles, I 769
Autry, Gene, I 619, 622, IV 258, 262, 287, V 120
Avakian, George, III 306
Avalon Ballroom, I 657
Avalon, Frankie, I 71, II 151, 184, III 425, IV 236, 618
Avary, Roger, IV 139
Avedon, Barbara, I 409
Aveling, Francis, IV 90
Avenger Magazine, IV 227
Avery, Cyrus, IV 284
Avery, Tex, I 384
Avildsen, John G., IV 247
Avon Books, IV 10
Axene, Harry, II 73
Ayers, Lemuel, I 677
Aykroyd, Dan, I 217, 293, III 451, IV 348
Ayres, Lew, I 52
Azor, Hurby "Luv Bug," IV 306
Aztec, V 15

"B" movies, I 644, II 100, IV 606
B-52s, I 416
Baa Baa Black Sheep, V 192
"Babalu," III 97
Babbitt, III 46, 155
Babies, Babies, Babies, III 228

Baby Boomers, II 98, 437, III 36, 136, 370, IV 446, 481
Baby Snooks, I 348
Babyland General Hospital, I 403
Bacall, Lauren, I 308
Bacchus, IV 669
Bach, J.S., II 66
Bacharach, Burt, I 352, 441, III 30, IV 84
Bachelor and the Bobbysoxer, IV 382
Bachman, Richard, III 37
Back Street, II 296
"Back to Africa" Movement, II 205
Back to the Beach, III 425
Back to the Future, I 416, IV 428
Backstreet Boys, III 511
Bad Lieutenant, III 13
Bad News is Coming, I 56
BADD (Bothered About Dungeons and Dragons), I 775
Baden-Powell, Robert Stephenson Smyth, I 334
Badlands, II 5
Badlands National Park, III 491
Baehr v. Lewin, II 209
Baekland, Leo H., IV 65
Baez, Joan, I 782, II 124, III 527
Bagdasarian, Jr., Ross, I 501
Bailey, Charles W. II, IV 364
Bailey, Deford, II 286
Bailey, F. Lee, I 325, II 179, IV 407
Bailey, James Anthony, IV 212
Bain, Conrad, I 709
Baio, Scott, II 358, IV 620
Baiul, Oksana, II 484
Bakelite, IV 65
Baker, Colin, I 739
Baker, George Pierce, I 574
Baker, Ginger, I 525
Baker, Jim, III 410
Baker, Lavern, IV 208
Baker League, III 398
Baker, Norma Jean. See Monroe, Marilyn
Baker, Ray Stannard, III 319
Baker, Rick, IV 642
Baker, Tom, I 739
Bakersfield, California, II 334
Bakersfield Sound, I 620
Bakker, Jim and Tammy Faye, III 337, IV 200, 367, 626
Balanchine, George, I 166, 180, III 413, IV 255, 256, 641
Baldwin, Alec, III 51
Baldwin, Faith, IV 271
Baldwin, James, III 327, V 196
Balenciaga, Cristobal, I 490
Balfe, Veronica, I 597
Balin, Marty, I 58, II 535
Ball, Lucille, I 117, II 157, 390, 477, III 505, IV 419
Ball Players Fraternity, I 540
Ballantine, I 212, IV 11
Ballard, Glen, III 414
Ballet, I 180, V 52
Bally's Las Vegas, III 281
Balmer, Edwin, IV 189
Balsam, Martin, I 458
Baltimore Colts, III 471, IV 116, 580, V 6
Baltimore Orioles, IV 7, 231
Balto, IV 44
Bambaataa, Afrika, IV 175
Bambi, III 169
Bamboo Harvester, III 377
Ban de Soliel, IV 604
Bancroft, Anne, II 280
Band That Plays the Blues, I 185
Band, The, I 782
Band-Aids, III 259
Banderas, Antonio, V 235
Bank Americard, I 628
Bank of America, I 628
Banks, Ernie, I 493
Bantam Books, I 738, IV 10
Bara, Theda, III 428, IV 369, 396
Baraka, Amiri, I 202, 520

Barbecue, I 239
Barber, Red, I 362, IV 345
Barbera, Joseph, II 355, IV 317
Barbie, I 68, 347, 589, II 229, IV 686
Barbour, Dave, III 121
Barcalo, Edward, III 106
"Barcalounger," III 106
Bardot, Brigitte, IV 370
Barefoot Contessa, II 200
Barenholtz, Ben, III 216
Bargain Basement, I 689
Barger, Sonny, I 58
Barker, Bob, II 16, 194, IV 108
Barkley, Alben, IV 28
Barkley, Charles, I 767, IV 485
Barlow, John, II 293
Barn Dance, II 286
Barnes & Noble, IV 514
Barnet, Charlie, I 248
Barnett, Ida B. Wells, I 32
Barnum and Bailey Circus, I 546
Barnum, P. T., I 130, II 158, IV 212
Baron of the Bluegrass, IV 290
Barr, Roseanne. See Roseanne
Barrilleaux, Doris, I 307
Barris, Chuck, II 194, III 526
Barris, George, II 456
Barron's, V 68
Barrow, Clyde, I 316
Barry, Jack, I 322
Barry, Joan, I 477
Barrymore, John, III 429, IV 396
Barrymore, Lionel, I 721
Bart, Peter, V 32
Barter syndication, IV 595
Barthes, Roland, IV 100
Bartholomew, Dave, I 743, III 513
Barton Fink, II 78
Barton, Lou Ann, V 37
Barton, Ralph, I 465
Barton, Steve, IV 49
Baryshnikov, Mikhail, IV 641
Barzun, Jacques, II 55
Baseball cards, I 182, V 59
Baseball Hall of Fame, I 234, 435, 528, 695, IV 231, 276, 298, V 59, 146, 217
Basie, Count, I 248, II 529, III 3, 214, 435, IV 207
Basketball Association of America (BAA), I 322, III 477
Basketball Hall of Fame, I 767, II 37, 158, IV 225
Basquiat, IV 82
Basquiat, Jean-Michel, V 82
Bass, Saul, II 416
Bass "Weejuns," III 182
Bates, Harry, I 666, IV 331
Bates, Norman, IV 130
Bathgate, Andy, II 417
Batman, I 561, 671, 703, 739
Batman, II 18
Batman, IV 141
Batman, IV 273
Batman, IV 350, 474
Batman & Robin, I 283, V 41
Battle Cry, V 191
Battle of the Bands, III 214
Battle of the Bulge, V 191
Battle of the Century, III 100
Battle of Midway, II 134
Battle of the Sexes, III 28
Battle Report, V 192
Bau, George, IV 642
Baudrillard, Jean, IV 100
Baugh, Sammy, IV 117
Bauhaus, II 492
Baum, L. Frank, V 162
Baum, W. Carter, I 714
Baxter, Anne, III 269, IV 635
Bay Area Bombers, IV 267
Baylor, Elgin, III 196
Baywatch, I 347, IV 596
Bazaar Book of Decorum, II 45
BBC, I 222, 442, III 404, V 198

Beach, Alfred Ely, IV 334
Beach Blanket Bingo, I 71
Beach Boys, I 355, III 251, IV 585
Beach Party, II 184
Beadle & Adams, I 717
Beadle, Irwin P., I 717
Beale, Howard, III 503
Beale Streeters, I 15
Beals, Jennifer, II 113
Bean, Leon Leonwood, III 180
Beard, Frank, V 236
Beard, Henry, III 487
Beard, Matthew "Stymie," III 578
Bearse, Amanda, III 278
Beastie Boys, IV 175, 305
Beat the Clock, II 193
Beat Generation, The, II 98, 239, III 176
Beatlemania, I 204
Beatles, I 4, 196, 354, 415, 576, II 48, 411, III 30, 131, 251, 262, 316, 435, 508, IV 84, 128, 234, 237, 313, 471, 496, 615, 621, 617, 619
Beatniks, I 168, II 98
Beatty, Clyde, IV 213
Beatty, Warren, I 54, 736, III 430, V 173
Beaumont, Charles, IV 714
Beaumont, Hugh, III 115
Beautiful America, I 310
Beauty and the Beast, I 730, III 460
Beavers, Louise, I 241
Beavis and Butthead, I 405, III 437
Bebble, Bert, III 174
Bebble, George, III 174
Bebop, II 530
Bechdel, Alison, I 780
Bechet, Sidney, I 559
Beck, Jeff, I 355, II 22, V 212
Beck, Martin, II 457
Becker, Marion Rombauer, II 572
Beckett, Samuel, II 50
Bee Gees, The, I 727, IV 85
Beemer, Brace, III 190
Beer, I 381
Beethoven, Ludwig von, II 67
Before Stonewall, IV 545
Beginner Books, I 758
Beiderbecke, Bix, I 436, 494, II 529, V 130
Bel Geddes, Barbara, I 653
Bel Geddes, Norman, II 492
Belafonte, Harry, II 15, IV 76
Belasco, David, I 357, IV 357
Beliveau, Jean, II 417
Bell, Alexander Graham, I 131, III 484, IV 53, 624
Bell, Bert, IV 118
Bell, James "Cool Papa," III 498
Bell, Jeanne, I 279
Bell System, I 130
Bell Telephone Orchestra, I 216
Bell, William, I 99, IV 446
Bellamann, Henry, IV 47
Bellamy, Edward, I 310, III 463
Bellamy, Ralph, IV 148
Bellas, Bruce Harry, IV 59
Bellisario, Donald, III 242
Bellows, George, I 122, 123
Beloved, III 414
Belushi, James, I 294
Belushi, John, I 89, 293, III 488, IV 286, 321, 348
Belushi, Judy Jacklin, I 218
Ben Casey, I 757
Benchley, Peter, II 527
Bencolin, Henri, I 442
Bendix, William, III 162
Benedict, Paul, II 536
Beneke, Tex, III 366
Ben-Hur, I 281, II 400, III 309
Benjamin, Benny, III 279
Benji, IV 44
Bennett, Joan, I 659
Bennett, Michael, III 459
Bennett, Tony, IV 84
Bennett, William, III 78
Benny Goodman Story, I 53

Benny, Jack, III 504, IV 1, 504, 643, V 22
Benson Murder Case, V 24
Benson, Robbie, IV 620
Benton, Robert, II 41
Benton, Thomas Hart, V 180
Bentyne, Cheryl, III 257
Berbick, Trevor, I 47
Berendt, John, II 41
Berg, Alan, V 130
Bergen, Candice, III 446
Bergen, Edgar, I 422, 478, II 90, III 504, V 22
Berger, Victor, IV 188
Bergman, Ingrid, I 448, II 415
Bergman, Peter, II 103
Berigan, Bunny, I 583
Berkeley, Busby, I 128, 423, II 142, V 228
Berle, Milton, I 85, 322, III 505, IV 504, V 219
Berlin, Irving, I 97, II 107, III 458, IV 439
Berlin Olympics, III 583
Berliner, Emile, IV 53
Berman, Shelley, IV 348
Bern, Paul, II 370
Bernabé, V 15
Bernard Hinault, III 130
Bernhardt, Sandra, III 428
Bernhardt, Sarah, I 357, IV 565
Bernstein, Carl, V 84, 86
Bernstein, Leonard, III 459, 561, V 116
Berra, Yogi, I 182, IV 523, V 184
Berry, Bill, IV 201
Berry, Chuck, I 354, 406, II 22, 430, IV 84, 207,
   208, 619, V 141
Berry, Jack, IV 151
Berryman, Clifford, IV 617
Bert and Ernie, IV 363
Bertinelli, Valerie, III 565, V 26
Berwanger, Jay, III 483, IV 117
Bessie, Alvah, II 434
Best, Pete, I 203
Best Years of Our Lives, III 3
Betamax, V 47
"Beth," III 42
Better Homes in America, Inc., I 239
Better World Society, IV 705
Betty Crocker Cookbook, I 237
Betty Ford Clinic, IV 615
Betty Furness, IV 565
Beulah, I 209, II 90, 580, IV 421
Beverly Hillbillies, I 422, II 122, III 505, IV 419
Bewitched, IV 419
Bey, Rahman, II 457
Biafra, Jello, I 675
Biberman, Herbert, II 434
Bible, The, II 182
Bickersons, III 278
Bickley, William, II 62
Bicycling, III 424
Biden, Joseph, I 93
Big 10, IV 275
Big Bird, IV 362
Big Bopper, I 354, II 430, 540
Big Boy, II 73
Big Chill, I 153
Big Heat, III 88
Big Little Books, II 113, 512, III 163, IV 88
Big One, III 409
Big Red One, V 191
Big River, III 368, 459
Big Sleep, II 99
Big Trail, V 91, 120
Big Valley, V 120
Bigelow, William Frederick, II 265
Bikini Atoll, I 311
Bikini Kill, III 414
Bill the Cat, I 284
Bill Haley and the Comets, I 268, II 344
Bill Haley and His Saddlemen, II 344
Bill Monroe and his Bluegrass Boys, II 287
Bill of Divorcement, II 394
*Billboard*Magazine Lifetime Achievement
   Award, II 312
Billings, Robert, IV 200

Billingsley, Barbara, III 115
Billy Jack, I 63
Bingham, Hiram, III 484
Biograph, IV 395, V 120
Biograph Company, II 313
Biograph studios, IV 357
Biograph Theater, I 714
Bionic Woman, I 721, IV 424
Birch, John, II 549
Bird, Larry, I 137, 187, 322, II 553, III 197, 478
Birds, II 415
Birdseye, Clarence, II 178
Birmingham, Frederic A., II 40
Birnbaum, Lisa, IV 105
Birth control, I 310, II 85, IV 374
Birth of a Nation, I 280, II 313, III 64, 309,
   428, IV 396
Bishop, Joey, I 344, IV 1
Bison, V 120
Blaché, Alice Guy, IV 396
Black Arts Movement, I 168
Black Belt Jones, I 279
Black Caesar, I 279
Black, Clint, I 620
Black Enterprise, I 32
Black Entertainment Television (BET), II 222
Black Filmmakers Hall of Fame, II 89
Black Flag, IV 143
Black Gunn, I 279
Black Mariah, IV 394
Black Mask, I 473, 694, III 65, IV 140
Black nationalism, I 168
Black Panther Party, I 152, 495, 520, II 197,
   444, III 245
Black Patti records, IV 155
Black Power, III 245
Black Sabbath, I 14, II 380, III 117, 575, IV 570
Black, Shirley Temple. See Temple, Shirley
"Black Sox" scandal, I 182, II 190, 521, V
   183, 276, 484
Black Swan records, IV 155
"Black Water," I 747
Blackboard Jungle, II 197, 344, 584, III 312, IV 76
Blackenstein, I 279
Blackface, I 721
Blacklist, II 393, III 315
Blackmail, II 415
Blackman, Honor, I 145
Black's Magic, IV 306
Blackstone, Milton, II 105
Blackton, J. Stuart, II 226, V 76
Blackwell, Robert "Bumps," III 178
Blacula, I 279
Blade Runner, I 701, III 558
Blades, Rubén, IV 304
Blair, Frank, IV 666
Blake, Amanda, II 327
Blake, Eubie, II 366
Blake, Robert, III 578
Blake, Tom, IV 585
Blake, William, I 748
Blakeney, Olive, II 393
Blakey, Art, I 19
Blanc, Mel, I 383, 422, IV 707
Blassie, Fred, III 9
Blasters, III 197
Blatty, William Peter, II 51
Blavatsky, Helena Petrovna, IV 129
Blaxploitation, II 312, 485, III 69, IV 283, 376
Blazing Publications, Inc., I 110
Blazing Saddles, I 366, V 121
Blimpie, II 73
Blind Date, II 150
Blind Faith, I 525
Blish, James, I 337
Bliven, Bruce, III 514
Blix, III 541
Bloch, Robert, IV 130, V 103
Block, Martin, I 725
Blocker, Dan, I 316
Blonde Venus, II 296
Blondie, III 516

Blood Feast, I 645
Blood in the Face, III 66
Blood, Johnny, IV 117
Bloom, Claire, I 477
Bloom County, I 722
Bloom, Vic, I 108
Bloomer, Amelia Jenks, IV 8
Bloomers, IV 8
Bloomingdale's, I 688
Blore, Chuck, IV 680
Blow, Kurtis, IV 288
Blue Dahlia, II 100, III 75
Blue Devils, I 184
Blue Grass Boys, The, I 288
Blue Jeans. See Jeans; Levi's; Wrangler Jeans
Blue laws, V 102
Blue Nun, IV 535
Blue Velvet, II 448, III 216
Bluegrass Boys, The, III 397
Blues, IV 236
Blues Brothers, V 94
Blues Brothers 2000, I 294
Blues Brothers Band, The, I 318
Blues Brothers, I 218, 413
Blues Incorporated, I 355
Bluesbreakers, I 355
Bluth, Don, I 91
Bly, Robert, III 345
Blyden, Larry, V 122
BMG, III 368
Bob Newhart Show, III 524
Bob Wills and his Texas Playboys, I 619
Bobbsey Twins, IV 548
Bobo, Willie, III 97
Bochco, Steven, II 406, III 71
Bodice rippers, IV 271
Bodkin, Herbert, II 436
Body Count, II 485
Body decoration, III 184
Bodybuilding, II 159, III 328, IV 309
Bodyguard, The, IV 18
Boetticher, Budd, IV 341
Bogart, Humphrey, I 33, 154, 226, 250, 448, II 471,
   III 195, 250, IV 162
Bohemian, I 168
Boitano, Brian, II 484
Bok, Edward, III 301
Bolan, Marc, I 86
Bolden, Buddy, I 247
Bolger, Ray, V 162
Bolshevik Revolution, IV 188
Bolt, Robert, III 105
Bolton, Judy. See Judy Bolton
Bomb, The, II 59
Bon Jovi, II 381
Bonaduce, Danny, IV 18
Bonanza, III 87
Bonanza, V 120
Bond, Ward, V 59, 120
Bonham, John, III 116
Bonnie and Clyde, I 69, 206, II 5, 122, V 133
Bono, II 329, III 27
Bono, Chastity, I 566, IV 457
Bono, Sonny, IV 207
Bono, Sonny. See also Sonny and Cher
Bonomo, Joe, I 307
Boob McNutt, II 257
Boogie Nights, IV 205, 206
Boogie-woogie, III 154
Book of Daniel, I 740
Bookends, IV 400
Booker T. and the MGs, III 26, IV 460
Book-of-the-Month Club, I 237, 375, II 55
Boone, Pat, II 251, IV 84, 619
Boorstin, Daniel, I 463
Booth, Edwin, I 357
Boothe, Clare, III 210
Borders, IV 514
Borg, Bjorn, V 150
Borges, Jorge Luis, I 695
Borglum, Gutzon, III 423
Borgnine, Ernest, II 434, III 327, V 59, 192

Bork, Robert, I 93
Borman, Frank, I 104
Born in the USA, IV 491
Born Innocent, II 584
''Born to Be Wild,'' IV 527
Born to Dance, IV 96
Born under a Bad Sign, III 26
Borne, Hal, I 128
Borscht Belt, V 219
Bosley, Tom, II 357
''Boss Radio,'' IV 681
Bosson, Barbara, II 407
Bostic, Earl, I 558
Boston Athletic Association, I 323
Boston Bruins, II 417, III 574
Boston Celtics, I 136, 186, 256, 323, II 571,
    III 196, 478
Boston marriages, III 141
Boston Pops, I 325
Boston Red Sox, II 87, V 145, 182, 217
Boston Strong Boy, IV 572
Boston Symphony Orchestra, II 400
Bostwick, Barry, I 644, IV 250
Botkin, Benjamin A., III 509
Bottin, Rob, IV 642
Boucher, Anthony, I 337
Boulder Dam Project, III 92
Boulle, Pierre, IV 63
Bourke-White, Margaret, I 508, III 159, 509
Bow, Clara, I 597, II 112, 432, IV 369, 396
Bowerman, Bill, III 535
Bowery Theatre, I 356
Bowie, David, I 86, 416, 746, II 247, III 279, IV 82,
    V 28, 37, 39, 82
Boy Council of Philadelphia, II 370
Boy George, I 86, 416, III 516
Boy in the Plastic Bubble, IV 694
A Boy Named Charlie Brown, II 323
Boy Scouts of America (BSA), I 334, 418, II 242
Boyce, William D., I 335
Boyd, William, II 444
Boyer, Charles, IV 616
Boys from Syracuse, IV 256
Boyz N the Hood, II 584
Bracco, Lorraine, II 269
Bracken, Eddie, II 393
Brackett, Charles, II 393, V 136
Brackett, Rogers, I 676
Bradbury, Ray, I 377, IV 332
Braddock, Benjamin, II 421
Braddock, James J., I 332, III 200
Bradham, Caleb, IV 36
Bradley, Bill, I 188
Bradley, Marion Zimmer, I 65
Bradshaw, Terry, IV 61, 118, 515, 589
Brady Bunch, IV 19, 289
Bragg, Billy, II 329
Brain, Robert, I 303
Branagh, Kenneth, II 153, III 557
Branca, Ralph, IV 648
Branch Davidians, The. See Koresh, David, and the
    Branch Davidians
Brand, Joshua, IV 495
Brand, Max, I 264, 756, IV 141
Branden, Nathaniel, III 547
Brando, Marlon, II 98, 202, 533, III 461,
    562, IV 3, 554
Branner, Martin, V 156
Branson, Missouri, IV 262
Brasington, Harold, IV 537
Brat Pack, I, 641, III 407
Braugher, Andre, III 53
Bray, John Randolph, II 226
Bray, Robert, III 96
Brazel, William ''Mac,'' IV 282
Breakfast at Tiffany's, I 427, II 394, III 173, 257
Breakfast Club, I 344
''Breakin' the Law,'' II 577
*Breathing Lessons: The Life and Work of Mark
    O'Brien*, I 722
Breathless, I 86
Brecht, Bertolt, I 748, III 195

Breisacher, George, III 463
Bremer, Lucille, III 340
Brennan, William, II 111
Brenner, David, III 47
Brenston, Jackie, IV 208
Breuer, Josef, II 167
Breuer, Marcel, II 492
Brewer, Carl, II 460
Brezhnev, Leonid, I 407
Brian's Song, I 492
Brice, Fanny, I 75, III 458, V 228
Bride of Frankenstein, II 152
Brideshead Revisited, IV 136
Bridge at Remagen., V 191
Bridge on the River Kwai, II 435, V 78, 191
Bridge Over Troubled Water, IV 400
Bridge Too Far, A, V 191
Bridges, Todd, I 709
Briefcase Full of Blues, I 218
Brigadoon, III 459
Briggs, Austin, II 113
Briggs Initiative, III 362
Briggs, Walter, I 695
Brigham, Carl Campbell, IV 502
Brightman, Sarah, IV 49
Brigman, June, I 348
Brillo, V 81
Bringing Up Baby, II 297, 394
Brinkley, David, I 636, II 469, IV 630
Briseno, Theodore, III 35
Brisson, Frederick, III 429
Bristol, Johnny, V 63
British Broadcasting Corporation (BBC), III 302
British hard rock, II 577
British Invasion, I 56, III 513
British monarchy, I 698
British Open, II 262
Britpop, IV 205
Britton, Vera, V 188
Britz, Chuck, I 196
Broadacre City, IV 433
Broadway, I 42, 730, II 338, 450, III 21, 97, 119,
    153, 177, 213, 259, 298, 458, IV 401, 535, 615
Broadway Melody of 1938, II 203
Broderick, Matthew, I 344
Brokaw, Tom, IV 666
Broken Lance, V 119
Brolin, James, III 269
Bronco Billy, V 121
Bronco Buster, IV 203
Bronner, Augusta Fox, II 583
Bronson, Charles, I 721, III 240
Brook, Louise, II 112
Brooklyn Dodgers, I 169, 182, 777, II 5, III 1, 94,
    263, IV 233, 345, 647
Brooks, Garth, I 262, 620, IV 29, V 141
Brooks, Herb, III 537
Brooks, James L., II 320, IV 611
Brooks, Joseph, I 220
Brooks, Mel, II 152, 227, III 216, IV 196, V 121
Brooks, Peter, II 19
Brooks, Richard, I 268
Brooks, Walter, III 376
Broomdusters, II 525
Brosnan, Pierce, II 524
Brotherhood of Sleeping Car Porters, III 72, 266
Brothers, Dr. Joyce, IV 151
Broun, Heywood, I 318
Brower, David, II 10
Brown, Bobby, II 458
Brown, Charles, I 15, IV 207
Brown, Charlie, IV 25
Brown, David, II 527
Brown, Father, I 693
Brown, Freddie, I 776
Brown, Helen Gurley, I 610, IV 366, 373
Brown, Helen Gurley. See *Cosmopolitan*; *Sex and the
    Single Girl*
Brown, Himan, I 463, II 494
Brown, James, I 294, II 184, 198, IV 460
Brown, Jim, I 279, IV 118
Brown, Kevin, I 183

Brown, Pat, II 162
Brown, Paul, IV 118
Brown, Piney, III 3
Brown Power Movement, II 19
Brown, Ruth, IV 208, 459
Brown, Tina, I 578, V 30
Brown v. Board of Education, I 93, 634, II 544
Brown, Willie, II 558
Browne, Allen Simpson, III 46
Browne, Bud, IV 585
Browne, Jackson, V 38
Browne, Stella, I 10
Brownie camera, III 52
Brownies' Book, II 79
Browning, Kurt, IV 430
Browning, Pete, III 202
Browning, Ricou, II 118
Browning, Tod, I 645, 760, II 159, IV 693
Bruce, Jack, I 355, 525
Bruce, Lenny, I 322, III 47, IV 220, 505
Bruce, Michael, I 595
Bruce of Los Angeles, IV 59
Bruner, Wally, V 122
Brunswick, John, I 329
Bryan, Clark W., II 265
Bryan, William Jennings, I 627, II 182, IV 336
Bryant, Anita, III 361
Bryant, Page, IV 349
Bryant, Paul ''Bear,'' I 556, III 471
Bryant, William Jennings, I 660
Brynner, Yul, III 85, 240, IV 635
BSkyB, II 438
Buchanan, Edgar, II 446
Buchanan, Pat, II 550
Buchinger, Matthew, II 158
Buchwald, Art, I 461
Buck and the Preacher, IV 76
Buck, John Lossing, I 376
Buck, Peter, IV 201
Buck, Robert, IV 638
Buck Rogers, I 64
Buck Rogers, II 113
Buckingham, Lindsey, II 114
Buckley, Thomas H., I 719
Buckley, William F., Jr., II 41
Bucyk, Johnny ''The Beast,'' II 417
Bud Bowl, IV 580
Budge, Don, III 103
Budweiser, I 210
Buena Vista, I 730
Buffalo Bill and the Indians, V 121
Buffalo Bills, IV 404, 581
Buffalo Bill's Wild West Show, I 622
Buffalo Springfield, I 639, V 217
Buffett, Jimmy, III 24
Bugliosi, Vincent, III 262
Bugs Bunny, I 85, 145, 276, IV 707, V 189
Builders Square, III 48
Bulimia, IV 211
Bullock, Annie Mae, IV 702
Bum, IV 692
Bundy, King Kong, III 278
Bundy, Ted, I 425
Bungalow, IV 173
Bunker, Archie, II 148, III 111, IV 441
Bunker Hill, II 227
Buntline, Ned, I 545
Bureau of Reclamation, II 30
Burger Chef, II 73
Burger King, II 73
Burger, Warren, IV 94
Burgess, Anthony, I 532
Burgess, Bobby, III 353, 425
Burke, Frank, II 328
Burke, Solomon, IV 208
Burlesque, IV 692
Burnett, Carol, I 96, III 106
Burnett, Chester. See Howlin' Wolf
Burnett, W.R., IV 230
Burning Bed, II 80
Burning Down the House, IV 602
Burns, Allan, IV 248

Burns and Allen, III 504
Burns, George, IV 197, 504
Burns, Jack, I 435
Burns, Tex, III 85
Burns, Tommy, I 332
Burr, Raymond, II 253, IV 41
Burroughs, Edgar Rice, IV 139, 330, 608
Burroughs, John, I 418
Burroughs, William S., I 16, 201, II 363
Burstyn, Ellen, I 47, IV 337
Burton, Richard, I 282, 414, II 105, IV 614
Burton, Tim, IV 287, V 173
Busch, Adolphus, I 210
Busey, Gary, I 374
Bush, George, I 93, II 326, 499, 546, 549,
    IV 147, 180
Buss, Jerry, III 197
Busse, Henry, V 130
Buster Brown, IV 686
Butch Cassidy and the Sundance Kid, II 402, IV
    190, V 118
Butkus, Dick, I 492, IV 118
Butler, Daws, II 253
Butler, Michael, II 339
Butler, Rhett, II 263
Buttafuoco, Joey, III 337
Butterfield 8, II 105, IV 614
Butterfly Kisses, I 592
Button, Dick, II 484
Buxton, Glen, I 595
Buzzi, Ruth, III 99
Bye, Bye Birdie, IV 572
Bye Bye Love, II 48
Byrd, Bobby, I 368
Byrd, Donald, II 184
Byrds, I 59, 204, 355, 639
Byrne, David, III 98, IV 602
Byrne, John, V 205

Cabaret, II 338, III 459
Cabaret, IV 114
Cabiria, I 280, IV 395
Cable channels, III 233
Cable, Lt. Joe, IV 465
Cable News Network (CNN), I 405, III 33,
    505, IV 704
Cable television, III 505
Cadillac Ranch, I 407
Caesar, Sid, I 540, IV 196, 402, V 221
Caesar's Hour, III 59
Caesar's Palace, III 48
Cafe Bizarre, V 39
Caffeine, I 546
Cage, John, I 648, IV 38
Cagney and Lacey, I 655, II 86
Cagney, James, V 207
Cahill, Holger, I 122, III 509
Cahners Publishing Company, V 32
Caidin, Martin, IV 425
Cain, James M., I 474, 751, III 359, IV 97
Cain, Paul, I 264
Cakewalk dancing, II 566
Caldwell, Erskine, II 40
Cale, John, IV 82, 192, V 39
Calhoun, George, II 300
California Angels, I 143, IV 231, 298
California Dreamin', III 251
California Highway Patrol, III 35
California International Exposition, III 169
Calkins, Dick, I 378
Call of the Wild, III 188
Callahan, John, I 722
Calley Jr., William, III 465
Calloway, Cab, I 240, 249, 293, 614, III 223
Calvin, John, I 414
Calypso, I 215
Camel (brand cigarette), I 511
Camelot, III 459
Cameras, III 52
Cameron, James, I 49, 283, 724, IV 330, 639, 663
Camille, IV 616
Camp, III 156

Camp, Walter, I 555
Campbell, Bruce, I 644
Campbell, E. Simms, II 40
Campbell, John W., I 125, 129, IV 141, 331
Campbell, Judy, IV 368
Campbell, Jule, IV 488
Campbell, Julie, IV 698
Campbell, Luther, IV 715
Campbell, Sir Malcolm, IV 537
Campbell's Soup, V 81
Camus, Albert, II 50
Canadian Bacon, III 408
Canby, Harry, I 318
Can-Can, IV 96
Cancer, III 76
Candeloro, Philippe, IV 430
Candid Camera, I 54, II 252
Candid Microphone, I 420
Candidate, IV 190
"Candle in the Wind," II 551
Candler, Asa, I 540
Candy, John, IV 348
Caniff, Milton, I 767, IV 640, V 191
Cannabis, III 272
Cannabis. See Marijuana
Cannonball Adderley Quintet, The, I 19
Cantor, Eddie, II 105, 542, III 504, IV 387, 644
Cape Canaveral, I 104
Cape Canaveral, Florida, III 475
Cape Cod, III 490
Cape Fear, III 381
Cape Fear (1991), IV 338
Capital Cities Inc., I 111
Capitol Records, I 204
Capone, Al, I 74, II 444, III 237, IV 218, 230
Capote, Truman, I 346, III 549, IV 663
Capp, Al, III 163
Capp, Al. See *Li'l Abner*
Capra, Frank, I 644, 758, II 297, 432, 504, 506, III
    294, 432, 450, IV 506, 533, V 189
Captain America, I 561, III 42, 285, V 190
Captain and the Kids. See Katzenjammer Kids
Captain Billy's Whiz Bang, I 582
Captain Blood, II 121
Captain Marvel, I 561, 672, III 229, 467
Captain Midnight, IV 686
Car 54, Where Are You?, IV 293
Carbine, Patricia, III 434
Carey, Harry, II 134, V 120
Carey, Harry, Jr., III 425
Carey, MacDonald, I 666
Carioca, I 128
Carlene Carter, I 445
Carlisle, Bob, I 592
Carlos, John, I 609, III 537, 560
Carlson, Emmons, II 323
Carlson, Raymond, I 110
Carmichael, Stokely, I 265, 585
Carne, Judy, III 98, IV 206
Carnegie, Andrew, I 440, IV 134
Carnegie, Dale, I 621, 779
Carnegie Hall, I 222, 248, 373, II 24, 353, III 156,
    165, IV 227, 440
Carnera, Primo, III 200
Carney, Art, II 246, III 60
Carol Burnett Show, I 391, 594, III 56
Carol, Sue, III 75
Carolina Alliance for Fair Employment, III 15
Caroline in the City, I 75
Caron, Glenn Gordon, III 406
Carothers, Wallace, III 544
Carousel, III 459, IV 255, 256
Carpenter, John, II 346, IV 642
Carpenters, I 57
Carpentier, George, I 686
Carpetbaggers, III 76
Carr, Eric, III 43
Carr, John Dickson, I 694
Carr, Leroy, IV 207
Carradine, David, III 68
Carradine, John, IV 635
Carrel, Alexis, III 167

Carrie, III 37, IV 694
Carroll, Diahann, I 784, II 580
Carroll, Joan, III 340
Carrol's, II 73
Carry Nation, IV 532
Cars, III 516
Carson, Johnny, I 460, III 132, 144, IV 220, 432, 677
Carson, Rachel, I 588, II 31
Carter administration, the, IV 137
Carter, Benny, I 19
Carter, Dick, I 57
Carter Family, I 618, II 315, IV 53
Carter, Jimmy, I 285, 299, II 155, III 151, 503,
    IV 198, 483
Carter, Lynda, IV 371
Carter, Ralph, II 267
Carter, T. K., IV 643
Cartier, IV 615
Cartwright, Angela, IV 645
Cartwright, Peggy, III 578
Cartwright, Veronica, I 48
Carver, Raymond, I 64, II 41
Carvey, Dana, IV 321, V 94
Casa Grande Ruin, III 491
Casablanca, I 226, III 75, IV 169
Casey, Robert, II 393
Cash, Johnny, I 446, III 154, 501, IV 558
Cash, June Carter, I 446
Casinos. See Gambling
Cass, Peggy, IV 1, 665
Cassady, Neal, I 201, II 292
Cassette, I 575
Cassidy, Butch, I 398
Cassidy, David, IV 18, 617, 619
Cassidy, Hopalong, V 120
Cassidy, Jack, I 452
Cassidy, Shaun, I 453, II 361, IV 620
Castelli, Leo, II 551, V 81
Castle, Irene and Vernon, III 449, IV 450
Castle Keep, V 191
Castle, White, II 72
Castro, Fidel, I 192
Cat Ballou, V 121
Cat on a Hot Tin Roof, IV 614
"Catch a Falling Star," I 575
Catch-22, I 42, V 191
Catholicism, IV 86
Catlow, III 85
Cats, III 181
Cavalcade of Stars, II 245
Cayce, Edgar, IV 129
CBGB's, IV 142
CBS Evening News, I 635
CBS Radio, I 574
CBS Sports, III 232
CBS's Radio Playhouse 3, III 143
Ceasar, Sid, I 322
Cecil B. DeMille, IV 395
Celebrities, II 275, III 564, IV 570
Celebrity, III 337
Cell 2455 Death Row, I 492
Cellophane, IV 65
Celluloid, IV 64
Celtic music, III 506
Censorship, IV 394, 715
Centennial, III 351
Centers for Disease Control, I 35
Central Intelligence Agency (CIA), I 192, III 208
Central Park, I 467, III 159, IV 591
Century Illustrated Monthly, IV 344
Cerf, Bennett, V 122
Chávez, César, II 19
Chad Mitchell Trio, I 687
Chaffee, Roger, I 104
Chagall, Marc, II 91
Challenge for Change, I 571
Challenger, III 476
Chamberlain, Richard, I 757
Chamberlain, Wilt, I 186, III 196, 197, 478
Chambers, Robert, IV 105
Chambers, Whittaker, II 413
Champion, Gower, II 384

Championship Auto Racing Teams League, II 491
Chan, Charlie. See Charlie Chan
Chancellor, John, I 353
Chandler, Albert Benjamin ''Happy,'' III 499, IV 232
Chandler, Chas., II 391
Chandler, Harry, II 431
Chandler, Raymond, I 250, 263, 694, 751, II 99, 359, IV 140
Chanel, I 111
Chanel, Coco, II 85, III 173
Chaney, Norman ''Chubby,'' III 578
Chaney, Sr., Lon, III 214, IV 50, 396, V 167
Chang and Eng, IV 212
Channing, Carol, II 223, 384, III 459
Chapbooks, IV 139
Chapin, Lauren, II 75
Chaplin, Charlie, I 499, 515, III 10, 101, 152, 389, 429, IV 357, 397, 692, 711, V 8
Chaplin, Geraldine, I 477
Chapman, Graham, III 403
Chapman, J. Wilburn, IV 578
Chappelle's Rabbit Foot Minstrels, IV 439
Charcot, Jean-Martin, II 166
Charisse, Cyd, I 129
Charles Addams, I 722
Charles Ranlegh Flint, II 481
Charles, Ray, I 293, II 155, III 311, IV 207, 208, 458
Charleston Bearcats, IV 322
A Charlie Brown Christmas, II 323
Charlie's Angels, I 298, II 79, III 505
Charlotte's Web, V 127
Charnin, Martin, I 96
Chartoff, Robert, IV 246
Chase, Alan, IV 446
Chase, Chevy, I 217, III 451, IV 320
Chase, Edna Woolman, I 577
Chastity, IV 457
Chaucer, Geoffrey, V 16
Chavez, Cesar, III 73
Chavis, Boozoo, V 236
Chayefsky, Paddy, III 60, 503, IV 50
Cheap Suit Serenaders, I 642
Checker, Chubby, I 165, 526
Cheech and Chong, I 485
Cheerios, III 190
Cheers, I 213, II 156, IV 422
''Cheeseheads,'' II 302
Cheever, Eddie, II 490
Chenier, Clifton, I 483, V 235
Cher, II 54
Cher. See Sonny and Cher
Chernobyl, I 311
Cherrill, Virginia, I 516
Cherryh, C. J., IV 333
Chesnutt, Charles, I 134
Chess, II 104
Chess, Leonard, I 1
Chess Records, I 292, IV 207
Chesterton, G. K., I 693
Chevalier, Maurice, III 224
Chevrolet, III 455
Chevy, IV 483
Cheyenne Autumn, V 119
Chez Mouquin, I 123
Chiang Kai Shek, III 211
Chicago, III 68
Chicago, III 459
Chicago, IV 307, 347, 453, V 152
Chicago Bears, I 731, II 342, III 483, IV 23, 117, 453
Chicago Blackhawks, II 417, 467
Chicago blues, I 292
Chicago Bulls, I 187, II 570, III 478, IV 259
Chicago Cubs, I 492, 778, III 110, V 182, 197
Chicago Daily News, IV 285
Chicago Defender, I 33
Chicago Democratic Convention, I 495, V 214
Chicago Hope, I 756, III 13, IV 19
Chicago jazz, I 734
Chicago Lions Club, II 77
Chicago Seven, II 420, III 62, IV 563
Chicago Sound, III 310

Chicago Sun-Times, I 27, IV 285
Chicago Tribune, I 348
Chicago White Sox, I 266, II 522, 571, V 183
Chicago White Stockings, IV 578
Chicago World's Fair (1893), I 305, IV 692
Chicanisma, II 19
Chicano Rock, III 71
Chicano theater, V 15
Chick Webb Orchestra, IV 322
Chico and the Man, III 439, IV 116
Child abuse, IV 391
Child is Waiting, A, II 204
Child, Julia, II 572
Child stars, II 203, IV 631
Childbirth, I 261
Childhood's End, IV 332
Children of An Loc, V 51
Childress, Alvin, I 74
China, I 375
China Beach, III 78, V 51
''China Girl,'' IV 82
China Syndrome, I 314
Chinese Theatre, III 427
Chinese Water Torture, II 457
Chitwood, Joey, III 48
Chomsky, Marvin, III 436
Chong, Tommy, I 485
Chong, Tommy. See Cheech and Chong
Chopra, Deepak, III 508
Chorus Line, III 459
Christian Broadcasting Network, III 505, IV 226, 626
Christian Coalition, II 183, IV 71, 125, 198, 226
Christian Identity, V 129
Christian Science, II 12
Christianity, II 46, IV 289
Christiansen, Ole Kirk, III 125
Christie, Agatha, I 693, II 282, III 445, IV 10
Christie, Julie, III 430
Christina's World, V 199
Christmas, I 541, 689, II 506, IV 685
Christmas Memory, I 427
Christy, Howard Chandler, IV 59
Chronicles of Narnia, III 150
Chrysler, II 534, III 455
Chrysler Building, II 28, IV 433
Chrysler Corporation, II 480, III 370
Chrysler, Walter Percy, I 507
Chuck D, IV 132
Chudd, Lew, IV 207
Chung, Connie, IV 176
Church of the Foursquare Gospel, III 332
Church of Latter Day Saints, I 646
Church of Scientology, II 42, IV 694
Churchill Downs, II 190, III 19
Church's Chicken, II 73
CIA, I 379
Cicero's Cat, III 463
Cicotte, Eddie, I 266
Cimarron, V 120
Cimino, Michael, I 681
Cincinnati Bengals, I 370, II 302, III 402
Cincinnati Reds, I 169, 219, 267, II 6, IV 230, 276, V 183
Cinderfella, III 152
Cinecittà, IV 614
CinemaScope, I 71
Cinerama, II 459
Cirque du Soleil, I 513, IV 214
Citizen Kane, II 100, 380, III 75, 429, IV 367, V 109
Citizens, III 145
Citizens' Commission to Investigate the FBI, II 444
City, III 30
City Lights Bookstore, I 201
City of New Orleans, II 328
Civil disobedience, II 10
Civil Rights, I 495, 585, 595, III 511, IV 76
Civil Rights Act, III 266
Civil Rights Movement, I 152, 162, 737, II 549, III 34, 186, 266, 310, IV 124, 545, 663
Civil War, I 259, 394, 761, II 263, 583, III 4, 491, IV 136, V 118
Clampett, Bob, I 146, 384

Clansman, I 258, IV 396
Clapton, Eric, I 355, II 22, 329, 391, III 25, V 38, 212
Clarabell the Clown, II 459
Claremont, Chris, V 205
Clarence O. Hurt, I 714
Clarence Thomas-Anita Hill Senate Hearings, IV 79
Clark, Candy, I 69
Clark, Colonel Meriwether Lewis, III 19
Clark, Dick, I 65, 165, 484, II 151, IV 619, 679
Clark, Dwight, III 402
Clark, Marcia, IV 407
Clark, Roy, II 381, 382
Clark, Russell, I 713
Clark, Stephen C., I 598
Clarke, Arthur C., IV 314, 332, 717
Clash, II 501, III 516, IV 142
Clay, Cassius, Jr., I 44
Clayton, Buck, I 185
Clayton, Jan, III 96
Cleargreen Inc., I 454
Clearwater, IV 352
Cleaver, Eldridge, I 264
Cleese, John, I 489, II 80, III 403
Clemens, Brian, I 145
Clemens, Roger, V 217
Cleopatra, I 282, II 105, IV 614, 681
Cleopatra Jones, I 279
Cleopatra Jones and the Casino of Gold, I 279
Cleveland Ballet Dancing Wheels, I 722
Cleveland Browns, I 369, 370, III 483, IV 118
Cleveland, George, III 96
Cleveland Indians, II 269, 522, III 371, IV 5
Cleveland, James, II 154, 274
Client, II 318
Clift, Montgomery, II 98, 175, IV 63, 613
Clinch Mountain Boys, IV 506
Cline, Patsy, III 219, 501
Clinton, Bill, I 89, 154, 314, II 115, 155, 471, 496, 499, III 149, 159, 337, 437, IV 368, 372, 516, 628, V 184
Clinton, George, II 185
Clinton, Hillary Rodham, IV 516
Clock, II 203
Clockwatchers, III 15
Cloisters, III 347
Close Encounters of the Third Kind, II 43
Clouseau, Inspector, IV 356
Clovers, IV 208
Clue, IV 13
Clyde, Andy, II 446
CNN (Cable News Network), IV 668
Coach, II 53
Coal Miner's Daughter, III 220
Coasters, IV 208, 233
Coat of Many Colors, IV 18
Cobain, Kurt, I 303, II 222, 321, III 204, 539, IV 27, V 218
Cobb, Joe, III 578
Cobb, Ty, I 695, IV 276
Coburn, Alvin Langdon, III 390
Coburn, James, III 240
Coca, Imogene, IV 196, V 221
Coca-Cola, I 543, IV 36, 82
Cochran, Eddie, IV 619
Cochran, John J., I 718
Cochran, Johnnie, IV 407
Cochrane, Mickey, III 262
Cocker, Joe, I 57
Cocktail parties, II 359
Codona, Alfredo, I 512
Cody, Buffalo Bill, II 488, IV 252, V 120
Cody, William F., I 545
Cody, William F. See Cody, Buffalo Bill, and his Wild West Show
Cody, William Frederick, I 717
Coe, Fred, IV 50
Coen Brothers, III 216
Coen, Joel and Ethan, II 69, III 135
Coffy, I 279
Cohan, George M., III 458, V 207
Cohen Collects a Debt, IV 358

Cohen, Herman, II 480
Cohen, Leonard, IV 471
Cohl, Emile, IV 395
Cohn, Harry, I 428, II 378, 504, III 432, 543, IV 566
Cohn, Nik, IV 320
Cohn, Roy, I 116
Coke Time, II 105
Colón, Willie, IV 304
Colbert, Claudette, I 28, 428, II 504
Cold War, I 102, 152, 313, 544, 766, 759, II 434, 549, III 208, IV 279, 313, 364, 493
Cole, Lester, II 434
Cole, Michael, III 386
Cole, Nat King, I 478, III 121, IV 285
Coleman, Gary, I 709
Coleman, Ornette, I 559, II 530
Colgate Comedy Hour, I 7, III 111
Collecting, IV 97
College Football Hall of Fame, IV 499
College Humour, V 103
Collier's, I 134
Collingwood, Charles, III 452, V 190
Collins, Bootsy, II 184
Collins, Joan, I 784, III 84
Collins, John, II 503
Collins, Judy, III 460
Collins, Max Allan, I 703
Collins, Michael, I 104
Collins, Phil, I 525
Collins, Ray, I 395
Collins, Ted, IV 440
Collins, Tommy, II 334
Collins, Wilkie, I 693
Collyer, Bud, IV 665
Colman, Ronald, I 207
Colonial Williamsburg, I 522
Color of Money, IV 338
Color Purple, IV 476, V 62
"Color Radio," IV 680
Colored American, I 32
Colorfield, I 12
Colston, Raleigh, III 20
Colt .45, II 103
Colt, Tim, V 120
Colter, Jessi, II 540
Columbia, I 149, II 122, 432
Columbia Amusement Company, I 389
Columbia Broadcasting System, I 75, 163, 242, 404, II 75, 447, 477, III 1, 111, 168, 185, 189, 241, 251, 504, IV 6, 419, 439
Columbia Pictures, I 428, III 432
Columbia Records, I 200, 583, II 155, 552, 558
Columbia Studios, I 504
Columbian Exposition, I 390
Columbo, I 302, III 53
Comaneci, Nadia, II 332
Combat, V 192
Combat Sergeant, V 192
Come Blow Your Horn, IV 402
Comedy Hour, I 423
Comet,, V 228
Comic books, IV 141
Comic Magazine Association of America, I 565
Comics Code, I 672, IV 600
Comics Code Authority, I 561, IV 350, V 4
Comics Code Authority, The, II 9
Comingore, Dorothy, I 272
Comique, I 107
Comique Studio, III 10
Comiskey, Charles A., I 266
Commission on Pornography, IV 34
Committee for the First Amendment, II 472
Committee on Social and Religious Surveys (CSRS), III 355
Committee to Re-Elect the President (CREEP), V 85
Communications Decency Act of 1996, II 497
Communism, I 116, 192, 424, 549, 569, II 97, 413, 549, III 314, 547, IV 188, 280
Communist Manifesto, I 569
Compañía Mexicana, III 540
Compact disc, IV 53
Company, III 459, IV 455

Company, Royal Shakespeare, III 139
Compass Players, The, III 529
Compulsion, III 139, 145
CompuServe, II 27, 497
Computer programming, III 353
Computers, II 492
Conan the Barbarian, V 103
Concentration camp, I 95
Concept musical, The, I 359
Condoms, IV 299
Condon, Eddie, I 494, 734
Condon, Jackie, III 578
Condon, Richard, I 551, III 254
Coney Island, I 77, II 454
Confessions of Nat Turner, IV 567
Confidential, II 469, III 157
Congress, Library of, II 329
Congress of Industrial Organizations (CIO), III 72
Congress of Racial Equality (CORE), II 163, 161, III 34, IV 124
Congressional Reconstruction Act, III 64
Conklin, Chester, III 24
Connecticut Yankee in King Arthur's Court, A, I 120
Connally, John, III 17
Connery, Sean, I 308, II 523, III 85
Connors, Chuck, I 322
Connors, Jimmy, II 49
Conrad, Joseph, I 102
Conrad, William, II 180, 326
Conried, Hans, IV 1, 645
Consciousness Raising groups, II 86, III 344
Conservation, I 310
Considine, Tim, III 425, 467
Conspiracy theories, III 17
Consumer groups, III 469
Consumer Reports, I 590
Consumer rights, III 469
Consumers' Research, I 588
Consumers Union, I 587, 590, IV 483
Consumers Union. See *Consumer Reports*
Continental Airlines, III 336
Continental Divide, I 218, IV 286
Contract with America, IV 201
Contras, II 499
Converse, IV 637
"Convoy", I 463
Convy, Bert, II 91
Conway, Gerry, IV 142
Conway, Tim, III 327, V 192
Coogan, Jackie, I 476, 499, II 278, III 577, IV 396
Cooke, Alistair, III 302, 561
Cooke, Jack Kent, III 197
Cooke, Janet, V 84
Cooke, Sam, II 155, IV 207, 459
Cookie Monster, IV 362
Cooking, I 497
Coolidge, Calvin, I 77, 205, IV 263
Coolio, V 210
Cooper, Alice, I 416, II 10, 249
Cooper, Charles, I 322
Cooper, Dr. Kenneth, II 547, IV 389
Cooper, Gary, I 207, IV 400, III 547, IV 102, 339, V 39, 120, 162
Cooper, Jackie, II 393
Cooper, James Fenimore, I 474, 598, II 309, V 120
Cooper, Kenneth H., I 30
Cooper, Meriam C., III 31
Cooper, Ralph, I 105
Cooper-Hewitt National Design Museum, IV 441
Cooperstown, New York, I 180
Coors, I 210
Coors, Adolph, I 599
Cop Killer, IV 176
Copacabana, II 105
Copas, Cowboy, I 531
Copeland, Douglas, I 303
Copeland, Harry, I 713
Coppertone, IV 604
Coppola, Francis Ford, I 69, 71, 101, II 250, IV 20, 346
Cops, IV 181
Corabi, John, III 419

Corbett, "Gentleman Jim," I 332
Corbett, Jim, IV 573
Corby, Ellen, V 74
Corday, Barbara, I 409
Corday, Ted, IV 446
Cordero, Angel, III 20
Corgan, Billy, I 443
Corio, Ann, I 390
Corman, Roger, I 71, 150, 645, III 250, IV 128
Cornelius, Don, IV 461
Cornell, Chris, II 321
Cornwell, Patricia, I 694
Coronet, II 40
Corporate sponsorship, III 527
Corporation for Public Broadcasting, IV 137
Correll, Charles, I 73
Corset, I 335
Corso, Gregory, I 201
Corvair, II 469
Corwin, Norman, IV 161
Coryell, Don, III 232
Cosby, Bill, II 479, IV 126, 318
Cosby Show, I 606, III 98, 277, IV 278, 422
Cosell, Howard, I 111, III 174, 393, V 1
Cosmic Connection, IV 300
Cosmopolitan, II 169, III 301, 443, IV 72, 367
COSMOS, IV 301
Costello, Elvis, I 222, III 515
Costello, Lou, I 5
Costner, Kevin, II 93
Cotler, Kami, V 74
Cotten, Joseph, II 415
Cotton Club, I 248, 412, 657, II 23, 449, 529, III 215, 223, 238
Cotton, Will, I 466
Couéism, I 615
Coughlin, Father Charles E., IV 159, 386, V 129
Coughlin, Paula, IV 372
Count Basie Band, IV 324
Counterculture, I 453, III 251, IV 223
Country Club Plaza, III 247
Country Gentlemen, IV 427
Country Music Association, II 562
Country Music Association Hall of Fame, IV 258
Country Music Hall of Fame, II 562, IV 28, 262
Coupland, Douglas, II 221
Couric, Katie, IV 667
Court, Margaret Smith, II 49, IV 636
Cousens, Charles, IV 669
Cousins, Morris, IV 701
Cousteau, Jacques, III 484
Cousy, Bob, I 137, III 478, IV 225
Covarrubias, Miguel, I 466
Cover, Franklin, II 536
Covered Wagon, V 120
Covey Leadership Center, I 621
Covey, Stephen, I 779
Cowen, Joshua Lionel, III 170
Cowher, Bill, IV 61
Cowley, Sam, I 714
Cowsills, IV 18
Cox, Billy, I 391
Cox, Courteney, II 172
Coxe, George Harmon, I 264
Crabbe, Buster, II 113
Crack cocaine, I 543
Craig, Gordon, I 774
Cramer, L. T., IV 546
Crandon, Mina (Margery), II 457
Crane, Bob, II 424
Crane, David, II 172
Crane, Hart, III 391
Crane, Mary, IV 130
Cranston, Lamont. See Shadow
Cravat, Nick, III 86
Craven, Wes, II 170, IV 341
Crawford, Cindy, III 89
Crawford, Joan, I 28, 128, II 56, 216, III 359, IV 544, 676
Crawford, Michael, III 460, IV 49
Crawford, Sam, I 695
Cray, Robert, V 38

Crazy Arms, III 154
Crazy Blues, I 292
Crazy Horse, V 218
Cream, I 265, 355, 525
Cream of Wheat, III 143
Creation Research Society, I 627
Creative Artists Agency (CAA), I 34
Creature From the Black Lagoon, III 256
Credit cards, I 591, 689
Creole dance music, I 380
Creole Jazz Band, I 494, 734
Crichton, Michael, II 33, 581
Crime Does Not Pay, I 561
Crimson Tide, I 375
Crisis, I 772, II 78
Criss, Peter, III 42
Critical Mass Energy Project, III 469
Croce, A. J., I 635
Croce, Jim, I 383
Croly, Herbert, III 514
Cronauer, Adrian, I 112
Cronkite, Walter, I 352, IV 176, 628, 630, 699
Cropper, Steve, III 26
Crosby, Bing, I 112, 769, III 84, 121, 504, IV
    411, V 139
Crosby, Bob, I 248, 583
Crosby, David, I 402
Crosby, Floyd, II 400
Crosby, Garry, I 638
Crosby, Mary, I 638
Crosby, Stills, and Nash, I 58, 382, 402, III 19
Crosland, Alan, II 531
Cross, Ben, I 660
Cross of Fire, III 66
Cross-dressing. See Drag
Crossroads, II 558
Crouse, Russel, IV 462
Crowd, V 49
Crowe, Robert, III 138
Crowninshield, Frank, II 45, V 28
Crucible, I 551, IV 280
Crumb, Robert, I 562, V 4, 225
Crump, Diane, III 20
Crusader Rabbit, IV 317
Cruz, Celia, IV 304
Cry Baby, IV 82
Cry Freedom, V 82
Cryer, John, I 344
Cuban Missile Crisis, I 193
Cugat, Xavier, I 117, III 97
Cukor, George, II 264
Cullen, Bill, IV 108
Cullen, Countee, IV 710
Cully, Zara, II 536
Culp, Robert, II 479
Cult films, I 448, IV 248
Culture Club, I 328, 416, III 516
Culture wars, IV 199, 374
Cummings, e. e., III 62, IV 710
Cumpanas, Ana, I 714
Cunard, Grace, IV 396
Cure, I 86
Curran, Mrs. John H., III 576
Current Affair, A, IV 182
Currie, Betty, IV 516
Curry, Tim, I 644, IV 250
Curse of Capistrano, V 234
Curtin, Jane, III 7, IV 321
Curtis, Dan, I 659
Curtis, Sonny, II 430
Curtis, Tony, I 325, IV 76, 453
Curwood, James Oliver, V 120
Cusack, John, I 344
Cushing, Maine, V 199
Cy Young Award, I 435, II 269, IV 298, V 19
Cyberporn, IV 95
Cyberpunk, I 274
Cyborg, IV 425
Czech Crisis, III 2

D, Chuck, IV 174
Dacron, IV 66

Daddy Warbucks, III 177
Daffy Duck, I 146, 276, V 189
Dafoe, Willem, IV 70, 338
Dahl, Gary, IV 42
Dahl, Steve, I 727
Daily, Bill, II 475
Daily Variety, V 31
Daily Worker, II 255
Dairy Queen, II 73, IV 560
Daisy: The Story of a Facelift, II 54
Dalai Lama, I 201, III 508
Dale, Dick, II 21, IV 585
Daley, Richard, I 495, II 420, IV 77, 286
Dallas, I 638, 783, III 50, IV 48, 447
Dallas Cowboys, I 731, III 87, 483, IV 520
Dalton, Timothy, II 524
Daly, Carroll John, I 263, 694, II 359, III 65
Daly, John, V 122
Daly, Tyne, I 409
D'Amato, Cus, I 332, IV 719
Damita, Lily, II 121
Damn Yankees, III 153, 459
Damned, I 86
Dance halls, IV 2
"Dance of the Hours," II 67
Dance, Stanley, I 185
Dancehall music, IV 196
Dances with Wolves, III 439, V 121
Dancing in the Street, III 279
Dandridge, Dorothy, I 215
Dandridge, Ruby, I 241
Danes, Claire, III 467
Dangerfield, Rodney, I 322, III 40
Dangerous Lady, III 250
Dangerous Men and Adventurous Women, IV 272
Daniels, Henry, III 340
Daniels, Jeff, I 54
Daniels, Jerry, II 493
Daniels, Mickey, III 578
Daniels, Stan, IV 611
Daniels, Yvonne, IV 681
Dannay, Frederic, I 694
Dannay, Frederic. See Queen, Ellery
Danny Thomas Show, I 656
D'Aquino, Iva Toguri, IV 669
D'Arcy MacManus, I 406
Darden, Chris, IV 407
Daredevil, the Man without Fear, I 562
Dark Shadows, IV 446
Dark Tower stories, III 38
Darling, Candy, I 416
Darlington Speedway, IV 47
Darnell, Linda, II 468
Darrow, Charles B., III 396
Darrow, Clarence, I 424, III 138, IV 336, 542
Darth Vader, IV 512
Darwin, Charles, I 627, IV 335
Darwinian theory, II 183
Dash for the Timber, IV 204
Dateline, IV 713
Dateline NBC, IV 182
Dating Game, III 526
Daughters of the American Revolution, I 82
Daughters of Bilitis, II 211, 213, IV 545
Daumier, Honoré, I 123
Dave Clark Five, I 355
Davenport, Harry, III 340
Davenport, Lester, I 704
David, Hal, I 352, III 30
Davidman, Joy, III 151
Davidson, Arthur, II 368
Davidson, Walter, II 369
Davidson, William, II 369
Davies, Arthur B., I 123
Davies, Cyril, I 355
Davies, Marion, IV 367
Davis, Al, III 547
Davis, Angela, III 35
Davis, Ann B., I 340
Davis, Bette, I 50, 625, II 328, III 250, IV
    544, 643, 694
Davis, Betty, II 185

Davis, Clive, II 458
Davis Cup team, I 124
Davis, David, IV 611
Davis, Geena, III 110
Davis, Harry, III 530
Davis, Jackie, III 578
Davis, Jacob, II 533
Davis, John, II 317
Davis, Miles, I 19, 558, II 350, 530, IV 82
Davis, Rennie, I 495
Davis, Sammy, Jr., I 344
Davis, Stuart, I 122
Davis, Willie, III 403
DAW, IV 11
Dawber, Pam, III 411
Dawson, Richard, II 424
Dawson's Creek, I 25
Day After, III 234
Day, Doris, I 370, II 463, IV 618
Day, Dorothy, IV 692
Day, Father's, III 418
Day of the Jackal, II 141
Daybreak, IV 17
Daybreakers, III 84
Days of Future Passed, I 576
Days of Our Lives, I 99, II 324, IV 446
"Days of Wine and Roses," III 256
Dayton, Tennessee, IV 335
Daytona, II 149
Daytona 500, II 149
Daytona Bike Week, II 370
Daytona International Speedway, IV 538
DC, I 565, IV 582
DC Comics, I 432, 561, 564, II 302, III 285, IV 307,
    470, 474, V 75, 171
DC Talk, I 592
De, Abhay Charan, II 362
De Camp, L. Sprague, I 125, 337, IV 331
De Carlo, Yvonne, IV 635
De Forest, Lee, IV 157
De Fornaro, Carlo, I 466
De Graff, Robert, IV 10
De Groot, Roy, I 707
De Guillebon, Jeanne-Claude, I 505
De Havilland, Olivia, II 264, III 429
De Kooning, Willem, I 11
De Leon, Millie, I 388
De Mave, Jack, III 96
De Mille, Agnes, III 553, IV 255
De Mille, Cecil B., I 280, IV 634
De Niro, Robert, I 71, III 153, 336, IV 165, 337, 611
De Palma, Brian, IV 694
De Stijl, III 158
De Tocqueville, Alexis, I 463, III 46
De Zayas, Marius, I 466
Dead End Kids, I 149
Dead Kennedys, IV 142
Dead Man, IV 82
Dead Man Walking, IV 312
Dean, James, I 342, II 98, 230, 533, III 60, 399, 430,
    IV 185, 371, 614, 618, V 173
Dean, John, V 86
Dean Martin Show, III 281
DeAngelis, Peter, IV 619
"Dear Abby," I 26
Dear America: Letters Home from Vietnam, V 52
"Dear Hagatha," I 28
Death Comes for the Archbishop, I 459
Death in the Afternoon, II 387
Death Row Records, IV 176
"Death Trip," IV 82
Death Wish, I 360
Debbie Reynolds, IV 614
DeBecque, Emile, IV 465
DeBont, Jan, II 255
Debs, Eugene V., I 660, IV 542, V 187
DeBurgh, Chris, III 436
Decca Records, I 185, II 430, III 215, 219
December 7, I 134
Declaration of Independence, I 464, II 146
Deconstructing Harry, I 54
Dee, Sandra, IV 618

Deep Purple, I 41, II 380, 544
Deep Throat (Watergate informant), V 86
Deer Hunter, IV 70, V 51, 78
Def Jam, I 200, 508, III 71, IV 175
Defense of Marriage Act (DOMA), II 209
Defiant Ones, IV 76
Deford, Frank, IV 487
DeGeneres, Ellen, III 89, 142, IV 423
Delaney and Bonnie, I 525
Delgado, Emilio, IV 363
Dell, IV 10
Dell'Abate, Gary, IV 531
Dellinger, David, I 495
Delmark, I 56
Delsarte, I 773
DeMar, Clarence, I 323
Demme, Jonathan, IV 393
Democracy in America, III 46
Democratic National Convention, II 419
Democratic Party, I 93
Dempsey, Jack, IV 485
Dempsey, Tom, I 722
Denis, Ruth, I 166
Denishawn, IV 381, 494
Denny, Reginald, IV 157
Denslow, W. W., I 191
Densmore, John, I 748
Dent, Lester, I 264, 738, IV 227
Denton, Sandy "Pepa," IV 305
Denver, Bob, I 735
Denver Broncos, II 25, 203
Denver, John, II 42
DePalma, Brian, IV 346
Department of Health Education and Welfare, I 565
Department of the Interior, III 490
Department stores, I 589
Depp, Johnny, V 173
Depression, I 569
Der Eigene, II 210
Der Verlorene, III 196
Derek and the Dominos, I 525
Derleth, August, V 103
Derrida, Jacques, IV 100
DeSalvo, Albert, I 324
Desert Solitaire, I 4
Desert Storm, II 325
Designing Woman, II 390
Desilu Studios, II 477, IV 251, 508
Desmond, Paul, I 372
Desperado, III 198
Destroyers, IV 649
Destry Rides Again, V 119
Detective Comics, I 561, 671, IV 582
Detective fiction, III 416
Detective Story, I 263
Detective story, IV 547
Detective Story Magazine, IV 140
Detroit, I 406
Detroit 9000, I 279
Detroit Lions, I 722, IV 118, 307
Detroit Pistons, IV 259, 645
Detroit Police Department, IV 157
Detroit Red Wings, II 417, 460
Detroit Tigers, II 302
Devine, Andy, V 120
DeVito, Danny, IV 610
Devlin, Dean, II 255, 487
Devlin, Johnny, II 257
Devo, III 516, 515
DeVol, Frank, I 583
DeVos, Richard M., I 80
DeWalt, Autry, II, V 63
Dewart, William T., I 110
Dewey, John, III 171, IV 131, 685
Dewey, Melvil, IV 134
Dewey, Thomas E., III 213
DeWitt, Joyce, IV 653
Dexter, Colin, I 694
Dey, Susan, IV 18
DeYoung, Dennis, II 544
Di Prima, Diane, I 201
Diaghilev, Serge, I 165

Diagnosis Murder, V 25
Dial M For Murder, IV 529
Diamond Records, III 280
Diana, Princess of Wales, IV 597, V 42
Dianetics, I 646, II 461
DiCaprio, Leonardo, IV 617, 663
Dick, Philip K., I 273, IV 332
Dick Van Dyke Show, I 74, III 272, 292, IV 197,
    422, 645, V 25
Dickens, Charles, IV 712
Dickey, James, I 134
Dickson, Carr, I 442
Dickson, Carter, I 442, 694
Didion, Joan, I 21
Didrikson, Babe, III 560, IV 486
Die Hard, III 406, V 147
Dietrich, Marlene, I 85, 168, V 55
Diller, Barry, II 438
Dillinger Days, I 316
Dillinger, John, II 103, 444
Dillon, Matt, I 344, II 326
DiMaggio, Joe, III 400, 520, V 144, 183, 208
Dimbleby, Jonathan, I 699
Dime Detective, I 264, 694
Dime Mystery Magazine, IV 140
Dime novels, II 488, IV 139
D'Indy, Vincent, IV 96
Diner, I 719
Diners Club, I 628
Dingbat Family, III 62
Dinosaur Jr., I 62
Dinsdale, Shirley, II 27
Dion and the Belmonts, II 430
Dion, Celine, IV 472, 663
Dionysus, IV 669
Dior, Christian, I 490, 633, II 390, III 512
Dirks, Rudolph, I 563, III 7
Dirt, IV 314
Dirty Dozen, III 52, V 191, 192
Disability, I 323, II 159, IV 471
Disc jockeys, IV 174, 679
Disch, Thomas M., I 65, 337
Disco, II 185, 214, 215, III 127, 516, IV 85,
    319, 575, 694
Discount stores, I 689
Discovery, III 476
Disney, I 79, 359, 405, III 115, 229, 291, 460,
    IV 73, 521
Disney Studio, IV 650
Disney, Roy, I 730
Disney, Walt, I 90, 561, 663, II 66, 83, 306, 355, III
    169, 351, 425, IV 445, 477, 686, V 155
Disneyland, I 77, 729, III 248
Ditka, Mike, I 493, IV 118
Ditko, Steve, I 561, III 124, IV 474
Dittoheads, III 165
Divine, I 644, II 469, V 88
Divorce American Style, III 111
Dix, Dorothy, I 26, II 45
Dixon, Jean, IV 129
Dixon, Thomas, Jr., I 258, III 64
Dixon, Willie, IV 208
DMC, IV 287
Dmytryk, Edward, II 434
Do Androids Dream of Electric Sheep?, I 273, 701
Doblin, Rick, III 209
Dobson, Bridget, IV 447
Dobson, Jerome, IV 447
Dobson, Tamara, I 279
Doc Savage, IV 141
Doc Savage Magazine, IV 227
Doc Wright, II 257
Doctors, II 218
Doda, Carol, I 347
Dodd, Jimmie, III 425
Dodd, Sonora Smart, II 77, III 418
Dodge, III 455
Dodsworth, III 155
Dogg, Snoop Doggy, II 198
Dogpatch, III 163
Dohanos, Stevan, V 190
Doherty, Denny, III 251

Dolenz, Micky, III 394
Dolly, IV 314
Dollywood, IV 18
Domino, Fats, I 484, III 154, 513, IV 207, V 141
Domino Theory, V 49
Domino's, IV 63
Domino's Pizza, II 73
Donahue, IV 126
Donahue, Elinor, II 75
Donahue, Phil, I 668, IV 646
Donald Duck, III 425
Donaldson, Sam, I 354
Donen, Stanley, IV 613
Donenfeld, Harry, I 671
Donerail, III 20
Donkey Kong, V 46
Donlevy, Brian, I 207
Donna Reed Show, II 53
"Donna," V 16
Donovan, Hedley, IV 659
Doohan, James, IV 508
Doom Patrol, IV 309
Doonesbury, I 285, IV 646, V 41
Doors, I 355
Dora, Mickey, IV 585
Doris Day Show, III 272, IV 420
Dorsett, Tony, I 654
Dorsey brothers, I 751, II 247
Dorsey, Jimmy, I 248, 751
Dorsey, Tommy, I 248, 751, II 274, 515, III 215,
    364, IV 410
Dos Passos, John, I 570, II 40, III 74, IV 710
Dostoevsky, Fyodor, II 50
Dotto, IV 151
Double Indemnity, I 474, IV 506
Double Trouble, V 37
Doubleday, Abner, I 598
Doucette, Dave, II 371
Dougherty, Jim, III 400
Douglas, Aaron, II 366, IV 710
Douglas, Gordon, IV 641
Douglas, Helen Gahagan, I 753
Douglas, Helen Gallagher, II 97
Douglas, Kirk, III 566, IV 468
Douglas, Michael, I 632, III 566
Douglas, Mike, I 668
Douglass, Frederick, I 32
Dow, Charles H., V 67
Dow Jones & Company, V 67
Dow, Tony, III 115
Dowling, Eddie, IV 440
Down Argentine Way, II 278
Downey, Morton, Jr., I 669
Downey, Robert, Jr., I 344
Downing, Andrew Jackson, I 239, 468, III 104
Downing, K.K., II 577
Downing the Nigh Leader, IV 204
Downs, Hugh, IV 1, 666, 712
Downs, Johnny, III 578
Doyle, Sir Arthur Conan, I 442, 693
Dozier, Lamont, III 422
Dr. Alex Comfort, II 573
Dr. Demento, V 209
Dr. Dre, II 485
Dr. Feelgood, III 418
Dr. J, I 187
Dr. J. See Erving, Julius "Dr. J"
Dr. No, II 523
Dr. Pepper, III 259
Dr. Seuss, II 578
*Dr. Strangelove or: How I Learned to Stop Worrying
    and Love the Bomb*, I 313, 550, 721, II
    55, IV 356
Dr. Who, IV 11
Dr. Zaius, IV 64
Dracula, III 5, 213, V 22
Drag, I 85, II 215, 339, IV 289, 682
Drag queen, I 731
Drag racing, II 455
Dragnet, III 505, V 99
Dragonflight, I 129
Dragonriders of Pern, III 313

Dragons of Eden, IV 301
Drake, Alfred, III 459, IV 96
Drake, Bill, IV 681
Drake, Tom, III 340
Drama Desk Award, III 216
Draper, Robert, IV 268
Dream Syndicate, IV 82
Dream Team, I 187, II 571, III 561, 568
Dreaming of You, IV 355
Dreamland, I 580
DreamWorks SKG, I 91, IV 477
Dreiser, Theodore, I 570, III 188, IV 63
Dreja, Chris, V 212
Dressed to Kill, I 703, II 415
Dressen, Charlie, IV 648
Drew Carey Show, I 213
Drew, Dennis, IV 638
Dreyfuss, Henry, II 492
Dreyfuss, Richard, I 69, II 528
Drifters, IV 208
Drifting Cowboys, V 142
Driggs, Franklin, I 184
Drinking Man's Diet, I 706
Driscoll, Paddy, IV 117
Drive-in restaurant, II 72
Drudge, Matt, II 276
Drug Enforcement Agency, I 771
Dryfuss, Richard, I 730
Du Pont, Coleman, II 28
Du Pont Company (E.I. du Pont de Nemours and
    Company), III 544
Du Pont, Pierre, II 28
DuBarry Was a Lady, IV 96
Dubin, Al, II 142
DuBois, Blanche, IV 554
Dubois, Ja'net, II 267
DuBois, W. E. B., I 32, 134, 215, 260, 633, II 367
Duchamp, Marcel, I 113, II 551, V 81
Duchovny, David, III 91, V 204
Duck and Cover, I 549
Dudley, Sumner F., I 418
Duel in the Sun, V 119
Dueling Banjos, IV 204
Duff, Howard, III 251
Duffey, John, I 617
Duffy, Patrick, I 652
Duffy, Richard, II 45
Dukas, Paul, II 66
Duke, David, III 66, V 130
Duke, Patty, III 234
Duke Records, I 15
Dulles, Allen, I 379
Dulles, John Foster, II 413
Dumas, Jennifer, III 470
DuMont, III 505
Dumont, Margaret, III 288
Dunaway, Faye, I 626
Dunbar, Paul Laurence, I 643
Duncan, Isadora, I 166, III 388
Dune, I 129, II 396, III 216
Dunhill Records, III 251
Dunn, Donald "Duck," III 26
Dunne, Finley Peter. See Mr. Dooley
Dunne, Irene, IV 343, 615
Dunne, Philip, III 431
Dunnway, Dennis, I 595
Dupin, C. Auguste, I 693
DuPont, IV 80
Dural, Stanley, Jr. See Buckwheat Zydeco
Duran Duran, I 416
Duran, Roberto, III 136
Durant, Billy, II 220
Durante, Jimmy, III 11, IV 96
Durbin, Deanna, IV 541
Durham, Eddie, I 185
Durham, Hal, II 287
Dust Brothers, I 201
Dutch Masters Cigars, III 59
Dutchman, I 168
Duvall, Evelyn, IV 45
DuValle, Reggie, I 436
Dworkin, Andrea, IV 94

Dyer Anti-Lynching Bill, III 218
Dyer, Wayne, III 335
Dying Inside, IV 332
Dykes, III 140
Dylan, Bob, I 157, 204, 355, II 69, 124, 328, 329, III
    379, 527, 549, IV 43, 234, V 217
Dynasty, I 653, IV 447, 472

E Street Band, IV 491
Eagles, I 383
Earl, Harley, I 406, 603, II 220
Earl Warren, IV 542
Earle, Steve, I 262, 620
Earnhardt, Dale, I 670
Earp, Wyatt, II 127
Earth Day, II 10
Earth First!, I 4, II 11, IV 125
Earth Liberation Front, II 11
East of Eden, I 677, IV 522
East Tremont, II 228
Easter Parade, II 203, IV 382
Eastern Colored League, III 497
Eastman, George, I 371, II 13, III 51
Eastman Kodak Company. See Kodak
Eastwood, Clint, I 350, II 107, 266, IV 380,
    467, V 5, 120
Easy Rider, II 43, 386, 448, IV 527, V 121, 176
Eaton, Rebecca, III 302
Ebb, Fred, III 459
Ebbets, Charles, I 362, II 5
Eberle, Ray, III 365
Eberly, Bob, I 751
Ebersol, Dick, III 8
Ebert, Roger. See Siskel and Ebert
Ebony, I 32, II 536
EC Comics, I 561, II 494, III 230, 285, IV 600
Ecce Homo, II 55
Eckstine, Billy, V 36
Ecodefense: A Field Guide to
    Monkeywrenching, II 11
Economic Research and Action Project, III 512
Eco-sabotage, II 11
Ed Sullivan Show, I 53, 204, 749, II 430, III 223, IV
    127, 535, 571, 619
Eddy, Mary Baker, I 646
Eddy, Nelson, III 224
Eden, Barbara, II 475
Edgerton, David, I 387, II 73
Edison bund, II 432
Edison, Harry, I 185
Edison, Thomas, I 307, II 226, III 52, IV 52,
    310, 334, 394
Edmonds, Kenneth. See Babyface
Edmunds, Dave, III 515
Edsel, II 137
Educational reform, I 310
Educational Television and Radio Center
    (ETRC), IV 135
Educational Testing Service (ETS), IV 503
Edward Scissorhands, IV 111
Edwards, Blake, III 256
Edwards, Bob, I 169
Edwards, Dennis, IV 633
Edwards, Gus, II 542
Edwards, Harry, III 538
Edwards, Jodie and Susie. See Butterbeans and Susie
Edwards, Ralph, IV 643
Eero Saarinen, I 38
Egan, Pierce, I 333
Ehrenburg, Ilya, I 95
Ehrlichman, John, V 85
Eight. See Ashcan School
8 ½, II 84
18th Amendment, IV 119
Einhorn, Ira, III 508
Einstein, Albert, I 134
Einstein, Harry "Parkyakarkus," I 423
Einstein War Resisters International Fund, II 17
Eisenhower, Dwight D., I 116, 141, 192, 312, II 97,
    402, III 165, 211, 225, 316, IV 285, 301, V 49
Eisenstein, Sergei, IV 398
Eisner, Michael, I 730, IV 328

Ekland, Britt, IV 356
El Capitan Theater, I 730
El Dorados, I 164
El Norte, III 465, 495
El Rancho, III 93
Eldridge, Roy, II 376
"Eleanor Rigby," III 316
Electra, Carmen, IV 259
Electric Horseman, IV 253, V 121
Electric Kool-Aid Acid Test, III 22, 208
Electricity, II 20
Electroconvulsive shock therapy, I 691
Electronic music, III 506
Elements of Style, V 127
Elephant Man, III 216
Eliot, T. S., I 460, IV 710
Ellen. See DeGeneres, Ellen
Ellery Queen's Mystery Magazine, I 442
Elliman, Yvonne, II 543
Ellington, Duke, I 247, 615, II 107, 108, 516, 529, III
    97, 223, 238, 459, IV 441
Elliot, Cass, III 251
Elliot, "Ramblin" Jack, II 329
Elliott, Bob, I 299
Elliott, Launceston, I 306
Elliott, Osborn, III 527
Ellis, Georgia, II 326
Ellison, Harlan, I 65
Ellison, James, II 445
Ellison, Ralph. See Invisible Man
Ellroy, James, I 694
Ellsberg, Daniel, V 85
Elmo, IV 363
Elvgren, Gil, IV 59
Elvira, IV 371
Emberg, Kate, II 579
Embinder, Donald, I 287
Emergency!, V 99
Emerson, Ralph Waldo, I 134
Emmerich, Roland, II 255, 486
Emmy Awards, I 43, II 245, 406, III 71, 234, 272,
    410, 558, IV 328, V 15
Emperor Jones, III 223
Emperor Maximilian, III 271
Empire State Building, I 507, III 31, IV 347,
    433, V 82, 196
Empire Strikes Back, IV 511
Empty Nest, IV 645
"End," I 749
Endino, Jack, II 322
Endless Summer, I 197
Endo, Mitsuye, II 526
Engels, Friedrich, I 549, 569
English, Diane, I 224, III 446
Eno, Brian, II 248, III 507, IV 602, V 39
Enola Gay, IV 441
Enright, Dan, IV 151
Enter Laughing, IV 197
Enterprise, IV 508
Entertainment Tonight, V 82
Environment, II 1
Environmental movement, I 4, II 1, 406, III
    166, IV 125
Environmental Protection Agency, II 1, 31
Epic of the Wheat, III 541
Epperson, Frank, IV 88
Epstein, Brian, I 203
Equal Rights Amendment, II 85, 209, IV 524
Equal Rights Movement, IV 415
ER, I 71, 631, 756
Eraserhead, III 216
Erdrich, Louise, I 134
Ergonomics, III 106
Erhard Seminar Training. See est
Erhard, Werner, II 42, III 335
Eric B. & Rakim, II 185
Ernst, Ken, III 295
Ernst, Paul, IV 227
Ertegun, Ahmet, I 1, 135, IV 208
Ertegun, Nesuhi, III 36, IV 208
Eruzione, Mike, III 537
Erving, Julius, I 187

Escalante, Jaime, IV 501
Escalona, Beatriz. See Noloesca, La Chata
ESPN, III 505, V 133, 203
Esquire, II 388, IV 94, V 30
Esquivel, Laura, III 162
Essanay film studios, I 476
Essence, I 32
Essmaker, Ronald, I 306
Est, III 335
Estefan, Gloria, IV 305
Estevez, Emilio, I 344, 347
Estrada, Alfredo J., II 412
Estrada, Fred, II 412
E.T. The Extra-Terrestrial, I 25, 273, III 57, IV 476
Etheridge, Melissa, III 89, 141
Etiquette, I 237
Etiquette: The Blue Book of Social Usage, I 680, II 45
Eubanks, Bob, III 526
European News Round-Up, IV 384
Evangelism, III 331
Evangelists. See Religious Right
Evans, Bill, I 222
Evans, Dale, IV 263, V 120
Evans, Ernest, I 484
Evans, Gil, III 306
Evans, Harry, II 60
Evans, Herschel, I 185, III 3
Evans, Linda, I 784, V 211
Evans, Maurice, IV 196
Evans, Walker, III 142, 509
Even Cowgirls Get the Blues, IV 223
Evening Graphic, V 152
Everly Brothers, II 315
Evert, Chris, I 584
"Everybody Loves Somebody," III 280
Everyday Etiquette, II 45
Evil Dead II, I 645
Evinrude, Ole, II 368
Evita, III 181, 216, 460
Evolution, IV 335
Ewbank, Weeb, IV 118
Ewell, Tom, IV 364
Examiner, II 169
Excellence in Broadcasting Network, III 164
Executioner's Song, I 425
Executive Order 9066, II 526
Exley, Frederick, II 236
Exodus, II 88, 435
Exorcist, IV 48
Extensions, III 258
Extreme Games, III 425, IV 429
Eye of the Needle, II 127

F/64, I 17
F-111, IV 81
Fabian, I 144, II 151, IV 236, 619
Fabio, IV 271
Fabulous Flamingo casino, III 93
Fabulous Thunderbirds, V 37
Face in the Crowd, III 503
Face the Nation, I 353
Factor, Max, II 450
Factory, IV 81, V 81
Facts of Life and Love for Teenagers, IV 45
Factsheet Five, V 228
Fail-Safe, I 550
Fair Housing Act, III 148
Fair Play Committee, III 321
Fairbanks, Douglas, III 429, IV 55, 397, 710, V 8, 235
Fairbanks, Douglas, Sr., I 13, II 55, V 75
Fairbanks, Jerry, IV 317
Fairfax, Beatrice, I 26
Falcon Crest, I 783
Falk, Peter, I 559, III 53
Falling Down, I 361
Falls, Mildred, II 516
Falsey, John, IV 495
Faltskog, Agnetha, I 4
Falwell, Jerry, I 11, II 471, III 409, IV 71, 198, 200, 314

Fame. See Celebrity
Family, III 262
Family Matters, III 503
Family Plot, II 416
Family Style, V 38
Family Ties, III 278
Famous Funnies, I 560
Famous Players-Lasky Co., IV 396
Fania Records, IV 304
Fantasia, IV 541
Fantastic Four, I 562, III 124, V 205
Fantasy, IV 671
Fantasy Island, III 203, 401
Fanzines, III 176, V 114
Far Side, I 722
Farewell to Arms, II 387
Farian, Frankie, III 368
Farley, Chris, IV 321, 348
Farm Aid, III 501
Farm Security Administration, III 509
Farmer, Philip Jose, I 738, IV 333
Farrakhan, Louis, III 368
Farrar, Jay, I 59
Farrell, Warren, III 344
Farrow, Mia, I 54, 86, IV 48
Fashion Café, I 625
Fassbinder, Rainer Werner, IV 673
Fassi, Carlo, II 117
Fast food, III 321, V 127
Fat Albert and the Cosby Kids, IV 318
"Fat farms," I 707
Father Goose, V 192
Father Knows Best, III 269, IV 419
Father of the Blues, II 352
Father of the Bride, IV 613
Fatty and Mabel, I 107
Faulkner, Heather, I 40
Faulkner, William, II 388, III 549, IV 11
Faust, Jessie, IV 710
Faustino, David, III 278
Favre, Brett, II 302
Fawcett Books, IV 11
Fawcett, Farrah, I 480, IV 370
Fawcett Publications, I 432, 561, 672
Faylen, Frank, I 735
FBI (Federal Bureau of Investigation), I 714, II 10, 443, 497, III 54
Fear of Flying, II 87, 565
Fear Street, IV 536
Fears, Tommie, IV 118
Feather, Leonard, III 526
Feathers, Beattie, IV 117
Feder, Robert Arthur, IV 651
Federal Art Project, II 296, III 509, V 179
Federal Bureau of Narcotics, III 273
Federal Communications Commission (FCC), I 41, 404, 462, IV 135, 531, 595, 626
Federal Housing Administration, III 147
Federal Records, I 164
Federal Theater Project, I 574, II 296, III 509
Federal Writers' Project, II 295, III 509
Feldstein, Al, II 9
Feliciano!, II 82
Feliz Navidad, II 83
Felker, Clay, II 41
Fell, Dr. Gideon, I 442
Fell, Norman, II 654
Felton, Norman, III 253
Female Jungle, III 260
Feminazis, III 164
Feminine Mystique, II 86, III 344, IV 260, 373
Feminism, I 336, 744, II 416, III 434, IV 4, 365, 373
Femme fatale, I 168
Fender, Leo, II 21
Fenholt, Jeff, II 544
Fennell, Albert, I 145
Ferber, Edna, I 237, IV 390
Ferguson, Maynard, I 249
Ferlinghetti, Lawrence, I 201
Fernwood 2-Night, III 91
Ferrar, Geraldine, I 684
Ferrigno, Lou, I 308

Ferry, Bryan, I 86, II 248
Fess Williams and His Royal Flush Orchestra, IV 322
Festival of Folklife, IV 441
Fetchit, Stepin, III 320
Fetzer, John, I 695
Fibber McGee and Molly, I 241, III 504, V 190
Fiddler on the Roof, II 338, III 459
Fidrych, Mark "Bird," I 696
Field, Sally, II 120
Fielder, Cecil, I 696
Fields, Verna, II 528
Fiennes, Ralph I 145
Fierstein, Harvey, II 487
Fifteenth Pelican, II 120
Fifty Million Frenchmen, IV 96
Fight For Your Right (To Party), I 200
Fighting Irish, IV 243
Figure skating, II 116, 360
Filene's, I 688
Filerman, Michael, III 50
Filling stations, IV 285
Fillmore Auditorium, II 283
Film Noir, I 168, II 131, 433, IV 97
Filmplay Journal, II 65
Final Four, IV 606
Fincher, David, I 49
Fine, Sylvia, III 9
Finest Physique Contest, I 306
Finger, Bill, I 189
Finian's Rainbow, III 459
Fink, David Harold, IV 90
Finley, Charles, III 68
Fire Next Time, I 162
Firm, II 318
Firpo, Luis, I 686
First Amendment, I 435, III 464
First Blood, I 283, IV 170, V 51
Fischer, Peter S., III 445
Fischinger, Oskar, II 67
Fisher, Amy, III 337
Fisher, Carrie, II 105
Fisher, Dorothy Canfield, I 318
Fisher, Eddie, IV 614
Fisher, Frances, II 3
Fisher, Fred, I 116
Fisher, Gary, III 424
Fisher, Harry "Bud," III 462
Fisher, Rudolph, III 416
Fisher, Terry Louise, I 302, III 71
Fisk Jubilee Singers, II 274
Fisk University, I 772
Fistful of Dollars, V 119
Fitness, IV 501
Fitzgerald, Ella, I 248, IV 322, V 37, 98
Fitzgerald, F. Scott, I 84, 140, II 40, 112, 387, IV 710
FitzGerald, John J., I 246
Fitzgerald, Zelda, II 109
Fitzhugh, Louise, I 294
Five Easy Pieces, I 69
500 Club, III 152
501, III 146
Five Royales, I 164
"Five-dollar day," II 132
Fixx, James (Jim), II 547, IV 389
Flagg, James Montgomery, V 190
Flame and the Flower, IV 271
Flamingo, IV 392
Flanagan, Edward, IV 692
Flanagan, Hallie, III 509
Flash, I 561, 672
Flash Gordon, I 298
Flatiron Building, III 390
Flatt, Lester. See also Foggy Mountain Boys
Fleetwood Mac, I 355
Fleetwood, Mick, I 355, II 114
Fleischer, Max, I 728, IV 287
Fleischer, Richard, IV 681
Fleischer Studio, I 239
Fleischmann, Raul, III 522
Fleming, Art, II 541
Fleming, Ian, II 523, III 253, IV 71

Fleming, Peggy, II 484, III 70, IV 430
Fleming, Victor, I 644, II 264, V 162
Fletcher, Adele Whitely, II 64
Fletcher, Rick, I 703
Flintstones, II 355, IV 317, 612
Flip books, IV 93
Flip Wilson Show, V 149
Flo, I 47
Flock brothers, IV 537
Flock of Seagulls, III 516
Flood, Curt, II 161
Flood geology, I 627
Flores, Tom, III 547
Flub-a-Dub, II 459
Flying Burrito Brothers, I 58
Flying Down to Rio, I 128
Flying High, IV 440
Flying Nun, IV 419
Flying Wallendas, IV 213
Flynn, Errol, III 461
Flynn, Joe, III 327
Flynt, Larry. See *Hustler*
Foch, Nina, IV 635
Fogerty, John, I 630
Fogerty, Tom, I 630
Foggy Mountain Boys, I 289, II 122, III 397,
    IV 345, 558
Foggy Mountain Breakdown, IV 345
Fogo Island project, I 571
Folger, Abigail, III 262
Folgers, I 547
Folies-Bergère, I 159, 389
Folkways Records, IV 441
Follies, III 459, IV 455
Follow the Girls, II 245
Fonda, Henry, I 325, 625, II 291, V 120
Fonda, Jane, I 31, 707, II 129, III 430, IV 705
Fonda, Peter, I 71, II 4, 448
Fontaine, Joan, II 415, III 429
Fonz and the Happy Days Gang, II 357
Fonzie, IV 441
Food and Drug Act, I 310
Foolish Questions, II 256
Football Hall of Fame, I 731, II 300
Foote, Horton, IV 50
For 3 to Get Ready, III 59
For the People, IV 623
''For What It's Worth,'' I 382
For Whom the Bell Tolls, I 226, 598, II 388
Foran, Thomas, I 496
Forbes, Malcolm, IV 615
Forbush, Nellie, IV 465
Ford, Daniel Sharp, V 222
Ford, Edsel, II 14
Ford, Ford Madox, II 387
Ford, Francis, II 134
Ford, Gerald, I 481, 599, II 526, IV 478, V 86
Ford, Glenn, I 268, II 378
Ford, Harrison, I 70, 273, II 180, IV 441
Ford, Henry, I 139, 245, 587, 616, II 135, 220, 491,
    III 387, IV 710, V 129
Ford, John, I 644, II 127, 290, 291, 311, 458, III 253,
    464, IV 346, 381, 497, V 119, 189
Ford, Mary, IV 22
Ford Motor Company, II 14, 16, 480, III 387, IV 483
Ford Mustang, III 455
Ford, Whitey, V 184
Fordham University, III 185
Foreman, Carl, II 400
Foreman, Dave, II 11
Foreman, George, I 46
Forest Lawn, I 467
Forgotten Man, V 51
Forman, Henry James, I 410
Forman, Milos, II 340, III 566
Formica, IV 66
Formula One World Championship, I 84
Forrest, Edwin, I 356
Forrest Gump, II 353, III 221
Forrester, ''Howdy, II 122
Forsythe, John, I 783
Fort Apache, IV 499

Forte, Fabiano, IV 619
Fortensky, Larry, IV 615
FORTRAN, II 482
Fortune, III 142, 211
Fortune 500, II 142
Fortune Tellers. See Psychics
48 Hours, IV 182
49ers, III 402
42nd Street, III 460
Foster, Andrew ''Rube,'' III 497
Foster, Jodie, IV 337, 393
Foster, William, I 279
Foucault, Michel, IV 100
Fountainhead, III 547
Four Aces of Western Swing, II 344
Four Tops, III 422
Fowler, Gene, IV 598
Fox, III 278
Fox After Breakfast, III 106
Fox Film Corporation, IV 396
Fox, Margaret, IV 129
Fox, Michael J., II 64
Fox News Corp., I 405
Fox Television Network, I 242, IV 408, 596
Foxx, Redd, IV 310, 413
Foxy Brown, I 71, 279
Foyt, A. J., V 9
Foyt, A. J., Jr., II 491
Fraddon, Ramona, I 348
Frakes, Jonathan, IV 509
France, William Henry ''Bill,'' IV 537
Francis, Arlene, V 122
Francis, Beverly, I 307, III 329
Francis, Connie, IV 620
Francis, Genie, II 219, IV 446
Francis, Kay, IV 103
Francis the Talking Mule, III 376
Frank, Otto, I 95
Frank, Robert, III 159
Franken, Al, III 165
Franken, Stephen, I 736
Frankenheimer, John, I 551, III 255, IV 364
Frankenstein, I 274, II 159, 582, III 4, 5, 214, IV
    330, V 103
Franklin, Aretha, I 293, II 516, IV 458
Franklin, Benjamin, IV 90, 346
Franklin, Bonnie, III 565
Franklin, Kirk, II 274
Franklin, Melvin, IV 633
Franklin, Reverend C. L., II 154
Franklin W. Dixon, II 360
Franks, Robert, III 138
Frantz, Chris, IV 602
Franz, Dennis, II 407, IV 442
Fraser, Margot, I 257
Frasier, I 489, IV 423
Frawley, William, II 27, 478, III 467, V 27
Frazier, Joe, I 20, 46, II 138
Freak Out!, I 576
Freak show, IV 693
Freaks, I 645, IV 693
Freckles, IV 550
Fred Waring and the Pennsylvanians, IV 20
''Free Bird,'' III 221
Free Jazz, I 557
Free speech, IV 715
Free Speech Movement, IV 562
Freed, Alan, I 485, 726, II 98, 430, III 154,
    IV 236, 679
Freedman, Al, IV 151
Freedman, Gerald, II 339
Freedom Forum, V 13
Freedom of Choice, I 697
Freedom of Speech, II 485
Freedom Riders, IV 124
Free-Lance Pallbearers, IV 191
Freeman, Bud, I 734
Freeman, Leonard, II 375
Freeman, R. Austin, I 694
Frehley, Ace, III 42
Frehm, Paul, IV 216
Frehm, Walter, IV 216

Freidan, Betty, III 344
Freleng, Friz, I 384, IV 707
Fremont, John C., III 92
French fries, II 71
French, Marilyn, II 87
French, Paul, I 126
French postcards, IV 93
French, Victor, II 327
Fresh, Doug E., IV 305
Fresh Prince of Bel Air, I 242
Fresno State, IV 607
Freud, Sigmund, I 691, IV 710, V 186
Frid, Jonathan, I 659
Friday Foster, I 279
Friday, Sgt. Joe, V 98
Friebus, Florida, I 736
Friedan, Betty, II 86, IV 260, 373
Friedkin, William, II 50, 165
Friedman, Benny, IV 117
Frieman, Joel, I 110
Friendly Fire, V 51
Friendly, Fred W., II 28, III 452
Friendship and Freedom, II 210
Fries, Kenny, I 722
Fritz the Cat, I 192, 562, 642, V 225
Frogs, IV 455, V 63
Froines, John, I 495
From Here to Eternity, III 86, IV 191, V 191
From Russia With Love, III 542
Frontier Marshall, III 464
Frost, David, III 403
Frost, Robert, I 427
Frueh, Al, I 466
Fruit Jar Drinkers, III 229
Fu Manchu, I 478
Fuhrman, Mark, IV 406
Fukasaku, Kinji, IV 683
Fukuda, Jun, II 254
Fuld, William, III 576
Full Metal Jacket, V 51
Fuller, Robert, V 59
Fuller, Sam, I 644, V 119, 191
Fullerton, Hugh, I 267
Functionalism, II 491
Fundamentals, II 182
Funhouse, IV 82
Funicello, Annette, I 71, 95, 144, III 352, 425
Funk, I 662
Funkadelic, I 532
Funny Face, II 390
Funny Girl, I 348, IV 557
*Funny Thing Happened on the Way to the
    Forum*, IV 454
Funt, Allen, I 420
Fuqua, Charles, II 493
Fuqua, Harvey, V 63
Furay, Richie, I 381
Furnier, Vincent, I 595
Future Shock, IV 668
Futuria Fantasia, I 337
Futurians, I 125

G. P. Putnam & Sons, III 183
G. W. ''Billy'' Bitzer, II 313
Gómez-Pena, Guillermo, II 185
Gabin, Jean, I 709
Gable, Clark, I 625, II 263, 504, III 429, 461,
    IV 102, 371
Gabor, Zsa Zsa, IV 1
Gaboriau, Emile, I 693
Gagarin, Yuri, I 104
Gage, Matilda Joslyn, I 191
Gage, Maud, I 191
Gaiman, Neil, I 597, IV 307
Gaines, Clarence ''Big House,'' III 398
Gaines, Jim, I 56
Gaines, Max C., I 560, II 9
Gaines, William M., I 564, II 9, III 230
Galaxie 500, V 39
Gale, Myra, III 154
Galewski, Moses, IV 322
Gallant Men, V 192

Gallipoli, V 188
Gambia, IV 274
Gambino crime family, II 277
"Gambler," IV 261
Gambling, II 520
Gance, Abel, IV 398
Gandhi, Mahatma, I 517
Gandil, Chick, I 267
Gang Green, IV 429
Gangsta Rap, II 197, 485, IV 132, 175, 176, IV 378
Gannett Company, V 11
Gantry, Elmer, III 86, 155
Ganz, Lowell, III 110
Gap, III 159, 555
Garand Semi-Automatic Rifle, II 102
Garbage, I 57
Garbage Pail Kids, III 308
Garbo, Greta, I 709, II 296, III 569, IV 369,
    396, 615, 710
Garcia, Andy, III 98
Garcia, Jerry, II 291
Garden of Allah, I 219
Gardner, Ava, III 86
Gardner, Erle Stanley, I 110, 263, 395, 694, IV 41
Garfield, IV 45
Garfield, John, II 435
Garfunkel, Art, I 458
Garis, Howard, IV 549, 674
Garland, Judy, I 191, II 212, 216, III 339, 340, IV
    441, 544, V 162, 164
Garlits, Don "Big Daddy," I 765
Garner, James, V 121
Garofolo, Janeane, III 91
Garretto, Paolo, I 466
Garrison, Jim, II 546, III 17, 33
Garrison, Wendell Phillips, III 476
Garrison's Gorillas, V 192
Garroway, Dave, IV 666
Garvey, Cynthia, II 206
Garvey, Marcus, I 772, II 366, III 244, 497
Gates, Bill, I 405, II 496, III 353, IV 134, 239
Gavin, Bill, IV 679
Gaxton, William, IV 96
Gay and Lesbian Press Association, II 211
Gay Divorcee, IV 96
Gay Liberation Front, IV 545
Gay Liberation Movement, II 211, III 141, 344,
    IV 374, 545
Gay Pride, IV 545
Gaye, Marvin, I 594, II 185, 272, 513, III 279, 420,
    422, IV 234, 460
Gaynor, Janet, I 13
Geary, Anthony, II 219, IV 446
Gebhard, Paul, III 41
Geddes, Norman Bel, I 141
Geer, Will, V 74
Geffen, David, I 371, 639, II 322
Gehrig, Lou, I 183, III 520, IV 214, V 208
Geisel, Theodor. See Dr. Seuss
Geisel, Theodor Seuss, I 757, II 578
Gelbart, Larry, III 297, IV 197
Genealogy, II 63
General, III 11
General Electric (GE), IV 312
General Foods, II 178, IV 706
General Hospital, I 99, 666, II 324, IV 446
General Mills, I 241, III 190
General Motors, I 406, 603, II 137, III 408, 455,
    469, IV 483
Generation gap, II 279
Generation X, I 209, 303, II 24, III 78, IV 181,
    447, V 229
*Generation X: Tales for an Accelerated
    Culture*, II 221
Genovese, Vito, III 238
Gentleman from Indiana, IV 607
Gentleman Prefer Blondes, III 194, 400 IV 293
Geodesic Dome, II 180, 181
Geoffrion, Bernie "Boom Boom," II 417, 467
George, Boy, II 249
George, Peter, I 759
George R. Smith College for Negroes, II 567

Georgetown University, IV 647
"Georgia on My Mind," I 436
Gerald McBoing-Boing, I 758
Gerber, Henry, II 210, 213
Gere, Richard, I 624
Geritol, IV 151
German Expressionist painting, III 88
German homosexual movement, II 210
Gernsback, Hugo, I 64, IV 141, 331
Gerry and the Pacemakers, I 355
Gershwin, George, I 27, 248, II 107, III 458, V 130
Gershwin, George and Ira, I 129
Gershwin, Ira, I 27
Gertie, the Trained Dinosaur, III 317, 318
Get Shorty, III 135, IV 694
Get Smart!, I 366, 551
Getty, Estelle, II 260
Gettysburg, III 490
Ghost Rider, I 562
G.I. Bill of Rights, III 147
Giacchetti, Ada, I 447
Giamatti, A. Bartlett, I 40, IV 276
Giant, I 677,II 448, 463, IV 614, V 121
Gibb, Andy, I 453, IV 620
Gibb, Barry, I 210
Gibb, Maurice, I 210
Gibb, Roberta, I 323
Gibb, Robin, I 210
Gibbons, Billy, V 236
Gibbs, Marla, II 536
*Gibbsville*Stories, IV 47
Gibson, Althea, V 150
Gibson, Charles Dana, II 233, 265, IV 59
Gibson, Debbie, III 413, IV 620
Gibson, Don, I 133
Gibson Girl, III 160, IV 59, V 30
Gibson Greetings, II 306
Gibson, Henry, III 99
Gibson, Hoot, IV 397, V 120
Gibson, Josh, I 182, III 498
Gibson, Kirk, V 184
Gibson, Walter, IV 375
Gibson, William, I 274
Gidget, II 94, IV 585
Giella, Joe, III 295
Gifford, Frank, I 609, III 393, IV 118
Gifford, Kathie Lee, I 668
Gift from the Sea, III 166
Gigantis the Fire Monster, II 253
Gigio, Topo, IV 571
Gilbert, Cass, IV 433
Gilbert, John, II 432, III 428
Gilbert, Ronnie, V 97
Gilda, II 131
Gilded Age, I 680
Gillen, Denver, IV 287
Gillespie, Dizzy, I 558, II 530, III 97, IV 138, 304
Gillette, IV 580
Gilliam, Terry, III 403, 404
Gillian, Ian, II 543
Gillies, Harold, IV 68
Gilligan's Island, I 298, IV 419
Gilmanton, New Hampshire, III 346
Gilmer, Elizabeth Meriwether, I 27
Gilmore, Gary, I 425
Gilmore, Patrick S., III 268
Gilmour, David, IV 58
Gimbel Brothers, IV 303
Gingold, Hermione, IV 1
Gingrich, Arnold, II 40
Gingrich, Newt, I 3, III 165
Ginsberg, Allen, I 61, 201, 397, II 535
Ginsburg, Ruth Bader, II 32
Ginzburg, Ralph, II 41
Gipp, George, I 556, IV 244
Girl Can't Help It, III 260
Girl Crazy, III 458
Girl groups, IV 384, 473
Girl Scouts, I 335, 418
Girl with Something Extra, II 120
"Girls Just Want to Have Fun," III 99
Giselle, I 180

Gish, Dorothy, I 258, II 244
Gish, Lillian, I 258, II 243, III 428
Gitlin, Todd, I 781
Givens, Robin, IV 719
Glackens, William, I 122
Gladys Knight and the Pips, IV 461
Glam, I 86
Glam rock, III 42
Glamour, I 578
Glaser, Joe, I 115
Glaser, Tompall, II 540
Gleason, Jackie, I 143, II 439, III 162, 505
Gleason, Lev, I 632
Glen or Glenda, III 214, V 172
Glengarry Glen Ross, III 252
Glenn, John, III 476
Glenn Miller Story, III 256
Gless, Sharon, I 409
Glickman, Marty, I 40
Glitter, Gary, II 248
Glitz, III 135
Glory for Me, III 3
Glover, Savion, IV 606
Glueck, Sheldon and Eleanor, II 583
Go Tell It on the Mountain, I 162
Go Tell the Spartans, V 51
"God Bless America," IV 439, V 190
Goddard, Henry, IV 502
Goddard, Paulette, I 476
Goddard, Robert, III 167
Godey's Lady's Book, I 239, II 45
Godfather, I 343, III 239, IV 3, 48
Godfrey, Arthur, I 668
Godspell, III 459
Godzilla, I 313, 724
Goffin, Gerry, I 351, III 30
Goin' South, I 217
Goines, David Lance, II 162
Gojira, II 252
Gold Diggers of 1933, II 296
Gold, Joe, III 454
Gold Medal, II 554, IV 11
Gold Rush, I 476
Goldberg, Leonard, I 480
Goldberg, Whoopi, II 434, III 224
Goldblum, Jeff, II 487
"Golden Age" of Hollywood, III 194
Golden Books, I 249, II 178
Golden Girls, I 119, IV 645, V 127
Golden Globe Award, III 13
Goldfish swallowing, I 553
Goldman, Gary, I 91
Goldman, William, I 398
Gold's Gym, III 454
Goldsmith, Cele, I 64
Goldsmith, Clifford, II 393
Goldstein, Baruch, II 545
Goldstein, Robert, V 187
Goldwater, Barry, I 53, II 549, V 130
Goldwyn Picture Corporation, IV 396
Goldwyn, Samuel, III 9, 309, V 198
Golf, I 704, II 231, III 194, 305, IV 7, 259, V 30, 90
Golfus, Billy, I 722
Gomer Pyle, IV 645
Gone with the Wind, I 13, 281, II 187, III 320, 332,
    380, IV 356
Gonna Be a Live One in Here Tonight!, I 56
Gonsalves, Virgil, III 306
Gonzalez, Pancho, I 584
Good Earth, I 376
Good Housekeeping, IV 189
Good Housekeeping Institute, II 265
Good Times, III 111, IV 265, 420, 457
Goodfellas, IV 337, V 219
Goodfriend, Lynda, II 358
Goodhue, Bertram, IV 433
Goodman, Benny, I 247, II 391, 525, 529, III 63,
    121, 214, 256, 364
Goodman, John, I 294
Goodman, Martin, III 124, 285
Goodman, Paul, III 512
Goodman, Theodesia, III 428

"Goodnight Irene," IV 351
Goodrich, William. See Arbuckle, Fatty
Good-roads movement, I 110
Goodson-Todman Productions, II 271
Goodstein, David B., I 29
Goodwill Games, IV 705
Goodwin, Archie, IV 546
Goon Show, IV 356
Goosebumps, IV 536
Gorbachev, Mikhail, I 570
Gordeeva, Ekaterina, II 484
Gordon, Bert, I 423
Gordon, Kim, III 205, 414
Gordon, Ruth, IV 279
Gordy, Berry, II 513, 518, III 279, 420, IV 233, 280,
    459, V 64, 111, 169
Gore, Al, I 405, II 496, III 33
Gore, Tipper, II 381, 577, III 419
Gorgeous George, I 44
Gorky, Arshile, V 180
Gorney, Karen Lynn, IV 320
Gosden, Freeman, I 73
Gospel music, II 154, 515, III 178
Gospel Music Workshop of America
    (GMWA), II 274
Gossard, Stone, IV 26
Gothic youth culture, V 24
Gottlieb, Carl, II 528
Gould, Chester "Chet," I 702
Goulding, Ray, I 299
Goulet, Robert, I 414
Goya, Francisco, I 123
Grable, Betty, IV 59, 370, V 75, 225
Graceland, IV 403
Graduate, I 716, II 420, IV 399
Grady, Don, III 467
Graffiti, IV 174
Grafl, Josef, I 307
Graham, Bill, III 26, IV 74
Graham, Billy, II 47, IV 200, 578, 587, 625
Graham, John, I 323
Graham, Katharine, III 527
Graham, Martha, I 166, 686, 773, IV 495
Graham, Otto, IV 118
Graham, Philip, V 83
Grammer, Kelsey, I 488, II 156
Gramophone, IV 53
Grand Canyon, I 310, III 491
"Grand Old Flag,," I 548
Grand Ole Opry, I 132, 619, II 122, 562, III 154,
    219, 229, IV 18, 28, 74, 111, V 142
Grand Royal, I 201
Grand Slam, III 103
Grand Tetons National Park, III 491
Grandin, Jules de, V 103
Grandmaster D.S.T., II 351
Grandmaster Flash, I 167, IV 174
Grandy, Fred, III 204
Grange, Red, I 492, 555, III 482, IV 117, 499
Granger, David, II 41
Grant, Amy, I 592, IV 29
Grant, Cary, II 415, III 541, IV 371, 618, V 192
Grant, John, I 6
Grant, Maxwell, IV 375
Grant, Ulysses S., I 419, II 499
Granz, Norman, II 108
Grapefruit diet, I 706
Grapes of Wrath, II 127, 134, 297, 329, III 74,
    IV 284, 522
Graphic, II 276, III 226
Graphical User Interface (GUI), III 354
Graser, Earl, III 190
Grateful Dead, I 57, 355, II 534, III 205
Graumann's Chinese Theater, II 433
Gravano, Sammy "the Bull," III 240
Graves, Jennie, II 239
Graves, Peter, I 39
Gravity's Rainbow, IV 145
Gray, Billy, II 75
Gray, Glen, I 583
Gray, Harold, I 96, III 177
Gray, John, IV 92

Graylisting, III 195
Grayson, David, I 159
Grayson, Kathryn, IV 96
Graziano, Rocky, V 219
Grease, I 144, IV 694
Great Balls of Fire, III 154
Great Depression, I 110, 128, 248, 713, 742, II 65,
    109, 291, 328, 482, 572, 579, 584, III 3, 177,
    396, 508, IV 229, 497, 539
Great Dictator, I 476
Great Escape, V 191
Great Gatsby, III 75, 103, 237
Great Gildersleeve, II 90
Great Smoky Mountains National Park, III 491
Great Train Robbery, II 488, IV 395, V 120
Great War. See World War I
Greatest Show on Earth, IV 634
Greek Revivalism, I 305
Green Acres, IV 419
Green, Al, I 594, II 185
Green Bay Packers, III 185, 483, IV 117, 515, 580
Green Berets, IV 70, V 50, 93
Green, Gerald, II 436
Green Grow the Lilacs, III 553
Green Hills of Africa, II 388
Green Hornet, II 296, III 191
Green, Jerome, I 704
Green Lantern, I 561, 672
Green, Mitzi, III 177
Green Monster, II 87
Green, Peter, I 355
Green, Tim, IV 581
Greenberg, Clement, I 12, IV 80
Greene, Freddie, I 185
Greene, Graham, III 75, 183
Greene, Joe, IV 521
Greene, Lorne, I 316
Greene, Pamela, IV 306
Greenfield, Howard, I 351
Greenfield Village, I 522
Greenlee, Gus, III 498
Greenpeace, II 11, 31, IV 125
Greenspan, Alan, III 548
Greenstreet, Sidney, III 250
Greenwich Village, I 168, 781, IV 544
Gregg, Forrest, II 302
Gregory, Dick, IV 127
Gretzky, Wayne, II 417, III 574
Grey, Brad, III 91
Grey, Lita, I 476
Grey, Zane, IV 141, 340
Greyhound, I 77
GRID (Gay Related Immunodeficiency), I 35
Grier, Pam, I 279, IV 371
Griese, Bob, IV 118
Griffin, G. Edward, I 586
Griffin, Merv, I 668, 745, II 194, V 123
Griffin, Richard, IV 132
Griffin, Rick, I 562
Griffin, William, III 481
Griffith, Andy, I 86
Griffith, Bill, V 230
Griffith, D. W., I 258, 280, II 244, 498, III 64, 428,
    IV 357, 395, 711, V 8, 76
Griffith, Martha, II 32
Griffith, Nanci, I 620
Griffith, Robert E., IV 114
Grimek, John, I 306, IV 541
Grimes, William Henry, V 67
Grimke, Angelina, II 84
Griot singers, I 291
Grisham, John, I 237
Grissom, Gus, I 104
Grobnik, Slats, IV 286
Groening, Matt, I 178, IV 409
Grofe, Ferde, V 130
Grohl, Dave, III 539
Gropius, Walter, II 492
Grosset & Dunlap, II 360, 578
Grossinger's, II 105
Grossman, Albert, II 124
Grosvenor, Gil, III 484

Grout, Jack, III 531
Grove, Lefty, V 217
Grover, IV 363
Growing Pains, III 278
Gruelle, Johnny, IV 163
Grundner, Tom, I 572
Grunge, I 265, 303, II 222, 577, III 43, 117, 414, IV
    82, V 217, 229
Gtech, III 199
Guantanamo Bay, I 299
Guard, Dave, III 40
Guazzoni, Enrico, I 280
Guccione, Bob, IV 34
Guerrero, Lalo, III 198
Guess, Don, II 430
Guess Who's Coming to Dinner, IV 76
Guest of Honor, II 568
Guiding Light, I 99, III 540, IV 446
Guillory, Ida, V 236
Guinness Book of World Records, IV 382, V 123
Guisewite, Cathy, I 460
Guitar Slim, II 330
Gulf War, II 10
Gumbel, Bryant, IV 666
Gund, Inc., IV 617
Gunderloy, Mike, V 228
Gundy, Elizabeth, III 56
Gunga Din, II 56
Gunn, Frederick William, I 418
Gunner and Sarge, V 191
Guns of the Magnificent Seven, III 241
Guns of Navarone, V 191
Gunsmoke, I 721, III 505, IV 205, V 120
Guth, Charles, IV 37
Guthrie, Arlo, II 329, III 527
Guthrie, Jack "Oklahoma," II 328
Guthrie, Steve, III 239
Guthrie, Woody, I 445, 781, II 124, 126, 328, III
    74, 509, V 97
Guy, Alice, IV 396
Guy, Buddy, I 56, V 38
Guys and Dolls, III 238, 459, IV 289
Gwynne, Fred, I 433
Gygax, Gary, I 775
Gymnastics, I 773, IV 210
Gypsy, I 655, III 119, 459, IV 454

Hackett, Buddy, I 322, IV 1
Hackett, James H., I 356
Hackman, Gene, II 164, 442
Hadden, Briton, IV 657
Hadley, Joan, II 399
Hagar, Sammy, V 26
Hagen, Jean, IV 644
Hagen, Walter, II 262
Haggard, Merle, I 450, 620, II 21, 335, III 501, 582
Hagman, Larry, I 652, II 475
Hahn, Jessica, IV 200
Haig, Alexander, V 86
Haight-Ashbury, II 240, 411, 534, III 208
Hailey, Arthur, I 238
Hailey, Royce, II 72
Hair, I 359, III 459, IV 166
Hair styles, III 79
Hairspray, I 732, III 78
HAL, I 527
Halas, George, I 400, 492, III 482, IV 117
Halas/Payton Foundation, IV 23
Haldeman, Bob, V 85
Haldeman-Julius, Emanuel, III 173
Hale, Barbara, I 395
Hale, Sarah Josepha Buell, II 45, IV 641
Halen, Eddie Van, V 26
Haley, Alex, IV 273
Haley, Bill, I 354
Haley, Jack, V 164
Halford, Rob, II 577
Hall, Adam, I 551
Hall, Anthony Michael, I 344, 347
Hall, Arsenio, IV 126
Hall, Daryl, II 345
Hall, Diedre, IV 447

Hall, Florence Howe, II 45
Hall, Floyd, III 48
Hall, G. Stanley, II 583
Hall, Glen, II 417
Hall, James Norman, III 461
Hall, Ruth, II 64
Hall, Stanley G., IV 685
Haller, Gordon, II 503
Halliday, Richard, IV 462
Hallmark Cards, II 306, 345, V 17
Halloween, II 170, IV 436
Hallucinogens, III 114
Halpin, Luke, II 118
Hals, Frans, I 122
Halston, V 82
Hamburger, II 71
Hamburger Hill, V 51
Hamel, Veronica, II 407
Hamer, Rusty, IV 645
Hamill, Dorothy, II 484, IV 430
Hamilton, Edmond, V 103
Hamilton, George, III 48, IV 604, 615, V 141, 235
Hamilton, John, I 713
Hamilton, Polly, I 714
Hamilton, Scott, II 484
Hamlisch, Marvin, III 459
Hammer, I 279
Hammer, Jan, III 349
Hammer, Mike, I 694
Hammerstein, Oscar, II, I 358, III 458, 553, IV 256, 389, 462, 465
Hammerstein, Oscar, II. See Rodgers and Hammerstein
Hammett, Dashiell, I 263, 473, 694, 751, II 40, 99, 359, 384, 435, III 134, 249, IV 103, 140
Hammond, John, I 1, 184, 781, II 155, III 3
Hammond, John, Sr., V 38
Hamner, Earl, Jr., V 74
Hampton, Lionel, I 248
Hamwi, Ernest, II 484
Hand guns, II 103
Handler, Ruth, I 171
Handy, W.C., I 247
Hanford, Washington, I 311
Hank Ballard and the Midnighters, I 485
Hanks, Tom, I 730, II 141, III 110
Hanna, William, II 355, IV 317
Hanna-Barbera, IV 317
Hannah and Her Sisters, I 54
Hannah, Darryl, I 371
Hansberry, Lorraine, I 358
Hanson, I 375, IV 620
Hanukkah, I 503
Happy Days, I 69, 298, III 103, IV 422, 441
Happy Mondays, I 746
Harburg, E. Y., III 459
Hard Copy, IV 182, 599
Hardaway, Anfernee "Penny", IV 225
Hardaway, Ben "Bugs", I 276, 383
Hard-boiled detective fiction, I 473, 694, IV 97
Hardcore (punk), IV 143
Hardee's, II 73
Harder They Come, IV 196
Harding, Tonya, II 484, III 21, IV 34, 430
Harding, Warren G., I 680, II 499
Hardwicke, Cedric, IV 635
Hardy Boys, III 473, IV 548
Hardy, Oliver, IV 397
Hardy, Thomas, V 223
Hare Krishnas, I 647
Hargitay, Mickey, I 307, III 260
Haring, Keith, II 282, V 82
Harlem, I 614, II 449, III 97, IV 157
Harlem Globetrotters, I 186
Harlem Nights, II 148
Harlem Renaissance, I 614, 643, II 78, 227, 465, 469, 555, III 182, 223, 327, 570, IV 710
Harlequin Enterprises, II 367, IV 11, 271
Harley, William, II 368
Harlow, Jean, IV 103, 369, V 8
Harmon, Hugh, I 729

Harmon, Mark, III 406
Harmonica Gang, II 371
Harmonica Rascals, II 371
Haroun, Ray, II 490
Harper, David W., V 74
Harper, Valerie, II 42, III 292
Harper Valley P.T.A., IV 48
Harper's Bazaar, II 55
Harrah's-Tahoe, III 281
Harrington, Michael, I 61
Harris, Addie "Micki", IV 384
Harris, Emmylou, I 59, III 572, IV 18, 427
Harris, Franco, IV 61
Harris, Mildred, I 476
Harris, Oren, IV 152
Harris, Richard, I 414
Harris, Susan, II 260
Harris, Thomas, IV 359, 393
Harris v. Forklift Systems, I 94
Harrison, Benjamin, I 545
Harrison, George, I 203, III 316
Harrison, Jerry, IV 602
Harrison Narcotics Act, I 543
Harrison, Rex, III 464
Harry, Deborah, I 284, III 516
Harry, Deborah. See Blondie
Harryhausen, Ray, III 32
Hart, Gary, III 482, IV 368
Hart, John, II 512
Hart, Kitty Carlisle, IV 665
Hart, Lorenz, III 458, IV 254
Hart, Lorenz. See Rodgers and Hart
Hart, Mickey, II 293
Hart to Hart, IV 382
Hart, William S., I 220, IV 397, V 120
Hartack, Bill, III 20
Hartford Whalers, II 460
Hartman, Lisa, III 51
Hartman, Phil, IV 321
Hartman, Sid, III 196
Hartnell, William, I 739
Harvard Medical School, I 631
Harvard Psilocybin Project, III 112
Harvard University, I 555, 772, IV 128
Harvey, Doug, II 417
Harvey, Paul, V 199
Hasbro, II 230, IV 686
Hasselhoff, David, I 193
Hatari!, III 257
Hathaway, Henry, II 458, IV 340
Hauer, Rutger, I 273
Haunted Tank, V 191
Haunting of Hill House, II 521
Hauptmann, Bruno, I 424, III 337
Hauser, Tim, III 257
Havana, IV 191
Have Gun, Will Travel, V 120
Havel, Václav, V 227
Havilland, Olivia de, II 121
Havlicek, John, III 49, IV 225
Hawaii Five-O, III 241, IV 585
Hawkins, Coleman, I 248, II 529, III 3
Hawkins, Connie, II 364
Hawkins, Edwin, II 274
Hawkins, Erskine, IV 322
Hawkins, Hawkshaw, I 531
Hawks, Howard, I 250, II 99, 223, IV 642
Hawn, Goldie, III 99, IV 326
Hawthorne, Nathaniel, I 134
Hay, George D., II 286
Haycox, Ernest, IV 497
Hayden, Palmer, II 367
Hayden, Sterling, II 435
Hayden, Tom, I 495, III 512, IV 563
Hayes, Elvin, I 8
Hayes, Gabby, II 445, IV 263, V 120
Hayes, Harold, II 41, IV 712
Hayes, John Michael, IV 184
Hayes, Woody, IV 275
Haynes, Marques, III 365
Haynes, Todd, II 249
Hays Code, V 116

Hays, Lee, V 97
Hays, Will, I 108, 240, IV 94
Hays, William, IV 398
Hays, William H., II 432
Hayward, Leland, IV 462
Hayworth, Rita, I 129, IV 370
HBO, III 91, 233
"He Stopped Loving Her Today," II 562
Head, Murray, II 543
Head of the Class, IV 299
Head Shops, V 4
Headlines and Bylines, III 2
Healer, II 441
Healy, William, II 583
Hearst Corporation, II 41
Hearst, William Randolph, I 27, 38, 514, III 7, 62, 481, IV 367, 598, V 109
Heart and Soul, I 436
Heart of Darkness, I 102
Hearts and Minds, V 50
Hearts of Darkness, I 102
Hearts of the World, V 76
Heaven's Gate, I 282
Heaven's Gate cult, I 648, V 3
Heavy Metal, I 92
Heavy Metal, I 86, II 577, III 575, V 26, 94
Heche, Anne, I 682
Hecht, Ben, IV 598
Hecht, Harold, III 86
Hecht, William, III 22
Hedley Donovan, III 211
Hee Haw, III 582
Hee Haw Honeys, II 382
Heebie Jeebie, I 400
Heflin, Hal, I 94
Hefner, Christie, IV 72
Hefner, Hugh, IV 59, 70, 72, V 31
Hegyes, Robert, V 105
Heinlein, Robert, I 125, 129, 337, III 261, IV 331
Heirich, Max, II 161
Held, James, II 438
Heldman, Gladys, III 28
Heller, Joseph, I 457, V 191
Heller with a Gun, III 85
Hellerman, Fred, V 97
Hellman, Lillian, I 570, II 350, 435
Hello, Dolly!, III 84, 459, V 138
Hell's Angels, II 464, V 8
Hell's Angels, I 57, II 368, 535, IV 646, V 135
Hell's Angels on Wheels, II 4
Helmet, I 266
Helms, Jesse, III 265, IV 94
Help!: An Absolutely Indispensable Guide to Life for Girls, I 68
Hemingway, Ernest, I 84, 134, 418, 474, 709, II 40, 100, III 24, 145, IV 710
Hemp, III 272
Hemsley, Sherman, II 536
Henderson, Fletcher, I 247, II 376, 529, IV 155, 168, 322
Henderson, Florence, I 340, IV 1
Henderson, Joe, IV 389
Hendricks, Jon, III 258
Hendrix, Jimi, II 22, V 37, 170
Hendry, Ian, I 144
Henesy, David, I 659
Henie, Sonja, II 484, III 560, IV 430
Henneberger, J. C., V 103
Henreid, Paul, I 448
Henri, Robert, I 122, II 448
Henry, Buck, I 366, 458, II 227, 281
Henry, Everett, V 190
Henschel, Georg, I 325
Henson, Jim, I 225, III 57, 444, IV 136, 362
Henson, Jim. See also Muppets, The
Hentoff, Nat, I 61
Hepburn, Audrey, III 464
Hepburn, Katharine, I 33, II 289, IV 76, 356, 688, V 72
Herbert, Don, III 433
Herbert, Frank, I 129, IV 332
Hercules, IV 194

Here, My Dear, II 216
Heritage Foundation, IV 125, 137, 199
Heritage of the Desert, II 309
Herlihy, James Leo, III 357
Herman, Bernard, IV 612
Herman, Jerry, II 384, III 459
Herman, Woody, I 185, IV 138
Herman's Hermits, I 355
Hernández, Little Joe, IV 623
Herriman, George, III 62
Herrmann, Bernard, I 514, 666, II 416
Hersh, Seymour, III 466
Hershey, Barbara, II 442
Hershey, John, V 191
Herskovitz, Marshall, III 467
Herzog, Whitey, I 40
Hester, Carolyn, II 315
Hester Street, I 123
Heston, Charlton, I 221, IV 564, 634
Hewitt, Don, IV 425
Hewitt, James, I 699
Heyer, Georgette, IV 271
Hey,There, It's Yogi Bear, II 355
Hickman, Dwayne, I 735
Higginson, Henry Lee, I 325
High Noon, I 597, V 119
High Performance Computing Act of 1991, II 496
High Plains Drifter, II 402
High Society, IV 96
Higher and Higher, I 321
Highsmith, Patricia, II 415
Highway to Heaven, III 87
Highwaymen, II 541, III 501
Highways, I 110, III 148, IV 285
Hiken, Nat, I 432
Hilfiger, Tommy, IV 81
Hilgemeier, Edward, Jr., IV 152
Hill, Anita, I 93, III 337, IV 371
Hill, Anita. See Anita Hill-Clarence Thomas Senate
     Hearings
Hill, Benny, I 222
Hill, Dusty, V 236
Hill, Grace Livingston, IV 271
Hill, Henry, II 269
Hill, Joe, III 74
Hill, Lauryn, IV 176
Hill, Lew, I 570
Hill Street Blues, I 71, 176, 302
Hillerich, Bud, III 201
Hills, L. Rust, II 41
Hi-Lo Country, V 121
Hilton, Lester, III 377
Hilton, Nicky, IV 613
Hilton-Jacobs, Lawrence, V 105
Himes, Chester, III 416
Hinckley, John, Jr., II 145
Hindenberg, V 159
Hindman, Earl, II 438
Hinduism, II 362
Hines, Connie, III 376
Hines, Earl, I 115, II 10, V 36
Hines, Gregory, IV 606
Hinkey, Frank, I 555
Hinwood, Peter, I 644
Hip-Hop. See Rap/Hip-Hop
Hippies, I 152, II 394, III 386
Hirabayashi, Gordon, II 526
Hiroshima, I 311, II 399
Hirsch, Elroy "Crazylegs," IV 118
Hirsch, Judd, II 487, IV 610
Hirschfeld, Al, I 467
Hirschfeld, Magnus, II 210
His Girl Friday, III 406
Hiss, Alger, II 97
History of the American Black Athlete, I 124
Hit the Deck, IV 440
Hitchcock, Alfred, II 24, III 139, 195, 541, 543, IV
     130, 184, 522, 532, 651, V 42
Hitchy-Koo, IV 96
Hitler, Adolf, I 95, 429, III 2, 560, 583
HIV (human immunodeficiency virus), I 36
Hobbes, Thomas, I 414

Hobbit, IV 671
Hobo. See Tramps
Hockenberry, John, I 722
Hockney, David, I 222
Hodges, Johnny, I 558
Hodges, Russ, IV 648
Hoff, Marcian, Jr., II 496
Hoffa, III 74
Hoffman, Abbie, I 495, V 176, 214
Hoffman, Albert, III 208
Hoffman, Dr. Richard, V 122
Hoffman, Dustin, II 279, III 358, IV 678
Hoffman, Harold, V 122
Hoffman, Robert (Bob), I 306, II 317, III 453
Hoffman-LaRoche, V 20
Hoffman, Julius, I 496
Hoffmeyer's Legacy, III 24
Hogan, Ben, II 262
Hogan, Hulk, IV 60
Hogan's Heroes, V 192
Hohner Company, II 370
Holabird & Roche, IV 453
Holden, William, IV 579
Hole, III 204
Holiday, Billie, I 248, II 108, III 422, IV 410
Holland, Brian, III 422
Holland, Eddie, III 422
Holland, Josiah Gilbert, IV 344
Hollander, Nicole, IV 594
Holley, Major, II 155
Holliday, Polly, I 47
Hollies, I 355, 639
Hollingshead, Richard, Jr., I 769
Hollis, Herman E., I 714
Holly, Buddy, I 249, 354, II 21, 251, 315,
     540, IV 619
Hollywood, II 56, 64, III 430, IV 507
Hollywood Bowl, III 156
Hollywood Production Code, I 240
Hollywood Reporter, V 31
Hollywood Shuffle, II 89
Hollywood Squares, III 272
Hollywood Talent Scouts, III 169
Hollywood Walk of Fame, III 6
Hollywood's Golden Age, IV 29
Holmes, John Clellon, I 201
Holmes, Larry, I 47
Holmes, Oliver Wendell, IV 529
Holmes, Sherlock, I 693, 755
Holmgren, Mike, II 302
Holocaust, I 95, III 308
Holyfield, Evander, I 333, II 139, IV 719
Hombre, III 135
Home Box Office (HBO), I 404, III 505
Home of the Brave, II 15
"Home Sweet Home," III 419
Homelessness, IV 692
Homer, Winslow, I 123
Homestead Grays, III 498
Hominy, II 319
Homophile Movement, II 210
Honda, Inoshiro, I 724, II 252
Hondo, III 84
Honeymoon Lane, IV 440
Honeymooners, II 118, 245, 246, III 74, 336, IV 610
Hoofers Club, IV 605
Hooks, Robert, I 279
Hoosiers, II 448
Hoover Dam, III 93
Hoover, Herbert, I 239, II 28, 443, III 92
Hoover, J. Edgar, I 162, 714, II 80, 216, III
     239, IV 188
*Hopalong Cassidy and the Riders of High
     Rock*, III 85
Hope, Bob, I 222, 638, II 90, III 84, 504, IV 96,
     V 106, 121
Hope Diamond, IV 441
Hopkins, Anthony, IV 393, V 235
Hopkins, Harry, III 508
Hopper, Dennis, II 4, 442, 485, III 216, V 121
Hopper, Edward, I 122
Hopper, Hedda, II 275, III 429, IV 54

Hopper, William, I 395
Hordines, Johnny, I 306
Horizons of Rock Developing Everywhere, III 184
Horn and Hardart, II 71
Horn, Bob, I 526
Hornung, Paul, IV 118
Horoscopes, I 130
Horse racing, II 190, III 238, IV 312
Horse Whisperer, IV 191
Horst, Louis, I 686
Horticulturalist, I 239
Horton, Robert, V 59
Horton, Willie, I 695
Hoskins, Allen Clayton "Farina," III 578
Hospital, I 484
Hot, Cool and Vicious, IV 305
Hot dogs, V 187
Hot rod, III 455
Hot Wheels, I 765
Houdini, Harry, V 103
Hound of the Baskervilles, I 237
House & Garden, I 577
House, Eddie "Son," II 558
House I Live In, IV 411
House Made of Dawn, III 392
House of Blues, I 294
House of Dark Shadows, I 659
House of Pizza, II 73
House of Representatives, III 438
House of Representatives Select Committee on
     Current Pornographic Materials, IV 11
House of Style, I 624
House of Usher, IV 110
House Party, III 168
House Un-American Activities Committee (HUAC), I
     272, 429, 550, 570, II 97, 384, 413, 434, III 251,
     563, IV 229, 351, V 98, 215
Houseman, John, V 79, 109
Houston Aeros, II 460
Houston Astros, I 778, IV 298
Houston, Cissy, II 458
Houston Rockets, III 568
Houston, Whitney, IV 18
Hovick, June, III 119
How Green Was My Valley, II 134
How to Marry a Millionaire, II 278
How to Succeed in Business without Really Trying,
     III 459, V 22
How to Win Friends and Influence People, I
     437, IV 10
Howard Johnson's, II 72
Howard, Leslie, II 264
Howard, Robert E., IV 141, V 103
Howard, Ron, I 70, II 354, 357
Howard, Sidney, II 264
Howdy Doody Show, II 459, IV 686
Howe, Gordie, II 417, 467, III 574
Howe, Julia Ward, II 45, 85
Howe, Maude, II 45
Howell, C. Thomas, I 344
Howells, William Dean, I 134
"Howl," I 201, II 239
Howland, Beth, I 47
Hoxie, Albert, II 370
H.R. Pufnstuf, IV 318
Hsieh, Teh-ching, IV 38
Hubbard, Gardiner Greene, III 484
Hubbard, L. Ron, I 646, II 42, III 508
Hud, V 121
Hudson, Rock, I 665, II 468, IV 371, 614
Huff, Sam, IV 118
Huggins, Roy, II 179
Hughes Aircraft Company, II 464
Hughes, Howard, III 93, IV 292, V 8
Hughes, John, I 344, 347
Hughes, Langston, II 40, 366, IV 710
Hughes, Ramsey "Randy," I 531
Hughes, Robert, IV 712
Hughes, Ted, V 69
Hugo award, III 313
Hugo, Victor, III 139
Hulk, III 124

Hulk Hogan, IV 322
Hull, Bobby, II 417, III 574
Hull, Brett, II 468
Hull House, I 17
Hulman, Anton "Tony," II 491
Human Sexual Response, III 303, IV 373
Humbert, Humbert, III 183
Hummert, Frank, II 512
Humphrey, Doris, I 686
Humphrey, Hubert, II 420, III 186
Huncke, Herbert, I 201
Hungry Again, IV 18
Hunt for Red October, I 524
Hunt, Howard, V 86
Hunt, Lamar, IV 118
Hunter, Evan. See McBain, Ed
Hunter, Jim "Catfish," IV 523
Hunter, Kim, IV 555
Hunter, Meredith, I 58
Hunter, Robert, II 125, 293
Hunter, Tab, IV 618
Huntley, Chet, I 636, IV 630
Huntley-Brinkley Report, I 352, II 469
Hupmobile, II 312
Hurley, Elizabeth, V 42
Hurok, Sol, I 82
Hursley, Bridget, II 219
Hursley, Doris, II 218
Hursley, Frank, II 218
Hurston, Zora Neale, II 366, III 223, IV 710, V 62
Hurt, John, I 48
Hurt, Marlin, II 90
Hurt, Michael, II 398
Hüsker Dü, III 516, IV 142
Hussein, Saddam, II 325
Hustead, Ted and Dorothy, V 67
"Hustle," I 727
Hustler, I 722, II 470, IV 94
Hustler (film), II 247
Huston, John, I 33, 96, III 196, 250, IV 695, V 189
Huston, Walter, II 472
Hutchins, Bobby "Wheezer," III 578
Hutson, Don, II 300, IV 117
Hutton, Bobby, I 265
Huxley, Aldous, II 41, III 208
Huyck, Willard, I 69
Hyatt, John Wesley, IV 64
Hynde, Chrissie, III 516
Hypertext markup languages (HTML), II 496

I Am Legend, III 532
I, Claudius, IV 136
I Could Go on Singing, II 204
I Dream of Jeannie, IV 382
"I Got You Babe," IV 456
I Hate Preppies Handbook: A Guide for the Rest of Us, IV 105
I, the Jury, IV 478
I Love a Mystery, III 415
I Love Adventure, II 476
I Love Lucy, I 163, 228, 490, II 157, 327, III 97, 103, IV 419, V 27
I Remember Mama, I 776
I Shot the Sheriff, III 276
I Spy, I 607
"I Want to Be a Cowboy's Sweetheart," III 403
I Want to Live, II 377
I Wanted Wings, III 79
I Was a Teenage Werewolf, I 71
Iacocca, Lee, I 438, 593, II 137, III 370
IBM, I 107, II 496, III 353
Ibuka, Masuru, V 66
Ice Capades, II 349, 484
Ice extravaganzas, I 730
Ice Follies, II 484
Ice skating, III 21
Ice Storm, III 335, IV 594
Ice T, IV 176
Iceberg Slim, II 485
Ideal Novelty and Toy Corporation, IV 617
Idle, Eric, III 403
If He Hollers, Let Him Go, I 279

Ifukube, Akira, II 253
Iger, Samuel "Jerry," II 18
Ignatz Mouse, III 62
I'll See You in My Dreams, IV 644
Ilitch, Mike, I 696
Ils Sont Partis Band, I 380
"I'm a Yankee Doodle Dandy," I 548
I'm Gonna Get You, Sucka, I 280
I'm in a Phone Booth, Baby, III 26
Image Comics, IV 470
Imbruglia, Natalie, III 414
Imitation of Life(1934), I 209
Imitation of Life(1959), II 516
Immigrants, II 228
Immigration Restriction Act of 1924, IV 502
Immoralist, I 677
Imperial Records, IV 207
Impressions, III 310
Imus, Don, III 164, IV 386, 531, 600, 601
In a Metal Mood: No More Mr. Nice Guy, I 320
In Caliente, I 422
In Cold Blood, I 427, IV 663
In Dahomey, V 63
In the Dark, II 292
"In Flanders Fields," V 186
In the Groove Boys, III 25
In the Heat of the Night, I 279, IV 76
In His Steps, I 238, V 198
In Living Color, I 85
IN Los Angeles, I 28
In Love and War, V 51
In Step, V 38
In Utero, III 539
In the Wake of the Bounty, III 461
Ince, Thomas, IV 358, 397
Inceville Studio, IV 397
Incident at Ogala, IV 190
Incredible Hulk, I 308, 562
Indecent Proposal, II 202
Independence Day, IV 282
Independent Artists, III 429
Independent comics, V 4
Independent News Company, I 671
Index of American Design, II 296, III 509
Indian Packing Company, II 300
Indiana Pacers, I 256, II 571
Indiana, Robert, V 82
Indiana University, III 40, 49
Indianapolis 500, I 84, II 148, V 8
Indianapolis Racing League, II 491
Indians, IV 346
Industrial Light & Magic, III 210
Industrial Workers of the World (IWW), III 74, IV 124, 188, V 165
Infante, Lindy, II 302
Information Please, II 192
Information, Please!, II 55
Information superhighway, I 405
Informer, II 133
Ingenue, III 89
Ingram, Billy, II 72
Ingram, Edward, V 127
Inherit the Wind, I 627, 661, IV 336
Inklings, IV 673
Inner Sanctum Mysteries, I 463
Inside Edition, IV 599
Institute for Sex Research, III 40
Institute for Social and Religious Research, III 355
Intel Corporation, II 496
Intercollegiate Athletic Association of the United States, III 479
Internal Revenue Service, I 426
International Amateur Basketball Federation, I 767
International Brotherhood of Teamsters, III 73
International Business Machines. See IBM (International Business Machines)
International Creative Management (ICM), I 34
International Exhibition of Modern Art. See Armory Show, The

International Federation of Bodybuilders (IFBB), I 307
International Gay Rodeo Association (IGRA), IV 254
International Group, I 415
International Harvester, IV 483
International Hot Rod Association (IHRA), I 764
International Olympic Committee, I 307
International Roller Derby League, IV 267
International Society for Krishna Consciousness (ISKCON), I 647, II 362
International Style, IV 433
International Weightlifting Federation, I 307
Internet, I 26, 319, 405, II 26, III 184, 355, IV 95
Interpretation of Dreams, II 168
Interstate Commerce Commission (ICC), II 164
Interstate Highway Act, I 141, II 404
Interview, V 81
Into the Woods, IV 455
Intolerance, I 280, II 314, IV 396
Invasion of the Body Snatchers, I 645
Invisible Man, II 498, IV 169
Ionesco, Eugene, II 50
Iooss, Walter, IV 487
Iran-Contra, I 544, III 338, IV 180
Ireland, Kathy, III 48
Iron John, I 296, III 345
Iron Maiden, II 381, III 117
Irons, Jack, IV 26
Ironside, I 395, 721
Irvin, Michael, I 654, IV 118
Irving Thalberg Award, II 416
Isaacson, Walter, IV 659
Isle of Wight Festival, II 392
Isuzu, IV 483
It, III 38
It Can't Happen Here, III 155
It Happened One Night, I 428, II 187, IV 343
'It' Girl, I 326
It, The Terror from Beyond Space, I 48
Ito, Lance, IV 406
It's a Gift, II 96
It's a Wonderful Life, I 428, 644, IV 534
"It's Like That," IV 288
Itzkowitz, Isadore, I 423
"I've Got to Live the Life I Sing About," II 515
Ivers, Julia Crawford, IV 396
Ives, Burl, IV 287
Ives, Charles, III 268
Iwerks, Ub, I 90, 728

J. G. Taylor Spink Award, IV 484
Jack Armstrong: The All-American Boy, II 296
Jack Benny Program, I 223, 277, IV 161, V 190
Jack Daniels, II 78
Jack in the Box, II 73
Jack LaLanne Show, III 81
Jack Ruby, III 16
Jackie Brown, III 135
Jackie Gleason Show, III 336
Jackpot, II 193
Jackson, Al, III 26
Jackson, Doris Kenner, IV 384
Jackson, Felix, IV 564
Jackson Five, II 517, III 422, 510
Jackson, George L., III 245
Jackson, Janet, II 267, 514
Jackson, Josephine, IV 90
Jackson, Kate, I 480, 660, II 79
Jackson, Keith, III 393
Jackson, Mahalia, II 154, 274
Jackson, Michael, I 328, 405, II 54, 159, 513, III 155, 235, 436, IV 85, 615, 617, V 209
Jackson, Millie, II 185
Jackson, Mississippi, II 164
Jackson, Peter, I 332, 601
Jackson, Phil, I 493, II 571
Jackson, Reggie, III 521, IV 523, V 184, 209
Jackson, Reverend Charles E. "Stoney," IV 152
Jackson, "Shoeless" Joe, I 266, V 183
Jackson State University, III 19, 512
Jackson, Wayne, III 26
Jacobs, David, III 50

Jacobs, Mary Phelps, I 335
Jacob's Pillow, IV 381
Jagger, Bianca, V 82
Jagger, Mick, I 58, 355, 416, III 159, 279, IV 269
Jam Master Jay, IV 287
Jamerson, James, III 279
James Bond, I 550, II 227, 523, III 52, 253, IV 71
James, Cheryl "Salt," IV 305
James, Frank, II 128
James, Harry, I 248, II 278, IV 410
James, Henry, I 134
James, Jesse, III 237, V 118
James Norris Trophy, III 574
James, P.D., I 694
James, Sheila, I 735
James Weldon Johnson Collection, V 27
James, William, IV 90
Jameson, House, II 393
Jamison, Judith, I 38
Jane, IV 314
Jane Eyre, IV 613
Janiger, Oscar, III 208
Jannings, Emil, I 13
Janssen, David, II 180
Japanese American Citizens League, IV 671
Jardine, Al, I 196
Jardinn, Ben, I 264
Jarmusch, Jim, III 216
Jars of Clay, I 592
Jarvis, Anna, III 417
Jastrow, Joseph, IV 90
Jaws, I 282, IV 11, 476
Jazz Age, I 159, 326, 507, II 109, 366, 464,
    V 166, 228
Jazz Singer, I 271, 729, II 542, 559, IV 644, 710
Jazzercise, I 30
Jeans, III 146
Jeep, IV 482
Jefferson Airplane, I 58
Jefferson, Blind Lemon, II 447, 558, III 26, 109
Jefferson, George, III 111
Jefferson, Thomas, II 29
Jeffersons, III 111, IV 420
Jeffries, James J., I 332, 602
Jeffries, Jim, II 554
Jell-O, I 191, 607
Jelly's Last Jam, III 459
Jenkins, Dan, IV 487
Jennings, Waylon, I 450, 620, III 501, V 141
Jenny Craig, I 707
Jeopardy, II 194, 313
Jerde, Jon, III 246
Jeremiah Johnson, IV 190
Jeremy, IV 26
Jerk, IV 197
Jerome, Steve, IV 638
Jerry Springer Show, I 668, III 79, IV 35, 181, 490
Jesse James, IV 340
Jesse Owens track and field award, IV 433
Jesus, I 219
Jesus Christ, Superstar, I 359, II 338, III 181, 459
Jet, I 32, II 7
Jethro Tull, I 355
Jetsons, IV 317
Jetsons: The Movie, II 355
Jewett, Sarah Orne, I 134
Jewish, I 95
Jewison, Norman, II 544
Jews, I 586, IV 325
JFK, II 82, III 17, IV 543
Jim Crow laws, I 32, III 162
Jim Jones, II 564
Jim, Jungle, V 104
Jimenez, Jose. See Dana, Bill
Jimi Hendrix Experience, II 391
Jiminy Cricket, III 425
Jimmy Dean Show, III 367
Jitterbug, IV 322, 592
Jobs, Steven, I 106, II 496
Joey Dee and the Starliters, IV 36
Jogging, I 324, III 335, IV 637
John Birch Society, V 129

John, Elton, I 86, 416, II 249, III 460, V 42
John Hancock Center, IV 433
John Mayall's Blues Breakers, Featuring Eric
    Clapton, I 525
John Paul II, Pope, IV 87
John Reed Club, III 314
John XXIII, Pope, IV 87
Johnny Mnemonic, II 236
Johnny's Greatest Hits, III 306
Johns, Jasper, I 415
Johnson, Arte, III 99
Johnson, Ban, IV 484
Johnson, Ben, III 151
Johnson, Byron "Ban," I 539
Johnson, Charles S., II 366, III 570
Johnson, Don, III 349
Johnson, Earvin "Magic," I 8, 187, 256, 767, II 571,
    III 196, 478, IV 225, 414
Johnson, Jack, I 332, III 200, V 129
Johnson, James Weldon, II 366, III 182, 327
Johnson, Jimmie, IV 118
Johnson, Jimmy, I 654
Johnson, John H., I 32, II 544
Johnson, Johnnie, III 25
Johnson, Julian, IV 53
Johnson, Junior, IV 537
Johnson, Kathie Lee, II 236
Johnson, Lonnie, III 26
Johnson, Lyndon Baines, I 93, 637, II 30, 411, 465,
    546, III 34, 171, 269, 518, IV 137, 314, V 75
Johnson, Mark, III 537
Johnson, Marv, III 420
Johnson, Pete, III 3
Johnson, Raymond Edward, II 494
Johnson, Robert, I 292
Johnson, Virginia, III 303, IV 373
Johnson, Virginia. See Masters and Johnson
Johnson, Walter, I 436, V 217
Johnson's Wax, II 90
Joker, I 703
Jolson, Al, I 271, II 531, 542, III 458
Jonathan Livingston Seagull, I 155
Jones, Bobby, II 262, 571, III 305
Jones, Brian, I 355, II 392
Jones, Buck, IV 397, V 120
Jones, Charles Jesse "Buffalo," II 309
Jones, Charles Price, II 274
Jones, Chuck, I 146, 384, 766, 758, IV 328
Jones, Davy, III 394
Jones, Edward D., V 67
Jones, George, I 620, II 335
Jones, Howard, IV 275
Jones, James, II 175, V 191
Jones, James Earl, II 93
Jones, Jennifer, IV 357
Jones, Jenny, I 668, 745
Jones, Jo, I 185
Jones, John Paul, III 116
Jones, Laurence C., IV 644
Jones, Leroi, I 202
Jones, Leroi. See Baraka, Amiri
Jones, Orville "Hoppy," II 493
Jones, Parnelli, II 491
Jones, Paul Corbin, IV 372
Jones, Paula, III 149, IV 34, 516
Jones, Ralph, II 516
Jones, Reverend Jim, I 646, IV 570
Jones, Shirley, I 452, IV 18
Jones, Terry, III 403
Jones, Tommy Lee, II 180, III 220
Jones v. Hallahan, II 209
Jonestown, I 646, IV 570
Jong, Erica, II 87
Joplin, Janis, II 392
Joplin, Scott, I 247, IV 450
Jordan, Jim, II 89
Jordan, Louis, III 27, 513, IV 207
Jordan, Marian, II 89
Jordan, Michael, I 187, 256, 493, 767, IV 37, 554, III
    478, 535, IV 61, 225, 235, 485, 488
Jordanaires, I 531
Jorden, Al, I 664

Joseph and the Amazing Technicolor
    Dreamcoat, III 181
Journal of Homosexuality, II 211
Journey, IV 312
Journeymen, III 251
Joy of Cooking, I 497
Joy of Gay Sex, II 574
Joyce, James, II 387
Joyner, Al, II 575
Jubilee, IV 96
Judas Priest, II 381
Judge, Mike, I 209
Judgment at Nuremberg, II 204
Judson, Edward, II 378
Judy Canova Show, I 422
Juilliard School of Music, III 166
Juke joints, II 580
Julia, II 384, IV 420
Juliet of the Spirits, II 84
Jump blues, IV 207, 236
Jump Jim Crow, I 270
Jun Fan Kung-Fu Institute, III 118
Jung, Carl, I 130
Jungle, III 73, IV 414
Jungle Princess, III 83
Jurado, Katy, II 401
Jurassic Park, II 43
Justice League of America, I 561
Justice Society of America, I 672
Juvenile delinquency, IV 350, V 113

Kael, Pauline, I 286, 150, III 523
Kafka, Franz, II 50
Kahanamoku, Duke, III 560, IV 585
Kahane, Rabbi Meir, II 545
Kahn, Jeanette, I 672
Kai-shek, Chiang, I 377
Kaline, Al, I 695
Kallet, Arthur, I 588
Kallus, Joseph, III 22
Kander, John, III 459
Kane, Bob, I 189, 703
Kane, Helen, I 240
Kanin, Garson, I 95
Kansas City Chiefs, III 403
Kansas City jazz, I 184
Kansas City Royals, III 164
Kantner, Paul, II 534
Kaplan, Gabriel, V 105
Karan, Donna, IV 81
Karenga, Ron, I 265, 520
Karloff, Boris, I 71, 266, II 494
Karno, Fred, I 476
Karpovich, Dr. Peter, II 317
Kate Smith Show, V 219
Katz, Gloria, I 69
Katzenberg, Jeffrey, I 91, 730
Kauffman, Marta, II 172
Kaufman, Andy, IV 505, 611
Kaufman, George S., III 287
Kaufman, "Murray the K," I 726
Kawasaki, II 545
Kay, John, IV 527
Kay, Monte, I 215
Kaye, Danny, I 322
Kazan, Elia, I 273, 342, 358, 677, II 435, III 562,
    IV 522, 554
KDKA, IV 158
Keane, Bil, II 61
Keane, Bob, V 16
Keane, Margaret, III 44
Kearns, Jack "Doc," I 685
Keaton, Buster, I 107, 477, II 218, III 152,
    IV 358, 397
Keaton, Diane, I 54, 98
Keel, Howard, IV 96
Keeler, Ruby, II 142
Keen, Sam, III 345
Keene, Carolyn, III 473
Keeshan, Bob, I 430, II 459
Kefauver, Estes, I 565, II 9, 191, IV 350
Kefauver investigation, IV 312

Keitel, Harvey, III 336, IV 337
Keith, Benjamin Franklin, V 34
Keith-Albee theater chain, V 31
Kelk, Jackie, II 393
Kell, George, I 695
Keller, David, I 64
Keller, Donald, III 96
Keller, Helen, I 310, 721
Kelley, David E., II 407, IV 49
Kelley, DeForest, IV 508
Kelley, Florence, II 583
Kellogg, Dr. John Harvey, III 453, IV 708
Kelly, Betty, III 279
Kelly, Brian, II 118
Kelly, Emmett, I 513, IV 214, 692
Kelly, Gene, II 203, 355, 384, IV 415, 605
Kelly, Grace, II 400, III 14, 60, V 12
Kelly, Walt, I 747, IV 73
Kelly, Walt. See *Pogo*
Kelly, William Russell, III 14
Kelton, Pert, II 246
Kemble, Fanny, V 161
Kemp, Harry, IV 692
Ken, I 171
Ken, II 40
Kendricks, Eddie, IV 633
Kennard, Charles, III 576
Kennedy, Bobby, IV 368
Kennedy, Edward, IV 368
Kennedy Foundation, IV 470
Kennedy, John F., I 104, 192, 313, 414, 586, 637, II
    59, 177, 516, 545, III 16, 60, 171, 223, 239, 245,
    254, 266, 338, 399, 475, 564, IV 1, 87, 302, 315,
    368, 411, 471, 628, V 49
Kennedy, Joseph P., V 35
Kennedy, Robert, I 162, 495, III 399
Kenney, Douglas, III 487
Kenny, Bill, II 493
Kenny, Kathryn, IV 698
Kent, Clark, IV 581
Kent, Frank, III 514
Kent State University, III 512
Kenton, Stan, I 249
Kentucky Fried Chicken, II 73
Keon, Dave, II 460
Kepner, Jim, I 29, II 211
Kermit the Frog, IV 362
Kern, Jerome, I 358, III 458, IV 254, 389
Kerouac, Jack, I 201, 397, III 561
Kerr, Clark, IV 179
Kerr, Deborah, IV 616
Kerrigan, Nancy, II 360, 484, III 70, IV 430
Kersee, Bobby, II 575
Kesey, Ken, III 208, 566
Kevorkian, Jack, III 408, IV 570
Key West, I 383
Keyes, Paul, III 98
Keystone film studio, I 107
Keystone Kops, IV 358, 397
Keystone View Company, IV 529
Khan, Chaka, II 458
Khan, Nusrat Fateh Ali, IV 28
Khrushchev, Nikita, I 193, IV 587
Kickapoo Indian Medicine Company, III 339
Kid Auto Races at Venice, I 475, IV 357
Kid Komedies, IV 358
Kid, I 476
Kidman, Nicole, I 641
Kids Say the Darndest Things, III 169
Kiel, Richard, II 524
Kieran, John, II 55
Kilgallen, Dorothy, IV 1, V 122
Kilgore, Barney "Bernard," V 67
Killers, II 100
Killian, Mike, I 703
Kilpatrick, James, IV 425
Kilrain, Jake, IV 573
Kilroy, II 281
Kinescopes, II 477, IV 394
King and I, I 375, III 459, IV 256
King, B. B., I 15, 56, 278, III 25, IV 207
King, Ben E., I 769

King, Billie Jean, I 124, II 49, III 337, IV 211,
    636, V 150
King, Carole, I 351, 352
King, Don, I 776
King Features Syndicate, II 380
King, Freddie, I 56
King, Martin Luther, Jr., I 135, 214, 478, 495, 517,
    519, II 155, 514, 515, III 244, 266, IV
    16, 125, 157
King Kong, II 252, V 196
King, Larry, IV 601, V 12
King, Maurice, III 420
King of Comedy, III 153
King of Jazz, V 130
King Records, I 165
King, Rodney, I 766, IV 157
King, Sonny, III 280
King, Stephen, II 10, 521, IV 694
King, Warren, II 257
King's Row, IV 47, 179
King-Size Canary, I 146
Kingsley, Charles, III 457
Kingston, Maxine Hong, I 375
Kingston Trio, II 124, IV 44
Kinison, Sam, III 278
Kinks, I 355, 576
Kinsella, W. P., II 93
Kinsey, Alfred, IV 374
Kinsey Report, IV 45
Kiowa, III 392
Kiowa Indian Medicine and Vaudeville
    Company, II 488
Kipling, Rudyard, V 161, 222
Kirby, Jack, I 429, 561, III 124, IV 474, 529,
    V 190, 205
Kirchner, Raphael, V 30
Kirchwey, Freda, III 477
Kirk, Andy, III 3
Kirk, Phyllis, I 401
Kirk, Tommy, III 425
Kirkland, Frank, I 704
Kirschner, Don, I 351
Kirstein, Lincoln, I 161, 166
Kiss, I 14, III 117
Kiss, IV 394
Kiss Me a Killer, IV 98
Kiss Me, Kate, III 459, IV 96
Kissinger, Henry, I 599
Kit Carson, V 120
Kitsch, I 12, II 264, IV 205
Kitty Foyle, I 129
Klein, Calvin, I 303, III 417, IV 205
Kling, Ken, III 463
Klugman, Jack, III 550
Knabusch, Ed, III 106
Knack, III 516, V 209
Knebel, Fletcher, IV 364
Knerr, Harold H., III 7
Knickerbockers, IV 84
Knight, Damon, I 337
Knight, Eric, III 95
Knight, Gladys, V 149
Knight, Jean, II 185
Knight, Phil, III 535
Knight, Ray, III 195
Knight, Ted, III 292, 294
Knock on Any Door, III 419
Knot's Landing, II 201, IV 48, 447
Knotts, Don, I 53, 87, IV 654
Knute Rockne, All American, IV 179
Koch, Howard, V 79
Kodachrome, I 110
Kodak, I 371, III 51
Koenig, Walter, IV 508
Kohner, Frederick, IV 585
Kong, Leslie, III 275
Kool DJ Herc, I 167, IV 174
Koon, Stacey, III 35
Koop, C. Everett, III 437, IV 200
Koppel, Ted, III 534
Koppell, Bernie, III 204
Korbut, Olga, II 332, IV 211

Korea, I 570
Korean War, I 761
Korematsu, Fred, II 526
Koresh, David, and the Branch Davidians, I 648, III
    54, IV 570
Korner, Alexis, I 355
Kornman, Mary, III 578
Koster, Henry, I 753
Kosuth, Joseph, I 577
Kotto, Yaphet, I 48
Kovic, Ron, I 722
Kowalski, Stanley, IV 554
Kozoll, Michael, I 302
Kraft Foods, V 39
Kraft Television Theater, III 213
Kraftwerk, III 516
Kramer, Peter D., IV 92
Kramer, Stanley, II 15, 204, V 135
Kramer vs. Kramer, I 733, II 87
Krantz, Grover, I 252
Krasner, Lee, IV 80
Krassner, Paul, I 61
Krauledat, Joachim, IV 527
Krauss, Alison, I 290
Krebs, Ernst, III 76
Krebs, Ernst, Jr.III 76
Kreutzmann, Bill, II 292
Krieger, Robbie, I 748
Kristofferson, Kris, II 540, III 501
Kroc, Ray A., II 72, III 321
Krupa, Gene, I 248
Kruschev, Nikita, II 20, III 282
Krusen, Dave, IV 26
Ku Klux Klan, I 258, II 163, III 218, V 129
Kubrick, Stanley, I 48, 527, 532, 759, IV 468,
    717, V 188
Kudrow, Lisa, II 172
Kuhn, Maggie, II 294
Kuklapolitans, III 68
Kundera, Milan, II 50
Kundun, IV 338
Kunstler, William, I 496
Kurosawa, Akira, II 252, III 240, IV 681
Kurtzman, Harvey, II 9, III 230
Kushner, Tony, I 36
Kushnick, Helen, III 132
Kuttner, Henry, V 103
Kwan, Michelle, II 484
Kwanzaa, I 503
Kyser, Kay, I 754

La Bamba, III 198, V 15
La Dolce Vita, II 84
La Huelga, I 483
La Jolla Playhouse, IV 30
L.A. Law, I 302, IV 442
LaBianca, Leno and Rosemary, III 262
Labine, Claire, II 219, IV 447
Labor Day Muscular Dystrophy Telethon, III 152
Labor unions, IV 124
Lachman, Edward, III 465
Lacoste, Rene, III 75
Ladd, Alan, III 80, IV 340
Ladd, Cheryl, I 480
Ladd, Diane, I 47
Ladder, II 210, IV 545
Ladies' Home Journal, I 310, 456, II 45, II 265, III
    301, IV 173, 189, 699
Ladies Professional Golf Association (LPGA), II 262,
    III 194, IV 388
Lady and the Tramp, III 121
Lady Eve, IV 507
Lady for a Day, III 294
Lady Sings the Blues, IV 127
Ladysmith Black Mambazo, IV 404
Laemmle, Carl, II 134
Laffel, Forrest, II 73
Lager, I 210
Lagerfeld, Karl, I 475
LaGuardia, Fiorello, I 389
Laguerre, Andre, IV 487
Lahr, Bert, IV 96, 440, V 162

Lake, Arthur, I 284
Lake Placid, New York, III 536
Lake, Ricki, I 668
Lake, Stuart, III 464
Lake, Veronica, III 75, IV 370
Lake Wobegon Days, III 12
LaLanne, Jack, I 308, III 453, 454
Lambada, III 449
Lambeau, Earl L. "Curly," II 300, III 483, IV 117
Lambert, Darrell "Pee Wee," IV 506
Lambert, Douglas, IV 72
LaMotta, Jake, I 332, IV 165, 234, 337
Lamour, Dorothy, IV 313
L'Amour, Louis, IV 11, 141
Lancaster, Burt, III 429
Lanchester, Elsa, II 152
Landau, Martin, V 173
Landers, Ann, I 27
Landis, John, I 89, 293, IV 642
Landis, Kennesaw Mountain, I 267, III 498, IV 232
Landlord's Game, III 396
Landmark Forum, II 42
Landon, Michael, I 316
Landry, George "Big Chief Jolley," III 514
Landry, Tom, I 654, 731, IV 118, 520
Lands' End, IV 81
"Landscape #20," I 675
Lane, Allan "Rocky," III 376
Lane, Lois, IV 582
Lane, Nathan, III 460
Lang, Fritz, II 99, 128, III 195, 347, IV 398, 566
Lang, k.d., I 222, 624, III 141
Lang, Michael, V 176
Langdon, Harry, I 428, IV 358, 397
Lange, Dorothea, III 509
Lange, Hope, IV 48
Lange, Jessica, IV 382, 554, 678
Lange, Ted, III 204
Langenheim Brothers, IV 529
Langham, Wallace, III 91
Langstroth, Bill, III 448
Lansbury, Angela, II 28, III 445, 460
Lansdowne, Helen, II 511
Lansky, Meyer, III 212
LAPD, I 766
Lapham, Lewis H., II 372
Lardner, Ring, Jr., II 434
Larger than Life, I 286
Larkin, John, II 13
Larry Sanders Show,, II 507
Larsen, Nella, II 366
Larsen, Roy E., III 211
Larson, Gary, I 722, II 69
Larson, Jonathan, III 459
Las Vegas, II 190, 563, III 156
Las Vendidas (The Sell-Outs), II 19
Lasky, Jesse L., I 684
Lasser, Louise, III 289
Lassie, IV 44, 419
Lassie Come Home, III 95, IV 613
Last Exit to Brooklyn, III 78
Last of the Plainsmen, II 309
Last Picture Show, III 331, V 121
Last Temptation of Christ, III 12, IV 338
Late Night With David Letterman, I 40, III 133
Late Show Starring Joan Rivers, IV 220
Lauer, Matt, IV 667
Laufer, Charles, IV 619
Laugh-In, I 153
Laughton, Charles, II 99, III 461, V 121
Lauper, Cyndi, III 235
Laurel and Hardy, III 24, IV 397
Lauren, Ralph, IV 205
Laver, Rod, V 150
Laverne and Shirley, I 69, 213
Lavin, Linda, I 47
LaVoe, Hector, IV 304
Law and Order, II 406
Law, Don, II 558
Lawford, Peter, I 344
Lawler, Jerry "The King," III 8
Lawless, Lucy, V 203

Lawrence, D.H., IV 11
Lawrence, James Duncan, IV 675
Lawrence, Jerome, I 112
Lawrence, Marjorie, I 721
Lawrence of Arabia, I 282
Lawrence, Pauline, I 686
Lawrence, Thomas Edward, III 104
Lawrence, Vera Brodsky, II 568
Lawson, Ernest, I 123
Lawson, John Howard, II 434
Lawyer's Guild, I 116
Layne, Bobby, IV 61, 118
Layton, Chris, V 313
Lazarus, Fred, I 689
Lazenby, George, II 523
Le Carré, John, I 551
Le Corbusier, IV 433
Le Guin, Ursula K., I 65
Le Mat, Paul, I 70
Le Morte D'Arthur, I 121
Le Parisienne, V 30
Leachman, Cloris, III 96, 292
Leadbelly, I 781, II 126, III 509
League of Conservative Citizens, V 130
League of Nations, I 310
Leakey, Louis, III 484
Lean Cuisine, I 707
Lean, David, III 105
Lear, Norman, I 50, 709, II 148, 156, 267, 536, III 91, 289, 306, 565, IV 310, 420
Learned, Michael, II 327, V 74
Leary, Timothy, III 208, IV 128
Leave It to Me!, IV 96
Leaves of Grass, III 157
Leavitt, Ron, III 278
LeBlanc, Matt, II 173
LeCarre, John, I 238
L'Ecole des Trois Gourmands, I 497
Lecter, Hannibal "The Cannibal," IV 393
Led Zeppelin, I 41, 265, 355, 746, II 380, III 527, V 212
Ledbetter, Huddie. See Leadbelly
Lee, B. Gentry, IV 301
Lee, Beverly, IV 384
Lee, Bruce, III 69
Lee, Gypsy Rose, I 390
Lee, Harper. See *To Kill a Mockingbird*
Lee, Manfred B. See Queen, Ellery, I 694
Lee, Michelle, III 51
Lee Middleton Original Dolls, III 22
Lee, Robert E., I 112
Lee, Russell, III 509
Lee, Spike, I 280, 735, III 66, 245
Lee, Stan, I 561, 565, III 42, 285, IV 399, 474, V 205
Lee, Tommy, III 419
Lee, Will, IV 136, 362
Left Hand of Darkness, III 108
Lego, III 126
LegoLand, III 126
Lehman, Ernest, III 541
Leiber, Jerry, I 351, III 30, 422
Leifer, Neil, IV 487
Leigh, Janet, IV 130
Leigh, Vivien, II 264, IV 554, 616
Leipzig Toy Fair, IV 617
Leisen, Mitchell, III 229
Leitch, Donovan, II 125
Leitzel, Lillian, I 512
Leland, Henry, I 406
Lemair, Lyn, II 503
Lemay, Harding, I 99, IV 446
Lemmings, I 217
Lemmon, Jack, III 60, 550, IV 453, 679
Lemon, Meadow "Meadowlark," II 364
Lemond, Greg, IV 684
Lenin, Vladimir, I 569, IV 188
Lennart, Isabel, II 435
Lennon, John, I 203, 754, III 30, 159, 316, IV 237
Lennon Sisters, The, V 106
Lenny, I 374
Leno, Jay, I 40, III 144, IV 677

Lensmen, I 129
Lenz, Kay, I 453
Leonard, Sheldon, IV 645
Leonard, Sugar Ray, I 673, 776, II 335
Leone, Sergio, II 3, 107, 266, IV 467, V 121
Leopard's Spots, I 258
Leopold, Aldo, II 405
Leopold, Nathan, I 424, 660, III 138
Leopold-Loeb murder case, III 146
Lerner, Alan Jay, I 414, III 459, 464
Leroux, Gaston, IV 49
Les, Don, II 371
Les Miserables, II 179, III 216, 460
Les Paul Trio, I 132
Lesbian rights, III 489
Lesbianism, II 86, III 88
Lesco Corporation, V 199
Lesh, Phil, II 292
LeSieg, Theo, I 758
Less Than Zero, II 24
"Let It Be," III 316
Let There Be Light, II 472
Let Us Now Praise Famous Men, III 509
Letterman, David, III 133
Letty Lynton dress, I 626
Levant, Oscar, II 55, IV 1
Levene, Philip, I 145
Levin, Jennifer, IV 105
Levin, Meyer, III 139
Levine, Joseph E., IV 194
Levinson, Barry, I 719
Levinson, Richard, I 559, III 445
Levi's, V 196
Levi-Strauss, I 455, III 146
Levi-Strauss, Claude, IV 100
Levitt, William, II 97, III 104, 247, IV 568
Levittown, I 457, II 97, IV 568
Levy, Maurice, III 171
Lewinsky, Monica, III 337, IV 11, 368, 372, 516
Lewis, Al, I 433
Lewis, Bob, I 552
Lewis, C. S., III 107
Lewis, Herschell Gordon, III 533
Lewis, Jerry, I 322, III 280, 502
Lewis, Jerry Lee, I 354, II 98, 430, IV 236, 587, 619
Lewis, John, III 306
Lewis Manufacturing Company, I 455
Lewis, Sinclair, I 140, 236, 418, II 388, III 46, IV 710, V 196
Lewis, Thomas H. A., I 112
Lewis, William B., V 190
Lewitt, Sol, I 577
Lewton, Val, I 149
Leyendecker, J(oseph) C(hristian), I 118
L.I.F.E. Bible College, III 331
Liat, IV 465
Liberation News Service, V 160
Liberation of L.B. Jones, I 279
Liberty Bonds, V 75
Liberty Loans, IV 464
Library of Congress, II 330
Librium, V 20
License To Ill, I 200
Lichtenstein, Roy, I 415, 591, IV 81
Liddy, G. Gordon, V 85, 86
Lido, IV 96
Lieber, Jerry, IV 208
Liebling, A.J., I 44, 332, IV 348
Liebman, Joshua Loth, IV 91
Liebovitz, Annie, IV 59
Liebowitz, Jack, I 671
Life, II 142, 578, III 211, IV 35
"Life During Wartime," IV 602
"Life in Hell," II 319, IV 409
Life of Riley, II 245
Life Plus 99 Years, III 139
Life with Luigi, II 90
Lifeboat, IV 522
LifeSavers, III 504
Lifetime Reading Plan, II 55
Lift Every Voice and Sing, II 556

Light that Failed, III 215
Lilies of the Field, I 279, IV 76
Lilith Fair, III 142, 184
Lilli doll, I 171
Lilly, Bob, I 654
Limbaugh, Rush, IV 387, 601
Limelight, I 477
Lincoln, Abraham, I 464, IV 307
Lincoln Center Jazz Orchestra, II 530
Lincoln, Elmo, I 307, IV 609
Lincoln Highway, II 402
Lincoln Memorial, III 266, V 83
Lind, Jenny, IV 212
Lindbergh, Anne Morrow, III 167
Lindbergh, Charles, I 38, II 464, III 166, 337,
    IV 485, 686
Lindley, Audra, IV 654
Lindsay, Howard, IV 462
Lindsay, "Terrible" Ted, II 417
Lindsey, Hal, III 96
Lindy Hop, IV 592
Link, William, I 559, III 445
Linkletter, Art, I 669
Lion King, I 91, II 31, III 460
Lion, Maro, I 708
Lion, the Witch, and the Wardrobe, III 150
Lions Gate, I 63
Liotta, Ray, II 93, 269
Lipinski, Tara, II 484
Lippmann, Walter, III 514
Lipscomb, Mance, I 56
Lipton, Peggy, III 386
Liquid Soul, III 527
Lish, Gordon, II 41
Liston, Sonny, I 44, 332
Lite Beer, I 212
Litel, John, II 393
Literary Digest, IV 177
Literary Guild, I 237
Literary naturalism, American, III 540
Little Big Man, II 421, V 119
Little Caesar, III 238, IV 230
Little Foxes, IV 615
Little House on the Prairie, III 87, V 137
Little Johnny Jones, V 207
Little League, I 156, IV 297
Little Leather Library, I 318
Little Mermaid, IV 686
Little Nemo, II 226
Little Nemo in Slumberland, III 317
Little Night Music, A, IV 455
Little Orphan Annie, I 96, 298, V 191
Little People, II 106
Little Rascals. See Our Gang
Little, Richard, I 354, IV 84
Little Theatre, I 573
Little Tramp, I 475
Little Women, I 67
Littlejohn, Johnny, III 154
Live Aid, II 283
Live Wire/Blues Power, III 26
Liverpool, England, IV 84
Lives of a Bengal Lancer, I 598
Living Theater, I 748
Livingston, Stanley, III 467
Livingstone, Bunny, IV 196
Livingstone, Mary, I 223
LL Cool J, IV 175
Lloyd, Christopher, IV 610
Lloyd, Harold, IV 397
Lloyd, John, II 49
Lloyd Webber, Andrew, I 359, 460, II 543, III 458,
    IV 49, 115, 579
Local Hero, IV 624
Locher, Dick, I 703
Locke, Alain, II 366, III 327
Locke, Sondra, II 3
Lockhart, Calvin, I 279
Lockhart, June, III 96
Locklear, Heather, III 419
"Loco-Motion," III 30
Lodger, II 415

Loeb, Philip, I 272
Loeb, Richard, I 424, 660, III 138
Loesser, Frank, III 459
Loew, Marcus, III 309
Loewe, Frederick, I 414, III 459, 464
Loewy, Raymond, II 492
Logan, Joshua, IV 465, 532
Lolita, IV 356
Lollobrigida, Gina, IV 370
Lomax, Alan, I 329
Lomax, John A., III 509
Lombard, Carole, IV 103
Lombardi, Vince, II 301, IV 118, 515
Lombardo, Guy, I 526, IV 710
London (record label), IV 306
London, Jack, I 332, IV 542, V 129, 223
Lone Ranger, I 298, II 296, V 118
Lone Star, V 121
Lonely Bull, I 57
Lonely Crowd, II 98
"Lonelyhearts" columns, I 26
Lonesome Dove, V 121
Long John Silver's, II 73
Long Riders, V 120
Longet, Claudine, V 139
Longfellow, Henry Wadsworth, I 134
Longley, Mitch, I 722
Long-Playing Record, I 575
Look Who's Talking, IV 694
Looking Backward, III 463
Looking for Mr. Goodbar, IV 416
Looney Tunes, I 146
Loos, Anita, II 223, 313, IV 396
Lopez, Robert. *See* El Vez
Lorca, Federico García, V 15
Lord, Jack, II 375
Lord, Marjorie, IV 645
Lord of the Rings, I 775, IV 332, 671
Loren, Sophia, II 469, III 85, IV 370
Lorenz, Anton, III 106
Lorraine, Lillian, V 228
Lorre, Peter, I 71, 448, II 494, III 250
Los Alamos, New Mexico, I 311
Los Angeles, V 123
Los Angeles Dodgers, I 778, III 93, IV 231, V 19
Los Angeles Lakers, I 8, II 553, 571, III 478,
    568, V 114
Los Angeles Police Department, III 35, IV 157, V 99
Los Angeles Rams, IV 118
Los Angeles. *See* City of Angels, The
Los Angeles T-Birds, IV 267
Losey, Joseph, I 272
Lost Generation, I 83, IV 710
Lost World, II 582
Lott, Trent, V 130
Lottery See also Gambling
Lou Grant, I 126
Louganis, Greg, IV 712
Louis, Joe, I 44, 332, III 238, IV 486
Louis-Dreyfus, Julia, IV 353
"Louisiana Man," III 21
Louisiana Purchase Exposition, II 567
Louvin Brothers, II 48
Love, American Style, IV 535
Love, Andrew, III 26
Love Boat, III 336, IV 535
Love, Courtney, I 303, III 414, 539
Love Me Tonight, IV 256
Love, Mike, I 196
Love of Life, IV 446
Love Parade, III 224
Love Story, IV 105
Love Unlimited Orchestra, V 125
Lovecraft, H. P., IV 141, V 103
Loved Dead, V 103
Lovell, James, I 104
Lovett, Lyle, I 262, 620
Lovitz, John, III 110
Lovksy, Celia, III 195
Lovullo, Sam, II 382
Low, Juliette Gordon, II 242

Lowe, Nick, III 515
Lowe, Rob, I 344
Loy, Myrna, IV 103
LSD, I 204, 453, III 112, 207, IV 128, 223
Lubitsch, Ernst, III 224, IV 566
Lucas, George, I 69, IV 166, 511
Lucas, Henry Lee, I 425
Lucas, Jerry, III 49
Lucas, Marcia, I 71
Lucas, Sam, I 271
Lucasfilm, IV 715
Lucci, Susan, I 52, II 28, IV 447
Luce, Henry, III 160, 527, IV 487, 657
Lucent Technologies, I 131
Luciano, Lucky, III 90, 237
"Lucille," IV 261
Luckman, Sid, I 492, IV 117
"Lucy in the Sky with Diamonds," III 209
Luddites, II 10
Ludlow Massacre, IV 241
Luft, Lorna, II 204
Luft, Sid, II 204
Lugosi, Bela, I 760, III 5, V 23, 172
Luks, George, I 122, V 213
Lumet, Sidney, III 503
Lumière, Louis, IV 395
Lunceford, Jimmy, I 248
Lupino, Ida, II 390
LuPone, Patti, III 139, 460
"Lust for Life," IV 82
Lust for Life: A Novel of Vincent Van Gogh, IV 542
Lusty Men, V 121
Luther, Martin, I 504
Luther's Blues, I 56
Lux Radio Theater, III 75
Luyendyk, Arie, II 490
Lydon, Jimmy, II 393
Lynch, David, I 286, III 572, IV 715
Lynd, Helen Merrell, III 355
Lynd, Robert, III 355
Lynde, Paul, II 434
Lyndon B. Johnson Space Center, III 475
Lyne, Adrian, II 74
Lyngstad, Frida, I 4
Lynn, Loretta, I 620
Lynyrd Skynyrd, I 42
Lyon, Lisa, I 307
Lyotard, Jean Francois, IV 100

M, II 100, III 195
M*A*S*H, I 42, 50, 63, II 71, 435, IV 420, 611
M1 rifle, II 102
M16 rifle, II 102
Ma Perkins, IV 446
Mabel Snow's Spectacular Burlesque Company, I 388
MacArthur, Charles, IV 598
MacArthur, James, II 375
Macbeth Gallery, I 122
MacDonald, Jeanette, II 13
MacDonald, John D., I 263
MacDonald, Ross, I 694, III 134
Macfadden, Bernarr, I 136, 306, 581, III 157,
    453, IV 699
Macfadden, Mary, III 228
MacGregor, I 20
Macheca, Joseph, III 237
Machine Gun Kelly, I 71
Macintosh, I 106
Macintosh, Cameron, I 359
Mack, I 279
Mack, Eddie, III 463
Mack, Nila, III 143
Mack Sennett Bathing Beauties, IV 358
Mack, Ted, I 668
MacKinnon, Catharine, IV 94
Mackintosh, Cameron, III 139, 460
MacLachlan, Kyle, III 216
MacLaine, Shirley, IV 614
MacLeod, Gavin, III 203
MacLise, Angus, V 39
MacMurray, Fred, III 467
Macnee, Patrick, I 144

Macon, Uncle Dave, I 620
MacPhail, Larry, I 169
Macroscope, I 100
Macy, Zaccheus, III 229
Macy's, I 688
Macy's Thanksgiving Day Parade, IV 248
Mad About You, II 468, IV 197
Mad Max, I 71, II 234
Madame Celeste's Female Minstrel Company, I 388
Madden, Dave, IV 18
Madden, John, III 547
Madden, Owney, I 614
*Mad*Magazine, I 564, II 9
Madonna, I 21, 168, 201, 305, 328, 337, 359, 405,
    708, II 224, 249, III 100, 110, 205, IV
    85, 259, 620
Mafia, II 269, 546, IV 409
Magazine culture, IV 14
Magazine of Fun, V 103
Magic Eye, IV 529
Magic of Believing, III 156
Magnificent Ambersons, IV 607
Magnificent Obsession, IV 616
Magnificent Seven Ride!, III 241
Magnificent Seven, I 375, III 334, V 119
Maharis, George, IV 72
Maharishi Mahesh Yogi, I 205, 746
Mahjong, III 148
Mahovlich, Frank, II 417
Maiden Form Brassiere Company, I 335
Mail order, II 494
Mailer, Norman, I 61, II 41, V 45, 191
Main, Marjorie, III 340
Main Street, III 155
Mainframe computers, II 482
Mairs, Nancy, I 722
Majestic, I 149
Major League Soccer, IV 449
Majors, Lee, II 79, IV 424
Make Room for Daddy, IV 419, 644
Making a Living, I 476
Makley, Charles, I 713
Malamud, Bernard, III 492
Malcolm X, I 45, 264, 520, II 343, III 123
Malden, Karl, IV 555
Mall of America, III 248
Malle, Louis, I 224
Malls, I 590
Malone, Karl, IV 486
Maltese Falcon, II 349, 471
Maltz, Albert, II 434
Mamas and the Papas, III 279
Mama's Family, III 56, 106
Mambo, IV 304
Mambo Kings, II 405, III 198
Mambo Kings Play Songs of Love, II 405
Man Amongst Men, I 704
Man Called Horse, V 119
Man in the Gray Flannel Suit, II 98
Man in the High Castle, I 702, IV 332
Man Nobody Knows, I 179
Man o' War, III 20
Man of the Forest, II 311
Man Who Knew Too Much, I 664, II 415
Man Who Shot Liberty Valance, IV 499, V 93, 119
Man With the Golden Arm, IV 104
Manassa Mauler, I 685
Manchester, William, III 62
Manchurian Candidate, I 551
Mancini, Henry, I 346, V 139
Manckiewicz, Joseph L., II 200, IV 614
Mandel, Babaloo, III 110
Mandel, Howie, I 670
Mandrake the Magician, I 475
Manet, Edouard, I 123
Maney, Mabel, I 491
Manfred Mann, I 355
Manhattan, I 54
Mankiewicz, Herman J., I 515, V 109
Mankiewicz, Joseph L., I 282
Mann Act, II 555
Mann, Anthony, V 120

Mann, Barry, I 351
Mann, Herbie, III 97
Manners and Social Usages, II 45
Manning, Marie, I 27
Mannix, I 9
Man's Woman, III 541
Mansfield, Jayne, IV 370
Manson, Charles, I 424
Manson, Marilyn, I 303, 597
Mantle, Burns, IV 54
Mantle, Mickey, I 326, II 138, 236, III 1, 521, IV
    485, V 184, 208
Many Loves of Dobie Gillis, I 202, IV 391
Manzano, Sonia, IV 363
Manzarek, Ray, I 748
Maple Leaf Rag, II 566
Mapplethorpe, Robert, IV 673
Maranzano, Salvatore, III 237
Marathon, III 559
Marble Dry Goods, I 688
Marcel, Jesse, IV 282
March, Colonel, I 442
March Madness, III 480
March of Time, IV 658
March on the Pentagon, V 214
March on Washington, I 157, III 34, IV 125
Marching bands, IV 463
Marchiony, Italo, II 484
Marconi, Guglielmo, IV 157
Marconi Wireless Telegraph Company, IV 312
Marcucci, Bob, IV 619
Margaritaville, I 383
Margo, III 97
Marie, Rose, I 75
Marielitos, I 299
Marilyn Diptych, IV 81
Marin, Richard "Cheech". See Cheech and Chong
Marino, Dan, II 26, III 402, IV 118
Marion, Frances, IV 396
Maris, Roger, I 169, 183, III 263, 326, 521, IV
    458, V 208
Mark Goodson-Bill Todman Productions, IV 664
Mark of Zorro, V 235
Markert, Russell, IV 242
Markoe, Merrill, III 144
Marks, Johnny, IV 287
Marks, Sadie, I 223
Marland, Douglas, II 219, 324
Marlette, Doug, III 66
Marley, Bob, IV 196
Marlowe, Philip, I 264, 474, 693
Marple, Miss, I 693
Marriage, V 10
Married . . . with Children, IV 278, 422
Mars, Mick, III 419
Marsalis, Wynton, II 530
Marshall, E. G., I 463
Marshall Field, I 688
Marshall, Garry, II 357, III 110, 169
Marshall, George, II 458
Marshall, Penny, II 354, III 103, 110
Marshall, Peter, II 434
Marshall, Thurgood, I 93, 553
Marshall, William, I 279
Marston, William Moulton, V 171
Martha and the Vandellas, III 279
Martha's Vineyard, II 528
Martial arts, III 117
Martin, Benny, II 122
Martin, Billy, II 138, 520, III 521, IV 523
Martin, Casey, I 722
Martin, Clyde, III 41
Martin, Dean, I 344, III 152
Martin, Dewey, I 381
Martin, Dick, III 98
Martin, George, I 203
Martin, Joe, I 44
Martin, John, II 73
Martin, Judith, II 45
Martin, Mary, III 459, IV 96, 462, 465
Martin, Pamela Sue, III 474
Martin, Quinn, II 180

Martin, Steve, IV 196, 197
Martinez, Dennis, III 272
Martinez, Yolanda, I 28
Martini, I 544
Martling, Jackie, IV 531
Marty, I 484
Martyn, Thomas J. C., III 527
Marvel, I 564
Marvel Comics, I 429, 561, 565, 659, 672, II 486, III
    42, 124, IV 399, 470, 474, V 75, 205
Marvelettes, III 279
Marvin, Lee, I 721, III 253, V 121, 191
Marx Brothers, I 773, II 297
Marx, Chico, III 287
Marx, Groucho, I 216, III 287, 504
Marx, Gummo, III 287
Marx, Harpo, III 287
Marx, Karl, I 549, 569, IV 188
Marx, Minna Palmer Schoenberg, III 287
Marx, Zeppo, III 287
Marxism. See Communism
Marxist revolutionary, I 168
Mary Hartman, Mary Hartman, III 111
Mary Tyler Moore Show, I 50, 126, II 86, 371, IV
    421, V 127
Mary Worth, II 257
Masculinity, II 40
Masekela, Hugh, I 215
Mask, IV 2
Maslow, Abraham, IV 92
Mason, Bobbie Ann, I 134
Mason, Charlotte Osgood, II 366
Mason, Marsha, IV 402
Mason-Dixon Line, II 163
Mass media, V 80
Mass Murderers. See Serial Killers
Mass production, II 491
Mass transit, II 220
Masseria, Giuseppe "The Boss," III 237
Master Charge, I 628
Master Comics, II 445
MasterCard, I 628
Mastering the Art of French Cooking, I 497
Masters Tournament, III 531
Masters, William, III 303, IV 373
Masucci, Jerry, IV 304
Masuda, Toshio, IV 683
Matchmaker, V 138
Mate swapping, IV 374
Matewan, III 74
Mather, Stephen T., III 490
Mathers, Jerry, III 115
Matheson, Richard, III 532, IV 714
Mathewson, Christy, V 182
Mathis, June, IV 396
Mathison, Melissa, II 44
Matlin, Marlee, I 722
Mattachine Society, IV 545
Mattachine Review, II 211
Mattachine Society, II 213
Mattel, Inc., I 68, 171, 765, II 106, IV 686
Matthau, Walter, I 156, II 384, III 550
Mattis, John, I 15
Matus, Don Juan, I 453
Maude, I 119, II 86, 267, III 111, IV 420
Maugham, W. Somerset, II 265
Mauldin, Bill, V 190
Mauldin, Joe B., II 430
Maus, I 562
Maverick, V 120
Max, Peter, IV 129
Maxson Food Systems, Inc., II 179
Maxwell, Elsa, IV 1
Maxwell House, I 547
May, Elaine, IV 348
May, Robert L., IV 287
Mayall, John, I 355, 525, II 391
Mayan, V 15
Mayberry, I 86
Mayer, Louis B., I 13, II 203, III 82, 225,
    347, IV 565
Mayes, Herbert, III 313

Mayfair, I 149
Mayfield, Curtis, I 594, II 184, 485
Mayfield, Percy, IV 207
Mays, Willie, III 1, 263
Mazes and Monsters, I 775
McAuliffe, Christa, I 472, III 476
McBain, Ed, I 268, 694
McCabe and Mrs. Miller, V 119
McCaffrey and McCall advertising agency, IV 328
McCaffrey, Anne, I 129
McCall, David, IV 328
McCall, James, III 313
McCall's, I 28, IV 189, 550
McCallum, David, III 253
McCambridge, Mercedes, I 463
McCarran Act, I 570
McCarran Internal Security Act, III 315
McCarroll, Marion Clyde, I 27
McCarthy, Andrew, I 344
McCarthy, Charlie, I 225, 422
McCarthy era, II 400
McCarthy, Jenny, III 437
McCarthy, Joseph, I 272, 550, II 81, 97, 549, III 314,
    452, 580, V 98
McCarthy, Senator Joseph, I 570
McCarthyism, II 9, 413, III 254, 363, IV 279
McCartney, Bill, IV 123, 201
McCartney, Kathleen, II 503
McCartney, Paul, I 203, 746, II 430, III 30, 121
McCarty, Jim, V 212
McCaughey septuplets, I 720
McCay, Winsor, II 226
McClanahan, Rue, II 260
McClintic, Guthrie, IV 30, 532
McClure, Samuel S., III 300, 318, 438
McClure's, III 301, 438, 443, IV 316, 521
McCoo, Marilyn, III 169
McCord, James, V 86
McCormick, Robert, V 192
McCorvey, Norma, I 11
McCoy, Horace, II 359
McCoy, Tim, V 120
McCrae, John, V 186
McCrea, Joel, V 120
McCready, Mike, IV 26
McCulley, Johnston, V 234
McCullough, John, II 73
McDaniel, Hattie, I 13, 241, II 264
McDermot, Galt, III 338
McDonald, Maurice, II 72
McDonald, Richard, II 72
McDonald, Ronald, III 321
McDonald's, I 387, 717, II 72, 166, 347, III
    259, IV 560
McDonnell, Mary, II 487
McDonough, Mary, V 74
McDormand, Frances, II 69
McDowall, Roddy, II 68
McDowell, Fred, I 56
McDowell, Malcolm, II 68
McEntire, Reba, I 620, 623
McEwen, Tom "Mongoose," I 765
McFarland, George "Spanky," III 578
McFarlane, Bud, II 499
McFarlane, Leslie, II 360
McFarlane, Todd, IV 470
McGoohan, Patrick, IV 116
McGovern, George, IV 401
McGrath, Bob, IV 363
McGrath, Frank, V 59
McGraw, John, V 182
McGuinn, Roger, I 402
McGuire, Barry, II 329
McGuire, Patti, I 585
McGuire Sisters, II 251
McGwire, Mark, I 183, IV 458, 486, V 209
McHale's Navy, II 424, V 192
McIlwraith, Dorothy, V 104
McIntire, John, V 59
McKay, Claude, IV 710
McKay, Jim, V 133
McKay, John, IV 275

McKay, Louis, II 428
McKenzie, Scott, III 251
McKernan, Ron "Pigpen," II 292
McKimson, Robert, I 384
McKinley, Ray, III 366
McLain, Denny, I 695
McLamore, James, I 387, II 73
McLaren, Malcolm, IV 142
McLean, Alistair, V 191
McLendon, Gordon, IV 680
McLeod, Gavin, III 292, 294
McLish, Rachel, I 307
McMahon, Ed, I 526, IV 677
McMahon, Vince, IV 60
McMahon, Vince, Jr., II 423, V 192
McManus, Louis, II 27
McNamara, Francis X., I 628
McNear, Howard, II 326
McNeill, Anna Matilda, V 125
McPartland, Jimmy, I 494, 734
McPhatter, Clyde, I 164, 769, IV 208
McPherson, Aimee Semple, I 646, IV 588
McQueen, Butterfly, I 241, II 264
McQueen, Steve, I 280, III 240
McShann, Jay, III 3
McTeague, II 298, III 541
McTiernan, John, V 147
McVeigh, Timothy, III 56
McVie, Christine, II 114
McVie, John, I 355, II 114
Meadows, Audrey, I 300
Mean Streets, IV 337
Mears, Rick, II 149, 490, V 9
Medicare, III 269
Medicine shows, II 488
Medved, Michael, IV 278
Meese Commission on Pornography, IV 71
Meese, Edwin, IV 34, 71, 94
Meet John Doe, II 297, III 503
Meet Me in St. Louis, II 203, III 201
Meet the Press, I 353
Meeting of Minds, I 53
Meisner, Randy, III 500
Melcher, Martin, I 665
Melcher, Terry, III 262
Méliès, Georges, IV 395
Melinda, I 279
Mellencamp, John, II 69, 329
Mellinger, Frederick N., I 159
Men and Religion Forward Movement, III 457
*Men Are From Mars, Women Are From
    Venus*, II 437
Men Dancers, IV 381
Menace, IV 86
Mencken, H. L., I 72, 263, 544, III 46, 119, IV 598
Menendez, Ramon, IV 502
Menjou, Adolphe, I 476
Menotti, Gian Carlo, II 345
Men's Center (Berkeley, California), III 344
Men's Rights, Inc., III 345
Menudo, IV 304, 620
Menzies, William Cameron, II 264
Mercedes-Benz, I 406
Mercer, Johnny, III 259, V 131
Merchant, Natalie, IV 638
Mercury Records, I 315
Mercury Theatre, V 79, 109
Mercury Theatre of the Air, IV 161
Mere Christianity, III 151
Meredith, Don, I 654
Meredith, Edwin T., I 238
Meridith, Don, I 609
Merlin, I 120
Merman, Ethel, I 97, 240, III 459, IV 96
Merrill, Charles E., II 60
Merrivale, Sir Henry, I 442
Merv Griffin Show, III 367, IV 127
Mesa Verde National Park, III 491
Mesmer, Franz Antoine, IV 129
Messick, Dale, I 348
Messmer, Otto, II 83
Metalious, Grace, IV 47

Metallica, II 381, III 117
Method Acting, II 420, IV 165, V 146
Method IV 554
Methot, Mayo, I 308
Metrecal, I 706
Metro-Goldwyn-Mayer (MGM), I 145, 191, 756, II
    449, III 82, 183, 339, IV 376, 532, 565, 640,
    711, V 162
Metropolitan Opera, I 446, III 166
Metzger, Tom, III 66
Mexican Americans, IV 623
Meyer, Carl, IV 398
Meyer, Eugene, V 83
Meyer, Katharine, V 83
Meyer, Mary Pinchot, IV 368
Meyer, Russ, II 321
Meyers, Mike, IV 321
MGM, I 87, 178, 625, 632, 721, II 199, 432, 458, III
    11, 225, 309, 579, IV 613, 616, V 8
Miami Bass, IV 715
Miami City Ballet, V 52
Miami Dolphins, III 402, IV 391
Miami Vice, III 558
Micah Clarke, I 755
Michael, George, II 155
Michaels, Al, III 537, V 133
Michaels, Lorne, III 451, IV 320
Micheaux, Oscar, I 279, IV 227, 396
Michener, James, IV 465
Michigan State University, II 553
Michtom, Morris, IV 617
Mickey Mouse, I 90, 729, II 66, 84, IV 521, 686
Mickey Mouse Club, II 184, III 425, IV 686
Mickey One, IV 676
Microbreweries, I 213
Microsoft, I 406, II 497
Microwave, II 20
Middlebrow culture, I 318
Middleton, Charles, II 113
Midler, Bette, I 188, 231, 348, 730, II 216, III
    259, IV 371
Midnight Cowboy, II 421, 435, V 118
Midnighters, The, I 164
Midwives, I 260
Mies Van der Rohe, Ludwig, II 492, III 369, IV 433
Mighty Morphin Power Rangers, IV 318
Mighty Mouse, IV 317
Mikan, George, I 186, III 196, 478
Mike Douglas Show, I 754
Milam, Lorenzo, I 571
Milam, Marin Scott, IV 72
Miles, Buddy, II 392
Miles, Vera, III 253
Miley, Bubber, I 249
Milhone, Kinsey, II 282
Military Honor and Decency Act, IV 34
Militias, I 761, II 549, III 55
Milius, John, II 528
Milk, Harvey, I 454
Mill, Andy, II 49
Millay, Edna St. Vincent, I 357, IV 710
Miller, I 210
Miller, Arthur, I 551, III 400
Miller, Dennis, IV 321
Miller, Frank, I 190, 562, 659
Miller, Frederick E., III 364
Miller, Glenn, I 248, III 214, 256
Miller, Henry, II 565, IV 373
Miller, Lewis, I 481
Miller, Mitch, I 533, III 306
Miller, Roger, III 459
Miller, Ron, I 730
Miller, Scott, V 59
Miller v. California, IV 94
Million Man March, III 345
Mills and Boon, IV 272
Mills, C. Wright, III 512
Mills, Donna, III 50
Mills, Mike, IV 201
Mills, Robert, V 83
Milne, Alan Alexander, V 155
Milstead, Harris Glenn. See Divine

Milton Berle Show, IV 419
Milton Bradley, I 298, IV 715
Milwaukee Brewers, V 1
Milwaukee Bucks, I 8
Milwaukee, Wisconsin, I 210, II 369
Mineo, Sal, III 60, IV 186
Miner, Worthington, IV 563
Minevitch, Borrah, II 371
Mingus, Charles, III 380
Miniskirt, II 390
Minnelli, Liza, II 204
Minnelli, Vincente, II 203, III 339
Minnesota Vikings, I 525
Minnow, Newton, IV 135
Minsky, Abe, I 389
Minsky, Morton, I 388
Minstrelsy, V 33
Minton's, II 530
Minute Man, II 101
Minutemen, V 129
Miracles, III 420, IV 233
Miramax, IV 341
Misery Train, II 20
Misfits, II 188
Miss America Pageant, I 133, 208, 585
Miss America Pageant. See also Beauty Queens
Miss Saigon, III 460
Miss U.S.A. Pageant, IV 109
Missett, Judi Sheppard, I 30
Missing in Action, V 51
Mississippi Burning, III 65
Mississippi delta blues, I 292
Mister Ed, II 152
Mister Roberts, V 192
Mister Rogers, I 430
"Misty," III 306
Mitch, Richard, I 29
Mitchell, Bill, I 603
Mitchell, John, V 86
Mitchell, John Ames, III 160
Mitchell, Joni, III 30, IV 615
Mitchell, Margaret, II 263
Mitchell, Mitch, II 391
Mitchell, Thomas, IV 497
Mitchum, Robert, II 426, 465, III 429
Mitty, Walter, IV 654
Mitzi the dolphin, II 118
Mix, Tom, III 428, IV 397, V 120
Mize, Billy, II 334
Mizer, Bob, I 132, IV 59
Mizer, Bob. See Athletic Model Guild
Mobil Corporation, III 302
Mobil Masterpiece Theatre. See *Masterpiece Theatre*
Mobile home, IV 689
Mod Squad, IV 645
Model T, I 139, II 132, 135
Modern dance, II 285, IV 495
Modern Electrics, II 225
Modern Lovers, V 39
Modern Maturity, I 3
Modern Records, IV 207
Modern Times, I 475
Modernaires, III 365
Modernism, IV 99, 331
Modesto Manifesto, II 284
Mods, V 131
Mogambo, II 201
Mojave Desert, III 92
Molinaro, Al, III 550
Molinsky, Joan, IV 220
Moltke, Alexandra, I 659
Molyneux, Tom, I 331
Monadnock Building, IV 433
Monaghan, Tom, I 696, II 73
Monday Night Blast, III 394
Monday Night Football, I 609
Monday Night Football, III 483, V 141
Monk, Thelonius, I 558
Monkees IV 84, 619, 622
Monkey Wrench Gang, I 4, II 11
Monogram, I 149
Monopoly, I 133, 297, IV 13

Monroe, Bill, I 287, II 122
Monroe Brothers, I 288, III 397
Monroe, Marilyn, I 168, 328, 346, 715, II 223, III
    259, 363, 400, 430, IV 59, 71, 364, 368, 370,
    453, 570, 643, V 81
Monsieur Verdoux, I 476
Monster, IV 528
Montalban, Ricardo, II 68
Montana, Bob, I 108
Montana, Joe, IV 118, 515
Monterey Pop Festival, II 283, 392, 411, III 251
Montessori, Maria, IV 685
Montgomery, Bob, II 430
Montgomery Bus Boycott, III 34
Montgomery, Elizabeth, I 243, III 234
Montgomery Improvement Association (MIA), IV 16
Montgomery Ward, I 455, IV 287, 446
Monty, Gloria, II 219
Monty Python and the Holy Grail, I 120
Monty Python's Flying Circus, IV 356
Monument Records, III 572
Monument Valley, II 134
Moody Blues, The, I 576
Moog synthesizer, II 22
Moon, I 102
Moon, Reverend Sun Myung, I 647
Moon River, V 139
Moon River Theatre, V 139
"Moon River," III 256
Moonies, I 647
Moonstruck, IV 457
Moore, C. L., V 103
Moore, Clayton, III 190
Moore, Clement Clark, I 504
Moore, Demi, I 344, III 159
Moore, Don, II 113
Moore, Mary Tyler, I 57, 127, III 292, IV
    190, 197, V 25
Moore, Roger, II 523
Moore, Rudy Ray, I 279
Moore, Sam. See Sam and Dave
Moore, Tim, I 74
Moore, Victor, IV 96
Moorehead, Agnes, I 244, 463
Moorer, Michael, II 139
Moral Majority, I 11, II 183, 209, 384, IV
    71, 125, 314
Moran, Earl, IV 59
Moran, Erin, II 357
Moran, Julie, V 133
Moran the Lady Letty, III 541
Moranis, Rick, IV 348
More Than Human, IV 332
Morenz, Howie, II 467
Morgan, Frank, V 164
Morgan, J.P., I 131
Morison, Patricia, IV 96
Morita, Akio, V 66
Morita, Pat, V 106
Mork and Mindy, I 298, II 357, V 143, 158
Morley, Christopher, I 318
Mormons, I 646
Moroder, Giorgio, III 347
Morrall, Earl, IV 118
Morricone, Ennio, II 266, IV 467
Morris, Garrett, IV 321
Morris, Henry M., I 627
Morris, Mark, I 166
Morris, Phillip, I 391
Morrison, Bret, I 463
Morrison, Ernie "Sunshine Sammy," III 577
Morrison, Jim, I 748, II 392
Morrison, Sterling, V 39
Morrison, Toni, III 441
Morrison, Van, I 355
Morrissey, Paul, V 82
Morrow, Vic, IV 715
Morse, Barry, II 180
Morse, Carlton E., II 476
Morse, Samuel F. B., II 495
Mortenson, Norma Jeane, III 399
Morton, Andrew, III 150

Morton, Benny, I 185
Morton, Jelly Roll, I 247, III 459, 513
Morvan, Fabrice, III 368
Moscone, Dave, I 454
Mosel, Tad, IV 50
Moses, IV 634
Moses, Robert, III 166
Mosley, Walter, I 694
Moss, Jerry, I 57
Moss, Julie, II 503
Moss, Kate, I 303, 624
Moss, Paul, I 389
Most, Donny, II 357
Most, Mickie, I 746
Mostel, Zero, II 91, III 459
Motels, IV 285
Moten, Bennie, I 184, III 3
Mother Jones, III 408
Mother Love Bone, II 321
Mother's Day, I 689, V 125
Mothers of Invention, V 226
Motherwell, Robert, I 11
Motion Picture, IV 507
Motion Picture Classic, II 65
Motion Picture Democratic Committee, I 753
*Motion Picture Story*Magazine, II 64
Motion pictures, I 65, III 52
Mötley Crüe, I 86, III 43
Motley, Marion, IV 118
Motown, II 272, 513, III 279, IV 233, V 111, 169
Motown Records, I 56, II 518, IV 459, 632
Mott the Hoople, II 248
Mott, Lucretia, II 84
Moulton, Charles, V 171
Mouly, Francoise, III 308
Mount Carmel, III 54
Move On Up A Little Higher, II 274, 515
Movie Brats, IV 337
Movie Weekly, II 65
Moye, Michael, III 278
Mozert, Zoe, IV 59
Mr. America, I 306, III 454, IV 194
Mr. Butts,, I 747
Mr. Deeds Goes to Town, I 428, 598, II 297
Mr. Dooley, I 177
"Mr. Natural," V 225
Mr. Smith Goes to Washington, I 428, II 297, IV 533
Mr. T, IV 423, IV 60
Mr. Twee Deedle, IV 163
Mr. Universe, I 308, IV 194
Ms., II 86
*Ms. Magazine's*Woman of the Year, III 99
Ms. Olympia, I 307, III 328
MSG Network, I 41
MSNBC, III 354
MTV (Music Television), I 67, 209, 221, 405, 443,
    508, II 222, III 43, 309, 349, 419, 467, 505, 516,
    IV 85, 181, 288, 306, 638, V 48 IV
Muckrakers, IV 521, 606
Muckraking, I 159, III 301, 318
Mudd, Roger, I 360
Mudhoney, II 321, III 117
Muehleisen, Maury, I 635
Muggs, J. Fred, IV 666
Muhammad, Elijah, I 46, III 244
Muir, Jean, II 393
Muir, John, I 134, 418, II 405, III 490
Muldowney, Shirley, I 765
Mulford, Clarence E., II 444
Mulholland, William, I 516
Mullin, Christopher, I 767
Mullin, John T., V 47
Multiculturalism, I 253
Multidisciplinary Association for Psychedelic
    Studies, III 209
Mummy, III 5
Mundy, Talbot, II 512
Munn & Company, IV 335
Munn, Orson Desaix, IV 334
Munsey, Frank A., I 109, III 300, 442, IV 139
Munsey's Magazine, I 109, III 301, 392
Munson, Thurman, V 208

Muppets, II 393, III 444, IV 136, 686, V 121
Murad, Jerry, II 371
Murder in Peyton Place, IV 48
Murder One, II 407
Murders in the Rue Morgue, III 214
Murdoch, Rupert, I 405, IV 226, 285, 597
Murnau, F.W., V 23
Murphy, Audie, V 120
Murphy Brown, I 225, IV 148, 278, 422
Murphy, Cullen, I 135
Murphy, Eddie, IV 126, 320
Murphy, Isaac, III 20
Murray, Bill, IV 320, 348
Murray, Will, I 738, IV 227
Murrow, Edward R., I 352, 636, IV 159, 630,
    699, V 190
Muscle & Fitness magazine, III 454
Muscle Beach, IV 541
Muscle Shoals studio, IV 459
Muscular Christianity, IV 178
Museum of Modern Art, I 72, II 551, V 82
Museum of Modern Art, The, I 17
Music Corporation of America (MCA), I 34
Music Man, III 459
Music, Roxy, I 86
Musician's Union, II 371
Mussolini, Benito, III 2
Mussorgsky, Modest, II 67
Mustang, II 137
Mutual Broadcasting System, III 504
Mutual film company, I 476
My Antonia, I 459
My Darling Clementine, V 119
My Fair Lady, I 643, III 459
My Family, III 495
My Father's House, III 145
My Favorite Husband, III 504
My Favorite Martian, IV 419
My Favorite Things, I 558
My Friend Irma, III 152, 504
My Song, I 15
My Three Sons, III 229
Mydland, Brent, II 293
Myers, Mike, IV 348, V 94
Myerson, Abraham, IV 90
Mystery Writers of America, IV 148

'N Sync, IV 617
NAACP, II 89, 366, III 34
NAACP (National Association for the Advancement
    of Colored People), I 241
Nabbie, Jim, II 493
Nabokov, Vladimir Vladimirovich, III 183
Nader, Ralph, I 141, 588, 590, II 220, 294
Nader's Raiders, III 469
Naess, Arne, II 10
Nagasaki, I 312
Nagurski, Bronko, I 492, IV 117
Naismith, James A., I 186, III 477
Naked and the Dead, V 191
Naked Spur, V 119
Namath, Joe, I 556, III 483, IV 118, 485, 580, V 7
Names Quilt, I 37
Nancy Drew, II 578, IV 548
Nanovic, John, I 738
Napier, John, I 252, 460
NASA (National Aeronautics and Space
    Administration, I 104, IV 530
Nash, Ogden, V 216
Nashville, I 63, 132, 530, 619, II 287, 334,
    391, III 572
Nast, Condé, V 29, 53
Nathan, George Jean, I 263
Nathan, Syd, I 164
Nation, II 55, IV 697
Nation Institute, III 476
Nation of Islam, I 46, 520, III 244, 368
Nation, III 514
National Academy of Design, I 122
National Aeronautics and Space Administration
    (NASA), IV 494
National Air and Space Museum, IV 441

National Association for the Advancement of Colored
    People (NAACP), I 73, 93, 258, 553, 633, 772, II
    555, III 73, 218, 266, 320, IV 15, 124
National Association of Colored Women, II 85
National Association of Stock Car Auto Racing
    (NASCAR), IV 46, 537
National Baseball Museum and Hall of Fame, I 598
National Basketball Association (NBA), I 8, 186,
    256, 493, 767, II 36, 364, 553, 570 III 568
National Basketball League (NBL), III 477
National Board of Censorship, IV 394
National Broadcasting Company (NBC), III 503,
    IV 48, 312
National Cancer Act, I 419
National Cartoonist Society, II 257
National Championship Stock Car Circuit
    (NCSCC), IV 537
National Cheerleader Association, I 487
National Collegiate Athletic Association, I 8,
    555, IV 606
National Comedy Hall of Fame, IV 28
National Committee for a Sane Nuclear Policy
    (SANE), IV 125
National Congress of Mothers, IV 131
National Cowboy Hall of Fame, II 328
National Educational Television (NET), IV 135
National Endowment for the Arts (NEA), I 574,
    IV 94, 493
National Enquirer, I 582
National Farm Workers Association, I 483
National Federation of Community Broadcasters
    (NFCB), I 571
National Football Conference, II 342, IV 580
National Football League (NFL), I 369, 492, 722, II
    300, III 185, 232, 472, IV 23, 117, 579
National Geographic Society, III 490
National Guard, III 359
National Highway Traffic Administration, IV 483
National Hispanic Foundation for the Arts, IV 441
National Historic Register of Places, V 199
National Hockey Association, II 417
National Hockey League (NHL), II 417, III 574
National Hockey League Hall of Fame, II 460
National Hot Rod Association (NHRA), I 764
National Jazz Ensemble, II 530
National Lampoon Magazine, I 217
National Lampoon Radio Hour, I 217, III 450
National Lampoon's Animal House, I 217
National League Pennant, I 647
National Mah-Jongg League, III 242
National Mobilization against the Vietnam War, I 495
National Motorsports Press Association's Hall of
    Fame, IV 46
National Museum of African Art, IV 441
National Museum of American Art, IV 441
National Museum of American History, IV 441
National Museum of the American Indian, IV 441
National Museum of Natural History, IV 441
National Observer, V 68
National Organization for Men, III 344
National Organization for the Reform of Marijuana
    Laws (NORML), III 273
National Organization for Women (NOW), II 86,
    416, III 344, IV 125
National Park Service, III 383, 491
National Physique Committee, I 307
National Portrait Gallery, IV 441
National Public Radio (NPR), I 37, 169, IV 601
National Reno Gay Rodeo, IV 254
National Retired Teachers Association, III 388
National Review, I 379
National Rifle Association, II 102, 400
National Roller Derby League, IV 267
National Science Foundation, II 496
National Theater of the Deaf, I 722
National Traffic and Motor Vehicle Safety Act, I
    141, III 469
National Urban League, II 366, III 570
National Velvet, IV 613
National Wheelchair Marathon Championships, I 323
National Women's Political Caucus, IV 525
National Women's Suffrage Association, II 85

National Zoo, IV 441
Native American literature, III 392
Native Americans, I 111, II 303
Native Dancer, III 20
Nativism, IV 86
Natural Born Killers, II 5, IV 543
Natwick, Grim, I 240
Naugahyde, IV 66
Naughty Marietta, III 225
Nava, Gregory, III 464
Naval Institute Press, I 524
Navarro, Ramon, I 220
Navasky, Victor, III 477
Navin Field, I 695
Navratilova, Martina, II 49, V 150
Naylor, Hazel Simpson, II 64
Nazi, I 95, II 436
NBA, IV 225, 259
NBC (National Broadcasting Company), I 40, 99,
    216, 228, 352, 404, II 33, 76, 406, 429, 436, 447,
    459, 469, III 8, 68, 133, 168, 251, 253, 354, 503,
    IV 108, 251, 310, 508, 639, 643, V 123
NBC Mystery Movie, I 559, III 234
NBA Playoffs, II 571
NCAA, II 36, 553, V 174
Neal, Patricia, I 597
Nebraska, IV 492
Nebula award, III 313
Needful Things, III 38
Neeley, Ted, II 544
Negro Digest, I 32, II 7
Negro Leagues, I 182, III 371, IV 5, 232
Negro National League, III 497
Negro Renaissance, II 365
''Negro vogue,'' II 367
Neighborhood Playhouse, IV 30
Neighbors, I 218
Neil, Vince, III 419
Nellis Air Force Base, III 93
Nelson, ''Baby Face,'' I 714
Nelson, Byron, II 422
Nelson, Gaylord, II 1
Nelson, Judd, I 344, 347
Nelson, Ricky, I 22, 23, III 280, IV 619
Nelson Riddle Orchestra, IV 644
Nelson, Willie, I 450, 620, II 69, 335, 540, V 141
Nemiroff, Robert, II 356
Nero, Franco, I 414
Nesmith, Mike, III 394
Nestor Film Company, II 432
Netscape Corporation, II 496
Network, I 484
Networks, I 404
Neuharth, Allen H., V 11
Neuromancer, II 235
Nevada Test Site, III 93
Nevermind, III 538
Nevers, Ernie, IV 117
Neville, Aaron, III 513
Nevins, Al, I 351
New Age, I 779, IV 350, V 210
New Age movement, I 152, 453, II 489
New age music, V 156
New American, II 550
New American Library, IV 11
New Christy Minstrels, IV 261
New Deal, II 30, III 266, 295
New Edition, III 510, IV 261
New England Patriots, IV 23
New Hollywood Cinema, I 63
New Journalism, I 427, V 166
New Kids on the Block, IV 617
New Leave It to Beaver, III 115
New Left, I 192, 585, V 214
New Look, II 390, III 400
New Masses, II 255, III 302
New Negro, III 182
New Negro Movement, II 365
New Orleans, II 189
New Orleans Rhythm Kings, I 734
New Orleans Saints, I 722
New Orleans sound, I 743

New religious right, II 183
New Republic, III 171
New Romantic movements, I 86
New World Pictures, I 150
New York City. See Big Apple
New York City Ballet, I 180
New York Daily Graphic, I 582
New York Dolls, I 416, II 248, IV 142, V 39
New York Giants, I 777, III 87, 263, 311, IV
   117, 118, 647
New York *Graphic, III 157*
New York Jets, III 471, IV 118, 580, V 7
New York Journal, I 27, II 379, III 7
New York Knicks, I 338, II 158
New York Mets, II 269, IV 297, 526
New York Philharmonic, I 325, III 166
New York Rangers, II 417
New York School of Art, I 122, IV 80
New York Shakespeare Festival, IV 339
New York Times, I 641, II 412, IV 36, 599, V 68
New York Titans, III 471
New York World, III 7, 171
New York World's Fair (1939), III 505
New York Yankees, I 233, 362, 715, 722, 777, II
   138, 217, 269, III 262, 274, IV 220, 523,
   526, V 182
New Yorker, I 88, 578, II 55, 521, IV 654, 697
New Yorkers, IV 96
Newark Airport, V 180
Newby-Fraser, Paula, II 503
Newcombe, Don, IV 648
Newell, Patrick, I 145
Newhall, Beaumont, I 17
Newhart, III 524
Newhart, Bob, I 458
Newkirk, Emma, I 306
Newman, Laraine, IV 321
Newman, Paul, I 342, 398, 599, III 60, IV 190
Newman, Sydney, I 144
Newport Folk Festival, I 157, 746, 781, II 328
Newport Jazz Festival, II 516, 530
News Corp., I 405
Newseum, V 13
Newsreels, V 189
Newsweek, IV 36
Newton, Huey, I 264
Next Plateau, IV 306
NFL, I 285
Niagara Falls, I 310, III 490
Niagara Movement, I 772
Niblo's Garden, I 388
Nichols, J. C., IV 568
Nichols, Mike, I 458, II 280, IV 348, 614
Nichols, Nichelle, IV 508
Nichols, Roger, I 441
Nichols, Wade, IV 189
Nicholson, Eliza, I 27
Nicholson, Jack, I 71, 217, 500, II 4, 448, III 566
Nicholson, James, I 71
Nick Carter Weekly, IV 139
Nickel weeklies, IV 139
Nickelodeon, I 245, III 426
Nickelodeons, IV 394
Nicklaus, Jack, II 262, III 305
Nicks, Stevie, II 114
Nico, I 371, V 40
Nielsen, Leslie, I 39
Niggaz with Attitude, IV 175
Nigger Heaven, V 26
Night Before Christmas, I 504
Night Gallery, IV 362
Night of Dark Shadows, I 659
Night of the Living Dead, I 645
"Night on a Bald Mountain," II 67
Night to Remember, A, IV 662
Nighthawks, II 448
Nightline, I 111
Nijinsky, Vaslav, I 166
Nike, I 20, II 571, IV 638
Nikisch, Arthur, I 326
Nimoy, Leonard, IV 508
Nin, Anaïs, I 61

Nine Inch Nails, I 597
9 to 5, IV 18
1984, I 107
1941, I 218
Nintendo, V 45
Nirvana, I 62, 266, 303, II 222, 321, III 117, 204, IV
   26, V 209, 218, 229
Nitty Gritty Dirt Band, I 371, 446
Nitzsche, Jack, IV 471
Nixon, Agnes, I 99, II 324, IV 446
Nixon, Richard, I 16, 162, 314, 407, 647, 753, 771, II
   20, 31, 77, 82, 97, 413, 420, 499, III 18, 186,
   225, 316, 518, IV 1, 45, 94, 108, 137, 279, 628,
   V 49, 85, 95
No Code, IV 27
"No Fun," IV 82
No, No, Nanette, III 459
No Place to Hide, I 312
Nobel Prize, I 17, II 17, 78, III 34, 153, 155
Noble, Edward, III 504
Noble, William, III 60
Nobody Knows My Name, I 162
Nolan, Bob, IV 262
Noll, Chuck, IV 61, 118
"Nonfiction novel," III 146
Norden, Tommy, II 118
Nordhoff, Charles, III 461
Norma Rae, III 74
Norman, Greg, II 262
Norman, Larry, I 591
Norman, Marsha, III 460
Norman, Peter, III 538
Normand, Mabel, I 107, 476, IV 357
Norris, Chuck, I 551
Norris, Frank, II 298, III 188
Norris, Fred, IV 531
Norris, Kathleen, IV 271
North American Soccer League (NASL), IV 449
North Bennington, Vermont, II 521
North by Northwest, II 415
North, Edward, IV 20
North, Oliver, II 499
Northern Exposure, I 71
Norton, Judy, V 74
Nosferatu: A Symphony of Horror, V 23
Nosotros, III 401
Notorious, II 415
Notre Dame University, I 556
Novak, Kim, II 415, IV 370
Novoselic, Chris, III 539
Nowlan, Philip Francis, I 64, 377
N'Sync, III 511
Nuclear winter, IV 300
Nude Descending a Staircase, I 113
Nugent, Elliott, IV 655
Numan, Gary, III 516
Nuova Cancion (New Song) movement, I 275
Nureyev, Rudolf, II 130
Nutcracker Suite," "The, II 67
Nutrilite, I 80
Nutty Professor, III 152
N.Y.P.D. Blue, I 302
Nyby, Christian, IV 642
Nye, Joseph, I 116
Nye, Louis, I 53
Nylon, IV 66, 80
NYPD Blue, II 407, IV 442, 518
Nyswander, Dr. Marie, V 21

O' Neill, Tip, I 3
O Pioneers!, I 459
O'Neal, Ryan, II 80
Oak Ridge, Tennessee, I 311
Oakland A's, V 184
Oakland Raiders, III 232
Oakley, Annie, I 545, V 120
Oates, John, II 345
Oates, Joyce Carol, I 134, IV 72
Oboler, Arch, IV 161
O'Brien, Margaret, III 340
O'Brien, Pat, I 411
O'Brien, Richard, IV 248

O'Brien, Willis H., II 253, III 31
Ocasek, Ric, I 442
Ocean's Eleven, III 280
Ochs, Adolph, III 518
Ochs, Phil, II 329
O'Connell, Helen, I 751
O'Connor, Frank, III 547
O'Connor, Reneé, V 203
Octopus, III 541
Odd Couple, IV 402
Odell, "Gorgeous" George, II 391
Odets, Clifford, I 570, II 435
O'Donnell, Rosie, I 668, 754, III 110
O'Donoghue, Mike, III 488
Oedipus complex, II 167
Of Mice and Men, IV 522
Office of Strategic Services, III 208
Office of War Information, V 190
Office of War Information (OWI), IV 669
Officer and a Gentleman, An, II 224
Officer Pupp, III 62
Official Preppy Handbook, IV 105
Oh, God!, IV 197
O'Hair, Madalyn Murray, I 745
O'Hara, John, I 237, IV 47, 256
O'Hara, Scarlett, I 633, II 263
O'Horgan, Tom, II 339
Oilers, Edmonton, II 417
O'Kanes, I 262
Okeh Records, I 184
OKeh records, IV 155
Oklahoma City bombing, III 360
Oklahoma!, III 459, IV 254, 256, V 120
Olajuwan, Hakeem, III 568
Olbermann, Keith, II 39
Old Boyfriends, I 218
Old Bunch, III 145
Old Man and the Sea, I 715, II 389
Old Yeller, IV 44
Oldenberg, Claes, IV 81
Oldsmobile, I 139
Oliver, Joe "King," I 115
Oliver, King, I 494, 734, II 529
Oliver, Sy, III 215
Olivier, Laurence, II 415, V 198
Olmos, Edward James, III 349, IV 501
Olmstead, John W., V 222
Olmsted, Frederick Law, I 467, 469, III 491
Olson, Johnny, IV 109
Olympia Press, III 183
Olympics, I 8, 20, 187, 323, 767, II 117, 293, 317,
   349, 576, III 21, 151, 536, 537, IV 388, 479,
   650, V 203
O'Malley, Walter, III 94
On a Roll, I 722
On the Beach, I 312
On Golden Pond, II 129
On the Road, II 4
On the Waterfront, I 342, III 74
On Wings of Eagles, IV 40
Once and Future King, I 414
ONE, IV 545
One Day at a Time, III 111, 252
One Down, Three to Go, I 280
One Flew Over the Cuckoo's Nest, III 22
ONE Institute Quarterly of Homophile Studies, II 211
One Life to Live, III 540
ONE Magazine, II 210
One Man's Family, III 415
O'Neal, Ron, I 279
O'Neal, Ryan, IV 48
O'Neal, Shaquille, III 197
O'Neal, Tatum, I 156
O'Neil, Buck, III 497
O'Neil, Dennis, I 190
O'Neill, Ed, III 278
O'Neill, Eugene, I 357, II 366
O'Neill, Rose, III 22
Onitsuka Tiger Company, III 535
Only Way, IV 712
Ono, Yoko, I 205, 754, II 42, III 132, 159, 205
Opera, I 446

Operation Desert Shield, IV 11
Operation Petticoat, V 192
Operation Rescue, I 10
Oppenheimer, J. Robert, I 311, III 452
Opper, Frederick, I 563
Oprah Winfrey Show, IV 35
Opryland, II 287
Opus, I 284
Order, V 130
Ordinary People, IV 190
Organization, I 279
Organized crime, I 332, II 277
Original Amateur Hour, I 668
Original Appalachian Artworks, I 403
Original Dixieland Jazz Band, I 214, 247, 494, 734, II 529
Original Gangster (O.G.), II 485
Orioles, IV 208
Orion Pictures, V 8
Orlan, IV 68
Orlando Magic, III 568
Orman, Roscoe, IV 363
Ornitz, Sam, I 272, II 434
O'Rourke, P. J., III 488
Orozco, Jose Clemente, V 180
Orr, Martha, III 294
Orson Welles, I 149
Ortega, Santos, I 463
Orteig, Raymond, I 38
O.S.S., V 192
Osbourne, Ozzy, I 266, II 321, 381
Oscar the Grouch, IV 363
Oscars See Academy Awards
Osmond, Donnie, IV 620
Osmond, Donny and Marie, I 670
Osmond, Humphrey, IV 128
Osmond, Ken, III 115
Osmond, Marie, IV 620
Ossessione, IV 98
Ossman, David, II 103
Ostertag, Greg, III 569
Ostman, Albert, I 252
O'Sullivan, Maureen, V 104
Oswald, Lee Harvey, II 546, III 16
Other Side of Midnight, IV 381
Other Voices, Other Rooms, I 427
Otis, Johnny, I 15
O'Toole, Peter, I 54, III 104
Ott, Mel, I 778
Our Bodies, Ourselves, I 261
Our Miss Brooks, III 504
Oursler, Fulton, III 158
Outcault, Richard, I 398, 563, V 212
Outlaw Josey Wales, V 121
Outlaw, II 464, IV 292, V 119
Ovaltine, III 177
"Over There," I 548
Overton, Aida, V 63
Ovitz, Michael, I 34
Owens, Bonnie, II 335
Owens, Buck, I 620, II 21, 334, 381, 382, III 219, V 216
Owens, Jesse, I 20, III 151, 538, 560
Owl and the Pussycat, III 213
Ox-Bow Incident, V 119
Oxford Group, IV 708
Oxydol, III 223
Oz, Frank, IV 364

Paar, Jack, I 460, IV 677, V 157
Pabst, I 210
Pace, Harry H., II 7, IV 155
Pacheco, Ferdie, I 47
Pachucos, V 234
Pacific 10, IV 275
Pacific Bell, I 710
Pacific Coast Hockey Association, II 417
Pacific Overtures, IV 455
Pacifica, I 571
Packard, Edward, I 502
Packard, Vance, IV 373
Paddington Bear, IV 617

Page, Betty, IV 59
Page, Geraldine, III 85
Page, Jimmy, I 355, III 116, V 212
Page, Walter, I 184, III 2
Paget, Debra, IV 635
Paglia, Camille, II 416, 471
Paige, Satchel, I 182, III 498, IV 231
Paint Your Wagon, V 120
Painted Dreams, IV 51, 446
Pajama Game, I 664, II 144
Pal Joey, III 459, IV 256
Pale Rider, IV 380, V 121
Paleface, V 121
Paley, William, II 327, III 504
Palillo, Ron, V 105
Palin, Michael, III 403
Palladium, III 97, IV 138
Palmer, A. Mitchell, IV 188
Palmer, Arnold, II 262, III 531
Palmer, Bruce, I 381
Palmer Raids, IV 188
Palmer, Ray, I 64
Palmieri, Eddie, IV 304
Pan, Hermes, I 128
Pandora's Box, I 365
Pantages theater, I 107
Panty raids, I 553
Paparazzi, I 699
Papp, Joseph, II 581
Paralympic Games, I 722
Paramount, I 149, 684, II 393 III 225, IV 155, 168, 340, 396, 509, 565, 634
Parental Music Resource Center, II 381, 577
Parent's Magazine, IV 686
Parents' Music Resource Center, III 419
Paretsky, Sara, I 694, II 359
Paris, IV 96
Park, Ida May, IV 396
Parker, Bonnie, I 316
Parker Brothers, I 297, III 396, 576
Parker, Charlie, I 19, II 237, 530, III 3, 97, IV 138
Parker, Colonel Tom, IV 107
Parker, Dorothy, I 219, II 112, III 283
Parker, Maceo, II 185
Parker, Peter, IV 474
Parker, Robert B., I 474
Parker, Trey, IV 466
Parker, William H., I 766
Parker-Bowles, Camilla, I 699
Parkinson, Dian, IV 109
Parks, Gordon, IV 376
Parks, Larry, I 272, II 435
Parks, Rosa, IV 124
Parliament, I 532
Parliament-Funkadelic, II 184, 198
Parrish, Leslie, I 155
Parrot Heads, I 382
Parsley, Sage, Rosemary and Thyme, IV 400
Parsons, Gram, I 59
Parsons, Louella, II 275, III 429, IV 54, 159
Parsons, Talcott, IV 99
Partisan Review, I 12
Partner Swapping. See Swinging
Parton, Dolly, I 620, IV 261
Partridge Family, I 75, 452
Passion, IV 456
Pasternak, Boris, I 740
Pastrone, Giovanni, I 280
Pat the Bunny, II 258
Pat Garrett and Billy the Kid, II 402, V 121
Patagonia, IV 81
Paterno, Joe, I 557
Paths of Glory, V 188
Patinkin, Mandy, III 460
Patrick, Dan, II 39
PATSY Award, II 119, III 96, 378
"Patterns," IV 362
Patterson, Floyd, I 44, 332, 333
Patterson, Joseph Medill, I 348
Patterson, Roger, I 252
Patton, IV 683, V 191
Patton, George S., II 102, IV 19, 339

Patty Duke Show, IV 382
Paul, Adrian, I 660
Paul, Alan, III 257
Paul, Frank R., II 225
Paul, Les, II 21
Paul Lynde Show, IV 535
Paul VI, Pope, IV 87
Pauley, Jane, IV 666
Paulsen, Pat, III 169
Paulucci, Jeno F., I 509
Pavitt, Bruce, II 322
Pavlova, Anna, I 166
Pawley, William Jr., IV 613
Payne Fund Studies, I 410
Payne, Virginia, III 223
Payola, I 42, 526, 726
Payton, Walter, I 492
Peace Corps, V 50
Peale, Norman Vincent, I 28, IV 90
Peanut Gallery, the, II 459
Peanuts, II 323
Pearl Harbor, II 526, IV 681, V 188
Pearl Jam, I 62, 303, II 321, III 117, V 218
Pearl, Minnie, II 287, 382
Pearlroth, Norbert, IV 216
Pearson, David, IV 47
Peary, Hal, II 90
Peary, Robert, III 484
Peck, M. Scott, III 508, IV 92
Peckinpah, Sam, IV 341, V 121, 133
Pee Wee's Playhouse, IV 318
Peeping Tom, IV 435
Peer, Ralph, I 1, 618
Peet's Coffee, I 547
"Peg O' My Heart," II 371
Pelé, IV 449
Pelican Brief, II 318
Pelley, William, V 129
Pendeltones, The, I 196
Pendergast, Tom, III 3, IV 77
Penguin, IV 10
Penis envy, II 167
Penn, Arthur, I 316, V 121
Penn, Irving, V 53
Pennies from Heaven, IV 44, 102
"Penny Lane," III 316
"Pentagon Papers," III 518, V 85
People Are Funny, III 168
People for the Ethical Treatment of Animals, III 89
People Magazine, IV 355
People of the Abyss, III 188
People United to Save Humanity, II 514
People Vs. Larry Flint, III 205
People's Classics, III 173
People's Court, II 16
People's Journal, IV 335
People's Princess, I 700
People's Songs Inc. (PSI), IV 351
People's Temple, II 563
Pep Comics, I 108
"Pep," IV 36
Percy, Walker, III 549
Pereira, Fernando, II 304
Perelman, S . J., II 578, III 287
Peress, Irving, I 116
Peretz, Martin, III 514
Perfect Stranger, IV 272
Performing Arts High School, IV 115
Perhach, Vanessa, I 40
Perkins, Anthony, I 458, III 60, IV 130
Perleman, Ronald, III 286
Perot, Ross, III 33, IV 278
Perrin, Vic, III 579
Perry, Bliss, I 135
Perry, Joe, I 32
Perry Mason, I 394, 694
Perry Mason. See also Burr, Raymond
Perry, Matthew, II 172
Persian Gulf War, IV 479
Personal Watercraft. See Jet Skis
Pesci, Joe, II 269
Pescow, Donna, IV 320

Pet Milk, II 90
Pet Sematary, III 38
Pet Sounds, I 196
Pete the Pup, III 578
Pete Seeger, I 781, III 74
Peter Gunn, III 256
Peter Pan, IV 211
Peter, Paul and Mary, I 354, 687, 746, II 125, 329
Peters, Bernadette, III 460
Peterson, Arthur, II 323
Petrenko, Viktor, II 484
Petrified Forest, III 491
Petronas Towers, IV 432
Pets or Meat: A Return to Flint, III 408
Petticoat Junction, IV 419
Pettiford, Oscar, I 19
Petty, George, IV 59, V 30
Petty girl, IV 94, V 30
Petty, Lee, I 670, IV 46
Petty, Norman, II 430
Petty, Richard, II 490
Peyton Place, III 346, IV 447
P-Funk All-Stars, I 532
Phair, Liz, III 414
Phantom Menace, IV 511, 686
Phantom of the Opera, III 182, 460
Phelps, Jill Farren, II 324
Phil Donahue Show, V 154
Phil Silvers Show, I 432
Philadelphia, I 36
Philadelphia Eagles, IV 117
Philadelphia Exposition, V 194
Philadelphia Flyers, IV 440
Philadelphia Harmonica Band, II 370
Philadelphia Negro: A Social Study, I 772
Philadelphia Orchestra, IV 541
Philadelphia Phillies, I 435, V 182
Philadelphia Story, II 297, IV 533
Philadelphia Tribune, I 33
Philbin, Regis, I 668
Philip Morris, I 212, 511
Philips Company, I 451
Phillips, V 66
Phillips, Dewey, II 98, IV 236
Phillips, Irna, I 99, II 323, III 539, IV 446
Phillips, John, III 251
Phillips, Lou Diamond, III 198
Phillips, Mackenzie, I 70, III 252, 565
Phillips, Michelle, III 251
Phillips, Sam, I 1, IV 106, 208, 236, 576
Phineas T. Bluster, II 459
Phoenix Suns, II 571
Phones, Judy Love, I 303
Photography, I 371
Photoplay, I 28, II 64, III 429, IV 507
Physical Culture, I 581, III 226
Physical fitness, IV 310
Physique Pictorial, IV 59
Physique Pictorial, IV 673
Physique Pictorial. See Athletic Model Guild
Piano, III 13
Piano smashing, I 553
Pic, IV 554
Piccolo, Brian, I 492
Picket Fences, III 13
Pickford, Mary, I 499, II 57, III 177, 428, IV 396,
     710, V 8, 235
Pickwick Records, V 39
Pierce, Jack, V 167
Pierpont, Harry, I 713
Pig Stand, II 72
Pigskin Parade, II 203
Pilatus, Rob, III 368
Pileggi, Nicholas, II 269
Pill, IV 374
Pillars of the Earth, II 127
Pillow Talk, I 665
Pillsbury, IV 446
Pinchback, P.B.S., I 32
Pinchot, Gifford, II 29
Pink Flamingos, I 416, 731
Pink Panther, III 256, IV 356

Pinkerton Detective Agency, I 263, II 350
Pinnacle, IV 11
Pinter, Harold, II 50, III 252
Pinup girls, II 277, III 82, IV 292
Pinza, Ezio, III 459, IV 465
Pippen, Scottie, I 493, II 571
Pirsig, Robert, IV 223
Pit, III 541
Pit and the Pendulum, I 71
Pittman, Robert, III 435
Pittsburgh Courier, I 32
Pittsburgh Pirates, I 528
Pittsburgh Steelers, I 285, III 483, IV 117, 521, 589
Pius X, Pope, IV 87
Pizza Hut, II 73, IV 63
Pizzeria Uno, IV 63
Pizzo, Angelo, II 442
Place in the Sun, IV 613
Plaisance, Midway, IV 692
Plan 9 from Outer Space, III 214, V 172
Planet of the Apes, II 400, IV 362
Plank Road Brewery, III 364
Planned Parenthood, I 9
Plant, Robert, III 116
Plante, Jacques, II 417
Plato, Dana, I 709
Platoon, IV 543, V 51, 93
Platters, I 164
Play It Again Sam, I 54
Playboy, I 722, II 41, 80, 223, 343, 383, III 401, 470,
     IV 34, 58, 72, 94, 370, V 31
Player, I 64
Pleasant Company, I 67
Plessey vs. Ferguson, III 497
Plexiglas, IV 66
Plow that Broke the Plains, II 30
Plummer, Christopher, IV 462
Plunkitt, George Washington, IV 77
Plymouth, III 455
Pocahontas, IV 686
Pocket Books, IV 9
Pocket Books. See Paperbacks
Pocket Classics, III 173
Pocket Series, III 173
Poe, Edgar Allan, I 64, 71, 693, 755, IV 148
Poffo, Randy, IV 322
Pogo, I 747
Poindexter, John, II 499
Poirot, Hercule, I 693
Poison, I 86
Poitier, Sidney, I 14, 268, 279, II 15, V 82
Poky Little Puppy, II 258
Polanski, Roman, III 262, IV 279
Polar fleece, IV 81
Polartec, IV 81
Police Surgeon, I 144
Police Tapes, II 406
Police, I 62, III 516
Police Woman, I 703
Polidori, John, V 22
Political correctness, III 441, 446
Pollack, Ben, III 525
Pollard, Fritz, IV 117
Pollock, Jackson, I 11
Pollyanna, IV 56
Polonsky, Abraham, II 435
Polsfuss, Lester, IV 20
Polyester, II 469
Polyester, IV 66
Polyester, IV 81
PolyGram, I 57, 584
Polyvinyl chloride, IV 66
Pomeroy, Wardell, III 41
Pomeroy, Wes, V 176
Pomus, Doc, I 351
Ponchielli, Amilcare, II 67
Poneman, Jonathan, II 322
Pong, V 45
Pontecorvo, Gilo, I 343
Pontiac GTO, III 455
Pony Express, I 545
Poole, William Frederick, IV 134

Poor People's Campaign, III 34
Pop Art, II 551, V 80, 131
Pop, Iggy, I 750, II 248
Pop Question Game, II 191
Pope, Albert, I 245
Pope, Generoso, III 480
Pope John XXIII, I 74
Popeye, II 71
Popular Electronics, II 225
Popular Library, IV 10
Popular Magazine, IV 553
Popular Publications, Inc., I 110, 264
Populist Party, IV 124
Porky Pig, I 146, 276
Pornography, II 470, IV 32, 300
Port Huron Statement, III 512, IV 125, 562, 563
Porter, Cole, II 107, III 458, IV 533, V 120
Porter, Edwin R., IV 395
Porter, Katherine Anne, I 61
Porter, Rufus, IV 334
Portfolio X, III 265
Portland Trailblazers, V 72
Posse Comitatus, III 360, V 129
Post, Emily, I 680, II 45, 265
Post, Wiley, IV 264
Posters, V 187
Postman Always Rings Twice, I 751
Postmodernism, I 740, IV 447
Pound, Ezra, II 177, 387, IV 710
Poverty, II 228
Powell, Adam Clayton, Jr., I 32
Powell, Dick, II 142
Powell, Eleanor, I 129
Powell, Laurence, III 35
Povich, Maury, I 668, IV 597
Powell, Maxine, III 420
Powell, William, III 207
Power, II 485
Power of Positive Thinking, IV 24
Powerwalking, IV 194
Powolny, Frank, IV 59
Pozner, Vladimir, I 745
Pozo, Charo, II 237
Prabhupada, A.C. Bhaktivedanta Swami, I 647, II 362
Practice, III 13
Prairie Home Companion, III 11
Prairie Ramblers, III 403
Prancela, Joseph, III 46
Pranksters, Merry, III 208
Prater, Dave. See Sam and Dave
Pratt, Jane, IV 314
Preacher, IV 309
Predator, V 41
Pregnancy, I 261
Premier, II 65
Preminger, Otto, III 100
Prendergast, Maurice, I 123
Preppie, III 181
Presidential Medal of Freedom, III 85
Presley, Elvis, I 53, 133, 319, 352, 354, 406, II 19,
     53, 98, 247, 251, 278, 344, 563, III 155, 280,
     571, IV 84, 210, 236, 371, 571, 576, 621, 617,
     V 141, 173
Presley, Lisa Marie, IV 108
Preston, John, I 29
Preston, Robert, III 459
Pretenders, The, III 516
Pretty in Pink, I 344
Pretty Woman, I 730, II 225, III 278, IV 300
Previn, Andre, IV 555
Price, George McCready, I 627
Price Is Right, I 298, II 194
Price, Ray, III 367
Price, Vincent, I 71, III 436, IV 635
Prickett, Charlene, I 31
Pride and Prejudice, IV 271
Pride, Charlie, I 133
Pride of the Yankees, I 598
Priest, Judas, IV 570
PrimeTimeLive, IV 713
Primitives, V 39
Prince, I 86, II 249, III 235

Prince Charles, I 699
Prince, Harold, II 91
Prince Valiant, I 121
Princess Diana. See Diana, Princess of Wales
Princess Summerfall Winterspring, II 459
Princeton University, I 338, 555
Principal, Victoria, I 652
Private Lives, IV 615
Private Parts, IV 531
Problem of Pain, III 151
Pro-choice, I 10
Procter & Gamble, I 99, IV 446
Proctor, Phil, II 103
Producers, I 366
Product placement, III 536
Production Code Administration, II 297
Production Code of the 1930s, I 108
Professional Golfers' Association (PGA), I
    722, II 262
Professor Longhair, III 513
Professor Quiz, II 192
Progressive Era, III 318, IV 131
Progressivism, III 443
Prohibition, I 210, 425, 544, II 197, 579, III 3, 237,
    283, IV 229, 709
Project Housing, II 228
Project Mercury, III 475
Project Vanguard, IV 494
Proletarian novel, III 73, 145
Pro-life, I 10
Promise Keepers, III 345, 457, IV 201
Propaganda, V 189
Prostitution, II 189, IV 32
Protestantism, II 46, 183
Provost, Jon, III 96
Prozac, I 691
Prudhomme, Don "The Snake," I 765
Prussian Cur, III 64
Pryor, Richard, IV 505
Psychedelia, IV 84
Psychedelic plants, I 453
Psychic Friends Network, IV 129
Psycho, II 414, IV 435
Psycho Killer, IV 602
Psychoanalysis, II 166
Psychologists, I 403
PTL Club, I 160
PTL Network, IV 626
Public Broadcasting Act, IV 137
Public Broadcasting Service (PBS), I 571,
    III 404, 561
Public Enemy, I 382, 410, 508, III 238, IV 175, 462
Public health, I 310
Public Opinion, III 171
Public service programming, IV 182
Public Works of Art Project, V 179
Publishers Weekly, I 237
Puck, II 578
Puelo, Johnny, II 371
Puente, Tito, III 97, IV 304
Pulitzer, Joseph, II 379, III 7, IV 598, V 101
Pulitzer Prize, I 310, 748, II 78, 290, III 3, 392,
    518, 556, IV 255, 285, 301, 338, 382, 554,
    607, 718, V 67
Pullman, Bill, II 487
Pullman porters, III 72
Pulp Fiction, III 13, IV 694
Pulp Fiction, V 148
Puma, I 20
Pumping Iron, III 454
Pumping Iron II: The Unprecedented Woman, I
    307, III 329
Punisher, I 562
Punk, I 303
Punk, V 228
Punk rock, III 516, IV 238
"Puppy Love," IV 18
Puritans, I 503
Purple Rain, IV 112
Purviance, Edna, I 476
Purvis, Melvin "Nervous," I 714

Push Comes to Shove, I 180
"Push It," IV 306
Puzo, Mario, II 250
PVC, IV 66
Pyle, C.C., IV 117
Pyne, Joe, I 669, IV 386

Quaid, Dennis, III 155
Quaid, Randy, II 487
Quant, Mary, I 415, II 390
Quarrymen, I 203
Quayle, Dan, I 225, IV 278
"Que Sera Sera," I 664, II 415
Queen, III 117, IV 274, V 28
Queen, Ellery, I 694
Queen for a Day, II 193
Queen Latifah, IV 176
Queen Victoria's Golden Jubilee, I 546
Queer in America, III 581
Questel, Mae, I 240
Quiet Man, II 134
Quigley, Joan, I 130
Quimby, Fred, II 355
Quinn, Anthony, III 85
Quinn, Don, II 89
Quirk, James, IV 53
Quivers, Robin, IV 531
Quiz Show, IV 152
Quiz show scandals, II 541, IV 427
Quiz Shows, IV 293
Quo Vadis?, I 280, IV 395
QVC cable shopping, I 689, IV 262

Rabbit, V 10
Rabbit Foot Minstrels, IV 168
Race records, II 552
Radford Architectural Company, The, I 456
Radio, IV 626
Radio City Music Hall, I 390, III 157, 426, IV 241
Radio Corporation of America (RCA), IV 312
Radio Daily, III 2
Radio Hall of Fame, III 6
Radner, Gilda, I 217, IV 321, 348
Rado, James. See Ragni, Gerome
Raffel, Leroy, II 73
Raffetto, Michael, III 415
Rage, III 37
Raging Bull, I 673, III 83, IV 337
Ragni, Gerome, II 338
Ragsdale, Phil, IV 254
Ragtime, II 566, 567, III 460
Ragtime Dance, II 569
Raiders of the Lost Ark, II 131, IV 441
Raimi, Sam, I 645, II 397
Rainbow Coalition, II 515
Rainbow Warrior, II 304
Rainer, Luise, I 13
Rainey, Ma, I 292, IV 439
Rainman, II 421
Rains, Claude, I 448
Raintree County, IV 614
Rainwater, Cederic, III 397
Raisch, Bill, II 180
Raisin in the Sun, II 356, IV 76
Raitt, John, III 459
Rakolta, Terry, III 278
Ralley's, II 73
Ralston, Henry, I 738
Rambaldi, Carlo, II 44
Rambo, I 283, 551, IV 500
Rambo: First Blood, V 51
Rambova, Natacha, V 18
Ramones, The, IV 82, 142, 471
Ramsaye, Terry, IV 54
Ramsey, Mary, IV 638
Rand, Asa, V 222
Rand, Ayn. See Objectivism/Ayn Rand
RAND Corporation, II 495
Rand, Sally, I 390
Randall, Tony, II 476, III 550
Randolph, A. Philip, III 72, 266
Random House, I 237

Range Drifters, The, II 344
Rankin, Jeannette, II 85
Rankin-Bass, IV 287
Rap Brown, I 495
Rap/Hip-Hop, I 200, II 222, 394, III 245,
    IV 287, 715
Raphael, Sally Jesse, I 668
Raphaelson, Samson, II 531
Rapp, William Jordan, I 582
Rappe, Virginia, I 107, IV 367
Rashbaum, David, I 315
Raskins, David, III 100
Raskob, John J., II 28
Rastafari, III 274
Rastus, IV 395
Rat Pack, I 344, III 280, IV 411
Rat Patrol, V 192
Rathbone, Basil, I 71
Rather, Dan, I 637, IV 426
Rau, Bill, I 29
Rauschenberg, Robert, I 648, II 551
Raven, IV 110
Raw, III 308
Raw Power, IV 82
Rawhide, V 120
Rawls, Lou, II 458
Ray, East Bay, I 675
Ray H. Bennett Lumber Company, I 456
Ray, Nicholas, IV 186
Ray of Light, I 305
Raymond, Alex, II 113
Raymond, Gene, III 225
Rayon, IV 66, 80
RCA, I 132, III 503, IV 107, 111
RCA Building, IV 433
RCA Victor, I 445, II 105, III 225
R.E.M., I 62, III 516, IV 638, V 39
Reade, Walter, III 532
Reagan administration, IV 329
Reagan, Nancy, I 130
Reagan, Ronald, I 11, 93, 314, 524, 551, 570, 608, II
    499, III 65, 225, 503, IV 29, 94, 137, 170, 244,
    260, 616, 628, 687, V 130
Realist, I 61, III 61
Realists, I 122
Rear Window, II 415, IV 534, 612
Rebecca, II 415
Rebecca of Sunnybrook Farm, IV 632
Rebel without a Cause, I 335, 677, II 197, 448,
    584, IV 622
Rebennack, Mac "Dr. John," III 514
Reconstruction, I 258
Red Alert, I 759
Red Barn, II 73
Red Dawn, I 551
Red Dust, II 296
Red Garters, V 120
Red, Hot and Blue!, IV 96
Red Hot Louisiana Band, I 491
Red Nightmare, I 549
Red River, V 93, 119
Red Ryder, V 119
Red Scare, III 315
Red Smiley, IV 204
Red Storm Entertainment, I 525
Red, White and Black, I 279
Redbook, II 265
Redding, Noel, II 391
Redding, Otis, IV 460
Redford, Robert, I 398, IV 253, 576
Redgrave, Vanessa, I 414, 774
Redman, Don, I 248
Redmond, Washington, III 355
Reds, I 207
Reebok, IV 638
Reed, Donna, I 653, II 175
Reed, Jerry, I 133
Reed, Jimmy, II 441, III 25
Reed, Lou, I 86, II 248, III 43, V 39, 81
Reed, Robert, I 340
Reed, Willis, I 40
Reese, Della, III 279

Reeve, Christopher, I 722, IV 185
Reeves, Jim, I 133
Reeves, Martha. See Martha and the Vandellas
Reeves, Shirley Alston, IV 384
Reeves, Steve, I 308, III 453
Reflections of Nazism: an Essay on Kitsch and Death, III 45
Refrigerator, II 20
Reggae, III 274
Regina v. Hicklin, IV 93
Reginald Rose, IV 564
Reid, Wallace, II 432, IV 398
Reilly, Hugh, III 96
Reilly, Jeanine C., IV 48
Reiner, Carl, I 75, V 25
Reiner, Rob, IV 197
Reinhardt, Django, III 27
Reisman, David, II 98
Relf, Keith, V 212
Remain in Light, IV 602
Remarque, Erich Maria, I 52, V 188
Rembrandt, I 123
Remembering Denny, IV 697
Remembrance Rock, IV 307
Remington, Frederic, I 622, II 379, V 120, 161
Renfro, Mel, I 654
Reno, Janet, III 54, IV 516
Rent, II 338, III 459
Replacements, I 62, IV 142
Reprise, III 280, IV 411
Republic of New Afrika, I 520
Republic Pictures, V 120
Republican Party, I 93, II 549
Reservoir Dogs, III 12
Resor, Stanley, II 511
Resurgence: The Movement for Equality vs. the Ku Klux Klan, III 65
Retro fashion, I 303
Rettig, Tommy, III 96
Return of the Jedi, III 216, IV 511
Return of the Seven, III 241
Return of Superfly, I 280
Return to Peyton Place, IV 48
Returning Home, III 4
Reubens, Paul, IV 32
Reuters, V 158
Revenge of the Nerds, III 502
Reville, Alma, II 414
Revival meetings, IV 578
Revlon, II 96
Revolution for the Hell of It, II 419
Revolutionary War, III 491
Revuers,'' ''The, II 429
Rexroth, Kenneth, II 201
Rey, H. A., I 649
Rey, Margaret, I 649
Reynolds, Burt, I 599, II 327, IV 371, 388
Reynolds, Debbie, II 105
Reynolds, Frank, III 534
Reynolds, Nick, III 40
Reynolds Wrap, II 90
Reza, Yasmina, III 369
Rhapsody in Blue, V 130
Rheingold, I 212
Rhinoplasty, IV 67
Rhoda, II 282, 371, III 292, IV 535
Rhodes, Hari, I 279
Rhodes, James, III 18
Rhumba, III 97, IV 304
Rhyme Pays, II 485
Rhythm and blues, II 162, IV 236
Rice, Anne, I 761
Rice, Grantland, I 556, 685, V 183
Rice, Jerry, IV 118
Rice, Linda Johnson, II 8
Rice, Thomas Dartmouth, I 270, III 371
Rice, Tim, II 543, III 459
Richard, Little, IV 207
Richard, Maurice ''Rocket,'' II 417, 467
Richards, Keith, I 58, 355, IV 237, 269
Richards, Michael, IV 353
Richardson, J(iles) P(erry). See Big Bopper

Richardson, Patricia, II 437
Richie, Lionel, I 566, III 422
Richman, Jonathan, I 442, III 515
Rich's, I 688
Rickenbacker, Eddie, I 38, II 491
Ricketts, John Bill, I 512
Rickey, Branch, I 362, II 6, III 497, IV 232
Riddle, Nelson, IV 411
Ride the High Country, IV 341
Ridenhour, Carlton, IV 132
''Rider from Nowhere,'' IV 378
Rider on the Rain, I 361
Riders of the Purple Sage, II 309
Riders of the Purple Sage, V 120
Rifkin, Joshua, II 568
Rigg, Diana, I 145, II 523
Riggs, Bobby, III 28, IV 636
Right Stuff, IV 382
Righteous Brothers, IV 472, 619
Riley, Pat, III 197
Rimbaud, Arthur, I 749
Ringling Brothers, IV 213
Ringling Brothers Barnum and Bailey, I 513
Ringwald, Molly, I 344, 347
Rio Bravo, III 280
Riordan, Bill, I 585
Riot Grrl movement, III 414
Ripken, Cal, Jr., I 183, II 218
Ripley, Alexandra, II 264
Ripley, Robert Le Roy, IV 215
Rising Sun, III 13
Riskin, Robert, I 428, II 504
Ritter, John, IV 653
Ritts, Herb, IV 59
Rivera, Chita, III 410, 459
Rivera, Diego, III 509, V 180
Rivera, Geraldo, I 668, 745
Rivers, Joan, I 348, II 434, IV 348, 678
Rizzo, Ratso, II 421
RKO, I 149, III 177, IV 565
Roach, Hal, I 428, III 576
''Road'' films, III 84
''Road Not Taken,'' II 177
Road Rules, IV 181
Road Runner, IV 707
Road, III 188
Rob & Fab, III 368
Robbins, Harold, I 237, 238
Robbins, Jerome, II 91, V 116
Robbins, Tod, II 159
Robbins, Trina, V 4
Robe, I 753
Robert-Houdin, II 457
Roberts, Clifford, III 305
Roberts, Cokie, I 354
Roberts, Julia, II 225, III 278
Roberts, Oral, IV 588, 625
Roberts, Pernell, I 316
Roberts, Tony, I 54
Roberts, Xavier, I 403
Robertson, Oscar, I 8
Robertson, Pat, II 183, III 410, 505, IV 71, 198, 626
Robeson, Kenneth, I 738
Robeson, Paul, I 215, IV 117
Robey, Don, IV 207
Robin Hood, III 189
Robin Hood, III 368
Robinson, Bill ''Bojangles,'' II 450, IV 605, V 22
Robinson, Eddie, IV 635
Robinson, Edward G., IV 635
Robinson, Jackie, I 169, 182, 362, 736, 777, II 6, III 497, IV 5, 193, 230, 486, V 183
Robinson, Ronnie, IV 267
Robinson, Shawna, IV 539
Robinson, ''Sugar Ray,'' I 332, III 83, 136
Robinson, William ''Smokey,'' III 420, IV 633, V 111
''Rock and Roll Summit, IV 312
Rock Around the Clock, II 163
''Rock Around the Clock,'' II 344
Rock 'n' roll, I 354, IV 53, 83, 412

Rock 'n' Roll Hall of Fame, I 165, 744, 769, II 154, 461, 493 III 30, 155, 252, 280, IV 22
Rock 'n' Roll High School, IV 171
Rock steady music, IV 195
''Rock Your Baby,'' I 727
Rockefeller Center, V 180
Rockefeller, John D., Sr., III 166
Rockefeller, John, IV 239, 606
Rockefeller, John D., Jr., III 165, IV 240, 242, V 180
Rockefeller, Nelson A., III 165, IV 239
Rocket 88, IV 236
''Rocket 88,'' II 344, IV 702
Rockettes, IV 605
Rockford Files, II 205
Rockford, Jim, I 474
Rockne, Knute, I 555, IV 117, 275
Rockwell, Norman, I 118, 541, II 306, III 44, 161, V 190
Rockwell, Tommy, I 115
Rocky, III 172, IV 500
Rocky III, I 25
Rocky IV, I 551
Rocky and Bullwinkle, IV 317
Rocky Horror Picture Show, I 416, 644, II 153, 249, III 426
Roddenberry, Gene, IV 508
Roddy, Rod, IV 109
Rodgers and Hart, II 107
Rodgers, Jimmie, I 445, 618, II 335, IV 53
Rodgers, Richard, III 458, 553, IV 462, 465
Rodgers, Richard. See Rodgers and Hammerstein; Rodgers and Hart
Rodman, Dennis, I 493, II 571
Rodriguez, Richard I 253
Rodriguez, Tito, III 97
Roe v. Wade, I 10, II 86
Roebuck, Alvah, IV 346
Roger & Me, III 408
Rogers, Fred McFeely, III 378
Rogers, Ginger, III 14
Rogers, Jean, II 113
Rogers, Mister, I 430
Rogers, ''Nature Boy'' Buddy, III 8
Rogers, Roy, I 619, 622, V 120
Rogers, Roy (blues musician), II 441
Rogers, Wayne, II 475
Rogers, Will, I 75, 139, II 89, III 458
Rohmer, Sax, II 179
Roker, Roxie, II 536
Rolle, Esther, II 267
Roller Super Stars, IV 267
Rollerball, IV 267
Rollergames, IV 267
Rolling Stone, I 58, 61, 452, II 38, III 159
Rolling Stones, I 56, 57, 204, 355, 415, II 391, 535, III 159, 220, 513, IV 84, V 89
Rolsten, Mathew, IV 205
Roman Catholic Church, IV 86
Roman, Charles, I 136
Roman Holiday, II 394
Romance on the High Seas, I 664
Romance Writers of America, IV 273
Rombauer, Irma S., II 572
Romberg, Sigmund, III 458
Romero, George, I 645, III 532
Ronstadt, Linda, III 572, IV 18
Rooney, Andy, IV 425
Rooney, Arthur J., IV 61, 117
Rooney, Frank, V 135
Rooney, Mickey, I 87, II 200, 203, III 577, IV 566
Roosevelt, Eleanor, I 28, 82, III 228, IV 669
Roosevelt, Franklin Delano, I 75, 721, II 28, 296, 371, 413, 526 III 158, 191, 266, 438, 499, 504, 508, IV 76, 159, V 188
Roosevelt, Theodore, I 122, 134, 622, II 29, 92, 405, III 188, 438, 443, 479, 491, 414, 521, 616, 685, V 162
Roots, II 343, 436, III 439
Rope, III 139
Roper, Deidre ''Dee Dee,'' IV 306
Rosa, Robby, IV 304
Rosalie, IV 96

Rose, III 356
Rose, Fred, I 619, V 142
Rose Marie, III 225
Rose, Pete, III 337
Roseanne, I 670, IV 278, 422, 504
Roseland, I 657
Roseland Ballroom Orchestra, I 248
Rosenbaum, Estelle, I 276
Rosenberg, Edgar, IV 220
Rosenberg, Ethel and Julius, I 570
Rosenberg, Julius and Ethel, I 424, V 113
Rosenberg, William, I 775
Rosenzweig, Barney, I 409
Rosie O'Donnell Show, III 552
''Rosie the Riveter,'' III 73
Ross, Diana, II 272, III 422
Ross, Harold, II 578, III 522
Ross, Joe E., I 433
Ross, Katherine, II 280
Ross, Lilian, II 389
Ross, Marion, II 357
Rossellini, Roberto, I 226
Rossen, Robert, II 435
Roswell incident, V 2
Roth, David Lee, V 26
Roth, Ed ''Big Daddy,'' II 455
Roth, Lillian, IV 644
Roth, Philip, I 134, II 268
Roth v. United States, IV 93
Rothafel, Samuel L. ''Roxy,'' III 426, IV 242
Rothko, Mark, I 11
Rothrock, Joseph Trimble, I 418
Rothstein, Arnold, I 267, III 237
Rothstein, Arthur, III 509
Rotten, Johnny, IV 142
Roundtree, Richard, I 279, IV 371, 376
Route 66, I 603, IV 285
Rover Boys, The, IV 548
Rowan and Martin's Laugh-In. See *Laugh-In*
Rowan, Dan, III 98
Rowland, Pleasant T., I 67
Roxy Music, II 247, III 426
Roy Roger's, II 73
Royal Canadians, III 187
Royal Castle, II 73
Royals, I 164
Rozelle, Pete, III 185, 472, 483, IV 118
Ru Paul, I 416, 764
Rube Goldberg Invention, II 256
Rubik, Erno, IV 286
Rubin, Jerry, I 495, II 420, V 214, 224
Rubin, Rick, I 200
Ruby Ridge, III 360
Rudolph, Wilma, III 560
Rudy Vallee, I 478
Ruf Records, I 56
Ruf, Thomas, I 56
Ruff and Reddy Show, II 355, IV 317
Ruffin, David, IV 633
Ruggles of Red Gap, V 121
Ruiz, Dina, II 3
Ruiz, Rosie, I 323
Rumble Records, I 56
Rumours, II 115
Run DMC, I 21, 32, IV 175, 305
Running Fence, I 506
Runyon, Damon, III 238, IV 266
Rupe, Art, IV 207
Rush, III 117
Rush, Otis, I 56
Rushing, Jimmy, I 184
Russell, Bill, I 137, 186, 322, 473, III 196, 478
Russell, Charles, V 120
Russell, Charley, I 622
Russell, Harold, I 721, III 4
Russell, Jane, II 223, III 260, IV 370, V 119
Russell, Kurt, IV 643
Russell, Rosalind, III 429
Rustin, Bayard, II 216, III 266
Ruth, Babe, I 2, 182, 362, 540, 617, 715, III 202, 263, 274, 520, IV 235, V 182, 198, 208
Ryan, Meg, II 354

Ryan, Nolan, I 435, II 161
Ryan, Paddy, IV 573
Rydell, Bobby, I 143, IV 236, 619
Ryder, Winona, III 155
Ryman Auditorium, II 287
Ryun, Jim, IV 389

S&H Green Stamp Co., IV 688
Sabich, Spider, V 139
SABRE reservation system, II 482
Sabrina, II 394
Sacco, Nicola, I 424
Sack, John, II 41
Sackler, Howard, II 528
Saddler, Joseph, II 286
Sado/masochism (s/m), III 141
Safer, Morley, IV 426
Sagal, Katey, III 278
Sage, Anna, I 714
Sahl, Mort, IV 263
Saint, Eva Marie, III 541
Saint James, Susan, III 7
Saint Laurent, Yves, I 490
Saint Nicholas, I 504
Sajak, Pat, V 123
Saks, Andrew, IV 302
Saldivar, Yolanda, IV 354
'Salem's Lot, III 37
Salinger, J. D., I 458
Salisbury, Harrison, III 518
Salk, Jonas, IV 77
Salsa music, I 275
Salt 'n' Pepa, IV 175
Salt of the Earth, III 74
Salt, Waldo, II 435
Salvador, IV 543
Sam, Magic, I 56
Sam Spade, II 296
Sambora, Richie, I 315
Sampson, Edgar, IV 323
Sampson, Will, III 567
Samurai Widow, I 218
Samwell-Smith, Paul, V 212
San Francisco, I 281
San Francisco, I 222, II 259, III 361
San Francisco 49ers, II 302, III 402, 483, IV 118, 209
San Francisco Giants, III 272, IV 231
San Francisco Mime Troupe, II 283
San Francisco Seals, I 715
San Francisco World's Fair, III 169
San Simeon, II 380
Sandberg, Ryne, I 493
Sandburg, Carl, IV 347
Sande, Earl, III 20
Sanders, Barry, IV 118
Sanders, ''Colonel'' Harlan, II 73, III 20, V 122
Sandinista, II 499
Sandler, Adam, I 422
Sandman, The, I 672
Sandow, Eugen, I 305
Sands of Iwo Jima, V 93, 191
Sands, Tommy, IV 619
Sandy, III 177
Sandy's, II 73
Sane, Aladdin, I 86
Sanford & Son, II 148, III 111, 439, IV 420
Sanford, Isabel, II 536
Sanger, Margaret, I 9, II 85
Sanitation, I 310
Sanka, I 547
Santa Ana Drags, I 764
Santa Barbara, IV 447
Santa Claus, I 505, 541
Santa Monica Track Club, III 151
Santana, I 58
Santana, Carlos, I 56, IV 138
Saperstein, Abe, I 186, II 364
Sappho, III 140
Saran wrap, IV 66
Sarandon, Susan, I 644, IV 250
Sarazen, Gene, II 262

Sargent Preston of the Yukon, II 296
Sartre, Jean-Paul, II 50, IV 100
Sasquatch. See Bigfoot
Sassy, IV 365
Satherly, Art, I 1
Satie, Erik, III 463
''Satisfaction,'' IV 270
Satrom, Leroy, III 18
Saturday Evening Post, I 134, 758, III 161, IV 244, 699
Saturday Night Fever, I 210, 727, IV 81, 85, 694
Saturday Night Live, I 217, 293, 480, 643, II 49, 345, III 7, 204, 282, 404, 450, 488, IV 162, 326, 442, V 94
Saturnalia, I 503
Saunders, Allen, III 294
Saunders, John, III 295
Savage, Augusta, IV 710
Savage, Don, I 29
Savalas, Telly, I 721, III 52
Savannah, IV 48
Save Our Children, Inc., III 362
Saving Private Ryan, V 78, 191
Savini, Tom, II 170
Savio, Mario, II 162
Savoy Ballroom, I 248, II 108, III 223
Savoy Sultans, IV 322
Sawchuk, Terry, II 417
Sawyer, Jack, III 344
Sayers, Dorothy L., I 693
Sayers, Gale, I 492, IV 118
Sayles, John, II 44
S.C.U.M., V 81
Scarface, III 238
''Scarsdale'' diet, I 707
Schaefer, I 212
Schaefer, Jack, IV 378
Schaffer, Paul, III 145
Schaffner, Franklin J., IV 20, 63
Schafly, Phyllis, IV 200
Schary, Dore, III 309
Scheider, Roy, II 528
Schenck, Joseph, I 107, III 347, V 8
Schenck, Nicholas, III 309
Scherman, Harry, I 318
Schifrin, Lalo, III 376
Schindler, Oskar, IV 325
Schine, David, I 116
Schlatter, George, III 98
Schlink, Frederick, I 588
Schlitz, I 210
Schmeling, Max, III 200
Schmidt, Gottfried, I 329
Schmidt, Otto, IV 693
Schoedsack, Ernest, III 31
Schoenstein, Ralph, IV 105
Scholastic Aptitude Test (SAT), IV 503
School House, II 333
Schoolhouse Rock, IV 319
Schrader, Paul, IV 338
Schufftan, Eugen, III 347
Schulberg, Budd, II 435, III 430, 562
Schuller, Gunther, I 19
Schultz, Dutch, III 213
Schultz, Howard, IV 514
Schulz, Charles, IV 25
Schuman, Mort, I 351
Schwartz, Sherwood, I 340, II 238
Schwartz, Stephen, III 459
Schwarzenegger, Arnold, I 307, III 453, IV 639
Schwimmer, David, II 172
Science and Health, II 12
Science and Inventions, IV 141
Science Fiction Achievement Awards, II 226
Scientific American, II 457
Scientology, I 646, III 508
Scientology. See Hubbard, L. Ron
Scooby Doo, II 355, III 6
Scopes, John T., IV 335
Scopes Monkey Trial, I 424, 627, 660 II 182, III 343, IV 712

Scorsese, Martin, I 71, 673, II 269, III 12, 153, 336,
    IV 165, 346, 611
Scotsboro Nine, the, III 218
Scott, Adrian, II 434
Scott, Bill, IV 248
Scott, Dave, II 503
Scott, Eric, V 74
Scott, George C., IV 19, V 191
Scott, Randolph, V 120
Scott, Ridley, I 273, IV 642
Scott, Willard, III 321
Scottie Pippen, I 767
Scream, Blacula, Scream, I 279
Scream, III 419
''Screamin' for Vengeance,'' II 577
Screen Actors Guild, I 34, II 28
Screenland, II 64
Screwball comedy, I 352, II 289, 504
Screwtape Letters, III 151
Scribner, Charles, IV 344
Scribner, Sam, I 389
Scruggs, Earl, I 288, II 122, III 397
Scruggs, Earl. See also Foggy Mountain Boys
Scruples, III 60
Sea Hunt, II 118
Sea Wolf, III 188
Seagram Building, IV 433
Seale, Bobby, I 264, 495
Search for Tomorrow, IV 446
Searchers, I 355
Searchers, I 644, V 119
Sears Point Speedway, I 57
Sears, Richard W., IV 346
Sears, Roebuck & Company, I 455, 689, III 48,
    IV 10, 347
Sears Tower, IV 432
Seattle Metropolitans, II 417
Seattle Slew, III 20
Seattle, Washington, II 321, IV 514
Seaver, Tom, II 232
Sebastian, John, V 106
Seberg, Jean, I 86
Seckler, John Ray ''Curly,'' II 122
Second Amendment, II 101
Second City, I 42, 217
Second Vatican Council, IV 87
Secret Agent, IV 116
Secret Garden, III 460
Secretariat, III 20
Sedaka, Neil, I 351, III 30
Sedalia, Missouri, II 567
Seduction of the Innocent, I 561, 565, V 111
See America First, IV 96
See It Now, III 452
Seeger, Pete, II 124, 329, V 96
Sega, V 46
Segar, E.C., IV 87
Segel, Joseph, II 438
Seidenberg, Sidney, III 27
Seifert, George, IV 118
Seinfeld, I 607, IV 262, 422, 535, 709
Seinfeld, Jerry, I 7, IV 352
Selchow and Righter, IV 698
Seldes, Gilbert, III 62
Selective Service, I 761
Selena, III 271
Selena, III 495
Self-Help, IV 708
Selig, William, II 432
Selleck, Tom, III 241
Sellers, Peter, I 760
Seltzer, Jerry, IV 267
Seltzer, Leo, IV 266
Selznick, David O., I 281, II 263, 415, 562, III 348
Senate Judiciary Committee, I 93
Sengstack, Robert, I 33
Sennett, Mack, I 107, 428, 476, III 24, IV 397
Sensuous Woman, IV 373
Sent for You Yesterday (Here You Come
    Today), I 185
''Sepia Bounce,'' III 3
Septic Death, IV 429

Sergeant York, I 598
Serial killers, I 384, II 82
Serling, Rod, III 60, IV 364, 713
Servello, Joe, III 56
Sesame Street, II 393, III 198, 444, IV 136, 328, 686
Seton, Ernest Thompson, I 334
Sevareid, Eric, III 452, V 190
Seven Brides for Seven Brothers, V 121
Seven Days in May, I 550
700 Club, IV 200, 225
Seven Lively Arts, III 62
Seven Pillars of Wisdom, III 105
Seven Words You Can Never Use on
    Television, I 435
Seven Year Bitch, III 414
Seven Year Itch, III 400
Seventeen, IV 313
Seventh Day Adventists, IV 708
Sex and the Office, IV 367
Sex and the Single Girl, I 610, IV 373
Sex Pistols, I 266, 416, II 501, IV 82, 142
Sex symbols, III 430
Sexton, Anne, IV 68
Sexual Behavior in the Human Female, IV 374
Sexual Behavior in the Human Male, IV 374
Sexual revolution, II 564, 573, III 303, 344,
    IV 57, 415
Sexually transmitted disease (STD), IV 299, 374
Seymour, Jane, III 234
Seymour, Lesley Jane, IV 189
Sergeant Pepper's Lonely Hearts Club Band, I 576,
    II 411, III 193, IV 84
Sgt. Rock, V 191
Shadow, A Detective Magazine, IV 141
Shadow, I 475, II 296, IV 379
Shaft, I 278, III 439, IV 282
Shaft in Africa, I 279
Shaft's Big Score, I 279
Shaggy, III 6
Shahn, Ben, III 509, V 190
''Shake, Rattle and Roll,'' II 344
Shakespeare, William, III 459, IV 564
Shakey's Pizza, II 73, IV 63
Shakur, Tupac, II 197, IV 176
Shalako, III 85
Shall We Dance, I 129
Shamu, IV 345
Shandling, Gary, II 507, III 91
Shane, III 75, V 119
Shane, Bob, III 40
Shanghai Express, V 172
Shannon, Frank, II 113
Shannon, Tommy, V 37
Sharif, Omar, III 104
Shatner, William, I 757, IV 508
Shaver, Billy Joe, II 540, III 501
Shaw, Artie, I 583, II 200
Shaw, Clay, II 546, III 17
Shaw, Irwin, V 191
Shaw, Joseph, I 263, 474
Shaw, Robert, II 528
Shaw, Wilbur, II 490
Shaw, Winifred, I 422
Shawn, Ted, I 166, 686, IV 494
Shawn, William, III 522, IV 697
She Done Him Wrong, V 115
''She Thinks I Still Care,'' II 562
She Wore a Yellow Ribbon, IV 499
Shearer, Norma, IV 640
Sheba Baby, I 279
Sheedy, Ally, I 344, 347
Sheen, Bishop Fulton, I 28
Sheen, Charlie, I 344, IV 69
Sheik, V 18
Shelby, Carroll, III 455
Sheldon, Charles M., V 198
Sheldon, Sidney, II 476
Shelley, Mary Wollstonecraft, II 152
Shelton, Gilbert, V 4
Shepard, Alan, I 104
Shepard, Sam, II 179
Shepherd, Cybill, III 406

Shepodd, Jon, III 96
Sherlock Holmes, I 149
Sherman, Allan, I 53
Sherman, Bobby, IV 620
Sherman, Eddie, I 6
Sherman, Harry, II 445
Sherrill, Billy, IV 209
Sherwood, Mary Elizabeth Wilson, II 45
Sherwood, Robert E., I 219
She's So Unusual III 100
Shields, Brooke, V 82
Shindle, Kate, IV 300
Shining, III 37
Shinn, Everett, I 122
Shirer, William L., III 452, V 190
Shirley and Lee, IV 207
Shoal Creek Country Club, Birmingham,
    Alabama, II 262
Shock Treatment, III 173
Shock Treatment, IV 250
Shoeless Joe, II 93
Shoemaker, Ed, III 106
Shoemaker, Willie, III 20
Sholes, Steve, I 132
Shootist, II 402, V 93, 119
Shopping malls, I 590
Shore, Dinah, I 668
Short Cuts, I 64
Short, Martin, IV 348
Shortridge, Stephen, V 106
Shout at the Devil, III 419
Showboat, I 358, III 21, 320, 459 IV 114, 227, 254
Shreve, Lamb and Harmon, II 29
Shrine of the Little Flower, I 617
Shriner, Kin, II 219
Shriver, Eunice Kennedy, IV 470
Shriver, Maria, IV 330
Shubert, Sam, Lee, and J.J., I 357
Shuffle Along, II 366
Shula, Don, I 370, IV 118
Shulman, Max, I 735
Shuster, Joe, I 561, IV 581
Siciliano, Angelo, I 135, 306
Side Show, II 257
Sideshows, IV 519
Sidney Janis Gallery, V 81
Siegel, Benjamin ''Bugsy,'' II 191, III 90, 93
Siegel, Don, II 3
Siegel, Janis, III 257
Siegel, Jerry, I 561, IV 581
Siembra, IV 304
Sierra Club, II 406
Signorile, Michelangelo, III 581
Silence of the Lambs, II 145, IV 359
Silent film, I 365, 721, IV 529
Silent Spring, II 1, 31
Silhouettes, The, V 16
Silk Stockings, IV 96
Silko, Leslie Marmon, III 441
Silkwood, IV 457
Siller, Sidney, III 344
Silver, III 190
Silver Shirts, V 129
Silver Surfer, I 562
Silverberg, Robert, IV 332
Silverheels, Jay, III 190
Silverman, Sime, I 389, V 31
Silverman, Syd, V 31
Silvers, Phil, I 432
Simmons, Al, IV 470
Simmons, Bob, IV 585
Simmons, Gene, III 42
Simmons, Matty, III 487
Simmons, Richard, I 31
Simmons, Russell, IV 175, 288
Simmons, William Joseph, III 64
Simon & Schuster, II 361, III 474, IV 549
Simon and Garfunkel, II 48, 125, 280, IV 403
Simon, Carly, IV 615
Simon, Danny, IV 401
Simon, George, I 185
Simon, Joe, I 429, III 42, V 190

Simon, Moises, III 97
Simon, Neil, I 43, III 550, IV 196
Simon, Paul, II 125
Simpson, Alan, I 3
Simpson, Don, II 433
Simpson murder trial, IV 130
Simpson, Nicole Brown, IV 404
Simpson, O. J., I 557, III 337, IV 11, 118, 275,
    405, 486, 597
Simpson, Red, II 334
Simpsons, I 53, 213, II 319, IV 248, 278, 422
Sims, Benny, II 122
Sinatra, Frank, I 95, 143, 222, 321, 344, 751, II 175,
    200, III 121, 153, 280, 460, IV 84, 387, 618
Sinatra, Nancy, I 71
Sinclair, Upton, III 73, 438
Singalong Jubilee, III 448
Singer, Isaac, II 491
"Singing Cowboy," I 142
Singing Detective, IV 102
Single bullet theory, III 17
Singles bars, IV 374
Singleton, John, I 280
Singleton, Linda Joy, II 579
Singleton, Shelby, IV 576
Siodmak, Curt, V 167
Siodmak, Robert, II 99, III 86
Siouxsie and the Banshees, I 86
Sipe, Brian, III 175
Sirk, Douglas, I 644
Siskel and Ebert, IV 18
Sissle, Noble, II 366
Sittin' on the Dock of the Bay, IV 190
Sitting Bull, I 545, II 488
Situation Comedy. See Sitcom
Six Flags, I 79
Six Million Dollar Man, I 255, 298, 721
Sixteen Candles, I 344
$64,000 Question, I 367, II 194, IV 151
60 Minutes, I 599, IV 712
Sixx, Nikki, III 419
Ska music, IV 195
Skaggs, Ricky, I 620
Skatemaster Tate, IV 429
Skelton, Red, I 222, 757, II 90, III 504
Skerrit, Tom, I 48
Skidmore, Owings and Merrill, IV 347
Skipper, I 171
Sky is Crying, V 39
Skylab, III 476
Skywalker, Luke, IV 512
Slam Dance, IV 577
Slapstick, I 39
Slash Records, III 198
Slater, Christian, I 344
Slaughter, I 279
Slaughter, Lenora, III 375
Slaughterhouse-Five, V 56, 191
Slavery, III 217, IV 124, 274
Sleeping Beauty, I 180
Sleepy Lagoon Case, IV 2
Slenderella, I 707
Slick, Grace, II 535
SlimFast, I 707
Slippery When Wet, I 315, II 381
Sliwa, Curtis, II 323
Sloan, Alfred, II 220
Sloan, John, I 122, II 448
Sloan, T. O'Connor, I 64
Sloane-Kettering Institute, III 76
Slot machines, II 189
Sly & the Family Stone, II 185
Smackout, II 89
Small Talk, III 579
Smart, David, II 40, V 30
Smart Set, I 263, III 343
SmartMoney, V 68
Smile, I 196
Smiles, Samuel, IV 708
Smith (Dr. Bob), Robert Holbrook, IV 708
Smith, Ada, I 23
Smith, Al, III 463

Smith, Alfred E., II 28
Smith, Anna, I 390
Smith, Aurlian, Jr., IV 223
Smith, Bessie, I 247, 292, II 515, III 414, 435,
    IV 155, 168
Smith, Buffalo Bob (Robert E.), II 459
Smith, Charles Martin, I 70
Smith, Dean, II 570
Smith, Dick, IV 642
Smith, E. E. "Doc," I 64, 129
Smith, Emmitt, I 654, IV 118
Smith, Fred, IV 441
Smith, G. Vance, II 549
Smith, Greg, I 722
Smith, Harry, II 126
Smith, Howard K., III 452
Smith, Jaclyn, I 480, II 79, III 48
Smith, James Todd, III 71
Smith, Joseph, I 646
Smith, Kate, I 6, IV 387, V 22, 75, 190
Smith, Mamie, I 292, II 529, IV 155
Smith, Margaret Chase, II 77
Smith, Michael W., II 288
Smith, Neal, I 595
Smith, Pat Falken, II 219
Smith, Patti, III 414, IV 201, V 39
Smith, Roger, III 408
Smith, Rosamond. See Oates, Joyce Carol
Smith, Susan, III 8
Smith, Tommie, I 609, III 537, 560
Smith, Will, II 487
Smithson, James, IV 441
Smithsonian Institute, I 479
Smokey and the Bandit, I 599, IV 205
Smothers Brothers, I 656, III 223, IV 22, 442
Smurfs, II 355, IV 318
Snead, Sam, II 262, IV 696
Sneakers, IV 637
Sneakers. See Tennis Shoes/Sneakers
Snider, Duke, III 263
Snoop Doggy Dogg, II 485, IV 176
Snoopy, IV 25
Snoopy, IV 45
Snow, Hank, I 133
Snow White and the Seven Dwarfs, I 90, 729
Snyder, Gary, II 535
Soccer moms, III 370
Social Security, I 3
Socialism, III 188
Socialist Party, I 679
Society for Human Rights, II 210, 213
Society for Psychical Research, IV 129
Society for the Suppression of Vice, III 227
Soda fountains, IV 592
Soda jerks, IV 453
Softball teams, III 141
Sokal, Alan, IV 101
Solanis, Valerie, V 81
Solberg, James, I 56
Soldier Blue, V 119
Some Like It Hot, II 398, IV 679
Somers, Brett, III 550
Somers, Suzanne, I 70, IV 371, 653
Somerset, I 99
Something about Amelia, III 234
"Somewhere Over the Rainbow," II 203
Sommers, Jamie, IV 424
Son of the Wolf, III 188
Sondheim, Stephen, I 359, III 458, IV 114
Song and Dance, IV 44
Songs for Sale, I 533
Sonic Youth, I 62, III 205, 414, V 39
Sonnenfeld, Barry, III 135
Sons of Daniel Boone, I 334
Sons of the Pioneers, IV 262, V 120
Sontag, Susan, I 415
Sony, V 46, 47, 66
Sophie's Choice, IV 567
Sophisticated Ladies, III 459
Sorbo, Kevin, II 397
"Sorcerer's Apprentice," II 67
Sorenson, Jackie, I 30

Sorvino, Paul, II 269
Sosa, Sammy, I 493, III 327
Soul Asylum, I 62
Soul Generals, I 369
"Soul Man," I 218
Soul music, I 477, II 154
Soul Stirrers, I 594
Soul Train, III 435, IV 451
Sound and the Fury, II 78
Sound of Music, I 282, III 459, IV 254
Sounder, I 279
Soundgarden, I 266, II 321, III 117
Sounds of Silence, IV 399
Sousa, John Philip, III 268
South Dakota, V 66
South Pacific, III 351, 459, IV 256
South Park, III 505
Southdale Mall, III 247
Southern Christian Leadership Conference (SCLC), I
    215, III 34, 266, IV 124
Southern cooking, II 319
Southern Publicity Association, III 64
Southern rock, III 220
Soviet Union, I 102, III 536
Space music, III 506
Space Needle, I 470
Spacek, Sissy, III 220
Spade, Sam, I 263, 693, III 249
Spader, James, I 344
Spaghetti Westerns, II 3, II 266, III 137, V 121
Spalding, A.G., I 329
Spam (unwanted e-mail), II 27
Spanier, Muggsy, II 525
Spanish Civil War, III 2
Spann, Otis, I 704
Spartacus, II 435
Spassky, Boris, II 104
Spawn, I 562
Speakeasy, IV 119
Special effects, III 210
Specialty Records, I 595, III 178, IV 207
Spector, Phil, I 1, 205, IV 619, 702
Speilberg, Steven, I 218
Spelling, Aaron, I 480, II 68, III 203, 386,
    IV 447, 645
Spencer Davis Group, I 355
Sperlich, Hal, III 370
Sperling, Abraham, IV 91
Spewack, Samuel and Bella, IV 96
Spheeris, Penelope, V 94
Spice Girls, IV 11, 620
Spider-Man, I 189, 562, II 486, III 124
Spider-Man, IV 470
Spider-Man, V 205
Spiegel, IV 10
Spiegel, Sam, II 472, III 105
Spiegelman, Art, I 562, III 308
Spiegelman, Art. See Maus
Spiegle, Dan, II 445
Spielberg, Steven, I 273, 534, II 43, 526, 581, IV
    166, 324, 715, V 191
Spike Jones Show, I 656
Spillane, Mickey, I 237, 551, 694, IV 11
Spiller, Bill, II 262
Spin, IV 34
"Spin the Black Circle," IV 27
Spinderella, IV 305
Spiner, Brent, II 487
Spink, Al, IV 483
Spink, C. C. Johnson, IV 484
Spink, Charlie, IV 484
Spink, J. G. Taylor, IV 484
Spinks, Leon, I 47
Spinney, Carol, IV 364
Spirit of '76, V 187
Spirit of St. Louis, III 167
Spirit, II 18
Spiritualists. See Psychics
Spock, Benjamin, IV 11, 173, 685
Spoilers, I 197
Sport utility vehicles, I 142
Sporting News, V 12

Sports Illustrated, I 285, III 211
Sportscenter, II 38
Sprecher, Jill, III 15
Sprecher, Karen, III 15
Springer, Jerry, I 668, 745, III 526
Springsteen, Bruce, I 782, II 329, III 73, 572, IV 471, 700
Sproul Hall, II 161
Sputnik, I 102, III 475, IV 314
Spy Who Came in from the Cold, I 238, 551, III 107
Squaw Man, V 120
Squeeze, V 41
Squier, George Owen, III 463
St. Denis, Ruth, I 686, IV 381
St. Elmo, IV 271
St. Elmo's Fire, I 344
St. Elsewhere, II 407
St. John, Adela Rogers, II 64, IV 54
St. Jude's Hospital, IV 645
St. Louis Blues, II 516
St. Louis Cardinals, I 435, 777, V 183, 217
St. Louis Exposition, II 484
St. Louis World's Fair, II 347
St. Martha of Bethany, II 572
St. Valentine's Day Massacre, I 426
Stafford, Jo, I 751
Stafford, Susan, V 123
Stag at Sharkey's, I 123
Stage, II 55
Stage Show, II 247
Stagecoach, II 134, 311, V 91, 119
Stagg, Amos Alonzo, Jr., I 555, IV 499
Stairway to Heaven, III 116
Stalag 17, II 426
Staley, A.E., I 492
Stalin, Joseph, I 569
Stalling, Carl, I 729
Stallone, Sylvester, IV 170, 246, 694
Stallworth, John, IV 61, 589
Stamos, John, IV 620
Stand, III 37
Standard Oil, I 758, IV 606
Stand-up comedy, III 144
Stanis, Bernadette, II 267
Stanislavsky Method, The, I 342
Stanley, II 333
Stanley Cup, II 417, 460, 467, III 574
Stanley, Paul, III 42
Stanley, Ralph, IV 427
Stanton, Elizabeth Cady, II 84
Stanton, Harry Dean, I 48
Stanwyck, Barbara, IV 615
Star is Born, II 204
Star Spangled Banner, IV 441
Star system, I 34, II 468
Star Trek, I 298, IV 11, 44, 251, V 203
Star Trek: The Next Generation, I 721, IV 509, 596
Star Wars, I 71
Star Wars, I 98, 153, 275, 282, 298, 643, II 131, III 209, IV 686, 715
Starbird, Daryl, II 456
Starbucks, I 547, 775
Starday Records, II 561
Stardust, I 436
Stardust, Ziggy, I 86
Stark, John, II 567
Starkweather, Charles, I 424
Starlight Express, III 181
Starr, Bart, I 339, II 301, III 185, IV 118
Starr, Kenneth, III 149, IV 372
Starr, Maurice, III 510
Starr, Ringo, I 203
Stars, IV 17
"Stars and Stripes Forever!," IV 465
Stars on Ice, II 484
Starstruck Entertainment, III 326
Staten Island Ferry, III 527
Statue of Liberty, III 490
Staubach, Roger, I 556, 654, IV 118
Stax/Volt Records, I 318, IV 189, 459, 460
Staying Alive, IV 694
Steamboat Willie, I 729

Stearns, George Luther, III 476
Steeger, Henry, I 110
Steel Magnolias, IV 18
Steele, Danielle, I 236
Stefano, Joseph, III 579, IV 130
Steffens, Lincoln, III 319
Steichen, Edward, III 390
Steichen, Lillian (Paula), IV 306
Steiff, Richard, IV 617
Steiger, Rod, IV 76
Stein, Gertrude, II 387, III 390
Stein, Joe, IV 196
Steinbeck, John, I 140, II 290, 388, III 74, IV 284
Steinbrenner III, George M., I 234, II 520, III 521, V 209
Steinem, Gloria, III 434, 489
Steiner, Max, II 264
Stella Dallas, II 56, IV 506
Stempel, Herbert, II 194, IV 151
Stengel, Casey, II 138, V 183
Steptoe & Son, II 148, IV 310
Stereographs. See Stereoscopes
Sterling, Annette, III 279
Sterling, Ford, III 24
Sterling Homes, I 455
Stern, David, I 256, III 478
Stern, Howard, III 164, IV 386, 600
Stern, Stewart, IV 186
Sternbach, Leo, V 20
Sternberg, Joseph von, I 708
Steve Allen Show, I 656
Steve Roper, III 294
Stevens, David, IV 274
Stevens, George, IV 613
Stevens, Leslie, III 579
Stevens, Morton, II 376
Stevens, Ray, IV 551
Stevens, Wallace, III 23
Stevenson, Mickey, III 420
Stevenson, Parker, II 361
Stewart, A. T., I 688
Stewart, Anita, III 309
Stewart, Bill, IV 679
Stewart, James, I 598, II 415, 506, III 253, IV 184, V 120
Stewart, John, III 40
Stewart, Martha, III 48
Stewart, Mel, II 536
Stewart, Michael, II 384
Stewart, Patrick, IV 509
Stewart, Potter, IV 93
Stewart, Sylvester, IV 437
Stewart, Wynn, II 335
Stickley, Gustav, I 387
Stieglitz, Alfred, I 466, III 390, 553
Still, Clyfford, I 11
Still Crazy After All These Years, IV 404
Stiller and Meara, IV 348
Stiller, Ben, IV 535
Stillman's Gym, I 332
Stills, Stephen, I 381
Stipe, Michael, IV 201
Stockton, Les, III 454
Stockton, Pudgy, III 453
Stohl, Ellen, I 722
Stojko, Elvis, IV 430
Stoker, Bram, I 760, V 22
Stokowski, Leopold, II 66
Stoller, Mike, I 351, III 30, 422, IV 208
Stoltz, Eric, I 344
Stompin' at the Savoy, IV 323
Stone Canyon Band, III 500
Stone, Ezra, II 393
Stone, Harry, II 286
Stone, Jesse, III 2, IV 208
Stone, Lucy, II 85
Stone, Matt, IV 466
Stone, Milburn, II 327
Stone Mountain, Georgia, III 64
Stone, Oliver, I 750, II 545, III 17, 493, IV 69
Stone, Sly, IV 198
Stonewall Rebellion, I 416, II 213, 215, IV 373

Stoney, George, I 571
Stooges, I 266, IV 82, 142
Stookey, Noel Paul, IV 42
Stop Making Sense, IV 602
Stop the Music, II 193
"Stopping by Woods on a Snowy Evening," II 177
Storyville, I 734
Storz, Todd, IV 679
Stotz, Carl, III 174
Stowe, Harriet Beecher, I 134, 271, V 222
Straight Alta-Pazz, III 35
Straight Talkin' American Government Party, IV 22
Straight, Willard D. and Dorothy, III 514
Strait, George, I 623
Strand Theater, III 426
Strange Brew, I 213
"Strange Brew," III 25
Strangers on a Train, II 415
Strasberg, Lee, II 120, III 400
Strassman, Marcia, V 105
Stratemeyer, Edna, IV 549
Stratemeyer, Edward, I 300, II 360, III 473
Stratemeyer Syndicate, I 300, II 579, III 474, IV 674
Stratemeyer Syndicate. See Stratemeyer, Edward
Stratton, Monty, I 722
Strauss, Joseph, II 259
Strauss, Levi, II 533
Stravinsky, Igor, II 67
Strawberry Field, III 159
Strawberry Shortcake, IV 686
Stray Cats, III 515
Strayhorn, Billy, II 24
Streamlined Cooking, II 572
Streamlining, II 492
Streep, Meryl, I 54, 350
Street and Smith, I 263, IV 139, 331, 375, 548
Streetcar Named Desire, I 342, V 146
Streisand, Barbra, I 231, 348, II 216, 384, III 460
Strength & Health, I 306, II 317
Strike It Rich, II 193
Striptease, III 119, IV 31
Strode, Woody, IV 118
Stroheim, Erich von, II 298
Strohs, I 210
Strong, Edward, II 161
Stuart, Mary, IV 346
Student League for Industrial Democracy, IV 563
Student Nonviolent Coordinating Committee (SNCC), I 164, 585, III 34, 245, 266, 511, IV 124, 561
Student Peace Union (SPU), IV 125
Students for a Democratic Society (SDS), I 495, 585, II 444, III 512, IV 125, 561, V 95, 215
Studio 54, I 727, V 82
Studio Basic Agreement, I 13
Studio One, III 213
Studio system, II 433
Studs' Place, IV 639
Study in Scarlet, I 755
Sturgeon, Theodore, IV 332
Sturges, John, III 240
Sturges, Preston, IV 343, V 22
Styne, Jule, III 459
Styrofoam, IV 67
Styron, William, I 461
Sub Pop Records, II 322
Suburbia, II 357, III 247
Such, Alec John, I 315
"Sucker MCs," IV 288
Suddenly Last Summer, IV 614
Sugarhill Gang, IV 174
Suicide, IV 540
Sullavan, Margaret, II 127, IV 532
Sullivan, Ed, III 259, 298, IV 1, 419
Sullivan, John L., I 330, 332, 601, II 555
Sullivan, Louis, II 491, IV 433
Sullivan, Maxine, V 22
Sullivan, Pat, II 83
Sullivan, Wiki, II 430
Sullivan's Travels, III 80
Summer camps, I 418
Summer of '42, I 70

"Summer of Love," I 454
Summer Stock, II 203
Summerall, Pat, III 232
Sun Also Rises, II 387
Sun Records, I 449, III 154, 572, IV 106
Suncoast Bargaineers, II 438
Sundance Film Festival, I 642
Sundance Institute, The, IV 190
Sunday, Billy, II 47, III 331
Sunday in the Park with George, IV 455
Sundblom, Haddon, I 541
Sunless tanning market, IV 604
Sunset Boulevard, II 99, 426, III 182, 216, 460, VI
    634, V 99, 136
Super Bowl, I 493, II 301, III 232, 309, 402, 471,
    483, IV 23, 118
Super Mario, V 46
Superfly, I 278, III 310, 439
Superfund site, I 311
Superior Physique Association, I 307
Superman, I 189, 432, 561, 671, 739, II 18, IV 141,
    350, 474, V 189
Supermodels, I 624, IV 488, V 54
Support Your Local Sheriff, V 121
Supreme Court, I 93, IV 607
Supremes, II 241, III 279
Surf music, I 196
Surfers, IV 585
Surfing, IV 585
Surprised by Joy, III 151
Survey Graphic, III 182
Susann, Jacqueline, IV 373
Suspense, I 463, IV 161
Suspicion, II 415
Sutcliffe, Stu, I 203
Sutherland, Donald, I 721
Sutherland, Kiefer, I 344
Sutton, Margaret, II 578
Suzy the dolphin, II 118
Swaggart, Jimmy, III 153, 337, 410, IV 71,
    IV 200, 626
Swan, Harry, III 143
Swann, Lynn, IV 61
Swanson, II 179, IV 706
Swanson, Gloria, I 685, III 428, IV 634
Swayze, John Cameron, I 352, IV 661
Sweeney Todd, The Demon Barber of Fleet Street, III
    460, IV 455
Sweet Charity, II 144
"Sweet Home Alabama," III 220
Sweet Jane, V 40
Sweet Jesus, Preacher Man, I 279
Sweet Sweetback's Baaadassss Song, I 279
Swift, Barton, IV 674
Swift, Wesley, V 129
Swing Era, II 23, III 364, IV 156
Swinging, IV 374
Swingtime Records, IV 459
Swit, Loretta, III 296
Switzer, Barry, I 654, IV 118
Switzer, Carl "Alfalfa," III 578
Swoon, III 139
Sydell, Rose, I 390
Sylvester and Tweety, I 277
Symphony, IV 464
Syncom II, IV 315
Syndicate theatre, I 573

T. Rex, II 249
Tabloid television, III 338
Taco Bell, II 73
Taco Time, II 73
Taco Tito's, II 73
Tailhook, IV 372
"Take Five," I 372
Take 6, II 274
Take It or Leave It, II 193
"Take Me to the River," IV 602
Take the Money and Run, I 54
Take Off Pounds Sensibly (TOPS), I 707
Takei, George, II 253, IV 508
Tale of Two Cities, IV 712

Tales from the Crypt, I 561
Tales of the City, III 307
Tales of the South Pacific, III 351
Talk shows, II 159
Talkartoons, I 239
Talkies, V 8
Talking Heads, III 516
Talman, William, I 395
Tambor, Jeffrey, III 91
Taming of the Shrew, III 406
Tanaka, Tomoyuki, II 252
Tandy, Jessica, IV 554
Tannen, Deborah, IV 92
Tanny, Vic, III 454
Tapert, Ron, II 397
Tapestry, III 30
Tarantino, Quentin, I 150, III 13, 135, 216, 494,
    IV 138, 694
Tarbell, Ida, III 318, IV 521
Target, III 47
Tarkington, Booth, II 265
Tarnower, Herbert, I 707
Tarzan, I 396, IV 139, V 104
A Taste of Honey, I 57
Tastee Freez, II 73
Tate, Sharon, III 262
Tate-LaBianca murders, III 262
Tatham, Julie, I 491
Tatum, Reece "Goose," II 364
Tauchnitz Books, IV 10
Taupin, Bernie, II 550
Tavernier, Jules, V 120
Taxi Driver, I 673, II 145, III 336, IV 337, V 51
Tayback, Vic, I 47
Tayi, Auda abu, III 105
Taylor, Buck, II 327
Taylor, Deems, II 66
Taylor, Eddie, II 441
Taylor, Elizabeth, I 282, II 105, 219, III 96,
    IV 63, 618
Taylor, Fred, III 49
Taylor, Jim, IV 118
Taylor, Mick, I 355
Taylor, Paul, I 166
Taylor, Ron and Valerie, II 528
Taylor, William Desmond, II 432, IV 398
Tchaikovsky, Peter Ilyich, II 67
Teague, Walter Dorwin, II 492
Teamsters, III 73
Technicolor, II 128, III 339
Ted Weems Orchestra, I 574
Teddy Bear, IV 685
Teds, III 384
Teen, IV 313
Teen idols, I 66, 243, 452, II 53, IV 298, 412
Teflon, IV 66
Tejano, III 270
Tejano music, IV 354
TeKanawa, Kiri, III 460
Telegraph, IV 624
Telephone, IV 53
Telephone-booth stuffing, I 553
Televangelism, II 47, 182, IV 587
Television, II 96
Tell Me a Riddle, III 558
Tell Me How Long the Train's Been Gone, I 162
Tell Them Willie Boy is Here, II 435
Telstar, IV 314
Temple, Shirley, I 498, III 577, IV 289, 605, V 225
Temptations, III 420, IV 234
Ten, IV 26
Ten Commandments, I 280, 375, II 400
Tenant farmers, III 142
"Tender Years," II 562
Tennessee Supreme Court, IV 336
Tennis, II 231
Teratology, II 158
Terkel, Studs, II 516
Term limitations, V 138
Terms of Endearment, I 365, III 331
"Terraplane Blues," II 558

Terry and the Pirates, I 767, V 191
Teschemacher, Frank, I 734
Tesh, John, V 211
Testorf, Helga, V 199
Tewes, Lauren, III 204
Texaco Star Theater, III 505
Texas, I 99
Texas Chainsaw Massacre, IV 435
Texas Rangers, IV 298
Texas v. Johnson, II 111
Tex-Mex, III 198
Tex-Mex Music. See Tejano Music
Thalberg, Irving, III 309, 347, IV 356
Thanksgiving, I 689
Tharp, Twyla, I 166, 180
That Girl, IV 420, 645
"That Silver-Haired Daddy of Mine," I 142
That Touch of Mink, III 336
That Was the Week That Was, I 42, 54
"That's Amore," III 280
Thaw, Evelyn Nesbit, V 129
Thaw, Harry, V 129
Theater of Pain, III 419
Theatre Syndicate, I 357
Thelma and Louise, II 5, III 13
Them, I 355
They Call Me MISTER Tibbs, I 279
They Shoot Horses, Don't They?, III 319
Thief of Bagdad, V 172
Thimble Theatre, IV 87
Thin Man, II 296, 349, III 207, IV 102
Thin Red Line, V 78, 191
Thinner, III 38
Third Reich, II 424
Third Wave, IV 668
Thirty-Nine Steps, II 415
This Gun For Hire, III 75
"This Guy's in Love with You," I 57
"This Land Is Your Land," I 445
This Week with David Brinkley, I 353
Thomas, Clarence, I 93, III 337, 548, IV 371
Thomas, Clarence. See Anita Hill-Clarence Thomas
    Senate Hearings
Thomas, Danny, III 111
Thomas, Dave, II 73
Thomas, Henry, II 44
Thomas, Irma, III 513
Thomas, Isiah, II 554
Thomas, J. Parnell, I 272
Thomas, Jonathan Taylor, IV 620
Thomas, Marlo, IV 645
Thomas, Philip Michael, III 349
Thomas, Richard, V 74
Thomas Show, Danny, IV 645
Thomas, Tony, IV 645
Thomas, William Henry "Buckwheat," III 578
Thompson and Her Blondes, Lydia, I 388
Thompson, Bill, II 90
Thompson, Daley, III 152
Thompson, Edward, III 211
Thompson, Hunter S., II 370, 385, IV 268, V 68
Thompson, Jack, IV 716
Thompson, James Walter, II 511
Thompson, Kay, V 139
Thompson, Ruth Plumly, I 191
Thompson, Scott, III 91
Thompson sextuplets, I 720
Thompson sub-machine gun, II 103
Thompson, Uncle Jimmy, II 286
Thomson, Bobby, I 778
Thor, III 124
Thoreau, Henry David, I 418, II 10
Thorndike, Dr., I 694
Thorpe, Jim, I 555, III 560, IV 117
Thorsen, Charles, I 383
Thorson, Linda, I 145
Thorson, Scott, III 157
Thrasher, IV 429
3-D Imagery. See Stereoscopes
Three Dimension Comics, IV 529
Three Mile Island, Pennsylvania, I 500
Three Stooges, The, III 24

Three's Company, III 505
Thriller, II 514, 519
Thum, Joe, I 329
Thumb, General Tom, IV 212
Thunder on Sycamore Street, IV 565
Thunder Road, IV 537
Thunderbird, II 137
Thurber, James, III 522
Thurman, Uma, I 145
Tibetan Freedom Festival, I 201
Ticketmaster, II 438, IV 27
Tickticktick, I 279
Tiegs, Cheryl, IV 488
Tiffany, Charles Lewis, IV 655
Tiffany, Louis Comfort, IV 656
''Tijuana Bibles,'' V 4
Till, Emmett, II 544
Till the Clouds Roll By, II 203
Tiller Girls, IV 242
Tillie the Toiler, V 156
Tillie's Punctured Romance, IV 358
Tillstrom, Burr, III 68
Time, III 160, 527, IV 36, 697
Time to Kill, II 318
Time Warner, I 319, 728, III 210, 211 IV 705
Timely Comics, III 124
Tin Pan Alley, I 247, 698, II 566, III 30, 460
Tinker, Grant, III 292
Tinklenberg, Janie, V 198
Tiny Tim, I 444
''Tip-Toe Thru' the Tulips with Me,'' IV 661
Tipton, Glenn, II 577
Titanic, I 283, 298, 700, IV 312, 663, V 159
Title IX, II 86, IV 211
Titletown, USA, II 300
TNT Jackson, I 279
To Have and Have Not, II 388
To Kill a Mockingbird, IV 30, 48
To Sir, with Love, IV 76
*To Wong Foo, Thanks for Everything, Julie
    Newmar*, I 764
Toast of the Town, IV 419, 571
Toasting (music style), IV 196
Toastmaster General, II 542
Tobacco Road, I 412
Today, I 668, III 59, IV 712
Today's Children, IV 446
Todd, John, III 190
Todd, Mike, II 105, IV 614
Toffler, Alvin, III 165
Toguri, Iva, IV 669
Toho Co. Ltd., II 252
Tokyo Rose, I 767
Toland, Gregg, I 514
Toland, John, I 316
Tolkien, J. R. R., III 108, IV 11, 332
Tom and Jerry, II 355
Tom of Finland, I 132, IV 59
Tom Swift, IV 548
Tomjanovich, Rudy, III 478
Tomlin, Lily, III 99, IV 197, 326
Tommy, I 576, II 543, V 131
Tommy gun, II 103
Tompkin, Dmitri, II 400
Tone, Franchot, I 625
Tonight Show, I 40, 52, 54, 95, 444, 668, II 507, III
    132, 144, IV 1, 220, V 139
''Tonight We Love,'' III 281
Tonto, III 189
Tony Award, I 655, III 216, 410, 446
Too Much Joy, IV 716
''Too Much, Too Little, Too Late,'' III 306
Toombs, Roderick, IV 60
Toomer, Jean, IV 710
Tooth of Crime, IV 383
Tootsie, II 421
Top 40, I 485, II 381
Topps Chewing Gum, Inc., I 194
Torch Song Trilogy, II 96, IV 678
Tork, Peter, III 394
Torme, Mel, II 108, III 259
Torn, Rip, III 91

Torrence, Frederick Ridgely, II 366
Torres, Tico, I 315
Torrio, Johnny, I 425, III 237
Tors, Ivan, II 118
Tosh, Peter, III 275, IV 196
Tosti, Don, IV 2
Totino's, IV 63
Touch of Evil, III 256
Tour de France, III 130
Tour of Duty, V 51
Tournament of the Americas, I 767
Tournament of Roses, IV 275
Toussaint, Allan, III 513
Towering Inferno, I 724
Town Hall Concerts, I 734
Townshend, Pete, II 21, IV 237, V 131
Toynbee, Arnold, V 187
Tracy, Spencer, II 395, 458, IV 76
Traf-o-Data, III 353
Trail of the Lonesome Pine, II 128
Trainspotting, IV 82
Transamerica Pyramid, IV 433
Transworld Skateboarding, IV 429
Transylvania, III 213
Trash TV, IV 218
Traubel, Helen, I 216
Travanti, Daniel J., II 407
Traveling Wilburys, I 783
Travers, Mary, IV 42
Travers, P. L. (Pamela Lyndon), III 291
Travis McGee series, III 226
Travis, Randy, I 262
Travolta, John, I 727, III 581, IV 81, 139, 320, 501,
    617, V 105
Treasure of the Sierra Madre, V 118
Treasury Relief Art Project, V 180
Trebek, Alex, II 541
Treemonisha, II 568
Treloar, Al, I 306
Tremaine, F. Orlin, IV 331
Tremayne, Les, I 463
Trendle, George W., III 189
Trevor, Clare, IV 497
Trevor, Elleston, I 551
T-Rex, I 86
Triangle Club, IV 532
Triangle Film Corporation, IV 358
Triangle Publications, IV 365
Tribune, IV 285
Trigger, IV 263
Trilling, Lionel, I 309
Trine, Ralph Waldo, IV 90
Trio, IV 18
Trip, II 4, IV 128
Triple Crown, The, III 19
Tripp, Linda, III 149, IV 516
Trivial Pursuit, I 297, IV 13
Trivouldas, Peter, I 323
Tropic of Cancer, III 367
Trouble Man, I 279
Troup, Bobby, IV 285
Trout Fishing in America, I 345
Trudeau, Gary, I 747, IV 646
Trudeau, Gary. See *Doonesbury*
True Colors, III 100
True Confessions, I 582
True Experiences, I 582
True Grit, V 93
True Love and Romances, I 582
True Romances, I 582
True Stories, I 581
True Story, III 226
Truffaut, François, IV 185
Truman Doctrine, I 549
Truman, Harry S., II 15, 58, III 2, 225, V 67, 159
Trumbo, Dalton, I 272, 429, II 434
Truth about De-evolution, I 697
Truth or Consequences, II 16, 193
TSR Inc., I 65
Tsuburaya, Eiji, II 253
Tubb, Ernest, III 219
Tucker, Benjamin Ricketson, III 157

Tucker, Karla Faye, I 425
Tucker, Maureen, V 39
Tucker, Wilson, IV 332
Tugwell, Rexford G., I 589
Tunnell, Emlen, IV 118
Tunney, Gene, I 685
Tupper, Earl, IV 700
Tupperware, IV 66
Turner and Hooch, IV 44
Turner, Big Joe, III 3, IV 207
Turner Classic Movies, IV 705
Turner, Francis, II 404
Turner, Frederick Jackson, III 188
Turner, Ike, III 27, IV 208, 236
Turner, Lana, IV 48, 370
Turner, Ted, I 404, 537, III 437, 505, V 207
Turow, Scott, II 318
Turpin, Ben, IV 397
Tuskegee Institute, I 260
TV Dinners, II 179
TV Nation, III 408
Twain, Mark, II 387, 424, III 342
Tweed, William W. ''Boss,'' IV 77
Tweedy, Jeff, I 59
Twelve Angry Men, II 127
Twenties, II 111
Twentieth Century-Fox, I 149, 282, II 487, III 260,
    IV 340, 565, 614, V 225
Twenty-One, II 194, IV 151
20/20, I 111, 754
21 Jump Street, I 9, III 386
21st Amendment, IV 119
Twerski, Abraham, IV 92
Twiggy, I 86, 415, IV 9
Twilight Zone, II 494, III 65, IV 361
Twin Peaks, III 217, IV 116
Twist, I 484, 485, IV 36, 592
Twister, I 297
Twitty, Conway, III 219
Twixt Twelve and Twenty, I 320
Two of Us, I 300
2001: A Space Odyssey, I 48, 527
2010: Odyssey Two, I 527
2,000 Year Old Man, IV 196
Two-Face, I 703
2Pacalypse Now, IV 377
Ty Corporation, I 198
Tyler, Steven, I 32
Tyson, Mike, I 330, II 436, III 337
Tytla, Vladimir, II 67

U2, I 62, III 27
UCLA Bruins, I 186
UFOs, III 476, IV 282, V 204
Ugly American, I 551, V 49
Ulrey, Dale Conner, III 294
Ultra High Frequency (UHF) television stations, I
    404, IV 595
Ultra Slim-Fast, III 94
Ulvaeus, Bjorn, I 4, III 460
Umbrellas, Japan--U.S.A. 1984-91, I 507
Unabomber, IV 34
Unbearable Lightness of Being, III 45
Uncle Jim's Question Bee, II 193
Uncle Tom's Cabin, I 209, 271, 357, IV 395
Uncle Tupelo, I 59
Uncle Wiggily, IV 549
Underground comics, I 562, 178, III 308
Understanding Media, III 329
Unforgiven, II 402, V 121
Unidentified Flying Objects. See UFOs (Unidentified
    Flying Objects)
Unification Church, I 647, III 405
Unified Against Genocide, III 35
Unitarian Church, III 508
Unitas, Johnny, IV 116
United Artists, I 476, III 348, IV 55, 246, 397, 711
United Farm Workers (UFW), I 482, III 73
United Nations, II 549
United Negro Improvement Association
    (UNIA), II 205
United Press International, I 352, V 160

United Service Organization, III 82
United Soccer Association (USA), IV 449
United States Football Association (USFA), IV 449
United States Football League (USFL), III 483, IV 118
United States Golf Association (USGA), II 262
United States Haitian immigration policy, I 125
United States Information Agency, IV 313
United States Justice Department, II 443, III 354
United States Marine Band, IV 463
United States Open, I 124, III 531
United States Science Pavilion, I 470
United States v. Dickerson, III 374
Univac, III 169
Universal Cheerleading Association, I 487
Universal Peace Mission Movement, II 75
Universal Product Code, II 482
Universal Studios, I 7, 149, 760, II 432, 438, 527, IV 340, 396, 565, 566
University of Alabama, III 471
University of California at Berkeley, II 161
University of California at Los Angeles (UCLA), I 8, V 174
University of Chicago, IV 499
University of Nevada-Las Vegas, IV 606
University of North Carolina, II 570
University of Notre Dame, IV 243
University of Washington, I 40
University of Wisconsin, IV 135
University Players, IV 532
UNIX, II 495
Unplugged, III 437
Unsafe at Any Speed, III 469
Unser, Al, II 149, 491
Unser, Bobby, I 84
Unsinkable Molly Brown, IV 662
Untermeyer, Louis, V 122
U.P. Trail, II 311
Updike, John, III 426
Upp, Virginia Vann, IV 396
Urban Cowboy, I 623, IV 694
Urban Outfitters, V 229
Uris, Leon, V 191
Urkel, II 62
U.S. Forest Service, II 30
U.S. Highway 66, IV 284
U.S. Olympic Basketball Team, IV 225
U.S. Olympic Dream Team, II 554
USA Basketball, I 767
USA Networks, Inc., II 438, 484
USSR, I 569
USA Today, I 124, III 33, IV 35, V 68

Vail, Theodore, I 131
Valachi, Joseph, III 239
Valdez, Luis, II 19, V 16
Valens, Ritchie, I 249, 354, II 430, III 71, 198, IV 619, V 15
Valentine, Helen, IV 365
Valentino, Rudolph, III 428, IV 369, 396, 710
Valiant Years, I 144
Vallee, Rudy, I 178, 240, II 393, IV 440, 618
Vallely, Henry E., II 512
Valley of the Dolls, IV 373, 586
Vampyre, V 22
Van Alen, William, I 507
Van Andel, Jay, I 80
Van Brocklin, Norm, III 232, IV 118
Van Buren, Abigail, I 26, 28
Van Damme, Jean-Claude, IV 259
Van Dine, S.S., I 694
Van Doren, Charles, II 194, IV 151
Van Doren, Mamie, III 259, IV 370
Van Dyke, Dick, III 292, IV 196
Van Dyke, W. S., IV 103
Van Dyne, Edith, I 191
Van Halen, II 381, III 279
Van Halen, Alex, V 26
Van Lierdes, Luc, II 503
Van Pebbles, Mario, I 265
Van Vechten, Carl, II 366
Van Zant, Ronnie, III 220

Vance, Philo, I 694, IV 103, V 24
Vance, Vivian, II 157, 478
Vancouver, Washington, II 76
Vanderbilt, Gloria, IV 541
Vanderbilt, Harold S., I 349
Vandover and the Brute, III 541
Vanilla Ice, III 510, IV 11
Vanishing American, II 311
Vanishing Point, II 5
Vanity Fair, I 219, 466, 578, 624, 758, II 45, III 89, 159, 407
Van-Tine, Gordon, I 455
Vanzetti, Bartolomeo, I 424
Varèse, Edgard, V 226
Vardon, Harry, II 262
Varga girl, IV 94
Vargas, Alberto, V 31
Vargas, Antonio, IV 59
Varsi, Diane, IV 48
Varsity Spirit Corporation, I 487
Vasko, Elmer ''Moose,'' II 417
Vatican II reforms, III 127
Vaudeville, I 423, II 226, III 59, IV 263, 578, 692, V 227
Vaughan, Jimmie, V 37
Vaughan, Sarah, II 10, III 259
Vaughan, Stevie Ray, I 56, 165, V 238
Vaughn, Robert, III 253
Vedder, Eddie, II 321, IV 26
Vee Jay label, I 164
Veeck, Bill, IV 5
Velcro, IV 66
Velez, Lupe, V 105
Velvet Goldmine, II 249
Velvet Underground, I 355, IV 82, 142, 192, 201, V 81
Venice Beach, III 455
Ventura, Jesse ''The Body,'' IV 60
Verdon, Gwen, III 459, IV 96
Vereen, Ben, II 544
Verne, Jules, I 64, IV 330
Versace, Gianni, I 303
Vertigo, II 415, IV 534
Vertigo comic books, IV 309
Verve, II 40
Very Necessary, IV 306
VH-1, I 67
Viacom, III 435, IV 595
Vice Versa, II 210
Vicious, Sid, IV 142
Victor Company, IV 312
Victor/Victoria, III 257, IV 678
Victoria, Queen, V 100
Vidal, Gore, II 41, III 243, IV 50
Video games, III 233
''Video Recordings Bill,'' IV 436
Vidor, King, I 280
Vietnam, I 152, 495, 570, II 447, III 241, IV 611
Vietnam: A Television History, IV 137
Vietnam veterans, I 721
Vietnam War, I 299, 681, 761, II 411, III 17, 34, 335, 512, IV 125, 170, 479, 562, 563, V 75, 123, 160
View-Master, IV 529
Viking Lander mission, IV 301
Villa, Beto, IV 623
Village People, I 727
Village Vanguard, V 97
Village Voice, I 61
Villard, Oscar Garrison, III 477
Villechaize, Herve, II 68
Vincent, John Heyl, I 481
Vinson, Eddie ''Cleanhead,'' I 558
Vinyl, IV 66
Virgil Tibbs, I 279
Virginia Minstrels, II 271
Virginia Slims International, III 28
Virginian, I 237, V 162
VISA, I 628
VistaVision, I 71
Vitamin B17. See Laetrile
Vitaphone, IV 711

Vitology, IV 27
Viva Zapata, IV 522
Vocalese, III 258
Vogue, I 577, 624, III 528, Vogue, V 29
Voice of America, IV 313
Voight, Jon, I 458, III 358
Volkswagen, III 370
Vollmer, Joan, I 397
Volstead Act, I 211, II 359, IV 119
Von Bingen, Abbess Hildegard, III 508
Von Ryan's Express, V 191
Von Sternberg, Josef, I 85
Von Stroheim, Erich, IV 566
Von Trapp, Maria, IV 462
Vonnegut, Kurt, Jr., I 488, IV 11, 223, V 191
Voorhees, Donald, I 216
Voting Rights Act of 1965, III 34, 266
Voyager spacecraft, IV 301
Vreeland, Diana, V 53
VS., IV 27

Wabash Cannonball, I 445
Wackiest Ship in the Army, V 192
Wacky Packages, III 308
Wade, Virginia, II 49
Wag the Dog, II 421
Waggoner, Lyle, IV 72
Wagner, Honus, I 183, III 202
Wagner, Lindsey, I 255
Wagoner, Porter, IV 18
Wahlberg, Donnie, III 510
Wahlberg, Garry, III 550
Wailers, III 275, IV 196
''Waist Deep in the Big Muddy,'' IV 352
Waite, Ralph, V 74
Waiting for Godot, III 77
Wake of the Ferry II, I 122
''Wake Up and Dream,'' IV 96
''Wake Up Little Susie,'' II 48
Walden Books, III 48
''Walk on the Wild Side,'' V 41
''Walk This Way,'' IV 288
Walken, Christopher, I 681, V 174
Walker, Alice, III 441
Walker, Doak, IV 118
Walker, Frank, I 1
Walker, George, V 61, 140
Walker, Jerry Jeff, I 383
Walker, Jimmie, II 267
Walker, John Brisben, III 301
Walker, Mickey, II 297
Walker Report, I 495
Walkman, I 575
Wall Street Journal, II 496, IV 35
Wallace, Edgar, III 31
Wallace, George, III 220, V 130
Wallace, Hal, III 250
Wallace, Lew, I 219
Wallace, Mike, IV 426
Wallace, William Roy DeWitt, IV 177
Wallach, Eli, II 266
Waller, Charlie, I 617
Waller, Fats, I 184, III 459, V 22
Waller, Robert James, I 350
Wallis, Hal, III 152
Wal-Mart, I 689, III 47
Walmsley, Jon, V 74
Walsh, Bill, I 370, IV 118
Walsh, Frank, IV 241
Walsh, John, II 38
Walsh, Lawrence, II 501
Walsh, Richard, I 375
Walters, Barbara, I 34, III 150, IV 666, 712
Walton, Bill, V 174
Walton, Sam, III 47, V 69
Wambaugh, Joseph, I 238
Wanamaker, John, I 689
Wandrei, Donald, I 692
WAR (White Aryan Resistance), V 130
War and Peace, I 280, V 49
War of the Worlds, I 724, II 296, III 2, 504, IV 159, 161, V 109

War Relocation Authority, II 525
Warbucks, Daddy, I 96
Ward, Burt, I 190
Ward, Clara, II 154
Ward, Evelyn, I 452
Ward, Jay, IV 248
Ward, Montgomery, IV 346
Wardell, Dave, IV 201
Warhol, Andy, I 415, 591, 648, II 152, 248, 363, III 204, 369, IV 81, 128, 192, 689, V 40
Warner Brothers, I 135, 145, 276, 149, 308, 410, 448, 564, II 33, 48, 56, 142, 202, 432, 531, III 250, 260, 429, IV 48, 112, 229, 641, 707
Warner, Glenn "Pop," I 556
Warner, Jack, I 108
Warner, John, IV 615
Warner, Marina, II 583
Warner, Pop, IV 275
Warner Records, V 229
Warner-Seven Arts, II 36
Warren Commission, II 545, III 17
Warren, Earl, I 185, III 225
Warren, Harry, II 142
Warren, Michael, II 62
Warren, Robert Penn, III 191
Warshawski, V. I., I 694, IV 12
Warwick, Dionne, II 458, IV 84
Washington, Booker T., I 260, 772, III 26
Washington, George, I 544, V 83
Washington, Kenny, IV 118
Washington, Kermit, III 478
Washington Post, III 527, IV 599, V 86
Washington Redskins, III 186, IV 117, 581
Watches, IV 661
Water Nymph, IV 358
Waterdance, I 722
Waterfield, Bob, IV 118
Watergate, I 430, II 499, III 337, 335, V 84
Waterloo, I 4
Waters, Ethel, I 209, 241, III 320, IV 421
Waters, John, I 416, 731, II 469, III 78, IV 81, 409
Waters, Muddy, I 292, II 21, 559, IV 208, 345
Waters, Roger, IV 58
Waterworld, I 283
Watson, Ivory, II 493
Watson, Thomas, Jr., II 482
Watson, Thomas J., Sr., II 481
Watson, Thomas, IV 624
Watson, Tom, II 262, IV 86
Watters, Lu, I 734
Watts, III 245, IV 157
Watts, Charlie, I 355, IV 269
Wax: Or the Discovery of Television Among the Bees, II 496
Way of All Flesh, IV 10
Way to Rainy Mountain, III 392
Way We Were, IV 190
Wayans, Damon, V 91
Wayans, Keenen Ivory, I 280, II 486, VI 126, V 91
Wayans, Kim, V 91
Wayans, Marlon, V 91
Wayans, Shawn, V 91
Wayne, John, II 134, 327, 426, 533, III 85, 253, IV 70, 339, 346, 381, 497, 499, V 77, 120, 191
Wayne's World, IV 321
"We Are the World," I 215
"We Hold These Truths," I 605
We Shall Overcome, IV 352
Weather Underground, IV 562
Weatherwax, Rudd, III 95
Weaver, Buck, I 267
Weaver, Dennis, II 327
Weaver, Pat, I 52
Weaver, Sigourney, I 48
Weaver, Sylvester "Pat," I 668, IV 666
Weavers, IV 351
Webb, Chick, I 248, II 108, IV 322
Webb, Jack, I 549, 766
Weber, Bruce, III 103, IV 673
Webster, Ben, III 3
Webster, Harold Tucker, I 450
Wedding Singer, IV 205

Weekly World News, III 482
Weider, Ben, I 307
Weider, Joe, I 306, II 317, III 453
Weidman, Charles, I 686
Weight Watchers, I 707
Weightlifting, II 317, IV 310
Weil, Cynthia, I 351
Weill, Kurt, I 748
Wein, George, III 526
Weinberg, Jack, II 161
Weinberger, Caspar, II 499
Weinberger, Ed, IV 611
Weiner, Lee, I 495
Weinglass, Leonard, I 496
Weir, Bob, II 292
Weird Tales, III 205, IV 141, 331
Weisinger, Mort, IV 583
Weissmuller, Johnny, III 560, IV 610, V 39
Welborn, Larry, II 430
Welch, Robert, II 549
Welcome Back Kotter, IV 694
Weld, Tuesday, I 736
Welles, Orson, I 514, 613, II 100, 135, 378, III 2, 256, 429, 504, 561, IV 159, 160, 376, V 22, 79
Wellman, William, I 207, V 77, 119
Wells, Dickie, I 185
Wells, H. G., I 64, III 581, IV 330, V 79
Wells, Helen, I 491
Wells, Kitty, III 219
Wells, Mary, III 279, 420, IV 233
Welty, Eudora, I 134, III 549
Wendy's, II 73
Wenner, Jann, IV 267
Wepner, Chuck, III 172, IV 247
Werblin, Sonny, III 471
Werewolves on Wheels, II 386
Wertham, Fredric, I 561, 564, 565, IV 350
West, Adam, I 190
West Coast Rock, II 534
West Edmonton Mall, III 248
West, Jerry, III 196, IV 225
West, Mae, I 240, II 297, IV 369
West, Nathanael, I 29
West Point, III 49
West side sound, III 30
West Side Story, I 282, II 197, 338, 584; III 410, 459, IV 454
Western Story Magazine, IV 141
Western Union, II 495
Westinghouse, IV 312
Weston, Joanie, IV 267
Westworld, I 632
Wetimer, Ned, II 536
Wexler, Haskell, I 70
Wexler, Jerry, I 135, II 155, V 37
Weyl, Walter, III 514
Weymouth, Tina, IV 602
Weyrich, Paul, IV 200
WGN, I 433
Whale, James, II 152
Wham-O Toy Company, II 174, 466
Wharton, Edith, IV 338
"What a Fool Believes," I 747
What Did You Do in the War, Daddy?, V 192
What a Life!, II 393
What Price Glory?, V 77
What Would Jesus Do?. See WWJD? (What Would Jesus Do?)
What's Going On, II 216
What's My Line?, I 53, II 193, 271
What's Up, Tiger Lily?, I 71
Wheaties, II 512, III 190
Wheel of Fortune, I 298, II 194, 313
Wheeler-Nicholson, Malcolm, I 560, 671
When Billy Broke His Head . . . and Other Tales of Wonder, I 722
When Hell Was in Session, V 51
"When the Moon Comes Over the Mountain," IV 439
When Worlds Collide, I 724
Where the Boys Are, II 151
Whip It, I 697

Whirlaway, III 20
Whiskey-a-Go-Go, I 748
Whist, I 349
Whistler, James Abbott McNeill, V 125
Whitcomb, John C., Jr., I 627
White, Betty, II 260, III 292, 294, IV 1
White, Bukka, III 27
White, Byron "Whizzer," IV 61
White Cargo, III 82
White Castle, II 347
White, Dan, I 454, III 362
White, E. B., III 522, IV 655
White, Edward, I 104
White Fang, III 188
White, Jaleel, II 62
White, John Sylvester, V 105
White, Kate, IV 189
White Light, White Heat, IV 192
White Night Riots, III 362
White, Randy, I 654
White Sox, Chicago, III 237, 371
White supremacy, III 217
White, Ted, I 65
White Tower, II 73
White, Trumbull, IV 189
White, Vanna, V 123
White, William Allen, I 318, III 319
Whiteman, Paul, I 143, 247, IV 710
Whitewater, II 499
Whitfield, Raoul, I 264
Whiting, Richard, V 130
Whitman Candy, I 318
Whitman, Walt, I 122, 774, III 390, IV 306, 344
Who, I 355, 576, III 220, 384
Who Framed Roger Rabbit?, I 240
"Whole Lotta Love," III 116
Whole Lotta Shakin' Goin' On, III 154
Whopper, I 387
Who's Next, V 131
Who's Tommy, III 459
Why We Fight, I 429, V 50, 189
Whyte, William H., III 572
Wickman, Carl Eric, II 312
Wiese, Otis, III 313
Wife Beware, I 769
Wigstock, I 416
Wilco, II 329
Wilcox, Harlow, II 90
Wilcox, Horace Henderson, II 431
Wild Angels, II 386
Wild at Heart, III 216
Wild Bunch, II 402, V 119
Wild One, I 343, 355, II 385
Wild, Wild West, I 551, V 120
Wildenberg, Harry I., I 560
Wilder, Billy, I 751, II 99, 393, III 229, IV 364, 453, 579
Wilder, Gene, IV 127, 162
Wilder, Thornton, II 384, 388
Wilding, Michael, IV 614
Wildwood Productions, IV 190
Wilford H. Fawcett, I 582
Will Success Spoil Rock Hunter?, III 260
Willard, Jesse, I 685
William Morris Agency, I 34
William Tell Overture, III 190
Williams, Andy, II 322, III 368
Williams, Anson, II 357
Williams, Barry, I 341
Williams, Bert, I 423, V 61, 62
Williams, Cindy, I 69, III 103
Williams, Clarence, III 386
Williams, Deniece, III 306
Williams, Gloria, III 279
Williams, Gluyas, I 219
Williams, Guy, V 235
Williams, Hank, I 619, II 287, III 154
Williams, J. "Mayo," IV 155
Williams, Jerry, IV 601
Williams, John, II 528, IV 512
Williams, Lefty, I 266
Williams, Mary Lou, III 3

Williams, Montel, I 668
Williams, Otis, IV 633
Williams, Paul, I 441, IV 633
Williams, Race, I 263, 694
Williams, Robert F., I 264
Williams, Robin, III 411
Williams, Roy, III 425
Williams, Spencer, Jr., I 74
Williams, Tennessee, I 358, II 245, III 549,
    IV 141, 554
Williams, Vanessa, III 375
Williams, William Carlos, I 201, III 391
Williamson, Fred, I 279
Williamson, Kevin, IV 341
Williamson, Sonny Boy, II 461, IV 345
Willie Dynamite, I 279
Willingham, Calder, II 281
Willis, Bill, IV 118
Willis, Bruce, III 406
Willis, Nathaniel, V 222
Wills, Bob, II 335, III 501
Wills, Chill, II 152
Wills, Gary, II 41
Willson, Henry, II 468
Willys-Overland Company, IV 483
Wilson, I 20
Wilson, Brian, I 195
Wilson, Carl, I 195
Wilson, Demond, IV 310
Wilson, Dennis, I 195, III 262
Wilson, Flip, I 435
Wilson, Gahan, I 722
Wilson, Jackie, II 272, III 420, IV 459
Wilson, Kemmons, II 428
Wilson Phillips, III 251
Wilson, S. Clay, V 4
Wilson, Sloan, II 98
Wilson, William Grifffith, (Bill W.), IV 708
Wilson, Woodrow, I 134, 258, II 77, III 171,
    491, V 186
Wimbledon, I 124, II 49, III 28, 495
Wimmer, Don, IV 216
Wimsey, Lord Peter, I 693
Winans, The, II 274
Winchell, Walter, I 159, II 275, 542, III 227, 238, IV
    1, 159, 671, V 13
Wind, Timothy, III 35
Windham Hill, III 506, V 157
Windows, I 107, III 354
Windsor, Henry Haven, Sr., IV 89
Winfield, Arthur M., IV 548
Winfrey, Oprah, I 591, 668, 745, III 78, IV 628
Winger, I 86
Wings, I 13, V 77
Winkler, Henry, II 357
Winkler, Irwin, IV 246
Winn, Matt, III 19
Winnie the Pooh, IV 617
Winningham, Mare, I 344
Winnipeg Jets, II 467
Winslet, Kate, IV 663
Winsor, Roy, IV 346, 446
Winstead, Charles B., I 714
Winston Cup, IV 46
Winston, Sam, I 29
Winston, Stan, IV 639
Winter Olympics, IV 430
Winter, Roger, I 28
Winters, Jonathan, III 411
Winters, Shelley, V 59
Wintour, Anna, I 577, V 54
Winwood, Steve, I 355, 525
Wire, Sidney, I 389
Wired, I 217
Wired Radio, III 463
Wirt, Mildred, III 473
Wirth, May, I 512
Wise, "Chubby," II 122, III 397
Wise, Robert, I 665, II 521
"Wise Use" movement, II 10
Wiseguy: Life in a Mafia Family, II 269
Wister, Owen, IV 141

Witchcraft, I 245
Witt, Katarina, IV 430
Wiz, V 164
Wizard of Oz, I 191, 644, II 203, III 77
Wizards of the Coast Inc., I 65
Wolfe, Nero, IV 546
Wolfe, Nero. See Stout, Rex
Wolfe, Tom, II 41, III 22, V 68
Wolfman Jack, I 70, IV 680
Wolfson, Lou, III 33
Womack, Bobby, I 594
Woman of Paris, A, I 476
Woman's Day, II 59
Women Against Pornography, IV 94
Women of Brewster Place, III 495
Women's Liberation Front, I 208
Women's Liberation Movement, I 585, 774, II 32,
    86, III 141, 344, 434, IV 373
Women's Liberation Party, I 336
Women's National Basketball Association
    (WNBA), I 187
Women's Prison, II 390
Women's Room, II 87
Women's Suffrage Movement, I 310, IV 124
Wonder, Stevie, II 185, 513, III 422, IV 234, 460
Wonder Woman, I 561, 672, IV 350, V 190
Wong, Anna May, I 767
Wood, Andrew, II 321
Wood, Ed, Jr., III 214, IV 194
Wood, Grant, I 69
Wood, Natalie, IV 186, 346
Wood, Robert D., IV 419
Wood, Sam, II 264
Woodcraft Indians, I 334
Wooden, John, I 186
Woodiwiss, Kathleen, IV 271
Woodlawn, Holly, I 416
Woodman, Marion, I 297
Woodruff, Ernest, I 541
Woodruff, John, IV 284
Woodruff, Robert, I 541
Woods, Robert, II 583
Woods, Rosemary, V 86
Woods, Tiger, II 262, III 305
Woodstock, I 58, 639, 782, II 283, 328, 392, 411,
    535, III 184, IV 311
Woodward, Bob, V 84, 86
Woodward, Joanne, III 60
Woody Woodpecker, I 276
Woolery, Chuck, V 123
Woolrich, Cornell, II 99, IV 184
Woolworth Building, IV 433
Woolworth, F. W., I 717
Workingman's Dead, II 293
Works Progress Administration (WPA), III 508, VI
    196, V 179
World Association for Community Broadcasters
    (AMARC), I 571
World Disarmament Conference, II 17
World Fantasy Award, IV 308
World Football League, IV 118
World Hockey Association (WHA), II 460, 467
World Magazine, III 484
World Road Race, III 130
World Series, I 169, 266, 362, 435, 539, 695, III 68,
    237, 263, 311, IV 231, 297, V 19, 217
World Skating League, IV 267
World Trade Center, II 28
World War I, I 52, 511, 761, V 75, 160
World War II, I 84, 95, 112, 152, 236, 239, 312, 358,
    428, 457, 742, II 229, 323, 447, 534, III 3, 82,
    110, 161, 177, 308, 560, IV 10, 187, 522, 534, V
    30, 75, 159, 171
World Wide Web, II 495, 496, III 354, IV 95
World Wrestling Federation (WWF), II 423, IV
    60, 223, 322
World's Columbian Exposition, Chicago, II
    567, V 153
World's Fair, I 77, III 119, 559
Worth, Patience, III 576
Worthy, James, III 197
Wozniak, Steven, I 106, II 496

Wray, Fay, III 30
Wren, Percival Christopher, I 207
Wrestling, II 159
Wright, Farnsworth, V 103
Wright, Frank Lloyd, I 387, II 491, IV 433
Wright, Orville and Wilbur, I 38, 245, IV 441
Wright, Richard, I 161, III 327
Wright, Willard Huntingdon, I 694
Wright-Patterson Air Force Base, IV 282
Wrigley, Philip K., III 110
Wrinkle in Time, III 131
WTBS, III 115
Wunder, George, IV 640
Wurlitzer, II 580
Wu-Tang Clan, IV 176
Wuthering Heights, IV 271
Wyatt Earp, V 121
Wyatt, Jane, II 75
Wyeth, Andrew, V 200
Wyler, William, I 221, V 189
Wylie, Paul, II 485
Wyman, Bill, IV 269
Wynette, Tammy, II 562
Wynn, Ed, III 504
Wynne, Arthur, I 641

X, Malcolm, I 45
Xena, Warrior Princess, II 398
X-Files, I 587, II 82, III 213, IV 116, 425
X-Men, I 562, III 124, IV 620
X-ray, III 52
XYZ Comics, I 642

Yahoo!, II 222, 497
Yale University, I 555, III 211
Yamaguchi, Kristi, II 484, III 70, IV 430
Yamaha, II 545
Yank, V 190
Yankee Doodle Dandy, I 411
Yankee Stadium, I 169
Yankovic, Frankie, V 209
Yarborough, Cale, IV 47
Yardbirds, I 204, 355, 525, III 116
Yarick, Ed, IV 193
Yarrow, Peter, IV 42
Yastrzemski, Carl, III 175
Yasui, Minoru, II 526
Yates, Herbert, V 120
Yeager, Chuck, IV 382
Year of the Quiet Sun, IV 332
Year of the Woman, I 94
Yellow journalism, II 379, V 213
Yellow Kid, II 379
Yellow Submarine, IV 128
Yellowstone National Park, II 29, III 48, 490
Yentl, IV 678
Yerba Buena Jazz Band, I 734
Yerkovich, Anthony, III 349
"Yesterday," III 316
Yeti, I 251
Yield, IV 28
Yippies, I 495, II 419, III 62
YM, IV 313
Yoakam, Dwight, I 262, IV 29
Yogi, Maharishi Mahesh, III 508
Yojimbo, II 107
York Barbell Club, II 317
York Barbell Company, I 306
Yorkin, Bud, II 148, III 111
Yosemite, II 29, III 490
Yost, Fielding H., I 555
You Bet Your Life, III 288, 289
You Can't Take it With You, IV 533
You Send Me, I 595
You'll Never Get Rich, I 432
Young, Alan, III 376
Young and the Restless, IV 446

Young, Brigham, III 92
Young, Buddy, IV 118
Young, Faron, III 367
Young Frankenstein, I 366
Young, Lester, I 185, III 3, 27
Young Lions, III 280, V 191
Young, Loretta, V 75
Young Men's Christian Association (YMCA), III 456
Young Mr. Lincoln, II 127, 128
Young, Murat "Chic," I 283
Young, Neil, I 381, 639, II 69, III 170, 220
Young, Robert, II 75, III 269
Youngman, Henny, I 322, IV 505
Your Physique, I 306
"Your Pretty Face Is Going to Hell," IV 82
Your Show of Shows, I 366, 408, 540, IV 196
You're in the Picture, II 247
"You're Nobody 'Til Somebody Loves You," III 280
Youth International Party. See Yippies

Yule, Doug, V 40
Yuppies, IV 105, 283

Zanuck, Darryl F., III 119
Zanuck, Richard, II 527
Zap, I 642
Zappa, Frank, I 355, 595
Zapruder film, II 546
Zaslow, Jeffery, I 29
Zecca, Ferdinand, IV 395
Zefferelli, Franco, III 557, IV 674
Zelazny, Roger, I 65
Zelig, I 54
Zemeckis, Robert, I 90, II 141
Zeppelin, II 409
Zeroes, II 19
Ziegfeld, Florenz, I 305, 357, 423, IV 310, 390, V 31, 227

Ziegfeld Follies, I 227, 348, II 95, III 119, 458, VI 263, V 140
Ziggy Stardust, II 248
Zimmerman, Robert, I 781
Zines, III 176
"Zing! Went the Strings of My Heart," II 203
Zinnemann, Fred, II 400
Zippy the Pinhead, I 562
Zmuda, Bob, III 9
Zoloft, I 691
Zombie, Rob, II 10
Zombies, I 355
Zoot Suit, II 19, IV 2
Zorro, IV 139
Zucker, David, I 39
Zukor, Adolph, III 428, IV 565
Zwick, Edward, III 467
Zwicker, Ralph W., I 116
Zwigoff, Terry, I 642
Zydeco, I 380, 483, 490